The Ornament Collector's™

Official Price Guide for Past Years'

Hallmark Ornaments

and Kiddie Car Classics

Check in with "Elvin the Elf"
in the next issue of
The Ornament Collector™
magazine for news, views,
collector ads and
collecting information on
Hallmark ornaments and
Christmas collectibles, plus other
companies' ornament offerings.

If you're looking for an older ornament...
Look to **The Ornament Collector**™
magazine's Classified ads!
1-800-455-8745

1997

11th Edition
Rosie Wells
Editor & Collector

Published by
Rosie Wells Enterprises, Inc.
22341 E. Wells Rd., Canton, IL 61520
Check us out on the World Wide Web!
http://www.RosieWells.com
E-Mail: Rosie@RosieWells.com
Ph. 1-800-445-8745

W9-CFV-008

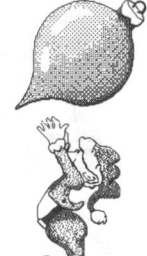

Rosalie "Rosie" Wells

Author, Editor, Collector, Wife, Mother, Grandma
Bringing Collectors Together Since 1983.

Rosie Wells lives in Central Illinois, "down on the farm," and has been a collector ever since she can remember. Even as a child, she cherished her comic books, pins, little steel cars (instead of dolls) and WWII bubble gum. She ordered by radio all the *Straight Arrow* drums she could get with Shredded Wheat box tops and collected Cracker Jack toys!

Rosie and her husband Dave have two children, Tim and Beth. They also have one precious, outstanding, super-smart, cute, little grandson named Hunter who will be four this year in June! Hunter and his mommy live with Gramma and Grampa. Tim was recently married to the former Kerrie Maurice, and now Rosie and Dave are very happy to have Kerrie as their very lovely daughter-in-law.

Rosie's career in publishing began at her kitchen table. Fifteen years later, with her dedicated staff of thirty-two employees, she works in a separate office building just across the road from the farm home. Rosie's love for animals is apparent as she enjoys her chickens, peacocks, swans, turkeys, rheas and ostriches, as well as Dave's White Park cattle. Three loyal dogs and a parrot also make their home with Rosie and Dave. Ask Dave sometime how he loves that parrot! Ha! Many species of woodland animals are seen on the farm and part of the fields are planted to provide winter food for wildlife. Canadian geese inhabit the land year 'round; whitetail deer are frequently spotted from the view at the office. Recently a log cabin was built in the woods to give us a hide-away to do some writing in a quiet calm, atmosphere with nature!

Rosie's Secondary Market Price Guides for Hallmark ornaments, Precious Moments® collectibles, Enesco's *Cherished Teddies®, The Boyds Collection, Ltd,* as well as the *Collectors' Bulletin™, The Ornament Collector™* and *Precious Collectibles®* are enjoyed by many all around the world. These three collector magazines are published to inform collectors of what is happening in the world of collecting. Rosie also publishes a *Weekly Collectors' Gazette™* filled with news on Hallmark collectibles and other limited edition collectibles. She and Dave also host the Midwest Collectibles Fest in Westmont, Illinois, twice a year (the largest in the nation with over 180 dealer tables each time!) and the annual LincolnLand Collectibles Show in Normal, Illinois.

Rosie is a noted authority on collectibles and can spot a "hot" collectible in the making almost from day one! She helps guide retailers each year in a retailer guide as to what ornament "picks" would be best to order for the current year! She has helped many collectibles gain recognition through her three international collectors' magazines and through shows and seminars throughout the United States. Having a sensational collectible knowledge, a sense of humor and a loving heart which collectors can relate to through the many articles she has written draws collectors to Rosie. Hallmark ornaments have always fascinated Rosie; she has a collection of several hundred ornaments. Rosie has also collected Hallmark Merry Miniatures, lapel pins, cookie cutters and magnets and has published guides for Hallmark Merry Miniatures, lapel pins and cookie cutters in the past.

Rosie says, "If I have only one life to live, then I hope to collect as much as my basement, shelves, drawers and walls can hold, then everyone will know I was a fun lovin', crazy collector! Collectors are fun folks, you know!"

Check us out on the World Wide Web at http://www.RosieWells.com or write our e-mail address Rosie@RosieWells.com. Our web site was honored with the Gold Service Award by The Public Eye, an internet watchdog group that gives this award out only to "Internet companies who demonstrate the highest and most extraordinary level of customer service excellence." This award is the ultimate symbol of distinction for any company doing business on the Internet, as it is only given to businesses that pass rigorous standards in the areas of "service," "accessibility," "warranties," "references" and "stability." We received this award after one of their people went "undercover" to purchase one of our products. They found our services to be exceptional and that made us happy, too!

THIS GUIDE IS ALSO AVAILABLE AS A CARRY ALONG POCKET GUIDE – JUST A SMALLER VERSION OF THIS GUIDE.
IT WILL BE EASY TO CARRY ALONG WHILE ATTENDING SHOWS AND SHOPPING SPREES! SEE PAGE 335 FOR MORE DETAILS.

Table of Contents

New Collector? – Read This!

Did you know that buying "just one more" Hallmark ornament is what thousands do to ease their Hallmark fever? There are many reasons to purchase Hallmark ornaments! People purchase their favorites! They purchase Hallmark ornaments for gifts! They purchase them for sentimental reasons and they purchase the ones which remind them of a special person, a special event or "just because." Boy, do I purchase for "just because!"

Yes, some people even purchase Hallmark ornaments as an investment in hopes of making a little extra cash later on. There's a good chance, if you're involved in the buyers' circle, you may double your money or more on the scarce ornaments and the "popular" first in series ornaments. For example, the 1993 *Holiday Barbie*, with a retail price of $14.75, went to $50 within two months on the secondary market; it has now risen to $100! (Not all first in series ornaments are a sure thing; some, like *Winter Surprise*, didn't do well on the secondary market.)

Of course, collectors and dealers were caught unaware of how popular the 1991 *Starship Enterprise* would become; the scarcity of this ornament caused the price to climb to the $300 mark, with seekers still out there looking. After a "hot" ornament is produced, don't get overly excited thinking that the second edition will be as scarce. Retailers remember the response to the "firsts" and usually order extra of "number two." Study the market carefully.

Fads come and go and "pop culture" ornaments are good sellers, such as the 1994 *Beatles* set. Retailers may not have ordered many of these because of the $48 retail price, but one must study the market! Someone, somewhere had over 1,000 of these to release on the secondary market and the 1994 *Beatles* secondary market was affected for a long period of time!

In my opinion, the only way the personalized ornaments will rise in value on the secondary market will be if you have a clever saying placed on it, maybe a famous name. For example, on the 1995 *Reindeer Rooters* (QP 605-6) I would put, "Hey Santa, may we ride too?" on the sign to be displayed with the 1993 *Cheery Cyclists* (QX 578-6) or "Vote for Clinton" - or "Vote for Dole" - or "Vote for Rosie!" Ha! That would be a real doozie!

Most light, motion and talking ornaments have not been favorites for secondary market folks to invest in. Many collectors are cautious about the life expectancy of the motors. Of course, if one holds these ornaments a year or two, one could easily make a few folks happy. I feel the 1996 *Chicken Coop Chorus* and the *Wizard of Oz* light and motion will be Hot soon!

If you're lucky to find ornaments from the '70s and early '80s at a bargain price, these would be great to resell on the secondary market. (Only a few of the ball ornaments are money makers. They're priced high but few buy!)

Before you decide to invest in ornaments, my advice is to attend several swap meets and watch what sells. **Although 99% of the listed ornaments in this guide have a higher value than their original retail, it's still not a guarantee they will all "sell" immediately at these prices. THESE PRICES ARE AVERAGED FROM SALE PRICES ACROSS THE COUNTRY AND SHOULD BE USED ONLY AS A GUIDE TO INSURE YOUR COLLECTION. WE MAKE NO WARRANTY ON THE PRICES CONTAINED IN THIS GUIDE.**

Write to me if you have any questions. We also may be able to help you locate a much sought after ornament. Thank you for purchasing our guide; we hope you enjoy reading and learning the values for your ornaments. Our goal is to "Bring Collectors Together." We know the family who prays together stays together and we've also found that when families collect together they enjoy being together. I hope to see you sometime at a Collectibles Show! (Ask about our three Collectibles Shows in Illinois for March, Sept. and Oct., 1997)

Don't forget... if you travel to shows and take your guide with you, you may want to order your carry along guide. See pg. 335.)

Insure Your Collection

You can be sure, this guide will be especially helpful when insuring your collection; many insurance companies use it as proof of value in settling claims. Collectibles usually are not covered with a general homeowner's insurance policy, but require a "rider" policy. Your agent may need additional documentation, such as photos of your collection and inventory records. Before appraising your collection for insuring, you may wish to contact your insurance agent and ask about the actual details which he/she requires. Be sure your agent insures your collection at today's replacement prices, not the original retail price.

In this guide, you will find space to record your ornament purchases as well as the condition of each ornament (mint in box, damaged box, etc.). It is very important to have a current inventory of your collection in the event you need to file a claim.

One should also be aware of the value of these ornaments in "estate planning." Sadly, many valuable Hallmark ornaments have been sold in a group for a very few dollars because of a lack of knowledge. Although you might never sell your collection, it's always best to keep a record of its monetary value.

Hallmark Ball Ornaments

Generally speaking, ball ornaments have not proven to be as collectible as the other Hallmark ornaments, although some are very difficult to locate, especially mint in box condition. Many older ball ornaments are found with discoloration, spotting and with no boxes.

According to an article written by Shirley Trexler which appeared in the June 1994 issue of **The Ornament Collector**™ magazine: "*Difficulty faces ball ornament collectors who try, in vain, to find ball ornaments that had low production and a high breakage and spotting potential. Few secondary market dealers have any ball or yarn ornaments listed on price lists or show tables. Many times collectors are unable to replace a broken, cherished ball ornament because these ornaments are so few in number anymore. A few examples of such rare older ball ornaments include: 1973* **Manger Scene** *and* **Christmas Is Love;** *1974* **Angel** *ball and* **Snow Goose** *ball; 1975* **Buttons and Bo** *collection and* **Little Miracles** *group of balls; 1976* **Rudolph and Santa;** *and the* **Baby's First Christmas** *and* **Drummer Boy** *balls; 1979* **Light of Christmas** *ball; 1980* **Christmas Choir** *ball and the 1983* **Christmas Wonderland** *ball. These are just a few of many which are fading from existence.*"

Some ball ornaments are scarce, not because of tremendous popularity but because of the reasons listed above, low production, breakage and spotting. Some of the older ball ornaments are sought after, but not many. If you're thinking of the future secondary market for ball ornaments, don't "go overboard." Three or four of each of the new ones per secondary market dealer would overload the supply, in my opinion. Ball ornaments are lovely and enjoyable, but not easy to hold for investment, in my opinion, unless they are extra rare or unusual.

What About The Boxes?

This guide is the first to research "no box" prices on the majority of the ornaments. **NB** prices are not given for ornaments produced in '93-'96 because it is very unlikely that these ornaments would be found without a box. When insuring '93 through '96 ornaments that do not have a box, deduct up to 15% of the secondary market value.

We have found that the older the ornament is the harder it becomes to find anywhere... so a collector wanting it badly will be happy to own it even without a box. Collectors will buy what they want with or without the box. Collectors do pay more for an older ornament with a box. Why? Because 20 years ago, many of those who bought Hallmark ornaments didn't keep the boxes and didn't know what boxes would mean to many in the future. It wasn't even in the minds of many that in 15 to 20 years a Hallmark ornament might be looked upon as a collectible valued at many times its original retail price! So having an older ornament, mint in box, can be reason enough to ask a higher price.

When you have an original box with a popular ornament such as the first in series *Here Comes Santa* you will be able to sell it for more than the same ornament without a box. Boxes are a plus with older ornaments, but we've found that, with or without the box, sought-after ornaments will still bring a good price and should be insured accordingly.

Most recent ornaments are easily found at shows and from secondary market dealers. So it's felt that collectors should be aware of keeping the boxes should there be a decision to sell in the future. These ornaments will be offered to a new generation of well-informed collectors who may want the boxes. This guide reflects selling prices of "no box" ornaments. Once an ornament becomes older, then you may find the "no box" price will escalate. There are differences of opinion on this subject, each with valid points to be made.

To locate an ornament/collectibles show in your area, search the ads in *The Ornament Collector*™ magazine! Shows are a lot of fun and you can find some of your favorite ornaments since secondary market dealers offer hundreds of ornaments for sale. In *The Ornament Collector*™ magazine *"We Bring Ornament Collectors Together"* to enjoy their collections. Ask about our shows.

Did You Know?

✭ Although the ball ornaments are not in demand, they are becoming harder to locate. Watch for age marks on ball ornaments.

✭ The 1980 *Cool Yule* is a very coveted ornament in the Hallmark line. *Here Comes Santa*, *Rocking Horse*, *Tin Locomotive*, *Classic American Cars* and *Barbie* are also very popular Hallmark series.

✭ Errors, such as missing decals, upside down sleeves on ball ornaments and missing painted parts, are sometimes found on ornaments. Errors are few; secondary market prices rise on these pieces, but there are few buyers for these errored pieces. An error found on an ornament is not highly sought after unless the error is corrected and the ornament re-released. (Example: *Mom* 1996. As of press time, we have not heard if the ornament will be changed.)

✭ A few ornaments through the years debuted in the *Dream Book* but were recalled due to production problems. Other ornaments were produced for retailers' displays and then pulled from production such as the 1990 *Country Angel* and the changed 1994 *Lion King*, with light and music.

✭ Usually attractive first editions increase in value immediately after Christmas. Always buy the first editions of the ornaments that you like as soon as they debut or the next year you'll pay more!

✭ There are local collector clubs in many states. Ask your favorite dealer, subscribe to *The Ornament Collector*™ magazine for locations or call the Hallmark Keepsake Ornament Club in Kansas City at 816/274-4000 or 816/274-7463.

✭ Many children, when they marry and leave home, leave the family dog and take their ornaments with them. ☺

✭ Remember, not all ornaments produced by Hallmark are "Keepsake Ornaments." Some are "Tree Trimmers." These are not in this guide and are not as sought after as the Keepsake Collection.

✭ It's best to put your favorite ornaments on layaway when they debut in July and August. Many people were accustomed to waiting for after Christmas sales to purchase their Hallmark ornaments but in the past three years some collectors have been very disappointed, finding that many ornaments were gone from the shelves forever.

✫ This guide is available on CD-Rom. See inside front and back covers.

✫ Many collectors display their ornaments all year 'round. *Many*, I say *many*, collectors put up three, four, five or even more trees at Christmas time! Each year we give a Collector of the Year award! You'd be amazed at the photo entries we receive.

✫ A collector found her 1995 *Holiday Barbie* ornament had two different earrings. One earring was red with silver on it and the other earring was silver with red on it.

✫ Back yard sales and auctions bring great finds to collectors. Advertise in your local paper for these collectibles!

✫ The *Rocking Horse* series ended with the 16th Edition dated 1996. This has been a very popular series sculpted by Linda Sickman. Also the 1997 *Springtime Barbie* will be the last in the *Springtime Barbie*™ Series.

✫ "Personalized" ornaments on which you have your own name or message placed usually do not escalate in value; they have only heirloom value.

✫ The 1987 Hallmark Crayola® ornament *Bright Christmas Dreams* was not actually a part of the Hallmark Crayola® Crayon series, which officially started in 1989 with *Bright Journey*, although many collectors consider it a "must have" to accompany this series.

✫ Be careful when packing and unpacking ornaments. The 1994 *Beatles* have been found with Ringo having broken drum sticks. Ornaments which become unglued can usually be repaired without loss in value. Those ornaments which actually become broken or which have loose parts suffer the most loss in value.

✫ Starting with the '96 ornaments, Hallmark included imprints of artists' signatures on many ornaments. There were some exceptions, of course. No signatures are found on miniature ornaments, on ornaments where there was no appropriate place that would not detract from the design of the ornament and no signatures were found on ornaments where the licensees did not give permission.

✫ In lieu of one large convention as in 1991 and 1993, Hallmark hosted one-day Ornament Expos across the country in 1994 and 1995 and Artist Signings in 1996. A special piece, *Mrs. Claus' Cupboard*, was available for purchase at the 1994 Expo, *Christmas Eve Bake-Off* was available at the 1995 Expo and *Santa's Toy Shop* was available at the 1996 Artist Signing. Hallmark also produced variations of popular ornaments which were given away at the Expos as door prizes and other special Expo offerings which collectors could purchase. (The 1995 miniature Pewter *Rocking Horse* is Hot!) Also, Artist Signing Events are held throughout the country each year, giving collectors a chance to meet Hallmark artists and have their favorite ornaments signed.

✫ There were three souvenir ornaments available only at Hallmark Expos in 1995. These included a Hallmark Artists' Caricature ball ornament, a miniature pewter *Rocking Horse* and a Cookie tree ornament. The three ornaments were limited to one each per registered membership. The pewter *Rocking Horse* was the most popular!

✫ There was no Expo in 1996; instead there were several scheduled artist signings at special locations. Available at the 1996 Artists Signings were *Toy Shop Santa* and a Gold Miniature *Rocking Horse*. The *Rocking Horse* commemorated the retirement of the *Rocking Horse* series.

✫ Sleepers are ornaments which sell out at dealers more quickly than originally predicted to do so. This is because there are usually fewer available.

✫ Generally, any train or Classic Car ornament is good for secondary market holdings. Just watch the market for the *700E Hudson Steam Locomotive,* the 1st in the *LIONEL®* Train series. I feel many LIONEL's were produced but value will go up after 1996.

✫ Did you know there are many channels through which you may find the older ornaments? These include ornament swap meets, secondary market dealers' ads; and some Hallmark stores have added rooms for older ornaments. Advertise; you'll probably find what you want! Check out our Web site at http://www.RosieWells.com! Call us – we'll try to help you!

✫ Know who you are dealing with when buying, selling and trading through the mail. Generally, most collectors are trustworthy folks but there's always that one bad onion! There's a very good method to use to mark your ornaments when selling. Use a blacklight marking pen to put a dot or two on each ornament in case a broken or scratched ornament is returned that is not yours. These marks will show up under a blacklight, proving whether or not the ornament that's returned is the one you sent. When shipping UPS, we advise shipping with the label AOD (Acknowledgment of Delivery). The recipient must "sign" for the package delivered by UPS. Or insure it through U.S. mail.

✫ In the future we may see new series of different dog breeds, cat breeds, actual nursery rhyme characters, more licensed product ornaments, bicycles, football stars, mermaids and computers, plus Victorian dolls, Nativity pieces, a special line of Santas, trains and definitely a new series of angels. The farmers have hoped for antique tractors; replicas of old toys and mechanical banks have been thought about as well as whimsical little vegetables! Mice will be around for years to come and surely, before the fad is over, a few black and white cows will debut. Hallmark artists plan designs several years ahead; as you read this in '97, this year's Christmas ornaments are well ahead on the production line in the Far East.

✫ The *Classic American Cars* series is very popular as many men receive them as gifts. In the future we may see a similar line of foreign cars. Car enthusiasts are offering these at their Swap 'n Sells also. Who knows? We may see lighthouses debut as ornaments. What about Harley Davidson motorcycles? A great suggestion, eh?!

✫ For Hallmark Artist interviews - read *The Ornament Collector*™ magazine. Subscribe NOW! 1-800-445-8745

✫ Read **"ROSIE'S PICKS"** in *The Ornament Collector*™ for **FUTURE** ornaments' popularity. She has a Retailer Guide each year, also! Tell your dealer!

✶ Sometimes the value of an ornament may fall after a peak, later to rise or level off. It pays to study the market.

✶ Many collectors feel that ornaments shouldn't be stored in the original bubble wrap packing as this bubble wrap may emit a gas which discolors the ornament. As of 1994, Hallmark replaced bubble wrap with tissue paper as packing material. One reason for this change is that tissue paper is more environmentally friendly. However, we saw bubble wrap used as packing again in 1995. Many collectors also store their ornaments in sectioned storage boxes, thus eliminating the wear and tear on individual ornament boxes, if they decide to keep them. This also makes it simpler when decorating or putting away ornaments for the year. Ornament boxes may then be carefully flattened and stored.

✶ Rosie has designed her own HoneyBee Bears and you just might love the "future" ornament.

✶ Many collectors want to know the relationship between Ambassador and Hallmark. Ambassador was a subsidiary of Hallmark and produced ornaments in the early '80s. Packaging for the Ambassador line consisted of white boxes with green inner boxes and a clear, see-through front. Printed on the outside of each box is *The Holiday House Collection*. It is difficult to find Ambassador ornaments in their original boxes.

✶ You have joined the National Hallmark Keepsake Collector's Club, haven't you? Pick up the forms from a Hallmark dealer.

✶ The 1986 *Cinnamon Teddy* has two different stock numbers. Hallmark was obtaining the ornament from more than one manufacturer and they identified them with different numerals to regulate inventory.

✶ Upside down decals sometimes are found on ornaments. Such was the case on the '94 third in series *Betsey's Country Christmas*.

✶ The large Keepsake ornament book which retailers offered for sale every two years will not be published again until 1998, when a 25th Anniversary book will be issued.

✶ Did you know Hallmark aired a very catchy television commercial featuring the *Solo in the Spotlight Barbie* ornament in the Fall of 1995?

✶ There will be two new series available in the '97 Easter ornaments. These include *Sidewalk Curisers - 1935 Steelcraft Streamline* and *Children Collector Barbie™ - Rapunzel.* Will we see *Little Bo Peep* as the second in series in '98?

✶ The 1995 *Tobin Fraley Holiday Carousel* had a manufacturing defect. The designed side of the horse is on the inside and the plain side of the horse is facing outside. Mr. Fraley is no longer with Hallmark but still designs carousel horses for other companies.

✶ The Hallmark at Home catalog features several of the ornaments found in the Dream Book. Look for the second in series 1996 "black" Rocking Horse (11" tall for $225) in that catalog.

✶ Six Keepsake Ornaments were issued in the 1996 *Olympic Spirit* Collection. They were: *Invitation to the Games,* two dated, trading-card size ceramic plaque ornaments; *Lighting the Flame,* a Magic Ornament which features flickering light and plays *Bugler's Dream; Olympic Triumph, Cloisonné Medallion, Parade of Nations* plate and *Izzy,* the 1996 Olympic mascot. The medallion and plate sold best.

✶ The 1994 *Here Comes Santa* ornament proved to be very popular among farm toy collectors. One collector in particular reported that he customized his with the John Deere colors and decal.

✶ Most of the 1994 *Holiday Barbie* ornament boxes sold in Canada had writing in French on the box. Not all ornaments sold in the USA are offered in Canada.

✶ *Troy Aikman*, *Larry Bird* and *Nolan Ryan* 1996 ornaments were allocated to retailers.

✶ The *Madame Alexander* series begins with *Cinderella,* and will continue with other storybook characters as well.

✶ The '97 Spring miniature ornament, *Rapunzel,* is sure to be a favorite among Barbie™ collectors. She is first in the Child*ren's Collector Barbie™* Ornament series and features long braided hair which touches the hem of her iridescent skirt. (See pg 286)

✶ 1996 *Mary Had a Little Lamb* does not have an error. According to Hallmark, this ornament is a figural book. When opened, there is a 3-D figure of Mary and her little lamb. Mary's face was left unpainted on all the ornaments. That's what I call a blank expression.

✶ Retailers (several) told me the Noah's ark elephants (miniature ornaments) are popular sellers to their Bingo fanatics! They say elephants, especially with trunks in the air, are "good luck!"

✶ The *1997 Springtime Barbie* ornament will be the last in the series. She retails for $12.95. To take over and continue will be the *Children's Collector Barbie* ornament series. Rapunzel will be the first with her braid to the hem of her iridescent dress. She is beautiful. This series may be more popular than the *Springtime Barbie* series.

✶ So many phone calls were received about us removing the series pages in the 10th Edition of The Ornament Collector's Price Guide for Hallmark Ornaments. They have been included again in this 11th Edition. Thanks for the input. We didn't know you liked it so much until we took it out!!

We have conducted extensive research in recording values for ornaments found in this guide. Use these values as a "guide" in insuring, as well as buying and selling. We make no warranty on the prices contained in this guide. Expect prices on recent years' ornaments to increase proportionally more in the next few years than ornaments from early years.

MIB Sec. Mkt. prices quoted are for ornaments which are in mint condition and in their original boxes with price tab still attached to the box. The price tab is the removable perforated price tag found on each Hallmark ornament box. There were also "strips" running across the box or "gift tags" on some earlier boxes (i.e. 1977-1978 Trimmer Collection). When purchasing new ornaments be sure the perforated price tab remains on the box if you plan to resell later. If you give Hallmark ornaments as gifts to friends or loved ones who are collectors, they may want you to leave the tabs on. (Normally, this would be considered a breach in good manners, but collectors are a rare breed!)

Photos of each ornament have been included next to each listing in this guide. Care has been taken to ensure the clarity of each photo, however some detail has been lost as the photos in this guide have been reduced from larger color photos. This guide includes all ornaments up through 1997 Easter. A secondary market price has been given for each ornament through 1995. Only a projected value has been given for 1996 ornaments through 1997 Easter ornaments. Looking at last year's guide, we were proven to be 99% correct on our projected values.

Read **The Ornament Collector**™ for price updates and current news on Hallmark ornaments! Each issue is packed with hot news on Hallmark ornaments and other Christmas theme collectibles, Collectors' Comments, classified ads, show listings, club information and much more!
$23.95 Yr/4 issues, 22341 E. Wells Rd., Dept. G, Canton, IL 61520
Phone: 1-800-445-8745; Fax: 309/668-2795
May be found on most newsstands!
Check us out on the Internet! http://www.RosieWells.com
E-Mail address: Rosie@RosieWells.com

This guide is arranged first by year of production, then each ornament is listed in alphabetical order by name.
Ornaments in a series or collection are listed
by the name of the series or collection.

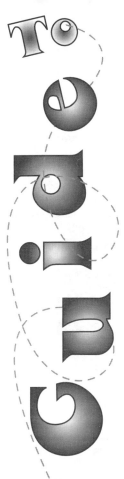

① ② QX 454-5   **MARY'S ANGELS: BLUEBELL** ③   ⑨ ☐
④ *Comments:*   **Second in Series,** Handcrafted/Acrylic, 3" tall. Bluebell kneels in prayer on a frosted acrylic cloud. She has a light blue gown. **Artist:** Robert Chad
⑤ ☐ Purchased 19 __ Pd $_____ MIB   NB   DB   BNT
☐ Want ⑥ Orig. Ret. $5.75
⑦ **NB** $35   ⑧ **MIB** Sec. Mkt. **$55-$60**

---

1 ....PHOTOGRAPH of the Ornament. If "Not Shown," then no photo of the piece was available. Photos welcomed!

2 ....NUMBER: Ornament's style number.

3 ....NAME of the Ornament. If the ornament is part of a series, the name of the series will appear first.

4 ....COMMENTS: Descriptions of each ornament include: Whether or not the ornament is part of a series and its standing in that series; if it is a ball ornament, acrylic, handcrafted, etc.; the size of the ornament (if available); whether or not it is dated; a short descriptive phrase; anything unusual or out of the ordinary.

5 ....This guide can also be used as a personal inventory book, keeping a record of ornaments you want or already own and the condition of your ornaments. MIB = mint in box, NB = no box, DB = damaged box and BNT = box with original price tab removed, NE = not established.

6 ....ORIG. RET.: Retail price of the ornament when it debuted.

7 ....NB: The value of the ornament without its original box. (NB-P signifies the fact that there is a plentiful supply of the ornament with No Box.)

8 ....MIB Sec. Mkt.: Today's secondary market price (collectors' and dealers' selling/buying prices). In most cases only one secondary market price was given, but there were cases where there was such a range in very high and very low selling prices for the ornament that only a range would do. Ninety-nine percent of the time you'll be able to find that special ornament at these prices. To sell a large collection quickly, expect to reduce your prices by 20%-30%. When selling to dealers, it may be necessary to deduct 50%-60% as they buy to resell. REMEMBER, USE THESE PRICES ONLY AS A GUIDE TO HELP YOU EVALUATE THE REPLACEMENT VALUE FOR INSURANCE PURPOSES ETC... YOU CAN ALSO RESEARCH PRICES BY STUDYING ADS BY COLLECTORS, ETC...

9 ....*NEW!*..........This box is for your convenience. You may mark the box so that you are able to tell immediately which ornaments you have and those which you do not have. Place a check in the box if it's in your collection

Collectible Ornament Series

All American Trucks, Dated

Series#	Year	Price	Item#
1	1995	$28	QX 552-7
2	1996	$20-22	QX 524-1

Complete series $48-50 MIB

Description
1956 Ford Truck
1955 Chevrolet Cameo

All God's Children, Dated

Series#	Year	Price	Item#
1	1996	$18-20	QX 556-4

Complete series $18-20 MIB

Description
Christy

Art Masterpiece, Padded Satin

Series#	Year	Price	Item#
1	1984	$18	QX 349-4
2	1985	$18	QX 377-2
3/Final	1986	$25	QX 350-6

Complete series $61 MIB

Description
Madonna and Child and St. John
Madonna of the Pomegranate
Madonna and Child w/Infant St. John

At the Ball Park, Dated

Series#	Year	Price	Item#
1	1996	$22 up	QXI 571-1

Complete series $22 up MIB

Description
Nolan Ryan

Barbie™, Dated

Series#	Year	Price	Item#
1	1994	$25-30	QX 500-6
2	1995	$28	QXI 504-9
3	1996	$20-22 up	QXI 654-1

Complete series $73-80 MIB

Description
Black and White Swimsuit
Solo in the Spotlight
Enchanting Evening

Baseball Heroes, Dated

Series#	Year	Price	Item#
1	1994	$35-40	QX 532-3
2	1995	$18	QX 502-9
3	1996	$18	QX 530-4

Complete series $71-76 MIB

Description
Babe Ruth
Lou Gehrig
Satchel Paige

Bellringers, The, Dated

Series#	Year	Price	Item#
1	1979	$250	QX 147-9
2	1980	$80	QX 157-4
3	1981	$85	QX 441-5
4	1982	$98	QX 455-6
5	1983	$130	QX 403-9
6/Final	1984	$40	QX 438-4

Complete series $683 MIB

Description
The Bellswinger (Elf on Bell Clapper)
The Bellringers (Angels w/ Stars)
Swingin' Bellringer (Mouse on Candy Cane)
Angel Bellringer
Teddy Bellringer
Elfin Artist

Betsey Clark, Dated Balls

Series#	Year	Price	Item#
1	1973	$130	QX 110-2
2	1974	$85	QX 108-1
3	1975	$65	QX 133-1
4	1976	$100	QX 195-1
5	1977	$425	QX 264-2
6	1978	$65	QX 201-6
7	1979	$38	QX 201-9
8	1980	$30	QX 215-4
9	1981	$27	QX 802-2
10	1982	$38	QX 215-6
11	1983	$30	QX 211-9
12	1984	$35	QX 249-4
13/Final	1985	$35	QX 263-2

Complete series $1,103 MIB

Description
Christmas 1973
Musicians
Caroling Trio
Christmas 1976
Truest Joys of Christmas
Christmas Spirit
Holiday Fun
Joy-in-the-Air
Christmas 1981
Joys of Christmas
Christmas Happiness
Days are Merry
Special Kind of Feeling

Betsey Clark: Home for Christmas, Dated

Series#	Year	Price	Item#
1	1986	$32	QX 277-6
2	1987	$24	QX 272-7
3	1988	$22	QX 271-4
4	1989	$32	QX 230-2
5	1990	$20	QX 203-3
6/Final	1991	$20	QX 210-9

Complete series $150 MIB

Description
Decorating the Christmas Tree
There's No Place Like Christmas
A Homemade Touch...
Filling Birdbath w/Water
Christmas Duet
Getting favorite friends together...

Betsey's Country Christmas, Dated

Series#	Year	Price	Item#
1	1992	$25	QX 210-4
2	1993	$15	QX 206-2
3/Final	1994	$15	QX 240-3

Complete series $55 MIB

Description
Christmas sets our hearts a dancing!
Happy is the memory of bringing home the Christmas tree!
It's the simple joys, the simple pleasures, the heart remembers and dearly treasures.

Carousel, Dated

Series#	Year	Price	Item#
1	1978	$410	QX 146-3
2	1979	$170	QX 146-7
3	1980	$160	QX 141-4
4	1981	$85	QX 427-5
5	1982	$105	QX 478-3
6/Final	1983	$50	QX 401-9

Complete series $980 MIB

Description
Antique Toys
Christmas Carousel
Merry Carousel
Skaters' Carousel
Snowman Carousel
Santa and Friends

Cat Naps, The, Dated

Series#	Year	Price	Item#
1	1994	$15	QX 531-3
2	1995	$12	QX 509-7
3	1996	$10	QX 564-1

Complete series $37 MIB

Description
Kitten Sleeping in Cookie Jar
Kitten Sleeping on Mitten

Celebration of Angels

	Year	Price	Item#
1	1995	$25	QX 507-7
2	1996	$16.50	QX 563-4

Complete series $41.50 MIB

Celebrates African-American holiday

Christmas Kitty, Porcelain

Series#	Year	Price	Item#
1	1989	$28	QX 544-5
2	1990	$28	QX 450-6
3/Final	1991	$32	QX 437-7

Complete series $88 MIB

Description
White/Yellow Kitten in White Dress
Grey Kitten in Blue/White Coat & Hat
Yellow Kitten in Pink NIghtgown

Christmas Visitors, Dated

	Year	Price	Item#
1	1995	$25	QX 508-7
2	1996	$16	QX 563-1

Complete series $41 MIB

St. Nicholas
Christkindl

Classic American Cars, The, Dated

Series#	Year	Price	Item#
1	1991	$175-195	QX 431-9
2	1992	$40-45	QX 428-4
3	1993	$30-35	QX 527-5
4	1994	$32	QX 542-2
5	1995	$18	QX 523-9
6	1996	$18-20	QX 538-4

Complete series $313-345 MIB

Description
1957 Corvette
1966 Mustang
1956 Thunderbird
1957 Chevrolet Bel Air
1969 Camaro
1959 Cadillac De Ville

Clothespin Soldier

Series#	Year	Price	Item#	Description
1	1982	$120	QX 458-3	British
2	1983	$50	QX 402-9	Early American
3	1984	$22	QX 447-1	Canadian Mountie
4	1985	$24	QX 471-5	Scottish Highlander
5	1986	$22	QX 406-3	French Officer
6/Final	1987	$22	QX 480-7	Sailor

Complete series $260 MIB

Collector's Plate, Dated on Back

Series#	Year	Price	Item#	Description
1	1987	$65-70	QX 481-7	Light Shines at Christmas
2	1988	$50	QX 406-1	Waiting for Santa
3	1989	$25	QX 461-2	Morning of Wonder
4	1990	$25	QX 443-6	Cookies for Santa
5	1991	$25	QX 436-9	Let It Snow!
6/Final	1992	$20-22	QX 446-1	Sweet Holiday Harmony

Complete series $210-217 MIB

CRAYOLA® Crayon

Series#	Year	Price	Item#	Description
1	1989	$48	QX 435-2	Bright Journey
2	1990	$44	QX 458-6	Bright Moving Colors
3	1991	$35	QX 421-9	Bright Vibrant Carols
4	1992	$35	QX 426-4	Bright Blazing Colors
5	1993	$25	QX 442-2	Bright Shining Castle
6	1994	$25	QX 527-3	Bright Playful Colors
7	1995	$18	QX 524-7	Bright 'n Sunny Tepee
8	1996	$16-18	QX 539-1	Bright Flying Colors

Complete series $246-248 MIB

Dickens' Caroler Bell Special Ed.

Series#	Year	Price	Item#	Description
1	1990	$35	QX 505-6	Mr. Ashbourne
2	1991	$48	QX 503-9	Mrs. Beaumont
3	1992	$45	QX 455-4	Lord Chadwick
4/Final	1993	$45	QX 550-5	Lady Daphne

Complete series $173 MIB

Dolls of the World, Dated

Series#	Year	Price	Item#	Description
1	1996	$25 up	QX 556-1	Native American Barbie

Complete series $25 up MIB

Fabulous Decade, Dated

Series#	Year	Price	Item#	Description
1	1990	$38	QX 446-6	Squirrel w/ Brass 1990
2	1991	$38	QX 411-9	Raccoon w/ Brass 1991
3	1992	$36	QX 424-4	Bear w/ Brass 1992
4	1993	$18	QX 447-5	Skunk w/ Brass 1993
5	1994	$20	QX 526-3	Rabbit w/ Brass 1994
6	1995	$16	QX 514-7	Otter w/ brass 1995
7	1996	$12.50	QX 566-1	Fox w/ brass 1996

Complete series $178.50 MIB

Football Legends, Dated

Series#	Year	Price	Item#	Description
1	1995	$35	QXI 575-9	Joe Montana
2	1996	$25-28 up	QXI 502-1	Troy Aikman

Complete series $60-63 MIB

Frosty Friends, Dated Eskimo

Series#	Year	Price	Item#	Description
1	1980	$550-650	QX 137-4	A Cool Yule
2	1981	$365	QX 433-5	Igloo
3	1982	$280	QX 452-3	Icicle
4	1983	$280	QX 400-7	Rubbing Noses w/ White Seal
5	1984	$80	QX 437-1	Ice Fishing/Gift
6	1985	$62	QX 482-2	Kayak
7	1986	$65	QX 405-3	Wreath Around Baby Reindeer's Neck
8	1987	$55	QX 440-9	Seal w/ Gift on Nose
9	1988	$65	QX 403-1	Wrapping Red Ribbon around North Pole
10	1989	$42	QX 457-2	Sled
11	1990	$30	QX 439-6	Sliding Down Iceberg
12	1991	$38	QX 432-7	Ice Hockey
13	1992	$25	QX 429-1	Whale
14	1993	$25	QX 414-2	Dog/Doghouse
15	1994	$24	QX 529-3	Polar Bear Jumping through Wreath
16	1995	$28	QX 516-9	Eskimo on snow mobile
17	1996	$14	QX 568-1	Playing Pool

Complete series $2,028-2,128 MIB

Gift Bringers, The, Dated Balls

Series#	Year	Price	Item#	Description
1	1989	$17	QX 279-5	St. Nicholas
2	1990	$15	QX 280-3	St. Lucia
3	1991	$20	QX 211-7	Christkindl
4	1992	$18	QX 212-4	Kolyada
5/Final	1993	$18	QX 206-5	The Magi

Complete series $88 MIB

Greatest Story, Dated

Series#	Year	Price	Item#	Description
1	1990	$26	QX 465-6	Brass Snowflake w/ White Porcelain Nativity
2	1991	$30	QX 412-9	Shepherds Gaze at the Star
3/Final	1992	$20	QX 425-1	Wise Men Offer their Gifts

Complete series $76 MIB

Hark! It's Herald, Dated

Series#	Year	Price	Item#	Description
1	1989	$25	QX 455-5	Elf w/ Xylophone
2	1990	$18	QX 446-3	Elf w/ Drum
3	1991	$24	QX 437-9	Elf w/ Golden Fife
4/Final	1992	$18	QX 446-4	Elf w/ Baritone

Complete series $85 MIB

Heart of Christmas, Dated

Series#	Year	Price	Item#	Description
1	1990	$75	QX 472-6	Santa Filing the Stockings
2	1991	$35	QX 435-7	Bringing Home the Tree
3	1992	$26	QX 441-1	Decorating the Tree
4	1993	$28	QX 448-2	Sleigh Ride
5/Final	1994	$21	QX 526-6	Family/Christmas Dinner

Complete series $185 MIB

Heavenly Angels, Dated

Series#	Year	Price	Item#	Description
1	1991	$32	QX 436-7	Baroque Angels, ivory antique
2	1992	$28	QX 445-4	Angel w/ Trumpet
3/Final	1993	$20	QX 494-5	Angel w/ Dove

Complete series $80 MIB

Collectible Ornament Series

Here Comes Santa, Dated

Complete series $2,103.50-2,106.50 MIB

Series#	Year	Price	Item#	Description
1	1979	$625	QX 155-9	Santa's Motorcar
2	1980	$185	QX 143-4	Santa's Express
3	1981	$265	QX 438-2	Rooftop Deliveries
4	1982	$130	QX 464-3	Jolly Trolley
5	1983	$280	QX 403-7	Santa Express
6	1984	$90	QX 432-4	Santa's Deliveries
7	1985	$57.50	QX 496-5	Santa's Fire Engines
8	1986	$60	QX 404-3	Kringle's Kool Treats
9	1987	$80	QX 484-7	Santa's Woody
10	1988	$42	QX 400-1	Kringle Koach
11	1989	$50	QX 458-5	Christmas Caboose
12	1990	$40	QX 492-3	Festive Surrey
13	1991	$45	QX 434-9	Antique Car
14	1992	$35	QX 434-1	Kringle Tours
15	1993	$32	QX 410-2	Happy Haul-idays
16	1994	$45	QX 529-6	Makin' Tractor Tracks
17	1995	$20	QX 517-9	Santa's Roadster
18	1996	$22-25	QX 568-4	Santa's 4x4

Holiday Barbie™, Dated

Complete series $235-237 MIB

Series#	Year	Price	Item#	Description
1	1993	$125	QX 572-5	Red Gown
2	1994	$55	QX 521-6	Gold/Ivory Gown
3	1995	$35	QXI 505-7	Green/White
4	1996	$20-22	QXI 537-1	Gold Gown w/ Red Overcoat trimmed in fur

Holiday Heirloom

Complete series $99 MIB

Series#	Year	Price	Item#	Description
1	1987	$32	QX 485-7	Glass Bell in Wreath
2	1988	$34	QX 406-4	Silver Angels Above Glass Bell
3/Final	1989	$33	QXC 460-5	Toys Above Glass Bell

Holiday Wildlife

Complete series $584 MIB

Series#	Year	Price	Item#	Description
1	1982	$395	QX 313-3	Cardinalis Cardinalis
2	1983	$78	QX 309-9	Black-Capped Chickadees
3	1984	$28	QX 347-4	Ring-Necked Pheasant
4	1985	$25	QX 376-5	California Partridge
5	1986	$25	QX 321-6	Cedar Waxwing
6	1987	$15	QX 371-7	Snow Goose
7/Final	1988	$18	QX 371-1	Purple Finch

Hoop Stars, Dated

Complete series $42-56 MIB

Series#	Year	Price	Item#	Description
1	1995	$20-30	QXI 551-7	Shaqille O'Neal
2	1996	$22-26	QXI 501-4	Larry Bird

Kiddie Car Classics, Dated

Complete series $98-114 MIB

Series#	Year	Price	Item#	Description
1	1994	$50-60	QX 542-6	Murray® Champion
2	1995	$30	QX 502-7	Murray® Fire Truck
3	1996	$18-24	QX 536-4	Murray® Airplane

Lionel®, Dated

Complete series $30-40 MIB

Series#	Year	Price	Item#	Description
1	1996	$30-40	QX 553-1	700E Hudson Steam Locomotive

Madame Alexander, Dated

Complete series $22-30 MIB

Series#	Year	Price	Item#	Description
1	1996	$22-30	QX 631-1	Cinderella

Mary's Angels

Complete series $271-278 MIB

Series#	Year	Price	Item#	Description
1	1988	$35	QX 407-4	Buttercup
2	1989	$55-60	QX 454-5	Bluebell
3	1990	$38	QX 442-3	Rosebud
4	1991	$38	QX 427-9	Iris
5	1992	$45	QX 427-4	Lily
6	1993	$20	QX 428-2	Ivy
7	1994	$15	QX 527-6	Jasmine
8	1995	$15	QX 514-9	Camellia
9	1996	$10-12	QX 566-4	Violet

Merry Olde Santa, Dated

Complete series $280-287 MIB

Series#	Year	Price	Item#	Description
1	1990	$65	QX 473-6	Santa Holding Mini Christmas Tree
2	1991	$85	QX 435-9	Santa w/ Bag of Toys, Cane w/ Bell
3	1992	$22-25	QX 441-4	Santa Filling a Stocking
4	1993	$30	QX 484-2	Santa w/ Bell and Ice Skates
5	1994	$30	QX 525-6	Santa w/ Wreath and Lantern
6	1995	$28	QX 513-9	Santa w/ bag of goodies
7	1996	$20-24	QX 565-4	Fourth of July Santa

Miniature creche

Complete series $152 MIB

Series#	Year	Price	Item#	Description
1	1985	$25	QX 482-5	Wood and Woven Straw
2	1986	$62	QX 407-6	Fine Porcelain
3	1987	$22	QX 481-9	Multi-Plated Brass
4	1988	$20	QX 403-4	Acrylic
5/Final	1989	$23	QX 459-2	Handcrafted

Mother Goose

Complete series $104-106 MIB

Series#	Year	Price	Item#	Description
1	1993	$28-30	QX 528-2	Humpty-Dumpty
2	1994	$38	QX 521-3	Hey Diddle, Diddle
3	1995	$22	QX 509-9	Jack and Jill
4	1996	$16	QX 564-4	Mary had a Little Lamb

Mr. and Mrs. Claus

Complete series $462 MIB

Series#	Year	Price	Item#	Description
1	1986	$100	QX 402-6	Merry Mistletoe Time
2	1987	$50	QX 483-7	Home Cooking
3	1988	$50	QX 401-1	Shall We Dance
4	1989	$52	QX 457-5	Holiday Duet
5	1990	$55	QX 439-3	Popcorn Party
6	1991	$35	QX 433-9	Checking His List
7	1992	$34	QX 429-4	Gift Exchange
8	1993	$35	QX 420-2	A Fitting Moment

9	1994	$29	QX 528-3	A Handwarming Present
10/Final	1995	$22	QX 515-7	Christmas Eve Kiss

Norman Rockwell

Series#	Year	Price	Item#	**Complete series $452 MIB**
				Description
1	1980	$220	QX 306-1	Santa's Visitors
2	1981	$45	QX 511-5	The Carolers
3	1982	$25	QX 305-3	Filling the Stockings
4	1983	$35	QX 300-7	Dress Rehearsal
5	1984	$35	QX 341-1	Caught Napping
6	1985	$30	QX 374-5	Jolly Postman
7	1986	$20	QX 321-3	Checking Up
8	1987	$22	QX 370-7	The Christmas Dance
9/Final	1988	$20	QX 370-4	And To All a Good Night

Nostalgic Houses and Shops

Series#	Year	Price	Item#	**Complete series $1002-1004 MIB**
				Description
1	1984	$180	QX 448-1	Victorian Doll house
2	1985	$110	QX 497-5	Old-Fashioned Toy Shop
3	1986	$260	QX 403-3	Christmas Candy Shoppe
4	1987	$70	QX 483-9	House on Main Street
5	1988	$50	QX 401-4	Hall Bro's Card Shop
6	1989	$60	QX 458-2	U.S. Post Office
7	1990	$60	QX 469-6	Holiday Home
8	1991	$62	QX 413-9	Fire Station
9	1992	$38	QX 425-4	Five-and-Ten-Cent Store
10	1993	$40	QX 417-5	Cozy Home
11	1994	$32	QX 528-6	Neighborhood Drugstore
12	1995	$22	QX 515-9	Town Church
13	1996	$18-20	QX 567-1	Victorian Painted Lady

Owliver

Series#	Year	Price	Item#	**Complete series $50 MIB**
				Description
1	1992	$16	QX 454-4	*Owliday Tales*
2	1993	$18	QX 542-5	Owliver Sleeping by Squirrel
3/Final	1994	$16	QX 522-6	Owliver/Woodpeckers Trimming Tree Stump

Peace On Earth, Dated

Series#	Year	Price	Item#	**Complete series $77 MIB**
				Description
1	1991	$30	QX 512-9	Italy
2	1992	$25	QX 517-4	Spain
3/Final	1993	$22	QX 524-2	Poland

Peanuts® Gang

Series#	Year	Price	Item#	**Complete series $117.50-120.50 MIB**
				Description
1	1993	$58	QX 531-5	Charlie Brown and Snow Man
2	1994	$22.50	QX 520-3	Lucy/Football w/ Red Ribbon
3	1995	$22	QX 505-9	Linus on sled
4/Final	1996	$15-18	QX 538-1	Sally making her list

Porcelain Bear

Series#	Year	Price	Item#	**Complete series $298.50 MIB**
				Description
1	1983	$70	QX 428-9	Cinnamon Bear w/ Top
2	1984	$35	QX 454-1	Cinnamon Bear w/ Jingle Bell
3	1985	$60	QX 479-2	Cinnamon Bear w/ Candy Cane
4	1986	$35	QX 405-6	Cinnamon Bear w/ Gift Behind Back
5	1987	$22.50	QX 442-7	Cinnamon Bear Digging in Sock
6	1988	$32	QX 404-4	Cinnamon Bear w/ Heart
7	1989	$24	QX 461-5	Cinnamon Bear Eating Candy
8/Final	1990	$20	QX 442-6	Cinnamon Bear w/ Christmas Tree

Puppy Love

Series#	Year	Price	Item#	**Complete series $151.50-154 MIB**
				Description
1	1991	$45	QX 537-9	Cocker Spaniel on Candy Cane
2	1992	$40	QX 448-4	Grey/White Terrier in Basket
3	1993	$24	QX 504-5	Golden Retriever on Sled
4	1994	$18.50	QX 525-3	White Poodle Tangled in Green Garland
5	1995	$14	QX 513-7	Puppy helping wrap presents
6	1996	$10-12.50	QX 565-1	Brown puppy begging for bone in stocking

Reindeer Champs

Series#	Year	Price	Item#	**Complete series $332-337 MIB**
				Description
1	1986	$125	QX 422-3	Dasher
2	1987	$45-50	QX 480-9	Dancer
3	1988	$35	QX 405-1	Prancer
4	1989	$18	QX 456-2	Vixen
5	1990	$24	QX 443-3	Comet
6	1991	$32	QX 434-7	Cupid
7	1992	$33	QX 528-4	Donder
8/Final	1993	$20	QX 433-1	Blitzen

Rocking Horse, Dated

Series#	Year	Price	Item#	**Complete series $1,743-1,747 MIB**
				Description
1	1981	$550	QX 422-2	Dappled
2	1982	$325	QX 502-3	Black
3	1983	$275	QX 417-7	Russet
4	1984	$65	QX 435-4	Appaloosa
5	1985	$65	QX 493-2	Pinto
6	1986	$60	QX 401-6	Palomino
7	1987	$58-60	QX 482-9	White
8	1988	$45	QX 402-4	Dappled Gray
9	1989	$38	QX 462-2	Bay
10	1990	$90	QX 464-6	Brown/White Dappled
11	1991	$37	QX 414-7	Buckskin
12	1992	$34	QX 426-1	Brown w/ White Feet
13	1993	$35	QX 416-2	Gray w/ White Feet
14	1994	$28	QX 501-6	Dark Brown w/ White Stockings
15	1995	$22	QX 516-7	Painted pony w/ red saddle
16/Final	1996	$16-18	QX 567-4	Black w/ White mane and tail

SNOOPY® and Friends, Dated

Series#	Year	Price	Item#	**Complete series $538 MIB**
				Description
1	1979	$128	QX 141-9	Ice-Hockey Holiday
2	1980	$115	QX 154-1	Ski Holiday
3	1981	$90	QX 436-2	SNOOPY® and Friends (Sledding)
4	1982	$120	QX 480-3	SNOOPY® and Friends (Sleigh on Chimney)
5/Final	1983	$85	QX 416-9	Santa SNOOPY®

Thimble

Series#	Year	Price	Item#		Complete series $1,012 MIB
					Description
1	1978	$300	QX 133-6		Mouse in a Thimble
2	1979	$150	QX 131-9		A Christmas Salute
3	1980	$150	QX 132-1		Thimble Elf
4	1981	$140	QX 413-5		Thimble Angel
5	1982	$60	QX 451-3		Thimble Mouse
6	1983	$35	QX 401-7		Thimble Elf
7	1984	$55	QX 430-4		Thimble Angel
8	1985	$35	QX 472-5		Thimble Santa
9	1986	$22	QX 406-6		Thimble Partridge
10	1987	$25	QX 441-9		Thimble Drummer
11	1988	$20	QX 405-4		Thimble Snowman
12/Final	1989	$20	QX 455-2		Thimble Puppy

Tin Locomotive

Series#	Year	Price	Item#		Complete series $1,120-1,130 MIB
					Description
1	1982	$500	QX 460-3		Blue
2	1983	$250	QX 404-9		Green and Red
3	1984	$80	QX 440-4		Red w/ Blue and Grey
4	1985	$70	QX 497-2		Black
5	1986	$65	QX 403-6		Red and Yellow
6	1987	$60-65	QX 484-9		Green and Blue
7	1988	$50	QX 400-4		Brown and Blue
8/Final	1989	$45-50	QX 460-2		Grey and Green

Tobin Fraley Carousel

Series#	Year	Price	Item#		Complete series $153-163 MIB
					Description
1	1992	$30-35	QX 489-1		White
2	1993	$30-35	QX 550-2		White
3	1994	$58	QX 522-3		White
4/Final	1995	$35	QX 506-9		White

Twelve Days of Christmas, Dated

Series#	Year	Price	Item#		Complete series $562 MIB
					Description
1	1984	$275	QX 348-4		Partridge in a Pear Tree
2	1985	$65	QX 371-2		Two Turtle Doves
3	1986	$44	QX 378-6		Three French Hens
4	1987	$30	QX 370-9		Four Colly Birds
5	1988	$26	QX 371-4		Five Golden Rings
6	1989	$16	QX 381-2		Six Geese A-Laying
7	1990	$22	QX 303-3		Seven Swans A Swimming
8	1991	$18	QX 308-9		Eight Maids A Milking
9	1992	$18	QX 303-1		Nine Ladies Dancing
10	1993	$20	QX 301-2		Ten Lords a Leaping
11	1994	$16	QX 318-3		Eleven Pipers Piping
12/Final	1995	$12	QX 300-9		Twelve Drummers drumming

U.S. Christmas Stamps

Series#	Year	Price	Item#		Complete series $59 MIB
					Description
1	1993	$26	QX 529-2		1983 Santa Stamp
2	1994	$22	QX 520-6		1982 Snow Scene from Snow, OK
3/Final	1995	$11	QX 506-7		.25 Greeting w/ Christmas tree

Windows of the World, Dated

Series#	Year	Price	Item#		Complete series $226 MIB
					Description
1	1985	$80	QX 490-2		Feliz Navidad
2	1986	$55	QX 408-3		Vrolyk Kerstfeest
3	1987	$20	QX 482-7		Mele Kalikimaka
4	1988	$27	QX 402-1		Joyeaux Noel
5	1989	$22	QX 462-5		Frohliche Weihnachten
6/Final	1990	$22	QX 463-6		Nollaig Shona

Winter Surprise

Series#	Year	Price	Item#		Complete series $92 MIB
					Description
1	1989	$18	QX 427-2		Decorating a Christmas tree
2	1990	$22	QX 444-3		Ice Skating
3	1991	$28	QX 427-7		Polar Carols
4/Final	1992	$24	QX 427-1		Building a Snowman

Wood Childhood Ornaments

Series#	Year	Price	Item#		Complete series $171 MIB
					Description
1	1984	$38	QX 439-4		Wood Lamb
2	1985	$48	QX 472-2		Wood Train
3	1986	$25	QX 407-3		Wood Reindeer
4	1987	$20	QX 441-7		Wood Horse
5	1988	$20	QX 404-1		Wood Airplane
6/Final	1989	$20	QX 459-5		Wood Truck

Yuletide Central, Dated

Series#	Year	Price	Item#		Complete series $91-98 MIB
					Description
1	1994	$45-52	QX 531-6		Locomotive
2	1995	$22	QX 507-9		Coal Car
3	1996	$24	QX 501-1		Mail Car

Lighted Ornament Series

Chris Mouse, Dated, Lighted

Series#	Year	Price	Item#		Complete series $521-526 MIB
					Description
1	1985	$75-80	QLX 703-2		Chris Mouse
2	1986	$65	QLX 705-6		Chris Mouse Dreams
3	1987	$57.50	QLX 705-7		Chris Mouse Glow
4	1988	$55	QLX 715-4		Chris Mouse Star
5	1989	$60	QLX 722-5		Chris Mouse Cookout
6	1990	$42.50	QLX 729-6		Chris Mouse Wreath
7	1991	$35	QLX 720-7		Chris Mouse Mail
8	1992	$30	QLX 707-4		Chris Mouse Tales
9	1993	$28	QLX 715-2		Chris Mouse Flight
10	1994	$28	QLX 739-3		Chris Mouse Jelly
11	1995	$25	QLX 730-7		Chris Mouse Tree
12	1996	$20	QLX 737-1		Chris Mouse Inn

Christmas Classics, Dated, Lighted

Series#	Year	Price	Item#		Complete series $246 MIB
					Description
1	1986	$85	QLX 704-3		The Nutcracker Ballet - Sugarplum Fairy
2	1987	$50	QLX 702-9		A Christmas Carol
3	1988	$30	QLX 716-1		Night Before Christmas
4	1989	$38	QLX 724-2		Little Drummer Boy
5/Final	1990	$43	QLX 730-3		The Littlest Angel

Forest Frolics, Dated, Lighted

Complete series $413 MIB

Series#	Year	Price	Item#	Description
1	1989	$90	QLX 728-2	Animals Skiing around Candy Cane
2	1990	$68	QLX 723-6	Animals in Tree House
3	1991	$65	QLX 721-9	Ice Show
4	1992	$60	QLX 725-4	Animals on Seesaw
5	1993	$50	QLX 716-5	Animals Decorating Christmas Tree
6	1994	$30	QLX 743-6	Animals Circle a Lighted Tree
7/Final	1995	$50	QLX 729-9	Forest Animals Swinging on a Wooden Swing

Journeys into Space, Dated

Complete series $35-38 MIB

Series#	Year	Price	Item#	Description
1	1996	$35-38	QLX 752-4	Freedom 7

Peanuts®, Dated, Lighted

Complete series $239 MIB

Series#	Year	Price	Item#	Description
1	1991	$55	QLX 722-9	*The stockings were hung by the chimney...*
2	1992	$50	QLX 721-4	Snoopy and Woodstock on Doghouse Roof
3	1993	$45	QLX 715-5	Snoopy and Woodstock Decorate the Tree
4	1994	$44	QLX 740-6	Snoopy and Woodstock Ringing Bells
5/Final	1995	$45	QLX 727-7	Snoopy Ice Skating

Santa and Sparky, Dated, Lighted

Complete series $185 MIB

Series#	Year	Price	Item#	Description
1	1986	$90	QLX 703-3	Lighting the Tree
2	1987	$60	QLX 701-9	Perfect Portrait
3/Final	1988	$35	QLX 719-1	On W/the Show

Tobin Fraley, Dated, Lighted & Music

Complete series $128-131 MIB

Series#	Year	Price	Item#	Description
1	1994	$48	QLX 749-6	*Skater's Waltz*
2	1995	$45	QLX 726-9	*Over the Waves*
3/Final	1996	$35-38	QLX 746-1	*On the Beautiful Blue Danube*

Show Case Ornaments

Language of Flowers, Dated

Complete series $35-40 MIB

Series#	Year	Price	Item#	Description
1	1996	$35-40	QK 117-1	Pansy

Turn of the Century Parade, Dated

Complete series $50.50-52.50 MIB

Series#	Year	Price	Item#	Description
1	1995	$32.50	QK 102-7	The Fireman
2	1996	$18-20	QK 108-4	Uncle Sam

Collectible Mini Ornament Series

Alice in Wonderland, Dated

Complete series $24 MIB

Series#	Year	Price	Item#	Description
1	1995	$13.50	QXM 477-7	Alice sitting on a thimble
2	1996	$10.50	QXM 407-4	Mad Hatter

Bearymores, The, Dated

Complete series $51 MIB

Series#	Year	Price	Item#	Description
1	1992	$18	QXM 554-4	Decorating the Tree

| 2 | 1993 | $16 | QXM 512-5 | Caroling |
| 3/Final | 1994 | $17 | QXM 513-3 | Building a Snowman |

Centuries of Santa, Dated

Complete series $44.75 MIB

Series#	Year	Price	Item#	Description
1	1994	$19.50	QXM 515-3	Santa w/ Tree
2	1995	$13.25	QXM 478-9	Santa w/ bunch of goodies
3	1996	$12	QXM 409-1	Santa w/ walking stick and lantern

Christmas Bells, Dated

Complete series $26-28 MIB

Series#	Year	Price	Item#	Description
1	1995	$16	QXM 400-7	Angel on top of bell
2	1996	$10-12	QXM 407-1	Santa on top of bell

Kittens in Toyland

Complete series $99.75 MIB

Series#	Year	Price	Item#	Description
1	1988	$24	QXM 562-1	Kitten w/ Locomotive
2	1989	$20	QXM 561-2	Kitten on Scooter
3	1990	$20	QXM 573-6	Kitten in Sailboat
4	1991	$19.50	QXM 563-9	Kitten in Airplane
5/Final	1992	$16.25	QXM 539-1	Kitten on Pogo Stick

Kringles, The, Dated

Complete series $112.50 MIB

Series#	Year	Price	Item#	Description
1	1989	$30	QXM 562-5	Santa w/ Package Behind Back
2	1990	$25	QXM 575-3	Santa Getting Ready to Leave
3	1991	$23	QXM 564-7	Mr. and Mrs. Kringle w/ Plate of Cookies
4	1992	$18.50	QXM 538-1	Mr. and Mrs. Kringle Caroling
5/Final	1993	$16	QXM 513-5	Mr. and Mrs. Kringle Holding Wreath

March of the Teddy Bears, Dated

Complete series $53.50 MIB

Series#	Year	Price	Item#	Description
1	1993	$18.50	QXM 400-5	Teddy Holding Baton
2	1994	$14	QXM 510-6	Teddy w/ Drum
3	1995	$12.50	QXM 479-9	Teddy Bear w/ Trumpet
4/Final	1996	$8.50	QXM 409-4	Teddy Bear w/ Horn

Miniature Clothespin Soldier

Complete series $21 MIB

Series#	Year	Price	Item#	Description
1	1995	$12.50	QXM 409-7	
2	1996	$8.50	QXM 414-4	

Miniature Kiddie Car Classics, Dated

Complete series $27.50 MIB

Series#	Year	Price	Item#	Description
1	1995	$15	QXM 404-9	Murray® Blue "Champion"
2	1996	$12.50 up	QXM 403-1	Murray® "Fire Truck"

Nature's Angels

Complete series $112 MIB

Series#	Year	Price	Item#	Description
1	1990	$26	QXM 573-3	Rabbit Angel in White
2	1991	$22	QXM 565-7	Puppy Angel in Blue
3	1992	$18	QXM 545-1	Bear Angel w/ Wreath
4	1993	$13.50	QXM 512-2	Kitty Angel
5	1994	$12	QXM 512-6	Skunk Angel
6	1995	$12.50	QXM 480-9	Bear Angel
7/Final	1996	$8	QXM 411-1	Squirrel Angel w/ Nut

Night Before Christmas, The, Dated — Complete series $84.50 MIB

Series#	Year	Price	Item#	Description
1	1992	$30-35	QXM 554-1	Tin House/Mouse in Rocking Chair
2	1993	$18	QXM 511-5	Children Sleeping in Bed
3	1994	$13	QXM 512-3	Pa in his Kerchief
4	1995	$16	QXM 480-7	Santa w/ bag of gifts
5/Final	1996	$7.50	QXM 410-4	Santa in Sleigh

Noel R.R., Dated — Complete series $178 MIB

Series#	Year	Price	Item#	Description
1	1989	$42.50	QXM 576-2	Blue Locomotive
2	1990	$28	QXM 575-6	Red Coal Car w/ Toys
3	1991	$25	QXM 564-9	Passenger Car
4	1992	$22.50	QXM 544-1	Box Car
5	1993	$20	QXM 510-5	Flatbed Car
6	1994	$16-20	QXM 511-3	Stock Car
7	1995	$16	QXM 481-7	Tank Car
8	1996	$8	QXM 411-4	Cookie Car

Nutcracker Ballet, Dated — Complete series $18.50 MIB

Series#	Year	Price	Item#	Description
1	1996	$18.50	QXM 406-4	Girl in Pink Dress

Nutcracker Guild, Dated — Complete series $41.95 MIB

Series#	Year	Price	Item#	Description
1	1994	$15	QXM 514-6	Nutcracker w/ Rolling Pin
2	1995	$14	QXM 478-7	Nutcracker w/ Gifts
3	1996	$12.95	QXM 408-4	Nutcracker w/ Fishing supplies

Old English Village Series, Dated — Complete series $209.50 MIB

Series#	Year	Price	Item#	Description
1	1988	$38	QXM 563-4	Family Home
2	1989	$35	QXM 561-5	Sweet Shop
3	1990	$23	QXM 576-3	School
4	1991	$27.50	QXM 562-7	Inn
5	1992	$28	QXM 538-4	Church
6	1993	$17.50	QXM 513-2	Toy Shop
7	1994	$17	QXM 514-3	Hat Shop
8	1995	$14	QXM 481-9	Tudor House
9	1996	$9.50	QXM 412-4	Village Mill

On the Road, Dated — Complete series $50.50 MIB

Series#	Year	Price	Item#	Description
1	1993	$15	QXM 400-2	Pressed Tin Station Wagon
2	1994	$14	QXM 510-3	Pressed Tin Van
3	1995	$12	QXM 479-7	Pressed Tin Fire Engine
4	1996	$9.50	QXM 410-1	Pressed Tin Truck

Penguin Pal — Complete series $75.50 MIB

Series#	Year	Price	Item#	Description
1	1988	$24	QXM 563-1	Penguin w/ Gift
2	1989	$18	QXM 560-2	Penguin w/ Candy Cane
3	1990	$18.50	QXM 574-6	Penguin on Green Skis
4/Final	1991	$15	QXM 562-9	Penguin on Ice Skates

Rocking Horse, Dated — Complete series $186 MIB

Series#	Year	Price	Item#	Description
1	1988	$42	QXM 562-4	Dappled horse w/ Red Rockers
2	1989	$28	QXM 560-5	Palomino w/ Blue Rockers
3	1990	$25	QXM 574-3	Pinto w/ Turquoise Rockers
4	1991	$25	QXM 563-7	Grey Arabian w/ Red Rockers
5	1992	$18	QXM 545-4	Brown w/ Green Rockers
6	1993	$14.50	QXM 511-2	Appalosa Black w/ Red Rockers
7	1994	$13	QXM 511-6	White w/ Tan Rockers
8	1995	$12-15	QXM 482-7	Brown Spotted Horse w/ Blue & Green Rocker
9	1996	$8.50	QXM 412-1	Spotted Horse w/ Red Rockers

Santa's Little Big Top, Dated — Complete series $21.50 MIB

Series#	Year	Price	Item#	Description
1	1995	$12-14	QXM 477-9	Santa is putting on his circus show
2	1996	$9.50	QXM 408-1	Clowns on Balls

Thimble Bells, Dated Porcelain — Complete series $80 MIB

Series#	Year	Price	Item#	Description
1	1990	$21	QXM 554-3	Rabbits
2	1991	$22.50	QXM 565-9	Year w/ Holly Enclosure
3	1992	$20.50	QXM 546-1	Teddy Bear and Holly
4/Final	1993	$16	QXM 514-2	Poinsettia

Woodland Babies — Complete series $39 MIB

Series#	Year	Price	Item#	Description
1	1991	$14.50	QXM 566-7	Baby Squirrel in Nutshell Cradle
2	1992	$12.50	QXM 544-4	Baby Raccoon Sleeping in a Leaf
3/Final	1993	$12	QXM 510-2	Baby Beaver on Tree Branch

Easter Ornament Series

Appple Blossom Lane, Dated — Complete series $39.45 MIB

Series#	Year	Price	Item#	Description
1	1995	$18.50	QEO 820-7	
2	1996	$12	QEO 808-4	Rabbit's house
3/Final	1997	$8.95	QEO 866-2	Apple Blossom Lane

Beatrix Potter — Complete series $63.95 MIB

Series#	Year	Price	Item#	Description
1	1996	$55-65	QEO 807-1	Peter Rabbit™
2	1997	$8.95	QEO 864-5	Jemima Puddle-duck™

Children's Collector Barbie™ — Complete series $29.90 MIB

Series#	Year	Price	Item#	Description
1	1997	$29.90	QEO 863-5	Barbie™ as Rapunzel

Collector's Plate, Dated, Porcelain — Complete series $69.95 MIB

Series#	Year	Price	Item#	Description
1	1994	$32	QEO 823-3	"Gathering Sunny Memories 1994"
2	1995	$18	QEO 821-9	Rabbits flying kites
3	1996	$12	QEO 822-1	"Keeping a secret"
4/Final	1997	$7.95	QEO 867-5	"Sunny Sunday Best"

Cotton Tail Express, Dated — Complete series $28.95 MIB

Series#	Year	Price	Item#	Description
1	1996	$20	QEO 807-4	Locomotive
2	1997	$8.95	QEO 865-2	Coal Car

Easter Parade, Dated — Complete series $67 MIB

Series#	Year	Price	Item#	Description
1	1992	$26	QEO 930-1	Rabbit Conductor
2	1993	$21	QEO 832-5	Rabbit playing xylophone
3/Final	1994	$20	QEO 813-6	Rabbit Trumpeter

Eggs in Sports — Complete series $78.50 MIB

Series#	Year	Price	Item#	Description
1	1992	$38	QEO 934-1	Baseball
2	1993	$18.50	QEO 833-2	Tennis
3/Final	1994	$22	QEO 813-3	Golf

Garden Club, Dated — Complete series $40.95 MIB

Series#	Year	Price	Item#	Description
1	1995	$21	QEO 820-9	Chipmunk w/ flowers
2	1996	$12	QEO 809-1	Skunk smelling flowers
3	1997	$7.95	QEO 866-5	Garden Club

Here Comes Easter, Dated — Complete series $68.95 MIB

Series#	Year	Price	Item#	Description
1	1994	$30	QEO 809-3	Rabbit in car
2	1995	$18.50	QEO 821-7	Helicopter
3	1996	$12.50	QEO 809-4	Rabbit w/ chick in bed of truck
4/Final	1997	$7.95	QEO 868-2	Duck in boat

Joyful Angels — Complete series $30.95 MIB

Series#	Year	Price	Item#	Description
1	1996	$20	QEO 818-4	Pink dress carrying flowers
2	1997	$10.95	QEO 865-5	Joyful Angels

Sidewalk Cruisers — Complete series $12.95 MIB

Series#	Year	Price	Item#	Description
1	1997	$12.95	QEO 863-2	1935 Velocipede by Murray®

Springtime Barbie, Dated — Complete series $78.45 MIB

Series#	Year	Price	Item#	Description
1	1995	$35	QEO 806-9	
2	1996	$17.50	QEO 808-1	Pink dress
3/Final	1997	$25.95	QEO 864-2	

Springtime Bonnets, Dated — Complete series $93.95 MIB

Series#	Year	Price	Item#	Description
1	1993	$32	QEO 832-2	Rabbit in purple and white dress
2	1994	$25	QEO 809-6	Rabbit in pink dress
3	1995	$14	QEO 822-7	
4	1996	$15-16	QEO 813-4	Rabbit in Dress/Umbrella
5/Final	1997	$7.95	QEO 867-2	

Hallmark Keepsake Ornament Collector's Club Ornaments

Year	Item #	Description	Comments	Price
1987	QXC 480-9	Wreath of Memories, Dated	Membership	$50
1987	QXC 581-7	Carousel Reindeer	Members Only	$60
1988	QXC 580-4	Our Clubhouse, Dated	Membership	$38
1988	QXC 570-4	Hold On Tight, Mini	Early Renewal Gift	$75
1988	QXC 580-1	Sleighful of Dreams	Members Only	$68
1988	QX 406-4	Holiday Heirloom, II	Club - LE 34,600	$34
1988	QX 408-4	Angelic Minstrel	Club - LE 49,900	$42.50
1988	QX 407-1	Christmas Is Sharing	Club - LE 49,900	$40
1989	QXC 580-2	Visit From Santa, Dated	Membership	$45
1989	QXC 428-5	Collect A Dream	Members Only	$55
1989	QXC 581-2	Sitting Purty, Mini	Special Gift	$30
1989	QXC 451-2	Christmas Is Peaceful	Club - LE 49,900	$40
1989	QXC 448-3	Noelle	Club - LE 49,900	$50
1989	QXC 460-5	Holiday Heirloom, III	Club - LE 34,600	$33
1990	QXC 445-6	Club Hollow, Dated	Membership	$35
1990	QXC 445-3	Armful of Joy	Members Only	$40
1990	QXC 560-3	Crown Prince, Mini	Special Gift	$34
1990	QXC 447-6	Dove of Peace	Club - LE 25,400	$70
1990	QXC 476-6	Christmas Limited	Club - LE 38,700	$105
1990	QXC 447-3	Sugar Plum Fairy	Club - LE 25,400	$55
1991	QXC 476-9	Hidden Treasure/Li'l Keeper	Membership	$38
1991	QXC 315-9	Five Years Together	Charter Member Gift	$45
1991	QXC 725-9	Beary Artistic (Lighted)	Members Only	$38
1991	QXC 479-7	Secrets for Santa	Club - LE 28,700	$60
1991	QXC 477-9	Galloping Into Christmas	Club - LE 28,400	$95
1992	QXC 508-1	Rodney Takes Flight	Membership	$20
1992	QXC 729-1	Santa's Club List	Members Only	$36
1992	QXC 519-4	Chipmunk Parcel Service, Mini	Special Gift	$18
1992	QXC 546-4	Christmas Treasures	Club - LE 15,500	$125-150
1992	QXC 406-7	Victorian Skater	Club - LE 14,700	$70
1993	QXC 527-2	It's in the Mail	Membership	$22.50
1993	QXC 543-2	Trimmed W/ Memories	Members Only	$32
1993	QXC 543-5	Sharing Christmas	Club - LE 16,500	$45
1993	QXC 544-2	Gentle Tidings	Club - LE 17,500	$48
1993	QXC 529-4	Forty Winks, Mini	Membership	$21
1994	QXC	First Hello	Membership	—
1994	QXC	Happy Collecting MM	Renewal Bonus	—
1994	QXC 482-3	Holiday Pursuit	Membership	$22
1994	QXC 483-3	Jolly Holly Santa	Club - LE	$50
1994	QXC 483-6	Majestic Deer	Club - LE	$45
1994	QXC 485-3	On Cloud Nine	Members Only	$28
1994	QXC 480-6	Sweet Bouquet - Mini	Membership	$20
1995	QXC 416-7	1958 Ford Edsel Citation Conv.	Members Only	$65

1995	QXC 539-7	Barbie™: Brunette Debut - 1959	Members Only	$40 up
1995	QXC 105-9	Home From The Woods	Members Only	$35
1995	QXC 412-9	A Gift From Rodney - Mini	Membership	$14
1995	QXM 411-7	Collecting Memories	Membership	$18
1995	QXM 445-7	Cool Santa - Mini	Membership	$16
1995	QXM 520-7	Fishing for Fun	Membership	$20
1996	QXC 416-4	Santa, Dated	Membership	$20-22
1996	QXC 734-1	Rudolph the Red-Nosed Reindeer®, Dated	Membership	$25-30
1996		Rudolph's Helper, Dated	Membership	$8.50
1996		Happy Holidays® Barbie®, Dated	Members Only	$25-30
1996	QX 536-4	Steelcraft Auburn by Murray®, Dated	Members Only	$18-22
1996		The Wizard of OZ™	Members Only	$50 up
1996		Airmail for Santa, Dated	Special Gift	$18

Special Edition Mini Ornaments

Year	Item#	Description	Price
1989	QXM 563-2	Santa's Magic Ride	$12.50
1990	QXM 553-3	Cloisonne Poinsettia	$17.50
1994	QXM 410-6	Noah's Ark	$55
1995	QXM 483-9	A Moustershire Christmas	$35
1996	QXM 420-4	O Holy Night	$26

Precious Edition Mini Ornaments

Year	Item #	Description	Price
1991	QXM 567-9	Silvery Santa	$21.50
1992	QXM 536-4	Holiday Holly, gold plated	$16
1993	QXM 401-2	Cloisonne Snowflake	$19
1994	QXM 402-6	Dazzling Reindeer	$17.50
1995	QXM 401-7	Cloisonne Partridge	$18
1996	QXM 426-4	Sparkling Crystal Angel	$14.95

Star Trek Ornaments

Year	Item#	Description	Price
1991	QLX 719-9	Starship Enterprise	$250-300
1992	QLX 733-1	Shuttlecraft Galileo	$40-45
1993	QLX 741-2	U.S.S. Enterprise™	$45
1994	QLX 738-6	Klingon Bird of Prey™	$38
1995	QXI 553-9	Captain James T. Kirk	$20
1995	QXI 573-7	Captain Jean-Luc Picard	$18
1995	QXI 726-7	Romulan Warbird™	$28
1996	QXI 554-4	Mr. Spock	$20-24
1996	QXI 753-4	U.S.S. Enterprise™ and Galileo Shuttlecraft™	$50-55
1996	QLX 555-1	Commander William T. Riker™	$18-20

Special Edition Ornaments

Year	Item#	Description	Price
1986	QX 429-6	Jolly St. Nick	$68
1987	QX 445-7	Favorite Santa	$30
1988	QX 411-4	The Wonderful Santacycle	$38
1989	QX 580-5	The Ornament Express	$40
1994	QX 481-3	Lucinda and Teddy	$42
1995	QX 525-9	Beverly and Teddy	$30
1996	QX 571-4	Evergreen Santa	$28

Limited Edition Ornaments

Year	Item #	Description	Size	Price
1984	QX 459-1	Classical Angel, Dated	24,700	$100
1985	QX 405-2	Heavenly Trumpeter	24,700	$95
1986	QX 429-3	Magical Unicorn	24,700	$85
1987	QX 444-9	Christmas Is Gentle	24,700	$80
1987	QX 442-9	Christmas Time Mime	24,700	$48

Lighted Special Edition

Year	Item#	Description	Price
1994	QLX 738-2	Dance of the Sugar Plum Fairy	$48-55
1995	QLX 735-7	Victorian toy Box	$50
1996	QLX 747-1	North Pole Volunteers	$65

**"Treasure map nothing!
This shows the location of the only
Hallmark store on the island."**

1973 Collection

(Deduct $15-$20 if there are "age spots.")
Ball ornaments are not in demand but would be hard to find if looking for one.

XHD 100-2   BETSEY CLARK ☐
Comments: White Glass Ball, 3-1/4" dia.
Five girls sing joyful carols as they gather around their Christmas tree.
☐ Purchased 19__Pd $_____MIB   NB   DB   BNT
☐ Want   Orig. Ret. $2.50   **NB** $70   **MIB** Sec. Mkt. **$90**

XHD 110-2   BETSEY CLARK SERIES ☐
Comments: ***FIRST IN SERIES***
Dated 1973, White Glass Ball, 3-1/4" dia.
One little girl is feeding a deer; the other is cuddling a lamb.
☐ Purchased 19__Pd $_____MIB   NB   DB   BNT
☐ Want   Orig. Ret. $2.50   **NB** $90   **MIB** Sec. Mkt. **$130**

XHD 106-2   CHRISTMAS IS LOVE ☐
Comments: White Glass Ball, 3-1/4" dia.
Two angels play mandolins; in shades of green and lavender. Caption:
"Christmas Is Love - Christmas Is You."
☐ Purchased 19__Pd $_____MIB   NB   DB   BNT
☐ Want   Orig. Ret. $2.50   **NB** $60   **MIB** Sec. Mkt. **$70**

XHD 103-5   ELVES ☐
Comments: White Glass Ball, 3-1/4" dia. Ice skating elves.
☐ Purchased 19__Pd $_____MIB   NB   DB   BNT
☐ Want   Orig. Ret. $2.50   **NB** $60   **MIB** Sec. Mkt. **$75**

XHD 102-2   MANGER SCENE ☐
Comments: White Glass Ball, 3-1/4" dia.
Designed scene on dark red background.
☐ Purchased 19__Pd $_____MIB   NB   DB   BNT
☐ Want   Orig. Ret. $2.50   **NB** $75   **MIB** Sec. Mkt. **$90**

XHD 101-5   SANTA WITH ELVES ☐
Comments: White Glass Ball, 3-1/4" dia.
☐ Purchased 19__Pd $_____MIB   NB   DB   BNT
☐ Want   Orig. Ret. $2.50   **NB** $65   **MIB** Sec. Mkt. **$85**

No secondary market value has been established for yarn and fabric ornaments found in original cellophane package.

XHD 78-5   YARN ORNAMENT - ANGEL ☐
Comments: 4-1/2" tall.
☐ Purchased 19 __Pd $_____MIB   NB   DB   BNT
☐ Want   Orig. Ret. $1.25   White Wings: **$30**
                                    Gold Wings: **$30**

XHD 85-2   YARN ORNAMENT - BLUE GIRL ☐
Comments: 4-1/2" tall.
☐ Purchased 19 __Pd $_____MIB   NB   DB   BNT
☐ Want   Orig. Ret. $1.25   Sec. Mkt. **$25**

XHD 83-2   YARN ORNAMENT - BOY CAROLER ☐
Comments: 4-1/2" tall. Blue hat and coat.
☐ Purchased 19 __Pd $_____MIB   NB   DB   BNT
☐ Want   Orig. Ret. $1.25   Sec. Mkt. **$25**

XHD 80-5   YARN ORNAMENT - CHOIR BOY ☐
Comments: 4-1/2" tall.
☐ Purchased 19   Pd $ MIB   NB   DB   BNT
☐ Want   Orig. Ret. $1.25   Sec. Mkt. **$25**

XHD 79-2   YARN ORNAMENT - ELF ☐
Comments: 4-1/2" tall.
☐ Purchased 19 __Pd $_____MIB   NB   DB   BNT
☐ Want   Orig. Ret. $1.25   Sec. Mkt. **$28**

XHD 84-5   YARN ORNAMENT - GREEN GIRL ☐
Comments: 4-1/2" tall. Green with red hat and song book.
☐ Purchased 19 __Pd $_____MIB   NB   DB   BNT
☐ Want   Orig. Ret. $1.25   Sec. Mkt. **$28**

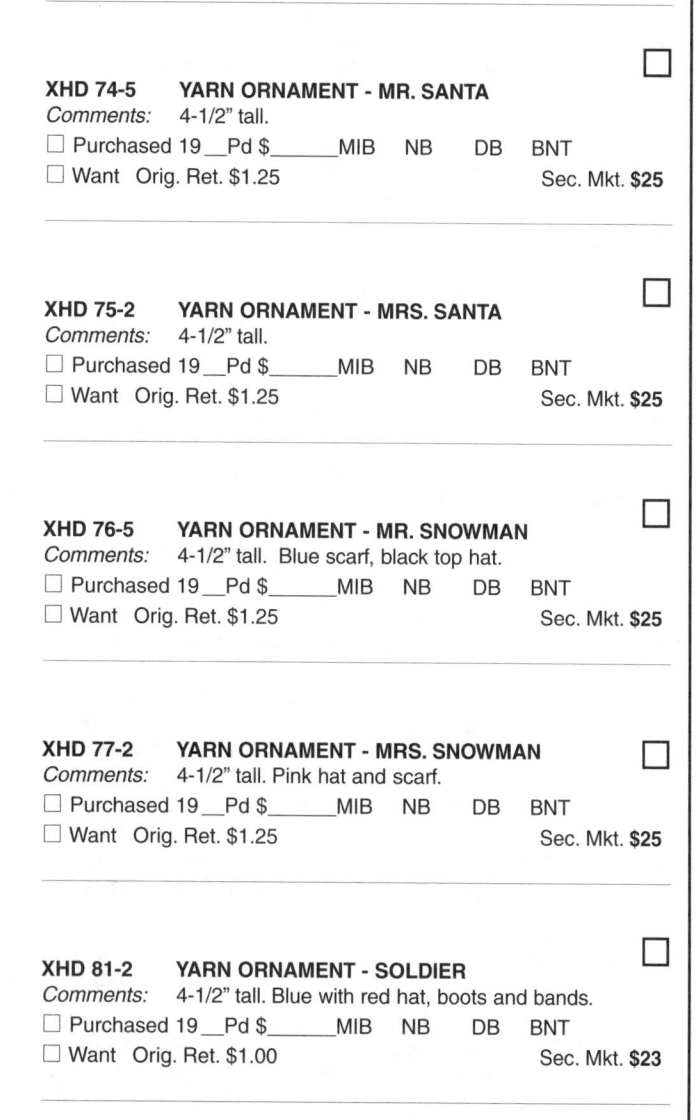

XHD 82-5   YARN ORNAMENT - LITTLE GIRL ☐
Comments: 4-1/2" tall. Pink dress, blond hair.
☐ Purchased 19 __ Pd $_____ MIB   NB   DB   BNT
☐ Want   Orig. Ret. $1.25   Sec. Mkt. **$25**

XHD 74-5   YARN ORNAMENT - MR. SANTA ☐
Comments: 4-1/2" tall.
☐ Purchased 19 __ Pd $_____ MIB   NB   DB   BNT
☐ Want   Orig. Ret. $1.25   Sec. Mkt. **$25**

XHD 75-2   YARN ORNAMENT - MRS. SANTA ☐
Comments: 4-1/2" tall.
☐ Purchased 19 __ Pd $_____ MIB   NB   DB   BNT
☐ Want   Orig. Ret. $1.25   Sec. Mkt. **$25**

XHD 76-5   YARN ORNAMENT - MR. SNOWMAN ☐
Comments: 4-1/2" tall. Blue scarf, black top hat.
☐ Purchased 19 __ Pd $_____ MIB   NB   DB   BNT
☐ Want   Orig. Ret. $1.25   Sec. Mkt. **$25**

XHD 77-2   YARN ORNAMENT - MRS. SNOWMAN ☐
Comments: 4-1/2" tall. Pink hat and scarf.
☐ Purchased 19 __ Pd $_____ MIB   NB   DB   BNT
☐ Want   Orig. Ret. $1.25   Sec. Mkt. **$25**

XHD 81-2   YARN ORNAMENT - SOLDIER ☐
Comments: 4-1/2" tall. Blue with red hat, boots and bands.
☐ Purchased 19 __ Pd $_____ MIB   NB   DB   BNT
☐ Want   Orig. Ret. $1.00   Sec. Mkt. **$23**

1974 Collection

QX 110-1   ANGEL ☐
Comments: White Glass Ball, 3-1/4" dia.
☐ Purchased 19 __ Pd $_____ MIB   NB   DB   BNT
☐ Want Orig. Ret. $2.50   **NB** $60   **MIB** Sec. Mkt. **$78**

QX 108-1   BETSEY CLARK SERIES ☐
Comments: **Second in Series,** Dated 1974.
White Glass Ball, 3-1/4" dia.
An orchestra and choir of youngsters prepare for a
Christmas celebration.
☐ Purchased 19 __ Pd $_____ MIB   NB   DB   BNT
☐ Want Orig. Ret. $2.50   **NB** $60   **MIB** Sec. Mkt. **$85**
ERROR - Sleeve Upside Down
Other ornaments have also been reported with the sleeves upside
down. Add $25-$30 over the secondary market to these.

QX 113-1   BUTTONS & BO ☐
Comments: White Glass Ball, 2-1/4" dia., Set of 2.
☐ Purchased 19 __ Pd $_____ MIB   NB   DB   BNT
☐ Want Orig. Ret. $3.50   **NB** $40   **MIB** Sec. Mkt. **$55**

QX 109-1   CHARMERS ☐
Comments: White Glass Ball, 3-1/4" dia., Dated 1974.
☐ Purchased 19 __ Pd $_____ MIB   NB   DB   BNT
☐ Want Orig. Ret. $2.50   **NB** $30   **MIB** Sec. Mkt. **$48**

QX 112-1   CURRIER & IVES ☐
Comments: White Glass Ball, 2-1/4" dia., Set of 2.
Country scenes of a winter farmstead and horse-drawn sleigh are
captured on two ornaments.
☐ Purchased 19 __ Pd $_____ MIB   NB   DB   BNT
☐ Want Orig. Ret. $3.50   **NB** $40   **MIB** Sec. Mkt. **$58**

QX 115-1   LITTLE MIRACLES ☐
Comments: White Glass Ball, 1-3/4" dia., Set of 4.
A little boy and his rabbit companion play together.
☐ Purchased 19 __ Pd $_____ MIB   NB   DB   BNT
☐ Want Orig. Ret. $4.50   **NB** $50   **MIB** Sec. Mkt. **$60**

QX 111-1   NORMAN ROCKWELL   ☐
Comments: White Glass Ball, 3-1/4" dia.
Santa wears an apron with tools in his pockets. He naps in a chair
while the elves work. The opposite side shows Santa with two boys.
☐ Purchased 19__Pd $_____MIB   NB   DB   BNT
☐ Want   Orig. Ret. $2.50   **NB** $65   **MIB** Sec. Mkt. **$82**

QX 106-1   NORMAN ROCKWELL SERIES   ☐
Comments: White Glass Ball, 3-1/4" dia., Dated 1974.
Two of Rockwell's famous illustrations on this ball include the "Jolly
Postman" and on the back, a father and son bringing home the perfect
Christmas tree.
☐ Purchased 19__Pd $_____MIB   NB   DB   BNT
☐ Want   Orig. Ret. $2.50   **NB** $65   **MIB** Sec. Mkt. **$95**

QX 114-1   RAGGEDY ANN™ AND RAGGEDY ANDY™   ☐
Comments: White Glass Ball, 1-3/4" dia.
A pretty set of 4.
☐ Purchased 19__Pd $_____MIB   NB   DB   BNT
☐ Want   Orig. Ret. $4.50   **NB** $75   **MIB** Sec. Mkt. **$88**

QX 107-1   SNOWGOOSE   ☐
Comments: White Glass Ball, 3-1/4" dia.
☐ Purchased 19__Pd $_____MIB   NB   DB   BNT
☐ Want   Orig. Ret. $2.50   **NB** $70   **MIB** Sec. Mkt. **$80**

No secondary market value has been established for yarn and fabric
ornaments found in original cellophane package.
Seldom found in original packaging.

QX 103-1   YARN ORNAMENT - ANGEL   ☐
Comments: 4-3/4" tall.
☐ Purchased 19__Pd $_____MIB   NB   DB   BNT
☐ Want   Orig. Ret. $1.50   Sec. Mkt. **$32**

QX 101-1   YARN ORNAMENT - ELF   ☐
Comments: 4-3/4" tall.
☐ Purchased 19__Pd $_____MIB   NB   DB   BNT
☐ Want   Orig. Ret. $1.50   Sec. Mkt. **$28**

QX 100-1   YARN ORNAMENT - MRS. SANTA   ☐
Comments: 4-3/4" tall. Red dress with white pinafore.
☐ Purchased 19__Pd $_____MIB   NB   DB   BNT
☐ Want   Orig. Ret. $1.50   Sec. Mkt. **$25**

QX 105-1   YARN ORNAMENT - SANTA   ☐
Comments: 4-3/4" tall. Traditional Santa in red.
☐ Purchased 19__Pd $_____MIB   NB   DB   BNT
☐ Want   Orig. Ret. $1.50   Sec. Mkt. **$26**

XHD 104-1   YARN ORNAMENT - SNOWMAN   ☐
Comments: 4-3/4" tall. Plaid scarf, black top hat.
☐ Purchased 19__Pd $_____MIB   NB   DB   BNT
☐ Want   Orig. Ret. $1.50   Sec. Mkt. **$24**

XHD 102-1   YARN ORNAMENT - SOLDIER   ☐
Comments: 4-3/4" tall. Blue with red hat and boots, white bands.
☐ Purchased 19__Pd $_____MIB   NB   DB   BNT
☐ Want   Orig. Ret. $1.50   Sec. Mkt. **$24**

1975 Collection

QX 157-1   ADORABLE ADORNMENTS: ☐
 BETSEY CLARK
Comments: 3-1/2" tall. **Artist:** Donna Lee
☐ Purchased 19__Pd $_____MIB   NB   DB   BNT
☐ Want   Orig. Ret. $2.5   **NB** $225   **MIB** Sec. Mkt. **$235**

QX 161-1   ADORABLE ADORNMENTS: ☐
 DRUMMER BOY
Comments: Handcrafted, 3-1/2" tall. **Artist:** Donna Lee
☐ Purchased 19__Pd $_____MIB   NB   DB   BNT
☐ Want   Orig. Ret. $2.50   **NB** $165   **MIB** Sec. Mkt **$235**

**If we fill our hours with regrets of yesterday and with worries
of tomorrow, we have no today in which to be thankful.**

QX 156-1 ADORABLE ADORNMENTS: MRS. SANTA ☐
Comments: Handcrafted, 3-1/2" tall.
This ornament came in an individual package. Reissued with Mr. Santa in 1981 in a box as "Mr. and Mrs. Claus." Only the original packaging proves whether or not this ornament is the 1975 version or the reissued 1981 ornament. This is why the no box price is considerably lower than MIB price. **Artist:** Donna Lee
☐ Purchased 19 __ Pd $_____ MIB NB DB BNT
☐ Want Orig. Ret. $2.50 **NB** $60 **MIB** Sec. Mkt. **$200**

QX 159-1 ADORABLE ADORNMENTS: RAGGEDY ANN™ ☐
Comments: Handcrafted, 3-1/2" tall.
RARE! Collectors are willing to pay nearly the same with or without the box. **Artist:** Donna Lee
☐ Purchased 19 __ Pd $_____ MIB NB DB BNT
☐ Want Orig. Ret. $2.50 **NB** $250 MIB Sec. Mkt. **$325**

QX 160-1 ADORABLE ADORNMENTS: RAGGEDY ANDY™ ☐
Comments: Handcrafted, 3-1/2" tall.
RARE! **Artist:** Donna Lee
☐ Purchased 19 __ Pd $_____ MIB NB DB BNT
☐ Want Orig. Ret. $2.50 **NB** $280 **MIB** Sec. Mkt. **$375**

QX 155-1 ADORABLE ADORNMENTS: SANTA ☐
Comments: Handcrafted, 3-1/2" tall.
This ornament came in an individual package. Reissued with Mrs. Santa in 1981 in box as "Mr. and Mrs. Claus." No real difference between these two years' ornaments. **Artist:** Donna Lee
☐ Purchased 19 __ Pd $_____ MIB NB DB BNT
☐ Want Orig. Ret. $2.50 **NB** $60 **MIB** Sec. Mkt. **$200**

QX 168-1 BETSEY CLARK ☐
Comments: White Satin Ball, Dated 1975, 2" dia., Set of 4.
Caption: "Christmas 1975." Four different scenes of children with the animals and birds.
☐ Purchased 19 __ Pd $_____ MIB NB DB BNT
☐ Want Orig. Ret. $4.50 **NB** $40 **MIB** Sec. Mkt. **$55**

QX 167-1 BETSEY CLARK ☐
Comments: White Satin Ball, 2-1/2" dia., Set of 2.
Caption: "Christmas 1975." Two skaters on one ornament and a girl wearing a stocking cap on the other ornament.
☐ Purchased 19 __ Pd $_____ MIB NB DB BNT
☐ Want Orig. Ret. $3.50 **NB** $25 **MIB** Sec. Mkt. **$45**

QX 163-1 BETSEY CLARK ☐
Comments: White Satin Ball, Dated 1975, 3" dia.
A youngster in pajamas says her bedtime prayers.
Artist: Linda Sickman
☐ Purchased 19 __ Pd $_____ MIB NB DB BNT
☐ Want Orig. Ret. $2.50 **NB** $25 **MIB** Sec. Mkt. **$38**

QX 133-1 BETSEY CLARK SERIES ☐
Comments: **Third in Series,** White Glass Ball, 3-1/4" dia.
Caption: "Christmas 1975" Three girls dressed in pink, blue and yellow calico sing carols.
☐ Purchased 19 __ Pd $_____ MIB NB DB BNT
☐ Want Orig. Ret. $3.00 **NB** $45 **MIB** Sec. Mkt. **$65**

QX 139-1 BUTTONS & BO ☐
Comments: White Glass Ball, 1-3/4" dia., Set of 4.
Dated 1975 on back.
☐ Purchased 19 __ Pd $_____ MIB NB DB BNT
☐ Want Orig. Ret. $5.00 **NB** $35 **MIB** Sec. Mkt. **$47.50**

QX 135-1 CHARMERS ☐
Comments: White Glass Ball, 3-1/2" dia. Dated 1975 on back.
☐ Purchased 19 __ Pd $_____ MIB NB DB BNT
☐ Want Orig. Ret. $3.00 **NB** $30 **MIB** Sec. Mkt. **$42.50**

QX 164-1 CURRIER & IVES ☐
Comments: White Satin Ball, 3" dia.
Winter scene of farm house and farm buildings.
Artist: Linda Sickman
☐ Purchased 19 __ Pd $_____ MIB NB DB BNT
☐ Want Orig. Ret. $2.50 **NB** $25 **MIB** Sec. Mkt. **$40**

QX 137-1 CURRIER & IVES ☐
Comments: White Glass Ball, 2-1/4" dia., Set of 2.
Snow scenes of Victorian ice skaters and old mill.
Artist: Linda Sickman
☐ Purchased 19 __ Pd $_____ MIB NB DB BNT
☐ Want Orig. Ret. $4.00 **NB** $28 **MIB** Sec. Mkt. **$40**

The key to willpower is want-power.
Those wanting something badly enough will find the willpower to do it.

QX 140-1   LITTLE MIRACLES ☐
Comments: White Glass Ball, 1-3/4" dia., Set of 4.
A cherub frolics with his forest friends. Caption on back: "Christmas 1975."
☐ Purchased 19 __ Pd $_____ MIB   NB   DB   BNT
☐ Want   Orig. Ret. $5.00   **NB** $35   **MIB** Sec. Mkt. **$42**

QX 136-1   MARTY LINKS™ ☐
Comments: White Glass Ball, 3-1/4" dia.
On back: "Merry Christmas 1975."
☐ Purchased 19 __ Pd $_____ MIB   NB   DB   BNT
☐ Want   Orig. Ret. $3.00   **NB** $35   **MIB** Sec. Mkt. **$45**

QX 166-1   NORMAN ROCKWELL ☐
Comments: White Satin Ball, 3" dia.
Front: Santa writes in book while checking on boys through his telescope. Back: Santa with bag of toys.
☐ Purchased 19 __ Pd $_____ MIB   NB   DB   BNT
☐ Want   Orig. Ret. $2.50   **NB** $35   **MIB** Sec. Mkt. **$40**

QX 134-1   NORMAN ROCKWELL ☐
Comments: White Glass Ball, 3-1/4" dia., Dated 1975.
Santa peeks at two small boys asleep in a chair. Back: A young child is kneeling at the bed, saying prayers. Price down from 1996.
☐ Purchased 19 __ Pd $_____ MIB   NB   DB   BNT
☐ Want   Orig. Ret. $3.00   **NB** $28   **MIB** Sec. Mkt. **$40**

QX 130-1   NOSTALGIA ORNAMENTS:
DRUMMER BOY ☐
Comments: 3-1/4" dia., Reissued in 1976.
A little boy marches to the beat of his drum. **Artist:** Linda Sickman
☐ Purchased 19 __ Pd $_____ MIB   NB   DB   BNT
☐ Want   Orig. Ret. $3.50   **NB** $100   **MIB** Sec. Mkt. **$170**

QX 132-1   NOSTALGIA ORNAMENTS:
JOY ☐
Comments: 3-1/4" dia.
Rare! Baby Jesus lies peacefully in the center of the word "Joy." **Artist:** Linda Sickman
☐ Purchased 19 __ Pd $_____ MIB   NB   DB   BNT
☐ Want   Orig. Ret. $3.50   **NB** $185   **MIB** Sec. Mkt. **$240**

QX 127-1   NOSTALGIA ORNAMENTS:
LOCOMOTIVE ☐
Comments: 3-1/4" dia., Dated 1975.
Price down from 1996. **Artist:** Linda Sickman
☐ Purchased 19 __ Pd $_____ MIB   NB   DB   BNT
☐ Want   Orig. Ret. $3.50   **NB** $125   **MIB** Sec. Mkt. **$165**

QX 131-1   NOSTALGIA ORNAMENTS:
PEACE ON EARTH ☐
Comments: 3-1/4" dia., Dated 1975.
"Peace On Earth" is the perfect caption for this snowy village scene.
Artist: Linda Sickman
☐ Purchased 19 __ Pd $_____ MIB   NB   DB   BNT
☐ Want   Orig. Ret. $3.50   **NB** $125   **MIB** Sec. Mkt. **$160**

QX 128-1   NOSTALGIA ORNAMENTS:
ROCKING HORSE ☐
Comments: 3-1/4" dia., Reissued in 1976.
Artist: Linda Sickman
☐ Purchased 19 __ Pd $_____ MIB   NB   DB   BNT
☐ Want   Orig. Ret. $3.50   **NB** $110   **MIB** Sec. Mkt. **$170**

QX 129-1   NOSTALGIA ORNAMENTS:
SANTA AND SLEIGH ☐
Comments: 3-1/4" dia., RARE!
Artist: Linda Sickman
☐ Purchased 19 __ Pd $_____ MIB   NB   DB   BNT
☐ Want   Orig. Ret. $3.50   **NB** $195   **MIB** Sec. Mkt. **$255**

QX 165-1   RAGGEDY ANN™ ☐
Comments: White Satin Ball, 3" dia., Dated 1975.
A cute one! **Artist:** Linda Sickman
☐ Purchased 19 __ Pd $_____ MIB   NB   DB   BNT
☐ Want   Orig. Ret. $2.50   **NB** $30   **MIB** Sec. Mkt. **$50**

QX 138-1   RAGGEDY ANN™ AND RAGGEDY ANDY™ ☐
Comments: White Glass Ball, 2-1/4" dia., Set of 2.
Front: Ann and Andy are seated beside each other; a green wreath encircles them. Back: They hold a "Merry Christmas" banner. Front of second ornament: "Decorating the tree" Back: "Christmas 1975."
Artist: Linda Sickman
☐ Purchased 19 __ Pd $_____ MIB   NB   DB   BNT
☐ Want   Orig. Ret. $4.00   **NB** $50   **MIB** Sec. Mkt. **$68**

No secondary market value has been established for yarn and fabric ornaments found in original cellophane package.

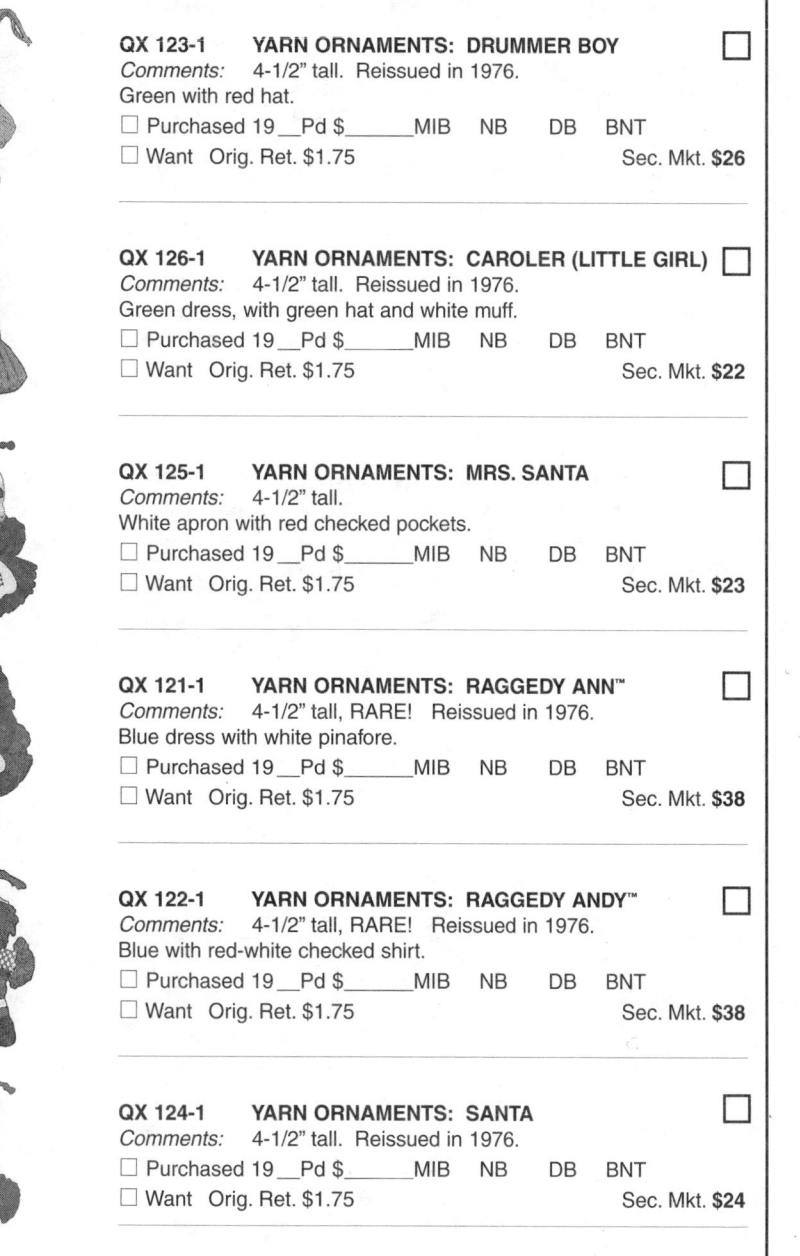

QX 123-1   YARN ORNAMENTS: DRUMMER BOY ☐
Comments: 4-1/2" tall. Reissued in 1976.
Green with red hat.
☐ Purchased 19__Pd $_____MIB   NB   DB   BNT
☐ Want   Orig. Ret. $1.75   Sec. Mkt. **$26**

QX 126-1   YARN ORNAMENTS: CAROLER (LITTLE GIRL) ☐
Comments: 4-1/2" tall. Reissued in 1976.
Green dress, with green hat and white muff.
☐ Purchased 19__Pd $_____MIB   NB   DB   BNT
☐ Want   Orig. Ret. $1.75   Sec. Mkt. **$22**

QX 125-1   YARN ORNAMENTS: MRS. SANTA ☐
Comments: 4-1/2" tall.
White apron with red checked pockets.
☐ Purchased 19__Pd $_____MIB   NB   DB   BNT
☐ Want   Orig. Ret. $1.75   Sec. Mkt. **$23**

QX 121-1   YARN ORNAMENTS: RAGGEDY ANN™ ☐
Comments: 4-1/2" tall, RARE! Reissued in 1976.
Blue dress with white pinafore.
☐ Purchased 19__Pd $_____MIB   NB   DB   BNT
☐ Want   Orig. Ret. $1.75   Sec. Mkt. **$38**

QX 122-1   YARN ORNAMENTS: RAGGEDY ANDY™ ☐
Comments: 4-1/2" tall, RARE! Reissued in 1976.
Blue with red-white checked shirt.
☐ Purchased 19__Pd $_____MIB   NB   DB   BNT
☐ Want   Orig. Ret. $1.75   Sec. Mkt. **$38**

QX 124-1   YARN ORNAMENTS: SANTA ☐
Comments: 4-1/2" tall. Reissued in 1976.
☐ Purchased 19__Pd $_____MIB   NB   DB   BNT
☐ Want   Orig. Ret. $1.75   Sec. Mkt. **$24**

1976 Collection

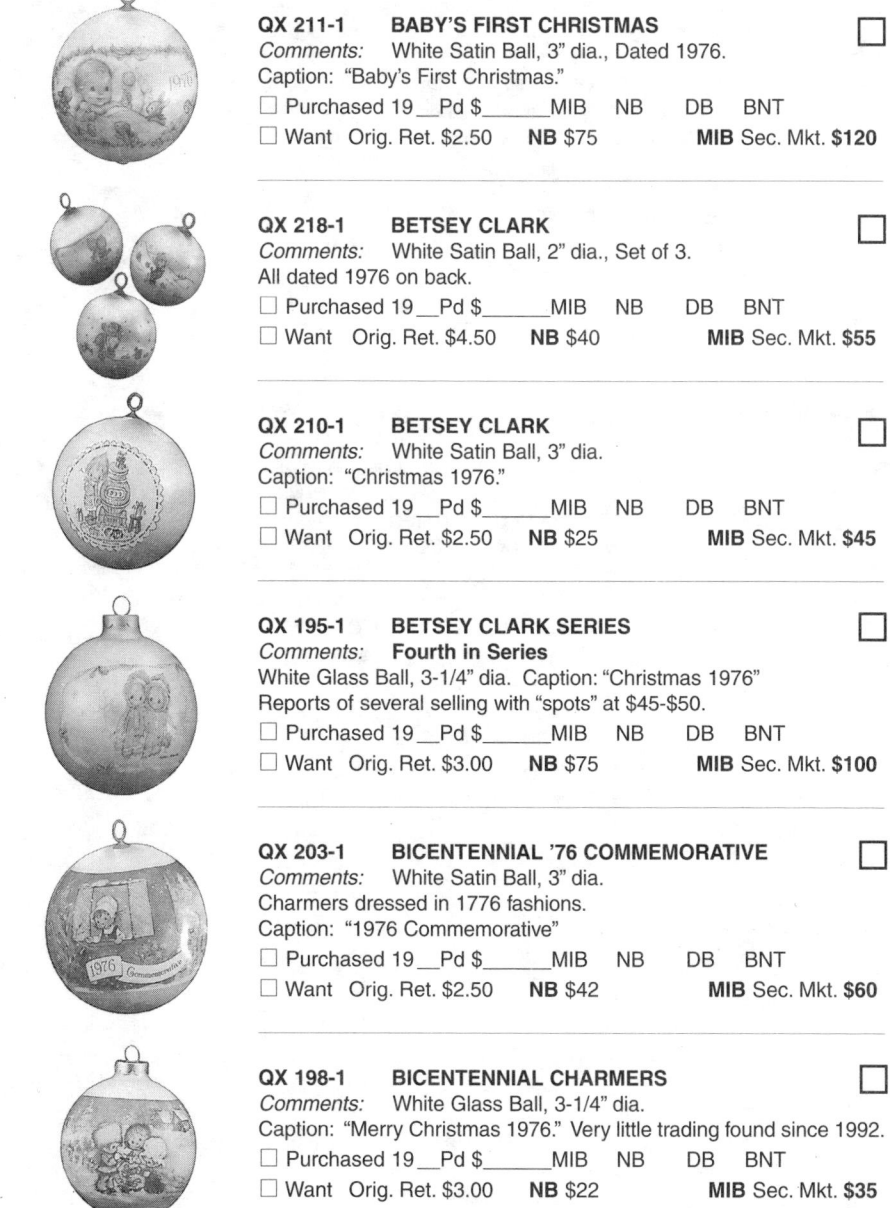

QX 211-1   BABY'S FIRST CHRISTMAS ☐
Comments: White Satin Ball, 3" dia., Dated 1976.
Caption: "Baby's First Christmas."
☐ Purchased 19__Pd $_____MIB   NB   DB   BNT
☐ Want   Orig. Ret. $2.50   **NB** $75   **MIB** Sec. Mkt. **$120**

QX 218-1   BETSEY CLARK ☐
Comments: White Satin Ball, 2" dia., Set of 3.
All dated 1976 on back.
☐ Purchased 19__Pd $_____MIB   NB   DB   BNT
☐ Want   Orig. Ret. $4.50   **NB** $40   **MIB** Sec. Mkt. **$55**

QX 210-1   BETSEY CLARK ☐
Comments: White Satin Ball, 3" dia.
Caption: "Christmas 1976."
☐ Purchased 19__Pd $_____MIB   NB   DB   BNT
☐ Want   Orig. Ret. $2.50   **NB** $25   **MIB** Sec. Mkt. **$45**

QX 195-1   BETSEY CLARK SERIES ☐
Comments: **Fourth in Series**
White Glass Ball, 3-1/4" dia. Caption: "Christmas 1976"
Reports of several selling with "spots" at $45-$50.
☐ Purchased 19__Pd $_____MIB   NB   DB   BNT
☐ Want   Orig. Ret. $3.00   **NB** $75   **MIB** Sec. Mkt. **$100**

QX 203-1   BICENTENNIAL '76 COMMEMORATIVE ☐
Comments: White Satin Ball, 3" dia.
Charmers dressed in 1776 fashions.
Caption: "1976 Commemorative"
☐ Purchased 19__Pd $_____MIB   NB   DB   BNT
☐ Want   Orig. Ret. $2.50   **NB** $42   **MIB** Sec. Mkt. **$60**

QX 198-1   BICENTENNIAL CHARMERS ☐
Comments: White Glass Ball, 3-1/4" dia.
Caption: "Merry Christmas 1976." Very little trading found since 1992.
☐ Purchased 19__Pd $_____MIB   NB   DB   BNT
☐ Want   Orig. Ret. $3.00   **NB** $22   **MIB** Sec. Mkt. **$35**

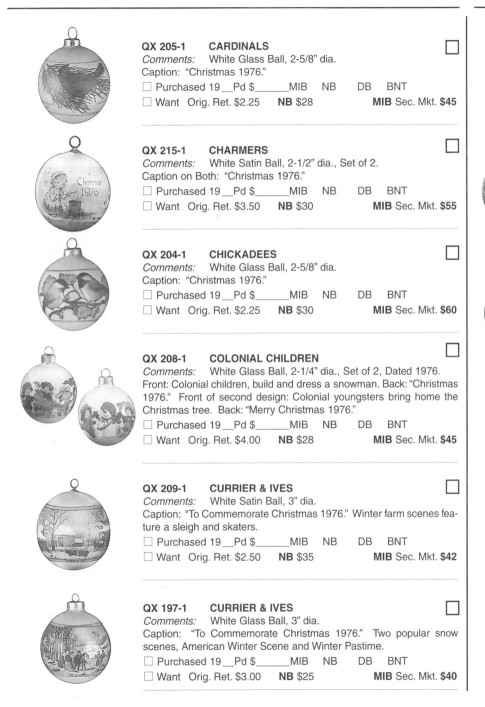

QX 205-1   CARDINALS
Comments: White Glass Ball, 2-5/8" dia.
Caption: "Christmas 1976."
☐ Purchased 19__ Pd $_____ MIB   NB   DB   BNT
☐ Want   Orig. Ret. $2.25   **NB** $28   **MIB** Sec. Mkt. **$45**

QX 215-1   CHARMERS
Comments: White Satin Ball, 2-1/2" dia., Set of 2.
Caption on Both: "Christmas 1976."
☐ Purchased 19__ Pd $_____ MIB   NB   DB   BNT
☐ Want   Orig. Ret. $3.50   **NB** $30   **MIB** Sec. Mkt. **$55**

QX 204-1   CHICKADEES
Comments: White Glass Ball, 2-5/8" dia.
Caption: "Christmas 1976."
☐ Purchased 19__ Pd $_____ MIB   NB   DB   BNT
☐ Want   Orig. Ret. $2.25   **NB** $30   **MIB** Sec. Mkt. **$60**

QX 208-1   COLONIAL CHILDREN
Comments: White Glass Ball, 2-1/4" dia., Set of 2, Dated 1976.
Front: Colonial children, build and dress a snowman. Back: "Christmas 1976." Front of second design: Colonial youngsters bring home the Christmas tree. Back: "Merry Christmas 1976."
☐ Purchased 19__ Pd $_____ MIB   NB   DB   BNT
☐ Want   Orig. Ret. $4.00   **NB** $28   **MIB** Sec. Mkt. **$45**

QX 209-1   CURRIER & IVES
Comments: White Satin Ball, 3" dia.
Caption: "To Commemorate Christmas 1976." Winter farm scenes feature a sleigh and skaters.
☐ Purchased 19__ Pd $_____ MIB   NB   DB   BNT
☐ Want   Orig. Ret. $2.50   **NB** $35   **MIB** Sec. Mkt. **$42**

QX 197-1   CURRIER & IVES
Comments: White Glass Ball, 3" dia.
Caption: "To Commemorate Christmas 1976." Two popular snow scenes, American Winter Scene and Winter Pastime.
☐ Purchased 19__ Pd $_____ MIB   NB   DB   BNT
☐ Want   Orig. Ret. $3.00   **NB** $25   **MIB** Sec. Mkt. **$40**

QX 225-1   HAPPY HOLIDAYS KISSING BALL
Comments: White Satin Ball, 5-6" dia.
Caption: "Happy Holidays." Decorated with red ribbon and green holly, this ball comes complete with mistletoe to hang in a doorway.
☐ Purchased 19__ Pd $_____ MIB   NB   DB   BNT
☐ Want   Orig. Ret. $5.00   **NB** $190   **MIB** Sec. Mkt. **$230**

QX 216-1   HAPPY THE SNOWMAN
Comments: White Satin Ball, 2-1/2" dia., Set of 2.
Captions: "Merry Christmas" on one side; "Happy Holidays" on the other. **Artist:** Linda Sickman
☐ Purchased 19__ Pd $_____ MIB   NB   DB   BNT
☐ Want   Orig. Ret. $3.50   **NB** $24   **MIB** Sec. Mkt. **$48**

QX 207-1   MARTY LINKS™
Comments: White Glass Ball, 2-1/2" dia., Set of 2.
Captions: "Noel 1976" and "Merry Christmas 1976."
☐ Purchased 19__ Pd $_____ MIB   NB   DB   BNT
☐ Want   Orig. Ret. $4.00   **NB** $26   **MIB** Sec. Mkt. **$40**

QX 196-1   NORMAN ROCKWELL
Comments: White Glass Ball, 3-1/4" dia.
Front: Santa convalesces from his travels. Back: Santa feeds his reindeer. Caption: "Christmas 1976."
☐ Purchased 19__ Pd $_____ MIB   NB   DB   BNT
☐ Want   Orig. Ret. $3.00   **NB** $45   **MIB** Sec. Mkt. **$75**

QX 130-1   NOSTALGIA ORNAMENTS: DRUMMER BOY
Comments: 3-1/4" dia. Reissued from 1975. **Artist:** Linda Sickman
☐ Purchased 19__ Pd $_____ MIB   NB   DB   BNT
☐ Want   1976 Ret. $4.00   **NB** $100   **MIB** Sec. Mkt. **$170**

QX 222-1   NOSTALGIA ORNAMENTS: LOCOMOTIVE
Comments: 3-1/4" dia., Dated 1976. Same design as 1975, but fewer available. **Artist:** Linda Sickman
☐ Purchased 19__ Pd $_____ MIB   NB   DB   BNT
☐ Want   Orig. Ret. $4.00   **NB** $120   **MIB** Sec. Mkt. **$165**

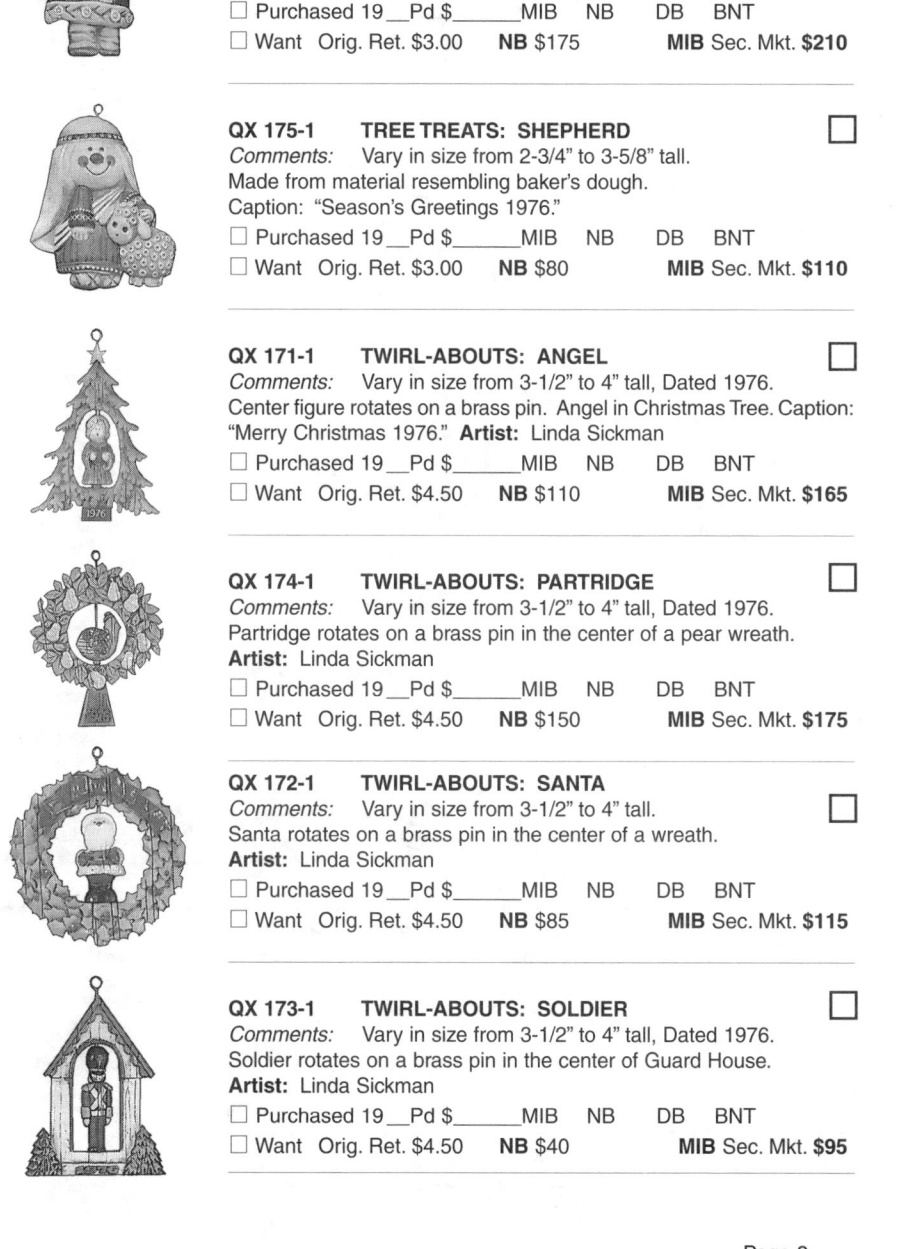

QX 223-1   NOSTALGIA ORNAMENTS:
PEACE ON EARTH ☐
Comments: 3-1/4" dia., Dated 1976. Same design as 1975.
Artist: Linda Sickman
☐ Purchased 19___Pd $_____MIB   NB   DB   BNT
☐ Want   Orig. Ret. $4.00   **NB** $60   **MIB** Sec. Mkt. **$160**

QX 128-1   NOSTALGIA ORNAMENTS:
ROCKING HORSE ☐
Comments: 3-1/4" dia. Reissued from 1975. **Artist:** Linda Sickman
☐ Purchased 19___Pd $_____MIB   NB   DB   BNT
☐ Want   1976 Retail $4.00 **NB** $110   **MIB** Sec. Mkt. **$170**

QX 212-1   RAGGEDY ANN™ ☐
Comments: White Satin Ball, 2-1/2" dia., Dated 1976.
Ann is hanging stockings at fireplace. Caption on back: "Merry
Christmas 1976."   Very cute!
☐ Purchased 19___Pd $_____MIB   NB   DB   BNT
☐ Want   Orig. Ret. $2.50   **NB** $40   **MIB** Sec. Mkt. **$65**

QX 213-1   RUDOLPH AND SANTA ☐
Comments: White Satin Ball, 2-1/2" dia., Dated 1976.
Front: "Rudolph the Red-Nosed Reindeer." Back: "Merry Christmas
1976."
☐ Purchased 19___Pd $_____MIB   NB   DB   BNT
☐ Want   Orig. Ret. $2.50   **NB** $65   **MIB** Sec. Mkt. **$80**

QX 176-1   TREE TREATS: ANGEL ☐
Comments: Vary in size from 2-3/4" to 3-5/8" tall.
Resembles baker's dough. Caption: "Merry Christmas 1976."
☐ Purchased 19___Pd $_____MIB   NB   DB   BNT
☐ Want   Orig. Ret. $3.00   **NB** $130   **MIB** Sec. Mkt. **$195**

QX 178-1   TREE TREATS: REINDEER ☐
Comments: Vary in size from 2-3/4" to 3-5/8" tall, Dated 1976.
Made from material resembling baker's dough.
Caption: "Merry Christmas 1976."
☐ Purchased 19___Pd $_____MIB   NB   DB   BNT
☐ Want   Orig. Ret. $3.00   **NB** $90   **MIB** Sec. Mkt. **$110**

QX 177-1   TREE TREATS: SANTA ☐
Comments: Vary in size from 2-3/4" to 3-5/8" tall, Dated 1976.
Made from material resembling baker's dough.
Caption: "Season's Greetings 1976."
☐ Purchased 19___Pd $_____MIB   NB   DB   BNT
☐ Want   Orig. Ret. $3.00   **NB** $175   **MIB** Sec. Mkt. **$210**

QX 175-1   TREE TREATS: SHEPHERD ☐
Comments: Vary in size from 2-3/4" to 3-5/8" tall.
Made from material resembling baker's dough.
Caption: "Season's Greetings 1976."
☐ Purchased 19___Pd $_____MIB   NB   DB   BNT
☐ Want   Orig. Ret. $3.00   **NB** $80   **MIB** Sec. Mkt. **$110**

QX 171-1   TWIRL-ABOUTS: ANGEL ☐
Comments: Vary in size from 3-1/2" to 4" tall, Dated 1976.
Center figure rotates on a brass pin. Angel in Christmas Tree. Caption:
"Merry Christmas 1976." **Artist:** Linda Sickman
☐ Purchased 19___Pd $_____MIB   NB   DB   BNT
☐ Want   Orig. Ret. $4.50   **NB** $110   **MIB** Sec. Mkt. **$165**

QX 174-1   TWIRL-ABOUTS: PARTRIDGE ☐
Comments: Vary in size from 3-1/2" to 4" tall, Dated 1976.
Partridge rotates on a brass pin in the center of a pear wreath.
Artist: Linda Sickman
☐ Purchased 19___Pd $_____MIB   NB   DB   BNT
☐ Want   Orig. Ret. $4.50   **NB** $150   **MIB** Sec. Mkt. **$175**

QX 172-1   TWIRL-ABOUTS: SANTA ☐
Comments: Vary in size from 3-1/2" to 4" tall.
Santa rotates on a brass pin in the center of a wreath.
Artist: Linda Sickman
☐ Purchased 19___Pd $_____MIB   NB   DB   BNT
☐ Want   Orig. Ret. $4.50   **NB** $85   **MIB** Sec. Mkt. **$115**

QX 173-1   TWIRL-ABOUTS: SOLDIER ☐
Comments: Vary in size from 3-1/2" to 4" tall, Dated 1976.
Soldier rotates on a brass pin in the center of Guard House.
Artist: Linda Sickman
☐ Purchased 19___Pd $_____MIB   NB   DB   BNT
☐ Want   Orig. Ret. $4.50   **NB** $40   **MIB** Sec. Mkt. **$95**

No secondary market value has been established for yarn and fabric ornaments found in original cellophane package.

QX 126-1   YARN ORNAMENTS: CAROLER (LITTLE GIRL)   ☐
Comments: 4-1/2" tall. Reissued from 1975.
Green, with white muff and green hat.
☐ Purchased 19 __ Pd $_____ MIB   NB   DB   BNT
☐ Want   Orig. Ret. $1.75   Sec. Mkt. **$22**

QX 123-1   YARN ORNAMENTS: DRUMMER BOY   ☐
Comments: 4-1/2" tall. Reissued from 1975.
Green with red hat.
☐ Purchased 19 __ Pd $_____ MIB   NB   DB   BNT
☐ Want   Orig. Ret. $1.75   Sec. Mkt. **$26**

QX 125-1   YARN ORNAMENTS: MRS. SANTA   ☐
Comments: 4-1/2" tall. Reissued from 1975.
White apron with red checked pockets.
☐ Purchased 19 __ Pd $_____ MIB   NB   DB   BNT
☐ Want   Orig. Ret. $1.75   Sec. Mkt. **$23**

QX 121-1   YARN ORNAMENTS: RAGGEDY ANN™   ☐
Comments: 4-1/2" tall, RARE!
Reissued from 1975. Blue dress with white pinafore.
☐ Purchased 19 __ Pd $_____ MIB   NB   DB   BNT
☐ Want   Orig. Ret. $1.75   Sec. Mkt. **$38**

QX 122-1   YARN ORNAMENTS: RAGGEDY ANDY™   ☐
Comments: 4-1/2" tall, RARE!
Reissued from 1975.   Blue with red-white checked shirt.
☐ Purchased 19 __ Pd $_____ MIB   NB   DB   BNT
☐ Want   Orig. Ret. $1.75   Sec. Mkt. **$38**

QX 124-1   YARN ORNAMENTS: SANTA   ☐
Comments: 4-1/2" tall. Reissued from 1975.
☐ Purchased 19 __ Pd $_____ MIB   NB   DB   BNT
☐ Want   Orig. Ret. $1.75   Sec. Mkt. **$24**

**If your foot slips, you may recover your balance,
but if your tongue slips, you cannot recall your words.**

QX 184-1   YESTERYEARS: DRUMMER BOY   ☐
Comments: Vary in size from 2-3/4" to 4" tall, Dated 1976.
This "wooden" soldier has been designed in "old world" tradition.
☐ Purchased 19 __ Pd $_____ MIB   NB   DB   BNT
☐ Want   Orig. Ret. $5.00   **NB** $90   **MIB** Sec. Mkt. **$155**

QX 183-1   YESTERYEARS: PARTRIDGE   ☐
Comments: Vary in size from 2-3/4" to 4" tall, Dated 1976.
"Wood look" design in "old world" character.
☐ Purchased 19 __ Pd $_____ MIB   NB   DB   BNT
☐ Want   Orig. Ret. $5.00   **NB** $75   **MIB** Sec. Mkt. **$120**

QX 182-1   YESTERYEARS: SANTA   ☐
Comments: Vary in size from 2-3/4" to 4" tall, Dated 1976.
Simulated wood design in "old world" character. Price down from 1996.
☐ Purchased 19 __ Pd $_____ MIB   NB   DB   BNT
☐ Want   Orig. Ret. $5.00   **NB** $95   **MIB** Sec. Mkt. **$155**

QX 181-1   YESTERYEARS: TRAIN   ☐
Comments: Vary in size from 2-3/4" to 4" tall, Dated 1976.
"Wood look" designs in "old world" character. Many sales found below $100 in my research.
☐ Purchased 19 __ Pd $_____ MIB   NB   DB   BNT
☐ Want   Orig. Ret. $5.00   **NB** $75   **MIB** Sec. Mkt. **$120**

1977 Collection

QX 220-2   ANGEL   ☐
Comments: 4" tall.
Quilted and stuffed doll made from silk-screened fabric.
☐ Purchased 19 __ Pd $_____ MIB   NB   DB   BNT
☐ Want   Orig. Ret. $1.75   **MIB** Sec. Mkt. **$52**

QSD 230-2   ANGEL TREE TOPPER   ☐
Comments: 3-1/2" tall. Country style simulated wood angel.
Dress is in cream, pink, turquoise and gold.
☐ Purchased 19 __ Pd $_____ MIB   NB   DB   BNT
☐ Want   Orig. Ret. $9.00   **NB** $225   **MIB** Sec. Mkt. **$410**

QX 131-5   BABY'S FIRST CHRISTMAS   ☐
Comments: White Satin Ball, 3-1/4" dia., Dated 1977.
Caption: "Baby's First Christmas"
☐ Purchased 19 __ Pd $_____ MIB   NB   DB   BNT
☐ Want   Orig. Ret. $3.50   **NB** $45   **MIB** Sec. Mkt. **$75**

QX 159-5   BEAUTY OF AMERICA COLLECTION: DESERT ☐
Comments: White Glass Ball, 2-5/8" dia.
A desert mission at sunset. Caption: "Ring Out Christmas Bells And Let All The World Hear Your Joyful Song."
☐ Purchased 19 __ Pd $_____ MIB   NB   DB   BNT
☐ Want Orig. Ret. $2.50   **NB** $15   **MIB** Sec. Mkt. **$30**

QX 158-2   BEAUTY OF AMERICA COLLECTION: MOUNTAINS ☐
Comments: White Glass Ball, 2-5/8" dia.
Caption: "The Spirit Of Christmas Is Peace... The Message Of Christmas Is Love." The beauty of the mountains is captured on this ornament.
☐ Purchased 19 __ Pd $_____ MIB   NB   DB   BNT
☐ Want Orig. Ret. $2.50   **NB** $15   **MIB** Sec. Mkt. **$30**

QX 160-2   BEAUTY OF AMERICA COLLECTION: SEASHORE ☐
Comments: White Glass Ball, 2-5/8" dia.
Caption: "Christmas Is - The Company Of Good Friends, The Warmth Of Goodwill And The Memory Of Good Times."
☐ Purchased 19 __ Pd $_____ MIB   NB   DB   BNT
☐ Want Orig. Ret. $2.50   **NB** $45   **MIB** Sec. Mkt. **$55**

QX 161-5   BEAUTY OF AMERICA COLLECTION: WHARF ☐
Comments: White Glass Ball, 2-5/8" dia.
Caption: "Christmas... When The World Stands Silent And The Spirit Of Hope Touches Every Heart."
☐ Purchased 19 __ Pd $_____ MIB   NB   DB   BNT
☐ Want Orig. Ret. $2.50   **NB** $20   **MIB** Sec. Mkt. **$38**

QX 264-2   BETSEY CLARK SERIES ☐
Comments: **Fifth in Series,** White Glass Ball, 3-1/4" dia.
Captions: "Christmas 1977" and "The Truest Joys Of Christmas Come From Deep Inside." Most scarce of Betsey Clark Series.
Very little trading for several years. Insure at price listed.
☐ Purchased 19 __ Pd $_____ MIB   NB   DB   BNT
☐ Want Orig. Ret. $3.50   **NB** $400   **MIB** Sec. Mkt. **$425**

QX 153-5   CHARMERS ☐
Comments: Gold Glass Ball, 3-1/4" dia. Dated 1977.
Caption: "We Wish You A Merry Christmas."
☐ Purchased 19 __ Pd $_____ MIB   NB   DB   BNT
☐ Want Orig. Ret. $3.50   **NB** $38   **MIB** Sec. Mkt. **$50**

QX 154-2   CHRISTMAS EXPRESSIONS: BELL ☐
Comments: White Glass Ball, 3-1/4" dia.
Caption: "I heard the bells on Christmas Day, Their old familiar carols play, And wild and sweet, the words repeat, Of peace on earth, good will to men." Henry Wadsworth Longfellow.
☐ Purchased 19 __ Pd $_____ MIB   NB   DB   BNT
☐ Want Orig. Ret. $3.50   **NB** $28   **MIB** Sec. Mkt. **$38**

QX 157-5   CHRISTMAS EXPRESSIONS: MANDOLIN ☐
Comments: White Glass Ball, 3-1/4" dia.
Caption: "Sing a song of seasons; Something bright in all..." Robert Louis Stevenson.
☐ Purchased 19 __ Pd $_____ MIB   NB   DB   BNT
☐ Want Orig. Ret. $3.50   **NB** $28   **MIB** Sec. Mkt. **$38**

QX 155-5   CHRISTMAS EXPRESSIONS: ORNAMENTS ☐
Comments: White Glass Ball, 3-1/4" dia.
Caption: "The Spirit of Christmas is Peace... The Message of Christmas is love." Marjorie Frances Ames.
☐ Purchased 19 __ Pd $_____ MIB   NB   DB   BNT
☐ Want Orig. Ret. $3.50   **NB** $28   **MIB** Sec. Mkt. **$38**

QX 156-2   CHRISTMAS EXPRESSIONS: WREATH ☐
Comments: White Glass Ball, 3-1/4" dia.
Caption: "Christmas Is A Special Time. A Season Set Apart - A Warm And Glad Remembering Time. A Season Of The Heart." Thomas Malloy.
☐ Purchased 19 __ Pd $_____ MIB   NB   DB   BNT
☐ Want Orig. Ret. $3.50   **NB** $22   **MIB** Sec. Mkt. **$35**

QX 134-2   CHRISTMAS MOUSE ☐
Comments: White Satin Ball, 3-1/4" dia.
Mice decorate their tree.   Caption: "Tinsel And Lights Make The Season So Bright."
☐ Purchased 19 __ Pd $_____ MIB   NB   DB   BNT
☐ Want Orig. Ret. $3.50   **NB** $45   **MIB** Sec. Mkt. **$65**

QX 200-2   COLORS OF CHRISTMAS: BELL ☐
Comments: Acrylic, 3-1/4" dia.
Stained glass look. Bell with green ribbon. **Artist:** Linda Sickman
☐ Purchased 19 __ Pd $_____ MIB   NB   DB   BNT
☐ Want Orig. Ret. $3.50   **NB** $42   **MIB** Sec. Mkt. **$50**

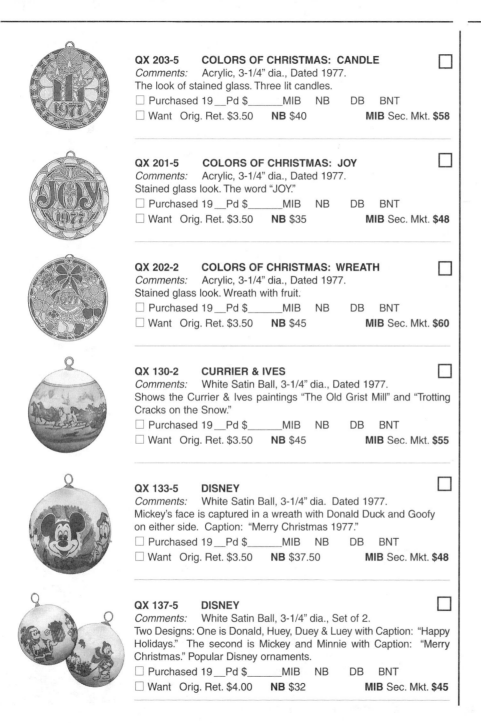

QX 203-5   COLORS OF CHRISTMAS: CANDLE ☐
Comments: Acrylic, 3-1/4" dia., Dated 1977.
The look of stained glass. Three lit candles.
☐ Purchased 19__Pd $_____MIB   NB   DB   BNT
☐ Want   Orig. Ret. $3.50   **NB** $40   **MIB** Sec. Mkt. **$58**

QX 201-5   COLORS OF CHRISTMAS: JOY ☐
Comments: Acrylic, 3-1/4" dia., Dated 1977.
Stained glass look. The word "JOY."
☐ Purchased 19__Pd $_____MIB   NB   DB   BNT
☐ Want   Orig. Ret. $3.50   **NB** $35   **MIB** Sec. Mkt. **$48**

QX 202-2   COLORS OF CHRISTMAS: WREATH ☐
Comments: Acrylic, 3-1/4" dia., Dated 1977.
Stained glass look. Wreath with fruit.
☐ Purchased 19__Pd $_____MIB   NB   DB   BNT
☐ Want   Orig. Ret. $3.50   **NB** $45   **MIB** Sec. Mkt. **$60**

QX 130-2   CURRIER & IVES ☐
Comments: White Satin Ball, 3-1/4" dia., Dated 1977.
Shows the Currier & Ives paintings "The Old Grist Mill" and "Trotting Cracks on the Snow."
☐ Purchased 19__Pd $_____MIB   NB   DB   BNT
☐ Want   Orig. Ret. $3.50   **NB** $45   **MIB** Sec. Mkt. **$55**

QX 133-5   DISNEY ☐
Comments: White Satin Ball, 3-1/4" dia. Dated 1977.
Mickey's face is captured in a wreath with Donald Duck and Goofy on either side. Caption: "Merry Christmas 1977."
☐ Purchased 19__Pd $_____MIB   NB   DB   BNT
☐ Want   Orig. Ret. $3.50   **NB** $37.50   **MIB** Sec. Mkt. **$48**

QX 137-5   DISNEY ☐
Comments: White Satin Ball, 3-1/4" dia., Set of 2.
Two Designs: One is Donald, Huey, Duey & Luey with Caption: "Happy Holidays." The second is Mickey and Minnie with Caption: "Merry Christmas." Popular Disney ornaments.
☐ Purchased 19__Pd $_____MIB   NB   DB   BNT
☐ Want   Orig. Ret. $4.00   **NB** $32   **MIB** Sec. Mkt. **$45**

QX 132-2   FIRST CHRISTMAS TOGETHER ☐
Comments: White Satin Ball, 3-1/4" dia., Dated 1977.
Caption: "Our First Christmas Together." Date and caption printed in gold.
☐ Purchased 19__Pd $_____MIB   NB   DB   BNT
☐ Want   Orig. Ret. $3.50   **NB** $35   **MIB** Sec. Mkt. **$60**

QX 263-5   FOR YOUR NEW HOME ☐
Comments: Gold Glass Ball, 3-1/4" dia.
Dated 1977 on doormat. Very little trading in past five years.
☐ Purchased 19__Pd $_____MIB   NB   DB   BNT
☐ Want   Orig. Ret. $3.50   **NB** $18   **MIB** Sec. Mkt. **$35**

QX 208-2   GRANDDAUGHTER ☐
Comments: White Satin Ball, 3-1/4" dia.
Caption: "A Granddaughter Is A Gift Whose Worth Cannot Be Measured Except By The Heart." Very little trading in past seven years.
☐ Purchased 19__Pd $_____MIB   NB   DB   BNT
☐ Want   Orig. Ret. $3.50   **NB** $18   **MIB** Sec. Mkt. **$25**

QX 150-2   GRANDMA MOSES ☐
Comments: White Glass Ball, 3-1/4" dia.
RARE! Two snow scenes from the paintings "Green Sleigh" and "Sugartime." A pamphlet giving the history of Grandma Moses and her paintings was included with each ornament.
☐ Purchased 19__Pd $_____MIB   NB   DB   BNT
☐ Want   Orig. Ret. $3.50   **NB** $45 (without pamphlet)
MIB Sec. Mkt. **$55**

QX 260-2   GRANDMOTHER ☐
Comments: Gold Glass Ball, 3-1/4" dia.
Caption: "Grandmother Is Another Word For Love."
☐ Purchased 19__Pd $_____MIB   NB   DB   BNT
☐ Want   Orig. Ret. $3.50   **NB** $25   **MIB** Sec. Mkt. **$40**

QX 209-5   GRANDSON ☐
Comments: White Satin Ball, 3-1/2" dia.
Caption: "A Grandson Is... A Joy Bringer... A Memory Maker... A Grandson Is Love."
☐ Purchased 19__Pd $_____MIB   NB   DB   BNT
☐ Want   Orig. Ret. $3.50   **NB** $15   **MIB** Sec. Mkt. **$25**

**A woman's age is like the speedometer on a used car...
you know it's been set back, but you don't know how far.**

QX 312-2   HOLIDAY HIGHLIGHTS: DRUMMER BOY ☐
Comments: Acrylic, 3-1/4" dia.
A drummer boy keeps the beat as he marches with his drum.
Caption repeated around border: "Rum-Pa-Pum-Pum."
☐ Purchased 19 __ Pd $_____ MIB   NB   DB   BNT
☐ Want   Orig. Ret. $3.50   **NB** $40   **MIB** Sec. Mkt. **$65**

QX 310-2   HOLIDAY HIGHLIGHTS: JOY ☐
Comments: Acrylic, 3-1/4" dia. Caption: "JOY 1977."
☐ Purchased 19 __ Pd $_____ MIB   NB   DB   BNT
☐ Want   Orig. Ret. $3.50   **NB** $20   **MIB** Sec. Mkt. **$45**

QX 311-5   HOLIDAY HIGHLIGHTS: PEACE ON EARTH ☐
Comments: Acrylic, 3-1/4" dia.
A picturesque village scene with snow-covered houses, pine trees and
a church in the center. Caption: "Peace On Earth, Good Will Toward
Men. 1977"
☐ Purchased 19 __ Pd $_____ MIB   NB   DB   BNT
☐ Want   Orig. Ret. $3.50   **NB** $40   **MIB** Sec. Mkt. **$55**

QX 313-5   HOLIDAY HIGHLIGHTS: STAR ☐
Comments: Acrylic, 3-1/4" dia.
A bright shining star radiates beams over the ornament's surface.
Caption: "Once For A Shining Hour Heaven Touched Earth."
☐ Purchased 19 __ Pd $_____ MIB   NB   DB   BNT
☐ Want   Orig. Ret. $3.50   **NB** $45   **MIB** Sec. Mkt. **$50**

OHD 320-2   HOLLY & POINSETTIA TABLE DECORATION ☐
Comments: With special base. Wood look.
☐ Purchased 19 __ Pd $_____ MIB   NB   DB   BNT
☐ Want   Orig. Ret. $8.00   **NB** $125   **MIB** Sec. Mkt. **$130**

QX 262-2   LOVE ☐
Comments: Gold Glass Ball, 3-1/4" dia. Caption: "Christmas 1977."
☐ Purchased 19 __ Pd $_____ MIB   NB   DB   BNT
☐ Want   Orig. Ret. $3.50   **NB** $10   **MIB** Sec. Mkt. **$25**

QX 210-2   METAL ORNAMENTS: SNOWFLAKES ☐
Comments: Chrome Plated Zinc, 2-1/8" dia., Set of 4 die-cast in
lightweight, chrome plated zinc. Packaged in peek-through gift box.
This is the only year the snowflake set was offered. This set is hard to
find. **Artist:** Linda Sickman
☐ Purchased 19 __ Pd $_____ MIB   NB   DB   BNT
☐ Want   Orig. Ret. $5.00   **NB** $70   **MIB** Sec. Mkt. **$95**

QX 261-5   MOTHER ☐
Comments: White Glass Ball, 3-1/4" dia.
Pink roses and green holly. Caption: "In a Mother's heart, there is
love... the very heart of Christmas."
☐ Purchased 19 __ Pd $_____ MIB   NB   DB   BNT
☐ Want   Orig. Ret. $3.50   **NB** $12   **MIB** Sec. Mkt. **$20**

Photo Needed

QX 225-2   MR. AND MRS. SNOWMAN KISSING BALL ☐
Comments: Photo welcomed.
☐ Purchased 19 __ Pd $_____ MIB   NB   DB   BNT
☐ Want   Orig. Ret. $5.00   **NB** $85   **MIB** Sec. Mkt. **$100**

QX 151-5   NORMAN ROCKWELL ☐
Comments: White Glass Ball, 3-1/4" dia., Dated 1977.
Four favorite Rockwell designs are reproduced in separate panels.
Caption: "Christmas 1977."
☐ Purchased 19 __ Pd $_____ MIB   NB   DB   BNT
☐ Want   Orig. Ret. $3.50   **NB** $50   **MIB** Sec. Mkt. **$65**

QX 182-2   NOSTALGIA COLLECTION: ANGEL ☐
Comments: Handcrafted, 3-1/4" dia.
An angel flies in the center of a wide outer ring which features the
caption: "Peace on earth" and "Good will toward men." Gift tag was
included. Several known sales below $100 reported. **Artist:** Donna Lee
☐ Purchased 19 __ Pd $_____ MIB   NB   DB   BNT
☐ Want   Orig. Ret. $5.00   **NB** $70   **MIB** Sec. Mkt. **$115**

QX 180-2   NOSTALGIA COLLECTION: ANTIQUE CAR ☐
Comments: Handcrafted, 3-1/4" dia.
Green car trimmed in red.   Caption: "Season's Greetings 1977."
Gift tag was included. **Artist:** Linda Sickman
☐ Purchased 19 __ Pd $_____ MIB   NB   DB   BNT
☐ Want   Orig. Ret. $5.00   **NB** $30   **MIB** Sec. Mkt. **$55**

QX 181-5   NOSTALGIA COLLECTION: NATIVITY
Comments: Handcrafted, 3-1/4" dia.
The Holy Family and animals in a stable with pine trees on either side. Caption: "O Come, Let Us Adore Him." Gift tag was included.
☐ Purchased 19 __ Pd $_____ MIB   NB   DB   BNT
☐ Want   Orig. Ret. $5.00   **NB** $100   **MIB** Sec. Mkt. **$140**

QX 183-5   NOSTALGIA COLLECTION: TOYS
Comments: Handcrafted, 3-1/4" dia., Dated 1977.
Toys in the center of a red and yellow ring. Gift tag was included.
Artist: Linda Sickman
☐ Purchased 19 __ Pd $_____ MIB   NB   DB   BNT
☐ Want   Orig. Ret. $5.00   **NB** $85   **MIB** Sec. Mkt. **$155**

QX 225-5   OLD FASHIONED CUSTOMS KISSING BALL
Comments: White Satin Ball.
☐ Purchased 19 __ Pd $_____ MIB   NB   DB   BNT
☐ Want   Orig. Ret. $5.00   **NB** $125   **MIB** Sec. Mkt. **$150**

QX 162-2   PEANUTS®
Comments: White Glass Ball, 2-5/8" dia.
Front: Charlie Brown and his sister Sally watch the stockings on the fireplace. Caption: "A Watched Stocking Never Fills." Back: Schroeder plays the piano as Lucy gives him a gift. Caption: "Merry Christmas." Packaged in Snoopy's Christmas-decorated doghouse.
☐ Purchased 19 __ Pd $_____ MIB   NB   DB   BNT
☐ Want   Orig. Ret. $2.50   **NB** $40   **MIB** Sec. Mkt. **$55**

QX 135-5   PEANUTS®
Comments: White Satin Ball, 3-1/4" dia., Dated 1977.
Front: Snoopy is tangled in Christmas tree lights. Back: Charlie Brown and Lucy.
☐ Purchased 19 __ Pd $_____ MIB   NB   DB   BNT
☐ Want   Orig. Ret. $3.50   **NB** $50   **MIB** Sec. Mkt. **$70**

QX 163-5   PEANUTS®
Comments: White Glass Ball, 2-1/4" dia., Set of 2, Dated 1977.
Two Designs: Santa Snoopy is pulled in a sleigh. Charlie Brown, Linus, Woodstock, Snoopy and Peppermint Patty play in the snow.
☐ Purchased 19 __ Pd $_____ MIB   NB   DB   BNT
☐ Want   Orig. Ret. $4.00   **NB** $60   **MIB** Sec. Mkt. **$80**

QX 139-5   RABBIT
Comments: White Satin Ball, 2-5/8" dia.
A rabbit looks at a little bird on a broken tree limb. Caption: "Nature's ever-changing beauty brings never-ending joy." Karl Lawrence.
☐ Purchased 19 __ Pd $_____ MIB   NB   DB   BNT
☐ Want   Orig. Ret. $2.50   **NB** $80   **MIB** Sec. Mkt. **$100**

QX 221-5   SANTA
Comments: 4" tall.   RARE!
Stuffed and quilted doll made from silk-screened fabric. A jingle bell is attached to his hat. Hard to find!
☐ Purchased 19 __ Pd $_____ MIB   NB   DB   BNT
☐ Want   Orig. Ret. $1.75   **NB** $50   **MIB** Sec. Mkt. **$60**

QX 138-2   SQUIRREL
Comments: White Satin Ball, 2-5/8" dia.
Caption: "Each Moment Of The Year Has Its Own Beauty..." Emerson.
☐ Purchased 19 __ Pd $_____ MIB   NB   DB   BNT
☐ Want   Orig. Ret. $2.50   **NB** $80   **MIB** Sec. Mkt. **$100**

QX 152-2   STAINED GLASS
Comments: Chrome Glass Ball, 3-1/4" dia.
A look of art deco stained glass. Caption: "Merry Christmas 1977."
☐ Purchased 19 __ Pd $_____ MIB   NB   DB   BNT
☐ Want   Orig. Ret. $3.50   **NB** $35   **MIB** Sec. Mkt. **$45**

QX 192-2   TWIRL-ABOUT COLLECTION: BELLRINGER
Comments: Handcrafted, 3-11/16" tall, Dated 1977.
A little boy strikes a bell as he rotates inside an arched gate decorated with red bows.
☐ Purchased 19 __ Pd $_____ MIB   NB   DB   BNT
☐ Want   Orig. Ret. $6.00   **NB-P** $25   **MIB** Sec. Mkt. **$55**

QX 193-5   TWIRL-ABOUT COLLECTION: DELLA ROBIA WREATH
Comments: Handcrafted, 3-9/16" tall, Dated 1977.
A little girl, kneeling in prayer, twirls in the center of the traditional Della Robia wreath. **Artist:** Donna Lee
☐ Purchased 19 __ Pd $_____ MIB   NB   DB   BNT
☐ Want   Orig. Ret. $4.50   **NB** $55   **MIB** Sec. Mkt. **$105**

QX 190-2   TWIRL-ABOUT COLLECTION: SNOWMAN ☐
Comments: Handcrafted, 3-3/4" tall, Dated 1977.
A snowman rotates in the center of a three-dimensional snowflake.
Artist: Linda Sickman

☐ Purchased 19___Pd $_____MIB   NB   DB   BNT
☐ Want   Orig. Ret. $4.50   **NB** $25   **MIB** Sec. Mkt. **$78**

**QX 191-5   TWIRL-ABOUT COLLECTION:
                    WEATHER HOUSE** ☐
Comments: Handcrafted, 3-15/16" tall, Dated 1977.
Swiss dressed boy and girl rotate through the doors of a country chalet.

☐ Purchased 19__ Pd $_____MIB   NB   DB   BNT
☐ Want   Orig. Ret. $6.00   **NB-P** $60   **MIB** Sec. Mkt. **$90**

QX 172-2   YESTERYEARS COLLECTION: ANGEL ☐
Comments: Handcrafted, 3-1/2" tall.
This lovely folk-art angel is similar to the Angel Tree Topper. Caption: "Joy to the world 1977."

☐ Purchased 19__Pd $_____MIB   NB   DB   BNT
☐ Want   Orig. Ret. $6.00   **NB-P** $60   **MIB** Sec. Mkt. **$98**

QX 170-2   YESTERYEARS COLLECTION: HOUSE ☐
Comments: Handcrafted, 3-11/16" tall.
This quaint cottage has a red roof and green shutters with painted designs. Caption: "Happy Holidays 1977."

☐ Purchased 19__Pd $_____MIB   NB   DB   BNT
☐ Want   Orig. Ret. $6.00   **NB** $95   **MIB** Sec. Mkt. **$110**

**QX 171-5   YESTERYEARS COLLECTION:
                    JACK-IN-THE-BOX** ☐
Comments: Handcrafted, 3-13/16" tall.
Green, blue and red Jack in a red and pink box. Caption: "Merry Christmas 1977." More readily available than most of 1970's ornaments. Price fell in 1996.

☐ Purchased 19__Pd $_____MIB   NB   DB   BNT
☐ Want   Orig. Ret. $6.00   **NB-P** $65   **MIB** Sec. Mkt. **$95**

QX 173-5   YESTERYEARS COLLECTION: REINDEER ☐
Comments: Handcrafted, 4-1/4" tall, Dated 1977.
Ivory painted reindeer on wheels has the look of a nostalgic child's toy.

☐ Purchased 19__Pd $_____MIB   NB   DB   BNT
☐ Want   Orig. Ret. $6.00   **NB** $65   **MIB** Sec. Mkt. **$135**

1978 Collection

QX 139-6   ANGEL ☐
Comments: Handcrafted, 2-15/16" tall, Reissued in 1981.
Made with the bread-dough look, a barefoot angel dressed in blue and white holds a star. **Artist:** Donna Lee

☐ Purchased 19 __Pd $_____MIB   NB   DB   BNT
☐ Want   Orig. Ret. $4.50   **NB** $65   **MIB** Sec. Mkt. **$85**

QX 150-3   ANGELS ☐
Comments: Handcrafted, 3-7/8" tall, Dated 1978.
Angels fly around decorating a Christmas tree. Price down from 1996.

☐ Purchased 19 __Pd $_____MIB   NB   DB   BNT
☐ Want   Orig. Ret. $8.00   **NB** $150   **MIB** Sec. Mkt. **$345**

QX 149-6   ANIMAL HOME ☐
Comments: Handcrafted, 2-9/16" tall.
A darling little mushroom has become "home sweet home" to a family of mice. **Artist:** Donna Lee

☐ Purchased 19 __Pd $_____MIB   NB   DB   BNT
☐ Want   Orig. Ret. $6.00   **NB** $100   **MIB** Sec. Mkt. **$160**

QX 200-3   BABY'S FIRST CHRISTMAS ☐
Comments: White Satin Ball, 3-1/4" dia.
A baby dressed in yellow plays with a stuffed teddy bear and a kitten. Caption: "Baby's First Christmas 1978."

☐ Purchased 19 __Pd $_____MIB   NB   DB   BNT
☐ Want   Orig. Ret. $3.50   **NB** $45   **MIB** Sec. Mkt. **$75**

QX 201-6   BETSEY CLARK SERIES ☐
Comments: **Sixth in series,** Ecru Soft-Sheen Satin Ball, 3-1/4" dia.
Dated 1978. A little girl wraps a gift and delivers it to a friend. Caption: "The Christmas Spirit Seems To Bring A Cheerful Glow To Everything."

☐ Purchased 19 __Pd $_____MIB   NB   DB   BNT
☐ Want   Orig. Ret. $3.50   **NB** $40   **MIB** Sec. Mkt. **$65**

QX 137-6   CALICO MOUSE ☐
Comments: Handcrafted, 3-7/16" tall.
Smiling red calico mouse, with green ears and nose, holds a sprig of holly. Similar to the Merry Miniature.

☐ Purchased 19 __Pd $_____MIB   NB   DB   BNT
☐ Want   Orig. Ret. $4.50   **NB** $110   **MIB** Sec. Mkt. **$185**

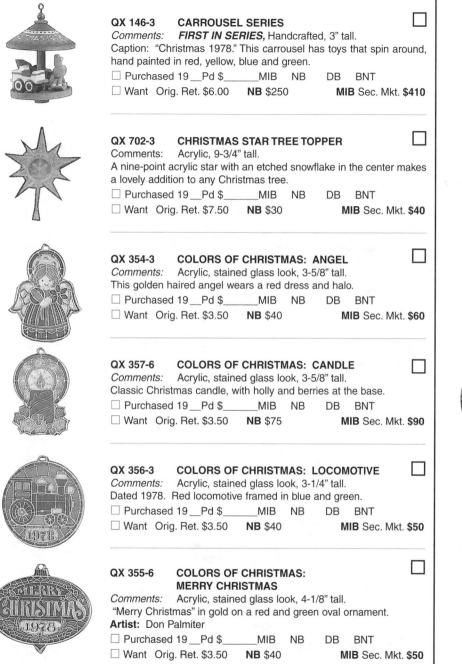

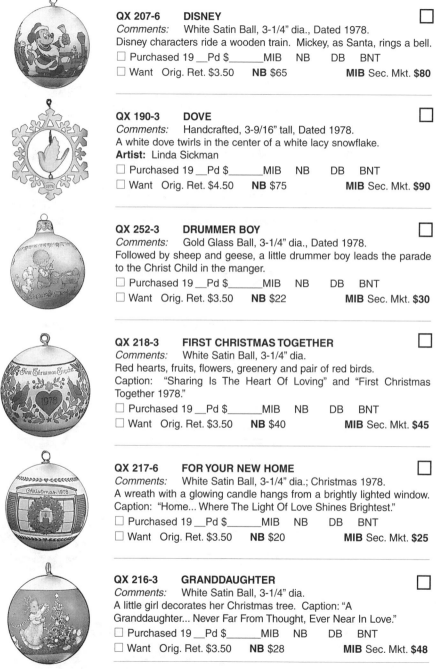

QX 146-3   CARROUSEL SERIES
Comments: **FIRST IN SERIES,** Handcrafted, 3" tall.
Caption: "Christmas 1978." This carrousel has toys that spin around, hand painted in red, yellow, blue and green.
☐ Purchased 19 __ Pd $_____ MIB   NB   DB   BNT
☐ Want   Orig. Ret. $6.00   **NB** $250   **MIB** Sec. Mkt. **$410**

QX 702-3   CHRISTMAS STAR TREE TOPPER
Comments: Acrylic, 9-3/4" tall.
A nine-point acrylic star with an etched snowflake in the center makes a lovely addition to any Christmas tree.
☐ Purchased 19 __ Pd $_____ MIB   NB   DB   BNT
☐ Want   Orig. Ret. $7.50   **NB** $30   **MIB** Sec. Mkt. **$40**

QX 354-3   COLORS OF CHRISTMAS: ANGEL
Comments: Acrylic, stained glass look, 3-5/8" tall.
This golden haired angel wears a red dress and halo.
☐ Purchased 19 __ Pd $_____ MIB   NB   DB   BNT
☐ Want   Orig. Ret. $3.50   **NB** $40   **MIB** Sec. Mkt. **$60**

QX 357-6   COLORS OF CHRISTMAS: CANDLE
Comments: Acrylic, stained glass look, 3-5/8" tall.
Classic Christmas candle, with holly and berries at the base.
☐ Purchased 19 __ Pd $_____ MIB   NB   DB   BNT
☐ Want   Orig. Ret. $3.50   **NB** $75   **MIB** Sec. Mkt. **$90**

QX 356-3   COLORS OF CHRISTMAS: LOCOMOTIVE
Comments: Acrylic, stained glass look, 3-1/4" tall.
Dated 1978. Red locomotive framed in blue and green.
☐ Purchased 19 __ Pd $_____ MIB   NB   DB   BNT
☐ Want   Orig. Ret. $3.50   **NB** $40   **MIB** Sec. Mkt. **$50**

QX 355-6   COLORS OF CHRISTMAS: MERRY CHRISTMAS
Comments: Acrylic, stained glass look, 4-1/8" tall.
"Merry Christmas" in gold on a red and green oval ornament.
Artist: Don Palmiter
☐ Purchased 19 __ Pd $_____ MIB   NB   DB   BNT
☐ Want   Orig. Ret. $3.50   **NB** $40   **MIB** Sec. Mkt. **$50**

QX 207-6   DISNEY
Comments: White Satin Ball, 3-1/4" dia., Dated 1978.
Disney characters ride a wooden train. Mickey, as Santa, rings a bell.
☐ Purchased 19 __ Pd $_____ MIB   NB   DB   BNT
☐ Want   Orig. Ret. $3.50   **NB** $65   **MIB** Sec. Mkt. **$80**

QX 190-3   DOVE
Comments: Handcrafted, 3-9/16" tall, Dated 1978.
A white dove twirls in the center of a white lacy snowflake.
Artist: Linda Sickman
☐ Purchased 19 __ Pd $_____ MIB   NB   DB   BNT
☐ Want   Orig. Ret. $4.50   **NB** $75   **MIB** Sec. Mkt. **$90**

QX 252-3   DRUMMER BOY
Comments: Gold Glass Ball, 3-1/4" dia., Dated 1978.
Followed by sheep and geese, a little drummer boy leads the parade to the Christ Child in the manger.
☐ Purchased 19 __ Pd $_____ MIB   NB   DB   BNT
☐ Want   Orig. Ret. $3.50   **NB** $22   **MIB** Sec. Mkt. **$30**

QX 218-3   FIRST CHRISTMAS TOGETHER
Comments: White Satin Ball, 3-1/4" dia.
Red hearts, fruits, flowers, greenery and pair of red birds.
Caption: "Sharing Is The Heart Of Loving" and "First Christmas Together 1978."
☐ Purchased 19 __ Pd $_____ MIB   NB   DB   BNT
☐ Want   Orig. Ret. $3.50   **NB** $40   **MIB** Sec. Mkt. **$45**

QX 217-6   FOR YOUR NEW HOME
Comments: White Satin Ball, 3-1/4" dia.; Christmas 1978.
A wreath with a glowing candle hangs from a brightly lighted window.
Caption: "Home... Where The Light Of Love Shines Brightest."
☐ Purchased 19 __ Pd $_____ MIB   NB   DB   BNT
☐ Want   Orig. Ret. $3.50   **NB** $20   **MIB** Sec. Mkt. **$25**

QX 216-3   GRANDDAUGHTER
Comments: White Satin Ball, 3-1/4" dia.
A little girl decorates her Christmas tree. Caption: "A Granddaughter... Never Far From Thought, Ever Near In Love."
☐ Purchased 19 __ Pd $_____ MIB   NB   DB   BNT
☐ Want   Orig. Ret. $3.50   **NB** $28   **MIB** Sec. Mkt. **$48**

QX 267-6   GRANDMOTHER
Comments: White Satin Ball, 3-1/4" dia.
Red American Beauty roses and holly. Caption: "A Grandmother Has A Special Way Of Bringing Joy To Every Day."
☐ Purchased 19___Pd $_____MIB   NB   DB   BNT
☐ Want   Orig. Ret. $3.50   **NB** $40   **MIB** Sec. Mkt. **$50**

QX 215-6   GRANDSON
Comments: White Satin Ball, 3-1/4" dia.
Raccoons have fun ice skating, building a snowman and sledding. Caption: "A Grandson Is Loved In A Special Way For The Special Joy He Brings."
☐ Purchased 19___Pd $_____MIB   NB   DB   BNT
☐ Want   Orig. Ret. $3.50   **NB** $30   **MIB** Sec. Mkt. **$40**

**QX 220-3   HALLMARK'S ANTIQUE
                CARD COLLECTION DESIGN**
Comments: Ecru Soft-Sheen Satin Ball, 3-1/4" dia.
Reproduced from an antique Hallmark card. Caption: "Christmas Is A Special Time, A Season Set Apart – A Warm And Glad Remembering Time, A Season Of The Heart." Very little trading.
☐ Purchased 19___Pd $_____MIB   NB   DB   BNT
☐ Want   Orig. Ret. $3.50   **NB** $35   **MIB** Sec. Mkt. **$40**

QHD 921-9   HEAVENLY MINSTREL TABLETOP
Comments: Very similar to the Heavenly Minstrel ornament.
Comes with walnut base with stained-glass look and brass background.
☐ Purchased 19___Pd $_____MIB   NB   DB   BNT
☐ Want   Orig. Ret. $35.00   **NB** $350   **MIB** Sec. Mkt. **$425**

QX 320-3   HOLIDAY CHIMES: REINDEER CHIMES
Comments: Reissued in 1979, Chrome plated brass, 5-1/2" tall. Three prancing reindeer are suspended from a large snowflake. **Artist:** Linda Sickman
☐ Purchased 19___Pd $_____MIB   NB   DB   BNT
☐ Want   Orig. Ret. $4.50   **NB** $25   **MIB** Sec. Mkt. **$38**

QX 310-3   HOLIDAY HIGHLIGHTS: DOVE
Comments: Acrylic with the look of hand-cut crystal.
Ranged from 2-11/16" to 3-5/8" tall. RARE! This dove in flight is produced in frosted acrylic with clear acrylic wing tips.
☐ Purchased 19___Pd $_____MIB   NB   DB   BNT
☐ Want   Orig. Ret. $3.50   **NB** $90   **MIB** Sec. Mkt. **$125**

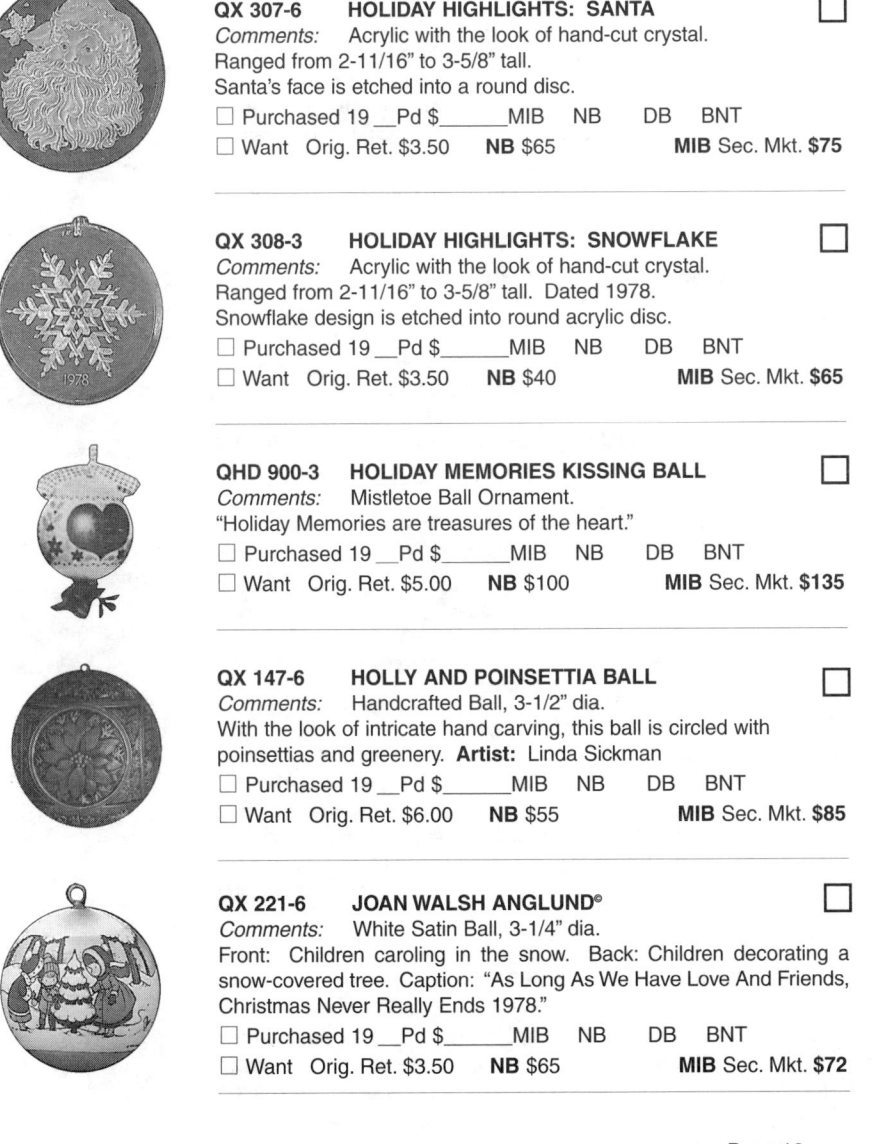

QX 309-6   HOLIDAY HIGHLIGHTS: NATIVITY
Comments: Acrylic with the look of hand-cut crystal.
Ranged from 2-11/16" to 3-5/8" tall. **Artist:** Don Palmiter
☐ Purchased 19___Pd $_____MIB   NB   DB   BNT
☐ Want   Orig. Ret. $3.50   **NB** $65   **MIB** Sec. Mkt. **$80**

QX 307-6   HOLIDAY HIGHLIGHTS: SANTA
Comments: Acrylic with the look of hand-cut crystal.
Ranged from 2-11/16" to 3-5/8" tall.
Santa's face is etched into a round disc.
☐ Purchased 19___Pd $_____MIB   NB   DB   BNT
☐ Want   Orig. Ret. $3.50   **NB** $65   **MIB** Sec. Mkt. **$75**

QX 308-3   HOLIDAY HIGHLIGHTS: SNOWFLAKE
Comments: Acrylic with the look of hand-cut crystal.
Ranged from 2-11/16" to 3-5/8" tall. Dated 1978.
Snowflake design is etched into round acrylic disc.
☐ Purchased 19___Pd $_____MIB   NB   DB   BNT
☐ Want   Orig. Ret. $3.50   **NB** $40   **MIB** Sec. Mkt. **$65**

QHD 900-3   HOLIDAY MEMORIES KISSING BALL
Comments: Mistletoe Ball Ornament.
"Holiday Memories are treasures of the heart."
☐ Purchased 19___Pd $_____MIB   NB   DB   BNT
☐ Want   Orig. Ret. $5.00   **NB** $100   **MIB** Sec. Mkt. **$135**

QX 147-6   HOLLY AND POINSETTIA BALL
Comments: Handcrafted Ball, 3-1/2" dia.
With the look of intricate hand carving, this ball is circled with poinsettias and greenery. **Artist:** Linda Sickman
☐ Purchased 19___Pd $_____MIB   NB   DB   BNT
☐ Want   Orig. Ret. $6.00   **NB** $55   **MIB** Sec. Mkt. **$85**

QX 221-6   JOAN WALSH ANGLUND®
Comments: White Satin Ball, 3-1/4" dia.
Front: Children caroling in the snow. Back: Children decorating a snow-covered tree. Caption: "As Long As We Have Love And Friends, Christmas Never Really Ends 1978."
☐ Purchased 19___Pd $_____MIB   NB   DB   BNT
☐ Want   Orig. Ret. $3.50   **NB** $65   **MIB** Sec. Mkt. **$72**

QX 254-3   JOY   ☐

Comments: Gold Glass Ball, 3-1/4" dia.
Front: A stained glass look complements the word "JOY."
Back: Christmas message in a matching oval.
Caption on back: "The Beauty Of Christmas Shines All Around Us."
☐ Purchased 19___Pd $_____MIB   NB   DB   BNT
☐ Want   Orig. Ret. $3.50   **NB** $35   **MIB** Sec. Mkt. **$48**

QX 138-3   JOY   ☐

Comments: Handcrafted, 4-3/16" tall.
Red "bread dough" letters spell the word "JOY" as a little blue-dressed elf pops through the "O."
☐ Purchased 19___Pd $_____MIB   NB   DB   BNT
☐ Want   Orig. Ret. $4.50   **NB** $38   **MIB** Sec. Mkt. **$80**

QX 136-3   LITTLE TRIMMERS: DRUMMER BOY   ☐

Comments: Handcrafted, 2-1/16" tall.
Drummer boy dressed in red, green and blue, plays his drum. Beware of missing or broken drumsticks.
☐ Purchased 19___Pd $_____MIB   NB   DB   BNT
☐ Want   Orig. Ret. $2.50   **NB** $45   **MIB** Sec. Mkt. **$65**

QX 134-3   LITTLE TRIMMERS: PRAYING ANGEL   ☐

Comments: Handcrafted, 2" tall.
A pink-clad angel kneels in prayer. **Artist:** Donna Lee
☐ Purchased 19___Pd $_____MIB   NB   DB   BNT
☐ Want   Orig. Ret. $2.50   **NB** $55   **MIB** Sec. Mkt. **$90**

QX 135-6   LITTLE TRIMMERS: SANTA   ☐

Comments: Handcrafted, 2-1/4" tall.
Reissued in 1979. Waving Santa, holding a gift.
☐ Purchased 19___Pd $_____MIB   NB   DB   BNT
☐ Want   Orig. Ret. $2.50   **NB** $32   **MIB** Sec. Mkt. **$55**

QX 133-6   LITTLE TRIMMERS: THIMBLE SERIES (MOUSE)   ☐

Comments: ***FIRST IN SERIES,*** Handcrafted, 1-3/4" tall.
A white mouse with a red cap peeks out of a silver thimble. Later known as Thimble Series.
☐ Purchased 19___Pd $_____MIB   NB   DB   BNT
☐ Want   Orig. Ret. $2.50   **NB** $250   **MIB** Sec. Mkt. **$300**

QX 132-3   LITTLE TRIMMER COLLECTION   ☐

Comments: Handcrafted, Set of 4.
Miniature versions of Thimble Mouse, Praying Angel, Drummer Boy and Santa. RARE!
☐ Purchased 19___Pd $_____MIB   NB   DB   BNT
☐ Want   Orig. Ret. $9.00   **NB** $300   **MIB** Sec. Mkt. **$340**

QX 268-3   LOVE   ☐

Comments: Gold Glass Ball, 3-1/4" dia., Dated 1978.
A heart which contains "1978" is surrounded by poinsettias and birds.
Caption: "Of Life's Many Treasures, The Most Beautiful Is Love."
☐ Purchased 19___Pd $_____MIB   NB   DB   BNT
☐ Want   Orig. Ret. $3.50   **NB** $40   **MIB** Sec. Mkt. **$55**

QX 202-3   MERRY CHRISTMAS (SANTA)   ☐

Comments: White Satin Ball, 3-1/4" dia., Dated 1978.
Santa with his pack of gifts is later seen flying over rooftops on Christmas eve. Caption: "Merry Christmas."
☐ Purchased 19___Pd $_____MIB   NB   DB   BNT
☐ Want   Orig. Ret. $3.50   **NB** $42   **MIB** Sec. Mkt. **$58**

QX 266-3   MOTHER   ☐

Comments: White Glass Ball, 3-1/4" dia.
Caption: "The Wonderful Meaning Of Christmas Is Found In A Mother's Love" and "Christmas 1978."
☐ Purchased 19___Pd $_____MIB   NB   DB   BNT
☐ Want   Orig. Ret. $3.50   **NB** $42   **MIB** Sec. Mkt. **$48**

QX 253-6   NATIVITY   ☐

Comments: White Glass Ball, 3-1/4" dia.
An "old world" Nativity scene. Caption: "The Joy Of Heaven Is Come To Earth."
☐ Purchased 19___Pd $_____MIB   NB   DB   BNT
☐ Want   Orig. Ret. $3.50   **NB** $35   **MIB** Sec. Mkt. **$60**

QX 145-6   PANORAMA BALL   ☐

Comments: Handcrafted Panorama Ball, 3-5/8" dia.
A little boy has fallen on the ice, viewed through a peek-through window in the ornament. Caption: "Merry Christmas 1978."
☐ Purchased 19___Pd $_____MIB   NB   DB   BNT
☐ Want   Orig. Ret. $6.00   **NB** $120   **MIB** Sec. Mkt. **$140**

QX 204-3   PEANUTS®
Comments: White Satin Ball, 2-5/8" dia., Dated 1978.
Snoopy and Woodstock decorate their freshly cut Christmas tree.
☐ Purchased 19 __ Pd $_____ MIB   NB   DB   BNT
☐ Want   Orig. Ret. $2.50   **NB** $55   **MIB** Sec. Mkt. **$68**

QX 205-6   PEANUTS®
Comments: White Satin Ball, 3-1/4" dia.
The gang sings while Linus holds a dated wreath. Caption: "Joy to the World 1978."
☐ Purchased 19 __ Pd $_____ MIB   NB   DB   BNT
☐ Want   Orig. Ret. $3.50   **NB** $55   **MIB** Sec. Mkt. **$62**

QX 206-3   PEANUTS®
Comments: White Satin Ball, 3-1/4" dia., Dated 1978.
Front: Snoopy, Woodstock and his flock are playing in a toy store. Back: Snoopy plays Santa.
☐ Purchased 19 __ Pd $_____ MIB   NB   DB   BNT
☐ Want   Orig. Ret. $3.50   **NB** $45   **MIB** Sec. Mkt. **$55**

QX 203-6   PEANUTS®
Comments: White Satin Ball, 2-5/8" dia.
Charlie Brown is wrapped up in the Christmas tree lights. Snoopy decorates his doghouse. Caption: "Have A Delightful Christmas."
☐ Purchased 19 __ Pd $_____ MIB   NB   DB   BNT
☐ Want   Orig. Ret. $2.50   **NB** $48   **MIB** Sec. Mkt. **$60**

QX 251-6   QUAIL, THE
Comments: Gold Glass Ball, 3-1/4" dia., Dated 1978.
Caption: "Nature Has A Wonderful Way Of Making A Wonder-filled World."
☐ Purchased 19 __ Pd $_____ MIB   NB   DB   BNT
☐ Want   Orig. Ret. $3.50   **NB** $38   **MIB** Sec. Mkt. **$45**

QX 144-3   RED CARDINAL
Comments: Handcrafted, 4" tall.
This cardinal clips on the branch of the tree.
☐ Purchased 19 __ Pd $_____ MIB   NB   DB   BNT
☐ Want   Orig. Ret. $4.50   **NB-P** $100   **MIB** Sec. Mkt. **$165**

QX 148-3   ROCKING HORSE
Comments: Handcrafted, 3-9/16" tall, Dated 1978.
Hand-painted polka-dot horse with white yarn mane and red rockers.
☐ Purchased 19 __ Pd $_____ MIB   NB   DB   BNT
☐ Want   Orig. Ret. $6.00   **NB** $80   **MIB** Sec. Mkt. **$95**

QX 152-3   SCHNEEBERG BELL
Comments: Handcrafted, 4" tall.
Reproduction of an intricate Schneeberg wood carving collage (82 decorating steps were required to achieve the natural wood look). Caption: "Christmas 1978."
☐ Purchased 19 __ Pd $_____ MIB   NB   DB   BNT
☐ Want   Orig. Ret. $8.00   **NB** $130   **MIB** Sec. Mkt. **$185**

QX 142-3   SKATING RACCOON
Comments: Handcrafted, 2-3/4" tall. Reissued in 1979.
Raccoon with red mittens and scarf wears real metal skates.
Artist: Donna Lee
☐ Purchased 19 __ Pd $_____ MIB   NB   DB   BNT
☐ Want   Orig. Ret. $6.00   **NB** $55   **MIB** Sec. Mkt. **$90**

QX 219-6   SPENCER™ SPARROW, ESQ.
Comments: Ecru Soft-Sheen Satin Ball, 3-1/4" dia.
A little sparrow named Spencer sits in a wreath and on the reverse, pulls a sled loaded with gifts. Caption: "Holly Days Are Jolly Days" and "Christmas 1978."
☐ Purchased 19 __ Pd $_____ MIB   NB   DB   BNT
☐ Want   Orig. Ret. $3.50   **NB** $45   **MIB** Sec. Mkt. **$50**

QX 133-6   THIMBLE SERIES: MOUSE
Comments: ***FIRST IN SERIES,*** Handcrafted, 1-3/4" tall.
Reissued from Little Trimmers Series - Thimble Mouse. No box price down from 1996.
☐ Purchased 19 __ Pd $_____ MIB   NB   DB   BNT
☐ Want   Orig. Ret. $2.50   **NB** $250   **MIB** Sec. Mkt. **$300**

QX 269-6   TWENTY-FIFTH CHRISTMAS TOGETHER
Comments: White Glass Ball, 3-1/4" dia., Dated 1978.
Front: Caption "25th Christmas Together."   Back: Caption "Time Endears But Cannot Fade The Memories That Love Has Made."
☐ Purchased 19 __ Pd $_____ MIB   NB   DB   BNT
☐ Want   Orig. Ret. $3.50   **NB** $20   **MIB** Sec. Mkt. **$25**

No secondary market value has been established for yarn and fabric ornaments found in original cellophane package.

QX 123-1   YARN ORNAMENTS: GREEN BOY
Comments: 4-1/2" tall. Green with red hat.
Slight changes from 1975. Reissued in 1979.
☐ Purchased 19__ Pd $_____ MIB   NB   DB   BNT
☐ Want Orig. Ret. $2.00   Sec. Mkt. **$22**

QX 126-1   YARN ORNAMENTS: GREEN GIRL
Comments: 4-1/2" tall. Green with white muff.
Slight changes from 1975. Reissued in 1979.
☐ Purchased 19__ Pd $_____ MIB   NB   DB   BNT
☐ Want Orig. Ret. $2.00   Sec. Mkt. **$20**

QX 340-3   YARN ORNAMENTS: MR. CLAUS
Comments: 4-1/2" tall. Identical to 1975. Reissued in 1979.
☐ Purchased 19__ Pd $_____ MIB   NB   DB   BNT
☐ Want Orig. Ret. $2.00   Sec. Mkt. **$22**

QX 125-1   YARN ORNAMENTS: MRS. CLAUS
Comments: 4-1/2" tall Identical to 1975. Reissued in 1979.
White apron with red checked pockets.
☐ Purchased 19__ Pd $_____ MIB   NB   DB   BNT
☐ Want Orig. Ret. $2.00   Sec. Mkt. **$22**

QX 250-3   YESTERDAY'S TOYS
Comments: Gold Glass Ball, 3-1/4" dia., Dated 1978.
Caption: "Every Joy Of Yesterday Is A Memory For Tomorrow. 1978"
☐ Purchased 19__ Pd $_____ MIB   NB   DB   BNT
☐ Want Orig. Ret. $3.50   **NB** $15   **MIB** Sec. Mkt. **$25**

1979 Collection

QX 134-7   A CHRISTMAS TREAT
Comments: Handcrafted, 4-3/4" tall. Reissued in 1980.
A teddy bear with a red cap and coat holds a giant candy cane.
The 1979 ornament has "grooves" around the candy cane; the 1980 ornament does not.
☐ Purchased 19__ Pd $_____ MIB   NB   DB   BNT
☐ Want Orig. Ret. $5.00   **NB** $40   **MIB** Sec. Mkt. **$65**

QX 343-9   ANGEL MUSIC
Comments: Sewn Fabric, 4-5" tall. Reissued in 1980.
Flying angel in blue flowered gown with pink and white wings, carrying a harp.
☐ Purchased 19__ Pd $_____ MIB   NB   DB   BNT
☐ Want Orig. Ret. $2.00   Sec. Mkt. **$20**

QX 208-7   BABY'S FIRST CHRISTMAS
Comments: White Satin Ball, 3-1/4" dia., Dated 1979.
Toys and gifts are pulled on a sleigh. Back: A Christmas tree is decorated by birds. Caption: "Baby's First Christmas 1979."
☐ Purchased 19__ Pd $_____ MIB   NB   DB   BNT
☐ Want Orig. Ret. $3.50   **NB** $15   **MIB** Sec. Mkt. **$30**

QX 154-7   BABY'S FIRST CHRISTMAS
Comments: Handcrafted, 4" tall, Dated 1979.
RARE!! Knitted stocking filled with toys. The first handcrafted ornament for Baby's First Christmas. Caption: "Baby's First Christmas 1979."
☐ Purchased 19__ Pd $_____ MIB   NB   DB   BNT
☐ Want Orig. Ret. $8.00   **NB** $100   **MIB** Sec. Mkt. **$125**

QX 255-9   BEHOLD THE STAR
Comments: White Satin Ball, 3-1/4" dia.
Caption: "And the light was for all time; And the love was for all men."
☐ Purchased 19__ Pd $_____ MIB   NB   DB   BNT
☐ Want Orig. Ret. $3.50   **NB** $20   **MIB** Sec. Mkt. **$35**

QX 147-9   BELLRINGER - "BELLSWINGER"
Comments: ***FIRST IN SERIES,*** Dated 1979.
Porcelain and Handcrafted, 4" tall. A happy elf swings on the clapper of a white porcelain bell decorated with a wreath. Price down from '96.
☐ Purchased 19__ Pd $_____ MIB   NB   DB   BNT
☐ Want Orig. Ret. $10.00   **NB** $195   **MIB** Sec. Mkt. **$250**

QX 201-9   BETSEY CLARK SERIES
Comments: **Seventh in Series,** White Satin Ball, 3-1/4" dia.
Children sit at home reading and then they pull a sled with a tree and gifts. Caption: "Holiday Fun Times Make Memories To Treasure. 1979"
☐ Purchased 19__ Pd $_____ MIB   NB   DB   BNT
☐ Want Orig. Ret. $3.50   **NB** $22   **MIB** Sec. Mkt. **$38**

QX 207-9   BLACK ANGEL   ☐
Comments: Gold Glass Ball, 3-1/4" dia., Dated 1979.
Young adult angel dressed in a red and white robe. Caption: "Merry Christmas 1979." **Artist:** Thomas Blackshear
☐ Purchased 19 __ Pd $_____ MIB   NB   DB   BNT
☐ Want   Orig. Ret. $3.50   **NB** $14   **MIB** Sec. Mkt. **$25**

QX 146-7   CARROUSEL SERIES: ☐
CHRISTMAS CARROUSEL
Comments: **Second in Series,** Handcrafted, 3-1/2" tall.
Four angel musicians revolve on a carrousel.
Caption: "Christmas 1979."
☐ Purchased 19 __ Pd $_____ MIB   NB   DB   BNT
☐ Want   Orig. Ret. $6.50   **NB** $135   **MIB** Sec. Mkt. **$170**

QX 204-7   CHRISTMAS CHICKADEES   ☐
Comments: Gold Glass Ball, 3-1/4" dia.
A pair of chickadees enjoy holly berries. Caption: "Beauty Is A Gift Nature Gives Every Day" and "Christmas 1979."
☐ Purchased 19 __ Pd $_____ MIB   NB   DB   BNT
☐ Want   Orig. Ret. $3.50   **NB** $18   **MIB** Sec. Mkt. **$35**

QX 257-9   CHRISTMAS COLLAGE   ☐
Comments: Gold Glass Ball, 3-1/4" dia., Dated 1979.
Old fashioned toys reproduced from a photograph of a Schneeberg collage. Caption: "Season's Greetings."
☐ Purchased 19 __ Pd $_____ MIB   NB   DB   BNT
☐ Want   Orig. Ret. $3.50   **NB** $12   **MIB** Sec. Mkt. **$35**

QX 157-9   CHRISTMAS EVE SURPRISE   ☐
Comments: Handcrafted, 4-1/4" tall, Dated 1979.
A wood-look shadow box shows Santa going down the chimney.
☐ Purchased 19 __ Pd $_____ MIB   NB   DB   BNT
☐ Want   Orig. Ret. $6.50   **NB** $45   **MIB** Sec. Mkt. **$65**

QX 140-7   CHRISTMAS HEART   ☐
Comments: Handcrafted, 3-1/2" tall, Dated 1979.
Two doves rotate through the center of this heart-shaped ornament.
Artist: Linda Sickman
☐ Purchased 19 __ Pd $_____ MIB   NB   DB   BNT
☐ Want   Orig. Ret. $6.50   **NB** $70   **MIB** Sec. Mkt. **$95**

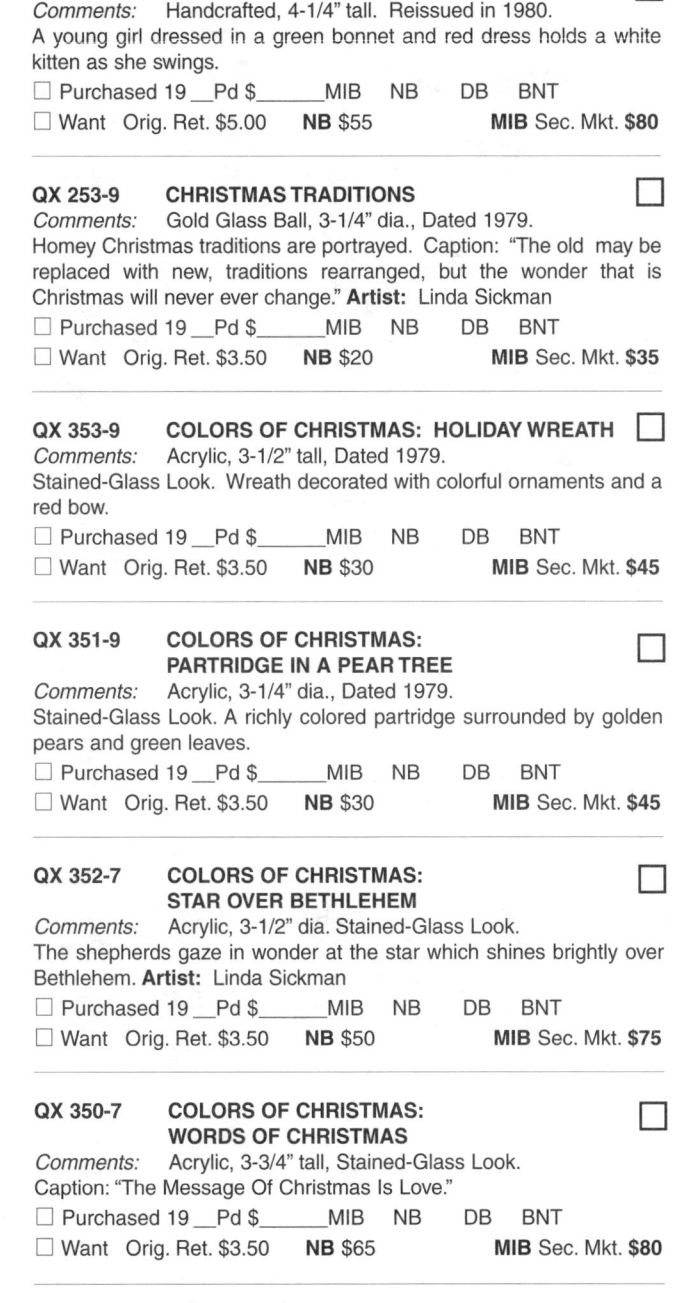

QX 135-9   CHRISTMAS IS FOR CHILDREN   ☐
Comments: Handcrafted, 4-1/4" tall. Reissued in 1980.
A young girl dressed in a green bonnet and red dress holds a white kitten as she swings.
☐ Purchased 19 __ Pd $_____ MIB   NB   DB   BNT
☐ Want   Orig. Ret. $5.00   **NB** $55   **MIB** Sec. Mkt. **$80**

QX 253-9   CHRISTMAS TRADITIONS   ☐
Comments: Gold Glass Ball, 3-1/4" dia., Dated 1979.
Homey Christmas traditions are portrayed. Caption: "The old may be replaced with new, traditions rearranged, but the wonder that is Christmas will never ever change." **Artist:** Linda Sickman
☐ Purchased 19 __ Pd $_____ MIB   NB   DB   BNT
☐ Want   Orig. Ret. $3.50   **NB** $20   **MIB** Sec. Mkt. **$35**

QX 353-9   COLORS OF CHRISTMAS: HOLIDAY WREATH   ☐
Comments: Acrylic, 3-1/2" tall, Dated 1979.
Stained-Glass Look. Wreath decorated with colorful ornaments and a red bow.
☐ Purchased 19 __ Pd $_____ MIB   NB   DB   BNT
☐ Want   Orig. Ret. $3.50   **NB** $30   **MIB** Sec. Mkt. **$45**

QX 351-9   COLORS OF CHRISTMAS: ☐
PARTRIDGE IN A PEAR TREE
Comments: Acrylic, 3-1/4" dia., Dated 1979.
Stained-Glass Look. A richly colored partridge surrounded by golden pears and green leaves.
☐ Purchased 19 __ Pd $_____ MIB   NB   DB   BNT
☐ Want   Orig. Ret. $3.50   **NB** $30   **MIB** Sec. Mkt. **$45**

QX 352-7   COLORS OF CHRISTMAS: ☐
STAR OVER BETHLEHEM
Comments: Acrylic, 3-1/2" dia. Stained-Glass Look.
The shepherds gaze in wonder at the star which shines brightly over Bethlehem. **Artist:** Linda Sickman
☐ Purchased 19 __ Pd $_____ MIB   NB   DB   BNT
☐ Want   Orig. Ret. $3.50   **NB** $50   **MIB** Sec. Mkt. **$75**

QX 350-7   COLORS OF CHRISTMAS: ☐
WORDS OF CHRISTMAS
Comments: Acrylic, 3-3/4" tall, Stained-Glass Look.
Caption: "The Message Of Christmas Is Love."
☐ Purchased 19 __ Pd $_____ MIB   NB   DB   BNT
☐ Want   Orig. Ret. $3.50   **NB** $65   **MIB** Sec. Mkt. **$80**

QHD 950-7   CRECHE TABLETOP DECORATION ☐
Comments: Frosted acrylic Creche on clear acrylic base.
Caption: "O Come Let Us Adore Him."
☐ Purchased 19__Pd $_____MIB   NB   DB   BNT
☐ Want Orig. Ret. $25.00 **NB** $120   **MIB** Sec. Mkt. **$175**

QX 145-9   DOWNHILL RUN, THE ☐
Comments: Handcrafted, 3" tall.
A rabbit in a blue scarf and a squirrel with a red cap make a downhill run on a red toboggan. **Artist:** Donna Lee
☐ Purchased 19__Pd $_____MIB   NB   DB   BNT
☐ Want Orig. Ret. $6.50 **NB** $140   **MIB** Sec. Mkt. **$160**

QX 143-9   DRUMMER BOY, THE ☐
Comments: Handcrafted Panorama Ball, 3-1/4" dia.
A red-capped drummer boy stands in the snow. A lamb and a duck listen as he plays his drum.
☐ Purchased 19__Pd $_____MIB   NB   DB   BNT
☐ Want Orig. Ret. $8.00 **NB** $90   **MIB** Sec. Mkt. **$130**

QX 209-9   FIRST CHRISTMAS TOGETHER, OUR ☐
Comments: Gold Glass Ball, 3-1/4" dia.
Caption: "Our First Christmas Together 1979" and "Christmas and Love are for Sharing."
☐ Purchased 19__Pd $_____MIB   NB   DB   BNT
☐ Want Orig. Ret. $3.50 **NB** $38   **MIB** Sec. Mkt. **$65**

QX 203-9   FRIENDSHIP ☐
Comments: White Glass Ball, 3-1/4" dia.
Ice skating and a sleigh ride. Caption: "There Is No Time Quite Like Christmas For Remembering Friendships We Cherish" and "Christmas 1979."
☐ Purchased 19__Pd $_____MIB   NB   DB   BNT
☐ Want Orig. Ret. $3.50 **NB** $20   **MIB** Sec. Mkt. **$32**

QX 211-9   GRANDDAUGHTER ☐
Comments: White Satin Ball, 3-1/4" dia., Dated 1979.
A little girl in a white cap and a red coat feeds the animals. Caption: "A Granddaughter Fills Each Day With Joy By Filling Hearts With Love."
☐ Purchased 19__Pd $_____MIB   NB   DB   BNT
☐ Want Orig. Ret. $3.50 **NB** $22   **MIB** Sec. Mkt. **$35**

QX 252-7   GRANDMOTHER ☐
Comments: White Glass Ball, 3-1/4" dia., Dated 1979.
Birds fly about a basket of Christmas flowers.
Caption: "Grandmothers Bring Happy Times — Time And Time Again."
☐ Purchased 19__Pd $_____MIB   NB   DB   BNT
☐ Want Orig. Ret. $3.50 **NB** $14   **MIB** Sec. Mkt. **$22**

QX 210-7   GRANDSON ☐
Comments: White Satin Ball, 3-1/4" dia.
Snoopy and Woodstock sledding in the snow.
Caption: "A Grandson... A Special Someone Whose Merry Ways Bring Extra Joy To The Holidays. Christmas 1979."
☐ Purchased 19__Pd $_____MIB   NB   DB   BNT
☐ Want Orig. Ret. $3.50 **NB** $21   **MIB** Sec. Mkt. **$28**

QX 155-9   HERE COMES SANTA SERIES: ☐
SANTA'S MOTORCAR
Comments: **FIRST IN SERIES,** Handcrafted, 3-1/2" tall, Dated 1979. Turning wheels on the antique car that Santa drives makes this a special ornament.
☐ Purchased 19__Pd $_____MIB   NB   DB   BNT
☐ Want Orig. Ret. $9.00 **NB** $425   **MIB** Sec. Mkt. **$625**

QX 320-3   HOLIDAY CHIMES: REINDEER CHIMES ☐
Comments: Chrome plated brass, 5-1/2" tall.
Issued in 1978, 1979 and 1980.
Artist: Linda Sickman
☐ Purchased 19__Pd $_____MIB   NB   DB   BNT
☐ Want Orig. Ret. $4.50 **NB** $32   **MIB** Sec. Mkt. **$40**

QX 137-9   HOLIDAY CHIMES: STAR CHIMES ☐
Comments: Chrome Plate, 4" tall, Dated 1979.
Stars circle within stars. Year date is in the center star.
Artist: Linda Sickman
☐ Purchased 19__Pd $_____MIB   NB   DB   BNT
☐ Want Orig. Ret. $4.50 **NB** $50   **MIB** Sec. Mkt. **$60**

QX 300-7   HOLIDAY HIGHLIGHTS: CHRISTMAS ANGEL ☐
Comments: Acrylic, 4-1/4" wide, Hard to Find.
Flying angel with long floral dress, feathery wings and halo, holding a nosegay of flowers. Caption: "Christmas 1979."
☐ Purchased 19__Pd $_____MIB   NB   DB   BNT
☐ Want Orig. Ret. $3.50 **NB** $62   **MIB** Sec. Mkt. **$95**

QX 303-9   **HOLIDAY HIGHLIGHTS: CHRISTMAS CHEER** ☐
Comments: Acrylic, 3-1/2" dia., Dated 1979.
A little bird with berries in its beak is perched on a holly bough.
☐ Purchased 19 __ Pd $_____ MIB   NB   DB   BNT
☐ Want   Orig. Ret. $3.50   **NB** $45   **MIB** Sec. Mkt. **$75**

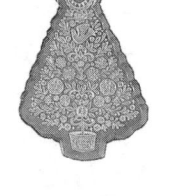

QX 302-7   **HOLIDAY HIGHLIGHTS: CHRISTMAS TREE** ☐
Comments: Acrylic, 4-1/2" tall, Dated 1979.
A tree of leaves and flowers with a dove near the top. The date is stamped in silver foil.
☐ Purchased 19 __ Pd $_____ MIB   NB   DB   BNT
☐ Want   Orig. Ret. $3.50   **NB** $45   **MIB** Sec. Mkt. **$75**

QX 304-7   **HOLIDAY HIGHLIGHTS: LOVE** ☐
Comments: Acrylic, 3-1/2" tall.
The caption is stamped in silver foil on this heart: "Time Of Memories And Dreams… Time Of Love. Christmas 1979."
☐ Purchased 19 __ Pd $_____ MIB   NB   DB   BNT
☐ Want   Orig. Ret. $3.50   **NB** $80   **MIB** Sec. Mkt. **$90**

QX 301-9   **HOLIDAY HIGHLIGHTS SNOWFLAKE** ☐
Comments: Acrylic, 3-1/2" dia., Dated 1979.
This lovely snowflake has the date "etched" in the center hexagon.
☐ Purchased 19 __ Pd $_____ MIB   NB   DB   BNT
☐ Want   Orig. Ret. $3.50   **NB** $30   **MIB** Sec. Mkt. **$40**

QX 152-7   **HOLIDAY SCRIMSHAW** ☐
Comments: Handcrafted, 3-1/2" tall.
Ivory angel with widespread wings resembles scrimshaw carving. Caption: "Peace - Love - Joy 1979."
☐ Purchased 19 __ Pd $_____ MIB   NB   DB   BNT
☐ Want   Orig. Ret. $4.00   **NB** $170   **MIB** Sec. Mkt. **$230**

QX 205-9   **JOAN WALSH ANGLUND©** ☐
Comments: White Satin Ball, 3-1/4" dia., Dated 1979.
Children hang their stockings by the fireplace. Back: Children with their gifts. Caption: "The Smallest Pleasure Is Big Enough To Share."
☐ Purchased 19 __ Pd $_____ MIB   NB   DB   BNT
☐ Want   Orig. Ret. $3.50   **NB** $27   **MIB** Sec. Mkt. **$38**

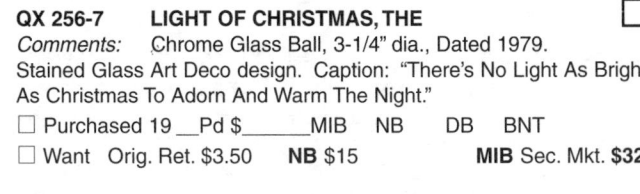

QX 256-7   **LIGHT OF CHRISTMAS, THE** ☐
Comments: Chrome Glass Ball, 3-1/4" dia., Dated 1979.
Stained Glass Art Deco design. Caption: "There's No Light As Bright As Christmas To Adorn And Warm The Night."
☐ Purchased 19 __ Pd $_____ MIB   NB   DB   BNT
☐ Want   Orig. Ret. $3.50   **NB** $15   **MIB** Sec. Mkt. **$32**

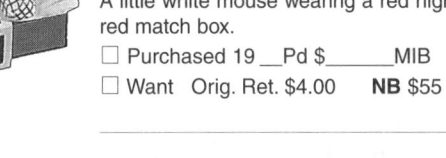

QX 132-7   **LITTLE TRIMMER COLLECTION:**
                A MATCHLESS CHRISTMAS ☐
Comments: Handcrafted, 2-1/2" long.
A little white mouse wearing a red nightcap makes a cozy bed from a red match box.
☐ Purchased 19 __ Pd $_____ MIB   NB   DB   BNT
☐ Want   Orig. Ret. $4.00   **NB** $55   **MIB** Sec. Mkt. **$78**

QX 130-7   **LITTLE TRIMMER COLLECTION:**
                ANGEL DELIGHT ☐
Comments: Handcrafted, 1-3/4" tall.
A little angel in a blue gown rides in her walnut shell.
☐ Purchased 19 __ Pd $_____ MIB   NB   DB   BNT
☐ Want   Orig. Ret. $3.00   **NB** $70   **MIB** Sec. Mkt. **$80**

QX 135-6   **LITTLE TRIMMERS: SANTA** ☐
Comments: Handcrafted, 2-1/4" tall. Reissued from 1978.
☐ Purchased 19 __ Pd $_____ MIB   NB   DB   BNT
☐ Want   1979 Retail $3.00   **NB** $32   **MIB** Sec. Mkt. **$55**

QX 133-6   **LITTLE TRIMMERS: THIMBLE SERIES** ☐
Comments: **FIRST IN SERIES,** Handcrafted, 1-3/4" tall. Reissued from 1978.
☐ Purchased 19 __ Pd $_____ MIB   NB   DB   BNT
☐ Want   1979 Retail $3.00   **NB** $250   **MIB** Sec. Mkt. **$300**

QX 159-9   **LITTLE TRIMMER SET** ☐
Comments: Handcrafted.
The Angel, Matchless Christmas and Soldier were packaged together as a trio of Trimmers.
☐ Purchased 19 __ Pd $_____ MIB   NB   DB   BNT
☐ Want   Orig. Ret. $9.00   **NB** $255   **MIB** Sec. Mkt. **$335**

QX 258-7   LOVE   ☐
Comments: White Glass Ball, 3-1/4" dia.
Caption: "Love... Warm As Candle Glow, Wondrous As Snowfall, Welcome As Christmas" and "Christmas 1979."
☐ Purchased 19__ Pd $_____ MIB   NB   DB   BNT
☐ Want   Orig. Ret. $3.50   **NB** $22   **MIB** Sec. Mkt. **$40**

QX 254-7   MARY HAMILTON   ☐
Comments: Ecru Soft-Sheen Satin Ball, 3-1/4" dia.
Dated 1979. A choir of angels sing to forest creatures.
Caption: "... And Heaven And Nature Sing."
☐ Purchased 19__ Pd $_____ MIB   NB   DB   BNT
☐ Want   Orig. Ret. $3.50   **NB** $18   **MIB** Sec. Mkt. **$28**

QX 342-7   MERRY SANTA   ☐
Comments: Fabric, 4"-5" tall. Reissued in 1980.
Whimsical Santa with a pack of toys on his back.
☐ Purchased 19__ Pd $_____ MIB   NB   DB   BNT
☐ Want   Orig. Ret. $2.00   Sec. Mkt. **$22**

QX 251-9   MOTHER   ☐
Comments: White Glass Ball, 3-1/4" dia.
Caption: "It's Love That Makes Christmas So Special - And Mother Who Makes Us Feel Loved."
☐ Purchased 19__ Pd $_____ MIB   NB   DB   BNT
☐ Want   Orig. Ret. $3.50   **NB** $18   **MIB** Sec. Mkt. **$25**

QX 212-7   NEW HOME   ☐
Comments: Ecru Soft-Sheen Satin Ball, 3-1/4" dia.
Dated 1979. A colorful snow-covered village and pond. Caption: "Christmas... When Love Fills The Heart, When Hearts Look To Home."
☐ Purchased 19__ Pd $_____ MIB   NB   DB   BNT
☐ Want   Orig. Ret. $3.50   **NB** $18   **MIB** Sec. Mkt. **$45**

QX 214-7   NIGHT BEFORE CHRISTMAS   ☐
Comments: White Satin Ball, 3-1/4" dia., Dated 1979.
Santa fills the stockings and continues on his journey. Caption: "... I Heard Him Exclaim, Ere He Drove Out Of Sight, Happy Christmas To All, And To All A Good Night." C. C. Moore
☐ Purchased 19__ Pd $_____ MIB   NB   DB   BNT
☐ Want   Orig. Ret. $3.50   **NB** $32   **MIB** Sec. Mkt. **$42**

QX 150-7   OUTDOOR FUN   ☐
Comments: Handcrafted, 3" tall.
A little girl swings between two fir trees. **Artist:** Linda Sickman
☐ Purchased 19__ Pd $_____ MIB   NB   DB   BNT
☐ Want   Orig. Ret. $8.00   **NB** $85   **MIB** Sec. Mkt. **$125**

QX 202-7   PEANUTS® (TIME TO TRIM)   ☐
Comments: White Satin Ball, 3-1/4" dia., Dated 1979.
Woodstock and his green-capped flock decorate their Christmas tree with candy canes Snoopy is giving them.
Caption: "Merry Christmas 1979."
☐ Purchased 19__ Pd $_____ MIB   NB   DB   BNT
☐ Want   Orig. Ret. $3.50   **NB** $28   **MIB** Sec. Mkt. **$42**

QX 133-9   READY FOR CHRISTMAS   ☐
Comments: Handcrafted, 3" tall, Dated 1979.
White birdhouse with snow-capped roof and green garland over the door. **Artist:** Donna Lee
☐ Purchased 19__ Pd $_____ MIB   NB   DB   BNT
☐ Want   Orig. Ret. $6.50   **NB** $80   **MIB** Sec. Mkt. **$135**

QX 340-7   ROCKING HORSE, THE   ☐
Comments: Quilted Fabric, 4" - 5" tall. Reissued in 1980.
A brown spotted rocking horse rides into Christmas on blue rockers. The ornament is trimmed in red.
☐ Purchased 19__ Pd $_____ MIB   NB   DB   BNT
☐ Want   Orig. Ret. $2.00   Sec. Mkt. **$25**

QX 138-7   SANTA'S HERE   ☐
Comments: Handcrafted, 4" dia., Dated 1979.
Santa, with his pack, waves as he rotates inside a white snowflake.
Artist: Linda Sickman
☐ Purchased 19__ Pd $_____ MIB   NB   DB   BNT
☐ Want   Orig. Ret. $5.00   **NB** $50   **MIB** Sec. Mkt. **$72**

QX 142-3   SKATING RACCOON   ☐
Comments: Handcrafted, 2" tall. Reissued from 1978.
Artist: Donna Lee
☐ Purchased 19__ Pd $_____ MIB   NB   DB   BNT
☐ Want   1979 Retail $6.50   **NB** $55   **MIB** Sec. Mkt. **$90**

QX 139-9   SKATING SNOWMAN, THE
Comments: Handcrafted, 4-1/4" tall, Reissued in 1980.
This happy snowman wears metal ice skates, a black top hat and a green and white scarf.
☐ Purchased 19 __Pd $_____MIB   NB   DB   BNT
☐ Want   Orig. Ret. $5.00   **NB** $60   **MIB** Sec. Mkt. **$80**

QX 141-9   SNOOPY & FRIENDS SERIES: ICE HOCKEY HOLIDAY
Comments: **FIRST IN SERIES**, 3-1/4" dia., Dated 1979.
Handcrafted Panorama Ball. Snoopy and Woodstock play ice hockey on a frozen pond.
☐ Purchased 19 __Pd $_____MIB   NB   DB   BNT
☐ Want   Orig. Ret. $8.00   **NB** $85   **MIB** Sec. Mkt. **$128**

QX 200-7   SPENCER™ SPARROW, ESQ.
Comments: Ecru Soft-Sheen Satin Ball, 3-1/4" dia.
Dated 1979. Spencer swings on a garland of popcorn and cranberries. Caption: "Christmas Time Means Decorating, Spreading Cheer And Celebrating."
☐ Purchased 19 __Pd $_____MIB   NB   DB   BNT
☐ Want   Orig. Ret. $3.50   **NB** $20   **MIB** Sec. Mkt. **$38**

QX 341-9   STUFFED FULL STOCKING
Comments: Quilted Fabric, 4" - 5" tall, Reissued in 1980.
Blue patchwork stocking holds a doll and other gifts to delight a child.
☐ Purchased 19 __Pd $_____MIB   NB   DB   BNT
☐ Want   Orig. Ret. $2.00   Sec. Mkt. **$24**

QX 213-9   TEACHER
Comments: White Satin Ball, 3-1/4" dia., Dated 1979.
Front: A raccoon writes a message to the teacher. Back: A sleigh with a gift. Caption: "To a Special Teacher" and "Merry Christmas 1979."
☐ Purchased 19 __Pd $_____MIB   NB   DB   BNT
☐ Want   Orig. Ret. $3.50   **NB** $10   **MIB** Sec. Mkt. **$20**

QX 131-9   THIMBLE SERIES: A CHRISTMAS SALUTE
Comments: **Second in Series,** Handcrafted, 2-1/4" tall.
Reissued in 1980. A cute soldier dressed in red and blue wears a thimble hat. Price down from 1996.
☐ Purchased 19 __Pd $_____MIB   NB   DB   BNT
☐ Want   Orig. Ret. $3.00   **NB** $90   **MIB** Sec. Mkt. **$150**

OX 703-7   TIFFANY ANGEL TREE TOPPER
Comments: This stained-glass look angel plays her lute.
Multicolored with silver "leading," she complements other stained-glass look ornaments.
☐ Purchased 19 __Pd $_____MIB   NB   DB   BNT
☐ Want   Orig. Ret. $10.00   **NB** $25   **MIB** Sec. Mkt. **$35**

QX 250-7   TWENTY-FIFTH ANNIVERSARY, OUR
Comments: White Glass Ball, 3-1/4" dia., Dated 1979.
Greenery and holly berries make a lovely background for white ribbon and wedding bells. Caption: "Year of our 25th Anniversary" and "Those Warm Times Shared In Past Decembers. The Mind Still Sees, The Heart Remembers."
☐ Purchased 19 __Pd $_____MIB   NB   DB   BNT
☐ Want   Orig. Ret. $3.50   **NB** $15   **MIB** Sec. Mkt. **$18**

QX 206-7   WINNIE-THE-POOH
Comments: White Satin Ball, 3-1/4" dia.
This Walt Disney design shows Winnie with his all-time favorite "hunny." Caption: "Merry Christmas 1979." Winnie is popular!
☐ Purchased 19 __Pd $_____MIB   NB   DB   BNT
☐ Want   Orig. Ret. $3.50   **NB** $30   **MIB** Sec. Mkt. **$45**

No secondary market value has been established for yarn and fabric ornaments found in original cellophane package.

QX 123-1   YARN ORNAMENTS: GREEN BOY
Comments: 4-1/2" tall, Slight changes from 1975.
Reissued from 1978. Green with red hat.
☐ Purchased 19 __Pd $_____MIB   NB   DB   BNT
☐ Want   Orig. Ret. $2.00   Sec. Mkt. **$22**

QX 126-1   YARN ORNAMENTS: GREEN GIRL
Comments: 4-1/2" tall, Slight changes from 1975.
Reissued from 1978. Green with white muff.
☐ Purchased 19 __Pd $_____MIB   NB   DB   BNT
☐ Want   Orig. Ret. $2.00   Sec. Mkt. **$20**

QX 340-3   YARN ORNAMENTS: MR. CLAUS
Comments: 4-1/2" tall. Identical to 1975. Reissued from 1978.
☐ Purchased 19 __Pd $_____MIB   NB   DB   BNT
☐ Want   Orig. Ret. $2.00   Sec. Mkt. **$22**

QX 125-1   YARN ORNAMENTS: MRS. CLAUS
Comments: 4-1/2" tall. Identical to 1975. Reissued from 1978.
☐ Purchased 19 __Pd $_____MIB   NB   DB   BNT
☐ Want   Orig. Ret. $2.00   Sec. Mkt. **$22**

1980 Collection

QX 134-7   A CHRISTMAS TREAT
Comments: Handcrafted, 4-3/4" tall.
Reissued from 1979. The 1979 ornament has "grooves" around the candy cane; the 1980 ornament does not.
☐ Purchased 19 __ Pd $_____ MIB   NB   DB   BNT
☐ Want   Orig. Retail $5.50   **NB** $40   **MIB** Sec. Mkt. **$65**

QX 144-1   A CHRISTMAS VIGIL
Comments: Handcrafted Panorama Ball, 3-13/16" tall.
A little boy and his dog look through a window in time to see Santa and his reindeer. Panorama Balls are usually not MIB.
Artist: Donna Lee
☐ Purchased 19 __ Pd $_____ MIB   NB   DB   BNT
☐ Want   Orig. Ret. $9.00   **NB** $85   **MIB** Sec. Mkt. **$100**

QX 139-4   A HEAVENLY NAP
Comments: Handcrafted, 3-1/2" tall. Reissued in 1981.
A frosted acrylic moon, sound asleep, holds a sleeping angel dressed in blue. **Artist:** Donna Lee
☐ Purchased 19 __ Pd $_____ MIB   NB   DB   BNT
☐ Want   Orig. Ret. $6.50   **NB** $25   **MIB** Sec. Mkt. **$55**

QX 153-4   A SPOT OF CHRISTMAS CHEER
Comments: Handcrafted, 2-47/64" tall, Dated 1980.
A chipmunk trims a Christmas tree inside a teapot decorated with green garland. **Artist:** Donna Lee
☐ Purchased 19 __ Pd $_____ MIB   NB   DB   BNT
☐ Want   Orig. Ret. $8.00   **NB** $80   **MIB** Sec. Mkt. **$145**

QX 343-9   ANGEL MUSIC
Comments: Quilted Fabric. Reissued from 1979.
☐ Purchased 19 __ Pd $_____ MIB   NB   DB   BNT
☐ Want   Orig. Ret. $2.00   Sec. Mkt. **$20**

Merry Christmas and a Happy New Year!

QX 150-1   ANIMALS' CHRISTMAS, THE
Comments: Handcrafted, 2-37/64" tall.
A brown rabbit and a brown bird decorate a tree with red ribbon and a gold star. **Artist:** Donna Lee
☐ Purchased 19 __ Pd $_____ MIB   NB   DB   BNT
☐ Want   Orig. Ret. $8.00   **NB** $45   **MIB** Sec. Mkt. **$55**

QX 200-1   BABY'S FIRST CHRISTMAS
Comments: White Satin Ball, 3-1/4" dia.
Santa stops to wish a Merry Christmas to baby. Caption: "Baby's First Christmas, 1980."
☐ Purchased 19 __ Pd $_____ MIB   NB   DB   BNT
☐ Want   Orig. Ret. $4.00   **NB** $18   **MIB** Sec. Mkt. **$30**

QX 156-1   BABY'S FIRST CHRISTMAS
Comments: Handcrafted, 3-57/64" tall, Dated 1980.
A shadow box in the shape of a Christmas tree is filled with baby's toys. Caption: "Baby's First Christmas." **Artist:** Linda Sickman
☐ Purchased 19 __ Pd $_____ MIB   NB   DB   BNT
☐ Want   Orig. Ret. $12.00   **NB** $38   **MIB** Sec. Mkt. **$45**

QX 303-4   BEAUTY OF FRIENDSHIP
Comments: Acrylic, 3-1/4" dia., Dated 1980.
Caption: "Friendship Brings Beauty To Our Days, Joy To Our World. Christmas 1980."
☐ Purchased 19 __ Pd $_____ MIB   NB   DB   BNT
☐ Want   Orig. Ret. $4.00   **NB** $40   **MIB** Sec. Mkt. **$45**

QX 157-4   BELLRINGERS SERIES
Comments: **Second in Series**, Handcrafted, 2-7/64" tall.
Dated 1980. Two angels in blue gowns circle and ring a white porcelain bell with the star "clappers" they are holding.
☐ Purchased 19 __ Pd $_____ MIB   NB   DB   BNT
☐ Want   Orig. Ret. $15.00   **NB** $65   **MIB** Sec. Mkt. **$80**

QX 215-4   BETSEY CLARK SERIES
Comments: **Eighth in Series**, White Glass Ball, 3-1/4" dia.
Two children sled past a sign that says "Christmas 1980." Caption: "It's Joy-In-The-Air Time, Love Everywhere Time, Good-Fun-To-Share Time, It's Christmas."
☐ Purchased 19 __ Pd $_____ MIB   NB   DB   BNT
☐ Want   Orig. Ret. $4.00   **NB** $21   **MIB** Sec. Mkt. **$30**

QX 307-4   BETSEY CLARK ☐

Comments: Lt. Blue Cameo, 3-3/8" dia., Dated 1980.
Angel is kneeling in prayer. Caption: "Love Came Down At Christmas, Love All Lovely, Love Divine: Love Was Born At Christmas, Star And Angels Gave The Sign" and "Christmas 1980."

☐ Purchased 19 __ Pd $_____ MIB   NB   DB   BNT
☐ Want   Orig. Ret. $6.50   **NB** $40   **MIB** Sec. Mkt. **$55**

QX 149-4   BETSEY CLARK'S CHRISTMAS ☐

Comments: Handcrafted, 4" tall, Dated 1980.
A shadow box trimmed in white and red shows a girl in a three-dimensional snow scene.

☐ Purchased 19 __ Pd $_____ MIB   NB   DB   BNT
☐ Want   Orig. Ret. $7.50   **NB** $22   **MIB** Sec. Mkt. **$30**

QX 229-4   BLACK BABY'S FIRST CHRISTMAS ☐

Comments: White Satin Ball, 3-1/4" dia., Dated 1980.
A black baby sits by a decorated tree that holds nested birds. Toys surround the tree. Caption: "Baby's First Christmas, 1980."

☐ Purchased 19 __ Pd $_____ MIB   NB   DB   BNT
☐ Want   Orig. Ret. $4.00   **NB** $18   **MIB** Sec. Mkt. **$28**

OX 705-4   BRASS STAR TREE TOPPER ☐

Comments: A lacy design was used for this interlocking brass star.

☐ Purchased 19 __ Pd $_____ MIB   NB   DB   BNT
☐ Want   Orig. Ret. $25.00   **NB** $45   **MIB** Sec. Mkt. **$65**

QX 140-1   CAROLING BEAR ☐

Comments: Handcrafted, 3-7/33" tall, Dated 1980.
A brown bear wearing a red and green striped scarf sings a duet with a red bird on his arm. Caption: "Carols 1980."
Artist: Donna Lee

☐ Purchased 19 __ Pd $_____ MIB   NB   DB   BNT
☐ Want   Orig. Ret. $7.50   **NB** $95   **MIB** Sec. Mkt. **$135**

QX 141-4   CARROUSEL SERIES: MERRY CARROUSEL ☐

Comments: **Third in Series**, Handcrafted, 3-1/8" tall, Dated 1980.
Santa and his reindeer make their "rounds."
Caption on top: "Christmas 1980."

☐ Purchased 19 __ Pd $_____ MIB   NB   DB   BNT
☐ Want   Orig. Ret. $7.50   **NB** $110   **MIB** Sec. Mkt. **$160**

QX 158-4   CHECKING IT TWICE ☐

Comments: Handcrafted, 5-15/16" tall, Special Edition.
Reissued in 1981. Santa checks his list. He wears spectacles of real metal. **Artist**: Thomas Blackshear

☐ Purchased 19 __ Pd $_____ MIB   NB   DB   BNT
☐ Want   Orig. Ret. $20.00   **NB** $165   **MIB** Sec. Mkt. **$200**

QX 210-1   CHRISTMAS AT HOME ☐

Comments: Gold Glass Ball, 3-1/4" dia., Dated 1980.
Caption: "A Home That's Filled With Christmas Glows With The Joyful Light Of The Special Warmth And Happiness That Makes The Season Bright. Christmas 1980."

☐ Purchased 19 __ Pd $_____ MIB   NB   DB   BNT
☐ Want   Orig. Ret. $4.00   **NB** $15   **MIB** Sec. Mkt. **$25**

QX 224-1   CHRISTMAS CARDINALS ☐

Comments: White Glass Ball, 3-1/4" dia., Dated 1980.
Two cardinals sit on berry-laden branches of holly. Caption: "Nature at Christmas... A Wonderland Of Wintry Art. Christmas 1980."

☐ Purchased 19 __ Pd $_____ MIB   NB   DB   BNT
☐ Want   Orig. Ret. $4.00   **NB** $15   **MIB** Sec. Mkt. **$30**

QX 228-1   CHRISTMAS CHOIR ☐

Comments: Gold Glass Ball, 3-1/4" dia., Dated 1980.
Three children dressed in choir robes sing the message of Christmas. Caption: "Go Tell It On The Mountain... Jesus Christ Is Born!" and "Christmas 1980."

☐ Purchased 19 __ Pd $_____ MIB   NB   DB   BNT
☐ Want   Orig. Ret. $4.00   **NB** $50   **MIB** Sec. Mkt. **$75**

QX 135-9   CHRISTMAS IS FOR CHILDREN ☐

Comments: Handcrafted, 4-1/4" tall.
Reissued from 1979.

☐ Purchased 19 __ Pd $_____ MIB   NB   DB   BNT
☐ Want   1980 Retail $5.50   **NB** $55   **MIB** Sec. Mkt. **$80**

QX 353-4   CHRISTMAS KITTEN TEST ORNAMENT ☐

Comments: *VERY RARE! ONLY 200 MADE..*
Very limited "known" sold prices in past years. Until recently we had not seen this ornament in a box. No sales found for two years.

☐ Purchased 19 __ Pd $_____ MIB   NB   DB   BNT
☐ Want   Orig. Ret. $4.00   **NB** $200   **MIB** Sec. Mkt. **$300**

QX 207-4   CHRISTMAS LOVE
Comments: White Glass Ball, 3-1/4" dia., Dated 1980.
Reproduction of a Schneeberg collage in pastels. Caption: "Love at Christmas... Happy Moments Spent Together, Memories To Be Shared Forever. Christmas 1980"
☐ Purchased 19 __ Pd $_____ MIB   NB   DB   BNT
☐ Want   Orig. Ret. $4.00   **NB** $25   **MIB** Sec. Mkt. **$40**

QX 226-1   CHRISTMAS TIME
Comments: Ecru Soft-Sheen Satin Ball, 3-1/4" dia., Dated 1980.
A stagecoach and a steaming mug of coffee. Caption: "These Are The Days Of Merrymaking Get-Togethers, Journey-Taking, Moments Of Delight And Love That Last In Memory. Christmas 1980."
☐ Purchased 19 __ Pd $_____ MIB   NB   DB   BNT
☐ Want   Orig. Ret. $4.00   **NB** $20   **MIB** Sec. Mkt. **$30**

QX 350-1   COLORS OF CHRISTMAS: JOY
Comments: Acrylic, 4" tall, Dated 1980.
With a look of leaded stained glass, the ornament is molded to spell "JOY" with the year on a gold ribbon scroll over the "O."
☐ Purchased 19 __ Pd $_____ MIB   NB   DB   BNT
☐ Want   Orig. Ret. $4.00   **NB** $15   **MIB** Sec. Mkt. **$22**

QX 214-1   DAD
Comments: Gold Glass Ball, 3-1/4" dia., Dated 1980.
"DAD" is printed on a red and green plaid background. Caption: "A Dad Is Always Caring, Always Sharing, Always Giving Of His Love. Christmas 1980."
☐ Purchased 19 __ Pd $_____ MIB   NB   DB   BNT
☐ Want   Orig. Ret. $4.00   **NB** $11   **MIB** Sec. Mkt. **$18**

QX 212-1   DAUGHTER
Comments: White Glass Ball, 3-1/4" dia., Dated 1980.
A white kitten naps near a potted plant while another plays with an ornament. Caption: "A Daughter Is The Sweetest Gift A Lifetime Can Provide. Christmas 1980."
☐ Purchased 19 __ Pd $_____ MIB   NB   DB   BNT
☐ Want   Orig. Ret. $4.00   **NB** $22   **MIB** Sec. Mkt. **$38**

QX 218-1   DISNEY
Comments: White Satin Ball, 3-1/4" dia., Dated 1980.
On one side, Mickey and Minnie Mouse ice skate. On the other, Mickey plays Santa. Caption: "Merry Christmas 1980."
☐ Purchased 19 __ Pd $_____ MIB   NB   DB   BNT
☐ Want   Orig. Ret. $4.00   **NB** $20   **MIB** Sec. Mkt. **$30**

QX 352-1   DOVE TEST ORNAMENT
Comments: *VERY RARE! ONLY 200 MADE..*
More of these in collectors' hands than Christmas Kitten, p. 26. This ornament should have a flat white back; some have been found without the back glued on. Not really sought after as in earlier years.
☐ Purchased 19 __ Pd $_____ MIB   NB   DB   BNT
☐.Want   Orig. Ret. $4.00 **NB** $115   **MIB** Sec. Mkt. **$200**

QX 147-4   DRUMMER BOY
Comments: Handcrafted, 3-3/64" tall, Dated 1980.
In bread-dough design, this drummer boy is dressed in green with brown sandals and stocking cap. He plays a red and gold drum.
Artist: Donna Lee
☐ Purchased 19 __ Pd $_____ MIB   NB   DB   BNT
☐ Want   Orig. Ret. $5.50   **NB** $70   **MIB** Sec. Mkt. **$90**

QX 142-1   ELFIN ANTICS
Comments: Hard to Find. Handcrafted. 4-9/16" tall.
Three elves swing down from your Christmas tree branch. The bottom elf rings a gold bell. Very popular!
☐ Purchased 19 __ Pd $_____ MIB   NB   DB   BNT
☐ Want   Orig. Ret. $9.00   **NB** $150   **MIB** Sec. Mkt. **$200**

QX 205-4   FIRST CHRISTMAS TOGETHER
Comments: White Glass Ball, 3-1/4" dia., Dated 1980.
A man and wife take a moonlight sleigh ride. Caption: "First Christmas Together. Christmas Is A Love Story Written In Our Hearts."
☐ Purchased 19 __ Pd $_____ MIB   NB   DB   BNT
☐ Want   Orig. Ret. $4.00   **NB** $18   **MIB** Sec. Mkt. **$35**

QX 305-4   FIRST CHRISTMAS TOGETHER
Comments: Acrylic, 3-1/2" tall, Dated 1980.
An acrylic heart has a floral and ribbon border surrounding the caption stamped in silver foil. Caption: "First Christmas Together 1980."
☐ Purchased 19 __ Pd $_____ MIB   NB   DB   BNT
☐ Want   Orig. Ret. $4.00   **NB** $40   **MIB** Sec. Mkt. **$55**

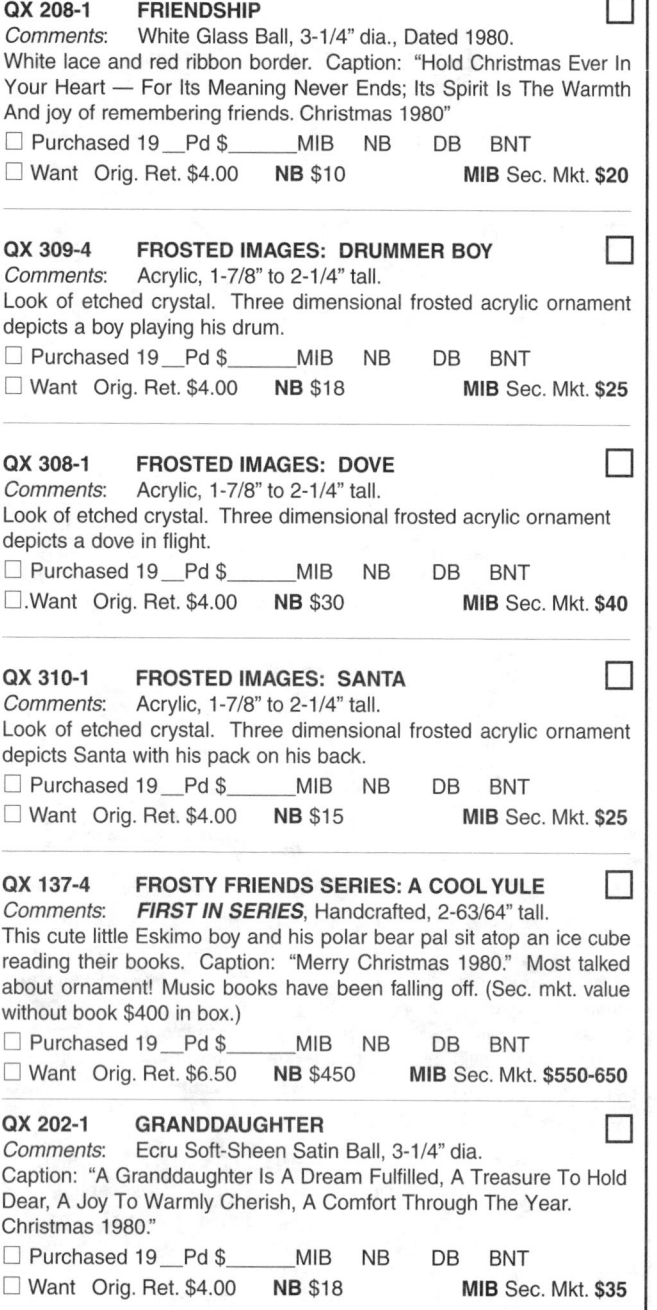

QX 208-1   FRIENDSHIP

Comments: White Glass Ball, 3-1/4" dia., Dated 1980.
White lace and red ribbon border. Caption: "Hold Christmas Ever In Your Heart — For Its Meaning Never Ends; Its Spirit Is The Warmth And Joy of remembering friends. Christmas 1980"

☐ Purchased 19___Pd $_____MIB   NB   DB   BNT
☐ Want   Orig. Ret. $4.00   **NB** $10   **MIB** Sec. Mkt. **$20**

QX 309-4   FROSTED IMAGES: DRUMMER BOY

Comments: Acrylic, 1-7/8" to 2-1/4" tall.
Look of etched crystal. Three dimensional frosted acrylic ornament depicts a boy playing his drum.

☐ Purchased 19___Pd $_____MIB   NB   DB   BNT
☐ Want   Orig. Ret. $4.00   **NB** $18   **MIB** Sec. Mkt. **$25**

QX 308-1   FROSTED IMAGES: DOVE

Comments: Acrylic, 1-7/8" to 2-1/4" tall.
Look of etched crystal. Three dimensional frosted acrylic ornament depicts a dove in flight.

☐ Purchased 19___Pd $_____MIB   NB   DB   BNT
☐.Want   Orig. Ret. $4.00   **NB** $30   **MIB** Sec. Mkt. **$40**

QX 310-1   FROSTED IMAGES: SANTA

Comments: Acrylic, 1-7/8" to 2-1/4" tall.
Look of etched crystal. Three dimensional frosted acrylic ornament depicts Santa with his pack on his back.

☐ Purchased 19___Pd $_____MIB   NB   DB   BNT
☐ Want   Orig. Ret. $4.00   **NB** $15   **MIB** Sec. Mkt. **$25**

QX 137-4   FROSTY FRIENDS SERIES: A COOL YULE

Comments: **FIRST IN SERIES**, Handcrafted, 2-63/64" tall.
This cute little Eskimo boy and his polar bear pal sit atop an ice cube reading their books. Caption: "Merry Christmas 1980." Most talked about ornament! Music books have been falling off. (Sec. mkt. value without book $400 in box.)

☐ Purchased 19___Pd $_____MIB   NB   DB   BNT
☐ Want   Orig. Ret. $6.50   **NB** $450   **MIB** Sec. Mkt. **$550-650**

QX 202-1   GRANDDAUGHTER

Comments: Ecru Soft-Sheen Satin Ball, 3-1/4" dia.
Caption: "A Granddaughter Is A Dream Fulfilled, A Treasure To Hold Dear, A Joy To Warmly Cherish, A Comfort Through The Year. Christmas 1980."

☐ Purchased 19___Pd $_____MIB   NB   DB   BNT
☐ Want   Orig. Ret. $4.00   **NB** $18   **MIB** Sec. Mkt. **$35**

QX 231-4   GRANDFATHER

Comments: White Glass Ball, 3-1/4" dia., Dated 1980.
Two snow scenes, one of a covered bridge and the other of an old wagon in a barn yard. Caption: "A Grandfather Is... Strong In His Wisdom, Gentle In His Love. Christmas 1980."

☐ Purchased 19___Pd $_____MIB   NB   DB   BNT
☐ Want   Orig. Ret. $4.00   **NB** $15   **MIB** Sec. Mkt. **$20**

QX 204-1   GRANDMOTHER

Comments: White Glass Ball, 3-1/4" dia., Dated 1980.
The caption and date are framed by flowers, birds and animals. Caption: "Love And Joy And Comfort And Cheer Are Gifts A Grandmother Gives All Year. Christmas 1980."

☐ Purchased 19___Pd $_____MIB   NB   DB   BNT
☐ Want   Orig. Ret. $4.00   **NB** $14   **MIB** Sec. Mkt. **$20**

QX 213-4   GRANDPARENTS

Comments: Gold Glass Ball, 3-1/4" dia., Dated 1980.
Reproduced from the Currier & Ives print, "Early Winter," the design is a large home by a pond. Caption: "Grandparents have beautiful ways of giving, of helping, of teaching... especially of loving."

☐ Purchased 19___Pd $_____MIB   NB   DB   BNT
☐ Want   Orig. Ret. $4.00   **NB** $20   **MIB** Sec. Mkt. **$35**

QX 201-4   GRANDSON

Comments: White Satin Ball, 3-1/4" dia.
Front: Raccoons pull a snowman on a sled. Back: A Snowman Adds A Candy Cane To A Tree. Caption: "Grandsons And Christmas Are Joys That Go Together. Christmas 1980."

☐ Purchased 19___Pd $_____MIB   NB   DB   BNT
☐ Want   Orig. Ret. $4.00   **NB** $18   **MIB** Sec. Mkt. **$32**

QX 222-1   HAPPY CHRISTMAS

Comments: Ecru Soft-Sheen Satin Ball, 3-1/4" dia.
A Koala bear waters a potted tree which grows into a "pear tree" with a small bird at the top. Caption: "Tis The Season When Hearts Are Glowing, Love Is Growing, And Happiness Rounds Out The Year!" and "Christmas 1980."

☐ Purchased 19___Pd $_____MIB   NB   DB   BNT
☐ Want   Orig. Ret. $4.00   **NB** $21   **MIB** Sec. Mkt. **$28**

It's better to sleep on what you plan to do than to lie awake because of what you've done.

QX 156-7　HEAVENLY MINSTREL
Comments:　**Special Edition**, Handcrafted, 6-1/4" tall.
A beautiful old world angel with widespread wings plays a lute.
Artist: Donna Lee
☐ Purchased 19__Pd $_____MIB　NB　　DB　BNT
☐ Want　Orig. Ret. $15.00　**NB** $250　　　　**MIB** Sec. Mkt. **$330**

QX 152-1　HEAVENLY SOUNDS
Comments:　Handcrafted, 3-30/64" tall, Dated 1980.
Angels dressed in pink and blue ring a gold metal bell as they twirl around in the center of a wood-look pink ring.
☐ Purchased 19__Pd $_____MIB　NB　　DB　BNT
☐ Want　Orig. Ret. $7.50　**NB** $60　　　　**MIB** Sec. Mkt. **$90**

QX 143-4　HERE COMES SANTA SERIES: SANTA'S EXPRESS
Comments:　**Second in Series**, Handcrafted, 3" tall.
Dated 1980. Santa waves from an old-fashioned locomotive in red and green; the wheels turn. Tends to be more NB sales than MIB.
☐ Purchased 19__Pd $_____MIB　NB　　DB　BNT
☐ Want　Orig. Ret. $12.00　**NB** $90　　　　**MIB** Sec. Mkt.**$185**

QX 320-3　HOLIDAY CHIMES: REINDEER CHIMES
Comments:　Chrome plated brass, 5-1/2" tall.
Issued in 1978, 1979 and 1980. Very few sales found recently to notice any change from 1996. **Artist**: Linda Sickman
☐ Purchased 19__Pd $_____MIB　NB　　DB　BNT
☐ Want　Orig. Retail $5.50　**NB** $35　　　　**MIB** Sec. Mkt. **$45**

QX 136-1　HOLIDAY CHIMES: SANTA MOBILE
Comments:　Chrome Plate, 3-57/64" tall. Reissued in 1981.
His sleigh pulled by three reindeer, Santa flies over three homes with smoking chimneys.
☐ Purchased 19__Pd $_____MIB　NB　　DB　BNT
☐ Want　Orig. Ret. $5.50　**NB** $35　　　　**MIB** Sec. Mkt. **$45**

QX 165-4　HOLIDAY CHIMES: SNOWFLAKE CHIMES
Comments:　Chrome Plate, 1-59/64" dia Reissued in 1981.
Three lacy snowflakes are suspended from a fourth snowflake.
Artist: Linda Sickman
☐ Purchased 19__Pd $_____MIB　NB　　DB　BNT
☐ Want　Orig. Ret. $5.50　**NB** $18　　　　**MIB** Sec. Mkt. **$30**

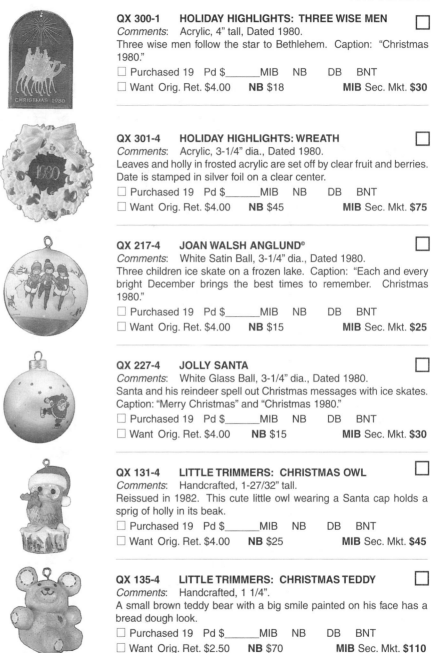

QX 300-1　HOLIDAY HIGHLIGHTS: THREE WISE MEN
Comments:　Acrylic, 4" tall, Dated 1980.
Three wise men follow the star to Bethlehem. Caption: "Christmas 1980."
☐ Purchased 19　Pd $_____MIB　NB　　DB　BNT
☐ Want　Orig. Ret. $4.00　**NB** $18　　　　**MIB** Sec. Mkt. **$30**

QX 301-4　HOLIDAY HIGHLIGHTS: WREATH
Comments:　Acrylic, 3-1/4" dia., Dated 1980.
Leaves and holly in frosted acrylic are set off by clear fruit and berries. Date is stamped in silver foil on a clear center.
☐ Purchased 19　Pd $_____MIB　NB　　DB　BNT
☐ Want　Orig. Ret. $4.00　**NB** $45　　　　**MIB** Sec. Mkt. **$75**

QX 217-4　JOAN WALSH ANGLUND©
Comments:　White Satin Ball, 3-1/4" dia., Dated 1980.
Three children ice skate on a frozen lake. Caption: "Each and every bright December brings the best times to remember. Christmas 1980."
☐ Purchased 19　Pd $_____MIB　NB　　DB　BNT
☐ Want　Orig. Ret. $4.00　**NB** $15　　　　**MIB** Sec. Mkt. **$25**

QX 227-4　JOLLY SANTA
Comments:　White Glass Ball, 3-1/4" dia., Dated 1980.
Santa and his reindeer spell out Christmas messages with ice skates. Caption: "Merry Christmas" and "Christmas 1980."
☐ Purchased 19　Pd $_____MIB　NB　　DB　BNT
☐ Want　Orig. Ret. $4.00　**NB** $15　　　　**MIB** Sec. Mkt. **$30**

QX 131-4　LITTLE TRIMMERS: CHRISTMAS OWL
Comments:　Handcrafted, 1-27/32" tall.
Reissued in 1982. This cute little owl wearing a Santa cap holds a sprig of holly in its beak.
☐ Purchased 19　Pd $_____MIB　NB　　DB　BNT
☐ Want　Orig. Ret. $4.00　**NB** $25　　　　**MIB** Sec. Mkt. **$45**

QX 135-4　LITTLE TRIMMERS: CHRISTMAS TEDDY
Comments:　Handcrafted, 1 1/4".
A small brown teddy bear with a big smile painted on his face has a bread dough look.
☐ Purchased 19　Pd $_____MIB　NB　　DB　BNT
☐ Want　Orig. Ret. $2.50　**NB** $70　　　　**MIB** Sec. Mkt. **$110**

QX 134-1   LITTLE TRIMMERS: CLOTHESPIN SOLDIER ☐
Comments: Handcrafted, 2-15/16" tall.
Blue and red clothespin style soldier stands at attention.
☐ Purchased 19 __ Pd $_____ MIB   NB   DB   BNT
☐ Want   Orig. Ret. $3.50   **NB** $22   **MIB** Sec. Mkt. **$38**

QX 160-1   LITTLE TRIMMERS: MERRY REDBIRD ☐
Comments: Handcrafted-Flocked, 1-27/32" long.
This little redbird wears flocked "feathers" and holds a sprig of holly in his bill.
☐ Purchased 19 __ Pd $_____ MIB   NB   DB   BNT
☐ Want   Orig. Ret. $3.50   **NB** $40   **MIB** Sec. Mkt. **$60**

QX 130-1   LITTLE TRIMMERS: SWINGIN' ON A STAR ☐
Comments: Handcrafted, 2-5/32" tall.
A tiny white mouse with a red and green striped cap swings on a brass star.
☐ Purchased 19 __ Pd $_____ MIB   NB   DB   BNT
☐ Want   Orig. Ret. $4.00   **NB** $50   **MIB** Sec. Mkt. **$80**

QX 302-1   LOVE ☐
Comments: Acrylic, 4" tall, Dated 1980.
The word LOVE is enhanced by silver foil stamping. Caption: "Where There Is Love, There Is The Spirit Of Christmas."
☐ Purchased 19 __ Pd $_____ MIB   NB   DB   BNT
☐ Want   Orig. Ret. $4.00   **NB** $50   **MIB** Sec. Mkt. **$65**

QX 221-4   MARTY LINKS™ ☐
Comments: White Satin Ball, 3-1/4" dia.
A little boy and animals carol in the snow under the direction of a little girl. Caption: "We Wish You A Merry Christmas And A Happy New Year" and "Christmas 1980."
☐ Purchased 19 __ Pd $_____ MIB   NB   DB   BNT
☐ Want   Orig. Ret. $4.00   **NB** $6   **MIB** Sec. Mkt. **$20**

QX 219-4   MARY HAMILTON ☐
Comments: Gold Glass Ball, 3-1/4" dia.
Caption: "Christmas – The Warmest, Brightest Season Of All" and "Christmas 1980."
☐ Purchased 19 __ Pd $_____ MIB   NB   DB   BNT
☐ Want   Orig. Ret. $4.00   **NB** $12   **MIB** Sec. Mkt. **$22**

QX 342-7   MERRY SANTA ☐
Comments: Quilted Fabric.
Reissued from 1979.
☐ Purchased 19 __ Pd $_____ MIB   NB   DB   BNT
☐ Want   Orig. Ret. $2.00   Sec. Mkt. **$22**

QX 203-4   MOTHER ☐
Comments: White Satin Ball, 3-1/4" dia., Dated 1980.
Large poinsettias and other Christmas flowers. Caption: "A Mother Has The Special Gift Of Giving Of Herself. Christmas 1980."
☐ Purchased 19 __ Pd $_____ MIB   NB   DB   BNT
☐ Want   Orig. Ret. $4.00   **NB** $14   **MIB** Sec. Mkt. **$22.50**

QX 304-1   MOTHER ☐
Comments: Acrylic, 3-1/2" tall, Dated 1980.
Heart-shaped with a ribbon tied floral border. Caption and date are stamped in silver foil: "Mother Is Another Word For Love. Christmas 1980."
☐ Purchased 19 __ Pd $_____ MIB   NB   DB   BNT
☐ Want   Orig. Ret. $4.00   **NB** $25   **MIB** Sec. Mkt. **$35**

QX 230-1   MOTHER & DAD ☐
Comments: White Glass Ball, 3-1/4" dia.
Sprigs of holly and berries. Caption: "When Homes Are Decked With Holly And Hearts Are Feeling Glad, It's A Wonderful Time To Remember A Wonderful Mother And Dad. Christmas 1980."
☐ Purchased 19 __ Pd $_____ MIB   NB   DB   BNT
☐ Want   Orig. Ret. $4.00   **NB** $14   **MIB** Sec. Mkt. **$22.50**

QX 220-1   MUPPETS™ ☐
Comments: White Satin Ball, 3-1/4" dia.
Kermit waves a greeting on the front. The Muppets sing carols. Caption: "Merry Christmas 1980."
☐ Purchased 19 __ Pd $_____ MIB   NB   DB   BNT
☐ Want   Orig. Ret. $4.00   **NB** $24   **MIB** Sec. Mkt. **$38**

QX 225-4   NATIVITY ☐
Comments: Gold Glass Ball, 3-1/4" dia.
Animals and birds draw near children in prayer at the manger. Caption: "Silent Night.. Holy Night..." and "Christmas 1980."
☐ Purchased 19 __ Pd $_____ MIB   NB   DB   BNT
☐ Want   Orig. Ret. $4.00   **NB** $21   **MIB** Sec. Mkt. **$32**

**QX 306-1   NORMAN ROCKWELL SERIES:
SANTA'S VISITORS**
Comments: **FIRST IN SERIES**, Cameo, 3-3/8" dia.
Rockwell's famous drawing is reproduced in white relief on a soft green background. Caption: "Santa's Visitors. The Norman Rockwell Collection, Christmas 1980."
☐ Purchased 19__Pd $_____MIB   NB   DB   BNT
☐ Want   Orig. Ret. $6.50   **NB** $170   **MIB** Sec. Mkt. **$220**

QX 216-1   PEANUTS®
Comments: White Satin Ball, 3-1/4" dia.; Christmas 1980.
Snoopy sings as Woodstock and his friends portray verses from a Christmas carol. Caption: "Four Colly Birds... Three French Hens... And A Partridge In A Pear Tree."
☐ Purchased 19__Pd $_____MIB   NB   DB   BNT
☐ Want   Orig. Ret. $4.00   **NB** $25   **MIB** Sec. Mkt. **$37.50**

QX 340-7   ROCKING HORSE, THE
Comments: Quilted Fabric.
Reissued from 1979.
☐ Purchased 19__Pd $_____MIB   NB   DB   BNT
☐ Want   Orig. Ret. $2.00   Sec. Mkt. **$25**

QX 146-1   SANTA 1980
Comments: Handcrafted, 4-5/32" tall, Dated 1980.
Dough-look material. Santa is seen popping into the chimney of a mouse's home. The date is incorporated into the design.
☐ Purchased 19__Pd $_____MIB   NB   DB   BNT
☐ Want   Orig. Ret. $5.50   **NB** $70   **MIB** Sec. Mkt. **$90**

QX 138-1   SANTA'S FLIGHT
Comments: Pressed Tin, 4" tall.
Santa makes his deliveries in a blue and gold dirigible decorated with a green garland and red ribbon. The propeller twirls around. Caption: "Merry Christmas 1980." **Artist**: Linda Sickman
☐ Purchased 19__Pd $_____MIB   NB   DB   BNT
☐ Want   Orig. Ret. $5.50   **NB** $90   **MIB** Sec. Mkt. **$110**

QX 223-4   SANTA'S WORKSHOP
Comments: White Satin Ball, 3-1/4" dia.
Santa adds a scarf to his usual costume and checks his list. Caption: "What Merriment Is All Around When Dear Old Santa Comes To Town" and "Christmas 1980."
☐ Purchased 19__Pd $_____MIB   NB   DB   BNT
☐ Want   Orig. Ret. $4.00   **NB** $15   **MIB** Sec. Mkt. **$28**

**QHD 925-4   SANTA'S WORKSHOP
TABLETOP DECORATIONS**
Comments: Handcrafted, 8" tall.
☐ Purchased 19__Pd $_____MIB   NB   DB   BNT
☐ Want   Orig. Ret. $40.00   **NB** $130   **MIB** Sec. Mkt. **$185**

QX 139-9   SKATING SNOWMAN, THE
Comments: Handcrafted, 4-1/4" tall.
Reissued from 1979.
Artist: Donna Lee
☐ Purchased 19__Pd $_____MIB   NB   DB   BNT
☐ Want   1980 Retail $5.50   **NB** $60   **MIB** Sec. Mkt. **$80**

**QX 154-1   SNOOPY AND FRIENDS SERIES:
SNOOPY SKI HOLIDAY**
Comments: **Second in Series**, Dated 1980.
Handcrafted Panorama Ball, 3-1/4" dia. Snoopy, on skis, wears a red and green stocking cap and Woodstock rides in Snoopy' personalized feeding bowl. Several of this style ornament have been found with scratched surfaces. **Artist**: John Francis (Collin)
☐ Purchased 19__Pd $_____MIB   NB   DB   BNT
☐ Want   Orig. Ret. $9.00   **NB** $95   **MIB** Sec. Mkt. **$115**

QX 133-4   SNOWFLAKE SWING, THE
Comments: Handcrafted, 3" tall.
An angel swings from an acrylic snowflake.
☐ Purchased 19__Pd $_____MIB   NB   DB   BNT
☐ Want   Orig. Ret. $4.00   **NB** $32   **MIB** Sec. Mkt. **$45**

QX 211-4   SON
Comments: Gold Glass Ball, 3-1/4" dia.
A scene of a boy's favorite toys. Caption: "A Son Is... A Maker Of Memories, A Source Of Pride... A Son Is Love" and "Christmas 1980."
☐ Purchased 19__Pd $_____MIB   NB   DB   BNT
☐ Want   Orig. Ret. $4.00   **NB** $21   **MIB** Sec. Mkt. **$35**

QX 341-9   STUFFED FULL STOCKING
Comments: Quilted Fabric.
Reissued from 1979.
☐ Purchased 19 __ Pd $_____ MIB   NB   DB   BNT
☐ Want   Orig. Ret. $2.00   Sec. Mkt. **$24**

QX 209-4   TEACHER
Comments: White Satin Ball, 3-1/4" dia.
Kitten dressed in warm clothing is walking to school with a gift.
Back: He's placing the gift on the teacher's desk.
Caption: "Merry Christmas, Teacher" and "Christmas 1980."
☐ Purchased 19 __ Pd $_____ MIB   NB   DB   BNT
☐ Want   Orig. Ret. $4.00   **NB** $12   **MIB** Sec. Mkt. **$20**

QX 131-9   THIMBLE SERIES: A CHRISTMAS SALUTE
Comments: **Second in Series,** Handcrafted, 2-1/4" tall.
Reissued from 1979.
☐ Purchased 19 __ Pd $_____ MIB   NB   DB   BNT
☐ Want   1980 Retail $4.00   **NB** $90   **MIB** Sec. Mkt. **$150**

QX 132-1   THIMBLE SERIES: THIMBLE ELF
Comments: **Third in Series,** Handcrafted, 2-31/32" tall.
Cute little elf dressed in red and green is swinging on a thimble "bell"
which hangs from a golden rope. Price down from the 1996 guide.
☐ Purchased 19 __ Pd $_____ MIB   NB   DB   BNT
☐ Want   Orig. Ret. $4.00   **NB** $90   **MIB** Sec. Mkt. **$150**

QX 206-1   TWENTY-FIFTH CHRISTMAS TOGETHER
Comments: White Glass Ball, 3-1/4" dia., Dated 1980.
Garlands, bells and ribbons frame the captions. "The good times of
the present blend with memories of the past to make each Christmas
season even dearer than the last" and "25th Christmas Together 1980."
A collector has reported this ball ornament being found without the
date.
☐ Purchased 19 __ Pd $_____ MIB   NB   DB   BNT
☐ Want   Orig. Ret. $4.00   **NB** $12   **MIB** Sec. Mkt. **$22**

QX 162-1   YARN & FABRIC: ANGEL
Comments: Yarn with lace and felt accents, 5" tall.
Reissued in 1981. This lovely blue angel with white wings, white
pinafore and golden hair holds a green wreath.
☐ Purchased 19 __ Pd $_____ MIB   NB   DB   BNT
☐ Want   Orig. Ret. $3.00   Sec. Mkt. **$10**

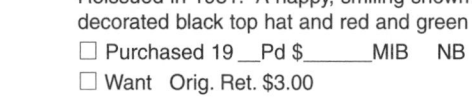

QX 161-4   YARN & FABRIC: SANTA
Comments: Yarn with lace and felt accents, 5" tall.
Reissued in 1981. Santa with felt hat and boots.
☐ Purchased 19 __ Pd $_____ MIB   NB   DB   BNT
☐ Want   Orig. Ret. $3.00   Sec. Mkt. **$10**

QX 163-4   YARN & FABRIC: SNOWMAN
Comments: Yarn with lace and felt accents, 5" tall.
Reissued in 1981. A happy, smiling snowman wears a holly-
decorated black top hat and red and green plaid scarf.
☐ Purchased 19 __ Pd $_____ MIB   NB   DB   BNT
☐ Want   Orig. Ret. $3.00   Sec. Mkt. **$10**

QX 164-1   YARN & FABRIC: SOLDIER
Comments: Yarn with lace and felt accents, 5" tall.
Reissued in 1981. This blue soldier is dressed with accents of red
and green.
☐ Purchased 19 __ Pd $_____ MIB   NB   DB   BNT
☐ Want   Orig. Ret. $3.00   Sec. Mkt. **$10**

1981 Collection

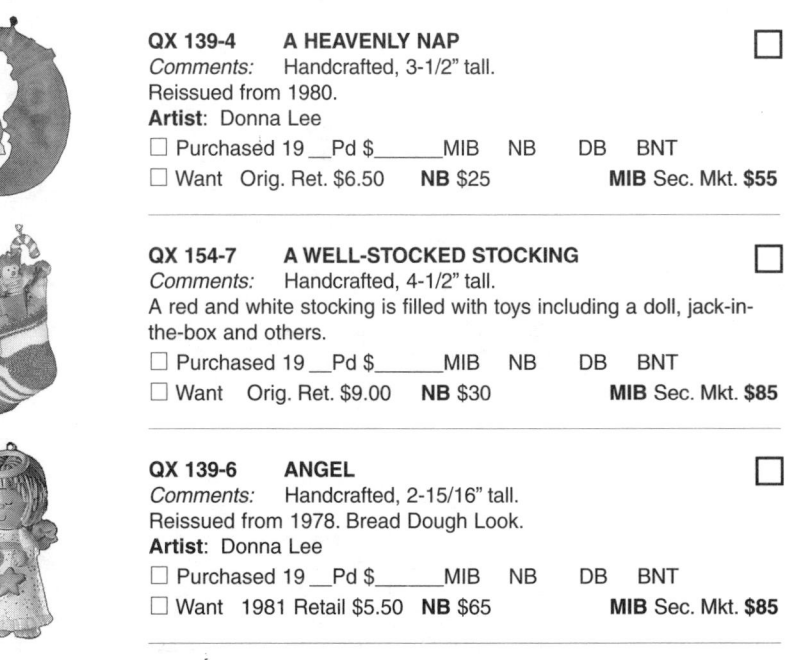

QX 139-4   A HEAVENLY NAP
Comments: Handcrafted, 3-1/2" tall.
Reissued from 1980.
Artist: Donna Lee
☐ Purchased 19 __ Pd $_____ MIB   NB   DB   BNT
☐ Want   Orig. Ret. $6.50   **NB** $25   **MIB** Sec. Mkt. **$55**

QX 154-7   A WELL-STOCKED STOCKING
Comments: Handcrafted, 4-1/2" tall.
A red and white stocking is filled with toys including a doll, jack-in-
the-box and others.
☐ Purchased 19 __ Pd $_____ MIB   NB   DB   BNT
☐ Want   Orig. Ret. $9.00   **NB** $30   **MIB** Sec. Mkt. **$85**

QX 139-6   ANGEL
Comments: Handcrafted, 2-15/16" tall.
Reissued from 1978. Bread Dough Look.
Artist: Donna Lee
☐ Purchased 19 __ Pd $_____ MIB   NB   DB   BNT
☐ Want   1981 Retail $5.50   **NB** $65   **MIB** Sec. Mkt. **$85**

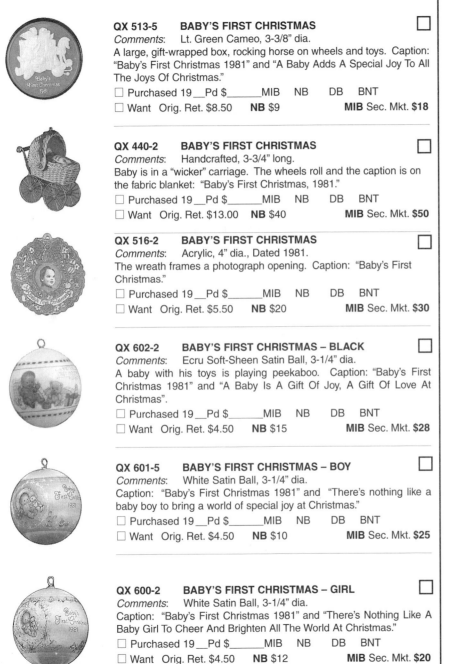

QX 513-5   BABY'S FIRST CHRISTMAS ☐
Comments: Lt. Green Cameo, 3-3/8" dia.
A large, gift-wrapped box, rocking horse on wheels and toys. Caption: "Baby's First Christmas 1981" and "A Baby Adds A Special Joy To All The Joys Of Christmas."
☐ Purchased 19__Pd $_____MIB   NB   DB   BNT
☐ Want   Orig. Ret. $8.50   **NB** $9   **MIB** Sec. Mkt. **$18**

QX 440-2   BABY'S FIRST CHRISTMAS ☐
Comments: Handcrafted, 3-3/4" long.
Baby is in a "wicker" carriage. The wheels roll and the caption is on the fabric blanket: "Baby's First Christmas, 1981."
☐ Purchased 19__Pd $_____MIB   NB   DB   BNT
☐ Want   Orig. Ret. $13.00   **NB** $40   **MIB** Sec. Mkt. **$50**

QX 516-2   BABY'S FIRST CHRISTMAS ☐
Comments: Acrylic, 4" dia., Dated 1981.
The wreath frames a photograph opening. Caption: "Baby's First Christmas."
☐ Purchased 19__Pd $_____MIB   NB   DB   BNT
☐ Want   Orig. Ret. $5.50   **NB** $20   **MIB** Sec. Mkt. **$30**

QX 602-2   BABY'S FIRST CHRISTMAS – BLACK ☐
Comments: Ecru Soft-Sheen Satin Ball, 3-1/4" dia.
A baby with his toys is playing peekaboo. Caption: "Baby's First Christmas 1981" and "A Baby Is A Gift Of Joy, A Gift Of Love At Christmas".
☐ Purchased 19__Pd $_____MIB   NB   DB   BNT
☐ Want   Orig. Ret. $4.50   **NB** $15   **MIB** Sec. Mkt. **$28**

QX 601-5   BABY'S FIRST CHRISTMAS – BOY ☐
Comments: White Satin Ball, 3-1/4" dia.
Caption: "Baby's First Christmas 1981" and "There's nothing like a baby boy to bring a world of special joy at Christmas."
☐ Purchased 19__Pd $_____MIB   NB   DB   BNT
☐ Want   Orig. Ret. $4.50   **NB** $10   **MIB** Sec. Mkt. **$25**

QX 600-2   BABY'S FIRST CHRISTMAS – GIRL ☐
Comments: White Satin Ball, 3-1/4" dia.
Caption: "Baby's First Christmas 1981" and "There's Nothing Like A Baby Girl To Cheer And Brighten All The World At Christmas."
☐ Purchased 19__Pd $_____MIB   NB   DB   BNT
☐ Want   Orig. Ret. $4.50   **NB** $12   **MIB** Sec. Mkt. **$20**

QX 441-5   BELLRINGER SERIIIES: ☐
SWINGIN' BELLRINGER
Comments: **Third in Series**, Handcrafted, 4" tall.
Dated 1981. A mouse swings on the candy cane clapper of this gold-rimmed bell.
☐ Purchased 19__Pd $_____MIB   NB   DB   BNT
☐ Want   Orig. Ret. $15.00   **NB** $65   MIB Sec. Mkt. **$85**

QX 802-2   BETSEY CLARK SERIES ☐
Comments: **Ninth in Series**, White Glass Ball, 3-1/4" dia.
A little girl leaves a gift for her friend. Back: She pulls a gift-filled sleigh. Caption: "Christmas 1981" and "The Greatest Joy Of Christmas Day Comes From The Joy We Give Away."
☐ Purchased 19__Pd $_____MIB   NB   DB   BNT
☐ Want   Orig. Ret. $4.50   **NB** $18   **MIB** Sec. Mkt. **$27**

QX 423-5   BETSEY CLARK ☐
Comments: Handcrafted, 3-9/32" tall.
Betsey and a fawn look at a tree topped with a brilliant star.
Artist: John Francis (Collin)
☐ Purchased 19__Pd $_____MIB   NB   DB   BNT
☐ Want   Orig. Ret. $9.00   **NB** $45   **MIB** Sec. Mkt. **$75**

QX 512-2   BETSEY CLARK BLUE CAMEO ☐
Comments: Cameo, 3-3/8" dia.
A little girl pets a fawn. Caption: "Christmas, When Hearts Reach Out To Give And Receive The Gentle Gifts Of Love" and "Christmas 1981."
☐ Purchased 19__Pd $_____MIB   NB   DB   BNT
☐ Want   Orig. Ret. $8.50   **NB** $18   **MIB** Sec. Mkt. **$25**

QX 403-5   CALICO KITTY ☐
Comments: Sewn Fabric, 3" tall.
Yellow Christmas fabric kitty has red bow.
☐ Purchased 19__Pd $_____MIB   NB   DB   BNT
☐ Want   Orig. Ret. $3.00   **NB** $12   Sec. Mkt. **$20**

QX 418-2   CANDYVILLE EXPRESS ☐
Comments: Handcrafted, 3" long.
Locomotive appears as if it has been crafted from gumdrops, cookies and licorice. Easily found Mint in Box.
☐ Purchased 19__Pd $_____MIB   NB   DB   BNT
☐ Want   Orig. Ret. $7.50   **NB** $75   **MIB** Sec. Mkt. **$110**

QX 400-2   CARDINAL CUTIE
Comments: Sewn Fabric, 3" tall.
Red fabric with white dots.
☐ Purchased 19 __Pd $_____MIB   NB   DB   BNT
☐Want   Orig. Ret. $3.00   **NB** $10   Sec. Mkt. **$22.50**

QX 427-5   CARROUSEL SERIES: SKATERS CARROUSEL ☐
Comments: **Fourth in Series**, Handcrafted, 2-15/32" tall.
A family of four ice skates around a green pole. Date "1981" stamped on the top of roof.
☐ Purchased 19 __Pd $_____MIB   NB   DB   BNT
☐ Want   Orig. Ret. $9.00   **NB** $70   **MIB** Sec. Mkt. **$85**

QX 158-4   CHECKING IT TWICE ☐
Comments: Special Edition, Handcrafted, 5-15/16" tall.
Reissued from 1980.
Artist: Thomas Blackshear
☐ Purchased 19 __Pd $_____MIB   NB   DB   BNT
☐ Want   1981 Ret. $22.50   **NB** $165   **MIB** Sec. Mkt. **$200**

QX 809-5   CHRISTMAS 1981 - SCHNEEBERG ☐
Comments: White Satin Ball, 3-1/4" dia., Dated 1981.
Schneeberg collage of a Christmas tree and sunburst of beads and colored glass.
☐ Purchased 19 __Pd $_____MIB   NB   DB   BNT
☐ Want   Orig. Ret. $4.50   **NB** $10   **MIB** Sec. Mkt. **$25**

QX 437-5   CHRISTMAS DREAMS ☐
Comments: Handcrafted Panorama Ball, 3-1/4" dia.
Little boy looks through a toy shop window. Caption: "Toy Shop 1981."
Artist: Donna Lee
☐ Purchased 19 __Pd $_____MIB   NB   DB   BNT
☐ Want   Orig. Ret. $12.00   **NB** $175   **MIB** Sec. Mkt. **$215**

QX 155-4   CHRISTMAS FANTASY ☐
Comments: Handcrafted, 3-3/4" long, Reissued in 1982.
An elf rides a white goose with a real brass ribbon in its bill.
☐ Purchased 19 __Pd $_____MIB   NB   DB   BNT
☐ Want   Orig. Ret. $13.00   **NB** $58   **MIB** Sec. Mkt. **$78**

QX 813-5   CHRISTMAS IN THE FOREST ☐
Comments: White Glass Ball, 3-1/4" dia., Dated 1981. RARE!
Caption: "Softly… Gently… Joyfully… Christmas Arrives In The Heart" and "Christmas 1981."
☐ Purchased 19 __Pd $_____MIB   NB   DB   BNT
☐ Want   Orig. Ret. $4.50   **NB** $80   **MIB** Sec. Mkt. **$130**

QX 810-2   CHRISTMAS MAGIC ☐
Comments: White Satin Ball, 3-1/4" dia., Dated 1981.
A gnome-like Santa ice skates with the animals. Caption: "Christmas 1981" and "It's here, there, everywhere... Christmas magic's in the air."
☐ Purchased 19 __Pd $_____MIB   NB   DB   BNT
☐ Want   Orig. Ret. $4.50   **NB** $12   **MIB** Sec. Mkt. **$25**

QX 404-2   CHRISTMAS TEDDY ☐
Comments: Plush, 4" tall, packed in gift box.
Cute little teddy with a green/red plaid bow and red stocking cap.
☐ Purchased 19 __Pd $_____MIB   NB   DB   BNT
☐ Want   Orig. Ret. $5.50   **NB** $15   **MIB** Sec. Mkt. **$22**

QX 507-5   CROWN CLASSICS COLLECTION: ANGEL ☐
Comments: Acrylic, 3-3/4" tall, stained glass look.
Golden-haired angel with white wings.
☐ Purchased 19 __Pd $_____MIB   NB   DB   BNT
☐ Want   Orig. Ret. $4.50   **NB** $20   **MIB** Sec. Mkt. **$26**

QX 515-5   CROWN CLASSICS COLLECTION: TREE PHOTOHOLDER ☐
Comments: Acrylic, 3-27/32" tall, Dated 1981.
Decorated tree has opening for photo. Caption: "Christmas 1981."
☐ Purchased 19 __Pd $_____MIB   NB   DB   BNT
☐ Want   Orig. Ret. $5.50   **NB** $16   **MIB** Sec. Mkt. **$24**

QX 516-5   CROWN CLASSICS COLLECTION: UNICORN ☐
Comments: Cameo, 3-3/8" dia., Dated 1981.
White unicorn on light green background. Caption: "A Time Of Magical Moments, Dreams Come True... Christmas 1981."
☐ Purchased 19 __Pd $_____MIB   NB   DB   BNT
☐ Want   Orig. Ret. $8.50   **NB** $15   **MIB** Sec. Mkt. **$26**

QX 607-5   DAUGHTER ☐
Comments: Ecru Soft-Sheen Satin Ball, 3-1/4" dia., Dated 1981.
"Wallpaper" design background shows a Christmas display. Caption:
"A Daughter Fills Each Day With Joy By Filling Hearts With Love" and
"Christmas 1981."
☐ Purchased 19 __Pd $_____MIB   NB   DB   BNT
☐ Want   Orig. Ret. $4.50   **NB** $22   **MIB** Sec. Mkt. **$38**

QX 805-5   DISNEY ☐
Comments: White Satin Ball, 3-1/4" dia., Dated 1981.
Sorcerer's apprentice Mickey.   Caption: "Christmas Is A Time Of
Magic, It's The Season Of Surprise, Everything Begins To Sparkle
Right Before Your Very Eyes" and "Christmas 1981."
☐ Purchased 19 __Pd $_____MIB   NB   DB   BNT
☐ Want   Orig. Ret. $4.50   **NB** $16   **MIB** Sec. Mkt. **$28**

QX 425-5   DIVINE MISS PIGGY, THE™ ☐
Comments: Handcrafted, 4" long, Reissued in 1982.
Miss Piggy poses as an angel with brass halo and white wings.
Artist: John Francis (Collin)
☐ Purchased 19 __Pd $_____MIB   NB   DB   BNT
☐ Want   Orig. Ret. $12.00   **NB** $65   **MIB** Sec. Mkt. **$95**

QX 148-1   DRUMMER BOY ☐
Comments: Wood, 3-1/2" tall.
Hand-painted drummer boy has moveable arms and legs.
☐ Purchased 19 __Pd $_____MIB   NB   DB   BNT
☐ Want   Orig. Ret. $2.50   **NB-P** $22   **MIB** Sec. Mkt. **$46**

QX 609-5   FATHER ☐
Comments: White Satin Ball, 3-1/4" dia., Dated 1981.
Caption: "Christmas 1981" and "Life Changes Season To Season, Year
To Year.. But A Father's Love Is For Always."
☐ Purchased 19 __Pd $_____MIB   NB   DB   BNT
☐ Want   Orig. Ret. $4.50   **NB** $8   **MIB** Sec. Mkt. **$20**

QX 708-2   FIFTIETH CHRISTMAS TOGETHER ☐
Comments: Gold Glass Ball, 3-1/4" dia., Dated 1981.
Poinsettias frame the captions: "Fifty Years Together, Christmas 1981"
and "A Treasure Of Memories Is A Very Special Happiness."
☐ Purchased 19 __Pd $_____MIB   NB   DB   BNT
☐ Want   Orig. Ret. $4.50   **NB** $10   **MIB** Sec. Mkt. **$20**

QX 706-2   FIRST CHRISTMAS TOGETHER ☐
Comments: Chrome Glass Ball, 3-1/4" dia., Dated 1981.
An 1800s couple ice skates against a red background. Caption: "First
Christmas Together 1981" and "Christmas... The Season For Sharing
The Spirit Of Love."
☐ Purchased 19 __Pd $_____MIB   NB   DB   BNT
☐ Want   Orig. Ret. $4.50   **NB** $12   **MIB** Sec. Mkt. **$30**

QX 505-5   FIRST CHRISTMAS TOGETHER ☐
Comments: Acrylic, 3" tall, Dated 1981.
Caption stamped in gold foil: "First Christmas Together 1981."
☐ Purchased 19 __Pd $_____MIB   NB   DB   BNT
☐ Want   Orig. Ret. $5.50   **NB** $10   **MIB** Sec. Mkt. **$24**

QX 434-2   FRIENDLY FIDDLER, THE ☐
Comments: Handcrafted, 3-5/32" tall.
A rabbit wearing a red and green scarf fiddles a Christmas tune.
Artist: Donna Lee
☐ Purchased 19 __Pd $_____MIB   NB   DB   BNT
☐ Want   Orig. Ret. $8.00   **NB** $50   **MIB** Sec. Mkt. **$70**

QX 704-2   FRIENDSHIP ☐
Comments: White Satin Ball, 3-1/4" dia., Dated 1981.
Fruit, flowers and holly border the caption: "The Beauty Of Friendship
Never Ends" and "Christmas 1981."
☐ Purchased 19 __Pd $_____MIB   NB   DB   BNT
☐ Want   Orig. Ret. $4.50   **NB** $12   **MIB** Sec. Mkt. **$25**

QX 503-5   FRIENDSHIP ☐
Comments: Acrylic, 3-1/4" dia., Dated 1981.
A squirrel and bird sing a duet. Caption: "Friends Put The "Merry"
In Christmas."
☐ Purchased 19 __Pd $_____MIB   NB   DB   BNT
☐ Want   Orig. Ret. $5.50   **NB** $18   **MIB** Sec. Mkt. **$30**

QX 509-5   FROSTED IMAGES: ANGEL ☐
Comments: Look of Etched Crystal, 1-15/32" – 1-19/32" tall.
Three-dimensional Angel has its hands folded.
☐ Purchased 19 __Pd $_____MIB   NB   DB   BNT
☐ Want   Orig. Ret. $4.00   **NB** $45   **MIB** Sec. Mkt. **$55**

QX 508-2   FROSTED IMAGES: MOUSE ☐
Comments: Look of Etched Crystal, 1-15/32" – 1-19/32" tall.
Three-dimensional Mouse holds a stocking.
☐ Purchased 19__Pd $_____MIB   NB   DB   BNT
☐ Want   Orig. Ret. $4.00   **NB** $15   **MIB** Sec. Mkt. **$25**

QX 510-2   FROSTED IMAGES: SNOWMAN ☐
Comments: Look of Etched Crystal, 1-15/32" – 1-19/32" tall.
Three-dimensional Snowman is waving.
☐ Purchased 19__Pd $_____MIB   NB   DB   BNT
☐ Want   Orig. Ret. $4.00   **NB** $16   **MIB** Sec. Mkt. **$25**

QX 433-5   FROSTY FRIENDS ☐
Comments: **Second in Series**, Handcrafted, 2" tall.
Dated 1981. An Eskimo and Husky puppy keep cozy in their igloo.
Many no box sales in '96 brought price down from previous years'. MIB
prices on this ornament down also by $35. It'll pay to shop around.
☐ Purchased 19__Pd $_____MIB   NB   DB   BNT
☐ Want   Orig. Ret. $8.00   **NB** $195   **MIB** Sec. Mkt. **$365**

QX 705-5   GIFT OF LOVE, THE ☐
Comments: Gold Glass Ball, 3-1/4" dia., Dated 1981.
Red roses and holly frame the date and caption: "Christmas 1981" and
"Love Is A Precious Gift, Priceless And Perfect, Cherished Above All
Life's Treasures."
☐ Purchased 19__Pd $_____MIB   NB   DB   BNT
☐ Want   Orig. Ret. $4.50   **NB** $10   **MIB** Sec. Mkt. **$25**

QX 402-2   GINGHAM DOG ☐
Comments: Sewn Fabric, 3" tall.
Cute blue/white gingham dog has a red bow.
☐ Purchased 19__Pd $_____MIB   NB   DB   BNT
☐ Want   Orig. Ret. $3.00   Sec. Mkt. **$20**

QX 603-5   GODCHILD ☐
Comments: White Satin Ball, 3-1/4" dia.
An angel and puppy on a cloud are placing stars in a bag. Caption:
"Christmas 1981" and "For A Special Godchild."
☐ Purchased 19__Pd $_____MIB   NB   DB   BNT
☐ Want   Orig. Ret. $4.50   **NB** $10   **MIB** Sec. Mkt. **$20**

**The safest way to double your money is to fold
it over and put it in your pocket.**

QX 605-5   GRANDDAUGHTER ☐
Comments: White Satin Ball, 3-1/4" dia., Dated 1981.
A white rocking horse and toys are featured. Caption: "A
Granddaughter Adds A Magical Touch To The Beauty And Joy Of
Christmas."
☐ Purchased 19__Pd $_____MIB   NB   DB   BNT
☐ Want   Orig. Ret. $4.50   **NB** $14   **MIB** Sec. Mkt. **$25**

QX 701-5   GRANDFATHER ☐
Comments: Gold Glass Ball, 3-1/4" dia.
The caption in red and gold is bordered by sprigs of holly: Grandfather
Holds A Special Place In The Heart" and "Christmas 1981."
☐ Purchased 19__Pd $_____MIB   NB   DB   BNT
☐ Want   Orig. Ret. $4.50   **NB** $10   **MIB** Sec. Mkt. **$20**

QX 702-2   GRANDMOTHER ☐
Comments: Ecru Soft-Sheen Satin Ball, 3-1/4" dia.
Caption: "Christmas 1981" and "A Grandmother Is So Loving And Dear
At Christmas And Throughout The Year."
☐ Purchased 19__Pd $_____MIB   NB   DB   BNT
☐ Want   Orig. Ret. $4.50   **NB** $12   **MIB** Sec. Mkt. **$20**

QX 703-5   GRANDPARENTS ☐
Comments: White Glass Ball, 3-1/4" dia., Dated 1981.
Caption: "Grandparents Give The Gift Of Love At Christmas And All
Year 'Round."
☐ Purchased 19__Pd $_____MIB   NB   DB   BNT
☐ Want   Orig. Ret. $4.50   **NB** $10   **MIB** Sec. Mkt. **$20**

QX 604-2   GRANDSON ☐
Comments: White Satin Ball, 3-1/4" dia.
Santa and reindeer are making toys. Caption: "A Grandson Makes
The 'Holly Days' Extra Bright And Jolly Days" and "Christmas 1981."
☐ Purchased 19__Pd $_____MIB   NB   DB   BNT
☐ Want   Orig. Ret. $4.50   **NB** $12   **MIB** Sec. Mkt. **$21**

QX 438-2   HERE COMES SANTA SERIES: ☐
ROOFTOP DELIVERIES
Comments: **Third in Series**, Handcrafted, 4-1/16" tall.
Santa's Making Deliveries In A Vehicle Which Resembles An Old Milk
Truck. Caption: "1981 S. Claus & Co. Rooftop Deliveries."
☐ Purchased 19__Pd $_____MIB   NB   DB   BNT
☐ Want   Orig. Ret. $13.00   **NB** $200   **MIB** Sec. Mkt. **$265**

QX 136-1   HOLIDAY CHIMES: SANTA MOBILE ☐
Comments: Chrome Plated.
Reissued from 1980.
☐ Purchased 19 __ Pd $_____ MIB   NB   DB   BNT
☐ Want   Orig. Ret. $5.50   **NB** $35   **MIB** Sec. Mkt. **$45**

QX 445-5   HOLIDAY CHIMES: SNOWMAN CHIMES ☐
Comments: Chrome Plate, 4" tall.
Mr. and Mrs. Snowman and Snowchild are suspended from a large snowflake.
☐ Purchased 19 __ Pd $_____ MIB   NB   DB   BNT
☐ Want   Orig. Ret. $5.50   **MIB** Sec. Mkt. **$30**

QX 165-4   HOLIDAY CHIMES: SNOWFLAKE CHIMES ☐
Comments: Chrome Plated.
Reissued from 1980. **Artist**: Linda Sickman
☐ Purchased 19 __ Pd $_____ MIB   NB   DB   BNT
☐ Want   Orig. Ret. $5.50   **NB** $18   **MIB** Sec. Mkt. **$30**

QX 501-5   HOLIDAY HIGHLIGHTS: CHRISTMAS STAR ☐
Comments: Clear Acrylic, 3-1/2" tall, Dated 1981.
Star with raised, faceted border has emerald shapes between the points. Caption stamped in silver foil: "Christmas 1981."
☐ Purchased 19 __ Pd $_____ MIB   NB   DB   BNT
☐ Want   Orig. Ret. $5.50   **NB** $12   **MIB** Sec. Mkt. **$20**

QX 500-2   HOLIDAY HIGHLIGHTS: SHEPHERD SCENE ☐
Comments: Clear Acrylic, 4" tall.
A shepherd and his sheep watch the star over Bethlehem.
☐ Purchased 19 __ Pd $_____ MIB   NB   DB   BNT
☐ Want   Orig. Ret. $5.50   **NB** $14   **MIB** Sec. Mkt. **$24**

QX 709-5   HOME ☐
Comments: White Satin Ball, 3-1/4" dia., Dated 1981.
Victorian winter village scene. Caption: "Christmas 1981" and "Love In The Home Puts Joy In The Heart."
☐ Purchased 19 __ Pd $_____ MIB   NB   DB   BNT
☐ Want   Orig. Ret. $4.50   **NB** $14   **MIB** Sec. Mkt. **$20**

Whether a boy ends up with a nest egg or a goose egg depends upon the chick he marries.

QX 431-5   ICE FAIRY ☐
Comments: Acrylic & Handcrafted, 4-1/8" tall.
A white frosted ice fairy with acrylic wings holds a clear acrylic snowflake. **Artist**: Donna Lee
☐ Purchased 19 __ Pd $_____ MIB   NB   DB   BNT
☐ Want   Orig. Ret. $6.50   **NB** $45   **MIB** Sec. Mkt. **$80**

QX 432-2   ICE SCULPTOR, THE ☐
Comments: Handcrafted, 3-1/32" tall.
A bear artist sculpts his self portrait in ice (clear acrylic).
Artist: Donna Lee
☐ Purchased 19 __ Pd $_____ MIB   NB   DB   BNT
☐ Want   Orig. Ret. $8.00   **NB** $70   **MIB** Sec. Mkt. **$80**

QX 804-2   JOAN WALSH ANGLUND© ☐
Comments: White Satin Ball, 3-1/4" dia.
Three children read a book together, then decorate the stair rail. Caption: " 'Tis The Time Of Dreams Come True. 'Tis The Time For Merrymaking" and "Christmas 1981."
☐ Purchased 19 __ Pd $_____ MIB   NB   DB   BNT
☐ Want   Orig. Ret. $4.50   **NB** $15   **MIB** Sec. Mkt. **$32**

QX 424-2   KERMIT THE FROG™ ☐
Comments: Handcrafted, 3-11/32" long.
Kermit, in a red stocking cap, races downhill on his sled.
Artist: John Francis (Collin)
☐ Purchased 19 __ Pd $_____ MIB   NB   DB   BNT
☐ Want   Orig. Ret. $9.00   **NB** $85   **MIB** Sec. Mkt. **$95**

QX 811-5   LET US ADORE HIM ☐
Comments: Gold Glass Ball, 3-1/4" dia.
Cherubs adore the Christ child on this lovely ball. Caption: "Christmas 1981" and "O Come Let Us Adore Him."
☐ Purchased 19 __ Pd $_____ MIB   NB   DB   BNT
☐ Want   Orig. Ret. $4.50   **NB** $45   **MIB** Sec. Mkt. **$57.50**

QX 408-2   LITTLE TRIMMERS: CLOTHESPIN DRUMMER BOY ☐
Comments: Handcrafted, 2-13/16" tall.
Drummer boy in black and brown beats a red drum.
☐ Purchased 19 __ Pd $_____ MIB   NB   DB   BNT
☐ Want   Orig. Ret. $4.50   **NB** $30   **MIB** Sec. Mkt. **$40**

QX 407-5   LITTLE TRIMMERS: JOLLY SNOWMAN ☐
Comments: Handcrafted, 2-7/32" tall.
Smiling snowman wears a black top hat and a fabric scarf.
☐ Purchased 19___Pd $_____MIB   NB   DB   BNT
☐ Want   Orig. Ret. $3.50   **NB** $20   **MIB** Sec. Mkt. **$50**

QX 409-5   LITTLE TRIMMERS: PERKY PENGUIN ☐
Comments: Handcrafted, 1-5/16" tall, Reissued in 1982.
Cute little penguin wears a red stocking cap and green and red striped scarf. Similar to Merry Miniature on disk.
☐ Purchased 19___Pd $_____MIB   NB   DB   BNT
☐ Want   Orig. Ret. $3.50   **NB** $35   **MIB** Sec. Mkt. **$55**

QX 406-2   LITTLE TRIMMERS: PUPPY LOVE ☐
Comments: Handcrafted, 1-5/32" tall, bread dough look.
This tan puppy has a red cord around his neck and a red heart on his chest.
☐ Purchased 19___Pd $_____MIB   NB   DB   BNT
☐ Want   Orig. Ret. $3.50   **NB** $26   **MIB** Sec. Mkt. **$38**

QX 412-2   LITTLE TRIMMERS: STOCKING MOUSE, THE ☐
Comments: Handcrafted, 2-1/4" tall.
A little white mouse with a white and blue night cap peeks out of a red and green striped stocking.
☐ Purchased 19___Pd $_____MIB   NB   DB   BNT
☐ Want   Orig. Ret. $4.50   **NB** $55   **MIB** Sec. Mkt. **$95**

QX 502-2   LOVE ☐
Comments: Acrylic, 3-1/2" tall.
Heart has a silver foil caption in center. "Love... the nicest gift of all. Christmas 1981."
☐ Purchased 19___Pd $_____MIB   NB   DB   BNT
☐ Want   Orig. Ret. $5.50   **NB** $40   **MIB** Sec. Mkt. **$50**

QX 425-2   LOVE AND JOY (PORCELAIN CHIMES) ☐
Comments: Porcelain, 3-3/4" tall, Dated 1981.
Three white doves are suspended from a while porcelain heart tied in red fabric ribbon. Caption: "Love and Joy."
☐ Purchased 19___Pd $_____MIB   NB   DB   BNT
☐ Want   Orig. Ret. $9.00   **NB** $80   **MIB** Sec. Mkt. **$90**

**Love is a little blind; when we love someone dearly
we unconsciously overlook many faults.**

QX 808-2   MARTY LINKS ☐
Comments: White Satin Ball, 3-1/4" dia.
Two children carry a large candy cane while another little girl holds mistletoe over her head. Caption: "Christmas 1981" and "Happy Hearts And Good Times Go Hand In Hand At Christmas."
☐ Purchased 19___Pd $_____MIB   NB   DB   BNT
☐ Want   Orig. Ret. $4.50   **NB** $12   **MIB** Sec. Mkt. **$20**

QX 806-2   MARY HAMILTON ☐
Comments: White Glass Ball, 3-1/4" dia.
Little angels take part in various activities. Caption: "Christmas 1981" and "Christmas Decorates The World With Wonder."
☐ Purchased 19___Pd $_____MIB   NB   DB   BNT
☐ Want   Orig. Ret. $4.50   **NB** $12   **MIB** Sec. Mkt. **$18**

QX 814-2   MERRY CHRISTMAS ☐
Comments: Gold Glass Ball, 3-1/4" dia., Dated 1981.
A burgundy diamond design on a green background frames the date. Caption: "Merry Christmas" is framed in same design, colors reversed.
☐ Purchased 19___Pd $_____MIB   NB   DB   BNT
☐ Want   Orig. Ret. $4.50   **NB** $12   **MIB** Sec. Mkt. **$22**

QX 608-2   MOTHER ☐
Comments: White Satin Ball, 3-1/4" dia., Dated 1981.
Red roses and Christmas greenery. Caption: "Christmas 1981" and "In A Mother's Heart There Is Love...The Very Heart Of Christmas."
☐ Purchased 19___Pd $_____MIB   NB   DB   BNT
☐ Want   Orig. Ret. $4.50   **NB** $12   **MIB** Sec. Mkt. **$18**

QX 700-2   MOTHER AND DAD ☐
Comments: Ecru Soft-Sheen Satin Ball, 3-1/4" dia., Dated 1981.
Caption: "For Mother And Dad, Christmas 1981." and "The Wonderful Meaning Of Christmas Is Found In The Circle Of Family Love."
☐ Purchased 19 Pd $_____MIB   NB   DB   BNT
☐ Want   Orig. Ret. $4.50   **NB** $10   **MIB** Sec. Mkt. **$15**

QX 448-5   MR. & MRS. CLAUS ☐
Comments: 3-1/2" tall, Handcrafted.
Boxed set of two ornaments. Originally issued in individual boxes in 1975 as Adorable Adornments: "Mrs. Santa" and "Santa." The only way to tell the difference is if you have the original packaging. There was an error in last year's prices. Oops sorry 'bout that!
☐ Purchased 19___Pd $_____MIB   NB   DB   BNT
☐ Want   Orig. Ret. $12.00   **NB** $60 ea.   **MIB** Sec. Mkt. **$120 pr.**

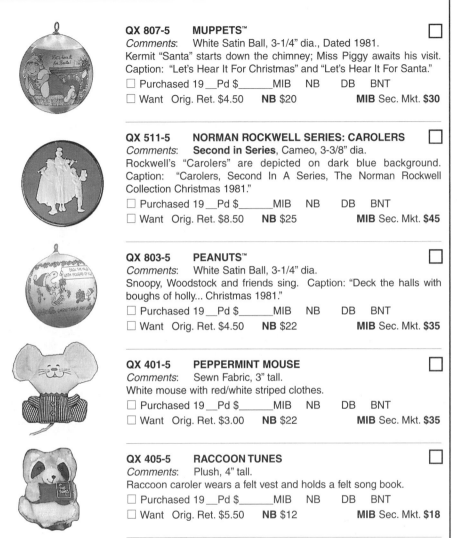

QX 807-5   MUPPETS™ ☐
Comments: White Satin Ball, 3-1/4" dia., Dated 1981.
Kermit "Santa" starts down the chimney; Miss Piggy awaits his visit.
Caption: "Let's Hear It For Christmas" and "Let's Hear It For Santa."
☐ Purchased 19 __Pd $_____MIB   NB   DB   BNT
☐ Want   Orig. Ret. $4.50   **NB** $20   **MIB** Sec. Mkt. **$30**

QX 511-5   NORMAN ROCKWELL SERIES: CAROLERS ☐
Comments: **Second in Series**, Cameo, 3-3/8" dia.
Rockwell's "Carolers" are depicted on dark blue background.
Caption: "Carolers, Second In A Series, The Norman Rockwell
Collection Christmas 1981."
☐ Purchased 19 __Pd $_____MIB   NB   DB   BNT
☐ Want   Orig. Ret. $8.50   **NB** $25   **MIB** Sec. Mkt. **$45**

QX 803-5   PEANUTS™ ☐
Comments: White Satin Ball, 3-1/4" dia.
Snoopy, Woodstock and friends sing. Caption: "Deck the halls with
boughs of holly... Christmas 1981."
☐ Purchased 19 __Pd $_____MIB   NB   DB   BNT
☐ Want   Orig. Ret. $4.50   **NB** $22   **MIB** Sec. Mkt. **$35**

QX 401-5   PEPPERMINT MOUSE ☐
Comments: Sewn Fabric, 3" tall.
White mouse with red/white striped clothes.
☐ Purchased 19 __Pd $_____MIB   NB   DB   BNT
☐ Want   Orig. Ret. $3.00   **NB** $22   **MIB** Sec. Mkt. **$35**

QX 405-5   RACCOON TUNES ☐
Comments: Plush, 4" tall.
Raccoon caroler wears a felt vest and holds a felt song book.
☐ Purchased 19 __Pd $_____MIB   NB   DB   BNT
☐ Want   Orig. Ret. $5.50   **NB** $12   **MIB** Sec. Mkt. **$18**

QX 422-2   ROCKING HORSE ☐
Comments: **FIRST IN SERIES**, Handcrafted 2" tall, Dated 1981.
Brown/white Palomino horse on red rockers. Very much sought after.
Price down from '96 more sales reported. **Artist**: Linda Sickman
☐ Purchased 19 __Pd $_____MIB   NB   DB   BNT
☐ Want   Orig. Ret. $9.00   **NB** $425   **MIB** Sec. Mkt. **$550**

**Truth exists;
only falsehood has to be invented.**

QX 439-5   SAILING SANTA ☐
Comments: Handcrafted, 5" tall, Dated 1981.
Santa sails away in a red hot air balloon. Caption: "Merry Christmas
1981."
☐ Purchased 19 __Pd $_____MIB   NB   DB   BNT
☐ Want   Orig. Ret. $13.00   **NB** $190   **MIB** Sec. Mkt. **$260**

QX 812-2   SANTA'S COMING ☐
Comments: White Satin Ball, 3-1/4" dia., Dated 1981.
Mrs. Santa makes sure Santa is ready for his trip and reindeer fly
through a moonlit night. Caption: "Christmas 1981" and "Hustle,
Bustle, Hurry, Scurry, Santa's Coming.. Never Worry."
☐ Purchased 19 __Pd $_____MIB   NB   DB   BNT
☐ Want   Orig. Ret. $4.50   **NB** $16   **MIB** Sec. Mkt. **$28**

QX 815-5   SANTA'S SURPRISE ☐
Comments: White Satin Ball, 3-1/4" dia., Dated 1981.
Santa uses the stars from the sky to decorate a small evergreen.
Caption: "Twinkle, Glimmer, Sparkle, Shimmer... Let The Christmas
Season Shine" and "Christmas 1981."
☐ Purchased 19 __Pd $_____MIB   NB   DB   BNT
☐ Want   Orig. Ret. $4.50   **NB** $14   **MIB** Sec. Mkt. **$25**

QX 436-2   SNOOPY AND FRIENDS ☐
Comments: **Third in Series**, Handcrafted Panorama Ball.
3-1/4" dia. Dated 1981. A "birdsled" pulls Snoopy past a snow Snoopy.
Artist: John Francis (Collin)
☐ Purchased 19 __Pd $_____MIB   NB   DB   BNT
☐ Want   Orig. Ret. $12.00   **NB** $65   **MIB** Sec. Mkt. **$90**

QX 606-2   SON ☐
Comments: White Satin Ball, 3-1/4" dia., Dated 1981.
A variety of Christmas scenes are shown in various colored
squares. Caption: "Christmas 1981" and "A Son Puts The Merry In
Christmas."
☐ Purchased 19 __Pd $_____MIB   NB   DB   BNT
☐ Want   Orig. Ret. $4.50   **NB** $15   **MIB** Sec. Mkt. **$32**

QX 430-2   SPACE SANTA ☐
Comments: Handcrafted, 3" tall, Dated 1981.
Santa flies in for a Christmas hello, wearing a silver space suit.
☐ Purchased 19 __Pd $_____MIB   NB   DB   BNT
☐ Want   Orig. Ret. $6.50   **NB** $70   **MIB** Sec. Mkt. **$100**

QX 446-2　ST. NICHOLAS
Comments:　Pressed Tin, 4-3/8" tall.
Traditional European St. Nicholas carries a lantern to light his way.
Artist: Linda Sickman

☐ Purchased 19__Pd $_____MIB　NB　　DB　　BNT
☐ Want　Orig. Ret. $5.50　**NB** $40　　**MIB** Sec. Mkt. **$50**

QX 421-5　STAR SWING
Comments:　Brass & Handcrafted, 3-5/8" tall, Dated 1981.
A little girl swings from a chrome-plated brass star.
Artist: Linda Sickman

☐ Purchased 19__Pd $_____MIB　NB　　DB　　BNT
☐ Want　Orig. Ret. $5.50　**NB** $22　　**MIB** Sec. Mkt. **$30**

QX 800-2　TEACHER
Comments:　White Satin Ball, 3-1/4" dia., Dated 1981.
Multi-colored stocking in white oval, red background. Caption: "For a special teacher 1981."

☐ Purchased 19__Pd $_____MIB　NB　　DB　　BNT
☐ Want　Orig. Ret. $4.50　**NB** $8　　**MIB** Sec. Mkt. **$14**

QX 413-5　THIMBLE SERIES: ANGEL
Comments:　**Fourth in Series,** Handcrafted, 1-1/2" dia.
Flying angel with white wings carries a tree that is potted in a thimble.
HARD TO FIND!

☐ Purchased 19__Pd $_____MIB　NB　　DB　　BNT
☐ Want　Orig. Ret. $4.50　**NB** $70　　**MIB** Sec. Mkt. **$140**

QX 429-5　TOPSY-TURVY TUNES
Comments:　Handcrafted, 3" tall.
An opossum hangs by his tail while a redbird sits on his book of Carols.
Artist: Donna Lee

☐ Purchased 19__Pd $_____MIB　NB　　DB　　BNT
☐ Want　Orig. Ret. $7.50　**NB** $50　　**MIB** Sec. Mkt. **$75**

QX 801-5　TRADITIONAL　(BLACK SANTA)
Comments:　RARE! White Satin Ball, 3-1/4" dia., Dated 1981.
A black Santa feeds the animals in the forest. Caption: "It's Christmas. It's time for Sharing... And dreaming, and caring and merry gift bearing..."

☐ Purchased 19__Pd $_____MIB　NB　　DB　　BNT
☐ Want　Orig. Ret. $4.50　**NB** $70　　**MIB** Sec. Mkt. **$95**

QX 504-2　TWENTY-FIFTH CHRISTMAS TOGETHER
Comments:　Clear Acrylic, 4-1/2" tall.
Two wedding bells with frosted border designs have caption in silver foil. "25 Years Together, Christmas 1981."

☐ Purchased 19__Pd $_____MIB　NB　　DB　　BNT
☐ Want　Orig. Ret. $5.50　**NB** $18　　**MIB** Sec. Mkt. **$22**

QX 707-5　TWENTY-FIFTH CHRISTMAS TOGETHER
Comments:　White Glass Ball, 3-1/4" dia.
White bells on a background of red ribbon and Christmas greenery. Caption: "25 Years Together, Christmas 1981" and "Christmas season of the heart, time of sweet remembrance."

☐ Purchased 19__Pd $_____MIB　NB　　DB　　BNT
☐ Want　Orig. Ret. $4.50　**NB** $12　　**MIB** Sec. Mkt. **$22**

QX 162-1　YARN & FABRIC ORNAMENT ANGEL
Comments:　Yarn with lace and felt accents, 5" tall.
Reissued from 1980.

☐ Purchased 19__Pd $_____MIB　NB　　DB　　BNT
☐ Want　Orig. Ret. $3.00　　　　　　　Sec. Mkt. **$10**

QX 161-4　YARN & FABRIC ORNAMENT SANTA
Comments:　Yarn with lace and felt accents, 5" tall.
Reissued from 1980.

☐ Purchased 19__Pd $_____MIB　NB　　DB　　BNT
☐ Want　Orig. Ret. $3.00　　　　　　　Sec. Mkt. **$10**

QX 163-4　YARN & FABRIC ORNAMENT SNOWMAN
Comments:　Yarn with lace and felt accents, 5" tall.
Reissued from 1980.

☐ Purchased 19__Pd $_____MIB　NB　　DB　　BNT
☐ Want　Orig. Ret. $3.00　　　　　　　Sec. Mkt. **$10**

QX 164-1　YARN & FABRIC ORNAMENT SOLDIER
Comments:　Yarn with lace and felt accents, 5" tall.
Reissued from 1980.

☐ Purchased 19__Pd $_____MIB　NB　　DB　　BNT
☐ Want　Orig. Ret. $3.00　　　　　　　Sec. Mkt. **$10**

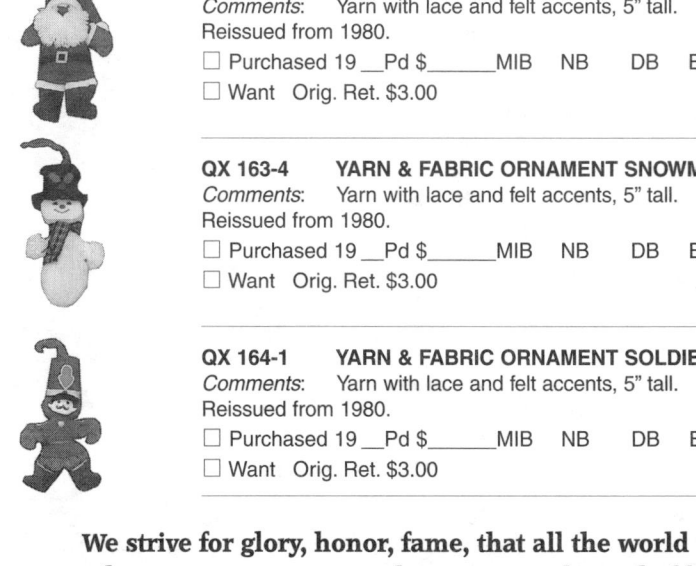

We strive for glory, honor, fame, that all the world may know our name... But when we near the end of life and look back o'er the years of strife, we find that happiness depends on none of these, but love of friends.

1982 Collection

QX 300-3　ARCTIC PENGUIN　☐
Comments:　Clear Acrylic, 1-1/2" tall.
Penguin molded to resemble an ice sculpture.
☐ Purchased 19__Pd $_____MIB　NB　　DB　　BNT
☐ Want　Orig. Ret. $4.00　**NB** $10　　　　**MIB** Sec. Mkt. **$20**

QX 455-3　BABY'S FIRST CHRISTMAS　☐
Comments:　Handcrafted, 3" tall, Dated 1982.
Baby's rattle with panorama window. Caption: "Baby's First Christmas." **Artist**: Ed Seale
☐ Purchased 19__Pd $_____MIB　NB　　DB　　BNT
☐ Want　Orig. Ret. $13.00　**NB** $25　　　　**MIB** Sec. Mkt. **$48**

QMB 900-7　BABY'S FIRST CHRISTMAS　☐
Comments:　Musical, Classic Shape, 4-1/2" tall, Dated 1982.
Caption: "First Christmas 1982." Plays Brahms' Lullaby.
☐ Purchased 19__Pd $_____MIB　NB　　DB　　BNT
☐ Want　Orig. Ret. $16.00　**NB** $50　　　　**MIB** Sec. Mkt. **$65**

QX 216-3　BABY'S FIRST CHRISTMAS (BOY)　☐
Comments:　Light Blue Satin Ball, 3-1/4" dia., Dated 1982.
Design was hand-embroidered, then photographed. Caption: "Baby's First Christmas 1982" and "A baby boy is a precious gift – a blessing from above."
☐ Purchased 19__Pd $_____MIB　NB　　DB　　BNT
☐ Want　Orig. Ret. $4.50　**NB** $12　　　　**MIB** Sec. Mkt. **$25**

QX 207-3　BABY'S FIRST CHRISTMAS (GIRL)　☐
Comments:　Light Pink Satin Ball, 3-1/4" dia., Dated 1982.
Embroidered toys form a quilt. Caption: "Baby's First Christmas 1982" and "A baby girl is the sweetest gift a lifetime can provide."
☐ Purchased 19__Pd $_____MIB　NB　　DB　　BNT
☐ Want　Orig. Ret. $4.50　**NB** $12　　　　**MIB** Sec. Mkt. **$28**

QX 312-6　BABY'S FIRST CHRISTMAS: PHOTOHOLDER　☐
Comments:　Acrylic, 4-1/4" tall, Dated 1982.
A stocking filled with toys. Caption: "Baby's First Christmas 1982" and "Oh what joy and sweet surprise Christmas brings to little eyes."
☐ Purchased 19__Pd $_____MIB　NB　　DB　　BNT
☐ Want　Orig. Ret. $6.50　**NB** $18　　　　**MIB** Sec. Mkt. **$25**

QX 302-3　BABY'S FIRST CHRISTMAS　☐
Comments:　Acrylic, 3-17/32" tall.
Teddy Bear in frosted acrylic with block. Caption: "Baby's First Christmas 1982." **Artist**: Ed Seale
☐ Purchased 19__Pd $_____MIB　NB　　DB　　BNT
☐ Want Orig. Ret. $5.50　**NB** $20　　　　**MIB** Sec. Mkt. **$38**

QX 456-6　BAROQUE ANGEL　☐
Comments:　Brass & Handcrafted, 4-7/16" tall.
A cherub flies with a brass banner. Caption: "Joyeux Noel."
Artist: Donna Lee
☐ Purchased 19__Pd $_____MIB　NB　　DB　　BNT
☐ Want　Orig. Ret. $15.00　**NB** $135　　　　**MIB** Sec. Mkt. **$165**

QX 455-6　BELLRINGER, THE: ANGEL　☐
Comments:　**Fourth in Series**, Handcrafted, 2-27/32" tall.
Dated 1982. The clapper is a red and green wreath with an angel in its center. **Artist**: Donna Lee
☐ Purchased 19__Pd $_____MIB　NB　　DB　　BNT
☐ Want Orig. Ret. $15.00　**NB** $75　　　　**MIB** Sec. Mkt. **$98**

QX 305-6　BETSEY CLARK　☐
Comments:　Blue Cameo, 3-3/8" dia.
Angel decorates a tree on a cloud. Caption: "Christmas 1982" and "'Tis The Season For Trimming Trees And Making Merry Memories."
☐ Purchased 19__Pd $_____MIB　NB　　DB　　BNT
☐ Want　Orig. Ret. $8.50　**NB** $20　　　　**MIB** Sec. Mkt. **$28**

QX 215-6　BETSEY CLARK SERIES　☐
Comments:　**Tenth in Series**, White Satin Ball, 3-1/4" dia.
Three children share a bedtime story. Caption: "Christmas 1982" and "The joys of Christmas are multiplied when shared with those we love."
☐ Purchased 19__Pd $_____MIB　NB　　DB　　BNT
☐ Want　Orig. Ret. $4.50　**NB** $18　　　　**MIB** Sec. Mkt. **$38**

QX 460-6　BRASS BELL　☐
Comments:　Polished Brass, 2-11/32" tall.
Design of holly leaves and berries are stamped into the bell. Red ribbon and bow for hanging. **Artist**: Donna Lee
☐ Purchased 19__Pd $_____MIB　NB　　DB　　BNT
☐ Want Orig. Ret. $12.00　**NB** $10　　　　**MIB** Sec. Mkt. **$24**

NO NUMBER BRASS PROMOTIONAL ORNAMENT ☐
Comments: Dimensional Brass, 2-3/8" tall.
24 k. gold tone coating. Victorian couple in sleigh are shown in front of a sleeping village.
☐ Purchased 19__ Pd $_____ MIB   NB   DB   BNT
☐ Want   Orig. Ret. $3.50   **NB** $35   **MIB** Sec. Mkt. **$45**

QX 478-3   CARROUSEL ☐
Comments: **Fifth in Series,** Handcrafted, 3" tall, Dated 1982.
Snowmen ice skate around a pole. Caption: "Merry Christmas 1982" on snow-covered top.   **Artist:** Ed Seale
☐ Purchased 19__ Pd $_____ MIB   NB   DB   BNT
☐ Want   Orig. Ret. $10.00   **NB** $80   **MIB** Sec. Mkt. **$105**

QX 220-6   CHRISTMAS ANGEL ☐
Comments: Gold Glass Ball, 3-1/4" dia., Dated 1982.
Angel shelters the flame of a glowing candle. Caption: "From Heaven above the light of love shines into our hearts at Christmas."
☐ Purchased 19__ Pd $_____ MIB   NB   DB   BNT
☐ Want   Orig. Ret. $4.50   **NB** $10   **MIB** Sec. Mkt. **$25**

QX 155-4   CHRISTMAS FANTASY ☐
Comments: Brass and Handcrafted, 3-3/4" long.
Reissued from 1981.
☐ Purchased 19__ Pd $_____ MIB   NB   DB   BNT
☐ Want   Orig. Ret. $13.00   **NB** $58   **MIB** Sec. Mkt. **$78**

QX 311-6   CHRISTMAS MEMORIES ☐
Comments: Acrylic, 4-1/8" tall, Dated 1982.
Square white photoholder with green holly leaves and red bow. Caption: "How bright the joys of Christmas, how warm the memories."
Artist: Linda Sickman
☐ Purchased 19__ Pd $_____ MIB   NB   DB   BNT
☐ Want   Orig. Ret. $6.50   **NB** $8   **MIB** Sec. Mkt. **$15**

QX 145-4   CLOISONNÉ ANGEL ☐
Comments: Cloisonné, 2-21/32" tall.
An angel flies in the center of an open heart. Caption: "Peace, Love, Joy."
☐ Purchased 19__ Pd $_____ MIB   NB   DB   BNT
☐ Want   Orig. Ret. $12.00   **NB** $70   **MIB** Sec. Mkt. **$95**

QX 458-3   CLOTHESPIN SOLDIER: BRITISH ☐
Comments: **FIRST IN SERIES**, Handcrafted, 3-5/32" tall.
This soldier has a black mustache, tall black hat, red/white/blue uniform and carries a black baton.   **Artist:** Linda Sickman
☐ Purchased 19__ Pd $_____ MIB   NB   DB   BNT
☐ Want   Orig. Ret. $5.00   **NB** $95   **MIB** Sec. Mkt. **$120**

QX 308-6   COLORS OF CHRISTMAS: SANTA'S FLIGHT ☐
Comments: Acrylic, 4-1/4" tall, Dated Christmas 1982.
Stained glass look; Santa in a hot air balloon.
☐ Purchased 19__ Pd $_____ MIB   NB   DB   BNT
☐ Want   Orig. Ret. $4.50   **NB** $25   **MIB** Sec. Mkt. **$48**

QX 308-3   COLORS OF CHRISTMAS: NATIVITY ☐
Comments: Acrylic, 4" tall, Stained glass look.
Traditional view of the Holy Family.
☐ Purchased 19__ Pd $_____ MIB   NB   DB   BNT
☐ Want   Orig. Ret. $4.50   **NB** $38   **MIB** Sec. Mkt. **$50**

QX 480-6   COWBOY SNOWMAN ☐
Comments: Handcrafted, 2-27/32" tall.
Snowman is dressed in red scarf, boots and hat with a candy cane "pistol."
☐ Purchased 19__ Pd $_____ MIB   NB   DB   BNT
☐ Want   Orig. Ret. $8.00   **NB** $40   **MIB** Sec. Mkt. **$50**

QX 201-3   CURRIER & IVES ☐
Comments: White Porcelain Glass Ball, 3-1/4" dia.
Reproduction of "The Road – Winter." Caption: "Christmas 1982" and "The Road – Winter" and "Currier and Ives." This print was "registered according to an Act of Congress in 1853."
☐ Purchased 19__ Pd $_____ MIB   NB   DB   BNT
☐ Want   Orig. Ret. $4.50   **NB** $10   **MIB** Sec. Mkt. **$22**

QX 435-5   CYCLING SANTA ☐
Comments: Handcrafted, 4-3/8" tall, Reissued in 1983.
Santa rides an old "velocipede" with his pack on the back. The wheels turn and three brass bells attached to his pack jingle. Price is down from '96.
☐ Purchased 19__ Pd $_____ MIB   NB   DB   BNT
☐ Want   Orig. Ret. $20.00   **NB** $90   **MIB** Sec. Mkt. **$125**

QX 204-6   DAUGHTER
Comments: Ecru Soft-Sheen Satin Ball, 3-1/4" dia., Dated 1982.
A selection of Christmas goodies are displayed.
Caption: "A Daughter's Love Makes Christmas Special."
☐ Purchased 19 __ Pd $_____ MIB   NB   DB   BNT
☐ Want   Orig. Ret. $4.50   **NB** $20   **MIB** Sec. Mkt. **$32**

QX 217-3   DISNEY®
Comments: White Satin Ball, 3-1/4" dia., Dated 1982.
Seven Dwarfs prepare for Christmas. Caption: "Christmas... Time For Surprises – In All Shapes And Sizes."
☐ Purchased 19 __ Pd $_____ MIB   NB   DB   BNT
☐ Want   Orig. Ret. $4.50   **NB** $22   **MIB** Sec. Mkt. **$38**

QX 425-5   DIVINE MISS PIGGY, THE™
Comments: Handcrafted, 4" long.
Reissued from 1981.   **Artist**: John Francis (Collin)
☐ Purchased 19 __ Pd $_____ MIB   NB   DB   BNT
☐ Want   Orig. Ret. $12.00   **NB** $65   **MIB** Sec. Mkt. **$95**

QX 457-3   ELFIN ARTIST
Comments: Handcrafted, 3" tall.
Bearded elf paints the stripes on ribbon candy while hanging onto his paint bucket. **Artist**: Linda Sickman
☐ Purchased 19 __ Pd $_____ MIB   NB   DB   BNT
☐ Want   Orig. Ret. $9.00   **NB** $35   **MIB** Sec. Mkt. **$45**

QX 494-6   EMBROIDERED TREE
Comments: Fabric, 4-9/16" tall.
Green fabric tree is decorated with embroidered flowers and trimmed in red braided cord.
☐ Purchased 19 __ Pd $_____ MIB   NB   DB   BNT
☐ Want   Orig. Ret. $6.50   Sec. Mkt. **$35**

QX 205-6   FATHER
Comments: Ecru Soft-Sheen Satin Ball, 3-1/4" dia.
Woodcut style. Caption: "Christmas 1982" and "A Father's Love Brightens The Season." **Artist**: Linda Sickman
☐ Purchased 19 __ Pd $_____ MIB   NB   DB   BNT
☐ Want   Orig. Ret. $4.50   **NB** $10   **MIB** Sec. Mkt. **$20**

QX 212-3   FIFTIETH CHRISTMAS TOGETHER
Comments: Gold Glass Ball, 3-1/4" dia., Dated 1982.
Burgundy lettering, highlighted with white. Caption: "50th Christmas Together 1982" and "We Measure Our Time, Not By Years Alone, But By The Love And Joy We've Known."
☐ Purchased 19 __ Pd $_____ MIB   NB   DB   BNT
☐ Want   Orig. Ret. $4.50   **NB** $14   **MIB** Sec. Mkt. **$22**

QMB 901-9   FIRST CHRISTMAS TOGETHER
Comments: Musical, Classic Shape, 4-1/2" tall, Dated 1982.
Plays "White Christmas" Caption: "First Christmas Together 1982."
☐ Purchased 19 __ Pd $_____ MIB   NB   DB   BNT
☐ Want   Orig. Ret. $16.00   **NB** $60   **MIB** Sec. Mkt. **$75**

QX 211-3   FIRST CHRISTMAS TOGETHER
Comments: Silver Chrome Glass Ball, 3-1/4" dia., Dated 1982.
Two redbirds soar against a frosty background.   Caption: "First Christmas Together 1982" and "Quiet Moments Together, Love That Lasts Forever."
☐ Purchased 19 __ Pd $_____ MIB   NB   DB   BNT
☐ Want   Orig. Ret. $4.50   **NB** $20   **MIB** Sec. Mkt. **$30**

QX 306-6   FIRST CHRISTMAS TOGETHER
Comments: Turquoise Cameo, 3-3/8" dia., Dated 1982.
A couple ice skates.   Caption: "First Christmas Together" and "Christmas Is For Sharing With The Special One You Love."
☐ Purchased 19 __ Pd $_____ MIB   NB   DB   BNT
☐ Want   Orig. Ret. $8.50   **NB** $20   **MIB** Sec. Mkt. **$38**

QX 456-3   FIRST CHRISTMAS TOGETHER – LOCKET
Comments: Polished Brass, 2-5/8" tall, Dated 1982.
Hinged, heart-shaped locket opens with inserts for two photos. Includes brass hanger. Caption: "First Christmas Together 1982."
Artist: Ed Seale
☐ Purchased 19 __ Pd $_____ MIB   NB   DB   BNT
☐ Want   Orig. Ret. $15.00   **NB** $20   **MIB** Sec. Mkt. **$30**

QX 302-6   FIRST CHRISTMAS TOGETHER
Comments: Acrylic, 4-1/4" tall, Dated 1982.
Tree. Caption: "First Christmas Together."
☐ Purchased 19 __ Pd $_____ MIB   NB   DB   BNT
☐ Want   Orig. Ret. $5.50   **NB** $8   **MIB** Sec. Mkt. **$18**

QX 208-6   FRIENDSHIP   ☐
Comments: White Satin Ball, 3-1/4" dia.
Happy animals ice skate together. Caption: "Christmas 1982" and "Hearts Are Happy When Friends Are Together."
☐ Purchased 19 __ Pd $_____ MIB   NB   DB   BNT
☐ Want   Orig. Ret. $4.50   **NB** $12   **MIB** Sec. Mkt. **$20**

QX 304-6   FRIENDSHIP   ☐
Comments: Acrylic, 3-1/4" tall, Dated 1982.
Kitten/puppy together. Caption: "Christmas Is For Friends."
☐ Purchased 19 __ Pd $_____ MIB   NB   DB   BNT
☐ Want   Orig. Ret. $5.50   **NB** $18   **MIB** Sec. Mkt. **$25**

QX 452-3   FROSTY FRIENDS   ☐
Comments: **Third in Series**, Handcrafted, 4-1/8" tall.
Dated 1982. A little Eskimo Climbs An Icicle "Mountain." His Husky puppy waits at the top. **Many no boxed ones out there. Artist**: Ed Seale
☐ Purchased 19 __ Pd $_____ MIB   NB   DB   BNT
☐ Want   Orig. Ret. $8.00   **NB** $80   **MIB** Sec. Mkt. **$280**

QX 222-6   GODCHILD   ☐
Comments: White Glass Ball, 3-1/4" dia., Dated 1982.
A little angel reaches for a snowflake. Caption: "Merry Christmas To A Special Godchild."
☐ Purchased 19 __ Pd $_____ MIB   NB   DB   BNT
☐ Want   Orig. Ret. $4.50   **NB** $8   **MIB** Sec. Mkt. **$22**

QX 224-3   GRANDDAUGHTER   ☐
Comments: White Satin Ball, 3-1/4" dia.
Puppies, teddy bears and bunnies carry a rope of green garland. Caption: "Christmas 1982" and "A Granddaughter Has A Special Gift For Giving Special Joy."
☐ Purchased 19 __ Pd $_____ MIB   NB   DB   BNT
☐ Want   Orig. Ret. $4.50   **NB** $5   **MIB** Sec. Mkt. **$24**

QX 207-6   GRANDFATHER   ☐
Comments: Dark Blue Satin Ball, 3-1/4" dia.
Caption: "Grandfather... In His Strength He Teaches, In His Gentleness He Loves" and "Christmas 1982."
☐ Purchased 19 __ Pd $_____ MIB   NB   DB   BNT
☐ Want   Orig. Ret. $4.50   **NB** $5   **MIB** Sec. Mkt. **$20**

QX 200-3   GRANDMOTHER   ☐
Comments: Dark Pink Satin Ball, 3-1/4" dia., Dated 1982.
Caption: "Christmas 1982" and "A Grandmother Is Love."
☐ Purchased 19 __ Pd $_____ MIB   NB   DB   BNT
☐ Want   Orig. Ret. $4.50   **NB** $10   **MIB** Sec. Mkt. **$18**

QX 214-6   GRANDPARENTS   ☐
Comments: White Glass Ball, 3-1/4" dia., Dated 1982.
Covered bridge and winter scenes. Caption: "Christmas 1982" and "With Thoughts Of Grandparents Come Thoughts Of Days The Heart Will Always Treasure."
☐ Purchased 19 __ Pd $_____ MIB   NB   DB   BNT
☐ Want   Orig. Ret. $4.50   **NB** $8   **MIB** Sec. Mkt. **$18**

QX 224-6   GRANDSON   ☐
Comments: White Satin Ball, 3-1/4" dia., Dated 1982.
Bunnies sled in the snow. Caption: "Christmas 1982" and "A Grandson... Makes Days Bright, Hearts Light And Christmas Time A Real Delight."
☐ Purchased 19 __ Pd $_____ MIB   NB   DB   BNT
☐ Want   Orig. Ret. $4.50   **NB** $18   **MIB** Sec. Mkt. **$30**

QX 464-3   HERE COMES SANTA: JOLLY TROLLEY   ☐
Comments: **Fourth in Series**, Handcrafted, 3-3/8" tall.
Santa's in the driver's seat of an old trolley car. Caption: "1982 Jolly Trolley." **Artist**: Linda Sickman
☐ Purchased 19 __ Pd $_____ MIB   NB   DB   BNT
☐ Want   Orig. Ret. $15.00   **NB** $85   **MIB** Sec. Mkt. **$130**

QX 502-6   HOLIDAY CHIMES: ANGEL CHIMES   ☐
Comments: Chrome-Plated Brass, 4-1/2" tall.
Three angels, each holding a poinsettia, are suspended from a large snowflake. Collectors have not been aware of these being produced until recent years.
☐ Purchased 19 __ Pd $_____ MIB   NB   DB   BNT
☐ Want   Orig. Ret. $5.50   **NB** $20   **MIB** Sec. Mkt. **$25**

QX 494-3   HOLIDAY CHIMES: BELL CHIMES   ☐
Comments: Chrome-Plated Brass, 3" tall.
Three stamped bells, each with different snowflake cutouts, hang from a snowflake. **Artist**: Linda Sickman
☐ Purchased 19 __ Pd $_____ MIB   NB   DB   BNT
☐ Want   Orig. Ret. $5.50   **NB** $18   **MIB** Sec. Mkt. **$28**

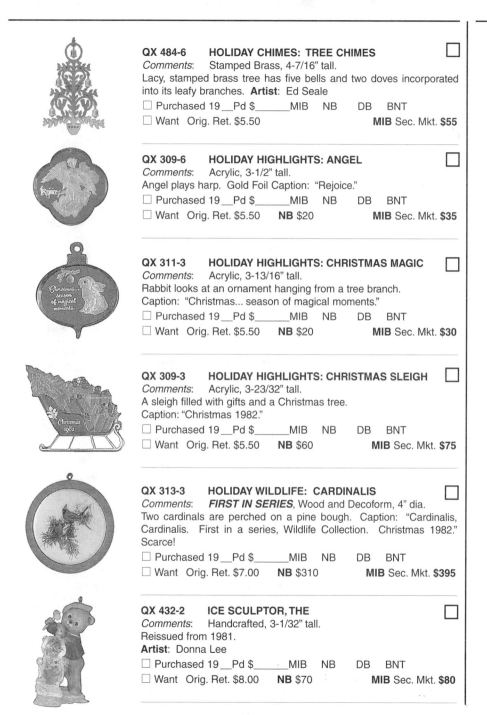

QX 484-6   HOLIDAY CHIMES: TREE CHIMES   ☐
Comments: Stamped Brass, 4-7/16" tall.
Lacy, stamped brass tree has five bells and two doves incorporated into its leafy branches. **Artist**: Ed Seale
☐ Purchased 19 __ Pd $_____ MIB   NB   DB   BNT
☐ Want   Orig. Ret. $5.50   **MIB** Sec. Mkt. **$55**

QX 309-6   HOLIDAY HIGHLIGHTS: ANGEL   ☐
Comments: Acrylic, 3-1/2" tall.
Angel plays harp. Gold Foil Caption: "Rejoice."
☐ Purchased 19 __ Pd $_____ MIB   NB   DB   BNT
☐ Want   Orig. Ret. $5.50   **NB** $20   **MIB** Sec. Mkt. **$35**

QX 311-3   HOLIDAY HIGHLIGHTS: CHRISTMAS MAGIC   ☐
Comments: Acrylic, 3-13/16" tall.
Rabbit looks at an ornament hanging from a tree branch.
Caption: "Christmas... season of magical moments."
☐ Purchased 19 __ Pd $_____ MIB   NB   DB   BNT
☐ Want   Orig. Ret. $5.50   **NB** $20   **MIB** Sec. Mkt. **$30**

QX 309-3   HOLIDAY HIGHLIGHTS: CHRISTMAS SLEIGH   ☐
Comments: Acrylic, 3-23/32" tall.
A sleigh filled with gifts and a Christmas tree.
Caption: "Christmas 1982."
☐ Purchased 19 __ Pd $_____ MIB   NB   DB   BNT
☐ Want   Orig. Ret. $5.50   **NB** $60   **MIB** Sec. Mkt. **$75**

QX 313-3   HOLIDAY WILDLIFE: CARDINALIS   ☐
Comments: **FIRST IN SERIES**, Wood and Decoform, 4" dia.
Two cardinals are perched on a pine bough. Caption: "Cardinalis, Cardinalis. First in a series, Wildlife Collection. Christmas 1982." Scarce!
☐ Purchased 19 __ Pd $_____ MIB   NB   DB   BNT
☐ Want   Orig. Ret. $7.00   **NB** $310   **MIB** Sec. Mkt. **$395**

QX 432-2   ICE SCULPTOR, THE   ☐
Comments: Handcrafted, 3-1/32" tall.
Reissued from 1981.
Artist: Donna Lee
☐ Purchased 19 __ Pd $_____ MIB   NB   DB   BNT
☐ Want   Orig. Ret. $8.00   **NB** $70   **MIB** Sec. Mkt. **$80**

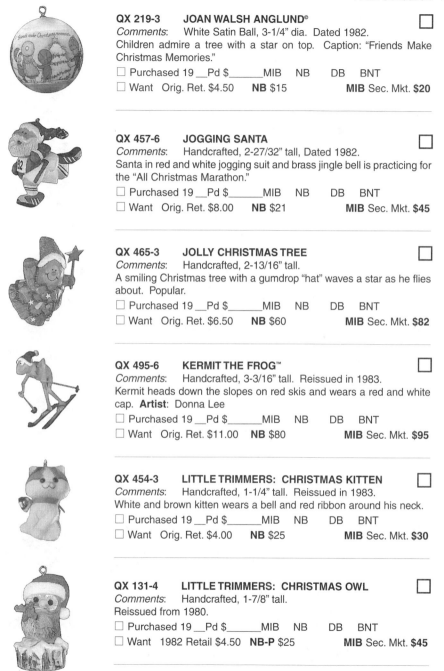

QX 219-3   JOAN WALSH ANGLUND®   ☐
Comments: White Satin Ball, 3-1/4" dia. Dated 1982.
Children admire a tree with a star on top. Caption: "Friends Make Christmas Memories."
☐ Purchased 19 __ Pd $_____ MIB   NB   DB   BNT
☐ Want   Orig. Ret. $4.50   **NB** $15   **MIB** Sec. Mkt. **$20**

QX 457-6   JOGGING SANTA   ☐
Comments: Handcrafted, 2-27/32" tall, Dated 1982.
Santa in red and white jogging suit and brass jingle bell is practicing for the "All Christmas Marathon."
☐ Purchased 19 __ Pd $_____ MIB   NB   DB   BNT
☐ Want   Orig. Ret. $8.00   **NB** $21   **MIB** Sec. Mkt. **$45**

QX 465-3   JOLLY CHRISTMAS TREE   ☐
Comments: Handcrafted, 2-13/16" tall.
A smiling Christmas tree with a gumdrop "hat" waves a star as he flies about. Popular.
☐ Purchased 19 __ Pd $_____ MIB   NB   DB   BNT
☐ Want   Orig. Ret. $6.50   **NB** $60   **MIB** Sec. Mkt. **$82**

QX 495-6   KERMIT THE FROG™   ☐
Comments: Handcrafted, 3-3/16" tall. Reissued in 1983.
Kermit heads down the slopes on red skis and wears a red and white cap. **Artist**: Donna Lee
☐ Purchased 19 __ Pd $_____ MIB   NB   DB   BNT
☐ Want   Orig. Ret. $11.00   **NB** $80   **MIB** Sec. Mkt. **$95**

QX 454-3   LITTLE TRIMMERS: CHRISTMAS KITTEN   ☐
Comments: Handcrafted, 1-1/4" tall. Reissued in 1983.
White and brown kitten wears a bell and red ribbon around his neck.
☐ Purchased 19 __ Pd $_____ MIB   NB   DB   BNT
☐ Want   Orig. Ret. $4.00   **NB** $25   **MIB** Sec. Mkt. **$30**

QX 131-4   LITTLE TRIMMERS: CHRISTMAS OWL   ☐
Comments: Handcrafted, 1-7/8" tall.
Reissued from 1980.
☐ Purchased 19 __ Pd $_____ MIB   NB   DB   BNT
☐ Want   1982 Retail $4.50   **NB-P** $25   **MIB** Sec. Mkt. **$45**

QX 454-6   LITTLE TRIMMERS: COOKIE MOUSE ☐
Comments: Handcrafted, 2-1/16" tall, Dated 1982.
A cute white mouse sits on top of a star shaped cookie, eating one of its "points." **Artist**: Linda Sickman
☐ Purchased 19 __Pd $_____MIB   NB   DB   BNT
☐ Want   Orig. Ret. $4.50   **NB** $40   **MIB** Sec. Mkt. **$58**

QX 462-3   LITTLE TRIMMERS: DOVE LOVE ☐
Comments: Acrylic, 2-1/16" tall.
A white dove swings in the center of an open red heart.
Artist: Linda Sickman
☐ Purchased 19 __Pd $_____MIB   NB   DB   BNT
☐ Want   Orig. Ret. $4.50   **NB** $42   **MIB** Sec. Mkt. **$55**

QX 477-6   LITTLE TRIMMERS: JINGLING TEDDY ☐
Comments: Flocked, Brass, 2-1/8" tall.
A brown flocked teddy bear holds a brass bell. **Artist**: Ed Seale
☐ Purchased 19 __Pd $_____MIB   NB   DB   BNT
☐ Want   Orig. Ret. $4.00   **NB** $27   **MIB** Sec. Mkt. **$40**

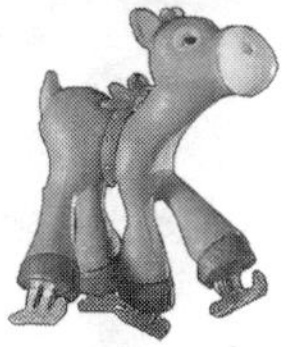

QX 415-5   LITTLE TRIMMERS: MERRY MOOSE ☐
Comments: Handcrafted, 1-3/4" tall.
Young moose on ice skates.
☐ Purchased 19 __Pd $_____MIB   NB   DB   BNT
☐ Want   Orig. Ret. $5.50   **NB** $40   **MIB** Sec. Mkt. **$50**

QX 459-6   LITTLE TRIMMERS: MUSICAL ANGEL ☐
Comments: Handcrafted, 1-15/16" tall.
A tiny angel wearing a brass halo, sits on a cloud playing his lyre.
Artist: Donna Lee
☐ Purchased 19 __Pd $_____MIB   NB   DB   BNT
☐ Want   Orig. Ret. $5.50   **NB** $80   **MIB** Sec. Mkt. **$160**

QX 409-5   LITTLE TRIMMERS: PERKY PENGUIN ☐
Comments: Handcrafted, 1-5/16" tall.
Reissued from 1981.
☐ Purchased 19 __Pd $_____MIB   NB   DB   BNT
☐ Want   1982 Retail $4.00 **NB** $35   **MIB** Sec. Mkt. **$55**

QX 209-6   LOVE ☐
Comments: Ecru Soft-Sheen Satin Ball, 3-1/4" dia., Dated 1982.
Wreaths of Christmas flowers and greenery.   Caption: "Christmas 1982" and "Christmas... Season Bright With Love."
☐ Purchased 19 __Pd $_____MIB   NB   DB   BNT
☐ Want   Orig. Ret. $4.50   **NB** $12   **MIB** Sec. Mkt. **$20**

QX 304-3   LOVE ☐
Comments: Acrylic – heart shaped, 4-1/8" tall, Dated 1982.
Caption in gold foil: "Love Is Forever Between Two Hearts That Share It. 1982"
☐ Purchased 19 __Pd $_____MIB   NB   DB   BNT
☐ Want   Orig. Ret. $5.50   **NB** $20   **MIB** Sec. Mkt. **$30**

QMB 900-9   LOVE ☐
Comments: Musical, Classic Shape, 4-1/2" tall, Dated 1982.
Plays "What The World Needs Now Is Love." Caption: "Love Puts The Warmth In Christmas."
☐ Purchased 19 __Pd $_____MIB   NB   DB   BNT
☐ Want   Orig. Ret. $16.00 **NB** $60   **MIB** Sec. Mkt. **$80**

QX 217-6   MARY HAMILTON ☐
Comments: Blue Soft-Sheen Satin Ball, 3-1/4" dia. Dated 1982.
Tiny angels ring bells and are perched on music notes as they sing.
Caption: "Joy To The World."
☐ Purchased 19 __Pd $_____MIB   NB   DB   BNT
☐ Want   Orig. Ret. $4.50   **NB** $14   **MIB** Sec. Mkt. **$24**

QX 225-6   MERRY CHRISTMAS ☐
Comments: Clear Glass Ball, 3-1/4" dia.
Red and gold fired-on decal. Captions: "Merry Christmas" and "Happy New Year."
☐ Purchased 19 __Pd $_____MIB   NB   DB   BNT
☐ Want   Orig. Ret. $4.50   **NB** $14   **MIB** Sec. Mkt. **$22**

QX 218-3   MISS PIGGY & KERMIT ™ ☐
Comments: White Satin Ball, 3-1/4" dia., Dated 1982.
Miss Piggy and Kermit in Christmas scenes. Caption: "Season's Greetings" and "Have Yourself A Lavish Little Christmas."
☐ Purchased 19 __Pd $_____MIB   NB   DB   BNT
☐ Want   Orig. Ret. $4.50   **NB** $35   **MIB** Sec. Mkt. **$45**

QX 209-3   MOMENTS OF LOVE ☐

Comments: Blue Soft-Sheen Satin Ball, 3-1/4" dia., Dated 1982.
A horse-drawn stagecoach is silhouetted in white. Caption:
"Christmas 1982" and "Each Moment Of Love Lives Forever In
Memory."

☐ Purchased 19___Pd $_____MIB   NB   DB   BNT

☐ Want   Orig. Ret. $4.50   **NB** $10   **MIB** Sec. Mkt. **$15**

QX 205-3   MOTHER ☐

Comments: White Glass Ball, 3-1/4" dia., Dated 1982.
Holly and pine garland and poinsettia bouquet. Caption: "Christmas
1982" and "The Spirit Of Christmas Lives In A Mother's Loving Heart."

☐ Purchased 19___Pd $_____MIB   NB   DB   BNT

☐ Want   Orig. Ret. $4.50   **NB** $8   **MIB** Sec. Mkt. **$18**

QX 222-3   MOTHER AND DAD ☐

Comments: White Porcelain Glass Ball, 3-1/4" dia., Dated 1982.
Holly leaves, berries and evergreens. Caption: "Christmas 1982" and
"A Mother And Dad Know So Many Ways To Warm A Heart With
Love."

☐ Purchased 19___Pd $_____MIB   NB   DB   BNT

☐ Want   Orig. Ret. $4.50   **NB** $8   **MIB** Sec. Mkt. **$18**

QX 218-6   MUPPETS™ PARTY ☐

Comments: White Satin Ball, 3-1/4" dia., Dated 1982.
The whole Muppets gang is gathered for a party. Caption: "Merry
Christmas 1982."

☐ Purchased 19___Pd $_____MIB   NB   DB   BNT

☐ Want   Orig. Ret. $4.50   **NB** $30   **MIB** Sec. Mkt. **$40**

QX 212-6   NEW HOME ☐

Comments: Dk. Blue Satin Ball, 3-1/4" dia., Dated 1982.
Snow covered village homes. Caption: "Christmas Time Fills Hearts
With Love And Homes With Warmth And Joy."

☐ Purchased 19___Pd $_____MIB   NB   DB   BNT

☐ Want   Orig. Ret. $4.50   **NB** $12   **MIB** Sec. Mkt. **$20**

**If you could turn back the clock,
where would you stop??**

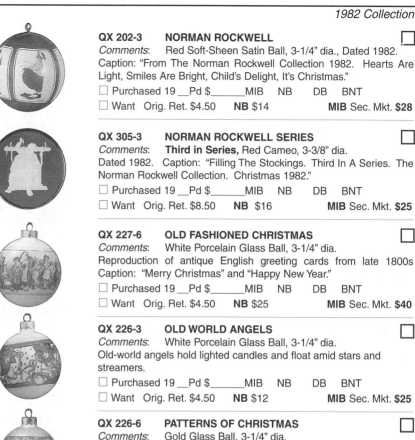

QX 202-3   NORMAN ROCKWELL ☐

Comments: Red Soft-Sheen Satin Ball, 3-1/4" dia., Dated 1982.
Caption: "From The Norman Rockwell Collection 1982. Hearts Are
Light, Smiles Are Bright, Child's Delight, It's Christmas."

☐ Purchased 19___Pd $_____MIB   NB   DB   BNT

☐ Want   Orig. Ret. $4.50   **NB** $14   **MIB** Sec. Mkt. **$28**

QX 305-3   NORMAN ROCKWELL SERIES ☐

Comments: **Third in Series,** Red Cameo, 3-3/8" dia.
Dated 1982. Caption: "Filling The Stockings. Third In A Series. The
Norman Rockwell Collection. Christmas 1982."

☐ Purchased 19___Pd $_____MIB   NB   DB   BNT

☐ Want   Orig. Ret. $8.50   **NB** $16   **MIB** Sec. Mkt. **$25**

QX 227-6   OLD FASHIONED CHRISTMAS ☐

Comments: White Porcelain Glass Ball, 3-1/4" dia.
Reproduction of antique English greeting cards from late 1800s
Caption: "Merry Christmas" and "Happy New Year."

☐ Purchased 19___Pd $_____MIB   NB   DB   BNT

☐ Want   Orig. Ret. $4.50   **NB** $25   **MIB** Sec. Mkt. **$40**

QX 226-3   OLD WORLD ANGELS ☐

Comments: White Porcelain Glass Ball, 3-1/4" dia.
Old-world angels hold lighted candles and float amid stars and
streamers.

☐ Purchased 19___Pd $_____MIB   NB   DB   BNT

☐ Want   Orig. Ret. $4.50   **NB** $12   **MIB** Sec. Mkt. **$25**

QX 226-6   PATTERNS OF CHRISTMAS ☐

Comments: Gold Glass Ball, 3-1/4" dia.
Oriental designs of poinsettias and holly are highlighted in gold.

☐ Purchased 19___Pd $_____MIB   NB   DB   BNT

☐ Want   Orig. Ret. $4.50   **NB** $14   **MIB** Sec. Mkt. **$22**

QX 200-6   PEANUTS® ☐

Comments: Light Blue Satin Ball, 3-1/4" dia., Dated 1982.
Snoopy, Woodstock and friends ride a tandem bike.
Caption: "Christmas 1982."

☐ Purchased 19___Pd $_____MIB   NB   DB   BNT

☐ Want   Orig. Ret. $4.50   **NB** $25   **MIB** Sec. Mkt. **$37.50**

QX 419-5   PEEKING ELF ☐

Comments: Handcrafted, 3-3/32" tall.
An elf peeks over the top of a silver ball ornament tied with a red
ribbon.

☐ Purchased 19___Pd $_____MIB   NB   DB   BNT

☐ Want   Orig. Ret. $6.50   **NB** $24   **MIB** Sec. Mkt. **$25**

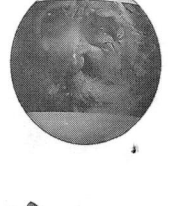

QX 461-3   PINECONE HOME
Comments: Handcrafted, 2-23/32" tall.
A small mouse in red pajamas looks out the shuttered window of his pinecone house. **Artist**: Donna Lee
☐ Purchased 19__ Pd $_____ MIB   NB   DB   BNT
☐ Want   Orig. Ret. $8.00   **NB** $100   **MIB** Sec. Mkt. **$165**

QX 479-3   RACCOON SURPRISES
Comments: Handcrafted, 3" tall.
A raccoon stands on a tree branch and raids a colorful Christmas stocking. **Artist**: Donna Lee
☐ Purchased 19__ Pd $_____ MIB   NB   DB   BNT
☐ Want   Orig. Ret. $9.00   **NB** $110   **MIB** Sec. Mkt. **$150**

QX 502-3   ROCKING HORSE
Comments: **Second in Series,** Handcrafted, 2" tall, Dated 1982.
Black stallion with maroon saddle and rockers. Harder to find in box than no box. Price down from '96. **Artist**: Linda Sickman
☐ Purchased 19__ Pd $_____ MIB   NB   DB   BNT
☐ Want   Orig. Ret. $10.00   **NB** $300   **MIB** Sec. Mkt. **$325**

QX 221-6   SANTA
Comments: White Porcelain Glass Ball, 3-1/4" dia., Dated 1982.
A close-up of Santa and Santa smoking his pipe. Caption: "Christmas 1982" and "His Eyes, How They Twinkled, His Dimples, How Merry."
Artist: Thomas Blackshear
☐ Purchased 19__ Pd $_____ MIB   NB   DB   BNT
☐ Want   Orig. Ret. $4.50   **NB** $10   **MIB** Sec. Mkt. **$15**

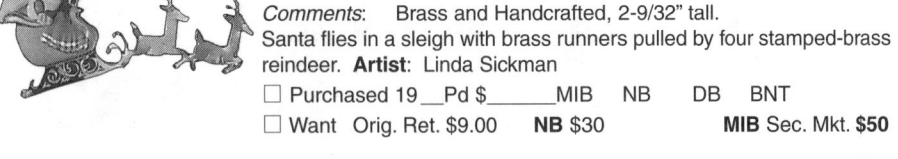

QX 467-6   SANTA AND REINDEER
Comments: Brass and Handcrafted, 2-9/32" tall.
Santa flies in a sleigh with brass runners pulled by four stamped-brass reindeer. **Artist**: Linda Sickman
☐ Purchased 19__ Pd $_____ MIB   NB   DB   BNT
☐ Want   Orig. Ret. $9.00   **NB** $30   **MIB** Sec. Mkt. **$50**

QX 148-7   SANTA BELL
Comments: Hand-decorated Porcelain, 3-11/16" tall.
Santa's black boots ring the bell.
☐ Purchased 19__ Pd $_____ MIB   NB   DB   BNT
☐ Want   Orig. Ret. $15.00   **NB** $45   **MIB** Sec. Mkt. **$55**

QX 478-6   SANTA'S SLEIGH
Comments: Polished Brass, 2-5/8" tall.
Stamped design of Santa in a sleigh full of toys. **Artist**: Ed Seale
☐ Purchased 19__ Pd $_____ MIB   NB   DB   BNT
☐ Want   Orig. Ret. $9.00   **NB** $12   **MIB** Sec. Mkt. **$30**

QX 450-3   SANTA'S WORKSHOP
Comments: Handcrafted, 3" tall. Reissued in 1983.
Santa paints a dollhouse in his snow-covered cottage. The inside of the cottage can be seen from three sides. **Artist**: Donna Lee
☐ Purchased 19__ Pd $_____ MIB   NB   DB   BNT
☐ Want   Orig. Ret. $10.00   **NB** $50   **MIB** Sec. Mkt. **$70**

QX 221-3   SEASON FOR CARING
Comments: Light Blue Soft-Sheen Satin Ball, 3-1/4" dia.
Dated 1982. Night scene: Bethlehem and the Star. Caption: "Christmas… Season For Caring."
☐ Purchased 19__ Pd $_____ MIB   NB   DB   BNT
☐ Want   Orig. Ret. $4.50   **NB** $12   **MIB** Sec. Mkt. **$22**

QX 208-3   SISTER
Comments: White Glass Ball, 3-1/4" dia., Dated 1982.
A small girl ice skates on a pond and pets a white bunny. Caption: "A Sister Brings The Beauty Of Memories And The Warmth Of Love To Christmas."
☐ Purchased 19__ Pd $_____ MIB   NB   DB   BNT
☐ Want   Orig. Ret. $4.50   **NB** $15   **MIB** Sec. Mkt. **$25**

QX 480-3   SNOOPY AND FRIENDS
Comments: **Fourth in Series**, Dated 1982.
Handcrafted Panorama Ball, 3-1/4" dia. Snoopy is flying in a sleigh drawn by Woodstock and his friends. **Artist**: Ed Seale
☐ Purchased 19__ Pd $_____ MIB   NB   DB   BNT
☐ Want   Orig. Ret. $13.00   **NB** $85   **MIB** Sec. Mkt. **$120**

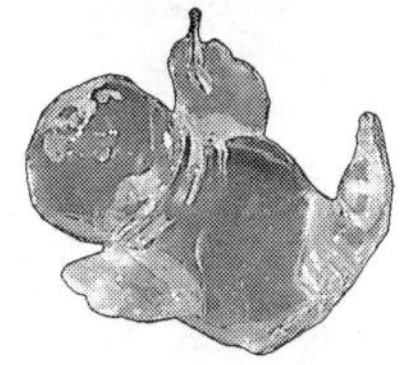

QX 300-6   SNOWY SEAL
Comments: Clear Acrylic, 1-19/32" tall.
Designed to resemble an ice sculpture.
☐ Purchased 19__ Pd $_____ MIB   NB   DB   BNT
☐ Want   Orig. Ret. $4.00   **NB** $14   **MIB** Sec. Mkt. **$20**

QX 204-3   SON
Comments: Caramel Soft-Sheen Satin Ball, 3-1/4" dia.
Marching band leads the way to Christmas. Caption: "Christmas 1982" and "A Son Is The Pride Of Your Heart, The Joy Of Your Life."
☐ Purchased 19 __Pd $_____MIB   NB   DB   BNT
☐ Want   Orig. Ret. $4.50   **NB** $12   **MIB** Sec. Mkt. **$20**

QX 452-6   SPIRIT OF CHRISTMAS, THE
Comments: Handcrafted, 1-29/32" tall, Dated 1982.
Santa flies in a silver and red biplane. Caption: "The Spirit Of Christmas." **Artist**: Linda Sickman
☐ Purchased 19 __Pd $_____MIB   NB   DB   BNT
☐ Want   Orig. Ret. $10.00   **NB** $55   **MIB** Sec. Mkt. **$130**

QX 228-3   STAINED GLASS
Comments: White Glass Ball, 3-1/4" dia.
Red poinsettia and green holly make a lovely contrast with lavender, blue and green panels.
☐ Purchased 19 __Pd $_____MIB   NB   DB   BNT
☐ Want   Orig. Ret. $4.50   **NB** $12   **MIB** Sec. Mkt. **$22**

QX 214-3   TEACHER
Comments: White Glass Ball, 3-1/4" dia., Dated 1982.
Elves cast shadows to spell "Christmas 1982." Caption: "To A Special Teacher."
☐ Purchased 19 __Pd $_____MIB   NB   DB   BNT
☐ Want   Orig. Ret. $4.50   **NB** $5   **MIB** Sec. Mkt. **$15**

QX 301-6   TEACHER
Comments: Acrylic Apple, 3-1/2" tall, Dated 1982.
Clear with green leaves and red print: "To A Special Teacher 1982." **Artist**: Ed Seale
☐ Purchased 19 __Pd $_____MIB   NB   DB   BNT
☐ Want   Orig. Ret. $5.50   **NB** $5   **MIB** Sec. Mkt. **$14**

QX 312-3   TEACHER
Comments: Acrylic, 3-15/16" tall, Dated 1982.
Snow covered red schoolhouse has a cutout for child's photo. Caption: "Merry Christmas To My Teacher." **Artist**: Linda Sickman
☐ Purchased 19 __Pd $_____MIB   NB   DB   BNT
☐ Want   Orig. Ret. $6.50   **NB** $8   **MIB** Sec. Mkt. **$15**

QX 451-3   THIMBLE – MOUSE
Comments: **Fifth in Series**, Handcrafted, 2-11/32" tall.
Little mouse "soldier" with big ears and silver needle "baton" wears a thimble as a hat.
☐ Purchased 19 __Pd $_____MIB   NB   DB   BNT
☐ Want   Orig. Ret. $5.00   **NB-P** $40   **MIB** Sec. Mkt. **$60**

QX 307-3   THREE KINGS
Comments: Blue Cameo, 3-3/8" dia., Dated 1982.
Caption: "By A Star Shining Brightly, Three Kings Set Their Course And Followed The Heavenly Light To Its Source." **Artist**: Thomas Blackshear
☐ Purchased 19 __Pd $_____MIB   NB   DB   BNT
☐ Want   Orig. Ret. $8.50   **NB** $12   **MIB** Sec. Mkt. **$25**

QX 460-3   TIN LOCOMOTIVE
Comments: **FIRST IN SERIES**, Pressed Tin, 3-5/8" tall.
Dated 1982. Decorated in red, blue and silver, with a brass bell that hangs in front of the cab. Price down from '96. **Artist**: Linda Sickman
☐ Purchased 19 __Pd $_____MIB   NB   DB   BNT
☐ Want   Orig. Ret. $13.00   **NB** $435   **MIB** Sec. Mkt. **$500**

QX 483-6   TIN SOLDIER
Comments: Pressed Tin, 4-7/8" tall.
A British soldier stands at stiff attention.
☐ Purchased 19 __Pd $_____MIB   NB   DB   BNT
☐ Want   Orig. Ret. $6.50   **NB** $40   **MIB** Sec. Mkt. **$45**

QX 203-6   TWELVE DAYS OF CHRISTMAS
Comments: White Pebbled Glass Ball, 3-1/4" dia., Dated 1982.
Illustration of the verses of the Christmas carol. Caption: "The Twelve Days Of Christmas 1982."
☐ Purchased 19 __Pd $_____MIB   NB   DB   BNT
☐ Want   Orig. Ret. $4.50   **NB** $15   **MIB** Sec. Mkt. **$25**

QX 211-6   TWENTY-FIFTH CHRISTMAS TOGETHER
Comments: White Porcelain Glass Ball, 3-1/4" dia., Dated 1982.
Caption: "Twenty-Fifth Christmas Together 1982" and "Christmas... As Timeless As Snow-Fall, As Forever As Candleglow, As Always As Love."
☐ Purchased 19 __Pd $_____MIB   NB   DB   BNT
☐ Want   Orig. Ret. $4.50   **NB** $10   **MIB** Sec. Mkt. **$15**

1983 Collection

When purchasing ball ornaments, watch for "spots." Deduct from price.

QX 220-9   1983
Comments: Raspberry Glass Ball, 3-1/4" dia.
Date is printed in gold on a narrow band. Trimmed in platinum colored stripes.
☐ Purchased 19 __ Pd $_____ MIB   NB   DB   BNT
☐ Want Orig. Ret. $4.50   **NB** $14   **MIB** Sec. Mkt. **$25**

QX 217-9   AN OLD FASHIONED CHRISTMAS
Comments: Green Porcelain Glass Ball, 3-1/4" dia.
Christmas scenes reminiscent of old greeting cards.
☐ Purchased 19 __ Pd $_____ MIB   NB   DB   BNT
☐ Want Orig. Ret. $4.50   **NB** $15   **MIB** Sec. Mkt. **$25**

QX 408-7   ANGEL MESSENGER
Comments: Brass, Handcrafted, 2" tall, Dated 1983.
The brass year date is carried by an angel dressed in a blue robe.
Artist: Ed Seale
☐ Purchased 19 __ Pd $_____ MIB   NB   DB   BNT
☐ Want Orig. Ret. $6.50   **NB** $80   **MIB** Sec. Mkt. **$95**

QX 219-7   ANGELS
Comments: Clear Glass Ball, 3-1/4" dia.
The inside of the ball has a gold tinsel starburst. Design is of old world angels in soft pastels.
☐ Purchased 19 __ Pd $_____ MIB   NB   DB   BNT
☐ Want Orig. Ret. $5.00   **NB** $12   **MIB** Sec. Mkt. **$25**

QX 216-7   ANNUNCIATION, THE
Comments: White Porcelain Glass Ball, 3-1/4" dia.
Reproduction of Fra Filippo Filippi of "The Annunciation."
Caption from Luke 1:35 (RSVB).
☐ Purchased 19 __ Pd $_____ MIB   NB   DB   BNT
☐ Want Orig. Ret. $4.50   **NB** $14   **MIB** Sec. Mkt. **$27.50**

QX 301-9   BABY'S FIRST CHRISTMAS
Comments: Red Cameo, 3-3/4" wide, Dated 1983.
Old fashioned rocking horse. Caption: "Baby's First Christmas 1983" and "A Baby Fills Each Day With Joy By Filling Hearts With Love."
Artist: Linda Sickman
☐ Purchased 19 __ Pd $_____ MIB   NB   DB   BNT
☐ Want Orig. Ret. $7.50   **NB** $8   **MIB** Sec. Mkt. **$12**

QX 402-7   BABY'S FIRST CHRISTMAS
Comments: Handcrafted, 3-5/32" tall, Dated 1983.
Cradle painted in folk art motif. Caption: "Baby's First Christmas."
Artist: Donna Lee
☐ Purchased 19 __ Pd $_____ MIB   NB   DB   BNT
☐ Want Orig. Ret. $14.00   **NB** $28   **MIB** Sec. Mkt. **$37.50**

QMB 903-9   BABY'S FIRST CHRISTMAS
Comments: Musical, Classic Shape, 4-1/2" tall, Dated 1983.
Babies crawl up and down the candy cane letters that form the caption: "Baby's First Christmas." Plays "Schubert's Lullaby."
☐ Purchased 19 __ Pd $_____ MIB   NB   DB   BNT
☐ Want Orig. Ret. $16.00   **NB** $50   **MIB** Sec. Mkt. **$90**

QX 200-9   BABY'S FIRST CHRISTMAS – BOY
Comments: Light Blue Soft-Sheen Satin Ball, 3-1/4" dia.
Dated 1983. Six teddies tumble around the ornament. Caption: "Baby's First Christmas 1983" and "A Baby Boy Is Love And Joy... And Pride That Lasts A Lifetime."
☐ Purchased 19 __ Pd $_____ MIB   NB   DB   BNT
☐ Want Orig. Ret. $4.50   **NB** $10   **MIB** Sec. Mkt. **$20**

QX 200-7   BABY'S FIRST CHRISTMAS – GIRL
Comments: White Soft-Sheen Satin Ball, 3-1/4" dia., Dated 1983.
Baby's red dress with white polka dots and pinafore. Caption: "Baby's First Christmas 1983" and "A Baby Girl Is A Special Gift Of Love."
☐ Purchased 19 __ Pd $_____ MIB   NB   DB   BNT
☐ Want Orig. Ret. $4.50   **NB** $14   **MIB** Sec. Mkt. **$18**

QX 302-9   BABY'S FIRST CHRISTMAS – PHOTOHOLDER
Comments: Acrylic, 3-7/8" tall, Dated 1983.
An open baby book holds baby's photo. Caption: "Baby's First Christmas 1983." and "A Baby Is A Dream Fulfilled, A Treasure To Hold Dear — A Baby Is A Love That Grows More Precious Every Year."
☐ Purchased 19 __ Pd $_____ MIB   NB   DB   BNT
☐ Want Orig. Ret. $7.00   **NB** $12   **MIB** Sec. Mkt. **$24**

QX 226-7   BABY'S SECOND CHRISTMAS
Comments: White Soft-Sheen Satin Ball, 3-1/4" dia.
Dated 1983. Caption: "Baby's Second Christmas 1983" and "A child knows such special ways to jolly up the holidays!"
☐ Purchased 19 __ Pd $_____ MIB   NB   DB   BNT
☐ Want Orig. Ret. $4.50   **NB** $16   **MIB** Sec. Mkt. **$35**

QX 422-9   BAROQUE ANGELS
Comments: Handcrafted, 2-1/2" tall.
Two angels with white wings and rose banners.
Artist: Donna Lee
☐ Purchased 19 __ Pd $_____ MIB   NB   DB   BNT
☐ Want   Orig. Ret. $13.00   **NB** $85   **MIB** Sec. Mkt. **$125**

QX 420-9   BELL WREATH
Comments: Brass, 3-13/16" tall.
Seven small bells jingle inside a holly wreath of solid brass.
Artist: Linda Sickman
☐ Purchased 19 __ Pd $_____ MIB   NB   DB   BNT
☐ Want   Orig. Ret. $6.50   **NB** $18   **MIB** Sec. Mkt. **$27.50**

QX 403-9   BELLRINGER, THE
Comments: **Fifth in Series,** Porcelain and Handcrafted.
2-27/32" tall, Dated 1983. Cute brown teddy bear holding a gold star
rings a porcelain bell decorated with holly and fir.
☐ Purchased 19 __ Pd $_____ MIB   NB   DB   BNT
☐ Want   Orig. Ret. $15.00   **NB** $100   **MIB** Sec. Mkt. **$130**

QX 440-1   BETSEY CLARK
Comments: Porcelain, 3-1/2" tall.
Betsey Clark angel on cloud has hooked a star with her pole.
☐ Purchased 19 __ Pd $_____ MIB   NB   DB   BNT
☐ Want   Orig. Ret. $9.00   **NB** $18   **MIB** Sec. Mkt. **$34**

QX 404-7   BETSEY CLARK
Comments: Handcrafted, 3" tall.
A child in blue sleeper is napping on a yellow flocked moon.
Artist: Ed Seale
☐ Purchased 19 __ Pd $_____ MIB   NB   DB   BNT
☐ Want   Orig. Ret. $6.50   **NB** $14   **MIB** Sec. Mkt. **$22**

QX 211-9   BETSEY CLARK SERIES
Comments: **Eleventh in Series,** White Glass Ball, 3-1/4" dia.
Dated 1983. Boys and girls ride a carousel. Caption: "Christmas
Happiness Is Found... Wherever Good Friends Gather Round."
☐ Purchased 19 __ Pd $_____ MIB   NB   DB   BNT
☐ Want   Orig. Ret. $4.50   **NB** $18   **MIB** Sec. Mkt. **$30**

QX 423-9   BRASS SANTA
Comments: Brass, 4" tall.
Front and back views of Santa's head have been created in polished
stamped brass and protectively coated.
Artist: Ed Seale
☐ Purchased 19 __ Pd $_____ MIB   NB   DB   BNT
☐ Want   Orig. Ret. $9.00   **NB** $12   **MIB** Sec. Mkt. **$20**

QX 411-7   CAROLING OWL
Comments: Handcrafted, 2-9/32" tall.
Small white owl holding a book of carols is perched on a brass ring.
Artist: Ed Seale
☐ Purchased 19 __ Pd $_____ MIB   NB   DB   BNT
☐ Want   Orig. Ret. $4.50   **NB** $25   **MIB** Sec. Mkt. **$38**

QX 401-9   CARROUSEL: SANTA & FRIENDS
Comments: **Sixth in Series,** Handcrafted, 3-3/32" tall.
Santa leads a marching band of children with their trumpets. Caption:
"Christmas 1983." **Artist:** Linda Sickman
☐ Purchased 19 __ Pd $_____ MIB   NB   DB   BNT
☐ Want   Orig. Ret. $11.00   **NB** $38   **MIB** Sec. Mkt. **$50**

QX 226-9   CHILD'S THIRD CHRISTMAS
Comments: White Satin Piqué Ball, 3-1/4" dia., Dated 1983.
Caption: "To Celebrate A Child's Third Christmas. How Merry
The Season, How Happy The Day When Santa Brings Christmas
Surprises Your Way."
☐ Purchased 19 __ Pd $_____ MIB   NB   DB   BNT
☐ Want   Orig. Ret. $4.50   **NB** $12   **MIB** Sec. Mkt. **$24**

QX 216-9   CHRISTMAS JOY
Comments: Ecru Soft-Sheen Satin Ball, 3-1/4" dia., Dated 1983.
Caption: "May All The Joy You Give Away... Return To You
On Christmas Day."
☐ Purchased 19 __ Pd $_____ MIB   NB   DB   BNT
☐ Want   Orig. Ret. $4.50   **NB** $16   **MIB** Sec. Mkt. **$28**

QX 454-3   CHRISTMAS KITTEN
Comments: Handcrafted, 1-1/4" tall.
Reissued from 1982 – Little Trimmers: Christmas Kitten
☐ Purchased 19 __ Pd $_____ MIB   NB   DB   BNT
☐ Want   Orig. Ret. $4.00   **NB** $25   **MIB** Sec. Mkt. **$30**

QX 419-9   CHRISTMAS KOALA   ☐
Comments: Handcrafted, 2-3/16" tall.
A flocked koala bear holds a sprig of evergreen. **Artist:** Ed Seale
☐ Purchased 19__Pd $_____MIB   NB   DB   BNT
☐ Want Orig. Ret. $4.00   **NB** $20   **MIB** Sec. Mkt. **$30**

QX 221-9   CHRISTMAS WONDERLAND   ☐
Comments: Clear Glass Ball, 3-1/4" dia., Rare!
The animals celebrate Christmas in the forest. Another scene
inside the ball may be seen through a "peek through" area of the
design.
☐ Purchased 19__Pd $_____MIB   NB   DB   BNT
☐ Want Orig. Ret. $4.50   **NB** $85   **MIB** Sec. Mkt. **$100**

QX 402-9   CLOTHESPIN SOLDIER: EARLY AMERICAN   ☐
Comments: **Second in Series,** Handcrafted, 2-7/16" tall.
American Revolutionary soldier beats his bass drum with arms that
move. **Artist:** Linda Sickman
☐ Purchased 19__Pd $_____MIB   NB   DB   BNT
☐ Want Orig. Ret. $5.00   **NB** $28   **MIB** Sec. Mkt. **$50**

QX 311-9   CROWN CLASSICS: ☐
ENAMELED CHRISTMAS WREATH
Comments: Enameled, 2-3/4" tall, Dated 1983.
Enameled patchwork wreath with a bezel of solid brass.
Caption: "Each Moment Of The Season Has Beauty All Its Own.
Christmas 1983."
☐ Purchased 19__Pd $_____MIB   NB   DB   BNT
☐ Want Orig. Ret. $9.00   **NB** $5   **MIB** Sec. Mkt. **$15**

QX 303-7   CROWN CLASSICS: ☐
MEMORIES TO TREASURE
Comments: Acrylic, 4-1/4" tall, Dated 1983.
Santa's beard holds your favorite photograph.
Caption: "Holiday Fun Times Make Memories To Treasure."
☐ Purchased 19__Pd $_____MIB   NB   DB   BNT
☐ Want Orig. Ret. $7.00   **NB** $20   **MIB** Sec. Mkt. **$24**

QX 302-7   CROWN CLASSICS: MOTHER & CHILD   ☐
Comments: Blue Oval Cameo, 3-3/4" tall.
Madonna and Child design with a translucent appearance. Caption:
"Come Let Us Celebrate His Love For This Is The Season Of
Rejoicing."
☐ Purchased 19__Pd $_____MIB   NB   DB   BNT
☐ Want Orig. Ret. $7.50   **NB** $21   **MIB** Sec. Mkt. **$40**

QX 215-9   CURRIER & IVES   ☐
Comments: White Porcelain Glass Ball, 3-1/4" dia., Dated 1983.
Caption: "Christmas 1983, Central Park Winter, The Skating Pond,
Currier and Ives."
☐ Purchased 19__Pd $_____MIB   NB   DB   BNT
☐ Want Orig. Ret. $4.50   **NB** $12   **MIB** Sec. Mkt. **$16**

QX 435-5   CYCLING SANTA   ☐
Comments: Handcrafted, 4-3/8" tall.
Reissued from 1982.
☐ Purchased 19__Pd $_____MIB   NB   DB   BNT
☐ Want Orig. Ret. $20.00   **NB** $90   **MIB** Sec. Mkt. **$125**

QX 203-7   DAUGHTER   ☐
Comments: Pink Glass Ball, 3-1/4" dia., Dated 1983.
Ribbons and pearls on lace and velvet form a lovely background for the
caption: "A Daughter's Love Makes Christmas Beautiful. 1983"
☐ Purchased 19__Pd $_____MIB   NB   DB   BNT
☐ Want Orig. Ret. $4.50   **NB** $20   **MIB** Sec. Mkt. **$40**

QX 423-7   DIANA DOLL   ☐
Comments: Porcelain Doll, 4-1/4" tall.
In the style of an antique doll, Diana's face is handpainted porcelain.
Artist: Donna Lee
☐ Purchased 19__Pd $_____MIB   NB   DB   BNT
☐ Want Orig. Ret. $9.00   **NB** $10   **MIB** Sec. Mkt. **$22**

QX 212-9   DISNEY   ☐
Comments: Chrome Glass Ball, 3-1/4" dia., Dated 1983.
Mickey's face is framed by a green wreath.
☐ Purchased 19__Pd $_____MIB   NB   DB   BNT
☐ Want Orig. Ret. $4.50   **NB** $35   **MIB** Sec. Mkt. **$40**

QX 421-7   EMBROIDERED HEART   ☐
Comments: Fabric, 4-13/16" tall, Reissued in 1984.
Trimmed with a green cord, this red heart has poinsettia and holly
embroidery.
☐ Purchased 19__Pd $_____MIB   NB   DB   BNT
☐ Want Orig. Ret. $6.50   **NB** $18   **MIB** Sec. Mkt. **$25**

Doctor: "Why do you have D 23650 tattooed on your back?"
Patient: "It's not a tattoo. That's where my wife ran into
me while I was trying to open the garage door."

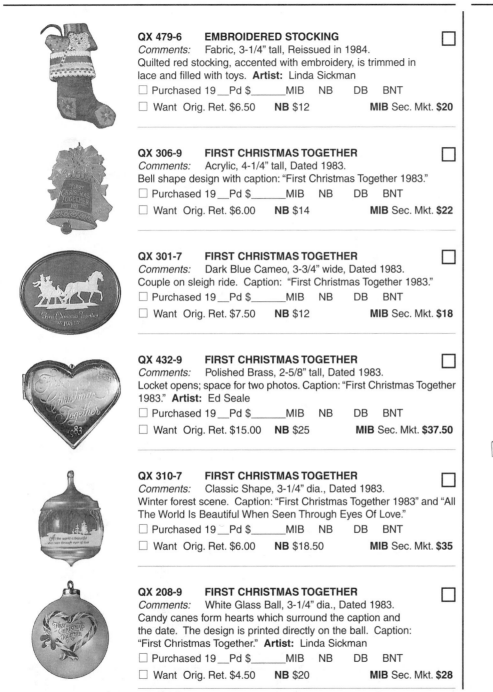

QX 479-6   EMBROIDERED STOCKING ☐
Comments: Fabric, 3-1/4" tall, Reissued in 1984.
Quilted red stocking, accented with embroidery, is trimmed in
lace and filled with toys. **Artist:** Linda Sickman
☐ Purchased 19 __ Pd $_____ MIB   NB   DB   BNT
☐ Want Orig. Ret. $6.50   **NB** $12   **MIB** Sec. Mkt. **$20**

QX 306-9   FIRST CHRISTMAS TOGETHER ☐
Comments: Acrylic, 4-1/4" tall, Dated 1983.
Bell shape design with caption: "First Christmas Together 1983."
☐ Purchased 19 __ Pd $_____ MIB   NB   DB   BNT
☐ Want Orig. Ret. $6.00   **NB** $14   **MIB** Sec. Mkt. **$22**

QX 301-7   FIRST CHRISTMAS TOGETHER ☐
Comments: Dark Blue Cameo, 3-3/4" wide, Dated 1983.
Couple on sleigh ride. Caption: "First Christmas Together 1983."
☐ Purchased 19 __ Pd $_____ MIB   NB   DB   BNT
☐ Want Orig. Ret. $7.50   **NB** $12   **MIB** Sec. Mkt. **$18**

QX 432-9   FIRST CHRISTMAS TOGETHER ☐
Comments: Polished Brass, 2-5/8" tall, Dated 1983.
Locket opens; space for two photos. Caption: "First Christmas Together
1983." **Artist:** Ed Seale
☐ Purchased 19 __ Pd $_____ MIB   NB   DB   BNT
☐ Want Orig. Ret. $15.00   **NB** $25   **MIB** Sec. Mkt. **$37.50**

QX 310-7   FIRST CHRISTMAS TOGETHER ☐
Comments: Classic Shape, 3-1/4" dia., Dated 1983.
Winter forest scene. Caption: "First Christmas Together 1983" and "All
The World Is Beautiful When Seen Through Eyes Of Love."
☐ Purchased 19 __ Pd $_____ MIB   NB   DB   BNT
☐ Want Orig. Ret. $6.00   **NB** $18.50   **MIB** Sec. Mkt. **$35**

QX 208-9   FIRST CHRISTMAS TOGETHER ☐
Comments: White Glass Ball, 3-1/4" dia., Dated 1983.
Candy canes form hearts which surround the caption and
the date. The design is printed directly on the ball. Caption:
"First Christmas Together." **Artist:** Linda Sickman
☐ Purchased 19 __ Pd $_____ MIB   NB   DB   BNT
☐ Want Orig. Ret. $4.50   **NB** $20   **MIB** Sec. Mkt. **$28**

QX 207-7   FRIENDSHIP ☐
Comments: White Classic Glass, 3-1/4" dia., Dated 1983.
Eskimo in Christmas scenes. Caption: "Christmas 1983" and
"Friendship Is A Special Gift That Gives Your Heart A Happy Lift."
☐ Purchased 19 __ Pd $_____ MIB   NB   DB   BNT
☐ Want Orig. Ret. $4.50   **NB** $12   **MIB** Sec. Mkt. **$20**

QX 305-9   FRIENDSHIP ☐
Comments: Acrylic, Classic shape, 5" tall, Dated 1983.
Caption: "Christmas 1983" and "Friendship Grows More
Beautiful With Each Passing Season."
☐ Purchased 19 __ Pd $_____ MIB   NB   DB   BNT
☐ Want Orig. Ret. $6.00   **NB** $10   **MIB** Sec. Mkt. **$20**

QMB 904-7   FRIENDSHIP ☐
Comments: Musical, Classic Shape, 4-1/2" tall.
Muffin celebrates Christmas. Caption: "It's Song-in-the-Air Time,
Lights-Everywhere Time, Good Fun-to-Share Time, It's Christmas."
Plays "We Wish You A Merry Christmas."
☐ Purchased 19 __ Pd $_____ MIB   NB   DB   BNT
☐ Want Orig. Ret. $16.00   **NB** $80   **MIB** Sec. Mkt. **$125**

QX 400-7   FROSTY FRIENDS ☐
Comments: **Fourth in Series,** Handcrafted, 1-59/64" tall.
Dated 1983. Frosty and his baby seal rub noses as they float on an
iceberg. Caption: "Merry Christmas 1983." Price down from '96.
Artist: Ed Seale
☐ Purchased 19 __ Pd $_____ MIB   NB   DB   BNT
☐ Want Orig. Ret. $8.00   **NB** $200   **MIB** Sec. Mkt. **$280**

QX 201-7   GODCHILD ☐
Comments: White Classical Glass, 3-1/4" dia., Dated 1983.
Angel and red bird sing a duet. Caption: "To Wish A Special Godchild
A Very Merry Christmas."
☐ Purchased 19 __ Pd $_____ MIB   NB   DB   BNT
☐ Want Orig. Ret. $4.50   **NB** $8   **MIB** Sec. Mkt. **$18**

QX 430-9   GRANDCHILD'S FIRST CHRISTMAS ☐
Comments: Handcrafted, 3-3/4" long, Dated 1983.
Baby rides in a white, wicker-look buggy. Caption: "Grandchild's First
Christmas 1983."
☐ Purchased 19 __ Pd $_____ MIB   NB   DB   BNT
☐ Want Orig. Ret. $14.00   **NB** $20   **MIB** Sec. Mkt. **$38**

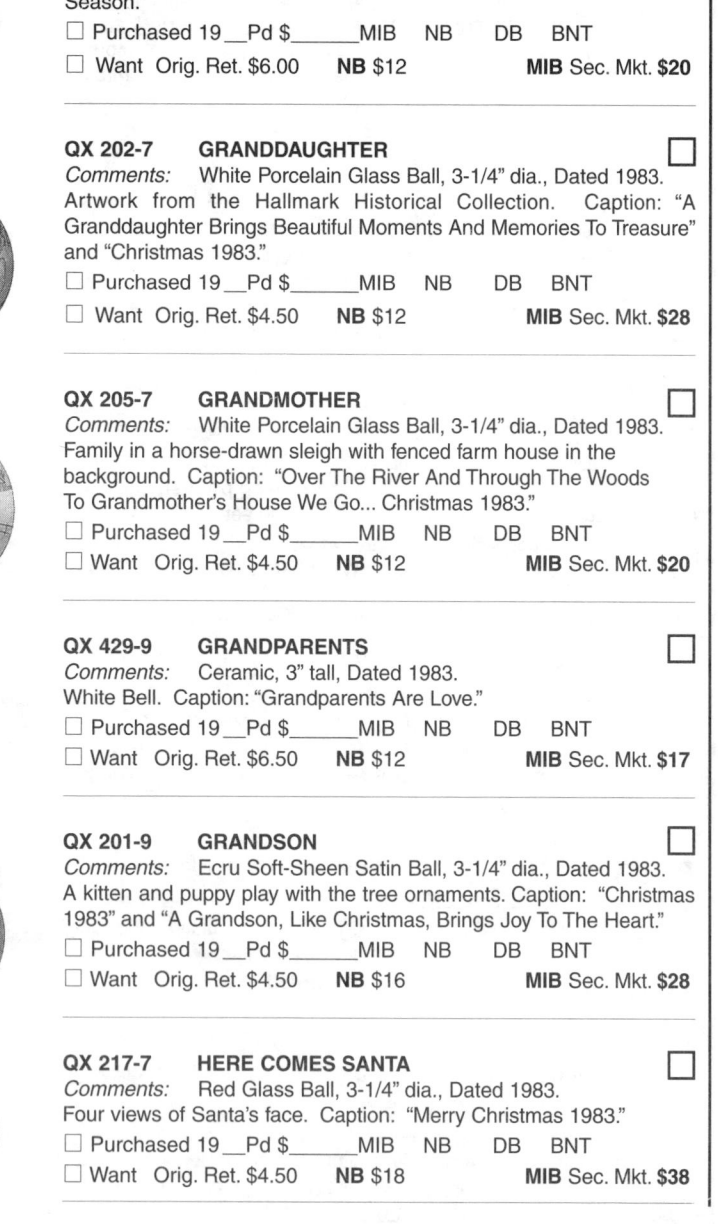

QX 312-9   GRANDCHILD'S FIRST CHRISTMAS   ☐
Comments: White Classic Shape, 3-1/4" dia., Dated 1983.
A baby and its toys. Caption: "Grandchild's First Christmas 1983" and "A Grandchild Is A Special Reason Why Christmas Is Such A Merry Season."

☐ Purchased 19 __ Pd $_____ MIB   NB   DB   BNT

☐ Want Orig. Ret. $6.00   **NB** $12   **MIB** Sec. Mkt. **$20**

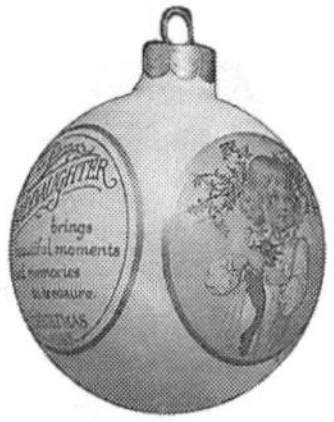

QX 202-7   GRANDDAUGHTER   ☐
Comments: White Porcelain Glass Ball, 3-1/4" dia., Dated 1983.
Artwork from the Hallmark Historical Collection.   Caption: "A Granddaughter Brings Beautiful Moments And Memories To Treasure" and "Christmas 1983."

☐ Purchased 19 __ Pd $_____ MIB   NB   DB   BNT

☐ Want Orig. Ret. $4.50   **NB** $12   **MIB** Sec. Mkt. **$28**

QX 205-7   GRANDMOTHER   ☐
Comments: White Porcelain Glass Ball, 3-1/4" dia., Dated 1983.
Family in a horse-drawn sleigh with fenced farm house in the background. Caption: "Over The River And Through The Woods To Grandmother's House We Go... Christmas 1983."

☐ Purchased 19 __ Pd $_____ MIB   NB   DB   BNT

☐ Want Orig. Ret. $4.50   **NB** $12   **MIB** Sec. Mkt. **$20**

QX 429-9   GRANDPARENTS   ☐
Comments: Ceramic, 3" tall, Dated 1983.
White Bell. Caption: "Grandparents Are Love."

☐ Purchased 19 __ Pd $_____ MIB   NB   DB   BNT

☐ Want Orig. Ret. $6.50   **NB** $12   **MIB** Sec. Mkt. **$17**

QX 201-9   GRANDSON   ☐
Comments: Ecru Soft-Sheen Satin Ball, 3-1/4" dia., Dated 1983.
A kitten and puppy play with the tree ornaments. Caption: "Christmas 1983" and "A Grandson, Like Christmas, Brings Joy To The Heart."

☐ Purchased 19 __ Pd $_____ MIB   NB   DB   BNT

☐ Want Orig. Ret. $4.50   **NB** $16   **MIB** Sec. Mkt. **$28**

QX 217-7   HERE COMES SANTA   ☐
Comments: Red Glass Ball, 3-1/4" dia., Dated 1983.
Four views of Santa's face. Caption: "Merry Christmas 1983."

☐ Purchased 19 __ Pd $_____ MIB   NB   DB   BNT

☐ Want Orig. Ret. $4.50   **NB** $18   **MIB** Sec. Mkt. **$38**

QX 403-7   HERE COMES SANTA: SANTA EXPRESS   ☐
Comments :   **Fifth in Series,** Handcrafted, 3-7/16" tall, Dated 1983.
Santa pumps a "wooden" railroad car with gifts. The wheels turn.
Artist: Donna Lee

☐ Purchased 19 __ Pd $_____ MIB   NB   DB   BNT

☐ Want   Orig. Ret. $13.00 **NB** $200   **MIB** Sec. Mkt. **$280**

QX 424-7   HITCHHIKING SANTA   ☐
Comments: Handcrafted, 2-21/32" tall.
Santa in sunglasses and white shorts is holding a sign that reads "Goin' South" as he "thumbs" a ride. **Artist:** Ed Seale

☐ Purchased 19 __ Pd $_____ MIB   NB   DB   BNT

☐ Want   Orig. Ret. $8.00 **NB** $30   **MIB** Sec. Mkt. **$42**

QX 303-9   HOLIDAY HIGHLIGHTS:
CHRISTMAS STOCKING   ☐
Comments: Acrylic, 4" tall, Dated 1983.
"Etched" argyle Christmas stocking is filled with gifts and toys. Caption: "Merry Christmas 1983."

☐ Purchased 19 __ Pd $_____ MIB   NB   DB   BNT

☐ Want   Orig. Ret. $6.00 **NB** $25   **MIB** Sec. Mkt. **$40**

QX 304-7   HOLIDAY HIGHLIGHTS: STAR OF PEACE   ☐
Comments: Acrylic, 4" tall.
A four-pointed star with "reflections" is centered in an oval shape.
Caption: "Peace." **Artist:** Ed Seale

☐ Purchased 19 __ Pd $_____ MIB   NB   DB   BNT

☐ Want   Orig. Ret. $6.00 **NB** $10   **MIB** Sec. Mkt. **$18**

QX 307-7   HOLIDAY HIGHLIGHTS: TIME FOR SHARING   ☐
Comments: Acrylic, 4" tall, Dated 1983.
Mary Hamilton scene of a little girl tying a scarf around a kitten's neck.
Caption: "Christmas Is A Time For Sharing, Smiling, Loving, Giving, Caring."

☐ Purchased 19 __ Pd $_____ MIB   NB   DB   BNT

☐ Want   Orig. Ret. $6.00 **NB** $25   **MIB** Sec. Mkt. **$40**

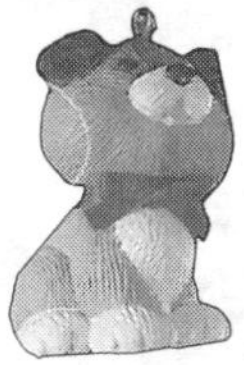

QX 412-7   HOLIDAY PUPPY   ☐
Comments: Handcrafted, 1-19/32" tall.
Cute brown and white puppy with black nose and ears has a red fabric bow around its neck.

☐ Purchased 19 __ Pd $_____ MIB   NB   DB   BNT

☐ Want   Orig. Ret. $3.50 **NB** $18   **MIB** Sec. Mkt. **$25**

QX 307-9   HOLIDAY SCULPTURE: HEART
Comments: Translucent Acrylic, 2" tall.
Red, three-dimensional heart. **Artist:** Linda Sickman
☐ Purchased 19___Pd $_____MIB   NB   DB   BNT
☐ Want   Orig. Ret. $4.00   **NB** $32   **MIB** Sec. Mkt. **$45**

QX 308-7   HOLIDAY SCULPTURE: SANTA
Comments: Translucent Red Acrylic.
Three-dimensional Santa.
☐ Purchased 19___Pd $_____MIB   NB   DB   BNT
☐ Want   Orig. Ret. $4.00   **NB** $18   **MIB** Sec. Mkt. **$32.50**

QX 309-9   HOLIDAY WILDLIFE: CHICKADEE
Comments: **Second in Series,** Decoform and Wood, 3" dia.
Dated 1983. Porcelain look insert of a chickadee on a branch.
Caption: "Black-Capped Chickadees, Parus Atricapillus" and
"Second In A Series, Wildlife Collection – Christmas 1983."
☐ Purchased 19___Pd $_____MIB   NB   DB   BNT
☐ Want   Orig. Ret. $7.00   **NB** $55   **MIB** Sec. Mkt. **$78**

QX 407-9   JACK FROST
Comments: Handcrafted, 3-3/4" tall.
Scrolls of frost on the window panes are evidence of Jack's special
artistry.
☐ Purchased 19___Pd $_____MIB   NB   DB   BNT
☐ Want   Orig. Ret. $9.00   **NB** $40   **MIB** Sec. Mkt. **$50**

QX 425-9   JOLLY SANTA
Comments: Handcrafted, 1-15/16" tall.
Merry Santa is posing with his pack of toys.
☐ Purchased 19___Pd $_____MIB   NB   DB   BNT
☐ Want   Orig. Ret. $3.50   **NB** $14   **MIB** Sec. Mkt. **$35**

QX 495-6   KERMIT THE FROG™
Comments: Handcrafted, 3-9/16" tall.
Reissued from 1982. **Artist:** Donna Lee
☐ Purchased 19___Pd $_____MIB   NB   DB   BNT
☐ Want   Orig. Ret. $11.00   **NB** $80   **MIB** Sec. Mkt. **$95**

QX 207-9   LOVE
Comments: Lt. Green Glass Ball, 3-1/4" dia., Dated 1983.
Woodland snow scene. Caption: "Love Makes Each Day A Joy, Each
Moment A Memory" And "Christmas 1983."
☐ Purchased 19___Pd $_____MIB   NB   DB   BNT
☐ Want   Orig. Ret. $4.50   **NB** $14   **MIB** Sec. Mkt. **$25**

QX 310-9   LOVE
Comments: Red Classic Shape Ball, 3-1/4" dia., Dated 1983.
Reproduced from needlework in sampler style. Caption:
"Christmas 1983" and "Love, The Spirit Which Enhances All The
Seasons Of Our Lives."
☐ Purchased 19___Pd $_____MIB   NB   DB   BNT
☐ Want   Orig. Ret. $6.00   **NB** $20   **MIB** Sec. Mkt. **$38**

QX 305-7   LOVE
Comments: Acrylic, 4" tall, Dated 1983.
Skaters form the word "Love" on this heart-shaped ornament. Caption:
"Christmas 1983."
☐ Purchased 19___Pd $_____MIB   NB   DB   BNT
☐ Want   Orig. Ret. $6.00   **NB** $12   **MIB** Sec. Mkt. **$20**

QX 422-7   LOVE
Comments: Porcelain, 3-1/8" tall, Dated 1983.
A small red heart hangs in the center of a larger open white heart.
Caption: "Love." **Artist:** Linda Sickman
☐ Purchased 19___Pd $_____MIB   NB   DB   BNT
☐ Want   Orig. Ret. $13.00   **NB** $20   **MIB** Sec. Mkt. **$30**

QX 223-9   LOVE IS A SONG
Comments: Silver Glass Bell, 2-1/2" tall, Dated 1983.
Dickens' characters are silhouetted in red, green and white. Caption:
"Christmas Is A Song Of Love For Every Heart To Sing."
☐ Purchased 19___Pd $_____MIB   NB   DB   BNT
☐ Want   Orig. Ret. $4.50   **NB** $18   **MIB** Sec. Mkt. **$28**

QX 428-7   MADONNA AND CHILD
Comments: Porcelain, 3-1/16" tall.
Madonna in blue and white holds the Christ Child.
☐ Purchased 19___Pd $_____MIB   NB   DB   BNT
☐ Want   Orig. Ret. $12.00   **NB** $28   **MIB** Sec. Mkt. **$38**

QX 415-7   MAILBOX KITTEN
Comments: Handcrafted, 1-9/16" tall, Dated 1983.
A kitten with letters in its paws peeks out of a red mailbox reading "1983 Peppermint Lane."
☐ Purchased 19__Pd $_____MIB   NB   DB   BNT
☐ Want   Orig. Ret. $6.50   **NB** $40   **MIB** Sec. Mkt. **$55**

QX 213-7   MARY HAMILTON
Comments: White Classical Glass, 3-1/2" tall, Dated 1983.
A little girl prays with forest creatures. Caption: "A Wee Little, Warm Little Christmas Time Prayer – May God bless us always with friendships to share."
☐ Purchased 19__Pd $_____MIB   NB   DB   BNT
☐ Want   Orig. Ret. $4.50   **NB** $18   **MIB** Sec. Mkt. **$30**

QX 405-7   MISS PIGGY™
Comments: Handcrafted, 4-9/16" tall.
Dressed in a lavender skating costume, Miss Piggy leaps gracefully on her ice skates. Price down from '96.
☐ Purchased 19__Pd $_____MIB   NB   DB   BNT
☐ Want   Orig. Ret. $13.00   **NB** $130   **MIB** Sec. Mkt. **$185**

QX 429-7   MOM & DAD
Comments: Ceramic Bell, 3" tall, Dated 1983.
Fired-on decals of poinsettias and holly frame the captions: "Mom and Dad" and "Christmas 1983." **Artist:** Sharon Pike
☐ Purchased 19__Pd $_____MIB   NB   DB   BNT
☐ Want   Orig. Ret. $6.50   **NB** $15   **MIB** Sec. Mkt. **$25**

QX 306-7   MOTHER
Comments: Acrylic, 4" tall, Dated 1983.
Heart-shaped design with white "etched" border carries the caption: "Mother... Always Caring, Always Sharing, Always There To Love."
☐ Purchased 19__Pd $_____MIB   NB   DB   BNT
☐ Want   Orig. Ret. $6.00   **NB** $12   **MIB** Sec. Mkt. **$20**

MDQ 340-7   MOTHER'S DAY – A MOTHER'S LOVE
Comments: Musical; White Glass Classical Ball.
Plays "Swan Lake."
☐ Purchased 19__Pd $_____MIB   NB   DB   BNT
☐ Want   Orig. Ret. $14.00   **NB** $60   **MIB** Sec. Mkt. **$90**

QX 407-7   MOUNTAIN CLIMBING SANTA
Comments: Handcrafted, 2-13/32" tall, Reissued in 1984.
Santa scales the cliffs using a real rope. **Artist:** Ed Seale
☐ Purchased 19__Pd $_____MIB   NB   DB   BNT
☐ Want   Orig. Ret. $6.50   **NB** $18   **MIB** Sec. Mkt. **$35**

QX 419-7   MOUSE IN BELL
Comments: Handcrafted-Glass, 4" tall.
A cute mouse with a leather tail and a brass ring in the top of his stocking cap is the "clapper" for this clear glass bell.
☐ Purchased 19__Pd $_____MIB   NB   DB   BNT
☐ Want   Orig. Ret. $10.00   **NB** $50   **MIB** Sec. Mkt. **$65**

QX 413-7   MOUSE ON CHEESE
Comments: Handcrafted, 2-37/64" tall.
An adorable gray mouse enjoys the gift-wrapped cheese on which he's sitting.
Artist: Linda Sickman
☐ Purchased 19__Pd $_____MIB   NB   DB   BNT
☐ Want   Orig. Ret. $6.50   **NB** $35   **MIB** Sec. Mkt. **$45**

QX 214-7   MUPPETS™, THE
Comments: Lt. Blue Satin Ball, 3-1/4" dia., Dated 1983.
Kermit and Miss Piggy are in a biplane skywriting "Merry Christmas" and Fozzie floats in a hot air balloon.
☐ Purchased 19__Pd $_____MIB   NB   DB   BNT
☐ Want   Orig. Ret. $4.50   **NB** $40   **MIB** Sec. Mkt. **$50**

QMB 904-9   NATIVITY
Comments: Musical, Classic Shape, Dark Blue, 4-1/2" tall.
Three Kings bring gifts for the Holy Child. Caption: "The star shone bright with a holy light as heaven came to earth that night." Plays "Silent Night."
☐ Purchased 19__Pd $_____MIB   NB   DB   BNT
☐ Want   Orig. Ret. $16.00   **NB** $30   **MIB** Sec. Mkt. **$45**

QX 210-7   NEW HOME
Comments: White Soft-Sheen Satin Ball, 3-1/4" dia.
Dated 1983. Carolers spread Christmas cheer on a snowy night. Caption: "Christmas Is The Perfect Way Of Rounding Out Each Year, For Every Heart And Home's Aglow With Love And Warmth And Cheer."
☐ Purchased 19__Pd $_____MIB   NB   DB   BNT
☐ Want   Orig. Ret. $4.50   **NB** $20   **MIB** Sec. Mkt. **$30**

QX 215-7   NORMAN ROCKWELL ☐
Comments: Light Green Glass Ball, 3-1/4" dia., Dated 1983.
Caption: "Things Are Humming, Santa's Coming, Hearts Are Full Of
Cheer. Lights Are Gleaming, Kids Are Dreaming... Christmas Time Is
Here." From the Norman Rockwell Collection.
☐ Purchased 19 __Pd $_____MIB   NB   DB   BNT
☐ Want   Orig. Ret. $4.50   **NB** $35   **MIB** Sec. Mkt. **$45**

QX 300-7   NORMAN ROCKWELL SERIES ☐
Comments: **Fourth in Series,** Dark Blue Cameo, 3" dia.
Dated 1983. Caption: "Dress Rehearsal. Fourth In A Series.
Christmas 1983." The Norman Rockwell Collection.
☐ Purchased 19 __Pd $_____MIB   NB   DB   BNT
☐ Want   Orig. Ret. $7.50   **NB** $21   **MIB** Sec. Mkt. **$35**

QX 409-9   OLD-FASHIONED SANTA ☐
Comments: Handcrafted, 5-9/64" tall.
Jointed, realistic interpretation. Santa wears a knee-length red suit
with red and white striped hose. His arms and legs are moveable.
Artist: Linda Sickman
☐ Purchased 19 __Pd $_____MIB   NB   DB   BNT
☐ Want   Orig. Ret. $11.00   **NB** $55   **MIB** Sec. Mkt. **$65**

QX 218-7   ORIENTAL BUTTERFLIES ☐
Comments: Turquoise Glass Ball, 3-1/4" dia.
Eight colorful butterflies; reproduced from original stitchery.
☐ Purchased 19 __Pd $_____MIB   NB   DB   BNT
☐ Want   Orig. Ret. $4.50   **NB** $20   **MIB** Sec. Mkt. **$27.50**

QX 212-7   PEANUTS® ☐
Comments: White Soft-Sheen Satin Ball, 3-1/4" dia.
Dated 1983. Comic strip panels show Snoopy bringing Woodstock and
his friends out of the cold. Caption: "Christmas 1983" and "May The Joy
Of The Season Warm Every Heart."
☐ Purchased 19 __Pd $_____MIB   NB   DB   BNT
☐ Want   Orig. Ret. $4.50   **NB** $22   **MIB** Sec. Mkt. **$35**

QX 408-9   PEPPERMINT PENGUIN ☐
Comments: Handcrafted, 2-3/4" tall.
A red capped penguin pedals his "peppermint candy" unicycle.
☐ Purchased 19 __Pd $_____MIB   NB   DB   BNT
☐ Want   Orig. Ret. $6.50   **NB** $20   **MIB** Sec. Mkt. **$38**

QX 428-9   PORCELAIN BEAR: CINNAMON TEDDY ☐
Comments: **FIRST IN SERIES,** Porcelain, 2-15/64" tall.
Made of fine porcelain and hand painted.
Artist: Peter Dutkin
☐ Purchased 19 __Pd $_____MIB   NB   DB   BNT
☐ Want   Orig. Ret. $7.00   **NB** $50   **MIB** Sec. Mkt. **$70**

QX 416-7   RAINBOW ANGEL ☐
Comments: Handcrafted, 2-15/16" tall.
Angel with a brass halo slides down a rainbow. Trading increase seen
on this ornament. **Artist:** Donna Lee
☐ Purchased 19 __Pd $_____MIB   NB   DB   BNT
☐ Want   Orig. Ret. $5.50   **NB** $65   **MIB** Sec. Mkt. **$100**

QX 417-7   ROCKING HORSE ☐
Comments: **Third in Series,** Handcrafted, 2-7/8" tall.
Dated 1983. Russet horse with green rockers.
Big price drop from 1996. **Artist:** Linda Sickman
☐ Purchased 19 __Pd $_____MIB   NB   DB   BNT
☐ Want   Orig. Ret. $10.00   **NB** $215   **MIB** Sec. Mkt. **$275**

QX 311-7   SANTA'S MANY FACES ☐
Comments: Red Classic Shape Ball, 3-1/4" dia., Dated 1983.
Six Santa scenes circle the ornament. Caption: "Merry Christmas."
☐ Purchased 19 __Pd $_____MIB   NB   DB   BNT
☐ Want   Orig. Ret. $6.00   **NB** $20   **MIB** Sec. Mkt. **$30**

QX 426-9   SANTA'S ON HIS WAY ☐
Comments: Handcrafted, 3" tall.
Four handcrafted openings show Santa in three-dimensional,
handpainted scenes.
☐ Purchased 19 __Pd $_____MIB   NB   DB   BNT
☐ Want   Orig. Ret. $10.00   **NB** $20   **MIB** Sec. Mkt. **$35**

QX 450-3   SANTA'S WORKSHOP ☐
Comments: Handcrafted, 3" tall. Reissued from 1982.
Artist: Donna Lee
☐ Purchased 19 __Pd $_____MIB   NB   DB   BNT
☐ Want   Orig. Ret. $10.00   **NB** $70   **MIB** Sec. Mkt. **$80**

QX 424-9   SCRIMSHAW REINDEER ☐
Comments: Handcrafted, 3-3/4" tall.
The leaping reindeer was created with the look of handcarved ivory scrimshaw accented in brown. **Artist:** Ed Seale
☐ Purchased 19 __Pd $_____MIB   NB   DB   BNT
☐ Want   Orig. Ret. $8.00   **NB** $20   **MIB** Sec. Mkt. **$35**

QX 219-9   SEASON'S GREETINGS ☐
Comments: Chrome Glass Ball, 3-1/4" dia.
The caption, "Season's Greetings," is formed with neon lettering on a dark background.
☐ Purchased 19 __Pd $_____MIB   NB   DB   BNT
☐ Want   Orig. Ret. $4.50   **NB** $12   **MIB** Sec. Mkt. **$22**

QX 214-9   SHIRT TALES™ ☐
Comments: White Classical Glass, 3-1/2" tall, Dated 1983.
A walrus, penguin and polar bear wear t-shirts that say, "Deck the Halls" and "Fa La-La-La-La" Caption: "Christmas 1983" and "Tis The Season To Be Jolly."
☐ Purchased 19 __Pd $_____MIB   NB   DB   BNT
☐ Want   Orig. Ret. $4.50   **NB** $15   **MIB** Sec. Mkt. **$25**

OX 110-9   SILVER BELL ☐
Comments: Silverplated.
Came with red ribbon; made for J. C. Penney.
☐ Purchased 19 __Pd $_____MIB   NB   DB   BNT
☐ Want   Orig. Ret. $12.00   **NB** $20   **MIB** Sec. Mkt. **$40**

QX 206-9   SISTER ☐
Comments: White Classical Glass, 3-1/4" dia., Dated 1983.
Wreath frames the caption: "A Sister Is A Forever Friend."
☐ Purchased 19 __Pd $_____MIB   NB   DB   BNT
☐ Want   Orig. Ret. $4.50   **NB** $14   **MIB** Sec. Mkt. **$22.50**

QX 409-7   SKATING RABBIT ☐
Comments: Handcrafted, 3-1/4" tall.
This happy rabbit has a real cotton tail and a specially designed stocking cap which covers each ear separately.
☐ Purchased 19 __Pd $_____MIB   NB   DB   BNT
☐ Want   Orig. Ret. $8.00   **NB** $35   **MIB** Sec. Mkt. **$45**

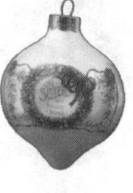

QX 418-7   SKI LIFT SANTA ☐
Comments: Handcrafted-Brass, 3-7/8" tall, Dated 1983.
Santa waves as he rides the ski lift. A brass bell is the pompon for his hat. Date is on his ski lift ticket.
☐ Purchased 19 __Pd $_____MIB   NB   DB   BNT
☐ Want   Orig. Ret. $8.00   **NB** $40   **MIB** Sec. Mkt. **$70**

QX 420-7   SKIING FOX ☐
Comments: Handcrafted, 2-5/32" tall.
A fox with a green muffler is showing great form as he races downhill.
Artist: Donna Lee
☐ Purchased 19 __Pd $_____MIB   NB   DB   BNT
☐ Want   Orig. Ret. $8.00   **NB** $25   **MIB** Sec. Mkt. **$40**

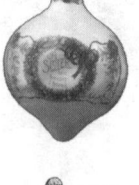

QX 400-9   SNEAKER MOUSE ☐
Comments: Handcrafted, 1-11/16" tall.
A cute white mouse has made his bed in a red and white sneaker.
Artist: Ed Seale
☐ Purchased 19 __Pd $_____MIB   NB   DB   BNT
☐ Want   Orig. Ret. $4.50   **NB-P** $20   **MIB** Sec. Mkt. **$30**

QX 416-9   SNOOPY AND FRIENDS ☐
Comments: **Fifth in Series,** Handcrafted Panorama Ball.
3-1/4" dia., Dated 1983. Snoopy is dressed as Santa and delivers a bag of gifts to Woodstock. **Artist:** Linda Sickman
☐ Purchased 19 __Pd $_____MIB   NB   DB   BNT
☐ Want   Orig. Ret. $13.00   **NB** $60   **MIB** Sec. Mkt. **$85**

QX 202-9   SON ☐
Comments: Deep Blue Satin Ball, 3-1/4" dia., Dated 1983.
A little boy, house, Christmas trees and a snowman riding a snowhorse are depicted. Caption: "A Son Brings A Bit Of Christmas Cheer To Every Day Throughout The Year."
☐ Purchased 19 __Pd $_____MIB   NB   DB   BNT
☐ Want   Orig. Ret. $4.50   **NB** $16   **MIB** Sec. Mkt. **$35**

QHD 406-9   ST. NICHOLAS ☐
Comments: Porcelain Table Decoration.
An Old-World Santa makes his rounds on Christmas Eve with his pack of toys and a walking stick.
☐ Purchased 19 __Pd $_____MIB   NB   DB   BNT
☐ Want   Orig. Ret. $27.50   **NB** $75   **MIB** Sec. Mkt. **$90**

QX 224-9   TEACHER
Comments: Silver Glass Bell, 2-1/2" tall, Dated 1983.
Schoolhouse and red and green lettering are bordered with green
bands. Caption: "For a Special Teacher at Christmas."
☐ Purchased 19 __Pd $_____MIB   NB   DB   BNT
☐ Want   Orig. Ret. $4.50   **NB** $12   **MIB** Sec. Mkt. **$18**

QX 304-9   TEACHER
Comments: Acrylic, 3-3/4" tall, Dated 1983.
A classic shape design shows a raccoon writing the caption: "Merry
Christmas, Merry Christmas, Merry Christmas, Teacher!"
☐ Purchased 19 __Pd $_____MIB   NB   DB   BNT
☐ Want   Orig. Ret. $6.00   **NB** $6   **MIB** Sec. Mkt. **$12**

QX 430-7   TENTH CHRISTMAS TOGETHER
Comments: Ceramic Bell, 3" tall, Dated 1983.
White ceramic bell is decorated with a golden French horn and hung
with red fabric ribbon. Caption: "Tenth Christmas Together 1983."
☐ Purchased 19 __Pd $_____MIB   NB   DB   BNT
☐ Want   Orig. Ret. $6.50   **NB** $10   **MIB** Sec. Mkt. **$25**

QX 401-7   THIMBLE SERIES: THIMBLE ELF
Comments: **Sixth in Series,** Handcrafted, 1-15/16" tall.
A little elf is licking his lips over a cherry-topped treat served
in a thimble.
☐ Purchased 19 __Pd $_____MIB   NB   DB   BNT
☐ Want   Orig. Ret. $5.00   **NB-P** $15   **MIB** Sec. Mkt. **$35**

QX 404-9   TIN LOCOMOTIVE
Comments: **Second in Series,** Pressed Tin, 3" tall, Dated 1983.
This early locomotive is lithographed in red and green and
trimmed in gold. **Artist:** Linda Sickman
☐ Purchased 19 __Pd $_____MIB   NB   DB   BNT
☐ Want   Orig. Ret. $13.00   **NB** $200   **MIB** Sec. Mkt. **$250**

QX 414-9   TIN ROCKING HORSE
Comments: Pressed Tin, 3-11/64" tall.
This three-dimensional lithographed tin rocking horse is a dappled gray
and resembles an Early American nursery toy. **Artist:** Linda Sickman
☐ Purchased 19 __Pd $_____MIB   NB   DB   BNT
☐ Want   Orig. Ret. $6.50   **NB** $38   **MIB** Sec. Mkt. **$50**

QMB 415-9   TWELVE DAYS OF CHRISTMAS MUSICAL
Comments: Musical, Handcrafted, 3-3/4" tall. Reissued in 1984.
Blue and white motifs of the song. Plays "Twelve Days of
Christmas." **Artist:** Ed Seale
☐ Purchased 19 __Pd $_____MIB   NB   DB   BNT
☐ Want   Orig. Ret. $15.00   **NB** $65   **MIB** Sec. Mkt. **$85**

QX 224-7   TWENTY-FIFTH CHRISTMAS TOGETHER
Comments: Silver Glass Bell, 2-1/2" tall, Dated 1983.
Bell with red print and white snowflakes. Caption: "25th
Christmas Together."
☐ Purchased 19 __Pd $_____MIB   NB   DB   BNT
☐ Want   Orig. Ret. $4.50   **NB** $15   **MIB** Sec. Mkt. **$20**

QX 426-7   UNICORN
Comments: Porcelain, 4" tall.
Beautiful white porcelain prancing unicorn has hand painted gold trim.
Don't confuse this with QX 429-3, 1986 *Magical Unicorn*.
☐ Purchased 19 __Pd $_____MIB   NB   DB   BNT
☐ Want   Orig. Ret. $10.00   **NB** $50   **MIB** Sec. Mkt. **$65**

QX 220-7   WISE MEN, THE
Comments: Gold Glass Ball, 3-1/4" dia.
Three kings raise their gifts to the star leading them.
☐ Purchased 19 __Pd $_____MIB   NB   DB   BNT
☐ Want   Orig. Ret. $4.50   **NB** $30   **MIB** Sec. Mkt. **$45**

1984 Collection

QX 246-1   A CHRISTMAS PRAYER
Comments: Blue Satin Ball, 2-7/8" dia.
Mary Hamilton's angels chase stars. Caption: "Little Prayer Be On Your
Way... Bless Our Friends On Christmas Day."
☐ Purchased 19 __Pd $_____MIB   NB   DB   BNT
☐ Want   Orig. Ret. $4.50   **NB** $15   **MIB** Sec. Mkt. **$22**

QX 260-4   A GIFT OF FRIENDSHIP
Comments: Peach Glass Ball, 3" dia.
Scenes of Muffin and her kitten. Caption: "Friendship Is The Happiest
Gift Of All."
☐ Purchased 19 __Pd $_____MIB   NB   DB   BNT
☐ Want   Orig. Ret. $4.50   **NB** $12   **MIB** Sec. Mkt. **$22**

QX 254-1   A SAVIOR IS BORN
Comments: Purple Glass Ball, 2-7/8" dia.
The Nativity flanks the caption which is printed in large gold lettering: "For Unto You Is Born This Day In The City Of David A Savior Which Is Christ The Lord. Luke 2:11."
☐ Purchased 19 __ Pd $_____ MIB   NB   DB   BNT
☐ Want   Orig. Ret. $4.50   **NB** $15   **MIB** Sec. Mkt. **$32**

QLX 704-4   ALL ARE PRECIOUS
Comments: Lighted Acrylic, 4" tall, Reissued in 1985.
A Shepherd, lamb and donkey watch the star. Caption in gold foil stamp: "All Are Precious In His Sight..."
☐ Purchased 19 __ Pd $_____ MIB   NB   DB   BNT
☐ Want   Orig. Ret. $8.00   **NB** $18   **MIB** Sec. Mkt. **$25**

QX 452-1   ALPINE ELF
Comments: Handcrafted, 3-1/2" wide.
A little elf dressed in a red coat and hat, plays a long curved horn.
Artist: Ed Seale
☐ Purchased 19 __ Pd $_____ MIB   NB   DB   BNT
☐ Want   Orig. Ret. $6.00   **NB** $25   **MIB** Sec. Mkt. **$32**

QX 432-1   AMANDA DOLL
Comments: Fabric, Handpainted Porcelain, 4-3/4" tall.
This doll is wearing a bright green ruffled dress and bonnet.
☐ Purchased 19 __ Pd $_____ MIB   NB   DB   BNT
☐ Want   Orig. Ret. $9.00   **NB** $15   **MIB** Sec. Mkt. **$25**

QTT 710-1   ANGEL TREE TOPPER
Comments: Fabric and Porcelain.
Golden accents on her wings and gown add to the charm of this lovely angel.
☐ Purchased 19 __ Pd $_____ MIB   NB   DB   BNT
☐ Want   Orig. Ret. $24.50   **NB** $30   **MIB** Sec. Mkt. **$40**

QX 349-4   ART MASTERPIECE
Comments: *FIRST IN SERIES,* Bezeled Satin, 2-3/4" dia.
Classic oil painting reproduced on padded satin. "Giuliano Bugiardini, Madonna And Child And St. John, (ca. 1505) The Nelson-Atkins Museum Of Art, Kansas City, Missouri (Nelson Fund)." **Artist:** Diana McGehee
☐ Purchased 19 __ Pd $_____ MIB   NB   DB   BNT
☐ Want   Orig. Ret. $6.50   **NB** $6   **MIB** Sec. Mkt. **$18**

QX 340-1   BABY'S FIRST CHRISTMAS
Comments: Acrylic, 3-3/4" tall, Dated 1984.
This etched teddy bear is holding a toy-filled stocking.
Caption: "Baby's First Christmas."
☐ Purchased 19 __ Pd $_____ MIB   NB   DB   BNT
☐ Want   Orig. Ret. $6.00   **NB** $30   **MIB** Sec. Mkt. **$40**

QX 240-4   BABY'S FIRST CHRISTMAS – BOY
Comments: White Satin Ball, 2-7/8" dia., Dated 1984.
A handcrafted mouse sits on top of the ornament. Caption: "Baby's First Christmas" and "A Baby Boy Is A Bundle Of Pleasure To Fill Every day With Love Beyond Measure."
☐ Purchased 19 __ Pd $_____ MIB   NB   DB   BNT
☐ Want   Orig. Ret. $4.50   **NB** $10   **MIB** Sec. Mkt. **$25**

QX 240-1   BABY'S FIRST CHRISTMAS – GIRL
Comments: Cream Satin Ball, 2-7/8" dia., Dated 1984.
A parade of little girls, animals and toys. Caption: "A Baby Girl Is Love That Grows In The Warmth Of Caring Hearts. Baby's First Christmas."
☐ Purchased 19 __ Pd $_____ MIB   NB   DB   BNT
☐ Want   Orig. Ret. $4.50   **NB** $12   **MIB** Sec. Mkt. **$28**

QX 438-1   BABY'S FIRST CHRISTMAS
Comments: Handcrafted, 3-1/2" wide, Dated 1984.
A brown bear rides a sled full of toys. Caption: "Baby's First Christmas."
☐ Purchased 19 __ Pd $_____ MIB   NB   DB   BNT
☐ Want   Orig. Ret. $14.00   **NB** $30   **MIB** Sec. Mkt. **$48**

QX 904-1   BABY'S FIRST CHRISTMAS
Comments: Musical, Classic Shape, 4-1/4" tall, Dated 1984.
"A Baby Is... Happiness, Pleasure, A Gift From Above... A Wonderful, Magical Treasure Of Love. Baby's First Christmas." Plays "Babes In Toyland." **Artist:** Donna Lee
☐ Purchased 19 __ Pd $_____ MIB   NB   DB   BNT
☐ Want   Orig. Ret. $16.00   **NB** $20   **MIB** Sec. Mkt. **$40**

QX 300-1   BABY'S FIRST CHRISTMAS PHOTOHOLDER
Comments: Fabric, 3-1/4" dia., Dated 1984.
Embroidered holly sprigs with a white fabric photoholder.
Caption: "Baby's First Christmas" and "A Baby Is A Special Dream Come True."
☐ Purchased 19 __ Pd $_____ MIB   NB   DB   BNT
☐ Want   Orig. Ret. $7.00   **NB** $14   **MIB** Sec. Mkt. **$18**

QX 241-1 BABY'S SECOND CHRISTMAS ☐
Comments: White Satin Ball, 2-7/8" dia., Dated 1984.
Pooh Bear and his friends share Christmas together. A gold crown tops the ornament. Caption: "Children And Christmas Are Joys That Go Together. Baby's Second Christmas."
☐ Purchased 19___ Pd $_____ MIB   NB   DB   BNT
☐ Want   Orig. Ret. $4.50   **NB** $10   **MIB** Sec. Mkt. **$22**

QX 253-1 BABY-SITTER ☐
Comments: Green Glass Ball, 3" dia.
A group of mice have fun with their baby-sitter. Caption: "Thank Heaven For Baby-Sitters Like You."
☐ Purchased 19___ Pd $_____ MIB   NB   DB   BNT
☐ Want   Orig. Ret. $4.50   **NB** $8   **MIB** Sec. Mkt. **$14**

QX 443-1 BELL RINGER SQUIRREL ☐
Comments: Glass, Handcrafted, 4" tall.
A handcrafted squirrel and acorn form the clapper for this clear glass bell. **Artist:** Ed Seale
☐ Purchased 19___ Pd $_____ MIB   NB   DB   BNT
☐ Want   Orig. Ret. $10.00   **NB** $18   **MIB** Sec. Mkt. **$32**

QX 438-4 BELLRINGER, THE: ELFIN ARTIST ☐
Comments: **Sixth and Final in Series,** Dated Christmas 1984.
Porcelain, 3-1/2" tall. An artistic elf has lettered his Christmas message on the bell in red paint.
☐ Purchased 19___ Pd $_____ MIB   NB   DB   BNT
☐ Want   Orig. Ret. $15.00   **NB** $25   **MIB** Sec. Mkt. **$40**

QX 249-4 BETSEY CLARK ☐
Comments: **Twelfth in Series,** Dated Christmas 1984.
White Frosted Glass, 3-1/4" Children decorate their homes for the holidays. Caption: "Days Are Merry, Hearts Are Light, And All The World's A Lovely Sight."
☐ Purchased 19___ Pd $_____ MIB   NB   DB   BNT
☐ Want   Orig. Ret. $5.00   **NB** $15   **MIB** Sec. Mkt. **$35**

QX 462-4 BETSEY CLARK ANGEL ☐
Comments: Porcelain, 3-1/2" tall.
Hand painted angel is dressed in a pink dress and white pinafore and plays a mandolin.
☐ Purchased 19___ Pd $_____ MIB   NB   DB   BNT
☐ Want   Orig. Ret. $9.00   **NB** $15   **MIB** Sec. Mkt. **$32**

QLX 707-1 BRASS CAROUSEL ☐
Comments: Lighted, Etched Brass, 3" tall, RARE!
Santa rides the carousel in his sleigh, pulled by one of his reindeer.
☐ Purchased 19___ Pd $_____ MIB   NB   DB   BNT
☐ Want   Orig. Ret. $9.00   **NB** $65   **MIB** Sec. Mkt. **$95**

QX 451-4 CHICKADEE ☐
Comments: Handpainted Porcelain, 3-1/4" wide.
Chickadee carries a sprig of mistletoe and has a clip to fasten him to the tree. **Artist:** Linda Sickman
☐ Purchased 19___ Pd $_____ MIB   NB   DB   BNT
☐ Want   Orig. Ret. $6.00   **NB** $25   **MIB** Sec. Mkt. **$42**

QX 261-1 CHILD'S THIRD CHRISTMAS ☐
Comments: Ecru Satin Ball, 2-7/8" dia., Dated 1984.
A small mouse sits on top of the ornament while teddy bears decorate for Christmas. Caption: "A Child's Third Christmas. Christmas Is A Time For Fun And Wonderful Surprises."
☐ Purchased 19___ Pd $_____ MIB   NB   DB   BNT
☐ Want   Orig. Ret. $4.50   **NB** $12   **MIB** Sec. Mkt. **$24**

QLX 703-4 CHRISTMAS IN THE FOREST ☐
Comments: Lighted Silver Classic Shape, 3-7/8" dia.
Lit from within, a moonlit night in a snowy forest is portrayed.
☐ Purchased 19___ Pd $_____ MIB   NB   DB   BNT
☐ Want   Orig. Ret. $8.00   **NB** $14   **MIB** Sec. Mkt. **$20**

QX 300-4 CHRISTMAS MEMORIES PHOTOHOLDER ☐
Comments: Fabric, 3" dia., Dated 1984.
Red, white and green holiday fabrics are stitched to create a charming photo wreath.
☐ Purchased 19___ Pd $_____ MIB   NB   DB   BNT
☐ Want   Orig. Ret. $6.50   **NB** $14   **MIB** Sec. Mkt. **$25**

QX 444-1 CHRISTMAS OWL ☐
Comments: Handcrafted, Acrylic, 3-3/4" tall.
A cute little owl, wearing a Santa cap, perches on an acrylic moon. His "stocking" hangs on the tip. **Artist:** Ed Seale
☐ Purchased 19___ Pd $_____ MIB   NB   DB   BNT
☐ Want   Orig. Ret. $6.00   **NB** $18   **MIB** Sec. Mkt. **$28**

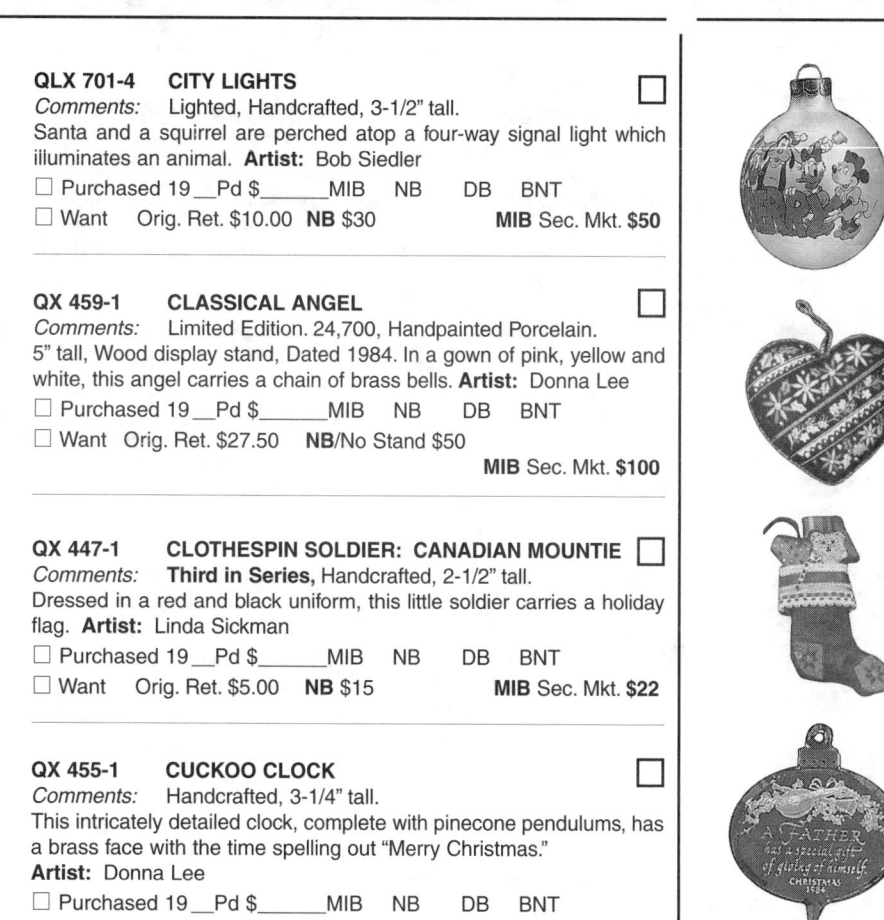

QLX 701-4   CITY LIGHTS   ☐

Comments: Lighted, Handcrafted, 3-1/2" tall.
Santa and a squirrel are perched atop a four-way signal light which illuminates an animal. **Artist:** Bob Siedler

☐ Purchased 19 __ Pd $_____ MIB   NB   DB   BNT

☐ Want   Orig. Ret. $10.00 **NB** $30   **MIB** Sec. Mkt. **$50**

QX 459-1   CLASSICAL ANGEL   ☐

Comments: Limited Edition. 24,700, Handpainted Porcelain.
5" tall, Wood display stand, Dated 1984. In a gown of pink, yellow and white, this angel carries a chain of brass bells. **Artist:** Donna Lee

☐ Purchased 19 __ Pd $_____ MIB   NB   DB   BNT

☐ Want   Orig. Ret. $27.50   **NB**/No Stand $50

MIB Sec. Mkt. **$100**

QX 447-1   CLOTHESPIN SOLDIER: CANADIAN MOUNTIE   ☐

Comments: **Third in Series,** Handcrafted, 2-1/2" tall.
Dressed in a red and black uniform, this little soldier carries a holiday flag. **Artist:** Linda Sickman

☐ Purchased 19 __ Pd $_____ MIB   NB   DB   BNT

☐ Want   Orig. Ret. $5.00   **NB** $15   **MIB** Sec. Mkt. **$22**

QX 455-1   CUCKOO CLOCK   ☐

Comments: Handcrafted, 3-1/4" tall.
This intricately detailed clock, complete with pinecone pendulums, has a brass face with the time spelling out "Merry Christmas."
Artist: Donna Lee

☐ Purchased 19 __ Pd $_____ MIB   NB   DB   BNT

☐ Want   Orig. Ret. $10.00 **NB** $35   **MIB** Sec. Mkt. **$45**

QX 250-1   CURRIER & IVES   ☐

Comments: White Blown Glass Ball, 2-7/8" dia., Dated 1984.
Caption: "American Winter Scenes, Evening, Christmas 1984."

☐ Purchased 19 __ Pd $_____ MIB   NB   DB   BNT

☐ Want   Orig. Ret. $4.50   **NB** $15   **MIB** Sec. Mkt. **$24**

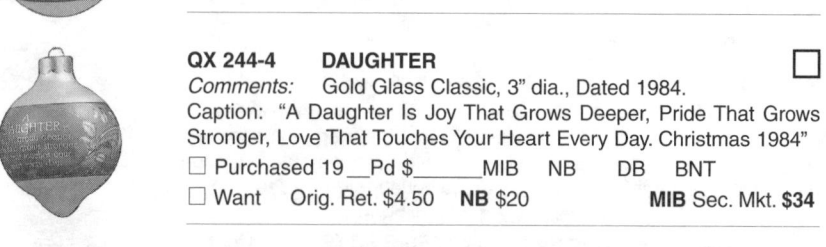

QX 244-4   DAUGHTER   ☐

Comments: Gold Glass Classic, 3" dia., Dated 1984.
Caption: "A Daughter Is Joy That Grows Deeper, Pride That Grows Stronger, Love That Touches Your Heart Every Day. Christmas 1984"

☐ Purchased 19 __ Pd $_____ MIB   NB   DB   BNT

☐ Want   Orig. Ret. $4.50   **NB** $20   **MIB** Sec. Mkt. **$34**

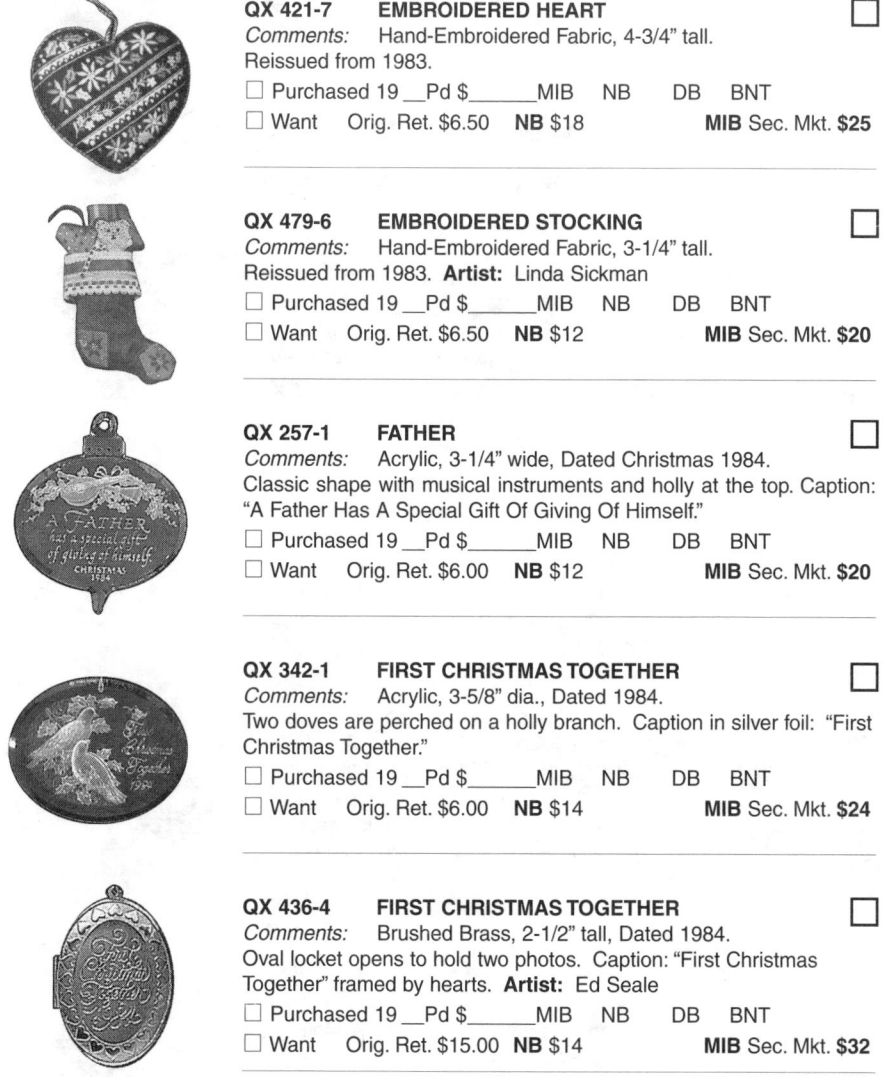

QX 250-4   DISNEY   ☐

Comments: White Glass Ball, 2-7/8" dia., Dated 1984.
The whole Disney gang sends Christmas greetings: "Friends Put The Merry In Christmas."

☐ Purchased 19 __ Pd $_____ MIB   NB   DB   BNT

☐ Want   Orig. Ret. $4.50   **NB** $25   **MIB** Sec. Mkt. **$40**

QX 421-7   EMBROIDERED HEART   ☐

Comments: Hand-Embroidered Fabric, 4-3/4" tall.
Reissued from 1983.

☐ Purchased 19 __ Pd $_____ MIB   NB   DB   BNT

☐ Want   Orig. Ret. $6.50   **NB** $18   **MIB** Sec. Mkt. **$25**

QX 479-6   EMBROIDERED STOCKING   ☐

Comments: Hand-Embroidered Fabric, 3-1/4" tall.
Reissued from 1983. **Artist:** Linda Sickman

☐ Purchased 19 __ Pd $_____ MIB   NB   DB   BNT

☐ Want   Orig. Ret. $6.50   **NB** $12   **MIB** Sec. Mkt. **$20**

QX 257-1   FATHER   ☐

Comments: Acrylic, 3-1/4" wide, Dated Christmas 1984.
Classic shape with musical instruments and holly at the top. Caption: "A Father Has A Special Gift Of Giving Of Himself."

☐ Purchased 19 __ Pd $_____ MIB   NB   DB   BNT

☐ Want   Orig. Ret. $6.00   **NB** $12   **MIB** Sec. Mkt. **$20**

QX 342-1   FIRST CHRISTMAS TOGETHER   ☐

Comments: Acrylic, 3-5/8" dia., Dated 1984.
Two doves are perched on a holly branch. Caption in silver foil: "First Christmas Together."

☐ Purchased 19 __ Pd $_____ MIB   NB   DB   BNT

☐ Want   Orig. Ret. $6.00   **NB** $14   **MIB** Sec. Mkt. **$24**

QX 436-4   FIRST CHRISTMAS TOGETHER   ☐

Comments: Brushed Brass, 2-1/2" tall, Dated 1984.
Oval locket opens to hold two photos. Caption: "First Christmas Together" framed by hearts. **Artist:** Ed Seale

☐ Purchased 19 __ Pd $_____ MIB   NB   DB   BNT

☐ Want   Orig. Ret. $15.00 **NB** $14   **MIB** Sec. Mkt. **$32**

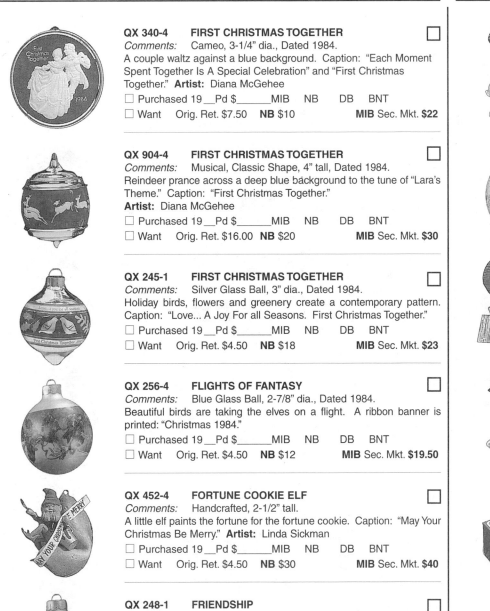

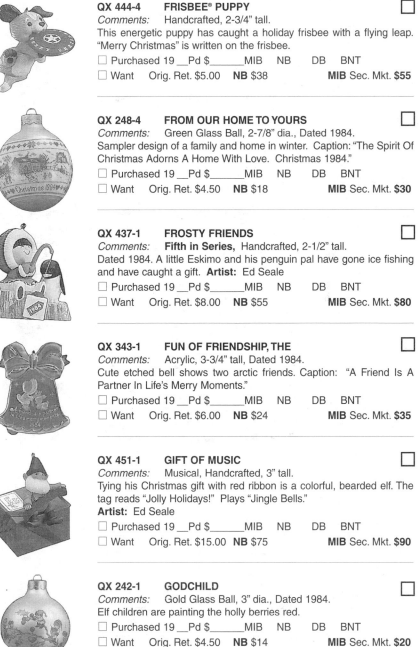

QX 340-4   FIRST CHRISTMAS TOGETHER
Comments: Cameo, 3-1/4" dia., Dated 1984.
A couple waltz against a blue background. Caption: "Each Moment Spent Together Is A Special Celebration" and "First Christmas Together." **Artist:** Diana McGehee
☐ Purchased 19 __ Pd $_____ MIB   NB   DB   BNT
☐ Want   Orig. Ret. $7.50 **NB** $10   **MIB** Sec. Mkt. **$22**

QX 904-4   FIRST CHRISTMAS TOGETHER
Comments: Musical, Classic Shape, 4" tall, Dated 1984.
Reindeer prance across a deep blue background to the tune of "Lara's Theme." Caption: "First Christmas Together."
Artist: Diana McGehee
☐ Purchased 19 __ Pd $_____ MIB   NB   DB   BNT
☐ Want   Orig. Ret. $16.00 **NB** $20   **MIB** Sec. Mkt. **$30**

QX 245-1   FIRST CHRISTMAS TOGETHER
Comments: Silver Glass Ball, 3" dia., Dated 1984.
Holiday birds, flowers and greenery create a contemporary pattern. Caption: "Love... A Joy For all Seasons. First Christmas Together."
☐ Purchased 19 __ Pd $_____ MIB   NB   DB   BNT
☐ Want   Orig. Ret. $4.50 **NB** $18   **MIB** Sec. Mkt. **$23**

QX 256-4   FLIGHTS OF FANTASY
Comments: Blue Glass Ball, 2-7/8" dia., Dated 1984.
Beautiful birds are taking the elves on a flight. A ribbon banner is printed: "Christmas 1984."
☐ Purchased 19 __ Pd $_____ MIB   NB   DB   BNT
☐ Want   Orig. Ret. $4.50 **NB** $12   **MIB** Sec. Mkt. **$19.50**

QX 452-4   FORTUNE COOKIE ELF
Comments: Handcrafted, 2-1/2" tall.
A little elf paints the fortune for the fortune cookie. Caption: "May Your Christmas Be Merry." **Artist:** Linda Sickman
☐ Purchased 19 __ Pd $_____ MIB   NB   DB   BNT
☐ Want   Orig. Ret. $4.50 **NB** $30   **MIB** Sec. Mkt. **$40**

QX 248-1   FRIENDSHIP
Comments: Blue-Green Glass Ball, 2-7/8" dia., Dated 1984.
Silhouettes of carolers against the snow. Caption: "Let Us Sing A Christmas Song Of Friendship, Joy And Cheer."
☐ Purchased 19 __ Pd $_____ MIB   NB   DB   BNT
☐ Want   Orig. Ret. $4.50 **NB** $8   **MIB** Sec. Mkt. **$20**

QX 444-4   FRISBEE® PUPPY
Comments: Handcrafted, 2-3/4" tall.
This energetic puppy has caught a holiday frisbee with a flying leap. "Merry Christmas" is written on the frisbee.
☐ Purchased 19 __ Pd $_____ MIB   NB   DB   BNT
☐ Want   Orig. Ret. $5.00 **NB** $38   **MIB** Sec. Mkt. **$55**

QX 248-4   FROM OUR HOME TO YOURS
Comments: Green Glass Ball, 2-7/8" dia., Dated 1984.
Sampler design of a family and home in winter. Caption: "The Spirit Of Christmas Adorns A Home With Love. Christmas 1984."
☐ Purchased 19 __ Pd $_____ MIB   NB   DB   BNT
☐ Want   Orig. Ret. $4.50 **NB** $18   **MIB** Sec. Mkt. **$30**

QX 437-1   FROSTY FRIENDS
Comments: **Fifth in Series,** Handcrafted, 2-1/2" tall.
Dated 1984. A little Eskimo and his penguin pal have gone ice fishing and have caught a gift. **Artist:** Ed Seale
☐ Purchased 19 __ Pd $_____ MIB   NB   DB   BNT
☐ Want   Orig. Ret. $8.00 **NB** $55   **MIB** Sec. Mkt. **$80**

QX 343-1   FUN OF FRIENDSHIP, THE
Comments: Acrylic, 3-3/4" tall, Dated 1984.
Cute etched bell shows two arctic friends. Caption: "A Friend Is A Partner In Life's Merry Moments."
☐ Purchased 19 __ Pd $_____ MIB   NB   DB   BNT
☐ Want   Orig. Ret. $6.00 **NB** $24   **MIB** Sec. Mkt. **$35**

QX 451-1   GIFT OF MUSIC
Comments: Musical, Handcrafted, 3" tall.
Tying his Christmas gift with red ribbon is a colorful, bearded elf. The tag reads "Jolly Holidays!" Plays "Jingle Bells."
Artist: Ed Seale
☐ Purchased 19 __ Pd $_____ MIB   NB   DB   BNT
☐ Want   Orig. Ret. $15.00 **NB** $75   **MIB** Sec. Mkt. **$90**

QX 242-1   GODCHILD
Comments: Gold Glass Ball, 3" dia., Dated 1984.
Elf children are painting the holly berries red.
☐ Purchased 19 __ Pd $_____ MIB   NB   DB   BNT
☐ Want   Orig. Ret. $4.50 **NB** $14   **MIB** Sec. Mkt. **$20**

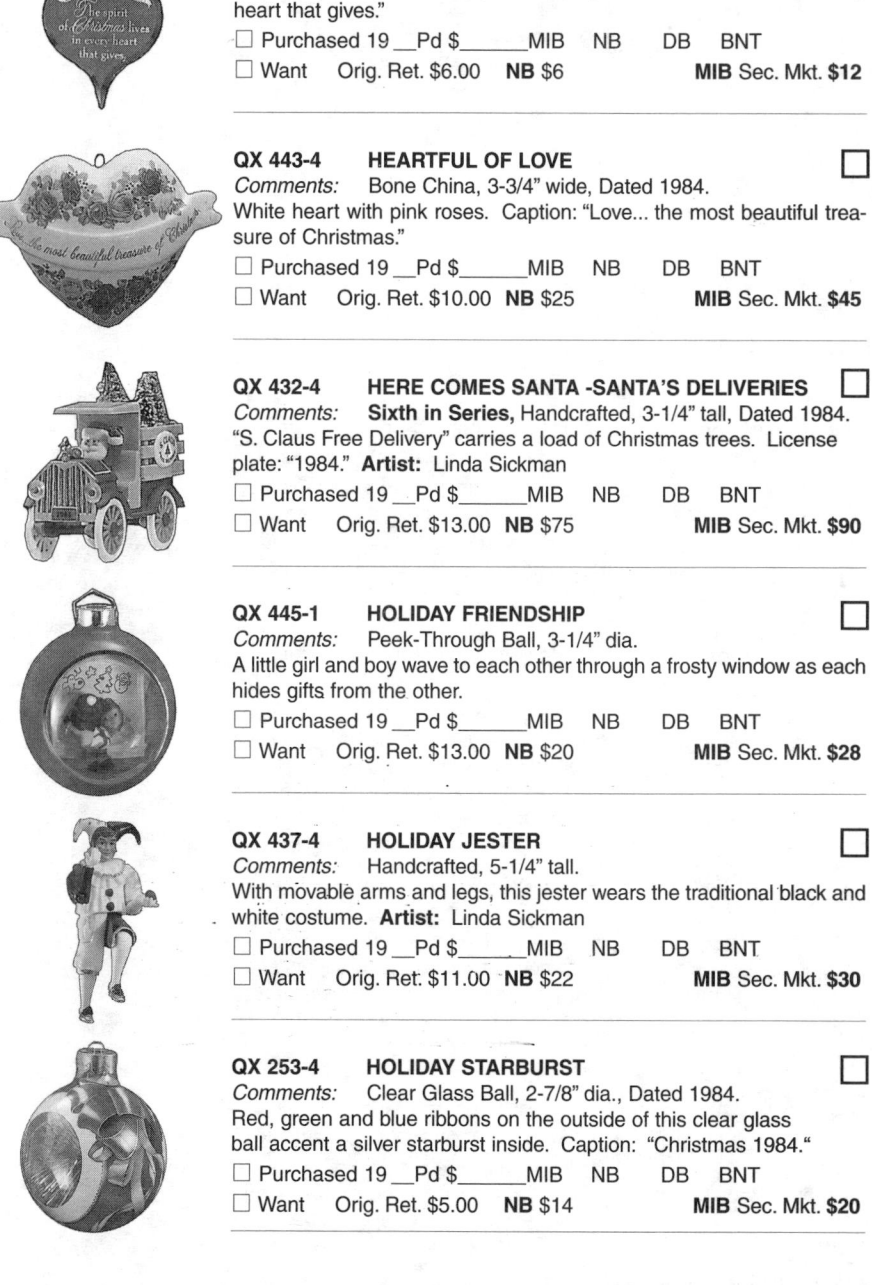

QX 257-4   GRANDCHILD'S FIRST CHRISTMAS ☐
Comments: Green Satin Ball, 2-7/8" dia., Dated 1984.
A "torn paper" scene of Santa loading toys into his bag. Handcrafted mouse sits atop the ornament. Caption: "A Baby Makes Christmas Delightfully Bright. Grandchild's First Christmas."
☐ Purchased 19__Pd $_____MIB   NB   DB   BNT
☐ Want   Orig. Ret. $4.50   **NB** $10   **MIB** Sec. Mkt. **$18**

QX 460-1   GRANDCHILD'S FIRST CHRISTMAS ☐
Comments: Handcrafted, 3-3/8" tall, Dated 1984.
A flocked white lamb stands on a colorful pull toy. Caption: "Grandchild's First Christmas."
☐ Purchased 19__Pd $_____MIB   NB   DB   BNT
☐ Want   Orig. Ret. $11.00   **NB** $14   **MIB** Sec. Mkt. **$20**

QX 243-1   GRANDDAUGHTER ☐
Comments: Green Glass Ball, 2-7/8" dia., Dated 1984.
Caption is written in a sampler design: "A Granddaughter Is Warmth, Hope And Promise. Christmas 1984."
☐ Purchased 19__Pd $_____MIB   NB   DB   BNT
☐ Want   Orig. Ret. $4.50   **NB** $14   **MIB** Sec. Mkt. **$27.50**

QX 244-1   GRANDMOTHER ☐
Comments: Lt. Blue Glass Ball, 2-7/8" dia., Dated 1984.
Pastel flowers frame the caption: "There's A Special Kind Of Beauty In A Grandmother's Special Love.   Christmas 1984."
☐ Purchased 19__Pd $_____MIB   NB   DB   BNT
☐ Want   Orig. Ret. $4.50   **NB** $14   **MIB** Sec. Mkt. **$18**

QX 256-1   GRANDPARENTS ☐
Comments: French Blue Glass Ball, 2-7/8" dia., Dated 1984.
"Stitched" snow scene. Caption: "Grandparents... Wherever They Are, There Is Love. Christmas 1984."
☐ Purchased 19__Pd $_____MIB   .NB   DB   BNT
☐ Want   Orig. Ret. $4.50   **NB** $8   **MIB** Sec. Mkt. **$12**

QX 242-4   GRANDSON ☐
Comments: Blue Glass Ball, 3" dia., Dated Christmas 1984.
A polar bear family enjoys Christmas together. Caption: "A Grandson Has A Wonderful Way Of Adding Love To Every Day."
☐ Purchased 19__Pd $_____MIB   NB   DB   BNT
☐ Want   Orig. Ret. $4.50   **NB** $14   **MIB** Sec. Mkt. **$28**

QX 344-4   GRATITUDE ☐
Comments: Acrylic, Teardrop shape, 4-1/2" tall.
Ribbon and sleigh bells. Caption: "The spirit of Christmas lives in every heart that gives."
☐ Purchased 19__Pd $_____MIB   NB   DB   BNT
☐ Want   Orig. Ret. $6.00   **NB** $6   **MIB** Sec. Mkt. **$12**

QX 443-4   HEARTFUL OF LOVE ☐
Comments: Bone China, 3-3/4" wide, Dated 1984.
White heart with pink roses. Caption: "Love... the most beautiful treasure of Christmas."
☐ Purchased 19__Pd $_____MIB   NB   DB   BNT
☐ Want   Orig. Ret. $10.00   **NB** $25   **MIB** Sec. Mkt. **$45**

QX 432-4   HERE COMES SANTA -SANTA'S DELIVERIES ☐
Comments: **Sixth in Series,** Handcrafted, 3-1/4" tall, Dated 1984.
"S. Claus Free Delivery" carries a load of Christmas trees. License plate: "1984." **Artist:** Linda Sickman
☐ Purchased 19__Pd $_____MIB   NB   DB   BNT
☐ Want   Orig. Ret. $13.00   **NB** $75   **MIB** Sec. Mkt. **$90**

QX 445-1   HOLIDAY FRIENDSHIP ☐
Comments: Peek-Through Ball, 3-1/4" dia.
A little girl and boy wave to each other through a frosty window as each hides gifts from the other.
☐ Purchased 19__Pd $_____MIB   NB   DB   BNT
☐ Want   Orig. Ret. $13.00   **NB** $20   **MIB** Sec. Mkt. **$28**

QX 437-4   HOLIDAY JESTER ☐
Comments: Handcrafted, 5-1/4" tall.
With movable arms and legs, this jester wears the traditional black and white costume. **Artist:** Linda Sickman
☐ Purchased 19__Pd $_____MIB   NB   DB   BNT
☐ Want   Orig. Ret. $11.00   **NB** $22   **MIB** Sec. Mkt. **$30**

QX 253-4   HOLIDAY STARBURST ☐
Comments: Clear Glass Ball, 2-7/8" dia., Dated 1984.
Red, green and blue ribbons on the outside of this clear glass ball accent a silver starburst inside. Caption: "Christmas 1984."
☐ Purchased 19__Pd $_____MIB   NB   DB   BNT
☐ Want   Orig. Ret. $5.00   **NB** $14   **MIB** Sec. Mkt. **$20**

QX 347-4   HOLIDAY WILDLIFE: PHEASANTS   ☐
Comments: **Third in Series,** 3" dia., Dated 1984.
Caption: "Ring-Necked Pheasant, Phasianus Torquatus, Third In A Series, Wildlife Collection, Christmas 1984."
☐ Purchased 19__Pd $_____MIB   NB   DB   BNT
☐ Want   Orig. Ret. $7.25   **NB** $17   **MIB** Sec. Mkt. **$28**

QX 463-1   KATYBETH   ☐
Comments: Handpainted Porcelain, 2-1/4" tall.
This freckle-faced angel holds a friendly, happy star.
☐ Purchased 19__Pd $_____MIB   NB   DB   BNT
☐ Want   Orig. Ret. $9.00   **NB** $14   **MIB** Sec. Mkt. **$28**

QX 453-4   KIT   ☐
Comments: Handcrafted, 2-3/4" tall.
Wearing his classic green cap, Muffin's friend Kit brings a candy cane to you.
☐ Purchased 19__Pd $_____MIB   NB   DB   BNT
☐ Want   Orig. Ret. $5.50   **NB** $16   **MIB** Sec. Mkt. **$24**

QX 255-4   LOVE   ☐
Comments: Chrome Glass Ball, 2-7/8" dia., Dated 1984.
Classic mimes share thoughts of love. Caption: "Love Can Say The Special Things That Words Alone Cannot. Christmas 1984."
☐ Purchased 19__Pd $_____MIB   NB   DB   BNT
☐ Want   Orig. Ret. $4.50   **NB** $15   **MIB** Sec. Mkt. **$25**

QX 247-4   LOVE... THE SPIRIT OF CHRISTMAS   ☐
Comments: Chrome Glass Ball, 2-7/8" dia., Dated 1984.
A bright fruit and flower design on a black band resembles a lacquer appearance. Caption: "Love, Which Is The Spirit And The Heart Of Christmas, Blossoms All Year Through."
☐ Purchased 19__Pd $_____MIB   NB   DB   BNT
☐ Want   Orig. Ret. $4.50   **NB** $20   **MIB** Sec. Mkt. **$40**

QX 344-1   MADONNA & CHILD   ☐
Comments: Acrylic, 4" tall.
This acrylic ornament features a beautifully etched design of the Holy Child cradled in the arms of the Madonna. Gold foil stamped caption: "All Is Calm, All Is Bright..." **Artist:** Don Palmiter
☐ Purchased 19__Pd $_____MIB   NB   DB   BNT
☐ Want   Orig. Ret. $6.00   **NB** $18   **MIB** Sec. Mkt. **$42**

QX 456-4   MARATHON SANTA   ☐
Comments: Handcrafted, 2-1/4" tall, Dated 1984.
Santa runs with the Olympic flame; let the games begin!
Artist: Ed Seale
☐ Purchased 19__Pd $_____MIB   NB   DB   BNT
☐ Want   Orig. Ret. $8.00   **NB** $22   **MIB** Sec. Mkt. **$38**

QX 342-4   MIRACLE OF LOVE, THE   ☐
Comments: Acrylic, 4" tall, Dated Christmas 1984.
Heart etched with festive ribbon and holly design. Gold foil Caption: "Love... A Miracle Of The Heart."
☐ Purchased 19__Pd $_____MIB   NB   DB   BNT
☐ Want   Orig. Ret. $6.00   **NB** $20   **MIB** Sec. Mkt. **$32**

QX 343-4   MOTHER   ☐
Comments: Acrylic, 3-1/4" wide, Dated 1984.
Etched fir branches help to highlight the caption: "A Mother Has A Beautiful Way Of Adding Love To Every Day."
☐ Purchased 19__Pd $_____MIB   NB   DB   BNT
☐ Want   Orig. Ret. $6.00   **NB** $8   **MIB** Sec. Mkt. **$15**

QX 258-1   MOTHER & DAD   ☐
Comments: Bone China Bell, 3" tall, Dated Christmas 1984.
White bell has decal of Christmas design motifs.
☐ Purchased 19__Pd $_____MIB   NB   DB   BNT
☐ Want   Orig. Ret. $6.50   **NB** $15   **MIB** Sec. Mkt. **$20**

QX 407-7   MOUNTAIN CLIMBING SANTA   ☐
Comments: Handcrafted, 2-1/2" tall.
Reissued from 1983. **Artist:** Ed Seale
☐ Purchased 19__Pd $_____MIB   NB   DB   BNT
☐ Want   Orig. Ret. $6.50   **NB** $18   **MIB** Sec. Mkt. **$35**

QX 442-1   MUFFIN   ☐
Comments: Handcrafted, 2-3/4" tall.
Muffin, wearing her trademark red, knitted cap, holds a gift behind her back.   **Artist:** Donna Lee
☐ Purchased 19__Pd $_____MIB   NB   DB   BNT
☐ Want   Orig. Ret. $5.50   **NB** $20   **MIB** Sec. Mkt. **$25**

Most highways have three lanes... a left lane, a right lane and the lane you're trapped in when you finally find your exit.

QX 251-4   MUPPETS™, THE   ☐
Comments: Chrome Glass Ball, 2-7/8" dia.
Kermit dons a Santa cap to wish us "Hoppy, Hoppy Holidays!" as Miss Piggy says, "Merry Kissmas!" Both are framed in wreaths.
☐ Purchased 19__Pd $_____MIB   NB   DB   BNT
☐ Want   Orig. Ret. $4.50   **NB** $24   **MIB** Sec. Mkt. **$38**

QX 434-4   MUSICAL ANGEL   ☐
Comments: Handcrafted, 1-1/4" tall.
This cute little angel, caught up by the hem of her dress, is playing a tune on her brass horn. The banner hanging from her horn says "Noel."
Artist: Donna Lee
☐ Purchased 19__Pd $_____MIB   NB   DB   BNT
☐ Want   Orig. Ret. $5.50   **NB** $50   **MIB** Sec. Mkt. **$70**

QX 435-1   NAPPING MOUSE   ☐
Comments: Handcrafted, 1-3/4" tall.
Sleeping soundly in a walnut shell, a little white mouse holds tightly onto his "teddy mouse."
☐ Purchased 19__Pd $_____MIB   NB   DB   BNT
☐ Want   Orig. Ret. $5.50   **NB** $35   **MIB** Sec. Mkt. **$50**

QLX 700-1   NATIVITY   ☐
Comments: Lighted Panorama Ball, 3-1/2" dia.
A beautiful vision of Bethlehem at night as seen by the three wise men. Caption: "Christmas... Light Through The Darkness... Love Through The Ages." **Artist:** Ed Seale
☐ Purchased 19__Pd $_____MIB   NB   DB   BNT
☐ Want   Orig. Ret. $12.00   **NB** $15   **MIB** Sec. Mkt. **$25**

QX 459-4   NEEDLEPOINT WREATH   ☐
Comments: Needlepoint-Fabric, 3-1/2" dia.
Bright holiday poinsettias have been stitched into a lovely wreath.
Artist: Sharon Pike
☐ Purchased 19__Pd $_____MIB   NB   DB   BNT
☐ Want   Orig. Ret. $6.50   **NB** $8   **MIB** Sec. Mkt. **$15**

QX 245-4   NEW HOME   ☐
Comments: Pearl Blue Glass Ball, 2-7/8" dia., Dated 1984.
Village holiday snow scene. Caption: "Home Is Where The Heart Is And A New Home Always Seems The Happiest Of Places, For It Is Filled With All Your Dreams. Christmas 1984."
☐ Purchased 19__Pd $_____MIB   NB   DB   BNT
☐ Want   Orig. Ret. $4.50   **NB** $40   **MIB** Sec. Mkt. **$55**

QX 251-1   NORMAN ROCKWELL   ☐
Comments: Gold Glass Ball, 2-7/8" dia., Dated 1984.
Dickens' Christmas characters. "Good Friends, Good Times, Good Health, Good Cheer And Happy Holidays Throughout The Year." From the Norman Rockwell Collection 1984.
Artist: Diana McGehee
☐ Purchased 19__Pd $_____MIB   NB   DB   BNT
☐ Want   Orig. Ret. $4.50   **NB** $20   **MIB** Sec. Mkt. **$30**

QX 341-1   NORMAN ROCKWELL: CAUGHT NAPPING   ☐
Comments: **Fifth in Series,** Cameo, 3" dia., Dated 1984.
"Caught Napping, Fifth In A Series, The Norman Rockwell Collection, Christmas 1984." **Artist:** Diana McGehee
☐ Purchased 19__Pd $_____MIB   NB   DB   BNT
☐ Want   Orig. Ret. $7.50   **NB** $22   **MIB** Sec. Mkt. **$35**

QX 448-1   NOSTALGIC HOUSES AND SHOPS: VICTORIAN DOLLHOUSE   ☐
Comments: **FIRST IN SERIES,** Handcrafted, 3-1/4" tall.
Fully decorated interior is complete with wallpaper, furniture, Christmas tree and a miniature dollhouse. **Artist:** Donna Lee
☐ Purchased 19__Pd $_____MIB   NB   DB   BNT
☐ Want   Orig. Ret. $13.00 **NB** $150   **MIB** Sec. Mkt. **$180**

QX 442-4   NOSTALGIC SLED   ☐
Comments: Handcrafted, 3-1/2" wide, Reissued in 1985.
Classic-style sled with real string rope and metal runners. Caption: "Season's Greetings." **Artist:** Linda Sickman
☐ Purchased 19__Pd $_____MIB   NB   DB   BNT
☐ Want   Orig. Ret. $6.00   **NB** $10   **MIB** Sec. Mkt. **$20**

QX 346-4   OLD FASHIONED ROCKING HORSE   ☐
Comments: Brass, Acrylic, 3-1/4" dia.
A finely-etched brass rocking horse is embedded in acrylic.
☐ Purchased 19__Pd $_____MIB   NB   DB   BNT
☐ Want   Orig. Ret. $7.50   **NB** $12   **MIB** Sec. Mkt. **$20**

QX 341-4   PEACE ON EARTH   ☐
Comments: Red Oval Cameo, 3" tall.
A beautiful old-world ivory angel plays a harp.
Caption: "Peace On Earth."
☐ Purchased 19__Pd $_____MIB   NB   DB   BNT
☐ Want   Orig. Ret. $7.50   **NB** $14   **MIB** Sec. Mkt. **$30**

QX 252-1   PEANUTS®
Comments: Light Blue Soft-Sheen Satin Ball, 2-7/8" dia.
Dated 1984. Woodstock and his friends build a gallery of snowmen as Snoopy watches. His red banner says, "Merry Christmas."
☐ Purchased 19 __Pd $_____MIB   NB   DB   BNT
☐ Want   Orig. Ret. $4.50   **NB** $28   **MIB** Sec. Mkt. **$35**

QX 456-1   PEPPERMINT 1984
Comments: Handcrafted, 2-3/4" wide, Dated 1984.
The year 1984 is designed from peppermint candy. Two birds sit atop the "9." **Artist:** Donna Lee
☐ Purchased 19 __Pd $_____MIB   NB   DB   BNT
☐ Want   Orig. Ret. $4.50   **NB** $42   **MIB** Sec. Mkt. **$50**

QX 430-1   POLAR BEAR DRUMMER
Comments: Handcrafted, 2-1/4" tall.
A white polar bear plays his red drum. **Artist:** Ed Seale
☐ Purchased 19 __Pd $_____MIB   NB   DB   BNT
☐ Want   Orig. Ret. $4.50   **NB** $10   **MIB** Sec. Mkt. **$25**

QX 454-1   PORCELAIN BEAR
Comments: **Second in Series,** Porcelain, 2-1/2" tall.
Handpainted Cinnamon Bear holds a gold jingle bell with a red bow. Price dropped from '96.
☐ Purchased 19 __Pd $_____MIB   NB   DB   BNT
☐ Want   Orig. Ret. $7.00   **NB** $15   **MIB** Sec. Mkt. **$35**

QX 447-4   RACCOON'S CHRISTMAS
Comments: Handcrafted, 2-3/4" tall.
A raccoon and his neighbor have hung their Christmas stockings outside their "homes." **Artist:** Ed Seale
☐ Purchased 19 __Pd $_____MIB   NB   DB   BNT
☐ Want   Orig. Ret. $9.00   **NB** $35   **MIB** Sec. Mkt. **$48**

QX 254-4   REINDEER RACETRACK
Comments: Red Glass Ball, 3" dia.
The race has started and they're off! Santa shouts his encouragement from the stands: "On Comet! On Cupid! On Donder! On Blitzen!"
☐ Purchased 19 __Pd $_____MIB   NB   DB   BNT
☐ Want   Orig. Ret. $4.50   **NB** $14   **MIB** Sec. Mkt. **$22**

QX 435-4   ROCKING HORSE
Comments: **Fourth in Series,** Handcrafted, 4" wide.
Dated 1984. Blue and red saddle and rockers are a striking contrast to this black and white Appaloosa with gray mane and tail. Many sales to obtain this lower price compared to a year ago.
☐ Purchased 19 __Pd $_____MIB   NB   DB   BNT
☐ Want   Orig. Ret. $10.00   **NB** $40   **MIB** Sec. Mkt. **$65**

QX 457-1   ROLLER SKATING RABBIT
Comments: Handcrafted, 2-1/2" wide, Reissued in 1985.
A white bunny has snuggled down into a green and white roller skate boot for a fun ride. The red wheels really turn!
Artist: Ed Seale
☐ Purchased 19 __Pd $_____MIB   NB   DB   BNT
☐ Want   Orig. Ret. $5.00   **NB** $18   **MIB** Sec. Mkt. **$28**

QX 458-4   SANTA
Comments: Hand-embroidered Fabric, 4" tall.
Santa rides a reindeer over lush green hillsides filled with blooming flowers.
☐ Purchased 19 __Pd $_____MIB   NB   DB   BNT
☐ Want   Orig. Ret. $7.50   **NB** $10   **MIB** Sec. Mkt. **$18**

QX 433-4   SANTA MOUSE
Comments: Handcrafted, 2" tall.
A cute little mouse has dressed up as Santa, complete with a furry "beard." **Artist:** Bob Siedler
☐ Purchased 19 __Pd $_____MIB   NB   DB   BNT
☐ Want   Orig. Ret. $4.50   **NB** $30   **MIB** Sec. Mkt. **$45**

QX 450-4   SANTA STAR
Comments: Handcrafted, 3-1/2" tall.
Santa is designed in the shape of a five-pointed star!
☐ Purchased 19 __Pd $_____MIB   NB   DB   BNT
☐ Want   Orig. Ret. $5.50   **NB** $28   **MIB** Sec. Mkt. **$38**

QX 436-1   SANTA SULKY DRIVER
Comments: Etched Brass, 1-3/4" tall.
Santa races along in his brass sulky rig. A banner reads "Season's Greetings."
☐ Purchased 19 __Pd $_____MIB   NB   DB   BNT
☐ Want   Orig. Ret. $9.00   **NB** $18   **MIB** Sec. Mkt. **$25**

QLX 702-4 SANTA'S ARRIVAL ☐
Comments: Lighted Peek-Through Ball, 3-1/2" dia.
Santa looks through a bedroom window to see a small child sleeping soundly. **Artist:** Donna Lee
☐ Purchased 19___Pd $_____MIB NB DB BNT
☐ Want Orig. Ret. $13.00 **NB** $50 **MIB** Sec. Mkt. **$65**

QLX 700-4 SANTA'S WORKSHOP ☐
Comments: Lighted Peek-Through Ball, 3-1/2" dia.
Reissued in 1985. Looking through the window into Santa's workshop, one can see him giving a toy bunny to the rabbit visiting outside.
☐ Purchased 19___Pd $_____MIB NB DB BNT
☐ Want Orig. Ret. $13.00 **NB** $40 **MIB** Sec. Mkt. **$55**

QX 252-4 SHIRT TALES ☐
Comments: Aqua-Blue Satin Ball, 2-7/8" dia.
It's a snowball fight with all the Shirt-Tales joining in on the fun! Caption: "Joy Is In The Air, Good Time To Share – Christmas, Christmas Everywhere."
☐ Purchased 19___Pd $_____MIB NB DB BNT
☐ Want Orig. Ret. $4.50 **NB** $15 **MIB** Sec. Mkt. **$22**

QX 259-4 SISTER ☐
Comments: Bone China Bell, 3" tall, Dated Christmas 1984.
A basket of poinsettias are cheerful and bright against a dark blue background. Caption: "For A Wonderful Sister."
☐ Purchased 19___Pd $_____MIB NB DB BNT
☐ Want Orig. Ret. $6.50 **NB** $16 **MIB** Sec. Mkt. **$26**

QX 439-1 SNOOPY® & WOODSTOCK ☐
Comments: Handcrafted, 4-1/4" wide.
Snoopy and Woodstock take to the slopes in their matching blue and green caps. **Artist:** Ed Seale
☐ Purchased 19___Pd $_____MIB NB DB BNT
☐ Want Orig. Ret. $7.50 **NB** $65 **MIB** Sec. Mkt. **$90**

QX 431-4 SNOWMOBILE SANTA ☐
Comments: Handcrafted, 2-3/4" wide.
Santa enjoys himself in a shiny silver snowmobile.
☐ Purchased 19___Pd $_____MIB NB DB BNT
☐ Want Orig. Ret. $6.50 **NB** $20 **MIB** Sec. Mkt. **$35**

QX 453-1 SNOWSHOE PENGUIN ☐
Comments: Handcrafted, 3" tall.
Santa's neighbor has donned his snowshoes and is on his way to deliver a present.
Artist: Linda Sickman
☐ Purchased 19___Pd $_____MIB NB DB BNT
☐ Want Orig. Ret. $6.50 **NB** $35 **MIB** Sec. Mkt. **$45**

QX 450-1 SNOWY SEAL ☐
Comments: Handcrafted, 1-1/2" wide, Reissued in 1985.
Dressed in a red fabric ribbon, this flocked white seal is ready for Christmas. **Artist:** Ed Seale
☐ Purchased 19___Pd $_____MIB NB DB BNT
☐ Want Orig. Ret. $4.00 **NB** $10 **MIB** Sec. Mkt. **$22**

QX 243-4 SON ☐
Comments: White Glass Ball, 3" dia., Dated Christmas 1984.
Cute Christmas designs form letters to spell "Merry Christmas." Caption: "For A Wonderful Son."
☐ Purchased 19___Pd $_____MIB NB DB BNT
☐ Want Orig. Ret. $4.50 **NB** $16 **MIB** Sec. Mkt. **$28**

QLX 703-1 STAINED GLASS ☐
Comments: Lighted, Golden Classic Shape, 3-7/8" dia.
Old-fashioned stained glass design glows like a beautiful stained-glass window when lit.
☐ Purchased 19___Pd $_____MIB NB DB BNT
☐ Want Orig. Ret. $8.00 **NB** $12 **MIB** Sec. Mkt. **$18.50**

QLX 701-1 SUGARPLUM COTTAGE ☐
Comments: Lighted, Handcrafted, 3" tall.
Reissued in 1985 and 1986. Sugarcoated gumdrops, lollipops and peppermint candy canes... mmm' good!
☐ Purchased 19___Pd $_____MIB NB DB BNT
☐ Want Orig. Ret. $11.00 **NB** $30 **MIB** Sec. Mkt. **$45**

QX 249-1 TEACHER ☐
Comments: White Glass Ball, 3" dia., Dated 1984.
Elves deliver a large apple to the teacher. Caption: "Merry Christmas, Teacher."
☐ Purchased 19___Pd $_____MIB NB DB BNT
☐ Want Orig. Ret. $4.50 **NB** $7 **MIB** Sec. Mkt. **$15**

**Bumper sticker: Beware of sudden stops...
collector looking for Hallmark ornaments at garage sales!**

QX 258-4   TEN YEARS TOGETHER
Comments: Bone China Bell, 3" tall, Dated Christmas 1984.
A frosty blue winter scene inside an oval is featured on this lovely bell.
Caption: "Ten Years Together."
☐ Purchased 19 __Pd $_____MIB   NB   DB   BNT
☐ Want   Orig. Ret. $6.50   **NB** $10   **MIB** Sec. Mkt. **$23**

QX 430-4   THIMBLE: ANGEL
Comments: **Seventh in Series,** Handcrafted, 1-3/4" tall.
A cute little angel has caught a thimbleful of stars.
Artist: Bob Siedler
☐ Purchased 19 __Pd $_____MIB   NB   DB   BNT
☐ Want   Orig. Ret. $5.00   **NB** $40   **MIB** Sec. Mkt. **$55**

QX 431-1   THREE KITTENS IN A MITTEN
Comments: Handcrafted, 3-1/2" tall, Reissued in 1985.
Three little kittens are hanging out of a knitted red and green mitten.
Artist: Donna Lee
☐ Purchased 19 __Pd $_____MIB   NB   DB   BNT
☐ Want   Orig. Ret. $8.00   **NB** $30   **MIB** Sec. Mkt. **$45**

QX 440-4   TIN LOCOMOTIVE
Comments: **Third in Series,** Pressed Tin, 2-1/2" tall.
Dated 1984. Antique design locomotive has movable wheels in red,
blue, and steel. **Artist:** Linda Sickman
☐ Purchased 19 __Pd $_____MIB   NB   DB   BNT
☐ Want   Orig. Ret. $14.00   **NB** $55   **MIB** Sec. Mkt. **$80**

QX 415-9   TWELVE DAYS OF CHRISTMAS
Comments: Musical, Handcrafted, 3-3/4" tall.
Issued in 1983 as part of the Musical Decoration line, it was reintro-
duced in 1984 as part of the Keepsake line.
Artist: Ed Seale
☐ Purchased 19 __Pd $_____MIB   NB   DB   BNT
☐ Want   Orig. Ret. $15.00   **NB** $65   **MIB** Sec. Mkt. **$85**

QX 348-4   TWELVE DAYS OF CHRISTMAS
Comments: *FIRST IN SERIES,* Acrylic, 3" tall, Dated 1984.
Etched partridge in a pear tree. Gold foil lettering: "The Twelve Days
Of Christmas" and "... And A Partridge In A Pear Tree."
☐ Purchased 19 __Pd $_____MIB   NB   DB   BNT
☐ Want   Orig. Ret. $6.00   **NB** $245   **MIB** Sec. Mkt. **$275**

QX 259-1   TWENTY-FIVE YEARS TOGETHER
Comments: Bone China Bell, 3" tall, Dated Christmas 1984.
A gold and silver sleigh filled with gifts graces this bone china bell.
Caption: "Twenty-Five Years Together."
☐ Purchased 19 __Pd $_____MIB   NB   DB   BNT
☐ Want   Orig. Ret. $6.50   **NB** $14   **MIB** Sec. Mkt. **$22**

QX 449-1   UNCLE SAM
Comments: Pressed Tin, 5" tall, Dated 1984.
Uncle Sam is decked out in red, white, and blue holding a teddy bear.
Artist: Linda Sickman
☐ Purchased 19 __Pd $_____MIB   NB   DB   BNT
☐ Want   Orig. Ret. $6.00   **NB** $35   **MIB** Sec. Mkt. **$40**

QLX 702-1   VILLAGE CHURCH
Comments: Lighted, Handcrafted, 4-5/8" tall.
Reissued in 1985. The tall steeple of this clapboard village church is
topped with a gold cross. Holiday carolers may be seen through the
open door. **Artist:** Donna Lee
☐ Purchased 19 __Pd $_____MIB   NB   DB   BNT
☐ Want   Orig. Ret. $15.00   **NB** $40   **MIB** Sec. Mkt. **$55**

QX 905-1   WHITE CHRISTMAS
Comments: Musical, Classic Shape, 4-1/2" tall.
A busy city at Christmas time. Plays White Christmas.
Caption: "At Christmas Time, Love Shines In Every Smile, glows in
Every Heart."
☐ Purchased 19 __Pd $_____MIB   NB   DB   BNT
☐ Want   Orig. Ret. $16.00   **NB** $60   **MIB** Sec. Mkt. **$90**

QX 439-4   WOOD CHILDHOOD ORNAMENTS: LAMB
Comments: *FIRST IN SERIES,* Wood, Handcrafted, 2-1/4" tall.
A little wooden lamb has red wheels and a fabric bow around its neck.
☐ Purchased 19 __Pd $_____MIB   NB   DB   BNT
☐ Want   Orig. Ret. $6.50   **NB** $22   **MIB** Sec. Mkt. **$38**

Ruth Moody has been collecting items pertaining to the post office for over 21 years and has quite a tree to show off her efforts.

1985 Collection

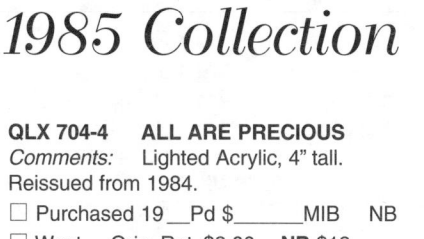

QLX 704-4   ALL ARE PRECIOUS
Comments: Lighted Acrylic, 4" tall.
Reissued from 1984.
☐ Purchased 19___ Pd $_____ MIB   NB   DB   BNT
☐ Want   Orig. Ret. $8.00   **NB** $18   **MIB** Sec. Mkt. **$25**

QX 377-2   ART MASTERPIECE
Comments: **Second in Series,** Bezeled Satin, 2-3/4" dia.
Caption: "Madonna of the Pomegranate (ca. 1487), The Uffizi Gallery, Florence, Italy." **Artist:** Diana McGehee
☐ Purchased 19___ Pd $_____ MIB   NB   DB   BNT
☐ Want   Orig. Ret. $6.75   **NB** $10   **MIB** Sec. Mkt. **$18**

QX 401-2   BABY LOCKET
Comments: Textured Brass, 2-1/4" dia.
Embossed toys and the word "Baby" decorate the locket. There is space for personalizing, as well as baby's photo.
Artist: Diana McGehee
☐ Purchased 19___ Pd $_____ MIB   NB   DB   BNT
☐ Want   Orig. Ret. $16.00   **NB** $15   **MIB** Sec. Mkt. **$22**

QX 370-2   BABY'S FIRST CHRISTMAS
Comments: Acrylic, 3-3/4" tall, Dated 1985.
Baby cup, filled with toys, carries the caption: "Baby's First Christmas."
Artist: Donna Lee
☐ Purchased 19___ Pd $_____ MIB   NB   DB   BNT
☐ Want   Orig. Ret. $5.75   **NB** $10   **MIB** Sec. Mkt. **$16**

QX 260-2   BABY'S FIRST CHRISTMAS
Comments: Green Soft-Sheen Satin Ball, 2-7/8" dia.
Dated 1985. Topped with a handcrafted mouse.
Caption: "A Baby Keeps The Season Bright And Warms The Heart With Sweet Delight. Baby's First Christmas."
☐ Purchased 19___ Pd $_____ MIB   NB   DB   BNT
☐ Want   Orig. Ret. $5.00   **NB** $14   **MIB** Sec. Mkt. **$22**

QX 478-2   BABY'S FIRST CHRISTMAS
Comments: Embroidered Fabric, 4-1/2" tall, Dated 1985.
Decorated with ribbon and lace, this hand embroidered tree says "Baby's First Christmas." **Artist:** LaDene Votruba
☐ Purchased 19___ Pd $_____ MIB   NB   DB   BNT
☐ Want   Orig. Ret. $7.00   **NB** $10   **MIB** Sec. Mkt. **$18**

QLX 700-5   BABY'S FIRST CHRISTMAS
Comments: Lighted, Handcrafted-Acrylic, 4" tall.
This cute carousel features teddy bears riding their frosted acrylic ponies. **Artist:** Ed Seale
☐ Purchased 19___ Pd $_____ MIB   NB   DB   BNT
☐ Want   Orig. Ret. $16.50   **NB** $30   **MIB** Sec. Mkt. **$42**

QX 499-5   BABY'S FIRST CHRISTMAS
Comments: Musical, Fabric, 3-1/4" tall, Dated 1985.
Embroidered satin baby block. Plays "Schubert's Lullaby."
Caption: "Baby's First Christmas."
☐ Purchased 19___ Pd $_____ MIB   NB   DB   BNT
☐ Want   Orig. Ret. $16.00   **NB** $30   **MIB** Sec. Mkt. **$42**

QX 499-2   BABY'S FIRST CHRISTMAS
Comments: Handcrafted, 3-3/4" tall, Dated 1985.
"Baby's First Christmas" is delightful in a rattan look stroller with lace trim and a red bow.
☐ Purchased 19___ Pd $_____ MIB   NB   DB   BNT
☐ Want   Orig. Ret. $15.00   **NB** $38   **MIB** Sec. Mkt. **$52**

QX 478-5   BABY'S SECOND CHRISTMAS
Comments: Handcrafted, 3-1/2' tall, Dated 1985.
Brown teddy in yellow t-shirt is riding his stick horse. Caption: "Baby's Second Christmas."
☐ Purchased 19___ Pd $_____ MIB   NB   DB   BNT
☐ Want   Orig. Ret. $6.00   **NB** $22   **MIB** Sec. Mkt. **$35**

QX 264-2   BABY-SITTER
Comments: Green Glass Ball, 3" dia., Dated 1985.
Panda bears are preparing for Christmas. Caption: "A Baby-Sitter Is A Special Kind Of Friend. Christmas 1985." **Artist:** Michele Pyda-Sevcik
☐ Purchased 19___ Pd $_____ MIB   NB   DB   BNT
☐ Want   Orig. Ret. $4.75   **NB** $5   **MIB** Sec. Mkt. **$12**

QX 491-2   BAKER ELF
Comments: Handcrafted, 3" tall, Dated 1985.
A cute elf uses red and green "icing" to decorate the bell-shaped cookie he has baked. **Artist:** Ed Seale
☐ Purchased 19___ Pd $_____ MIB   NB   DB   BNT
☐ Want   Orig. Ret. $5.75   **NB** $20   **MIB** Sec. Mkt. **$30**

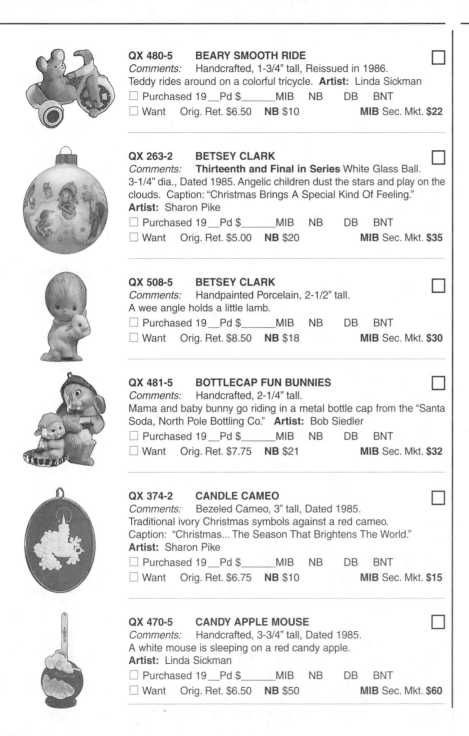

QX 480-5   BEARY SMOOTH RIDE ☐
Comments: Handcrafted, 1-3/4" tall, Reissued in 1986.
Teddy rides around on a colorful tricycle. **Artist:** Linda Sickman
☐ Purchased 19__ Pd $_____ MIB   NB   DB   BNT
☐ Want   Orig. Ret. $6.50   **NB** $10   **MIB** Sec. Mkt. **$22**

QX 263-2   BETSEY CLARK ☐
Comments: **Thirteenth and Final in Series** White Glass Ball.
3-1/4" dia., Dated 1985. Angelic children dust the stars and play on the clouds. Caption: "Christmas Brings A Special Kind Of Feeling."
Artist: Sharon Pike
☐ Purchased 19__ Pd $_____ MIB   NB   DB   BNT
☐ Want   Orig. Ret. $5.00   **NB** $20   **MIB** Sec. Mkt. **$35**

QX 508-5   BETSEY CLARK ☐
Comments: Handpainted Porcelain, 2-1/2" tall.
A wee angle holds a little lamb.
☐ Purchased 19__ Pd $_____ MIB   NB   DB   BNT
☐ Want   Orig. Ret. $8.50   **NB** $18   **MIB** Sec. Mkt. **$30**

QX 481-5   BOTTLECAP FUN BUNNIES ☐
Comments: Handcrafted, 2-1/4" tall.
Mama and baby bunny go riding in a metal bottle cap from the "Santa Soda, North Pole Bottling Co." **Artist:** Bob Siedler
☐ Purchased 19__ Pd $_____ MIB   NB   DB   BNT
☐ Want   Orig. Ret. $7.75   **NB** $21   **MIB** Sec. Mkt. **$32**

QX 374-2   CANDLE CAMEO ☐
Comments: Bezeled Cameo, 3" tall, Dated 1985.
Traditional ivory Christmas symbols against a red cameo.
Caption: "Christmas... The Season That Brightens The World."
Artist: Sharon Pike
☐ Purchased 19__ Pd $_____ MIB   NB   DB   BNT
☐ Want   Orig. Ret. $6.75   **NB** $10   **MIB** Sec. Mkt. **$15**

QX 470-5   CANDY APPLE MOUSE ☐
Comments: Handcrafted, 3-3/4" tall, Dated 1985.
A white mouse is sleeping on a red candy apple.
Artist: Linda Sickman
☐ Purchased 19__ Pd $_____ MIB   NB   DB   BNT
☐ Want   Orig. Ret. $6.50   **NB** $50   **MIB** Sec. Mkt. **$60**

QX 512-5   CHARMING ANGEL: HEIRLOOM COLLECTION ☐
Comments: Fabric, 3-3/4" tall.
This angel has yarn hair, sheer net wings and is wearing a hand-sewn lace dress. **Artist:** Michele Pyda-Sevcik
☐ Purchased 19__ Pd $_____ MIB   NB   DB   BNT
☐ Want   Orig. Ret. $9.75   **NB** $14   **MIB** Sec. Mkt. **$24**

QX 475-5   CHILD'S THIRD CHRISTMAS ☐
Comments: Handcrafted, 2-1/4" tall, Dated 1985.
A red and white sneaker with green laces holds a brown teddy bear.
Caption: "A Child's Third Christmas '85."
Artist: Ed Seale
☐ Purchased 19__ Pd $_____ MIB   NB   DB   BNT
☐ Want   Orig. Ret. $6.00   **NB** $18   **MIB** Sec. Mkt. **$33**

QX 490-5   CHILDREN IN THE SHOE ☐
Comments: Handcrafted, 3-1/4" tall.
This old shoe with a snow-capped roof has children everywhere depicting the nursery rhyme. **Artist:** Ed Seale
☐ Purchased 19__ Pd $_____ MIB   NB   DB   BNT
☐ Want   Orig. Ret. $9.50   **NB** $28   **MIB** Sec. Mkt. **$40**

QLX 703-2   CHRIS MOUSE ☐
Comments: **FIRST IN SERIES,** Lighted, 3-7/8" tall, Dated 1985.
This ornament attaches to the tree with a clip and shows Chris, dressed for bed, sitting in the base of a candle, reading a story.
Artist: Bob Siedler
☐ Purchased 19__ Pd $_____ MIB   NB   DB   BNT
☐ Want   Orig. Ret. $12.50   **NB-P** $45   **MIB** Sec. Mkt. **$75-80**

QLX 710-5   CHRISTMAS EVE VISIT ☐
Comments: Lighted, Etched Brass, 2" tall.
Santa and his reindeer make their rounds on Christmas Eve. First stop – a brightly lit house.
☐ Purchased 19__ Pd $_____ MIB   NB   DB   BNT
☐ Want   Orig. Ret. $12.00   **NB** $15   **MIB** Sec. Mkt. **$28**

QX 507-5   CHRISTMAS TREATS ☐
Comments: Bezeled Glass, 3-1/4" tall.
Colorful candy canes and Christmas candies on white creates a stained glass effect.
☐ Purchased 19__ Pd $_____ MIB   NB   DB   BNT
☐ Want   Orig. Ret. $5.50   **NB** $10   **MIB** Sec. Mkt. **$17**

QX 471-5   CLOTHESPIN SOLDIER: SCOTTISH   ☐
Comments: **Fourth in Series,** Handcrafted, 2-1/2" tall.
The Scottish Highlander is dressed in a colorful fabric kilt with a blue pom-pom on his red tam. **Artist:** Linda Sickman

☐ Purchased 19__Pd $_____MIB   NB   DB   BNT
☐ Want   Orig. Ret. $5.50   **NB** $17   **MIB** Sec. Mkt. **$24**

QX 518-5   COUNTRY GOOSE   ☐
Comments: Wood, 3" dia.
A goose with a Christmas wreath around its neck graces this wood ornament. Caption: "This Original Design, Styled In The American Country Tradition, Has Been Printed On Hardwood."
Artist: Michele Pyda-Sevcik

☐ Purchased 19__Pd $_____MIB   NB   DB   BNT
☐ Want   Orig. Ret. $7.75   **NB** $8   **MIB** Sec. Mkt. **$12**

QX 477-2   DAPPER PENGUIN   ☐
Comments: Handcrafted, 2-1/4" tall.
This cute little fellow is all decked out with a red top hat, green bow tie and gold cane. **Artist:** Ed Seale

☐ Purchased 19__Pd $_____MIB   NB   DB   BNT
☐ Want   Orig. Ret. $5.00   **NB** $16   **MIB** Sec. Mkt. **$28**

QX 503-2   DAUGHTER   ☐
Comments: Wood, 3-1/4" dia., Dated Christmas 1985.
"Silk-screened" design in an embroidery hoop. Caption: "A Daughter Decorates The Holidays With Love."

☐ Purchased 19__Pd $_____MIB   NB   DB   BNT
☐ Want   Orig. Ret. $5.50   **NB** $8   **MIB** Sec. Mkt. **$14**

QX 271-2   DISNEY® CHRISTMAS   ☐
Comments: Pearl Blue Glass, 3" dia., Dated 1985.
Mice hang their stockings for Christmas as Mickey dons a Santa suit.

☐ Purchased 19__Pd $_____MIB   NB   DB   BNT
☐ Want   Orig. Ret. $4.75   **NB** $15   **MIB** Sec. Mkt. **$23**

QX 481-2   DO NOT DISTURB BEAR   ☐
Comments: Handcrafted, 3" wide, Reissued in 1986.
A flocked bear snoozes comfortably in his hollow log with his "Do Not Disturb 'Til Christmas" sign. **Artist:** Ed Seale

☐ Purchased 19__Pd $_____MIB   NB   DB   BNT
☐ Want   Orig. Ret. $7.75   **NB** $18   **MIB** Sec. Mkt. **$25**

QX 474-2   DOGGY IN A STOCKING   ☐
Comments: Handcrafted, 3" tall.
A cute tan terrier is poking his head out of the red and green striped stocking.

☐ Purchased 19__Pd $_____MIB   NB   DB   BNT
☐ Want   Orig. Ret. $5.50   **NB** $20   **MIB** Sec. Mkt. **$35**

QX 473-5   ENGINEERING MOUSE   ☐
Comments: Handcrafted, 2" tall.
Designed to look like a windup toy, a little white mouse engineers a red and green locomotive. **Artist:** Bob Siedler

☐ Purchased 19__Pd $_____MIB   NB   DB   BNT
☐ Want   Orig. Ret. $5.50   **NB** $12   **MIB** Sec. Mkt. **$21**

QX 376-2   FATHER   ☐
Comments: Wood, 3" dia., Dated Christmas 1985.
Printed on wood to resemble hand painting is an old-fashioned sleigh filled with gifts and a Christmas tree. Caption: "A Father Sees Through The Eyes Of Love And Listens With His Heart."
Artist: LaDene Votruba

☐ Purchased 19__Pd $_____MIB   NB   DB   BNT
☐ Want   Orig. Ret. $6.50   **NB** $2   **MIB** Sec. Mkt. **$10**

QX 370-5   FIRST CHRISTMAS TOGETHER   ☐
Comments: Acrylic, 3-1/2" wide, Dated 1985.
Doves carry a banner with the caption: "First Christmas Together." Framed in brass.

☐ Purchased 19__Pd $_____MIB   NB   DB   BNT
☐ Want   Orig. Ret. $6.75   **NB** $5   **MIB** Sec. Mkt. **$16**

QX 261-2   FIRST CHRISTMAS TOGETHER   ☐
Comments: Lt. Blue Glass Ball, 2-7/8" dia., Dated 1985.
Silhouettes of a couple at Christmas are shown in heart frames tied with red ribbons. Caption: "Love Is A Gift From Heart To Heart. First Christmas Together."

☐ Purchased 19__Pd $_____MIB   NB   DB   BNT
☐ Want   Orig. Ret. $4.75   **NB** $10   **MIB** Sec. Mkt. **$22**

QX 507-2   FIRST CHRISTMAS TOGETHER   ☐
Comments: Fabric and Wood, 2-1/2" tall, Dated 1985.
Red and white hearts are woven in a wooden frame.
Caption: "First Christmas Together."

☐ Purchased 19__Pd $_____MIB   NB   DB   BNT
☐ Want   Orig. Ret. $8.00   **NB** $6   **MIB** Sec. Mkt. **$12**

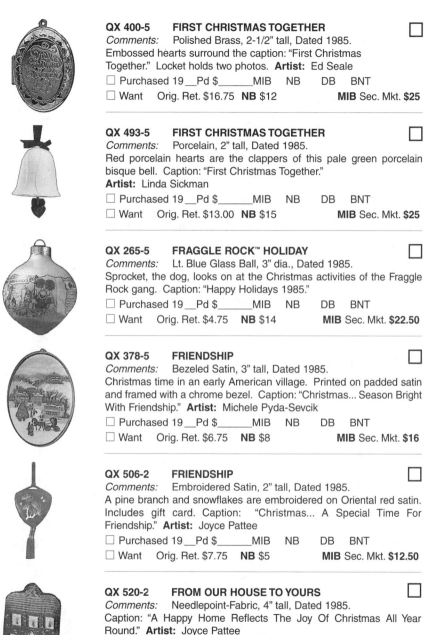

QX 400-5   FIRST CHRISTMAS TOGETHER ☐
Comments: Polished Brass, 2-1/2" tall, Dated 1985.
Embossed hearts surround the caption: "First Christmas
Together." Locket holds two photos. **Artist:** Ed Seale

☐ Purchased 19___Pd $_____MIB   NB   DB   BNT
☐ Want   Orig. Ret. $16.75 **NB** $12   **MIB** Sec. Mkt. **$25**

QX 493-5   FIRST CHRISTMAS TOGETHER ☐
Comments: Porcelain, 2" tall, Dated 1985.
Red porcelain hearts are the clappers of this pale green porcelain
bisque bell. Caption: "First Christmas Together."
Artist: Linda Sickman

☐ Purchased 19___Pd $_____MIB   NB   DB   BNT
☐ Want   Orig. Ret. $13.00 **NB** $15   **MIB** Sec. Mkt. **$25**

QX 265-5   FRAGGLE ROCK™ HOLIDAY ☐
Comments: Lt. Blue Glass Ball, 3" dia., Dated 1985.
Sprocket, the dog, looks on at the Christmas activities of the Fraggle
Rock gang. Caption: "Happy Holidays 1985."

☐ Purchased 19___Pd $_____MIB   NB   DB   BNT
☐ Want   Orig. Ret. $4.75 **NB** $14   **MIB** Sec. Mkt. **$22.50**

QX 378-5   FRIENDSHIP ☐
Comments: Bezeled Satin, 3" tall, Dated 1985.
Christmas time in an early American village. Printed on padded satin
and framed with a chrome bezel. Caption: "Christmas... Season Bright
With Friendship." **Artist:** Michele Pyda-Sevcik

☐ Purchased 19___Pd $_____MIB   NB   DB   BNT
☐ Want   Orig. Ret. $6.75 **NB** $8   **MIB** Sec. Mkt. **$16**

QX 506-2   FRIENDSHIP ☐
Comments: Embroidered Satin, 2" tall, Dated 1985.
A pine branch and snowflakes are embroidered on Oriental red satin.
Includes gift card. Caption: "Christmas... A Special Time For
Friendship." **Artist:** Joyce Pattee

☐ Purchased 19___Pd $_____MIB   NB   DB   BNT
☐ Want   Orig. Ret. $7.75 **NB** $5   **MIB** Sec. Mkt. **$12.50**

QX 520-2   FROM OUR HOUSE TO YOURS ☐
Comments: Needlepoint-Fabric, 4" tall, Dated 1985.
Caption: "A Happy Home Reflects The Joy Of Christmas All Year
Round." **Artist:** Joyce Pattee

☐ Purchased 19___Pd $_____MIB   NB   DB   BNT
☐ Want   Orig. Ret. $7.75 **NB** $3   **MIB** Sec. Mkt. **$10**

QX 482-2   FROSTY FRIENDS ☐
Comments: **Sixth in Series,** Handcrafted, 2" tall, Dated 1985.
The little Eskimo and friend are paddling a red dated kayak.
Artist: Ed Seale

☐ Purchased 19___Pd $_____MIB   NB   DB   BNT
☐ Want   Orig. Ret. $8.50 **NB** $50   **MIB** Sec. Mkt. **$62**

QX 380-2   GODCHILD ☐
Comments: Bezeled Satin, 2-3/4" dia., Dated Christmas 1985.
From Hallmark's Antique Greeting Card Collection. Caption: "A
Godchild Is A Loving Gift To Treasure Through The Years."
Artist: Diana McGehee

☐ Purchased 19___Pd $_____MIB   NB   DB   BNT
☐ Want   Orig. Ret. $6.75 **NB** $4   **MIB** Sec. Mkt. **$12**

QX 265-2   GOOD FRIENDS ☐
Comments: White Frosted Glass, 3" dia., Dated 1985.
Penguins play in the snow. Caption: "Good Times With Good Friends
Make Life's Merriest Moments."

☐ Purchased 19___Pd $_____MIB   NB   DB   BNT
☐ Want   Orig. Ret. $4.75 **NB** $14   **MIB** Sec. Mkt. **$25**

QX 260-5   GRANDCHILD'S FIRST CHRISTMAS ☐
Comments: Ecru Satin Ball, 2-7/8" dia., Dated 1985.
Elves keep busy making Christmas toys, while Santa holds a baby on
his lap. Handcrafted mouse sits at the top of the ornament. Caption:
"Baby's First Christmas."

☐ Purchased 19___Pd $_____MIB   NB   DB   BNT
☐ Want   Orig. Ret. $5.00 **NB** $8   **MIB** Sec. Mkt. **$15**

QX 495-5   GRANDCHILD'S FIRST CHRISTMAS ☐
Comments: Handcrafted, 3-1/4" tall, Dated 1985.
White knitted baby bootie holds baby's block and other toys. Caption:
"Baby's First Christmas." **Artist:** LaDene Votruba

☐ Purchased 19___Pd $_____MIB   NB   DB   BNT
☐ Want   Orig. Ret. $11.00 **NB** $10   **MIB** Sec. Mkt. **$20**

QX 263-5   GRANDDAUGHTER ☐
Comments: Ivory Glass Ball, 2-7/8" dia., Dated 1985.
Caption: "There's Nothing Like A Granddaughter To Warm The World At
Christmas."

☐ Purchased 19___Pd $_____MIB   NB   DB   BNT
☐ Want   Orig. Ret. $4.75 **NB** $14   **MIB** Sec. Mkt. **$27.50**

QX 262-5 GRANDMOTHER

Comments: Red Glass Ball, 3" dia., Dated Christmas 1985.
Floral design and scroll banner decorate this red transparent ball.
Caption: "A Grandmother Gives The Gift Of Love."
Artist: Joyce Pattee

☐ Purchased 19___Pd $_____MIB   NB   DB   BNT
☐ Want   Orig. Ret. $4.75   **NB** $8   **MIB** Sec. Mkt. **$20**

QX 380-5 GRANDPARENTS

Comments: Bezeled Lacquer-Look, 2-3/4" wide, Dated 1985.
A white poinsettia against a red background is framed in brass and
accented with gold. Caption: "Grandparents Have Beautiful Ways Of
Adding Love To The Holidays. Christmas 1985."
Artist: Sharon Pike

☐ Purchased 19___Pd $_____MIB   NB   DB   BNT
☐ Want   Orig. Ret. $7.00   **NB** $2   **MIB** Sec. Mkt. **$8**

QX 262-2 GRANDSON

Comments: Green Glass Ball, 2-7/8" dia., Dated 1985.
A bright red, green and yellow train circles the ball. Caption: "A
Grandson Makes Holiday Joys Shine Even Brighter! Christmas 1985."
Artist: LaDene Votruba

☐ Purchased 19___Pd $_____MIB   NB   DB   BNT
☐ Want   Orig. Ret. $4.75   **NB** $18   **MIB** Sec. Mkt. **$30**

QX 378-2 HEART FULL OF LOVE

Comments: Bezeled Satin, 3" tall, Dated Christmas 1985.
Winter scene is framed with a chrome ring. Caption: "The World Is Full
Of Beauty When Hearts Are Full Of Love."

☐ Purchased 19___Pd $_____MIB   NB   DB   BNT
☐ Want   Orig. Ret. $6.75   **NB** $6   **MIB** Sec. Mkt. **$16**

QX 405-2 HEAVENLY TRUMPETER

Comments: Porcelain, 5" tall, Limited Edition of 24,700.
Comes with a wooden display stand. A handpainted porcelain angel
plays her golden trumpet.

☐ Purchased 19___Pd $_____MIB   NB   DB   BNT
☐ Want   Orig. Ret. $27.50   **NB** $65   **MIB** Sec. Mkt. **$95**

QX 496-5 HERE COMES SANTA: SANTA'S FIRE ENGINE

Comments: **Seventh in Series,** Handcrafted, 3" tall.
Dated 1985. Santa's Fire Engine from the "North Pole Fire
Department" has Santa in the driver's seat once again.
Artist: Linda Sickman

☐ Purchased 19___Pd $_____MIB   NB   DB   BNT
☐ Want   Orig. Ret. $14.00   **NB** $45   **MIB** Sec. Mkt. **$57.50**

QX 498-2 HOLIDAY HEART

Comments: Porcelain, 2" tall.
Christmas greenery decorates a white porcelain puffed heart. Caption:
"Love."

☐ Purchased 19___Pd $_____MIB   NB   DB   BNT
☐ Want   Orig. Ret. $8.00   **NB** $14   **MIB** Sec. Mkt. **$25**

QX 376-5 HOLIDAY WILDLIFE: PARTRIDGE

Comments: **Fourth in Series,** Wood, 3" dia.
Caption: "California Partridge, Lophortyx Californica, Fourth in a
Series, Wildlife Collection, Christmas 1985."

☐ Purchased 19___Pd $_____MIB   NB   DB   BNT
☐ Want   Orig. Ret. $7.50   **NB** $16   **MIB** Sec. Mkt. **$25**

QX 271-5 HUGGA BUNCH™

Comments: Lt. Blue Glass Ball, 2-7/8" dia.
Children share hugs and fun as they decorate the house for Christmas.
Caption: "Huggy Holidays!"

☐ Purchased 19___Pd $_____MIB   NB   DB   BNT
☐ Want   Orig. Ret. $5.00   **NB** $12   **MIB** Sec. Mkt. **$28**

QX 476-5 ICE-SKATING OWL

Comments: Handcrafted, 2" tall.
A white owl with a red and white hat, tries out his ice skates.
Artist: Bob Siedler

☐ Purchased 19___Pd $_____MIB   NB   DB   BNT
☐ Want   Orig. Ret. $5.00   **NB** $12   **MIB** Sec. Mkt. **$20**

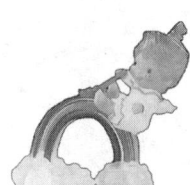

QLX 710-2 KATYBETH

Comments: Lighted, Handcrafted-Acrylic, 3-5/8" tall.
Katybeth is busy painting the rainbow on which she is sitting. The
rainbow and clouds light up.

☐ Purchased 19___Pd $_____MIB   NB   DB   BNT
☐ Want   Orig. Ret. $10.75   **NB** $25   **MIB** Sec. Mkt. **$40**

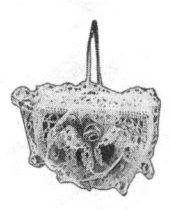

QX 514-5 KEEPSAKE BASKET: HEIRLOOM COLLECTION

Comments: Fabric, 2-1/2" tall.
A rose-scented sachet is enclosed in a hand-crocheted basket trimmed
with satin and lace. **Artist:** Sharon Pike

☐ Purchased 19___Pd $_____MIB   NB   DB   BNT
☐ Want   Orig. Ret. $15.00   **NB** $10   **MIB** Sec. Mkt. **$19**

QX 484-5   KIT THE SHEPHERD ☐
Comments: Handcrafted, 2-1/2" tall.
Kit has traded in his green cap for a shepherd's headdress for the Christmas play. **Artist:** Bob Siedler

☐ Purchased 19 __ Pd $_____ MIB   NB   DB   BNT
☐ Want   Orig. Ret. $5.75   **NB** $15   **MIB** Sec. Mkt. **$25**

QX 474-5   KITTY MISCHIEF ☐
Comments: Handcrafted, 2" tall, Reissued in 1986.
A ball of real yarn is used with this yellow and white kitten.
Artist: Peter Dutkin

☐ Purchased 19 __ Pd $_____ MIB   NB   DB   BNT
☐ Want   Orig. Ret. $5.00   **NB** $12   **MIB** Sec. Mkt. **$20**

QX 511-2   LACY HEART: HEIRLOOM COLLECTION ☐
Comments: Fabric, 3" tall.
A padded white satin heart is trimmed with lace.
Scented with a rose sachet.

☐ Purchased 19 __ Pd $_____ MIB   NB   DB   BNT
☐ Want   Orig. Ret. $8.75   **NB** $10   **MIB** Sec. Mkt. **$24**

QX 480-2   LAMB IN LEGWARMERS ☐
Comments: Handcrafted, 3" tall.
Green, red and white crocheted legwarmers keep this little flocked lamb warm and cozy.

☐ Purchased 19 __ Pd $_____ MIB   NB   DB   BNT
☐ Want   Orig. Ret. $7.00   **NB** $12.50   **MIB** Sec. Mkt. **$22**

QLX 711-2   LITTLE RED SCHOOLHOUSE ☐
Comments: Lighted, Handcrafted 2-5/8" tall.
Inside, three parents watch the children perform in a school Christmas pageant. There is a great amount of detail on this ornament.
Artist: Donna Lee

☐ Purchased 19 __ Pd $_____ MIB   NB   DB   BNT
☐ Want   Orig. Ret. $15.75   **NB** $75   **MIB** Sec. Mkt. **$80**

QX 371-5   LOVE AT CHRISTMAS ☐
Comments: Acrylic, 3-1/4" wide.
This acrylic heart is raining red foil hearts. Caption: "The Spirit Of Christmas Is Love." **Artist:** Diana McGehee

☐ Purchased 19 __ Pd $_____ MIB   NB   DB   BNT
☐ Want   Orig. Ret. $5.75   **NB** $25   **MIB** Sec. Mkt. **$38**

QLX 702-5   LOVE WREATH ☐
Comments: Lighted, Acrylic, 3-1/2" tall.
A wreath, hearts and ribbon is etched in clear acrylic. Caption: "Christmas Happens In The Heart." **Artist:** LaDene Votruba

☐ Purchased 19 __ Pd $_____ MIB   NB   DB   BNT
☐ Want   Orig. Ret. $8.50   **NB** $20   **MIB** Sec. Mkt. **$28**

QX 403-2   MERRY MOUSE ☐
Comments: Handcrafted, 2-1/2" tall, Reissued in 1986.
This happy little fellow wears a Santa hat. His tail is made of leather.
Artist: Peter Dutkin

☐ Purchased 19 __ Pd $_____ MIB   NB   DB   BNT
☐ Want   Orig. Ret. $4.50   **NB** $15   **MIB** Sec. Mkt. **$25**

QX 267-2   MERRY SHIRT TALES™ ☐
Comments: Lt. Blue Glass, 3" dia., Dated Christmas 1985.
The Shirt Tales gang is sledding, skating and skiing. Caption: "Every Day's A Holiday When Good Friends Get Together."

☐ Purchased 19 __ Pd $_____ MIB   NB   DB   BNT
☐ Want   Orig. Ret. $4.75   **NB** $14   **MIB** Sec. Mkt. **$21**

QX 482-5   MINIATURE CRECHE ☐
Comments: ***FIRST IN SERIES,*** Wood and Straw, 3-1/2" tall.
Wooden figures of the Holy Family grace the straw "stable."
Price down from last guide. **Artist:** Ed Seale

☐ Purchased 19 __ Pd $_____ MIB   NB   DB   BNT
☐ Want   Orig. Ret. $8.75   **NB** $10   **MIB** Sec. Mkt. **$25**

QX 372-2   MOTHER ☐
Comments: Acrylic, 3-3/8" tall, Dated Christmas 1985.
Acrylic teardrop framed in gold, has a caption which reads: "Mother Is The Heart Of Our Happiest Holiday Memories."
Artist: Sharon Pike

☐ Purchased 19 __ Pd $_____ MIB   NB   DB   BNT
☐ Want   Orig. Ret. $6.75   **NB** $6   **MIB** Sec. Mkt. **$10**

QX 509-2   MOTHER & DAD ☐
Comments: Porcelain Bell, 3" tall, Dated Christmas 1985.
White porcelain bell has a bas relief paisley design. Caption in soft blue: "Mother And Dad." **Artist:** LaDene Votruba

☐ Purchased 19 __ Pd $_____ MIB   NB   DB   BNT
☐ Want   Orig. Ret. $7.75   **NB** $10   **MIB** Sec. Mkt. **$18**

QX 476-2   MOUSE WAGON ☐
Comments: Handcrafted, 2" tall, Dated 1985.
Little white mouse rides his little red wagon bearing a gift of cheese.
☐ Purchased 19 __Pd $_____MIB   NB   DB   BNT
☐ Want   Orig. Ret. $5.75   **NB** $45   **MIB** Sec. Mkt. **$65**

QLX 705-2   MR. AND MRS. SANTA ☐
Comments: Lighted, Handcrafted, 3" tall, Reissued in 1986.
Mrs. Santa decorates her Christmas tree while Santa waves to people passing by. Price lower than last year.
☐ Purchased 19 __Pd $_____MIB   NB   DB   BNT
☐ Want   Orig. Ret. $14.50   **NB** $45   **MIB** Sec. Mkt. **$75**

QX 483-5   MUFFIN THE ANGEL ☐
Comments: Handcrafted, 2-1/2" tall.
Muffin is dressed as an angel and is ready for the Christmas play.
Artist: Bob Siedler
☐ Purchased 19 __Pd $_____MIB   NB   DB   BNT
☐ Want   Orig. Ret. $5.75   **NB** $16   **MIB** Sec. Mkt. **$24**

QLX 700-1   NATIVITY ☐
Comments: Lighted Panorama Ball, 3-1/2" dia.
Reissued from 1984. **Artist:** Ed Seale
☐ Purchased 19 __Pd $_____MIB   NB   DB   BNT
☐ Want   Orig. Ret. $12.00   **NB** $20   **MIB** Sec. Mkt. **$32**

QX 264-5   NATIVITY SCENE ☐
Comments: Lt. Blue Glass Ball, 3" dia., Dated Christmas 1985.
Hard to Find! Little angels welcome the Christ Child. Caption:
"O Come, All Ye Faithful... Christmas 1985."
☐ Purchased 19 __Pd $_____MIB   NB   DB   BNT
☐ Want   Orig. Ret. $4.75   **NB** $12   **MIB** Sec. Mkt. **$30**

QX 269-5   NEW HOME ☐
Comments: Blue Glass Ball, 3" dia., Dated Christmas 1985.
Victorian homes, decorated for Christmas, circle this blue tear-drop ball. Caption: "New Home, New Joys, New Memories To Cherish."
Artist: Michele Pyda-Sevcik
☐ Purchased 19 __Pd $_____MIB   NB   DB   BNT
☐ Want   Orig. Ret. $4.75   **NB** $9   **MIB** Sec. Mkt. **$30**

QX 520-5   NIECE ☐
Comments: Acrylic, 3-3/4" tall, Dated Christmas 1985.
Caption stamped in silver foil on teardrop shape: "A Niece Fills Hearts With A Special Kind Of Love."
☐ Purchased 19 __Pd $_____MIB   NB   DB   BNT
☐ Want   Orig. Ret. $5.75   **NB** $5   **MIB** Sec. Mkt. **$8**

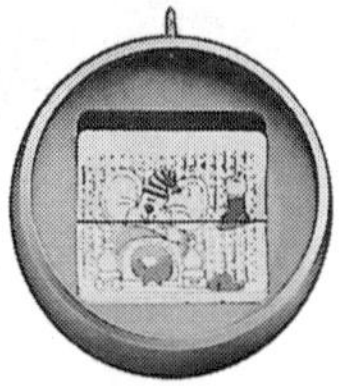

QX 449-4   NIGHT BEFORE CHRISTMAS ☐
Comments: Panorama Ball, 3-1/4" dia.
Push the button and the pages of this favorite Christmas story flip over (30 pages). Comes with special stand for off-tree display.
Artist: Ed Seale
☐ Purchased 19 __Pd $_____MIB   NB   DB   BNT
☐ Want   Orig. Ret. $13.00   **NB** $28   **MIB** Sec. Mkt. **$38**

QX 266-2   NORMAN ROCKWELL ☐
Comments: White Glass Ball, 2-7/8" dia., Dated 1985.
Caption: "... He Was Chubby And Plump, A Right Jolly Old Elf, And I Laughed When I Saw Him, In Spite Of Myself... C.C. Moore From the Norman Rockwell Collection 1985."
Artist: Diana McGehee
☐ Purchased 19 __Pd $_____MIB   NB   DB   BNT
☐ Want   Orig. Ret. $4.75   **NB** $15   **MIB** Sec. Mkt. **$25**

QX 374-5   NORMAN ROCKWELL: JOLLY POSTMAN ☐
Comments: **Sixth in Series,** Light Green Cameo, 3" dia.
Dated 1985. Caption: "Jolly Postman, Sixth In A Series, Christmas 1985, The Norman Rockwell Collection."
Artist: Diana McGehee
☐ Purchased 19 __Pd $_____MIB   NB   DB   BNT
☐ Want   Orig. Ret. $7.50   **NB** $10   **MIB** Sec. Mkt. **$30**

QX 497-5   NOSTALGIC HOUSES AND SHOPS: TOY SHOP ☐
Comments: **Second in Series,** Handcrafted, 2-1/2" tall.
Dated 1985. This Old-Fashioned Toy Shop boasts a counter, cash register, dollhouse and toy truck downstairs and the owner's furnished apartment upstairs.
Artist: Donna Lee
☐ Purchased 19 __Pd $_____MIB   NB   DB   BNT
☐ Want   Orig. Ret. $13.75   **NB** $85   **MIB** Sec. Mkt. **$110**

QX 442-4   NOSTALGIC SLED ☐
Comments: Handcrafted, 3-1/2" wide.
Reissued from 1984. **Artist:** Linda Sickman
☐ Purchased 19 __Pd $_____MIB   NB   DB   BNT
☐ Want   Orig. Ret. $6.00   **NB** $12   **MIB** Sec. Mkt. **$28**

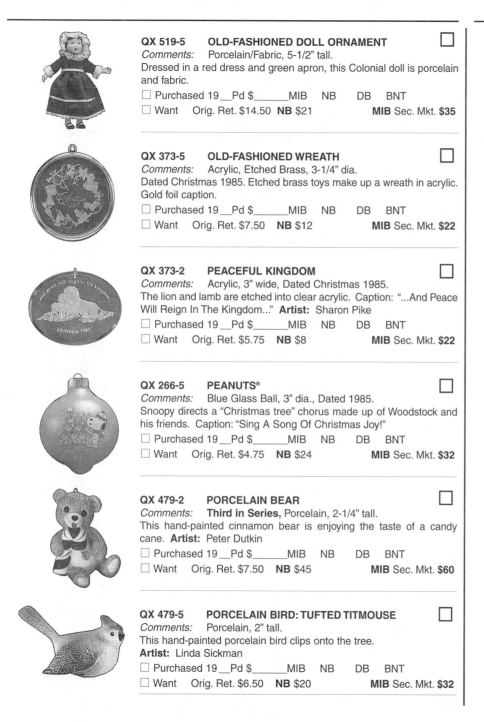

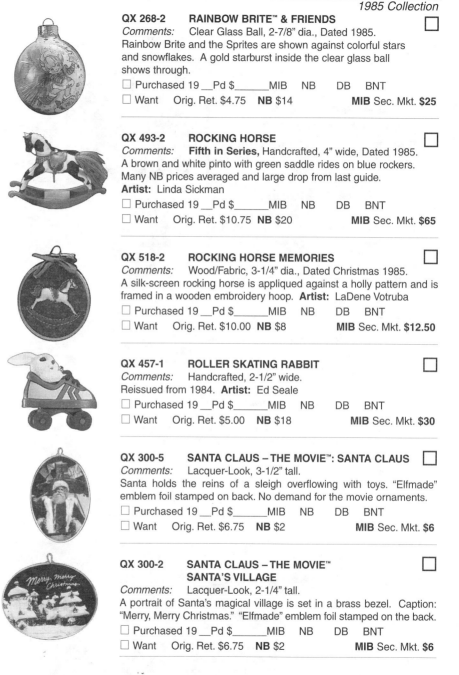

QX 519-5   OLD-FASHIONED DOLL ORNAMENT   ☐
Comments: Porcelain/Fabric, 5-1/2" tall.
Dressed in a red dress and green apron, this Colonial doll is porcelain and fabric.
☐ Purchased 19 __ Pd $_____ MIB   NB   DB   BNT
☐ Want   Orig. Ret. $14.50 **NB** $21   **MIB** Sec. Mkt. **$35**

QX 373-5   OLD-FASHIONED WREATH   ☐
Comments: Acrylic, Etched Brass, 3-1/4" dia.
Dated Christmas 1985. Etched brass toys make up a wreath in acrylic. Gold foil caption.
☐ Purchased 19 __ Pd $_____ MIB   NB   DB   BNT
☐ Want   Orig. Ret. $7.50 **NB** $12   **MIB** Sec. Mkt. **$22**

QX 373-2   PEACEFUL KINGDOM   ☐
Comments: Acrylic, 3" wide, Dated Christmas 1985.
The lion and lamb are etched into clear acrylic. Caption: "...And Peace Will Reign In The Kingdom..." **Artist:** Sharon Pike
☐ Purchased 19 __ Pd $_____ MIB   NB   DB   BNT
☐ Want   Orig. Ret. $5.75 **NB** $8   **MIB** Sec. Mkt. **$22**

QX 266-5   PEANUTS®   ☐
Comments: Blue Glass Ball, 3" dia., Dated 1985.
Snoopy directs a "Christmas tree" chorus made up of Woodstock and his friends. Caption: "Sing A Song Of Christmas Joy!"
☐ Purchased 19 __ Pd $_____ MIB   NB   DB   BNT
☐ Want   Orig. Ret. $4.75 **NB** $24   **MIB** Sec. Mkt. **$32**

QX 479-2   PORCELAIN BEAR   ☐
Comments: **Third in Series,** Porcelain, 2-1/4" tall.
This hand-painted cinnamon bear is enjoying the taste of a candy cane. **Artist:** Peter Dutkin
☐ Purchased 19 __ Pd $_____ MIB   NB   DB   BNT
☐ Want   Orig. Ret. $7.50 **NB** $45   **MIB** Sec. Mkt. **$60**

QX 479-5   PORCELAIN BIRD: TUFTED TITMOUSE   ☐
Comments: Porcelain, 2" tall.
This hand-painted porcelain bird clips onto the tree.
Artist: Linda Sickman
☐ Purchased 19 __ Pd $_____ MIB   NB   DB   BNT
☐ Want   Orig. Ret. $6.50 **NB** $20   **MIB** Sec. Mkt. **$32**

QX 268-2   RAINBOW BRITE™ & FRIENDS   ☐
Comments: Clear Glass Ball, 2-7/8" dia., Dated 1985.
Rainbow Brite and the Sprites are shown against colorful stars and snowflakes. A gold starburst inside the clear glass ball shows through.
☐ Purchased 19 __ Pd $_____ MIB   NB   DB   BNT
☐ Want   Orig. Ret. $4.75 **NB** $14   **MIB** Sec. Mkt. **$25**

QX 493-2   ROCKING HORSE   ☐
Comments: **Fifth in Series,** Handcrafted, 4" wide, Dated 1985.
A brown and white pinto with green saddle rides on blue rockers. Many NB prices averaged and large drop from last guide.
Artist: Linda Sickman
☐ Purchased 19 __ Pd $_____ MIB   NB   DB   BNT
☐ Want   Orig. Ret. $10.75 **NB** $20   **MIB** Sec. Mkt. **$65**

QX 518-2   ROCKING HORSE MEMORIES   ☐
Comments: Wood/Fabric, 3-1/4" dia., Dated Christmas 1985.
A silk-screen rocking horse is appliqued against a holly pattern and is framed in a wooden embroidery hoop. **Artist:** LaDene Votruba
☐ Purchased 19 __ Pd $_____ MIB   NB   DB   BNT
☐ Want   Orig. Ret. $10.00 **NB** $8   **MIB** Sec. Mkt. **$12.50**

QX 457-1   ROLLER SKATING RABBIT   ☐
Comments: Handcrafted, 2-1/2" wide.
Reissued from 1984. **Artist:** Ed Seale
☐ Purchased 19 __ Pd $_____ MIB   NB   DB   BNT
☐ Want   Orig. Ret. $5.00 **NB** $18   **MIB** Sec. Mkt. **$30**

QX 300-5   SANTA CLAUS – THE MOVIE™: SANTA CLAUS   ☐
Comments: Lacquer-Look, 3-1/2" tall.
Santa holds the reins of a sleigh overflowing with toys. "Elfmade" emblem foil stamped on back. No demand for the movie ornaments.
☐ Purchased 19 __ Pd $_____ MIB   NB   DB   BNT
☐ Want   Orig. Ret. $6.75 **NB** $2   **MIB** Sec. Mkt. **$6**

**QX 300-2   SANTA CLAUS – THE MOVIE™
SANTA'S VILLAGE**   ☐
Comments: Lacquer-Look, 2-1/4" tall.
A portrait of Santa's magical village is set in a brass bezel. Caption: "Merry, Merry Christmas." "Elfmade" emblem foil stamped on the back.
☐ Purchased 19 __ Pd $_____ MIB   NB   DB   BNT
☐ Want   Orig. Ret. $6.75 **NB** $2   **MIB** Sec. Mkt. **$6**

QX 494-2   SANTA PIPE
Comments: Handcrafted, 4-1/2" tall.
This pipe, with the look of carved antique meerschaum, depicts Santa and the reindeer on Christmas eve.
Artist: Peter Dutkin

☐ Purchased 19 __Pd $_____MIB   NB   DB   BNT
☐ Want   Orig. Ret. $9.50   **NB** $12   **MIB** Sec. Mkt. **$20**

QX 496-2   SANTA'S SKI TRIP
Comments: Handcrafted, 3-3/4" tall, Dated 1985.
Santa rides a green cable car to the top of "Snowflake Mountain No. 1985." Don't drop your hat, Santa! **Artist:** Ed Seale

☐ Purchased 19 __Pd $_____MIB   NB   DB   BNT
☐ Want   Orig. Ret. $12.00   **NB** $48   **MIB** Sec. Mkt. **$55-$60**

QLX 700-4   SANTA'S WORKSHOP
Comments: Lighted, Peek-Through Ball, 3-1/2" dia.
Reissued from 1984.

☐ Purchased 19 __Pd $_____MIB   NB   DB   BNT
☐ Want   Orig. Ret. $13.00   **NB** $40   **MIB** Sec. Mkt. **$55**

QLX 712-2   SEASON OF BEAUTY
Comments: Lighted, Red and Gold Classic Shape, 3-1/4" dia.
A wintry scene reflects peace and beauty. Caption: "May Joy Come Into Your World As Christmas Comes Into Your Heart."
Artist: Joyce A. Lyle

☐ Purchased 19 __Pd $_____MIB   NB   DB   BNT
☐ Want   Orig. Ret. $8.00   **NB** $12   **MIB** Sec. Mkt. **$25**

QX 379-5   SEWN PHOTOHOLDER
Comments: Embroidered Fabric, 3-1/4" dia.
Dated Christmas 1985. Red fabric photoholder is embroidered with holiday designs and hearts. Caption: "Cherished Times That Mean The Most Are Kept In Memory Ever Close."
Artist: Sharon Pike

☐ Purchased 19 __Pd $_____MIB   NB   DB   BNT
☐ Want   Orig. Ret. $7.00   **NB** $15   **MIB** Sec. Mkt. **$30**

QX 517-5   SHEEP AT CHRISTMAS
Comments: Handcrafted, 3-1/4" tall, Dated 1985.
This wood-look sheep wears a bell. Caption: "Season's Greetings."   **Artist:** Linda Sickman

☐ Purchased 19 __Pd $_____MIB   NB   DB   BNT
☐ Want   Orig. Ret. $8.25   **NB** $12   **MIB** Sec. Mkt. **$22**

QX 506-5   SISTER
Comments: Porcelain, 2-3/4" tall, Dated Christmas 1985.
White porcelain bell with red ribbon is designed with hearts and holly. Caption: "For Sister, With Love." **Artist:** Joyce Pattee

☐ Purchased 19 __Pd $_____MIB   NB   DB   BNT
☐ Want   Orig. Ret. $7.25   **NB** $11   **MIB** Sec. Mkt. **$22**

QX 473-2   SKATEBOARD RACCOON
Comments: Handcrafted, 2-1/2" tall, Reissued in 1986.
A flocked raccoon is riding a red skateboard with green moveable wheels. **Artist:** Peter Dutkin

☐ Purchased 19 __Pd $_____MIB   NB   DB   BNT
☐ Want   Orig. Ret. $6.50   **NB** $20   **MIB** Sec. Mkt. **$30**

QX 491-5   SNOOPY® AND WOODSTOCK
Comments: Handcrafted, 1-3/4" tall.
Snoopy and Woodstock are practicing their hockey moves.
Artist: Bob Siedler

☐ Purchased 19 __Pd $_____MIB   NB   DB   BNT
☐ Want   Orig. Ret. $7.50   **NB** $45   **MIB** Sec. Mkt. **$58**

QX 470-2   SNOW-PITCHING SNOWMAN
Comments: Handcrafted, 2" tall, Reissued in 1986.
A cute little snowman, dressed in a red and green baseball cap, is captured in the middle of pitching his snowball.
Artist: Donna Lee

☐ Purchased 19 __Pd $_____MIB   NB   DB   BNT
☐ Want   Orig. Ret. $4.50   **NB** $14   **MIB** Sec. Mkt. **$22.50**

Decorating tip…

**Linda Gilden has her tree loaded
with nativity ornaments
from top to bottom.**

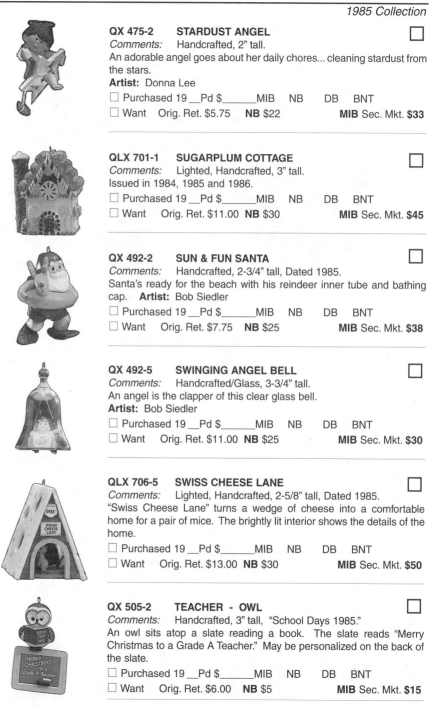

QX 510-5   SNOWFLAKE: HEIRLOOM COLLECTION ☐
Comments: Fabric, 4-1/4" dia.
Hand-crocheted snowflake covers padded burgundy satin.
Artist: Joyce Pattee
☐ Purchased 19 __ Pd $_____ MIB   NB   DB   BNT
☐ Want   Orig. Ret. $6.50   **NB** $6   **MIB** Sec. Mkt. **$20**

QX 450-1   SNOWY SEAL ☐
Comments: Handcrafted, 1-1/2" wide.
Reissued from 1984. **Artist:** Ed Seale
☐ Purchased 19 __ Pd $_____ MIB   NB   DB   BNT
☐ Want   Orig. Ret. $4.00   **NB** $10   **MIB** Sec. Mkt. **$22**

QX 477-5   SOCCER BEAVER ☐
Comments: Handcrafted, 2-1/2" tall, Reissued in 1986.
This little fellow, dressed in a red shirt, is ready to play!
Artist: Peter Dutkin
☐ Purchased 19 __ Pd $_____ MIB   NB   DB   BNT
☐ Want   Orig. Ret. $6.50   **NB** $9   **MIB** Sec. Mkt. **$22**

QX 502-5   SON ☐
Comments: Handcrafted, 2" tall, Dated 1985.
This charming little terrier with red bow, holds a message,
"Merry Christmas Son." **Artist:** Bob Siedler
☐ Purchased 19 __ Pd $_____ MIB   NB   DB   BNT
☐ Want   Orig. Ret. $5.50   **NB** $20   **MIB** Sec. Mkt. **$38**

QX 372-5   SPECIAL FRIENDS ☐
Comments: Acrylic, 3" wide, Dated 1985.
A doll and a bear are etched with the message: "Special friends bring
special joys to Christmas." **Artist:** Don Palmiter
☐ Purchased 19 __ Pd $_____ MIB   NB   DB   BNT
☐ Want   Orig. Ret. $5.75   **NB** $2   **MIB** Sec. Mkt. **$10**

QX 498-5   SPIRIT OF SANTA CLAUS, THE ☐
Comments: Special Ed., Handcrafted, 4-3/4" tall.
This elaborate reindeer and sleigh with Santa at the reins is beautiful!
Came with a wishbone-shaped hanger. Many sales below $65 were
found, dropping the value from last year. **Artist:** Donna Lee
☐ Purchased 19 __ Pd $_____ MIB   NB   DB   BNT
☐ Want   Orig. Ret. $22.50   **NB** $70   **MIB** Sec. Mkt. **$80**

QX 475-2   STARDUST ANGEL ☐
Comments: Handcrafted, 2" tall.
An adorable angel goes about her daily chores... cleaning stardust from
the stars.
Artist: Donna Lee
☐ Purchased 19 __ Pd $_____ MIB   NB   DB   BNT
☐ Want   Orig. Ret. $5.75   **NB** $22   **MIB** Sec. Mkt. **$33**

QLX 701-1   SUGARPLUM COTTAGE ☐
Comments: Lighted, Handcrafted, 3" tall.
Issued in 1984, 1985 and 1986.
☐ Purchased 19 __ Pd $_____ MIB   NB   DB   BNT
☐ Want   Orig. Ret. $11.00   **NB** $30   **MIB** Sec. Mkt. **$45**

QX 492-2   SUN & FUN SANTA ☐
Comments: Handcrafted, 2-3/4" tall, Dated 1985.
Santa's ready for the beach with his reindeer inner tube and bathing
cap.   **Artist:** Bob Siedler
☐ Purchased 19 __ Pd $_____ MIB   NB   DB   BNT
☐ Want   Orig. Ret. $7.75   **NB** $25   **MIB** Sec. Mkt. **$38**

QX 492-5   SWINGING ANGEL BELL ☐
Comments: Handcrafted/Glass, 3-3/4" tall.
An angel is the clapper of this clear glass bell.
Artist: Bob Siedler
☐ Purchased 19 __ Pd $_____ MIB   NB   DB   BNT
☐ Want   Orig. Ret. $11.00   **NB** $25   **MIB** Sec. Mkt. **$30**

QLX 706-5   SWISS CHEESE LANE ☐
Comments: Lighted, Handcrafted, 2-5/8" tall, Dated 1985.
"Swiss Cheese Lane" turns a wedge of cheese into a comfortable
home for a pair of mice. The brightly lit interior shows the details of the
home.
☐ Purchased 19 __ Pd $_____ MIB   NB   DB   BNT
☐ Want   Orig. Ret. $13.00   **NB** $30   **MIB** Sec. Mkt. **$50**

QX 505-2   TEACHER - OWL ☐
Comments: Handcrafted, 3" tall, "School Days 1985."
An owl sits atop a slate reading a book. The slate reads "Merry
Christmas to a Grade A Teacher." May be personalized on the back of
the slate.
☐ Purchased 19 __ Pd $_____ MIB   NB   DB   BNT
☐ Want   Orig. Ret. $6.00   **NB** $5   **MIB** Sec. Mkt. **$15**

QX 472-5   THIMBLE SERIES: SANTA ☐
Comments: **Eighth in Series,** Handcrafted, 2-3/8" tall.
Santa carries a thimble "backpack" with a Christmas tree.
Artist: Bob Siedler

☐ Purchased 19 __ Pd $_____ MIB   NB   DB   BNT
☐ Want   Orig. Ret. $5.50   **NB** $20   **MIB** Sec. Mkt. **$35**

QX 431-1   THREE KITTENS IN A MITTEN ☐
Comments: Handcrafted, 3-1/2" tall.
Reissued from 1984. **Artist:** Donna Lee

☐ Purchased 19 __ Pd $_____ MIB   NB   DB   BNT
☐ Want   Orig. Ret. $8.00   **NB** $30   **MIB** Sec. Mkt. **$45**

QX 497-2   TIN LOCOMOTIVE ☐
Comments: **Fourth in Series,** 3-1/2" tall, Dated 1985.
This black locomotive is embellished with colors and designs and
a jingle bell. **Artist:** Linda Sickman

☐ Purchased 19 __ Pd $_____ MIB   NB   DB   BNT
☐ Want   Orig. Ret. $14.75   **NB** $55   **MIB** Sec. Mkt. **$70**

QX 471-2   TRUMPET PANDA ☐
Comments: Handcrafted, 2" tall.
A flocked panda plays a red trumpet. **Artist:** Ed Seale

☐ Purchased 19 __ Pd $_____ MIB   NB   DB   BNT
☐ Want   Orig. Ret. $4.50   **NB** $10   **MIB** Sec. Mkt. **$18**

QX 371-2   TWELVE DAYS OF CHRISTMAS ☐
Comments: **Second in Series,** Acrylic, 3" tall, Dated 1985.
Two turtle doves are represented for the Second Day of
Christmas. Caption: "...two turtle doves." **Artist:** Sharon Pike

☐ Purchased 19 __ Pd $_____ MIB   NB   DB   BNT
☐ Want   Orig. Ret. $6.50   **NB** $45   **MIB** Sec. Mkt. **$65**

QX 500-5   TWENTY-FIVE YEARS TOGETHER ☐
Comments: Porcelain, 3-1/4" dia., Dated 1985.
A white porcelain plate is decorated with a blue, silver and gold wreath
of holly and firs. Caption: "Twenty-Five Years Together."

☐ Purchased 19 __ Pd $_____ MIB   NB   DB   BNT
☐ Want   Orig. Ret. $8.00   **NB** $8   **MIB** Sec. Mkt. **$18**

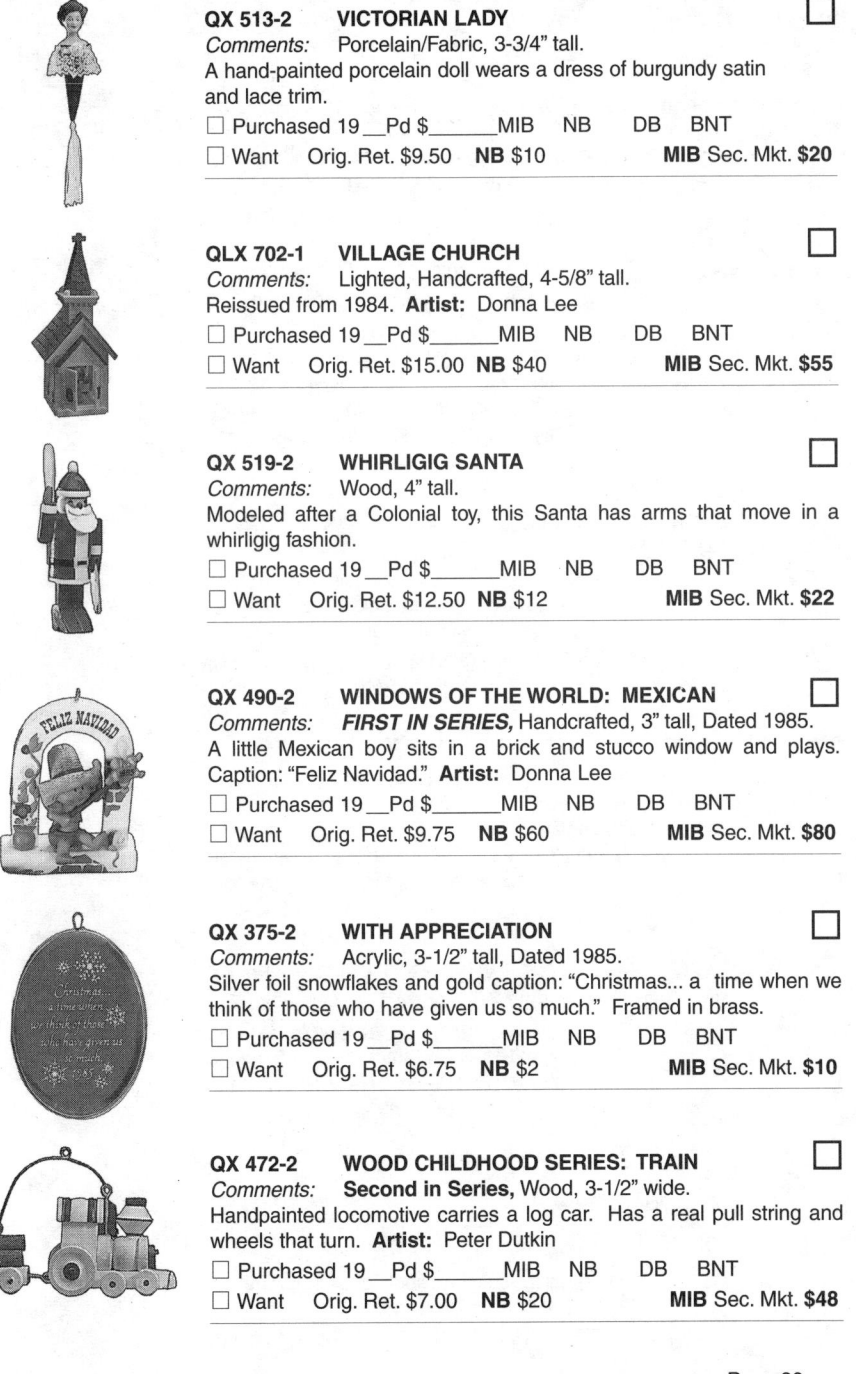

QX 513-2   VICTORIAN LADY ☐
Comments: Porcelain/Fabric, 3-3/4" tall.
A hand-painted porcelain doll wears a dress of burgundy satin
and lace trim.

☐ Purchased 19 __ Pd $_____ MIB   NB   DB   BNT
☐ Want   Orig. Ret. $9.50   **NB** $10   **MIB** Sec. Mkt. **$20**

QLX 702-1   VILLAGE CHURCH ☐
Comments: Lighted, Handcrafted, 4-5/8" tall.
Reissued from 1984. **Artist:** Donna Lee

☐ Purchased 19 __ Pd $_____ MIB   NB   DB   BNT
☐ Want   Orig. Ret. $15.00 **NB** $40   **MIB** Sec. Mkt. **$55**

QX 519-2   WHIRLIGIG SANTA ☐
Comments: Wood, 4" tall.
Modeled after a Colonial toy, this Santa has arms that move in a
whirligig fashion.

☐ Purchased 19 __ Pd $_____ MIB   NB   DB   BNT
☐ Want   Orig. Ret. $12.50   **NB** $12   **MIB** Sec. Mkt. **$22**

QX 490-2   WINDOWS OF THE WORLD: MEXICAN ☐
Comments: **FIRST IN SERIES,** Handcrafted, 3" tall, Dated 1985.
A little Mexican boy sits in a brick and stucco window and plays.
Caption: "Feliz Navidad." **Artist:** Donna Lee

☐ Purchased 19 __ Pd $_____ MIB   NB   DB   BNT
☐ Want   Orig. Ret. $9.75   **NB** $60   **MIB** Sec. Mkt. **$80**

QX 375-2   WITH APPRECIATION ☐
Comments: Acrylic, 3-1/2" tall, Dated 1985.
Silver foil snowflakes and gold caption: "Christmas... a time when we
think of those who have given us so much." Framed in brass.

☐ Purchased 19 __ Pd $_____ MIB   NB   DB   BNT
☐ Want   Orig. Ret. $6.75   **NB** $2   **MIB** Sec. Mkt. **$10**

QX 472-2   WOOD CHILDHOOD SERIES: TRAIN ☐
Comments: **Second in Series,** Wood, 3-1/2" wide.
Handpainted locomotive carries a log car. Has a real pull string and
wheels that turn. **Artist:** Peter Dutkin

☐ Purchased 19 __ Pd $_____ MIB   NB   DB   BNT
☐ Want   Orig. Ret. $7.00   **NB** $20   **MIB** Sec. Mkt. **$48**

1986 Collection

QX 424-3   ACORN INN   ☐
Comments: Handcrafted, 2" tall.
Using a green wreath a squirrel decorates his snow-capped inn.
Artist: Duane Unruh
☐ Purchased 19 __ Pd $_____ MIB   NB   DB   BNT
☐ Want   Orig. Ret. $8.50   **NB** $20   **MIB** Sec. Mkt. **$30**

QX 350-6   ART MASTERPIECE: MADONNA & CHILD   ☐
Comments: **Third and Final in Series,** Bezeled Satin, 3-1/4" tall.
Caption: "Lorenzo Di Cridi, Madonna and Child with the Infant St. John, The Nelson-Atkins Museum Of Art, Kansas City, MO (Nelson Fund)."
Artist: Diana McGehee
☐ Purchased 19 __ Pd $_____ MIB   NB   DB   BNT
☐ Want   Orig. Ret. $6.75   **NB** $12   **MIB** Sec. Mkt. **$25**

QX 412-3   BABY LOCKET   ☐
Comments: Textured Brass, 2-1/4" dia., Dated 1986.
This brass locket includes embossed lettering and baby toy designs. Opens for Baby's photo and personalizing. Caption: "Baby."
Artist: Diana McGehee
☐ Purchased 19 __ Pd $_____ MIB   NB   DB   BNT
☐ Want   Orig. Ret. $16.00 **NB** $15   **MIB** Sec. Mkt. **$25**

QX 271-3   BABY'S FIRST CHRISTMAS   ☐
Comments: Ecru Satin Ball 2-7/8" dia., Dated 1986.
Caption: "A Baby's A Bundle Of Hope And Joy" and "Baby's First Christmas."
☐ Purchased 19 __ Pd $_____ MIB   NB   DB   BNT
☐ Want   Orig. Ret. $5.50   **NB** $15   **MIB** Sec. Mkt. **$25**

QLX 710-3   BABY'S FIRST CHRISTMAS   ☐
Comments: Lighted Panorama Ball, 3-5/8" tall.
Baby's First Christmas 1986. Caption: "There's Someone New On Santa's List, Someone Small And Dear, Someone Santa's Sure To Love And Visit Every Year!" **Artist:** Ken Crow
☐ Purchased 19 __ Pd $_____ MIB   NB   DB   BNT
☐ Want   Orig. Ret. $19.50 **NB** $32   **MIB** Sec. Mkt. **$45**

QX 412-6   BABY'S FIRST CHRISTMAS   ☐
Comments: Handcrafted, 3-1/2" tall, Dated 1986.
Miniature mobile has a duck, Santa, teddy bear and stocking hanging from an acrylic cloud and star with the caption: "Baby's First Christmas." **Artist:** Linda Sickman
☐ Purchased 19 __ Pd $_____ MIB   NB   DB   BNT
☐ Want   Orig. Ret. $9.00   **NB** $28   **MIB** Sec. Mkt. **$42**

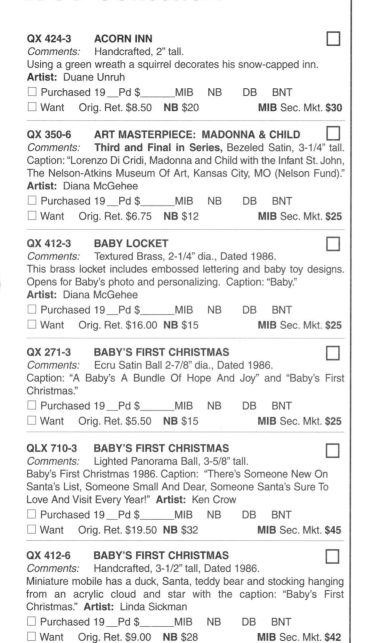

QX 380-3   BABY'S FIRST CHRISTMAS   ☐
Comments: Acrylic, 3-3/4" tall, Dated 1986.
A lamb with curly etched "wool" carries a stocking for "Baby's First Christmas." **Artist:** Don Palmiter
☐ Purchased 19 __ Pd $_____ MIB   NB   DB   BNT
☐ Want   Orig. Ret. $6.00   **NB** $8   **MIB** Sec. Mkt. **$25**

QX 379-2   BABY'S FIRST CHRISTMAS PHOTOHOLDER   ☐
Comments: Fabric, 3-3/4" tall, Dated 1986.
Green and white gingham photoholder. Caption: "Baby's First Christmas" and "A Baby Puts Special Magic In Holiday Moments."
Artist: Joyce Pattee
☐ Purchased 19 __ Pd $_____ MIB   NB   DB   BNT
☐ Want   Orig. Ret. $8.00   **NB** $15   **MIB** Sec. Mkt. **$20**

QX 413-3   BABY'S SECOND CHRISTMAS   ☐
Comments: Handcrafted, 1-3/4" tall, Dated 1986.
A little mouse with a diaper delivers a stocking that says "Baby's 2nd Christmas." **Artist:** Bob Siedler
☐ Purchased 19 __ Pd $_____ MIB   NB   DB   BNT
☐ Want   Orig. Ret. $6.50   **NB** $10   **MIB** Sec. Mkt. **$25**

QX 275-6   BABY-SITTER   ☐
Comments: Gold Glass Ball, 3" dia., Dated Christmas 1986.
Antique toys circle the ball. Caption: "For Being The Best Friend A Child Could Ever Have." Baby sitter ornaments usually never go up on the Secondary Market.
☐ Purchased 19 __ Pd $_____ MIB   NB   DB   BNT
☐ Want   Orig. Ret. $4.75   **NB** $4   **MIB** Sec. Mkt. **$10**

QX 480-5   BEARY SMOOTH RIDE   ☐
Comments: Handcrafted, 1-3/4" tall.
Reissued from 1985. **Artist:** Linda Sickman
☐ Purchased 19 __ Pd $_____ MIB   NB   DB   BNT
☐ Want   Orig. Ret. $6.50   **NB** $12   **MIB** Sec. Mkt. **$22**

QX 277-6   BETSEY CLARK: HOME FOR CHRISTMAS   ☐
Comments: **FIRST IN SERIES,** Pink Glass Ball, 2-7/8" dia.
Dated 1986. Betsey and her friends are busy decorating.
Caption: "May Christmas Love Fill Every Little Corner Of Your World."
Artist: Sharon Pike
☐ Purchased 19 __ Pd $_____ MIB   NB   DB   BNT
☐ Want   Orig. Ret. $5.00   **NB** $20   **MIB** Sec. Mkt. **$32**

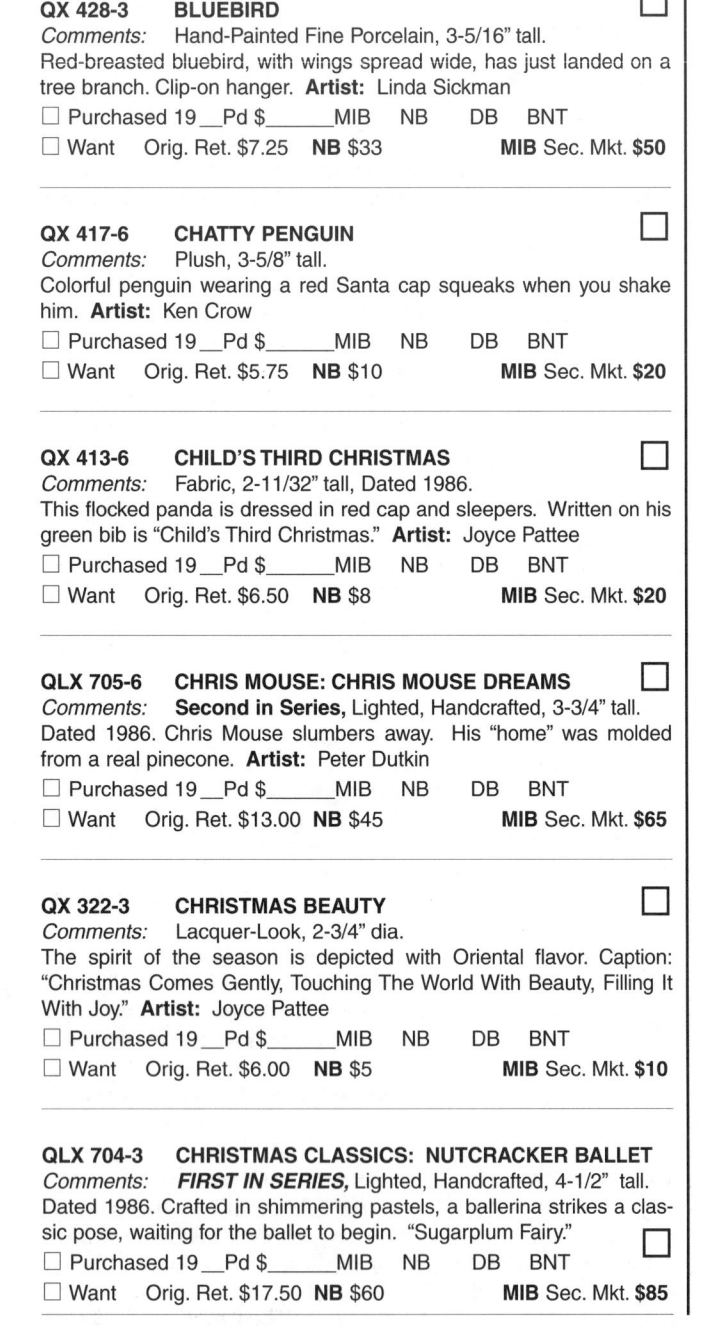

QX 428-3   BLUEBIRD ☐
Comments: Hand-Painted Fine Porcelain, 3-5/16" tall.
Red-breasted bluebird, with wings spread wide, has just landed on a tree branch. Clip-on hanger. **Artist:** Linda Sickman
☐ Purchased 19 __Pd $_____MIB   NB   DB   BNT
☐ Want   Orig. Ret. $7.25   **NB** $33   **MIB** Sec. Mkt. **$50**

QX 417-6   CHATTY PENGUIN ☐
Comments: Plush, 3-5/8" tall.
Colorful penguin wearing a red Santa cap squeaks when you shake him. **Artist:** Ken Crow
☐ Purchased 19 __Pd $_____MIB   NB   DB   BNT
☐ Want   Orig. Ret. $5.75   **NB** $10   **MIB** Sec. Mkt. **$20**

QX 413-6   CHILD'S THIRD CHRISTMAS ☐
Comments: Fabric, 2-11/32" tall, Dated 1986.
This flocked panda is dressed in red cap and sleepers. Written on his green bib is "Child's Third Christmas." **Artist:** Joyce Pattee
☐ Purchased 19 __Pd $_____MIB   NB   DB   BNT
☐ Want   Orig. Ret. $6.50   **NB** $8   **MIB** Sec. Mkt. **$20**

QLX 705-6   CHRIS MOUSE: CHRIS MOUSE DREAMS ☐
Comments: **Second in Series,** Lighted, Handcrafted, 3-3/4" tall.
Dated 1986. Chris Mouse slumbers away. His "home" was molded from a real pinecone. **Artist:** Peter Dutkin
☐ Purchased 19 __Pd $_____MIB   NB   DB   BNT
☐ Want   Orig. Ret. $13.00   **NB** $45   **MIB** Sec. Mkt. **$65**

QX 322-3   CHRISTMAS BEAUTY ☐
Comments: Lacquer-Look, 2-3/4" dia.
The spirit of the season is depicted with Oriental flavor. Caption: "Christmas Comes Gently, Touching The World With Beauty, Filling It With Joy." **Artist:** Joyce Pattee
☐ Purchased 19 __Pd $_____MIB   NB   DB   BNT
☐ Want   Orig. Ret. $6.00   **NB** $5   **MIB** Sec. Mkt. **$10**

QLX 704-3   CHRISTMAS CLASSICS: NUTCRACKER BALLET
Comments: **FIRST IN SERIES,** Lighted, Handcrafted, 4-1/2" tall.
Dated 1986. Crafted in shimmering pastels, a ballerina strikes a classic pose, waiting for the ballet to begin. "Sugarplum Fairy." ☐
☐ Purchased 19 __Pd $_____MIB   NB   DB   BNT
☐ Want   Orig. Ret. $17.50   **NB** $60   **MIB** Sec. Mkt. **$85**

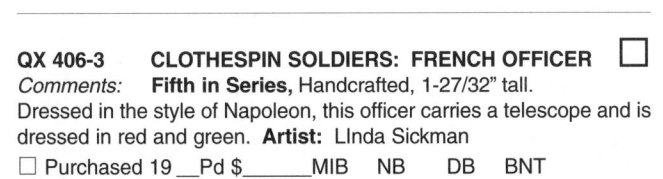

QX 512-6   CHRISTMAS GUITAR ☐
Comments: Handcrafted, 3" tall, Dated 1986.
This miniature guitar is decorated with green and red holly. Hangs from fabric guitar strap. **Artist:** Duane Unruh
☐ Purchased 19 __Pd $_____MIB   NB   DB   BNT
☐ Want   Orig. Ret. $7.00   **NB** $12   **MIB** Sec. Mkt. **$22**

QLX 701-2   CHRISTMAS SLEIGH RIDE ☐
Comments: Light and Motion, Handcrafted, 3-3/4" tall.
A couple rides in a horse-drawn sleigh. The clear dome is sprinkled with "snow." Caption: "Love's Precious Moments Shine Forever In The Heart." **Artist:** Ed Seal
☐ Purchased 19 __Pd $_____MIB   NB   DB   BNT
☐ Want   Orig. Ret. $24.50   **NB** $100   **MIB** Sec. Mkt. **$125**

QX 406-3   CLOTHESPIN SOLDIERS: FRENCH OFFICER ☐
Comments: **Fifth in Series,** Handcrafted, 1-27/32" tall.
Dressed in the style of Napoleon, this officer carries a telescope and is dressed in red and green. **Artist:** LInda Sickman
☐ Purchased 19 __Pd $_____MIB   NB   DB   BNT
☐ Want   Orig. Ret. $5.50   **NB** $15   **MIB** Sec. Mkt. **$22**

QXO279-6   COCA-COLA SANTA: OPEN HOUSE ORNAMENT
Comments: Porcelain White Glass Ball, 2-7/8" dia. ☐
Three nostalgic paintings of Santa. Special offering for dealers' "Open House" events.
☐ Purchased 19 __Pd $_____MIB   NB   DB   BNT
☐ Want   Orig. Ret. $4.75   **NB** $12   **MIB** Sec. Mkt. **$22**

QX 414-6   COOKIES FOR SANTA ☐
Comments: Handcrafted, 2-3/4" dia., Dated 1986.
A plate carries a sign "For Santa" and holds a star shaped cookie and a gingerbread man. **Artist:** Diana McGehee
☐ Purchased 19 __Pd $_____MIB   NB   DB   BNT
☐ Want   Orig. Ret. $4.50   **NB** $14   **MIB** Sec. Mkt. **$26**

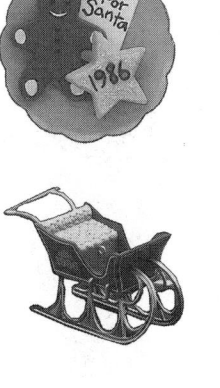

QX 511-3   COUNTRY SLEIGH ☐
Comments: Handcrafted, 2" tall, Dated 1986.
This red and gold sleigh was modeled after an antique sleigh and holds a plaid fabric blanket. **Artist:** Linda Sickman
☐ Purchased 19 __Pd $_____MIB   NB   DB   BNT
☐ Want   Orig. Ret. $10.00   **NB** $12   **MIB** Sec. Mkt. **$22**

QX 430-6   DAUGHTER
Comments: Handcrafted, 3-1/2" tall, Dated 1986.
A "wooden" doll, resembling an Old-World European toy, is in a red and green knit stocking. Caption: "For Daughter." **Artist:** Ed Seale
☐ Purchased 19 __Pd $_____MIB   NB   DB   BNT
☐ Want   Orig. Ret. $5.75   **NB** $22   **MIB** Sec. Mkt. **$40**

QX 481-2   DO NOT DISTURB BEAR
Comments: Handcrafted, 3" wide.
Reissued from 1985. **Artist:** Ed Seale
☐ Purchased 19 __Pd $_____MIB   NB   DB   BNT
☐ Want   Orig. Ret. $7.75   **NB** $18   **MIB** Sec. Mkt. **$25**

QX 431-3   FATHER
Comments: Wood, 3-1/4" dia., Dated Christmas 1986.
A silver French horn, tied with a festive bow, decorates this wooden disc. Caption: "Nothing Can Ever Replace The Wisdom, Guidance And Love Of A Father." **Artist:** LaDene Votruba
☐ Purchased 19 __Pd $_____MIB   NB   DB   BNT
☐ Want   Orig. Ret. $6.50   **NB** $10   **MIB** Sec. Mkt. **$15**

QX 514-3   FAVORITE TIN DRUM
Comments: Tin, 2" dia, Dated 1986.
The top and bottom of this drum are decorated with holly and gold cord bindings. Don't forget the drumsticks. **Artist:** Linda Sickman
☐ Purchased 19 __Pd $_____MIB   NB   DB   BNT
☐ Want   Orig. Ret. $8.50   **NB** $15   **MIB** Sec. Mkt. **$26**

QX 513-3   FESTIVE TREBLE CLEF
Comments: Handcrafted, 3-7/8" tall.
A golden treble clef is accented with translucent red, a brass bell and a striped ribbon. **Artist:** Bob Siedler
☐ Purchased 19 __Pd $_____MIB   NB   DB   BNT
☐ Want   Orig. Ret. $8.75   **NB** $12   **MIB** Sec. Mkt. **$20**

QX 400-6   FIFTY YEARS TOGETHER
Comments: Fine Porcelain, 3-13/32" tall.
Dated Christmas 1986. White porcelain bell has a bas-relief holly design and a sculpted "50" as the handle. Caption: "Fifty Years Together."
☐ Purchased 19 __Pd $_____MIB   NB   DB   BNT
☐ Want   Orig. Ret. $10.00   **NB** $10   **MIB** Sec. Mkt. **$18**

QX 379-3   FIRST CHRISTMAS TOGETHER
Comments: Acrylic, 3-11/32" tall, Dated 1986.
Two hearts are entwined on teardrop-shaped acrylic.
Caption: "First Christmas Together."
☐ Purchased 19 __Pd $_____MIB   NB   DB   BNT
☐ Want   Orig. Ret. $7.00   **NB** $8   **MIB** Sec. Mkt. **$20**

QLX 707-3   FIRST CHRISTMAS TOGETHER
Comments: Lighted, Handcrafted, 5-1/4" tall, Dated 1986.
Mr. and Mrs. Teddy are up and away in a brightly lit hot air balloon. The date is on a brass heart hanging from the basket. Caption: "First Christmas Together." **Artist:** Ed Seale
☐ Purchased 19 __Pd $_____MIB   NB   DB   BNT
☐ Want   Orig. Ret. $14.00   **NB** $20   **MIB** Sec. Mkt. **$36**

QX 400-3   FIRST CHRISTMAS TOGETHER LOCKET
Comments: Textured Brass, 2-1/4" tall, Dated 1986.
Brass Locket opens to hold two photographs. Caption: "First Christmas Together."
☐ Purchased 19 __Pd $_____MIB   NB   DB   BNT
☐ Want   Orig. Ret. $16.00   **NB** $10   **MIB** Sec. Mkt. **$18**

QX 270-3   FIRST CHRISTMAS TOGETHER
Comments: Light Green Glass Ball, 2-7/8" dia., Dated 1986.
Two redbirds fly against a wintry landscape. Caption: "First Christmas Together" and "How Beautiful The Season When It's Filled With Love."
☐ Purchased 19 __Pd $_____MIB   NB   DB   BNT
☐ Want   Orig. Ret. $4.75   **NB** $10   **MIB** Sec. Mkt. **$18**

QX 409-6   FIRST CHRISTMAS TOGETHER
Comments: Handcrafted, 4" tall, Dated 1986.
Two turtledoves swing together in a miniature bird cage with polished brass bars. Caption: "First Christmas Together."
Artist: Linda Sickman
☐ Purchased 19 __Pd $_____MIB   NB   DB   BNT
☐ Want   Orig. Ret. $12.00   **NB** $10   **MIB** Sec. Mkt. **$25**

QX 272-3   FRIENDS ARE FUN
Comments: Light Blue Glass Ball, 2-7/8" dia.
Dated Christmas 1986. Eskimo children are riding their dog sled through the snow. Caption: "It's Fun Having Friends To Go 'Round With." **Artist:** Ken Crow
☐ Purchased 19 __Pd $_____MIB   NB   DB   BNT
☐ Want   Orig. Ret. $4.75   **NB** $20   **MIB** Sec. Mkt. **$36**

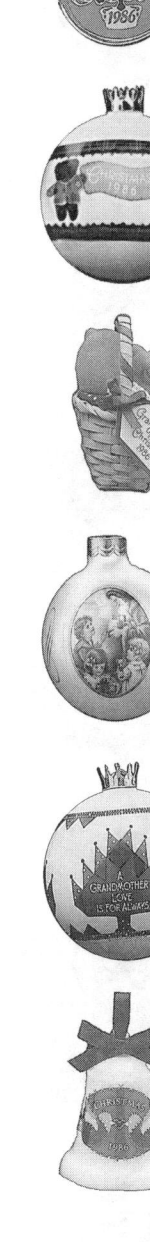

QX 427-3   FRIENDSHIP GREETING
Comments: Fabric, 2-3/4" tall, Dated 1986.
Silk-screened fabric is stitched to create a colorful envelope orna-
ment. Enclosed card reads: "Friends are forever." Back of envelope
says "Merry Christmas."
☐ Purchased 19 __ Pd $_____ MIB   NB   DB   BNT
☐ Want   Orig. Ret. $8.00   **NB** $5   **MIB** Sec. Mkt. **$15**

QX 381-6   FRIENDSHIP'S GIFT
Comments: Acrylic, 3" tall, Dated Christmas 1986.
A little mouse helps Santa deliver a gift. Caption: "Friendship
Is A Gift."
☐ Purchased 19 __ Pd $_____ MIB   NB   DB   BNT
☐ Want   Orig. Ret. $6.00   **NB** $5   **MIB** Sec. Mkt. **$12.50**

QX 383-3   FROM OUR HOME TO YOURS
Comments: Acrylic, 3-1/4" tall, Dated Christmas 1986.
A fruit-filled wicker basket graces this teardrop shaped ornament.
Caption: "From Our Home To Yours."
☐ Purchased 19 __ Pd $_____ MIB   NB   DB   BNT
☐ Want   Orig. Ret. $6.00   **NB** $8   **MIB** Sec. Mkt. **$15**

QX 405-3   FROSTY FRIENDS
Comments: **Seventh in Series,** Handcrafted, 2-1/4" tall.
Dated 1986. A flocked baby reindeer and the cute little Eskimo sit on
an acrylic ice flow. NB price down from '96. **Artist:** Bob Siedler
☐ Purchased 19 __ Pd $_____ MIB   NB   DB   BNT
☐ Want   Orig. Ret. $8.50   **NB** $22   **MIB** Sec. Mkt. **$65**

QLX 705-3   GENERAL STORE
Comments: Lighted, Handcrafted, 2-11/16" tall.
The store is bright with light and open for holiday business as it adver-
tises "Christmas Trees 50¢." **Artist:** Donna Lee
☐ Purchased 19 __ Pd $_____ MIB   NB   DB   BNT
☐ Want   Orig. Ret. $15.75   **NB** $35   **MIB** Sec. Mkt. **$48**

QLX 708-3   GENTLE BLESSINGS
Comments: Lighted Panorama Ball, 3-5/8" tall.
A glowing light shines on the Christ Child as the animals in the stable
watch over Him. **Artist:** Linda Sickman
☐ Purchased 19 __ Pd $_____ MIB   NB   DB   BNT
☐ Want   Orig. Ret. $15.00   **NB** $100   **MIB** Sec. Mkt. **$150**

QX 428-6   GLOWING CHRISTMAS TREE
Comments: Embedded Acrylic, 3-1/4," Dated 1986.
A brass Christmas tree, complete with colorful stars, is embedded in
teardrop shaped acrylic. **Artist:** Joyce Pattee
☐ Purchased 19 __ Pd $_____ MIB   NB   DB   BNT
☐ Want   Orig. Ret. $7.00   **NB** $10   **MIB** Sec. Mkt. **$14**

QX 271-6   GODCHILD
Comments: White Satin Ball, 2-7/8" dia.
Dated Christmas 1986. Colorful teddy bears circle the ornament
capped with a gold crown. Caption: "A Godchild Is A Very Special
Someone."
☐ Purchased 19 __ Pd $_____ MIB   NB   DB   BNT
☐ Want   Orig. Ret. $4.75   **NB** $8   **MIB** Sec. Mkt. **$16**

QX 411-6   GRANDCHILD'S FIRST CHRISTMAS
Comments: Handcrafted, 2-1/4" tall, Dated 1986.
A flocked bear is sound asleep in a basket ready for "Baby's First
Christmas."
☐ Purchased 19 __ Pd $_____ MIB   NB   DB   BNT
☐ Want   Orig. Ret. $10.00   **NB** $10   **MIB** Sec. Mkt. **$16**

QX 273-6   GRANDDAUGHTER
Comments: White Glass Ball, 2-7/8" dia.
Dated Christmas 1986. Old-fashioned scenes of children and
Christmas. Caption: "Season After Season, A Granddaughter Grows
Dearer And Dearer." **Artist:** Joyce Lyle
☐ Purchased 19 __ Pd $_____ MIB   NB   DB   BNT
☐ Want   Orig. Ret. $4.75   **NB** $10   **MIB** Sec. Mkt. **$18**

QX 274-3   GRANDMOTHER
Comments: Ivory Satin Ball, 2-7/8" dia.
Dated Christmas 1986. A country quilt design of Christmas trees
carries the message: "A Grandmother's Love Is For Always."
Artist: Joyce Pattee
☐ Purchased 19 __ Pd $_____ MIB   NB   DB   BNT
☐ Want   Orig. Ret. $4.75   **NB** $8   **MIB** Sec. Mkt. **$15**

QX 432-3   GRANDPARENTS
Comments: Porcelain, 5-1/2" tall, Dated Christmas 1986.
Two doves in a Christmas stitch design decorate a white
porcelain bell. Caption: "Grandparents Are Never Far From Thought...
Ever Near In Love."
☐ Purchased 19 __ Pd $_____ MIB   NB   DB   BNT
☐ Want   Orig. Ret. $7.50   **NB** $10   **MIB** Sec. Mkt. **$20**

QX 273-3   GRANDSON ☐
Comments: Blue Glass Ball, 3" dia., Dated Christmas 1986.
Forest animals enjoy Christmas. "A Grandson is a bringer of a very special kind of love." **Artist:** LaDene Votruba
☐ Purchased 19 __Pd $_____MIB   NB   DB   BNT
☐ Want   Orig. Ret. $4.75 **NB** $12   **MIB** Sec. Mkt. **$22**

QX 432-6   GRATITUDE ☐
Comments: Satin and Wood, 5" tall, Dated 1986.
A bright red cardinal sits on a branch of holly, framed in an embroidery hoop. Caption: "Especially To Thank You... Especially At Christmas."
Artist: Sharon Pike
☐ Purchased 19 __Pd $_____MIB   NB   DB   BNT
☐ Want   Orig. Ret. $6.00 **NB** $6   **MIB** Sec. Mkt. **$8**

QX 418-3   HAPPY CHRISTMAS TO OWL ☐
Comments: Handcrafted, 3" tall.
Owl reads "Christmas Stories" to a small friend, "I Heard Him Exclaim, Ere He Drove Out Of Sight, Happy Christmas To Owl, And To Owl A Good-nite." **Artist** Duane Unruh
☐ Purchased 19 __Pd $_____MIB   NB   DB   BNT
☐ Want   Orig. Ret. $6.00 **NB** $10   **MIB** Sec. Mkt. **$15**

QX 436-3   HEATHCLIFF ☐
Comments: Handcrafted, 3-3/32" tall.
Heathcliff has his own little angel reminding him to be good. His letter reads: "Dear Santa, I've Been Exceptional. Heathcliff."
Artist: Ed Seale
☐ Purchased 19 __Pd $_____MIB   NB   DB   BNT
☐ Want   Orig. Ret. $7.50 **NB** $12   **MIB** Sec. Mkt. **$25**

QX 417-3   HEAVENLY DREAMER ☐
Comments: Handcrafted, 1-3/8" tall.
A little angel, wearing a brass halo, has fallen asleep on a billowy acrylic cloud. **Artist:** Donna Lee
☐ Purchased 19 __Pd $_____MIB   NB   DB   BNT
☐ Want   Orig. Ret. $5.75 **NB** $19   **MIB** Sec. Mkt. **$32**

QX 515-3   HEIRLOOM SNOWFLAKE ☐
Comments: Fabric, 4-3/4" tall.
Lavender-blue padded satin is covered with lacy, hand-crocheted snowflakes. **Artist:** Joyce Pattee
☐ Purchased 19 __Pd $_____MIB   NB   DB   BNT
☐ Want   Orig. Ret. $6.75 **NB** $10   **MIB** Sec. Mkt. **$15**

QX 404-3   HERE COMES SANTA:
          KRINGLE'S KOOL TREATS ☐
Comments: **Eighth in Series,** Handcrafted, 3-15/18" tall.
Dated 1986. Santa cycles his "Ice Cream" and "Snow Cones" complete with a bell. **Artist:** Bob Siedler
☐ Purchased 19 __Pd $_____MIB   NB   DB   BNT
☐ Want   Orig. Ret. $14.00 **NB** $45   **MIB** Sec. Mkt. **$60**

QX 514-6   HOLIDAY HORN ☐
Comments: Bisque Porcelain, 3" tall.
This ivory horn is trimmed with a delicate holly design and tied with red and green ribbon. **Artist:** Duane Unruh
☐ Purchased 19 __Pd $_____MIB   NB   DB   BNT
☐ Want   Orig. Ret. $8.00 **NB** $18   **MIB** Sec. Mkt. **$33**

QX 404-6   HOLIDAY JINGLE BELL ☐
Comments: Musical, Handcrafted, 2-3/4" dia.
Blue and white musical ornament plays "Jingle Bells" and has white prancing reindeer circling the blue band in the center.
☐ Purchased 19 __Pd $_____MIB   NB   DB   BNT
☐ Want   Orig. Ret. $16.00 **NB** $30   **MIB** Sec. Mkt. **$48**

QX 321-6   HOLIDAY WILDLIFE: CEDAR WAXWING ☐
Comments: **Fifth in Series,** Wood, 2-1/2" dia., Dated 1986.
Caption: "Cedar Waxwing, (Cedarbird), BOMBYCILLA CEDORUM, Fifth in a Series, Wildlife Collection, Christmas 1986."
☐ Purchased 19 __Pd $_____MIB   NB   DB   BNT
☐ Want   Orig. Ret. $7.50 **NB** $16   **MIB** Sec. Mkt. **$25**

QX 383-6   HUSBAND ☐
Comments: Cameo, 2-3/4" dia., Dated Christmas 1986.
An intricately detailed duck decoy and wreath decorate this ornament. Caption: "A Husband Is A Forever Friend." **Artist:** Sharon Pike
☐ Purchased 19 __Pd $_____MIB   NB   DB   BNT
☐ Want   Orig. Ret. $8.00 **NB** $8   **MIB** Sec. Mkt. **$14**

QX 483-2   JOLLY HIKER ☐
Comments: Handcrafted, 2" tall, Reissued in 1987.
Santa's ready for his hike with his backpack, bedroll and candy cane walking stick. **Artist:** Bob Siedler
☐ Purchased 19 __Pd $_____MIB   NB   DB   BNT
☐ Want   Orig. Ret. $5.00 **NB** $10   **MIB** Sec. Mkt. **$20**

QX 429-6   JOLLY ST. NICK ☐
Comments: Hand-Painted Fine Porcelain, 5-1/2" tall.
Special Edition. Crafted from a Thomas Nast St. Nicholas introduced in the 1800s. **Artist:** Duane Unruh

☐ Purchased 19__Pd $_____MIB   NB   DB   BNT
☐ Want   Orig. Ret. $22.50 **NB** $45   **MIB** Sec. Mkt. **$68**

QX 382-3   JOY OF FRIENDS ☐
Comments: Bezeled Satin, 2-3/4" tall.
Ice skaters, printed on padded satin, resemble American folk art. Framed in chrome. Caption: "Friends Make The Heart Warmer, The Day Merrier, The Season More Memorable." **Artist:** Joyce Pattee

☐ Purchased 19__Pd $_____MIB   NB   DB   BNT
☐ Want   Orig. Ret. $6.75 **NB** $10   **MIB** Sec. Mkt. **$18**

QX 513-6   JOYFUL CAROLERS ☐
Comments: Handcrafted, 3-1/4" dia., Dated 1986.
Designed similar to the Nostalgia ornaments, carolers dressed in Dickens' style share their joy. Caption: "Joy To The World."
Artist: Linda Sickman

☐ Purchased 19__Pd $_____MIB   NB   DB   BNT
☐ Want   Orig. Ret. $9.75 **NB** $24   **MIB** Sec. Mkt. **$30**

QX 435-3   KATYBETH WITH STAR ☐
Comments: Hand-Painted Fine Porcelain, 2-19/32" tall.
Katybeth plays with a star that is passing by.

☐ Purchased 19__Pd $_____MIB   NB   DB   BNT
☐ Want   Orig. Ret. $7.00 **NB** $12   **MIB** Sec. Mkt. **$22**

QLX 707-6   KEEP ON GLOWIN'! ☐
Comments: Lighted, Handcrafted, 2-7/16" tall.
Reissued in 1987. This bright icicle proves a source of fun for one of Santa's elves. **Artist:** Ken Crow

☐ Purchased 19__Pd $_____MIB   NB   DB   BNT
☐ Want   Orig. Ret. $10.00 **NB** $30   **MIB** Sec. Mkt. **$44**

QX 474-5   KITTY MISCHIEF ☐
Comments: Handcrafted, 2" tall.
Reissued from 1985. **Artist:** Peter Dutkin

☐ Purchased 19__Pd $_____MIB   NB   DB   BNT
☐ Want   Orig. Ret. $5.00 **NB** $15   **MIB** Sec. Mkt. **$25**

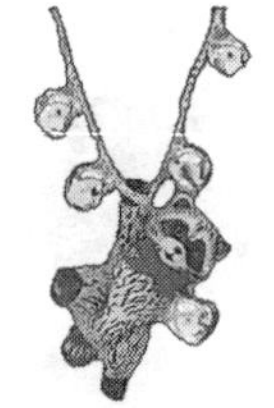

QX 419-3   LI'L JINGLER ☐
Comments: Handcrafted, 2" tall, Reissued in 1987.
A cute little raccoon in a red bow-tie hangs onto a stringer of brass jingle bells. Cute piece! **Artist:** Ed Seale

☐ Purchased 19__Pd $_____MIB   NB   DB   BNT
☐ Want   Orig. Ret. $6.75 **NB** $25   **MIB** Sec. Mkt. **$38**

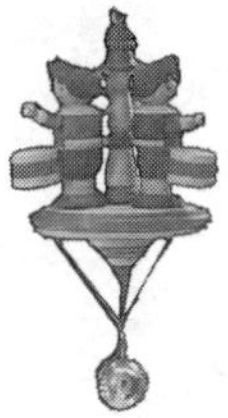

QX 511-6   LITTLE DRUMMERS ☐
Comments: Handcrafted, 4" tall, Real Drumming Motion.
Three little drummer boys play their drums when you tap or shake their platform. **Artist:** Ken Crow

☐ Purchased 19__Pd $_____MIB   NB   DB   BNT
☐ Want   Orig. Ret. $12.50 **NB** $18   **MIB** Sec. Mkt. **$23**

QX 409-3   LOVING MEMORIES ☐
Comments: Handcrafted, 5-1/4" tall, Dated 1986.
A heart-shaped shadow box holds a brass bell, teddy bear and Christmas gift. **Artist:** Ed Seale

☐ Purchased 19__Pd $_____MIB   NB   DB   BNT
☐ Want   Orig. Ret. $9.00 **NB** $18   **MIB** Sec. Mkt. **$28**

QX 272-6   MAGI, THE ☐
Comments: Gold Glass Teardrop Ball, 3" dia.
Dated Christmas 1986. The Magi bring their gifts to the Child. Caption: "O Come Let Us Adore Him." **Artist:** Sharon Pike

☐ Purchased 19__Pd $_____MIB   NB   DB   BNT
☐ Want   Orig. Ret. $4.75 **NB** $12   **MIB** Sec. Mkt. **$18.50**

QX 429-3   MAGICAL UNICORN ☐
Comments: Limited Edition 24,700, Wooden Display Stand.
Hand-Painted Fine Porcelain, 4-1/2" tall. White porcelain unicorn has hand-painted pastel flowers and pastel ribbons. Beautiful!
Artist: Duane Unruh

☐ Purchased 19__Pd $_____MIB   NB   DB   BNT
☐ Want   Orig. Ret. $27.50 **NB** $75   **MIB** Sec. Mkt. **$85**

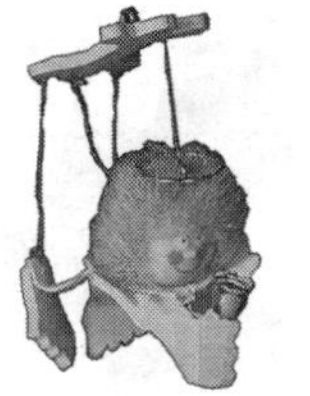

QX 402-3   MARIONETTE ANGEL ☐
Comments: Handcrafted, 3-9/16" tall, Very rare!
This whimsical little angel has authentic marionette features. Appeared in retailers' catalogs but was pulled from production.

☐ Purchased 19__Pd $_____MIB   NB   DB   BNT
☐ Want   Orig. Ret. $8.50 **NB** $350   **MIB** Sec. Mkt. **$410**

QX 275-2   MARY EMMERLING:
AMERICAN COUNTRY COLLECTION ☐
Comments: Glass Balls, 2-7/8" dia., Set of 4.
These four blue and white glass balls feature motifs from 19th Century American homes.

☐ Purchased 19__Pd $_____MIB   NB   DB   BNT
☐ Want   Orig. Ret. $7.95   **NB** $12   **MIB** Sec. Mkt. **$25**

QX 427-6   MEMORIES TO CHERISH: PHOTOHOLDER ☐
Comments: Ceramic, 3-1/8" tall, Dated Christmas 1986.
A white, braided wreath sports holly and a big red bow. Caption: "A Memory To Cherish."

☐ Purchased 19__Pd $_____MIB   NB   DB   BNT
☐ Want   Orig. Ret. $7.50   **NB** $15   **MIB** Sec. Mkt. **$28**

QLX 709-3   MERRY CHRISTMAS BELL ☐
Comments: Lighted Acrylic, 5-9/16" tall.
Bell-shaped acrylic has etched Christmas flowers.
Caption: "Merry Christmas." **Artist:** LaDene Votruba

☐ Purchased 19__Pd $_____MIB   NB   DB   BNT
☐ Want   Orig. Ret. $8.50   **NB** $12.50   **MIB** Sec. Mkt. **$22**

QX 415-3   MERRY KOALA ☐
Comments: Handcrafted, 2" tall, Reissued in 1987.
Flocked koala is wearing an oversized Santa cap.
Artist: Linda Sickman

☐ Purchased 19__Pd $_____MIB   NB   DB   BNT
☐ Want   Orig. Ret. $5.00   **NB** $10   **MIB** Sec. Mkt. **$22**

QX 403-2   MERRY MOUSE ☐
Comments: Handcrafted, 2-1/2" tall.
Reissued from 1985. **Artist:** Peter Dutkin

☐ Purchased 19__Pd $_____MIB   NB   DB   BNT
☐ Want   Orig. Ret. $4.50   **NB** $15   **MIB** Sec. Mkt. **$25**

QX 407-6   MINIATURE CRECHE ☐
Comments: **Second in Series,** Fine Porcelain, 3-3/4" tall.
Porcelain bisque figures of the Holy Family are set off beautifully with the graceful arch and brass star shining brightly above.
Artist: Ed Seale

☐ Purchased 19__Pd $_____MIB   NB   DB   BNT
☐ Want   Orig. Ret. $9.00   **NB** $45   **MIB** Sec. Mkt. **$62**

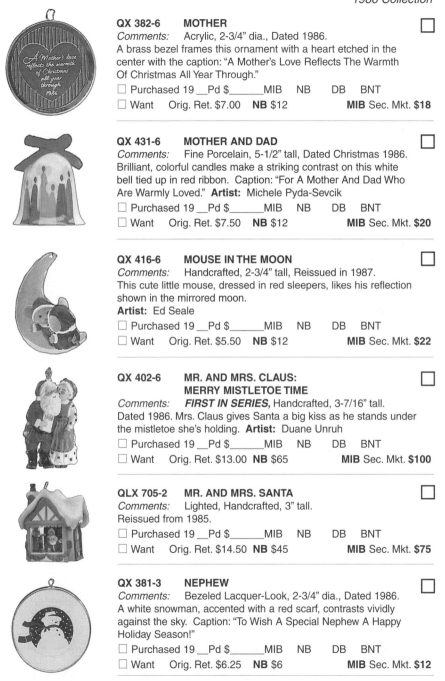

QX 382-6   MOTHER ☐
Comments: Acrylic, 2-3/4" dia., Dated 1986.
A brass bezel frames this ornament with a heart etched in the center with the caption: "A Mother's Love Reflects The Warmth Of Christmas All Year Through."

☐ Purchased 19__Pd $_____MIB   NB   DB   BNT
☐ Want   Orig. Ret. $7.00   **NB** $12   **MIB** Sec. Mkt. **$18**

QX 431-6   MOTHER AND DAD ☐
Comments: Fine Porcelain, 5-1/2" tall, Dated Christmas 1986.
Brilliant, colorful candles make a striking contrast on this white bell tied up in red ribbon. Caption: "For A Mother And Dad Who Are Warmly Loved." **Artist:** Michele Pyda-Sevcik

☐ Purchased 19__Pd $_____MIB   NB   DB   BNT
☐ Want   Orig. Ret. $7.50   **NB** $12   **MIB** Sec. Mkt. **$20**

QX 416-6   MOUSE IN THE MOON ☐
Comments: Handcrafted, 2-3/4" tall, Reissued in 1987.
This cute little mouse, dressed in red sleepers, likes his reflection shown in the mirrored moon.
Artist: Ed Seale

☐ Purchased 19__Pd $_____MIB   NB   DB   BNT
☐ Want   Orig. Ret. $5.50   **NB** $12   **MIB** Sec. Mkt. **$22**

QX 402-6   MR. AND MRS. CLAUS:
MERRY MISTLETOE TIME ☐
Comments: **FIRST IN SERIES,** Handcrafted, 3-7/16" tall.
Dated 1986. Mrs. Claus gives Santa a big kiss as he stands under the mistletoe she's holding. **Artist:** Duane Unruh

☐ Purchased 19__Pd $_____MIB   NB   DB   BNT
☐ Want   Orig. Ret. $13.00   **NB** $65   **MIB** Sec. Mkt. **$100**

QLX 705-2   MR. AND MRS. SANTA ☐
Comments: Lighted, Handcrafted, 3" tall.
Reissued from 1985.

☐ Purchased 19__Pd $_____MIB   NB   DB   BNT
☐ Want   Orig. Ret. $14.50   **NB** $45   **MIB** Sec. Mkt. **$75**

QX 381-3   NEPHEW ☐
Comments: Bezeled Lacquer-Look, 2-3/4" dia., Dated 1986.
A white snowman, accented with a red scarf, contrasts vividly against the sky. Caption: "To Wish A Special Nephew A Happy Holiday Season!"

☐ Purchased 19__Pd $_____MIB   NB   DB   BNT
☐ Want   Orig. Ret. $6.25   **NB** $6   **MIB** Sec. Mkt. **$12**

QX 274-6   NEW HOME ☐
Comments: White Glass Ball, 3" dia., Dated 1986.
Gingerbread people and animals run through a neighborhood of sweets. Caption: "Christmas Is So Special When It's Spent In A New Home." **Artist:** Ken Crow

☐ Purchased 19__ Pd $_____ MIB   NB   DB   BNT
☐ Want   Orig. Ret. $4.75   **NB** $22   **MIB** Sec. Mkt. **$38**

QX 426-6   NIECE ☐
Comments: Fabric and Wood, 4-1/2" tall.
Dated Christmas 1986. A white cat with a big red bow around its neck sits on red and green cushions. Caption: "Nieces Give The Nicest Gifts... Beauty, Joy And Love."

☐ Purchased 19__ Pd $_____ MIB   NB   DB   BNT
☐ Want   Orig. Ret. $6.00   **NB** $5   **MIB** Sec. Mkt. **$10**

QX 276-3   NORMAN ROCKWELL ☐
Comments: Green Glass Ball, 2-7/8" dia.
Christmas scenes reflect the excitement of Christmas. Caption: "Christmas Time Is Filled With Joy And Glad Anticipation, And All The Loving Reasons For A Happy Celebration."

☐ Purchased 19__ Pd $_____ MIB   NB   DB   BNT
☐ Want   Orig. Ret. $4.75   **NB** $14   **MIB** Sec. Mkt. **$28**

QX 321-3   NORMAN ROCKWELL: CHECKING UP ☐
Comments: **Seventh in Series,** Red Cameo, 3-1/4" dia.
Caption: "Checking Up, Seventh In A Series, Christmas 1986, The Norman Rockwell Collection." **Artist:** Sharon Pike

☐ Purchased 19__ Pd $_____ MIB   NB   DB   BNT
☐ Want   Orig. Ret. $7.75   **NB** $12   **MIB** Sec. Mkt. **$20**

QX 403-3   NOSTALGIC HOUSES AND SHOPS: CHRISTMAS CANDY SHOPPE ☐
Comments: **Third in Series,** Handcrafted, 4-5/16" tall.
Dated 1986. The baking is done upstairs and the candies are sold downstairs. Very popular ornament. Harder to find than the 1985 issue. **Artist:** Donna Lee

☐ Purchased 19__ Pd $_____ MIB   NB   DB   BNT
☐ Want   Orig. Ret. $13.75   **NB** $185   **MIB** Sec. Mkt. **$260**

QX 512-3   NUTCRACKER SANTA ☐
Comments: Handcrafted, 3-3/8" tall.
Crafted to look like a nutcracker, Santa's mouth pops open when you lift the tassel on his cap. **Artist:** Duane Unruh

☐ Purchased 19__ Pd $_____ MIB   NB   DB   BNT
☐ Want   Orig. Ret. $10.00   **NB** $35   **MIB** Sec. Mkt. **$50**

QXO440-3   OLD-FASHIONED SANTA: OPEN HOUSE ORN. ☐
Comments: Handcrafted, 4-1/2" tall.
Old World Santa, looking like hand-carved wood, carries a bag of toys. Special offering for dealers' "Open House" events.
Artist: Linda Sickman

☐ Purchased 19__ Pd $_____ MIB   NB   DB   BNT
☐ Want   Orig. Ret. $12.75 **NB** $35   **MIB** Sec. Mkt. **$52.50**

QSP 420-1   ON THE RIGHT TRACK: GOLD CROWN ORN. ☐
Comments: Hand-Painted Fine Porcelain, 4-3/4" tall.
The artist signed his name to this special promotional Santa. Santa, in his shirt sleeves, puts the finishing touches on a locomotive. **Artist:** Peter Dutkin

☐ Purchased 19__ Pd $_____ MIB   NB   DB   BNT
☐ Want   Orig. Ret. $15.00 **NB** $25   **MIB** Sec. Mkt. **$38**

QX 422-6   OPEN ME FIRST ☐
Comments: Handcrafted, 2-15/16" tall, Dated 1986.
A child is delighted with the kitten inside a gift box titled "Open Me First."

☐ Purchased 19__ Pd $_____ MIB   NB   DB   BNT
☐ Want   Orig. Ret. $7.25   **NB** $18   **MIB** Sec. Mkt. **$28**

QX 435-6   PADDINGTON™ BEAR ☐
Comments: Handcrafted, 2-9/16" tall.
This favorite bear is dressed in a bright blue coat and yellow hat, and carries a jar of honey. **Artist:** Bob Siedler

☐ Purchased 19__ Pd $_____ MIB   NB   DB   BNT
☐ Want   Orig. Ret. $6.00   **NB** $25   **MIB** Sec. Mkt. **$37**

QX 276-6   PEANUTS® ☐
Comments: Blue Glass Ball, 3" dia., Dated 1986.
Snoopy, Woodstock and his feathered friends go ice skating. Caption: "Merry Christmas."

☐ Purchased 19__ Pd $_____ MIB   NB   DB   BNT
☐ Want   Orig. Ret. $4.75   **NB** $20   **MIB** Sec. Mkt. **$32**

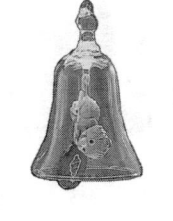

QX 425-3   PLAYFUL POSSUM ☐
Comments: Handcrafted/Glass, 3-23/32" tall.
An opossum is the clapper in a clear glass bell.
Artist: Ken Crow

☐ Purchased 19__ Pd $_____ MIB   NB   DB   BNT
☐ Want   Orig. Ret. $11.00   **NB** $18   **MIB** Sec. Mkt. **$22**

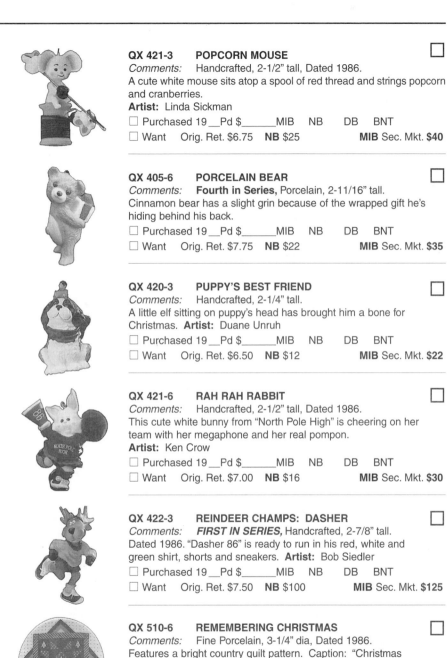

QX 421-3   POPCORN MOUSE
Comments: Handcrafted, 2-1/2" tall, Dated 1986.
A cute white mouse sits atop a spool of red thread and strings popcorn and cranberries.
Artist: Linda Sickman
☐ Purchased 19 __Pd $_____MIB   NB   DB   BNT
☐ Want   Orig. Ret. $6.75   **NB** $25   **MIB** Sec. Mkt. **$40**

QX 405-6   PORCELAIN BEAR
Comments: **Fourth in Series,** Porcelain, 2-11/16" tall.
Cinnamon bear has a slight grin because of the wrapped gift he's hiding behind his back.
☐ Purchased 19 __Pd $_____MIB   NB   DB   BNT
☐ Want   Orig. Ret. $7.75   **NB** $22   **MIB** Sec. Mkt. **$35**

QX 420-3   PUPPY'S BEST FRIEND
Comments: Handcrafted, 2-1/4" tall.
A little elf sitting on puppy's head has brought him a bone for Christmas. **Artist:** Duane Unruh
☐ Purchased 19 __Pd $_____MIB   NB   DB   BNT
☐ Want   Orig. Ret. $6.50   **NB** $12   **MIB** Sec. Mkt. **$22**

QX 421-6   RAH RAH RABBIT
Comments: Handcrafted, 2-1/2" tall, Dated 1986.
This cute white bunny from "North Pole High" is cheering on her team with her megaphone and her real pompon.
Artist: Ken Crow
☐ Purchased 19 __Pd $_____MIB   NB   DB   BNT
☐ Want   Orig. Ret. $7.00   **NB** $16   **MIB** Sec. Mkt. **$30**

QX 422-3   REINDEER CHAMPS: DASHER
Comments: **FIRST IN SERIES,** Handcrafted, 2-7/8" tall.
Dated 1986. "Dasher 86" is ready to run in his red, white and green shirt, shorts and sneakers. **Artist:** Bob Siedler
☐ Purchased 19 __Pd $_____MIB   NB   DB   BNT
☐ Want   Orig. Ret. $7.50   **NB** $100   **MIB** Sec. Mkt. **$125**

QX 510-6   REMEMBERING CHRISTMAS
Comments: Fine Porcelain, 3-1/4" dia, Dated 1986.
Features a bright country quilt pattern. Caption: "Christmas Memories Are Keepsakes Of The Heart." Plate stand included.
☐ Purchased 19 __Pd $_____MIB   NB   DB   BNT
☐ Want   Orig. Ret. $8.75   **NB** $12   **MIB** Sec. Mkt. **$28**

QX 401-6   ROCKING HORSE
Comments: **Sixth in Series,** Handcrafted, 4" wide, Dated 1986.
A golden palomino rides into the holidays on green rockers. Some collectors found this ornament with the number "QX 436-6." Others have found a gold sticker on the box stating "Made in Macau."
Artist: Linda Sickman
☐ Purchased 19 __Pd $_____MIB   NB   DB   BNT
☐ Want   Orig. Ret. $10.75   **NB** $25   **MIB** Sec. Mkt. **$60**

QXO440-6   SANTA & HIS REINDEER: OPEN HOUSE ORNAMENT
Comments: Handcrafted, 2" tall and 14" wide.
Two reindeer pull Santa in his sleigh full of toys. Special offering for "Open House" events. Very nice ornament!
☐ Purchased 19 __Pd $_____MIB   NB   DB   BNT
☐ Want   Orig. Ret. $9.75   **NB** $22   **MIB** Sec. Mkt. **$35**

QLX 703-3   SANTA & SPARKY
Comments: **FIRST IN SERIES,** Light and Motion, Handcrafted. 4-1/16" tall, Dated 1986. Santa lights the Christmas tree and moves backwards to admire this work, as Sparky penguin watches with excitement.
☐ Purchased 19 __Pd $_____MIB   NB   DB   BNT
☐ Want   Orig. Ret. $22.00   **NB** $60   **MIB** Sec. Mkt. **$90**

QT 700-6   SANTA TREE TOPPER
Comments: Open House, Fabric.
This whimsical Santa is all set in his red and white suit with green mittens. He holds a gold wand.
☐ Purchased 19 __Pd $_____MIB   NB   DB   BNT
☐ Want   Orig. Ret. $18.00   **NB** $28   **MIB** Sec. Mkt. **$38**

QX 426-3   SANTA'S HOT TUB
Comments: Handcrafted, 3" tall.
Santa and one of his reindeer are enjoying themselves in a hot tub from the "Polar Barrel Hot Tub Co."
Artist: Ed Seale
☐ Purchased 19 __Pd $_____MIB   NB   DB   BNT
☐ Want   Orig. Ret. $12.00   **NB** $30   **MIB** Sec. Mkt. **$55**

QLX 711-5   SANTA'S ON HIS WAY
Comments: Light and Hologram Panorama Ball, 3-5/8" tall.
Laser photography creates a three-dimensional effect of Santa and his reindeer flying above the city.
Artist: Duane Unruh
☐ Purchased 19 __Pd $_____MIB   NB   DB   BNT
☐ Want   Orig. Ret. $15.00   **NB** $50   **MIB** Sec. Mkt. **$65**

QXO 441-3   SANTA'S PANDA PAL: OPEN HOUSE ORN. ☐
Comments: Handcrafted, 2-1/4" tall.
Cute flocked panda wears a Santa hat. Special offering for dealers' "Open House" events.
☐ Purchased 19 __Pd $_____MIB   NB   DB   BNT
☐ Want   Orig. Ret. $5.00 **NB** $10   **MIB** Sec. Mkt. **$22**

QLX 706-6   SANTA'S SNACK ☐
Comments: Lighted, Handcrafted, 2-15/16" tall.
Santa's midnight snack is a "mile-high" sandwich. Santa is dressed in reindeer slippers and a green striped nightshirt.
Artist: Ken Crow
☐ Purchased 19 __Pd $_____MIB   NB   DB   BNT
☐ Want   Orig. Ret. $10.00 **NB** $40   **MIB** Sec. Mkt. **$55**

QX 270-6   SEASON OF THE HEART ☐
Comments: Red Glass Ball, 2-7/8" dia.
A family enjoys a ride through the snow-covered countryside in a horse-drawn sleigh. Caption: "Christmas... Season Of The Heart, Time Of Fond Remembrance."
☐ Purchased 19 __Pd $_____MIB   NB   DB   BNT
☐ Want   Orig. Ret. $4.75 **NB** $5   **MIB** Sec. Mkt. **$18**

QLX 706-3   SHARING FRIENDSHIP ☐
Comments: Lighted Acrylic, 5-5/16" tall, Dated 1986.
A poinsettia etched into clear acrylic accents the caption: "Friendship Is A Special Kind Of Sharing."
Artist: LaDene Votruba
☐ Purchased 19 __Pd $_____MIB   NB   DB   BNT
☐ Want   Orig. Ret. $8.50 **NB** $12   **MIB** Sec. Mkt. **$18**

QLT 709-6   SHINING STAR TREE TOPPER ☐
Comments: Lighted, Acrylic.
A partridge graces the center of this five-pointed star. Each of the five points include a design of a pear and leaf.
☐ Purchased 19 __Pd $_____MIB   NB   DB   BNT
☐ Want   Orig. Ret. $17.50 **NB** $14   **MIB** Sec. Mkt. **$25**

QX 277-3   SHIRT TALES™ PARADE ☐
Comments: Gold Glass Ball, 2-7/8" dia.
The Shirt Tales Band parades around the ball. Caption: "Here Comes Christmas!" and "Merriment Is All Around Whenever Christmas Comes To Town!"
☐ Purchased 19 __Pd $_____MIB   NB   DB   BNT
☐ Want   Orig. Ret. $4.75 **NB** $8   **MIB** Sec. Mkt. **$18**

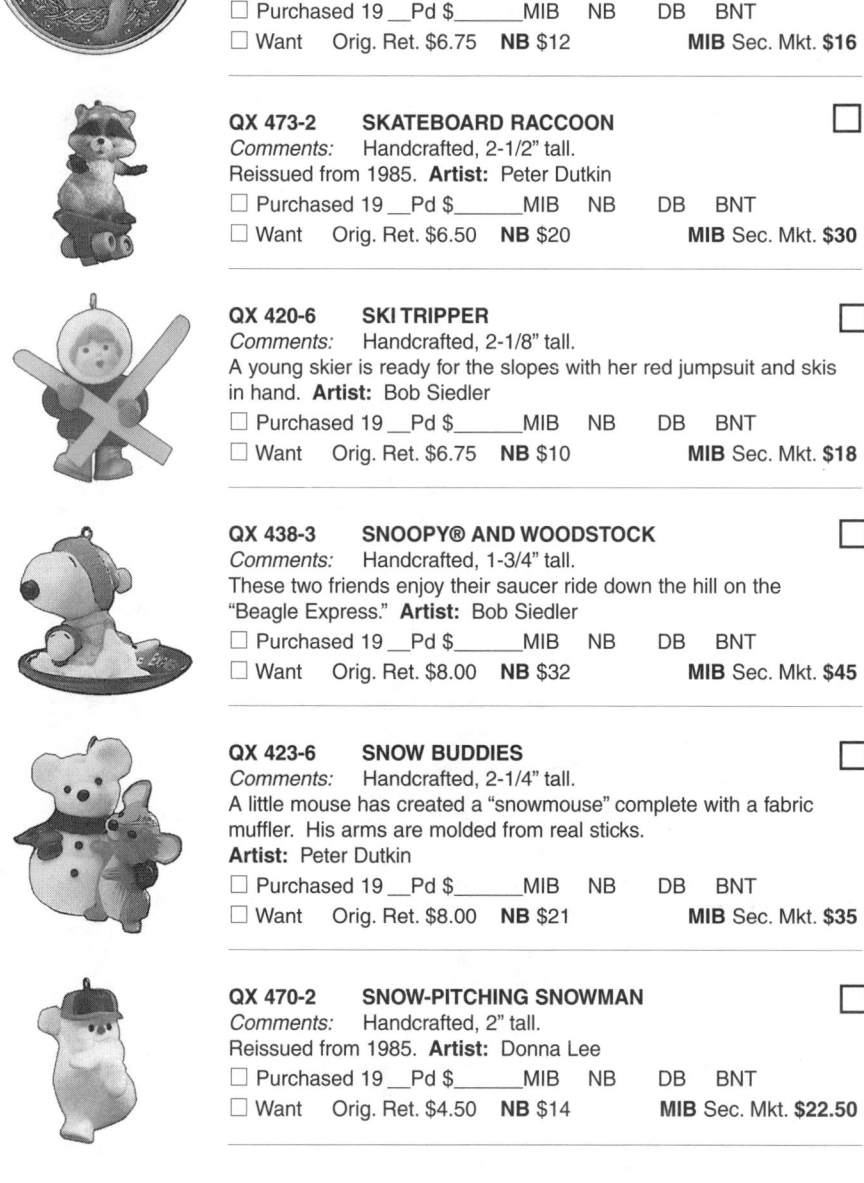

QX 380-6   SISTER ☐
Comments: Bezeled Satin, 2-3/4" dia., Dated 1986.
Red padded satin carries a design of a grapevine wreath entwined with holly and ribbon, with a teddy bear for company. Caption: "With Every Christmas, Every Year, A Sister Grows More Loved... More Dear." **Artist:** LaDene Votruba
☐ Purchased 19 __Pd $_____MIB   NB   DB   BNT
☐ Want   Orig. Ret. $6.75 **NB** $12   **MIB** Sec. Mkt. **$16**

QX 473-2   SKATEBOARD RACCOON ☐
Comments: Handcrafted, 2-1/2" tall.
Reissued from 1985. **Artist:** Peter Dutkin
☐ Purchased 19 __Pd $_____MIB   NB   DB   BNT
☐ Want   Orig. Ret. $6.50 **NB** $20   **MIB** Sec. Mkt. **$30**

QX 420-6   SKI TRIPPER ☐
Comments: Handcrafted, 2-1/8" tall.
A young skier is ready for the slopes with her red jumpsuit and skis in hand. **Artist:** Bob Siedler
☐ Purchased 19 __Pd $_____MIB   NB   DB   BNT
☐ Want   Orig. Ret. $6.75 **NB** $10   **MIB** Sec. Mkt. **$18**

QX 438-3   SNOOPY® AND WOODSTOCK ☐
Comments: Handcrafted, 1-3/4" tall.
These two friends enjoy their saucer ride down the hill on the "Beagle Express." **Artist:** Bob Siedler
☐ Purchased 19 __Pd $_____MIB   NB   DB   BNT
☐ Want   Orig. Ret. $8.00 **NB** $32   **MIB** Sec. Mkt. **$45**

QX 423-6   SNOW BUDDIES ☐
Comments: Handcrafted, 2-1/4" tall.
A little mouse has created a "snowmouse" complete with a fabric muffler. His arms are molded from real sticks.
Artist: Peter Dutkin
☐ Purchased 19 __Pd $_____MIB   NB   DB   BNT
☐ Want   Orig. Ret. $8.00 **NB** $21   **MIB** Sec. Mkt. **$35**

QX 470-2   SNOW-PITCHING SNOWMAN ☐
Comments: Handcrafted, 2" tall.
Reissued from 1985. **Artist:** Donna Lee
☐ Purchased 19 __Pd $_____MIB   NB   DB   BNT
☐ Want   Orig. Ret. $4.50 **NB** $14   **MIB** Sec. Mkt. **$22.50**

QX 477-5   SOCCER BEAVER

Comments: Handcrafted, 2-1/2" tall.
Reissued from 1985. **Artist:** Peter Dutkin

☐ Purchased 19 __ Pd $_____ MIB   NB   DB   BNT

☐ Want   Orig. Ret. $6.50   **NB** $9   **MIB** Sec. Mkt. **$22**

QX 430-3   SON

Comments: Handcrafted, 4" tall, Dated 1986.
A wooden boy toy is poking out of the top of a red and green
striped knit stocking "For Son."

Artist: Ed Seale

☐ Purchased 19 __ Pd $_____ MIB   NB   DB   BNT

☐ Want   Orig. Ret. $5.75   **NB** $18   **MIB** Sec. Mkt. **$35**

QX 415-6   SPECIAL DELIVERY

Comments: Handcrafted, 2" tall.
This little penguin is on his way to deliver a gift of sardines to one
of his friends. **Artist:** Bob Siedler

☐ Purchased 19 __ Pd $_____ MIB   NB   DB   BNT

☐ Want   Orig. Ret. $5.00   **NB** $12   **MIB** Sec. Mkt. **$20**

QX 322-6   STAR BRIGHTENERS

Comments: Acrylic, 2-3/4" dia., Dated 1986.
Two etched angels are polishing a star. Caption: "Joy At
Christmas." **Artist:** LaDene Votruba

☐ Purchased 19 __ Pd $_____ MIB   NB   DB   BNT

☐ Want   Orig. Ret. $6.00   **NB** $6   **MIB** Sec. Mkt. **$12.50**

QX 384-3   STATUE OF LIBERTY, THE

Comments: Acrylic, 3-9/16" tall, Dated 1986.
This special commemorative shows "The Lady" etched in clear
acrylic and was created in honor of the statue's 100th birthday.
Caption: "1886 Centennial 1986." **Artist:** Michele Pyda-Sevcik

☐ Purchased 19 __ Pd $_____ MIB   NB   DB   BNT

☐ Want   Orig. Ret. $6.00   **NB** $11   **MIB** Sec. Mkt. **$24**

QLX 701-1   SUGARPLUM COTTAGE

Comments: Lighted, Handcrafted, 3" tall.
Issued in 1984, 1985 and 1986.

☐ Purchased 19 __ Pd $_____ MIB   NB   DB   BNT

☐ Want   Orig. Ret. $11.00   **NB** $30   **MIB** Sec. Mkt. **$45**

QX 408-6   SWEETHEART

Comments: Handcrafted, 3-1/2" tall, Dated Christmas 1986.
An ivory gazebo with red shingled roof has a Christmas tree in the
center and two squirrels sitting on the railing. Sign reads, "To My
Sweetheart With Love." May be personalized.

Artist: Joyce Pattee

☐ Purchased 19 __ Pd $_____ MIB   NB   DB   BNT

☐ Want   Orig. Ret. $11.00 **NB** $30   **MIB** Sec. Mkt. **$55**

QX 275-3   TEACHER

Comments: White Glass Ball, 2-7/8" dia., Dated Christmas 1986.
A little mouse sits next to a bright red apple, from which he has
nibbled a star. Caption: "For My Teacher."

☐ Purchased 19 __ Pd $_____ MIB   NB   DB   BNT

☐ Want   Orig. Ret. $4.75   **NB** $8   **MIB** Sec. Mkt. **$12**

QX 401-3   TEN YEARS TOGETHER

Comments: Fine Porcelain, 3" tall, Dated 1986.
Roses and holly, accented with gold, create a cloisonne look.
Caption: "Ten Years Together" and "More Than Yesterday...
Less Than Tomorrow."

☐ Purchased 19 __ Pd $_____ MIB   NB   DB   BNT

☐ Want   Orig. Ret. $7.50   **NB** $10   **MIB** Sec. Mkt. **$18**

QX 406-6   THIMBLE SERIES: PARTRIDGE

Comments: **Ninth in Series,** Handcrafted, 1-21/32" tall.
A sweet little partridge has made its nest in a thimble full of
greenery and fruit.

☐ Purchased 19 __ Pd $_____ MIB   NB   DB   BNT

☐ Want   Orig. Ret. $5.75   **NB** $12   **MIB** Sec. Mkt. **$22**

QX 379-6   TIMELESS LOVE

Comments: Acrylic, 3" tall, Dated Christmas 1986.
Caption in gold foil: "Love... Comes Not In Moments Of Time
But In Timeless Moments." **Artist:** LaDene Votruba

☐ Purchased 19 __ Pd $_____ MIB   NB   DB   BNT

☐ Want   Orig. Ret. $6.00   **NB** $6   **MIB** Sec. Mkt. **$25**

QX 403-6   TIN LOCOMOTIVE

Comments: **Fifth in Series,** Pressed Tin, 3-17/32" tall.
Dated 1986. A stenciled holly design adorns the yellow and red
cab of this locomotive. **Artist:** Linda Sickman

☐ Purchased 19 __ Pd $_____ MIB   NB   DB   BNT

☐ Want   Orig. Ret. $14.75   **NB** $50   **MIB** Sec. Mkt. **$65**

QX 418-6   TIPPING THE SCALES ☐

Comments: Handcrafted, 2-11/16" tall, Dated 1986.
Santa, in his red monogrammed robe, checks out his weight...
"1986" while holding a cookie. **Artist:** Peter Dutkin

☐ Purchased 19 ___ Pd $_____ MIB   NB   DB   BNT
☐ Want   Orig. Ret. $6.75   **NB** $15   **MIB** Sec. Mkt. **$22**

QX 423-3   TOUCHDOWN SANTA ☐

Comments: Handcrafted, 2-15/16" tall, Dated 1986.
Santa has the ball and he's headed for a touchdown! His red jersey is
'86. **Artist:** Peter Dutkin

☐ Purchased 19 ___ Pd $_____ MIB   NB   DB   BNT
☐ Want   Orig. Ret. $8.00   **NB** $21   **MIB** Sec. Mkt. **$32**

QX 425-6   TREETOP TRIO/BLUEBIRDS ☐

Comments: Handcrafted, 2" tall, Reissued in 1987.
The bluebird trio is chirping out a Christmas carol in a nest of
real straw. **Artist:** Donna Lee

☐ Purchased 19 ___ Pd $_____ MIB   NB   DB   BNT
☐ Want   Orig. Ret. $11.00 **NB** $16   **MIB** Sec. Mkt. **$28**

QX 378-6   TWELVE DAYS OF CHRISTMAS: ☐
THREE FRENCH HENS

Comments: **Third in Series,** Acrylic, 3-3/8" tall, Dated 1986.
This acrylic teardrop has captions in gold and pictures three hens on
holly leaves. **Artist:** LaDene Votruba

☐ Purchased 19 ___ Pd $_____ MIB   NB   DB   BNT
☐ Want   Orig. Ret. $6.50   **NB** $20   **MIB** Sec. Mkt. **$44**

QX 410-3   TWENTY-FIVE YEARS TOGETHER ☐

Comments: Fine Porcelain Plate, 3-1/4" tall.
Dated Christmas 1986. Blue and silver bells tied up with ribbon
and holly. Comes with acrylic stand. Caption: "Twenty-Five
Years Together" and "Love Lights All The Seasons Of Our
Years." **Artist:** LaDene Votruba

☐ Purchased 19 ___ Pd $_____ MIB   NB   DB   BNT
☐ Want   Orig. Ret. $8.00   **NB** $10   **MIB** Sec. Mkt. **$22**

QLX 707-2   VILLAGE EXPRESS ☐

Comments: Light/Motion, Handcrafted, 3-1/2" tall.
Reissued in 1987. A train chugs through a peaceful mountain
village and a tunnel. **Artist:** Linda Sickman

☐ Purchased 19 ___ Pd $_____ MIB   NB   DB   BNT
☐ Want   Orig. Ret. $24.50 **NB** $60   **MIB** Sec. Mkt. **$115**

QX 419-6   WALNUT SHELL RIDER ☐

Comments: Handcrafted, 1-3/4" tall, Reissued in 1987.
An elf dressed in blue rides downhill in his walnut shell sled.
Artist: Ed Seale

☐ Purchased 19 ___ Pd $_____ MIB   NB   DB   BNT
☐ Want   Orig. Ret. $6.00   **NB** $12   **MIB** Sec. Mkt. **$20**

QX 510-3   WELCOME, CHRISTMAS ☐

Comments: Handcrafted, 2-5/8" tall, Dated 1986.
A precious little angel dangles inside a wooden heart with holly
and heart stencils. Caption: "Welcome, Christmas!"
Artist: Ken Crow

☐ Purchased 19 ___ Pd $_____ MIB   NB   DB   BNT
☐ Want   Orig. Ret. $8.25   **NB** $12   **MIB** Sec. Mkt. **$25**

QX 408-3   WINDOWS OF THE WORLD: DUTCH ☐

Comments: **Second in Series,** Handcrafted, 3" tall, Dated 1986.
A little Dutch girl looks through the top half of the double door of her
home. Caption: "Vrolyk Kerstfeest." **Artist:** Bob Siedler

☐ Purchased 19 ___ Pd $_____ MIB   NB   DB   BNT
☐ Want   Orig. Ret. $10.00 **NB** $30   **MIB** Sec. Mkt. **$55**

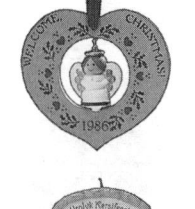

QX 407-3   WOOD CHILDHOOD: REINDEER ☐

Comments: **Third in Series,** Wood, 2-1/2" tall, Dated 1986.
This cute hand-painted wooden reindeer makes a galloping
motion as he rolls along on his wagon. **Artist:** Ken Crow

☐ Purchased 19 ___ Pd $_____ MIB   NB   DB   BNT
☐ Want   Orig. Ret. $7.50   **NB** $14   **MIB** Sec. Mkt. **$25**

QX 424-6   WYNKEN, BLYNKEN AND NOD ☐

Comments: Handcrafted, 2-7/8" tall.
The nursery rhyme has come to life as the three set sail in a small
boat with silver nets. **Artist:** Donna Lee

☐ Purchased 19 ___ Pd $_____ MIB   NB   DB   BNT
☐ Want   Orig. Ret. $9.75   **NB** $32   **MIB** Sec. Mkt. **$42**

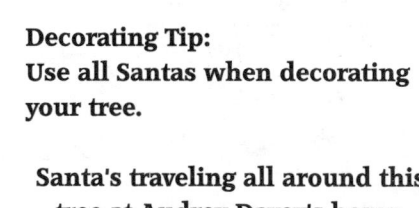

Decorating Tip:
**Use all Santas when decorating
your tree.**

**Santa's traveling all around this
tree at Audrey Davey's home.**

1987 Collection

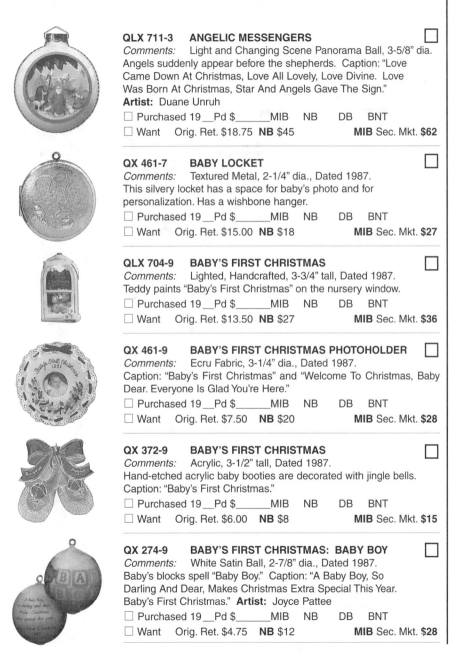

QLX 711-3   ANGELIC MESSENGERS ☐
Comments: Light and Changing Scene Panorama Ball, 3-5/8" dia.
Angels suddenly appear before the shepherds. Caption: "Love
Came Down At Christmas, Love All Lovely, Love Divine. Love
Was Born At Christmas, Star And Angels Gave The Sign."
Artist: Duane Unruh

☐ Purchased 19 __ Pd $_____ MIB   NB   DB   BNT
☐ Want   Orig. Ret. $18.75 **NB** $45   **MIB** Sec. Mkt. **$62**

QX 461-7   BABY LOCKET ☐
Comments: Textured Metal, 2-1/4" dia., Dated 1987.
This silvery locket has a space for baby's photo and for
personalization. Has a wishbone hanger.

☐ Purchased 19 __ Pd $_____ MIB   NB   DB   BNT
☐ Want   Orig. Ret. $15.00 **NB** $18   **MIB** Sec. Mkt. **$27**

QLX 704-9   BABY'S FIRST CHRISTMAS ☐
Comments: Lighted, Handcrafted, 3-3/4" tall, Dated 1987.
Teddy paints "Baby's First Christmas" on the nursery window.

☐ Purchased 19 __ Pd $_____ MIB   NB   DB   BNT
☐ Want   Orig. Ret. $13.50 **NB** $27   **MIB** Sec. Mkt. **$36**

QX 461-9   BABY'S FIRST CHRISTMAS PHOTOHOLDER ☐
Comments: Ecru Fabric, 3-1/4" dia., Dated 1987.
Caption: "Baby's First Christmas" and "Welcome To Christmas, Baby
Dear. Everyone Is Glad You're Here."

☐ Purchased 19 __ Pd $_____ MIB   NB   DB   BNT
☐ Want   Orig. Ret. $7.50 **NB** $20   **MIB** Sec. Mkt. **$28**

QX 372-9   BABY'S FIRST CHRISTMAS ☐
Comments: Acrylic, 3-1/2" tall, Dated 1987.
Hand-etched acrylic baby booties are decorated with jingle bells.
Caption: "Baby's First Christmas."

☐ Purchased 19 __ Pd $_____ MIB   NB   DB   BNT
☐ Want   Orig. Ret. $6.00 **NB** $8   **MIB** Sec. Mkt. **$15**

QX 274-9   BABY'S FIRST CHRISTMAS: BABY BOY ☐
Comments: White Satin Ball, 2-7/8" dia., Dated 1987.
Baby's blocks spell "Baby Boy." Caption: "A Baby Boy, So
Darling And Dear, Makes Christmas Extra Special This Year.
Baby's First Christmas." **Artist:** Joyce Pattee

☐ Purchased 19 __ Pd $_____ MIB   NB   DB   BNT
☐ Want   Orig. Ret. $4.75 **NB** $12   **MIB** Sec. Mkt. **$28**

QX 274-7   BABY'S FIRST CHRISTMAS: BABY GIRL ☐
Comments: White Satin Ball, 2-7/8" dia., Dated 1987.
Caption: "A Baby Girl, So Dear And Sweet, Makes Your
Christmas Joy Complete. Baby's First Christmas." More
"girls" than "boys." **Artist:** Joyce Pattee

☐ Purchased 19 __ Pd $_____ MIB   NB   DB   BNT
☐ Want   Orig. Ret. $4.75 **NB** $8   **MIB** Sec. Mkt. **$15**

QX 411-3   BABY'S FIRST CHRISTMAS ☐
Comments: Handcrafted, 4-1/4" tall, Dated 1987.
Baby has lots of fun in this real spring seat. Caption: "Baby's
First Christmas." **Artist:** Donna Lee

☐ Purchased 19 __ Pd $_____ MIB   NB   DB   BNT
☐ Want   Orig. Ret. $9.75 **NB** $14   **MIB** Sec. Mkt. **$26**

QX 460-7   BABY'S SECOND CHRISTMAS ☐
Comments: Handcrafted, 2-3/4" tall, Dated 1987.
A "Clown-in-the-Box" greets "Baby's 2nd Christmas." Attaches to
the tree with a clip. **Artist:** Donna Lee

☐ Purchased 19 __ Pd $_____ MIB   NB   DB   BNT
☐ Want   Orig. Ret. $5.75 **NB** $15   **MIB** Sec. Mkt. **$29**

QX 279-7   BABYSITTER ☐
Comments: Porcelain White Glass Ball, 3" dia., Dated 1987.
Caption: "For Bringing Children Such Special Gifts... Gentleness,
Caring, And Love. Merry Christmas."   **Artist:** Sharon Pike

☐ Purchased 19 __ Pd $_____ MIB   NB   DB   BNT
☐ Want   Orig. Ret. $4.75 **NB** $8   **MIB** Sec. Mkt. **$16**

QX 455-7   BEARY SPECIAL ☐
Comments: Handcrafted, 2-1/2" tall.
A flocked brown bear reaches up to hang an ornament on the
tree – it has his picture on it! **Artist:** Bob Siedler

☐ Purchased 19 __ Pd $_____ MIB   NB   DB   BNT
☐ Want   Orig. Ret. $4.75 **NB** $8   **MIB** Sec. Mkt. **$20**

QX 272-7   BETSEY CLARK: HOME FOR CHRISTMAS ☐
Comments: **Second in Series,** Gold Glass Ball, 2-7/8" dia.
Dated 1987. Betsey and her friends add final holiday decorating
touches. Captions: "There's No Place Like Christmas" and
"Noel." **Artist:** Sharon Pike

☐ Purchased 19 __ Pd $_____ MIB   NB   DB   BNT
☐ Want   Orig. Ret. $5.00 **NB** $15   **MIB** Sec. Mkt. **$24**

QX 473-7   BRIGHT CHRISTMAS DREAMS ☐
Comments: Handcrafted 4" tall, Dated Christmas 1987.
Four white mice with brightly colored nightcaps have fallen asleep
in a box of Crayola Crayons. The Crayola series began in '88. **Artist:**
Bob Siedler

☐ Purchased 19__Pd $_____MIB   NB   DB   BNT
☐ Want   Orig. Ret. $7.25   **NB** $75   **MIB** Sec. Mkt. **$88**

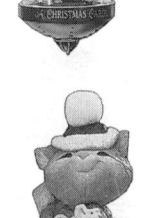

QLX 705-9   BRIGHT NOEL ☐
Comments: Lighted Acrylic, 5-1/2" tall.
An outline of an acrylic star is the framework for a bright red Noel
in the center. **Artist:** LaDene Votruba

☐ Purchased 19__Pd $_____MIB   NB   DB   BNT
☐ Want   Orig. Ret. $7.00   **NB** $20   **MIB** Sec. Mkt. **$32**

QXC 581-7   CAROUSEL REINDEER:
**   CHARTER CLUB MEMBERSHIP ORNAMENT** ☐
Comments: Handcrafted, 3-3/4" tall, Dated 1987.
A prancing reindeer rides a brass post inside a hoop. Caption:
"1987 Charter Member." Club logo is printed in gold on bottom
of hoop. **Artist:** Linda Sickman

☐ Purchased 19__Pd $_____MIB   NB   DB   BNT
☐ Want   Orig. Ret. $8.00   **NB** $40   **MIB** Sec. Mkt. **$60**

QX 459-9   CHILD'S THIRD CHRISTMAS ☐
Comments: Handcrafted, 3" tall, Dated 1987.
A child dressed in red rides a reindeer, which makes a galloping
motion when it is tapped. Caption: "My 3rd Christmas."
Artist: Ken Crow

☐ Purchased 19__Pd $_____MIB   NB   DB   BNT
☐ Want   Orig. Ret. $5.75   **NB** $10   **MIB** Sec. Mkt. **$25**

QX 456-7   CHOCOLATE CHIPMUNK ☐
Comments: Handcrafted, 2" tall.
This cute little fellow sits happily on a chocolate chip cookie and
holds a chip in his paws. **Artist:** Ed Seale

☐ Purchased 19__Pd $_____MIB   NB   DB   BNT
☐ Want   Orig. Ret. $6.00   **NB** $28   **MIB** Sec. Mkt. **$50**

QLX 705-7   CHRIS MOUSE GLOW ☐
Comments: **Third in Series,** Lighted, Handcrafted, 4-1/8" tall.
Dated 1987. In a blue nightshirt and red cap, Chris Mouse swings
happily from his "stained glass" lamp. **Artist:** Bob Siedler

☐ Purchased 19__Pd $_____MIB   NB   DB   BNT
☐ Want   Orig. Ret. $11.00   **NB** $45   **MIB** Sec. Mkt. **$57.50**

QLX 702-9   CHRISTMAS CLASSICS:
**   A CHRISTMAS CAROL** ☐
Comments: **Second in Series,** Lighted, Handcrafted, 4-3/16" tall.
Dated 1987. In this scene, Scrooge gives gifts to Tiny Tim while his
parents look on. Setting is a stage draped in elegant curtains.

☐ Purchased 19__Pd $_____MIB   NB   DB   BNT
☐ Want   Orig. Ret. $16.00   **NB** $35   **MIB** Sec. Mkt. **$50**

QX 453-7   CHRISTMAS CUDDLE ☐
Comments: Handcrafted, 2-3/4" tall.
A kitten and a white mouse, in matching Santa caps, snuggle together.

☐ Purchased 19__Pd $_____MIB   NB   DB   BNT
☐ Want   Orig. Ret. $5.75   **NB** $16   **MIB** Sec. Mkt. **$28**

QX 467-9   CHRISTMAS FUN PUZZLE ☐
Comments: Handcrafted, 2-1/2" dia.
A Santa, mouse and reindeer take on new shapes and designs as this
ornament is rotated to mix or match the characters.
Artist: Donna Lee

☐ Purchased 19__Pd $_____MIB   NB   DB   BNT
☐ Want   Orig. Ret. $8.00   **NB** $12   **MIB** Sec. Mkt. **$18**

QX 444-9   CHRISTMAS IS GENTLE ☐
Comments: Limited Edition 24,700, Hand numbered.
Handpainted Bone China, 3" tall. Two lambs sit peacefully in a basket
edged with gold. **Artist:** Ed Seale

☐ Purchased 19__Pd $_____MIB   NB   DB   BNT
☐ Want   Orig. Ret. $17.50   **NB** $38   **MIB** Sec. Mkt. **$80**

QX 473-9   CHRISTMAS KEYS ☐
Comments: Handcrafted, 2" tall.
An ivory upright piano is decorated with sprigs of bright green holly and
red berries. **Artist:** Duane Unruh

☐ Purchased 19__Pd $_____MIB   NB   DB   BNT
☐ Want   Orig. Ret. $5.75   **NB** $18   **MIB** Sec. Mkt. **$30**

QLX 701-3   CHRISTMAS MORNING ☐
Comments: Light and Motion, Handcrafted, 4-5/16" tall.
Reissued in 1988. Two children slide down the banister in anticipation
of their Christmas gifts. **Artist:** Ken Crow

☐ Purchased 19__Pd $_____MIB   NB   DB   BNT
☐ Want   Orig. Ret. $24.50   **NB** $28   **MIB** Sec. Mkt. **$40**

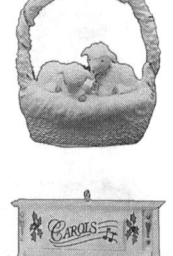

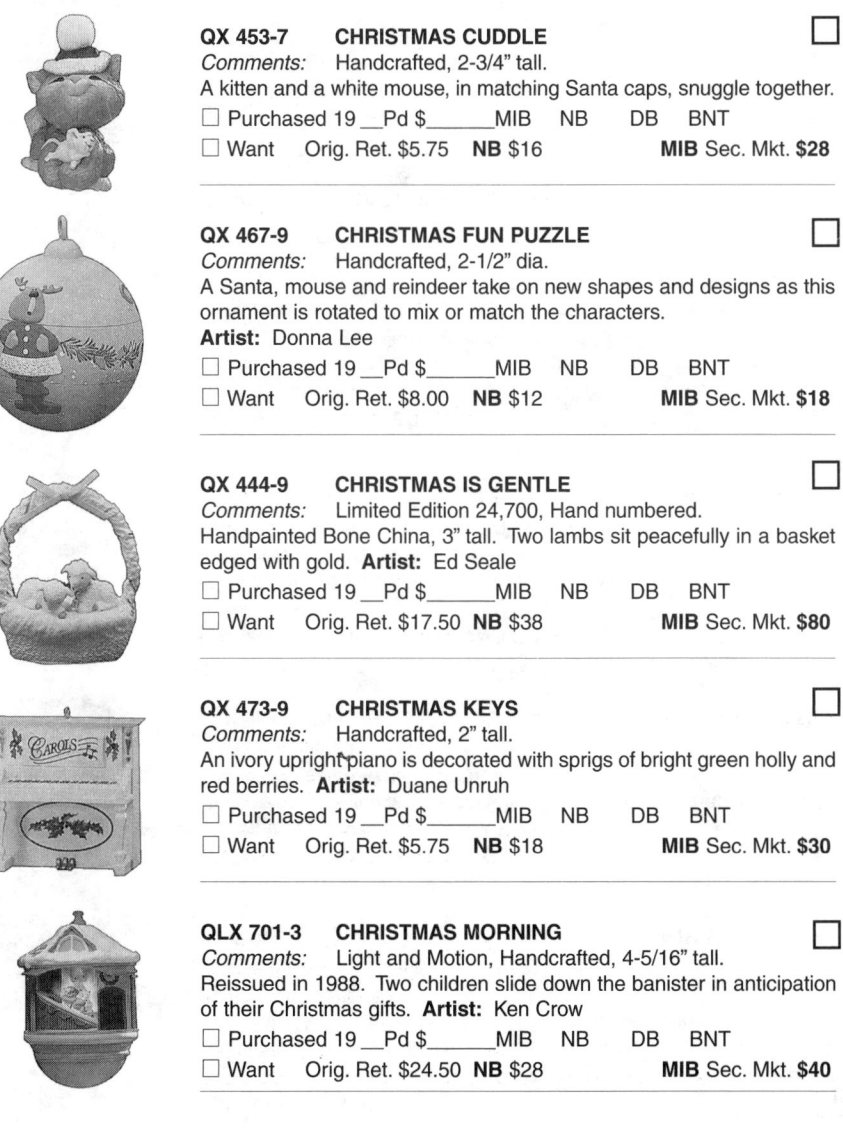

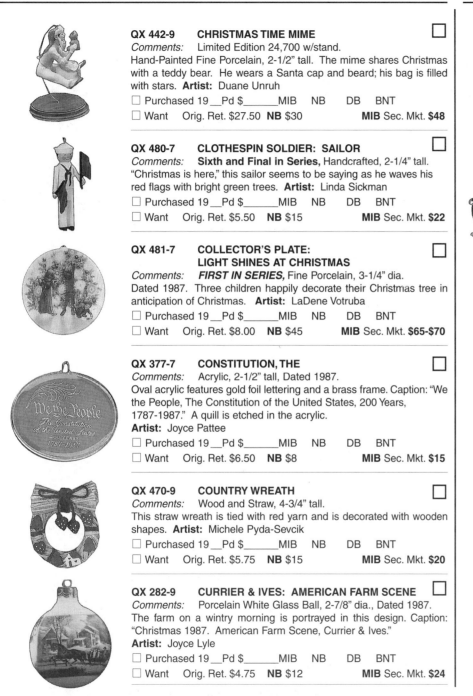

QX 442-9   CHRISTMAS TIME MIME ☐
Comments: Limited Edition 24,700 w/stand.
Hand-Painted Fine Porcelain, 2-1/2" tall. The mime shares Christmas with a teddy bear. He wears a Santa cap and beard; his bag is filled with stars. **Artist:** Duane Unruh
☐ Purchased 19 __Pd $_____MIB   NB   DB   BNT
☐ Want   Orig. Ret. $27.50 **NB** $30   **MIB** Sec. Mkt. **$48**

QX 480-7   CLOTHESPIN SOLDIER: SAILOR ☐
Comments: **Sixth and Final in Series,** Handcrafted, 2-1/4" tall.
"Christmas is here," this sailor seems to be saying as he waves his red flags with bright green trees. **Artist:** Linda Sickman
☐ Purchased 19 __Pd $_____MIB   NB   DB   BNT
☐ Want   Orig. Ret. $5.50 **NB** $15   **MIB** Sec. Mkt. **$22**

QX 481-7   COLLECTOR'S PLATE: ☐
LIGHT SHINES AT CHRISTMAS
Comments: **FIRST IN SERIES,** Fine Porcelain, 3-1/4" dia.
Dated 1987. Three children happily decorate their Christmas tree in anticipation of Christmas. **Artist:** LaDene Votruba
☐ Purchased 19 __Pd $_____MIB   NB   DB   BNT
☐ Want   Orig. Ret. $8.00 **NB** $45   **MIB** Sec. Mkt. **$65-$70**

QX 377-7   CONSTITUTION, THE ☐
Comments: Acrylic, 2-1/2" tall, Dated 1987.
Oval acrylic features gold foil lettering and a brass frame. Caption: "We the People, The Constitution of the United States, 200 Years, 1787-1987." A quill is etched in the acrylic.
Artist: Joyce Pattee
☐ Purchased 19 __Pd $_____MIB   NB   DB   BNT
☐ Want   Orig. Ret. $6.50 **NB** $8   **MIB** Sec. Mkt. **$15**

QX 470-9   COUNTRY WREATH ☐
Comments: Wood and Straw, 4-3/4" tall.
This straw wreath is tied with red yarn and is decorated with wooden shapes. **Artist:** Michele Pyda-Sevcik
☐ Purchased 19 __Pd $_____MIB   NB   DB   BNT
☐ Want   Orig. Ret. $5.75 **NB** $15   **MIB** Sec. Mkt. **$20**

QX 282-9   CURRIER & IVES: AMERICAN FARM SCENE ☐
Comments: Porcelain White Glass Ball, 2-7/8" dia., Dated 1987.
The farm on a wintry morning is portrayed in this design. Caption: "Christmas 1987. American Farm Scene, Currier & Ives."
Artist: Joyce Lyle
☐ Purchased 19 __Pd $_____MIB   NB   DB   BNT
☐ Want   Orig. Ret. $4.75 **NB** $12   **MIB** Sec. Mkt. **$24**

QX 462-9   DAD ☐
Comments: Handcrafted, 3" tall, Dated Christmas 1987.
This polar bear papa may be living at the North Pole, but his new tie is from the South Pacific. Caption: "For Dad."
Artist: Bob Siedler
☐ Purchased 19 __Pd $_____MIB   NB   DB   BNT
☐ Want   Orig. Ret. $6.00 **NB** $24   **MIB** Sec. Mkt. **$37.50**

QX 463-7   DAUGHTER ☐
Comments: Handcrafted, 1-1/4" tall, Dated 1987.
A graceful swan sleigh is pulled by two reindeer. Caption: "Daughter."
Looks like wood. **Artist:** Linda Sickman
☐ Purchased 19 __Pd $_____MIB   NB   DB   BNT
☐ Want   Orig. Ret. $5.75 **NB** $14   **MIB** Sec. Mkt. **$22**

QX 448-7   DECEMBER SHOWERS ☐
Comments: Handcrafted, 2-1/2" tall.
A little angel dressed in pink, checks out from under her umbrella to see if the rain has quit. **Artist:** Donna Lee
☐ Purchased 19 __Pd $_____MIB   NB   DB   BNT
☐ Want   Orig. Ret. $5.50 **NB** $16   **MIB** Sec. Mkt. **$25**

QX 467-7   DOC HOLIDAY ☐
Comments: Handcrafted, 4" tall.
"Doc Holiday," as noted on his shirt, rides a spring-powered mechanical reindeer. Giddyap! Hard to find.
Artist: Ed Seale
☐ Purchased 19 __Pd $_____MIB   NB   DB   BNT
☐ Want   Orig. Ret. $8.00 **NB** $30   **MIB** Sec. Mkt. **$45**

QX 278-3   DR. SEUSS: THE GRINCH'S CHRISTMAS ☐
Comments: Glass Ball, 2-7/8" dia.
A happy grinch smiles inside a green wreath as the Whos sing carols around him. Caption: "A Very Merry Wish For A Merry, Merry Christmas."
☐ Purchased 19 __Pd $_____MIB   NB   DB   BNT
☐ Want   Orig. Ret. $4.75 **NB** $28   **MIB** Sec. Mkt. **$50**

QSP 930-9   ELVES – EMIL PAINTER ELF – FIGURINE ☐
Comments: Hand-Painted Porcelain.
☐ Purchased 19 __Pd $_____MIB   NB   DB   BNT
☐ Want   Orig. Ret. $10.00 **NB** $25   **MIB** Sec. Mkt. **$38**

QSP 930-7   ELVES - HANS CARPENTER ELF - FIGURINE ☐
Comments: Hand-Painted Porcelain.
☐ Purchased 19__ Pd $_____ MIB   NB   DB   BNT
☐ Want   Orig. Ret. $10.00 **NB** $25   **MIB** Sec. Mkt. **$38**

QSP 931-7   ELVES - KURT BLUE PRINT ELF - FIGURINE ☐
Comments: Hand-Painted Porcelain.
☐ Purchased 19__ Pd $_____ MIB   NB   DB   BNT
☐ Want   Orig. Ret. $10.00 **NB** $25   **MIB** Sec. Mkt. **$38**

QX 445-7   FAVORITE SANTA ☐
Comments: Special Edition, Hand-Painted Fine Porcelain, 5-1/2" tall.
A "Jolly Old Elf" indeed – Santa carries a long green, patched
stocking full of gifts. **Artist:** Peter Dutkin
☐ Purchased 19__ Pd $_____ MIB   NB   DB   BNT
☐ Want   Orig. Ret. $22.50 **NB** $18   **MIB** Sec. Mkt. **$30**

QX 443-7   FIFTY YEARS TOGETHER ☐
Comments: Fine Porcelain, 5" tall, Dated Christmas 1987.
This lovely bell shows off a bas relief poinsettia and is rimmed in
gold. Caption: "Fifty Years Together." Handle is a sculpted "50."
Artist: Ed Seale
☐ Purchased 19__ Pd $_____ MIB   NB   DB   BNT
☐ Want   Orig. Ret. $8.00 **NB** $10   **MIB** Sec. Mkt. **$25**

QX 272-9   FIRST CHRISTMAS TOGETHER ☐
Comments: White Glass Ball, 2-7/8" dia., Dated 1987.
This ornament has a delicate design of lovebirds in a garden of
pastel poinsettias. Caption: "First Christmas Together" and "To
All Who Love, Love Is All The World." **Artist:** Joyce A. Lyle
☐ Purchased 19__ Pd $_____ MIB   NB   DB   BNT
☐ Want   Orig. Ret. $4.75 **NB** $12   **MIB** Sec. Mkt. **$20**

QX 371-9   FIRST CHRISTMAS TOGETHER ☐
Comments: Acrylic, 2-1/2" tall, Dated 1987.
Two etched swans glide gracefully among the tall grasses.
Caption: "First Christmas Together."
☐ Purchased 19__ Pd $_____ MIB   NB   DB   BNT
☐ Want   Orig. Ret. $6.50 **NB** $8   **MIB** Sec. Mkt. **$16**

**Hallmark Ornaments make excellent
Christmas presents for all.
Remember to buy extra for
summer wedding gifts!**

QX 446-9   FIRST CHRISTMAS TOGETHER ☐
Comments: Textured Brass, 2-1/4" tall, Dated 1987.
Heart-shaped brass locket is decorated with embossed lovebirds
and caption.
☐ Purchased 19__ Pd $_____ MIB   NB   DB   BNT
☐ Want   Orig. Ret. $15.00 **NB** $15   **MIB** Sec. Mkt. **$28**

QLX 708-7   FIRST CHRISTMAS TOGETHER ☐
Comments: Lighted, Handcrafted, 2-5/8" tall, Dated 1987.
Two polar bears celebrate Christmas in their snow-capped igloo.
☐ Purchased 19__ Pd $_____ MIB   NB   DB   BNT
☐ Want   Orig. Ret. $11.50 **NB** $35   **MIB** Sec. Mkt. **$48**

QX 445-9   FIRST CHRISTMAS TOGETHER ☐
Comments: Handcrafted, 2-1/2" tall, Dated 1987.
Two raccoons "share" a red fabric sweatshirt. Caption: "First
Christmas Together."
☐ Purchased 19__ Pd $_____ MIB   NB   DB   BNT
☐ Want   Orig. Ret. $8.00 **NB** $10   **MIB** Sec. Mkt. **$28**

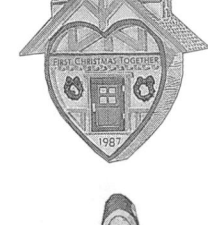

QX 446-7   FIRST CHRISTMAS TOGETHER ☐
Comments: Handcrafted, 3" tall, Dated 1987.
Just add an attic and a roof to the heart and you have a cozy
cottage for two! Sampler inside reads "Love, Sweet Love."
Artist: Donna Lee
☐ Purchased 19__ Pd $_____ MIB   NB   DB   BNT
☐ Want   Orig. Ret. $9.50 **NB** $15   **MIB** Sec. Mkt. **$22**

QX 474-9   FOLK ART SANTA ☐
Comments: Handcrafted, 4" tall.
This Old-World Santa has been painted and antiqued to resemble folk
art. His coat is accented with gold. **Artist:** Linda Sickman
☐ Purchased 19__ Pd $_____ MIB   NB   DB   BNT
☐ Want   Orig. Ret. $5.25 **NB** $20   **MIB** Sec. Mkt. **$30**

QX 279-9   FROM OUR HOME TO YOURS ☐
Comments: White Glass Ball, 3" dia., Dated 1987.
Holiday decorated doorways circle this frosted ball ornament.
Caption: "From Our Home... To Yours... At Christmas."
Artist: Michele Pyda-Sevcik
☐ Purchased 19__ Pd $_____ MIB   NB   DB   BNT
☐ Want   rig. Ret. $4.75   **NB** $10   **MIB** Sec. Mkt. **$25**

QX 440-9   FROSTY FRIENDS ☐
Comments: **Eighth in Series,** Handcrafted, 2" tall, Dated 1987.
The little Eskimo is receiving a bright red gift from a flocked seal who has jumped up through a hole in the ice.
Artist: Ed Seale

☐ Purchased 19__Pd $_____MIB   NB   DB   BNT
☐ Want   Orig. Ret. $8.50   **NB** $40   **MIB** Sec. Mkt. **$55**

QX 449-7   FUDGE FOREVER ☐
Comments: Handcrafted, 3" tall.
A little white mouse has filled his tummy with the fudge in this blue spatterware ladle. **Artist:** Peter Dutkin

☐ Purchased 19__Pd $_____MIB   NB   DB   BNT
☐ Want   Orig. Ret. $5.00   **NB** $20   **MIB** Sec. Mkt. **$35**

QX 276-7   GODCHILD ☐
Comments: Blue Glass Ball, 2-7/8" dia., Dated 1987.
A contemporary green tree with red balls and gold star are painted against a "snowy" blue ball. Caption: "A Godchild Makes Christmas Glow A Little Brighter." **Artist:** Michele Pyda-Sevcik

☐ Purchased 19__Pd $_____MIB   NB   DB   BNT
☐ Want   Orig. Ret. $4.75   **NB** $12   **MIB** Sec. Mkt. **$18**

QX 464-9   GOLDFINCH ☐
Comments: Hand-Painted Fine Porcelain, 2-1/2" tall.
Poised in flight, this goldfinch is so realistically painted, you'd think it could fly away. Has a hook.
Artist: Linda Sickman

☐ Purchased 19__Pd $_____MIB   NB   DB   BNT
☐ Want   Orig. Ret. $7.00   **NB** $24   **MIB** Sec. Mkt. **$65**

QLX 704-6   GOOD CHEER BLIMP ☐
Comments: Blinking Lights, Handcrafted, 3-1/16" tall.
Santa leans over the side of his gondola to see where his next stop will be. **Artist:** Linda Sickman

☐ Purchased 19__Pd $_____MIB   NB   DB   BNT
☐ Want   Orig. Ret. $16.00   **NB** $30   **MIB** Sec. Mkt. **$60**

QX 460-9   GRANDCHILD'S FIRST CHRISTMAS ☐
Comments: Handcrafted, 1-3/4" tall, Dated 1987.
A teddy bear sits on a red and green quilt inside a Jenny Lind style playpen. "Grandchild's First Christmas" is on the blanket over the side. **Artist:** Ed Seale

☐ Purchased 19__Pd $_____MIB   NB   DB   BNT
☐ Want   Orig. Ret. $9.00   **NB** $12   **MIB** Sec. Mkt. **$20**

QX 374-7   GRANDDAUGHTER ☐
Comments: Bezeled Satin, 2-3/4" dia., Dated Christmas 1987.
A snowy background holds a sleigh full of toys. Caption: "A Granddaughter Makes Each Day A Holiday In The Heart."
Artist: LaDene Votruba

☐ Purchased 19__Pd $_____MIB   NB   DB   BNT
☐ Want   Orig. Ret. $6.00   **NB** $5   **MIB** Sec. Mkt. **$18**

QX 277-9   GRANDMOTHER ☐
Comments: Pink Glass Ball, 3" dia., Dated Christmas 1987.
Roses and carnations add a delicate touch. Caption: "Grandmothers, Like Flowers, Fill The World With Beauty, The Heart With Joy."

☐ Purchased 19__Pd $_____MIB   NB   DB   BNT
☐ Want   Orig. Ret. $4.75   **NB** $8   **MIB** Sec. Mkt. **$15**

QX 277-7   GRANDPARENTS ☐
Comments: Porcelain White Glass Ball, 2-7/8" dia.
Dated 1987. Children are depicted in winter activities. Caption: "Grandparents... So Warm, So Loving, So Like The Christmas Season." **Artist:** Sharon Pike

☐ Purchased 19__Pd $_____MIB   NB   DB   BNT
☐ Want   Orig. Ret. $4.75   **NB** $8   **MIB** Sec. Mkt. **$18**

QX 276-9   GRANDSON ☐
Comments: Blue Glass Ball, 3" dia., Dated Christmas 1987.
A marching band parades around the center of this ball. Caption: "Grandsons Have A Talent For Making Wonderful Memories."
Artist: LaDene Votruba

☐ Purchased 19__Pd $_____MIB   NB   DB   BNT
☐ Want   Orig. Ret. $4.75   **NB** $16   **MIB** Sec. Mkt. **$24**

EPCA   HALLIS STAR - ORNAMENT TREE TOPPER ☐
Comments: Acrylic, 9-7/8" tall.

☐ Purchased 19__Pd $_____MIB   NB   DB   BNT
☐ Want   Orig. Ret. Unknown   **NB** $25   **MIB** Sec. Mkt. **$35-$40**

QX 471-7   HAPPY HOLIDATA ☐
Comments: Handcrafted, 1-1/2" tall, Reissued in 1988.
Two white mice send their message, "Happy Holidata," on this computer which flashes the words and background in alternating colors. **Artist:** Bob Siedler

☐ Purchased 19__Pd $_____MIB   NB   DB   BNT
☐ Want   Orig. Ret. $6.50   **NB** $18   **MIB** Sec. Mkt. **$28**

QX 456-9   HAPPY SANTA   ☐
Comments: Handcrafted, 2-1/2" tall.
Santa hangs onto the tree branch with his candy cane. He also holds a gold jingle bell. **Artist:** Ken Crow

☐ Purchased 19 __ Pd $_____ MIB   NB   DB   BNT
☐ Want   Orig. Ret. $4.75   **NB** $15   **MIB** Sec. Mkt. **$26**

QX 372-7   HEART IN BLOSSOM   ☐
Comments: Acrylic, 2-3/4" tall, Dated Christmas 1987.
An acrylic etched rose is growing around the edge of the heart shaped ornament and blooming into the center. "Love Is The Heart In Blossom."
Artist: LaDene Votruba

☐ Purchased 19 __ Pd $_____ MIB   NB   DB   BNT
☐ Want   Orig. Ret. $6.00   **NB** $12   **MIB** Sec. Mkt. **$22.50**

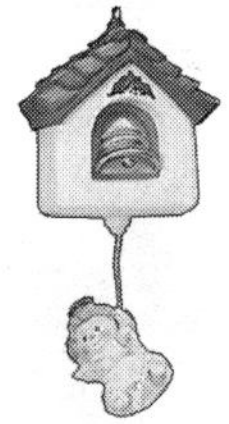

QX 465-9   HEAVENLY HARMONY   ☐
Comments: Musical, Handcrafted, 4-1/4" tall.
A little angel rings out "Joy To The World" as she pulls the rope to the bell tower. A key at the back activates the music.
Artist: Ken Crow

☐ Purchased 19 __ Pd $_____ MIB   NB   DB   BNT
☐ Want   Orig. Ret. $15.00   **NB** $24   **MIB** Sec. Mkt. **$32**

QX 484-7   HERE COMES SANTA: SANTA'S WOODY   ☐
Comments: **Ninth in Series,** Handcrafted, 2" tall, Dated 1987.
Santa's new car sports whitewall tires, custom paneling and a license plate that says "JOY-2-U." **Artist:** Ken Crow

☐ Purchased 19 __ Pd $_____ MIB   NB   DB   BNT
☐ Want   Orig. Ret. $14.00   **NB** $60   **MIB** Sec. Mkt. **$80**

QX 375-7   HOLIDAY GREETINGS   ☐
Comments: Bezeled Foil, 2-3/4" dia., Dated 1987.
A silver tree and lettering against blue foil. Caption: "Season's Greetings" and "Wishing You Happiness At This Beautiful Time Of Year."

☐ Purchased 19 __ Pd $_____ MIB   NB   DB   BNT
☐ Want   Orig. Ret. $6.00   **NB** $8   **MIB** Sec. Mkt. **$14**

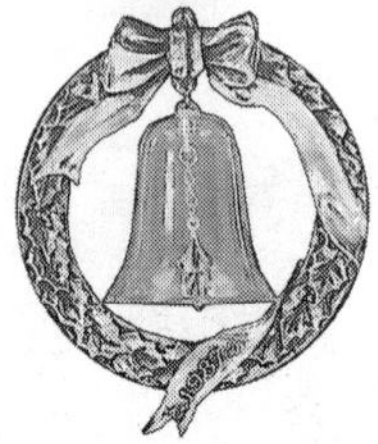

QX 485-7   HOLIDAY HEIRLOOM   ☐
Comments: **FIRST IN SERIES,** Limited Edition 34,600, Dated 1987.
Lead Crystal, Silver Plating, 3-1/4" tall.
Hanging in the center of a silver-plated wreath is this clear crystal bell with bow and ribbon. Many were "bought up" in 1987 for the secondary market. **Artist:** Duane Unruh

☐ Purchased 19 __ Pd $_____ MIB   NB   DB   BNT
☐ Want   Orig. Ret. $25.00   **NB** $20   **MIB** Sec. Mkt. **$32**

QX 470-7   HOLIDAY HOURGLASS   ☐
Comments: Handcrafted, 3" tall.
This snowman changes holidays as you turn him over - "Merry Christmas" and "Happy New Year." **Artist:** Duane Unru

☐ Purchased 19 __ Pd $_____ MIB   NB   DB   BNT
☐ Want   Orig. Ret. $8.00   **NB** $10   **MIB** Sec. Mkt. **$22**

QX 371-7   HOLIDAY WILDLIFE: SNOW GOOSE   ☐
Comments: **Sixth in Series,** Wood, 2-1/2" dia.
Caption: "Snow Goose, CHEN HYPERBOREA, Sixth In A Series, Wildlife Collection, Christmas 1987."
Artist: LaDene Votruba

☐ Purchased 19 __ Pd $_____ MIB   NB   DB   BNT
☐ Want   Orig. Ret. $7.50   **NB** $10   **MIB** Sec. Mkt. **$15**

QX 471-9   HOT DOGGER   ☐
Comments: Handcrafted, 2-1/2" tall.
Santa's a real "hot dogger" in his red ski suit, and has proven that he is a real champion. **Artist:** Duane Unruh

☐ Purchased 19 __ Pd $_____ MIB   NB   DB   BNT
☐ Want   Orig. Ret. $6.50   **NB** $14   **MIB** Sec. Mkt. **$25**

QX 373-9   HUSBAND   ☐
Comments: Blue Cameo, 3-1/4" dia., Dated 1987.
A couple sit together in an ivory sleigh. Caption: "For My Husband" and "The Nicest Part Of Christmas Is Sharing It With You." **Artist:** LaDene Votruba

☐ Purchased 19 __ Pd $_____ MIB   NB   DB   BNT
☐ Want   Orig. Ret. $7.00   **NB** $6   **MIB** Sec. Mkt. **$10**

QX 278-9   I REMEMBER SANTA   ☐
Comments: Porcelain White Glass Ball, 2-7/8" dia.
Dated 1987. Three antique postcard reproductions of Santa are captured on this porcelain ball. Caption: "At Christmastime, Especially, Those Magic Memories Start... Those Memories Of Yesterday That So Delight The Heart." **Artist:** Joyce A. Lyle

☐ Purchased 19 __ Pd $_____ MIB   NB   DB   BNT
☐ Want   Orig. Ret. $4.75   **NB** $15   **MIB** Sec. Mkt. **$28**

QX 450-9   ICY TREAT   ☐
Comments: Handcrafted, 2-1/4" tall.
A penguin in a green stocking cap is enjoying his icy cherry treat.
Artist: Bob Siedler

☐ Purchased 19 __ Pd $_____ MIB   NB   DB   BNT
☐ Want   Orig. Ret. $4.50   **NB** $10   **MIB** Sec. Mkt. **$18**

QX 469-7   IN A NUTSHELL   ☐
Comments: Handcrafted, 1-1/2" tall, Reissued in 1988.
Open the walnut and inside are detailed Christmas scenes.
Artist: Duane Unruh

☐ Purchased 19__Pd $_____MIB   NB   DB   BNT
☐ Want   Orig. Ret. $5.50   **NB** $10   **MIB** Sec. Mkt. **$20**

QX 449-9   JACK FROSTING   ☐
Comments: Handcrafted, 2-1/2" tall.
Jack brushes a glittery frost onto each leaf to make the Christmas
season sparkle. **Artist:** Ed Seale

☐ Purchased 19__Pd $_____MIB   NB   DB   BNT
☐ Want   Orig. Ret. $7.00   **NB** $45   **MIB** Sec. Mkt. **$60**

QX 283-9   JAMMIE PIES™   ☐
Comments: Porcelain White Glass Ball, 2-7/8" dia., Dated 1987.
A child waits for the swan; it is bringing a visitor who knows
many stories. Caption: "When Jammie Pies Are Close To You,
All Your Christmas Dreams Come True."

☐ Purchased 19__Pd $_____MIB   NB   DB   BNT
☐ Want   Orig. Ret. $4.75   **NB** $5   **MIB** Sec. Mkt. **$15**

QX 457-7   JOGGING THROUGH THE SNOW   ☐
Comments: Handcrafted, 3" tall, Dated 1987.
This perky rabbit is wearing his jogging shirt and shorts and has
his radio and earphones on. **Artist:** Peter Dutkin

☐ Purchased 19__Pd $_____MIB   NB   DB   BNT
☐ Want   Orig. Ret. $7.25   **NB** $12   **MIB** Sec. Mkt. **$24**

QX 466-9   JOLLY FOLLIES   ☐
Comments: Handcrafted, 2" tall.
When you pull the string three penguins in top hats, spats and red bow
ties dance at the "Jolly Follies." **Artist:** Ken Crow

☐ Purchased 19__Pd $_____MIB   NB   DB   BNT
☐ Want   Orig. Ret. $8.50   **NB** $16   **MIB** Sec. Mkt. **$38**

QX 483-2   JOLLY HIKER   ☐
Comments: Handcrafted, 2" tall.
Reissued from 1986. **Artist:** Bob Siedler

☐ Purchased 19__Pd $_____MIB   NB   DB   BNT
☐ Want   Orig. Ret. $5.00   **NB** $10   **MIB** Sec. Mkt. **$22**

QX 440-7   JOY RIDE   ☐
Comments: Handcrafted, 3-1/2" tall, Dated 1987.
Santa's taking one of his reindeer for a ride on his new green
motorcycle. The front fender says "Joy Ride."

☐ Purchased 19__Pd $_____MIB   NB   DB   BNT
☐ Want   Orig. Ret. $11.50 **NB** $55   **MIB** Sec. Mkt. **$80**

QX 465-7   JOYOUS ANGELS   ☐
Comments: Handcrafted, 4" tall.
A trio of angels dance beneath a brass star. The trim on their
gowns and halos is gold.
Artist: Ed Seale

☐ Purchased 19__Pd $_____MIB   NB   DB   BNT
☐ Want   Orig. Ret. $7.75   **NB** $10   **MIB** Sec. Mkt. **$22**

QLX 707-6   KEEP ON GLOWIN'!   ☐
Comments: Lighted, Handcrafted, 2-7/16" tall.
Reissued from 1986. **Artist:** Ken Crow

☐ Purchased 19__Pd $_____MIB   NB   DB   BNT
☐ Want   Orig. Ret. $10.00 **NB** $35   **MIB** Sec. Mkt. **$45**

QLX 704-7   KEEPING COZY   ☐
Comments: Lighted, Handcrafted, 2-1/2" tall.
Santa in his flocked long johns is joined at the potbelly stove by
a little mouse. **Artist:** Ken Crow

☐ Purchased 19__Pd $_____MIB   NB   DB   BNT
☐ Want   Orig. Ret. $11.75 **NB** $20   **MIB** Sec. Mkt. **$30**

QLX 709-7   LACY BRASS SNOWFLAKE   ☐
Comments: Lighted, Brass, 2-1/2" tall.
Two snowflakes, one solid with an etched design and one a lacy
filigree, reflect lights to create a sparkling snowflake.

☐ Purchased 19__Pd $_____MIB   NB   DB   BNT
☐ Want   Orig. Ret. $11.50 **NB** $12   **MIB** Sec. Mkt. **$24**

QX 458-9   LET IT SNOW   ☐
Comments: Handcrafted, 3" tall.
Christmas is for children, and this little one is ready for winter
weather. He's wearing a green and red stocking cap, coat,
mittens and knit muffler.

☐ Purchased 19__Pd $_____MIB   NB   DB   BNT
☐ Want   Orig. Ret. $6.50   **NB** $10   **MIB** Sec. Mkt. **$18**

QX 419-3 LI'L JINGLER ☐
Comments: Handcrafted, 2" tall. ·
Reissued from 1986. **Artist:** Ed Seale
☐ Purchased 19__ Pd $_____ MIB   NB   DB   BNT
☐ Want   Orig. Ret. $6.75   **NB** $38   **MIB** Sec. Mkt. **$50**

QX 469-9 LITTLE WHITTLER ☐
Comments: Handcrafted, 3" tall.
With the look of hand-carved wood, this Santa is happy with the
reindeer toy he is carving. **Artist:** Peter Dutkin
☐ Purchased 19__ Pd $_____ MIB   NB   DB   BNT
☐ Want   Orig. Ret. $6.00   **NB** $20   **MIB** Sec. Mkt. **$30**

QX 278-7 LOVE IS EVERYWHERE ☐
Comments: Chrome and Frosted Blue Glass Ball, 2-7/8" dia.
Dated 1987. Two redbirds fly against a wintry landscape.
Caption: "Beautifully, Peacefully, Christmas Touches Our Lives... Love
Is Everywhere." **Artist:** Joyce A. Lyle
☐ Purchased 19__ Pd $_____ MIB   NB   DB   BNT
☐ Want Orig. Ret. $4.75   **NB** $11   **MIB** Sec. Mkt. **$22**

QLX 701-6 LOVING HOLIDAY ☐
Comments: Light and Motion, Handcrafted, 3-5/8" tall.
A couple move out of the house and meet under the clock in
this reproduction of an old-fashioned glockenspiel. Caption:
"Precious Times Are Spent With Those We Love."
Artist: Ed Seale
☐ Purchased 19__ Pd $_____ MIB   NB   DB   BNT
☐ Want   Orig. Ret. $22.00 **NB** $24   **MIB** Sec. Mkt. **$50**

QLX 706-7 MEMORIES ARE FOREVER PHOTOHOLDER ☐
Comments: Lighted, Handcrafted, 3-7/8" tall.
The design of this ornament illuminates your favorite photo.
Caption: "Memory Keeps Each Christmas Forever Warm And
Bright." **Artist:** Ed Seale
☐ Purchased 19__ Pd $_____ MIB   NB   DB   BNT
☐ Want   Orig. Ret. $8.50   **NB** $15   **MIB** Sec. Mkt. **$32**

QLX 708-9 MEOWY CHRISTMAS ☐
Comments: Lighted, Handcrafted, 2-1/2" tall.
Two kittens play with the white fabric bow on a glowing red
heart. **Artist:** Sharon Pike
☐ Purchased 19__ Pd $_____ MIB   NB   DB   BNT
☐ Want   Orig. Ret. $10.00 **NB** $40   **MIB** Sec. Mkt. **$60**

QX 415-3 MERRY KOALA ☐
Comments: Handcrafted, 2" tall.
Reissued from 1986. **Artist:** Linda Sickman
☐ Purchased 19__ Pd $_____ MIB   NB   DB   BNT
☐ Want   Orig. Ret. $5.00   **NB** $12   **MIB** Sec. Mkt. **$22**

QX 481-9 MINIATURE CRECHE ☐
Comments: **Third in Series,** Multi-plated Brass, 3-1/2" tall.
Etched brass, washed in nickel, gold and copper, form a
beautiful Nativity. **Artist:** Ed Seale
☐ Purchased 19__ Pd $_____ MIB   NB   DB   BNT
☐ Want   Orig. Ret. $9.00   **NB** $14   **MIB** Sec. Mkt. **$22**

QX 468-7 MISTLETOAD ☐
Comments: Handcrafted, 3-3/4" tall, Reissued in 1988.
This little green fellow croaks when you pull his cord. His red hat
has his name. **Artist:** Ken Crow
☐ Purchased 19__ Pd $_____ MIB   NB   DB   BNT
☐ Want   Orig. Ret. $7.00   **NB** $14   **MIB** Sec. Mkt. **$24**

QX 373-7 MOTHER ☐
Comments: Acrylic, 3-1/2" tall, Dated Christmas 1987.
Caption: "Mother Is Another Word For Love" is etched in acrylic
with a beveled edge. **Artist:** Sharon Pike
☐ Purchased 19__ Pd $_____ MIB   NB   DB   BNT
☐ Want   Orig. Ret. $6.50   **NB** $8   **MIB** Sec. Mkt. **$10**

QX 462-7 MOTHER & DAD ☐
Comments: Porcelain, 4-3/4" tall, Dated Christmas 1987.
This deep blue bell features a Christmas tree with two gifts and
two red hearts. Caption: "For A Mother And Dad Who Give The
Gift Of Love." **Artist:** Sharon Pike
☐ Purchased 19__ Pd $_____ MIB   NB   DB   BNT
☐ Want   Orig. Ret. $7.00   **NB** $16   **MIB** Sec. Mkt. **$23**

QX 416-6 MOUSE IN THE MOON ☐
Comments: Handcrafted, 2-3/4" tall.
Reissued from 1986. **Artist:** Ed Seale
☐ Purchased 19__ Pd $_____ MIB   NB   DB   BNT
☐ Want   Orig. Ret. $5.50   **NB** $12   **MIB** Sec. Mkt. **$22**

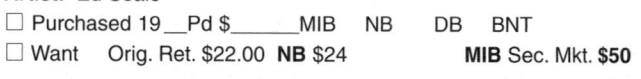
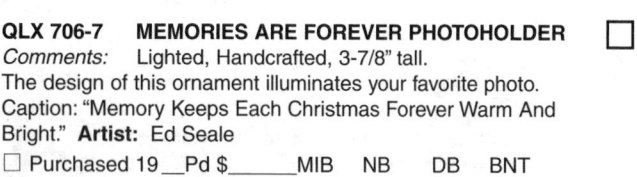

QX 483-7   MR. AND MRS. CLAUS: HOME COOKING ☐
Comments: **Second in Series,** Handcrafted, 3" tall.
Dated 1987. Dec. 24. Mrs. Claus won't let Santa leave on his
journey without a plate of cookies (chocolate chip, probably).
Artist: Duane Unruh

☐ Purchased 19 __ Pd $_____MIB   NB   DB   BNT
☐ Want   Orig. Ret. $13.25 **NB** $40   **MIB** Sec. Mkt. **$50**

QX 273-9   NATURE'S DECORATIONS ☐
Comments: Blue Glass Ball, 2-7/8" dia., Dated 1987.
Forest animals enjoy the winter season. Caption: "The Nicest
Christmas Decorations Start With Nature's Own Creations."
Artist: LaDene Votruba

☐ Purchased 19 __ Pd $_____MIB   NB   DB   BNT
☐ Want   Orig. Ret. $4.75 **NB** $10   **MIB** Sec. Mkt. **$28**

QX 376-7   NEW HOME ☐
Comments: Mirrored Acrylic, 2-3/4" dia., Dated Christmas 1987.
Caption: "A New Home Is A Wonderful
Beginning To Wonderful Memories."
Artist: Joyce Pattee

☐ Purchased 19 __ Pd $_____MIB   NB   DB   BNT
☐ Want   Orig. Ret. $6.00 **NB** $14   **MIB** Sec. Mkt. **$23**

QX 275-9   NIECE ☐
Comments: Turquoise Blue Glass Ball, 3" dia., Dated 1987.
White fluffy sheep, accented in red, frolic around the ball.
Caption: "Christmas Is Happier... Merrier... Cheerier... Because
Of A Niece's Love."

☐ Purchased 19 __ Pd $_____MIB   NB   DB   BNT
☐ Want   Orig. Ret. $4.75 **NB** $6   **MIB** Sec. Mkt. **$12**

QX 451-7   NIGHT BEFORE CHRISTMAS ☐
Comments: Handcrafted, 2-3/4" tall, Reissued in 1988.
'Twas the night before Christmas... not a creature was stirring, espe-
cially not this little mouse! He's got his teddy and some cheese and is
all tucked away in Santa's flocked hat.
Artist: Ken Crow

☐ Purchased 19 __ Pd $_____MIB   NB   DB   BNT
☐ Want   Orig. Ret. $6.50 **NB** $18   **MIB** Sec. Mkt. **$30**

QX 282-7   NORMAN ROCKWELL: CHRISTMAS SCENES ☐
Comments: Gold Glass Ball, 2-7/8" dia., Dated 1987.
Caption: "O Gather Friends, At Christmastime, To Sing A Song Of
Cheer, To Reminisce The Days Gone By, To Toast The Bright New Year.
From The Norman Rockwell Collection."
Artist: Joyce A. Lyle

☐ Purchased 19 __ Pd $_____MIB   NB   DB   BNT
☐ Want   Orig. Ret. $4.75 **NB** $12   **MIB** Sec. Mkt. **$23**

QX 370-7   NORMAN ROCKWELL: CHRISTMAS DANCE ☐
Comments: **Eighth in Series,** Light Blue Cameo, 3-1/4" dia.
Caption: "The Christmas Dance, Eighth In A Series, Christmas
1987, The Norman Rockwell Collection." **Artist:** Don Palmiter

☐ Purchased 19 __ Pd $_____MIB   NB   DB   BNT
☐ Want   Orig. Ret. $7.75 **NB** $8   **MIB** Sec. Mkt. **$22**

XPR 933-3   NORTH POLE POWER & LIGHT: OPEN HOUSE ☐
Comments: Handcrafted, 3" tall.
A colorful elf is on 24-hour call to keep the lights on your Christmas
tree in good order. He carries three replacement bulbs in his
backpack. **Artist:** Ken Crow

☐ Purchased 19 __ Pd $_____MIB   NB   DB   BNT
☐ Want   Orig. Ret. $2.95 **NB** $12   **MIB** Sec. Mkt. **$25**

QX 483-9   NOSTALGIC HOUSES AND SHOPS: ☐
HOUSE ON MAIN ST.
Comments: **Fourth in Series,** Handcrafted, 4-1/4" tall.
Dated 1987. This lovely Victorian home includes a lavender and
mauve bedroom upstairs and a parlor decorated for Christmas.
Artist: Donna Lee

☐ Purchased 19 __ Pd $_____MIB   NB   DB   BNT
☐ Want   Orig. Ret. $14.00 **NB** $55   **MIB** Sec. Mkt. **$70**

QX 468-9   NOSTALGIC ROCKER ☐
Comments: Wood, 2-1/2" tall.
Rocking horse is handcrafted in wood with fabric ears.
Artist: Linda Sickman

☐ Purchased 19 __ Pd $_____MIB   NB   DB   BNT
☐ Want   Orig. Ret. $6.50 **NB** $16   **MIB** Sec. Mkt. **$24**

QX 455-9   "OWLIDAY" WISH ☐
Comments: Handcrafted, 2" tall Reissued in 1988.
This cute white owl in spectacles is pointing to the holiday
message written on the eye chart: "Seasons Greetings To You."
Artist: Sharon Pike

☐ Purchased 19   Pd $ MIB   NB   DB   BNT
☐ Want   Orig. Ret. $6.50 **NB** $10   **MIB** Sec. Mkt. **$20**

QX 472-7   PADDINGTON™ BEAR ☐
Comments: Handcrafted, 3" tall.
Paddington wears a red apron and white chef's cap. On his hat is a tag
that says, "Please Look After This Bear. Thank You."
Artist: Sharon Pike

☐ Purchased 19 __ Pd $_____MIB   NB   DB   BNT
☐ Want   Orig. Ret. $5.50 **NB** $15   **MIB** Sec. Mkt. **$24**

QX 281-9   PEANUTS®
Comments: Chrome Glass Ball, 3" dia., Dated 1987.
"Everyone's Cool At Christmastime!" is depicted by Snoopy,
Woodstock and his friends, as well as a snowman, all wearing
their "shades."

☐ Purchased 19___Pd $_____MIB   NB   DB   BNT
☐ Want   Orig. Ret. $4.75   **NB** $18   **MIB** Sec. Mkt. **$30**

QX 442-7   PORCELAIN BEAR
Comments: **Fifth in Series,** Fine Porcelain, 2-1/8" tall.
This hand-painted Cinnamon Bear is searching for something
in the toe of his red stocking.

☐ Purchased 19___Pd $_____MIB   NB   DB   BNT
☐ Want   Orig. Ret. $7.75   **NB** $15   **MIB** Sec. Mkt. **$22.50**

QX 448-9   PRETTY KITTY
Comments: Handcrafted/Glass, 3-1/2" tall.
A clear glass bell is a perfect display for a little kitten tangled in
a red bead garland. **Artist:** Ken Crow

☐ Purchased 19___Pd $_____MIB   NB   DB   BNT
☐ Want   Orig. Ret. $11.00   **NB** $12   **MIB** Sec. Mkt. **$23**

QX 374-9   PROMISE OF PEACE
Comments: Acrylic, 2-3/4" dia., Framed in brass.
A dove with a gold foil olive branch. The caption, "A Season Of Hope,
A Reminder Of Miracles, A Promise Of Peace," is etched in the bevel
in the front. **Artist:** Ken Crow

☐ Purchased 19___Pd $_____MIB   NB   DB   BNT
☐ Want   Orig. Ret. $11.00   **NB** $14   **MIB** Sec. Mkt. **$22**

QX 458-7   RACCOON BIKER
Comments: Handcrafted, 3" tall, Dated 1987.
This little raccoon is pedaling his bicycle to deliver his special
Christmas present. **Artist:** Bob Siedler

☐ Purchased 19___Pd $_____MIB   NB   DB   BNT
☐ Want   Orig. Ret. $7.00   **NB** $12   **MIB** Sec. Mkt. **$20**

QX 480-9   REINDEER CHAMPS: DANCER
Comments: **Second in Series,** Handcrafted, 3-1/2" tall.
Dated 1987. Dancer is a vision of loveliness as she ice skates her
way into the hearts and homes of collectors.
Artist: Bob Siedler

☐ Purchased 19___Pd $_____MIB   NB   DB   BNT
☐ Want   Orig. Ret. $7.50   **NB** $35   **MIB** Sec. Mkt. **$45-$50**

QX 452-7   REINDOGGY
Comments: Handcrafted, 2-3/4" tall, Reissued in 1988.
This puppy is wearing antlers fashioned from real sticks, tied to
his head with red satin ribbon.
Artist: Bob Siedler

☐ Purchased 19___Pd $_____MIB   NB   DB   BNT
☐ Want   Orig. Ret. $5.75   **NB** $20   **MIB** Sec. Mkt. **$30**

QX 482-9   ROCKING HORSE
Comments: **Seventh in Series,** Handcrafted, 3-3/4" wide.
Dated 1987. A white charger on purple rockers makes a fine
steed for any boy or girl.
Artist: Linda Sickman

☐ Purchased 19___Pd $_____MIB   NB   DB   BNT
☐ Want   Orig. Ret. $10.75   **NB** $28   **MIB** Sec. Mkt. **$58-$60**

QLX 701-9   SANTA & SPARKY: PERFECT PORTRAIT
Comments: **Second in Series,** Light and Motion, Dated 1987.
Handcrafted, 4-1/16" tall. Sparky has sculpted a perfect likeness of
Santa in ice. He moves forward to light the statue.

☐ Purchased 19___Pd $_____MIB   NB   DB   BNT
☐ Want   Orig. Ret. $19.50   **NB** $30   **MIB** Sec. Mkt. **$60**

QX 457-9   SANTA AT THE BAT
Comments: Handcrafted, 3-1/4" tall, Dated 1987.
Wearing a uniform for the "North Pole Nicks 87," Santa swings
and hits the snowball. Highs and lows out there on this one.

☐ Purchased 19___Pd $_____MIB   NB   DB   BNT
☐ Want   Orig. Ret. $7.75   **NB** $12   **MIB** Sec. Mkt. **$22**

QLX 706-9   SEASON FOR FRIENDSHIP
Comments: Lighted Acrylic, 5-5/16" tall.
Christmas greenery is etched above the caption: "How Lovely
The Season When It's Filled With Friendship." Bevels in the
teardrop reflect light.

☐ Purchased 19___Pd $_____MIB   NB   DB   BNT
☐ Want   Orig. Ret. $8.50   **NB** $10   **MIB** Sec. Mkt. **$20**

QX 454-9   SEASONED GREETINGS
Comments: Handcrafted, 2" tall.
A little elf does his job very well. He salts all the holiday pretzels
from a silvery shaker which is labeled, "Seasoned Greetings
SALT." **Artist:** Ed Seale

☐ Purchased 19___Pd $_____MIB   NB   DB   BNT
☐ Want   Orig. Ret. $6.25   **NB** $12   **MIB** Sec. Mkt. **$25**

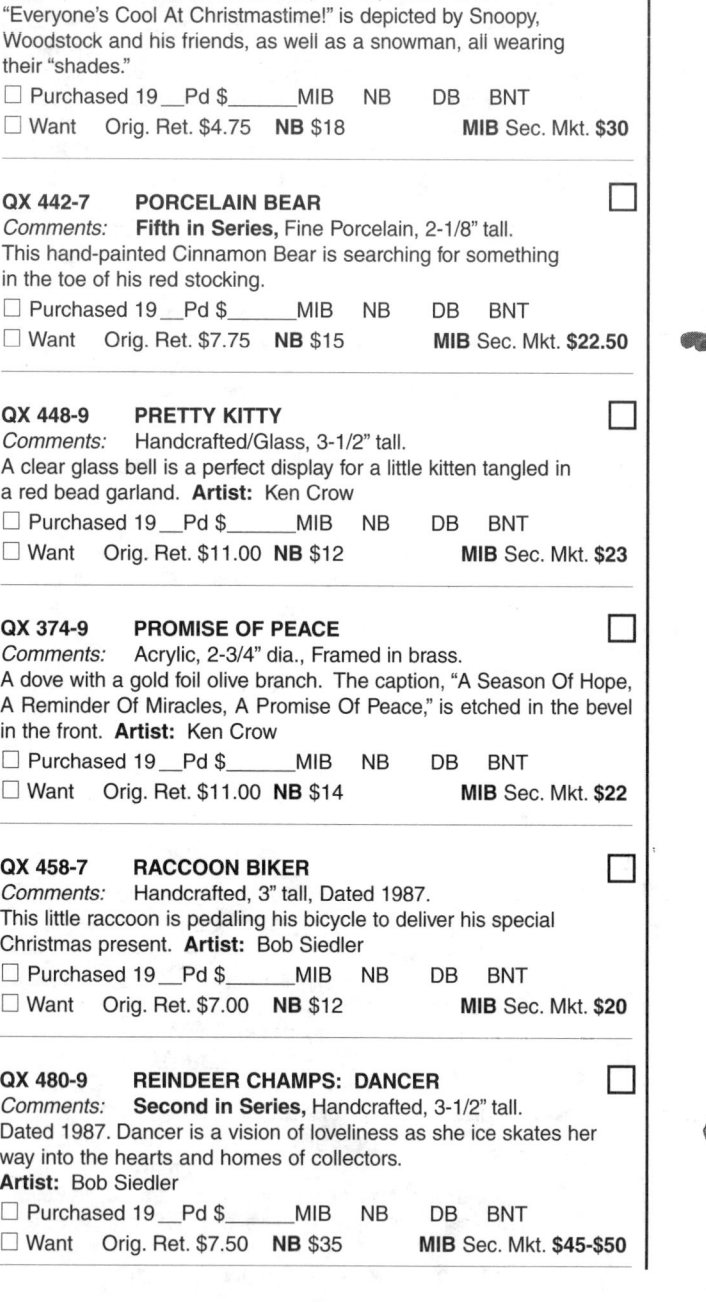

QX 474-7   SISTER ☐

Comments: Wood, 2-3/4" tall, Dated Christmas 1987.
This wooden heart has a basket of brightly stenciled poinsettias on the front. Caption: "A Sister Brings Happiness Wrapped In Love." **Artist:** Linda Sickman

☐ Purchased 19 __Pd $_____MIB   NB   DB   BNT
☐ Want   Orig. Ret. $6.00   **NB** $7   **MIB** Sec. Mkt. **$13**

QX 450-7   SLEEPY SANTA ☐

Comments: Handcrafted, 2-3/4" tall.
Santa relaxes in his favorite chair and soaks his feet — it's Dec. 26 and he deserves his rest!
Artist: Ken Crow

☐ Purchased 19 __Pd $_____MIB   NB   DB   BNT
☐ Want   Orig. Ret. $6.25   **NB** $22   **MIB** Sec. Mkt. **$38**

QX 472-9   SNOOPY & WOODSTOCK ☐

Comments: Handcrafted, 2-1/2" tall.
Woodstock plays "Angel" and perches on the top of Snoopy's bottle-brush tree. **Artist:** Bob Siedler

☐ Purchased 19 __Pd $_____MIB   NB   DB   BNT
☐ Want   Orig. Ret. $7.25   **NB** $25   **MIB** Sec. Mkt. **$45**

QX 463-9   SON ☐

Comments: Handcrafted, 1" tall, Dated Christmas 1987.
Hanging from a red cord is an old-fashioned toy train with the words "For Son" painted in bright colors. **Artist:** Linda Sickman

☐ Purchased 19 __Pd $_____MIB   NB   DB   BNT
☐ Want   Orig. Ret. $5.75   **NB** $18   **MIB** Sec. Mkt. **$42**

QX 464-7   SPECIAL MEMORIES PHOTOHOLDER ☐

Comments: Fabric, 3-1/4" dia., Dated 1987.
This fabric wreath with red satin rosette and green satin ribbon features embroidery and needlepoint. Caption: "Every Christmas Brings Special Moments To Remember."

☐ Purchased 19 __Pd $_____MIB   NB   DB   BNT
☐ Want   Orig. Ret. $6.75   **NB** $12   **MIB** Sec. Mkt. **$23**

QX 452-9   SPOTS 'N STRIPES ☐

Comments: Handcrafted, 2-1/4" tall.
This little Dalmatian pup has received a red and white striped candy cane in the shape of a bone.

☐ Purchased 19 __Pd $_____MIB   NB   DB   BNT
☐ Want   Orig. Ret. $5.50   **NB** $10   **MIB** Sec. Mkt. **$18**

QX 453-9   ST. LOUIE NICK ☐

Comments: Handcrafted, 3-1/2" tall, Reissued in 1988.
Santa plays the blues with his jazzy sax— he's also a cool cat in his spats, beret and dark glasses. **Artist:** Peter Dutkin

☐ Purchased 19 __Pd $_____MIB   NB   DB   BNT
☐ Want   Orig. Ret. $7.75   **NB** $12   **MIB** Sec. Mkt. **$28**

QX 447-9   SWEETHEART ☐

Comments: Handcrafted, 3-1/8" tall, Dated Christmas 1987.
This lovely surrey with red fabric fringe contains a present "For My Sweetheart." On the back, "Sweet" is printed above two entwined hearts. **Artist:** Linda Sickman

☐ Purchased 19 __Pd $_____MIB   NB   DB   BNT
☐ Want   Orig. Ret. $11.00   **NB** $15   **MIB** Sec. Mkt. **$28**

QX 466-7   TEACHER ☐

Comments: Handcrafted, 2" tall, Dated 1987.
Teddy has taken time to write a Christmas greeting: "Merry Christmas Teacher From (name)."
Artist: Bob Siedler

☐ Purchased 19 __Pd $_____MIB   NB   DB   BNT
☐ Want   Orig. Ret. $5.75   **NB** $12   **MIB** Sec. Mkt. **$20**

QX 444-7   TEN YEARS TOGETHER ☐

Comments: Porcelain/Bell, 4-3/4" tall, Dated Christmas 1987.
A heart-shaped green wreath decorated with red ribbon, berries and flowers frames the words "Ten Years Together." Tied with satin ribbon. **Artist:** LaDene Votruba

☐ Purchased 19 __Pd $_____MIB   NB   DB   BNT
☐ Want   Orig. Ret. $7.00   **NB** $16   **MIB** Sec. Mkt. **$25**

QX 441-9   THIMBLE SERIES: DRUMMER ☐

Comments: **Tenth in Series,** 2" tall.
A brown bunny with a fluffy pom-pom tail plays his thimble drum.
Artist: Bob Siedler

☐ Purchased 19 __Pd $_____MIB   NB   DB   BNT
☐ Want   Orig. Ret. $5.75   **NB** $16   **MIB** Sec. Mkt. **$25**

QX 454-7   THREE MEN IN A TUB ☐

Comments: Handcrafted, 3" tall.
The butcher, the baker and the candlestick maker are all sitting in a small tub which says "Rub A Dub Dub." **Artist:** Donna Lee

☐ Purchased 19 __Pd $_____MIB   NB   DB   BNT
☐ Want   Orig. Ret. $8.00   **NB** $12   **MIB** Sec. Mkt. **$28**

QX 280-7 TIME FOR FRIENDS ☐
Comments: Red Glass Ball, 3" dia., Dated Christmas 1987.
Two white mice decorate with a green holly garland. Caption: "When Good Friends Meet, Good Times Are Complete!"
Artist: LaDene Votruba
☐ Purchased 19__Pd $_____MIB NB DB BNT
☐ Want Orig. Ret. $4.75 NB $8 MIB Sec. Mkt. **$22**

QX 484-9 TIN LOCOMOTIVE ☐
Comments: **Sixth in Series,** Pressed Tin, 3-1/2" tall, Dated 1987.
With red wheels that really roll and a brass bell that rings, this locomotive is a delight for collectors of all ages. **Artist:** Linda Sickman
☐ Purchased 19__Pd $_____MIB NB DB BNT
☐ Want Orig. Ret. $14.75 **NB** $50 **MIB** Sec. Mkt. **$60-$65**

QLX 703-9 TRAIN STATION ☐
Comments: Lighted, Handcrafted, 3-3/16" tall.
The Merriville station is open for business. A mother and child are waiting for the next train to arrive and a ticket taker stands at his station.
Artist: Donna Lee
☐ Purchased 19__Pd $_____MIB NB DB BNT
☐ Want Orig. Ret. $12.75 **NB** $25 **MIB** Sec. Mkt. **$42**

QX 459-7 TREETOP DREAMS ☐
Comments: Handcrafted, 3" tall, Reissued in 1988.
This little squirrel will find a pleasant surprise when he wakes. Santa has left an acorn in his green stocking. His bed is a vine wreath.
Artist: Ed Seale
☐ Purchased 19__Pd $_____MIB NB DB BNT
☐ Want Orig. Ret. $6.75 **NB** $15 **MIB** Sec. Mkt. **$25**

QX 425-6 TREETOP TRIO/BLUEBIRDS ☐
Comments: Handcrafted, 2" tall.
Reissued from 1986. **Artist:** Donna Lee
☐ Purchased 19__Pd $_____MIB NB DB BNT
☐ Want Orig. Ret. $11.00 **NB** $16 **MIB** Sec. Mkt. **$28**

QX 370-9 TWELVE DAYS OF CHRISTMAS: FOUR COLLY BIRDS ☐
Comments: **Fourth in Series,** Acrylic, 4" tall, Dated 1987.
The diamond acrylic shape features four etched colly birds in the center, with gold foil captions. **Artist:** Sharon Pike
☐ Purchased 19__Pd $_____MIB NB DB BNT
☐ Want Orig. Ret. $6.50 **NB** $20 **MIB** Sec. Mkt. **$30**

QX 443-9 TWENTY-FIVE YEARS TOGETHER ☐
Comments: Porcelain Plate, 3-1/4" dia., Acrylic stand.
Dated Christmas 1987. Two bright red cardinals perch on a pine branch above silver lettering "25 Years Together." Caption: "Love Is For Always."
☐ Purchased 19__Pd $_____MIB NB DB BNT
☐ Want Orig. Ret. $7.50 **NB** $16 **MIB** Sec. Mkt. **$25**

QLX 707-2 VILLAGE EXPRESS ☐
Comments: Light and Motion, Handcrafted, 3-1/2" tall.
Reissued from 1986.
Artist: Linda Sickman
☐ Purchased 19__Pd $_____MIB NB DB BNT
☐ Want Orig. Ret. $24.50 **NB** $60 **MIB** Sec. Mkt. **$115**

QX 419-6 WALNUT SHELL RIDER ☐
Comments: Handcrafted, 1-3/4" tall.
Reissued from 1986. **Artist:** Ed Seale
☐ Purchased 19__Pd $_____MIB NB DB BNT
☐ Want Orig. Ret. $6.00 **NB** $12 **MIB** Sec. Mkt. **$20**

QX 375-9 WARMTH OF FRIENDSHIP ☐
Comments: Acrylic, 3-3/4" tall, Dated 1987.
Ornament-shaped acrylic features the caption in gold foil calligraphy: "As Christmas Warms The World, Friendship Warms Our Hearts."
☐ Purchased 19__Pd $_____MIB NB DB BNT
☐ Want Orig. Ret. $6.00 **NB** $5 **MIB** Sec. Mkt. **$10**

QX 451-9 WEE CHIMNEY SWEEP ☐
Comments: Handcrafted, 3" tall.
This little white mouse is cleaning the chimneys so Santa won't get soot all over himself when he makes his rounds Christmas Eve. **Artist:** Ed Seale
☐ Purchased 19__Pd $_____MIB NB DB BNT
☐ Want Orig. Ret. $6.25 **NB** $12 **MIB** Sec. Mkt. **$25**

QX 482-7 WINDOWS OF THE WORLD: HAWAIIAN ☐
Comments: **Third in Series,** Handcrafted, 3" tall, Dated 1987.
A little Hawaiian girl sits in the comfort of her thatched hut strumming her ukulele. Caption: "Mele Kalikimaka." Easily found.
Artist: Donna Lee
☐ Purchased 19__Pd $_____MIB NB DB BNT
☐ Want Orig. Ret. $10.00 **NB** $14 **MIB** Sec. Mkt. **$20**

QX 441-7   WOOD CHILDHOOD: HORSE   ☐
Comments: **Fourth in Series,** Wood, 2-1/4" tall, Dated 1987.
This little horse, with a plush mane and yarn tail, is standing on a cart with wheels that turn. He sports a hand painted red and green saddle.
Artist: Bob Siedler

☐ Purchased 19__Pd $_____MIB   NB   DB   BNT
☐ Want   Orig. Ret. $7.50   **NB** $10   **MIB** Sec. Mkt. **$20**

QX 447-7   WORD OF LOVE   ☐
Comments: Porcelain, 2-1/8" tall, Dated Christmas 1987.
The word "Love" is sculpted into a contemporary design. A small red heart dangles inside the "o."

☐ Purchased 19__Pd $_____MIB   NB   DB   BNT
☐ Want   Orig. Ret. $8.00   **NB** $8   **MIB** Sec. Mkt. **$18**

QXC 580-9   WREATH OF MEMORIES
CHARTER CLUB MEMBERSHIP ORN.   ☐
Comments: Handcrafted, 3-1/8" tall, Dated 1987.
This detailed green wreath is decorated with Hallmark ornaments. Caption: "1987 Charter Member." Club logo is engraved in brass.
Artist: Duane Unruh

☐ Purchased 19__Pd $_____MIB   NB   DB   BNT
☐ Want   Orig. Ret.: Gift to Charter Members.
                    NB $35   MIB Sec. Mkt. **$50**

"It's a Christmas Club."

Collectors prove you don't need a tree to display ornaments all year round!

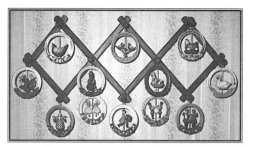

N. Albritton shows off her Nostalgia Ornaments.

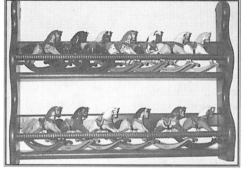

B.K. Dreyer has the entire collection of Rocking Horses from 1981-1994 on display all year!

Joy M. has the complete *Here Comes Santa* Series.

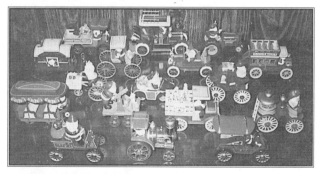

You can watch Santa take flight from Audrey D.'s shelf!

Page 105

1988 Collection

QX 482-1   A KISS™ FROM SANTA

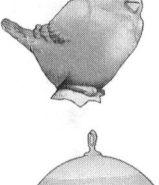

Comments: Handcrafted, 3-1/4" tall.
A "chocolate" Santa holds a Hershey's Kiss. His hat is red with a silvery trim. **Artist:** Duane Unruh

☐ Purchased 19__ Pd $_____ MIB   NB   DB   BNT

☐ Want   Orig. Ret. $4.50   **NB** $15   **MIB** Sec. Mkt. **$28**

QX 488-1   AMERICANA DRUM

Comments: Tin, 2" dia., Dated 1988.
An American eagle and banner design is portrayed against a vivid blue background. Caption: "Merry Christmas U.S.A."
Artist: Linda Sickman

☐ Purchased 19__ Pd $_____ MIB   NB   DB   BNT

☐ Want   Orig. Ret. $7.75   **NB** $14   **MIB** Sec. Mkt. **$26**

QX 408-4   ANGELIC MINSTREL: KEEPSAKE CLUB

Comments: Limited Edition 49,900, Wood Display Stand. Hand-Painted Fine Porcelain, 5" tall.
This blue gowned angel plays a golden lyre. Offered only to members of the Hallmark Keepsake Ornament Club. Some say this was overproduced for a Limited Edition.
Artist: Donna Lee

☐ Purchased 19__ Pd $_____ MIB   NB   DB   BNT

☐ Want   Orig. Ret. $29.50   **NB** $30   **MIB** Sec. Mkt. **$42.50**

QX 472-1   ARCTIC TENOR

Comments: Handcrafted, 1-3/4" tall.
This penguin is in great voice for his solo. He's wearing spats and a green bow tie and has his song book of "Arctic Arias" open.
Artist: Bob Siedler

☐ Purchased 19__ Pd $_____ MIB   NB   DB   BNT

☐ Want   Orig. Ret. $4.00   **NB** $8   **MIB** Sec. Mkt. **$18**

QX 410-1   BABY REDBIRD

Comments: Handcrafted, 2-5/8" tall.
This baby resembles the cardinals who feast throughout the winter at bird feeders. **Artist:** Robert Chad

☐ Purchased 19__ Pd $_____ MIB   NB   DB   BNT

☐ Want   Orig. Ret. $5.00   **NB** $7   **MIB** Sec. Mkt. **$15**

QX 272-1   BABY'S FIRST CHRISTMAS: BOY

Comments: White Satin Ball, 2-7/8" dia., Dated 1988.
Caption: "From The Moment A New Baby Boy Arrives, He's The Love Of Your Heart, The Light In Your Eyes. Baby's First Christmas."

☐ Purchased 19__ Pd $_____ MIB   NB   DB   BNT

☐ Want   Orig. Ret. $4.75   **NB** $8   **MIB** Sec. Mkt. **$22**

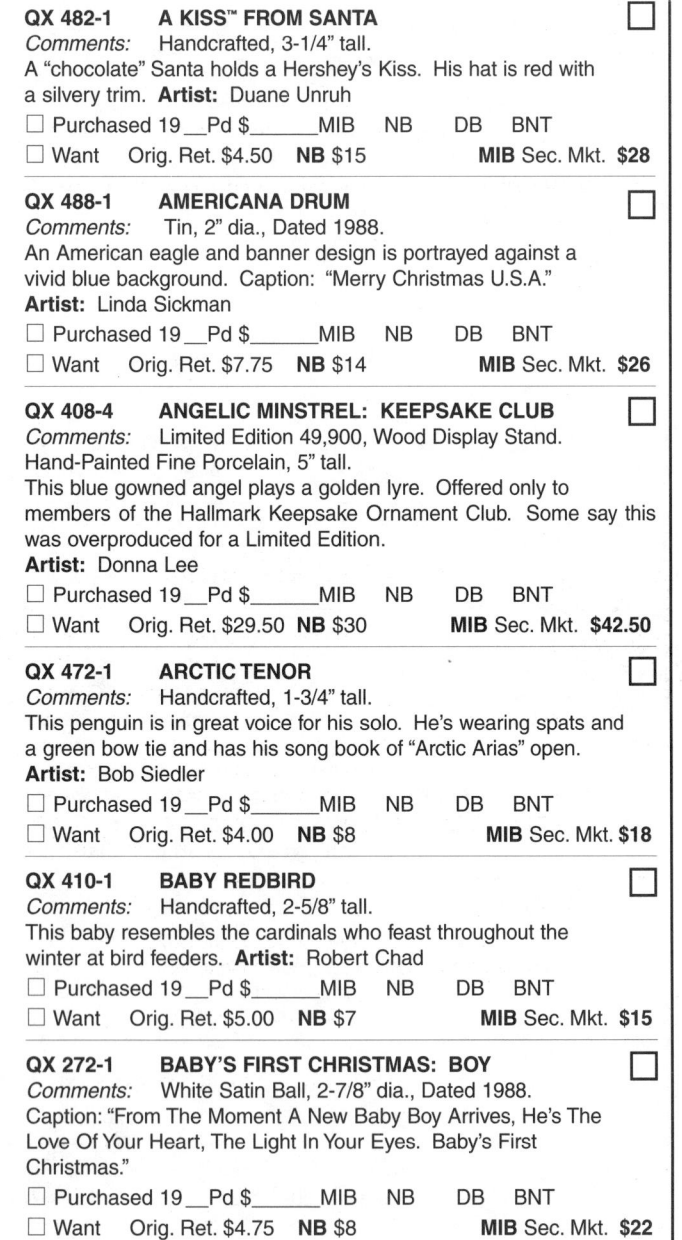

QX 272-4   BABY'S FIRST CHRISTMAS: GIRL

Comments: White Satin Ball, 2-7/8" dia., Dated 1988.
Caption: "A Sweet Baby Girl, So Tiny And New, Is A Bundle Of Joy And A Dream Come True. Baby's First Christmas."

☐ Purchased 19__ Pd $_____ MIB   NB   DB   BNT

☐ Want   Orig. Ret. $4.75   **NB** $6   **MIB** Sec. Mkt. **$22**

QLX 718-4   BABY'S FIRST CHRISTMAS

Comments: Light and Motion, Handcrafted, 4" tall, Dated 1988.
A carousel of prancing horses under a blue and white canopy celebrates Baby's First Christmas. **Artist:** Ed Seale

☐ Purchased 19__ Pd $_____ MIB   NB   DB   BNT

☐ Want   Orig. Ret. $24.00   **NB** $25   **MIB** Sec. Mkt. **$50**

QX 372-1   BABY'S FIRST CHRISTMAS

Comments: Acrylic, 4" tall, Dated 1988.
"Baby's First Christmas" in gold foil letters is framed by a heart made from two candy canes and is held by an intricately etched bunny. **Artist:** Sharon Pike

☐ Purchased 19__ Pd $_____ MIB   NB   DB   BNT

☐ Want   Orig. Ret. $6.00   **NB** $12   **MIB** Sec. Mkt. **$21**

QX 470-1   BABY'S FIRST CHRISTMAS

Comments: Handcrafted, 3-5/8" tall, Dated 1988.
Baby's all wrapped up in white bunting and a green blanket trimmed with lace for a ride in a cute rocking horse trimmed in red and green. **Artist:** Ken Crow

☐ Purchased 19__ Pd $_____ MIB   NB   DB   BNT

☐ Want   Orig. Ret. $9.75   **NB** $20   **MIB** Sec. Mkt. **$40**

QX 470-4   BABY'S FIRST CHRISTMAS PHOTOHOLDER

Comments: Fabric, 5" tall, Dated 1988.
Embroidered angels and holly decorate this heart-shaped photo holder. Caption: "Baby's First Christmas" and "A Baby Is A Gift Of Joy, A Gift Of Love At Christmas."

☐ Purchased 19__ Pd $_____ MIB   NB   DB   BNT

☐ Want   Orig. Ret. $7.50   **NB** $14   **MIB** Sec. Mkt. **$25**

QX 471-1   BABY'S SECOND CHRISTMAS

Comments: Handcrafted, 1-3/4" tall, Dated 1988.
A flocked bear enjoys pounding the blocks on a child's toy.
"Baby's 2nd Christmas" on side. **Artist:** Sharon Pike

☐ Purchased 19__ Pd $_____ MIB   NB   DB   BNT

☐ Want   Orig. Ret. $6.00   **NB** $20   **MIB** Sec. Mkt. **$33**

QX 279-1   BABYSITTER   ☐
Comments: Green Glass Ball, 2-7/8" dia., Dated 1988.
Childlike drawings portray winter fun in the snow.   Caption: "May
The Love You Show Children Return To You This Holiday."
Artist: Linda Sickman

☐ Purchased 19 __Pd $_____MIB   NB   DB   BNT
☐ Want   Orig. Ret. $4.75   **NB** $6   **MIB** Sec. Mkt. **$10**

QLX 715-1   BEARLY REACHING   ☐
Comments: Light, Handcrafted, 4" tall.
This tiny little bear must stand on the candle holder with his candle
snuffer in hand to put out the candle at night. **Artist:** Linda Sickman

☐ Purchased 19 __Pd $_____MIB   NB   DB   BNT
☐ Want   Orig. Ret. $9.50   **NB** $14   **MIB** Sec. Mkt. **$38**

QX 271-4   BETSEY CLARK: HOME FOR CHRISTMAS   ☐
Comments: **Third in Series,** Light Blue Glass Ball, 2-7/8" dia.
Dated 1988. Betsey and her friends show love: pressing a
stocking, baking cookies and stitching a quilt. Caption: "A
Homemade Touch Can Do So Much To Make Each Christmas
Special." **Artist:** Sharon Pike

☐ Purchased 19 __Pd $_____MIB   NB   DB   BNT
☐ Want   Orig. Ret. $5.00   **NB** $12   **MIB** Sec. Mkt. **$22**

QX 471-4   CHILD'S THIRD CHRISTMAS   ☐
Comments: Handcrafted, 2-1/2" tall, Dated 1988.
Riding a red reindeer bounce ball is a lot of fun for this tyke. Ball
says "My 3rd Christmas."
Artist: Robert Chad

☐ Purchased 19 __Pd $_____MIB   NB   DB   BNT
☐ Want   Orig. Ret. $6.00   **NB** $12   **MIB** Sec. Mkt. **$25**

QLX 715-4   CHRIS MOUSE STAR   ☐
Comments: **Fourth in Series,** Light, Handcrafted, 2-1/2" tall.
Dated 1988. Chris, in his red nightcap and blue nightshirt, is
shining and cleaning a golden star.
Artist: Bob Siedler

☐ Purchased 19 __Pd $_____MIB   NB   DB   BNT
☐ Want   Orig. Ret. $8.75   **NB** $40   **MIB** Sec. Mkt. **$55**

QX 494-1   CHRISTMAS CARDINAL   ☐
Comments: Handcrafted, 2-7/8" tall.
A little cardinal suspended from golden beads twirls inside an
outline of an evergreen.
Artist: Anita Marra Rogers

☐ Purchased 19 __Pd $_____MIB   NB   DB   BNT
☐ Want   Orig. Ret. $4.75   **NB** $8   **MIB** Sec. Mkt. **$14**

**QLX 716-1   CHRISTMAS CLASSICS:
                       NIGHT BEFORE CHRISTMAS**   ☐
Comments: **Third in Series.** Light, Handcrafted, 4-1/2" tall.
Dated 1988. While everyone sleeps snugly upstairs, Santa is filling the
stockings in the decorated living room downstairs. No series number
on this ornament. **Artist:** Donna Lee

☐ Purchased 19 __Pd $_____MIB   NB   DB   BNT
☐ Want   Orig. Ret. $15.00 **NB** $20   **MIB** Sec. Mkt. **$30**

QX 480-1   CHRISTMAS CUCKOO   ☐
Comments: Handcrafted, 4-7/8" tall.
Tap the pendulum and watch for two surprises. The clock
changes from 12:00 to 3:00 and the little door opens to show a
blue bird inside. **Artist:** Ken Crow

☐ Purchased 19 __Pd $_____MIB   NB   DB   BNT
☐ Want   Orig. Ret. $8.00   **NB** $15   **MIB** Sec. Mkt. **$22**

QLX 717-1   CHRISTMAS IS MAGIC   ☐
Comments: Light, Handcrafted, 3-1/4" tall.
Santa uses the light from a table lantern and his puppy's bones
to create a reindeer silhouette on the window. "Christmas Is
Magic!" **Artist:** Ken Crow

☐ Purchased 19 __Pd $_____MIB   NB   DB   BNT
☐ Want   Orig. Ret. $12.00 **NB** $35   **MIB** Sec. Mkt. **$45-$50**

QX 407-1   CHRISTMAS IS SHARING: KEEPSAKE CLUB   ☐
Comments: Limited Edition, 49,900, Hand Numbered.
Hand-Painted Bone China, 2-1/4" tall.
Two little rabbits sit in the arch of a tree bowed down with
the weight of the snowfall.   **Artist:** Ed Seale

☐ Purchased 19 __Pd $_____MIB   NB   DB   BNT
☐ Want   Orig. Ret. $17.50 **NB** $28   **MIB** Sec. Mkt. **$40**

QX 372-4   CHRISTMAS MEMORIES PHOTOHOLDER   ☐
Comments: Acrylic, 3-3/4" tall, Dated 1988.
This acrylic wreath is circled with silver foil snowflakes. Caption:
"Christmas Is More Than A Day In December... It's The Magic
And Love We'll Always Remember." **Artist:** Joyce Pattee

☐ Purchased 19 __Pd $_____MIB   NB   DB   BNT
☐ Want   Orig. Ret. $6.50   **NB** $14   **MIB** Sec. Mkt. **$24**

QLX 701-3   CHRISTMAS MORNING   ☐
Comments: Light and Motion, Handcrafted, 4-5/16" tall.
Reissued from 1987. **Artist:** Ken Crow

☐ Purchased 19 __Pd $_____MIB   NB   DB   BNT
☐ Want   Orig. Ret. $24.50 **NB** $28   **MIB** Sec. Mkt. **$40**

QLX 712-4   CIRCLING THE GLOBE
Comments: Light, Handcrafted, 2-3/4" tall.
Santa is charting his delivery route by using a large lighted globe.
Artist: Ken Crow

☐ Purchased 19 __Pd $_____MIB   NB   DB   BNT
☐ Want   Orig. Ret. $10.50 **NB** $25   **MIB** Sec. Mkt. **$35**

QX 406-1   COLLECTOR'S PLATE: WAITING FOR SANTA
Comments: **Second in Series,** Fine Porcelain, 3-1/4" dia.
Dated 1988. A brother and sister have fallen asleep in the chair
as they watch for Santa.   **Artist:** LaDene Votruba

☐ Purchased 19 __Pd $_____MIB   NB   DB   BNT
☐ Want   Orig. Ret. $8.00 **NB** $32   **MIB** Sec. Mkt. **$50**

QX 487-4   COOL JUGGLER
Comments: Handcrafted, 4-3/4" tall.
This fellow has it all figured out — juggling, that is. Just tap the
snowball below and watch the snowman's arms move as he
juggles three snowballs. **Artist:** Ken Crow

☐ Purchased 19 __Pd $_____MIB   NB   DB   BNT
☐ Want   Orig. Ret. $6.50 **NB** $12   **MIB** Sec. Mkt. **$20**

QLX 721-1   COUNTRY EXPRESS
Comments: Light and Motion, Handcrafted, 3-1/2" tall.
An engine, boxcar and caboose travel round and round a country
village as it travels over a trestle and through a mountain tunnel.
 Artist: Linda Sickman

☐ Purchased 19 __Pd $_____MIB   NB   DB   BNT
☐ Want   Orig. Ret. $24.50 **NB** $50   **MIB** Sec. Mkt. **$65**

QX 411-1   CYMBALS OF CHRISTMAS
Comments: Handcrafted, 2-1/8" tall.
This little angel is so happy, she's letting everyone know. She's
made cymbals from two gold stars she's pulled from the sky.
Artist: Donna Lee

☐ Purchased 19 __Pd $_____MIB   NB   DB   BNT
☐ Want   Orig. Ret. $5.50 **NB** $14   **MIB** Sec. Mkt. **$28**

QX 414-1   DAD
Comments: Handcrafted, 2-3/4" tall, Dated 1988.
The gift box "For Dad" held new socks. Hey, these red and green
ones are really warm! **Artist:** Bob Siedler

☐ Purchased 19 __Pd $_____MIB   NB   DB   BNT
☐ Want   Orig. Ret. $7.00 **NB** $12   **MIB** Sec. Mkt. **$20**

QX 415-1   DAUGHTER
Comments: Handcrafted, 3-5/8" tall, Dated 1988.
A cookie girl has baked up a batch of even more cookies for
"Daughter." **Artist:** Joyce Pattee

☐ Purchased 19 __Pd $_____MIB   NB   DB   BNT
☐ Want   Orig. Ret. $5.75 **NB** $40   **MIB** Sec. Mkt. **$50**

QX 416-1   FELIZ NAVIDAD
Comments: Handcrafted, 2-7/8" tall.
This little gray burro in a Mexican sombrero, carries a wrapped
package and a bottle brush tree in his saddlebags. "Feliz
Navidad!" **Artist:** Duane Unruh

☐ Purchased 19 __Pd $_____MIB   NB   DB   BNT
☐ Want   Orig. Ret. $6.75 **NB** $18   **MIB** Sec. Mkt. **$30**

QLX 720-4   FESTIVE FEEDER
Comments: Light, Handcrafted, 3" tall.
These birds will be well-fed all winter with their bird feeder full of
food. Red and green Christmas lights shine on the top.
Artist: Linda Sickman

☐ Purchased 19 __Pd $_____MIB   NB   DB   BNT
☐ Want   Orig. Ret. $11.50 **NB** $32   **MIB** Sec. Mkt. **$50**

QX 374-1   FIFTY YEARS TOGETHER
Comments: Acrylic, 3-1/8" tall, Dated Christmas 1988.
"50 Years Together" caption is stamped in gold foil. Brass
frame accents the design.

☐ Purchased 19 __Pd $_____MIB   NB   DB   BNT
☐ Want   Orig. Ret. $6.75 **NB** $12   **MIB** Sec. Mkt. **$20**

QX 419-1   FILLED WITH FUDGE
Comments: Handcrafted, 3-3/8" tall.
A little mouse has found the tastiest treat in the house. It's a cone
filled with chocolate fudge. **Artist:** Ed Seale

☐ Purchased 19 __Pd $_____MIB   NB   DB   BNT
☐ Want   Orig. Ret. $4.75 **NB** $15   **MIB** Sec. Mkt. **$30**

QX 373-1   FIRST CHRISTMAS TOGETHER
Comments: Acrylic, 4" tall, Dated 1988.
A brass frame and art nouveau design make this acrylic
ornament a lovely ornament. Caption: "Our First Christmas
Together." **Artist:** LaDene Votruba

☐ Purchased 19 __Pd $_____MIB   NB   DB   BNT
☐ Want   Orig. Ret. $6.75 **NB** $20   **MIB** Sec. Mkt. **$29**

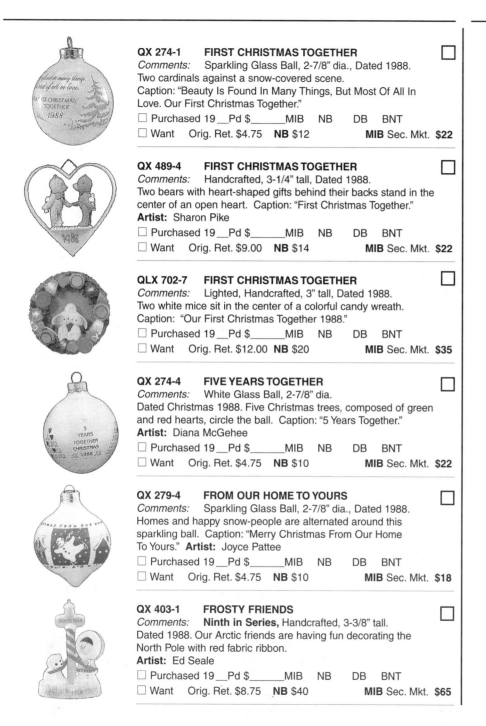

QX 274-1   FIRST CHRISTMAS TOGETHER ☐
Comments: Sparkling Glass Ball, 2-7/8" dia., Dated 1988.
Two cardinals against a snow-covered scene.
Caption: "Beauty Is Found In Many Things, But Most Of All In Love. Our First Christmas Together."

☐ Purchased 19 __Pd $_____MIB   NB   DB   BNT
☐ Want   Orig. Ret. $4.75   **NB** $12   **MIB** Sec. Mkt. **$22**

QX 489-4   FIRST CHRISTMAS TOGETHER ☐
Comments: Handcrafted, 3-1/4" tall, Dated 1988.
Two bears with heart-shaped gifts behind their backs stand in the center of an open heart. Caption: "First Christmas Together."
Artist: Sharon Pike

☐ Purchased 19 __Pd $_____MIB   NB   DB   BNT
☐ Want   Orig. Ret. $9.00   **NB** $14   **MIB** Sec. Mkt. **$22**

QLX 702-7   FIRST CHRISTMAS TOGETHER ☐
Comments: Lighted, Handcrafted, 3" tall, Dated 1988.
Two white mice sit in the center of a colorful candy wreath.
Caption: "Our First Christmas Together 1988."

☐ Purchased 19 __Pd $_____MIB   NB   DB   BNT
☐ Want   Orig. Ret. $12.00   **NB** $20   **MIB** Sec. Mkt. **$35**

QX 274-4   FIVE YEARS TOGETHER ☐
Comments: White Glass Ball, 2-7/8" dia.
Dated Christmas 1988. Five Christmas trees, composed of green and red hearts, circle the ball. Caption: "5 Years Together."
Artist: Diana McGehee

☐ Purchased 19 __Pd $_____MIB   NB   DB   BNT
☐ Want   Orig. Ret. $4.75   **NB** $10   **MIB** Sec. Mkt. **$22**

QX 279-4   FROM OUR HOME TO YOURS ☐
Comments: Sparkling Glass Ball, 2-7/8" dia., Dated 1988.
Homes and happy snow-people are alternated around this sparkling ball. Caption: "Merry Christmas From Our Home To Yours." **Artist:** Joyce Pattee

☐ Purchased 19 __Pd $_____MIB   NB   DB   BNT
☐ Want   Orig. Ret. $4.75   **NB** $10   **MIB** Sec. Mkt. **$18**

QX 403-1   FROSTY FRIENDS ☐
Comments: **Ninth in Series,** Handcrafted, 3-3/8" tall.
Dated 1988. Our Arctic friends are having fun decorating the North Pole with red fabric ribbon.
Artist: Ed Seale

☐ Purchased 19 __Pd $_____MIB   NB   DB   BNT
☐ Want   Orig. Ret. $8.75   **NB** $40   **MIB** Sec. Mkt. **$65**

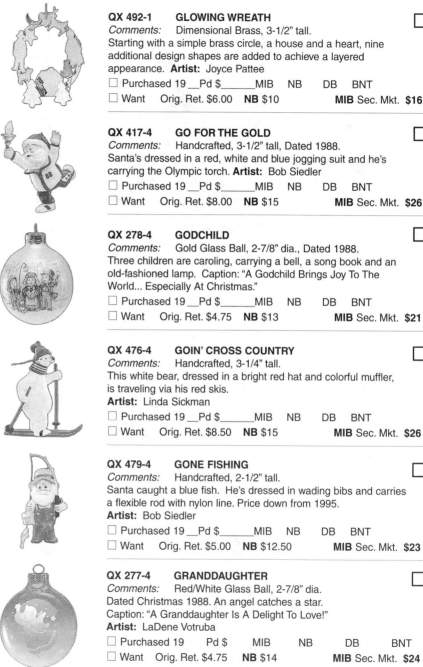

QX 492-1   GLOWING WREATH ☐
Comments: Dimensional Brass, 3-1/2" tall.
Starting with a simple brass circle, a house and a heart, nine additional design shapes are added to achieve a layered appearance. **Artist:** Joyce Pattee

☐ Purchased 19 __Pd $_____MIB   NB   DB   BNT
☐ Want   Orig. Ret. $6.00   **NB** $10   **MIB** Sec. Mkt. **$16**

QX 417-4   GO FOR THE GOLD ☐
Comments: Handcrafted, 3-1/2" tall, Dated 1988.
Santa's dressed in a red, white and blue jogging suit and he's carrying the Olympic torch. **Artist:** Bob Siedler

☐ Purchased 19 __Pd $_____MIB   NB   DB   BNT
☐ Want   Orig. Ret. $8.00   **NB** $15   **MIB** Sec. Mkt. **$26**

QX 278-4   GODCHILD ☐
Comments: Gold Glass Ball, 2-7/8" dia., Dated 1988.
Three children are caroling, carrying a bell, a song book and an old-fashioned lamp. Caption: "A Godchild Brings Joy To The World... Especially At Christmas."

☐ Purchased 19 __Pd $_____MIB   NB   DB   BNT
☐ Want   Orig. Ret. $4.75   **NB** $13   **MIB** Sec. Mkt. **$21**

QX 476-4   GOIN' CROSS COUNTRY ☐
Comments: Handcrafted, 3-1/4" tall.
This white bear, dressed in a bright red hat and colorful muffler, is traveling via his red skis.
Artist: Linda Sickman

☐ Purchased 19 __Pd $_____MIB   NB   DB   BNT
☐ Want   Orig. Ret. $8.50   **NB** $15   **MIB** Sec. Mkt. **$26**

QX 479-4   GONE FISHING ☐
Comments: Handcrafted, 2-1/2" tall.
Santa caught a blue fish. He's dressed in wading bibs and carries a flexible rod with nylon line. Price down from 1995.
Artist: Bob Siedler

☐ Purchased 19 __Pd $_____MIB   NB   DB   BNT
☐ Want   Orig. Ret. $5.00   **NB** $12.50   **MIB** Sec. Mkt. **$23**

QX 277-4   GRANDDAUGHTER ☐
Comments: Red/White Glass Ball, 2-7/8" dia.
Dated Christmas 1988. An angel catches a star.
Caption: "A Granddaughter Is A Delight To Love!"
Artist: LaDene Votruba

☐ Purchased 19   Pd $ MIB   NB   DB   BNT
☐ Want   Orig. Ret. $4.75   **NB** $14   **MIB** Sec. Mkt. **$24**

QX 276-4   GRANDMOTHER
Comments: Gold Glass Ball, 2-7/8" dia., Dated 1988.
With the look of crewel embroidery, the caption is bordered with
the partridge and pear tree theme.
Caption: "Grandmother Makes Love A Christmas Tradition."
☐ Purchased 19 __Pd $_____MIB   NB   DB   BNT
☐ Want   Orig. Ret. $4.75   **NB** $12   **MIB** Sec. Mkt. **$19**

QX 277-1   GRANDPARENTS
Comments: Red Glass Ball, 2-7/8" dia., Dated Christmas 1988.
A cozy Christmas scene with a tree and a cat napping on a rug.
All depicted wiith the caption: "Grandparents Are The Heart Of So
Many Treasured Memories." **Artist:** Joyce Pattee
☐ Purchased 19 __Pd $_____MIB   NB   DB   BNT
☐ Want   Orig. Ret. $4.75   **NB** $10   **MIB** Sec. Mkt. **$19**

QX 278-1   GRANDSON
Comments: Green/White Glass Ball, 2-7/8" tall, Dated 1988.
Santa's catching snowflakes! Caption: "A Grandson Makes
Christmas Merry!" **Artist:** LaDene Votruba
☐ Purchased 19 __Pd $_____MIB   NB   DB   BNT
☐ Want   Orig. Ret. $4.75   **NB** $12   **MIB** Sec. Mkt. **$22**

QX 375-4   GRATITUDE
Comments: Acrylic, 3-3/8" tall, Dated 1988.
A snow-covered evergreen tree and snowflakes. Caption:
"Christmas Fills Our Hearts With Thoughts Of Those Who Care."
Artist: Joyce Pattee
☐ Purchased 19 __Pd $_____MIB   NB   DB   BNT
☐ Want   Orig. Ret. $6.00   **NB** $6   **MIB** Sec. Mkt. **$12.50**

QX 471-4   HAPPY HOLIDATA
Comments: Handcrafted, 1-1/2" tall.
Reissued from 1987. **Artist:** Bob Siedler
☐ Purchased 19 __Pd $_____MIB   NB   DB   BNT
☐ Want   Orig. Ret. $6.50   **NB** $18   **MIB** Sec. Mkt. **$25**

QLX 711-4   HEAVENLY GLOW
Comments: Light, Brass, 3" tall.
A delicately etched brass angel holds a Christmas star. Lighted
from within. **Artist:** Michele Pyda-Sevcik
☐ Purchased 19 __Pd $_____MIB   NB   DB   BNT
☐ Want   Orig. Ret. $11.75   **NB** $16   **MIB** Sec. Mkt. **$24**

QX 400-1   HERE COMES SANTA: KRINGLE KOACH
Comments: **Tenth in Series,** Handcrafted, 3-1/4" tall.
Dated 1988. Santa's delivering presents by way of the "Kringle
Koach." He's wearing a ten-gallon hat and carrying a teddy bear
passenger. **Artist:** Ken Crow
☐ Purchased 19 __Pd $_____MIB   NB   DB   BNT
☐ Want   Orig. Ret. $14.00   **NB** $30   **MIB** Sec. Mkt. **$42**

QX 422-1   HOE-HOE-HOE!
Comments: Handcrafted, 2-3/8" tall.
Santa's all ready to work in the garden. He's wearing a red visor
and green coveralls.
Artist: Bob Siedler
☐ Purchased 19 __Pd $_____MIB   NB   DB   BNT
☐ Want   Orig. Ret. $5.00   **NB** $10   **MIB** Sec. Mkt. **$14**

QX 406-4   HOLIDAY HEIRLOOM: KEEPSAKE CLUB
Comments: **Second in Series,** Limited Edition 34,600.
Lead Crystal/Silver Plating, 3-1/2" tall, Dated 1988.
The second crystal bell has two angels in flight holding a silver-
plated star. The second in series was offered only to Club Members.
Artist: Duane Unruh
☐ Purchased 19 __Pd $_____MIB   NB   DB   BNT
☐ Want   Orig. Ret. $25.00   **NB** $20   **MIB** Sec. Mkt. **$34**

QX 423-1   HOLIDAY HERO
Comments: Handcrafted, 2-5/8" tall.
Whether on the field or off, S. Claus is number "1". He's ready to
pass the football for a win! **Artist:** Bob Siedler
☐ Purchased 19 __Pd $_____MIB   NB   DB   BNT
☐ Want   Orig. Ret. $5.00   **NB** $10   **MIB** Sec. Mkt. **$14**

QX 371-1   HOLIDAY WILDLIFE: PURPLE FINCH
Comments: **Seventh and Final in Series,** Wood, 2-1/2" dia.
Dated Christmas 1988. Caption: "Purple Finch, CARPODACUS
PURPUREUS, Seventh In A Series, Wildlife Collection."
☐ Purchased 19 __Pd $_____MIB   NB   DB   BNT
☐ Want   Orig. Ret. $7.75   **NB** $8.50   **MIB** Sec. Mkt. **$18**

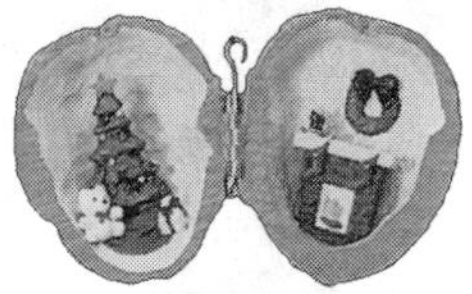

QX 469-7   IN A NUTSHELL
Comments: Handcrafted, 1-1/2" tall, Reissued from 1987.
Artist: Duane Unruh
☐ Purchased 19 __Pd $_____MIB   NB   DB   BNT
☐ Want   Orig. Ret. $5.50   **NB** $10   **MIB** Sec. Mkt. **$20**

QX 477-4   JINGLE BELL CLOWN
Comments: Musical/Handcrafted, 3" tall, Dated 1988.
This happy clown likes to ring his brass jingle bell as he rides
along in his reindeer cart. Tune: "Jingle Bells."
☐ Purchased 19__Pd $_____MIB   NB   DB   BNT
☐ Want   Orig. Ret. $15.00   **NB** $14   **MIB** Sec. Mkt. **$28**

QX 473-1   JOLLY WALRUS
Comments: Handcrafted, 1-7/8" tall.
This cute walrus has quite a toothy smile. He also has a green foil
wreath tied with red satin ribbon.
Artist: Anita Marra Rogers
☐ Purchased 19__Pd $_____MIB   NB   DB   BNT
☐ Want   Orig. Ret. $4.50   **NB** $7   **MIB** Sec. Mkt. **$20**

QX 486-1   KISS THE CLAUS
Comments: Handcrafted, 2-3/4" tall.
Santa's apron says to "Kiss the Claus." But he's serving up
cheeseburgers right now.
Artist: Duane Unruh
☐ Purchased 19__Pd $_____MIB   NB   DB   BNT
☐ Want   Orig. Ret. $5.00   **NB** $10   **MIB** Sec. Mkt. **$14**

QLX 716-4   KITTY CAPERS
Comments: Blinking Lights, Handcrafted, 1-1/2" tall.
Kitty has gotten himself all tangled up in the Christmas tree lights.
Fastens with a clip. **Artist:** Sharon Pike
☐ Purchased 19__Pd $_____MIB   NB   DB   BNT
☐ Want   Orig. Ret. $13.00   **NB** $22   **MIB** Sec. Mkt. **$42**

QX 495-1   KRINGLE MOON
Comments: Handcrafted, 3-3/8" tall.
Santa has been sculpted in the shape of a quarter moon. He's
napping away with a brass jingle bell at the top of his hat.
Artist: Anita Marra Rogers
☐ Purchased 19__Pd $_____MIB   NB   DB   BNT
☐ Want   Orig. Ret. $5.50   **NB** $22   **MIB** Sec. Mkt. **$30**

QX 421-4   KRINGLE PORTRAIT
Comments: Handcrafted, 3-1/4" tall.
Santa's face and beard are circled by a wreath. His sleigh, along with
a tree and teddy bear are sculpted on the back. Some color differences
have been noted.
☐ Purchased 19__Pd $_____MIB   NB   DB   BNT
☐ Want   Orig. Ret. $7.50   **NB** $18   **MIB** Sec. Mkt. **$28**

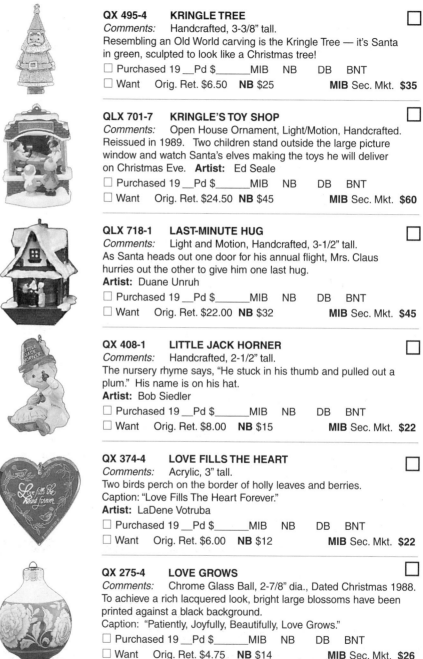

QX 495-4   KRINGLE TREE
Comments: Handcrafted, 3-3/8" tall.
Resembling an Old World carving is the Kringle Tree — it's Santa
in green, sculpted to look like a Christmas tree!
☐ Purchased 19__Pd $_____MIB   NB   DB   BNT
☐ Want   Orig. Ret. $6.50   **NB** $25   **MIB** Sec. Mkt. **$35**

QLX 701-7   KRINGLE'S TOY SHOP
Comments: Open House Ornament, Light/Motion, Handcrafted.
Reissued in 1989.   Two children stand outside the large picture
window and watch Santa's elves making the toys he will deliver
on Christmas Eve.   **Artist:** Ed Seale
☐ Purchased 19__Pd $_____MIB   NB   DB   BNT
☐ Want   Orig. Ret. $24.50   **NB** $45   **MIB** Sec. Mkt. **$60**

QLX 718-1   LAST-MINUTE HUG
Comments: Light and Motion, Handcrafted, 3-1/2" tall.
As Santa heads out one door for his annual flight, Mrs. Claus
hurries out the other to give him one last hug.
Artist: Duane Unruh
☐ Purchased 19__Pd $_____MIB   NB   DB   BNT
☐ Want   Orig. Ret. $22.00   **NB** $32   **MIB** Sec. Mkt. **$45**

QX 408-1   LITTLE JACK HORNER
Comments: Handcrafted, 2-1/2" tall.
The nursery rhyme says, "He stuck in his thumb and pulled out a
plum." His name is on his hat.
Artist: Bob Siedler
☐ Purchased 19__Pd $_____MIB   NB   DB   BNT
☐ Want   Orig. Ret. $8.00   **NB** $15   **MIB** Sec. Mkt. **$22**

QX 374-4   LOVE FILLS THE HEART
Comments: Acrylic, 3" tall.
Two birds perch on the border of holly leaves and berries.
Caption: "Love Fills The Heart Forever."
Artist: LaDene Votruba
☐ Purchased 19__Pd $_____MIB   NB   DB   BNT
☐ Want   Orig. Ret. $6.00   **NB** $12   **MIB** Sec. Mkt. **$22**

QX 275-4   LOVE GROWS
Comments: Chrome Glass Ball, 2-7/8" dia., Dated Christmas 1988.
To achieve a rich lacquered look, bright large blossoms have been
printed against a black background.
Caption: "Patiently, Joyfully, Beautifully, Love Grows."
☐ Purchased 19__Pd $_____MIB   NB   DB   BNT
☐ Want   Orig. Ret. $4.75   **NB** $14   **MIB** Sec. Mkt. **$26**

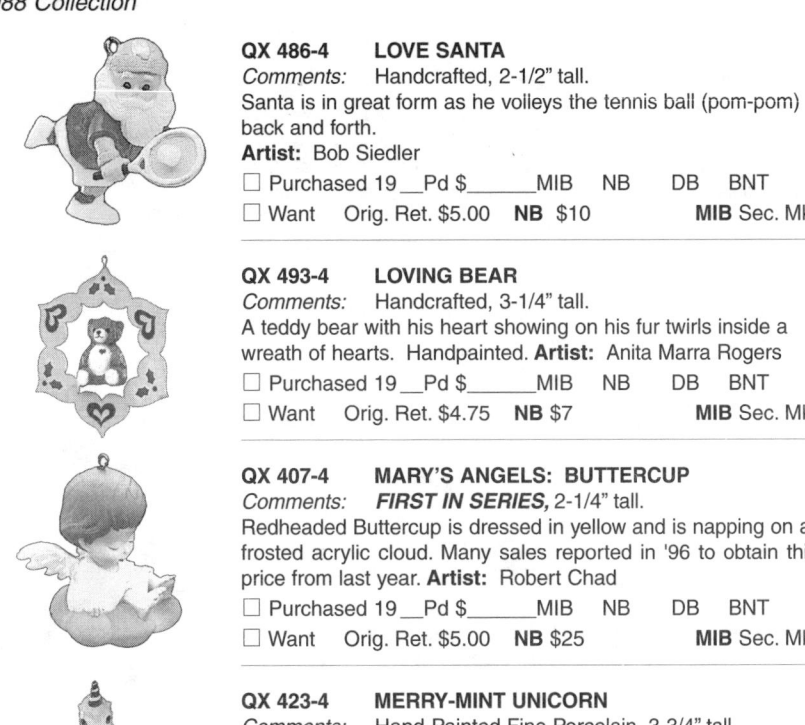

QX 486-4   LOVE SANTA ☐
Comments: Handcrafted, 2-1/2" tall.
Santa is in great form as he volleys the tennis ball (pom-pom)
back and forth.
Artist: Bob Siedler
☐ Purchased 19___Pd $_____MIB   NB   DB   BNT
☐ Want   Orig. Ret. $5.00   **NB** $10   **MIB** Sec. Mkt. **$15**

QX 493-4   LOVING BEAR ☐
Comments: Handcrafted, 3-1/4" tall.
A teddy bear with his heart showing on his fur twirls inside a
wreath of hearts. Handpainted. **Artist:** Anita Marra Rogers
☐ Purchased 19___Pd $_____MIB   NB   DB   BNT
☐ Want   Orig. Ret. $4.75   **NB** $7   **MIB** Sec. Mkt. **$16**

QX 407-4   MARY'S ANGELS: BUTTERCUP ☐
Comments: ***FIRST IN SERIES,*** 2-1/4" tall.
Redheaded Buttercup is dressed in yellow and is napping on a
frosted acrylic cloud. Many sales reported in '96 to obtain this lower
price from last year. **Artist:** Robert Chad
☐ Purchased 19___Pd $_____MIB   NB   DB   BNT
☐ Want   Orig. Ret. $5.00   **NB** $25   **MIB** Sec. Mkt. **$35**

QX 423-4   MERRY-MINT UNICORN ☐
Comments: Hand-Painted Fine Porcelain, 3-3/4" tall.
This lovely white unicorn has a red and white striped horn and is
balancing on a peppermint candy.
Artist: Anita Marra Rogers
☐ Purchased 19___Pd $_____MIB   NB   DB   BNT
☐ Want   Orig. Ret. $8.50   **NB** $12   **MIB** Sec. Mkt. **$15**

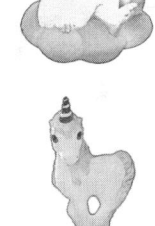

QX 410-4   MIDNIGHT SNACK ☐
Comments: Handcrafted, 2-1/2" tall.
Donuts make the perfect nighttime snack and this little white
mouse agrees as he nibbles away.
Artist: Bob Siedler
☐ Purchased 19___Pd $_____MIB   NB   DB   BNT
☐ Want   Orig. Ret. $6.00   **NB** $15   **MIB** Sec. Mkt. **$18**

QX 403-4   MINIATURE CRECHE ☐
Comments: **Fourth in Series,** Acrylic, 2-3/4" tall.
The Holy Family is depicted in frosted acrylic which has been set
in a clear acrylic star. The edges of the star are faceted and
painted gold. **Artist:** Duane Unruh
☐ Purchased 19___Pd $_____MIB   NB   DB   BNT
☐ Want   Orig. Ret. $8.50   **NB** $8.50   **MIB** Sec. Mkt. **$20**

QX 468-7   MISTLETOAD ☐
Comments: Handcrafted, 3-3/4" tall, Reissued from 1987.
Artist: Ken Crow
☐ Purchased 19___Pd $_____MIB   NB   DB   BNT
☐ Want   Orig. Ret. $7.00   **NB** $14   **MIB** Sec. Mkt. **$24**

QLX 713-4   MOONLIT NAP ☐
Comments: Light, Handcrafted, 2-3/4" tall.
A little angel, dressed in a blue gown and white wings, has hung
his stocking on the tip of the brightly glowing moon awaiting Santa's
visit. **Artist:** Robert Chad
☐ Purchased 19___Pd $_____MIB   NB   DB   BNT
☐ Want   Orig. Ret. $8.75   **NB** $15   **MIB** Sec. Mkt. **$24**

QX 375-1   MOTHER ☐
Comments: Acrylic, 3-3/4" tall, Dated 1988.
Heart shaped acrylic with gold foil heart outline and caption:
"Mother Puts Love Inside Each Moment Of Christmas."
☐ Purchased 19___Pd $_____MIB   NB   DB   BNT
☐ Want   Orig. Ret. $6.50   **NB** $10   **MIB** Sec. Mkt. **$14**

QX 414-4   MOTHER AND DAD ☐
Comments: Fine Porcelain, 3" tall, Dated 1988.
A candle and holly design bring light to this bell. Caption: "Mother
And Dad" and "You Give Christmas A Special Warmth And
Glow." **Artist:** Joyce A. Lyle
☐ Purchased 19___Pd $_____MIB   NB   DB   BNT
☐ Want   Orig. Ret. $8.00   **NB** $14   **MIB** Sec. Mkt. **$18**

QX 401-1   MR. AND MRS. CLAUS: SHALL WE DANCE? ☐
Comments: **Third in Series,** Handcrafted, 4-1/4" tall.
Dated 1988. Santa always has time for a dance with his
sweetheart. **Artist:** Duane Unruh
☐ Purchased 19___Pd $_____MIB   NB   DB   BNT
☐ Want   Orig. Ret. $13.00   **NB** $30   **MIB** Sec. Mkt. **$50**

QX 376-1   NEW HOME ☐
Comments: Acrylic, 2-1/2" tall, Dated 1988.
Santa and his reindeer fly over a wintry home scene. Caption in
gold foil: "A New Home Makes Christmas Merry And Bright."
Artist: LaDene Votruba
☐ Purchased 19___Pd $_____MIB   NB   DB   BNT
☐ Want   Orig. Ret. $6.00   **NB** $10   **MIB** Sec. Mkt. **$20**

QX 422-4   NICK THE KICK ☐
Comments: Handcrafted, 2-1/4" tall.
Santa's playing soccer for the "Blizzard" team. The number on the
back of his shirt is "OO." **Artist:** Bob Siedler
☐ Purchased 19 __ Pd $_____ MIB   NB   DB   BNT
☐ Want   Orig. Ret. $5.00   **NB** $12   **MIB** Sec. Mkt. **$20**

QX 451-7   NIGHT BEFORE CHRISTMAS ☐
Comments: Handcrafted, 2-3/4" tall. Reissued from 1987.
Artist: Ken Crow
☐ Purchased 19 __ Pd $_____ MIB   NB   DB   BNT
☐ Want   Orig. Ret. $6.50   **NB** $18   **MIB** Sec. Mkt. **$30**

QX 490-4   NOAH'S ARK ☐
Comments: Pressed Tin, 2-1/8" tall.
Similar to antique pull toys with wheels that turn and a metallic pull
cord. This vessel is also filled with passengers. Tin ornaments are
popular. **Artist:** Linda Sickman
☐ Purchased 19 __ Pd $_____ MIB   NB   DB   BNT
☐ Want   Orig. Ret. $8.50   **NB** $22   **MIB** Sec. Mkt. **$30**

QX 273-1   NORMAN ROCKWELL: CHRISTMAS SCENES ☐
Comments: White Glass Ball, 2-7/8" dia., Dated 1988.
Caption: "Christmas.. The Season That Blesses The World"
and "Christmas…The Season That Touches The Heart. From the
Norman Rockwell Collection." **Artist:** Joyce A. Lyle
☐ Purchased 19 __ Pd $_____ MIB   NB   DB   BNT
☐ Want   Orig. Ret. $4.75   **NB** $12   **MIB** Sec. Mkt. **$20**

QX 370-4   NORMAN ROCKWELL: ☐
AND TO ALL A GOOD NIGHT
Comments: **Ninth and Final in Series,** Red Cameo, 3-1/4" dia.
Caption: "And To All A Good Night, Ninth In A Series, Christmas
1988, The Norman Rockwell Collection."
☐ Purchased 19 __ Pd $_____ MIB   NB   DB   BNT
☐ Want   Orig. Ret. $7.75   **NB** $12   **MIB** Sec. Mkt. **$20**

QX 401-4   NOSTALGIC HOUSES AND SHOPS: ☐
HALL BRO'S CARD SHOP
Comments: **Fifth in Series,** 4-1/4" tall, Dated 1988.
An old-fashioned cash register sits on a counter in this card shop
and a greeting card display is nearby. The second floor is an
artist's studio. **Artist:** Donna Lee
☐ Purchased 19 __ Pd $_____ MIB   NB   DB   BNT
☐ Want   Orig. Ret. $14.50 **NB** $35   **MIB** Sec. Mkt. **$50**

QX 498-1   OLD-FASHIONED CHURCH ☐
Comments: Wood, 4-1/2" tall.
In American country motif, this small white church boasts a
steeple with a cross at the top.
Artist: Linda Sickman
☐ Purchased 19 __ Pd $_____ MIB   NB   DB   BNT
☐ Want   Orig. Ret. $4.00   **NB** $10   **MIB** Sec. Mkt. **$18**

QX 497-1   OLD-FASHIONED SCHOOLHOUSE ☐
Comments: Wood, 3" tall.
The little red schoolhouse is reminiscent of early country with
its flag and bell tower.
Artist: Linda Sickman
☐ Purchased 19 __ Pd $_____ MIB   NB   DB   BNT
☐ Want   Orig. Ret. $4.00   **NB** $10   **MIB** Sec. Mkt. **$20**

QX 481-4   OREO® ☐
Comments: Handcrafted, 1-7/8" dia.
Cookie opens to show frosting inside. Santa's face is part of
the frosting. "Ho Ho Ho!" **Artist:** Duane Unruh
☐ Purchased 19 __ Pd $_____ MIB   NB   DB   BNT
☐ Want   Orig. Ret. $4.00   **NB** $8   **MIB** Sec. Mkt. **$12**

QXC 580-4   OUR CLUBHOUSE: KEEPSAKE CLUB ☐
Comments: Handcrafted, 2-1/2" tall, Dated 1988.
"For Club Members Only" is a cute little clubhouse with a mouse
inside. He's decorated the inside for Christmas. The Club logo
is on the bottom. **Artist:** Bob Siedler
☐ Purchased 19 __ Pd $_____ MIB   NB   DB   BNT
☐ Want   Price: Came with Club Membership of $_____
                NB $30   **MIB** Sec. Mkt. **$38**

QX 455-9   "OWLIDAY" WISH ☐
Comments: Handcrafted, 2" tall. Reissued from 1987.
Artist: Sharon Pike
☐ Purchased 19 __ Pd $_____ MIB   NB   DB   BNT
☐ Want   Orig. Ret. $6.50   **NB** $10   **MIB** Sec. Mkt. **$20**

QX 479-1   PAR FOR SANTA ☐
Comments: Handcrafted, 2-5/8" tall.
Santa's waiting for the St. Nick Open to begin and he's ready to
tee off in this golf design.
Artist: Bob Siedler
☐ Purchased 19 __ Pd $_____ MIB   NB   DB   BNT
☐ Want   Orig. Ret. $5.00   **NB** $11   **MIB** Sec. Mkt. **$16**

QLX 719-4   PARADE OF THE TOYS

Comments: Light and Motion, Handcrafted, 3-1/2" tall.
The toys are on parade. A toy soldier pulls a red wagon with a jack-in-the-box which pops up and down, a doll pushes a baby carriage and three ducks all circle a lighted Christmas tree.
Artist: Linda Sickman

☐ Purchased 19 __ Pd $_____ MIB NB DB BNT
☐ Want   Orig. Ret. $24.50 **NB** $22   **MIB** Sec. Mkt. **$35**

QX 476-1   PARTY LINE

Comments: Handcrafted, 1-3/4" tall.
Two little raccoons have solved their communication problems; they've created their own telephone from two miniature cans of "Campbell's Chicken Noodle Soup." Campbell's Collectibles are very popular. **Artist:** Sharon Pike

☐ Purchased 19 __ Pd $_____ MIB NB DB BNT
☐ Want   Orig. Ret. $8.75 **NB** $18   **MIB** Sec. Mkt. **$28**

QX 280-1   PEANUTS®

Comments: Blue Glass Ball, 2-7/8" dia., Dated Christmas 1988.
Santa Snoopy flies across the sky on a sled loaded with gifts, and pulled by Woodstock and his friends.

☐ Purchased 19 __ Pd $_____ MIB NB DB BNT
☐ Want   Orig. Ret. $4.75 **NB** $22   **MIB** Sec. Mkt. **$35**

QX 487-1   PEEK-A-BOO KITTIES

Comments: Handcrafted, 5" tall.
While a kitten plays with a ball of yarn, two more peek out of the basket when the string is pulled.
Artist: Ken Crow

☐ Purchased 19 __ Pd $_____ MIB NB DB BNT
☐ Want   Orig. Ret. $7.50 **NB** $15   **MIB** Sec. Mkt. **$20**

QX 478-4   POLAR BOWLER

Comments: Handcrafted, 2-1/4" tall.
Santa shows great form with his polished green bowling ball at the "North Pole Bowl."
Artist: Bob Siedler

☐ Purchased 19 __ Pd $_____ MIB NB DB BNT
☐ Want   Orig. Ret. $5.00 **NB** $12   **MIB** Sec. Mkt. **$16.50**

QX 404-4   PORCELAIN BEAR

Comments: **Sixth in Series,** Fine Porcelain, 2-1/4" tall.
This year's cinnamon bear is thrilled with his gift! It's wrapped inside a red heart-shaped box with a green bow.
Artist: Sharon Pike

☐ Purchased 19 __ Pd $_____ MIB NB DB BNT
☐ Want   Orig. Ret. $8.00 **NB** $20   **MIB** Sec. Mkt. **$32**

QX 474-4   PURRFECT SNUGGLE

Comments: Handcrafted, 2" tall.
A gray and white striped kitten has found a new friend - a brown teddy bear with a holiday bow.
Artist: Anita Marra Rogers

☐ Purchased 19 __ Pd $_____ MIB NB DB BNT
☐ Want   Orig. Ret. $6.25 **NB** $15   **MIB** Sec. Mkt. **$25**

QLX 712-1   RADIANT TREE

Comments: Light, Brass, 3-1/4" tall.
Ten cutout triangular panels form this brass tree which radiates light from all sides.
Artist: Joyce A. Lyle

☐ Purchased 19 __ Pd $_____ MIB NB DB BNT
☐ Want   Orig. Ret. $11.75 **NB** $12   **MIB** Sec. Mkt. **$18**

QX 405-1   REINDEER CHAMPS: PRANCER

Comments: **Third in Series,** Handcrafted, 3-1/2" tall, Dated 1988.
"Prancer 88" is a basketball champion with his white sport shoes and shooting technique.
Artist: Bob Siedler

☐ Purchased 19 __ Pd $_____ MIB NB DB BNT
☐ Want   Orig. Ret. $7.50 **NB** $22   **MIB** Sec. Mkt. **$35**

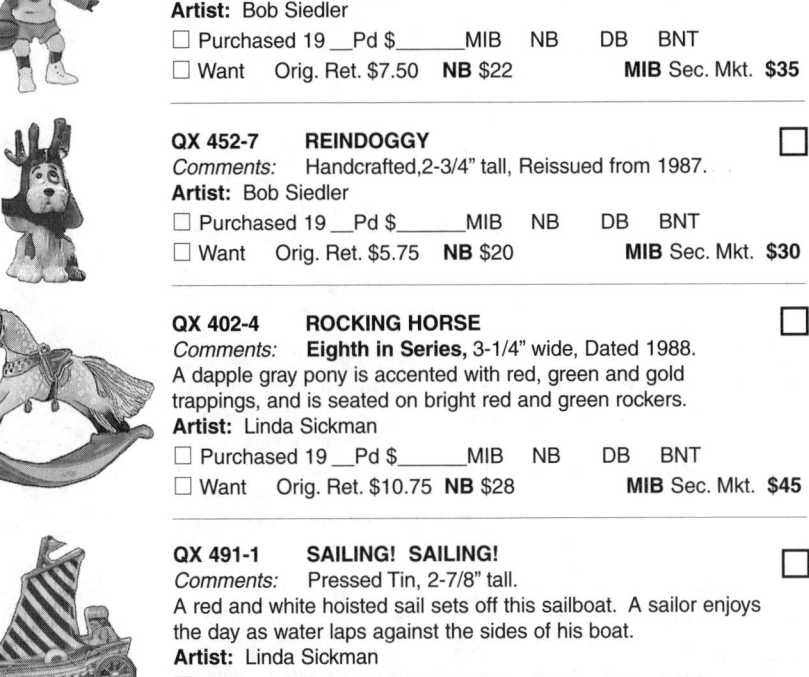

QX 452-7   REINDOGGY

Comments: Handcrafted, 2-3/4" tall, Reissued from 1987.
Artist: Bob Siedler

☐ Purchased 19 __ Pd $_____ MIB NB DB BNT
☐ Want   Orig. Ret. $5.75 **NB** $20   **MIB** Sec. Mkt. **$30**

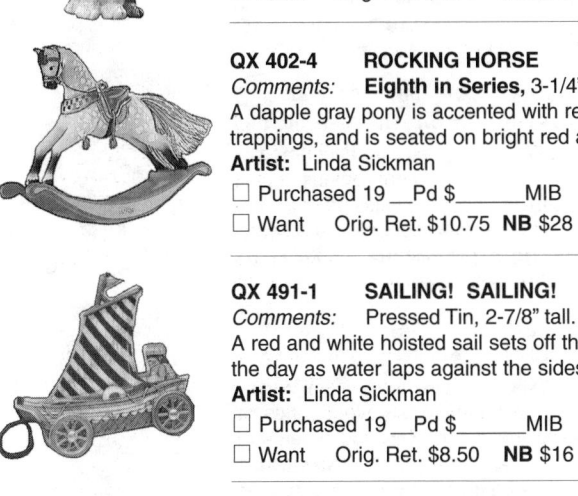

QX 402-4   ROCKING HORSE

Comments: **Eighth in Series,** 3-1/4" wide, Dated 1988.
A dapple gray pony is accented with red, green and gold trappings, and is seated on bright red and green rockers.
Artist: Linda Sickman

☐ Purchased 19 __ Pd $_____ MIB NB DB BNT
☐ Want   Orig. Ret. $10.75 **NB** $28   **MIB** Sec. Mkt. **$45**

QX 491-1   SAILING! SAILING!

Comments: Pressed Tin, 2-7/8" tall.
A red and white hoisted sail sets off this sailboat. A sailor enjoys the day as water laps against the sides of his boat.
Artist: Linda Sickman

☐ Purchased 19 __ Pd $_____ MIB NB DB BNT
☐ Want   Orig. Ret. $8.50 **NB** $16   **MIB** Sec. Mkt. **$25**

QLX 719-1   SANTA & SPARKY: ON WITH THE SHOW ☐
Comments: **Third in Series,** Light and Motion, Handcrafted, 4" tall.
Dated 1988. Santa steps forward and waves his magic wand and
presto! A penguin pops out of his hat!
☐ Purchased 19 __ Pd $_____ MIB   NB   DB   BNT
☐ Want   Orig. Ret. $19.50 **NB** $28   **MIB** Sec. Mkt. **$35**

QX 483-4   SANTA FLAMINGO ☐
Comments: Handcrafted, 5-1/2" tall.
This pink flamingo stands tall among others due to his long legs
(which really move). He wears a red fabric Santa hat with furry
white trim. **Artist:** Michele Pyda-Sevcik
☐ Purchased 19 __ Pd $_____ MIB   NB   DB   BNT
☐ Want   Orig. Ret. $4.75 **NB** $15   **MIB** Sec. Mkt. **$28**

QX 492-4   SHINY SLEIGH ☐
Comments: Dimensional Brass, 1-3/8" tall.
The multidimensional design of Santa and his reindeer has been
achieved by bending and shaping one continuous piece of
brass. **Artist:** Joyce Pattee
☐ Purchased 19 __ Pd $_____ MIB   NB   DB   BNT
☐ Want   Orig. Ret. $5.75 **NB** $12   **MIB** Sec. Mkt. **$18**

QX 499-4   SISTER ☐
Comments: Fine Porcelain Bell, 3" tall, Dated 1988.
A little girl places a star on the top of her Christmas tree. Caption:
"Sisters Know So Many Ways To Brighten Up The Holidays!"
Artist: LaDene Votruba
☐ Purchased 19 __ Pd $_____ MIB   NB   DB   BNT
☐ Want   Orig. Ret. $8.00 **NB** $12   **MIB** Sec. Mkt. **$30**

QLX 720-1   SKATER'S WALTZ ☐
Comments: Light and Motion, Handcrafted, 3-1/2" tall.
Two Victorian couples ice skate around snow covered
evergreens and a lamppost. **Artist:** Duane Unruh
☐ Purchased 19 __ Pd $_____ MIB   NB   DB   BNT
☐ Want   Orig. Ret. $24.50 **NB** $35   **MIB** Sec. Mkt. **$50**

QXC 580-1   SLEIGHFUL OF DREAMS: KEEPSAKE CLUB ☐
Comments: Handcrafted, 2-1/8" tall, Dated 1988.
Designed to resemble an old-fashioned wooden sleigh, this
creation features bas relief designs of favorite past Keepsake
ornaments. **Artist:** Linda Sickman
☐ Purchased 19 __ Pd $_____ MIB   NB   DB   BNT
☐ Want   Orig. Ret. $8.00 **NB** $42   **MIB** Sec. Mkt. **$68**

QX 472-4   SLIPPER SPANIEL ☐
Comments: Handcrafted, 3" tall.
This little brown and white puppy has fallen asleep in a red
flocked slipper. **Artist:** Ken Crow
☐ Purchased 19 __ Pd $_____ MIB   NB   DB   BNT
☐ Want   Orig. Ret. $4.25 **NB** $7   **MIB** Sec. Mkt. **$16**

QX 474-1   SNOOPY® AND WOODSTOCK ☐
Comments: Handcrafted, 2-3/8" tall.
These two friends have tucked themselves into a red and white
knit stocking which includes a bone with a green bow.
Artist: Duane Unruh
☐ Purchased 19 __ Pd $_____ MIB   NB   DB   BNT
☐ Want   Orig. Ret. $6.00 **NB** $22   **MIB** Sec. Mkt. **$40**

QX 475-1   SOFT LANDING ☐
Comments: Handcrafted, 3" tall.
If Santa falls down on his ice skates, he won't get hurt — he's tied
a green pillow to his waist.
Artist: Robert Chad
☐ Purchased 19 __ Pd $_____ MIB   NB   DB   BNT
☐ Want   Orig. Ret. $7.00 **NB** $12   **MIB** Sec. Mkt. **$22**

QX 415-4   SON ☐
Comments: Handcrafted, 3-5/8" tall, Dated 1988.
Similar to the Daughter ornament, a cookie boy is carrying a
cookie sheet full of more cookies.
Artist: Joyce Pattee
☐ Purchased 19 __ Pd $_____ MIB   NB   DB   BNT
☐ Want   Orig. Ret. $5.75 **NB** $31   **MIB** Sec. Mkt. **$40**

QLX 711-1   SONG OF CHRISTMAS ☐
Comments: Light, Acrylic, 3-1/2" tall.
The beveled, faceted edge sets off the exquisite etched cardinal.
Caption: "Song Of Christmas."
☐ Purchased 19 __ Pd $_____ MIB   NB   DB   BNT
☐ Want   Orig. Ret. $8.50 **NB** $15   **MIB** Sec. Mkt. **$24**

QX 493-1   SPARKLING TREE ☐
Comments: Dimensional Brass, 3-3/8" tall.
A brass Christmas tree is layered with brass silhouettes of a
home, reindeer, doves, heart and star. There are also cutouts
in the tree. Artist: Joyce Pattee
☐ Purchased 19   Pd $ MIB   NB   DB   BNT
☐ Want   Orig. Ret. $6.00 **NB** $12   **MIB** Sec. Mkt. **$18**

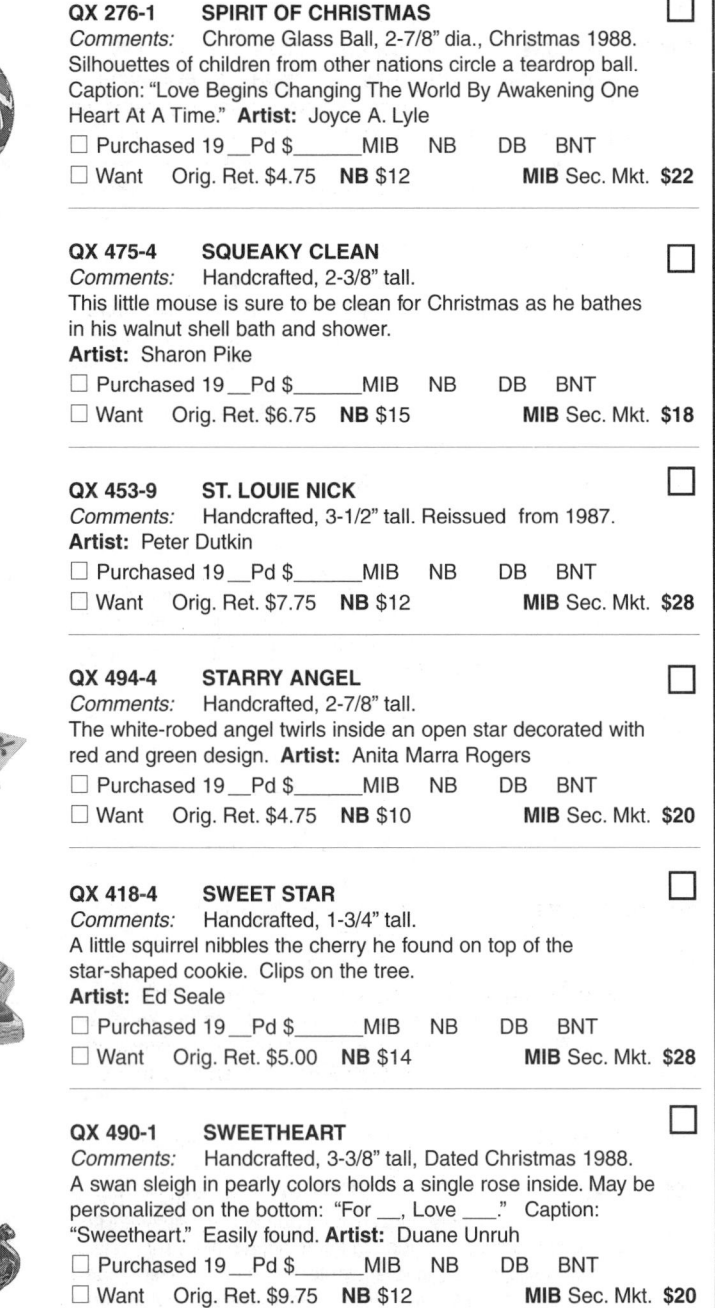

QX 276-1   SPIRIT OF CHRISTMAS   ☐
Comments: Chrome Glass Ball, 2-7/8" dia., Christmas 1988.
Silhouettes of children from other nations circle a teardrop ball.
Caption: "Love Begins Changing The World By Awakening One
Heart At A Time." **Artist:** Joyce A. Lyle

☐ Purchased 19 __ Pd $_____ MIB   NB   DB   BNT
☐ Want   Orig. Ret. $4.75   **NB** $12   **MIB** Sec. Mkt. **$22**

QX 475-4   SQUEAKY CLEAN   ☐
Comments: Handcrafted, 2-3/8" tall.
This little mouse is sure to be clean for Christmas as he bathes
in his walnut shell bath and shower.
Artist: Sharon Pike

☐ Purchased 19 __ Pd $_____ MIB   NB   DB   BNT
☐ Want   Orig. Ret. $6.75   **NB** $15   **MIB** Sec. Mkt. **$18**

QX 453-9   ST. LOUIE NICK   ☐
Comments: Handcrafted, 3-1/2" tall. Reissued from 1987.
Artist: Peter Dutkin

☐ Purchased 19 __ Pd $_____ MIB   NB   DB   BNT
☐ Want   Orig. Ret. $7.75   **NB** $12   **MIB** Sec. Mkt. **$28**

QX 494-4   STARRY ANGEL   ☐
Comments: Handcrafted, 2-7/8" tall.
The white-robed angel twirls inside an open star decorated with
red and green design. **Artist:** Anita Marra Rogers

☐ Purchased 19 __ Pd $_____ MIB   NB   DB   BNT
☐ Want   Orig. Ret. $4.75   **NB** $10   **MIB** Sec. Mkt. **$20**

QX 418-4   SWEET STAR   ☐
Comments: Handcrafted, 1-3/4" tall.
A little squirrel nibbles the cherry he found on top of the
star-shaped cookie. Clips on the tree.
Artist: Ed Seale

☐ Purchased 19 __ Pd $_____ MIB   NB   DB   BNT
☐ Want   Orig. Ret. $5.00   **NB** $14   **MIB** Sec. Mkt. **$28**

QX 490-1   SWEETHEART   ☐
Comments: Handcrafted, 3-3/8" tall, Dated Christmas 1988.
A swan sleigh in pearly colors holds a single rose inside. May be
personalized on the bottom: "For __, Love ___." Caption:
"Sweetheart." Easily found. **Artist:** Duane Unruh

☐ Purchased 19 __ Pd $_____ MIB   NB   DB   BNT
☐ Want   Orig. Ret. $9.75   **NB** $12   **MIB** Sec. Mkt. **$20**

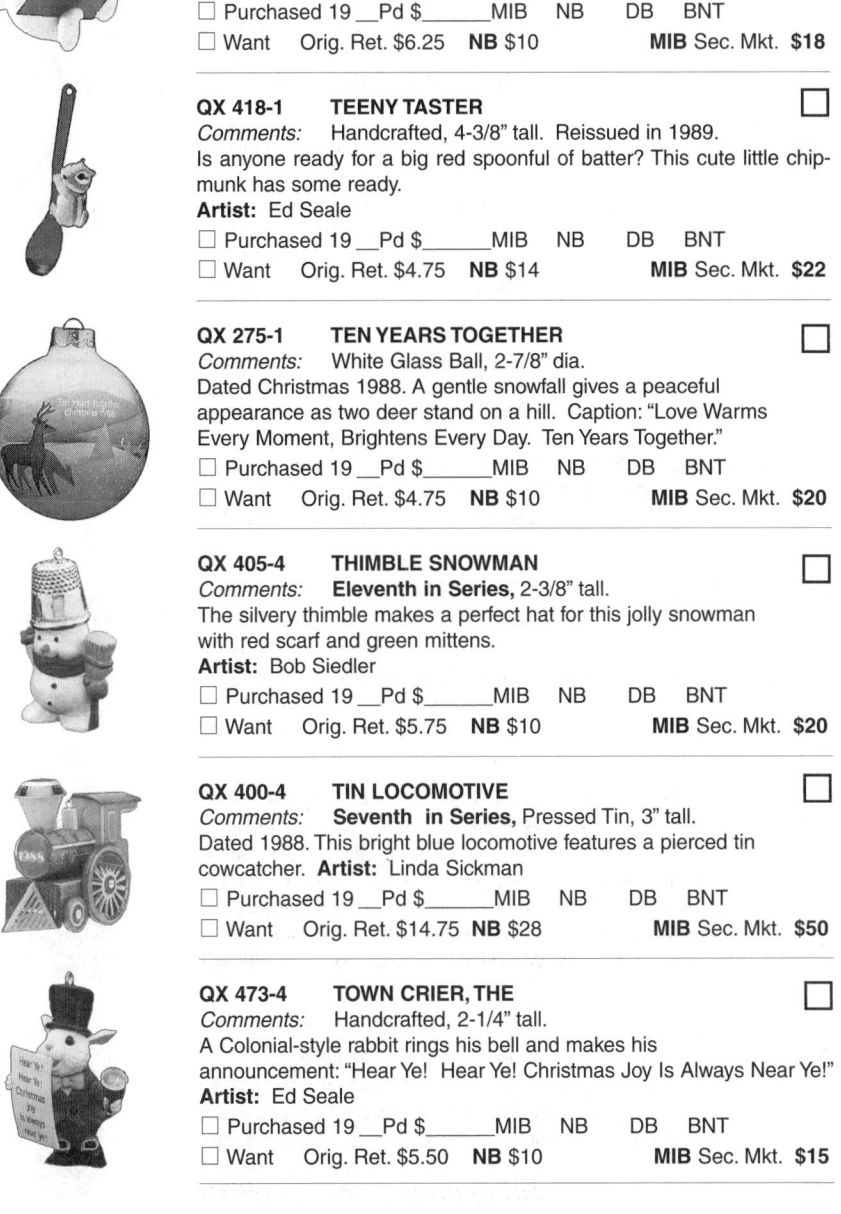

QX 417-1   TEACHER   ☐
Comments: Handcrafted, 2-1/4" tall, Dated 1988.
This flocked bunny has created a card for his favorite teacher at
Christmas. Caption: "For Teacher" and "Merry Christmas 1988."
Artist: Sharon Pike

☐ Purchased 19 __ Pd $_____ MIB   NB   DB   BNT
☐ Want   Orig. Ret. $6.25   **NB** $10   **MIB** Sec. Mkt. **$18**

QX 418-1   TEENY TASTER   ☐
Comments: Handcrafted, 4-3/8" tall. Reissued in 1989.
Is anyone ready for a big red spoonful of batter? This cute little chip-
munk has some ready.
Artist: Ed Seale

☐ Purchased 19 __ Pd $_____ MIB   NB   DB   BNT
☐ Want   Orig. Ret. $4.75   **NB** $14   **MIB** Sec. Mkt. **$22**

QX 275-1   TEN YEARS TOGETHER   ☐
Comments: White Glass Ball, 2-7/8" dia.
Dated Christmas 1988. A gentle snowfall gives a peaceful
appearance as two deer stand on a hill. Caption: "Love Warms
Every Moment, Brightens Every Day. Ten Years Together."

☐ Purchased 19 __ Pd $_____ MIB   NB   DB   BNT
☐ Want   Orig. Ret. $4.75   **NB** $10   **MIB** Sec. Mkt. **$20**

QX 405-4   THIMBLE SNOWMAN   ☐
Comments: **Eleventh in Series,** 2-3/8" tall.
The silvery thimble makes a perfect hat for this jolly snowman
with red scarf and green mittens.
Artist: Bob Siedler

☐ Purchased 19 __ Pd $_____ MIB   NB   DB   BNT
☐ Want   Orig. Ret. $5.75   **NB** $10   **MIB** Sec. Mkt. **$20**

QX 400-4   TIN LOCOMOTIVE   ☐
Comments: **Seventh in Series,** Pressed Tin, 3" tall.
Dated 1988. This bright blue locomotive features a pierced tin
cowcatcher. **Artist:** Linda Sickman

☐ Purchased 19 __ Pd $_____ MIB   NB   DB   BNT
☐ Want   Orig. Ret. $14.75 **NB** $28   **MIB** Sec. Mkt. **$50**

QX 473-4   TOWN CRIER, THE   ☐
Comments: Handcrafted, 2-1/4" tall.
A Colonial-style rabbit rings his bell and makes his
announcement: "Hear Ye! Hear Ye! Christmas Joy Is Always Near Ye!"
Artist: Ed Seale

☐ Purchased 19 __ Pd $_____ MIB   NB   DB   BNT
☐ Want   Orig. Ret. $5.50   **NB** $10   **MIB** Sec. Mkt. **$15**

QX 477-1   TRAVELS WITH SANTA   ☐

Comments: Handcrafted, 2" tall.
Santa's license plate proclaims "B MERRY" to all who pass him in his shiny travel trailer. Look through the picture window and you'll see his TV and bottlebrush Christmas tree.
Artist: Donna Lee

☐ Purchased 19 __ Pd $_____ MIB   NB   DB   BNT
☐ Want   Orig. Ret. $10.00 **NB** $16   **MIB** Sec. Mkt. **$36**

QLX 710-4   TREE OF FRIENDSHIP   ☐

Comments: Lighted Acrylic, 4-1/4" tall.
This tree-shaped acrylic has beveled edges and etched snowflakes and caption: "Friends Decorate The Holiday With Love."

☐ Purchased 19 __ Pd $_____ MIB   NB   DB   BNT
☐ Want   Orig. Ret. $8.50 **NB** $12   **MIB** Sec. Mkt. **$24**

QX 459-7   TREETOP DREAMS   ☐

Comments: Handcrafted, 3" tall.
Reissued from 1987. **Artist:** Ed Seale

☐ Purchased 19 __ Pd $_____ MIB   NB   DB   BNT
☐ Want   Orig. Ret. $6.75 **NB** $15   **MIB** Sec. Mkt. **$25**

QX 371-4   TWELVE DAYS OF CHRISTMAS: FIVE GOLDEN RINGS   ☐

Comments: **Fifth in Series,** Acrylic, 3" tall, Dated 1988.
With gold foil captions, a design of five rings is etched into this quatrefoil designed acrylic.
Artist: Sharon Pike

☐ Purchased 19 __ Pd $_____ MIB   NB   DB   BNT
☐ Want   Orig. Ret. $6.50 **NB** $18   **MIB** Sec. Mkt. **$26**

QX 373-4   TWENTY-FIVE YEARS TOGETHER   ☐

Comments: Acrylic, 3-1/8" tall, Dated Christmas 1988.
The caption, "25 Years Together" is stamped in silver foil on a silver bezeled acrylic ornament.
Artist: Joyce Pattee

☐ Purchased 19 __ Pd $_____ MIB   NB   DB   BNT
☐ Want   Orig. Ret. $6.75 **NB** $10   **MIB** Sec. Mkt. **$16**

QX 488-4   UNCLE SAM NUTCRACKER   ☐

Comments: Handcrafted, 5-1/4" tall, Dated 1988.
When you lift Uncle Sam's ponytail, his mouth moves in real nutcracker fashion. **Artist:** Donna Lee

☐ Purchased 19 __ Pd $_____ MIB   NB   DB   BNT
☐ Want   Orig. Ret. $7.00   **NB** $16   **MIB** Sec. Mkt. **$28**

QX 409-1   VERY STRAWBEARY   ☐

Comments: Handcrafted, 2-1/4" tall.
This flocked teddy bear has a special treat - a strawberry snow-cone. Includes the artist's initials, "PDII"
Artist: Peter Dutkin

☐ Purchased 19 __ Pd $_____ MIB   NB   DB   BNT
☐ Want   Orig. Ret. $4.75 **NB** $8   **MIB** Sec. Mkt. **$15**

QX 402-1   WINDOWS OF THE WORLD: FRENCH   ☐

Comments: **Fourth in Series,** Handcrafted, 3-1/2" tall.
Dated 1988. A little boy plays with his poodle near a fireplace waiting for Santa. A banner overhead proclaims "Joyeux Noel."
Artist: Donna Lee

☐ Purchased 19 __ Pd $_____ MIB   NB   DB   BNT
☐ Want   Orig. Ret. $10.00 **NB** $15   **MIB** Sec. Mkt. **$27**

QX 478-1   WINTER FUN   ☐

Comments: Handcrafted, 2" tall.
Three children are racing downhill on a fast toboggan. One child faces backwards. **Artist:** Robert Chad

☐ Purchased 19 __ Pd $_____ MIB   NB   DB   BNT
☐ Want   Orig. Ret. $8.50 **NB** $14   **MIB** Sec. Mkt. **$20**

QX 411-4   WONDERFUL SANTACYCLE, THE   ☐

Comments: Special Edition, Handcrafted, 4-1/4" tall.
Santa's fancy three-wheeler has replaced the normal seat and handlebars with a rocking horse! Includes golden spoked wheels. Easily found. **Artist:** Ed Seale

☐ Purchased 19 __ Pd $_____ MIB   NB   DB   BNT
☐ Want   Orig. Ret. $22.50 **NB** $24   **MIB** Sec. Mkt. **$38**

QX 404-1   WOOD CHILDHOOD: AIRPLANE   ☐

Comments: **Fifth in Series,** Wood, 1-5/8" tall, Dated 1988.
This toy wooden airplane is painted red and green and has a cord to pull it along. **Artist:** Peter Dutkin

☐ Purchased 19 __ Pd $_____ MIB   NB   DB   BNT
☐ Want   Orig. Ret. $7.50 **NB** $12   **MIB** Sec. Mkt. **$20**

QX 416-4   YEAR TO REMEMBER   ☐

Comments: Ceramic, 3-3/4" tall, Dated 1988.
The year date has been designed in ivory ceramic and incorporates holly, berries and an oval frame. It is tied with a red satin ribbon.

☐ Purchased 19 __ Pd $_____ MIB   NB   DB   BNT
☐ Want   Orig. Ret. $7.00 **NB** $12   **MIB** Sec. Mkt. **$18**

1988 Miniature Ornament Collection

A   QXM 574-4   **BABY'S FIRST CHRISTMAS**
Handcrafted, 2-1/2" tall, Dated 1988. **Artist:** Donna Lee
☐ Purchased 19___ Pd $_____   MIB   NB   DB   BNT
☐ Want   Orig. Retail $5.00
         NB $10   **MIB** Sec. Mkt. **$14**

B   QXM 567-1   **BRASS ANGEL**
Brass, 1-1/4" tall. **Artist:** Joyce A. Lyle
☐ Purchased 19___ Pd $_____   MIB   NB   DB   BNT
☐ Want   Orig. Retail $1.50
         NB $14   **MIB** Sec. Mkt. **$20**

C   QXM 566-4   **BRASS STAR**
Brass, 1-1/4" tall. **Artist:** Joyce A. Lyle
☐ Purchased 19___ Pd $_____   MIB   NB   DB   BNT
☐ Want   Orig. Retail $1.50
         NB $14   **MIB** Sec. Mkt. **$20**

D   QXM 567-4   **BRASS TREE**
Brass, 1-1/4" tall. **Artist:** Joyce A. Lyle
☐ Purchased 19___ Pd $_____   MIB   NB   DB   BNT
☐ Want   Orig. Retail $1.50
         NB $14   **MIB** Sec. Mkt. **$20**

E   QXM 570-1   **CANDY CANE ELF**
Handcrafted, 7/8" tall. **Artist:** Bob Siedler
☐ Purchased 19___ Pd $_____   MIB   NB   DB   BNT
☐ Want   Orig. Retail $3.00
         NB $14   **MIB** Sec. Mkt. **$19**

F   QXM 573-1   **COUNTRY WREATH**
Handcrafted, 1-1/2" tall. Reissued in 1989. **Artist:** Anita Marra Rogers
☐ Purchased 19___ Pd $_____   MIB   NB   DB   BNT
☐ Want   Orig. Retail $4.00
         NB $6   **MIB** Sec. Mkt. **$12**

G   QXM 574-1   **FIRST CHRISTMAS TOGETHER**
Wood/Straw Wreath, 1-3/4" tall, Dated 1988. **Artist:** Diana McGehee
☐ Purchased 19___ Pd $_____   MIB   NB   DB   BNT
☐ Want   Orig. Retail $4.00
         NB $6   **MIB** Sec. Mkt. **$12**

H   QXM 576-4   **FRIENDS SHARE JOY**
Faceted Acrylic, 1-1/4" tall. **Artist:** Joyce Pattee
☐ Purchased 19___ Pd $_____   MIB   NB   DB   BNT
☐ Want   Orig. Retail $2.00
         NB $9   **MIB** Sec. Mkt. **$15**

I   QXM 577-1   **GENTLE ANGEL**
Acrylic, 1-1/2" tall. **Artist:** LaDene Votruba
☐ Purchased 19___ Pd $_____   MIB   NB   DB   BNT
☐ Want   Orig. Retail $2.00
         NB $10   **MIB** Sec. Mkt. **$18.50**

J   QXM 561-4   **HAPPY SANTA**
Frosted Glass Ball, 3/4" dia. **Artist:** Joyce Pattee
☐ Purchased 19___ Pd $_____   MIB   NB   DB   BNT
☐ Want   Orig. Retail $4.50
         NB $10   **MIB** Sec. Mkt. **$18.50**

K   QXM 566-1   **HEAVENLY GLOW TREE TOPPER**
Brass. Reissued in 1989.
☐ Purchased 19___ Pd $_____   MIB   NB   DB   BNT
☐ Want   Orig. Retail $9.75
         NB $9   **MIB** Sec. Mkt. **$18.50**

L   QXC 570-4   **HOLD ON TIGHT: KEEPSAKE CLUB**
Handcrafted, 15/16" tall. **Artist:** Bob Siedler
☐ Purchased 19___ Pd $_____   MIB   NB   DB   BNT
☐ Want   Orig. Retail - Free to Renewing Members
         NB $40   **MIB** Sec. Mkt. **$75**

M   QXM 561-1   **HOLY FAMILY**
Handcrafted, 1-3/4" tall, Reissued in 1989. **Artist:** Duane Unruh
☐ Purchased 19___ Pd $_____   MIB   NB   DB   BNT
☐ Want   Orig. Retail $8.50
         NB $9   **MIB** Sec. Mkt. **$11.50**

N   QXM 572-1   **JOLLY ST. NICK**
Handcrafted Santa, 1-3/8" tall. **Artist:** Duane Unruh
☐ Purchased 19___ Pd $_____   MIB   NB   DB   BNT
☐ Want   Orig. Retail $8.00
         NB $25   **MIB** Sec. Mkt. **$32**

A   QXM 569-1   **JOYOUS HEART** ☐
Wood, 1-1/8" tall. **Artist:** Diana McGehee
☐ Purchased 19___ Pd $_____ MIB NB DB BNT
☐ Want   Orig. Retail $3.50
           NB $15   **MIB** Sec. Mkt. **$29.50**

B   QXM 568-1   **FOLK ART LAMB** ☐
Wood, 1" tall. **Artist:** Joyce Pattee
☐ Purchased 19___ Pd $_____ MIB NB DB BNT
☐ Want   Orig. Retail $2.75
           NB $12   **MIB** Sec. Mkt. **$22**

C   QXM 568-4   **FOLK ART REINDEER** ☐
Wood, 1-1/8" tall. **Artist:** Joyce Pattee
☐ Purchased 19___ Pd $_____ MIB NB DB BNT
☐ Want   Orig. Retail $3.00
           NB $12   **MIB** Sec. Mkt. **$18**

D   QXM 562-1   **KITTENS IN TOYLAND; TRAIN** ☐
FIRST IN SERIES, Handcrafted, 3/4" tall. Price down from 96 guide. **Artist:** Ken Crow
☐ Purchased 19___ Pd $_____ MIB NB DB BNT
☐ Want   Orig. Retail $5.00
           NB $12   **MIB** Sec. Mkt. **$24**

E   QXM 578-4   **LITTLE DRUMMER BOY** ☐
Handcrafted, 1-1/4" tall. **Artist:** Bob Siedler
☐ Purchased 19___ Pd $_____ MIB NB DB BNT
☐ Want   Orig. Retail $4.50
           NB $12   **MIB** Sec. Mkt. **$25**

F   QXM 577-4   **LOVE IS FOREVER** ☐
Acrylic, 1" tall. **Artist:** Joyce Pattee
☐ Purchased 19___ Pd $_____ MIB NB DB BNT
☐ Want   Orig. Retail $2.00
           NB $8   **MIB** Sec. Mkt. **$15**

G   QXM 572-4   **MOTHER** ☐
Handcrafted Heart, 1-1/4" tall, Dated 1988. **Artist:** Sharon Pike
☐ Purchased 19___ Pd $_____ MIB NB DB BNT
☐ Want   Orig. Retail $3.00
           NB $6   **MIB** Sec. Mkt. **$12**

H   QXM 563-4   **OLD ENGLISH VILLAGE: FAMILY HOME** ☐
FIRST IN SERIES, Handcrafted, 1-1/4" tall, Dated 1988. **Artist:** Donna Lee
☐ Purchased 19___ Pd $_____ MIB NB DB BNT
☐ Want   Orig. Retail $8.50
           NB $25   **MIB** Sec. Mkt. **$38**

I   QXM 563-1   **PENGUIN PAL: GIFT** ☐
FIRST IN SERIES, Handcrafted, 1" tall. **Artist:** Bob Siedler
☐ Purchased 19___ Pd $_____ MIB NB DB BNT
☐ Want   Orig. Retail $3.75
           NB $15   **MIB** Sec. Mkt. **$24**

J   QXM 562-4   **ROCKING HORSE: DAPPLED** ☐
FIRST IN SERIES, Handcrafted, 1-1/8" tall, Dated 1988. **Artist:** Linda Sickman
☐ Purchased 19___ Pd $_____ MIB NB DB BNT
☐ Want   Orig. Retail $4.50
           NB $24   **MIB** Sec. Mkt. **$42**

K   QXM 560-1   **SKATER'S WALTZ** ☐
Handcrafted, 1-3/8" tall. **Artist:** Duane Unruh
☐ Purchased 19___ Pd $_____ MIB NB DB BNT
☐ Want   Orig. Retail $7.00
           NB $12   **MIB** Sec. Mkt. **$20**

L   QXM 571-1   **SNEAKER MOUSE** ☐
Handcrafted, 1/2" tall.
☐ Purchased 19___ Pd $_____ MIB NB DB BNT
☐ Want   Orig. Retail $4.00
           NB $9   **MIB** Sec. Mkt. **$18.50**

M   QXM 571-4   **SNUGGLY SKATER** ☐
Handcrafted, 1-1/8" tall. **Artist:** Bob Siedler
☐ Purchased 19___ Pd $_____ MIB NB DB BNT
☐ Want   Orig. Retail $4.50
           NB $16   **MIB** Sec. Mkt. **$28**

N   QXM 560-4   **SWEET DREAMS** ☐
Handcrafted, 1-1/2" tall.
☐ Purchased 19___ Pd $_____ MIB NB DB BNT
☐ Want   Orig. Retail $7.00
           NB $10   **MIB** Sec. Mkt. **$20**

O   QXM 569-4   **THREE LITTLE KITTIES** ☐
Handcrafted/Willow, 15/16" tall, Reissued in 1989. **Artist:** Sharon Pike
☐ Purchased 19___ Pd $_____ MIB NB DB BNT
☐ Want   Orig. Retail $6.00
           NB $10   **MIB** Sec. Mkt. **$18.50**

1989 Collection

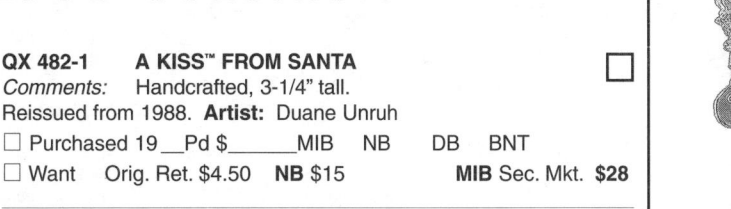

QX 482-1 A KISS™ FROM SANTA
Comments: Handcrafted, 3-1/4" tall.
Reissued from 1988. **Artist:** Duane Unruh
☐ Purchased 19 __ Pd $_____ MIB NB DB BNT
☐ Want Orig. Ret. $4.50 **NB** $15 **MIB** Sec. Mkt. **$28**

QLX 720-2 ANGEL MELODY
Comments: Lighted Acrylic, 5-7/16" tall.
Etched and faceted to reflect the light, an angel in the center joyfully plays her trumpet.
Artist: LaDene Votruba
☐ Purchased 19 __ Pd $_____ MIB NB DB BNT
☐ Want Orig. Ret. $9.50 **NB** $15 **MIB** Sec. Mkt. **$24**

QLX 723-2 ANIMALS SPEAK, THE
Comments: Lighted Panorama Ball, 3-5/8" tall.
The story of Christmas is illustrated. Caption: "The Animals Rejoiced And Spoke, The Star Shone Bright Above, For On This Day A Child Was Born To Touch The World With Love."
Artist: John Francis (Collin)
☐ Purchased 19 __ Pd $_____ MIB NB DB BNT
☐ Want Orig. Ret. $13.50 **NB** $85 **MIB** Sec. Mkt. **$115**

QX 452-5 BABY PARTRIDGE
Comments: Handcrafted, 2-3/4" tall.
This sweet little bird attaches to your tree with a special clip.
Artist: John Francis (Collin)
☐ Purchased 19 __ Pd $_____ MIB NB DB BNT
☐ Want Orig. Ret. $6.75 **NB** $10 **MIB** Sec. Mkt. **$14**

QX 272-5 BABY'S FIRST CHRISTMAS: BOY
Comments: Blue Satin Ball, 2-7/8" dia., Dated 1989.
Caption: "A New Baby Boy To Love. Baby's First Christmas."
Artist: LaDene Votruba
☐ Purchased 19 __ Pd $_____ MIB NB DB BNT
☐ Want Orig. Ret. $4.75 **NB** $8 **MIB** Sec. Mkt. **$19**

QX 272-2 BABY'S FIRST CHRISTMAS: GIRL
Comments: Pink Satin Ball, 2-7/8" dia., Dated 1989.
Caption: "A New Baby Girl To Love. Baby's First Christmas."
Artist: LaDene Votruba
☐ Purchased 19 __ Pd $_____ MIB NB DB BNT
☐ Want Orig. Ret. $4.75 **NB** $8 **MIB** Sec. Mkt. **$19**

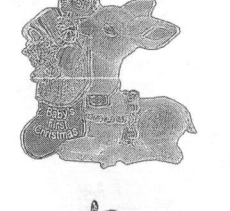

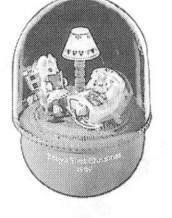

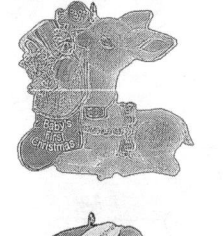
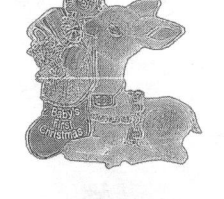

QX 381-5 BABY'S FIRST CHRISTMAS
Comments: Acrylic, 3-7/16" tall, Dated 1989.
An etched reindeer holds a stocking full of toys for baby. "Baby's First Christmas" in gold foil. **Artist:** John Francis (Collin)
☐ Purchased 19 __ Pd $_____ MIB NB DB BNT
☐ Want Orig. Ret. $6.75 **NB** $9 **MIB** Sec. Mkt. **$16**

QX 449-2 BABY'S FIRST CHRISTMAS
Comments: Handcrafted, 2-5/8" tall, Dated 1989.
A flocked teddy bear wearing a green bow and red Santa cap holds a candy cane "1." Hat says "Baby's 1st Christmas."
Artist: Robert Chad
☐ Purchased 19 __ Pd $_____ MIB NB DB BNT
☐ Want Orig. Ret. $7.25 **NB** $60 **MIB** Sec. Mkt. **$75**

QLX 727-2 BABY'S FIRST CHRISTMAS
Comments: Light, Motion and Music, Handcrafted, 4-1/2" tall.
Dated 1989. Mama mouse rocks baby's cradle as she rocks back and forth. Caption: "Baby's First Christmas" and "Christmas And Babies Fill A Home With Love." Plays "Brahms' Lullaby."
Artist: Ed Seale
☐ Purchased 19 __ Pd $_____ MIB NB DB BNT
☐ Want Orig. Ret. $30.00 **NB** $50 **MIB** Sec. Mkt. **$65**

QX 468-2 BABY'S FIRST CHRISTMAS PHOTOHOLDER
Comments: Handcrafted, 3-3/4" tall, Dated 1989.
Caption: "A New Star On The Family Tree!" says it all!
Decorated with colorful toys. **Artist:** LaDene Votruba
☐ Purchased 19 __ Pd $_____ MIB NB DB BNT
☐ Want Orig. Ret. $6.25 **NB** $20 **MIB** Sec. Mkt. **$45**

QX 449-5 BABY'S SECOND CHRISTMAS
Comments: Handcrafted, 2-13/16" tall, Dated 1989.
"Baby's 2nd Christmas" is celebrated by a cute polar bear holding a red, white and green "2." **Artist:** John Francis (Collin)
☐ Purchased 19 __ Pd $_____ MIB NB DB BNT
☐ Want Orig. Ret. $6.75 **NB** $24 **MIB** Sec. Mkt. **$35**

QLX 721-5 BACKSTAGE BEAR
Comments: Lighted, Handcrafted, 3-3/8" tall.
A teddy checks his appearance in the lighted mirror before a performance. Caption: "Beary Christmas!" and on the script: "Beary Christmas To All And To All A Good Night." A mold production sample was found at a garage sale!
Artist: Bob Siedler
☐ Purchased 19 __ Pd $_____ MIB NB DB BNT
☐ Want Orig. Ret. $13.50 **NB** $15 **MIB** Sec. Mkt. **$35**

QX 489-5   BALANCING ELF
Comments: Handcrafted, 4-3/8" tall.
Look at this! Santa's elf holds two brass bells as he balances
on one leg.
Artist: Robert Chad
☐ Purchased 19 __ Pd $_____ MIB   NB   DB   BNT
☐ Want   Orig. Ret. $6.75   **NB** $16   **MIB** Sec. Mkt. **$22**

QX 454-2   BEAR-I-TONE
Comments: Handcrafted, 2-1/4" tall.
An adorable flocked bear plays a real metal triangle in the
Christmas band.
Artist: Bob Siedler
☐ Purchased 19 __ Pd $_____ MIB   NB   DB   BNT
☐ Want   Orig. Ret. $4.75   **NB** $10   **MIB** Sec. Mkt. **$16**

QX 230-2   BETSEY CLARK: HOME FOR CHRISTMAS
Comments: **Fourth in Series,** 2-7/8" dia., Dated 1989.
Betsey and her friends remember the animals outdoors at
Christmas. Caption: "Fun And Friendship Are The Things The
Christmas Season Always Brings!"
☐ Purchased 19 __ Pd $_____ MIB   NB   DB   BNT
☐ Want   Orig. Ret. $5.00   **NB** $15   **MIB** Sec. Mkt. **$32**

QX 445-2   BROTHER
Comments: Handcrafted, 3-1/4" tall, Dated 1989.
A puppy has jumped into this red and white high-top tennis shoe
and is playing with the green laces. Caption: "Brother" and "No
One Else Can Fill Your Shoes!" **Artist:** Joyce A. Lyle
☐ Purchased 19 __ Pd $_____ MIB   NB   DB   BNT
☐ Want   Orig. Ret. $7.25   **NB** $10   **MIB** Sec. Mkt. **$16**

QLX 724-5   BUSY BEAVER
Comments: Light, Handcrafted, 2-7/8" tall.
A beaver warms his paws over a fire in a barrel on a cold night.
He's selling "Fresh Cut Trees."
Artist: Donna Lee
☐ Purchased 19 __ Pd $_____ MIB   NB   DB   BNT
☐ Want   Orig. Ret. $17.50 **NB** $40   **MIB** Sec. Mkt. **$52**

QX 411-2   CACTUS COWBOY
Comments: Handcrafted, 3-1/2" tall, Dated 1989.
Not an easy ornament to locate. A smiling green cactus is
wrapped up in red lights and wears a red cowboy hat. Not
easy to locate. **Artist:** Peter Dutkin
☐ Purchased 19 __ Pd $_____ MIB   NB   DB   BNT
☐ Want   Orig. Ret. $6.75   **NB** $25   **MIB** Sec. Mkt. **$40**

QX 546-5   CAMERA CLAUS
Comments: Handcrafted, 2-3/8" tall.
Say "Cheese" because Santa is here with his camera and he's
ready to take your picture. **Artist:** Bob Siedler
☐ Purchased 19 __ Pd $_____ MIB   NB   DB   BNT
☐ Want   Orig. Ret. $5.75   **NB** $10   **MIB** Sec. Mkt. **$15**

QX 451-5   CAROUSEL ZEBRA
Comments: Handcrafted, 2-3/4" tall, Dated 1989.
The zebra is a striking contrast to the colorful saddle and gold
pole which it rides. **Artist:** Linda Sickman
☐ Purchased 19 __ Pd $_____ MIB   NB   DB   BNT
☐ Want   Orig. Ret. $9.25   **NB** $14   **MIB** Sec. Mkt. **$15**

QX 453-2   CHERRY JUBILEE
Comments: Handcrafted, 2-1/4" tall.
A little white mouse sits in the middle of a cherry pie and enjoys
his tasty treat. **Artist:** Linda Sickman
☐ Purchased 19 __ Pd $_____ MIB   NB   DB   BNT
☐ Want   Orig. Ret. $5.00   **NB** $15   **MIB** Sec. Mkt. **$25**

QX 543-5   CHILD'S FIFTH CHRISTMAS
Comments: Handcrafted, 2-3/8" tall, Dated 1989.
A little koala in a red Santa cap grins merrily as he hangs from
the candy-striped "5." **Artist:** Dill Rhodus
☐ Purchased 19 __ Pd $_____ MIB   NB   DB   BNT
☐ Want   Orig. Ret. $6.75   **NB** $12   **MIB** Sec. Mkt. **$18**

QX 543-2   CHILD'S FOURTH CHRISTMAS
Comments: Handcrafted, 3" tall, Dated 1989.
A panda shoulders its candy cane "4" in proper military fashion
as he marches along. **Artist:** John Francis (Collin)
☐ Purchased 19 __ Pd $_____ MIB   NB   DB   BNT
☐ Want   Orig. Ret. $6.75   **NB** $12   **MIB** Sec. Mkt. **$18**

QX 469-5   CHILD'S THIRD CHRISTMAS
Comments: Handcrafted, 2-1/2" tall, Dated 1989.
A honey bear hugs a red, white and green candy cane "3." "My
3rd Christmas" is on his Santa hat.
Artist: John Francis (Collin)
☐ Purchased 19 __ Pd $_____ MIB   NB   DB   BNT
☐ Want   Orig. Ret. $6.75   **NB** $15   **MIB** Sec. Mkt. **$20**

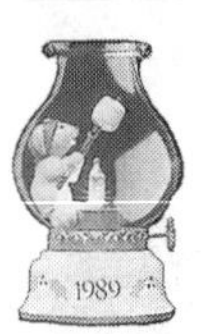

QLX 722-5 CHRIS MOUSE COOKOUT ☐
Comments: **Fifth in Series,** Handcrafted, 4-1/2" tall.
Dated 1989. Chris, dressed in a red nightcap and green night
shirt, toasts his marshmallow. **Artist:** Anita Marra Rogers
☐ Purchased 19___ Pd $_____ MIB   NB   DB   BNT
☐ Want   Orig. Ret. $9.50   **NB** $45   **MIB** Sec. Mkt. **$60**

XPR 972-1 CHRISTMAS CAROUSEL HORSE ☐
            COLLECTION: GINGER
Comments: Special Offer, Handcrafted/Brass, 3-3/16" tall.
Dated 1989. Palomino with white mane and tail. Caption:
"Ginger, 4 In A Collection Of Four." **Artist:** Julia Lee
☐ Purchased 19___ Pd $_____ MIB   NB   DB   BNT
☐ Want   Orig. Ret. $3.95 w/$10 Hallmark purchase.
                         NB $15   **MIB** Sec. Mkt. **$20**

XPR 972-2 CHRISTMAS CAROUSEL HORSE ☐
            COLLECTION: HOLLY
Comments: Special Offer, Handcrafted/Brass, 3-3/16" tall.
Dated 1989. Gray horse with red, gold and green saddle.
Caption: "Holly, 2 In A Collection Of Four." **Artist:** Julia Lee
☐ Purchased 19___ Pd $_____ MIB   NB   DB   BNT
☐ Want   Orig. Ret. $3.95 w/$10 Hallmark purchase.
                         NB $15   **MIB** Sec. Mkt. **$20**

XPR 971-9 CHRISTMAS CAROUSEL HORSE ☐
            COLLECTION: SNOW   (MOST POPULAR)
Comments: Special Offer, Handcrafted/Brass, 3-3/16" tall.
Dated 1989. White horse with golden mane and tail.
Caption: "Snow, 1 In A Collection Of Four." **Artist:** Julia Lee
☐ Purchased 19___ Pd $_____ MIB   NB   DB   BNT
☐ Want   Orig. Ret. $3.95 w/$10 Hallmark purchase.
                         NB $22   **MIB** Sec. Mkt. **$29**

XPR 972-0 CHRISTMAS CAROUSEL HORSE ☐
            COLLECTION: STAR
Comments: Special Offer, Handcrafted/Brass, 3-3/16" tall.
Dated 1989. Brown horse with white mane and tail.
Caption: "Star, 3 In A Collection Of Four." **Artist:** Julia Lee
☐ Purchased 19___ Pd $_____ MIB   NB   DB   BNT
☐ Want   Orig. Ret. $3.95 w/$10 Hallmark purchase.
                         NB $15   **MIB** Sec. Mkt. **$20**

XPR 972-3 CHRISTMAS CAROUSEL HORSE ☐
            COLLECTION: CAROUSEL DISPLAY STAND
Comments: Special Offer, Handcrafted/Brass, 4-5/8" tall.
Dated 1989. Brass pole w/red and green ribbons in center.
Stand did not include horses.
☐ Purchased 19___ Pd $_____ MIB   NB   DB   BNT
☐ Want   Orig. Ret. $1.00 w/any Hallmark purchase.
                         NB $5   **MIB** Sec. Mkt. **$10**

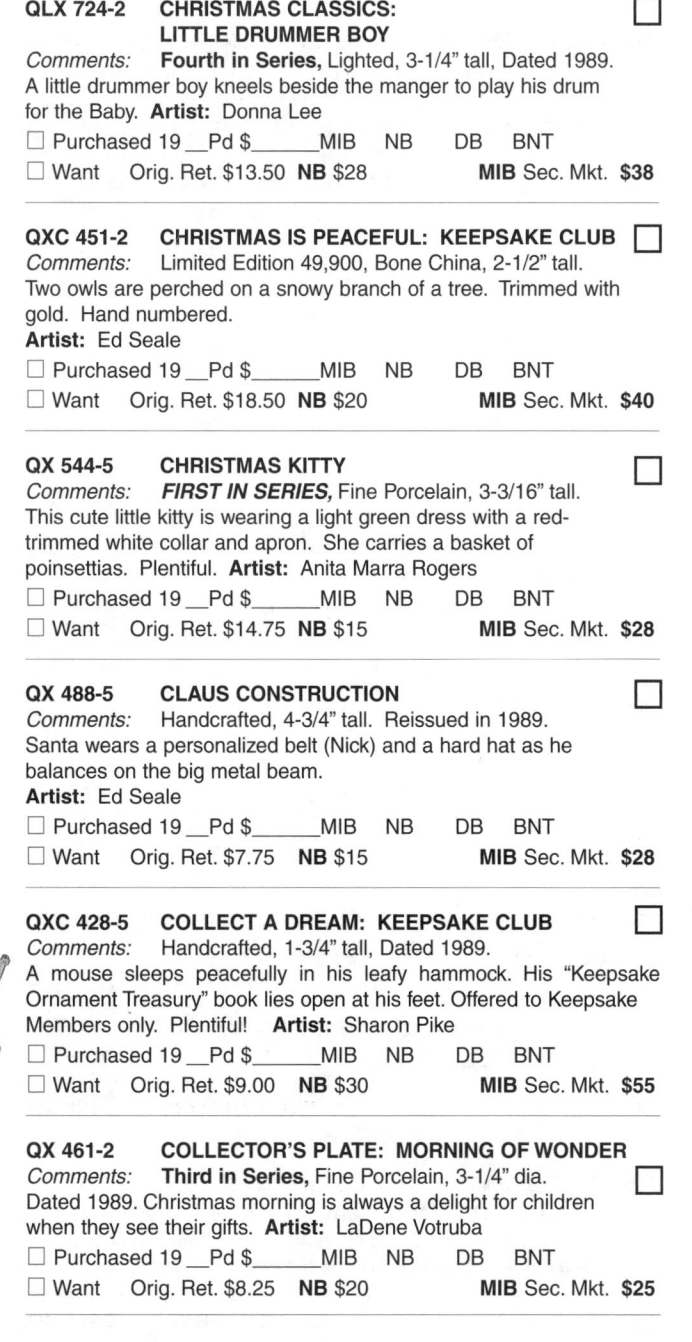

QLX 724-2 CHRISTMAS CLASSICS: ☐
            LITTLE DRUMMER BOY
Comments: **Fourth in Series,** Lighted, 3-1/4" tall, Dated 1989.
A little drummer boy kneels beside the manger to play his drum
for the Baby. **Artist:** Donna Lee
☐ Purchased 19___ Pd $_____ MIB   NB   DB   BNT
☐ Want   Orig. Ret. $13.50 **NB** $28   **MIB** Sec. Mkt. **$38**

QXC 451-2 CHRISTMAS IS PEACEFUL: KEEPSAKE CLUB ☐
Comments: Limited Edition 49,900, Bone China, 2-1/2" tall.
Two owls are perched on a snowy branch of a tree. Trimmed with
gold. Hand numbered.
Artist: Ed Seale
☐ Purchased 19___ Pd $_____ MIB   NB   DB   BNT
☐ Want   Orig. Ret. $18.50 **NB** $20   **MIB** Sec. Mkt. **$40**

QX 544-5 CHRISTMAS KITTY ☐
Comments: **FIRST IN SERIES,** Fine Porcelain, 3-3/16" tall.
This cute little kitty is wearing a light green dress with a red-
trimmed white collar and apron. She carries a basket of
poinsettias. Plentiful. **Artist:** Anita Marra Rogers
☐ Purchased 19___ Pd $_____ MIB   NB   DB   BNT
☐ Want   Orig. Ret. $14.75 **NB** $15   **MIB** Sec. Mkt. **$28**

QX 488-5 CLAUS CONSTRUCTION ☐
Comments: Handcrafted, 4-3/4" tall. Reissued in 1989.
Santa wears a personalized belt (Nick) and a hard hat as he
balances on the big metal beam.
Artist: Ed Seale
☐ Purchased 19___ Pd $_____ MIB   NB   DB   BNT
☐ Want   Orig. Ret. $7.75   **NB** $15   **MIB** Sec. Mkt. **$28**

QXC 428-5 COLLECT A DREAM: KEEPSAKE CLUB ☐
Comments: Handcrafted, 1-3/4" tall, Dated 1989.
A mouse sleeps peacefully in his leafy hammock. His "Keepsake
Ornament Treasury" book lies open at his feet. Offered to Keepsake
Members only. Plentiful! **Artist:** Sharon Pike
☐ Purchased 19___ Pd $_____ MIB   NB   DB   BNT
☐ Want   Orig. Ret. $9.00   **NB** $30   **MIB** Sec. Mkt. **$55**

QX 461-2 COLLECTOR'S PLATE: MORNING OF WONDER
Comments: **Third in Series,** Fine Porcelain, 3-1/4" dia. ☐
Dated 1989. Christmas morning is always a delight for children
when they see their gifts. **Artist:** LaDene Votruba
☐ Purchased 19___ Pd $_____ MIB   NB   DB   BNT
☐ Want   Orig. Ret. $8.25   **NB** $20   **MIB** Sec. Mkt. **$25**

QX 487-5   COOL SWING
Comments: Handcrafted/Acrylic, 3-1/2" tall.
A penguin in a red stocking cap has fun swinging on his ice cube which says "Have A Cool Christmas."
Artist: Ken Crow

☐ Purchased 19___Pd $_____MIB   NB   DB   BNT
☐ Want   Orig. Ret. $6.25   **NB** $20   **MIB** Sec. Mkt. **$30**

QX 467-2   COUNTRY CAT
Comments: Handcrafted, 2-1/4" tall.
This black and white fat cat is ready to ride. He's seated in an old-fashioned red wagon.
Artist: Michele Pyda-Sevcik

☐ Purchased 19___Pd $_____MIB   NB   DB   BNT
☐ Want   Orig. Ret. $6.25   **NB** $14   **MIB** Sec. Mkt. **$16**

QX 426-2   CRANBERRY BUNNY
Comments: Handcrafted, 2-5/8" tall.
A cute, white, flocked bunny is wearing a green stocking hat and is stringing cranberries.
Artist: Anita Marra Rogers

☐ Purchased 19___Pd $_____MIB   NB   DB   BNT
☐ Want   Orig. Ret. $5.75   **NB** $10   **MIB** Sec. Mkt. **$16**

QX 435-2   CRAYOLA® CRAYON: BRIGHT JOURNEY
Comments: **FIRST IN SERIES,** Handcrafted, 3" tall, Dated 1989.
Bear has built a raft with a sail made from a Crayola crayon box. Nice series... many first editions were bought up for secondary market.
Artist: Linda Sickman

☐ Purchased 19___Pd $_____MIB   NB   DB   BNT
☐ Want   Orig. Ret. $8.75   **NB** $35   **MIB** Sec. Mkt. **$48**

QX 441-2   DAD
Comments: Handcrafted, 2-7/8" tall, Dated 1989.
Dad's red and white shorts are just a wee bit big.
Captioned: "For Dad." **Artist:** Julia Lee

☐ Purchased 19___Pd $_____MIB   NB   DB   BNT
☐ Want   Orig. Ret. $7.25   **NB** $8   **MIB** Sec. Mkt. **$14**

QX 443-2   DAUGHTER
Comments: Handcrafted, 3" tall, Dated Christmas 1989.
This little wood-look doll is dressed in bright red and carries a hat box for "Daughter." **Artist:** Linda Sickman

☐ Purchased 19___Pd $_____MIB   NB   DB   BNT
☐ Want   Orig. Ret. $6.25   **NB** $10   **MIB** Sec. Mkt. **$18**

QX 426-5   DEER DISGUISE
Comments: Handcrafted, 1-3/4" tall.
Two children peek out from under their reindeer costume to see where they're going. **Artist:** Bob Siedler

☐ Purchased 19___Pd $_____MIB   NB   DB   BNT
☐ Want   Orig. Ret. $5.75   **NB** $12   **MIB** Sec. Mkt. **$22**

QX 439-2   FELIZ NAVIDAD
Comments: Handcrafted, 2" tall.
Resembling a piñata, this colorful bull carries the Spanish Christmas greeting. Tail is real yarn. Feliz Navidad ornaments are collected exclusively by many.
Artist: Michele Pyda-Sevcik

☐ Purchased 19___Pd $_____MIB   NB   DB   BNT
☐ Want   Orig. Ret. $6.75   **NB** $18   **MIB** Sec. Mkt. **$29**

QX 463-5   FESTIVE ANGEL
Comments: Dimensional Brass, 3-5/16" tall.
This beautiful angel is created from etched layers of brass; her wings are arched together.

☐ Purchased 19___Pd $_____MIB   NB   DB   BNT
☐ Want   Orig. Ret. $6.75   **NB** $14   **MIB** Sec. Mkt. **$22**

QX 384-2   FESTIVE YEAR
Comments: Acrylic, 2-13/16" tall, Dated 1989.
The date is captured in silver foil in the center of this ornament resembling stained glass. **Artist:** LaDene Votruba

☐ Purchased 19___Pd $_____MIB   NB   DB   BNT
☐ Want   Orig. Ret. $7.75   **NB** $10   **MIB** Sec. Mkt. **$20**

QX 486-2   FIFTY YEARS TOGETHER PHOTOHOLDER
Comments: Porcelain, 3-3/4" tall, Dated Christmas 1989.
A lovely white wreath, accented with green holly and red berries, holds a photo. Caption: "50 Years Together."
Artist: Anita Marra Rogers

☐ Purchased 19___Pd $_____MIB   NB   DB   BNT
☐ Want   Orig. Ret. $8.75   **NB** $10   **MIB** Sec. Mkt. **$20**

QX 547-5   FIRST CHRISTMAS, THE
Comments: Blue Cameo, 3-1/8" tall.
Caption: "For Unto You Is Born This Day In The City Of David A Saviour, Which Is Christ The Lord."

☐ Purchased 19___Pd $_____MIB   NB   DB   BNT
☐ Want   Orig. Ret. $7.75   **NB** $8   **MIB** Sec. Mkt. **$16**

QX 383-2   FIRST CHRISTMAS TOGETHER
Comments: Acrylic, 2-7/16" tall, Dated 1989.
Etched deer in the forest make a lovely ornament; gold foil
lettering "Our First Christmas." **Artist:** Dill Rhodus
☐ Purchased 19 __ Pd $_____ MIB   NB   DB   BNT
☐ Want   Orig. Ret. $6.75   **NB** $16   **MIB** Sec. Mkt. **$24**

QLX 734-2   FIRST CHRISTMAS TOGETHER
Comments: Light, Handcrafted, 3-3/4" tall, Dated 1989.
The flickering light from the fireplace casts a warm glow for the
"First Christmas Together." **Artist:** Donna Lee
☐ Purchased 19 __ Pd $_____ MIB   NB   DB   BNT
☐ Want   Orig. Ret. $17.50   **NB** $22   **MIB** Sec. Mkt. **$42**

QX 485-2   FIRST CHRISTMAS TOGETHER
Comments: Handcrafted, 3-1/2" tall, Dated 1989.
A heart-shaped wreath decorated with holly, berries and red
hearts makes the perfect support for a swing for these loving
chipmunks. **Artist:** Anita Marra Rogers
☐ Purchased 19 __ Pd $_____ MIB   NB   DB   BNT
☐ Want   Orig. Ret. $9.75   **NB** $16   **MIB** Sec. Mkt. **$24**

QX 273-2   FIRST CHRISTMAS TOGETHER
Comments: White Glass Ball, 2-7/8" dia., Dated 1989.
Mr. Polar Bear holds a sprig of mistletoe over his sweetheart's
head as they rub noses. Caption: "Our First Christmas Together"
and "Tis The Season To Be Cuddly."
☐ Purchased 19 __ Pd $_____ MIB   NB   DB   BNT
☐ Want   Orig. Ret. $4.75   **NB** $12   **MIB** Sec. Mkt. **$22**

QX 273-5   FIVE YEARS TOGETHER
Comments: Blue/Green Glass, 2-7/8" dia.
Dated Christmas 1989. Caption: "Five Years Together" and
"Love Makes The World A Beautiful Place To Be."
☐ Purchased 19 __ Pd $_____ MIB   NB   DB   BNT
☐ Want   Orig. Ret. $4.75   **NB** $12   **MIB** Sec. Mkt. **$22**

QLX 728-2   FOREST FROLICS
Comments: ***FIRST IN SERIES,*** Light and Motion, Dated 1989.
Handcrafted, 4-7/16" tall. A candy cane in the center has a sign
that reads "Merry Christmas" while forest animals ski the trail that
circles it. **Artist:** Sharon Pike
☐ Purchased 19 __ Pd $_____ MIB   NB   DB   BNT
☐ Want   Orig. Ret. $24.50   **NB** $65   **MIB** Sec. Mkt. **$90**

QX 545-2   FORTY YEARS TOGETHER PHOTOHOLDER
Comments: Porcelain, 3-3/4" tall, Dated Christmas 1989.
White wreath with green holly and red berries holds a couple's
favorite photo. Caption: "40 Years Together."
Artist: Anita Marra Rogers
☐ Purchased 19 __ Pd $_____ MIB   NB   DB   BNT
☐ Want   Orig. Ret. $8.75   **NB** $12   **MIB** Sec. Mkt. **$18**

QX 413-2   FRIENDSHIP TIME
Comments: Handcrafted, 2-1/2" tall, Dated Christmas 1989.
Two delightful mice, in red and green, take time out to chat in a
teacup. Caption: "... Always Time For Friendship."
Artist: Julia Lee
☐ Purchased 19 __ Pd $_____ MIB   NB   DB   BNT
☐ Want   Orig. Ret. $9.75   **NB** $21   **MIB** Sec. Mkt. **$32**

QX 384-5   FROM OUR HOME TO YOURS
Comments: Acrylic, 3-1/2" tall, Dated 1989.
A beautifully detailed mailbox full of gifts is etched onto oval
acrylic. Caption: "From Our Home To Yours At Christmas."
☐ Purchased 19 __ Pd $_____ MIB   NB   DB   BNT
☐ Want   Orig. Ret. $6.25   **NB** $8   **MIB** Sec. Mkt. **$16**

QX 457-2   FROSTY FRIENDS
Comments: **Tenth in Series,** Handcrafted, 2-1/2" tall.
Dated 1989. The little Eskimo and his husky puppy are rushing
over the ice to deliver a gift.
Artist: Ed Seale
☐ Purchased 19 __ Pd $_____ MIB   NB   DB   BNT
☐ Want   Orig. Ret. $9.25   **NB** $25   **MIB** Sec. Mkt. **$42**

QX 548-5   GENTLE FAWN
Comments: Handcrafted, 2-5/16" tall.
This flocked fawn has large shiny eyes that tug at your heart.
He wears holly in his ribbon.
☐ Purchased 19 __ Pd $_____ MIB   NB   DB   BNT
☐ Want   Orig. Ret. $7.75   **NB** $10   **MIB** Sec. Mkt. **$17.50**

QX 386-2   GEORGE WASHINGTON BICENTENNIAL
Comments: Acrylic, 3-9/16" tall, Dated 1989.
The likeness of George Washington is etched into clear acrylic.
Caption: "1789-1989 American Bicentennial, George
Washington, First Presidential Inauguration."
☐ Purchased 19 __ Pd $_____ MIB   NB   DB   BNT
☐ Want   Orig. Ret. $6.25   **NB** $6   **MIB** Sec. Mkt. **$15**

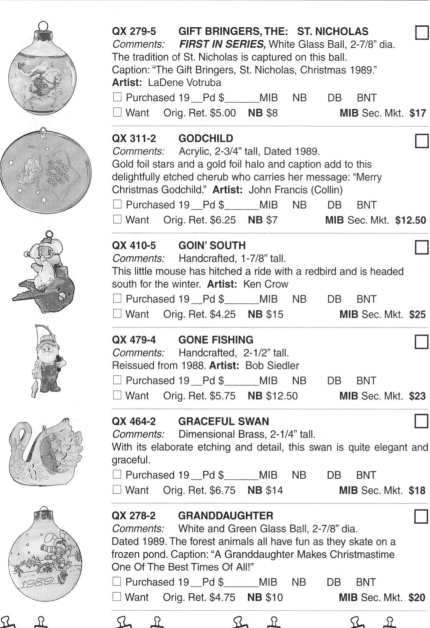

QX 279-5 GIFT BRINGERS, THE: ST. NICHOLAS □
Comments: **FIRST IN SERIES,** White Glass Ball, 2-7/8" dia.
The tradition of St. Nicholas is captured on this ball.
Caption: "The Gift Bringers, St. Nicholas, Christmas 1989."
Artist: LaDene Votruba

□ Purchased 19 __Pd $_____MIB NB DB BNT
□ Want Orig. Ret. $5.00 **NB** $8 **MIB** Sec. Mkt. **$17**

QX 311-2 GODCHILD □
Comments: Acrylic, 2-3/4" tall, Dated 1989.
Gold foil stars and a gold foil halo and caption add to this
delightfully etched cherub who carries her message: "Merry
Christmas Godchild." **Artist:** John Francis (Collin)

□ Purchased 19 __Pd $_____MIB NB DB BNT
□ Want Orig. Ret. $6.25 **NB** $7 **MIB** Sec. Mkt. **$12.50**

QX 410-5 GOIN' SOUTH □
Comments: Handcrafted, 1-7/8" tall.
This little mouse has hitched a ride with a redbird and is headed
south for the winter. **Artist:** Ken Crow

□ Purchased 19 __Pd $_____MIB NB DB BNT
□ Want Orig. Ret. $4.25 **NB** $15 **MIB** Sec. Mkt. **$25**

QX 479-4 GONE FISHING □
Comments: Handcrafted, 2-1/2" tall.
Reissued from 1988. **Artist:** Bob Siedler

□ Purchased 19 __Pd $_____MIB NB DB BNT
□ Want Orig. Ret. $5.75 **NB** $12.50 **MIB** Sec. Mkt. **$23**

QX 464-2 GRACEFUL SWAN □
Comments: Dimensional Brass, 2-1/4" tall.
With its elaborate etching and detail, this swan is quite elegant and
graceful.

□ Purchased 19 __Pd $_____MIB NB DB BNT
□ Want Orig. Ret. $6.75 **NB** $14 **MIB** Sec. Mkt. **$18**

QX 278-2 GRANDDAUGHTER □
Comments: White and Green Glass Ball, 2-7/8" dia.
Dated 1989. The forest animals all have fun as they skate on a
frozen pond. Caption: "A Granddaughter Makes Christmastime
One Of The Best Times Of All!"

□ Purchased 19 __Pd $_____MIB NB DB BNT
□ Want Orig. Ret. $4.75 **NB** $10 **MIB** Sec. Mkt. **$20**

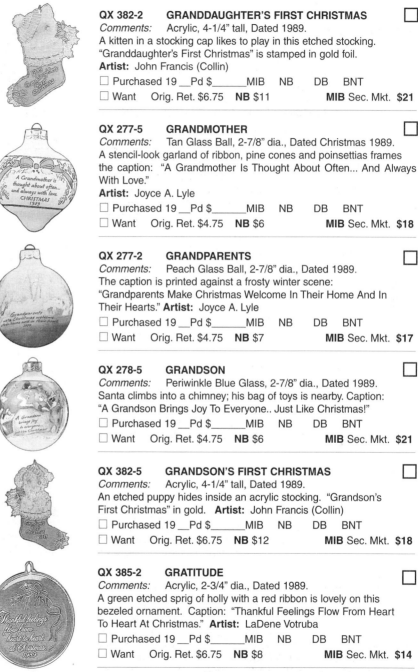

QX 382-2 GRANDDAUGHTER'S FIRST CHRISTMAS □
Comments: Acrylic, 4-1/4" tall, Dated 1989.
A kitten in a stocking cap likes to play in this etched stocking.
"Granddaughter's First Christmas" is stamped in gold foil.
Artist: John Francis (Collin)

□ Purchased 19 __Pd $_____MIB NB DB BNT
□ Want Orig. Ret. $6.75 **NB** $11 **MIB** Sec. Mkt. **$21**

QX 277-5 GRANDMOTHER □
Comments: Tan Glass Ball, 2-7/8" dia., Dated Christmas 1989.
A stencil-look garland of ribbon, pine cones and poinsettias frames
the caption: "A Grandmother Is Thought About Often... And Always
With Love."
Artist: Joyce A. Lyle

□ Purchased 19 __Pd $_____MIB NB DB BNT
□ Want Orig. Ret. $4.75 **NB** $6 **MIB** Sec. Mkt. **$18**

QX 277-2 GRANDPARENTS □
Comments: Peach Glass Ball, 2-7/8" dia., Dated 1989.
The caption is printed against a frosty winter scene:
"Grandparents Make Christmas Welcome In Their Home And In
Their Hearts." **Artist:** Joyce A. Lyle

□ Purchased 19 __Pd $_____MIB NB DB BNT
□ Want Orig. Ret. $4.75 **NB** $7 **MIB** Sec. Mkt. **$17**

QX 278-5 GRANDSON □
Comments: Periwinkle Blue Glass, 2-7/8" dia., Dated 1989.
Santa climbs into a chimney; his bag of toys is nearby. Caption:
"A Grandson Brings Joy To Everyone.. Just Like Christmas!"

□ Purchased 19 __Pd $_____MIB NB DB BNT
□ Want Orig. Ret. $4.75 **NB** $6 **MIB** Sec. Mkt. **$21**

QX 382-5 GRANDSON'S FIRST CHRISTMAS □
Comments: Acrylic, 4-1/4" tall, Dated 1989.
An etched puppy hides inside an acrylic stocking. "Grandson's
First Christmas" in gold. **Artist:** John Francis (Collin)

□ Purchased 19 __Pd $_____MIB NB DB BNT
□ Want Orig. Ret. $6.75 **NB** $12 **MIB** Sec. Mkt. **$18**

QX 385-2 GRATITUDE □
Comments: Acrylic, 2-3/4" dia., Dated 1989.
A green etched sprig of holly with a red ribbon is lovely on this
bezeled ornament. Caption: "Thankful Feelings Flow From Heart
To Heart At Christmas." **Artist:** LaDene Votruba

□ Purchased 19 __Pd $_____MIB NB DB BNT
□ Want Orig. Ret. $6.75 **NB** $8 **MIB** Sec. Mkt. **$14**

QX 418-5   GYM DANDY
Comments: Handcrafted, 2-1/2" tall.
"Kringle's Gym" finds Santa in red and gray sweats working out with dumbbells. **Artist:** Bob Siedler
☐ Purchased 19__Pd $_____MIB   NB   DB   BNT
☐ Want   Orig. Ret. $5.75   **NB** $10   **MIB** Sec. Mkt. **$18**

QX 430-5   HANG IN THERE
Comments: Handcrafted, 3" tall.
A little mouse is hanging on to his red Santa cap, even though it's too big for him. He has a green ribbon tied to his leather tail.
Artist: Ken Crow
☐ Purchased 19__Pd $_____MIB   NB   DB   BNT
☐ Want   Orig. Ret. $5.25   **NB** $24   **MIB** Sec. Mkt. **$34**

QX 455-5   HARK! IT'S HERALD
Comments: **FIRST IN SERIES,** Handcrafted, 2" tall, Dated 1989.
Herald, dressed in a green jacket and red hat, plays a Christmas tune on his xylophone. **Artist:** Ken Crow
☐ Purchased 19__Pd $_____MIB   NB   DB   BNT
☐ Want   Orig. Ret. $6.75   **NB** $12   **MIB** Sec. Mkt. **$25**

QX 458-5   HERE COMES SANTA: CHRISTMAS CABOOSE
Comments: **Eleventh in Series,** Handcrafted, 3-1/2" tall.
Dated 1989. This delightful caboose has movable wheels and shows Santa leaning out the window to wave at everyone as he passes. **Artist:** Ken Crow
☐ Purchased 19__Pd $_____MIB   NB   DB   BNT
☐ Want   Orig. Ret. $14.75   **NB** $25   **MIB** Sec. Mkt. **$50**

QX 545-5   HERE'S THE PITCH
Comments: Handcrafted, 2-3/8" tall.
Santa's playing the majors in his red baseball cap, cleated shoes and uniform. His name and number: "Santa 1." What else?!
Artist: Bob Siedler
☐ Purchased 19__Pd $_____MIB   NB   DB   BNT
☐ Want   Orig. Ret. $5.75   **NB** $12   **MIB** Sec. Mkt. **$16**

QLX 722-2   HOLIDAY BELL
Comments: Lighted, Lead Crystal, 3-1/2" tall, Dated 1989.
With a specially designed brass cap, the many facets give this bell the look of hand-cut glass.
☐ Purchased 19__Pd $_____MIB   NB   DB   BNT
☐ Want   Orig. Ret. $17.50   **NB** $21   **MIB** Sec. Mkt. **$34**

QXC 460-5   HOLIDAY HEIRLOOM: KEEPSAKE CLUB
Comments: **Third and Final in Series,** Limited Edition 34,600.
Lead Crystal/Silver Plating, 2-1/2" tall, Dated 1989. A crystal bell hangs from a tree surrounded by old-fashioned toys. Offered only to Keepsake Club Members. **Artist:** Duane Unruh
☐ Purchased 19__Pd $_____MIB   NB   DB   BNT
☐ Want   Orig. Ret. $25.00 **NB** $18   **MIB** Sec. Mkt. **$33**

QX 469-2   HOPPY HOLIDAYS
Comments: Handcrafted, 2-3/4" tall, Dated 1989.
This little flocked bunny has hopped right into a shopping cart.
He has two gifts in his red cart.
Artist: Bob Siedler
☐ Purchased 19__Pd $_____MIB   NB   DB   BNT
☐ Want   Orig. Ret. $7.75   **NB** $12   **MIB** Sec. Mkt. **$21**

QX 463-2   HORSE WEATHERVANE
Comments: Handcrafted, 3" tall.
A white and brown horse, galloping into the wind, has been designed to resemble carved wood.
Artist: Linda Sickman
☐ Purchased 19__Pd $_____MIB   NB   DB   BNT
☐ Want   Orig. Ret. $5.75   **NB** $10   **MIB** Sec. Mkt. **$17**

QX 437-2   JOYFUL TRIO
Comments: Handcrafted, 2-1/4" tall.
Holding a blue banner proclaiming "Joy To You," this delightful trio of angels sing out for peace and harmony.
Artist: John Francis (Collin)
☐ Purchased 19__Pd $_____MIB   NB   DB   BNT
☐ Want   Orig. Ret. $9.75   **NB** $10   **MIB** Sec. Mkt. **$17.50**

QLX 729-5   JOYOUS CAROLERS
Comments: Light, Motion and Music, Handcrafted, 4-11/16" tall.
Victorian carolers sing under a lamppost to the melody of a violin.
Plays "We Wish You A Merry Christmas." **Artist:** Duane Unruh
☐ Purchased 19__Pd $_____MIB   NB   DB   BNT
☐ Want   Orig. Ret. $30.00   **NB** $45   **MIB** Sec. Mkt. **$68**

QLX 701-7   KRINGLE'S TOY SHOP
Comments: Light and Motion, Handcrafted, 3-5/8" tall.
Reissued from 1988.
Artist: Ed Seale
☐ Purchased 19__Pd $_____MIB   NB   DB   BNT
☐ Want   Orig. Ret. $24.50   **NB** $45   **MIB** Sec. Mkt. **$60**

QX 424-5   KRISTY CLAUS
Comments: Handcrafted, 2-15/16" tall.
Wearing green earmuffs, Santa's lovely wife is ready to show her grace and style on the ice.
Artist: Bob Siedler

☐ Purchased 19 __Pd $_____MIB   NB   DB   BNT
☐ Want   Orig. Ret. $5.75   **NB** $8   **MIB** Sec. Mkt. **$14**

QX 383-5   LANGUAGE OF LOVE
Comments: Acrylic, 3" tall, Dated 1989.
The etched outline of poinsettias is lovely on this heart-shaped ornament. Caption: "Together... The Most Caring Word In The Language Of Love."

☐ Purchased 19 __Pd $_____MIB   NB   DB   BNT
☐ Want   Orig. Ret. $6.25   **NB** $9   **MIB** Sec. Mkt. **$22**

QX 488-2   LET'S PLAY
Comments: Handcrafted, 2-3/4" tall, Dated 1989.
Tap this ornament and the puppy and kitten play and move. Kitten sits on the pup's red doghouse.
Artist: Ken Crow

☐ Purchased 19 __Pd $_____MIB   NB   DB   BNT
☐ Want   Orig. Ret. $7.25   **NB** $12   **MIB** Sec. Mkt. **$28**

QLX 726-2   LOVING SPOONFUL
Comments: Light and Motion, Handcrafted, 3-1/2" tall.
Two little mice have turned the teaspoon at the sugar bowl into a seesaw. Caption: "Sugar."
Artist: Bob Siedler

☐ Purchased 19 __Pd $_____MIB   NB   DB   BNT
☐ Want   Orig. Ret. $19.50 **NB** $25   **MIB** Sec. Mkt. **$35**

QX 452-2   MAIL CALL
Comments: Handcrafted, 3" tall.
A raccoon mail carrier delivers mail from the "Branch Office" to a redbird's "branch." **Artist:** Ed Seale

☐ Purchased 19 __Pd $_____MIB   NB   DB   BNT
☐ Want   Orig. Ret. $8.75   **NB** $10   **MIB** Sec. Mkt. **$16**

QX 454-5   MARY'S ANGELS: BLUEBELL
Comments: **Second in Series,** Handcrafted/Acrylic, 3" tall.
Bluebell kneels in prayer on a frosted acrylic cloud. She wears a light blue gown. **Artist:** Robert Chad

☐ Purchased 19 __Pd $_____MIB   NB   DB   BNT
☐ Want   Orig. Ret. $5.75   **NB** $35   **MIB** Sec. Mkt. **$55-$60**

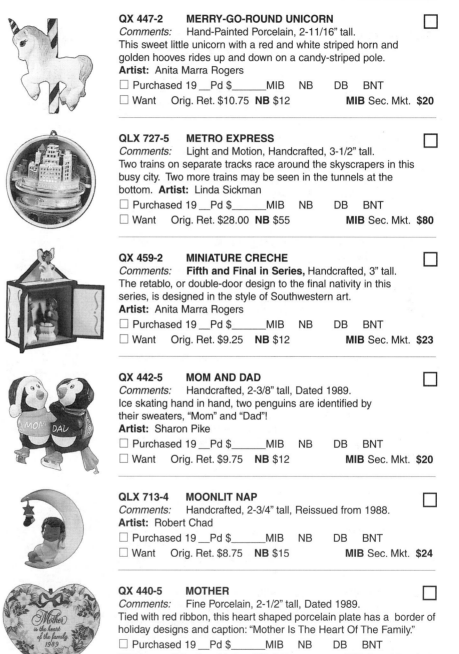

QX 447-2   MERRY-GO-ROUND UNICORN
Comments: Hand-Painted Porcelain, 2-11/16" tall.
This sweet little unicorn with a red and white striped horn and golden hooves rides up and down on a candy-striped pole.
Artist: Anita Marra Rogers

☐ Purchased 19 __Pd $_____MIB   NB   DB   BNT
☐ Want   Orig. Ret. $10.75 **NB** $12   **MIB** Sec. Mkt. **$20**

QLX 727-5   METRO EXPRESS
Comments: Light and Motion, Handcrafted, 3-1/2" tall.
Two trains on separate tracks race around the skyscrapers in this busy city. Two more trains may be seen in the tunnels at the bottom. **Artist:** Linda Sickman

☐ Purchased 19 __Pd $_____MIB   NB   DB   BNT
☐ Want   Orig. Ret. $28.00 **NB** $55   **MIB** Sec. Mkt. **$80**

QX 459-2   MINIATURE CRECHE
Comments: **Fifth and Final in Series,** Handcrafted, 3" tall.
The retablo, or double-door design to the final nativity in this series, is designed in the style of Southwestern art.
Artist: Anita Marra Rogers

☐ Purchased 19 __Pd $_____MIB   NB   DB   BNT
☐ Want   Orig. Ret. $9.25   **NB** $12   **MIB** Sec. Mkt. **$23**

QX 442-5   MOM AND DAD
Comments: Handcrafted, 2-3/8" tall, Dated 1989.
Ice skating hand in hand, two penguins are identified by their sweaters, "Mom" and "Dad"!
Artist: Sharon Pike

☐ Purchased 19 __Pd $_____MIB   NB   DB   BNT
☐ Want   Orig. Ret. $9.75   **NB** $12   **MIB** Sec. Mkt. **$20**

QLX 713-4   MOONLIT NAP
Comments: Handcrafted, 2-3/4" tall, Reissued from 1988.
Artist: Robert Chad

☐ Purchased 19 __Pd $_____MIB   NB   DB   BNT
☐ Want   Orig. Ret. $8.75   **NB** $15   **MIB** Sec. Mkt. **$24**

QX 440-5   MOTHER
Comments: Fine Porcelain, 2-1/2" tall, Dated 1989.
Tied with red ribbon, this heart shaped porcelain plate has a border of holiday designs and caption: "Mother Is The Heart Of The Family."

☐ Purchased 19 __Pd $_____MIB   NB   DB   BNT
☐ Want   Orig. Ret. $9.75   **NB** $18   **MIB** Sec. Mkt. **$28**

QX 457-5   MR. AND MRS. CLAUS: HOLIDAY DUET
Comments: **Fourth in Series,** Handcrafted, 3-1/4" tall.
Dated 1989. Santa and his wife sing "We Wish You A Merry
Christmas And A Happy New Year."
Artist: Duane Unruh
☐ Purchased 19___Pd $_____MIB   NB   DB   BNT
☐ Want   Orig. Ret. $13.25 **NB** $35   **MIB** Sec. Mkt. **$52**

QX 275-5   NEW HOME
Comments: Lavender and White Glass Ball, 2-7/8" dia.
Dated Christmas 1989. A home is nestled among the trees in a
wintry landscape. Caption: "Love Is The Light In The Window Of
Your New Home." **Artist:** LaDene Votruba
☐ Purchased 19___Pd $_____MIB   NB   DB   BNT
☐ Want   Orig. Ret. $4.75 **NB** $12   **MIB** Sec. Mkt. **$22**

QXC 448-3   NOELLE: KEEPSAKE CLUB
Comments: Limited Edition 49,900, Fine Porcelain, 3-3/4" tall.
This elegant cat has a red bow with a jingle bell and sprig of holly.
Comes with wooden display stand. Available to Club Members
only. **Artist:** Duane Unruh
☐ Purchased 19___Pd $_____MIB   NB   DB   BNT
☐ Want   Orig. Ret. $19.75 **NB** $28   **MIB** Sec. Mkt. **$50**

QX 276-2   NORMAN ROCKWELL
Comments: Gold Glass Ball, 2-7/8" dia., Dated 1989.
"Norman Rockwell, Famous Holiday Covers From The Saturday
Evening Post" - "Santa's Seen In The Smiles The Whole World
Is Sharing, He's Found Where There's Friendship And Loving
And Caring." **Artist:** Joyce A. Lyle
☐ Purchased 19___Pd $_____MIB   NB   DB   BNT
☐ Want   Orig. Ret. $4.75 **NB** $12   **MIB** Sec. Mkt. **$20**

QX 546-2   NORTH POLE JOGGER
Comments: Handcrafted, 2-1/4" tall.
Santa's jogging suit reads "North Pole 1K." Santa jogs along while he
listens to his favorite music. **Artist:** Bob Siedler
☐ Purchased 19___Pd $_____MIB   NB   DB   BNT
☐ Want   Orig. Ret. $5.75 **NB** $8   **MIB** Sec. Mkt. **$15**

**QX 458-2   NOSTALGIC HOUSES AND SHOPS:
U.S. POST OFFICE**
Comments: **Sixth in Series,** Handcrafted, 4-1/4" tall.
Dated 1989. Designed as a red brick building.
The upstairs has a furnished office.
Artist: Donna Lee
☐ Purchased 19___Pd $_____MIB   NB   DB   BNT
☐ Want   Orig. Ret. $14.25 **NB** $40   **MIB** Sec. Mkt. **$60**

QX 466-5   NOSTALGIC LAMB
Comments: Handcrafted, 1-3/4" tall.
This lamb has been sculpted to show its curly wool. He rides in
a red wagon with wheels that turn.
Artist: Michele Pyda-Sevcik
☐ Purchased 19___Pd $_____MIB   NB   DB   BNT
☐ Want   Orig. Ret. $6.75 **NB** $10   **MIB** Sec. Mkt. **$12**

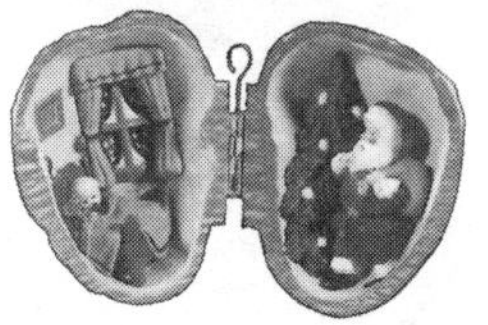

QX 465-5   NUTSHELL DREAMS
Comments: Handcrafted, 1-1/2" tall.
A child sleeping in his bedroom dreams of the toys Santa will
leave; in another room, Santa motions quiet so as not to
wake the child. **Artist:** Robert Chad
☐ Purchased 19___Pd $_____MIB   NB   DB   BNT
☐ Want   Orig. Ret. $5.75 **NB** $12   **MIB** Sec. Mkt. **$18**

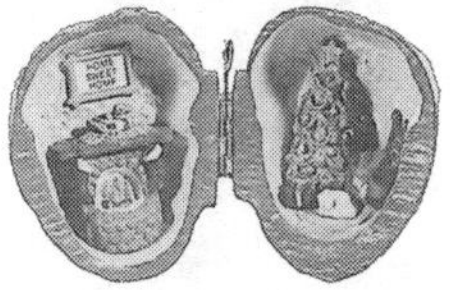

QX 465-2   NUTSHELL HOLIDAY
Comments: Handcrafted, 1-1/2" tall. Reissued in 1990.
Open this tiny nutshell and you will find a home decorated and
waiting for Santa's arrival.
Artist: Anita Marra Rogers
☐ Purchased 19___Pd $_____MIB   NB   DB   BNT
☐ Want   Orig. Ret. $5.75 **NB** $15   **MIB** Sec. Mkt. **$25**

QX 487-2   NUTSHELL WORKSHOP
Comments: Handcrafted, 1-1/2" tall.
Santa's elves keep busy building new toys in the tiny workshop
inside. **Artist:** Robert Chad
☐ Purchased 19___Pd $_____MIB   NB   DB   BNT
☐ Want   Orig. Ret. $5.75 **NB** $15   **MIB** Sec. Mkt. **$18**

QX 434-5   OLD WORLD GNOME
Comments: Handcrafted, 3-1/4" tall.
This friendly gnome has been created to resemble a European
wood carving.
☐ Purchased 19___Pd $_____MIB   NB   DB   BNT
☐ Want   Orig. Ret. $7.75 **NB** $18   **MIB** Sec. Mkt. **$24**

QX 419-2   ON THE LINKS
Comments: Handcrafted, 2-1/2" tall.
Santa's golf swing is perfect. He's wearing red slacks and
sunshade and a green shirt.
Artist: Bob Siedler
☐ Purchased 19___Pd $_____MIB   NB   DB   BNT
☐ Want   Orig. Ret. $5.75 **NB** $12   **MIB** Sec. Mkt. **$20**

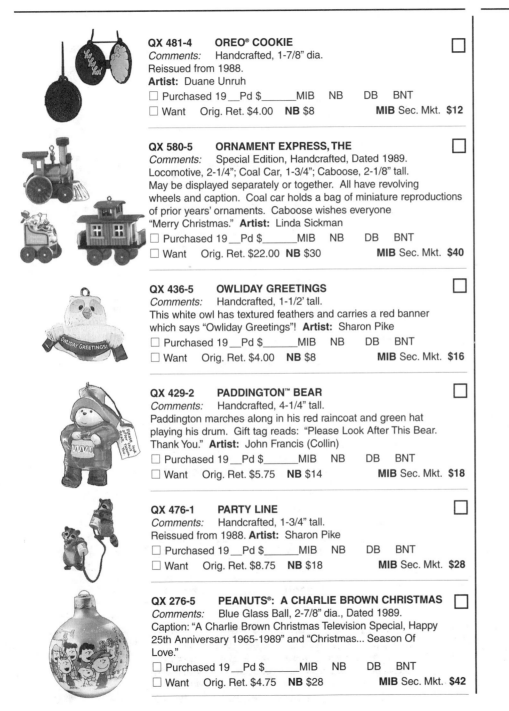

QX 481-4　OREO® COOKIE ☐
Comments:　Handcrafted, 1-7/8" dia.
Reissued from 1988.
Artist: Duane Unruh
☐ Purchased 19___Pd $_____MIB　NB　　DB　BNT
☐ Want　Orig. Ret. $4.00　**NB** $8　　　**MIB** Sec. Mkt. **$12**

QX 580-5　ORNAMENT EXPRESS, THE ☐
Comments:　Special Edition, Handcrafted, Dated 1989.
Locomotive, 2-1/4"; Coal Car, 1-3/4"; Caboose, 2-1/8" tall.
May be displayed separately or together. All have revolving
wheels and caption. Coal car holds a bag of miniature reproductions
of prior years' ornaments. Caboose wishes everyone
"Merry Christmas." **Artist:** Linda Sickman
☐ Purchased 19___Pd $_____MIB　NB　　DB　BNT
☐ Want　Orig. Ret. $22.00 **NB** $30　　　**MIB** Sec. Mkt. **$40**

QX 436-5　OWLIDAY GREETINGS ☐
Comments:　Handcrafted, 1-1/2' tall.
This white owl has textured feathers and carries a red banner
which says "Owliday Greetings"! **Artist:** Sharon Pike
☐ Purchased 19___Pd $_____MIB　NB　　DB　BNT
☐ Want　Orig. Ret. $4.00　**NB** $8　　　**MIB** Sec. Mkt. **$16**

QX 429-2　PADDINGTON™ BEAR ☐
Comments:　Handcrafted, 4-1/4" tall.
Paddington marches along in his red raincoat and green hat
playing his drum. Gift tag reads: "Please Look After This Bear.
Thank You." **Artist:** John Francis (Collin)
☐ Purchased 19___Pd $_____MIB　NB　　DB　BNT
☐ Want　Orig. Ret. $5.75　**NB** $14　　　**MIB** Sec. Mkt. **$18**

QX 476-1　PARTY LINE ☐
Comments:　Handcrafted, 1-3/4" tall.
Reissued from 1988. **Artist:** Sharon Pike
☐ Purchased 19___Pd $_____MIB　NB　　DB　BNT
☐ Want　Orig. Ret. $8.75　**NB** $18　　　**MIB** Sec. Mkt. **$28**

QX 276-5　PEANUTS®: A CHARLIE BROWN CHRISTMAS ☐
Comments:　Blue Glass Ball, 2-7/8" dia., Dated 1989.
Caption: "A Charlie Brown Christmas Television Special, Happy
25th Anniversary 1965-1989" and "Christmas... Season Of
Love."
☐ Purchased 19___Pd $_____MIB　NB　　DB　BNT
☐ Want　Orig. Ret. $4.75　**NB** $28　　　**MIB** Sec. Mkt. **$42**

QX 487-1　PEEK-A-BOO KITTIES ☐
Comments:　Handcrafted, 5" tall.
Reissued from 1988. **Artist:** Ken Crow
☐ Purchased 19___Pd $_____MIB　NB　　DB　BNT
☐ Want　Orig. Ret. $7.50　**NB** $15　　　**MIB** Sec. Mkt. **$20**

QX 450-5　PEPPERMINT CLOWN ☐
Comments:　Hand-Painted Fine Porcelain, 5-1/32" tall.
This hand-painted porcelain clown rides a peppermint unicycle.
Artist: Peter Dutkin
☐ Purchased 19___Pd $_____MIB　NB　　DB　BNT
☐ Want　Orig. Ret. $24.75 **NB** $20　　　**MIB** Sec. Mkt. **$35**

QX 453-5　PLAYFUL ANGEL ☐
Comments:　Handcrafted/Acrylic, 3-1/8" tall.
A little angel plays in a swing attached to an acrylic cloud.
She wears a brass halo. **Artist:** Donna Lee
☐ Purchased 19___Pd $_____MIB　NB　　DB　BNT
☐ Want　Orig. Ret. $6.75　**NB** $18　　　**MIB** Sec. Mkt. **$23**

QX 478-4　POLAR BOWLER ☐
Comments:　Handcrafted, 2-1/4" tall.
Reissued from 1988. **Artist:** Bob Siedler
☐ Purchased 19___Pd $_____MIB　NB　　DB　BNT
☐ Want　1989 Retail $5.75 **NB** $12　　　**MIB** Sec. Mkt. **$16.50**

QX 461-5　PORCELAIN BEAR ☐
Comments:　**Seventh in Series,** Fine Porcelain, 2" tall.
This hand-painted cinnamon bear is enjoying his special treat
from Santa - a bag of candy! **Artist:** Sharon Pike
☐ Purchased 19___Pd $_____MIB　NB　　DB　BNT
☐ Want　Orig. Ret. $8.75　**NB** $14　　　**MIB** Sec. Mkt. **$24**

QX 456-2　REINDEER CHAMPS: VIXEN ☐
Comments:　**Fourth in Series,** Handcrafted, 3-1/4" tall.
Dated 1989. "Vixen" wears a sporty tennis outfit in red and white
and a green visor. Price down from '96. **Artist:** Bob Siedler
☐ Purchased 19___Pd $_____MIB　NB　　DB　BNT
☐ Want　Orig. Ret. $7.75　**NB** $14　　　**MIB** Sec. Mkt. **$18**

It easy to make a mountain out of a molehill ...
just add more dirt.

QX 462-2   ROCKING HORSE ☐
Comments: **Ninth in Series,** Handcrafted, 4" wide.
Dated 1989. A russet and black bay horse is fitted with brass
stirrups and red yarn rein. **Artist:** Linda Sickman
☐ Purchased 19 __ Pd $_____ MIB   NB   DB   BNT
☐ Want   Orig. Ret. $10.75 **NB** $24   **MIB** Sec. Mkt. **$38**

QX 407-2   RODNEY REINDEER ☐
Comments: Handcrafted, 5" tall, Dated 1989.
Rodney is checking the route for Christmas Eve on his "Reindeer
Route 89." He's made of a flexible material which allows him to
be bent into many positions. **Artist:** Bob Siedler
☐ Purchased 19 __ Pd $_____ MIB   NB   DB   BNT
☐ Want   Orig. Ret. $6.75 **NB** $7   **MIB** Sec. Mkt. **$14**

QX 467-5   ROOSTER WEATHERVANE ☐
Comments: Handcrafted, 3-1/2" tall.
With the design of American folk art, this bright, colorful rooster
is crowing good morning to everyone.
☐ Purchased 19 __ Pd $_____ MIB   NB   DB   BNT
☐ Want   Orig. Ret. $5.75 **NB** $6   **MIB** Sec. Mkt. **$14**

QLX 725-2   RUDOLPH THE RED-NOSED REINDEER ☐
Comments: Lighted, Handcrafted, 2-1/2" tall.
Rudolph's nose glows to light Santa's way, in addition to the
blinking lights on Santa's sleigh. Price down from '96, many
sales found below $50. **Artist:** Robert Chad
☐ Purchased 19 __ Pd $_____ MIB   NB   DB   BNT
☐ Want   Orig. Ret. $19.50 **NB** $40   **MIB** Sec. Mkt. **$55**

QX 415-2   SEA SANTA ☐
Comments: Handcrafted, 2-1/2" tall.
Santa's ready to do some diving for underwater treasure in his
scuba gear. Caption: "Sea Santa."
Artist: Bob Siedler
☐ Purchased 19 __ Pd $_____ MIB   NB   DB   BNT
☐ Want   Orig. Ret. $5.75 **NB** $14   **MIB** Sec. Mkt. **$24**

QX 279-2   SISTER ☐
Comments: Porcelain White Glass Ball, 2-7/8" dia.
Dated Christmas 1989. Caption: "Having A Sister Means
Happiness. Loving A Sister Means Joy."
☐ Purchased 19 __ Pd $_____ MIB   NB   DB   BNT
☐ Want   Orig. Ret. $4.75 **NB** $9   **MIB** Sec. Mkt. **$18**

QX 433-2   SNOOPY® AND WOODSTOCK ☐
Comments: Handcrafted, 3" tall.
In matching top hats, bow ties and candy canes, this twosome
perform a soft-shoe routine for their fans.
Artist: Dill Rhodus
☐ Purchased 19 __ Pd $_____ MIB   NB   DB   BNT
☐ Want   Orig. Ret. $6.75 **NB** $18   **MIB** Sec. Mkt. **$30**

QX 420-5   SNOWPLOW SANTA ☐
Comments: Handcrafted, 2-5/16" tall.
Santa loves to ski, and says so on his shirt: "I ♥ Skiing." He has
white skis and green gloves.
Artist: Bob Siedler
☐ Purchased 19 __ Pd $_____ MIB   NB   DB   BNT
☐ Want   Orig. Ret. $5.75 **NB** $10   **MIB** Sec. Mkt. **$18**

QX 444-5   SON ☐
Comments: Handcrafted, 3" tall, Dated Christmas 1989.
This old-fashioned wood look ornament shows a boy dressed for
winter weather. He carries a gift addressed to "Son."
Artist: Linda Sickman
☐ Purchased 19 __ Pd $_____ MIB   NB   DB   BNT
☐ Want   Orig. Ret. $6.25 **NB** $10   **MIB** Sec. Mkt. **$18**

QX 547-2   SPARKLING SNOWFLAKE ☐
Comments: Brass, 3-3/8" tall, Dated 1989.
This lacy snowflake was created with separate, etched layers of
brass. **Artist:** Joyce A. Lyle
☐ Purchased 19 __ Pd $_____ MIB   NB   DB   BNT
☐ Want   Orig. Ret. $7.75 **NB** $10   **MIB** Sec. Mkt. **$20**

QX 432-5   SPECIAL DELIVERY ☐
Comments: Handcrafted, 2" tall.
This flocked seal has been "Signed, Sealed & Delivered" but he's
not waiting until Christmas to announce his arrival. May be
personalized. **Artist:** Anita Marra Rogers
☐ Purchased 19 __ Pd $_____ MIB   NB   DB   BNT
☐ Want   Orig. Ret. $5.75 **NB** $10   **MIB** Sec. Mkt. **$19**

QX 431-2   SPENCER® SPARROW, ESQ. ☐
Comments: Handcrafted, 1-3/4" tall. Reissued in 1990.
Spencer's treat is a sesame cracker. The Spencer Sparrow logo
is on the bottom. **Artist:** Sharon Pike
☐ Purchased 19 __ Pd $_____ MIB   NB   DB   BNT
☐ Want   Orig. Ret. $6.75 **NB** $12   **MIB** Sec. Mkt. **$20**

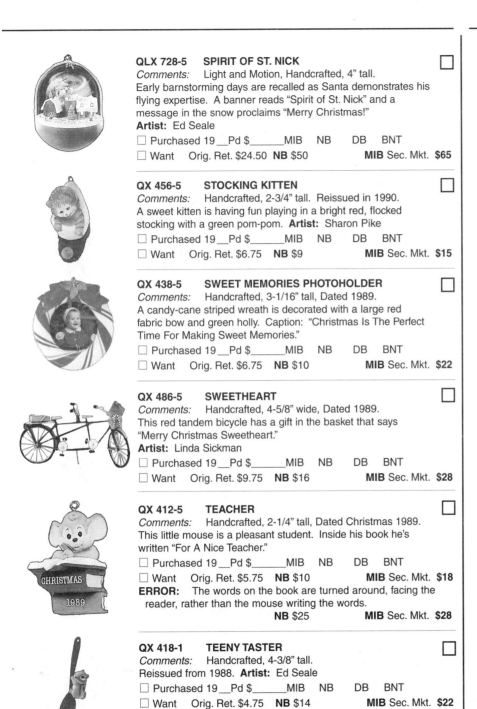

QLX 728-5   SPIRIT OF ST. NICK
Comments: Light and Motion, Handcrafted, 4" tall.
Early barnstorming days are recalled as Santa demonstrates his
flying expertise. A banner reads "Spirit of St. Nick" and a
message in the snow proclaims "Merry Christmas!"
Artist: Ed Seale
☐ Purchased 19 __Pd $_____MIB   NB   DB   BNT
☐ Want   Orig. Ret. $24.50 **NB** $50   **MIB** Sec. Mkt. **$65**

QX 456-5   STOCKING KITTEN
Comments: Handcrafted, 2-3/4" tall. Reissued in 1990.
A sweet kitten is having fun playing in a bright red, flocked
stocking with a green pom-pom. **Artist:** Sharon Pike
☐ Purchased 19 __Pd $_____MIB   NB   DB   BNT
☐ Want   Orig. Ret. $6.75 **NB** $9   **MIB** Sec. Mkt. **$15**

QX 438-5   SWEET MEMORIES PHOTOHOLDER
Comments: Handcrafted, 3-1/16" tall, Dated 1989.
A candy-cane striped wreath is decorated with a large red
fabric bow and green holly. Caption: "Christmas Is The Perfect
Time For Making Sweet Memories."
☐ Purchased 19 __Pd $_____MIB   NB   DB   BNT
☐ Want   Orig. Ret. $6.75 **NB** $10   **MIB** Sec. Mkt. **$22**

QX 486-5   SWEETHEART
Comments: Handcrafted, 4-5/8" wide, Dated 1989.
This red tandem bicycle has a gift in the basket that says
"Merry Christmas Sweetheart."
Artist: Linda Sickman
☐ Purchased 19 __Pd $_____MIB   NB   DB   BNT
☐ Want   Orig. Ret. $9.75 **NB** $16   **MIB** Sec. Mkt. **$28**

QX 412-5   TEACHER
Comments: Handcrafted, 2-1/4" tall, Dated Christmas 1989.
This little mouse is a pleasant student. Inside his book he's
written "For A Nice Teacher."
☐ Purchased 19 __Pd $_____MIB   NB   DB   BNT
☐ Want   Orig. Ret. $5.75 **NB** $10   **MIB** Sec. Mkt. **$18**
ERROR: The words on the book are turned around, facing the
        reader, rather than the mouse writing the words.
                    NB $25   **MIB** Sec. Mkt. **$28**

QX 418-1   TEENY TASTER
Comments: Handcrafted, 4-3/8" tall.
Reissued from 1988. **Artist:** Ed Seale
☐ Purchased 19 __Pd $_____MIB   NB   DB   BNT
☐ Want   Orig. Ret. $4.75 **NB** $14   **MIB** Sec. Mkt. **$22**

QX 274-2   TEN YEARS TOGETHER
Comments: White Glass Ball, 2-7/8" dia.
Dated Christmas 1989. A couple rides in a horse-drawn sleigh.
Caption: "There's Joy In Each Season When There's Love In Our
Hearts" and "Ten Years Together." **Artist:** Joyce A. Lyle
☐ Purchased 19 __Pd $_____MIB   NB   DB   BNT
☐ Want   Orig. Ret. $4.75 **NB** $15   **MIB** Sec. Mkt. **$25**

QX 455-2   THIMBLE SERIES: PUPPY
Comments: **Twelfth and Final in Series,** Handcrafted, 1-3/4" tall.
This adorable puppy with a big red bow, captures everyone's
attention as he sits inside a thimble.
Artist: Anita Marra Rogers
☐ Purchased 19 __Pd $_____MIB   NB   DB   BNT
☐ Want   Orig. Ret. $5.75 **NB** $12   **MIB** Sec. Mkt. **$20**

QX 460-2   TIN LOCOMOTIVE
Comments: **Eighth and Final in Series,** Dated 1989. Pressed Tin.
3-3/16" tall. The last locomotive in the series is also
one of the most complex. A brass bell jingles as the wheels turn.
Artist: Linda Sickman
☐ Purchased 19 __Pd $_____MIB   NB   DB   BNT
☐ Want   Orig. Ret. $14.75 **NB** $40   **MIB** Sec. Mkt. **$45-$50**

QLX 717-4   TINY TINKER
Comments: Light and Motion, Handcrafted, 3" tall.
This little elf is burning the midnight oil to repair a shoe. A toy
locomotive also waits for repair. **Artist:** Ken Crow
☐ Purchased 19 __Pd $_____MIB   NB   DB   BNT
☐ Want   Orig. Ret. $19.50 **NB** $35   **MIB** Sec. Mkt. **$45-$50**

QX 409-2   TV BREAK
Comments: Handcrafted, 3" tall.
Santa watches his favorite TV programs while relaxing in his
hammock. **Artist:** Donna Lee
☐ Purchased 19 __Pd $_____MIB   NB   DB   BNT
☐ Want   Orig. Ret. $6.25 **NB** $10   **MIB** Sec. Mkt. **$18**

QX 381-2   TWELVE DAYS OF CHRISTMAS:
            SIX GEESE-A-LAYING
Comments: **Sixth in Series,** Acrylic, 3" tall, Dated 1989.
Six geese are etched into heart-shaped acrylic. Captions are
printed in gold foil.
☐ Purchased 19 __Pd $_____MIB   NB   DB   BNT
☐ Want   Orig. Ret. $6.75 **NB** $10   **MIB** Sec. Mkt. **$16**

QX 485-5   TWENTY-FIVE YEARS TOGETHER PHOTOHOLDER
Comments: Porcelain, 3-3/4" tall, Dated Christmas 1989.
A wreath decorated with holly and berries carries the silver caption: "25 Years Together." **Artist:** Anita Marra Rogers

☐ Purchased 19___Pd $_____MIB   NB   DB   BNT
☐ Want   Orig. Ret. $8.75   **NB** $7   **MIB** Sec. Mkt. **$14**

QLX 723-5   UNICORN FANTASY
Comments: Lighted, Handcrafted, 4-1/2" tall.
A shimmering unicorn prances inside a lighted, crystal gazebo.
Artist: Dill Rhodus

☐ Purchased 19___Pd $_____MIB   NB   DB   BNT
☐ Want   Orig. Ret. $9.50   **NB** $12   **MIB** Sec. Mkt. **$28**

QXC 580-2   VISIT FROM SANTA: KEEPSAKE CLUB
Comments: Handcrafted, 4" tall, Dated 1989.
Santa with toys and "personalized" sled or "Merry Christmas."
Sled was personalized with the name of the Club member.
Personalized ornaments are selling for less than the Merry Christmas verse. **Artist:** Ken Crow

☐ Purchased 19___Pd $_____MIB   NB   DB   BNT
☐ Want   Price: Came with Club Membership of $_____
                       NB $24   **MIB** Sec. Mkt. **$45**

QX 489-2   WIGGLY SNOWMAN
Comments: Handcrafted, 4-3/4" tall.
This pearly snowman wiggles and jiggles his head for you when you tap him. What fun!
Artist: Dill Rhodus

☐ Purchased 19___Pd $_____MIB   NB   DB   BNT
☐ Want   Orig. Ret. $6.75   **NB** $14   **MIB** Sec. Mkt. **$20**

QX 462-5   WINDOWS OF WORLD: GERMAN
Comments: **Fifth in Series,** Handcrafted, 3-3/4" tall.
Dated 1989. Caption: "Frohliche Weihnachten." A little German boy sits near his Christmas tree in his Alpine cottage, playing his concertina. **Artist:** Donna Lee

☐ Purchased 19___Pd $_____MIB   NB   DB   BNT
☐ Want   Orig. Ret. $10.75 **NB** $18   **MIB** Sec. Mkt. **$22**

QX 427-2   WINTER SURPRISE
Comments: **FIRST IN SERIES,** Handcrafted, 3-1/4" tall.
Dated 1989. Inside an egg-shaped peek-through ornament, two penguins decorate their white frosted Christmas tree with tiny ornaments. Series ended in 1992. Price drop from '96. Was up to $26.

☐ Purchased 19___Pd $_____MIB   NB   DB   BNT
☐ Want   Orig. Ret. $10.75 **NB** $15   **MIB** Sec. Mkt. **$18**

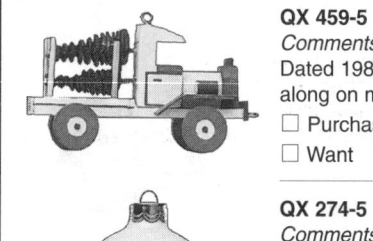

QX 459-5   WOOD CHILDHOOD: TRUCK
Comments: **Sixth and Final in Series,** Wood, 2" tall.
Dated 1989. This truck is hauling a cargo of Christmas trees as it rolls along on movable wheels.

☐ Purchased 19___Pd $_____MIB   NB   DB   BNT
☐ Want   Orig. Ret. $7.75 **NB** $12   **MIB** Sec. Mkt. **$20**

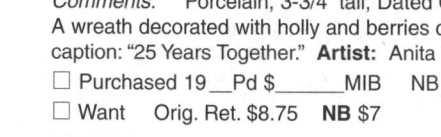

QX 274-5   WORLD OF LOVE
Comments: Silver Blue Glass Ball, 2-7/8" dia., Dated 1989.
Children from around the world enjoy the holiday season.
Caption: "Christmas Is Here, And The Sound Of Love Echoes All Over The World."

☐ Purchased 19___Pd $_____MIB   NB   DB   BNT
☐ Want   Orig. Ret. $4.75 **NB** $16   **MIB** Sec. Mkt. **$30**

"That price was too low.
Come on, we can do better than that."

—R. STUBLER—

1989 Miniature Ornament Collection

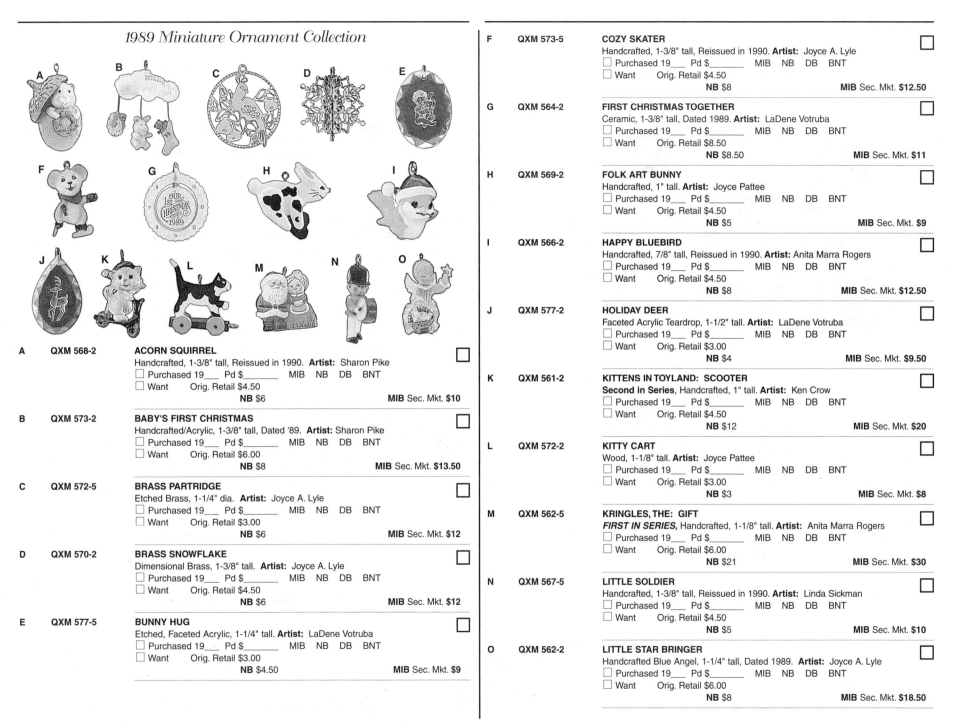

A QXM 568-2 **ACORN SQUIRREL**
Handcrafted, 1-3/8" tall, Reissued in 1990. **Artist:** Sharon Pike
☐ Purchased 19___ Pd $_____ MIB NB DB BNT
☐ Want Orig. Retail $4.50
NB $6 **MIB** Sec. Mkt. **$10**

B QXM 573-2 **BABY'S FIRST CHRISTMAS**
Handcrafted/Acrylic, 1-3/8" tall, Dated '89. **Artist:** Sharon Pike
☐ Purchased 19___ Pd $_____ MIB NB DB BNT
☐ Want Orig. Retail $6.00
NB $8 **MIB** Sec. Mkt. **$13.50**

C QXM 572-5 **BRASS PARTRIDGE**
Etched Brass, 1-1/4" dia. **Artist:** Joyce A. Lyle
☐ Purchased 19___ Pd $_____ MIB NB DB BNT
☐ Want Orig. Retail $3.00
NB $6 **MIB** Sec. Mkt. **$12**

D QXM 570-2 **BRASS SNOWFLAKE**
Dimensional Brass, 1-3/8" tall. **Artist:** Joyce A. Lyle
☐ Purchased 19___ Pd $_____ MIB NB DB BNT
☐ Want Orig. Retail $4.50
NB $6 **MIB** Sec. Mkt. **$12**

E QXM 577-5 **BUNNY HUG**
Etched, Faceted Acrylic, 1-1/4" tall. **Artist:** LaDene Votruba
☐ Purchased 19___ Pd $_____ MIB NB DB BNT
☐ Want Orig. Retail $3.00
NB $4.50 **MIB** Sec. Mkt. **$9**

F QXM 573-5 **COZY SKATER**
Handcrafted, 1-3/8" tall, Reissued in 1990. **Artist:** Joyce A. Lyle
☐ Purchased 19___ Pd $_____ MIB NB DB BNT
☐ Want Orig. Retail $4.50
NB $8 **MIB** Sec. Mkt. **$12.50**

G QXM 564-2 **FIRST CHRISTMAS TOGETHER**
Ceramic, 1-3/8" tall, Dated 1989. **Artist:** LaDene Votruba
☐ Purchased 19___ Pd $_____ MIB NB DB BNT
☐ Want Orig. Retail $8.50
NB $8.50 **MIB** Sec. Mkt. **$11**

H QXM 569-2 **FOLK ART BUNNY**
Handcrafted, 1" tall. **Artist:** Joyce Pattee
☐ Purchased 19___ Pd $_____ MIB NB DB BNT
☐ Want Orig. Retail $4.50
NB $5 **MIB** Sec. Mkt. **$9**

I QXM 566-2 **HAPPY BLUEBIRD**
Handcrafted, 7/8" tall, Reissued in 1990. **Artist:** Anita Marra Rogers
☐ Purchased 19___ Pd $_____ MIB NB DB BNT
☐ Want Orig. Retail $4.50
NB $8 **MIB** Sec. Mkt. **$12.50**

J QXM 577-2 **HOLIDAY DEER**
Faceted Acrylic Teardrop, 1-1/2" tall. **Artist:** LaDene Votruba
☐ Purchased 19___ Pd $_____ MIB NB DB BNT
☐ Want Orig. Retail $3.00
NB $4 **MIB** Sec. Mkt. **$9.50**

K QXM 561-2 **KITTENS IN TOYLAND: SCOOTER**
Second in Series, Handcrafted, 1" tall. **Artist:** Ken Crow
☐ Purchased 19___ Pd $_____ MIB NB DB BNT
☐ Want Orig. Retail $4.50
NB $12 **MIB** Sec. Mkt. **$20**

L QXM 572-2 **KITTY CART**
Wood, 1-1/8" tall. **Artist:** Joyce Pattee
☐ Purchased 19___ Pd $_____ MIB NB DB BNT
☐ Want Orig. Retail $3.00
NB $3 **MIB** Sec. Mkt. **$8**

M QXM 562-5 **KRINGLES, THE: GIFT**
FIRST IN SERIES, Handcrafted, 1-1/8" tall. **Artist:** Anita Marra Rogers
☐ Purchased 19___ Pd $_____ MIB NB DB BNT
☐ Want Orig. Retail $6.00
NB $21 **MIB** Sec. Mkt. **$30**

N QXM 567-5 **LITTLE SOLDIER**
Handcrafted, 1-3/8" tall, Reissued in 1990. **Artist:** Linda Sickman
☐ Purchased 19___ Pd $_____ MIB NB DB BNT
☐ Want Orig. Retail $4.50
NB $5 **MIB** Sec. Mkt. **$10**

O QXM 562-2 **LITTLE STAR BRINGER**
Handcrafted Blue Angel, 1-1/4" tall, Dated 1989. **Artist:** Joyce A. Lyle
☐ Purchased 19___ Pd $_____ MIB NB DB BNT
☐ Want Orig. Retail $6.00
NB $8 **MIB** Sec. Mkt. **$18.50**

A QXM 574-5 **LOAD OF CHEER**
Handcrafted, 7/8" tall, Dated 1989. **Artist:** Dill Rhodus
☐ Purchased 19___ Pd $_____ MIB NB DB BNT
☐ Want Orig. Retail $6.00
NB $8 **MIB** Sec. Mkt. **$18**

B QXM 563-5 **LOVEBIRDS**
Handcrafted/Brass, 1-1/8" tall. **Artist:** Sharon Pike
☐ Purchased 19___ Pd $_____ MIB NB DB BNT
☐ Want Orig. Retail $6.00
NB $8 **MIB** Sec. Mkt. **$14**

C QXM 575-5 **MERRY SEAL**
Hand Painted Porcelain, 7/8" tall. **Artist:** John Francis (Collin)
☐ Purchased 19___ Pd $_____ MIB NB DB BNT
☐ Want Orig. Retail $6.00
NB $8 **MIB** Sec. Mkt. **$15**

D QXM 564-5 **MOTHER**
Blue Cameo, Chrome Bezel, 1-1/4" dia., Dated 1989.
☐ Purchased 19___ Pd $_____ MIB NB DB BNT
☐ Want Orig. Retail $6.00
NB $5 **MIB** Sec. Mkt. **$12**

E QXM 576-2 **NOEL R.R.: LOCOMOTIVE**
FIRST IN SERIES, Handcrafted, 1" tall, Dated 1989.
Artist: Linda Sickman
☐ Purchased 19___ Pd $_____ MIB NB DB BNT
☐ Want Orig. Retail $8.50
NB $25 **MIB** Sec. Mkt. **$42.50**

F QXM 561-5 **OLD ENGLISH VILLAGE: SWEET SHOP**
Second in Series, Handcrafted, 1-1/4" tall, Dated 1989.
Artist: Julia Lee
☐ Purchased 19___ Pd $_____ MIB NB DB BNT
☐ Want Orig. Retail $8.50
NB $18 **MIB** Sec. Mkt. **$35**

G QXM 569-5 **OLD WORLD SANTA**
Handcrafted, 1-3/8" tall. Reissued in 1990. **Artist:** Bob Siedler
☐ Purchased 19___ Pd $_____ MIB NB DB BNT
☐ Want Orig. Retail $3.00
NB $3 **MIB** Sec. Mkt. **$8.50**

H QXM 560-2 **PENGUIN PAL: CANDY CANE**
Second in Series, Handcrafted/Acrylic, 1-3/8" tall.
☐ Purchased 19___ Pd $_____ MIB NB DB BNT
☐ Want Orig. Retail $4.50
NB $12 **MiB** Sec. Mkt. **$18**

I QXM 573-4 **PINECONE BASKET**
Handcrafted, 7/8" tall. **Artist:** Dill Rhodus
☐ Purchased 19___ Pd $_____ MIB NB DB BNT
☐ Want Orig. Retail $4.50
NB $4.50 **MIB** Sec. Mkt. **$7**

J QXM 571-5 **PUPPY CART**
Wood, 1-1/4" tall. **Artist:** Linda Sickman
☐ Purchased 19___ Pd $_____ MIB NB DB BNT
☐ Want Orig. Retail $3.00
NB $3 **MIB** Sec. Mkt. **$7**

K QXM 578-2 **REJOICE**
Faceted Acrylic, 1" tall. **Artist:** LaDene Votruba
☐ Purchased 19___ Pd $_____ MIB NB DB BNT
☐ Want Orig. Retail $3.00
NB $3 **MIB** Sec. Mkt. **$9**

L QXM 560-5 **ROCKING HORSE: PALOMINO**
Second in Series, Handcrafted, 1-1/8" tall, Dated 1989.
Artist: Linda Sickman
☐ Purchased 19___ Pd $_____ MIB NB DB BNT
☐ Want Orig. Retail $4.50
NB $18 **MIB** Sec. Mkt. **$28**

M QXM 573-1 **COUNTRY WREATH**
Handcrafted, 1-1/2" tall. **Artist:** Anita Marra Rogers
Reissued from 1988.
☐ Purchased 19___ Pd $_____ MIB NB DB BNT
☐ Want Orig. Retail $4.50
NB $6 **MIB** Sec. Mkt. **$12**

N QXM 561-1 **HOLY FAMILY**
Handcrafted, 1-3/4" tall. **Artist:** Duane Unruh
Reissued from 1988.
☐ Purchased 19___ Pd $_____ MIB NB DB BNT
☐ Want Orig. Retail $8.50
NB $9 **MIB** Sec. Mkt. **$11.50**

A

B

C

D

E

F

G

H

I

J

K

L

M

N

A QXM 571-2 **ROLY-POLY PIG**
Handcrafted, 7/8" tall, Reissued in 1990. **Artist:** Sharon Pike
☐ Purchased 19___ Pd $_____ MIB NB DB BNT
☐ Want Orig. Retail $3.00
NB $8 **MIB** Sec. Mkt. **$15**

B QXM 570-5 **ROLY-POLY RAM**
Handcrafted, Handcrafted, 7/8" tall.
☐ Purchased 19___ Pd $_____ MIB NB DB BNT
☐ Want Orig. Retail $3.00
NB $6 **MIB** Sec. Mkt. **$14**

C QXM 563-2 **SANTA'S MAGIC RIDE**
Special Edition, Handcrafted, 1-3/16" tall. **Artist:** Anita Marra Rogers
☐ Purchased 19___ Pd $_____ MIB NB DB BNT
☐ Want Orig. Retail $8.50
NB $8 **MIB** Sec. Mkt. **$12.50**

D QXM 566-5 **SANTA'S ROADSTER**
Handcrafted, 15/16" tall, Dated 1989. **Artist:** Ken Crow
☐ Purchased 19___ Pd $_____ MIB NB DB BNT
☐ Want Orig. Retail $6.00
NB $10 **MIB** Sec. Mkt. **$18.50**

E QXM 568-5 **SCRIMSHAW REINDEER**
Handcrafted, 15/16" tall. **Artist:** LaDene Votruba
☐ Purchased 19___ Pd $_____ MIB NB DB BNT
☐ Want Orig. Retail $4.50
NB $5 **MIB** Sec. Mkt. **$9**

F QXM 576-5 **SHARING A RIDE**
Handcrafted, 1-1/4" tall. **Artist:** Peter Dutkin
☐ Purchased 19___ Pd $_____ MIB NB DB BNT
☐ Want Orig. Retail $8.50
NB $10 **MIB** Sec. Mkt. **$15**

G QXC 581-2 **SITTING PURRTY: KEEPSAKE CLUB**
Handcrafted, 1-1/4" tall, Dated 1989.
Artist: Peter Dutkin
☐ Purchased 19___ Pd $_____ MIB NB DB BNT
☐ Want Orig. Retail -- Free to Club Members
NB $15 **MIB** Sec. Mkt. **$30**

H QXM 575-2 **SLOW MOTION**
Handcrafted, 1" tall. **Artist:** Bob Siedler
☐ Purchased 19___ Pd $_____ MIB NB DB BNT
☐ Want Orig. Retail $6.00
NB $6 **MIB** Sec. Mkt. **$15**

I QXM 565-2 **SPECIAL FRIEND**
Handcrafted/Willow, 1-3/8" tall, Dated 1989.
☐ Purchased 19___ Pd $_____ MIB NB DB BNT
☐ Want Orig. Retail $4.50
NB $8 **MIB** Sec. Mkt. **$14**

J QXM 565-5 **STARLIT MOUSE**
Handcrafted, 1-3/16" tall, Dated 1989. **Artist:** Dill Rhodus
☐ Purchased 19___ Pd $_____ MIB NB DB BNT
☐ Want Orig. Retail $4.50
NB $10 **MIB** Sec. Mkt. **$17**

K QXM 567-2 **STOCKING PAL**
Handcrafted, 1" tall, Reissued in 1990. **Artist:** Julia Lee
☐ Purchased 19___ Pd $_____ MIB NB DB BNT
☐ Want Orig. Retail $4.50
NB $5 **MIB** Sec. Mkt. **$8.50**

L QXM 574-2 **STROLLIN' SNOWMAN**
Hand Painted Fine Porcelain, 1-1/4" tall. **Artist:** Bob Siedler
☐ Purchased 19___ Pd $_____ MIB NB DB BNT
☐ Want Orig. Retail $4.50
NB $6 **MIB** Sec. Mkt. **$16**

M QXM 569-4 **THREE LITTLE KITTIES**
Handcrafted, 15/16" tall **Artist:** Sharon Pike
Reissued from 1988.
☐ Purchased 19___ Pd $_____ MIB NB DB BNT
☐ Want Orig. Retail $6.00
NB $10 **MIB** Sec. Mkt. **$18.50**

N QXM 566-1 **HEAVENLY GLOW TREE TOPPER**
Reissued from 1988.
☐ Purchased 19___ Pd $_____ MIB NB DB BNT
☐ Want Orig. Retail $9.75
NB $9 **MIB** Sec. Mkt. **$18.50**

**Remember:
You can't judge a book
by its movie.**

Page 135

1990 Collection

QX 317-3 ACROSS THE MILES ☐
Comments: Acrylic, 3-1/2" tall.
Etched into this oval acrylic a happy raccoon carries a large poinsettia.
Caption: "Christmas Smiles Across The Miles."
Artist: LaDene Votruba

☐ Purchased 19 __ Pd $_____ MIB NB DB BNT
☐ Want Orig. Ret. $6.75 **NB** $10 **MIB** Sec. Mkt. **$14**

QX 474-6 ANGEL KITTY ☐
Comments: Handcrafted, 2-9/16" tall, Dated 1990.
The artist used her own cat as the model for this ornament,
dressed in a blue dress and slippers with sparkling net wings,
a brass halo and brass star wand. **Artist:** Michele Pyda-Sevcik

☐ Purchased 19 __ Pd $_____ MIB NB DB BNT
☐ Want Orig. Ret. $8.75 **NB** $12 **MIB** Sec. Mkt. **$20**

QXC 445-3 ARMFUL OF JOY: KEEPSAKE CLUB ☐
Comments: Handcrafted, 2-13/16" tall, Dated 1990.
This wide-eyed elf has quite a job. He's trying to balance a stack
of colorful gifts. Top box is labeled "1990 Membership Kit." Club
logo is on the elf's shopping bag. Available to Club Members
only. **Artist:** John Francis (Collin)

☐ Purchased 19 __ Pd $_____ MIB NB DB BNT
☐ Want Orig. Ret. $9.75 **NB** $20 **MIB** Sec. Mkt. **$40**

QX 548-6 BABY UNICORN ☐
Comments: Fine Porcelain, 2" tall.
This iridescent unicorn watches from large, dark eyes. His horn
and hooves are painted gold. **Artist:** Anita Marra Rogers

☐ Purchased 19 __ Pd $_____ MIB NB DB BNT
☐ Want Orig. Ret. $9.75 **NB** $12 **MIB** Sec. Mkt. **$18**

QX 303-6 BABY'S FIRST CHRISTMAS ☐
Comments: Acrylic, 4-7/32" tall, Dated 1990.
A fluffy etched puppy takes a ride in a hot air balloon.
Caption: "Baby's First Christmas." **Artist:** Anita Marra Rogers

☐ Purchased 19 __ Pd $_____ MIB NB DB BNT
☐ Want Orig. Ret. $6.75 **NB** $15 **MIB** Sec. Mkt. **$20**

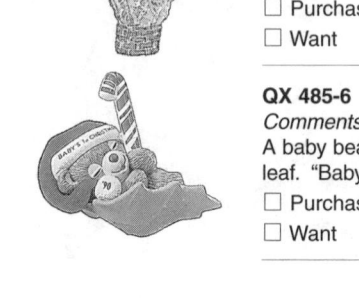

QX 485-6 BABY'S FIRST CHRISTMAS ☐
Comments: Handcrafted, 2-3/8" tall, Dated 1990.
A baby bear dreams sweetly, with candy cane in hand, on a green
leaf. "Baby's First Christmas" **Artist:** John Francis (Collin)

☐ Purchased 19 __ Pd $_____ MIB NB DB BNT
☐ Want Orig. Ret. $7.75 **NB** $20 **MIB** Sec. Mkt. **$35**

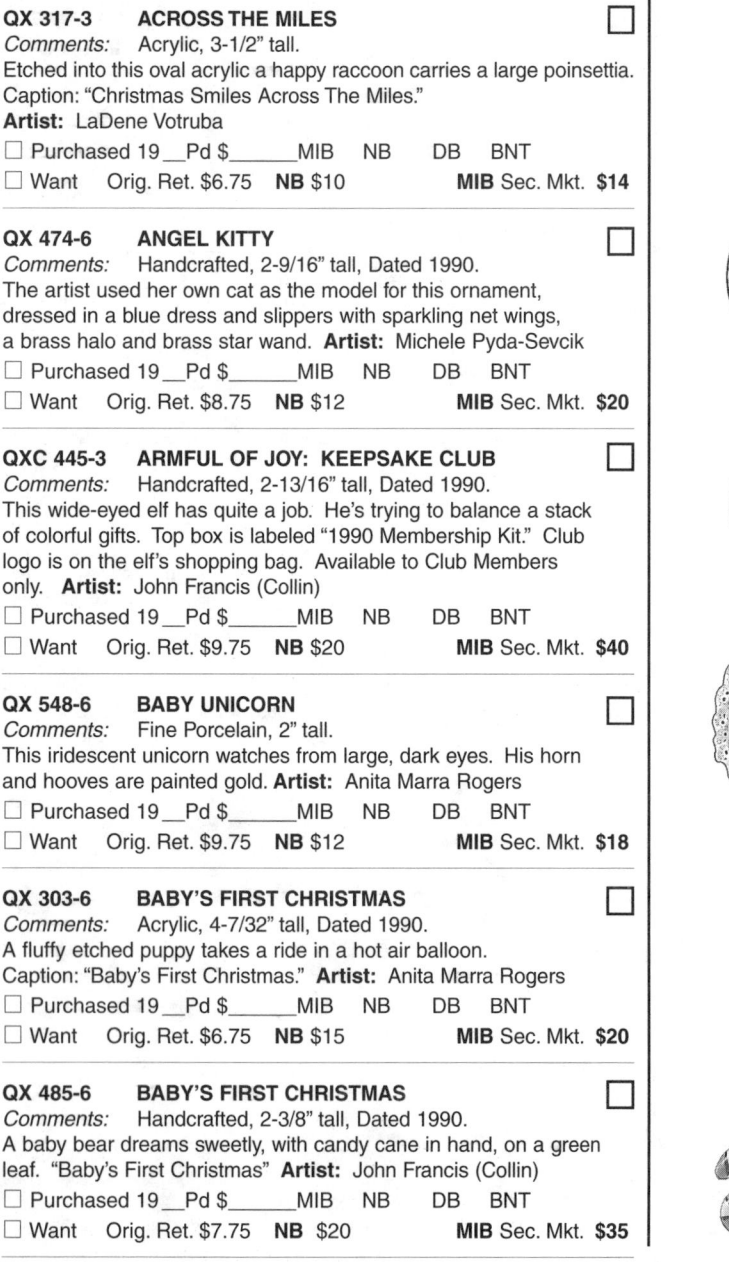

QLX 724-6 BABY'S FIRST CHRISTMAS ☐
Comments: Light and Motion, Handcrafted, 3-3/4" tall.
Dated 1990. The stork flies above the snow-covered village with his
precious bundle. Caption: "Baby's First Christmas."
Artist: Don Palmiter

☐ Purchased 19 __ Pd $_____ MIB NB DB BNT
☐ Want Orig. Ret. $28.00 **NB** $38 **MIB** Sec. Mkt. **$60**

QX 206-3 BABY'S FIRST CHRISTMAS: BABY BOY ☐
Comments: Blue Satin Ball, 2-7/8" dia., Dated 1990.
Caption: "Baby's First Christmas" and "Joy Comes Into Your
Heart When A Baby Boy Comes Into Your World." Usually it's
harder to locate the boy than the girl.

☐ Purchased 19 __ Pd $_____ MIB NB DB BNT
☐ Want Orig. Ret. $4.75 **NB** $12 **MIB** Sec. Mkt. **$18**

QX 206-6 BABY'S FIRST CHRISTMAS: BABY GIRL ☐
Comments: Pink Satin Ball, 2-7/8" dia., Dated 1990.
Caption: "Baby's First Christmas" and "Joy Comes Into Your
Heart When A Baby Girl Comes Into Your World."

☐ Purchased 19 __ Pd $_____ MIB NB DB BNT
☐ Want Orig. Ret. $4.75 **NB** $12 **MIB** Sec. Mkt. **$19**

QX 484-3 BABY'S FIRST CHRISTMAS PHOTOHOLDER ☐
Comments: Fabric, 3-1/2" dia., Dated 1990.
Embroidered bunnies scamper among the holly. Caption:
"Baby's First Christmas" and "There Are So Many Moments To
Cherish With A Beautiful Baby To Love."

☐ Purchased 19 __ Pd $_____ MIB NB DB BNT
☐ Want Orig. Ret. $7.75 **NB** $15 **MIB** Sec. Mkt. **$22**

QX 485-3 BABY'S FIRST CHRISTMAS ☐
Comments: Handcrafted, 3-3/8" tall, Dated 1990.
This little baby is sure to keep happy in his red and white baby walker.
"Baby's 1st Christmas." **Artist:** John Francis (Collin)

☐ Purchased 19 __ Pd $_____ MIB NB DB BNT
☐ Want Orig. Ret. $9.75 **NB** $14 **MIB** Sec. Mkt. **$18**

QX 486-3 BABY'S SECOND CHRISTMAS ☐
Comments: Handcrafted, 2-3/16" tall, Dated 1990.
Identical to 1989; only date has changed.
Artist: John Francis (Collin)

☐ Purchased 19 __ Pd $_____ MIB NB DB BNT
☐ Want · Orig. Ret. $6.75 **NB** $24 **MIB** Sec. Mkt. **$35**

QX 548-3   BEARBACK RIDER ☐
Comments: Handcrafted, 3-1/4" tall, Dated 1990.
A perky penguin with a red hat is riding "bear-back" on a polar bear on red and white rockers.
Artist: Ken Crow

☐ Purchased 19 __Pd $_____MIB   NB   DB   BNT
☐ Want   Orig. Ret. $9.75   **NB** $14   **MIB** Sec. Mkt. **$23**

QX 473-3   BEARY GOOD DEAL ☐
Comments: Handcrafted, 2" tall.
This cute flocked bear is playing with "Santa" cards and he must have a good hand by the smile on his face.
Artist: Bob Siedler

☐ Purchased 19 __Pd $_____MIB   NB   DB   BNT
☐ Want   Orig. Ret. $6.75   **NB** $10   **MIB** Sec. Mkt. **$14**

QLX 732-6   BEARY SHORT NAP ☐
Comments: Lighted, Handcrafted, 2-3/8" tall, Dated 1990.
Tomorrow is Dec. 25 so this Santa bear cannot nap too long. A little mouse also naps in a drawer of his desk.
Artist: Bob Siedler

☐ Purchased 19 __Pd $_____MIB   NB   DB   BNT
☐ Want   Orig. Ret. $10.00 **NB** $18   **MIB** Sec. Mkt. **$26**

QX 203-3   BETSEY CLARK – HOME FOR CHRISTMAS ☐
Comments: **Fifth in Series,** Pink Glass Ball, 2-7/8" dia.
Dated 1990. Betsey's children are making holiday music.
Caption: "Merry Christmas" and "Tis The Season When Hearts Are Singing!"

☐ Purchased 19 __Pd $_____MIB   NB   DB   BNT
☐ Want   Orig. Ret. $5.00   **NB** $10   **MIB** Sec. Mkt. **$20**

QX 519-6   BILLBOARD BUNNY ☐
Comments: Handcrafted, 2-3/8" tall.
The Easter bunny is wearing a bright red sandwich board proclaiming his thoughts about the Christmas season:
"Bah Hum Bug" and "Ban Fruit Cake."
Artist: Julia Lee

☐ Purchased 19 __Pd $_____MIB   NB   DB   BNT
☐ Want   Orig. Ret. $7.75   **NB** $12   **MIB** Sec. Mkt. **$14**

QLX 736-3   BLESSINGS OF LOVE ☐
Comments: Lighted Panorama Ball, 4-3/4" tall.
The barn animals watch the Baby Jesus sleeping in the manger.
Caption: "His Humble Birth Blessed All The Earth With Love And Joy Forever."

☐ Purchased 19 __Pd $_____MIB   NB   DB   BNT
☐ Want   Orig. Ret. $14.00 **NB** $28   **MIB** Sec. Mkt. **$50**

QX 504-3   BORN TO DANCE ☐
Comments: Handcrafted, 2-9/16" tall.
This little ballerina mouse is wearing a pink lacy tutu and is very flexible. She may be bent into various dance positions.
Artist: Sharon Pike

☐ Purchased 19 __Pd $_____MIB   NB   DB   BNT
☐ Want   Orig. Ret. $7.75   **NB** $12   **MIB** Sec. Mkt. **$19**

QX 449-3   BROTHER ☐
Comments: Handcrafted, 2-3/16" tall, Dated 1990.
The baseball glove claims "M.V.B. Most Valuable Brother" and the puppy sitting in the middle of the glove thinks so, too.
Artist: Bob Siedler

☐ Purchased 19 __Pd $_____MIB   NB   DB   BNT
☐ Want   Orig. Ret. $5.75   **NB** $6   **MIB** Sec. Mkt. **$10.50**

QX 316-6   CHILD CARE GIVER ☐
Comments: Acrylic, 3" tall, Dated Christmas 1990.
Etched onto this quatrefoil shaped ornament is a teddy bear hugging a bunny. Gold foil caption: "A Special Person Like You Is Every Child's Dream."

☐ Purchased 19 __Pd $_____MIB   NB   DB   BNT
☐ Want   Orig. Ret. $6.75   **NB** $8   **MIB** Sec. Mkt. **$12**

QX 487-6   CHILD'S FIFTH CHRISTMAS ☐
Comments: Handcrafted, 2-3/8" tall, Dated 1990.
Identical to 1989; only date has changed.
Artist: Dill Rhodus

☐ Purchased 19 __Pd $_____MIB   NB   DB   BNT
☐ Want   Orig. Ret. $6.75   **NB** $12   **MIB** Sec. Mkt. **$18**

QX 487-3   CHILD'S FOURTH CHRISTMAS ☐
Comments: Handcrafted, 3" tall, Dated 1990.
Identical to 1989; only date has changed.
Artist: John Francis (Collin)

☐ Purchased 19 __Pd $_____MIB   NB   DB   BNT
☐ Want   Orig. Ret. $6.75   **NB** $12   **MIB** Sec. Mkt. **$18**

QX 486-6   CHILD'S THIRD CHRISTMAS ☐
Comments: Handcrafted, 2-1/2" tall, Dated 1990.
Identical to 1989; only date has changed.
Artist: John Francis (Collin)

☐ Purchased 19 __Pd $_____MIB   NB   DB   BNT
☐ Want   Orig. Ret. $6.75   **NB** $15   **MIB** Sec. Mkt. **$20**

QLX 724-3 CHILDREN'S EXPRESS ☐
Comments: Light and Motion, Handcrafted, 3-3/4" tall.
Two children have fun playing with a train set. The little boy swings his legs and moves his head back and forth as he watches the train. **Artist:** Linda Sickman

☐ Purchased 19___ Pd $_____ MIB NB DB BNT
☐ Want Orig. Ret. $28.00 **NB** $48 **MIB** Sec. Mkt. **$65**

QX 436-6 CHIMING IN ☐
Comments: Handcrafted/Brass, 5" tall, Dated 1990.
A little squirrel is standing on top of the chimes waiting for his cue to ring the chimes with his candy cane mallet.
Artist: Sharon Pike

☐ Purchased 19___ Pd $_____ MIB NB DB BNT
☐ Want Orig. Ret. $9.75 **NB** $12 **MIB** Sec. Mkt. **$21**

QLX 729-6 CHRIS MOUSE WREATH ☐
Comments: **Sixth in Series,** Handcrafted, 4-1/2" tall.
Dated 1990. Chris lights the candle inside a lovely green wreath decorated with gold ball ornaments.
Artist: Anita Marra Rogers

☐ Purchased 19___ Pd $_____ MIB NB DB BNT
☐ Want Orig. Ret. $10.00 **NB** $24 **MIB** Sec. Mkt. **$42.50**

QLX 730-3 CHRISTMAS CLASSICS: THE LITTLEST ANGEL ☐
Comments: **Fifth and Final in Series,** Lighted, Handcrafted.
4-1/2" tall, Dated 1990. The Littlest Angel kneels in awe as his gift to the Child is transformed into the Star of Bethlehem. Caption: "The Littlest Angel." **Artist:** John Francis (Collin)

☐ Purchased 19___ Pd $_____ MIB NB DB BNT
☐ Want Orig. Ret. $14.00 **NB** $30 **MIB** Sec. Mkt. **$43**

QX 437-3 CHRISTMAS CROC ☐
Comments: Handcrafted, 1-1/18" tall.
This bright green crocodile wears a Christmas red smile and a fabric muffler to match. Twist the tip of his tail and he'll open his mouth for you. **Artist:** Michele Pyda-Sevcik

☐ Purchased 19___ Pd $_____ MIB NB DB BNT
☐ Want Orig. Ret. $7.75 **NB** $12 **MIB** Sec. Mkt. **$18**

QX 450-6 CHRISTMAS KITTY ☐
Comments: **Second in Series,** Fine Porcelain, 3" tall.
This hand-painted grey kitten is lovely in her pale blue and white coat, hat and muff with sprigs of holly.
Artist: Anita Marra Rogers

☐ Purchased 19___ Pd $_____ MIB NB DB BNT
☐ Want Orig. Ret. $14.75 **NB** $18 **MIB** Sec. Mkt. **$28**

QXC 476-6 CHRISTMAS LIMITED: KEEPSAKE CLUB ☐
Comments: Limited Edition 38,700, Wood Display Stand.
Cast Metal, 2-5/8" tall. This blue and red, brass-trimmed locomotive has a brass bell that rings and wheels that turn. Available to Members only. **Artist:** Linda Sickman

☐ Purchased 19___ Pd $_____ MIB NB DB BNT
☐ Want Orig. Ret. $19.75 **NB** $85 **MIB** Sec. Mkt. **$105**

QLX 727-6 CHRISTMAS MEMORIES ☐
Comments: Light and Motion, Handcrafted, 4-1/4" tall.
A Clydesdale horse pulls a family in a sleigh as they bring home their Christmas tree. Caption: "The Joy Is In Remembering..."
Artist: Duane Unruh

☐ Purchased 19___ Pd $_____ MIB NB DB BNT
☐ Want Orig. Ret. $25.00 **NB** $40 **MIB** Sec. Mkt. **$50**

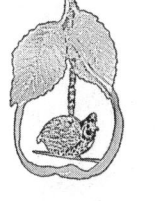

QX 524-6 CHRISTMAS PARTRIDGE ☐
Comments: Dimensional Brass, 3-1/4" tall.
A delicately etched partridge dangles inside the silhouette of a pear with large etched leaves.
Artist: Linda Sickman

☐ Purchased 19___ Pd $_____ MIB NB DB BNT
☐ Want Orig. Ret. $7.75 **NB** $10 **MIB** Sec. Mkt. **$18.50**

QX 488-5 CLAUS CONSTRUCTION ☐
Comments: Handcrafted, 4-3/4" tall.
Reissued from 1989. **Artist:** Ed Seale

☐ Purchased 19___ Pd $_____ MIB NB DB BNT
☐ Want Orig. Ret. $7.75 **NB** $15 **MIB** Sec. Mkt. **$28**

QXC 445-6 CLUB HOLLOW: KEEPSAKE CLUB ☐
Comments: Handcrafted, 1-7/8" tall, Dated 1990.
This feathered owl is reading "Whoo's Whoo" in the "Courier 1990," snug inside his snow-capped home. "Collectors Club + Me" is carved in the back of the tree. Club logo on the bottom.
Artist: Ken Crow

☐ Purchased 19___ Pd $_____ MIB NB DB BNT
☐ Want Price: Came with Club Membership of $_____
NB $20 **MIB** Sec. Mkt. **$35**

QX 443-6 COLLECTOR'S PLATE: COOKIES FOR SANTA ☐
Comments: **Fourth in Series,** Fine Porcelain, 3-1/4" dia.
Dated 1990. Two children have set out a plate of cookies and are writing their wish list for Santa. Caption "Cookies For Santa" on back. **Artist:** LaDene Votruba

☐ Purchased 19___ Pd $_____ MIB NB DB BNT
☐ Want Orig. Ret. $8.75 **NB** $18 **MIB** Sec. Mkt. **$25**

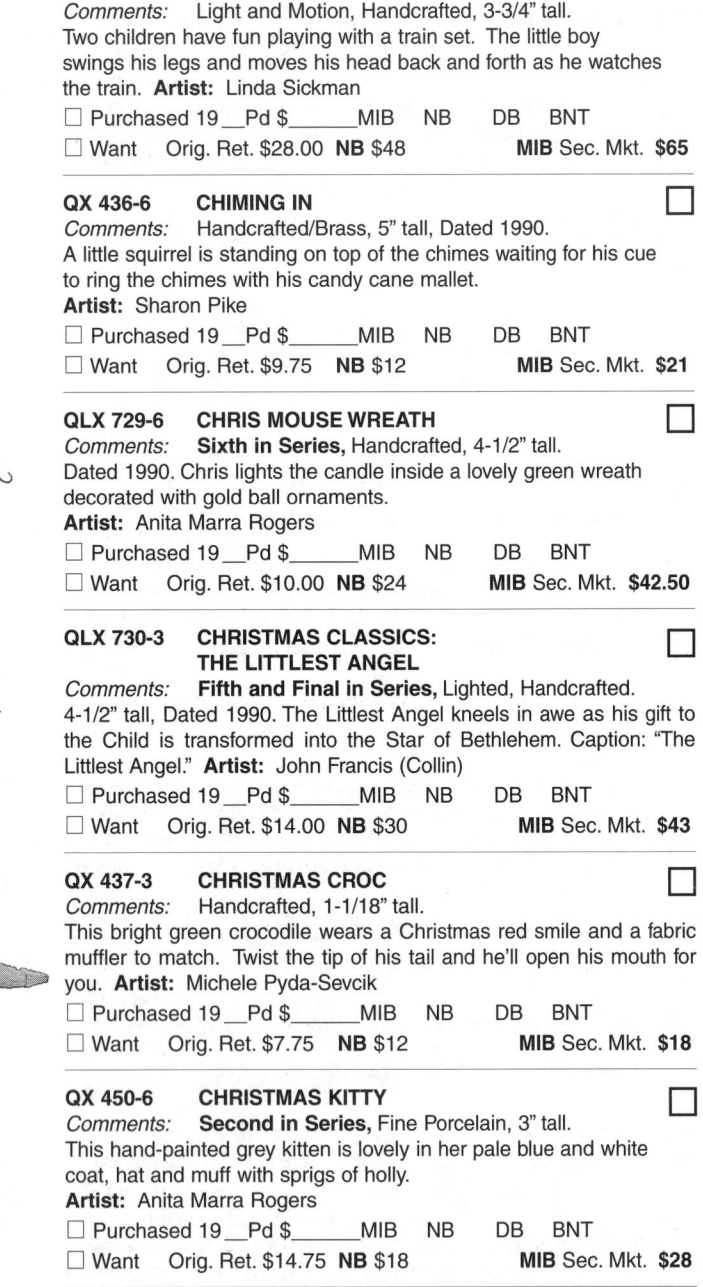

QX 448-6 COPY OF CHEER
Comments: Handcrafted, 2-1/16" tall, Dated 1990.
A little mouse is making copies of his "Merry Christmas" message to distribute to everyone! **Artist:** Bob Siedler

☐ Purchased 19__Pd $_____MIB NB   DB   BNT
☐ Want   Orig. Ret. $7.75 **NB** $10   **MIB** Sec. Mkt. **$16**

QX 504-6 COUNTRY ANGEL
Comments: Handcrafted, Limited amount of trading reported.
Sculpted to resemble hand-carved wood, the Country Angel was pulled from the line due to production problems. The only pieces produced were the retailers' display items.

☐ Purchased 19__Pd $_____MIB NB   DB   BNT
☐ Want   Orig. Ret. $6.75 **NB** $80   **MIB** Sec. Mkt. **$90**

QX 499-3 COYOTE CAROLS
Comments: Handcrafted, 3" tall.
These coyotes love to howl a few bars of their favorite Christmas carols. Could it be "Home on the Range at Christmas"?
Artist: Julia Lee

☐ Purchased 19__Pd $_____MIB NB   DB   BNT
☐ Want   Orig. Ret. $8.75 **NB** $14   **MIB** Sec. Mkt. **$21**

QX 496-6 COZY GOOSE
Comments: Handcrafted, 3-1/8" tall.
This goose wants to make sure he's warm throughout the holidays in his goose-down vest.
Artist: Sharon Pike

☐ Purchased 19__Pd $_____MIB NB   DB   BNT
☐ Want   Orig. Ret. $5.75 **NB** $7   **MIB** Sec. Mkt. **$12**

**QX 458-6 CRAYOLA® CRAYON:
             BRIGHT MOVING COLORS**
Comments: **Second in Series,** Handcrafted, 2-1/4" tall.
This little white mouse has ingeniously crafted a sled using red and blue crayon runners and the box forms the sled.
Artist: Ken Crow

☐ Purchased 19__Pd $_____MIB NB   DB   BNT
☐ Want   Orig. Ret. $8.75 **NB** $35   **MIB** Sec. Mkt. **$44**

QX 453-3 DAD
Comments: Handcrafted, 2-1/2" tall, Dated 1990.
Dad is one happy king, whether of forest or home in his oversized sweater. **Artist:** Julia Lee

☐ Purchased 19__Pd $_____MIB NB   DB   BNT
☐ Want   Orig. Ret. $6.75 **NB** $8   **MIB** Sec. Mkt. **$12**

QX 491-3 DAD-TO-BE
Comments: Handcrafted, 3" tall, Dated Christmas 1990.
A proud papa to be is ready with suitcase in hand and a book of instructions, "Tips for Dads." **Artist:** Bob Siedler

☐ Purchased 19__Pd $_____MIB NB   DB   BNT
☐ Want   Orig. Ret. $5.75 **NB** $14   **MIB** Sec. Mkt. **$18**

QX 449-6 DAUGHTER
Comments: Handcrafted, 2-1/4" tall, Dated 1990.
This snow "Daughter" shows graceful form on her ice skates.
Red skirt and tam, green muffler. **Artist:** Bob Siedler

☐ Purchased 19__Pd $_____MIB NB   DB   BNT
☐ Want   Orig. Ret. $5.75 **NB** $10   **MIB** Sec. Mkt. **$16**

QLX 721-3 DEER CROSSING
Comments: Blinking Lights, Handcrafted, 3-15/16" tall.
Just in case you miss the blinking red lights on this "Deer Crossing" sign, a little beaver with a stop sign will remind you to watch for the deer. **Artist:** Bob Siedler

☐ Purchased 19__Pd $_____MIB NB   DB   BNT
☐ Want   Orig. Ret. $18.00 **NB** $30   **MIB** Sec. Mkt. **$40**

QX 505-6 DICKENS CAROLER BELL: MR. ASHBOURNE
Comments: ***FIRST IN SERIES,*** Fine Porcelain, 4-1/4" tall, Dated 1990. First in Collection. Special Edition. This bell combines the look of a figurine with the charm of a bell. Mr. Ashbourne opens his song book and sings. His jacket is trimmed in gold.
Artist: Robert Chad

☐ Purchased 19__Pd $_____MIB NB   DB   BNT
☐ Want   Orig. Ret. $21.75 **NB** $20   **MIB** Sec. Mkt. **$35**

QX 482-3 DONDER'S DINER
Comments: Handcrafted, 2-3/8" tall, Dated 1990.
Peek into this streetcar converted into a diner and you'll see Donder serving Santa a hamburger. Signs on the walls advertise the fare. **Artist:** Donna Lee

☐ Purchased 19__Pd $_____MIB NB   DB   BNT
☐ Want   Orig. Ret. $13.75 **NB** $12   **MIB** Sec. Mkt. **$18**

QXC 447-6 DOVE OF PEACE: KEEPSAKE CLUB
Comments: Limited Edition 25,400, Wood Display Stand.
Hand-Painted Fine Porcelain, 2-3/8" tall
This beautiful dove in flight carries a golden brass banner with the words "Peace," "Hope" and "Love." Available to Club Members only. **Artist:** Linda Sickman

☐ Purchased 19__Pd $_____MIB NB   DB   BNT
☐ Want   Orig. Ret. $24.75 **NB** $35   **MIB** Sec. Mkt. **$70**

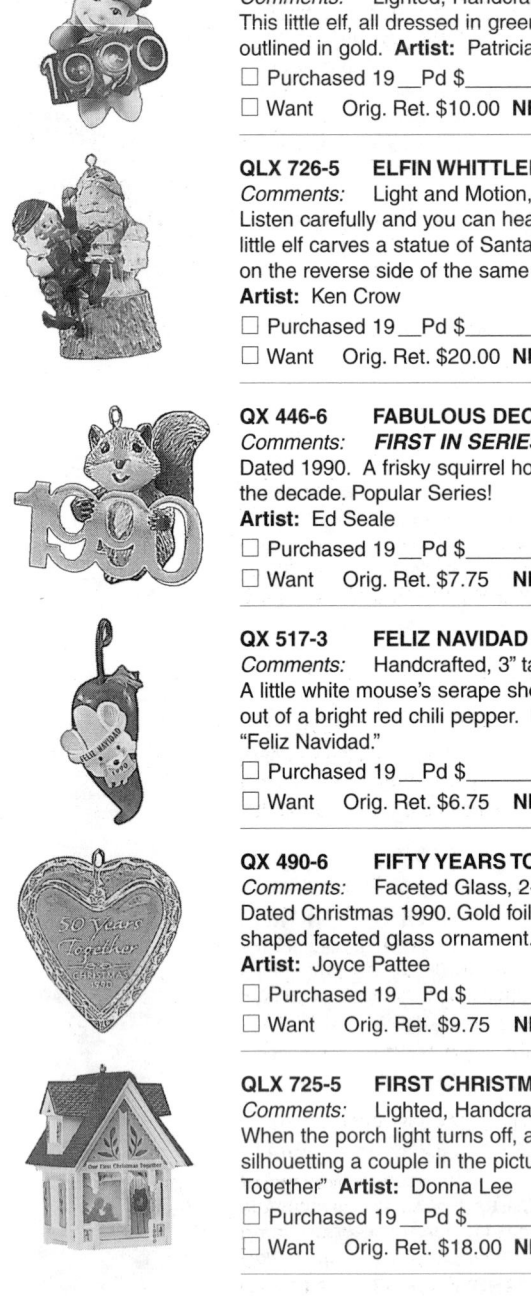

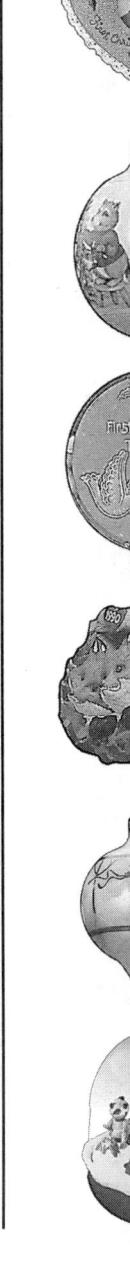

QLX 735-6   ELF OF THE YEAR
Comments: Lighted, Handcrafted, 2-15/16" tall, Dated 1990.
This little elf, all dressed in green, holds a glowing red 1990
outlined in gold. **Artist:** Patricia Andrews
☐ Purchased 19 __ Pd $_____ MIB   NB   DB   BNT
☐ Want   Orig. Ret. $10.00 **NB** $15   **MIB** Sec. Mkt. **$20**

QLX 726-5   ELFIN WHITTLER
Comments: Light and Motion, Handcrafted, 3-1/8" tall.
Listen carefully and you can hear a tapping sound as this busy
little elf carves a statue of Santa. A teddy bear has been whittled
on the reverse side of the same stump.
Artist: Ken Crow
☐ Purchased 19 __ Pd $_____ MIB   NB   DB   BNT
☐ Want   Orig. Ret. $20.00 **NB** $35   **MIB** Sec. Mkt. **$50**

QX 446-6   FABULOUS DECADE
Comments: ***FIRST IN SERIES,*** Handcrafted/Brass, 1-3/8" tall.
Dated 1990. A frisky squirrel holds up a brass 1990 to usher in
the decade. Popular Series!
Artist: Ed Seale
☐ Purchased 19 __ Pd $_____ MIB   NB   DB   BNT
☐ Want   Orig. Ret. $7.75 **NB** $22   **MIB** Sec. Mkt. **$38**

QX 517-3   FELIZ NAVIDAD
Comments: Handcrafted, 3" tall, Dated 1990.
A little white mouse's serape shows the year as this fellow peeks
out of a bright red chili pepper. His sombrero wishes everyone
"Feliz Navidad."
☐ Purchased 19 __ Pd $_____ MIB   NB   DB   BNT
☐ Want   Orig. Ret. $6.75 **NB** $12   **MIB** Sec. Mkt. **$24**

QX 490-6   FIFTY YEARS TOGETHER
Comments: Faceted Glass, 2-9/16" tall.
Dated Christmas 1990. Gold foil lettering is lovely on this heart-
shaped faceted glass ornament. Caption: "50 Years Together."
Artist: Joyce Pattee
☐ Purchased 19 __ Pd $_____ MIB   NB   DB   BNT
☐ Want   Orig. Ret. $9.75 **NB** $12   **MIB** Sec. Mkt. **$18**

QLX 725-5   FIRST CHRISTMAS TOGETHER
Comments: Lighted, Handcrafted, 3-5/8" tall, Dated 1990.
When the porch light turns off, a light inside the house turns on,
silhouetting a couple in the picture window. "Our First Christmas
Together" **Artist:** Donna Lee
☐ Purchased 19 __ Pd $_____ MIB   NB   DB   BNT
☐ Want   Orig. Ret. $18.00 **NB** $30   **MIB** Sec. Mkt. **$42**

**QX 488-6   FIRST CHRISTMAS TOGETHER
                  PHOTOHOLDER**
Comments: Fabric, 3-1/4" tall, Dated 1990.
Caption: "First Christmas Together" and "Loving Memories Are
Celebrations Of The Heart." **Artist:** LaDene Votruba
☐ Purchased 19 __ Pd $_____ MIB   NB   DB   BNT
☐ Want   Orig. Ret. $7.75 **NB** $10   **MIB** Sec. Mkt. **$18**

QX 213-6   FIRST CHRISTMAS TOGETHER
Comments: Light Gold Glass Ball, 2-7/8" dia., Dated 1990.
Inside a cozy living room, a raccoon couple trim their tree. "Our
First Christmas Together" and "Love Decorates Our Lives With
Joy!" **Artist:** LaDene Votruba
☐ Purchased 19 __ Pd $_____ MIB   NB   DB   BNT
☐ Want   Orig. Ret. $4.75
                                        NB $10   **MIB** Sec. Mkt. **$21**

QX 314-6   FIRST CHRISTMAS TOGETHER
Comments: Acrylic, 2-3/4" tall, Dated 1990.
Two etched doves and a heart-shaped holly wreath are set off
with gold foil caption: "Our First Christmas Together."
Artist: LaDene Votruba
☐ Purchased 19 __ Pd $_____ MIB   NB   DB   BNT
☐ Want   Orig. Ret. $6.75 **NB** $10   **MIB** Sec. Mkt. **$20**

QX 488-3   FIRST CHRISTMAS TOGETHER
Comments: Handcrafted, 1-9/16" tall, Dated 1990.
Two happy foxes snuggle together inside a cozy, snow-covered
log. Caption: "Our First Christmas Together" and "Isn't Love
Wonderful!" **Artist:** Michele Pyda-Sevcik
☐ Purchased 19 __ Pd $_____ MIB   NB   DB   BNT
☐ Want   Orig. Ret. $9.75 **NB** $12   **MIB** Sec. Mkt. **$17**

QX 210-3   FIVE YEARS TOGETHER
Comments: Light Silver Glass Ball, 2-7/8" dia.
Dated Christmas 1990. Two deer prance around this teardrop
ball. Caption: "5 Years Together" and "Loves Makes You
Happy!" **Artist:** LaDene Votruba
☐ Purchased 19 __ Pd $_____ MIB   NB   DB   BNT
☐ Want   Orig. Ret. $4.75 **NB** $10   **MIB** Sec. Mkt. **$18**

QLX 723-6   FOREST FROLICS
Comments: **Second in Series,** Light and Motion, Dated 1990.
Handcrafted, 4-1/2" tall. The forest friends have gathered
together for fun and play. Caption: "Merry Christmas 1990."
Artist: Sharon Pike
☐ Purchased 19 __ Pd $_____ MIB   NB   DB   BNT
☐ Want   Orig. Ret. $25.00 **NB** $45   **MIB** Sec. Mkt. **$68**

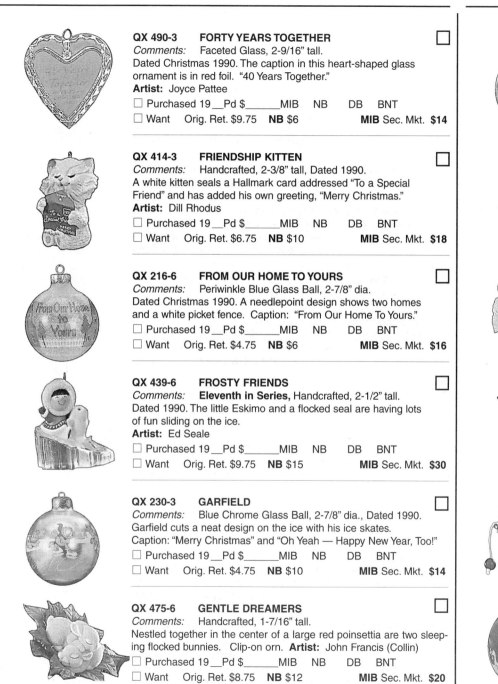
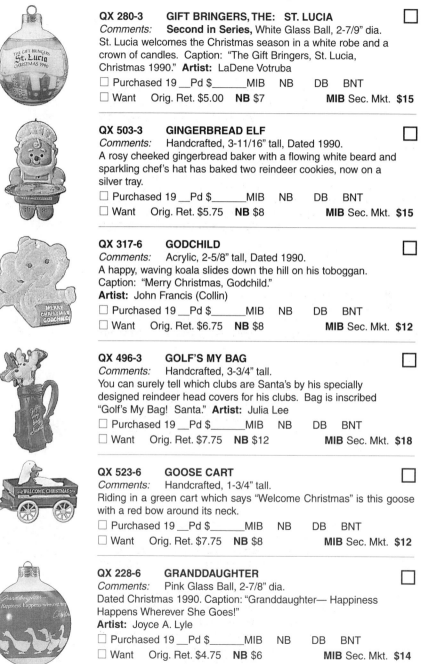

QX 490-3   FORTY YEARS TOGETHER ☐
Comments: Faceted Glass, 2-9/16" tall.
Dated Christmas 1990. The caption in this heart-shaped glass
ornament is in red foil. "40 Years Together."
Artist: Joyce Pattee

☐ Purchased 19 __Pd $_____MIB   NB   DB   BNT
☐ Want   Orig. Ret. $9.75   **NB** $6   **MIB** Sec. Mkt. **$14**

QX 414-3   FRIENDSHIP KITTEN ☐
Comments: Handcrafted, 2-3/8" tall, Dated 1990.
A white kitten seals a Hallmark card addressed "To a Special
Friend" and has added his own greeting, "Merry Christmas."
Artist: Dill Rhodus

☐ Purchased 19 __Pd $_____MIB   NB   DB   BNT
☐ Want   Orig. Ret. $6.75   **NB** $10   **MIB** Sec. Mkt. **$18**

QX 216-6   FROM OUR HOME TO YOURS ☐
Comments: Periwinkle Blue Glass Ball, 2-7/8" dia.
Dated Christmas 1990. A needlepoint design shows two homes
and a white picket fence. Caption: "From Our Home To Yours."

☐ Purchased 19 __Pd $_____MIB   NB   DB   BNT
☐ Want   Orig. Ret. $4.75   **NB** $6   **MIB** Sec. Mkt. **$16**

QX 439-6   FROSTY FRIENDS ☐
Comments: **Eleventh in Series,** Handcrafted, 2-1/2" tall.
Dated 1990. The little Eskimo and a flocked seal are having lots
of fun sliding on the ice.
Artist: Ed Seale

☐ Purchased 19 __Pd $_____MIB   NB   DB   BNT
☐ Want   Orig. Ret. $9.75   **NB** $15   **MIB** Sec. Mkt. **$30**

QX 230-3   GARFIELD ☐
Comments: Blue Chrome Glass Ball, 2-7/8" dia., Dated 1990.
Garfield cuts a neat design on the ice with his ice skates.
Caption: "Merry Christmas" and "Oh Yeah — Happy New Year, Too!"

☐ Purchased 19 __Pd $_____MIB   NB   DB   BNT
☐ Want   Orig. Ret. $4.75   **NB** $10   **MIB** Sec. Mkt. **$14**

QX 475-6   GENTLE DREAMERS ☐
Comments: Handcrafted, 1-7/16" tall.
Nestled together in the center of a large red poinsettia are two sleep-
ing flocked bunnies. Clip-on orn. **Artist:** John Francis (Collin)

☐ Purchased 19 __Pd $_____MIB   NB   DB   BNT
☐ Want   Orig. Ret. $8.75   **NB** $12   **MIB** Sec. Mkt. **$20**

QX 280-3   GIFT BRINGERS, THE: ST. LUCIA ☐
Comments: **Second in Series,** White Glass Ball, 2-7/9" dia.
St. Lucia welcomes the Christmas season in a white robe and a
crown of candles. Caption: "The Gift Bringers, St. Lucia,
Christmas 1990." **Artist:** LaDene Votruba

☐ Purchased 19 __Pd $_____MIB   NB   DB   BNT
☐ Want   Orig. Ret. $5.00   **NB** $7   **MIB** Sec. Mkt. **$15**

QX 503-3   GINGERBREAD ELF ☐
Comments: Handcrafted, 3-11/16" tall, Dated 1990.
A rosy cheeked gingerbread baker with a flowing white beard and
sparkling chef's hat has baked two reindeer cookies, now on a
silver tray.

☐ Purchased 19 __Pd $_____MIB   NB   DB   BNT
☐ Want   Orig. Ret. $5.75   **NB** $8   **MIB** Sec. Mkt. **$15**

QX 317-6   GODCHILD ☐
Comments: Acrylic, 2-5/8" tall, Dated 1990.
A happy, waving koala slides down the hill on his toboggan.
Caption: "Merry Christmas, Godchild."
Artist: John Francis (Collin)

☐ Purchased 19 __Pd $_____MIB   NB   DB   BNT
☐ Want   Orig. Ret. $6.75   **NB** $8   **MIB** Sec. Mkt. **$12**

QX 496-3   GOLF'S MY BAG ☐
Comments: Handcrafted, 3-3/4" tall.
You can surely tell which clubs are Santa's by his specially
designed reindeer head covers for his clubs. Bag is inscribed
"Golf's My Bag! Santa." **Artist:** Julia Lee

☐ Purchased 19 __Pd $_____MIB   NB   DB   BNT
☐ Want   Orig. Ret. $7.75   **NB** $12   **MIB** Sec. Mkt. **$18**

QX 523-6   GOOSE CART ☐
Comments: Handcrafted, 1-3/4" tall.
Riding in a green cart which says "Welcome Christmas" is this goose
with a red bow around its neck.

☐ Purchased 19 __Pd $_____MIB   NB   DB   BNT
☐ Want   Orig. Ret. $7.75   **NB** $8   **MIB** Sec. Mkt. **$12**

QX 228-6   GRANDDAUGHTER ☐
Comments: Pink Glass Ball, 2-7/8" dia.
Dated Christmas 1990. Caption: "Granddaughter— Happiness
Happens Wherever She Goes!"
Artist: Joyce A. Lyle

☐ Purchased 19 __Pd $_____MIB   NB   DB   BNT
☐ Want   Orig. Ret. $4.75   **NB** $6   **MIB** Sec. Mkt. **$14**

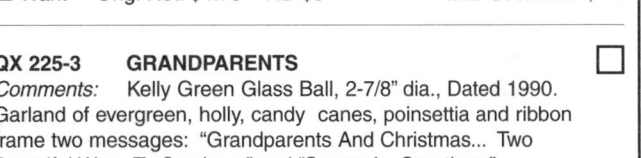

QX 310-6 GRANDDAUGHTER'S FIRST CHRISTMAS

Comments: Acrylic, 3-9/16" tall, Dated 1990.
A little mouse of frosted, textured acrylic is sitting inside a hat box. Pink foil lettering announces "Granddaughter's First Christmas."
Artist: John Francis (Collin)

☐ Purchased 19 __ Pd $_____ MIB   NB   DB   BNT
☐ Want   Orig. Ret. $6.75   **NB** $8   **MIB** Sec. Mkt. **$14**

QX 223-6 GRANDMOTHER

Comments: Blue/White Glass Ball, 2-7/8" dia.
Dated Christmas 1990. A little mouse writes a message: "Grandmother... You're Wonderful!" on a tall wooden fence.
Artist: LaDene Votruba

☐ Purchased 19 __ Pd $_____ MIB   NB   DB   BNT
☐ Want   Orig. Ret. $4.75   **NB** $8   **MIB** Sec. Mkt. **$14**

QX 225-3 GRANDPARENTS

Comments: Kelly Green Glass Ball, 2-7/8" dia., Dated 1990.
Garland of evergreen, holly, candy canes, poinsettia and ribbon frame two messages: "Grandparents And Christmas... Two Beautiful Ways To Say Love" and "Season's Greetings."

☐ Purchased 19 __ Pd $_____ MIB   NB   DB   BNT
☐ Want   Orig. Ret. $4.75   **NB** $6   **MIB** Sec. Mkt. **$15**

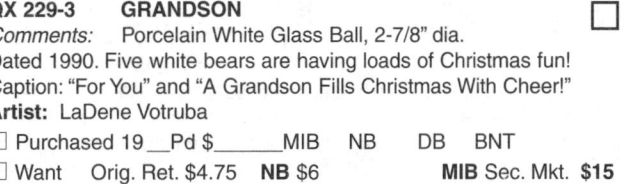

QX 229-3 GRANDSON

Comments: Porcelain White Glass Ball, 2-7/8" dia.
Dated 1990. Five white bears are having loads of Christmas fun! Caption: "For You" and "A Grandson Fills Christmas With Cheer!"
Artist: LaDene Votruba

☐ Purchased 19 __ Pd $_____ MIB   NB   DB   BNT
☐ Want   Orig. Ret. $4.75   **NB** $6   **MIB** Sec. Mkt. **$15**

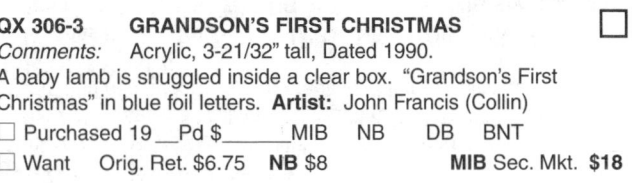

QX 306-3 GRANDSON'S FIRST CHRISTMAS

Comments: Acrylic, 3-21/32" tall, Dated 1990.
A baby lamb is snuggled inside a clear box. "Grandson's First Christmas" in blue foil letters. **Artist:** John Francis (Collin)

☐ Purchased 19 __ Pd $_____ MIB   NB   DB   BNT
☐ Want   Orig. Ret. $6.75   **NB** $8   **MIB** Sec. Mkt. **$18**

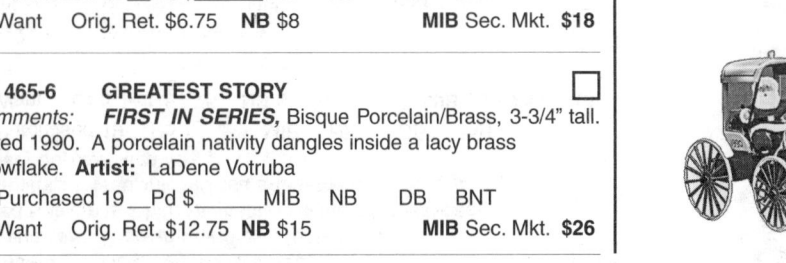

QX 465-6 GREATEST STORY

Comments: **FIRST IN SERIES,** Bisque Porcelain/Brass, 3-3/4" tall.
Dated 1990. A porcelain nativity dangles inside a lacy brass snowflake. **Artist:** LaDene Votruba

☐ Purchased 19 __ Pd $_____ MIB   NB   DB   BNT
☐ Want   Orig. Ret. $12.75   **NB** $15   **MIB** Sec. Mkt. **$26**

QX 471-3 HANG IN THERE

Comments: Handcrafted, 2-1/4" tall.
A charming little raccoon in his green cap is hanging on tightly to a branch so as not to miss anything.
Artist: Ed Seale

☐ Purchased 19 __ Pd $_____ MIB   NB   DB   BNT
☐ Want   Orig. Ret. $6.75   **NB** $10   **MIB** Sec. Mkt. **$20**

QX 464-5 HAPPY VOICES

Comments: Wood, 3-1/8" tall.
A shadow box provides a perfect setting for two carolers and their dog. Caption: "Happy Voices Fill The Air!"
Artist: LaDene Votruba

☐ Purchased 19 __ Pd $_____ MIB   NB   DB   BNT
☐ Want   Orig. Ret. $6.75   **NB** $8   **MIB** Sec. Mkt. **$12**

QX 476-3 HAPPY WOODCUTTER

Comments: Handcrafted, 2" tall, Dated 1990.
This little fellow with the big toothy smile has cut a Christmas tree for his home... with a chain saw. **Artist:** Julia Lee

☐ Purchased 19 __ Pd $_____ MIB   NB   DB   BNT
☐ Want   Orig. Ret. $9.75   **NB** $14   **MIB** Sec. Mkt. **$22**

QX 446-3 HARK! IT'S HERALD

Comments: **Second in Series,** Handcrafted, 2-1/8" tall.
Dated 1990. Herald is ready to celebrate the holidays with his new bass drum. **Artist:** Ken Crow

☐ Purchased 19 __ Pd $_____ MIB   NB   DB   BNT
☐ Want   Orig. Ret. $6.75   **NB** $14   **MIB** Sec. Mkt. **$18**

QX 472-6 HEART OF CHRISTMAS

Comments: **FIRST IN SERIES,** Handcrafted, 2" tall, Dated 1990.
This double-hinged heart opens to reveal Santa filling the stockings. One child watches from behind the Christmas tree and another from the stairs. "Keep The Magic Of Christmas In Your Heart."
Artist: Ed Seale

☐ Purchased 19 __ Pd $_____ MIB   NB   DB   BNT
☐ Want   Orig. Ret. $13.75   **NB** $45   **MIB** Sec. Mkt. **$75**

QX 492-3 HERE COMES SANTA: FESTIVE SURREY

Comments: **Twelfth in Series,** Handcrafted, 3-1/8" tall.
Dated 1990. Santa's surrey has wheels that revolve and is decorated with a wreath on the back of the seat. A bag of toys is at Santa's feet. **Artist:** Linda Sickman

☐ Purchased 19 __ Pd $_____ MIB   NB   DB   BNT
☐ Want   Orig. Ret. $14.75   **NB** $30   **MIB** Sec. Mkt. **$40**

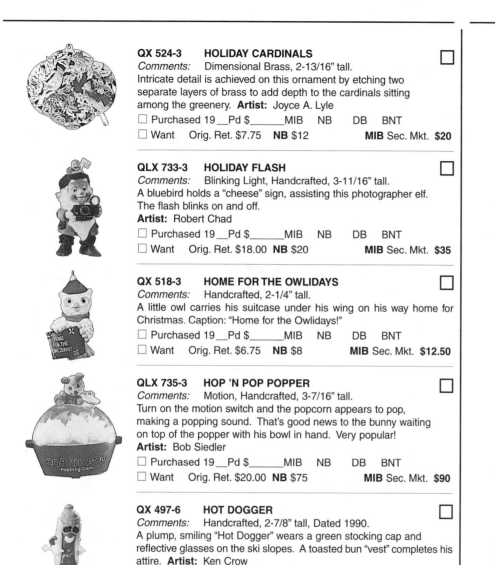

QX 524-3   HOLIDAY CARDINALS

Comments: Dimensional Brass, 2-13/16" tall.
Intricate detail is achieved on this ornament by etching two separate layers of brass to add depth to the cardinals sitting among the greenery. **Artist:** Joyce A. Lyle

☐ Purchased 19 __ Pd $_____ MIB   NB   DB   BNT
☐ Want   Orig. Ret. $7.75   **NB** $12   **MIB** Sec. Mkt. **$20**

QLX 733-3   HOLIDAY FLASH

Comments: Blinking Light, Handcrafted, 3-11/16" tall.
A bluebird holds a "cheese" sign, assisting this photographer elf. The flash blinks on and off.
Artist: Robert Chad

☐ Purchased 19 __ Pd $_____ MIB   NB   DB   BNT
☐ Want   Orig. Ret. $18.00 **NB** $20   **MIB** Sec. Mkt. **$35**

QX 518-3   HOME FOR THE OWLIDAYS

Comments: Handcrafted, 2-1/4" tall.
A little owl carries his suitcase under his wing on his way home for Christmas. Caption: "Home for the Owlidays!"

☐ Purchased 19 __ Pd $_____ MIB   NB   DB   BNT
☐ Want   Orig. Ret. $6.75   **NB** $8   **MIB** Sec. Mkt. **$12.50**

QLX 735-3   HOP 'N POP POPPER

Comments: Motion, Handcrafted, 3-7/16" tall.
Turn on the motion switch and the popcorn appears to pop, making a popping sound. That's good news to the bunny waiting on top of the popper with his bowl in hand. Very popular!
Artist: Bob Siedler

☐ Purchased 19 __ Pd $_____ MIB   NB   DB   BNT
☐ Want   Orig. Ret. $20.00 **NB** $75   **MIB** Sec. Mkt. **$90**

QX 497-6   HOT DOGGER

Comments: Handcrafted, 2-7/8" tall, Dated 1990.
A plump, smiling "Hot Dogger" wears a green stocking cap and reflective glasses on the ski slopes. A toasted bun "vest" completes his attire. **Artist:** Ken Crow

☐ Purchased 19 __ Pd $_____ MIB   NB   DB   BNT
☐ Want   Orig. Ret. $7.75   **NB** $10   **MIB** Sec. Mkt. **$16**

QX 315-6   JESUS LOVES ME

Comments: Acrylic, 2-3/4" dia.
A happy bunny shows his joy in this etched frosted design. Caption: "Jesus Loves Me." **Artist:** Joyce Pattee

☐ Purchased 19 __ Pd $_____ MIB   NB   DB   BNT
☐ Want   Orig. Ret. $6.75   **NB** $9   **MIB** Sec. Mkt. **$12**

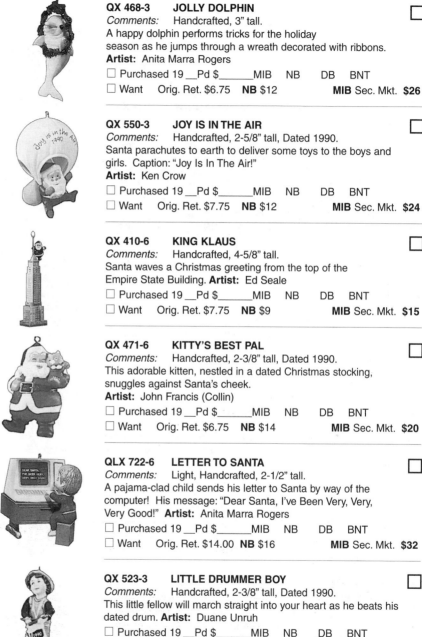

QX 468-3   JOLLY DOLPHIN

Comments: Handcrafted, 3" tall.
A happy dolphin performs tricks for the holiday season as he jumps through a wreath decorated with ribbons.
Artist: Anita Marra Rogers

☐ Purchased 19 __ Pd $_____ MIB   NB   DB   BNT
☐ Want   Orig. Ret. $6.75   **NB** $12   **MIB** Sec. Mkt. **$26**

QX 550-3   JOY IS IN THE AIR

Comments: Handcrafted, 2-5/8" tall, Dated 1990.
Santa parachutes to earth to deliver some toys to the boys and girls. Caption: "Joy Is In The Air!"
Artist: Ken Crow

☐ Purchased 19 __ Pd $_____ MIB   NB   DB   BNT
☐ Want   Orig. Ret. $7.75   **NB** $12   **MIB** Sec. Mkt. **$24**

QX 410-6   KING KLAUS

Comments: Handcrafted, 4-5/8" tall.
Santa waves a Christmas greeting from the top of the Empire State Building. **Artist:** Ed Seale

☐ Purchased 19 __ Pd $_____ MIB   NB   DB   BNT
☐ Want   Orig. Ret. $7.75   **NB** $9   **MIB** Sec. Mkt. **$15**

QX 471-6   KITTY'S BEST PAL

Comments: Handcrafted, 2-3/8" tall, Dated 1990.
This adorable kitten, nestled in a dated Christmas stocking, snuggles against Santa's cheek.
Artist: John Francis (Collin)

☐ Purchased 19 __ Pd $_____ MIB   NB   DB   BNT
☐ Want   Orig. Ret. $6.75   **NB** $14   **MIB** Sec. Mkt. **$20**

QLX 722-6   LETTER TO SANTA

Comments: Light, Handcrafted, 2-1/2" tall.
A pajama-clad child sends his letter to Santa by way of the computer! His message: "Dear Santa, I've Been Very, Very, Very Good!" **Artist:** Anita Marra Rogers

☐ Purchased 19 __ Pd $_____ MIB   NB   DB   BNT
☐ Want   Orig. Ret. $14.00 **NB** $16   **MIB** Sec. Mkt. **$32**

QX 523-3   LITTLE DRUMMER BOY

Comments: Handcrafted, 2-3/8" tall, Dated 1990.
This little fellow will march straight into your heart as he beats his dated drum. **Artist:** Duane Unruh

☐ Purchased 19 __ Pd $_____ MIB   NB   DB   BNT
☐ Want   Orig. Ret. $7.75   **NB** $8   **MIB** Sec. Mkt. **$18**

QX 470-3   LONG WINTER'S NAP

Comments: Handcrafted, 1-3/8" tall, Dated 1990.
A dachshund wearing a Santa cap sleeps soundly in an open-ended gift box. He fastens to the tree with a special clip.
Artist: Anita Marra Rogers

☐ Purchased 19 __Pd $_____MIB   NB   DB   BNT
☐ Want   Orig. Ret. $6.75   **NB** $8   **MIB** Sec. Mkt. **$18**

QX 547-6   LOVABLE DEARS

Comments: Handcrafted, 2-5/16" tall.
A little girl, dressed in a bright red coat and blue muffler, shares a hug with her pet fawn.   **Artist:** Duane Unruh

☐ Purchased 19 __Pd $_____MIB   NB   DB   BNT
☐ Want   Orig. Ret. $8.75   **NB** $10   **MIB** Sec. Mkt. **$16**

QX 442-3   MARY'S ANGELS: ROSEBUD

Comments: **Third in Series,** Handcrafted and Acrylic, 3-1/8" tall.
Rosebud, in a pink gown and with wings spread, holds a candle for all to see. She stands on a frosted acrylic cloud.
Artist: Robert Chad

☐ Purchased 19 __Pd $_____MIB   NB   DB   BNT
☐ Want   Orig. Ret. $5.75   **NB** $28   **MIB** Sec. Mkt **$38**

QX 444-6   MEOW MART

Comments: Handcrafted, 1-1/4" tall.
What does it take to make a playful kitten happy? Only a sack from the "Meow Mart" and a ball of red yarn!
Artist: Sharon Pike

☐ Purchased 19 __Pd $_____MIB   NB   DB   BNT
☐ Want   Orig. Ret. $7.75   **NB** $10   **MIB** Sec. Mkt. **$23**

QX 473-6   MERRY OLDE SANTA

Comments: ***FIRST IN SERIES,*** Handcrafted, 4-3/4" tall.
Dated 1990. An old-fashioned German Santa has toys tucked into his pockets and carries a small Christmas tree in his hand.
Artist: Ed Seale

☐ Purchased 19 __Pd $_____MIB   NB   DB   BNT
☐ Want   Orig. Ret. $14.75   **NB** $50   **MIB** Sec. Mkt. **$65**

QX 459-3   MOM AND DAD

Comments: Handcrafted, 2-1/2" tall, Dated 1990.
These smiling bears are mailing a Hallmark card in their mailbox which is sitting on a tree stump. Mailbox reads "Mom And Dad."
Artist: Robert Chad

☐ Purchased 19 __Pd $_____MIB   NB   DB   BNT
☐ Want   Orig. Ret. $8.75   **NB** $12   **MIB** Sec. Mkt. **$22**

QX 491-6   MOM-TO-BE

Comments: Handcrafted, 2-7/8" tall, Dated Christmas 1990.
First to debut for Mom-To-Be. This Momma bunny is happily awaiting a new little bundle. **Artist:** Bob Siedler

☐ Purchased 19 __Pd $_____MIB   NB   DB   BNT
☐ Want   Orig. Ret. $5.75   **NB** $22   **MIB** Sec. Mkt. **$34**

QX 493-3   MOOY CHRISTMAS

Comments: Handcrafted, 2-1/16" tall.
This little holstein wears a bright red scarf with its Christmas greeting: "Mooy Christmas."

☐ Purchased 19 __Pd $_____MIB   NB   DB   BNT
☐ Want   Orig. Ret. $6.75   NB $10   MIB Sec. Mkt. **$24**

QX 453-6   MOTHER

Comments: Ceramic w/Bisque Finish, 2-7/8 dia., Dated 1990.
Delicate filigree lettering confirms that "Mother Is Love." Tied with red ribbon.   **Artist:** LaDene Votruba

☐ Purchased 19 __Pd $_____MIB   NB   DB   BNT
☐ Want   Orig. Ret. $8.75   **NB** $12   **MIB** Sec. Mkt. **$20**

QX 475-3   MOUSEBOAT

Comments: Handcrafted, 3" tall, Dated 1990.
A whimsical sailor mouse is headed out to sea in his walnut shell boat. The sail contains the signature of the artist, "Seale" and the date. **Artist:** Ed Seale

☐ Purchased 19 __Pd $_____MIB   NB   DB   BNT
☐ Want   Orig. Ret. $7.75   **NB** $8   **MIB** Sec. Mkt. **$12**

QX 439-3   MR. AND MRS. CLAUS: POPCORN PARTY

Comments: **Fifth in Series,** Handcrafted, 3" tall, Dated 1990.
Santa and his Mrs. have popped a big pan of popcorn and are busy stringing it to put on their Christmas tree.
Artist: Duane Unruh

☐ Purchased 19 __Pd $_____MIB   NB   DB   BNT
☐ Want   Orig. Ret. $13.75   **NB** $35   **MIB** Sec. Mkt. **$55**

QLX 726-3   MRS. SANTA'S KITCHEN

Comments: Light and Motion, Handcrafted, 4-3/4" tall.
Dated 1990. Mrs. Santa's special recipe gingerbread cookies dance around her kitchen. Caption: "Christmas Cookies Dance And Play To Celebrate The Holiday!" **Artist:** Dill Rhodus

☐ Purchased 19 __Pd $_____MIB   NB   DB   BNT
☐ Want   Orig. Ret. $25.00   **NB** $55   **MIB** Sec. Mkt. **$70**

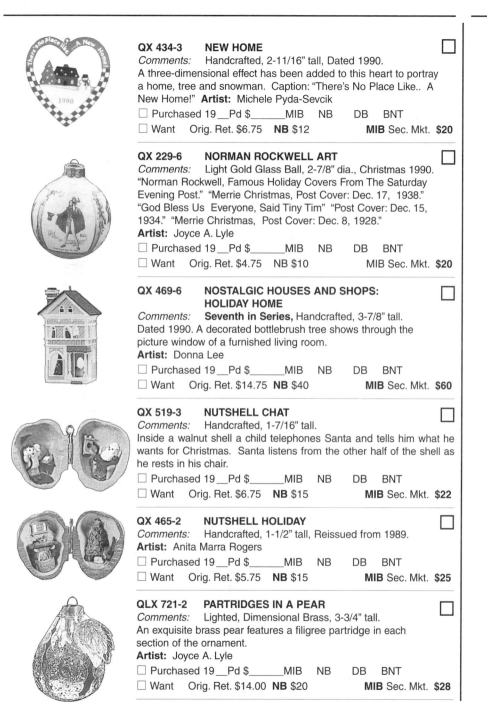

QX 434-3   NEW HOME

Comments: Handcrafted, 2-11/16" tall, Dated 1990.
A three-dimensional effect has been added to this heart to portray a home, tree and snowman. Caption: "There's No Place Like.. A New Home!" **Artist:** Michele Pyda-Sevcik

☐ Purchased 19 __ Pd $_____ MIB   NB   DB   BNT

☐ Want   Orig. Ret. $6.75   **NB** $12   **MIB** Sec. Mkt. **$20**

QX 229-6   NORMAN ROCKWELL ART

Comments: Light Gold Glass Ball, 2-7/8" dia., Christmas 1990. "Norman Rockwell, Famous Holiday Covers From The Saturday Evening Post." "Merrie Christmas, Post Cover: Dec. 17, 1938." "God Bless Us Everyone, Said Tiny Tim" "Post Cover: Dec. 15, 1934." "Merrie Christmas, Post Cover: Dec. 8, 1928."
Artist: Joyce A. Lyle

☐ Purchased 19 __ Pd $_____ MIB   NB   DB   BNT

☐ Want   Orig. Ret. $4.75   NB $10   MIB Sec. Mkt. **$20**

QX 469-6   NOSTALGIC HOUSES AND SHOPS: HOLIDAY HOME

Comments: **Seventh in Series,** Handcrafted, 3-7/8" tall. Dated 1990. A decorated bottlebrush tree shows through the picture window of a furnished living room.
Artist: Donna Lee

☐ Purchased 19 __ Pd $_____ MIB   NB   DB   BNT

☐ Want   Orig. Ret. $14.75   **NB** $40   **MIB** Sec. Mkt. **$60**

QX 519-3   NUTSHELL CHAT

Comments: Handcrafted, 1-7/16" tall.
Inside a walnut shell a child telephones Santa and tells him what he wants for Christmas. Santa listens from the other half of the shell as he rests in his chair.

☐ Purchased 19 __ Pd $_____ MIB   NB   DB   BNT

☐ Want   Orig. Ret. $6.75   **NB** $15   **MIB** Sec. Mkt. **$22**

QX 465-2   NUTSHELL HOLIDAY

Comments: Handcrafted, 1-1/2" tall, Reissued from 1989.
Artist: Anita Marra Rogers

☐ Purchased 19 __ Pd $_____ MIB   NB   DB   BNT

☐ Want   Orig. Ret. $5.75   **NB** $15   **MIB** Sec. Mkt. **$25**

QLX 721-2   PARTRIDGES IN A PEAR

Comments: Lighted, Dimensional Brass, 3-3/4" tall.
An exquisite brass pear features a filigree partridge in each section of the ornament.
Artist: Joyce A. Lyle

☐ Purchased 19 __ Pd $_____ MIB   NB   DB   BNT

☐ Want   Orig. Ret. $14.00   **NB** $20   **MIB** Sec. Mkt. **$28**

QX 210-6   PEACEFUL KINGDOM

Comments: Light Gold Glass Ball, 2-7/8" dia.
Dated Christmas 1990. A lion cub snuggles with a lamb. Caption: "And Peace Will Reign In The Kingdom — The Lion Will Lie Down With The Lamb." Very nice!

☐ Purchased 19 __ Pd $_____ MIB   NB   DB   BNT

☐ Want   Orig. Ret. $4.75   **NB** $14   **MIB** Sec. Mkt. **$21**

QX 223-3   PEANUTS®

Comments: Chrome Glass Ball, 2-7/8" dia., Dated 1990. Schroeder plays a lively Christmas melody while the rest of the gang dances merrily. Caption: "Christmas Is The Merriest, Lightest, Jolliest, Brightest, Happiest Time Of The Year!" Peanuts anniversary logo is on the box with the words "40 Years Of Happiness."

☐ Purchased 19 __ Pd $_____ MIB   NB   DB   BNT

☐ Want   Orig. Ret. $4.75   **NB** $18   **MIB** Sec. Mkt. **$25**

QX 497-3   PEPPERONI MOUSE

Comments: Handcrafted, 1-3/4" tall.
Since mice like cheese, why not pizza!? This little mouse especially likes pepperoni pizza! **Artist:** Bob Siedler

☐ Purchased 19 __ Pd $_____ MIB   NB   DB   BNT

☐ Want   Orig. Ret. $6.75   **NB** $10   **MIB** Sec. Mkt. **$15**

QX 469-3   PERFECT CATCH

Comments: Handcrafted, 3-13/16" tall, Dated 1990.
Santa proves that he's a man for all seasons as he catches the fly ball to win the game! His team is the "North Pole Nicks." Go Santa! **Artist:** Bob Siedler

☐ Purchased 19 __ Pd $_____ MIB   NB   DB   BNT

☐ Want   Orig. Ret. $7.75   **NB** $11   **MIB** Sec. Mkt. **$19**

QX 466-6   POLAR JOGGER

Comments: Handcrafted, 1-5/8" tall.
This chubby fellow is waddling away some extra calories. To keep warm, he's donned a red sweat shirt from "Polar College."
Artist: Bob Siedler

☐ Purchased 19 __ Pd $_____ MIB   NB   DB   BNT

☐ Want   Orig. Ret. $5.75   **NB** $10   **MIB** Sec. Mkt. **$12**

QX 462-6   POLAR PAIR

Comments: Handcrafted, 2" tall.
What's more fun than one penguin? Why, it's two! And everywhere the parent goes, baby tags along in his own special backpack. **Artist:** Bob Siedler

☐ Purchased 19 __ Pd $_____ MIB   NB   DB   BNT

☐ Want   Orig. Ret. $5.75   **NB** $8   **MIB** Sec. Mkt. **$15**

QX 515-6   POLAR SPORT

Comments: Handcrafted 1-3/4" tall.
Our dapper penguin draws looks from everyone around wearing a scarf and beret and driving his red convertible sports car.
Artist: Bob Siedler

☐ Purchased 19 __ Pd $_____ MIB   NB   DB   BNT
☐ Want   Orig. Ret. $7.75   **NB** $10   **MIB** Sec. Mkt. **$18**

QX 516-6   POLAR TV

Comments: Handcrafted 1-5/8" tall.
Life can be great! This penguin relaxes on a shimmery iceberg and sips a cool drink as he watches the "Polar News" on television. **Artist:** Bob Siedler

☐ Purchased 19 __ Pd $_____ MIB   NB   DB   BNT
☐ Want   Orig. Ret. $7.75   **NB** $8   **MIB** Sec. Mkt. **$12**

QX 466-3   POLAR V.I.P.

Comments: Handcrafted, 2" tall.
This fellow must be a "Very Important Penguin." He carries a briefcase and cordless phone to keep in touch with his clientele.
Artist: Bob Siedler

☐ Purchased 19 __ Pd $_____ MIB   NB   DB   BNT
☐ Want   Orig. Ret. $5.75   **NB** $8   **MIB** Sec. Mkt. **$12**

QX 463-3   POLAR VIDEO

Comments: Handcrafted, 2" tall.
Go ahead and behave naturally... our perky penguin is going to capture all the holiday fun on his new camcorder.
Artist: Bob Siedler

☐ Purchased 19 __ Pd $_____ MIB   NB   DB   BNT
☐ Want   Orig. Ret. $5.75   **NB** $8   **MIB** Sec. Mkt. **$12**

QX 498-6   POOLSIDE WALRUS

Comments: Handcrafted, 1-3/4" tall.
What fun! This walrus wears a red swimming suit and sits on his reindeer float. **Artist:** Julia Lee

☐ Purchased 19 __ Pd $_____ MIB   NB   DB   BNT
☐ Want   Orig. Ret. $7.75   **NB** $10   **MIB** Sec. Mkt. **$18**

QX 442-6   PORCELAIN BEAR

Comments: **Eighth and Final in Series,** Fine Porcelain, 1-9/16" tall.
The final cinnamon bear finishes his holiday decorating by placing a star on the top of his tree.

☐ Purchased 19 __ Pd $_____ MIB   NB   DB   BNT
☐ Want   Orig. Ret. $8.75   **NB** $10   **MIB** Sec. Mkt. **$20**

QX 443-3   REINDEER CHAMPS: COMET

Comments: **Fifth in Series,** Handcrafted, 3-3/16" tall.
Dated 1990. Comet scores again. He's wearing a sporty soccer uniform of red and green and is set to kick the soccer ball.
Artist: Bob Siedler

☐ Purchased 19 __ Pd $_____ MIB   NB   DB   BNT
☐ Want   Orig. Ret. $7.75   **NB** $15   **MIB** Sec. Mkt. **$24**

QX 464-6   ROCKING HORSE

Comments: **Tenth in Series,** Handcrafted, 4" wide.
Dated 1990. **Scarce.** This Appaloosa has a festive look with a red and green saddle and matching rockers.
Artist: Linda Sickman

☐ Purchased 19 __ Pd $_____ MIB   NB   DB   BNT
☐ Want   Orig. Ret. $10.75   **NB** $35   **MIB** Sec. Mkt. **$90**

QX 468-6   S. CLAUS TAXI

Comments: Handcrafted, 2" tall, Dated 12-25-1990.
Santa's taxi is in constant demand. He has a teddy bear passenger in the front seat. The taxi's wheels revolve.
License: "Santa." **Artist:** Peter Dutkin

☐ Purchased 19 __ Pd $_____ MIB   NB   DB   BNT
☐ Want   Orig. Ret. $11.75   **NB** $18   **MIB** Sec. Mkt. **$25**

QX 498-3   SANTA SCHNOZ

Comments: Handcrafted, 2-1/2" tall.
Santa sports a phony pair of glasses, mustache and schnoz! He's hiding a gift behind his back.
Artist: Ken Crow

☐ Purchased 19 __ Pd $_____ MIB   NB   DB   BNT
☐ Want   Orig. Ret. $6.75   **NB** $10   **MIB** Sec. Mkt. **$23**

QLX 725-6   SANTA'S HO-HO-HOEDOWN

Comments: Light and Motion, Handcrafted, 4-3/8" tall.
"Ho-Ho-Ho! Doe-See-Doe! Grab Your Partner — And 'Round We Go!" calls Santa as four reindeer couples twirl around at the barn dance. **Artist:** Ken Crow

☐ Purchased 19 __ Pd $_____ MIB   NB   DB   BNT
☐ Want   Orig. Ret. $25.00   **NB** $70   **MIB** Sec. Mkt. **$90**

QX 227-3   SISTER

Comments: Porcelain White Glass Ball, 2-7/8" dia., Dated 1990.
Large colorful poinsettias add charm. Caption: "A Sister Adds Her Own Special Touch To The Beauty And Joy Of Christmas."

☐ Purchased 19 __ Pd $_____ MIB   NB   DB   BNT
☐ Want   Orig. Ret. $4.75   **NB** $8   **MIB** Sec. Mkt. **$15**

QX 472-3   SNOOPY® AND WOODSTOCK ☐
Comments: Handcrafted, 2-1/4" tall.
Snoopy and Woodstock share a special hug between friends.
The slogan "40 Years Of Happiness" appears on the ornament
box. **Artist:** Dill Rhodus

☐ Purchased 19 __ Pd $_____ MIB   NB   DB   BNT
☐ Want   Orig. Ret. $6.75 **NB** $18   **MIB** Sec. Mkt. **$38**

QX 451-6   SON ☐
Comments: Handcrafted, 1-7/8" tall, Dated 1990.
A warmly dressed "snowboy" loves to play hockey. His cap
reads "Son" and his jersey announces the year.
Artist: Bob Siedler

☐ Purchased 19 __ Pd $_____ MIB   NB   DB   BNT
☐ Want   Orig. Ret. $5.75 **NB** $7   **MIB** Sec. Mkt. **$16**

QLX 725-3   SONG & DANCE ☐
Comments: Motion and Music, Handcrafted, 4-1/8" tall.
A mouse couple spins around and around on a record as it plays
"Jingle Bells" on the old phonograph. Caption: "Love And
Christmas... Two Reasons To Celebrate!"
Artist: Anita Marra Rogers

☐ Purchased 19 __ Pd $_____ MIB   NB   DB   BNT
☐ Want   Orig. Ret. $20.00 **NB** $65   **MIB** Sec. Mkt. **$95**

QX 431-2   SPENCER® SPARROW, ESQ. ☐
Comments: Handcrafted, 1-3/4" tall, Reissued from 1989.
Artist: Sharon Pike

☐ Purchased 19 __ Pd $_____ MIB   NB   DB   BNT
☐ Want   Orig. Ret. $6.75 **NB** $12   **MIB** Sec. Mkt. **$18**

QX 549-6   SPOON RIDER ☐
Comments: Handcrafted, 2-2/4" tall.
A couple of mischievous elves are ready to go sledding — in a
teaspoon. Where's the snow?
Artist: Patricia Andrews

☐ Purchased 19 __ Pd $_____ MIB   NB   DB   BNT
☐ Want   Orig. Ret. $9.75 **NB** $12   **MIB** Sec. Mkt. **$18**

QLX 730-6   STARLIGHT ANGEL ☐
Comments: Lighted, Handcrafted, 2-3/4" tall.
A sweet angel wearing a blue robe and shiny brass halo is
carrying a bag full of bright, shinny stars.
Artist: Anita Marra Rogers

☐ Purchased 19 __ Pd $_____ MIB   NB   DB   BNT
☐ Want   Orig. Ret. $14.00 **NB** $20   **MIB** Sec. Mkt. **$34**

QLX 733-6   STARSHIP CHRISTMAS ☐
Comments: Blinking Lights, Handcrafted, 2-1/4" tall.
Dated 1990. Santa and one of his reindeer fly off in their "Starship
Christmas S.S." to deliver a bag of toys to children in other
galaxies. **Artist:** Bob Siedler

☐ Purchased 19 __ Pd $_____ MIB   NB   DB   BNT
☐ Want   Orig. Ret. $18.00 **NB** $32   **MIB** Sec. Mkt. **$45**

QX 518-6   STITCHES OF JOY ☐
Comments: Handcrafted, 2-1/2" tall.
A blue-gowned mama rabbit is working her needlepoint sampler
with a special Christmas message: "Joy."
Artist: Julia Lee

☐ Purchased 19 __ Pd $_____ MIB   NB   DB   BNT
☐ Want   Orig. Ret. $7.75 **NB** $15   **MIB** Sec. Mkt. **$25**

QX 456-5   STOCKING KITTEN ☐
Comments: Handcrafted, 2-3/4" tall.
Reissued from 1989. **Artist:** Sharon Pike

☐ Purchased 19 __ Pd $_____ MIB   NB   DB   BNT
☐ Want   Orig. Ret. $6.75 **NB** $9   **MIB** Sec. Mkt. **$15**

QX 549-3   STOCKING PALS ☐
Comments: Handcrafted, 3-1/4" tall, Dated 1990.
A dated gift balances in the top of a knit stocking. Two koalas hold
the yarn ends to the stocking.
Artist: Ed Seale

☐ Purchased 19 __ Pd $_____ MIB   NB   DB   BNT
☐ Want   Orig. Ret. $10.75 **NB** $12   **MIB** Sec. Mkt. **$22**

QXC 447-3   SUGAR PLUM FAIRY: KEEPSAKE CLUB ☐
Comments: Limited Edition 25,400, Wood display stand.
Hand-Painted Fine Porcelain, 5-1/2" tall
This prime ballerina dances gracefully on her toes in her pearly white
tutu. She's a lovely addition to the Keepsake line. Available to
Members only. **Artist:** Patricia Andrews

☐ Purchased 19 __ Pd $_____ MIB   NB   DB   BNT
☐ Want   Orig. Ret. $27.75 **NB** $30   **MIB** Sec. Mkt. **$55**

QX 489-3   SWEETHEART ☐
Comments: Handcrafted, 3-1/8" tall, Dated 1990.
Two gifts sit next to a snowy wishing well "For Sweethearts."
The well is filled with acrylic "water." **Artist:** Dill Rhodus

☐ Purchased 19 __ Pd $_____ MIB   NB   DB   BNT
☐ Want   Orig. Ret. $11.75 **NB** $15   **MIB** Sec. Mkt. **$20**

QX 448-3   TEACHER ☐
Comments: Handcrafted, 2-3/8" tall, Dated Dec. 25, 1990.
An adorable chipmunk points to the lessons he has learned,
along with a message, "We ♥ Teacher." **Artist:** Ed Seale

☐ Purchased 19 __Pd $_____MIB   NB   DB   BNT
☐ Want   Orig. Ret. $7.75   **NB** $6   **MIB** Sec. Mkt. **$14**

QX 215-3   TEN YEARS TOGETHER ☐
Comments: White Glass Ball, 2-7/8" dia.
Dated Christmas 1990. Redbirds enjoy an early winter snowfall.
Caption: "Love Wraps The World In Wonder.   10 Years Together."
Artist: Joyce A. Lyle

☐ Purchased 19 __Pd $_____MIB   NB   DB   BNT
☐ Want   Orig. Ret. $4.75   **NB** $8   **MIB** Sec. Mkt. **$16**

QX 499-6   THREE LITTLE PIGGIES ☐
Comments: Handcrafted, 2-5/8" tall.
A red and blue five-toed stocking holds these happy chaps in
their colorful nightcaps.
Artist: Ken Crow

☐ Purchased 19 __Pd $_____MIB   NB   DB   BNT
☐ Want   Orig. Ret. $7.75   **NB** $10   **MIB** Sec. Mkt. **$20**

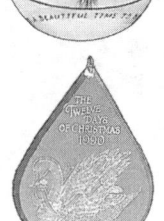

QX 213-3   TIME FOR LOVE: CARDINALS ☐
Comments: Light Gold Glass Ball, 2-7/8" dia., Dated 1990.
A pair of cardinals perch on evergreen and holly branches.
Caption: "Christmas Is A Beautiful Time To Be In Love."
Artist: Joyce A. Lyle

☐ Purchased 19 __Pd $_____MIB   NB   DB   BNT
☐ Want   Orig. Ret. $4.75   **NB** $8   **MIB** Sec. Mkt. **$20**

QX 303-3   TWELVE DAYS OF CHRISTMAS: ☐
SEVEN SWANS A-SWIMMING
Comments: **Seventh in a Series,** Acrylic, 3-3/8" tall.
Dated 1990. An etched swan swims on this acrylic teardrop, symbolic
of the gifts given on the seventh day. Captions in gold foil.

☐ Purchased 19 __Pd $_____MIB   NB   DB   BNT
☐ Want   Orig. Ret. $6.75   **NB** $12   **MIB** Sec. Mkt. **$22**

QX 489-6   TWENTY-FIVE YEARS TOGETHER ☐
Comments: Faceted Glass , 2-9/16" tall, Dated Christmas 1990.
The faceted glass heart has a silver caption: "25 Years
Together." **Artist:** Joyce Pattee

☐ Purchased 19 __Pd $_____MIB   NB   DB   BNT
☐ Want   Orig. Ret. $9.75   **NB** $10   **MIB** Sec. Mkt. **$16**

QX 492-6   TWO PEAS IN A POD ☐
Comments: Handcrafted, 3-3/4" tall.
This pea pod houses two smiling peas who are looking through
an opening in the pod. Tied with red satin ribbon.
Artist: Patricia Andrews

☐ Purchased 19 __Pd $_____MIB   NB   DB   BNT
☐ Want   Orig. Ret. $4.75   **NB** $22   **MIB** Sec. Mkt. **$35**

QX 477-3   WELCOME, SANTA ☐
Comments: Handcrafted, 2-5/8" tall.
Press the candle and Santa starts up the chimney. Caption:
"Welcome Santa" and "With A Wink And A Grin And A Big 'Ho Ho
Ho,' Santa Drops In With A Christmas Hello!" **Artist:** Ken Crow

☐ Purchased 19 __Pd $_____MIB   NB   DB   BNT
☐ Want   Orig. Ret. $11.75   **NB** $18   **MIB** Sec. Mkt. **$25**

QX 463-6   WINDOWS OF THE WORLD: IRISH ☐
Comments: **Sixth and Final in Series,** Handcrafted, 3" tall.
Dated 1990. An Irish child leans out her window to see a
leprechaun holding a gift. The caption "Nollaig Shona" means
Merry Christmas. **Artist:** Donna Lee

☐ Purchased 19 __Pd $_____MIB   NB   DB   BNT
☐ Want   Orig. Ret. $10.75   **NB** $10   **MIB** Sec. Mkt. **$22**

QX 444-3   WINTER SURPRISE ☐
Comments: **Second in Series,** Handcrafted, 3-1/4" tall.
Dated 1990. Two penguins ice skate on a frozen lake. The scene
is completed by two bottle brush trees and a glittering blue sky.
Artist: John Francis (Collin)

☐ Purchased 19 __Pd $_____MIB   NB   DB   BNT
☐ Want   Orig. Ret. $10.75   **NB** $12   **MIB** Sec. Mkt. **$22**

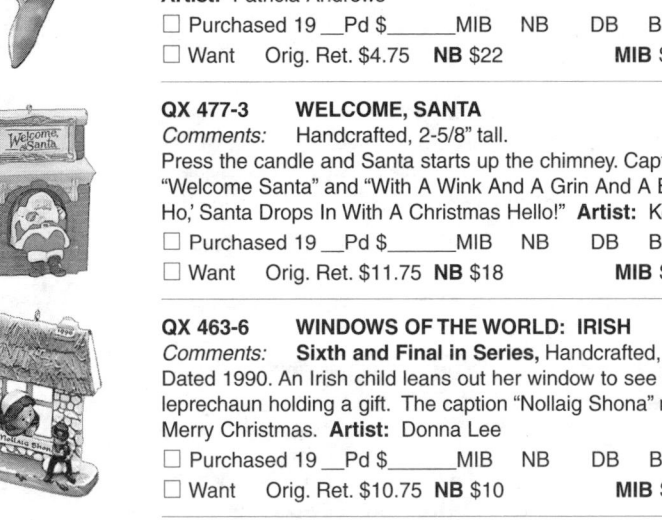

**How much would you
say this tree weighs?!
Pat Spakes must have a few hours extra
to hang all of these ornaments.**

A QXM 568-6 **ACORN WREATH**
Handcrafted, 1-1/4" tall. **Artist:** Ken Crow
☐ Purchased 19___ Pd $_____ MIB NB DB BNT
☐ Want Orig. Retail $6.00
NB $7 **MIB** Sec. Mkt. **$12**

B QXM 565-6 **AIR SANTA**
Handcrafted, 1/2" tall, Dated 1990.
☐ Purchased 19___ Pd $_____ MIB NB DB BNT
☐ Want Orig. Retail $4.50
NB $7 **MIB** Sec. Mkt. **$12.50**

C QXM 570-3 **BABY'S FIRST CHRISTMAS**
Handcrafted Cradle, 1-1/8" tall, Dated 1990. **Artist:** John Francis (Collin)
☐ Purchased 19___ Pd $_____ MIB NB DB BNT
☐ Want Orig. Retail $8.50
NB $10 **MIB** Sec. Mkt. **$17**

D QXM 569-6 **BASKET BUDDY**
Handcrafted, 1-3/16" tall. **Artist:** Anita Marra Rogers
☐ Purchased 19___ Pd $_____ MIB NB DB BNT
☐ Want Orig. Retail $6.00
NB $8 **MIB** Sec. Mkt. **$12**

E QXM 563-3 **BEAR HUG**
Handcrafted, 15/16" tall. **Artist:** Don Palmiter
☐ Purchased 19___ Pd $_____ MIB NB DB BNT
☐ Want Orig. Retail $6.00
NB $7 **MIB** Sec. Mkt. **$14**

F QXM 577-6 **BRASS BOUQUET**
Antiqued Brass Medallion, 1-1/4" tall. **Artist:** Joyce A. Lyle
☐ Purchased 19___ Pd $_____ MIB NB DB BNT
☐ Want Orig. Retail $6.00
NB $4 **MIB** Sec. Mkt. **$6.50**

G QXM 579-3 **BRASS HORN.**
Etched, Pierced Brass, 3/4" tall, Dated 1990.
☐ Purchased 19___ Pd $_____ MIB NB DB BNT
☐ Want Orig. Retail $3.00
NB $3 **MIB** Sec. Mkt. **$7**

H QXM 579-6 **BRASS PEACE**
Filigree Brass, 1-1/4" tall.
☐ Purchased 19___ Pd $_____ MIB NB DB BNT
☐ Want Orig. Retail $3.00
NB $3 **MIB** Sec. Mkt. **$7**

I QXM 578-6 **BRASS SANTA**
Etched, Pierced Brass, 1-1/4" tall, Dated 1990. **Artist:** Joyce Pattee
☐ Purchased 19___ Pd $_____ MIB NB DB BNT
☐ Want Orig. Retail $3.00
NB $3 **MIB** Sec. Mkt. **$8**

J QXM 583-3 **BRASS YEAR**
Etched Brass, 3/4" tall, Dated 1990.
☐ Purchased 19___ Pd $_____ MIB NB DB BNT
☐ Want Orig. Retail $3.00
NB $4 **MIB** Sec. Mkt. **$7.50**

K QXM 567-3 **BUSY CARVER**
Handcrafted, 3/4" tall, Dated 1990. **Artist:** Ken Crow
☐ Purchased 19___ Pd $_____ MIB NB DB BNT
☐ Want Orig. Retail $4.50
NB $5 **MIB** Sec. Mkt. **$8.50**

L QXM 563-6 **CHRISTMAS DOVE**
Handcrafted, 1-1/16" tall. **Artist:** Bob Siedler
☐ Purchased 19___ Pd $_____ MIB NB DB BNT
☐ Want Orig. Retail $4.50
NB $6 **MIB** Sec. Mkt. **$13.50**

M QXM 553-3 **CLOISONNÉ POINSETTIA**
Precious Edition, Cloisonné/Brass, 1" dia. **Artist:** LaDene Votruba
☐ Purchased 19___ Pd $_____ MIB NB DB BNT
☐ Want Orig. Retail $10.50
NB $14 **MIB** Sec. Mkt. **$17.50**

N QXM 569-3 **COUNTRY HEART**
Handcrafted, 1-3/8" tall. **Artist:** Anita Marra Rogers
☐ Purchased 19___ Pd $_____ MIB NB DB BNT
☐ Want Orig. Retail $4.50
NB $5 **MIB** Sec. Mkt. **$10**

O QXM 568-2 **ACORN SQUIRREL**
Handcrafted, 1-3/8" tall. **Artist:** Sharon Pike
Reissued from 1989.
☐ Purchased 19___ Pd $_____ MIB NB DB BNT
☐ Want Orig. Retail $4.50
NB $6 **MIB** Sec. Mkt. **$10**

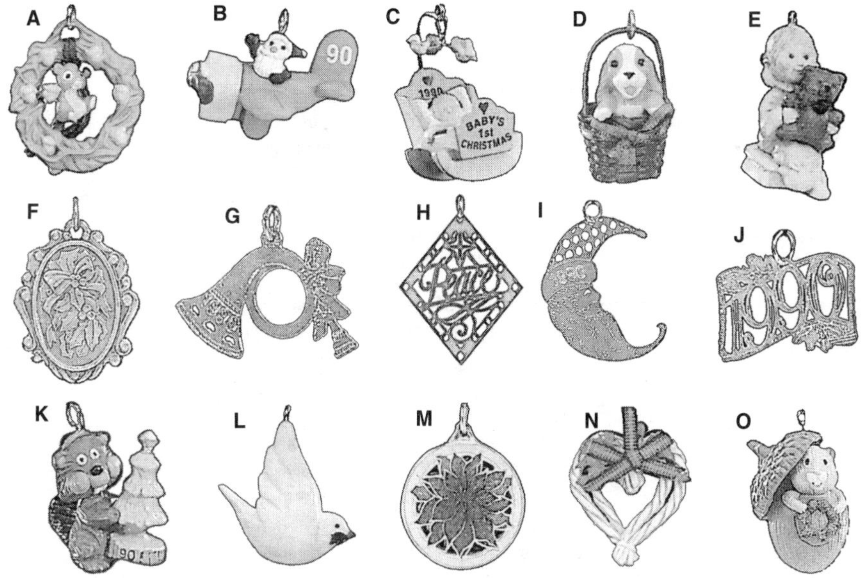

A B C D E
F G H I J
K L M N O

A QXC 560-3 **CROWN PRINCE: KEEPSAKE CLUB** ☐
Handcrafted, 1-3/8" tall, Dated 1990.
Artist: Anita Marra Rogers
☐ Purchased 19___ Pd $_____ MIB NB DB BNT
☐ Want Orig. Retail --- Gift to all Club Members
NB $20 **MIB** Sec. Mkt. **$34**

B QXM 578-3 **FESTIVE ANGEL TREE TOPPER** ☐
Glass/Brass.
☐ Purchased 19___ Pd $_____ MIB NB DB BNT
☐ Want Orig. Retail $9.75
NB $12 **MIB** Sec. Mkt. **$28**

C QXM 553-6 **FIRST CHRISTMAS TOGETHER** ☐
Hand-Painted Fine Porcelain, 1" tall, Dated 1990.
Artist: Patricia Andrews
☐ Purchased 19___ Pd $_____ MIB NB DB BNT
☐ Want Orig. Retail $6.00
NB $7 **MIB** Sec. Mkt. **$14**

D QXM 568-3 **GOING SLEDDING** ☐
Handcrafted, 13/16" tall. **Artist:** Julia Lee
☐ Purchased 19___ Pd $_____ MIB NB DB BNT
☐ Want Orig. Retail $4.50
NB $6 **MIB** Sec. Mkt. **$12.50**

E QXM 572-3 **GRANDCHILD'S FIRST CHRISTMAS** ☐
Handcrafted High Chair, 1-1/4" tall, Dated 1990.
Artist: Bob Siedler
☐ Purchased 19___ Pd $_____ MIB NB DB BNT
☐ Want Orig. Retail $6.00
NB $7 **MIB** Sec. Mkt. **$12**

F QXM 552-6 **HOLIDAY CARDINAL** ☐
Faceted, Etched Acrylic, 1-1/2" tall. **Artist:** John Francis (Collin)
☐ Purchased 19___ Pd $_____ MIB NB DB BNT
☐ Want Orig. Retail $3.00
NB $5 **MIB** Sec. Mkt. **$12**

G QXM 573-6 **KITTENS IN TOYLAND: SAILBOAT** ☐
Third in Series, Handcrafted, 13/16" tall. **Artist:** Ken Crow
☐ Purchased 19___ Pd $_____ MIB NB DB BNT
☐ Want Orig. Retail $4.50
NB $14 **MIB** Sec. Mkt. **$20**

H QXM 575-3 **KRINGLES, THE** ☐
Second in Series, Handcrafted, 1" tall. **Artist:** Anita Marra Rogers
☐ Purchased 19___ Pd $_____ MIB NB DB BNT
☐ Want Orig. Retail $6.00
NB $18 **MIB** Sec. Mkt. **$25**

I QXM 567-6 **LION & LAMB** ☐
Wood, 1-1/8" tall. **Artist:** Linda Sickman
☐ Purchased 19___ Pd $_____ MIB NB DB BNT
☐ Want Orig. Retail $4.50
NB $5 **MIB** Sec. Mkt. **$10**

J XPR 972-3 **LITTLE FROSTY FRIENDS: LITTLE BEAR** ☐
Handcrafted, 1" tall, Dated 1990.
Artist: Bob Siedler
☐ Purchased 19___ Pd $_____ MIB NB DB BNT
☐ Want Orig. Retail $2.95 w/$5 purchase.
NB $5 **MIB** Sec. Mkt. **$10**

K XPR 972-0 **LITTLE FROSTY FRIENDS: LITTLE FROSTY** ☐
Handcrafted, 1-7/16" tall, Dated 1990. **Artist:** Bob Siedler
☐ Purchased 19___ Pd $_____ MIB NB DB BNT
☐ Want Orig. Retail $2.95 w/$5 purchase.
NB $5 **MIB** Sec. Mkt. **$10**

L XPR 972-2 **LITTLE FROSTY FRIENDS: LITTLE HUSKY** ☐
Handcrafted, 1-1/8" tall, Dated 1990. **Artist:** Ed Seale
☐ Purchased 19___ Pd $_____ MIB NB DB BNT
☐ Want Orig. Retail $2.95 w/$5 purchase.
NB $4 **MIB** Sec. Mkt. **$9.50**

M QXM 567-5 **LITTLE SOLDIER** ☐
Handcrafted, 1-3/8" tall. **Artist:** Linda Sickman
Reissued from 1989.
☐ Purchased 19___ Pd $_____ MIB NB DB BNT
☐ Want Orig. Retail $4.50
NB $5 **MIB** Sec. Mkt. **$10**

N QXM 573-5 **COZY SKATER** ☐
Handcrafted, 1-3/8" tall. **Artist:** Joyce A. Lyle
Reissued from 1989.
☐ Purchased 19___ Pd $_____ MIB NB DB BNT
☐ Want Orig. Retail $4.50
NB $8 **MIB** Sec. Mkt. **$10**

A B C D E

F G H I J

K L M N

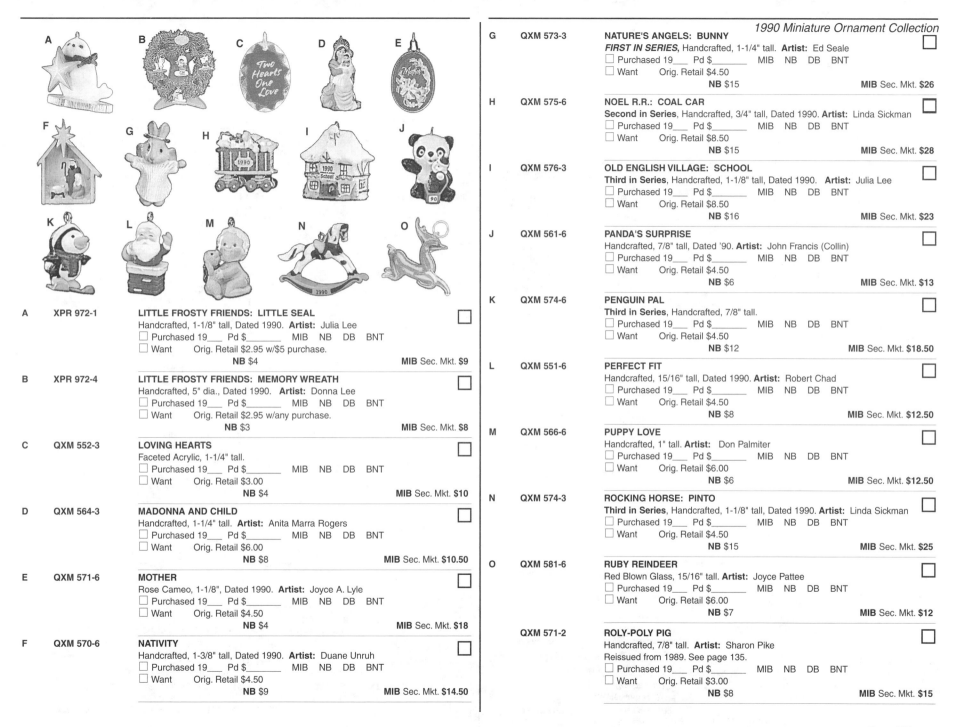

A XPR 972-1 | **LITTLE FROSTY FRIENDS: LITTLE SEAL**
Handcrafted, 1-1/8" tall, Dated 1990. **Artist:** Julia Lee
☐ Purchased 19___ Pd $_____ MIB NB DB BNT
☐ Want   Orig. Retail $2.95 w/$5 purchase.
NB $4   **MIB** Sec. Mkt. **$9**

B XPR 972-4 | **LITTLE FROSTY FRIENDS: MEMORY WREATH**
Handcrafted, 5" dia., Dated 1990. **Artist:** Donna Lee
☐ Purchased 19___ Pd $_____ MIB NB DB BNT
☐ Want   Orig. Retail $2.95 w/any purchase.
NB $3   **MIB** Sec. Mkt. **$8**

C QXM 552-3 | **LOVING HEARTS**
Faceted Acrylic, 1-1/4" tall.
☐ Purchased 19___ Pd $_____ MIB NB DB BNT
☐ Want   Orig. Retail $3.00
NB $4   **MIB** Sec. Mkt. **$10**

D QXM 564-3 | **MADONNA AND CHILD**
Handcrafted, 1-1/4" tall. **Artist:** Anita Marra Rogers
☐ Purchased 19___ Pd $_____ MIB NB DB BNT
☐ Want   Orig. Retail $6.00
NB $8   **MIB** Sec. Mkt. **$10.50**

E QXM 571-6 | **MOTHER**
Rose Cameo, 1-1/8", Dated 1990. **Artist:** Joyce A. Lyle
☐ Purchased 19___ Pd $_____ MIB NB DB BNT
☐ Want   Orig. Retail $4.50
NB $4   **MIB** Sec. Mkt. **$18**

F QXM 570-6 | **NATIVITY**
Handcrafted, 1-3/8" tall, Dated 1990. **Artist:** Duane Unruh
☐ Purchased 19___ Pd $_____ MIB NB DB BNT
☐ Want   Orig. Retail $4.50
NB $9   **MIB** Sec. Mkt. **$14.50**

G QXM 573-3 | **NATURE'S ANGELS: BUNNY**
FIRST IN SERIES, Handcrafted, 1-1/4" tall. **Artist:** Ed Seale
☐ Purchased 19___ Pd $_____ MIB NB DB BNT
☐ Want   Orig. Retail $4.50
NB $15   **MIB** Sec. Mkt. **$26**

H QXM 575-6 | **NOEL R.R.: COAL CAR**
Second in Series, Handcrafted, 3/4" tall, Dated 1990. **Artist:** Linda Sickman
☐ Purchased 19___ Pd $_____ MIB NB DB BNT
☐ Want   Orig. Retail $8.50
NB $15   **MIB** Sec. Mkt. **$28**

I QXM 576-3 | **OLD ENGLISH VILLAGE: SCHOOL**
Third in Series, Handcrafted, 1-1/8" tall, Dated 1990. **Artist:** Julia Lee
☐ Purchased 19___ Pd $_____ MIB NB DB BNT
☐ Want   Orig. Retail $8.50
NB $16   **MIB** Sec. Mkt. **$23**

J QXM 561-6 | **PANDA'S SURPRISE**
Handcrafted, 7/8" tall, Dated '90. **Artist:** John Francis (Collin)
☐ Purchased 19___ Pd $_____ MIB NB DB BNT
☐ Want   Orig. Retail $4.50
NB $6   **MIB** Sec. Mkt. **$13**

K QXM 574-6 | **PENGUIN PAL**
Third in Series, Handcrafted, 7/8" tall.
☐ Purchased 19___ Pd $_____ MIB NB DB BNT
☐ Want   Orig. Retail $4.50
NB $12   **MIB** Sec. Mkt. **$18.50**

L QXM 551-6 | **PERFECT FIT**
Handcrafted, 15/16" tall, Dated 1990. **Artist:** Robert Chad
☐ Purchased 19___ Pd $_____ MIB NB DB BNT
☐ Want   Orig. Retail $4.50
NB $8   **MIB** Sec. Mkt. **$12.50**

M QXM 566-6 | **PUPPY LOVE**
Handcrafted, 1" tall. **Artist:** Don Palmiter
☐ Purchased 19___ Pd $_____ MIB NB DB BNT
☐ Want   Orig. Retail $6.00
NB $6   **MIB** Sec. Mkt. **$12.50**

N QXM 574-3 | **ROCKING HORSE: PINTO**
Third in Series, Handcrafted, 1-1/8" tall, Dated 1990. **Artist:** Linda Sickman
☐ Purchased 19___ Pd $_____ MIB NB DB BNT
☐ Want   Orig. Retail $4.50
NB $15   **MIB** Sec. Mkt. **$25**

O QXM 581-6 | **RUBY REINDEER**
Red Blown Glass, 15/16" tall. **Artist:** Joyce Pattee
☐ Purchased 19___ Pd $_____ MIB NB DB BNT
☐ Want   Orig. Retail $6.00
NB $7   **MIB** Sec. Mkt. **$12**

QXM 571-2 | **ROLY-POLY PIG**
Handcrafted, 7/8" tall. **Artist:** Sharon Pike
Reissued from 1989. See page 135.
☐ Purchased 19___ Pd $_____ MIB NB DB BNT
☐ Want   Orig. Retail $3.00
NB $8   **MIB** Sec. Mkt. **$15**

A QXM 582-6   **SANTA'S JOURNEY** ☐
Handcrafted/Brass, 1" tall, Dated 1990. **Artist:** Linda Sickman
☐ Purchased 19___ Pd $_____ MIB NB DB BNT
☐ Want   Orig. Retail $8.50
       NB $10   **MIB** Sec. Mkt. **$16.50**

B QXM 576-6   **SANTA'S STREETCAR** ☐
Handcrafted, 1-1/4" wide, Dated 1990. **Artist:** Donna Lee
☐ Purchased 19___ Pd $_____ MIB NB DB BNT
☐ Want   Orig. Retail $8.50
       NB $10   **MIB** Sec. Mkt. **$15**

C QXM 577-3   **SNOW ANGEL** ☐
Handcrafted, 1-1/8" tall. **Artist:** Julia Lee
☐ Purchased 19___ Pd $_____ MIB NB DB BNT
☐ Want   Orig. Retail $6.00
       NB $8   **MIB** Sec. Mkt. **$12**

D QXM 572-6   **SPECIAL FRIENDS** ☐
Handcrafted, 15/16" tall. **Artist:** Sharon Pike
☐ Purchased 19___ Pd $_____ MIB NB DB BNT
☐ Want   Orig. Retail $6.00
       NB $8   **MIB** Sec. Mkt. **$13**

E QXM 562-3   **STAMP COLLECTOR** ☐
Handcrafted, 7/8" tall. Dated Christmas 1990. **Artist:** Ken Crow
☐ Purchased 19___ Pd $_____ MIB NB DB BNT
☐ Want   Orig. Retail $4.50
       NB $5   **MIB** Sec. Mkt. **$9**

F QXM 560-6   **STRINGING ALONG** ☐
Handcrafted, 1-1/8" tall. **Artist:** Ed Seale
☐ Purchased 19___ Pd $_____ MIB NB DB BNT
☐ Want   Orig. Retail $8.50
       NB $10   **MIB** Sec. Mkt. **$14**

G QXM 566-3   **SWEET SLUMBER** ☐
Handcrafted, 9/16" tall. **Artist:** Bob Siedler
☐ Purchased 19___ Pd $_____ MIB NB DB BNT
☐ Want   Orig. Retail $4.50
       NB $5   **MIB** Sec. Mkt. **$8.50**

H QXM 565-3   **TEACHER** ☐
Handcrafted owl/pencil, 7/8" tall, Dated 1990. **Artist:** Sharon Pike
☐ Purchased 19___ Pd $_____ MIB NB DB BNT
☐ Want   Orig. Retail $4.50
       NB $4   **MIB** Sec. Mkt. **$8**

I QXM 554-3   **THIMBLE BELLS** ☐
FIRST IN SERIES, Fine Porcelain, 1-1/8" tall, Dated 1990.
Artist: Michele Pyda-Sevcik
☐ Purchased 19___ Pd $_____ MIB NB DB BNT
☐ Want   Orig. Retail $6.00
       NB $10   **MIB** Sec. Mkt. **$21**

J QXM 564-6   **TYPE OF JOY** ☐
Handcrafted, 11/16" tall. **Artist:** Robert Chad
☐ Purchased 19___ Pd $_____ MIB NB DB BNT
☐ Want   Orig. Retail $4.50
       NB $5   **MIB** Sec. Mkt. **$9.50**

K QXM 571-3   **WARM MEMORIES** ☐
Handcrafted, 1-1/8" tall, Dated 1990. **Artist:** Ed Seale
☐ Purchased 19___ Pd $_____ MIB NB DB BNT
☐ Want   Orig. Retail $4.50
       NB $7.50   **MIB** Sec. Mkt. **$10.50**

L QXM 584-3   **WEE NUTCRACKER** ☐
Handcrafted, 1-1/4" tall, Dated 1990. **Artist:** Bob Siedler
☐ Purchased 19___ Pd $_____ MIB NB DB BNT
☐ Want   Orig. Retail $8.50
       NB $10   **MIB** Sec. Mkt. **$15**

M QXM 567-2   **STOCKING PAL** ☐
Handcrafted, 1" tall. **Artist:** Julia Lee
Reissued from 1989.
☐ Purchased 19___ Pd $_____ MIB NB DB BNT
☐ Want   Orig. Retail $4.50
       NB $5   **MIB** Sec. Mkt. **$8.50**

N QXM 566-2   **HAPPY BLUEBIRD** ☐
Handcrafted, 7/8" tall. **Artist:** Anita Marra Rogers
Reissued from 1989.
☐ Purchased 19___ Pd $_____ MIB NB DB BNT
☐ Want   Orig. Retail $4.50
       NB $8   **MIB** Sec. Mkt. **$12.50**

O QXM 569-5   **OLD WORLD SANTA** ☐
Handcrafted, 1-3/8" tall. **Artist:** Bob Siedler
Reissued from 1989.
☐ Purchased 19___ Pd $_____ MIB NB DB BNT
☐ Want   Orig. Retail $3.00
       NB $3   **MIB** Sec. Mkt. **$8.50**

1991 Collection

QX 488-7   A CHILD'S CHRISTMAS

Comments: Handcrafted, 2-3/8" tall, Dated 1991.
A wide-eyed child in a red sleeper with his old-fashioned wood-style blocks is seated on a braided rug captioned "A Child's Christmas." **Artist:** John Francis (Collin)

☐ Purchased 19__Pd $_____MIB   NB   DB   BNT
☐ Want   Orig. Ret. $9.75   **NB** $10   **MIB** Sec. Mkt. **$16**

QX 499-7   A CHRISTMAS CAROL COLLECTION: BOB CRATCHIT

Comments: Hand-Painted Fine Porcelain, 3-15/16" tall.
Caption: "Bob Cratchit 1991." Holding a Ledger and quill pen, Bob Cratchit wears the dress of a Victorian bookkeeper. **Artist:** Duane Unruh

☐ Purchased 19__Pd $_____MIB   NB   DB   BNT
☐ Want   Orig. Ret. $13.75   **NB** $16   **MIB** Sec. Mkt. **$30**

QX 498-9   A CHRISTMAS CAROL COLLECTION: EBENEZER SCROOGE

Comments: Hand-Painted Fine Porcelain, 4-1/16" tall.
Caption: "Ebenezer Scrooge 1991." A content, smiling Scrooge has found the real source of happiness in giving to others. **Artist:** Duane Unruh

☐ Purchased 19__Pd $_____MIB   NB   DB   BNT
☐ Want   Orig. Ret. $13.75   **NB** $15   **MIB** Sec. Mkt. **$42**

QX 479-9   A CHRISTMAS CAROL COLLECTION: MERRY CAROLERS

Comments: Hand-Painted Fine Porcelain, 4-1/8" tall.
Caption: "Merry Carolers 1991." A man and woman sing the story of Christmas. Caption on pages: "Joy To The World! The Lord Is Come." Prices down from last year. **Artist:** Duane Unruh

☐ Purchased 19__Pd $_____MIB   NB   DB   BNT
☐ Want   Orig. Ret. $29.75   **NB** $28   **MIB** Sec. Mkt. **$45**

QX 499-9   A CHRISTMAS CAROL COLLECTION: MRS. CRATCHIT

Comments: Hand-Painted Fine Porcelain, 3-7/8" tall.
Caption: "Mrs. Cratchit 1991." In a ruffled dress, Mrs. Cratchit serves a Christmas turkey provided by a generous Scrooge. **Artist:** Duane Unruh

☐ Purchased 19__Pd $_____MIB   NB   DB   BNT
☐ Want   Orig. Ret. $13.75   **NB** $14   MIB Sec. Mkt. **$30**

QX 503-7   A CHRISTMAS CAROL COLLECTION: TINY TIM ☐

Comments: Hand-Painted Fine Porcelain, 2-1/8" tall.
Caption: "Tiny Tim 1991." The child sits on a wooden bench with his crutches nearby. **Artist:** Duane Unruh

☐ Purchased 19__Pd $_____MIB   NB   DB   BNT
☐ Want   Orig. Ret. $10.75   **NB** $15   **MIB** Sec. Mkt. **$38**

QX 315-7   ACROSS THE MILES ☐

Comments: Acrylic, 2-5/8" tall, Dated 1991.
Sparkling acrylic, framed in brass, is etched with holly leaves and ribbons. "There's No Such Thing As Far Away When Christmas Draws Us Close." **Artist:** Joyce Lyle

☐ Purchased 19__Pd $_____MIB   NB   DB   BNT
☐ Want   Orig. Ret. $6.75   **NB** $8   **MIB** Sec. Mkt. **$14**

QX 532-9   ALL STAR ☐

Comments: Handcrafted, 2-1/8" tall, Dated 1991.
This two-toned turtle is "All Star 91" as shown by his umpire's cap and his catcher's mitt. **Artist:** Bob Siedler

☐ Purchased 19__Pd $_____MIB   NB   DB   BNT
☐ Want   Orig. Ret. $6.75   **NB** $14   **MIB** Sec. Mkt. **$22**

QLX 711-7   ARCTIC DOME ☐

Comments: Light and Motion, Handcrafted, 2-15/16" tall.
Dated 1991. Santa and his North Stars reindeer are playing the polar bear South Paws. The lines move back and forth across the field and Santa spins away from the defenders.
Artist: Ken Crow

☐ Purchased 19__Pd $_____MIB   NB   DB   BNT
☐ Want   Orig. Ret. $25.00   **NB** $40   **MIB** Sec. Mkt. **$55**

QX 510-7   BABY'S FIRST CHRISTMAS ☐

Comments: Silver-Plated, 2-5/8" tall, Dated 1991.
An intricately sculpted bear peeks out of the top of a baby bootie. A silver tag detaches for engraving and personalization.
Artist: John Francis (Collin)

☐ Purchased 19__Pd $_____MIB   NB   DB   BNT
☐ Want   Orig. Ret. $17.75   **NB** $15   **MIB** Sec. Mkt. **$28**

QLX 724-7   BABY'S FIRST CHRISTMAS ☐

Comments: Lighted, Handcrafted, 4-1/2" tall, Dated 1991.
Santa takes time from his busy schedule. Plays Rock-A-Bye-Baby. Caption: "Baby's First Christmas" and "Rock-A-Bye-Baby." **Artist:** Ed Seale

☐ Purchased 19__Pd $_____MIB   NB   DB   BNT
☐ Want   Orig. Ret. $30.00   **NB** $45   **MIB** Sec. Mkt. **$80**

QX 488-9   BABY'S FIRST CHRISTMAS
Comments: Handcrafted, 2-1/2" tall, Dated 1991.
This adorable teddy hugs his big candy cane "1." His flocked cap
says "Baby's First Christmas." **Artist:** John Francis (Collin)
☐ Purchased 19__Pd $_____MIB   NB   DB   BNT
☐ Want   Orig. Ret. $7.75   **NB** $24   **MIB** Sec. Mkt. **$32**

QX 221-7   BABY'S FIRST CHRISTMAS: BABY BOY
Comments: Blue Satin Ball, 2-7/8" dia., Dated 1991.
Caption: "A Baby Boy's World... Soft With Lullabies, Sweet
With Hugs, Bright With Wonder, Warm With Love. Baby's
First Christmas." **Artist:** Mary Hamilton
☐ Purchased 19__Pd $_____MIB   NB   DB   BNT
☐ Want   Orig. Ret. $4.75   **NB** $16   **MIB** Sec. Mkt. **$20**

QX 222-7   BABY'S FIRST CHRISTMAS: BABY GIRL
Comments: Pink Satin Ball, 2-7/8" dia., Dated 1991.
Caption: "A Baby Girl's World... Soft With Lullabies, Sweet
With Hugs, Bright With Wonder, Warm With Love. Baby's
First Christmas." **Artist:** Mary Hamilton
☐ Purchased 19__Pd $_____MIB   NB   DB   BNT
☐ Want   Orig. Ret. $4.75   **NB** $10   **MIB** Sec. Mkt. **$20**

QX 486-9   BABY'S FIRST CHRISTMAS PHOTOHOLDER
Comments: Fabric, 4-3/8" dia., Dated 1991.
Embroidered teddy bears and holly frame baby's photo. Caption:
"Baby's First Christmas" and "The Cutest Grins, The Brightest
Eyes, Always Come In Baby Size." **Artist:** LaDene Votruba
☐ Purchased 19__Pd $_____MIB   NB   DB   BNT
☐ Want   Orig. Ret. $7.75   **NB** $14   **MIB** Sec. Mkt. **$23**

QX 489-7   BABY'S SECOND CHRISTMAS
Comments: Handcrafted, 2-3/16" tall, Dated 1991.
Identical to 1989; only date has changed.
Artist: John Francis (Collin)
☐ Purchased 19__Pd $_____MIB   NB   DB   BNT
☐ Want   Orig. Ret. $6.75   **NB** $24   **MIB** Sec. Mkt. **$32**

QX 537-7   BASKET BELL PLAYERS
Comments: Handcrafted and Wicker, 2" tall, Dated 1991.
Two adorable kittens are having fun playing with the shiny brass
bell tied to the handle of their basket. **Artist:** Ed Seale
☐ Purchased 19__Pd $_____MIB   NB   DB   BNT
☐ Want   Orig. Ret. $7.75   **NB** $12   **MIB** Sec. Mkt. **$20**

QXC 725-9   BEARY ARTISTIC: KEEPSAKE CLUB
Comments: Lighted, Handcrafted and Acrylic, 2-1/2" tall.
This little bear is carving the word "JOY" from a chunk of "ice."
The "O" contains the logo for the Keepsake Ornament Club.
Club Members only. **Artist:** Bob Siedler
☐ Purchased 19__Pd $_____MIB   NB   DB   BNT
☐ Want   Orig. Ret. $10.00 **NB** $28   **MIB** Sec. Mkt. **$38**

QX 210-9   BETSEY CLARK: HOME FOR CHRISTMAS
Comments: **Sixth and Final in Series,** Dated 1991.
Light Blue Glass Ball, 2-7/8" dia. Betsey and her friends love the snow!
Caption: "Getting Favorite Friends Together Is Extra Fun In Frosty
Weather!" The box notes a new series will begin in 1992.
☐ Purchased 19__Pd $_____MIB   NB   DB   BNT
☐ Want   Orig. Ret. $5.00 **NB** $10   **MIB** Sec. Mkt. **$20**

QX 532-7   BIG CHEESE, THE
Comments: Handcrafted, 1-7/8" tall.
Dated Merry Christmas 1991. "The Big Cheese" has stuffed
himself with Swiss cheese and has curled up in the hole he has
nibbled. **Artist:** Bob Siedler
☐ Purchased 19__Pd $_____MIB   NB   DB   BNT
☐ Want   Orig. Ret. $6.75 **NB** $10   **MIB** Sec. Mkt. **$16**

QLX 724-9   BRINGING HOME THE TREE
Comments: Light and Motion, Handcrafted, 4-3/8" tall.
Dated 1991. A man and child emerge from the forest with their
tree. The door to the home swings open and they go inside, their
dog following closely behind. Caption: "Merry Christmas."
Artist: Duane Unruh
☐ Purchased 19__Pd $_____MIB   NB   DB   BNT
☐ Want   Orig. Ret. $28.00 **NB** $45   **MIB** Sec. Mkt. **$60**

QX 547-9   BROTHER
Comments: Handcrafted, 2-3/4" tall, Dated 1991.
Designed especially for a "Superstar Brother" is a puppy hanging
onto the rim of the basketball hoop. **Artist:** Bob Siedler
☐ Purchased 19__Pd $_____MIB   NB   DB   BNT
☐ Want   Orig. Ret. $6.75 **NB** $8   **MIB** Sec. Mkt. **$15**

QX 490-9   CHILD'S FIFTH CHRISTMAS
Comments: Handcrafted, 2-3/8" tall, Dated 1991.
Identical to 1989; only date has changed.
Artist: Dill Rhodus
☐ Purchased 19__Pd $_____MIB   NB   DB   BNT
☐ Want   Orig. Ret. $6.75 **NB** $12   **MIB** Sec. Mkt. **$18**

QX 490-7 CHILD'S FOURTH CHRISTMAS ☐
Comments: Handcrafted, 3" tall, Dated 1991.
Identical to 1989; only date has changed.
Artist: John Francis (Collin)
☐ Purchased 19__Pd $_____MIB   NB   DB   BNT
☐ Want   Orig. Ret. $6.75 **NB** $12   **MIB** Sec. Mkt. **$18**

QX 489-9 CHILD'S THIRD CHRISTMAS ☐
Comments: Handcrafted, 2-1/2" tall, Dated 1991.
Identical to 1989; only date has changed.
Artist: John Francis (Collin)
☐ Purchased 19__Pd $_____MIB   NB   DB   BNT
☐ Want   Orig. Ret. $6.75 **NB** $16   **MIB** Sec. Mkt. **$25**

QX 533-9 CHILLY CHAP ☐
Comments: Handcrafted, 3-3/4" tall, Dated 1991.
This double-dip ice cream cone snowman is adorable in pearly
colors. He wears a sparkly hat decorated with a dated holly leaf.
Artist: Donna Lee
☐ Purchased 19__Pd $_____MIB   NB   DB   BNT
☐ Want   Orig. Ret. $6.75 **NB** $10   **MIB** Sec. Mkt. **$18**

QLX 720-7 CHRIS MOUSE MAIL ☐
Comments: **Seventh in Series,** Lighted, Handcrafted, 3" tall.
Dated 1991. Chris has made a comfy home inside a red mail box.
His "Welcome" mat is out and he reads a message "JOY" with a
flashlight. **Artist:** Bob Siedler
☐ Purchased 19__Pd $_____MIB   NB   DB   BNT
☐ Want   Orig. Ret. $10.00 **NB** $20   **MIB** Sec. Mkt. **$35**

QX 437-7 CHRISTMAS KITTY ☐
Comments: **Third and Final in Series,** Fine Porcelain, 3-1/16" tall.
Wearing a ruffled gown and carrying two red and white candy canes is
this pretty hand-painted kitten. This series is not in demand.
Artist: Anita Marra Rogers
☐ Purchased 19__Pd $_____MIB   NB   DB   BNT
☐ Want   Orig. Ret. $14.75 **NB** $10   **MIB** Sec. Mkt. **$32**

QX 529-9 CHRISTMAS WELCOME ☐
Comments: Handcrafted, 3-3/8" tall, Dated 1991.
This basket of fruit, sitting inside a ring wrapped with red "ribbon"
is reminiscent of the nostalgia ornaments from 1975.
Artist: Linda Sickman
☐ Purchased 19__Pd $_____MIB   NB   DB   BNT
☐ Want   Orig. Ret. $9.75 **NB** $10   **MIB** Sec. Mkt. **$20**

QX 431-9 CLASSIC AMERICAN CARS: 1957 CORVETTE ☐
Comments: ***FIRST IN SERIES,*** Handcrafted, 1-5/16" tall.
Dated 1991. Very popular. Some are found with green Christmas
tree, some with brown. No difference in value between the two.
Artist: Don Palmiter
☐ Purchased 19__Pd $_____MIB   NB   DB   BNT
☐ Want   Orig. Ret. $12.75 **NB** $150   **MIB** Sec. Mkt. **$175-$195**

XPR 973-3 CLAUS & CO. R.R. ORNAMENTS: CABOOSE ☐
Comments: Handcrafted, Dated 1991.
Santa waves happily to one and all as the train passes through.
Artist: Don Palmiter
☐ Purchased 19__Pd $_____MIB   NB   DB   BNT
☐ Want   Orig. Ret. $3.95 w/$5 Hallmark purchase.
                    NB $5   **MIB** Sec. Mkt. **$15**

XPR 973-1 CLAUS & CO. R.R. ORNAMENTS: GIFT CAR ☐
Comments: Handcrafted, Dated 1991. **Artist:** Don Palmiter
This coal car carries an overflowing load of brightly wrapped gifts.
☐ Purchased 19__Pd $_____MIB   NB   DB   BNT
☐ Want   Orig. Ret. $3.95 w/$5 Hallmark purchase.
                    NB $5   **MIB** Sec. Mkt. **$15**

**XPR 973-0 CLAUS & CO. R.R. ORNAMENTS:
LOCOMOTIVE** ☐
Comments: Handcrafted, Dated 1991. **Artist:** Don Palmiter
☐ Purchased 19__Pd $_____MIB   NB   DB   BNT
☐ Want   Orig. Ret. $3.95 w/$5 Hallmark purchase.
                    NB $8   **MIB** Sec. Mkt. **$33**

**XPR 973-2 CLAUS & CO. R.R. ORNAMENTS:
PASSENGER CAR** ☐
Comments: Handcrafted, Dated 1991. **Artist:** Don Palmiter
☐ Purchased 19__Pd $_____MIB   NB   DB   BNT
☐ Want   Orig. Ret. $3.95 w/$5 Hallmark purchase.
                    NB $5   **MIB** Sec. Mkt. **$15**

**XPR 973-4 CLAUS & CO. R.R. ORNAMENTS:
TRESTLE** ☐
Comments: Handcrafted, Dated 1991. **Artist:** Don Palmiter
Holds four ornament cars in the series. Train cars not included.
☐ Purchased 19__Pd $_____MIB   NB   DB   BNT
☐ Want   Orig. Ret. $2.95 w/any Hallmark purchase
                    NB $5   **MIB** Sec. Mkt. **$12**

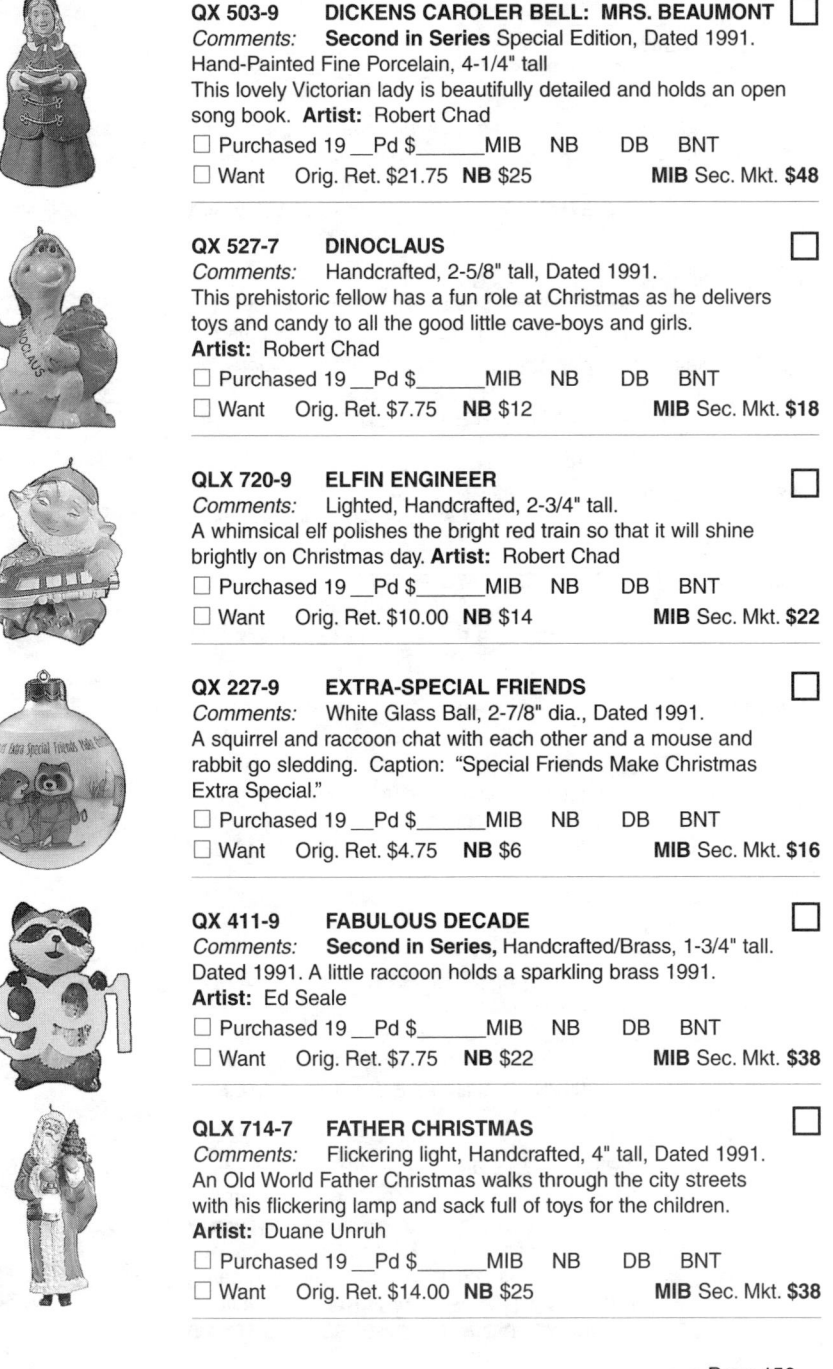

QX 436-9   COLLECTOR'S PLATE: LET IT SNOW ☐
Comments: **Fifth in Series,** Fine Porcelain, 3-1/4" dia.
Dated 1991. Two children and their dog have fun on a snowy
day building a snowman. **Artist:** LaDene Votruba
☐ Purchased 19 __Pd $_____MIB   NB   DB   BNT
☐ Want   Orig. Ret. $8.75 **NB** $16   **MIB** Sec. Mkt. **$25**

QX 421-9   CRAYOLA® CRAYON: ☐
BRIGHT VIBRANT CAROLS
Comments: **Third in Series,** Handcrafted, 3-1/4" tall.
Dated 1991. A red teddy bear is seated at a pipe organ created
from an open box of crayons. The sheet music is titled "Bright
Vibrant Carols" and the words... "Jingle Bears! Jingle Bears!"
Artist: Ken Crow
☐ Purchased 19 __Pd $_____MIB   NB   DB   BNT
☐ Want   Orig. Ret. $9.75 **NB** $20   **MIB** Sec. Mkt. **$35**

QX 519-9   CUDDLY LAMB ☐
Comments: Handcrafted, 1-7/8" tall.
Detailed texturing and white flocking give this lamb the look and
feel of wool. **Artist:** Anita Marra Rogers
☐ Purchased 19 __Pd $_____MIB   NB   DB   BNT
☐ Want   Orig. Ret. $6.75 **NB** $8   **MIB** Sec. Mkt. **$14**

QX 512-7   DAD ☐
Comments: Handcrafted, 2-1/4" tall, Dated Dad 1991.
A white polar bear dad, with wrench in hand, reads his "Easy To
Assemble!" Instruction Sheet, but the directions appear to be
complex. **Artist:** Julia Lee
☐ Purchased 19 __Pd $_____MIB   NB   DB   BNT
☐ Want   Orig. Ret. $7.75 **NB** $10   **MIB** Sec. Mkt. **$17**

QX 487-9   DAD-TO-BE ☐
Comments: Handcrafted, 2-3/8" tall, Dated Christmas 1991.
This kangaroo papa-to-be proudly announces the fact on his
shirt. **Artist:** Julia Lee
☐ Purchased 19 __Pd $_____MIB   NB   DB   BNT
☐ Want   Orig. Ret. $5.75 **NB** $8   **MIB** Sec. Mkt. **$16**

QX 547-7   DAUGHTER ☐
Comments: Handcrafted, 3-1/16" tall, Dated Daughter 1991.
A little white mouse with a red hair bow snuggles peacefully in a
pink slipper. **Artist:** Bob Siedler
☐ Purchased 19 __Pd $_____MIB   NB   DB   BNT
☐ Want   Orig. Ret. $5.75 **NB** $12   **MIB** Sec. Mkt. **$20**

QX 503-9   DICKENS CAROLER BELL: MRS. BEAUMONT ☐
Comments: **Second in Series** Special Edition, Dated 1991.
Hand-Painted Fine Porcelain, 4-1/4" tall
This lovely Victorian lady is beautifully detailed and holds an open
song book. **Artist:** Robert Chad
☐ Purchased 19 __Pd $_____MIB   NB   DB   BNT
☐ Want   Orig. Ret. $21.75 **NB** $25   **MIB** Sec. Mkt. **$48**

QX 527-7   DINOCLAUS ☐
Comments: Handcrafted, 2-5/8" tall, Dated 1991.
This prehistoric fellow has a fun role at Christmas as he delivers
toys and candy to all the good little cave-boys and girls.
Artist: Robert Chad
☐ Purchased 19 __Pd $_____MIB   NB   DB   BNT
☐ Want   Orig. Ret. $7.75 **NB** $12   **MIB** Sec. Mkt. **$18**

QLX 720-9   ELFIN ENGINEER ☐
Comments: Lighted, Handcrafted, 2-3/4" tall.
A whimsical elf polishes the bright red train so that it will shine
brightly on Christmas day. **Artist:** Robert Chad
☐ Purchased 19 __Pd $_____MIB   NB   DB   BNT
☐ Want   Orig. Ret. $10.00 **NB** $14   **MIB** Sec. Mkt. **$22**

QX 227-9   EXTRA-SPECIAL FRIENDS ☐
Comments: White Glass Ball, 2-7/8" dia., Dated 1991.
A squirrel and raccoon chat with each other and a mouse and
rabbit go sledding. Caption: "Special Friends Make Christmas
Extra Special."
☐ Purchased 19 __Pd $_____MIB   NB   DB   BNT
☐ Want   Orig. Ret. $4.75 **NB** $6   **MIB** Sec. Mkt. **$16**

QX 411-9   FABULOUS DECADE ☐
Comments: **Second in Series,** Handcrafted/Brass, 1-3/4" tall.
Dated 1991. A little raccoon holds a sparkling brass 1991.
Artist: Ed Seale
☐ Purchased 19 __Pd $_____MIB   NB   DB   BNT
☐ Want   Orig. Ret. $7.75 **NB** $22   **MIB** Sec. Mkt. **$38**

QLX 714-7   FATHER CHRISTMAS ☐
Comments: Flickering light, Handcrafted, 4" tall, Dated 1991.
An Old World Father Christmas walks through the city streets
with his flickering lamp and sack full of toys for the children.
Artist: Duane Unruh
☐ Purchased 19 __Pd $_____MIB   NB   DB   BNT
☐ Want   Orig. Ret. $14.00 **NB** $25   **MIB** Sec. Mkt. **$38**

QX 527-9   FELIZ NAVIDAD

Comments: Handcrafted, 2" tall, Dated Feliz Navidad 1991.
Santa's taking his afternoon siesta south of the border. He's
added a sombrero and a colorful fabric serape to his traditional
costume. **Artist:** Julia Lee

☐ Purchased 19___ Pd $_____ MIB   NB   DB   BNT
☐ Want   Orig. Ret. $6.75   **NB** $15   **MIB** Sec. Mkt. **$23**

QLX 717-9   FESTIVE BRASS CHURCH

Comments: Lighted, Dimensional Brass, 3-1/8" tall.
Light sparkles and shines from this intricately etched brass
church. All the windows are trimmed with wreaths to celebrate
the holidays. **Artist:** Diana McGehee

☐ Purchased 19___ Pd $_____ MIB   NB   DB   BNT
☐ Want   Orig. Ret. $14.00 **NB** $16   **MIB** Sec. Mkt. **$30**

QX 438-7   FIDDLIN' AROUND

Comments: Handcrafted, 2-7/8" tall.
This little fellow is multi-talented... He does a little dance while
playing his fiddle.   **Artist:** LaDene Votruba

☐ Purchased 19___ Pd $_____ MIB   NB   DB   BNT
☐ Want   Orig. Ret. $7.75   **NB** $10   **MIB** Sec. Mkt. **$18**

QX 494-7   FIFTY YEARS TOGETHER PHOTOHOLDER

Comments: Handcrafted and Brass, 3-1/4" dia., Dated 1991.
"50 Years Together" is framed with pearly white roses. Caption:
"Golden Christmas Memories.. Golden Years Of Love."
Artist: LaDene Votruba

☐ Purchased 19___ Pd $_____ MIB   NB   DB   BNT
☐ Want   Orig. Ret. $8.75   **NB** $10   **MIB** Sec. Mkt. **$18**

QX 491-9   FIRST CHRISTMAS TOGETHER

Comments: Handcrafted, 3-1/8" tall, Dated 1991.
A twirl-about couple dances inside the center of their heart-
shaped vine wreath. Caption: "Our First Christmas Together."
Artist: Linda Sickman

☐ Purchased 19___ Pd $_____ MIB   NB   DB   BNT
☐ Want   Orig. Ret. $8.75   **NB** $12   **MIB** Sec. Mkt. **$23**

QX 313-9   FIRST CHRISTMAS TOGETHER

Comments: Acrylic, 3-3/16" tall, Dated 1991.
A heart-shaped frosted acrylic wreath shows two sculpted doves
and the caption in gold foil: "Our First Christmas Together."
Artist: Sharon Pike

☐ Purchased 19___ Pd $_____ MIB   NB   DB   BNT
☐ Want   Orig. Ret. $6.75   **NB** $10   **MIB** Sec. Mkt. **$24**

QX 222-9   FIRST CHRISTMAS TOGETHER

Comments: White Glass Ball, 2-7/8" dia., Dated 1991.
A romantic Victorian couple is ice skating. Caption: "Our First
Christmas Together" and "Christmas Is For Sharing With The
Special One You Love."

☐ Purchased 19___ Pd $_____ MIB   NB   DB   BNT
☐ Want   Orig. Ret. $4.75   **NB** $6   **MIB** Sec. Mkt. **$16**

QLX 713-7   FIRST CHRISTMAS TOGETHER

Comments: Light and Motion, Handcrafted, 4-1/8" tall.
Dated 1991. A large red heart proclaims "Our First Christmas
Together" as a loving teddy bear couple snuggle in a swan-shaped
car at the "Tunnel of Love." **Artist:** Linda Sickman

☐ Purchased 19___ Pd $_____ MIB   NB   DB   BNT
☐ Want   Orig. Ret. $25.00 **NB** $35   **MIB** Sec. Mkt. **$55**

QX 491-7   FIRST CHRISTMAS TOGETHER PHOTOHOLDER

Comments: Handcrafted and Brass, 3-1/4" dia., Dated 1991.
"1st Christmas Together" written on a banner is carried by two
ivory doves. Caption: "Of Life's Many Treasures, The Most
Beautiful Is Love." **Artist:** LaDene Votruba

☐ Purchased 19___ Pd $_____ MIB   NB   DB   BNT
☐ Want   Orig. Ret. $8.75   **NB** $8   **MIB** Sec. Mkt. **$25**

QX 492-7   FIVE YEARS TOGETHER

Comments: Faceted Glass, 2-9/16" tall, Dated 1991.
Caption in red foil.

☐ Purchased 19___ Pd $_____ MIB   NB   DB   BNT
☐ Want   Orig. Ret. $7.75   **NB** $8   **MIB** Sec. Mkt. **$20**

QXC 315-9   FIVE YEARS TOGETHER: KEEPSAKE CLUB CHARTER MEMBER

Comments: Acrylic, 3" tall, Dated 1991.
A red quatrefoil with gold lettering has the Keepsake Ornament
Club logo and "Charter Member, Five Years Together."

☐ Purchased 19___ Pd $_____ MIB   NB   DB   BNT
☐ Want   Price: Free Gift to Charter Members
                    NB $25   **MIB** Sec. Mkt. **$45**

QX 535-9   FOLK ART REINDEER

Comments: Hand Painted Wood and Brass, 2-5/16" tall.
Dated 1991. This hand-carved, hand-painted reindeer is
wearing a collar with the date in brass. No two ornaments will be
exactly alike. **Artist:** LaDene Votruba

☐ Purchased 19___ Pd $_____ MIB   NB   DB   BNT
☐ Want   Orig. Ret. $8.75   **NB** $10   **MIB** Sec. Mkt. **$15**

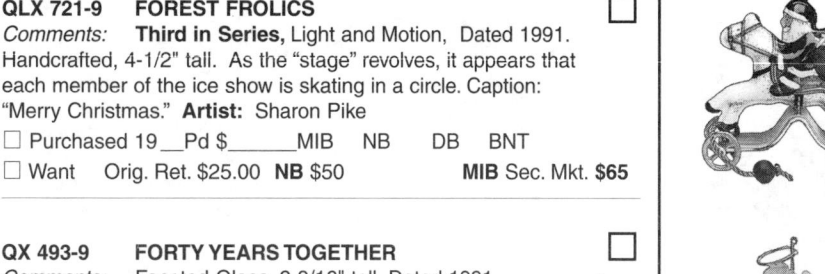

QLX 721-9   FOREST FROLICS

Comments: **Third in Series,** Light and Motion, Dated 1991.
Handcrafted, 4-1/2" tall. As the "stage" revolves, it appears that
each member of the ice show is skating in a circle. Caption:
"Merry Christmas." **Artist:** Sharon Pike

☐ Purchased 19 __ Pd $_____ MIB   NB   DB   BNT

☐ Want   Orig. Ret. $25.00 **NB** $50   **MIB** Sec. Mkt. **$65**

QX 493-9   FORTY YEARS TOGETHER

Comments: Faceted Glass, 2-9/16" tall, Dated 1991.
Identical to 1990 with date change.

☐ Purchased 19 __ Pd $_____ MIB   NB   DB   BNT

☐ Want   Orig. Ret. $7.75 **NB** $6   **MIB** Sec. Mkt. **$14**

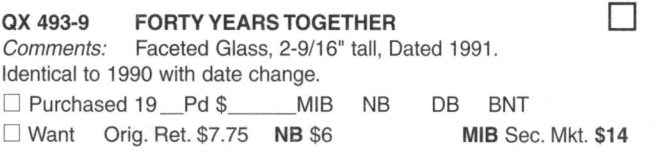

QX 528-9   FRIENDS ARE FUN

Comments: Handcrafted, 2-15/16" tall.
Dated Christmas 1991. Give one of these bunnies a push on the
teeter-totter and they move up and down; the package moves
back and forth. Caption: "Friends Are For Fun!" **Artist:** Ken Crow

☐ Purchased 19 __ Pd $_____ MIB   NB   DB   BNT

☐ Want   Orig. Ret. $9.75 **NB** $13   **MIB** Sec. Mkt. **$23**

QLX 716-9   FRIENDSHIP TREE

Comments: Lighted, Handcrafted, 3-1/8" tall, Dated 1991.
Sharing homes in the same snow-covered tree makes it easy to
exchange gifts. **Artist:** Peter Dutkin

☐ Purchased 19 __ Pd $_____ MIB   NB   DB   BNT

☐ Want   Orig. Ret. $10.00 **NB** $14   **MIB** Sec. Mkt. **$25**

QX 228-7   FROM OUR HOME TO YOURS

Comments: Midnight Blue and White Glass Ball, 2-7/8" dia.
Dated Christmas 1991. A bright red cardinal delivers a message
of JOY from the bears to the mice. Caption: "From Our Home To
Yours." **Artist:** LaDene Votruba

☐ Purchased 19 __ Pd $_____ MIB   NB   DB   BNT

☐ Want   Orig. Ret. $4.75 **NB** $12   **MIB** Sec. Mkt. **$22**

QX 432-7   FROSTY FRIENDS

Comments: **Twelfth in Series,** Handcrafted and Acrylic, 1-7/8" tall.
Dated 1991. Ice hockey is fun when you have a little penguin
friend to play with you. **Artist:** Sharon Pike

☐ Purchased 19 __ Pd $_____ MIB   NB   DB   BNT

☐ Want   Orig. Ret. $9.75 **NB** $21   **MIB** Sec. Mkt. **$38**

QXC 477-9   GALLOPING INTO CHRISTMAS: KEEPSAKE CLUB

Comments: Limited Edition 28,400, Wood Display Stand.
Pressed Tin, 3" tall. A carefully painted and detailed Santa on
horseback rolls along on wheels that move. Available to
Members only. **Artist:** Linda Sickman

☐ Purchased 19 __ Pd $_____ MIB   NB   DB   BNT

☐ Want   Orig. Ret. $19.75 **NB** $50   **MIB** Sec. Mkt. **$95**

QX 517-7   GARFIELD

Comments: Handcrafted, 3-3/4" tall, Dated 1991.
Garfield is an angel in his brass halo and white wings. He sits on
a dated star. **Artist:** Dill Rhodus

☐ Purchased 19 __ Pd $_____ MIB   NB   DB   BNT

☐ Want   Orig. Ret. $7.75 **NB** $18   **MIB** Sec. Mkt. **$30**

QX 211-7   GIFT BRINGERS, THE: CHRISTKINDL

Comments: **Third in Series,** White Glass Ball, 2-7/8" dia.
Christmas 1991. Symbolizing the Christ Child, Christkindl travels
through the countryside on a tiny deer delivering gifts.
Artist: LaDene Votruba

☐ Purchased 19 __ Pd $_____ MIB   NB   DB   BNT

☐ Want   Orig. Ret. $5.00 **NB** $12   **MIB** Sec. Mkt. **$20**

QX 531-9   GIFT OF JOY

Comments: Brass, Chrome and Copper, 4" tall, Christmas 1991.
A brass "J," chrome "O," and copper "Y" in die-cut design spell
JOY on all four sides. Each letter revolves.
Artist: Diana McGehee

☐ Purchased 19 __ Pd $_____ MIB   NB   DB   BNT

☐ Want   Orig. Ret. $8.75 **NB** $14   **MIB** Sec. Mkt. **$24**

QX 548-9   GODCHILD

Comments: Handcrafted, 2-1/16" tall, Dated 1991.
A little angel in white playing her trumpet, is suspended from a
golden banner which reads: "Merry Christmas, Godchild!"
Artist: Ron Bishop

☐ Purchased 19 __ Pd $_____ MIB   NB   DB   BNT

☐ Want   Orig. Ret. $6.75 **NB** $10   **MIB** Sec. Mkt. **$20**

QX 229-9   GRANDDAUGHTER

Comments: Porcelain White Glass Ball, 2-7/8" dia.
Dated Christmas 1991. Knit-look bunnies prance on a pink
background. Caption: "A Granddaughter Is A Special Joy!"
Artist: Michele Pyda-Sevcik

☐ Purchased 19 __ Pd $_____ MIB   NB   DB   BNT

☐ Want   Orig. Ret. $4.75 **NB** $12   **MIB** Sec. Mkt. **$24**

QX 511-9   GRANDDAUGHTER'S FIRST CHRISTMAS ☐
Comments: Handcrafted, 4-1/4" tall, Dated 1991.
A little bear dressed in a pink frock holds a chain of raised letters
that spell "Granddaughter." Pink foil caption on her hat says,
"My First Christmas." **Artist:** Robert Chad
☐ Purchased 19__ Pd $_____ MIB   NB   DB   BNT
☐ Want   Orig. Ret. $6.75   **NB** $10   **MIB** Sec. Mkt. **$22**

QX 230-7   GRANDMOTHER ☐
Comments: Light Gold Glass Ball, 2-7/8" dia.
Dated Christmas 1991. Christmas flowers and greenery frame
the caption: "A Grandmother Grows Ever More Loving..
Ever More Loved."
☐ Purchased 19__ Pd $_____ MIB   NB   DB   BNT
☐ Want   Orig. Ret. $4.75   **NB** $8.50   **MIB** Sec. Mkt. **$15**

QX 230-9   GRANDPARENTS ☐
Comments: White Glass Ball, 2-7/8" dia.
Dated Christmas 1991. A wintry village scene. Caption:
"Grandparents Add So Many Beautiful Pages To Your Album Of
Memories." **Artist:** Michele Pyda-Sevcik
☐ Purchased 19__ Pd $_____ MIB   NB   DB   BNT
☐ Want   Orig. Ret. $4.75   **NB** $8   **MIB** Sec. Mkt. **$14**

QX 229-7   GRANDSON ☐
Comments: Porcelain White Glass Ball, 2-7/8" dia.
Dated 1991. Resembling hand-knit sweaters, prancing reindeer
frame the caption: "A Grandson Makes Christmas Even More
Wonderful!" **Artist:** Michele Pyda-Sevcik
☐ Purchased 19__ Pd $_____ MIB   NB   DB   BNT
☐ Want   Orig. Ret. $4.75   **NB** $10   **MIB** Sec. Mkt. **$20**

QX 511-7   GRANDSON'S FIRST CHRISTMAS ☐
Comments: Handcrafted, 4-1/4" tall, Dated 1991.
Similar to the Granddaughter ornament, this bear is dressed in
blue, holding the letters "Grandson." "My First Christmas" is
lettered in blue foil. **Artist:** Robert Chad
☐ Purchased 19__ Pd $_____ MIB   NB   DB   BNT
☐ Want   Orig. Ret. $6.75   **NB** $10   **MIB** Sec. Mkt. **$22**

QX 412-9   GREATEST STORY ☐
Comments: **Second in Series,** Dated 1991.
Fine Bisque Porcelain and Brass, 3-3/4" tall
The shepherds stare in awe at the Star of Bethlehem.
Artist: LaDene Votruba
☐ Purchased 19__ Pd $_____ MIB   NB   DB   BNT
☐ Want   Orig. Ret. $12.75   **NB** $18   **MIB** Sec. Mkt. **$30**

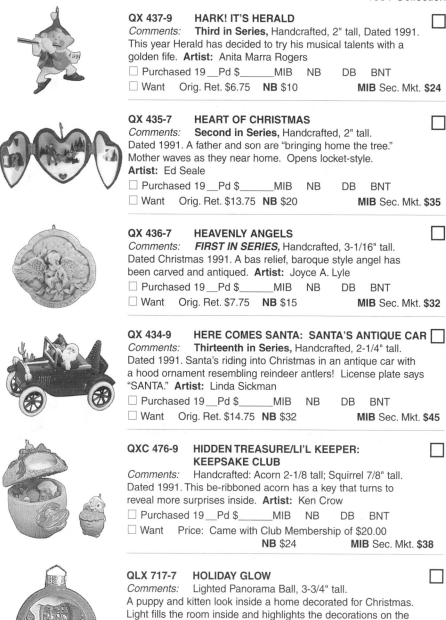

QX 437-9   HARK! IT'S HERALD ☐
Comments: **Third in Series,** Handcrafted, 2" tall, Dated 1991.
This year Herald has decided to try his musical talents with a
golden fife. **Artist:** Anita Marra Rogers
☐ Purchased 19__ Pd $_____ MIB   NB   DB   BNT
☐ Want   Orig. Ret. $6.75   **NB** $10   **MIB** Sec. Mkt. **$24**

QX 435-7   HEART OF CHRISTMAS ☐
Comments: **Second in Series,** Handcrafted, 2" tall.
Dated 1991. A father and son are "bringing home the tree."
Mother waves as they near home. Opens locket-style.
Artist: Ed Seale
☐ Purchased 19__ Pd $_____ MIB   NB   DB   BNT
☐ Want   Orig. Ret. $13.75   **NB** $20   **MIB** Sec. Mkt. **$35**

QX 436-7   HEAVENLY ANGELS ☐
Comments: *FIRST IN SERIES,* Handcrafted, 3-1/16" tall.
Dated Christmas 1991. A bas relief, baroque style angel has
been carved and antiqued. **Artist:** Joyce A. Lyle
☐ Purchased 19__ Pd $_____ MIB   NB   DB   BNT
☐ Want   Orig. Ret. $7.75   **NB** $15   **MIB** Sec. Mkt. **$32**

QX 434-9   HERE COMES SANTA: SANTA'S ANTIQUE CAR ☐
Comments: **Thirteenth in Series,** Handcrafted, 2-1/4" tall.
Dated 1991. Santa's riding into Christmas in an antique car with
a hood ornament resembling reindeer antlers! License plate says
"SANTA." **Artist:** Linda Sickman
☐ Purchased 19__ Pd $_____ MIB   NB   DB   BNT
☐ Want   Orig. Ret. $14.75   **NB** $32   **MIB** Sec. Mkt. **$45**

QXC 476-9   HIDDEN TREASURE/LI'L KEEPER: KEEPSAKE CLUB ☐
Comments: Handcrafted: Acorn 2-1/8 tall; Squirrel 7/8" tall.
Dated 1991. This be-ribboned acorn has a key that turns to
reveal more surprises inside. **Artist:** Ken Crow
☐ Purchased 19__ Pd $_____ MIB   NB   DB   BNT
☐ Want   Price: Came with Club Membership of $20.00
    NB $24   **MIB** Sec. Mkt. **$38**

QLX 717-7   HOLIDAY GLOW ☐
Comments: Lighted Panorama Ball, 3-3/4" tall.
A puppy and kitten look inside a home decorated for Christmas.
Light fills the room inside and highlights the decorations on the
tree. **Artist:** Sharon Pike
☐ Purchased 19__ Pd $_____ MIB   NB   DB   BNT
☐ Want   Orig. Ret. $14.00   **NB** $15   **MIB** Sec. Mkt. **$25**

QX 410-9 HOOKED ON SANTA ☐
Comments: Handcrafted, 4" tall.
Santa's hooked a big one this time... himself! His hook has gotten caught in his green waders. **Artist:** Julia Lee

☐ Purchased 19__Pd $_____MIB NB DB BNT
☐ Want Orig. Ret. $7.75 **NB** $14 **MIB** Sec. Mkt. **$22**

QLX 723-7 IT'S A WONDERFUL LIFE ☐
Comments: Blinking Lights, Handcrafted, 3-3/16" tall.
Dated 1991. A nostalgic movie theater is now showing a classic, It's A Wonderful Life. The marquee proclaims "Happy Holidays" and on a poster: "Coming Soon: A Christmas Carol."
Artist: Donna Lee

☐ Purchased 19__Pd $_____MIB NB DB BNT
☐ Want Orig. Ret. $20.00 **NB** $50 **MIB** Sec. Mkt. **$65**

QX 314-7 JESUS LOVES ME ☐
Comments: Blue Cameo, 2-3/4" dia., Christmas 1991.
A baby squirrel kneels beside his bed to say his nighttime prayers. Caption: "Jesus Loves Me." **Artist:** Dill Rhodus

☐ Purchased 19__Pd $_____MIB NB DB BNT
☐ Want Orig. Ret. $7.75 **NB** $9 **MIB** Sec. Mkt. **$16.50**

QLX 732-3 JINGLE BEARS ☐
Comments: Light, Music and Motion, Handcrafted, 4-3/8" tall.
Papa bear plays the tune "Jingle Bells" and mama sways from side to side. Caption: "Happy Family Memories Make The Season Bright." **Artist:** Julia Lee

☐ Purchased 19__Pd $_____MIB NB DB BNT
☐ Want Orig. Ret. $25.00 **NB** $35 **MIB** Sec. Mkt. **$55**

QX 541-9 JOLLY WOLLY SANTA ☐
Comments: Handcrafted, 3-3/4" tall, Dated 1991.
With his sack of toys and jingle bells, this whimsical Santa is ready for Christmas. **Artist:** Linda Sickman

☐ Purchased 19__Pd $_____MIB NB DB BNT
☐ Want Orig. Ret. $7.75 **NB** $10 **MIB** Sec. Mkt. **$30**

QX 542-7 JOLLY WOLLY SNOWMAN ☐
Comments: Handcrafted, 3-3/4" tall, Dated 1991.
A well-rounded fellow, for sure! The snowman design lithographed on this tin container has a corncob pipe and eyes made out of coal. **Artist:** Linda Sickman

☐ Purchased 19__Pd $_____MIB NB DB BNT
☐ Want Orig. Ret. $7.75 **NB** $12 **MIB** Sec. Mkt. **$22.50**

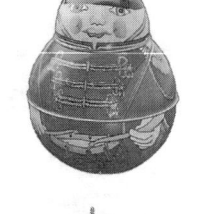

QX 542-9 JOLLY WOLLY SOLDIER ☐
Comments: Pressed Tin, 3-3/4" tall, Dated 1991.
This tin soldier, dressed in his elaborate red and blue uniform, keeps everyone in step with the beat of his drum.
Artist: Linda Sickman

☐ Purchased 19 __Pd $_____MIB NB DB BNT
☐ Want Orig. Ret. $7.75 **NB** $10 **MIB** Sec. Mkt. **$22**

QX 536-9 JOYOUS MEMORIES PHOTOHOLDER ☐
Comments: Hand-Painted Handcrafted, 3-3/8" dia.
Dated 1991. A bas-relief holly design sculpted and painted white on white frames a favorite photograph. Caption: "Each Joy Of Christmas Becomes A Precious Memory."
Artist: LaDene Votruba

☐ Purchased 19 __Pd $_____MIB NB DB BNT
☐ Want Orig. Ret. $6.75 **NB** $12 **MIB** Sec. Mkt. **$24**

QLX 711-9 KRINGLE'S BUMPER CARS ☐
Comments: Blinking Lights and Motion, Handcrafted, 3-3/4" tall.
Santa, one of his elves and a reindeer have a bit of fun playing in the bumper cars. **Artist:** Linda Sickman

☐ Purchased 19 __Pd $_____MIB NB DB BNT
☐ Want Orig. Ret. $25.00 **NB** $45 **MIB** Sec. Mkt. **$55**

QX 223-7 MARY ENGELBREIT ☐
Comments: Porcelain White Glass Ball, 2-7/8" dia.
Dated Christmas 1991. Santa leads a parade of elves, dove, bunny and reindeer. More Engelbreit products debuting may influence her ornament prices.

☐ Purchased 19 __Pd $_____MIB NB DB BNT
☐ Want Orig. Ret. $4.75 **NB** $14 **MIB** Sec. Mkt. **$25**

QX 427-9 MARY'S ANGELS: IRIS ☐
Comments: **Fourth in Series,** Handcrafted and Acrylic, 2" tall.
Iris sleeps comfortably on her frosted acrylic cloud. She's wearing a lavender dress. This is a popular series. **Artist:** Robert Chad

☐ Purchased 19 __Pd $_____MIB NB DB BNT
☐ Want Orig. Ret. $6.75 **NB** $20 **MIB** Sec. Mkt. **$38**

QX 538-9 MATCHBOX MEMORIES: EVERGREEN INN ☐
Comments: Handcrafted, 1-7/16" tall, Dated 1991.
The proprietor of this country inn looks surprisingly like Santa! Caption: "Evergreen Inn 1991" **Artist:** Ed Seale

☐ Purchased 19 __Pd $_____MIB NB DB BNT
☐ Want Orig. Ret. $8.75 **NB** $15 **MIB** Sec. Mkt. **$20**

QX 539-9   MATCHBOX MEMORIES: HOLIDAY CAFE ☐
Comments: Handcrafted, 1-7/16" tall, Dated 1991.
A couple sit at a table by the window and hold hands. Lettering
on the "window" is reversed. **Artist:** Ed Seale
☐ Purchased 19__Pd $_____MIB   NB   DB   BNT
☐ Want   Orig. Ret. $8.75 **NB** $12   **MIB** Sec. Mkt. **$17.50**

QX 539-7   MATCHBOX MEMORIES: SANTA'S STUDIO ☐
Comments: Handcrafted, 1-7/16" tall, Dated 1991.
Santa chisels and sculpts a likeness of one of his elves. Statue
has the appearance of marble. **Artist:** Ed Seale
☐ Purchased 19__Pd $_____MIB   NB   DB   BNT
☐ Want   Orig. Ret. $8.75 **NB** $12   **MIB** Sec. Mkt. **$18**

QX 435-9   MERRY OLDE SANTA ☐
Comments: **Second in Series,** Handcrafted, 4" tall.
Dated 1991. This Old World Santa carries a walking stick with a
brass bell to announce his arrival. He wears a long red coat.
Artist: Julia Lee
☐ Purchased 19__Pd $_____MIB   NB   DB   BNT
☐ Want   Orig. Ret. $14.75 **NB** $60   **MIB** Sec. Mkt. **$85**

QLX 714-9   MOLE FAMILY HOME ☐
Comments: Flickering Light, Handcrafted, 3-3/8" tall.
Dated 1991. All that may be seen above ground is a snow-
covered tree stump and red door, but underground mother bakes
cookies while father and child read a story. **Artist:** Julia Lee
☐ Purchased 19__Pd $_____MIB   NB   DB   BNT
☐ Want   Orig. Ret. $20.00 **NB** $22   **MIB** Sec. Mkt. **$45**

QX 546-7   MOM AND DAD ☐
Comments: Handcrafted, 3-5/8" tall, Dated 1991.
Two raccoons are snuggling together in a real knit stocking. The
stocking carries the caption: "Mom And Dad."
☐ Purchased 19__Pd $_____MIB   NB   DB   BNT
☐ Want   Orig. Ret. $9.75 **NB** $14   **MIB** Sec. Mkt. **$24**

QX 487-7   MOM-TO-BE ☐
Comments: Handcrafted, 2-3/8" tall, Dated Christmas 1991.
The lady kangaroo carries a wrapped gift in her pouch. Her
sweat shirt reads "Mom-To-Be." **Artist:** Julia Lee
☐ Purchased 19__Pd $_____MIB   NB   DB   BNT
☐ Want   Orig. Ret. $5.75 **NB** $10   **MIB** Sec. Mkt. **$18**

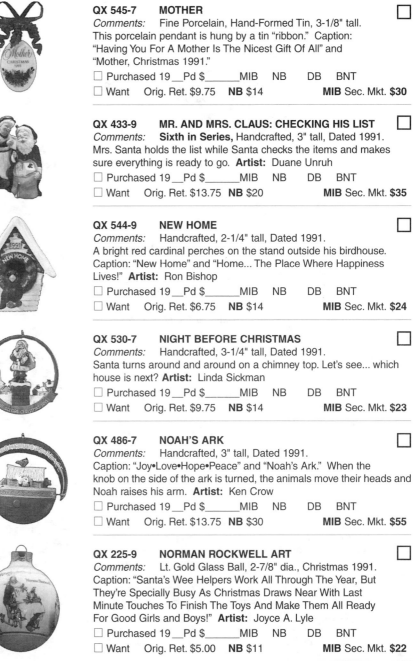

QX 545-7   MOTHER ☐
Comments: Fine Porcelain, Hand-Formed Tin, 3-1/8" tall.
This porcelain pendant is hung by a tin "ribbon." Caption:
"Having You For A Mother Is The Nicest Gift Of All" and
"Mother, Christmas 1991."
☐ Purchased 19__Pd $_____MIB   NB   DB   BNT
☐ Want   Orig. Ret. $9.75 **NB** $14   **MIB** Sec. Mkt. **$30**

QX 433-9   MR. AND MRS. CLAUS: CHECKING HIS LIST ☐
Comments: **Sixth in Series,** Handcrafted, 3" tall, Dated 1991.
Mrs. Santa holds the list while Santa checks the items and makes
sure everything is ready to go. **Artist:** Duane Unruh
☐ Purchased 19__Pd $_____MIB   NB   DB   BNT
☐ Want   Orig. Ret. $13.75 **NB** $20   **MIB** Sec. Mkt. **$35**

QX 544-9   NEW HOME ☐
Comments: Handcrafted, 2-1/4" tall, Dated 1991.
A bright red cardinal perches on the stand outside his birdhouse.
Caption: "New Home" and "Home... The Place Where Happiness
Lives!" **Artist:** Ron Bishop
☐ Purchased 19__Pd $_____MIB   NB   DB   BNT
☐ Want   Orig. Ret. $6.75 **NB** $14   **MIB** Sec. Mkt. **$24**

QX 530-7   NIGHT BEFORE CHRISTMAS ☐
Comments: Handcrafted, 3-1/4" tall, Dated 1991.
Santa turns around and around on a chimney top. Let's see... which
house is next? **Artist:** Linda Sickman
☐ Purchased 19__Pd $_____MIB   NB   DB   BNT
☐ Want   Orig. Ret. $9.75 **NB** $14   **MIB** Sec. Mkt. **$23**

QX 486-7   NOAH'S ARK ☐
Comments: Handcrafted, 3" tall, Dated 1991.
Caption: "Joy•Love•Hope•Peace" and "Noah's Ark." When the
knob on the side of the ark is turned, the animals move their heads and
Noah raises his arm. **Artist:** Ken Crow
☐ Purchased 19__Pd $_____MIB   NB   DB   BNT
☐ Want   Orig. Ret. $13.75 **NB** $30   **MIB** Sec. Mkt. **$55**

QX 225-9   NORMAN ROCKWELL ART ☐
Comments: Lt. Gold Glass Ball, 2-7/8" dia., Christmas 1991.
Caption: "Santa's Wee Helpers Work All Through The Year, But
They're Specially Busy As Christmas Draws Near With Last
Minute Touches To Finish The Toys And Make Them All Ready
For Good Girls and Boys!" **Artist:** Joyce A. Lyle
☐ Purchased 19__Pd $_____MIB   NB   DB   BNT
☐ Want   Orig. Ret. $5.00 **NB** $11   **MIB** Sec. Mkt. **$22**

QX 413-9   NOSTALGIC HOUSES AND SHOPS:
FIRE STATION
Comments: **Eighth in Series,** Handcrafted, 4" tall.
Dated 1991. Awaiting the return of the fireman at "Fire Co. 1991" are an old-time fire engine, Christmas tree and two dalmatians.
Artist: Donna Lee

☐ Purchased 19__Pd $_____MIB   NB   DB   BNT
☐ Want   Orig. Ret. $14.75 **NB** $40   **MIB** Sec. Mkt. **$62**

QX 535-7   NOTES OF CHEER
Comments: Handcrafted, 1-3/4" tall, Dated 1991.
This flocked brown bear seems to be asking "any requests?" as he plays his special keyboard. **Artist:** Bob Siedler

☐ Purchased 19__Pd $_____MIB   NB   DB   BNT
☐ Want   Orig. Ret. $5.75 **NB** $10   **MIB** Sec. Mkt. **$14**

QX 517-6   NUTSHELL NATIVITY
Comments: Handcrafted, 1-7/16" tall.
The three kings (left) kneel before the Baby in the manger (right) and present their gifts. **Artist:** Anita M. Rogers

☐ Purchased 19__Pd $_____MIB   NB   DB   BNT
☐ Want   Orig. Ret. $6.75 **NB** $15   **MIB** Sec. Mkt. **$24**

QX 483-3   NUTTY SQUIRREL
Comments: Handcrafted, 1-3/4" tall.
The detailed sculpting on this little fellow makes him a prize. He Is delivering an acorn tied with a bright red handcrafted bow.
Artist: Sharon Pike

☐ Purchased 19__Pd $_____MIB   NB   DB   BNT
☐ Want   Orig. Ret. $5.75 **NB** $10   **MIB** Sec. Mkt. **$14**

QX 431-7   OLD FASHIONED SLED
Comments: Handcrafted, 1-5/16" tall, Dated 1991.
This authentically detailed sled pictures winter scenery. Tiny gold bells are on the front of the Bentwood-style runners.
Artist: Linda Sickman

☐ Purchased 19__Pd $_____MIB   NB   DB   BNT
☐ Want   Orig. Ret. $8.75 **NB** $10   **MIB** Sec. Mkt. **$18.50**

QX 534-7   ON A ROLL
Comments: Handcrafted, 5" tall, Merry Christmas 1991.
A little mouse swings on a strand of green fabric ribbon, scissors in hand. The red spool fastens to the tree with a wishbone hanger.
Artist: Ken Crow

☐ Purchased 19__Pd $_____MIB   NB   DB   BNT
☐ Want   Orig. Ret. $6.75 **NB** $12   **MIB** Sec. Mkt. **$20**

QX 529-7   PARTRIDGE IN A PEAR TREE
Comments: Handcrafted, 3-5/16" tall, Dated 1991.
This ornament of a partridge sitting in the top of a pear tree has the look of carved wood. **Artist:** Linda Sickman

☐ Purchased 19__Pd $_____MIB   NB   DB   BNT
☐ Want   Orig. Ret. $9.75 **NB** $15   **MIB** Sec. Mkt. **$21**

QX 512-9   PEACE ON EARTH: ITALY
Comments: **FIRST IN SERIES,** Handcrafted, 3" tall, Dated 1991.
This intricately detailed ornament features two children in costume holding a globe. In bas-relief on the front of the ornament are famous scenes from Italy and the caption "Pace Al Mondo."
Artist: Linda Sickman

☐ Purchased 19__Pd $_____MIB   NB   DB   BNT
☐ Want   Orig. Ret. $11.75 **NB** $15   **MIB** Sec. Mkt. **$30**

QX 225-7   PEANUTS®
Comments: Chrome Glass Ball, 2-7/8" dia., Dated 1991.
The gang decorates Snoopy's doghouse.   Caption: "It's The Time Of The Year For Sharing Good Cheer!"

☐ Purchased 19__Pd $_____MIB   NB   DB   BNT
☐ Want   Orig. Ret. $5.00 **NB** $12   **MIB** Sec. Mkt. **$24**

QLX 722-9   PEANUTS®
Comments: **FIRST IN SERIES,** Flickering Light, Handcrafted, 3" tall.
Dated 1991. Snoopy and Woodstock wait for Santa -- inside the stocking on the fireplace. The mantel holds a plate of cookies "For Santa." **Artist:** Dill Rhodus

☐ Purchased 19__Pd $_____MIB   NB   DB   BNT
☐ Want   Orig. Ret. $18.00 **NB** $40   **MIB** Sec. Mkt. **$55**

QX 439-9   POLAR CIRCUS WAGON
Comments: Handcrafted, 2-7/8" tall, Dated 1991.
The circus has come to the North Pole; a polar bear rides in a cage designed to resemble an antique pull toy.
Artist: Linda Sickman

☐ Purchased 19__Pd $_____MIB   NB   DB   BNT
☐ Want   Orig. Ret. $13.75 **NB** $16   **MIB** Sec. Mkt. **$28**

QX 528-7   POLAR CLASSIC
Comments: Handcrafted, 3" tall, Dated 1991.
A white bear with a red shirt and green visor that says "Polar Classic 91" has a perfect swing. **Artist:** Bob Siedler

☐ Purchased 19__Pd $_____MIB   NB   DB   BNT
☐ Want   Orig. Ret. $6.75 **NB** $11   **MIB** Sec. Mkt. **$20**

QX 537-9   PUPPY LOVE
Comments: **FIRST IN SERIES,** Handcrafted and Brass.
3-1/8" tall, Dated 1991. A golden cocker spaniel rides a candy
cane. He wears a brass identification tag on a red ribbon
around his neck. **Artist:** Anita Marra Rogers
☐ Purchased 19__ Pd $_____ MIB   NB   DB   BNT
☐ Want   Orig. Ret. $7.75   **NB** $25   **MIB** Sec. Mkt. **$45**

QX 434-7   REINDEER CHAMPS: CUPID
Comments: **Sixth in Series,** Handcrafted, 3-1/8" tall.
Dated 1991. Cupid serves on the volleyball court with style and
grace. Her name is on her shirt. **Artist:** Bob Siedler
☐ Purchased 19__ Pd $_____ MIB   NB   DB   BNT
☐ Want   Orig. Ret. $7.75   **NB** $15   **MIB** Sec. Mkt. **$32**

QX 414-7   ROCKING HORSE
Comments: **Eleventh in Series,** Handcrafted, 4" wide.
Dated 1991. A buckskin wears a patterned saddle that
resembles hand-tooled leather with shiny brass stirrups. His
mane and tail are black. **Artist:** Linda Sickman
☐ Purchased 19__ Pd $_____ MIB   NB   DB   BNT
☐ Want   Orig. Ret. $10.75   **NB** $20   **MIB** Sec. Mkt. **$37**

QLX 727-3   SALVATION ARMY BAND
Comments: Light, Motion and Music, Handcrafted, 4-5/8" tall.
Standing on a brick street beneath a lighted lamp, a band plays
"Joy To The World." Includes the familiar kettle and sign:
"The Salvation Army®, Sharing Is Caring." **Artist:** Duane Unruh
☐ Purchased 19__ Pd $_____ MIB   NB   DB   BNT
☐ Want   Orig. Ret. $30.00   **NB** $55   **M IB** Sec. Mkt. **$80**

QX 438-9   SANTA SAILOR
Comments: Handcrafted and Metal, 3-3/8" tall, Dated 1991.
Santa's dressed in nautical dress blues and stands with his pack
of toys on a metal anchor. **Artist:** Ed Seale
☐ Purchased 19__ Pd $_____ MIB   NB   DB   BNT
☐ Want   Orig. Ret. $9.75   **NB** $12   **MIB** Sec. Mkt. **$25**

QLX 716-7   SANTA SPECIAL
Comments: Light, Motion and Sound, Handcrafted, 3-1/8" tall.
This locomotive looks, acts and sounds like a real train. The
headlight is lighted; it whistles and chugs. The wheels and drive
rods turn. Engineer Santa waves. Reissued in 1992.
Artist: Ed Seale
☐ Purchased 19__ Pd $_____ MIB   NB   DB   BNT
☐ Want   Orig. Ret. $40.00   **NB** $60   **MIB** Sec. Mkt. **$75**

QLX 715-9   SANTA'S HOT LINE
Comments: Blinking Lights, Handcrafted, 3-7/8" tall.
Dated 1991. A busy elf answers calls on this old-fashioned
switchboard and adds to his list: "Sara - Train, Paul - Puppy."
Artist: Ken Crow
☐ Purchased 19__ Pd $_____ MIB   NB   DB   BNT
☐ Want   Orig. Ret. $18.00   **NB** $26   **MIB** Sec. Mkt. **$43**

QX 523-7   SANTA'S PREMIERE: GOLD CROWN ORNAMENT
Comments: Hand-Painted Fine Porcelain, 3-1/4" tall.
Dated 1991. The handle of this gold-rimmed porcelain bell is a
finely crafted Santa in a long red coat. Caption: "Hallmark
Keepsake Ornament Premiere, Gold Crown Exclusive."
☐ Purchased 19__ Pd $_____ MIB   NB   DB   BNT
☐ Want   Orig. Ret. $10.75   **NB** $25   **MIB** Sec. Mkt. **$40**

QXC 479-7   SECRETS FOR SANTA: KEEPSAKE CLUB
Comments: Limited Edition 28,700, Wood Display Stand.
Hand-Painted, Handcrafted, 3-1/2" tall
A child seated on Santa's lap whispers a wish in his ear. Available
to Club Members only. **Artist:** Anita Marra Rogers
☐ Purchased 19__ Pd $_____ MIB   NB   DB   BNT
☐ Want   Orig. Ret. $23.75   **NB** $30   **MIB** Sec. Mkt. **$60**

QX 548-7   SISTER
Comments: Handcrafted, 3-3/4" tall, Dated 1991.
This cookie angel has been lavishly decorated with pearly "icing"
to serve up a lovely treat for "Sister," as noted on the star she is
holding. **Artist:** Joyce A. Lyle
☐ Purchased 19__ Pd $_____ MIB   NB   DB   BNT
☐ Want   Orig. Ret. $6.75   **NB** $14   **MIB** Sec. Mkt. **$18**

QX 544-7   SKI LIFT BUNNY
Comments: Handcrafted, 2-3/4" tall, Dated 1991.
With a white pom-pom tail, this colorfully dressed bunny loves to
ride the ski lift. **Artist:** Julia Lee
☐ Purchased 19__ Pd $_____ MIB   NB   DB   BNT
☐ Want   Orig. Ret. $6.75   **NB** $12   **MIB** Sec. Mkt. **$20**

QLX 726-6   SKI TRIP
Comments: Light and Motion, Handcrafted, 4-1/4" tall.
In this snow-covered village, skiers ride the ski lift to the top of the
hill then glide down the slopes. Lights shine through the lodge's
windows. **Artist:** Ed Seale
☐ Purchased 19__ Pd $_____ MIB   NB   DB   BNT
☐ Want   Orig. Ret. $28.00   **NB** $45   **MIB** Sec. Mkt. **$60**

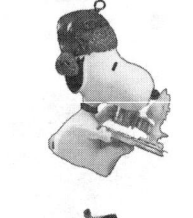

QX 519-7   SNOOPY® AND WOODSTOCK

Comments: Handcrafted, 2-1/8" tall, Dated 1991.
Snoopy and Woodstock enjoy a Christmas meal of pepperoni pizza and "Root Beer." **Artist:** Dill Rhodus

☐ Purchased 19__Pd $_____MIB   NB   DB   BNT

☐ Want   Orig. Ret. $6.75   **NB** $20   **MIB** Sec. Mkt. **$35**

QX 526-9   SNOWY OWL

Comments: Handcrafted, 3" tall
The distinctive markings for this wide-eyed owl make it very impressive as well as beautiful. **Artist:** Linda Sickman

☐ Purchased 19__Pd $_____MIB   NB   DB   BNT

☐ Want   Orig. Ret. $7.75   **NB** $12   **MIB** Sec. Mkt. **$20**

QX 546-9   SON

Comments: Handcrafted, 3-3/16" tall, Dated Son 1991.
This flocked red slipper holds a flocked white mouse that is fast asleep on a green pillow. **Artist:** Bob Siedler

☐ Purchased 19__Pd $_____MIB   NB   DB   BNT

☐ Want   Orig. Ret. $5.75   **NB** $12   **MIB** Sec. Mkt. **$15**

QLX 715-7   SPARKLING ANGEL

Comments: Blinking Lights, Handcrafted, 3-13/16" tall.
The stars on this little angel's glittering gold tinsel garland twinkle off and on. **Artist:** Robert Chad

☐ Purchased 19__Pd $_____MIB   NB   DB   BNT

☐ Want   Orig. Ret. $18.00 **NB** $24   **MIB** Sec. Mkt. **$34**

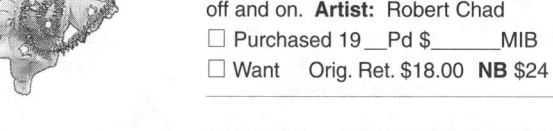

QLX 719-9   STAR TREK: STARSHIP ENTERPRISE

Comments: Blinking Lights, Handcrafted, 1-5/8" tall.
Dated 1991. Commemorating the 25th anniversary of the television series Star Trek. Many Star Trek collectors were unaware of its debut. Production was much less than 92's Shuttlecraft Galileo, which was abundant. **Artist:** Lynn Norton

☐ Purchased 19__Pd $_____MIB   NB   DB   BNT

☐ Want   Orig. Ret. $20.00   **Lights Not Working** $100
                                NB $250   **MIB** Sec. Mkt. **$250-$300**

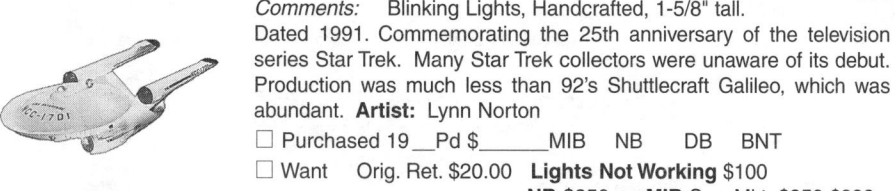

QX 536-7   SWEET TALK

Comments: Handcrafted, 2-1/8" tall.
A little girl's love for her pony is evident… aren't candy canes just as good for ponies as sugar cubes? **Artist:** Duane Unruh

☐ Purchased 19__Pd $_____MIB   NB   DB   BNT

☐ Want   Orig. Ret. $8.75   **NB** $10   **MIB** Sec. Mkt. **$18**

QX 495-7   SWEETHEART

Comments: Fine Porcelain, 2-1/2" tall, Dated 1991.
An old-fashioned sleigh ride has been reproduced on a heart-shaped porcelain ornament. Caption: "Merry Christmas, Sweetheart" and "Gently Comes The Season Of Love."

☐ Purchased 19__Pd $_____MIB   NB   DB   BNT

☐ Want   Orig. Ret. $9.75   **NB** $14   **MIB** Sec. Mkt. **$24**

QX 228-9   TEACHER

Comments: Porcelain White Glass Ball, 2-7/8" dia.
Dated Christmas 1991. This ornament has the look of a child's drawing. "For My Teacher" is written on this ornament and it pictures a tree with gifts and wreath.
Artist: Anita Marra Rogers

☐ Purchased 19__Pd $_____MIB   NB   DB   BNT

☐ Want   Orig. Ret. $4.75   **NB** $7   **MIB** Sec. Mkt. **$12**

QX 492-9   TEN YEARS TOGETHER

Comments: Faceted Glass, 2-9/16" tall, Dated 1991.
Caption in red foil.

☐ Purchased 19__Pd $_____MIB   NB   DB   BNT

☐ Want   Orig. Ret. $7.75   **NB** $10   **MIB** Sec. Mkt. **$20**

QX 533-7   TENDER TOUCHES COLLECTION:
FANFARE BEAR

Comments: Hand-Painted and Handcrafted, 2-7/16" tall.
Dated 1991. The "Little Drummer Bear" plays his drum with real wooden drumsticks. **Artist:** Ed Seale

☐ Purchased 19__Pd $_____MIB   NB   DB   BNT

☐ Want   Orig. Ret. $8.75   **NB** $12   **MIB** Sec. Mkt. **$18**

QX 496-9   TENDER TOUCHES COLLECTION:
GLEE CLUB BEARS

Comments: Hand-Painted and Handcrafted, 2" tall, Dated 1991.
Three brown bears in ivory choir robes sing carols from their "Deck the Halls" song book. **Artist:** Ed Seale

☐ Purchased 19__Pd $_____MIB   NB   DB   BNT

☐ Want   Orig. Ret. $8.75   **NB** $15   **MIB** Sec. Mkt. **$18**

QX 495-9   TENDER TOUCHES COLLECTION:
LOOK OUT BELOW

Comments: Hand-Painted and Handcrafted, 1-3/4" tall.
Dated 1991. A little grey mouse waves to his friends as he sleds down the hill. **Artist:** Ed Seale

☐ Purchased 19__Pd $_____MIB   NB   DB   BNT

☐ Want   Orig. Ret. $8.75   **NB** $15   **MIB** Sec. Mkt. **$20**

QX 498-7   TENDER TOUCHES COLLECTION: LOVING STITCHES ☐

Comments: Hand-Painted and Handcrafted, 2-1/4" tall. Dated 1991. A darling chipmunk rocks in her high-back rocking chair and stitches a heart sampler for a special friend.
Artist: Ed Seale

☐ Purchased 19__ Pd $_____ MIB   NB   DB   BNT
☐ Want   Orig. Ret. $8.75   **NB** $22   **MIB** Sec. Mkt. **$30**

QX 497-7   TENDER TOUCHES COLLECTION: PLUM DELIGHTFUL ☐

Comments: Hand-Painted and Handcrafted, 2-1/4" tall. Dated 1991. Mrs. Raccoon has prepared a delicious plum pudding to serve her Christmas guests. Her white lace apron has a dated heart. **Artist:** Ed Seale

☐ Purchased 19__ Pd $_____ MIB   NB   DB   BNT
☐ Want   Orig. Ret. $8.75   **NB** $12   **MIB** Sec. Mkt. **$20**

QX 497--9   TENDER TOUCHES COLLECTION: SNOW TWINS ☐

Comments: Hand-Painted and Handcrafted, 2-1/8" tall. Dated 1991. Don't all snowmen have long ears and a carrot for a nose? The little fellow in the red suit thinks so.
Artist: Ed Seale

☐ Purchased 19__ Pd $_____ MIB   NB   DB   BNT
☐ Want   Orig. Ret. $8.75   **NB** $12   **MIB** Sec. Mkt. **$20**

QX 496-7   TENDER TOUCHES COLLECTION: YULE LOGGER ☐

Comments: Hand-Painted and Handcrafted, 2" tall, Dated 1991. This adorable beaver in his red sweater, jeans and yellow muffler, has gnawed his own tree. **Artist:** Ed Seale

☐ Purchased 19__ Pd $_____ MIB   NB   DB   BNT
☐ Want   Orig. Ret. $8.75   **NB** $18   **MIB** Sec. Mkt. **$27**

QX 530-9   TERRIFIC TEACHER ☐

Comments: Handcrafted, 2-1/4" tall, Dated Christmas 1991. This cute little owl has a special rubber stamp created for his Terrific Teacher. **Artist:** Linda Sickman

☐ Purchased 19__ Pd $_____ MIB   NB   DB   BNT
☐ Want   Orig. Ret. $6.75   **NB** $8   **MIB** Sec. Mkt. **$14**

QLX 712-9   TOYLAND TOWER ☐

Comments: Motion, Handcrafted, 3-13/16" tall. A teddy bear sits and beats a drum at the gate entrance as a colorful soldier guards the tower. **Artist:** Ken Crow

☐ Purchased 19__ Pd $_____ MIB   NB   DB   BNT
☐ Want   Orig. Ret. $20.00 **NB** $27   **MIB** Sec. Mkt. **$38**

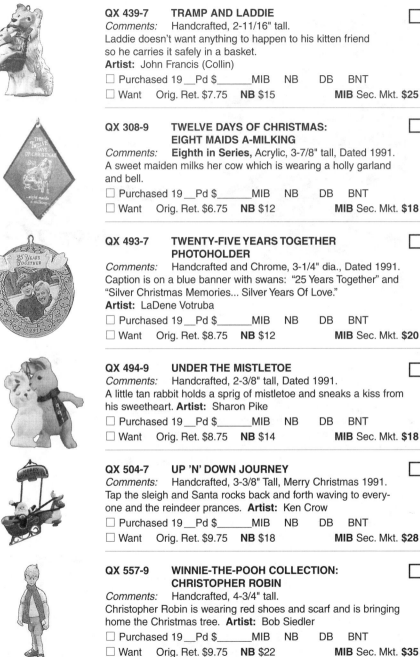

QX 439-7   TRAMP AND LADDIE ☐

Comments: Handcrafted, 2-11/16" tall. Laddie doesn't want anything to happen to his kitten friend so he carries it safely in a basket.
Artist: John Francis (Collin)

☐ Purchased 19__ Pd $_____ MIB   NB   DB   BNT
☐ Want   Orig. Ret. $7.75   **NB** $15   **MIB** Sec. Mkt. **$25**

QX 308-9   TWELVE DAYS OF CHRISTMAS: EIGHT MAIDS A-MILKING ☐

Comments: **Eighth in Series,** Acrylic, 3-7/8" tall, Dated 1991. A sweet maiden milks her cow which is wearing a holly garland and bell.

☐ Purchased 19__ Pd $_____ MIB   NB   DB   BNT
☐ Want   Orig. Ret. $6.75   **NB** $12   **MIB** Sec. Mkt. **$18**

QX 493-7   TWENTY-FIVE YEARS TOGETHER PHOTOHOLDER ☐

Comments: Handcrafted and Chrome, 3-1/4" dia., Dated 1991. Caption is on a blue banner with swans: "25 Years Together" and "Silver Christmas Memories... Silver Years Of Love."
Artist: LaDene Votruba

☐ Purchased 19__ Pd $_____ MIB   NB   DB   BNT
☐ Want   Orig. Ret. $8.75   **NB** $12   **MIB** Sec. Mkt. **$20**

QX 494-9   UNDER THE MISTLETOE ☐

Comments: Handcrafted, 2-3/8" tall, Dated 1991. A little tan rabbit holds a sprig of mistletoe and sneaks a kiss from his sweetheart. **Artist:** Sharon Pike

☐ Purchased 19__ Pd $_____ MIB   NB   DB   BNT
☐ Want   Orig. Ret. $8.75   **NB** $14   **MIB** Sec. Mkt. **$18**

QX 504-7   UP 'N' DOWN JOURNEY ☐

Comments: Handcrafted, 3-3/8" Tall, Merry Christmas 1991. Tap the sleigh and Santa rocks back and forth waving to everyone and the reindeer prances. **Artist:** Ken Crow

☐ Purchased 19__ Pd $_____ MIB   NB   DB   BNT
☐ Want   Orig. Ret. $9.75   **NB** $18   **MIB** Sec. Mkt. **$28**

QX 557-9   WINNIE-THE-POOH COLLECTION: CHRISTOPHER ROBIN ☐

Comments: Handcrafted, 4-3/4" tall. Christopher Robin is wearing red shoes and scarf and is bringing home the Christmas tree. **Artist:** Bob Siedler

☐ Purchased 19__ Pd $_____ MIB   NB   DB   BNT
☐ Want   Orig. Ret. $9.75   **NB** $22   **MIB** Sec. Mkt. **$35**

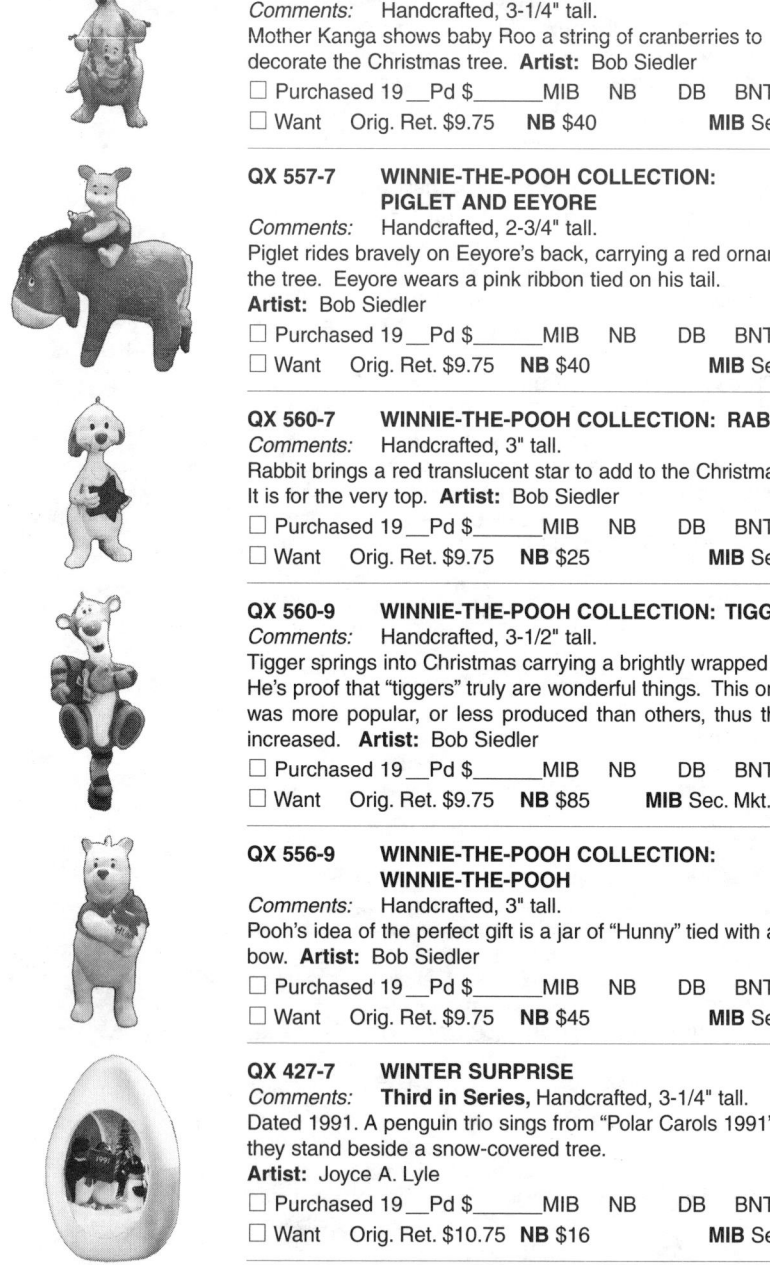

QX 561-7   WINNIE-THE-POOH COLLECTION:
KANGA AND ROO   ☐
Comments: Handcrafted, 3-1/4" tall.
Mother Kanga shows baby Roo a string of cranberries to
decorate the Christmas tree. **Artist:** Bob Siedler

☐ Purchased 19__Pd $_____MIB   NB   DB   BNT
☐ Want   Orig. Ret. $9.75   **NB** $40   **MIB** Sec. Mkt. **$55**

QX 557-7   WINNIE-THE-POOH COLLECTION:
PIGLET AND EEYORE   ☐
Comments: Handcrafted, 2-3/4" tall.
Piglet rides bravely on Eeyore's back, carrying a red ornament for
the tree. Eeyore wears a pink ribbon tied on his tail.
Artist: Bob Siedler

☐ Purchased 19__Pd $_____MIB   NB   DB   BNT
☐ Want   Orig. Ret. $9.75   **NB** $40   **MIB** Sec. Mkt. **$55**

QX 560-7   WINNIE-THE-POOH COLLECTION: RABBIT   ☐
Comments: Handcrafted, 3" tall.
Rabbit brings a red translucent star to add to the Christmas tree.
It is for the very top. **Artist:** Bob Siedler

☐ Purchased 19__Pd $_____MIB   NB   DB   BNT
☐ Want   Orig. Ret. $9.75   **NB** $25   **MIB** Sec. Mkt. **$35**

QX 560-9   WINNIE-THE-POOH COLLECTION: TIGGER   ☐
Comments: Handcrafted, 3-1/2" tall.
Tigger springs into Christmas carrying a brightly wrapped gift.
He's proof that "tiggers" truly are wonderful things. This ornament
was more popular, or less produced than others, thus the value has
increased. **Artist:** Bob Siedler

☐ Purchased 19__Pd $_____MIB   NB   DB   BNT
☐ Want   Orig. Ret. $9.75   **NB** $85   **MIB** Sec. Mkt. **$100-$110**

QX 556-9   WINNIE-THE-POOH COLLECTION:
WINNIE-THE-POOH   ☐
Comments: Handcrafted, 3" tall.
Pooh's idea of the perfect gift is a jar of "Hunny" tied with a big red
bow. **Artist:** Bob Siedler

☐ Purchased 19__Pd $_____MIB   NB   DB   BNT
☐ Want   Orig. Ret. $9.75   **NB** $45   **MIB** Sec. Mkt. **$60**

QX 427-7   WINTER SURPRISE   ☐
Comments: **Third in Series,** Handcrafted, 3-1/4" tall.
Dated 1991. A penguin trio sings from "Polar Carols 1991" as
they stand beside a snow-covered tree.
Artist: Joyce A. Lyle

☐ Purchased 19__Pd $_____MIB   NB   DB   BNT
☐ Want   Orig. Ret. $10.75 **NB** $16   **MIB** Sec. Mkt. **$28**

Specialty Ornaments

QX 524-9   FLAG OF LIBERTY   ☐
Comments: Handcrafted, 3-5/16" tall, Dated 1991.
A pearlized yellow banner carries the caption: "God Bless America
1991" on this commemorative ornament of Desert Shield/Desert
Storm. For each ornament sold, Hallmark donated $1.00 to the
American Red Cross. The first shipment in June was very limited but
Hallmark began shipping the ornaments again in August. **Artist:**
Donna Lee

☐ Purchased 19__Pd $_____MIB   NB   DB   BNT
☐ Want Orig. Retail $6.75 **NB** $4   **MIB** Sec. Mkt. **$10**

Convention Ornaments

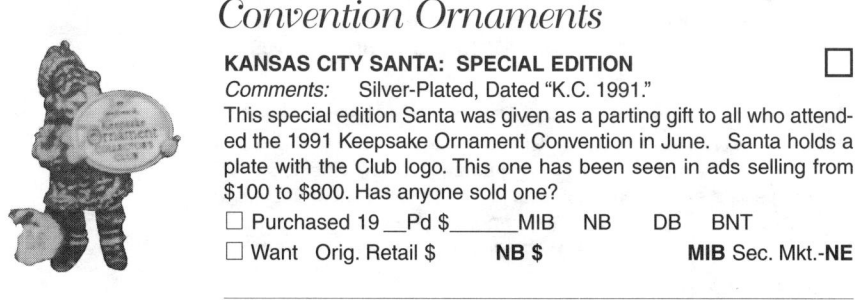

KANSAS CITY SANTA: SPECIAL EDITION   ☐
Comments: Silver-Plated, Dated "K.C. 1991."
This special edition Santa was given as a parting gift to all who attended the 1991 Keepsake Ornament Convention in June.   Santa holds a
plate with the Club logo. This one has been seen in ads selling from
$100 to $800. Has anyone sold one?

☐ Purchased 19__Pd $_____MIB   NB   DB   BNT
☐ Want Orig. Retail $ **NB** $ **MIB** Sec. Mkt.-**NE**

Season's
Greetings

Anna Lysenko's angel tree topper is
watching over all her collection.
What a tree!

1991 Miniature Ornament Collection

A · B · C · D · E · F · G · H · I · J · K · L · M · N · O

A   QXM 586-9   ALL ABOARD
Handcrafted, 1" tall, Dated 1991. **Artist:** Robert Chad
☐ Purchased 19___ Pd $_____   MIB   NB   DB   BNT
☐ Want   Orig. Retail $4.50
                          NB $5   **MIB** Sec. Mkt. **$15**

B   QXM 579-9   BABY'S FIRST CHRISTMAS
Handcrafted Carriage, 1" tall, Dated 1991.
Artist: John Francis (Collin)
☐ Purchased 19___ Pd $_____   MIB   NB   DB   BNT
☐ Want   Orig. Retail $6.00
                          NB $10   **MIB** Sec. Mkt. **$22**

C   QXM 597-7   BRASS BELLS
Etched, Pierced Brass, 1-1/4" tall, Dated 1991. **Artist:** Patricia Andrews
☐ Purchased 19___ Pd $_____   MIB   NB   DB   BNT
☐ Want   Orig. Retail $3.00
                          NB $3.50   **MIB** Sec. Mkt. **$8.50**

D   QXM 597-9   BRASS CHURCH
Etched Brass, 1-1/4" tall, Dated 1991.
☐ Purchased 19___ Pd $_____   MIB   NB   DB   BNT
☐ Want   Orig. Retail $3.00
                          NB $4   **MIB** Sec. Mkt. **$8.50**

E   QXM 598-7   BRASS SOLDIER
Etched Brass, 1-1/4" tall, Dated 1991.
☐ Purchased 19___ Pd $_____   MIB   NB   DB   BNT
☐ Want   Orig. Retail $3.00
                          NB $4   **MIB** Sec. Mkt. **$8.50**

F   QXM 587-7   BRIGHT BOXERS
Handcrafted, 1" tall, Dated 1991. **Artist:** Dill Rhodus
☐ Purchased 19___ Pd $_____   MIB   NB   DB   BNT
☐ Want   Orig. Retail $4.50
                          NB $8   **MIB** Sec. Mkt. **$16**

G   QXM 593-9   BUSY BEAR
Wood, 1-7/16" tall. **Artist:** Dill Rhodus
☐ Purchased 19___ Pd $_____   MIB   NB   DB   BNT
☐ Want   Orig. Retail $4.50
                          NB $5   **MIB** Sec. Mkt. **$11.25**

H   QXM 595-7   CARDINAL CAMEO
Handcrafted, 1-7/16" tall, Dated "Season's Greetings 1991." **Artist:** Joyce A. Lyle
☐ Purchased 19___ Pd $_____   MIB   NB   DB   BNT
☐ Want   Orig. Retail $6.00
                          NB $8   **MIB** Sec. Mkt. **$16.50**

I   QXM 594-9   CARING SHEPHERD
Hand-Painted Porcelain, 1-1/16" tall. **Artist:** John Francis (Collin)
☐ Purchased 19___ Pd $_____   MIB   NB   DB   BNT
☐ Want   Orig. Retail $6.00
                          NB $9   **MIB** Sec. Mkt. **$17**

J   QXM 586-7   COOL 'N' SWEET
Hand-Painted Fine Porcelain, 1-3/16" tall, Dated 1991. **Artist:** Sharon Pike
☐ Purchased 19___ Pd $_____   MIB   NB   DB   BNT
☐ Want   Orig. Retail $4.50
                          NB $10   **MIB** Sec. Mkt. **$20**

K   QXM 599-9   COUNTRY SLEIGH
Enamel, 1" tall, Dated 1991. **Artist:** LaDene Votruba
☐ Purchased 19___ Pd $_____   MIB   NB   DB   BNT
☐ Want   Orig. Retail $4.50
                          NB $5   **MIB** Sec. Mkt. **$12.50**

L   QXM 585-7   COURIER TURTLE
Handcrafted, 1-1/8" tall. **Artist:** Sharon Pike
☐ Purchased 19___ Pd $_____   MIB   NB   DB   BNT
☐ Want   Orig. Retail $4.50
                          NB $8   **MIB** Sec. Mkt. **$13**

M   QXM 591-7   FANCY WREATH
Handcrafted, 1-1/16" tall. **Artist:** Joyce A. Lyle
☐ Purchased 19___ Pd $_____   MIB   NB   DB   BNT
☐ Want   Orig. Retail $4.50
                          NB $7   **MIB** Sec. Mkt. **$13.25**

N   QXM 588-7   FELIZ NAVIDAD
Handcrafted/Straw, 1" tall, Dated 1991. **Artist:** Anita Marra Rogers
☐ Purchased 19___ Pd $_____   MIB   NB   DB   BNT
☐ Want   Orig. Retail $6.00
                          NB $8   **MIB** Sec. Mkt. **$14**

O   QXM 581-9   FIRST CHRISTMAS TOGETHER
Handcrafted/Brass, 1-1/8" tall, Dated 1991. **Artist:** Duane Unruh
☐ Purchased 19___ Pd $_____   MIB   NB   DB   BNT
☐ Want   Orig. Retail $6.00
                          NB $8   **MIB** Sec. Mkt. **$14**

A QXM 585-9 **FLY BY**
Handcrafted, 7/8" tall, Dated 1991. **Artist:** Ken Crow
☐ Purchased 19___ Pd $_____ MIB NB DB BNT
☐ Want Orig. Retail $4.50
NB $6 **MIB** Sec. Mkt. **$17.50**

B QXM 594-7 **FRIENDLY FAWN**
Handcrafted, 1-1/8" tall, Dated 1991. **Artist:** Julia Lee
☐ Purchased 19___ Pd $_____ MIB NB DB BNT
☐ Want Orig. Retail $6.00
NB $8 **MIB** Sec. Mkt. **$14**

C QXM 569-7 **GRANDCHILD'S FIRST CHRISTMAS**
Hand-Painted Fine Porcelain, 1-1/16", Dated 1991.
Artist: Anita Marra Rogers
☐ Purchased 19___ Pd $_____ MIB NB DB BNT
☐ Want Orig. Retail $4.50
NB $7 **MIB** Sec. Mkt. **$14**

D QXM 568-7 **HEAVENLY MINSTREL**
Handcrafted, 1-3/16" tall. **Artist:** Donna Lee
☐ Purchased 19___ Pd $_____ MIB NB DB BNT
☐ Want Orig. Retail $9.75
NB $12 **MIB** Sec. Mkt. **$22**

E QXM 599-7 **HOLIDAY SNOWFLAKE**
Etched, Faceted Acrylic, 1-15/32" tall, 1991. **Artist:** Dill Rhodus
☐ Purchased 19___ Pd $_____ MIB NB DB BNT
☐ Want Orig. Retail $3.00
NB $5 **MIB** Sec. Mkt. **$10**

F QXM 568-9 **KEY TO LOVE**
Handcrafted, 1" tall, Dated "Love 1991." **Artist:** Ken Crow
☐ Purchased 19___ Pd $_____ MIB NB DB BNT
☐ Want Orig. Retail $4.50
NB $10 **MIB** Sec. Mkt. **$15**

G QXM 563-9 **KITTENS IN TOYLAND: AIRPLANE**
Fourth in Series, Handcrafted, 7/8" tall. **Artist:** Ken Crow
☐ Purchased 19___ Pd $_____ MIB NB DB BNT
☐ Want Orig. Retail $4.50
NB $10 **MIB** Sec. Mkt. **$19.50**

H QXM 587-9 **KITTY IN A MITTY**
Handcrafted, 1" tall, Dated 1991. **Artist:** Patricia Andrews
☐ Purchased 19___ Pd $_____ MIB NB DB BNT
☐ Want Orig. Retail $4.50
NB $5 **MIB** Sec. Mkt. **$9.50**

I QXM 564-7 **KRINGLES, THE: PLATE OF COOKIES**
Third in Series, Handcrafted, 1" tall. **Artist:** Anita Marra Rogers
☐ Purchased 19___ Pd $_____ MIB NB DB BNT
☐ Want Orig. Retail $6.00
NB $12 **MIB** Sec. Mkt. **$23**

J QXM 589-7 **LI'L POPPER**
Handcrafted, 1-3/4" tall. **Artist:** Linda Sickman
☐ Purchased 19___ Pd $_____ MIB NB DB BNT
☐ Want Orig. Retail $4.50
NB $10.50 **MIB** Sec. Mkt. **$16.25**

K QXM 595-9 **LOVE IS BORN**
Fine Porcelain, 1-1/16" dia., Dated 1991. **Artist:** LaDene Votruba
☐ Purchased 19___ Pd $_____ MIB NB DB BNT
☐ Want Orig. Retail $6.00
NB $8 **MIB** Sec. Mkt. **$16**

L QXM 567-7 **LULU & FAMILY**
Handcrafted, 7/8" tall. **Artist:** Anita Marra Rogers
☐ Purchased 19___ Pd $_____ MIB NB DB BNT
☐ Want Orig. Retail $6.00
NB $9 **MIB** Sec. Mkt. **$12.50**

M QXM 569-9 **MOM**
Handcrafted, 1-3/16" tall, Dated "Mom 1991." **Artist:** Bob Siedler
☐ Purchased 19___ Pd $_____ MIB NB DB BNT
☐ Want Orig. Retail $6.00
NB $10 **MIB** Sec. Mkt. **$16.25**

N QXM 592-7 **N. POLE BUDDY**
Handcrafted, 1" tall, Dated 1991. **Artist:** Don Palmiter
☐ Purchased 19___ Pd $_____ MIB NB DB BNT
☐ Want Orig. Retail $4.50
NB $6 **MIB** Sec. Mkt. **$16.50**

O QXM 565-7 **NATURE'S ANGELS: PUPPY**
Second in Series, Handcrafted/Brass, 1-1/8" tall. **Artist:** Sharon Pike
☐ Purchased 19___ Pd $_____ MIB NB DB BNT
☐ Want Orig. Retail $4.50
NB $11 **MIB** Sec. Mkt. **$22**

A	QXM 598-9	**NOEL**

A   QXM 598-9   **NOEL**
Faceted Acrylic, 31/32" tall, Dated 1991. **Artist:** Linda Sickman
☐ Purchased 19___   Pd $_____   MIB   NB   DB   BNT
☐ Want   Orig. Retail $3.00
        NB $6   **MIB** Sec. Mkt. **$11.50**

B   QXM 564-9   **NOEL R.R.: PASSENGER CAR**
Third in Series, Handcrafted, 13/16" tall, Dated 1991.
Artist: Linda Sickman
☐ Purchased 19___   Pd $_____   MIB   NB   DB   BNT
☐ Want   Orig. Retail $8.50
        NB $13   **MIB** Sec. Mkt. **$25**

C   QXM 562-7   **OLD ENGLISH VILLAGE: COUNTRY INN**
Fourth in Series, Handcrafted, 1-1/8" tall, Dated 1991.
Artist: Julia Lee.
☐ Purchased 19___   Pd $_____   MIB   NB   DB   BNT
☐ Want   Orig. Retail $8.50
        NB $15   **MIB** Sec. Mkt. **$27.50**

D   QXM 562-9   **PENGUIN PAL**
Fourth & Final in Series, Handcrafted, 3/4" tall. **Artist:** Bob Siedler
☐ Purchased 19___   Pd $_____   MIB   NB   DB   BNT
☐ Want   Orig. Retail $4.50
        NB $8   **MIB** Sec. Mkt. **$15**

E   QXM 566-9   **RING-A-DING ELF**
Handcrafted/Brass, 1-1/4' tall, Dated 1991. **Artist:** Robert Chad
☐ Purchased 19___   Pd $_____   MIB   NB   DB   BNT
☐ Want   Orig. Retail $8.50
        NB $12   **MIB** Sec. Mkt. **$17.50**

F   QXM 563-7   **ROCKING HORSE: GREY ARABIAN**
Fourth in Series, Handcrafted, 1-1/8" tall, Dated 1991.
Popular Series. **Artist:** Linda Sickman
☐ Purchased 19___   Pd $_____   MIB   NB   DB   BNT
☐ Want   Orig. Retail $4.50
        NB $14   **MIB** Sec. Mkt. **$25**

G   QXM 590-9   **SEASIDE OTTER**
Handcrafted, 7/8" tall. **Artist:** Bob Siedler
☐ Purchased 19___   Pd $_____   MIB   NB   DB   BNT
☐ Want   Orig. Retail $4.50
        NB $6.50   **MIB** Sec. Mkt. **$12**

H   QXM 567-9   **SILVERY SANTA**
Precious Edition, Silver-Plated, 1-1/8" tall, Dated 1991.
Artist: Julia Lee
☐ Purchased 19___   Pd $_____   MIB   NB   DB   BNT
☐ Want   Orig. Retail $9.75
        NB $15   **MIB** Sec. Mkt. **$21.50**

I   QXM 579-7   **SPECIAL FRIENDS**
Handcrafted/Wicker, 13/16" tall, Dated 1991. **Artist:** Julia Lee
☐ Purchased 19___   Pd $_____   MIB   NB   DB   BNT
☐ Want   Orig. Retail $8.50
        NB $12   **MIB** Sec. Mkt. **$18**

J   QXM 565-9   **THIMBLE BELLS**
Second in Series, Handcrafted, 1-1/8" tall, Dated 1991.
Artist: Michele Pyda-Sevcik
☐ Purchased 19___   Pd $_____   MIB   NB   DB   BNT
☐ Want   Orig. Retail $6.00
        NB $12   **MIB** Sec. Mkt. **$22.50**

K   QXM 588-9   **TOP HATTER**
Handcrafted, 1" tall, Dated 1991. **Artist:** Ed Seale
☐ Purchased 19___   Pd $_____   MIB   NB   DB   BNT
☐ Want   Orig. Retail $6.00
        NB $10   **MIB** Sec. Mkt. **$17**

L   QXM 589-9   **TREELAND TRIO**
Handcrafted, 7/8" tall, Dated 1991. **Artist:** Robert Chad
☐ Purchased 19___   Pd $_____   MIB   NB   DB   BNT
☐ Want   Orig. Retail $8.50
        NB $12   **MIB** Sec. Mkt. **$16.50**

M   QXM 590-7   **UPBEAT BEAR**
Handcrafted/Metal, 1-1/16" tall, Dated 1991.
Artist: John Francis (Collin)
☐ Purchased 19___   Pd $_____   MIB   NB   DB   BNT
☐ Want   Orig. Retail $6.00
        NB $10   **MIB** Sec. Mkt. **$16**

N   QXM 593-7   **VISION OF SANTA**
Handcrafted, 1-1/16" tall, Dated 1991. **Artist:** Robert Chad
☐ Purchased 19___   Pd $_____   MIB   NB   DB   BNT
☐ Want   Orig. Retail $4.50
        NB $9   **MIB** Sec. Mkt. **$13.50**

Miniature Collections

The Shearer's shelves (right) are packed with miniature ornaments.

A	QXM 582-7	**TINY TEA PARTY SET**

Fine **Porcelain**/Handcrafted, Dated 1991. Other mini sets not porcelain. These porcelain ornaments were "first of their kind." They were not bought up on the secondary market due to the inital retail. Following sets were artplas, not porcelain. The second issue was over-ordered and plentiful. Hope to see these mini sets continue for years to come! Bring back the porcelain! More! More!

Artist: Ed Seale

Cookie Plate, 11/16" tall.	Teacup Lounger, 5/8" tall.
Teacup Taster, 13/16" tall.	Teapot, 1" tall.
Creamer, 1-3/16" tall.	Sugar Bowl, 15/16" tall.

☐ Purchased 19___ Pd $_____ MIB NB DB BNT

☐ Want Orig. Retail $29.00

NB $100 **MIB** Sec. Mkt. **$140-$155**

B.K. Breyer (above) has her Thimble Series ornaments '78-'89 above her sewing machine. How clever!

B	QXM 596-7	**WEE TOYMAKER**

Handcrafted, 1" tall, Dated 1991. **Artist:** Ron Bishop

☐ Purchased 19___ Pd $_____ MIB NB DB BNT

☐ Want Orig. Retail $8.50

NB $10 **MIB** Sec. Mkt. **$17**

C	QXM 566-7	**WOODLAND BABIES**

FIRST IN SERIES, Handcrafted, 1" tall. **Artist:** Ken Crow

☐ Purchased 19___ Pd $_____ MIB NB DB BNT

☐ Want Orig. Retail $6.00

NB $5 **MIB** Sec. Mkt. **$14.50**

Clara Ashley made this tree out of blocks with miniature ornaments.

Carolyn Brown (left) displays her "mini" collection on this tree.

1991 Easter Ornament Collection

Prices up from '96 guide! Easter Ornaments becoming more sought after!

A   QEO 518-9   **BABY'S FIRST EASTER**   ☐
Hand-Painted/Handcrafted, 1-1/2" tall, Dated 1991.
☐ Purchased 19___   Pd $_____   MIB   NB   DB   BNT
☐ Want   Original Retail $8.75
         NB $14   **MIB** Sec. Mkt. **$25**

B   QEO 517-9   **DAUGHTER**   ☐
Hand-Painted/Handcrafted, 1-1/2" tall.
☐ Purchased 19___   Pd $_____   MIB   NB   DB   BNT
☐ Want   Original Retail $5.75
         NB $15   **MIB** Sec. Mkt. **$32**

C   QEO 513-7   **EASTER MEMORIES PHOTOHOLDER**   ☐
Fabric, 2-1/2" tall, Dated 1991.
☐ Purchased 19___   Pd $_____   MIB   NB   DB   BNT
☐ Want   Original Retail $7.75
         NB $12   **MIB** Sec. Mkt. **$16**

D   QEO 514-9   **FULL OF LOVE**   ☐
Hand-Painted/Handcrafted, 2" tall, Dated 1991.
☐ Purchased 19___   Pd $_____   MIB   NB   DB   BNT
☐ Want   Original Retail $7.75
         NB $21   **MIB** Sec. Mkt. **$42.50**

E   QEO 515-9   **GENTLE LAMB**   ☐
Hand-Painted/Handcrafted, 2" tall, Dated '91.
☐ Purchased 19___   Pd $_____   MIB   NB   DB   BNT
☐ Want   Original Retail $6.75
         NB $12   **MIB** Sec. Mkt. **$19.50**

F   QEO 517-7   **GRANDCHILD**   ☐
Hand-Painted/Handcrafted, 2-1/2" tall, Dated 1991.
☐ Purchased 19___   Pd $_____   MIB   NB   DB   BNT
☐ Want   Original Retail $6.75
         NB $12   **MIB** Sec. Mkt. **$20**

G   QEO 514-7   **LI'L DIPPER**   ☐
Hand-Painted/Handcrafted, 2-1/2" tall.
☐ Purchased 19___   Pd $_____   MIB   NB   DB   BNT
☐ Want   Original Retail $6.75
         NB $15   **MIB** Sec. Mkt. **$24**

H   QEO 513-9   **LILY EGG**   ☐
Hand-Painted Fine Porcelain, 2" tall, Dated 1991.
☐ Purchased 19___   Pd $_____   MIB   NB   DB   BNT
☐ Want   Original Retail $9.75
         NB $10   **MIB** Sec. Mkt. **$22.50**

I   QEO 518-7   **SON**   ☐
Hand-Painted/Handcrafted, 1-1/2" tall.
☐ Purchased 19___   Pd $_____   MIB   NB   DB   BNT
☐ Want   Original Retail $5.75
         NB $12   **MIB** Sec. Mkt. **$25**

J   QEO 516-9   **SPIRIT OF EASTER**   ☐
Hand-Painted/Handcrafted, 2" tall, Dated 1991.
☐ Purchased 19___   Pd $_____   MIB   NB   DB   BNT
☐ Want   Original Retail $7.75
         NB $18   **MIB** Sec. Mkt. **$35**

K   QEO 5167   **SPRINGTIME STROLL**   ☐
Hand-Painted/Handcrafted, 2-1/2" tall, Dated 1991.
☐ Purchased 19___   Pd $_____   MIB   NB   DB   BNT
☐ Want   Original Retail $6.75
         NB $14   **MIB** Sec. Mkt. **$22**

1992 Collection

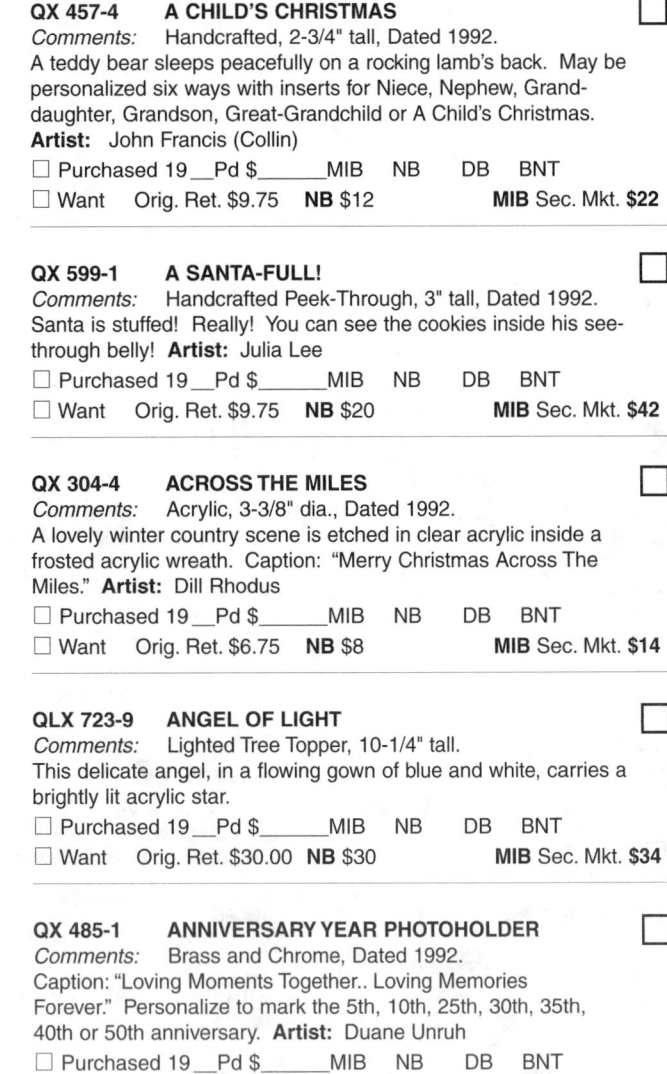

QX 457-4   A CHILD'S CHRISTMAS
Comments: Handcrafted, 2-3/4" tall, Dated 1992.
A teddy bear sleeps peacefully on a rocking lamb's back. May be personalized six ways with inserts for Niece, Nephew, Granddaughter, Grandson, Great-Grandchild or A Child's Christmas.
Artist: John Francis (Collin)

☐ Purchased 19 __ Pd $_____ MIB   NB   DB   BNT
☐ Want   Orig. Ret. $9.75   **NB** $12   **MIB** Sec. Mkt. **$22**

QX 599-1   A SANTA-FULL!
Comments: Handcrafted Peek-Through, 3" tall, Dated 1992.
Santa is stuffed! Really! You can see the cookies inside his see-through belly! **Artist:** Julia Lee

☐ Purchased 19 __ Pd $_____ MIB   NB   DB   BNT
☐ Want   Orig. Ret. $9.75   **NB** $20   **MIB** Sec. Mkt. **$42**

QX 304-4   ACROSS THE MILES
Comments: Acrylic, 3-3/8" dia., Dated 1992.
A lovely winter country scene is etched in clear acrylic inside a frosted acrylic wreath. Caption: "Merry Christmas Across The Miles." **Artist:** Dill Rhodus

☐ Purchased 19 __ Pd $_____ MIB   NB   DB   BNT
☐ Want   Orig. Ret. $6.75   **NB** $8   **MIB** Sec. Mkt. **$14**

QLX 723-9   ANGEL OF LIGHT
Comments: Lighted Tree Topper, 10-1/4" tall.
This delicate angel, in a flowing gown of blue and white, carries a brightly lit acrylic star.

☐ Purchased 19 __ Pd $_____ MIB   NB   DB   BNT
☐ Want   Orig. Ret. $30.00   **NB** $30   **MIB** Sec. Mkt. **$34**

QX 485-1   ANNIVERSARY YEAR PHOTOHOLDER
Comments: Brass and Chrome, Dated 1992.
Caption: "Loving Moments Together.. Loving Memories Forever." Personalize to mark the 5th, 10th, 25th, 30th, 35th, 40th or 50th anniversary. **Artist:** Duane Unruh

☐ Purchased 19 __ Pd $_____ MIB   NB   DB   BNT
☐ Want   Orig. Ret. $9.75   **NB** $16   **MIB** Sec. Mkt. **$25**

The best mirror is an old friend.

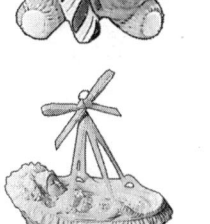

QX 464-4   BABY'S FIRST CHRISTMAS
Comments: Handcrafted, 2-1/8" tall, Dated 1992.
This cute light brown bear holds a red, white and green striped candy-cane "1" in celebration of its first Christmas.
Artist: John Francis (Collin)

☐ Purchased 19 __ Pd $_____ MIB   NB   DB   BNT
☐ Want   Orig. Ret. $7.75   **NB** $16   **MIB** Sec. Mkt. **$25**

QX 458-1   BABY'S FIRST CHRISTMAS
Comments: Hand-Painted Fine Porcelain, 3-1/2" tall, Dated 1992.
A tiny baby sleeps soundly in a wicker-look basket tied with pale green ribbon. **Artist:** Trish Andrews

☐ Purchased 19 __ Pd $_____ MIB   NB   DB   BNT
☐ Want   Orig. Ret. $18.75   **NB** $22   **MIB** Sec. Mkt. **$40**

QLX 728-1   BABY'S FIRST CHRISTMAS
Comments: Light and Music, Handcrafted, 3-7/16" tall.
Dated 1992. Baby sleeps soundly in this white, lace-trimmed crib. Plays "Silent Night." **Artist:** Ken Crow

☐ Purchased 19 __ Pd $_____ MIB   NB   DB   BNT
☐ Want   Orig. Ret. $22.00   **NB** $65   **MIB** Sec. Mkt. **$80**

QX 219-1   BABY'S FIRST CHRISTMAS - BABY BOY
Comments: Blue Satin Ball, 2-7/8" dia.,Dated 1992.
Forest animals decorate a Christmas tree.
Caption: "To Love, Spoil, Play With, Adore -- That's What Baby Boys Are For!" **Artist:** LaDene Votruba

☐ Purchased 19 __ Pd $_____ MIB   NB   DB   BNT
☐ Want   Orig. Ret. $4.75   **NB** $6   **MIB** Sec. Mkt. **$15**

QX 220-4   BABY'S FIRST CHRISTMAS - BABY GIRL
Comments: Pink Satin Ball, 2-7/8" dia.,Dated 1992.
Forest animals decorate a Christmas tree. Caption: "To Love, Spoil, Play With, Adore -- That's What Baby Girls Are For!"
Artist: LaDene Votruba

☐ Purchased 19 __ Pd $_____ MIB   NB   DB   BNT
☐ Want   Orig. Ret. $4.75   **NB** $8   **MIB** Sec. Mkt. **$15**

QX 464-1   BABY'S FIRST CHRISTMAS PHOTOHOLDER
Comments: Embroidered Fabric, 3-3/16" tall, Dated 1992.
White eyelet lace and embroidered designs frame baby's photo. Caption: "With Every Small Discovery, Baby Makes A Merry Memory." **Artist:** LaDene Votruba

☐ Purchased 19 __ Pd $_____ MIB   NB   DB   BNT
☐ Want   Orig. Ret. $7.75   **NB** $14   **MIB** Sec. Mkt. **$20**

QX 465-1   BABY'S SECOND CHRISTMAS

Comments: Handcrafted, 2-3/16" tall, Dated 1992.
Identical to 1989, only date has changed.
Artist: John Francis (Collin)

☐ Purchased 19___ Pd $_____ MIB   NB   DB   BNT
☐ Want   Orig. Ret. $6.75   **NB** $15   **MIB** Sec. Mkt. **$24**

QX 507-1   BEAR BELL CHAMP

Comments: Handcrafted, 2-3/16" tall, Dated 1992.
This champion lifts real bells -- jingle bells, that is!
1992 Commemorative. **Artist:** Ed Seale

☐ Purchased 19___ Pd $_____ MIB   NB   DB   BNT
☐ Want   Orig. Ret. $7.75   **NB** $10   **MIB** Sec. Mkt. **$24**

QX 210-4   BETSEY'S COUNTRY CHRISTMAS

Comments: **FIRST IN SERIES,** Aqua Teardrop Ball, 2-7/8" tall.
Dated 1992. Caption: "Christmas Sets Our Hearts A-Dancing!"

☐ Purchased 19___ Pd $_____ MIB   NB   DB   BNT
☐ Want   Orig. Ret. $5.00   **NB** $15   **MIB** Sec. Mkt. **$25**

QX 468-4   BROTHER

Comments: Handcrafted, 4-1/8" tall, Dated 1992.
Pull the ball on this ornament and the drummer beats a rhythm on
his drum. **Artist:** Ken Crow

☐ Purchased 19___ Pd $_____ MIB   NB   DB   BNT
☐ Want   Orig. Ret. $6.75   **NB** $10   **MIB** Sec. Mkt. **$13.50**

QX 515-4   CHEERFUL SANTA

Comments: Handcrafted, 3-1/8" tall, Dated 1992.
Bearing the date on his pack, this African-American Santa waves
a very Merry Christmas to all.
Artist: Duane Unruh

☐ Purchased 19___ Pd $_____ MIB   NB   DB   BNT
☐ Want   Orig. Ret. $9.75   **NB** $20   **MIB** Sec. Mkt. **$30**

QX 466-4   CHILD'S FIFTH CHRISTMAS

Comments: Handcrafted, 2-3/8" tall, Dated 1992.
Identical to 1989, only date has changed.
Artist: Dill Rhodus

☐ Purchased 19___ Pd $_____ MIB   NB   DB   BNT
☐ Want   Orig. Ret. $6.75   **NB** $12   **MIB** Sec. Mkt. **$18**

QX 466-1   CHILD'S FOURTH CHRISTMAS

Comments: Handcrafted, 3" tall, Dated 1992.
Identical to 1989, only date has changed.
Artist: John Francis (Collin)

☐ Purchased 19___ Pd $_____ MIB   NB   DB   BNT
☐ Want   Orig. Ret. $6.75   **NB** $12   **MIB** Sec. Mkt. **$23**

QX 465-4   CHILD'S THIRD CHRISTMAS

Comments: Handcrafted, 2-1/2" tall, Dated 1992.
Identical to 1989, only date has changed.
Artist: John Francis (Collin)

☐ Purchased 19___ Pd $_____ MIB   NB   DB   BNT
☐ Want   Orig. Ret. $6.75   **NB** $10   **MIB** Sec. Mkt. **$20**

QLX 707-4   CHRIS MOUSE TALES

Comments: **Eighth in Series,** Light, Handcrafted, 3-9/16" tall.
Dated 1992. Chris Mouse opens the shutters of his brightly lit
shoe-house. A "Chris Mouse Tales" story book forms the roof for
his "house." **Artist:** Anita Marra Rogers

☐ Purchased 19___ Pd $_____ MIB   NB   DB   BNT
☐ Want   Orig. Ret. $12.00   **NB** $22   **MIB** Sec. Mkt. **$30**

QLX 727-1   CHRISTMAS PARADE

Comments: Light and Motion, Handcrafted, 3-3/8" tall, Dated 1992.
It's Christmas time in the city as evidenced by the decorations
atop the skyscrapers and the parade marching 'round the city.
Artist: Linda Sickman

☐ Purchased 19___ Pd $_____ MIB   NB   DB   BNT
☐ Want   Orig. Ret. $30.00   **NB** $50   **MIB** Sec. Mkt. **$62**

QX 532-1   CHRISTMAS SKY LINE COLLECTION: CABOOSE

Comments: Die Cast Metal, 2" tall, Dated 1992.
The traditional red caboose brings up the tail of the Christmas Sky
Line Collection. May be displayed hanging or standing.
Artist: Linda Sickman

☐ Purchased 19___ Pd $_____ MIB   NB   DB   BNT
☐ Want   Orig. Ret. $9.75   **NB** $18   **MIB** Sec. Mkt. **$25**

QX 540-1   CHRISTMAS SKY LINE COLLECTION: COAL CAR

Comments: Die Cast Metal, 1-7/8" tall, Dated 1992.
"Christmas Sky Line" proudly proclaims the name of the line on
the side of the coal car. **Artist:** Linda Sickman

☐ Purchased 19___ Pd $_____ MIB   NB   DB   BNT
☐ Want   Orig. Ret. $9.75   **NB** $15   **MIB** Sec. Mkt. **$21**

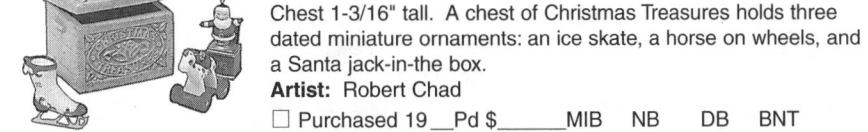

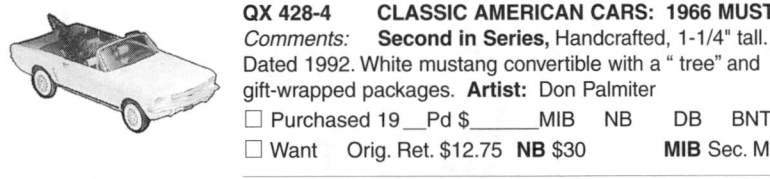

**QX 531-1   CHRISTMAS SKY LINE COLLECTION:
LOCOMOTIVE**

Comments: Die Cast Metal, 1-3/4" tall, Dated 1992.
This cheery locomotive is bright blue with red wheels and a red
cabin. **Artist:** Linda Sickman

☐ Purchased 19 __ Pd $_____ MIB   NB   DB   BNT
☐ Want   Orig. Ret. $9.75   **NB** $32   **MIB** Sec. Mkt. **$45**

**QX 531-4   CHRISTMAS SKY LINE COLLECTION:
STOCK CAR**

Comments: Die Cast Metal, 1-7/8" tall, Dated 1992.
The stock car is painted a bright yellow with black stripes.
Artist: Linda Sickman

☐ Purchased 19 __ Pd $_____ MIB   NB   DB   BNT
☐ Want   Orig. Ret. $9.75   **NB** $15   **MIB** Sec. Mkt. **$21**

QXC 546-4   CHRISTMAS TREASURES: KEEPSAKE CLUB

Comments: Limited Edition 15,500, Handcrafted, Dated 1992.
Chest 1-3/16" tall. A chest of Christmas Treasures holds three
dated miniature ornaments: an ice skate, a horse on wheels, and
a Santa jack-in-the box.
Artist: Robert Chad

☐ Purchased 19 __ Pd $_____ MIB   NB   DB   BNT
☐ Want   Orig. Ret. $22.00   **NB** $120   **MIB** Sec. Mkt. **$125-$150**

QX 428-4   CLASSIC AMERICAN CARS: 1966 MUSTANG

Comments: **Second in Series,** Handcrafted, 1-1/4" tall.
Dated 1992. White mustang convertible with a " tree" and
gift-wrapped packages. **Artist:** Don Palmiter

☐ Purchased 19 __ Pd $_____ MIB   NB   DB   BNT
☐ Want   Orig. Ret. $12.75   **NB** $30   **MIB** Sec. Mkt. **$40-$45**

**QX 446-1   COLLECTOR'S PLATE:
SWEET HOLIDAY HARMONY**

Comments: **Sixth and Final in Series** Porcelain, 3-1/4" dia.
Dated 1992. Includes Acrylic Display Stand. This brother and
sister duet becomes a trio when their puppy joins his voice with
theirs. **Artist:** LaDene Votruba

☐ Purchased 19 __ Pd $_____ MIB   NB   DB   BNT
☐ Want   Orig. Ret. $8.75   **NB** $14   **MIB** Sec. Mkt. **$20-$22**

QLX 726-4   CONTINENTAL EXPRESS

Comments: Light and Motion, Handcrafted, 3-3/4" tall.
Dated 1992. Two trains circle a village going in opposite directions.
Artist: Linda Sickman

☐ Purchased 19 __ Pd $_____ MIB   NB   DB   BNT
☐ Want   Orig. Ret. $32.00   **NB** $55   **MIB** Sec. Mkt. **$65**

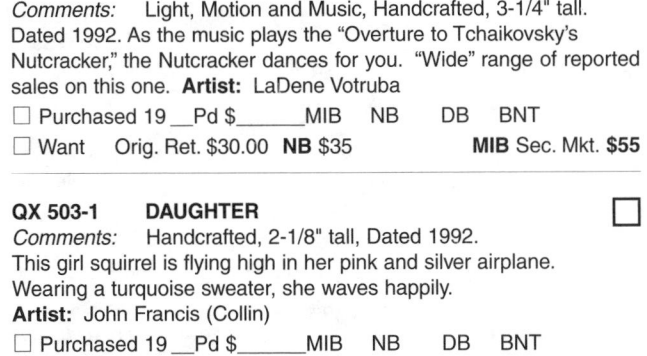

QX 547-4   COOL FLIERS

Comments: Handcrafted, 3-1/2" tall, Dated 1992.
These two can really swing! A snowman and snow woman on
trapezes may be hung on separate branches; their hands inter-
lock to complete their act. **Artist:** Julia Lee

☐ Purchased 19 __ Pd $_____ MIB   NB   DB   BNT
☐ Want   Orig. Ret. $10.75   **NB** $14   **MIB** Sec. Mkt. **$20**

**QX 426-4   CRAYOLA® CRAYON:
BRIGHT BLAZING COLORS**

Comments: **Fourth in Series,** Handcrafted, 2-1/8" tall.
Dated 1992. A dalmatian, wearing a bright red fireman's helmet,
races to the rescue. **Artist:** Ken Crow

☐ Purchased 19 __ Pd $_____ MIB   NB   DB   BNT
☐ Want   Orig. Ret. $9.75   **NB** $16   **MIB** Sec. Mkt. **$35**

QX 467-4   DAD

Comments: Handcrafted, 2-5/16" tall, Dated 1992.
It's official! "Dad's A Winner!" Dad naps comfortably in his
recliner with a smile on his face as the newspaper declares that
it's been a "Banner Year For Dad!" **Artist:** Bob Siedler

☐ Purchased 19 __ Pd $_____ MIB   NB   DB   BNT
☐ Want   Orig. Ret. $7.75   **NB** $14   **MIB** Sec. Mkt. **$18**

QX 461-1   DAD-TO-BE

Comments: Handcrafted, 2-3/8" tall, Dated 1992.
Dad rooster crows out the good news -- he'll be a father soon!
Artist: Julia Lee

☐ Purchased 19 __ Pd $_____ MIB   NB   DB   BNT
☐ Want   Orig. Ret. $6.75   **NB** $10   **MIB** Sec. Mkt. **$15**

QLX 726-1   DANCING NUTCRACKER, THE

Comments: Light, Motion and Music, Handcrafted, 3-1/4" tall.
Dated 1992. As the music plays the "Overture to Tchaikovsky's
Nutcracker," the Nutcracker dances for you. "Wide" range of reported
sales on this one. **Artist:** LaDene Votruba

☐ Purchased 19 __ Pd $_____ MIB   NB   DB   BNT
☐ Want   Orig. Ret. $30.00   **NB** $35   **MIB** Sec. Mkt. **$55**

QX 503-1   DAUGHTER

Comments: Handcrafted, 2-1/8" tall, Dated 1992.
This girl squirrel is flying high in her pink and silver airplane.
Wearing a turquoise sweater, she waves happily.
Artist: John Francis (Collin)

☐ Purchased 19 __ Pd $_____ MIB   NB   DB   BNT
☐ Want   Orig. Ret. $6.75   **NB** $12   **MIB** Sec. Mkt. **$18**

QX 520-4   DECK THE HOGS
Comments: Handcrafted, 3-1/8" tall, Dated 1992.
"Deck The Hogs With Boughs Of Holly" sings a happy fellow
decorated with red ribbon and holly.
Artist: John Francis (Collin)

☐ Purchased 19__ Pd $_____ MIB   NB   DB   BNT
☐ Want   Orig. Ret. $8.75   **NB** $12   **MIB** Sec. Mkt. **$18**

QX 455-4   DICKENS CAROLER BELL: LORD CHADWICK ☐
Comments: **Third in Collection,** Hand-Painted Porcelain.
4-5/8" tall, Dated 1992, inside bell. Lord Chadwick depicts a
Victorian gentleman with his pale blue coat and a sprig of
Christmas ivy in his hat. **Artist:** Robert Chad

☐ Purchased 19__ Pd $_____ MIB   NB   DB   BNT
☐ Want   Orig. Ret. $21.75 **NB** $25   **MIB** Sec. Mkt. **$45**

QX 514-4   DOWN-UNDER HOLIDAY
Comments: Handcrafted, 2-7/8" tall, Dated 1992.
A koala has hopped a ride on the back of a kangaroo in his red and
white sneakers. He also carries a wrapped gift in his pouch and
a dated boomerang. **Artist:** Ken Crow

☐ Purchased 19__ Pd $_____ MIB   NB   DB   BNT
☐ Want   Orig. Ret. $7.75   **NB** $14   **MIB** Sec. Mkt. **$20**

QX 512-1   EGG NOG NEST
Comments: Handcrafted, 2-1/2" tall, Dated 1992.
A cute little bluebird has made his home in an Egg Nog carton;
he's trimmed the "roof" with lights and is hanging out his stocking
for Santa. "Vitamins And Cheer Added. Enjoy By 12-25-92."

☐ Purchased 19__ Pd $_____ MIB   NB   DB   BNT
☐ Want   Orig. Ret. $7.75   **NB** $10   **MIB** Sec. Mkt. **$16**

QX 593-1   ELFIN MARIONETTE
Comments: Handcrafted, 3-15/16" tall, Dated 1992.
This wood-look marionette works just like the real thing! Move the
crossbar and the elf moves his arms and legs.
Artist: Robert Chad

☐ Purchased 19__ Pd $_____ MIB   NB   DB   BNT
☐ Want   Orig. Ret. $11.75 **NB** $12   **MIB** Sec. Mkt. **$22**

QX 562-4   ELVIS
Comments: Brass-plated, 4-1/2" tall, Dated 1992.
Taken from his early years, Elvis strikes a classic pose, guitar in
hand. This special issue Keepsake ornament has a bronze-cast
finish. Was not well received by the consumer or collector.
Artist: Dill Rhodus/Joyce A. Lyle

☐ Purchased 19__ Pd $_____ MIB   NB   DB   BNT
☐ Want   Orig. Ret. $14.75 **NB** $5   **MIB** Sec. Mkt. **$10-$12**

QLX 727-4   ENCHANTED CLOCK ☐
Comments: Light and Motion, Handcrafted, 3-15/16" tall.
Caption: "When This Enchanted Clock Strikes Twelve Each
Starry Christmas Eve, The Magic Toys Will Dance And Play, If
Only You Believe." Several found below retail. **Artist:** Ken Crow

☐ Purchased 19__ Pd $_____ MIB   NB   DB   BNT
☐ Want   Orig. Ret. $30.00 **NB** $35   **MIB** Sec. Mkt. **$60**

QX 424-4   FABULOUS DECADE ☐
Comments: **Third in Series,** 1-7/8" tall, Handcrafted and Brass.
Dated 1992. A light brown bear with a red neck ribbon holds
a shiny brass "1992." **Artist:** Ed Seale

☐ Purchased 19__ Pd $_____ MIB   NB   DB   BNT
☐ Want   Orig. Ret. $7.7   **NB** $22   **MIB** Sec. Mkt. **$36**

QLX 709-1   FEATHERED FRIENDS ☐
Comments: Light, Handcrafted, 1-15/16" tall, Dated 1992.
A favorite pastime for many during the winter months is to watch
the birds at outdoor feeders. **Artist:** Linda Sickman

☐ Purchased 19__ Pd $_____ MIB   NB   DB   BNT
☐ Want   Orig. Ret. $14.00 **NB** $22   **MIB** Sec. Mkt. **$30**

QX 518-1   FELIZ NAVIDAD ☐
Comments: Handcrafted, 2-7/8" tall, Dated 1992.
A merry mouse rides his guitar and wishes everyone "Feliz
Navidad" ... Merry Christmas! **Artist:** Trish Andrews

☐ Purchased 19__ Pd $_____ MIB   NB   DB   BNT
☐ Want   Orig. Ret. $6.75   **NB** $14   **MIB** Sec. Mkt. **$20**

QX 301-1   FIRST CHRISTMAS TOGETHER, OUR ☐
Comments: Acrylic, 3" tall, Dated 1992.
Red hearts and gold foil lettering decorate this clear acrylic heart.
Caption: "Our First Christmas Together 1992."
Artist: LaDene Votruba

☐ Purchased 19__ Pd $_____ MIB   NB   DB   BNT
☐ Want   Orig. Ret. $6.75   **NB** $10   **MIB** Sec. Mkt. **$14**

QX 506-1   FIRST CHRISTMAS TOGETHER, OUR ☐
Comments: Handcrafted, 2-7/8" tall, Dated 1992.
Two little mice share a sugar heart inside a silvery sugar bowl.
Caption: "Our First Christmas Together 1992."
Artist: Julia Lee

☐ Purchased 19__ Pd $_____ MIB   NB   DB   BNT
☐ Want   Orig. Ret. $9.75   **NB** $12   **MIB** Sec. Mkt. **$20**

QX 469-4 FIRST CHRISTMAS TOGETHER PHOTOHOLDER

Comments: Handcrafted, 3-1/2" tall, Dated 1992.
Slide your favorite photo into the shutter-framed window of this snow-capped home. Captions: "Our First Christmas Together" and "Home Is Where The Heart Is." **Artist:** Ed Seale

☐ Purchased 19___Pd $_____MIB NB DB BNT
☐ Want Orig. Ret. $8.75 **NB** $12 **MIB** Sec. Mkt. **$24**

QX 518-4 FOR MY GRANDMA PHOTOHOLDER

Comments: Embroidered Fabric, 3-1/8" tall, Dated 1992.
Hearts and holly decorate this heart-shaped ivory photo holder for Grandma. Caption: "Merry Christmas -- With Love And Kisses From XOXO."

☐ Purchased 19___Pd $_____MIB NB DB BNT
☐ Want Orig. Ret. $7.75 **NB** $8 **MIB** Sec. Mkt. **$12**

QX 484-4 FOR THE ONE I LOVE

Comments: Hand-Painted Fine Porcelain, 2-3/8" tall, Dated 1992.
This ivory heart is filled with lovely pink roses in full bloom. Captions: "For The One I Love." and "Having Your Love Makes Christmas Perfect 1992." **Artist:** Joyce A. Lyle

☐ Purchased 19___Pd $_____MIB NB DB BNT
☐ Want Orig. Ret. $9.75 **NB** $12 **MIB** Sec. Mkt. **$20**

QLX 725-4 FOREST FROLICS

Comments: **Fourth in Series,** Handcrafted, 4-1/8" tall, Dated 1992.
Light and Motion. Forest friends have fun together on a seesaw which moves up and down. **Artist:** Sharon Pike

☐ Purchased 19___Pd $_____MIB NB DB BNT
☐ Want Orig. Ret. $28.00 **NB** $38 **MIB** Sec. Mkt. **$60**

QX 504-1 FRIENDLY GREETINGS

Comments: Handcrafted, 2-5/16" tall, Dated 1992.
A yellow and white kitten shares "A Friendly Christmas Greeting." Caption: "Friendship -- Tis The Reason To Be Jolly!" Add your own message inside the card as well. **Artist:** Robert Chad

☐ Purchased 19___Pd $_____MIB NB DB BNT
☐ Want Orig. Ret. $7.75 **NB** $8 **MIB** Sec. Mkt. **$12**

QX 503-4 FRIENDSHIP LINE

Comments: Handcrafted, 4-1/2" tall, Dated 1992.
Two chipmunks converse gaily on a red telephone receiver.
Artist: Ed Seale

☐ Purchased 19___Pd $_____MIB NB DB BNT
☐ Want Orig. Ret. $9.75 **NB** $14 **MIB** Sec. Mkt. **$28**

QX 213-1 FROM OUR HOME TO YOURS

Comments: White Glass Ball, 2-7/8" dia., Dated 1992.
A whimsical Christmas scene of snow-capped houses decorates this glass ball. **Artist:** LaDene Votruba

☐ Purchased 19___Pd $_____MIB NB DB BNT
☐ Want Orig. Ret. $4.75 **NB** $6 **MIB** Sec. Mkt. **$12**

QX 429-1 FROSTY FRIENDS

Comments: **Thirteenth in Series,** 2-11/16" tall, Dated 1992.
Handcrafted and Acrylic. Our little Eskimo friend shares his bright red and white candy canes with a little whale which has popped his head through the ice. **Artist:** Julia Lee

☐ Purchased 19___Pd $_____MIB NB DB BNT
☐ Want Orig. Ret. $9.75 **NB** $15 **MIB** Sec. Mkt. **$25**

QX 513-4 FUN ON A BIG SCALE

Comments: Handcrafted, 3-3/16" tall, Dated 1992.
Fun is exactly what this little hamster is having! Press down gently on the dish of candy and the scale tips.
Artist: Ken Crow

☐ Purchased 19___Pd $_____MIB NB DB BNT
☐ Want Orig. Ret. $10.75 **NB** $12 **MIB** Sec. Mkt. **$22**

QX 537-4 GARFIELD

Comments: Handcrafted, 2-7/16" tall, Dated 1992.
That cool cat is ready for bed; he's wearing a Santa nightcap, his special slippers and has his book and blanket in hand.
Artist: Don Palmiter

☐ Purchased 19___Pd $_____MIB NB DB BNT
☐ Want Orig. Ret. $7.75 **NB** $12 **MIB** Sec. Mkt. **$17**

QX 537-1 GENIUS AT WORK

Comments: Handcrafted, 2-3/8" tall, Dated 1992.
Watch the elf work as he pounds his hammer and jiggles the wrench. **Artist:** Ken Crow

☐ Purchased 19___Pd $_____MIB NB DB BNT
☐ Want Orig. Ret. $10.75 **NB** $12 **MIB** Sec. Mkt. **$22**

QX 212-4 GIFT BRINGERS, THE: KOLYADA

Comments: **Fourth in Series,** White Glass Ball, 2-7/8" dia.
Dated Christmas 1992. The elf maiden Kolyada brings Christmas to Russian children. **Artist:** LaDene Votruba

☐ Purchased 19___Pd $_____MIB NB DB BNT
☐ Want Orig. Ret. $5.00 **NB** $8 **MIB** Sec. Mkt. **$18**

QX 594-1   GODCHILD

Comments: Handcrafted, 1-5/8" tall, Dated 1992.
The love of the Godparent and Godchild for each other is portrayed on the faces of these sheep. **Artist:** Duane Unruh

☐ Purchased 19 __ Pd $_____ MIB   NB   DB   BNT
☐ Want   Orig. Ret. $6.75   **NB** $10   **MIB** Sec. Mkt. **$18**

QX 598-4   GOLF'S A BALL

Comments: Handcrafted, 3-1/2" tall, Dated 1992.
This cheery snowman is fashioned from golf balls and has golf clubs for arms.
Artist: Lee Schuler

☐ Purchased 19 __ Pd $_____ MIB   NB   DB   BNT
☐ Want   Orig. Ret. $6.75   **NB** $10   **MIB** Sec. Mkt. **$25**

QX 517-1   GONE WISHIN'

Comments: Handcrafted, 1-11/16" tall, Dated 1992.
While Santa naps in his silver motorboat, he has hooked a green package on his line. **Artist:** Donna Lee

☐ Purchased 19 __ Pd $_____ MIB   NB   DB   BNT
☐ Want   Orig. Ret. $8.75   **NB** $9   **MIB** Sec. Mkt. **$18.50**

QLX 724-4   GOOD SLEDDING AHEAD

Comments: Light and Motion, Handcrafted, 3-9/16" tall, Dated 1992.
A dog follows closely behind as the children sled 'round and 'round their house. Many pieces found below original retail! **Artist:** Don Palmiter

☐ Purchased 19 __ Pd $_____ MIB   NB   DB   BNT
☐ Want   Orig. Ret. $28.00   **NB** $35   **MIB** Sec. Mkt. **$55**

QX 560-4   GRANDDAUGHTER

Comments: Handcrafted, 1-3/4" tall, Dated 1992.
A little mouse, with pink frock and a bow on her head, naps in the core of the red apple she has been nibbling. Caption: "Granddaughter, You're The Apple Of My Eye." **Artist:** Ed Seale

☐ Purchased 19 __ Pd $_____ MIB   NB   DB   BNT
☐ Want   Orig. Ret. $6.75   **NB** $10   **MIB** Sec. Mkt. **$18**

QX 463-4   GRANDDAUGHTER'S FIRST CHRISTMAS

Comments: Handcrafted, 2-3/16" tall, Dated 1992.
This little girl cub loves the toys and ice skates tucked inside her Christmas bag. **Artist:** Bob Siedler

☐ Purchased 19 __ Pd $_____ MIB   NB   DB   BNT
☐ Want   Orig. Ret. $6.75   **NB** $10   **MIB** Sec. Mkt. **$18**

QX 201-1   GRANDMOTHER

Comments: Pink Glass Ball, 2-7/8" dia., Dated 1992.
The caption: "A Grandmother's World... A World Of Love And Cherished Memories. Christmas 1992," is framed with decorative holly and Christmas memorabilia.

☐ Purchased 19 __ Pd $_____ MIB   NB   DB   BNT
☐ Want   Orig. Ret. $4.75   **NB** $6   **MIB** Sec. Mkt. **$16**

QX 200-4   GRANDPARENTS

Comments: Silver Glass Ball, 2-7/8" dia., Dated 1992.
Christmas themes frame the caption: "Grandparents Have A Special Way Of Brightening Up The Holiday! Christmas 1992."

☐ Purchased 19 __ Pd $_____ MIB   NB   DB   BNT
☐ Want   Orig. Ret. $4.75   **NB** $6   **MIB** Sec. Mkt. **$15**

QX 561-1   GRANDSON

Comments: Handcrafted, 1-3/4" tall, Dated 1992.
A stuffed little mouse in a blue nightshirt naps against the core of a green apple he's eaten. Caption: "Grandson, You're The Apple Of My Eye." **Artist:** Ed Seale

☐ Purchased 19 __ Pd $_____ MIB   NB   DB   BNT
☐ Want   Orig. Ret. $6.75   **NB** $14   **MIB** Sec. Mkt. **$15**

QX 462-1   GRANDSON'S FIRST CHRISTMAS

Comments: Handcrafted, 2-1/4" tall, Dated 1992.
A little boy bear cub, wearing a red ball cap, happily opens his sack of Christmas toys. **Artist:** Bob Siedler

☐ Purchased 19 __ Pd $_____ MIB   NB   DB   BNT
☐ Want   Orig. Ret. $6.75   **NB** $12   **MIB** Sec. Mkt. **$15**

QX 425-1   GREATEST STORY

Comments: **Third and Final in Series**
Porcelain and Brass, 3-3/4" tall, Dated 1992.
The traditional picture of the birth of Christ is portrayed in white porcelain. **Artist:** LaDene Votruba

☐ Purchased 19 __ Pd $_____ MIB   NB   DB   BNT
☐ Want   Orig. Ret. $12.75   **NB** $14   **MIB** Sec. Mkt. **$20**

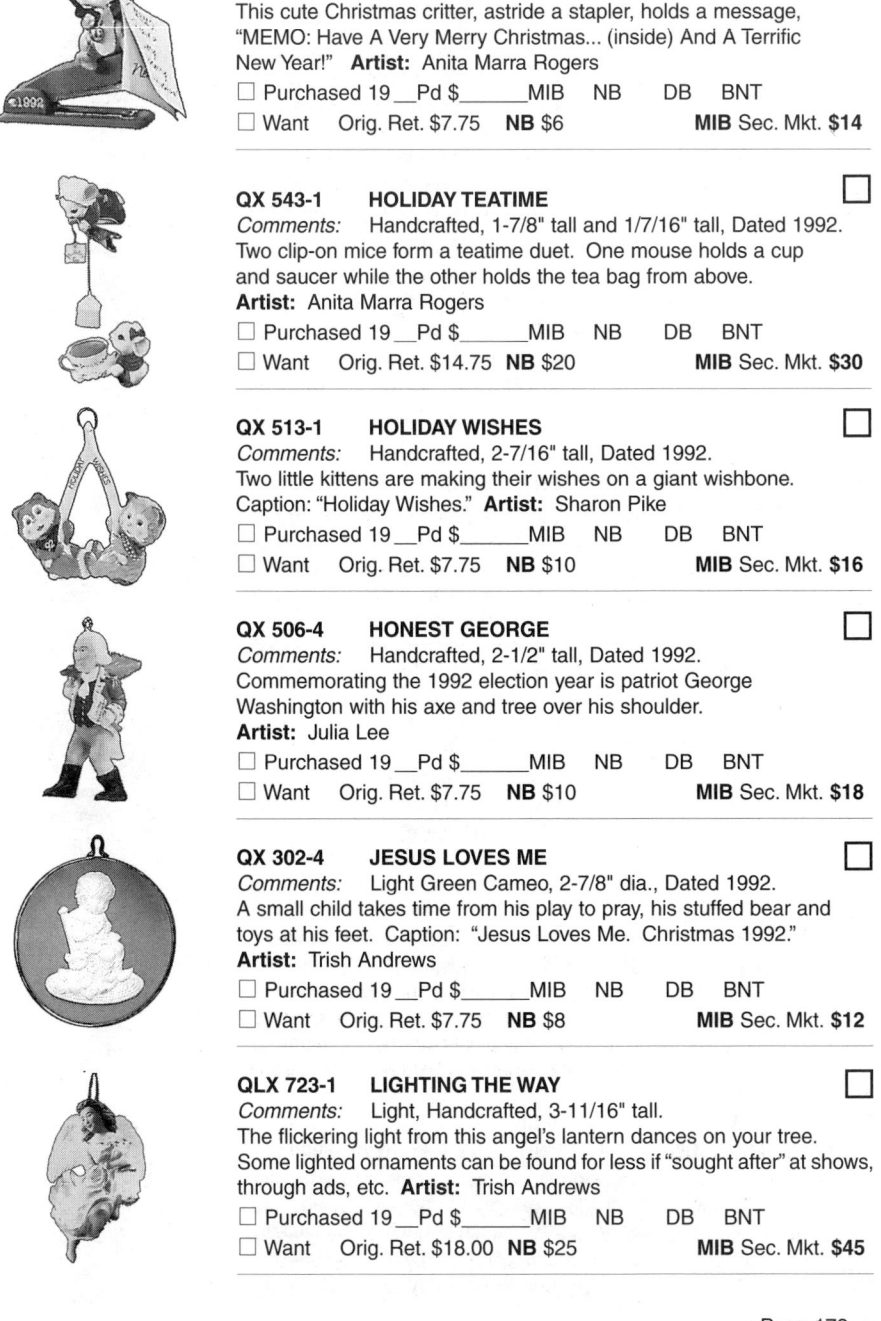

QX 510-1   GREEN THUMB SANTA   ☐
Comments: Handcrafted, 2-3/16" tall, Dated 1992.
Santa is wearing a red visor and giving his Christmas tree a drink,
using a watering can dated '92.
Artist: Don Palmiter

☐ Purchased 19 __ Pd $_____ MIB   NB   DB   BNT
☐ Want   Orig. Ret. $7.75   **NB** $10   **MIB** Sec. Mkt. **$15**

QX 446-4   HARK! IT'S HERALD   ☐
Comments: **Fourth and Final in Series** Edition, Handcrafted, 2-1/16" tall.
Dated 1992. Completing the series, Herald blows a Merry
Christmas melody on his baritone.   **Artist:** Julia Lee

☐ Purchased 19 __ Pd $_____ MIB   NB   DB   BNT
☐ Want   Orig. Ret. $7.75   **NB** $12   **MIB** Sec. Mkt. **$18**

QX 441-1   HEART OF CHRISTMAS   ☐
Comments: **Third in Series,** Handcrafted, 2" tall, Dated 1992.
This heart opens to reveal a family preparing for Christmas at
home. Caption: "Christmas Traditions Warm Every Heart."
Artist: Ed Seale

☐ Purchased 19 __ Pd $_____ MIB   NB   DB   BNT
☐ Want   Orig. Ret. $13.75   **NB** $18   **MIB** Sec. Mkt. **$26**

QX 445-4   HEAVENLY ANGELS   ☐
Comments: **Second in Series,** Handcrafted, 3" tall, Dated 1992.
This lovely bas-relief angel heralds the season of Christmas.
Artist: Joyce A. Lyle

☐ Purchased 19 __ Pd $_____ MIB   NB   DB   BNT
☐ Want   Orig. Ret. $7.75   **NB** $18   **MIB** Sec. Mkt. **$28**

QX 514-1   HELLO-HO-HO   ☐
Comments: Handcrafted, 3-15/16" tall, Dated 1992.
Santa opens the doors and comes out to greet you when you pull
the ball. **Artist:** Ken Crow

☐ Purchased 19 __ Pd $_____ MIB   NB   DB   BNT
☐ Want   Orig. Ret. $9.75   **NB** $14   **MIB** Sec. Mkt. **$22**

QX 434-1   HERE COMES SANTA: KRINGLE TOURS   ☐
Comments: **Fourteenth in Series,** Handcrafted, 2-5/8" tall.
Dated 1992. Santa makes the perfect tour guide as he leads the
Christmas tour. This is the longest-running Keepsake Ornament
series.   **Artist:** Linda Sickman

☐ Purchased 19 __ Pd $_____ MIB   NB   DB   BNT
☐ Want   Orig. Ret. $14.75   **NB** $20   **MIB** Sec. Mkt. **$35**

QX 504-4   HOLIDAY MEMO   ☐
Comments: Handcrafted, 2-7/16" tall, Dated 1992.
This cute Christmas critter, astride a stapler, holds a message,
"MEMO: Have A Very Merry Christmas... (inside) And A Terrific
New Year!"   **Artist:** Anita Marra Rogers

☐ Purchased 19 __ Pd $_____ MIB   NB   DB   BNT
☐ Want   Orig. Ret. $7.75   **NB** $6   **MIB** Sec. Mkt. **$14**

QX 543-1   HOLIDAY TEATIME   ☐
Comments: Handcrafted, 1-7/8" tall and 1/7/16" tall, Dated 1992.
Two clip-on mice form a teatime duet. One mouse holds a cup
and saucer while the other holds the tea bag from above.
Artist: Anita Marra Rogers

☐ Purchased 19 __ Pd $_____ MIB   NB   DB   BNT
☐ Want   Orig. Ret. $14.75   **NB** $20   **MIB** Sec. Mkt. **$30**

QX 513-1   HOLIDAY WISHES   ☐
Comments: Handcrafted, 2-7/16" tall, Dated 1992.
Two little kittens are making their wishes on a giant wishbone.
Caption: "Holiday Wishes." **Artist:** Sharon Pike

☐ Purchased 19 __ Pd $_____ MIB   NB   DB   BNT
☐ Want   Orig. Ret. $7.75   **NB** $10   **MIB** Sec. Mkt. **$16**

QX 506-4   HONEST GEORGE   ☐
Comments: Handcrafted, 2-1/2" tall, Dated 1992.
Commemorating the 1992 election year is patriot George
Washington with his axe and tree over his shoulder.
Artist: Julia Lee

☐ Purchased 19 __ Pd $_____ MIB   NB   DB   BNT
☐ Want   Orig. Ret. $7.75   **NB** $10   **MIB** Sec. Mkt. **$18**

QX 302-4   JESUS LOVES ME   ☐
Comments: Light Green Cameo, 2-7/8" dia., Dated 1992.
A small child takes time from his play to pray, his stuffed bear and
toys at his feet. Caption: "Jesus Loves Me. Christmas 1992."
Artist: Trish Andrews

☐ Purchased 19 __ Pd $_____ MIB   NB   DB   BNT
☐ Want   Orig. Ret. $7.75   **NB** $8   **MIB** Sec. Mkt. **$12**

QLX 723-1   LIGHTING THE WAY   ☐
Comments: Light, Handcrafted, 3-11/16" tall.
The flickering light from this angel's lantern dances on your tree.
Some lighted ornaments can be found for less if "sought after" at shows,
through ads, etc. **Artist:** Trish Andrews

☐ Purchased 19 __ Pd $_____ MIB   NB   DB   BNT
☐ Want   Orig. Ret. $18.00   **NB** $25   **MIB** Sec. Mkt. **$45**

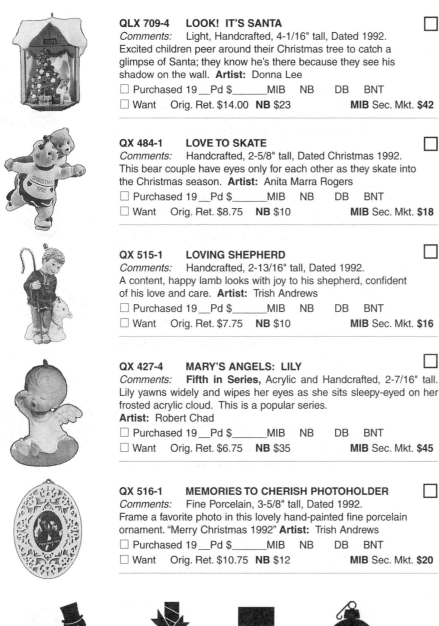

QLX 709-4   LOOK! IT'S SANTA ☐

Comments: Light, Handcrafted, 4-1/16" tall, Dated 1992.
Excited children peer around their Christmas tree to catch a
glimpse of Santa; they know he's there because they see his
shadow on the wall. **Artist:** Donna Lee

☐ Purchased 19 __ Pd $_____ MIB   NB   DB   BNT

☐ Want   Orig. Ret. $14.00 **NB** $23   **MIB** Sec. Mkt. **$42**

QX 484-1   LOVE TO SKATE ☐

Comments: Handcrafted, 2-5/8" tall, Dated Christmas 1992.
This bear couple have eyes only for each other as they skate into
the Christmas season. **Artist:** Anita Marra Rogers

☐ Purchased 19 __ Pd $_____ MIB   NB   DB   BNT

☐ Want   Orig. Ret. $8.75 **NB** $10   **MIB** Sec. Mkt. **$18**

QX 515-1   LOVING SHEPHERD ☐

Comments: Handcrafted, 2-13/16" tall, Dated 1992.
A content, happy lamb looks with joy to his shepherd, confident
of his love and care. **Artist:** Trish Andrews

☐ Purchased 19 __ Pd $_____ MIB   NB   DB   BNT

☐ Want   Orig. Ret. $7.75 **NB** $10   **MIB** Sec. Mkt. **$16**

QX 427-4   MARY'S ANGELS: LILY ☐

Comments: **Fifth in Series,** Acrylic and Handcrafted, 2-7/16" tall.
Lily yawns widely and wipes her eyes as she sits sleepy-eyed on her
frosted acrylic cloud. This is a popular series.
Artist: Robert Chad

☐ Purchased 19 __ Pd $_____ MIB   NB   DB   BNT

☐ Want   Orig. Ret. $6.75 **NB** $35   **MIB** Sec. Mkt. **$45**

QX 516-1   MEMORIES TO CHERISH PHOTOHOLDER ☐

Comments: Fine Porcelain, 3-5/8" tall, Dated 1992.
Frame a favorite photo in this lovely hand-painted fine porcelain
ornament. "Merry Christmas 1992" **Artist:** Trish Andrews

☐ Purchased 19 __ Pd $_____ MIB   NB   DB   BNT

☐ Want   Orig. Ret. $10.75 **NB** $12   **MIB** Sec. Mkt. **$20**

QX 441-4   MERRY OLDE SANTA ☐

Comments: **Third in Series,** Handcrafted, 4-1/8" tall, Dated 1992.
While a teddy sits nearby on a toy drum, Santa is filling a red stocking
with a horn. Price down from '96. **Artist:** Duane Unruh

☐ Purchased 19 __ Pd $_____ MIB   NB   DB   BNT

☐ Want   Orig. Ret. $14.75 **NB** $15   **MIB** Sec. Mkt. **$22-$25**

QX 511-4   MERRY "SWISS" MOUSE ☐

Comments: Handcrafted, 1-13/16" tall, Dated 1992.
This little white mouse and his all-time favorite Swiss cheese clips
to your tree or wreath. **Artist:** Ed Seale

☐ Purchased 19 __ Pd $_____ MIB   NB   DB   BNT

☐ Want   Orig. Ret. $7.75 **NB** $10   **MIB** Sec. Mkt. **$15**

QX 516-4   MOM ☐

Comments: Handcrafted, 2-3/8" tall, Dated 1992.
Mama rabbit closes her eyes and reflects on "Mom's Christmas
Memories." Sweet dreams! **Artist:** Anita Marra Rogers

☐ Purchased 19 __ Pd $_____ MIB   NB   DB   BNT

☐ Want   Orig. Ret. $7.75 **NB** $10   **MIB** Sec. Mkt. **$16**

QX 467-1   MOM AND DAD ☐

Comments: Handcrafted, 1-15/16" tall, Dated 1992.
Mom and Dad beavers are hanging the lights on the tree. This
stringer ornament may be hung on one branch or two different
branches of your tree. **Artist:** Bob Siedler

☐ Purchased 19 __ Pd $_____ MIB   NB   DB   BNT

☐ Want   Orig. Ret. $9.75 **NB** $24   **MIB** Sec. Mkt. **$40**

QX 461-4   MOM-TO-BE ☐

Comments: Handcrafted, 2-5/16" tall, Dated 1992.
A happy hen sits on her, as yet, unhatched egg which sports a
gold bow. **Artist:** Julia Lee

☐ Purchased 19 __ Pd $_____ MIB   NB   DB   BNT

☐ Want   Orig. Ret. $6.75 **NB** $12   **MIB** Sec. Mkt. **$18**

QX 498-4   MOTHER GOOSE ☐

Comments: Handcrafted, 3-1/2" tall, Dated 1992.
Mother Goose reads her Nursery Rhymes while gliding on a large
white goose. Swing the ornament back and forth; the head, tail
and wings of the goose move up and down.
Artist: Ken Crow

☐ Purchased 19 __ Pd $_____ MIB   NB   DB   BNT

☐ Want   Orig. Ret. $13.75 **NB** $20   **MIB** Sec. Mkt. **$25**

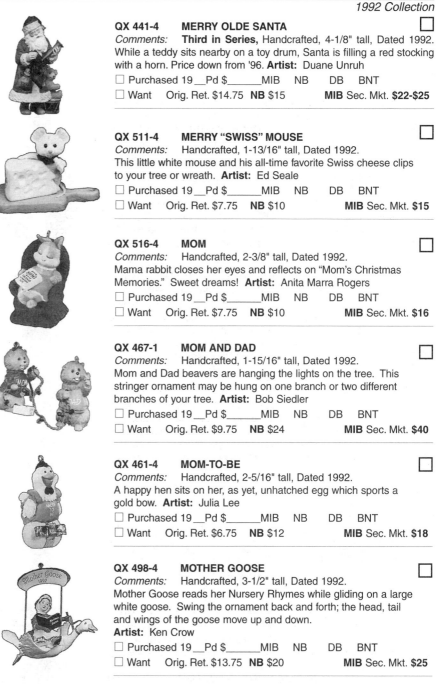

QX 429-4   MR. AND MRS. CLAUS: GIFT EXCHANGE   ☐
Comments: **Seventh in Series,** Handcrafted, 3-1/8" tall.
Dated 1992. Taking time out from their busy Christmas schedules, this
loving couple exchanges gifts. **Artist:** Duane Unruh
☐ Purchased 19 __Pd $_____MIB   NB   DB   BNT
☐ Want   Orig. Ret. $14.75 **NB** $20   **MIB** Sec. Mkt. **$34**

QX 519-1   NEW HOME   ☐
Comments: Handcrafted, 2-1/2" tall, Dated 1992.
A little mouse looks out the door of his cupcake home, topped with
pink frosting "snow" and a cherry. Caption: "Home Sweet
Home." **Artist:** Sharon Pike
☐ Purchased 19 __Pd $_____MIB   NB   DB   BNT
☐ Want   Orig. Ret. $8.75 **NB** $10   **MIB** Sec. Mkt. **$16**

QX 222-4   NORMAN ROCKWELL ART   ☐
Comments: White Glass Ball, 2-7/8" dia., Dated 1992.
Captions: "Christmas Sing Merrily." and "In Each Of Our Hearts
Lives An Ideal Christmas... A Season Of Snow-Covered Trees,
Smiling Carolers, And Santa Claus, A Season Of Memories And
Dreams." **Artist:** Joyce A. Lyle
☐ Purchased 19 __Pd $_____MIB   NB   DB   BNT
☐ Want   Orig. Ret. $5.00 **NB** $ 8.50   **MIB** Sec. Mkt. **$20**

QX 510-4   NORTH POLE FIRE FIGHTER   ☐
Comments: Handcrafted, 3-3/4" tall, Dated 1992.
Santa is on his way to rescue Christmas as he slides down the
"North Pole" with his pack on his back. **Artist:** Ed Seale
☐ Purchased 19 __Pd $_____MIB   NB   DB   BNT
☐ Want   Orig. Ret. $9.75 **NB** $14   **MIB** Sec. Mkt. **$21**

QX 524-4   NORTH POLE NUTCRACKERS: ☐
ERIC THE BAKER
Comments: Handcrafted, 4-3/8" tall, Dated on Bottom - 1992.
Yum! Eric's been in the kitchen again. What tasty treat is he
serving today? **Artist:** Linda Sickman
☐ Purchased 19 __Pd $_____MIB   NB   DB   BNT
☐ Want   Orig. Ret. $8.75 **NB** $10   **MIB** Sec. Mkt. **$20**

QX 526-1   NORTH POLE NUTCRACKERS: ☐
FRANZ THE ARTIST
Comments: Handcrafted, 4-5/8" tall, Dated on Bottom - 1992.
Franz is ready to paint your portrait! He carries his brush and
palette with him. **Artist:** Linda Sickman
☐ Purchased 19 __Pd $_____MIB   NB   DB   BNT
☐ Want   Orig. Ret. $8.75 **NB** $15   **MIB** Sec. Mkt. **$24**

QX 526-4   NORTH POLE NUTCRACKERS: ☐
FRIEDA THE ANIMALS' FRIEND
Comments: Handcrafted, 4-3/8" tall, Dated on Bottom - 1992.
The animals know of Frieda's love for them and they happily come
to her. **Artist:** Linda Sickman
☐ Purchased 19 __Pd $_____MIB   NB   DB   BNT
☐ Want   Orig. Ret. $8.75 **NB** $15   **MIB** Sec. Mkt. **$20**

QX 528-1   NORTH POLE NUTCRACKERS: ☐
LUDWIG THE MUSICIAN
Comments: Handcrafted, 4-7/8" tall, Dated on Bottom - 1992.
Ludwig's talents are readily seen by his sheet music and French
Horn. **Artist:** Linda Sickman
☐ Purchased 19 __Pd $_____MIB   NB   DB   BNT
☐ Want   Orig. Ret. $8.75 **NB** $15   **MIB** Sec. Mkt. **$20**

QX 525-1   NORTH POLE NUTCRACKERS: ☐
MAX THE TAILOR
Comments: Handcrafted, 4-3/8" tall, Dated on Bottom - 1992.
Max comes complete with needle and thread to stitch a torn teddy
bear. **Artist:** Linda Sickman
☐ Purchased 19 __Pd $_____MIB   NB   DB   BNT
☐ Want   Orig. Ret. $8.75 **NB** $12   **MIB** Sec. Mkt. **$22**

QX 525-4   NORTH POLE NUTCRACKERS: ☐
OTTO THE CARPENTER
Comments: Handcrafted, 4-3/8" tall, Dated on Bottom - 1992.
Otto is ready for business with his mallet in one hand and his
masterpiece in the other. **Artist:** Linda Sickman
☐ Purchased 19 __Pd $_____MIB   NB   DB   BNT
☐ Want   Orig. Ret. $8.75 **NB** $12   **MIB** Sec. Mkt. **$20**

QX 425-4   NOSTALGIC HOUSES AND SHOPS: ☐
FIVE-AND-TEN-CENT STORE
Comments: **Ninth in Series,** Handcrafted, 3-5/8" tall, Dated 1992.
This old-fashioned shop recreates yesteryear, down to the bubble gum
machine in front of the store.
Artist: Donna Lee
☐ Purchased 19 __Pd $_____MIB   NB   DB   BNT
☐ Want   Orig. Ret. $14.75 **NB** $25   **MIB** Sec. Mkt. **$38**

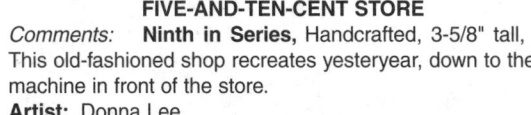

QLX 708-1   NUT, SWEET NUT
Comments: Light, Handcrafted, 2-1/16" tall, Dated 1992.
A cute little chipmunk peeks through the door of his snow-covered walnut home. **Artist:** Ken Crow
☐ Purchased 19__Pd $_____MIB   NB   DB   BNT
☐ Want   Orig. Ret. $10.00 **NB** $15   **MIB** Sec. Mkt. **$24**

QX 541-1   O CHRISTMAS TREE
Comments: Porcelain Bell, Dated 1992.
A Christmas tree sits atop this Hallmark Keepsake Premiere Bell.
Artist: LaDene Votruba
☐ Purchased 19__Pd $_____MIB   NB   DB   BNT
☐ Want   Orig. Ret. $10.75 **NB** $12   **MIB** Sec. Mkt. **$32**

QLX 722-1   OUR FIRST CHRISTMAS
Comments: Light, Panorama Ball, 3-5/8" tall, Dated 1992.
The view inside this blue panorama ball reveals a couple enjoying a cozy, flickering fireplace. Caption: "Christmas Is A Magic Time Of Sweet, Romantic Moments." **Artist:** Robert Chad
☐ Purchased 19__Pd $_____MIB   NB   DB   BNT
☐ Want   Orig. Ret. $20.00 **NB** $22   **MIB** Sec. Mkt. **$43**

QX 561-4   OWL
Comments: Handcrafted, 2-7/8" tall.
Owl is getting ready for Christmas with his string of colored lights. An addition to the Winnie-the-Pooh collection.   **Artist:** Bob Siedler
☐ Purchased 19__Pd $_____MIB   NB   DB   BNT
☐ Want   Orig. Ret. $9.75 **NB** $15   **MIB** Sec. Mkt. **$25**

QX 454-4   OWLIVER
Comments: **FIRST IN SERIES,** Handcrafted, 2-1/16" tall.
Dated 1992. Owliver reads from a book. This first in series ornament is still not showing an increase on the secondary market.
Artist: Bob Siedler
☐ Purchased 19__Pd $_____MIB   NB   DB   BNT
☐ Want   Orig. Ret. $7.75 **NB** $11   **MIB** Sec. Mkt. **$16**

"My sister got in a lot of trouble yesterday,"
Ernie said to Ruth.
"What did she do?"
"She was feeding the tropical fish."
"What's wrong with that?" Ruth asked.
Ernie said, "She was feeding them to our cat."

QX 523-4   PARTRIDGE IN A PEAR TREE
Comments: Handcrafted, 4-1/8" tall, Dated 1992.
The pear at the top of this tree, planted in a gift box, opens to reveal an embarrassed partridge in his boxer shorts. Tree trunk is dated. **Artist:** Bob Siedler
☐ Purchased 19__Pd $_____MIB   NB   DB   BNT
☐ Want   Orig. Ret. $8.75 **NB** $9   **MIB** Sec. Mkt. **$16**

QX 517-4   PEACE ON EARTH: SPAIN
Comments: **Second in Series,** Handcrafted, 3" dia., Dated 1992.
Two Spanish children wish to all "Paz Sobre La Tierra."
Artist: Linda Sickman
☐ Purchased 19__Pd $_____MIB   NB   DB   BNT
☐ Want   Orig. Ret. $11.75 **NB** $15   **MIB** Sec. Mkt. **$25**

QX 224-4   PEANUTS®
Comments: Chrome Ball, 2-7/8" dia., Christmas 1992.
Charlie Brown, Lucy and the rest of the Peanuts gang act out the Nativity. Caption: "... Behold, I Bring You Good Tidings Of Great Joy, Which Shall Be To All People."
☐ Purchased 19__Pd $_____MIB   NB   DB   BNT
☐ Want   Orig. Ret. $5.00 **NB** $15   **MIB** Sec. Mkt. **$25**

QLX 721-4   PEANUTS®
Comments: **Second in Series,** Handcrafted, 3-15/16" tall.
Dated 1992. Lights blink merrily on the wreath as Snoopy and Woodstock sit cozily on the roof of Snoopy's doghouse.
Caption: "Happy Holidays."   **Artist:** Dill Rhodus
☐ Purchased 19__Pd $_____MIB   NB   DB   BNT
☐ Want   Orig. Ret. $18.00 **NB** $30   **MIB** Sec. Mkt. **$50**

QX 529-1   PLEASE PAUSE HERE
Comments: Handcrafted, 4" tall, Dated 1992.
Santa's note reads, "Dear Santa, Please Pause Here. Your PAL." Santa holds his Coca-Cola and does just that. Clips onto a tree branch or garland. **Artist:** Donna Lee
☐ Purchased 19__Pd $_____MIB   NB   DB   BNT
☐ Want   Orig. Ret. $14.75 **NB** $16   **MIB** Sec. Mkt. **$32.50**

Some folks would sleep better at night if they'd get down on their knees by the bed before they hopped into the bed!

QX 491-4   POLAR POST ☐
Comments: Handcrafted, 2-7/8" tall, Dated 1992.
This polar mail carrier, dressed in a red scarf, holds a real working compass to help find the North Pole. **Artist:** Ed Seale
☐ Purchased 19__ Pd $_____ MIB   NB   DB   BNT
☐ Want   Orig. Ret. $8.75   **NB** $10   **MIB** Sec. Mkt. **$20**

QX 448-4   PUPPY LOVE ☐
Comments: **Second in Series,** 2-5/8" tall, Handcrafted/Brass. Dated 1992. A gray and white terrier wags a Merry Christmas from his wicker basket. **Artist:** Anita Marra Rogers
☐ Purchased 19__ Pd $_____ MIB   NB   DB   BNT
☐ Want   Orig. Ret. $7.75   **NB** $22   **MIB** Sec. Mkt. **$40**

QX 509-4   RAPID DELIVERY ☐
Comments: Handcrafted, 1-7/8" tall, Dated 1992.
The Christmas deliveries must be made... so this cute little elf braves the rapids in his blue raft. **Artist:** Don Palmiter
☐ Purchased 19__ Pd $_____ MIB   NB   DB   BNT
☐ Want   Orig. Ret. $8.75   **NB** $12   **MIB** Sec. Mkt. **$20**

QX 528-4   REINDEER CHAMPS: DONDER ☐
Comments: **Seventh in Series,** Handcrafted, 3-1/16" tall. Dated 1992. Donder is ready to strike out the opposing team. He's wearing his team colors: white with red socks and a green shirt. **Artist:** Bob Siedler
☐ Purchased 19__ Pd $_____ MIB   NB   DB   BNT
☐ Want   Orig. Ret. $8.75   **NB** $14   **MIB** Sec. Mkt. **$33**

QX 426-1   ROCKING HORSE ☐
Comments: **Twelfth in Series,** Handcrafted, 3" tall, Dated 1992. This brown horse wears a lacy white saddle blanket with a green saddle trimmed in red. **Artist:** Linda Sickman
☐ Purchased 19__ Pd $_____ MIB   NB   DB   BNT
☐ Want   Orig. Ret. $10.75 **NB** $14   **MIB** Sec. Mkt. **$34**

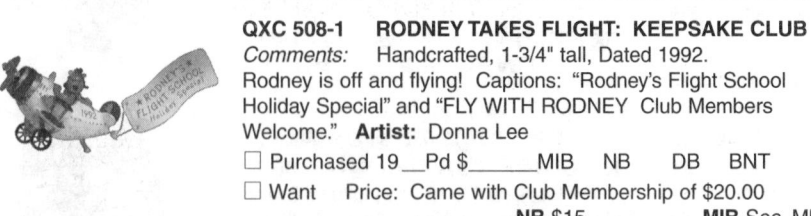

QXC 508-1   RODNEY TAKES FLIGHT: KEEPSAKE CLUB ☐
Comments: Handcrafted, 1-3/4" tall, Dated 1992.
Rodney is off and flying! Captions: "Rodney's Flight School Holiday Special" and "FLY WITH RODNEY Club Members Welcome." **Artist:** Donna Lee
☐ Purchased 19__ Pd $_____ MIB   NB   DB   BNT
☐ Want   Price: Came with Club Membership of $20.00
                NB $15   **MIB** Sec. Mkt. **$20**

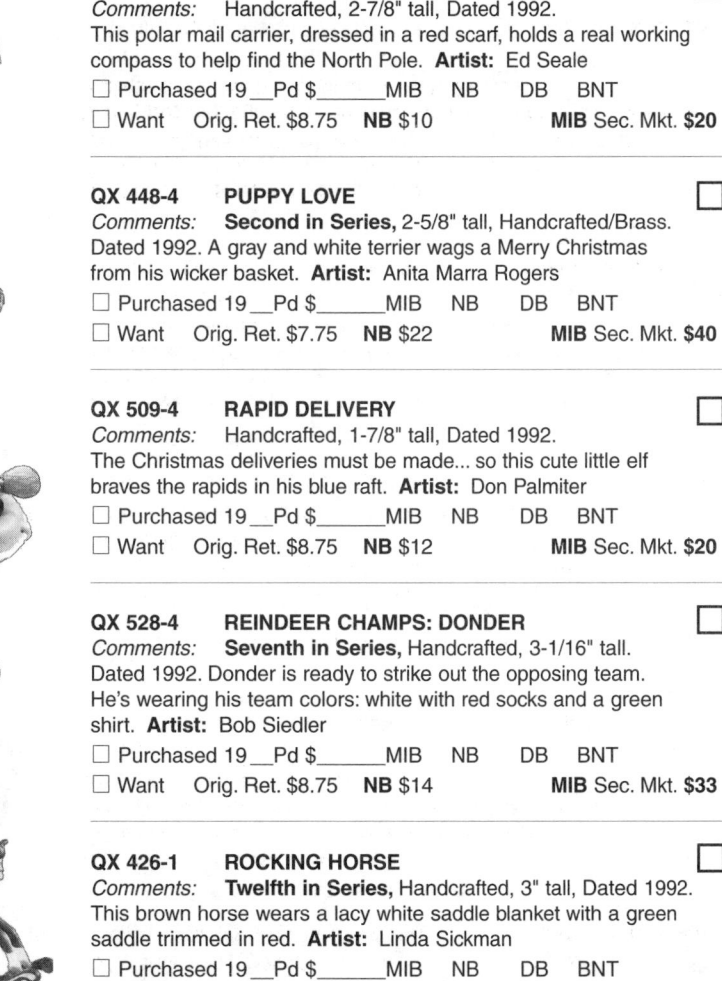

QX 507-4   SANTA MARIA ☐
Comments: Handcrafted, 3-1/8" tall, Dated 1992.
Santa spies land as he stands aboard the Santa Maria, commemorating the 500th anniversary of Columbus' arrival in America. Plenty out there on the secondary market! **Artist:** Ken Crow
☐ Purchased 19__ Pd $_____ MIB   NB   DB   BNT
☐ Want   Orig. Ret. $12.75 **NB** $8   **MIB** Sec. Mkt. **$18**

XPR 973-5   SANTA & HIS REINDEER COLLECTION: DASHER & DANCER (SLEIGH ON PAGE 169) ☐
Comments: Handcrafted, 3-15/64" tall.
Dasher and Dancer lead the way to Hallmark's Christmas Open House Promotional ornaments. **Artist:** Ken Crow
☐ Purchased 19__ Pd $_____ MIB   NB   DB   BNT
☐ Want   Orig. Ret. $4.95 with any $5 Hallmark purchase
                NB $11   **MIB** Sec. Mkt. **$25**

XPR 973-6   SANTA & HIS REINDEER COLLECTION: PRANCER & VIXEN ☐
Comments: Handcrafted, 3-15/64" tall.
Artist: Ken Crow
☐ Purchased 19__ Pd $_____ MIB   NB   DB   BNT
☐ Want   Orig. Ret. $4.95 with any $5 Hallmark purchase
                NB $8   **MIB** Sec. Mkt. **$16**

XPR 973-7   SANTA & HIS REINDEER COLLECTION: COMET & CUPID ☐
Comments: Handcrafted, 3-3/64" tall.
Artist: Ken Crow
☐ Purchased 19__ Pd $_____ MIB   NB   DB   BNT
☐ Want   Orig. Ret. $4.95 with any $5 Hallmark purchase
                NB $8   **MIB** Sec. Mkt. **$16**

XPR 973-8   SANTA & HIS REINDEER COLLECTION: DONDER & BLITZEN ☐
Comments: Handcrafted, 3-5/32" tall.
Artist: Ken Crow
☐ Purchased 19__ Pd $_____ MIB   NB   DB   BNT
☐ Want   Orig. Ret. $4.95 with any $5 Hallmark purchase
                NB $11   **MIB** Sec. Mkt. **$25**

Collectible Shows: A place to make new friends and find that special ornament.

XPR 973-9 SANTA & HIS REINDEER COLLECTION: SANTA & SLEIGH ☐
Comments: Handcrafted, 2-9/16" tall, Dated 1992.
Santa and his sleigh complete the Collection. All ornaments in this set link together. **Artist:** Ken Crow

☐ Purchased 19__Pd $_____MIB NB DB BNT
☐ Want Orig. Ret. $4.95 with any $5 Hallmark purchase
NB $10 **MIB** Sec. Mkt. **$24**

QLX 716-7 SANTA SPECIAL ☐
Comments: Light, Motion and Sound, Handcrafted, 3-1/8" tall. Reissued from 1991. **Artist:** Ed Seale

☐ Purchased 19__Pd $_____MIB NB DB BNT
☐ Want Orig. Ret. $40.00 **NB** $60 **MIB** Sec. Mkt. **$80**

QLX 732-1 SANTA SUB ☐
Comments: Blinking Lights, Handcrafted, 2-3/4" tall, Dated 1992. Santa's safe in the USS Peppermint, red and white striped submarine. **Artist:** Ken Crow

☐ Purchased 19__Pd $_____MIB NB DB BNT
☐ Want Orig. Ret. $18.00 **NB** $30 **MIB** Sec. Mkt. **$45**

QLX 724-1 SANTA'S ANSWERING MACHINE ☐
Comments: Voice, Sound and Blinking Light, 1-7/8" tall. Dated 1992. Santa's not in, but when you press the button you will hear his Christmas message to you, along with the jingling of bells. **Artist:** Julia Lee

☐ Purchased 19__Pd $_____MIB NB DB BNT
☐ Want Orig. Ret. $22.00 **NB** $12 **MIB** Sec. Mkt. **$25**

QXC 729-1 SANTA'S CLUB LIST: KEEPSAKE CLUB ☐
Comments: Members Only, Light, Handcrafted, 2-1/8" tall. Dressed as Santa, a small raccoon holds a lighted candle and reads from "Santa's Club List." **Artist:** Ed Seale

☐ Purchased 19__Pd $_____MIB NB DB BNT
☐ Want Orig. Ret. $15.00 **NB** $20 **MIB** Sec. Mkt. **$36**

QX 543-4 SANTA'S HOOK SHOT ☐
Comments: Handcrafted, 2" tall, Dated 1992. Santa's "Hooked on Christmas!" Set of two ornaments includes Santa, wearing a green dated jersey and red shorts and a clip-on basketball hoop with basketball. **Artist:** Ed Seale

☐ Purchased 19__Pd $_____MIB NB DB BNT
☐ Want Orig. Ret. $12.75 **NB** $18 **MIB** Sec. Mkt. **$28**

QX 508-4 SANTA'S ROUNDUP ☐
Comments: Handcrafted, 3-3/4" tall, Dated 1992. Wearing his white-tassled cowboy hat, Santa performs the best rope tricks. His green rope is in the shape of a Christmas tree! **Artist:** Julia Lee

☐ Purchased 19__Pd $_____MIB NB DB BNT
☐ Want Orig. Ret. $8.75 **NB** $14 **MIB** Sec. Mkt. **$24**

QX 542-4 SECRET PAL ☐
Comments: Handcrafted, 2-3/4" tall, Dated 1992. A chipper raccoon dressed in blue and red tips his hat as he delivers a gift "From Your Secret Pal." **Artist:** Anita Marra Rogers

☐ Purchased 19__Pd $_____MIB NB DB BNT
☐ Want Orig. Ret. $7.75 **NB** $10 **MIB** Sec. Mkt. **$14**

QLX 733-1 SHUTTLECRAFT GALILEO ☐
Comments: Voice and Light, Handcrafted, Dated 1992. This Special Issue gives an authentic greeting in the voice of Mr. Spock. Many more Galileos produced than the '91 Starship Enterprise. Easily found on the secondary market. **Artist:** Dill Rhodus

☐ Purchased 19__Pd $_____MIB NB DB BNT
☐ Want Orig. Ret. $21.00 **NB** $18 **MIB** Sec. Mkt. **$40-$45**

QX 532-4 SILVER STAR ☐
Comments: Die-Cast Metal, each 1-1/2" tall, Dated 1992. The sleek streamliner includes a locomotive, luggage car and dome car. May be hung on tree or displayed standing. **Artist:** Linda Sickman

☐ Purchased 19__Pd $_____MIB NB DB BNT
☐ Want Orig. Ret. $28.00 **NB** $20 **MIB** Sec. Mkt. **$40-$45**

QX 468-1 SISTER ☐
Comments: Handcrafted, 4" tall, Dated 1992. When the ball is pulled gently, sister's basket opens and a little kitten peeks out. **Artist:** Ken Crow

☐ Purchased 19__Pd $_____MIB NB DB BNT
☐ Want Orig. Ret. $6.75 **NB** $8 **MIB** Sec. Mkt. **$16**

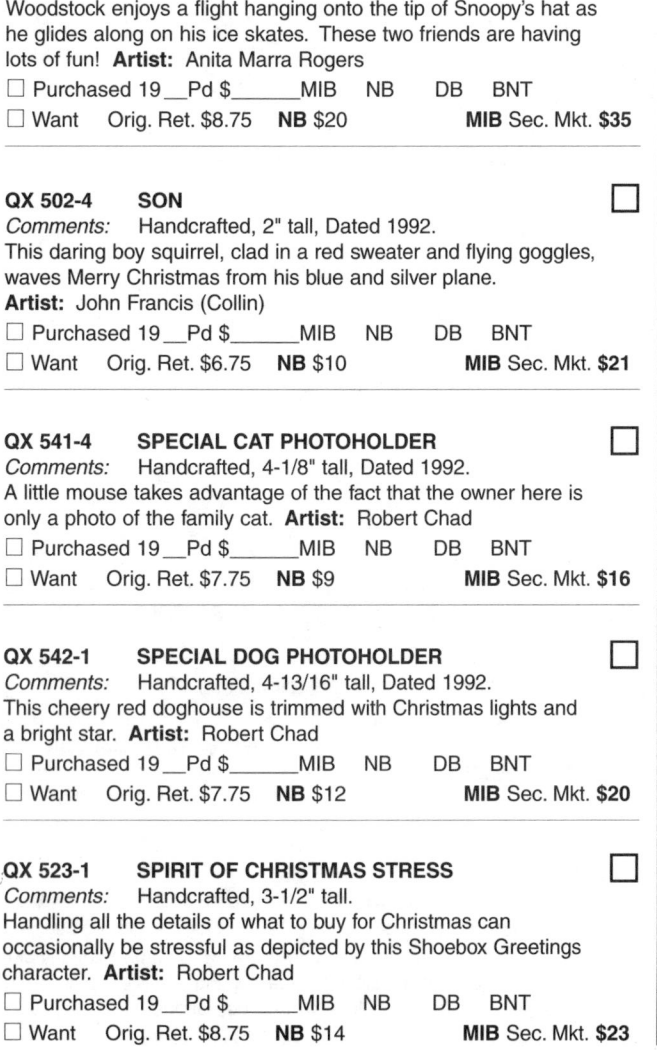

QX 521-4   SKIING 'ROUND

Comments: Handcrafted, 3-5/8" tall, Dated 1992.
This fellow has gotten himself all bound up in the middle of a snowball. **Artist:** Julia Lee

☐ Purchased 19 __Pd $_____MIB   NB   DB   BNT
☐ Want   Orig. Ret. $8.75   **NB** $12   **MIB** Sec. Mkt. **$18**

QX 595-4   SNOOPY® AND WOODSTOCK

Comments: Handcrafted, 2-3/4" tall, Dated 1992.
Woodstock enjoys a flight hanging onto the tip of Snoopy's hat as he glides along on his ice skates. These two friends are having lots of fun! **Artist:** Anita Marra Rogers

☐ Purchased 19 __Pd $_____MIB   NB   DB   BNT
☐ Want   Orig. Ret. $8.75   **NB** $20   **MIB** Sec. Mkt. **$35**

QX 502-4   SON

Comments: Handcrafted, 2" tall, Dated 1992.
This daring boy squirrel, clad in a red sweater and flying goggles, waves Merry Christmas from his blue and silver plane.
Artist: John Francis (Collin)

☐ Purchased 19 __Pd $_____MIB   NB   DB   BNT
☐ Want   Orig. Ret. $6.75   **NB** $10   **MIB** Sec. Mkt. **$21**

QX 541-4   SPECIAL CAT PHOTOHOLDER

Comments: Handcrafted, 4-1/8" tall, Dated 1992.
A little mouse takes advantage of the fact that the owner here is only a photo of the family cat. **Artist:** Robert Chad

☐ Purchased 19 __Pd $_____MIB   NB   DB   BNT
☐ Want   Orig. Ret. $7.75   **NB** $9   **MIB** Sec. Mkt. **$16**

QX 542-1   SPECIAL DOG PHOTOHOLDER

Comments: Handcrafted, 4-13/16" tall, Dated 1992.
This cheery red doghouse is trimmed with Christmas lights and a bright star. **Artist:** Robert Chad

☐ Purchased 19 __Pd $_____MIB   NB   DB   BNT
☐ Want   Orig. Ret. $7.75   **NB** $12   **MIB** Sec. Mkt. **$20**

QX 523-1   SPIRIT OF CHRISTMAS STRESS

Comments: Handcrafted, 3-1/2" tall.
Handling all the details of what to buy for Christmas can occasionally be stressful as depicted by this Shoebox Greetings character. **Artist:** Robert Chad

☐ Purchased 19 __Pd $_____MIB   NB   DB   BNT
☐ Want   Orig. Ret. $8.75   **NB** $14   **MIB** Sec. Mkt. **$23**

QX 593-4   STOCKED WITH JOY

Comments: Pressed Tin, 4-3/4" tall, Dated 1992.
A horse, checker board and other toys stuffed into a blue stocking would delight any child. Tin ornaments are becoming very popular.
Artist: Linda Sickman

☐ Purchased 19 __Pd $_____MIB   NB   DB   BNT
☐ Want   Orig. Ret. $7.75   **NB** $12   **MIB** Sec. Mkt. **$20**

QX 599-4   TASTY CHRISTMAS

Comments: Handcrafted, 2-5/16" tall.
Decorated with silver garland, the shark's jaws open and close when you turn his tail. Caption: "It's Beginning To Taste A Lot Like Christmas!" **Artist:** Julia Lee

☐ Purchased 19 __Pd $_____MIB   NB   DB   BNT
☐ Want   Orig. Ret. $9.75   **NB** $12   **MIB** Sec. Mkt. **$20**

QX 226-4   TEACHER

Comments: Red Glass Ball, 2-7/8" dia., Dated Dec. 25, 1992.
Costumed children spell "Christmas" with the letters on their hats. Mary Engelbreit design. Caption: "For Teacher -- Thanks For Making Learning Lots Of Fun!"

☐ Purchased 19 __Pd $_____MIB   NB   DB   BNT
☐ Want   Orig. Ret. $4.75   **NB** $9   **MIB** Sec. Mkt. **$14**

QX 489-1   TOBIN FRALEY CAROUSEL

Comments: *FIRST IN SERIES,* Porcelain and Brass, 5-1/4" tall.
Dated 1992. A beautiful white horse decorated in red and green rides a brass carousel pole. Many, many advertised for less. Sales of this signed ornament have reached $50. **Artist:** Tobin Fraley

☐ Purchased 19 __Pd $_____MIB   NB   DB   BNT
☐ Want   Orig. Ret. $28.00 **NB** $18   **MIB** Sec. Mkt. **$30-$35**

QX 545-9   TOBOGGAN TAIL

Comments: Handcrafted, 2-1/2" tall, Dated 1992.
Who needs a separate sled when you have one that's built-in? With her tail tucked beneath her, mama beaver gives her son a thrilling ride. **Artist:** Trish Andrews

☐ Purchased 19 __Pd $_____MIB   NB   DB   BNT
☐ Want   Orig. Ret. $7.75   **NB** $14   **MIB** Sec. Mkt. **$18**

" I just love my carry along Hallmark Ornament Guide." (See page 335)

QX 509-1   TREAD BEAR ☐
Comments: Handcrafted, 2-1/4" tall, Dated 1992.
Swinging happily in his tire swing, this little white bear is dressed warmly in his red scarf.   Caption: "Bear Paws 1992 Road Gripper."
Artist: Ed Seale

☐ Purchased 19 __Pd $_____MIB   NB   DB   BNT
☐ Want   Orig. Ret. $8.75   **NB** $12   **MIB** Sec. Mkt. **$22**

QX 499-1   TURTLE DREAMS ☐
Comments: Handcrafted, 1-13/16" tall, Dated 1992.
Open the shell and find this little fellow all tucked in, complete with a red stocking cap! Caption: "Don't Open Till Christmas."
Artist: Julia Lee

☐ Purchased 19 __Pd $_____MIB   NB   DB   BNT
☐ Want   Orig. Ret. $8.75   **NB** $14   **MIB** Sec. Mkt. **$22**

QX 303-1   TWELVE DAYS OF CHRISTMAS: ☐
                   NINE LADIES DANCING
Comments: **Ninth in Series,** Acrylic, 3" tall, Dated 1992.
A lovely maiden with holly decorations on her skirt dances on a quatrefoil shaped acrylic. This series needs a scarce one!
Artist: Michele Pyda-Sevcik

☐ Purchased 19 __Pd $_____MIB   NB   DB   BNT
☐ Want   Orig. Ret. $6.75   **NB** $12   **MIB** Sec. Mkt. **$18**

QX 500-1   UNCLE ART'S ICE CREAM ☐
Comments: Handcrafted, 3-1/4" tall, Dated 1992.
A cute little mouse seems to be having fun turning the crank on this old fashioned ice cream maker.
Artist: Bob Siedler

☐ Purchased 19 __Pd $_____MIB   NB   DB   BNT
☐ Want   Orig. Ret. $8.75   **NB** $14   **MIB** Sec. Mkt. **$24**

QLX 732-4   UNDER CONSTRUCTION ☐
Comments: Light, Handcrafted, 3-1/2" tall, Dated 1992.
A little beaver flashes his red light to warn that you're nearing the tree-trimming zone. Caption: "Caution, Tree-Trimming Zone, 1992 Branch Under Construction." **Artist:** Don Palmiter

☐ Purchased 19 __Pd $_____MIB   NB   DB   BNT
☐ Want   Orig. Ret. $18.00   **NB** $20   **MIB** Sec. Mkt. **$38**

QX 505-1   V.P. OF IMPORTANT STUFF ☐
Comments: Handcrafted, 2-1/16" tall, Dated 1992.
A penguin eats his donut from inside a white coffee cup.
Caption in green print. **Artist:** Bob Siedler

☐ Purchased 19 __Pd $_____MIB   NB   DB   BNT
☐ Want   Orig. Ret. $6.75   **NB** $8   **MIB** Sec. Mkt. **$15**

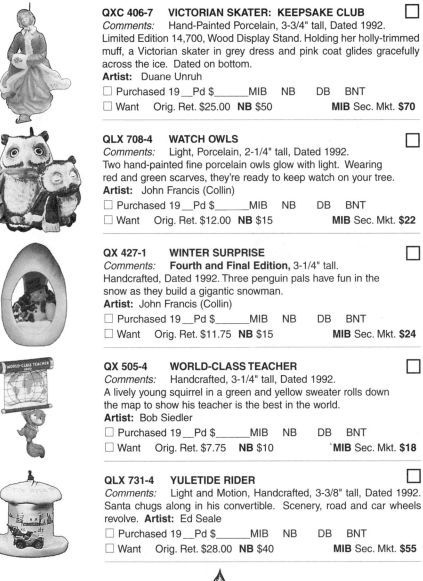

QXC 406-7   VICTORIAN SKATER: KEEPSAKE CLUB ☐
Comments: Hand-Painted Porcelain, 3-3/4" tall, Dated 1992.
Limited Edition 14,700, Wood Display Stand. Holding her holly-trimmed muff, a Victorian skater in grey dress and pink coat glides gracefully across the ice. Dated on bottom.
Artist: Duane Unruh

☐ Purchased 19 __Pd $_____MIB   NB   DB   BNT
☐ Want   Orig. Ret. $25.00   **NB** $50   **MIB** Sec. Mkt. **$70**

QLX 708-4   WATCH OWLS ☐
Comments: Light, Porcelain, 2-1/4" tall, Dated 1992.
Two hand-painted fine porcelain owls glow with light. Wearing red and green scarves, they're ready to keep watch on your tree.
Artist: John Francis (Collin)

☐ Purchased 19 __Pd $_____MIB   NB   DB   BNT
☐ Want   Orig. Ret. $12.00   **NB** $15   **MIB** Sec. Mkt. **$22**

QX 427-1   WINTER SURPRISE ☐
Comments: **Fourth and Final Edition,** 3-1/4" tall.
Handcrafted, Dated 1992. Three penguin pals have fun in the snow as they build a gigantic snowman.
Artist: John Francis (Collin)

☐ Purchased 19 __Pd $_____MIB   NB   DB   BNT
☐ Want   Orig. Ret. $11.75   **NB** $15   **MIB** Sec. Mkt. **$24**

QX 505-4   WORLD-CLASS TEACHER ☐
Comments: Handcrafted, 3-1/4" tall, Dated 1992.
A lively young squirrel in a green and yellow sweater rolls down the map to show his teacher is the best in the world.
Artist: Bob Siedler

☐ Purchased 19 __Pd $_____MIB   NB   DB   BNT
☐ Want   Orig. Ret. $7.75   **NB** $10   `**MIB** Sec. Mkt. **$18**

QLX 731-4   YULETIDE RIDER ☐
Comments: Light and Motion, Handcrafted, 3-3/8" tall, Dated 1992.
Santa chugs along in his convertible. Scenery, road and car wheels revolve. **Artist:** Ed Seale

☐ Purchased 19 __Pd $_____MIB   NB   DB   BNT
☐ Want   Orig. Ret. $28.00   **NB** $40   **MIB** Sec. Mkt. **$55**

1992 Miniature Ornament Collection

A   QXM 551-1   **A+ TEACHER** ☐
Handcrafted, 1-1/8" tall, Dated 1992. **Artist:** Duane Unruh
☐ Purchased 19___ Pd $_____   MIB   NB   DB   BNT
☐ Want   Orig. Retail $3.75
           NB $4   **MIB** Sec. Mkt. **$6.50**

B   QXM 552-4   **ANGELIC HARPIST** ☐
Handcrafted, 1-1/4" tall. **Artist:** Joyce A. Lyle
☐ Purchased 19___ Pd $_____   MIB   NB   DB   BNT
☐ Want   Orig. Retail $4.50
           NB $8   **MIB** Sec. Mkt. **$14**

C   QXM 549-4   **BABY'S FIRST CHRISTMAS** ☐
Handcrafted, 1-1/4" tall, Dated 1992.
Artist: Joyce A. Lyle
☐ Purchased 19___ Pd $_____   MIB   NB   DB   BNT
☐ Want   Orig. Retail $4.50
           NB $8   **MIB** Sec. Mkt. **$16.50**

D   QXM 554-4   **BEARYMORES, THE** ☐
FIRST IN SERIES, Handcrafted, 1-1/8" tall, Dated 1992.
Artist: Anita Marra Rogers
☐ Purchased 19___ Pd $_____   MIB   NB   DB   BNT
☐ Want   Orig. Retail $5.75
           NB $10   **MIB** Sec. Mkt. **$18**

E   QXM 548-4   **BLACK-CAPPED CHICKADEE** ☐
Handcrafted, 1-3/8" tall, Dated 1992.
Artist: John Francis (Collin)
☐ Purchased 19___ Pd $_____   MIB   NB   DB   BNT
☐ Want   Orig. Retail $3.00
           NB $8   **MIB** Sec. Mkt. **$14**

F   QXM 584-1   **BRIGHT STRINGERS** ☐
Handcrafted, 1-1/8" tall. **Artist:** Ed Seale
☐ Purchased 19___ Pd $_____   MIB   NB   DB   BNT
☐ Want   Orig. Retail $3.75
           NB $8   **MIB** Sec. Mkt. **$14**

G   QXM 581-4   **BUCK-A-ROO** ☐
Handcrafted, 1-1/8" tall, Dated 1993. **Artist:** Ken Crow
☐ Purchased 19___ Pd $_____   MIB   NB   DB   BNT
☐ Want   Orig. Retail $4.50
           NB $8   **MIB** Sec. Mkt. **$12.50**

H   QXC 519-4   **CHIPMUNK PARCEL SERVICE: KEEPSAKE CLUB** ☐
Handcrafted, Dated 1992. **Artist:** Ed Seale
☐ Purchased 19___ Pd $_____   MIB   NB   DB   BNT
☐ Want   Early Renewal Gift to Keepsake Orn. Club Members
           NB $14   **MIB** Sec. Mkt. **$18**

I   QXM 581-1   **CHRISTMAS BONUS** ☐
Handcrafted, 1-3/16" tall, Dated 1992. **Artist:** Don Palmiter
☐ Purchased 19___ Pd $_____   MIB   NB   DB   BNT
☐ Want   Orig. Retail $3.00
           NB $3   **MIB** Sec. Mkt. **$7.50**

J   QXM 584-4   **CHRISTMAS COPTER** ☐
Handcrafted, 7/8" tall, Dated 1992. **Artist:** John Francis (Collin)
☐ Purchased 19___ Pd $_____   MIB   NB   DB   BNT
☐ Want   Orig. Retail $5.75
           NB $8   **MIB** Sec. Mkt. **$12.50**

K   QXM 588-4   **COCA-COLA SANTA** ☐
Handcrafted, 1-3/16" tall. **Artist:** Duane Unruh
☐ Purchased 19___ Pd $_____   MIB   NB   DB   BNT
☐ Want   Orig. Retail $5.75
           NB $9   **MIB** Sec. Mkt. **$16**

L   QXM 556-1   **COOL UNCLE SAM** ☐
Handcrafted, 1" tall, Dated '92. **Artist:** Julia Lee
Election Year Commemorative
☐ Purchased 19___ Pd $_____   MIB   NB   DB   BNT
☐ Want   Orig. Retail $3.00
           NB $8   **MIB** Sec. Mkt. **$11.50**

M   QXM 555-1   **COZY KAYAK** ☐
Handcrafted, 3/4" tall, Dated 1992. **Artist:** Julia Lee
☐ Purchased 19___ Pd $_____   MIB   NB   DB   BNT
☐ Want   Orig. Retail $3.75
           NB $8   **MIB** Sec. Mkt. **$11**

N   QXM 589-1   **DANCING ANGELS TREE TOPPER** ☐
Dimensional Brass, 2-7/8" tall. Reissued in 1993.
☐ Purchased 19___ Pd $_____   MIB   NB   DB   BNT
☐ Want   Orig. Retail $9.75
           NB $10   **MIB** Sec. Mkt. **$12**

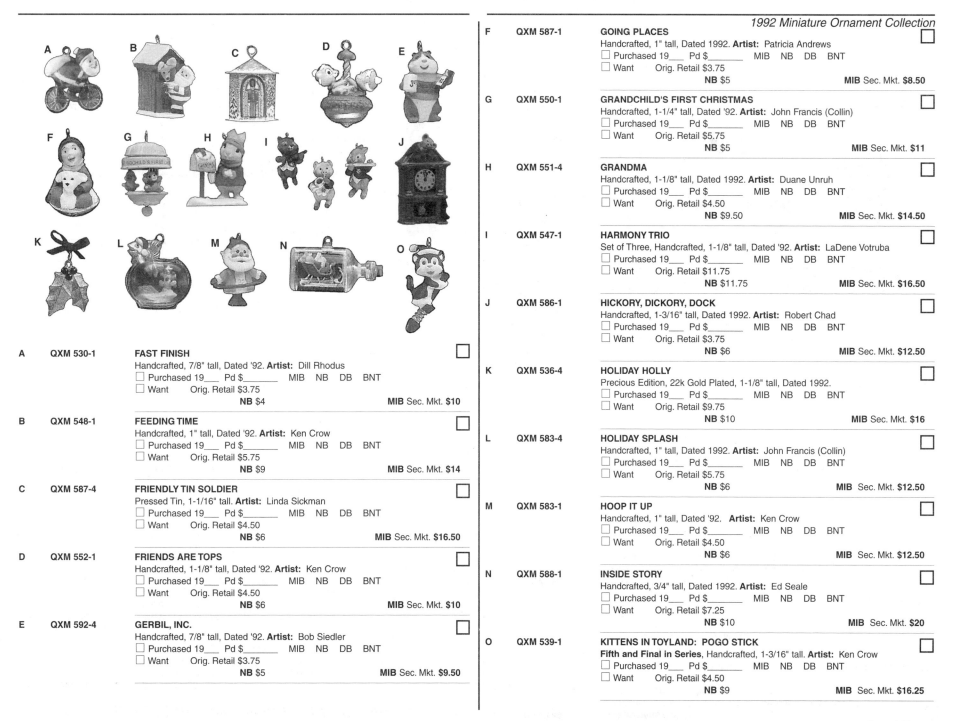

A QXM 530-1   **FAST FINISH**
Handcrafted, 7/8" tall, Dated '92. **Artist:** Dill Rhodus
☐ Purchased 19___ Pd $_____   MIB   NB   DB   BNT
☐ Want   Orig. Retail $3.75
                NB $4   **MIB** Sec. Mkt. **$10**

B QXM 548-1   **FEEDING TIME**
Handcrafted, 1" tall, Dated '92. **Artist:** Ken Crow
☐ Purchased 19___ Pd $_____   MIB   NB   DB   BNT
☐ Want   Orig. Retail $5.75
                NB $9   **MIB** Sec. Mkt. **$14**

C QXM 587-4   **FRIENDLY TIN SOLDIER**
Pressed Tin, 1-1/16" tall. **Artist:** Linda Sickman
☐ Purchased 19___ Pd $_____   MIB   NB   DB   BNT
☐ Want   Orig. Retail $4.50
                NB $6   **MIB** Sec. Mkt. **$16.50**

D QXM 552-1   **FRIENDS ARE TOPS**
Handcrafted, 1-1/8" tall, Dated '92. **Artist:** Ken Crow
☐ Purchased 19___ Pd $_____   MIB   NB   DB   BNT
☐ Want   Orig. Retail $4.50
                NB $6   **MIB** Sec. Mkt. **$10**

E QXM 592-4   **GERBIL, INC.**
Handcrafted, 7/8" tall, Dated '92. **Artist:** Bob Siedler
☐ Purchased 19___ Pd $_____   MIB   NB   DB   BNT
☐ Want   Orig. Retail $3.75
                NB $5   **MIB** Sec. Mkt. **$9.50**

F QXM 587-1   **GOING PLACES**
Handcrafted, 1" tall, Dated 1992. **Artist:** Patricia Andrews
☐ Purchased 19___ Pd $_____   MIB   NB   DB   BNT
☐ Want   Orig. Retail $3.75
                NB $5   **MIB** Sec. Mkt. **$8.50**

G QXM 550-1   **GRANDCHILD'S FIRST CHRISTMAS**
Handcrafted, 1-1/4" tall, Dated '92. **Artist:** John Francis (Collin)
☐ Purchased 19___ Pd $_____   MIB   NB   DB   BNT
☐ Want   Orig. Retail $5.75
                NB $5   **MIB** Sec. Mkt. **$11**

H QXM 551-4   **GRANDMA**
Handcrafted, 1-1/8" tall, Dated 1992. **Artist:** Duane Unruh
☐ Purchased 19___ Pd $_____   MIB   NB   DB   BNT
☐ Want   Orig. Retail $4.50
                NB $9.50   **MIB** Sec. Mkt. **$14.50**

I QXM 547-1   **HARMONY TRIO**
Set of Three, Handcrafted, 1-1/8" tall, Dated '92. **Artist:** LaDene Votruba
☐ Purchased 19___ Pd $_____   MIB   NB   DB   BNT
☐ Want   Orig. Retail $11.75
                NB $11.75   **MIB** Sec. Mkt. **$16.50**

J QXM 586-1   **HICKORY, DICKORY, DOCK**
Handcrafted, 1-3/16" tall, Dated 1992. **Artist:** Robert Chad
☐ Purchased 19___ Pd $_____   MIB   NB   DB   BNT
☐ Want   Orig. Retail $3.75
                NB $6   **MIB** Sec. Mkt. **$12.50**

K QXM 536-4   **HOLIDAY HOLLY**
Precious Edition, 22k Gold Plated, 1-1/8" tall, Dated 1992.
☐ Purchased 19___ Pd $_____   MIB   NB   DB   BNT
☐ Want   Orig. Retail $9.75
                NB $10   **MIB** Sec. Mkt. **$16**

L QXM 583-4   **HOLIDAY SPLASH**
Handcrafted, 1" tall, Dated 1992. **Artist:** John Francis (Collin)
☐ Purchased 19___ Pd $_____   MIB   NB   DB   BNT
☐ Want   Orig. Retail $5.75
                NB $6   **MIB** Sec. Mkt. **$12.50**

M QXM 583-1   **HOOP IT UP**
Handcrafted, 1" tall, Dated '92. **Artist:** Ken Crow
☐ Purchased 19___ Pd $_____   MIB   NB   DB   BNT
☐ Want   Orig. Retail $4.50
                NB $6   **MIB** Sec. Mkt. **$12.50**

N QXM 588-1   **INSIDE STORY**
Handcrafted, 3/4" tall, Dated 1992. **Artist:** Ed Seale
☐ Purchased 19___ Pd $_____   MIB   NB   DB   BNT
☐ Want   Orig. Retail $7.25
                NB $10   **MIB** Sec. Mkt. **$20**

O QXM 539-1   **KITTENS IN TOYLAND: POGO STICK**
Fifth and Final in Series, Handcrafted, 1-3/16" tall. **Artist:** Ken Crow
☐ Purchased 19___ Pd $_____   MIB   NB   DB   BNT
☐ Want   Orig. Retail $4.50
                NB $9   **MIB** Sec. Mkt. **$16.25**

A   QXM 538-1   **KRINGLES, THE** ☐
Fourth in Series, Handcrafted, 1" tall. **Artist:** Anita Marra Rogers
☐ Purchased 19___ Pd $_____ MIB NB DB BNT
☐ Want   Orig. Retail $6.00
       NB $12   **MIB** Sec. Mkt. **$18.50**

B   QXM 586-4   **LITTLE TOWN OF BETHLEHEM** ☐
Handcrafted, 1" dia., Dated 1992. **Artist:** Linda Sickman
☐ Purchased 19___ Pd $_____ MIB NB DB BNT
☐ Want   Orig. Retail $3.00
       NB $10   **MIB** Sec. Mkt. **$19.50**

C   QXM 585-4   **MINTED FOR SANTA** ☐
Copper, 1" dia., Dated 1992. **Artist:** Duane Unruh
☐ Purchased 19___ Pd $_____ MIB NB DB BNT
☐ Want   Orig. Retail $3.75
       NB $6   **MIB** Sec. Mkt. **$11.50**

D   QXM 550-4   **MOM** ☐
Handcrafted, 1-3/16" tall, Dated 1992. **Artist:** Patricia Andrews
☐ Purchased 19___ Pd $_____ MIB NB DB BNT
☐ Want   Orig. Retail $4.50
       NB $9   **MIB** Sec. Mkt. **$15.50**

E   QXM 545-1   **NATURE'S ANGELS** ☐
Third in Series, Handcrafted, 1" tall. **Artist:** Sharon Pike
☐ Purchased 19___ Pd $_____ MIB NB DB BNT
☐ Want   Orig. Retail $4.50
       NB $10   **MIB** Sec. Mkt. **$18**

F   QXM 554-1   **NIGHT BEFORE CHRISTMAS, THE: HOUSE** ☐
FIRST IN SERIES, Tin/Handcrafted
Tin Display House, 8" tall x 5-1/2" wide; Rocker w/Mouse, 1-1/8" tall.
Due to the house being produced only in '92 this series will not be as popular, as there are too many "new" buyers each year who will not have the house for the remaining pieces in the series.
Artists: LaDene Votruba and Duane Unruh
☐ Purchased 19___ Pd $_____ MIB NB DB BNT
☐ Want   Orig. Retail $13.75
       NB $22   **MIB** Sec. Mkt. **$30-$35**

G   QXM 544-1   **NOEL R.R.: BOX CAR** ☐
Fourth in Series, Handcrafted, 13/16" tall, Dated 1992.
Artist: Linda Sickman
☐ Purchased 19___ Pd $_____ MIB NB DB BNT
☐ Want   Orig. Retail $7.00
       NB $16   **MIB** Sec. Mkt. **$22.50**

H   QXM 538-4   **OLD ENGLISH VILLAGE: CHURCH** ☐
Fifth in Series, Handcrafted, 1-5/16" tall, Dated 1992.
Artist: Julia Lee
☐ Purchased 19___ Pd $_____ MIB NB DB BNT
☐ Want   Orig. Retail $7.00
       NB $15   **MIB** Sec. Mkt. **$28**

I   QXM 557-1   **PERFECT BALANCE** ☐
Handcrafted, 1-1/4" tall, Dated '92. **Artist:** Anita Marra Rogers
☐ Purchased 19___ Pd $_____ MIB NB DB BNT
☐ Want   Orig. Retail $3.00
       NB $8   **MIB** Sec. Mkt. **$14**

J   QXM 553-4   **POLAR POLKA** ☐
Handcrafted, 1-13/16" tall, Dated 1992. **Artist:** Ed Seale
☐ Purchased 19___ Pd $_____ MIB NB DB BNT
☐ Want   Orig. Retail $4.50
       NB $8   **MIB** Sec. Mkt. **$14.50**

K   QXM 557-4   **PUPPET SHOW** ☐
Handcrafted, 1" tall, Dated '92. **Artist:** Bob Siedler
☐ Purchased 19___ Pd $_____ MIB NB DB BNT
☐ Want   Orig. Retail $3.00
       NB $6   **MIB** Sec. Mkt. **$12.50**

L   QXM 545-4   **ROCKING HORSE: BROWN HORSE** ☐
Fifth in Series, Handcrafted, 1-1/8" tall, Dated 1992.
Artist: Linda Sickman
☐ Purchased 19___ Pd $_____ MIB NB DB BNT
☐ Want   Orig. Retail $4.50
       NB $10   **MIB** Sec. Mkt. **$18**

M   QXM 579-4   **SEW, SEW TINY** ☐
Handcrafted, Dated 1992. Not Porcelain. **Artist:** Ed Seale
A. Basket Break, 1-1/8" tall   D. Cutting Edge, 7/8" tall
B. Threaded Thru, 1-1/4" tall   E. Buttoned Up, 3/4" tall
C. Pinned On, 1-1/8" tall   F. Thimble Full, 13/16" tall
☐ Purchased 19___ Pd $_____ MIB NB DB BNT
☐ Want   Orig. Retail $29.00
       NB $28   **MIB** Sec. Mkt. **$48**

A   QXM 582-1   **SKI FOR TWO**
Handcrafted, 15/16" tall, Dated '92. **Artist:** Patricia Andrews
☐ Purchased 19___ Pd $_____ MIB NB DB BNT
☐ Want   Orig. Retail $4.50
                     NB $6   **MIB** Sec. Mkt. **$12.50**

B   QXM 556-4   **SNOWSHOE BUNNY**
Handcrafted, 1-1/16" tall. **Artist:** LaDene Votruba
☐ Purchased 19___ Pd $_____ MIB NB DB BNT
☐ Want   Orig. Retail $3.75
                     NB $5   **MIB** Sec. Mkt. **$9.50**

C   QXM 555-4   **SNUG KITTY**
Handcrafted, 1" tall, Dated '92. **Artist:** Sharon Pike
☐ Purchased 19___ Pd $_____ MIB NB DB BNT
☐ Want   Orig. Retail $3.75
                     NB $5   **MIB** Sec. Mkt. **$12.50**

D   QXM 592-1   **SPUNKY MONKEY**
Handcrafted, 1-3/8" tall, Dated '92. **Artist:** Robert Chad
☐ Purchased 19___ Pd $_____ MIB NB DB BNT
☐ Want   Orig. Retail $3.00
                     NB $9.50   **MIB** Sec. Mkt. **$15**

E   QXM 546-1   **THIMBLE BELLS**
Third in Series, Porcelain, 1-1/8" tall, Dated 1992.
Artist: Joyce A. Lyle
☐ Purchased 19___ Pd $_____ MIB NB DB BNT
☐ Want   Orig. Retail $6.00
                     NB $10   **MIB** Sec. Mkt. **$20.50**

F   QXM 585-1   **VISIONS OF ACORNS**
Handcrafted, 1-3/16" tall, Dated '92. **Artist:** Patricia Andrews
☐ Purchased 19___ Pd $_____ MIB NB DB BNT
☐ Want   Orig. Retail $4.50
                     NB $8   **MIB** Sec. Mkt. **$10.50**

G   QXM 553-1   **WEE THREE KINGS**
Handcrafted, 1-3/16" tall, Dated 1991. **Artist:** Don Palmiter
☐ Purchased 19___ Pd $_____ MIB NB DB BNT
☐ Want   Orig. Retail $5.75
                     NB $10   **MIB** Sec. Mkt. **$20**

H   QXM 544-4   **WOODLAND BABIES**
Second in Series, Handcrafted, 1" tall, Dated 1992.
Artist: Don Palmiter
☐ Purchased 19___ Pd $_____ MIB NB DB BNT
☐ Want   Orig. Retail $6.00
                     NB $9   **MIB** Sec. Mkt. **$12.50**

N. Albritton's tree is decorated solely with Hallmark's ball ornament's.

Kristin Smith has up to 500 ornaments placed on her tree, many of which are intertwined within the branches.

Brenda Brannon has more ornaments than you can count!

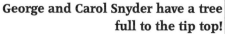

George and Carol Snyder have a tree full to the tip top!

1992 Easter Ornament Collection

A QEO 927-1 **BABY'S FIRST EASTER**
Handcrafted, 3" tall, Dated 1992. **Artist:** John Francis (Collin)

☐ Purchased 19___ Pd $_____ MIB NB DB BNT

☐ Want Original Retail $6.75

NB $10 **MIB** Sec. Mkt. **$22**

B QEO 935-4 **BELLE BUNNY**
Porcelain, 3" tall, Dated '92. **Artist:** LaDene Votruba

☐ Purchased 19___ Pd $_____ MIB NB DB BNT

☐ Want Original Retail $9.75

NB $12 **MIB** Sec. Mkt. **$21**

C QEO 929-1 **BLESS YOU**
Handcrafted, 3" tall. **Artist:** John Francis (Collin)

☐ Purchased 19___ Pd $_____ MIB NB DB BNT

☐ Want Original Retail $6.75

NB $9 **MIB** Sec. Mkt. **$24**

D QEO 936-4 **COSMIC RABBIT**
Handcrafted, 3" tall, Dated '92. **Artist:** Bob Siedler

☐ Purchased 19___ Pd $_____ MIB NB DB BNT

☐ Want Original Retail $7.75

NB $9 **MIB** Sec. Mkt. **$20**

E QEO 930-4 **CRAYOLA® BUNNY**
Handcrafted, 3" tall, Dated '92. **Artist:** Anita Marra Rogers

☐ Purchased 19___ Pd $_____ MIB NB DB BNT

☐ Want Original Retail $7.75

NB $20 **MIB** Sec. Mkt. **$27.50**

F QEO 935-1 **CULTIVATED GARDENER**
Handcrafted, 3" tall, Caption: "Carrots 92." **Artist:** Bob Siedler

☐ Purchased 19___ Pd $_____ MIB NB DB BNT

☐ Want Original Retail $5.75

NB $8 **MIB** Sec. Mkt. **$15**

G QEO 928-4 **DAUGHTER**
Handcrafted, 3" tall, Dated 1992. **Artist:** Anita Marra Rogers

☐ Purchased 19___ Pd $_____ MIB NB DB BNT

☐ Want Original Retail $5.75

NB $12 **MIB** Sec. Mkt. **$18**

H QEO 930-1 **EASTER PARADE**
FIRST IN SERIES, 3" tall, Handcrafted, Dated '92. **Artist:** Ken Crow

☐ Purchased 19___ Pd $_____ MIB NB DB BNT

☐ Want Original Retail $6.75

NB $15 **MIB** Sec. Mkt. **$26**

I QEO 934-1 **EGGS IN SPORTS**
FIRST IN SERIES, 3" tall, Handcrafted, Caption: "Grade A's 92."
Series ended in 1994. **Artist:** Bob Siedler

☐ Purchased 19___ Pd $_____ MIB NB DB BNT

☐ Want Original Retail $6.75

NB $20 **MIB** Sec. Mkt. **$38**

J QEO 936-1 **EGGSPERT PAINTER**
Handcrafted, 3" tall, Dated '92. **Artist:** Bob Siedler

☐ Purchased 19___ Pd $_____ MIB NB DB BNT

☐ Want Original Retail $6.75

NB $14 **MIB** Sec. Mkt. **$22.50**

K QEO 933-1 **EVERYTHING'S DUCKY!**
Handcrafted, 3" tall, Dated '92. **Artist:** Sharon Pike

☐ Purchased 19___ Pd $_____ MIB NB DB BNT

☐ Want Original Retail $6.75

NB $13.50 **MIB** Sec. Mkt. **$19**

L QEO 927-4 **GRANDCHILD**
Handcrafted, 3" tall. **Artist:** Ken Crow

☐ Purchased 19___ Pd $_____ MIB NB DB BNT

☐ Want Original Retail $6.75

NB $12 **MIB** Sec. Mkt. **$20**

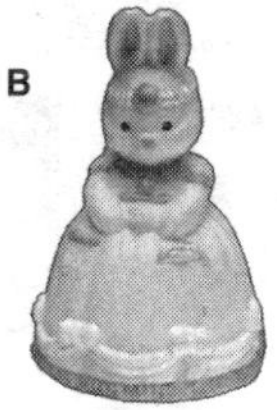

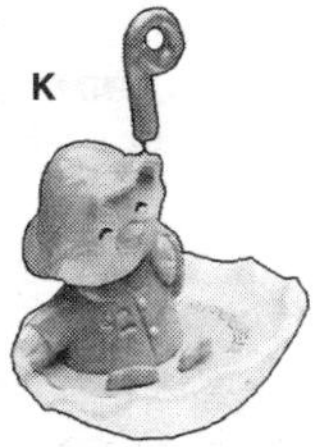

A QEO 933-4 **JOY BEARER**
Handcrafted, Dated '92. **Artist:** Don Palmiter
☐ Purchased 19___ Pd $_____ MIB NB DB BNT
☐ Want   Original Retail $8.75
NB $14   **MIB** Sec. Mkt. **$24**

B QEO 931-4 **PROMISE OF EASTER**
Porcelain, 3" tall, Dated 1992. **Artist:** Joyce A. Lyle
Caption: "God's love shines everywhere."
☐ Purchased 19___ Pd $_____ MIB NB DB BNT
☐ Want   Original Retail $8.75
NB $14   **MIB** Sec. Mkt. **$18**

C QEO 932-4 **ROCKING BUNNY**
Handcrafted and Nickel-Plated, 3" tall. **Artist:** LaDene Votruba
Caption: "Happy Easter 1992."
☐ Purchased 19___ Pd $_____ MIB NB DB BNT
☐ Want   Original Retail $9.75
NB $14   **MIB** Sec. Mkt. **$23**

D QEO 929-4 **SOMEBUNNY LOVES YOU**
Handcrafted, 3" tall. **Artist:** John Francis (Collin)
☐ Purchased 19___ Pd $_____ MIB NB DB BNT
☐ Want   Original Retail $6.75
NB $12   **MIB** Sec. Mkt. **$28**

E QEO 928-1 **SON**
Handcrafted, 3" tall, Dated 1992. **Artist:** Anita Marra Rogers
☐ Purchased 19___ Pd $_____ MIB NB DB BNT
☐ Want   Original Retail $5.75
NB $8   **MIB** Sec. Mkt. **$18**

F QEO 932-1 **SPRINGTIME EGG**
Handcrafted, 3" tall, Dated 1992. **Artist:** Julia Lee
☐ Purchased 19___ Pd $_____ MIB NB DB BNT
☐ Want   Original Retail $8.75
NB $10   **MIB** Sec. Mkt. **$20**

G QEO 934-4 **SUNNY WISHER**
Handcrafted, 3" tall. **Artist:** Sharon Pike
Caption: "Sunny Easter Wishes."
☐ Purchased 19___ Pd $_____ MIB NB DB BNT
☐ Want   Original Retail $5.75
NB $10   **MIB** Sec. Mkt. **$18**

H QEO 931-1 **WARM MEMORIES**
Embroidered Fabric Photoholder, 4: tall, Dated 1992.
Artist: LaDene Votruba. Caption: "Easter brings warm memories."
☐ Purchased 19___ Pd $_____ MIB NB DB BNT
☐ Want   Original Retail $7.75
NB $12   MIB Sec. Mkt. **$16**

—R.STUBLER—

**"Excuse me officer. Could you please hurry?
This garage sale I'm going to has Hallmark Ornaments!"**

1993 Collection

QX 568-2   20TH ANNIVERSARY: FROSTY FRIENDS
Comments: Handcrafted, 2-1/2" tall, Dated 1993.
Frosty and his penguin pal decorate their igloo for a Merry
Christmas. This anniversary edition complements the
Frosty Friends Series.   **Artist:** Ed Seale
☐ Purchased 19__Pd $_____MIB   NB   DB   BNT
☐ Want   Orig. Ret. $20.00   **MIB** Sec. Mkt. **$50**

QX 530-2   20TH ANNIVERSARY:
               GLOWING PEWTER WREATH
Comments: Fine Pewter, 3-11/16" tall, Dated 1993.
Images of Santa, musical instruments, a star and a dated stocking
are part of the design on this pewter wreath. Seek and ye shall find for
even less.
Artist: Duane Unruh
☐ Purchased 19__Pd $_____MIB   NB   DB   BNT
☐ Want   Orig. Ret. $18.75   **MIB** Sec. Mkt. **$35-$38**

QX 567-5   20TH ANNIVERSARY: SHOPPING WITH SANTA
Comments: Handcrafted, 3-1/2" tall, Dated 1993.
Santa drives into Christmas in this vintage car. Let's go
Hallmarking! This ornament complements the Here Comes Santa
Series. **Artist:** Linda Sickman
☐ Purchased 19__Pd $_____MIB   NB   DB   BNT
☐ Want   Orig. Ret. $24.00   **MIB** Sec. Mkt. **$45**

QX 561-2   20TH ANNIVERSARY:
               TANNENBAUM'S DEPT. STORE
Comments: Handcrafted, 4-15/16" tall, Dated 1993.
Tannenbaum's three-story shop complements the Nostalgic
Houses and Shops Series. **Artist:** Donna Lee
☐ Purchased 19__Pd $_____MIB   NB   DB   BNT
☐ Want   Orig. Ret. $26.00   **MIB** Sec. Mkt. **$55**

QX 588-2   A CHILD'S CHRISTMAS
Comments: Handcrafted, 2-5/16" tall, Dated 1993.
A light brown teddy has popped out of a brightly striped gift box
to wish happy holidays. May be personalized for Niece, Nephew,
Granddaughter, Grandson, Great-Grandchild, or A Child's
Christmas. **Artist:** John Francis (Collin)
☐ Purchased 19__Pd $_____MIB   NB   DB   BNT
☐ Want   Orig. Ret. $9.75   **MIB** Sec. Mkt. **$18**

QX 591-2   ACROSS THE MILES
Comments: Handcrafted, 1-11/16" tall, Dated 1993.
This white bear is sprawled on the ice reading a journal from
"Across the Miles." **Artist:** John Francis (Collin)
☐ Purchased 19__Pd $_____MIB   NB   DB   BNT
☐ Want   Orig. Ret. $8.75   **MIB** Sec. Mkt. **$18**

QX 597-2   ANNIVERSARY YEAR PHOTOHOLDER
Comments: Brass and Chrome, 3-13/16" tall, Dated 1993.
This ornate photo holder may be personalized eight ways to mark
anniversaries for 5, 10, 25, 30, 35, 40, 50 and 60 years.
Artist: Joyce A. Lyle
☐ Purchased 19__Pd $_____MIB   NB   DB   BNT
☐ Want   Orig. Ret. $9.75   **MIB** Sec. Mkt. **$18**

QX 590-2   APPLE FOR TEACHER
Comments: Handcrafted, 2-3/8" tall, Dated 1993.
Open the apple and view two mice students at their desks and
a chalkboard which may be personalized. Caption: "A Is For
Apple, A+ Is For Teacher." **Artist:** Ed Seale
☐ Purchased 19__Pd $_____MIB   NB   DB   BNT
☐ Want   Orig. Ret. $7.75   **MIB** Sec. Mkt. **$14**

QX 551-2   BABY'S FIRST CHRISTMAS
Comments: Silver plated, 3-1/16" tall, Dated 1993.
This silver-plated baby rattle is all tied up in a red bow and comes
with a silver tag which may be engraved for personalization.
Artist: Don Palmiter
☐ Purchased 19__Pd $_____MIB   NB   DB   BNT
☐ Want   Orig. Ret. $18.75   **MIB** Sec. Mkt. **$35**

QX 551-5   BABY'S FIRST CHRISTMAS
Comments: Handcrafted, 3-3/16" tall, Dated 1993.
An adorable baby squirrel plays merrily in its walnut shell
"swing."   **Artist:** Trish Andrews
☐ Purchased 19__Pd $_____MIB   NB   DB   BNT
☐ Want   Orig. Ret. $10.75   **MIB** Sec. Mkt. **$20**

QX 552-2   BABY'S FIRST CHRISTMAS PHOTOHOLDER
Comments: Handcrafted, 4-3/4" dia., Dated 1993.
Christmas and baby designs adorn this "quilted" lace-trimmed
photoholder.   Caption: "Christmas And Babies Fill A Home With
Special Joys." **Artist:** Anita Marra Rogers
☐ Purchased 19__Pd $_____MIB   NB   DB   BNT
☐ Want   Orig. Ret. $7.75   **MIB** Sec. Mkt. **$20**

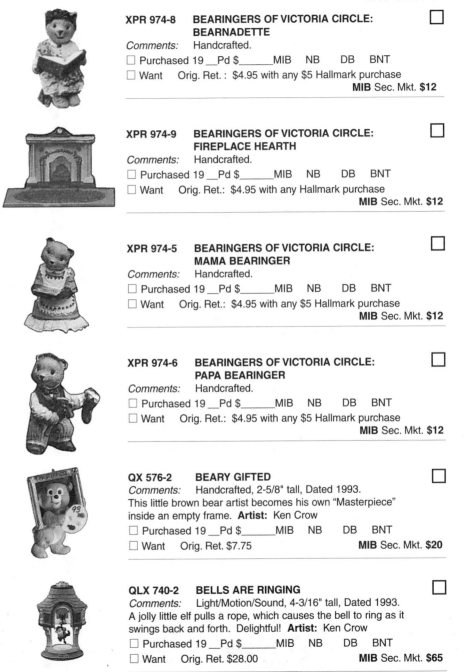

QX 552-5   BABY'S FIRST CHRISTMAS
Comments: Handcrafted, 2-3/16" dia., Dated 1993.
Also known as the "Teddy Bear Years," a tan teddy holds a red
stocking filled with a large cookie star, as he enjoys his pacifier.
Artist: Ken Crow

☐ Purchased 19 __Pd $_____MIB   NB   DB   BNT
☐ Want   Orig. Ret. $7.75   **MIB** Sec. Mkt. **$28**

QLX 736-5   BABY'S FIRST CHRISTMAS
Comments: Light and Music, 3-7/8" tall, Dated 1993.
Baby sleeps soundly in the nursery on Christmas Eve.
Plays "Brahms' Lullaby." Caption: "There's A New Little Stocking
For Santa To Fill!" **Artist:** John Francis (Collin)

☐ Purchased 19 __Pd $_____MIB   NB   DB   BNT
☐ Want   Orig. Ret. $22.00   **MIB** Sec. Mkt. **$44**

QX 210-5   BABY'S FIRST CHRISTMAS-BOY
Comments: Light Blue Glass Ball, 2-7/8" dia., Dated 1993.
Toy animals sit side by side around this glass ball. Caption:
"A Baby Boy Is A Bundle Of Delight." **Artist:** LaDene Votruba

☐ Purchased 19 __Pd $_____MIB   NB   DB   BNT
☐ Want   Orig. Ret. $4.75   **MIB** Sec. Mkt. **$13**

QX 209-2   BABY'S FIRST CHRISTMAS-GIRL
Comments: Pink Glass Ball, 2-7/8" dia., Dated 1993.
Toy animals sit side by side around this glass ball. Caption:
"A Baby Girl Is A Bundle Of Delight." **Artist:** LaDene Votruba

☐ Purchased 19 __Pd $_____MIB   NB   DB   BNT
☐ Want   Orig. Ret. $4.75   **MIB** Sec. Mkt. **$14**

QX 599-2   BABY'S SECOND CHRISTMAS
Comments: Handcrafted, 2-3/16" dia., Dated 1993.
Identical to 1989 except for date. **Artist:** John Francis (Collin)

☐ Purchased 19 __Pd $_____MIB   NB   DB   BNT
☐ Want   Orig. Ret. $6.75   **MIB** Sec. Mkt. **$18**

XPR 974-7   BEARINGERS OF VICTORIA CIRCLE:
                     ABEARNATHY
Comments: Handcrafted.

☐ Purchased 19 __Pd $_____MIB   NB   DB   BNT
☐ Want   Orig. Ret.: $4.95 with any $5 Hallmark purchase
                                           MIB Sec. Mkt. **$12**

XPR 974-8   BEARINGERS OF VICTORIA CIRCLE:
                     BEARNADETTE
Comments: Handcrafted.

☐ Purchased 19 __Pd $_____MIB   NB   DB   BNT
☐ Want   Orig. Ret. : $4.95 with any $5 Hallmark purchase
                                           MIB Sec. Mkt. **$12**

XPR 974-9   BEARINGERS OF VICTORIA CIRCLE:
                     FIREPLACE HEARTH
Comments: Handcrafted.

☐ Purchased 19 __Pd $_____MIB   NB   DB   BNT
☐ Want   Orig. Ret.: $4.95 with any Hallmark purchase
                                           MIB Sec. Mkt. **$12**

XPR 974-5   BEARINGERS OF VICTORIA CIRCLE:
                     MAMA BEARINGER
Comments: Handcrafted.

☐ Purchased 19 __Pd $_____MIB   NB   DB   BNT
☐ Want   Orig. Ret.: $4.95 with any $5 Hallmark purchase
                                           MIB Sec. Mkt. **$12**

XPR 974-6   BEARINGERS OF VICTORIA CIRCLE:
                     PAPA BEARINGER
Comments: Handcrafted.

☐ Purchased 19 __Pd $_____MIB   NB   DB   BNT
☐ Want   Orig. Ret.: $4.95 with any $5 Hallmark purchase
                                           MIB Sec. Mkt. **$12**

QX 576-2   BEARY GIFTED
Comments: Handcrafted, 2-5/8" tall, Dated 1993.
This little brown bear artist becomes his own "Masterpiece"
inside an empty frame. **Artist:** Ken Crow

☐ Purchased 19 __Pd $_____MIB   NB   DB   BNT
☐ Want   Orig. Ret. $7.75   **MIB** Sec. Mkt. **$20**

QLX 740-2   BELLS ARE RINGING
Comments: Light/Motion/Sound, 4-3/16" tall, Dated 1993.
A jolly little elf pulls a rope, which causes the bell to ring as it
swings back and forth. Delightful! **Artist:** Ken Crow

☐ Purchased 19 __Pd $_____MIB   NB   DB   BNT
☐ Want   Orig. Ret. $28.00   **MIB** Sec. Mkt. **$65**

QX 206-2   BETSEY'S COUNTRY CHRISTMAS ☐
Comments: **Second in Series,** Teardrop Ball, 2-7/8" tall.
Dated 1993. Caption: "Happy Is The Memory Of Bringing
Home The Christmas Tree!"
☐ Purchased 19__Pd $_____MIB   NB   DB   BNT
☐ Want   Orig. Ret. $5.00   **MIB** Sec. Mkt. **$15**

QX 584-2   BIG ON GARDENING ☐
Comments: Handcrafted, 2-1/2" tall, Dated 1993.
This cute little elephant in a red gardening apron is holding a red pot-
ted flower and gardening tools. **Artist:** LaDene Votruba
☐ Purchased 19__Pd $_____MIB   NB   DB   BNT
☐ Want   Orig. Ret. $9.75   **MIB** Sec. Mkt. **$18**

QX 535-2   BIG ROLLER ☐
Comments: Handcrafted, 3-1/16" tall, Dated 1993.
This little creature, dressed for winter, runs on a nickel-plated exercise
wheel that really spins. **Artist:** Bob Siedler
☐ Purchased 19__Pd $_____MIB   NB   DB   BNT
☐ Want   Orig. Ret. $8.75   **MIB** Sec. Mkt. **$15**

QX 525-2   BIRD WATCHER ☐
Comments: Handcrafted, 2-7/16" tall, Dated 1993.
All set with his sneakers, camera and binoculars, a bluebird has
its eyes on Santa and his reindeer. **Artist:** Julia Lee
☐ Purchased 19__Pd $_____MIB   NB   DB   BNT
☐ Want   Orig. Ret. $9.75   **MIB** Sec. Mkt. **$18**

QX 556-5   BOWLING FOR ZZZS ☐
Comments: Handcrafted, 1-13/16" tall, Dated 1993.
A little mouse naps under a hand towel captioned "Santa Claus
Lanes," which is tucked inside a green bowling bag.
Artist: John Francis (Collin)
☐ Purchased 19__Pd $_____MIB   NB   DB   BNT
☐ Want   Orig. Ret. $7.75   **MIB** Sec. Mkt. **$18**

QX 554-2   BROTHER ☐
Comments: Handcrafted, 2-3/8" tall, Dated 1993.
Sporting a red, white and green football helmet, this pup is
sure to score big! **Artist:** Anita Marra Rogers
☐ Purchased 19__Pd $_____MIB   NB   DB   BNT
☐ Want   Orig. Ret. $6.75   **MIB** Sec. Mkt. **$12**

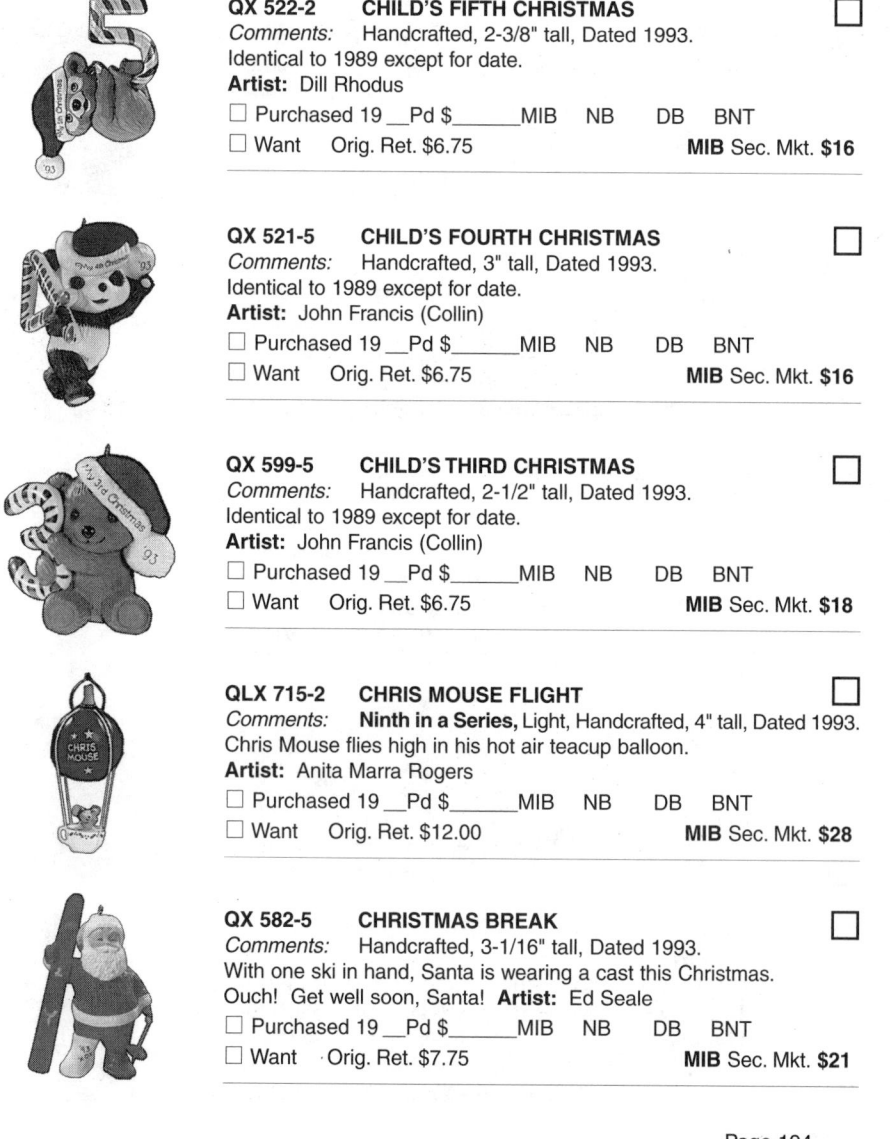

QX 578-5   CARING NURSE ☐
Comments: Handcrafted, 1-1/4" tall, Dated 1993.
This little bear nurse specializes in "TLC" as she checks her
patient with a stethoscope. **Artist:** John Francis (Collin)
☐ Purchased 19__Pd $_____MIB   NB   DB   BNT
☐ Want   Orig. Ret. $6.75   **MIB** Sec. Mkt. **$18**

QX 522-2   CHILD'S FIFTH CHRISTMAS ☐
Comments: Handcrafted, 2-3/8" tall, Dated 1993.
Identical to 1989 except for date.
Artist: Dill Rhodus
☐ Purchased 19__Pd $_____MIB   NB   DB   BNT
☐ Want   Orig. Ret. $6.75   **MIB** Sec. Mkt. **$16**

QX 521-5   CHILD'S FOURTH CHRISTMAS ☐
Comments: Handcrafted, 3" tall, Dated 1993.
Identical to 1989 except for date.
Artist: John Francis (Collin)
☐ Purchased 19__Pd $_____MIB   NB   DB   BNT
☐ Want   Orig. Ret. $6.75   **MIB** Sec. Mkt. **$16**

QX 599-5   CHILD'S THIRD CHRISTMAS ☐
Comments: Handcrafted, 2-1/2" tall, Dated 1993.
Identical to 1989 except for date.
Artist: John Francis (Collin)
☐ Purchased 19__Pd $_____MIB   NB   DB   BNT
☐ Want   Orig. Ret. $6.75   **MIB** Sec. Mkt. **$18**

QLX 715-2   CHRIS MOUSE FLIGHT ☐
Comments: **Ninth in a Series,** Light, Handcrafted, 4" tall, Dated 1993.
Chris Mouse flies high in his hot air teacup balloon.
Artist: Anita Marra Rogers
☐ Purchased 19__Pd $_____MIB   NB   DB   BNT
☐ Want   Orig. Ret. $12.00   **MIB** Sec. Mkt. **$28**

QX 582-5   CHRISTMAS BREAK ☐
Comments: Handcrafted, 3-1/16" tall, Dated 1993.
With one ski in hand, Santa is wearing a cast this Christmas.
Ouch! Get well soon, Santa! **Artist:** Ed Seale
☐ Purchased 19__Pd $_____MIB   NB   DB   BNT
☐ Want   ·Orig. Ret. $7.75   **MIB** Sec. Mkt. **$21**

QX 527-5   CLASSIC AMERICAN CARS:
1956 FORD THUNDERBIRD
Comments: **Third in Series,** Handcrafted, 2-5/16" tall, Dated 1993.
This blue T-bird is guaranteed to delight car collectors of all ages!
Artist: Don Palmiter
☐ Purchased 19 __Pd $_____MIB   NB   DB   BNT
☐ Want   Orig. Ret. $12.75   **MIB** Sec. Mkt. **$30-$35**

QX 566-2   CLEVER COOKIE
Comments: Handcrafted and Tin, 3-1/8" tall, Dated 1993.
Clever is the right word, as this gingerbread cookie girl decides
to leave her cutter frame. **Artist:** Linda Sickman
☐ Purchased 19 __Pd $_____MIB   NB   DB   BNT
☐ Want   Orig. Ret. $7.75   **MIB** Sec. Mkt. **$18**

QX 593-5   COACH
Comments: Handcrafted, 2-1/2" tall, Dated 1993.
A new commemorative ornament to the line, this penguin,
wearing a red cap, holds onto his clipboard as he blows a silver
whistle. **Artist:** Don Palmiter
☐ Purchased 19 __Pd $_____MIB   NB   DB   BNT
☐ Want   Orig. Ret. $6.75   **MIB** Sec. Mkt. **$15**

QX 442-2   CRAYOLA® CRAYON:
BRIGHT SHINING CASTLE
Comments: **Fifth in Series,** Handcrafted, 3-5/8" tall, Dated 1993.
A bear trumpet player welcomes everyone to his colorful castle.
Artist: Ken Crow
☐ Purchased 19 __Pd $_____MIB   NB   DB   BNT
☐ Want   Orig. Ret. $10.75   **MIB** Sec. Mkt. **$25**

QX 528-5   CURLY 'N' KINGLY
Comments: Handcrafted, 4-1/8" tall, Dated 1993.
A lion and a lamb work together to ring the bell and wish you a
Merry Christmas. **Artist:** Ken Crow
☐ Purchased 19 __Pd $_____MIB   NB   DB   BNT
☐ Want   Orig. Ret. $10.75   **MIB** Sec. Mkt. **$20**

QX 585-5   DAD
Comments: Handcrafted, 2-5/8" tall, Dated 1993.
Dad is all set to make something special in his workshop with his
saw and his tool belt. **Artist:** Julia Lee
☐ Purchased 19 __Pd $_____MIB   NB   DB   BNT
☐ Want   Orig. Ret. $7.75   **MIB** Sec. Mkt. **$18**

QX 553-2   DAD-TO-BE
Comments: Handcrafted, 2-1/8" tall, Dated 1993.
"Dad-To-Bee," wearing a red and white cap, is buzzing to his
honey with a bouquet of flowers. **Artist:** Julia Lee
☐ Purchased 19 __Pd $_____MIB   NB   DB   BNT
☐ Want   Orig. Ret. $6.75   **MIB** Sec. Mkt. **$15**

QX 587-2   DAUGHTER
Comments: Handcrafted, 4-7/16" tall, Dated 1993.
This giraffe with bendable neck and legs is wearing a green sweater
and red ice skates. **Artist:** LaDene Votruba
☐ Purchased 19 __Pd $_____MIB   NB   DB   BNT
☐ Want   Orig. Ret. $6.75   **MIB** Sec. Mkt. **$18**

QX 550-5   DICKENS CAROLER BELL: LADY DAPHNE
Comments: **Fourth and Final in Collection,** Porcelain Bell.
4-1/4" tall, Dated 1993. Lady Daphne is ready for caroling in her red and
white coat, hat, and songbook in hand.
Artist: Robert Chad
☐ Purchased 19 __Pd $_____MIB   NB   DB   BNT
☐ Want   Orig. Ret. $21.75   **MIB** Sec. Mkt. **$45**

QLX 717-2   DOG'S BEST FRIEND
Comments: Light, 3" tall.
A black and white pooch adorns a fire hydrant with Christmas
lights and an acrylic star. **Artist:** Julia Lee
☐ Purchased 19 __Pd $_____MIB   NB   DB   BNT
☐ Want   Orig. Ret. $12.00   **MIB** Sec. Mkt. **$24**

QLX 737-2   DOLLHOUSE DREAMS
Comments: Light, 3-5/16" tall, Dated 1993.
A little girl plays with her dollhouse which is complete with a
flickering fire in the hearth and lights which blink on upstairs.
Artist: Ken Crow
☐ Purchased 19 __Pd $_____MIB   NB   DB   BNT
☐ Want   Orig. Ret. $22.00   **MIB** Sec. Mkt. **$48**

QX 557-5   DUNKIN' ROO
Comments: Handcrafted, 3-7/8" tall, Dated 1993.
Wearing red tennis shoes and a green shirt, this kangaroo is sure
to get his ball into the basket. **Artist:** Bob Siedler
☐ Purchased 19 __Pd $_____MIB   NB   DB   BNT
☐ Want   Orig. Ret. $7.75   **MIB** Sec. Mkt. **$16**

QX 447-5 FABULOUS DECADE
Comments: **Fourth in Series,** Handcrafted and Brass.
1-13/16" tall, Dated 1993.
A perky skunk carries a brass "1993" by its tail.
Artist: Sharon Pike
☐ Purchased 19__ Pd $_____ MIB   NB   DB   BNT
☐ Want   Orig. Ret. $7.75   **MIB** Sec. Mkt. **$18**

QX 578-2 FAITHFUL FIRE FIGHTER
Comments: Handcrafted, 2-3/4" tall.
A little Dalmatian, in a fireman's hat and yellow raincoat, is ready
to go with a water hose in paw. **Artist:** LaDene Votruba
☐ Purchased 19__ Pd $_____ MIB   NB   DB   BNT
☐ Want   Orig. Ret. $8   **MIB** Sec. Mkt. **$18**

QX 536-5 FELIZ NAVIDAD
Comments: Handcrafted Brass, 2-15/16" tall, Dated 1993.
A monk stands at the entrance of a Spanish mission, complete
with a gold bell in the tower. **Artist:** Donna Lee
☐ Purchased 19__ Pd $_____ MIB   NB   DB   BNT
☐ Want   Orig. Ret. $8.75   **MIB** Sec. Mkt. **$18**

QX 557-2 FILLS THE BILL
Comments: Handcrafted, 3-7/8" tall, Dated 1993.
Pole in hand, a pelican sitting at "Pier 93" is casting his fishing line
for a Christmas nibble. **Artist:** Bob Siedler
☐ Purchased 19__ Pd $_____ MIB   NB   DB   BNT
☐ Want   Orig. Ret. $8.75   **MIB** Sec. Mkt. **$15**

QLX 716-5 FOREST FROLICS
Comments: **Fifth in a Series,** Light/Motion, Handcrafted.
4-3/16" tall, Dated 1993. Woodland animals scamper around a snow
coated tree adorned with a lighted gold star.
Artist: Sharon Pike
☐ Purchased 19__ Pd $_____ MIB   NB   DB   BNT
☐ Want   Orig. Ret. $25.00   **MIB** Sec. Mkt. **$50**

QX 414-2 FROSTY FRIENDS
Comments: **Fourteenth in Series,** Handcrafted, 2-7/8" tall.
Dated 1993. Frosty's little husky puppy snuggles into his icy doghouse.
Artist: Julia Lee
☐ Purchased 19__ Pd $_____ MIB   NB   DB   BNT
☐ Want   Orig. Ret. $9.75   **MIB** Sec. Mkt. **$25**

QXC 544-2 GENTLE TIDINGS: KEEPSAKE CLUB
Comments: Hand-painted Porcelain, 4-9/16" dia., Dated 1993.
A delicate porcelain angel cradles a lamb in her arms. Available
to Club Members only. **Artist:** Trish Andrews
☐ Purchased 19__ Pd $_____ MIB   NB   DB   BNT
☐ Want   Orig. Ret. $25.00   **MIB** Sec. Mkt. **$48**

QX 206-5 GIFT BRINGERS, THE: THE MAGI
Comments: **Fifth and Final in Series,** White Glass Ball.
2-7/8" dia., Dated 1993. Three wise men from the East bring their gifts
of gold, frankincense and myrrh to the Baby Jesus.
Artist: LaDene Votruba
☐ Purchased 19__ Pd $_____ MIB   NB   DB   BNT
☐ Want   Orig. Ret. $5.00   **MIB** Sec. Mkt. **$18**

QX 587-5 GODCHILD
Comments: Handcrafted, 2" tall, Dated 1993.
A small child kneels in prayer by his pillow which reads, "Bless
You, Godchild 1993." **Artist:** Robert Chad
☐ Purchased 19__ Pd $_____ MIB   NB   DB   BNT
☐ Want   Orig. Ret. $8.75   **MIB** Sec. Mkt. **$18.50**

QX 555-2 GRANDCHILD'S FIRST CHRISTMAS
Comments: Handcrafted, 1-7/8" tall, Dated 1993.
With the wonder of its first Christmas, this adorable baby raccoon's
eyes are aglow. **Artist:** John Francis (Collin)
☐ Purchased 19__ Pd $_____ MIB   NB   DB   BNT
☐ Want   Orig. Ret. $6.75   **MIB** Sec. Mkt. **$15**

QX 563-5 GRANDDAUGHTER
Comments: Handcrafted, 3-5/8" tall, Dated 1993.
A little koala girl with a pink bow in her hair, waves hello from her
stand on a red telephone. **Artist:** Robert Chad
☐ Purchased 19__ Pd $_____ MIB   NB   DB   BNT
☐ Want   Orig. Ret. $6.75   **MIB** Sec. Mkt. **$15**

QX 566-5 GRANDMOTHER
Comments: Handcrafted, 2-9/16" tall, Dated 1993.
A card reading "Grandmother 1993" sits atop a lovely basket
filled with poinsettias. **Artist:** Trish Andrews
☐ Purchased 19__ Pd $_____ MIB   NB   DB   BNT
☐ Want   Orig. Ret. $6.75   **MIB** Sec. Mkt. **$14**

QX 208-5   GRANDPARENTS
Comments: Gold Glass Ball, 2-7/8" Dia., Dated 1993. Christmas flowers and green bands against a white sleeve are graced with the words: "The Christmas Traditions, Loving And Giving Are Kept By Grandparents All Year, 1993."
Artist: LaDene Votruba
☐ Purchased 19 __Pd $_____MIB   NB   DB   BNT
☐ Want   Orig. Ret. $4.75   **MIB** Sec. Mkt. **$14**

QX 563-2   GRANDSON
Comments: Handcrafted, 3-11/16" tall, Dated 1993. An active koala bear, dressed in a bright red shirt with matching cap, waves and swings on a green telephone receiver.
Artist: Robert Chad
☐ Purchased 19 __Pd $_____MIB   NB   DB   BNT
☐ Want   Orig. Ret. $6.75   **MIB** Sec. Mkt. **$15**

QX 540-2   GREAT CONNECTIONS
Comments: Handcrafted, 3-5/8" tall, Dated 1993. Two little redbirds, with their blue and green ski hats, are busy making a paper chain garland for the tree. (Set of two hang-together ornaments.)   **Artist:** Anita Marra Rogers
☐ Purchased 19 __Pd $_____MIB   NB   DB   BNT
☐ Want   Orig. Ret. $10.75   **MIB** Sec. Mkt. **$22**

QX 536-2   HE IS BORN
Comments: Handcrafted, 3-9/16" tall, Dated Christmas 1993. A touching Nativity scene is engraved on this bisque-look ornament. Caption: "For Unto Us A Child Is Born... Isaiah 9:6."
Artist: Joyce A. Lyle
☐ Purchased 19 __Pd $_____MIB   NB   DB   BNT
☐ Want   Orig. Ret. $9.75   **MIB** Sec. Mkt. **$35**

QX 448-2   HEART OF CHRISTMAS
Comments: **Fourth in Series,** Handcrafted, 2" tall, Dated 1993. Open this Christmas heart and view the lovely wintry landscape inside. Caption: "Christmas Brings A Gentle Peace That Enters Every Heart." **Artist:** Ed Seale
☐ Purchased 19 __Pd $_____MIB   NB   DB   BNT
☐ Want   Orig. Ret. $14.75   **MIB** Sec. Mkt. **$28**

QX 494-5   HEAVENLY ANGELS
Comments: **Third and Final in Series,** Handcrafted, 3" tall. Dated 1993. An angel cradles a dove in her hands.
Artist: Joyce A. Lyle
☐ Purchased 19 __Pd $_____MIB   NB   DB   BNT
☐ Want   Orig. Ret. $7.75   **MIB** Sec. Mkt. **$20**

QX 410-2   HERE COMES SANTA: HAPPY HAUL-IDAYS
Comments: **Fifteenth in Series,** Handcrafted, 2-7/8" tall. Dated 1993. Santa is delivering toys rather than hauling things away in his truck. **Artist:** Linda Sickman
☐ Purchased 19 __Pd $_____MIB   NB   DB   BNT
☐ Want   Orig. Ret. $14.75   **MIB** Sec. Mkt. **$32**

QX 533-2   HIGH TOP-PURR
Comments: Handcrafted, 2-3/16" tall, Dated 1993. Tucked inside a red sneaker is a little brown kitten that enjoys playing with the shoe strings. **Artist:** Ed Seale
☐ Purchased 19 __Pd $_____MIB   NB   DB   BNT
☐ Want   Orig. Ret. $8.75   **MIB** Sec. Mkt. **$22.50**

QX 572-5   HOLIDAY BARBIE™
Comments: **FIRST IN SERIES,** Handcrafted, 3-1/2" tall, Dated 1993. Patterned after 1993 Holiday Barbie doll. 1996 saw prices fall on this ornament. Check around before you buy. May go higher in mid '97.
Artist: Trish Andrews
☐ Purchased 19 __Pd $_____MIB   NB   DB   BNT
☐ Want   Orig. Ret. $14.75   **MIB** Sec. Mkt. **$125**

QX 562-2   HOLIDAY FLIERS: TIN AIRPLANE
Comments: Handcrafted, 1-5/16" tall, Dated 1993. Santa pilots a red and grey airplane with a message to all, "Season's Greetings." **Artist:** Linda Sickman
☐ Purchased 19 __Pd $_____MIB   NB   DB   BNT
☐ Want   Orig. Ret. $7.75   **MIB** Sec. Mkt. **$26**

QX 562-5   HOLIDAY FLIERS: TIN BLIMP
Comments: Handcrafted, 1-11/16" tall, Dated 1993. "Happy Holidays 1993" are wished to all on the sides of his holiday decorated blimp. **Artist:** Linda Sickman
☐ Purchased 19 __Pd $_____MIB   NB   DB   BNT
☐ Want   Orig. Ret. $7.75   **MIB** Sec. Mkt. **$18**

QX 561-5   HOLIDAY FLIERS: TIN HOT AIR BALLOON
Comments: Handcrafted, 2-5/8" tall, Dated 1993. A golden colored hot air balloon decorated with holly and red bows wishes everyone a "Merry Christmas."
Artist: Linda Sickman
☐ Purchased 19 __Pd $_____MIB   NB   DB   BNT
☐ Want   Orig. Ret. $7.75   **MIB** Sec. Mkt. **$18**

QX 556-2 HOME FOR CHRISTMAS

Comments: Handcrafted, 1-3/4" tall, Dated 1993.
A little ball player slides to home plate. Cute!
Artist: Bob Siedler

☐ Purchased 19 __ Pd $_____ MIB   NB   DB   BNT
☐ Want   Orig. Ret. $7.75   **MIB** Sec. Mkt. **$15**

QLX 739-5 HOME ON THE RANGE

Comments: Light/Motion/Music, Handcrafted, 4-1/8" tall.
Dated 1993. Plays "Home On The Range." Santa's rocking horse is hitched to one cactus, and Christmas lights and star adorn another "Christmas Cactus." Santa and horse rock.
Artist: Linda Sickman

☐ Purchased 19 __ Pd $_____ MIB   NB   DB   BNT
☐ Want   Orig. Ret. $32.00   **MIB** Sec. Mkt. **$65**

QX 525-5 HOWLING GOOD TIME

Comments: Handcrafted, 3" tall, Dated 1993.
In a Texan mood, Santa dons his cowboy hat and sings a duet with his good pal, a brown dog. **Artist:** Anita Marra Rogers

☐ Purchased 19 __ Pd $_____ MIB   NB   DB   BNT
☐ Want   Orig. Ret. $9.75   **MIB** Sec. Mkt. **$18**

QX 583-5 ICICLE BICYCLE

Comments: Handcrafted, 2-1/2" tall, Dated 1993.
A snowman races his cool cycle with wheels that really turn.
Artist: Julia Lee

☐ Purchased 19 __ Pd $_____ MIB   NB   DB   BNT
☐ Want   Orig. Ret. $9.75   **MIB** Sec. Mkt. **$19.50**

QXC 527-2 IT'S IN THE MAIL: KEEPSAKE CLUB

Comments: Handcrafted, 2-5/8" tall, Dated 1993.
A little "Post Mouse" is sending you a copy of the "Collector's Courier," but only if you are a member of the Keepsake Ornament Club! **Artist:** Ed Seale

☐ Purchased 19 __ Pd $_____ MIB   NB   DB   BNT
☐ Want   Orig. Ret. Comes w/Membership
                                              MIB Sec. Mkt. **$22.50**

QX 529-5 JULIANNE AND TEDDY

Comments: Handcrafted and Fabric, 2-3/4" tall, Dated 1993.
This Special Edition ornament is a dark-haired Victorian child with her favorite teddy. **Artist:** Duane Unruh

☐ Purchased 19 __ Pd $_____ MIB   NB   DB   BNT
☐ Want   Orig. Ret. $21.75   **MIB** Sec. Mkt. **$42**

QLX 719-2 LAMPLIGHTER, THE

Comments: Light, 4-3/16" tall, Dated 1993.
A little bear lights an old-fashioned street lantern to make Christmas bright for everyone. **Artist:** Don Palmiter

☐ Purchased 19 __ Pd $_____ MIB   NB   DB   BNT
☐ Want   Orig. Ret. $18.00   **MIB** Sec. Mkt. **$38**

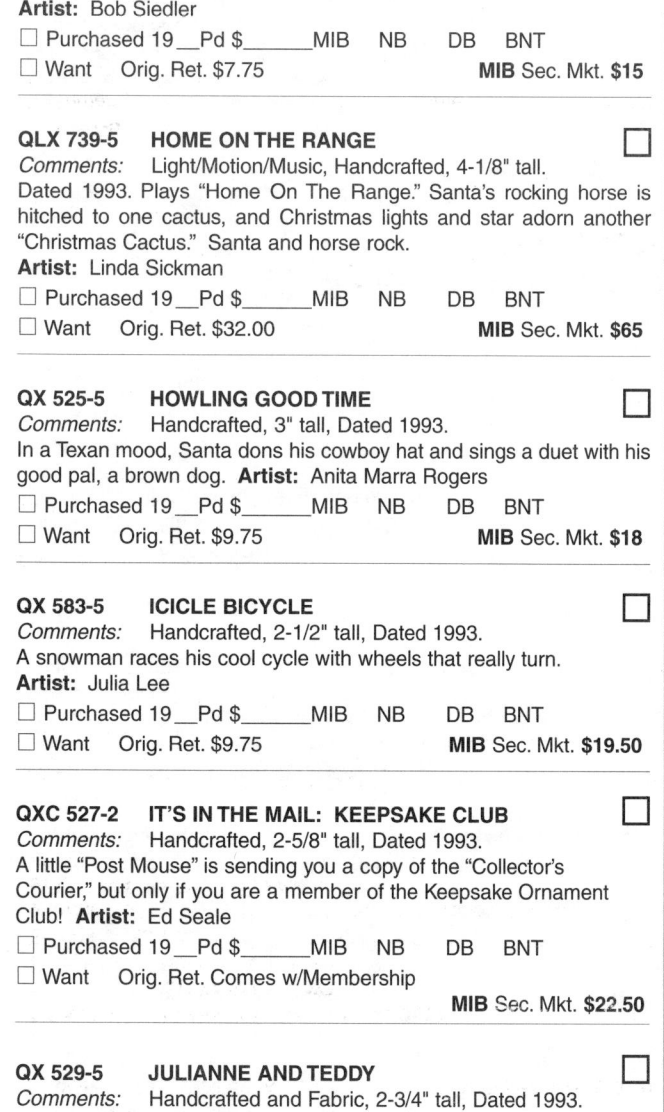

QLX 738-5 LAST MINUTE SHOPPING

Comments: Light/Motion, Handcrafted, 4-1/8" tall, Dated 1993.
Shoppers scurry through the shops, making their last-minute purchases. **Artist:** LaDene Votruba

☐ Purchased 19 __ Pd $_____ MIB   NB   DB   BNT
☐ Want   Orig. Ret. $28.00   **MIB** Sec. Mkt. **$58**

QX 537-2 LITTLE DRUMMER BOY

Comments: Handcrafted, 2-3/4" tall, Dated 1993.
A little African-American boy merrily plays his drum.
Artist: Don Palmiter

☐ Purchased 19 __ Pd $_____ MIB   NB   DB   BNT
☐ Want   Orig. Ret. $8.75   **MIB** Sec. Mkt. **$18.50**

QX 568-5 LOOK FOR THE WONDER

Comments: Handcrafted, 3-1/2" tall, Dated 1993.
Designed from a Ukrainian holiday tradition, Grandma points toward heaven. This ornament may be used as an Advent calendar by sliding the angel along the window frame.
Artist: Donna Lee

☐ Purchased 19 __ Pd $_____ MIB   NB   DB   BNT
☐ Want   Orig. Ret. $12.75   **MIB** Sec. Mkt. **$25**

QX 541-2 LOONEY TUNES COLLECTION: BUGS BUNNY

Comments: Handcrafted, 3-9/16" tall.
Bugs is all set for Christmas with his bag full of his favorite holiday treat... carrots! **Artist:** Linda Sickman

☐ Purchased 19 __ Pd $_____ MIB   NB   DB   BNT
☐ Want   Orig. Ret. $8.75   **MIB** Sec. Mkt. **$22**

QX 549-5 LOONEY TUNES COLLECTION: ELMER FUDD

Comments: Handcrafted, 2-7/8" tall.
Elmer plays Santa and brings lots of goodies to the rest of the Looney Tunes family. **Artist:** Joyce A. Lyle

☐ Purchased 19 __ Pd $_____ MIB   NB   DB   BNT
☐ Want   Orig. Ret. $8.75   **MIB** Sec. Mkt. **$18.50**

QX 565-2   LOONEY TUNES COLLECTION: PORKY PIG ☐
Comments: Handcrafted, 2-9/18" tall.
Santa's coming! Porky is ready for bed dressed in his nightshirt
and slippers, but he's getting Santa's treats ready first!
Artist: Trish Andrews

☐ Purchased 19__Pd $_____MIB   NB   DB   BNT
☐ Want   Orig. Ret. $8.75   **MIB** Sec. Mkt. **$18.50**

**QX 540-5   LOONEY TUNES COLLECTION:
SYLVESTER AND TWEETY** ☐
Comments: Handcrafted, 3-9/16" tall.
Sylvester and Tweety get into the spirit of Christmas. Tweety is
wearing a red Santa cap and Sylvester is sporting antlers and
sleigh bells. **Artist:** Don Palmiter

☐ Purchased 19__Pd $_____MIB   NB   DB   BNT
☐ Want   Orig. Ret. $9.75   **MIB** Sec. Mkt. **$28**

QX 574-5   LOU RANKIN POLAR BEAR ☐
Comments: Handcrafted, 3-15/16" tall.
This unique bear is sculpted after the style of artist, Lou Rankin.
Artist: Dill Rhodus

☐ Purchased 19__Pd $_____MIB   NB   DB   BNT
☐ Want   Orig. Ret. $9.75   **MIB** Sec. Mkt. **$26**

QX 532-5   MAKIN' MUSIC ☐
Comments: Handcrafted and Brass, 2" tall.
A little mouse plays his violin as he stands atop a brass music staff.
Artist: Ed Seale

☐ Purchased 19__Pd $_____MIB   NB   DB   BNT
☐ Want   Orig. Ret. $9.75   **MIB** Sec. Mkt. **$20**

QX 577-5   MAKING WAVES ☐
Comments: Handcrafted, 2-1/2" tall, Dated 1993.
Santa and one of his reindeer are racing into Christmas in a speedboat.
Artist: Don Palmiter

☐ Purchased 19__Pd $_____MIB   NB   DB   BNT
☐ Want   Orig. Ret. $9.75   **MIB** Sec. Mkt. **$25**

QX 207-5   MARY ENGELBREIT ☐
Comments: Red Glass Ball, 2-7/8" dia., Dated 1993.
Christmas morning is a delight for all children, as depicted on
this ball ornament. Caption: "Christmas Morning 1993."
©1993 Mary Engelbreit

☐ Purchased 19__Pd $_____MIB   NB   DB   BNT
☐ Want   Orig. Ret. $5.00   **MIB** Sec. Mkt. **$15**

QX 428-2   MARY'S ANGELS: IVY ☐
Comments: **Sixth in Series,** Handcrafted, 2-3/8" tall.
Many collectors have reported finding the box with Joy instead of Ivy;
this is because of hard-to-read script writing. The box is not
misprinted. **Artist:** Robert Chad

☐ Purchased 19__Pd $_____MIB   NB   DB   BNT
☐ Want   Orig. Ret. $6.75   **MIB** Sec. Mkt. **$20**

QX 538-5   MAXINE ☐
Comments: Handcrafted, 3-7/16" tall.
Maxine has a style all her own with a Santa coat and beard
and bunny slippers on her feet. **Artist:** Linda Sickman

☐ Purchased 19__Pd $_____MIB   NB   DB   BNT
☐ Want   Orig. Ret. $8.75   **MIB** Sec. Mkt. **$22**

QX 484-2   MERRY OLDE SANTA ☐
Comments: **Fourth in Series,** Handcrafted, 4-5/16" tall.
Dated 1993. Santa announces his arrival with the golden
bell he rings, his pack on his back and a pair of ice skates for a
lucky boy or girl. **Artist:** Anita Marra Rogers

☐ Purchased 19__Pd $_____MIB   NB   DB   BNT
☐ Want   Orig. Ret. $14.75   **MIB** Sec. Mkt. **$30**

QLX 747-6   MESSAGES OF CHRISTMAS ☐
Comments: Special Issue, Handcrafted, Recordable, 4-1/2" tall.
Dated 1993. Collectors were able to record their own Christmas
message on this ornament. **Artist:** Bob Siedler

☐ Purchased 19__Pd $_____MIB   NB   DB   BNT
☐ Want   Orig. Ret. $35.00   **MIB** Sec. Mkt. **$40**

QX 585-2   MOM ☐
Comments: Handcrafted, 2-5/8" tall, Dated 1993.
Mom is ready to go shopping. **Artist:** Julia Lee

☐ Purchased 19__Pd $_____MIB   NB   DB   BNT
☐ Want   Orig. Ret. $7.75   **MIB** Sec. Mkt. **$18**

QX 584-5   MOM AND DAD ☐
Comments: Handcrafted, 2-11/16" tall, Dated 1993.
Two lovable red foxes open their gift. Love their slippers!
Artist: Don Palmiter

☐ Purchased 19__Pd $_____MIB   NB   DB   BNT
☐ Want   Orig. Ret. $9.75   **MIB** Sec. Mkt. **$18.50**

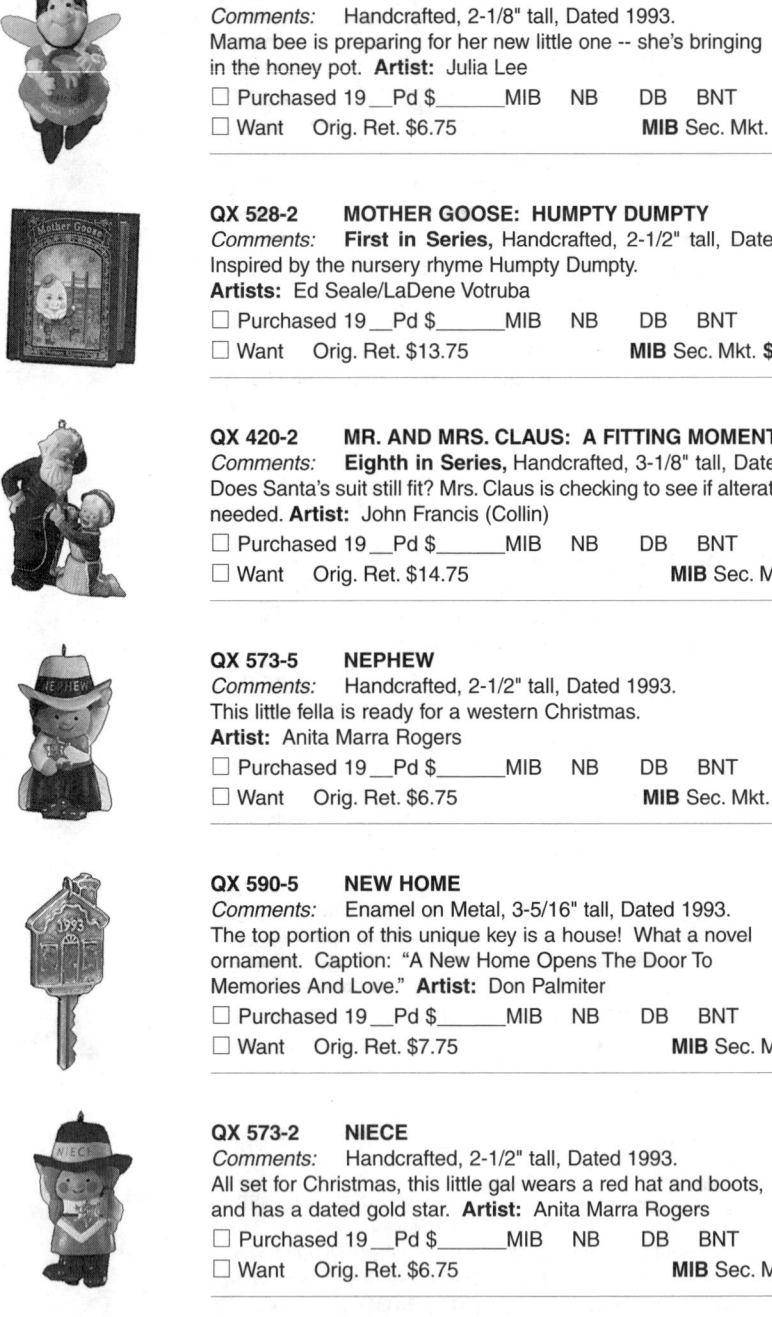
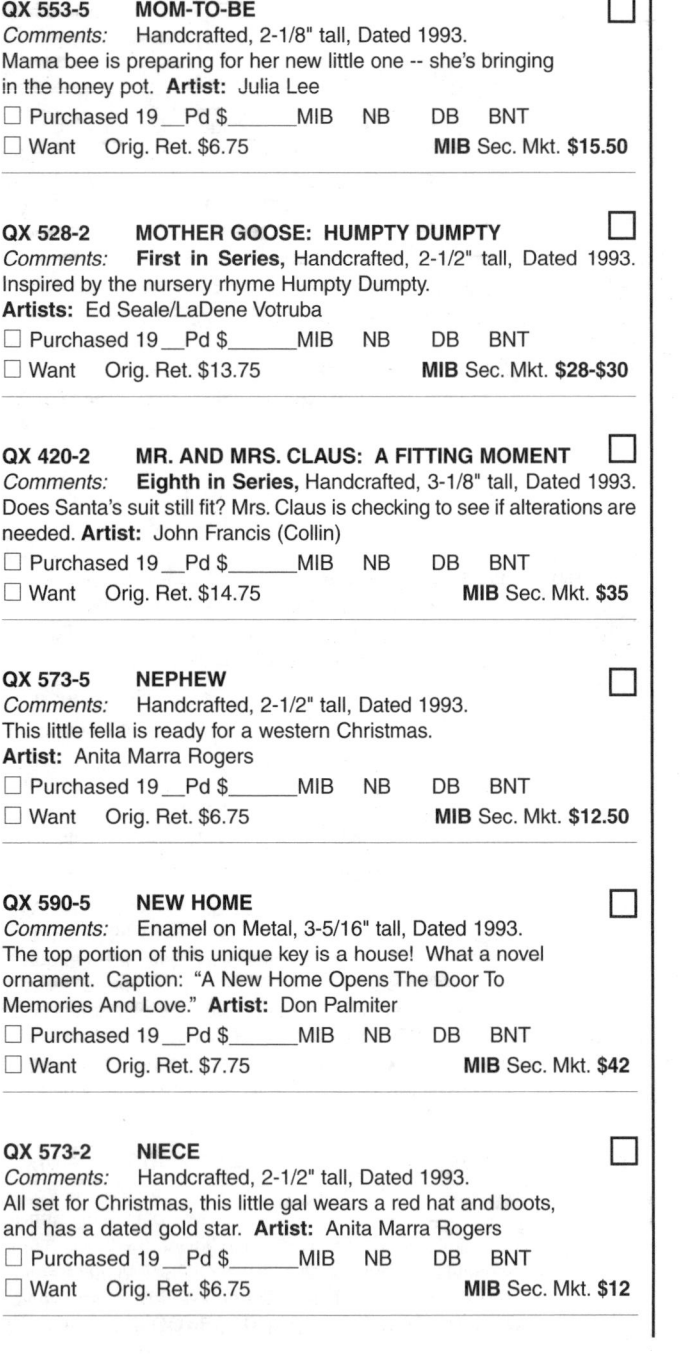

QX 553-5   MOM-TO-BE
Comments: Handcrafted, 2-1/8" tall, Dated 1993.
Mama bee is preparing for her new little one -- she's bringing
in the honey pot. **Artist:** Julia Lee
☐ Purchased 19___Pd $_____MIB   NB   DB   BNT
☐ Want   Orig. Ret. $6.75   **MIB** Sec. Mkt. **$15.50**

QX 528-2   MOTHER GOOSE: HUMPTY DUMPTY
Comments: **First in Series,** Handcrafted, 2-1/2" tall, Dated 1993.
Inspired by the nursery rhyme Humpty Dumpty.
Artists: Ed Seale/LaDene Votruba
☐ Purchased 19___Pd $_____MIB   NB   DB   BNT
☐ Want   Orig. Ret. $13.75   **MIB** Sec. Mkt. **$28-$30**

QX 420-2   MR. AND MRS. CLAUS: A FITTING MOMENT
Comments: **Eighth in Series,** Handcrafted, 3-1/8" tall, Dated 1993.
Does Santa's suit still fit? Mrs. Claus is checking to see if alterations are
needed. **Artist:** John Francis (Collin)
☐ Purchased 19___Pd $_____MIB   NB   DB   BNT
☐ Want   Orig. Ret. $14.75   **MIB** Sec. Mkt. **$35**

QX 573-5   NEPHEW
Comments: Handcrafted, 2-1/2" tall, Dated 1993.
This little fella is ready for a western Christmas.
Artist: Anita Marra Rogers
☐ Purchased 19___Pd $_____MIB   NB   DB   BNT
☐ Want   Orig. Ret. $6.75   **MIB** Sec. Mkt. **$12.50**

QX 590-5   NEW HOME
Comments: Enamel on Metal, 3-5/16" tall, Dated 1993.
The top portion of this unique key is a house! What a novel
ornament. Caption: "A New Home Opens The Door To
Memories And Love." **Artist:** Don Palmiter
☐ Purchased 19___Pd $_____MIB   NB   DB   BNT
☐ Want   Orig. Ret. $7.75   **MIB** Sec. Mkt. **$42**

QX 573-2   NIECE
Comments: Handcrafted, 2-1/2" tall, Dated 1993.
All set for Christmas, this little gal wears a red hat and boots,
and has a dated gold star. **Artist:** Anita Marra Rogers
☐ Purchased 19___Pd $_____MIB   NB   DB   BNT
☐ Want   Orig. Ret. $6.75   **MIB** Sec. Mkt. **$12**

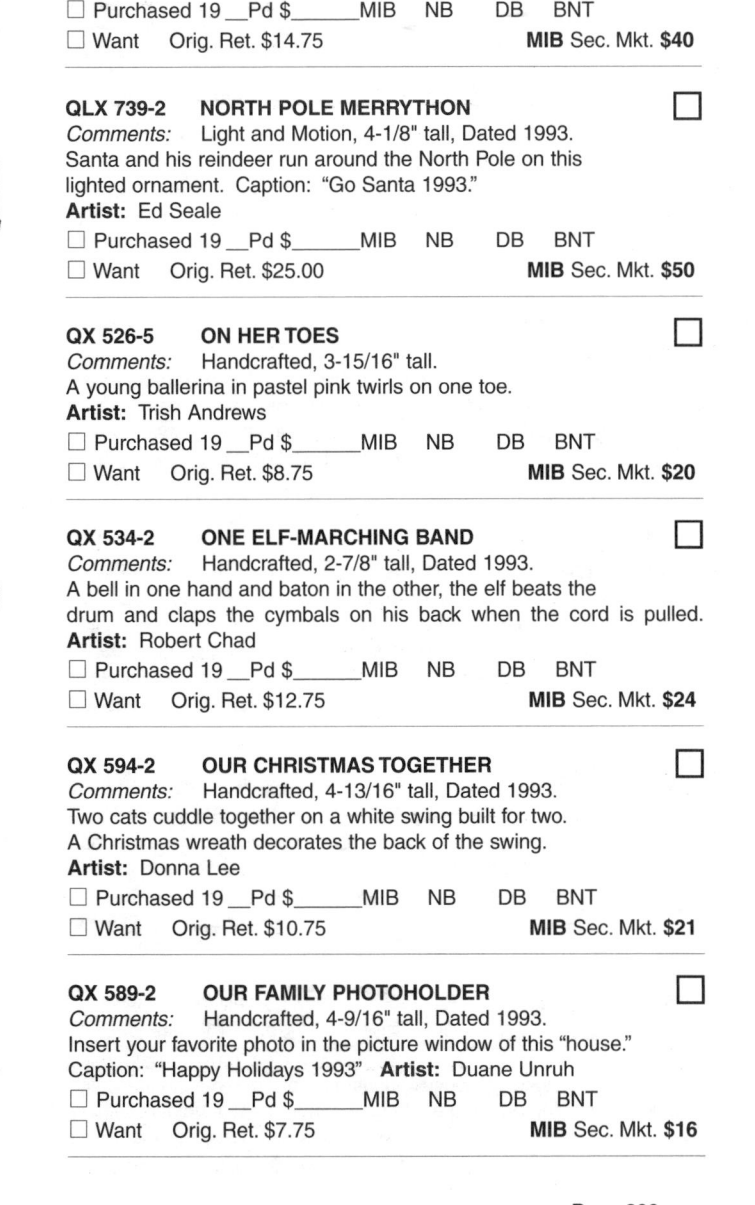

**QX 417-5   NOSTALGIC HOUSES AND SHOPS:
                    COZY HOME**
Comments: **Tenth in Series,** Handcrafted, 3-13/16" tall, Dated 1993.
What a lovely home! A veranda covers the old-
fashioned porch and welcomes all inside.
Artist: Donna Lee
☐ Purchased 19 __Pd $_____MIB   NB   DB   BNT
☐ Want   Orig. Ret. $14.75   **MIB** Sec. Mkt. **$40**

QLX 739-2   NORTH POLE MERRYTHON
Comments: Light and Motion, 4-1/8" tall, Dated 1993.
Santa and his reindeer run around the North Pole on this
lighted ornament. Caption: "Go Santa 1993."
Artist: Ed Seale
☐ Purchased 19 __Pd $_____MIB   NB   DB   BNT
☐ Want   Orig. Ret. $25.00   **MIB** Sec. Mkt. **$50**

QX 526-5   ON HER TOES
Comments: Handcrafted, 3-15/16" tall.
A young ballerina in pastel pink twirls on one toe.
Artist: Trish Andrews
☐ Purchased 19 __Pd $_____MIB   NB   DB   BNT
☐ Want   Orig. Ret. $8.75   **MIB** Sec. Mkt. **$20**

QX 534-2   ONE ELF-MARCHING BAND
Comments: Handcrafted, 2-7/8" tall, Dated 1993.
A bell in one hand and baton in the other, the elf beats the
drum and claps the cymbals on his back when the cord is pulled.
Artist: Robert Chad
☐ Purchased 19 __Pd $_____MIB   NB   DB   BNT
☐ Want   Orig. Ret. $12.75   **MIB** Sec. Mkt. **$24**

QX 594-2   OUR CHRISTMAS TOGETHER
Comments: Handcrafted, 4-13/16" tall, Dated 1993.
Two cats cuddle together on a white swing built for two.
A Christmas wreath decorates the back of the swing.
Artist: Donna Lee
☐ Purchased 19 __Pd $_____MIB   NB   DB   BNT
☐ Want   Orig. Ret. $10.75   **MIB** Sec. Mkt. **$21**

QX 589-2   OUR FAMILY PHOTOHOLDER
Comments: Handcrafted, 4-9/16" tall, Dated 1993.
Insert your favorite photo in the picture window of this "house."
Caption: "Happy Holidays 1993" **Artist:** Duane Unruh
☐ Purchased 19 __Pd $_____MIB   NB   DB   BNT
☐ Want   Orig. Ret. $7.75   **MIB** Sec. Mkt. **$16**

QX 595-5   OUR FIRST CHRISTMAS TOGETHER
Comments: Brass and Silver Plated, 3-1/4" tall, Dated 1993.
A silver-plated man and woman dance and spin in the center
of a brass heart etched with holly and "Our First Christmas 1993."
Artist: Anita Marra Rogers

☐ Purchased 19 __Pd $_____MIB   NB   DB   BNT
☐ Want   Orig. Ret. $18.75   **MIB** Sec. Mkt. **$38**

QX 564-2   OUR FIRST CHRISTMAS TOGETHER
Comments: Handcrafted, 2-3/16" tall, Dated 1993.
A raccoon couple celebrate their first Christmas around their
Christmas tree.   **Artist:** Joyce A. Lyle

☐ Purchased 19 __Pd $_____MIB   NB   DB   BNT
☐ Want   Orig. Ret. $9.75   **MIB** Sec. Mkt. **$15**

QLX 735-5   OUR FIRST CHRISTMAS TOGETHER
Comments: Light, 2-3/4" tall, Dated 1993.
A couple sit side by side in front of a flickering fire inside this
peek-through ball.   **Artist:** Robert Chad

☐ Purchased 19 __Pd $_____MIB   NB   DB   BNT
☐ Want   Orig. Ret. $20.00   **MIB** Sec. Mkt. **$38**

**QX 595-2   OUR FIRST CHRISTMAS TOGETHER
                PHOTOHOLDER**
Comments: Handcrafted, 3-5/8" tall, Dated 1993.
Red hearts adorn an oval green wreath for this photo frame.
Caption: "Love Is The Heart's Most Cherished Treasure."
Artist: Duane Unruh

☐ Purchased 19 __Pd $_____MIB   NB   DB   BNT
☐ Want   Orig. Ret. $8.75   **MIB** Sec. Mkt. **$16**

QX 301-5   OUR FIRST CHRISTMAS TOGETHER
Comments: Acrylic, 3-3/8" tall, Dated 1993.
Two frosted swans snuggle together inside a frosted heart
frame.   **Artist:** Trish Andrews

☐ Purchased 19 __Pd $_____MIB   NB   DB   BNT
☐ Want   Orig. Ret. $6.75   **MIB** Sec. Mkt. **$15**

QX 542-5   OWLIVER
Comments: **Second in Series,** Handcrafted, 2-3/8" tall, Dated 1993.
Owliver naps on a tree stump while a little
squirrel delivers a present. **Artist:** Bob Siedler

☐ Purchased 19 __Pd $_____MIB   NB   DB   BNT
☐ Want   Orig. Ret. $7.75   **MIB** Sec. Mkt. **$18**

QX 524-2   PEACE ON EARTH: POLAND
Comments: **Third and Final in Series,** Handcrafted, 3" dia.
Dated 1993. Children in native dress portray a message
for all mankind; one of peace. Caption: "Pokój Ludziom
Dobrej Wol." **Artist:** Linda Sickman

☐ Purchased 19 __Pd $_____MIB   NB   DB   BNT
☐ Want   Orig. Ret. $11.75   **MIB** Sec. Mkt. **$22**

QLX 715-5   PEANUTS®
Comments: **Third in Series,** Blinking Lights, Handcrafted.
3-1/2" tall, Dated 1993. Snoopy and Woodstock admire their
Christmas tree; its lights blink off and on.   **Artist:** Dill Rhodus

☐ Purchased 19 __Pd $_____MIB   NB   DB   BNT
☐ Want   Orig. Ret. $18.00   **MIB** Sec. Mkt. **$45**

QX 207-2   PEANUTS®
Comments: Silver Glass Ball, 2-7/8" dia., Dated 1993.
The Peanuts characters are wishing you a Merry Christmas
in Spanish, German, Italian, French and English.

☐ Purchased 19 __Pd $_____MIB   NB   DB   BNT
☐ Want   Orig. Ret. $5.00   **MIB** Sec. Mkt. **$24**

QX 531-5   PEANUTS® GANG
Comments: *FIRST IN SERIES,* Handcrafted, 2-3/8" tall, Dated 1993.
Charlie Brown has a twin! It's a "snow boy" he built himself!
Artist: Dill Rhodus

☐ Purchased 19 __Pd $_____MIB   NB   DB   BNT
☐ Want   Orig. Ret. $9.75   **MIB** Sec. Mkt. **$58**

QX 524-5   PEEK-A-BOO TREE
Comments: Handcrafted, 4-3/16" tall, Dated 1993.
Little animals peek in and out of the tree when you turn the
pinecone knob. **Artist:** Ken Crow

☐ Purchased 19 __Pd $_____MIB   NB   DB   BNT
☐ Want   Orig. Ret. $10.75   **MIB** Sec. Mkt. **$22**

QX 532-2   PEEP INSIDE
Comments: Handcrafted, 2-7/16" tall, Dated 1993.
A birdhouse opens to reveal mama's babies inside on the
nest, waiting for their Christmas dinner.
Artist: Donna Lee

☐ Purchased 19 __Pd $_____MIB   NB   DB   BNT
☐ Want   Orig. Ret. $13.75   **MIB** Sec. Mkt. **$23**

QX 593-2   PEOPLE FRIENDLY
Comments: Handcrafted, 2-5/16" tall, Dated 1993.
A raccoon sits atop the keys of a computer terminal decorated with Christmas lights. Was personalized four ways: "Secretary Friendly," "Student Friendly," "VIP Friendly" or blank which one could sign. **Artist:** Ed Seale

☐ Purchased 19___Pd $_____MIB   NB   DB   BNT
☐ Want   Orig. Ret. $8.75   **MIB** Sec. Mkt. **$14**

QX 577-2   PERFECT MATCH
Comments: Handcrafted, 3-1/3" tall, Dated 1993.
A little bear sits between two yellow tennis balls in a canister captioned "Perfect Match Tennis Balls 93." **Artist:** Bob Siedler

☐ Purchased 19___Pd $_____MIB   NB   DB   BNT
☐ Want   Orig. Ret. $8.75   **MIB** Sec. Mkt. **$17**

QX 575-5   PINK PANTHER, THE
Comments: Handcrafted, 3" tall, Dated 1993.
Dressed as Santa and carrying his pack on his back, the Pink Panther prepares to climb down the chimney.
Artist: Don Palmiter

☐ Purchased 19___Pd $_____MIB   NB   DB   BNT
☐ Want   Orig. Ret. $12.75   **MIB** Sec. Mkt. **$24**

QX 574-2   PLAYFUL PALS: COCA-COLA SANTA
Comments: Handcrafted, 3-7/8" tall, Dated 1993.
A little black French poodle sits up and begs for Santa's cookie. The gift-wrapped doghouse is dated. **Artist:** Anita Marra Rogers

☐ Purchased 19___Pd $_____MIB   NB   DB   BNT
☐ Want   Orig. Ret. $14.75   **MIB** Sec. Mkt. **$32**

QX 539-2   POPPING GOOD TIMES
Comments: Handcrafted, 2" tall, Dated 1993.
Two individual mice, one with a bag of popcorn and the other with a popcorn popper, create a set of hang-together ornaments.
Artist: Robert Chad

☐ Purchased 19___Pd $_____MIB   NB   DB   BNT
☐ Want   Orig. Ret. $14.75   **MIB** Sec. Mkt. **$28**

QX 504-5   PUPPY LOVE
Comments: **Third in Series,** Handcrafted, 1-9/16" tall,Dated 1993.
A golden retriever is enjoying a speedy trip downhill on a toboggan.
Artist: Anita Marra Rogers

☐ Purchased 19___Pd $_____MIB   NB   DB   BNT
☐ Want   Orig. Ret. $7.75   **MIB** Sec. Mkt. **$24**

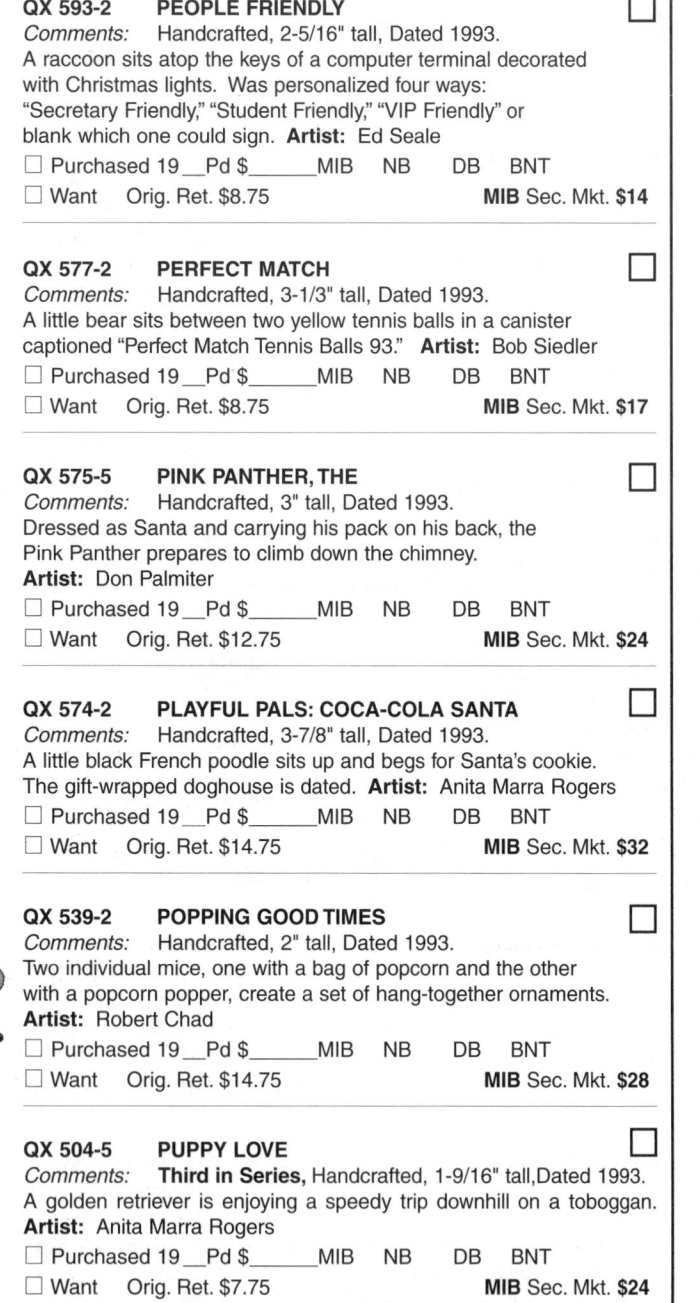

QX 579-5   PUTT-PUTT PENGUIN
Comments: Handcrafted, 3" tall, Dated 1993.
A perky penguin in a blue hat rides to the next hole in his red golf cart. The words "Putt-Putt" are on both sides of the cart.
Artist: Julia Lee

☐ Purchased 19___Pd $_____MIB   NB   DB   BNT
☐ Want   Orig. Ret. $9.75   **MIB** Sec. Mkt. **$18**

QX 579-2   QUICK AS A FOX
Comments: Handcrafted, 2-5/8" tall, Dated 1993.
This little postal fox handles his deliveries with speed and ingenuity. He has fastened his package to a pair of ice skate blades and rides his way into Christmas. **Artist:** Ken Crow

☐ Purchased 19___Pd $_____MIB   NB   DB   BNT
☐ Want   Orig. Ret. $8.75   **MIB** Sec. Mkt. **$16**

QLX 736-2   RADIO NEWS FLASH
Comments: Light and Sound, 3-3/16" tall, Dated 1993.
A kitten listens to the sounds of Christmas on this holly trimmed old-fashioned radio. Caption: "Christmas Is In The Air!"
Artist: Donna Lee

☐ Purchased 19___Pd $_____MIB   NB   DB   BNT
☐ Want   Orig. Ret. $22.00   **MIB** Sec. Mkt. **$48**

QLX 718-5   RAIDING THE FRIDGE
Comments: Light, 3-7/16" tall, Dated 1993.
Santa's catching a late-night snack. The refrigerator light is on because he has the door open. Caption: "Cold Milk And Cool Cookies For Santa!" **Artist:** Anita Marra Rogers

☐ Purchased 19___Pd $_____MIB   NB   DB   BNT
☐ Want   Orig. Ret. $16.00   **MIB** Sec. Mkt. **$32**

QX 512-4   READY FOR FUN
Comments: Handcrafted and Tin, 3-1/8" tall, Dated 1993.
A gingerbread cookie boy moves out of his cookie cutter frame so that he might join in the Christmas festivities.
Artist: Joyce A. Lyle

☐ Purchased 19___Pd $_____MIB   NB   DB   BNT
☐ Want   Orig. Ret. $7.75   **MIB** Sec. Mkt. **$16.50**

QX 433-1   REINDEER CHAMPS: BLITZEN
Comments: **Eighth and Final in Series,** Handcrafted. 3-1/8" tall, Dated 1993. Blitzen scores again! Santa's reindeer team wins this football game! **Artist:** Bob Siedler

☐ Purchased 19___Pd $_____MIB   NB   DB   BNT
☐ Want   Orig. Ret. $8.75   **MIB** Sec. Mkt. **$20**

QLX 741-5　ROAD RUNNER AND WILE E. COYOTE™
Comments:　Light/Motion, Handcrafted, 4-1/8" tall, Dated 1993.
Wile E. Coyote will never learn as he chases the Road Runner
through a cave. Caption: "Have A Dynamite Christmas!"
Artist: Robert Chad

☐ Purchased 19 __Pd $_____MIB　NB　DB　BNT
☐ Want　Orig. Ret. $30.00　　　　**MIB** Sec. Mkt. **$75**

QX 416-2　ROCKING HORSE
Comments:　**Thirteenth in Series,** Handcrafted, 3" tall, Dated 1993.
Dark grey with white stockings and a white star on its forehead, this
horse also sports a white tail. **Artist:** Linda Sickman

☐ Purchased 19 __Pd $_____MIB　NB　DB　BNT
☐ Want　Orig. Ret. $10.75　　　　**MIB** Sec. Mkt. **$35**

QX 538-2　ROOM FOR ONE MORE
Comments:　Handcrafted, 3-3/16" tall, Dated 1993.
How many reindeer can squeeze into the telephone booth
with Santa? Count them and see! Proclaimed as a sleeper by many in
'94, thus many bought up extras. Easily found now.
Artist: Ken Crow

☐ Purchased 19 __Pd $_____MIB　NB　DB　BNT
☐ Want　Orig. Ret. $8.75　　　　**MIB** Sec. Mkt. **$48**

QLX 735-2　SANTA'S SNOW-GETTER
Comments:　Light, 3-5/16" tall, Dated 1993.
Santa is making his Christmas deliveries with the help of a
red and white snowmobile. **Artist:** Ken Crow

☐ Purchased 19 __Pd $_____MIB　NB　DB　BNT
☐ Want　Orig. Ret. $18.00　　　　**MIB** Sec. Mkt. **$35**

QLX 737-5　SANTA'S WORKSHOP
Comments:　Light/Motion, Handcrafted, 4-1/16" tall, Dated 1993.
It's December 23 and Santa is busy with last-minute toys. The
ballerina twirls, the blades of the helicopter revolve and the ball
and top spin around as the toys circle on a conveyor belt.
Artist: Bob Siedler

☐ Purchased 19 __Pd $_____MIB　NB　DB　BNT
☐ Want　Orig. Ret. $28.00　　　　**MIB** Sec. Mkt. **$55**

QXC 543-5　SHARING CHRISTMAS: KEEPSAKE CLUB
Comments:　Limited Edition Porcelain, 3-3/4" tall, Dated 1993.
A boy and girl sit on a bench and share a Christmas gift.
Delicate holly designs enhance the beauty of this ornament.
Caption: "Christmas, A Beautiful Season For Sharing."
Artist: Joyce A. Lyle

☐ Purchased 19 __Pd $_____MIB　NB　DB　BNT
☐ Want　Orig. Ret. $20.00　　　　**MIB** Sec. Mkt. **$45**

QX 530-5　SILVERY NOEL
Comments:　Silver-plated, 2" tall, Dated 1993.
Decorative letters "N-O-E-L" make up the sides of this silver-
plated block with a dated, hinged lid that opens.
Artist: Joyce A. Lyle

☐ Purchased 19 __Pd $_____MIB　NB　DB　BNT
☐ Want　Orig. Ret. $12.75　　　　**MIB** Sec. Mkt. **$30**

QX 554-5　SISTER
Comments:　Handcrafted, 2-1/4" tall, Dated 1993.
A Cheerleader kitten cheers for Christmas with her red and
yellow pom-poms. **Artist:** Anita Marra Rogers

☐ Purchased 19 __Pd $_____MIB　NB　DB　BNT
☐ Want　Orig. Ret. $6.75　　　　**MIB** Sec. Mkt. **$18**

QX 588-5　SISTER TO SISTER
Comments:　Handcrafted, 2-5/16" tall, Dated 1993.
Two mice sit together in a compact. The lipstick message on the
mirror reads, "Sisters Are Forever Friends!" Somewhat scarce due to
production problems. **Artist:** Ed Seale

☐ Purchased 19 __Pd $_____MIB　NB　DB　BNT
☐ Want　Orig. Ret. $9.75　　　　**MIB** Sec. Mkt. **$45**

QX 533-5　SMILE! IT'S CHRISTMAS PHOTOHOLDER
Comments:　Handcrafted Photoholder, 4" tall, Dated 1993.
A little mouse pulls on the end of the film to see what's developed!
This ornament holds two photos. Caption: "Develop By December
25th, 35 mm Merry Memories (Double Exposure), CHRISTMAS
COLOR, ASA 93." **Artist:** Ed Seale

☐ Purchased 19 __Pd $_____MIB　NB　DB　BNT
☐ Want　Orig. Ret. $9.75　　　　**MIB** Sec. Mkt. **$20**

**My wife told me not to come home until
I brought her the next issue of
The Ornament Collector.
Guess I won't go back in the house!**

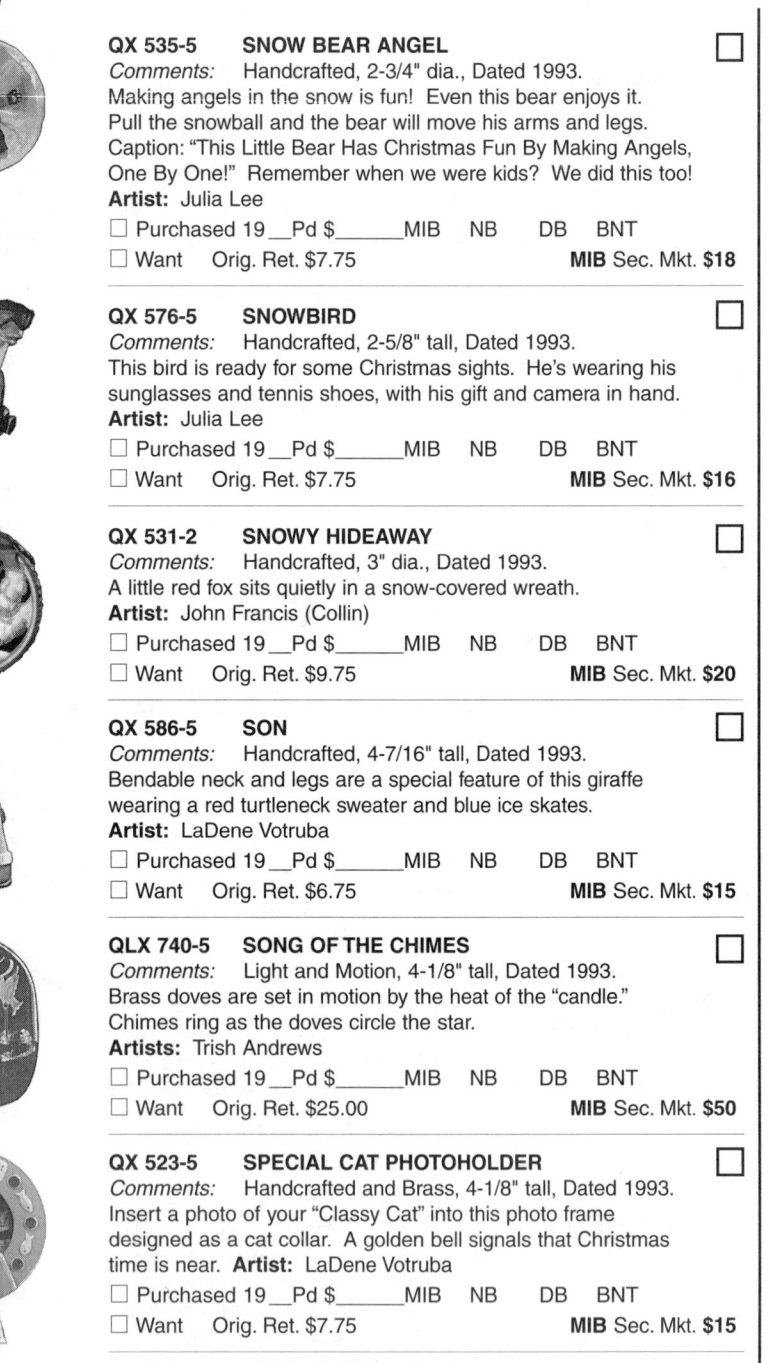

QX 535-5   SNOW BEAR ANGEL □
Comments: Handcrafted, 2-3/4" dia., Dated 1993.
Making angels in the snow is fun! Even this bear enjoys it.
Pull the snowball and the bear will move his arms and legs.
Caption: "This Little Bear Has Christmas Fun By Making Angels,
One By One!" Remember when we were kids? We did this too!
Artist: Julia Lee

□ Purchased 19 __Pd $_____MIB   NB   DB   BNT
□ Want   Orig. Ret. $7.75   **MIB** Sec. Mkt. **$18**

QX 576-5   SNOWBIRD □
Comments: Handcrafted, 2-5/8" tall, Dated 1993.
This bird is ready for some Christmas sights. He's wearing his
sunglasses and tennis shoes, with his gift and camera in hand.
Artist: Julia Lee

□ Purchased 19 __Pd $_____MIB   NB   DB   BNT
□ Want   Orig. Ret. $7.75   **MIB** Sec. Mkt. **$16**

QX 531-2   SNOWY HIDEAWAY □
Comments: Handcrafted, 3" dia., Dated 1993.
A little red fox sits quietly in a snow-covered wreath.
Artist: John Francis (Collin)

□ Purchased 19 __Pd $_____MIB   NB   DB   BNT
□ Want   Orig. Ret. $9.75   **MIB** Sec. Mkt. **$20**

QX 586-5   SON □
Comments: Handcrafted, 4-7/16" tall, Dated 1993.
Bendable neck and legs are a special feature of this giraffe
wearing a red turtleneck sweater and blue ice skates.
Artist: LaDene Votruba

□ Purchased 19 __Pd $_____MIB   NB   DB   BNT
□ Want   Orig. Ret. $6.75   **MIB** Sec. Mkt. **$15**

QLX 740-5   SONG OF THE CHIMES □
Comments: Light and Motion, 4-1/8" tall, Dated 1993.
Brass doves are set in motion by the heat of the "candle."
Chimes ring as the doves circle the star.
Artists: Trish Andrews

□ Purchased 19 __Pd $_____MIB   NB   DB   BNT
□ Want   Orig. Ret. $25.00   **MIB** Sec. Mkt. **$50**

QX 523-5   SPECIAL CAT PHOTOHOLDER □
Comments: Handcrafted and Brass, 4-1/8" tall, Dated 1993.
Insert a photo of your "Classy Cat" into this photo frame
designed as a cat collar. A golden bell signals that Christmas
time is near. **Artist:** LaDene Votruba

□ Purchased 19 __Pd $_____MIB   NB   DB   BNT
□ Want   Orig. Ret. $7.75   **MIB** Sec. Mkt. **$15**

QX 596-2   SPECIAL DOG PHOTOHOLDER □
Comments: Handcrafted and Brass, 4-13/16" tall, Dated 1993.
This photo frame resembles a dog collar with bones and includes a
"Perfect Pooch 1993" tag.
Artist: LaDene Votruba

□ Purchased 19 __Pd $_____MIB   NB   DB   BNT
□ Want   Orig. Ret. $7.75   **MIB** Sec. Mkt. **$15**

QX 598-2   STAR OF WONDER □
Comments: Handcrafted, 3-1/4" tall, Dated 1993.
Forest animals take time to gaze at the Star in the wintry sky.
Artist: Joyce A. Lyle

□ Purchased 19 __Pd $_____MIB   NB   DB   BNT
□ Want   Orig. Ret. $6.75   **MIB** Sec. Mkt. **$35**

QX 564-5   STAR TEACHER PHOTOHOLDER □
Comments: Handcrafted, 2-15/16" tall, Dated 1993.
A little white bear holds up a gold star photo frame. Captions:
"1993 For A Star Teacher." and "Have A Beary Merry Christmas!"
Artist: Trish Andrews

□ Purchased 19 __Pd $_____MIB   NB   DB   BNT
□ Want   Orig. Ret. $5.75   **MIB** Sec. Mkt. **$14**

QX 596-5   STRANGE AND WONDERFUL LOVE □
Comments: Handcrafted, 2-13/16" tall, Dated 1993.
A porcupine cozies up to a flowering cactus. Caption: "Ours Is A
Strange And Wonderful Relationship." **Artist:** Linda Sickman

□ Purchased 19 __Pd $_____MIB   NB   DB   BNT
□ Want   Orig. Ret. $8.75   **MIB** Sec. Mkt. **$18**

QX 575-2   SUPERMAN □
Comments: Handcrafted, 6" tall.
Look! Up in the sky! It's a bird, it's Santa... no, it's Superman!
Plenty available on secondary market. Price dropped early in '96.
Artist: Robert Chad

□ Purchased 19 __Pd $_____MIB   NB   DB   BNT
□ Want   Orig. Ret. $12.75   **MIB** Sec. Mkt. **$38**

QX 539-5   SWAT TEAM, THE □
Comments: Handcrafted, 1-9/16" tall, Dated 1993.
Hang-together ornaments. Two white kittens play swat games
with a ball of red yarn. **Artist:** Trish Andrews

□ Purchased 19 __Pd $_____MIB   NB   DB   BNT
□ Want   Orig. Ret. $12.75   **MIB** Sec. Mkt. **$26**

QX 534-5   THAT'S ENTERTAINMENT

Comments: Handcrafted, 2-15/16" tall, Dated 1993.
Watch as Santa pulls a rabbit out of his hat!
Artist: Bob Siedler

☐ Purchased 19 __Pd $_____MIB   NB   DB   BNT
☐ Want   Orig. Ret. $8.75   **MIB** Sec. Mkt. **$18**

QX 555-5   TO MY GRANDMA

Comments: Handcrafted, 3-5/16" tall, Dated 1993.
A red note pad doubles as a photo holder. May be personalized.
Captions: "To My Grandma XOXO, 1993 XOXO" and "I May Be
Little, But I Love You Great Big!" **Artist:** Donna Lee

☐ Purchased 19 __Pd $_____MIB   NB   DB   BNT
☐ Want   Orig. Ret. $7.75   **MIB** Sec. Mkt. **$16**

QX 550-2   TOBIN FRALEY CAROUSEL

Comments: **Second in Series,** Porcelain and Brass, 5-1/4" tall.
Dated 1993. A white horse decorated in Christmas finery gallops into
Christmas. Secondary market buyers bought less of this ornament than
the first, so this is the reason for the higher value. (Supply and
demand.)

☐ Purchased 19 __Pd $_____MIB   NB   DB   BNT
☐ Want   Orig. Ret. $28.00   **MIB** Sec. Mkt. **$30-$35**

QX 592-5   TOP BANANA

Comments: Handcrafted, 2-7/16" tall, Dated 1993.
This perky little monkey, dressed in a Santa suit and sitting on top of a
bunch of bananas, is sure to perk up anyone's Christmas.
Artist: Anita Marra Rogers

☐ Purchased 19 __Pd $_____MIB   NB   DB   BNT
☐ Want   Orig. Ret. $7.75   **MIB** Sec. Mkt. **$17.50**

QXC 543-2   TRIMMED WITH MEMORIES:
KEEPSAKE CLUB ANNIVERSARY EDITION

Comments: Handcrafted, 3-7/8" tall, Dated 1993 and 1973.
A blue spruce is decorated with small gold replicas of Keepsake
ornaments, as well as candles and garland. **Artist:** Linda Sickman

☐ Purchased 19 __Pd $_____MIB   NB   DB   BNT
☐ Want   Orig. Ret. $12.00   **MIB** Sec. Mkt. **$32**

QX 301-2   TWELVE DAYS OF CHRISTMAS:
TEN LORDS A-LEAPIN

Comments: **Tenth in Series,** Acrylic, 3" tall, Dated 1993.
One of the ten lords leaps among holly leaves on this heart-
shaped acrylic ornament. **Artist:** Robert Chad

☐ Purchased 19 __Pd $_____MIB   NB   DB   BNT
☐ Want   Orig. Ret. $6.75   **MIB** Sec. Mkt. **$20**

QX 529-2   U. S. CHRISTMAS STAMPS

Comments: **FIRST IN SERIES,** Enamel on Copper, 2-5/16" tall.
Dated 1993. Inspired by a Christmas stamp issued in 1983 in
Santa Claus, Indiana. Display stand included. This series ended
with the 1995 ornament. **Artist:** Linda Sickman

☐ Purchased 19 __Pd $_____MIB   NB   DB   BNT
☐ Want   Orig. Ret. $10.75 **NB** $16   **MIB** Sec. Mkt. **$26**

QLX 741-2   U. S. S. ENTERPRISE™

Comments: Handcrafted, Blinking Light, Stardated 1993.
This special promotional ornament was the third ornament to
be produced with the Star Trek theme. This Enterprise is from
Star Trek® The Next Generation™. **Artist:** Lynn Norton

☐ Purchased 19 __Pd $_____MIB   NB   DB   BNT
☐ Want   Orig. Ret. $24.00 **NB** $37   **MIB** Sec. Mkt. **$45**

QX 526-2   WAKE-UP CALL

Comments: Handcrafted, 1-7/18" tall, Dated 1993.
It's Christmas morning and junior can't wait til dad wakes up.
Artist: Duane Unruh

☐ Purchased 19 __Pd $_____MIB   NB   DB   BNT
☐ Want   Orig. Ret. $8.75   **MIB** Sec. Mkt. **$18**

QX 589-5   WARM AND SPECIAL FRIENDS

Comments: Handcrafted and Stamped Metal, 2-1/8" tall.
Dated 1993. Two mice sit atop a can of "Hershey's Cocoa."
Artist: Linda Sickman

☐ Purchased 19 __Pd $_____MIB   NB   DB   BNT
☐ Want   Orig. Ret. $10.75   **MIB** Sec. Mkt. **$22**

QX 537-5   WATER BED SNOOZE

Comments: Handcrafted, 1-3/4" tall, Dated 1993.
A bear sleeping on the "Polar Water Bed" is actually sleeping
on top of an ice cube tray! **Artist:** Julia Lee

☐ Purchased 19 __Pd $_____MIB   NB   DB   BNT
☐ Want   Orig. Ret. $9.75   **MIB** Sec. Mkt. **$20**

QLX 742-2   WINNIE THE POOH

Comments: Voice, Handcrafted, 3-5/8" tall, Dated 1993.
Pooh sits on a tree stump with his pot of "Hunny." This ornament
features the voice of Sterling Holloway (who has always been the
voice of Pooh and passed away in 1993.) Somewhat plentiful.
Artist: Bob Siedler

☐ Purchased 19 __Pd $_____MIB   NB   DB   BNT
☐ Want   Orig. Ret. $24.00   **MIB** Sec. Mkt. **$48**

QX 571-2 **WINNIE THE POOH COLLECTION:**
EEYORE ☐

Comments: Handcrafted, 2" tall.
Hang on Eeyore!
Artist: Bob Siedler

☐ Purchased 19__Pd $_____MIB   NB   DB   BNT
☐ Want   Orig. Ret. $9.75   **MIB** Sec. Mkt. **$20**

QX 567-2 **WINNIE THE POOH COLLECTION:**
KANGA AND ROO ☐

Comments: Handcrafted, 3-3/8" tall.
Roo peeks out from Kanga's pouch for a better view.
Artist: Bob Siedler

☐ Purchased 19__Pd $_____MIB   NB   DB   BNT
☐ Want   Orig. Ret. $9.75   **MIB** Sec. Mkt. **$22**

QX 569-5 **WINNIE THE POOH COLLECTION:**
OWL ☐

Comments: Handcrafted, 3-5/8" tall.
Owl stays warm in winter by strapping a hot water bottle to his
stomach. **Artist:** Bob Siedler

☐ Purchased 19__Pd $_____MIB   NB   DB   BNT
☐ Want   Orig. Ret. $9.75   **MIB** Sec. Mkt. **$20**

QX 570-2 **WINNIE THE POOH COLLECTION:**
RABBIT ☐

Comments: Handcrafted, 3-1/2" tall.
Rabbit finds that frying pans make great snowshoes!
Artist: Bob Siedler

☐ Purchased 19__Pd $_____MIB   NB   DB   BNT
☐ Want   Orig. Ret. $9.75   **MIB** Sec. Mkt. **$20**

QX 570-5 **WINNIE THE POOH COLLECTION:**
TIGGER AND PIGLET ☐

Comments: Handcrafted, 3-3/4" tall.
As Tigger glides on his ice skates, Piglet grabs a ride on his tail.
Artist: Bob Siedler

☐ Purchased 19__Pd $_____MIB   NB   DB   BNT
☐ Want   Orig. Ret. $9.75   **MIB** Sec. Mkt. **$48**

QX 571-5 **WINNIE THE POOH COLLECTION:**
WINNIE THE POOH ☐

Comments: Handcrafted, 3-3/8" tall.
Pooh is an expert skier!
Artist: Bob Siedler

☐ Purchased 19__Pd $_____MIB   NB   DB   BNT
☐ Want   Orig. Ret. $9.75   **MIB** Sec. Mkt. **$28**

QXC 569-2 **YOU'RE ALWAYS WELCOME** ☐

Comments: Handcrafted, 2-1/2" tall, Dated 1993.
A Tender Touches bear puts out her special "Welcome 1993"
door mat. The Tender Touches logo and Keepsake Ornament
Premiere is on the base of this ornament. Plentiful in '94 and '95!
Artist: Ed Seale

☐ Purchased 19__Pd $_____MIB   NB   DB   BNT
☐ Want   Orig. Ret. $9.75   **MIB** Sec. Mkt. **$60**

Hallmark Keepsake
Personalized Ornaments

These ornaments may not escalate in value on the secondary market unless, perhaps, they are personalized with a well-known name or saying. No sales on these have been reported or found advertised.

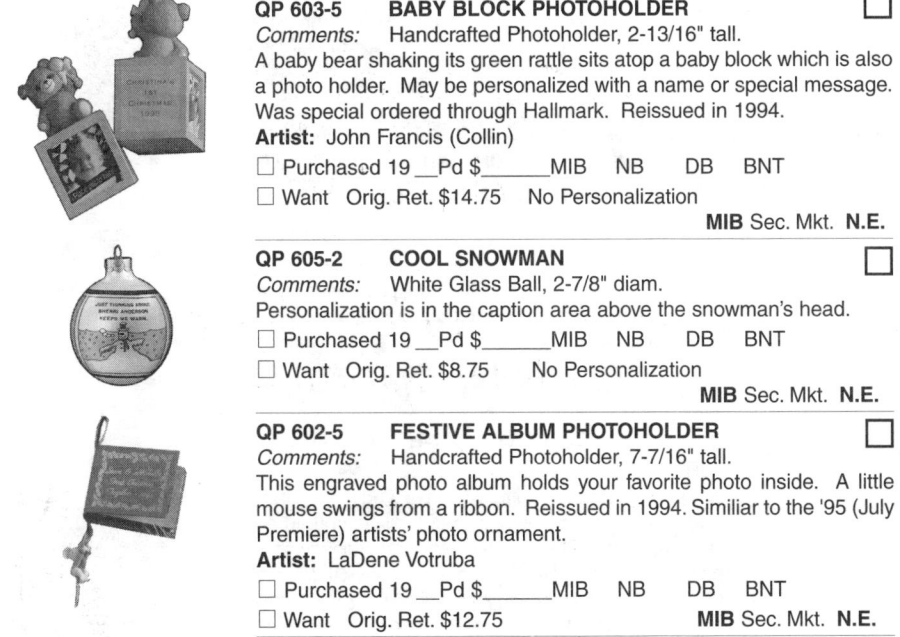

QP 603-5 **BABY BLOCK PHOTOHOLDER** ☐

Comments: Handcrafted Photoholder, 2-13/16" tall.
A baby bear shaking its green rattle sits atop a baby block which is also
a photo holder. May be personalized with a name or special message.
Was special ordered through Hallmark. Reissued in 1994.
Artist: John Francis (Collin)

☐ Purchased 19__Pd $_____MIB   NB   DB   BNT
☐ Want   Orig. Ret. $14.75   No Personalization
                                          MIB Sec. Mkt. **N.E.**

QP 605-2 **COOL SNOWMAN** ☐

Comments: White Glass Ball, 2-7/8" diam.
Personalization is in the caption area above the snowman's head.

☐ Purchased 19__Pd $_____MIB   NB   DB   BNT
☐ Want   Orig. Ret. $8.75   No Personalization
                                          MIB Sec. Mkt. **N.E.**

QP 602-5 **FESTIVE ALBUM PHOTOHOLDER** ☐

Comments: Handcrafted Photoholder, 7-7/16" tall.
This engraved photo album holds your favorite photo inside. A little
mouse swings from a ribbon. Reissued in 1994. Similiar to the '95 (July
Premiere) artists' photo ornament.
Artist: LaDene Votruba

☐ Purchased 19__Pd $_____MIB   NB   DB   BNT
☐ Want   Orig. Ret. $12.75   **MIB** Sec. Mkt. **N.E.**

QP 604-2 **FILLED WITH COOKIES** ☐

Comments: Handcrafted, 2-1/8" tall.
An acorn-designed cookie jar is being raided by a little squirrel. Shh!
Don't tell! Reissued in '95. **Artist:** Anita Marra Rogers

☐ Purchased 19__Pd $_____MIB   NB   DB   BNT
☐ Want   Orig. Ret. $12.75   **MIB** Sec. Mkt. **N.E.**

QP 601-2   GOING GOLFIN' ☐
Comments: Handcrafted, 2-13/16" tall.
This little beaver is ready to go, golf club in hand, as he sits on a large golf ball. Reissued in 1994.
Artist: Don Palmiter
☐ Purchased 19 __Pd $_____MIB   NB   DB   BNT
☐ Want   Orig. Ret. $12.75   **MIB** Sec. Mkt. **N.E.**

QP 600-2   HERE'S YOUR FORTUNE ☐
Comments: Handcrafted,1-13/16" tall.
Fortune cookie anyone? Send your own message to someone special on the fortune cookie strip. **Artist:** Ed Seale
☐ Purchased 19 __Pd $_____MIB   NB   DB   BNT
☐ Want   Orig. Ret. $10.75   **MIB** Sec. Mkt. **N.E.**

QP 601-5   MAILBOX DELIVERY ☐
Comments: Handcrafted, 1-7/8" tall.
A cheery raccoon inside the red mailbox holds an envelope with the message "Merry Christmas." Reissued in 1994 and 1995.
Artist: Ken Crow
☐ Purchased 19 __Pd $_____MIB   NB   DB   BNT
☐ Want   Orig. Ret. $14.75   **MIB** Sec. Mkt. **N.E.**

QP 602-2   ON THE BILLBOARD ☐
Comments: Handcrafted, 2-1/8" tall.
A little elf from the "Santa Sign Co." will paint your message on the billboard. Reissued in 1994 and 1995. **Artist:** Ken Crow
☐ Purchased 19 __Pd $_____MIB   NB   DB   BNT
☐ Want   Orig. Ret. $12.75   **MIB** Sec. Mkt. **N.E.**

QP 604-5   PEANUTS® ☐
Comments: White Glass Ball, 2-7/8" dia.
The Peanuts gang is here to send a special Christmas wish.
☐ Purchased 19 __Pd $_____MIB   NB   DB   BNT
☐ Want   Orig. Ret. $9.00   **MIB** Sec. Mkt. **N.E.**

QP 603-2   PLAYING BALL ☐
Comments: Handcrafted, 3-11/16" tall.
An adorable bear cub is ready to play ball. The personalized message is written on his bat. Reissued in 1994 and 1995.
Artist: John Francis (Collin)
☐ Purchased 19 __Pd $_____MIB   NB   DB   BNT
☐ Want   Orig. Ret. $12.75   **MIB** Sec. Mkt. **N.E.**

QP 605-5   REINDEER IN THE SKY ☐
Comments: White Glass Ball, 2-7/8" dia.
Santa's reindeer hold a conversation of your design!
☐ Purchased 19 __Pd $_____MIB   NB   DB   BNT
☐ Want   Orig. Ret. $8.75   **MIB** Sec. Mkt. **N.E.**

QP 600-5   SANTA SAYS ☐
Comments: Handcrafted, 2-15/16" tall.
What does Santa say? Pull the cord and the message pops out of the pack on his back. Reissued in 1994. **Artist:** Ed Seale
☐ Purchased 19 __Pd $_____MIB   NB   DB   BNT
☐ Want   Orig. Ret. $12.75   **MIB** Sec. Mkt. **$15**

Hallmark Keepsake Showcase Ornaments
Found at Gold Crown Stores only

Folk Art Americana

QK 105-2   ANGEL IN FLIGHT ☐
Comments: Wood Look, 3-1/4" tall, Dated 1993.
This angel appears to be hand-chiseled in wood.
Artist: Linda Sickman
☐ Purchased 19 __Pd $_____MIB   NB   DB   BNT
☐ Want   Orig. Ret. $15.75   **MIB** Sec. Mkt. **$50**

QK 105-5   POLAR BEAR ADVENTURE ☐
Comments: Wood Look, 2-15/16" tall, Dated 1993.
A small elf brings home the tree. **Artist:** Linda Sickman
☐ Purchased 19 __Pd $_____MIB   NB   DB   BNT
☐ Want   Orig. Ret. $15.00   **MIB** Sec. Mkt. **$65**

Have you checked your mailbox lately for your next issue of the *Weekly Collectors' Gazette?* Won't be long... We'll tell you before the others what some of the '97 ornaments are going to be!!

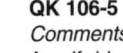
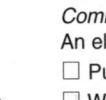

QK 106-5   RIDING IN THE WOODS   ☐
Comments: Wood Look, 2-13/16" tall, Dated 1993.
An elf rides astride a red fox. **Artist:** Linda Sickman

☐ Purchased 19 __Pd $_____MIB   NB   DB   BNT
☐ Want   Orig. Ret. $15.75   **MIB** Sec. Mkt. **$70**

QK 104-5   RIDING THE WIND   ☐
Comments: Wood Look, 2-1/16" tall, Dated 1993.
An elf flies on the back of a white goose. **Artist:** Linda Sickman

☐ Purchased 19 __Pd $_____MIB   NB   DB   BNT
☐ Want   Orig. Ret. $15.75   **MIB** Sec. Mkt. **$60**

QK 107-2   SANTA CLAUS   ☐
Comments: Wood Look, 4-5/8" tall, Dated 1993.
Santa delivers lots of toys to children.   Santa collectors love him!
Artist: Linda Sickman

☐ Purchased 19 __Pd $_____MIB   NB   DB   BNT
☐ Want   Orig. Ret. $16.75   **MIB** Sec. Mkt. **$220**

Holiday Enchantment

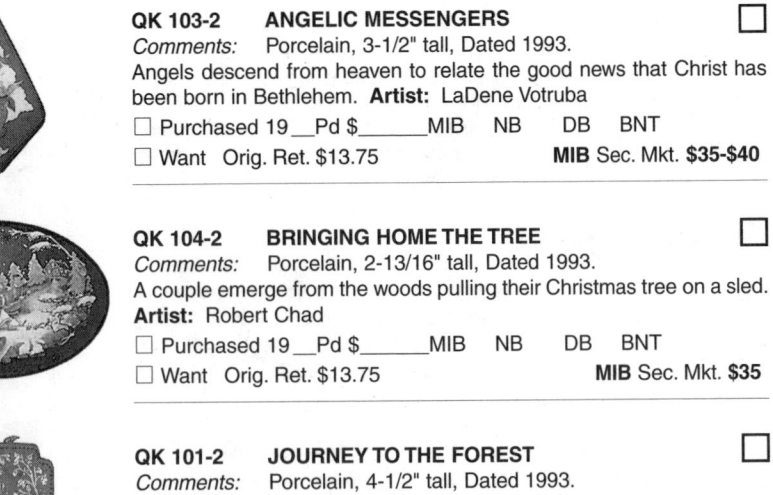

QK 103-2   ANGELIC MESSENGERS   ☐
Comments: Porcelain, 3-1/2" tall, Dated 1993.
Angels descend from heaven to relate the good news that Christ has
been born in Bethlehem. **Artist:** LaDene Votruba

☐ Purchased 19 __Pd $_____MIB   NB   DB   BNT
☐ Want   Orig. Ret. $13.75   **MIB** Sec. Mkt. **$35-$40**

QK 104-2   BRINGING HOME THE TREE   ☐
Comments: Porcelain, 2-13/16" tall, Dated 1993.
A couple emerge from the woods pulling their Christmas tree on a sled.
Artist: Robert Chad

☐ Purchased 19 __Pd $_____MIB   NB   DB   BNT
☐ Want   Orig. Ret. $13.75   **MIB** Sec. Mkt. **$35**

QK 101-2   JOURNEY TO THE FOREST   ☐
Comments: Porcelain, 4-1/2" tall, Dated 1993.
Santa goes into the forest to check on his reindeer.

☐ Purchased 19 __Pd $_____MIB   NB   DB   BNT
☐ Want   Orig. Ret. $13.75   **MIB** Sec. Mkt. **$32.50**

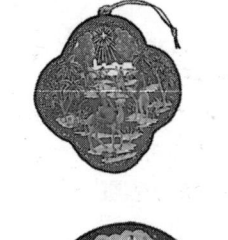

QK 102-5   MAGI, THE   ☐
Comments: Porcelain, 3-3/4" tall, Dated 1993.
The wise men follow the star to Bethlehem to find the Christ Child.
Caption: "We Three Kings Of Orient Are, Bearing Gifts We Traverse
Afar, Field And Fountain, Moor And Mountain, Following Yonder Star."

☐ Purchased 19 __Pd $_____MIB   NB   DB   BNT
☐ Want   Orig. Ret. $13.75   **MIB** Sec. Mkt. **$36**

QK 100-5   VISIONS OF SUGARPLUMS   ☐
Comments: Fine Porcelain, 3-1/2" dia, Dated 1993.
A child dreams of Christmas treats and toys on Christmas Eve.
Caption: "The Children Were Nestled All Snug In Their Beds, While
Visions Of Sugarplums Danced In Their Heads."
Artist: LaDene Votruba

☐ Purchased 19 __Pd $_____MIB   NB   DB   BNT
☐ Want   Orig. Ret. $13.75   **MIB** Sec. Mkt. **$35**

Old-World Silver

QK 107-5   SILVER DOVE OF PEACE   ☐
Comments: Silver-Plated, 3-3/16" tall, Dated 1993.
A dove of peace is intricately engraved on the sides of this silver orna-
ment in European style. Caption: "Silver Dove Of Peace."
Artist: Don Palmiter

☐ Purchased 19 __Pd $_____MIB   NB   DB   BNT
☐ Want   Orig. Ret. $24.75   **MIB** Sec. Mkt. **$35**

QK 109-2   SILVER SANTA   ☐
Comments: Silver-Plated, 3-5/16" tall, Dated 1993.
A design of Santa's head circles the sides of this ornament.
Artist: Duane Unruh

☐ Purchased 19 __Pd $_____MIB   NB   DB   BNT
☐ Want   Orig. Ret. $24.75   **MIB** Sec. Mkt. **$56**

QK 108-2   SILVER SLEIGH   ☐
Comments: Silver-Plated, 3-1/8" tall, Dated 1993.
Detailed engraving on this ornament portrays a sleigh.
Artist: Don Palmiter

☐ Purchased 19 __Pd $_____MIB   NB   DB   BNT
☐ Want   Orig. Ret. $24.75   **MIB** Sec. Mkt. **$38**

QK 108-5   SILVER STAR AND HOLLY   ☐
Comments: Silver-Plated, 3-1/16" tall, Dated 1993.
Lavishly engraved stars and holly decorate this unique Christmas orna-
ment. **Artist:** Don Palmiter

☐ Purchased 19 __Pd $_____MIB   NB   DB   BNT
☐ Want   Orig. Ret. $24.75   **MIB** Sec. Mkt. **$35**

Portraits in Bisque

QK 115-2   CHRISTMAS FEAST   ☐
Comments: Porcelain Bisque, 3-1/2" tall, Dated 1993.
Two little girls look on as mother carries the roasted turkey to the table.
Artist: Sharon Pike
☐ Purchased 19__Pd $_____MIB   NB   DB   BNT
☐ Want   Orig. Ret. $15.75   **MIB** Sec. Mkt. **$35**

QK 114-2   JOY OF SHARING   ☐
Comments: Porcelain Bisque, 3-1/2" tall, Dated 1993.
Two friends exchange Christmas gifts during this season of giving.
☐ Purchased 19__Pd $_____MIB   NB   DB   BNT
☐ Want   Orig. Ret. $15.75   **MIB** Sec. Mkt. **$35**

QK 114-5   MISTLETOE KISS   ☐
Comments: Porcelain Bisque, 3-5/6" tall.
A gentleman prepares to kiss his favorite lady as he holds a sprig of mistletoe over her head. **Artist:** Sharon Pike
☐ Purchased 19__Pd $_____MIB   NB   DB   BNT
☐ Want   Orig. Ret. $15.75   **MIB** Sec. Mkt. **$35**

QK 116-2   NORMAN ROCKWELL: JOLLY POSTMAN   ☐
Comments: Porcelain Bisque, 3-1/4" tall.
Children crowd around a happy postman who is delivering the Christmas mail. **Artist:** Peter Dutkin
☐ Purchased 19__Pd $_____MIB   NB   DB   BNT
☐ Want   Orig. Ret. $15.75   **MIB** Sec. Mkt. **$35**

**QK 115-5   NORMAN ROCKWELL:
                FILLING THE STOCKINGS**   ☐
Comments: Porcelain Bisque, 3-9/16" tall.
Santa is busy at his chores on Christmas Eve. **Artist:** Peter Dutkin
☐ Purchased 19__Pd $_____MIB   NB   DB   BNT
☐ Want   Orig. Ret. $15.75   **MIB** Sec. Mkt. **$35**

Convention Ornaments

KANSAS CITY ANGEL: SPECIAL EDITION   ☐
Comments: Silver-Plated, Dated "K.C. 1993."
This special edition Angel was given as a parting gift to all who attended the 1993 Keepsake Ornament Conventions in June and September.
☐ Purchased 19__Pd $_____MIB   NB   DB   BNT
☐ Want   **MIB** Sec. Mkt.-**NE**

Keepsake Signature Collection

SANTA'S FAVORITE STOP   ☐
Comments: Handcrafted, 1993 with removable Santa ornament. Sculpted by 14 artists, this tabletop was available only at Hallmark stores hosting special 1993 Artist's Appearances; only 200 per event were available. **Artists:** Removable Santa, Ken Crow; Stocking Holder Snowman, Trish Andrews; Elf on Mantel, Robert Chad; Hearth/Puppy, John Francis (Collin); Cat, Julia Lee; Victorian Doll, Joyce A. Lyle; Santa's Bag, Don Palmiter; Fireplace, Dill Rhodus; Cookies and Milk for Santa/Garland, Anita Marra Rogers; Stocking Holder Teddy Bear, Ed Seale; Toy Train/Kindling Box, Linda Sickman; Stocking Holder Mouse, Bob Siedler; Clock on the Mantel, Duane Unruh; and Teddy Bear, LaDene Votruba.
☐ Purchased 19___ Pd $_____   MIB NB DB BNT
☐ Want   Orig. Ret. $55 with $25 purchase of Keepsake Ornaments
                    MIB Sec. Mkt. **$250-$275** if signed by all

**Pat B. decorates her home with a
Hallmark ornament tree. Her little
snow covered village surrounds the
base of the tree.**

1993 Miniature Ornament Collection

A   QXM 514-5   **BABY'S FIRST CHRISTMAS**
Handcrafted, 1-1/16" tall, Dated 1993. **Artist:** LaDene Votruba
☐ Purchased 19___ Pd $_____   MIB   NB   DB   BNT
☐ Want   Orig. Retail $5.75
  MIB Sec. Mkt. **$13.50**

B   QXM 512-5   **BEARYMORES, THE**
Second in Series, Handcrafted, 1-1/8" tall, Dated 1993.
Artist: Anita Marra Rogers
☐ Purchased 19___ Pd $_____   MIB   NB   DB   BNT
☐ Want   Orig. Retail $5.75
  MIB Sec. Mkt. **$16**

C   QXM 407-2   **CHEESE PLEASE**
Handcrafted, 1-1/4" tall, Dated 1993. **Artist:** Bob Siedler
☐ Purchased 19___ Pd $_____   MIB   NB   DB   BNT
☐ Want   Orig. Retail $3.75
  MIB Sec. Mkt. **$9.50**

D   QXM 408-5   **CHRISTMAS CASTLE**
Handcrafted, 1-1/8" tall, Dated 1993. **Artist:** Ed Seale
☐ Purchased 19___ Pd $_____   MIB   NB   DB   BNT
☐ Want   Orig. Retail $5.75
  MIB Sec. Mkt. **$12**

E   QXM 401-2   **CLOISONNÉ SNOWFLAKE**
Precious Edition. Cloisonné/Brass, 1" dia. Being used as earrings and necklaces.
Artist: LaDene Votruba
☐ Purchased 19___ Pd $_____   MIB   NB   DB   BNT
☐ Want   Orig. Retail $9.75
  MIB Sec. Mkt. **$19**

F   QXM 406-2   **COUNTRY FIDDLING**
Handcrafted, 1" tall, Dated '93. **Artist:** John Francis (Collin)
☐ Purchased 19___ Pd $_____   MIB   NB   DB   BNT
☐ Want   Orig. Retail $3.75
  MIB Sec. Mkt. **$9**

G   QXM 401-5   **CRYSTAL ANGEL**
Full lead crystal and gold-plated, 1" tall, Dated '93. Being used as a necklace!
Another debuted in '96 being "green". **Artist:** Don Palmiter
☐ Purchased 19___ Pd $_____   MIB   NB   DB   BNT
☐ Want   Orig. Retail $9.75
  MIB Sec. Mkt. **$65**

H   QXM 589-1   **DANCING ANGELS TREE-TOPPER**
Dimensional brass 2-7/8" tall, Reissued from 1992.
☐ Purchased 19___ Pd $_____   MIB   NB   DB   BNT
☐ Want   Orig. Retail $9.75
  MIB Sec. Mkt. **$12**

I   QXM 407-5   **EARS TO PALS**
Handcrafted, 1-3/16" tall, Dated '93. **Artist:** Patricia Andrews
☐ Purchased 19___ Pd $_____   MIB   NB   DB   BNT
☐ Want   Orig. Retail $3.75
  MIB Sec. Mkt. **$8.50**

J   QXC 529-4   **FORTY WINKS: KEEPSAKE CLUB**
Handcrafted, 1-3/16" tall. **Artist:** John Francis (Collin)
☐ Purchased 19___ Pd $_____   MIB   NB   DB   BNT
☐ Want   Orig. Retail---Free with Membership
  MIB Sec. Mkt. **$21**

K   QXM 516-2   **GRANDMA**
Handcrafted, 1" tall, Dated 1993. **Artist:** Ed Seale
☐ Purchased 19___ Pd $_____   MIB   NB   DB   BNT
☐ Want   Orig. Retail $4.50
  MIB Sec. Mkt. **$12.50**

L   QXM 405-5   **I DREAM OF SANTA**
Handcrafted, 1-1/8" tall, Dated 1993. **Artist:** Linda Sickman
☐ Purchased 19___ Pd $_____   MIB   NB   DB   BNT
☐ Want   Orig. Retail $3.75
  MIB Sec. Mkt. **$13.50**

M   QXM 404-5   **INTO THE WOODS**
Handcrafted, 1" tall, Dated '93. **Artist:** Ed Seale
☐ Purchased 19___ Pd $_____   MIB   NB   DB   BNT
☐ Want   Orig. Retail $3.75
  MIB Sec. Mkt. **$8.50**

N   QXM 513-5   **KRINGLES, THE: WREATH**
Fifth and Final in Series, Handcrafted, 1" tall. **Artist:** Anita Marra Rogers
☐ Purchased 19___ Pd $_____   MIB   NB   DB   BNT
☐ Want   Orig. Retail $5.75
  MIB Sec. Mkt. **$16**

A   B   C   D   E
F   G   H   I   J
K   L   M   N

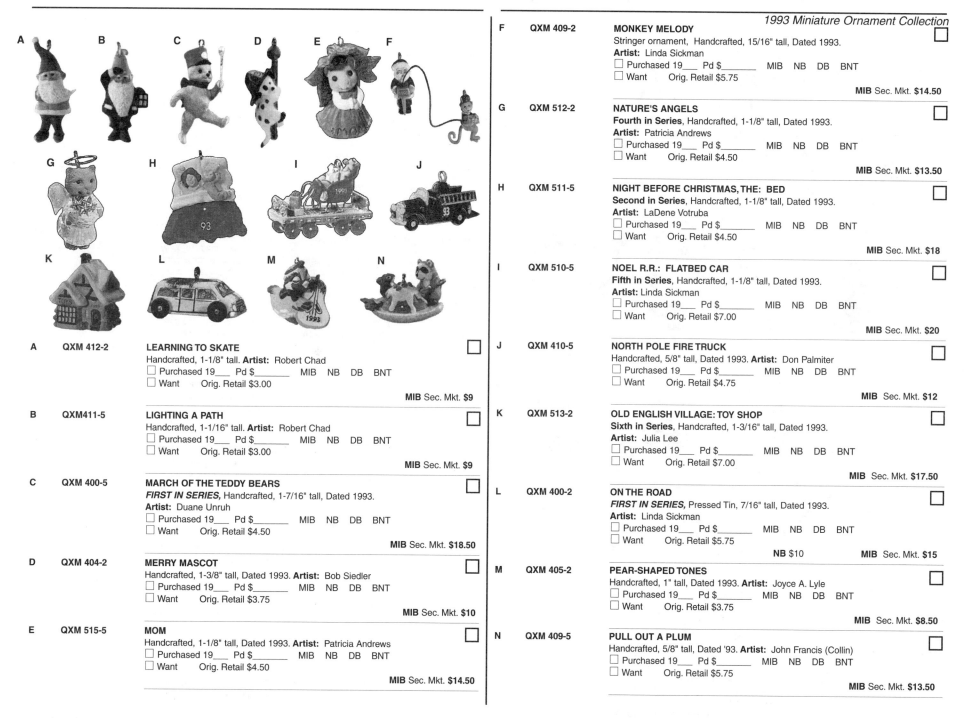

F QXM 409-2   **MONKEY MELODY**
Stringer ornament, Handcrafted, 15/16" tall, Dated 1993.
Artist: Linda Sickman
☐ Purchased 19___ Pd $_____   MIB   NB   DB   BNT
☐ Want   Orig. Retail $5.75

MIB Sec. Mkt. **$14.50**

G QXM 512-2   **NATURE'S ANGELS**
Fourth in Series, Handcrafted, 1-1/8" tall, Dated 1993.
Artist: Patricia Andrews
☐ Purchased 19___ Pd $_____   MIB   NB   DB   BNT
☐ Want   Orig. Retail $4.50

MIB Sec. Mkt. **$13.50**

H QXM 511-5   **NIGHT BEFORE CHRISTMAS, THE: BED**
Second in Series, Handcrafted, 1-1/8" tall, Dated 1993.
Artist: LaDene Votruba
☐ Purchased 19___ Pd $_____   MIB   NB   DB   BNT
☐ Want   Orig. Retail $4.50

MIB Sec. Mkt. **$18**

I QXM 510-5   **NOEL R.R.: FLATBED CAR**
Fifth in Series, Handcrafted, 1-1/8" tall, Dated 1993.
Artist: Linda Sickman
☐ Purchased 19___ Pd $_____   MIB   NB   DB   BNT
☐ Want   Orig. Retail $7.00

MIB Sec. Mkt. **$20**

J QXM 410-5   **NORTH POLE FIRE TRUCK**
Handcrafted, 5/8" tall, Dated 1993. **Artist:** Don Palmiter
☐ Purchased 19___ Pd $_____   MIB   NB   DB   BNT
☐ Want   Orig. Retail $4.75

MIB Sec. Mkt. **$12**

K QXM 513-2   **OLD ENGLISH VILLAGE: TOY SHOP**
Sixth in Series, Handcrafted, 1-3/16" tall, Dated 1993.
Artist: Julia Lee
☐ Purchased 19___ Pd $_____   MIB   NB   DB   BNT
☐ Want   Orig. Retail $7.00

MIB Sec. Mkt. **$17.50**

L QXM 400-2   **ON THE ROAD**
FIRST IN SERIES, Pressed Tin, 7/16" tall, Dated 1993.
Artist: Linda Sickman
☐ Purchased 19___ Pd $_____   MIB   NB   DB   BNT
☐ Want   Orig. Retail $5.75

NB $10   **MIB** Sec. Mkt. **$15**

M QXM 405-2   **PEAR-SHAPED TONES**
Handcrafted, 1" tall, Dated 1993. **Artist:** Joyce A. Lyle
☐ Purchased 19___ Pd $_____   MIB   NB   DB   BNT
☐ Want   Orig. Retail $3.75

MIB Sec. Mkt. **$8.50**

N QXM 409-5   **PULL OUT A PLUM**
Handcrafted, 5/8" tall, Dated '93. **Artist:** John Francis (Collin)
☐ Purchased 19___ Pd $_____   MIB   NB   DB   BNT
☐ Want   Orig. Retail $5.75

MIB Sec. Mkt. **$13.50**

A QXM 412-2   **LEARNING TO SKATE**
Handcrafted, 1-1/8" tall. **Artist:** Robert Chad
☐ Purchased 19___ Pd $_____   MIB   NB   DB   BNT
☐ Want   Orig. Retail $3.00

MIB Sec. Mkt. **$9**

B QXM411-5   **LIGHTING A PATH**
Handcrafted, 1-1/16" tall. **Artist:** Robert Chad
☐ Purchased 19___ Pd $_____   MIB   NB   DB   BNT
☐ Want   Orig. Retail $3.00

MIB Sec. Mkt. **$9**

C QXM 400-5   **MARCH OF THE TEDDY BEARS**
FIRST IN SERIES, Handcrafted, 1-7/16" tall, Dated 1993.
Artist: Duane Unruh
☐ Purchased 19___ Pd $_____   MIB   NB   DB   BNT
☐ Want   Orig. Retail $4.50

MIB Sec. Mkt. **$18.50**

D QXM 404-2   **MERRY MASCOT**
Handcrafted, 1-3/8" tall, Dated 1993. **Artist:** Bob Siedler
☐ Purchased 19___ Pd $_____   MIB   NB   DB   BNT
☐ Want   Orig. Retail $3.75

MIB Sec. Mkt. **$10**

E QXM 515-5   **MOM**
Handcrafted, 1-1/8" tall, Dated 1993. **Artist:** Patricia Andrews
☐ Purchased 19___ Pd $_____   MIB   NB   DB   BNT
☐ Want   Orig. Retail $4.50

MIB Sec. Mkt. **$14.50**

A QXM 411-2 REFRESHING FLIGHT
Handcrafted, 7/8" tall. **Artist:** Robert Chad
☐ Purchased 19___ Pd $_____   MIB NB DB BNT
☐ Want   Orig. Retail $5.75
MIB Sec. Mkt. **$14.50**

B QXM 545-2 REVOLVING TREE BASE: HOLIDAY EXPRESS
Train circles on track. Free miniature tree w/purchase.
Reissued in '94 and '95.
☐ Purchased 19___ Pd $_____   MIB NB DB BNT
☐ Want   Orig. Retail $50.00
MIB Sec. Mkt. **$74**

C QXM 511-2 ROCKING HORSE: APPALOOSA
Sixth in Series, Handcrafted, 1-1/8" tall, Dated 1993.
Artist: Linda Sickman
☐ Purchased 19___ Pd $_____   MIB NB DB BNT
☐ Want   Orig. Retail $4.50
MIB Sec. Mkt. **$14.50**

D QXM 402-5 'ROUND THE MOUNTAIN
Handcrafted, 1-11/16" tall, Dated 1993. **Artist:** Ken Crow
☐ Purchased 19___ Pd $_____   MIB NB DB BNT
☐ Want   Orig. Retail $7.25
MIB Sec. Mkt. **$18**

E QXM 517-2 SECRET PAL
New Commemorative, Handcrafted, 1" tall, Dated 1993.
Artist: Anita Marra Rogers
☐ Purchased 19___ Pd $_____   MIB NB DB BNT
☐ Want   Orig. Retail $3.75
MIB Sec. Mkt. **$8.50**

F QXM 518-2 SNUGGLE BIRDS
Handcrafted, 1-9/16" tall, Dated 1993. **Artist:** Patricia Andrews
☐ Purchased 19___ Pd $_____   MIB NB DB BNT
☐ Want   Orig. Retail $5.75
MIB Sec. Mkt. **$12.50**

G QXM 516-5 SPECIAL FRIENDS
Handcrafted, 1" tall, Dated 1993. **Artist:** John Francis (Collin)
☐ Purchased 19___ Pd $_____   MIB NB DB BNT
☐ Want   Orig. Retail $4.50
MIB Sec. Mkt. **$10**

H QXM 514-2 THIMBLE BELLS
Fourth and Final in Series, Handcrafted, 1-1/8" tall, Dated 1993.
Artist: LaDene Votruba
☐ Purchased 19___ Pd $_____   MIB NB DB BNT
☐ Want   Orig. Retail $5.75
MIB Sec. Mkt. **$16**

I QXM 403-2 TINY GREEN THUMBS
(Porcelain Sew Sew Tiny is the most popular set.)
Set of Six, Handcrafted, Dated 1993. **Artist:** Ed Seale
A. Here We Grow, 1-1/4" tall.   D. Ever Green, 13/16" tall.
B. Teeny Clips, 1-1/8" tall.   E. Keep on Hoein', 11/16" tall.
C. Li'l Sprinkler, 13/16" tall.   F. Just Resting, 11/16" tall.
☐ Purchased 19___ Pd $_____   MIB NB DB BNT
☐ Want   Orig. Retail $29.00
MIB Sec. Mkt. **$45**

J QXM 402-2 VISIONS OF SUGARPLUMS
Pewter, 1-3/8" tall, Dated 1993. **Artist:** Don Palmiter
☐ Purchased 19___ Pd $_____   MIB NB DB BNT
☐ Want   Orig. Retail $7.25
MIB Sec. Mkt. **$15**

K QXM 510-2 WOODLAND BABIES
Third and Final in Series, Handcrafted, 1-1/8" tall, Dated 1993.
Artist: John Francis (Collin)
☐ Purchased 19___ Pd $_____   MIB NB DB BNT
☐ Want   Orig. Retail $5.75
MIB Sec. Mkt. **$12**

Can somebody stop this thing!?!

1993 Easter Ornament Collection

A   QEO 834-5   **BABY'S FIRST EASTER**
Handcrafted, 1-1/4" tall, Dated 1993. **Artist:** Don Palmiter
☐ Purchased 19___ Pd $_____   MIB   NB   DB   BNT
☐ Want   Original Retail $6.75
       MIB Sec. Mkt. **$16**

B   QEO 840-5   **BACKYARD BUNNY**
Handcrafted, 2" tall, Dated 1993. **Artist:** Linda Sickman
☐ Purchased 19___ Pd $_____   MIB   NB   DB   BNT
☐ Want   Original Retail $6.75
       MIB Sec. Mkt. **$17.50**

C   QEO 840-2   **BARROW OF GIGGLES**
Handcrafted, 1-7/8" tall, Dated 1993. **Artist:** Patricia Andrews
☐ Purchased 19___ Pd $_____   MIB   NB   DB   BNT
☐ Want   Original Retail $8.75
       MIB Sec. Mkt. **$20**

D   QEO 836-2   **BEAUTIFUL MEMORIES**
Handcrafted Photoholder, 2-1/2" tall. **Artist:** Duane Unruh
Caption: "1993 Beautiful Easter Memories."
☐ Purchased 19___ Pd $_____   MIB   NB   DB   BNT
☐ Want   Original Retail $6.75
       MIB Sec. Mkt. **$12.50**

E   QEO 839-2   **BEST-DRESSED TURTLE**
Handcrafted, 1-7/8" tall. **Artist:** Julia Lee
☐ Purchased 19___ Pd $_____   MIB   NB   DB   BNT
☐ Want   Original Retail $5.75
       MIB Sec. Mkt. **$14**

F   QEO 837-5   **CHICKS-ON-A-TWIRL**
Handcrafted Twirl-About, 3" tall, Dated 1993.
Artist: Joyce A. Lyle
☐ Purchased 19___ Pd $_____   MIB   NB   DB   BNT
☐ Want   Original Retail $7.75
       MIB Sec. Mkt. **$15**

G   QEO 834-2   **DAUGHTER**
Handcrafted, 2-1/2" tall, Dated 1993. **Artist:** Patricia Andrews
☐ Purchased 19___ Pd $_____   MIB   NB   DB   BNT
☐ Want   Original Retail $5.75
       MIB Sec. Mkt. **$17**

H   QEO 832-5   **EASTER PARADE**
Second in Series, Handcrafted, 2-7/8" tall, Dated 1993.
Artist: Julia Lee
☐ Purchased 19___ Pd $_____   MIB   NB   DB   BNT
☐ Want   Original Retail $6.75
       MIB Sec. Mkt. **$21**

I   QEO 833-2   **EGGS IN SPORTS**
Second in Series, Handcrafted, 2" tall. **Artist:** Bob Siedler
Caption: "Tennis 93 Ace"
☐ Purchased 19___ Pd $_____   MIB   NB   DB   BNT
☐ Want   Original Retail $6.75
       MIB Sec. Mkt. **$18.50**

J   QEO 835-2   **GRANDCHILD**
Handcrafted, 1-7/8" tall, Dated 1993. **Artist:** Bob Siedler
☐ Purchased 19___ Pd $_____   MIB   NB   DB   BNT
☐ Want   Original Retail $6.75
       MIB Sec. Mkt. **$18.50**

K   QEO 831-2   **LI'L PEEPER**
Handcrafted, 1-7/8" tall. **Artist:** Julia Lee
☐ Purchased 19___ Pd $_____   MIB   NB   DB   BNT
☐ Want   Original Retail $7.75
       MIB Sec. Mkt. **$21**

L   QEO 831-5   **LOP-EARED BUNNY**
Handcrafted, 7/8" tall. **Artist:** Linda Sickman
☐ Purchased 19___ Pd $_____   MIB   NB   DB   BNT
☐ Want   Original Retail $5.75
       MIB Sec. Mkt. **$19.50**

A

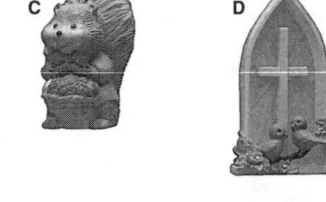
B

C

D

E

F

G

A QEO 837-2 **LOVELY LAMB**
Porcelain, 3" tall, Dated 1993. **Artist:** LaDene Votruba
☐ Purchased 19___ Pd $_____   MIB NB DB BNT
☐ Want   Original Retail $9.75

MIB Sec. Mkt. **$22.50**

B QEO 839-5 **MAYPOLE STROLL**
Handcrafted. **Artists:** John Francis (Collin) and Robert Chad
Dollie Duck, Ricky Rabbit and Chester Chipmunk, 2" - 2-1/2" tall.
Basket, 4-1/4" tall.
☐ Purchased 19___ Pd $_____   MIB NB DB BNT
☐ Want   Original Retail $28.00

MIB Sec. Mkt. **$48**

C QEO 838-2 **NUTTY EGGS**
Handcrafted, 1-7/8" tall. **Artist:** Julia Lee
☐ Purchased 19___ Pd $_____   MIB NB DB BNT
☐ Want   Original Retail $6.75

MIB Sec. Mkt. **$15**

D QEO 836-5 **RADIANT WINDOW**
Handcrafted, 3-1/4" tall. **Artist:** Duane Unruh
☐ Purchased 19___ Pd $_____   MIB NB DB BNT
☐ Want   Original Retail $7.75

MIB Sec. Mkt. **$18**

E QEO 832-2 **SPRINGTIME BONNETS**
FIRST IN SERIES, Handcrafted, 2-1/4" tall, Dated 1993. Very popular.
Artist: Donna Lee
☐ Purchased 19___ Pd $_____   MIB NB DB BNT
☐ Want   Original Retail $7.75

MIB Sec. Mkt. **$32**

F QEO 833-5 **SON**
Handcrafted, 2-1/2" tall, Dated 1993. **Artist:** Patricia Andrews
☐ Purchased 19___ Pd $_____   MIB NB DB BNT
☐ Want   Original Retail $5.75

MIB Sec. Mkt. **$15**

G QEO 838-5 **TIME FOR EASTER**
Handcrafted, 3-1/2" tall. **Artist:** Robert Chad
Caption: "1993 Time for Easter Fun!"
☐ Purchased 19___ Pd $_____   MIB NB DB BNT
☐ Want   Original Retail $8.75

MIB Sec. Mkt. **$21**

Midwest Collectibles Fest XII

—R.STUBLER—

"Yes, it does say the price is 98¢ but that's a 1930's catalog."

1994 Collection

QX 581-6   A FELINE OF CHRISTMAS ☐
Comments: Handcrafted, 3-1/16" tall, Dated 1994.
Dangling from a string of lights, this silly cat, a Shoebox Greetings design, holds tightly to a Christmas tree ball ornament.
Artist: Patricia Andrews

☐ Purchased 19 __Pd $_____MIB   NB   DB   BNT
☐ Want   Orig. Ret. $8.95   **MIB** Sec. Mkt. **$28**

QX 577-3   A SHARP FLAT ☐
Comments: Handcrafted, 3-3/4" tall, Dated 1994.
A virtuoso mouse lives in the back of this violin. His "flat" is complete with a fireplace and Christmas tree. The front of the ornament resembles a classical violin. **Artist:** Ken Crow

☐ Purchased 19 __Pd $_____MIB   NB   DB   BNT
☐ Want   Orig. Ret. $10.95   **MIB** Sec. Mkt. **$23**

QX 565-6   ACROSS THE MILES ☐
Comments: Handcrafted, 2-9/16" tall, Dated 1994.
This cheery raccoon is sending his Christmas greeting via a note in a bottle. **Artist:** Patricia Andrews

☐ Purchased 19 __Pd $_____MIB   NB   DB   BNT
☐ Want   Orig. Ret. $8.95   **MIB** Sec. Mkt. **$18**

QX 592-3   ALL PUMPED UP ☐
Comments: Handcrafted, 2-7/16" tall, Dated 1994.
A little elf sits atop an air pump; he has just filled the football for "Santa's Football League." **Artist:** Dill Rhodus

☐ Purchased 19 __Pd $_____MIB   NB   DB   BNT
☐ Want   Orig. Ret. $8.95   **MIB** Sec. Mkt. **$20**

QX 589-6   ANGEL HARE ☐
Comments: Handcrafted/Brass Halo, 2-1/2" tall, Dated 1994.
A whimsical bunny angel is putting the final touch to the Christmas tree -- Angel Hair. **Artist:** Linda Sickman

☐ Purchased 19 __Pd $_____MIB   NB   DB   BNT
☐ Want   Orig. Ret. $8.95   **MIB** Sec. Mkt. **$20**

QX 568-3   ANNIVERSARY YEAR: PHOTOHOLDER ☐
Comments: Brass/Chrome, 3-13/16" tall, Dated 1994.
Delicately etched with holly and ribbon, this photoholder may be personalized to mark 5, 10, 20, 25, 30, 35, 40, 45, 50 and 60 years. Caption: "Loving moments together... Loving memories forever."
Artist: Ron Bishop

☐ Purchased 19 __Pd $_____MIB   NB   DB   BNT
☐ Want   Orig. Ret. $10.95   **MIB** Sec. Mkt. **$18**

QLX 738-3   AWAY IN A MANGER ☐
Comments: Light, Handcrafted, 3-7/16" tall Dated 1994.
The Star of Bethlehem is aglow and casts its light on Baby Jesus lying in his manger bed. Caption: "Away in a manger, no crib for a bed. The little Lord Jesus laid down His sweet head." **Artist:** Joyce Lyle

☐ Purchased 19 __Pd $_____MIB   NB   DB   BNT
☐ Want   Orig. Ret. $16.00   **MIB** Sec. Mkt. **$40**

QX 563-3   BABY'S FIRST CHRISTMAS ☐
Comments: Porcelain/Brass, 2-9/16" tall, Dated 1994.
A brass tag, bell and green satin ribbon grace porcelain "knitted" booties. **Artist:** Duane Unruh

☐ Purchased 19 __Pd $_____MIB   NB   DB   BNT
☐ Want   Orig. Ret. $18.95   **MIB** Sec. Mkt. **$36**

QX 574-3   BABY'S FIRST CHRISTMAS ☐
Comments: Handcrafted, 1-7/8" tall, Dated 1994.
Pull the safety pin to open the baby block; shh... a baby teddy is sound asleep inside. **Artist:** Ed Seale

☐ Purchased 19 __Pd $_____MIB   NB   DB   BNT
☐ Want   Orig. Ret. $12.95   **MIB** Sec. Mkt. **$25**

QLX 746-6   BABY'S FIRST CHRISTMAS ☐
Comments: Light and Music, Handcrafted, 2-11/16" tall Dated 1994.
Mama and Papa squirrels check on their tiny infant, sound asleep in his cradle. Plays "Rock-a-Bye Baby."
Artist: John Francis (Collin)

☐ Purchased 19 __Pd $_____MIB   NB   DB   BNT
☐ Want   Orig. Ret. $20.00   **MIB** Sec. Mkt. **$38**

QX 571-3   BABY'S FIRST CHRISTMAS: ☐
TEDDY BEAR YEARS COLLECTION
Comments: Handcrafted, 2-3/16" tall, Dated 1994.
Baby celebrates its first Christmas with a stocking and star-shaped Christmas cookie. Design is repeated from 1993.
Artist: Ken Crow

☐ Purchased 19 __Pd $_____MIB   NB   DB   BNT
☐ Want   Orig. Ret. $7.95   **MIB** Sec. Mkt. **$28**

QX 243-6   BABY'S FIRST CHRISTMAS: BABY BOY ☐
Comments: Blue Glass Ball, 2-7/8" dia., Dated 1994.
As Santa peeks through the window, a baby boy is bouncing in his crib. Caption: "Santa's excited for he'll soon get to meet a new baby boy who's precious and sweet."

☐ Purchased 19 __Pd $_____MIB   NB   DB   BNT
☐ Want   Orig. Ret. $5.00   **MIB** Sec. Mkt. **$14**

QX 243-3   BABY'S FIRST CHRISTMAS: BABY GIRL   ☐
Comments: Pink Glass Ball, 2-7/8" dia., Dated 1994.
Santa peeks through a window and watches a baby girl in her crib.
Caption: "Santa's excited for he'll soon get to meet a new baby girl
who's precious and sweet."
☐ Purchased 19 __ Pd $_____ MIB   NB   DB   BNT
☐ Want   Orig. Ret. $5.00   **MIB** Sec. Mkt. **$15**

QX 563-6   BABY'S FIRST CHRISTMAS PHOTOHOLDER   ☐
Comments: Handcrafted, 3-5/16" tall, Dated 1994.
Baby's photo is framed appropriately with stars, a teddy bear and rock-
ing horse. Caption: "There's a new little star on your horizon."
Artist: LaDene Votruba
☐ Purchased 19 __ Pd $_____ MIB   NB   DB   BNT
☐ Want   Orig. Ret. $7.95   **MIB** Sec. Mkt. **$21**

QX 571-6   BABY'S SECOND CHRISTMAS:
TEDDY BEAR YEARS COLLECTION   ☐
Comments: Handcrafted, 2-3/8" tall, Dated 1994.
This teddy wears a red and white bow tie and holds a green Christmas
stocking with a tree-shaped cookie. **Artist:** Ken Crow
☐ Purchased 19 __ Pd $_____ MIB   NB   DB   BNT
☐ Want   Orig. Ret. $7.95   **MIB** Sec. Mkt. **$18**

QX 500-6   BARBIE™   ☐
Comments: **FIRST IN SERIES,** Handcrafted, 4-7/16" tall.
Dated 1994. Barbie is back in her original black and white swimsuit, mark-
ing the 35th anniversary of her debut in 1959. May go higher late '97.
☐ Purchased 19 __ Pd $_____ MIB   NB   DB   BNT
☐ Want   Orig. Ret. $14.95   **MIB** Sec. Mkt. **$25-$30**

QLX 750-6   BARNEY™   ☐
Comments: Light and Motion, Handcrafted, 4-1/8" tall.
Dated 1994. Barney and his rabbit friend sled around a snowman.
Caption: "Sledding is simply Stu-u-u-pendous."
☐ Purchased 19 __ Pd $_____ MIB   NB   DB   BNT
☐ Want   Orig. Ret. $24.00   **MIB** Sec. Mkt. **$45**

QX 596-6   BARNEY™   ☐
Comments: Handcrafted, 3-15/16" tall, Dated 1994.
A favorite of many small children, this popular purple dinosaur skates
into Christmas wearing a Santa cap.
☐ Purchased 19 __ Pd $_____ MIB   NB   DB   BNT
☐ Want   Orig. Ret. $9.95   **MIB** Sec. Mkt. **$18**

QX 532-3   BASEBALL HEROES: BABE RUTH   ☐
Comments: **FIRST IN SERIES,** Handcrafted, 3-3/8" Dia.
Dated 1994. Caption: "714 Career Home Runs, 60 Home Runs in 1927;
.342 Lifetime Batting Average; Inducted into Hall of Fame 1936." This
new series features baseball greats, first of which is "The Babe."
Artist: Dill Rhodus
☐ Purchased 19 __ Pd $_____ MIB   NB   DB   BNT
☐ Want   Orig. Ret. $12.95   **MIB** Sec. Mkt. **$35-$40**

QX 585-3   BATMAN   ☐
Comments: Handcrafted, 5-11/16" tall, Dated 1994.
Batman swings from the Batarang. The size is complementary to
Superman which was issued in 1993. **Artist:** Robert Chad
☐ Purchased 19 __ Pd $_____ MIB   NB   DB   BNT
☐ Want   Orig. Ret. $12.95   **MIB** Sec. Mkt. **$18-$20**

QX 537-3   BEATLES GIFT SET   ☐
Comments: Handcrafted, Dated 1994.
Set includes four ornaments plus microphones, stage and drum set. An
abundance is waiting to be sold on the secondary market! Many sales
in '96. **Artist:** Anita Marra Rogers
A. Paul McCartney, 4-9/16"   F. Drum Set, 2-3/4"
B. John Lennon, 4-1/2"   G. Floor Tom-Tom, 2-13/16"
C. George Harrison, 4-9/16"   H. Top Hat Cymbal, 2-7/16"
D. Ringo Starr, 3-3/4"I.   Stage, 2-3/16"
E. Stand with Two Microphones, 3-15/16"
☐ Purchased 19 __ Pd $_____ MIB   NB   DB   BNT
☐ Want Orig. Ret. $48.00   **MIB** Sec. Mkt. **$70**

QX 240-3   BETSEY'S COUNTRY CHRISTMAS   ☐
Comments: **Third and Final in Series,** Teardrop Ball,2-7/8" dia.
Dated 1994. Betsey and her friends gather together to decorate the
house for the Christmas holidays. Caption: "It's the simple joys, the
simple pleasures, the heart remembers and dearly treasures."
☐ Purchased 19 __ Pd $_____ MIB   NB   DB   BNT
☐ Want   Orig. Ret. $5.00   **MIB** Sec. Mkt. **$15**

QX 587-3   BIG SHOT   ☐
Comments: Handcrafted, 2-7/8" tall, Dated 1994.
This little fellow actually spins the basketball on his finger!
Artist: Bob Siedler
☐ Purchased 19 __ Pd $_____ MIB   NB   DB   BNT
☐ Want   Orig. Ret. $7.95   **MIB** Sec. Mkt. **$15**

QX 551-6   BROTHER

Comments: Handcrafted, 1-15/16" tall, Dated 1994.
"Super Terrific Brother" zips around town in his sports car.
Artist: Sharon Pike

☐ Purchased 19___Pd $_____MIB   NB   DB   BNT

☐ Want   Orig. Ret. $6.95   **MIB** Sec. Mkt. **$15**

QX 587-6   BUSY BATTER

Comments: Handcrafted, 2-5/8" tall, Dated 1994.
The "Wood Sox" are up to bat. Someone pitch the ball to this busy beaver before he chews his bat to pieces! **Artist:** Bob Siedler

☐ Purchased 19___Pd $_____MIB   NB   DB   BNT

☐ Want   Orig. Ret. $7.95   **MIB** Sec. Mkt. **$12**

QLX 737-6   CANDY CANE LOOKOUT

Comments: Light and Voice, Handcrafted, 4-1/4" tall, Dated 1994.
A penguin at the top of the lighthouse keeps a lookout while Santa, Mrs. Claus and another penguin sing carols below.   **Artist:**   John Francis (Collin)

☐ Purchased 19___Pd $_____MIB   NB   DB   BNT

☐ Want   Orig. Ret. $18.00   **MIB** Sec. Mkt. **$50**

QX 577-6   CANDY CAPER

Comments: Handcrafted, 2-11/16" tall, Dated 1994.
A glass jar full of red and green peppermint candies is just too irresistible!   **Artist:** Patricia Andrews

☐ Purchased 19___Pd $_____MIB   NB   DB   BNT

☐ Want   Orig. Ret. $8.95   **MIB** Sec. Mkt. **$20**

QX 582-3   CARING DOCTOR

Comments: Handcrafted, 2-5/16" tall, Dated 1994.
The doctor dates the cast on his cookie patient.
Artist: Anita Marra Rogers

☐ Purchased 19___Pd $_____MIB   NB   DB   BNT

☐ Want   Orig. Ret. $8.95   **MIB** Sec. Mkt. **$18**

♪ ♪ ♪

♪   **Oh Christmas tree,**
oh Christmas tree. . .
How lovely are your branches. ♪

♪

QX 531-3   CAT NAPS

Comments: ***FIRST IN SERIES,*** Handcrafted, 1-15/16" tall.
Dated 1994. Kitty naps in her very own cookie jar. Not all 1st in series increase in value quickly. **Artist:** Dill Rhodus

☐ Purchased 19___Pd $_____MIB   NB   DB   BNT

☐ Want   Orig. Ret. $7.75   **MIB** Sec. Mkt. **$15**

QX 583-6   CHAMPION TEACHER

Comments: Handcrafted, 1-11/16" tall, Dated 1994.
A cute little worm pokes his head out of a bright red apple to give his opinion of his teacher.   **Artist:** Bob Siedler

☐ Purchased 19___Pd $_____MIB   NB   DB   BNT

☐ Want   Orig. Ret. $6.95   **MIB** Sec. Mkt. **$14**

QX 579-6   CHEERS TO YOU!

Comments: Handcrafted/Brass Bell, 3-1/16" tall.
"Frohliche Weihnacten," the German Merry Christmas, is inscribed on this stein.   **Artist:** Ken Crow

☐ Purchased 19___Pd $_____MIB   NB   DB   BNT

☐ Want   Orig. Ret. $10.95   **MIB** Sec. Mkt. **$22**

QX 578-6   CHEERY CYCLISTS

Comments: Handcrafted, 3-3/16" tall, Dated 1994.
Santa and his reindeer are riding a motorcycle built for five!
Artist: Ken Crow

☐ Purchased 19___Pd $_____MIB   NB   DB   BNT

☐ Want   Orig. Ret. $12.95   **MIB** Sec. Mkt. **$28**

QX 590-6   CHILD CARE GIVER

Comments: Handcrafted, 2-1/8" tall, Dated 1994.
A little raccoon sits entranced by the "Holiday Stories" being read by the child care giver. **Artist:** LaDene Votruba

☐ Purchased 19___Pd $_____MIB   NB   DB   BNT

☐ Want   Orig. Ret. $7.95   **MIB** Sec. Mkt. **$14**

QX 573-3   CHILD'S FIFTH CHRISTMAS:
TEDDY BEAR YEARS COLLECTION
Comments: Handcrafted, 2-3/8" tall, Dated 1994.
Design is repeated from 1993.   **Artist:** Dill Rhodus
☐ Purchased 19__Pd $_____MIB   NB   DB   BNT
☐ Want   Orig. Ret. $6.95   **MIB** Sec. Mkt. **$14**

QX 572-6   CHILD'S FOURTH CHRISTMAS:
TEDDY BEAR YEARS COLLECTION
Comments: Handcrafted, 3" tall, Dated 1994.
Design is repeated from 1993.   **Artist:** John Francis (Collin)
☐ Purchased 19__Pd $_____MIB   NB   DB   BNT
☐ Want   Orig. Ret. $6.95   **MIB** Sec. Mkt. **$17**

QX 572-3   CHILD'S THIRD CHRISTMAS:
TEDDY BEAR YEARS COLLECTION
Comments: Handcrafted, 2-1/2" tall, Dated 1994.
Design is repeated from 1993.   **Artist:** John Francis (Collin)
☐ Purchased 19__Pd $_____MIB   NB   DB   BNT
☐ Want   Orig. Ret. $6.95   **MIB** Sec. Mkt. **$16**

QLX 739-3   CHRIS MOUSE JELLY
Comments: **Tenth in Series,** Lighted, Handcrafted, 2-13/16" tall.
Dated 1994. Chris Mouse dips into "Lite Jelly From the Kitchen of Chris
Mouse" to add a bread and jelly sandwich to his evening cheese snack.
Artist: Anita Marra Rogers
☐ Purchased 19__Pd $_____MIB   NB   DB   BNT
☐ Want   Orig. Ret. $12.00   **MIB** Sec. Mkt. **$28**

QX 542-2   CLASSIC AMERICAN CARS:
1957 CHEVROLET BEL AIR
Comments: **Fourth in Series,** Handcrafted, 1-3/8" tall, Dated 1994.
A well-liked addition to a very popular series.
Artist: Don Palmiter
☐ Purchased 19__Pd $_____MIB   NB   DB   BNT
☐ Want   Orig. Ret. $12.95   **MIB** Sec. Mkt. **$32**

QX 593-3   COACH
Comments: Handcrafted, 3-1/8" tall, Dated 1994.
A happy coach is ready to go with his green gym bag and whistle.
Artist: Duane Unruh
☐ Purchased 19__Pd $_____MIB   NB   DB   BNT
☐ Want   Orig. Ret. $7.95   **MIB** Sec. Mkt. **$12.50**

QX 539-6   COCK-A-DOODLE CHRISTMAS
Comments: Handcrafted, 3-3/16" tall, Dated 1994.
A rooster crows his Christmas greeting from atop a pony.
Artist: LaDene Votruba
☐ Purchased 19__Pd $_____MIB   NB   DB   BNT
☐ Want   Orig. Ret. $8.95   **MIB** Sec. Mkt. **$20**

QX 589-3   COLORS OF JOY
Comments: Handcrafted, 2-3/16" tall, Dated 1994.
A little mouse stands in a tray of paints and adds his holiday sentiment
to the cover.   **Artist:** Ed Seale
☐ Purchased 19__Pd $_____MIB   NB   DB   BNT
☐ Want   Orig. Ret. $7.95   **MIB** Sec. Mkt. **$22.50**

QLX 742-6   CONVERSATIONS WITH SANTA
Comments: Motion and Voice, Handcrafted, 3-1/8" tall, Dated 1994.
Santa's mouth moves as he speaks one of four messages.
Artist: Ed Seale
☐ Purchased 19__Pd $_____MIB   NB   DB   BNT
☐ Want   Orig. Ret. $28.00   **MIB** Sec. Mkt. **$50**

QLX 741-6   COUNTRY SHOWTIME
Comments: Blinking Lights and Motion, Handcrafted 4-3/16" tall.
Dated 1994. This jointed "wooden" Santa dances at center stage.
Artist: Linda Sickman
☐ Purchased 19__Pd $_____MIB   NB   DB   BNT
☐ Want   Orig. Ret. $22.00   **MIB** Sec. Mkt. **$46**

QX 527-3   CRAYOLA® CRAYON:
BRIGHT PLAYFUL COLORS
Comments: **Sixth in Series,** Handcrafted, 3-3/8" tall, Dated 1994.
A Teddy Bear swings on his colorful playground set while waiting for
Santa. Popular series. **Artist:** Ken Crow
☐ Purchased 19__Pd $_____MIB   NB   DB   BNT
☐ Want   Orig. Ret. $10.95   **MIB** Sec. Mkt. **$25**

**There is no such thing as bad weather . . .
there are just different kinds of
good weather.**

QX 546-3   DAD ☐
Comments: Handcrafted, 2-5/16" tall, Dated 1994.
Dad has won a loving cup. Of course he's the "World's Greatest Dad!"
Artist: Anita Marra Rogers

☐ Purchased 19 __ Pd $_____ MIB   NB   DB   BNT
☐ Want   Orig. Ret. $7.95   **MIB** Sec. Mkt. **$16**

QX 547-3   DAD-TO-BE ☐
Comments: Handcrafted, 2-9/16" tall, Dated 1994.
The soon-to-be papa, dressed in his red and white striped night shirt, holds a package entitled "All Night Takeout" in one hand and his car keys in the other. **Artist:** Sharon Pike

☐ Purchased 19 __ Pd $_____ MIB   NB   DB   BNT
☐ Want   Orig. Ret. $7.95   **MIB** Sec. Mkt. **$16**

QX 562-3   DAUGHTER ☐
Comments: Handcrafted, 2-13/16" tall, Dated 1994.
Daughter dinosaur is having lots of Christmas fun on her new roller blades. **Artist:** Patricia Andrews

☐ Purchased 19 __ Pd $_____ MIB   NB   DB   BNT
☐ Want   Orig. Ret. $6.95   **MIB** Sec. Mkt. **$14**

QX 580-6   DEAR SANTA MOUSE ☐
Comments: Handcrafted, 2-15/16" tall and 1-11/16" tall, Dated 1994.
Set of two hang-together ornaments. While one mouse holds the ink bottle, the other writes their letter, "Dear Santa, We know you're very busy and we'd help you if we could, but we really thought you'd want to hear -- this year we've been real good! X" **Artist:** Ken Crow

☐ Purchased 19 __ Pd $_____ MIB   NB   DB   BNT
☐ Want   Orig. Ret. $14.95   **MIB** Sec. Mkt. **$28**

QX533-6   EAGER FOR CHRISTMAS ☐
Comments: Handcrafted
The whimsical Tender Touches beaver chats happily with a little blue-bird perched atop his Christmas tree. This exclusive Premiere ornament was available for purchase during the Keepsake Ornament Premiere in July, 1994. **Artist:** Ed Seale

☐ Purchased 19 __ Pd $_____ MIB   NB   DB   BNT
☐ Want   Orig. Ret. $15.00   **MIB** Sec. Mkt. **$24**

QLX 748-6   EAGLE HAS LANDED, THE ☐
Comments: Light and Voice, Handcrafted, 4-1/2" tall, Dated 1994.
An American astronaut places the American flag on the surface of the moon. Commemorates the 25th anniversary of the first lunar landing. Caption: "Here men from the planet earth first set foot upon the moon, July 1969 A.D. We came in peace for all mankind." Features astronaut Neil Armstrong repeating his message, "Houston, Tranquility Base here. The Eagle has landed... One small step for man, one giant leap for mankind." **Artist:** Ed Seale

☐ Purchased 19 __ Pd $_____ MIB   NB   DB   BNT
☐ Want   Orig. Ret. $24.00   **MIB** Sec. Mkt. **$32**

QX 583-3   EXTRA-SPECIAL DELIVERY ☐
Comments: Handcrafted, 2-1/8" tall, Dated 1994.
This special mail carrier truly is "First Class."
Artist: Ken Crow

☐ Purchased 19 __ Pd $_____ MIB   NB   DB   BNT
☐ Want   Orig. Ret. $7.95   **MIB** Sec. Mkt. **$18**

QX 526-3   FABULOUS DECADE ☐
Comments: **Fifth in Series,** Handcrafted and Brass, 2" tall. Dated 1994. A white Christmas bunny heralds the year.
Artist: Ed Seale

☐ Purchased 19 __ Pd $_____ MIB   NB   DB   BNT
☐ Want   Orig. Ret. $7.95   **MIB** Sec. Mkt. **$20**

QX 595-3   FEELIN' GROOVY ☐
Comments: Handcrafted, 2-11/16" tall, Dated 1994.
Santa is wearin' his shades and flashing a peace sign to all he meets.

☐ Purchased 19 __ Pd $_____ MIB   NB   DB   BNT
☐ Want   Orig. Ret. $7.95   **MIB** Sec. Mkt. **$21**

QX 579-3   FELIZ NAVIDAD ☐
Comments: Handcrafted, 2-13/16" tall, Dated 1994.
A little Spanish Chihuahua in his sombrero awakens from his siesta and pops up from a gaily painted Mexican pot.
Artist: Anita Marra Rogers

☐ Purchased 19 __ Pd $_____ MIB   NB   DB   BNT
☐ Want   Orig. Ret. $8.95   **MIB** Sec. Mkt. **$18.50**

**Cleaning your house while the kids
are still growing is like shoveling the sidewalks
while it's still snowing.**

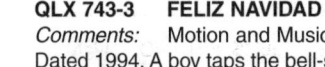

QLX 743-3   FELIZ NAVIDAD

Comments: Motion and Music, Handcrafted, 3-1/8" tall.
Dated 1994. A boy taps the bell-shaped piñata with a stick and the children dance around the sombrero. Plays "Feliz Navidad."
Artist: Linda Crow

☐ Purchased 19 __ Pd $_____ MIB   NB   DB   BNT
☐ Want   Orig. Ret. $28.00   **MIB** Sec. Mkt. **$35**

QX 584-6   FOLLOW THE SUN

Comments: Handcrafted, 3-13/16" tall, Dated 1994.
Riding a reindeer and sleigh weather vane, this bird is following "Route 94" to "Lake Wannagothere." **Artist:** Ken Crow

☐ Purchased 19 __ Pd $_____ MIB   NB   DB   BNT
☐ Want   Orig. Ret. $8.95   **MIB** Sec. Mkt. **$18**

QX 561-3   FOR MY GRANDMA: PHOTOHOLDER

Comments: Handcrafted, 3-9/16" tall, Dated 1994.
Grandma will be delighted with this brightly decorated Christmas tree photoholder. Caption: "1994 I Love you! From _____"
Artist: Donna Lee

☐ Purchased 19 __ Pd $_____ MIB   NB   DB   BNT
☐ Want   Orig. Ret. $6.95   **MIB** Sec. Mkt. **$14**

QLX 743-6   FOREST FROLICS

Comments: **Sixth in Series,** Light and Motion, Handcrafted.
4-1/8" tall, Dated 1994.The forest animals play happily around the Christmas tree. **Artist:** Sharon Pike

☐ Purchased 19 __ Pd $_____ MIB   NB   DB   BNT
☐ Want   Orig. Ret. $28.00   **MIB** Sec. Mkt. **$30**

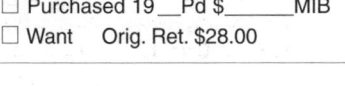

QX 500-3   FRED AND BARNEY: THE FLINTSTONES®

Comments: Handcrafted, 2-5/8" tall, Dated 1994.
The ever-popular duo are headed out in their Stone Age car.
Artist: Dill Rhodus

☐ Purchased 19 __ Pd $_____ MIB   NB   DB   BNT
☐ Want   Orig. Ret. $14.95   **MIB** Sec. Mkt. **$25**

QX 568-6   FRIENDLY PUSH

Comments: Handcrafted, 3-1/8" tall, Dated 1994.
As one little brown mouse sits inside an ice skate, another little gray mouse gives a friendly little push. **Artist:** Bob Seidler

☐ Purchased 19 __ Pd $_____ MIB   NB   DB   BNT
☐ Want   Orig. Ret. $8.95   **MIB** Sec. Mkt. **$17**

QX 476-6   FRIENDSHIP SUNDAE

Comments: Handcrafted, 3-1/4" tall, Dated 1994.
These two white mice must love lots of Hershey's chocolate on their ice cream! Yum, yum! **Artist:** Linda Sickman

☐ Purchased 19 __ Pd $_____ MIB   NB   DB   BNT
☐ Want   Orig. Ret. $10.95   **MIB** Sec. Mkt. **$23**

QX 529-3   FROSTY FRIENDS

Comments: **Fifteenth in Series,** Handcrafted, 2-1/8" tall.
Dated 1994. Little Eskimo holds a wreath while his polar bear friend jumps through. **Artist:** Ed Seale

☐ Purchased 19 __ Pd $_____ MIB   NB   DB   BNT
☐ Want   Orig. Ret. $9.95   **MIB** Sec. Mkt. **$24**

QX 598-6   GARDEN ELVES COLLECTION: DAISY DAYS

Comments: Handcrafted, 2-7/8" tall.
Summer daisies always brighten up a room, and this blond haired lass is bringing some home to share. **Artist:** Robert Chad

☐ Purchased 19 __ Pd $_____ MIB   NB   DB   BNT
☐ Want   Orig. Ret. $9.95   **MIB** Sec. Mkt. **$12**

QX 599-3   GARDEN ELVES COLLECTION: HARVEST JOY

Comments: Handcrafted, 2-13/16" tall.
This little lad, dressed in green and tan, is bringing home the bounty of a good autumn harvest. **Artist:** Robert Chad

☐ Purchased 19 __ Pd $_____ MIB   NB   DB   BNT
☐ Want   Orig. Ret. $9.95   **MIB** Sec. Mkt. **$12**

QX 598-3   GARDEN ELVES COLLECTION:
TULIP TIME

Comments: Handcrafted, 2-5/16" tall.
A pot full of red tulips testifies to this young lady's green thumb. She represents Spring. **Artist:** Robert Chad

☐ Purchased 19 __ Pd $_____ MIB   NB   DB   BNT
☐ Want   Orig. Ret. $9.95   **MIB** Sec. Mkt. **$12**

QX 597-6   GARDEN ELVES COLLECTION:
YULETIDE CHEER

Comments: Handcrafted, 2-13/16" tall.
This little lad is getting ready for Christmas. He has a miniature tree in one hand and a holly leaf in the other. **Artist:** Robert Chad

☐ Purchased 19 __ Pd $_____ MIB   NB   DB   BNT
☐ Want   Orig. Ret. $9.95   **MIB** Sec. Mkt. **$14**

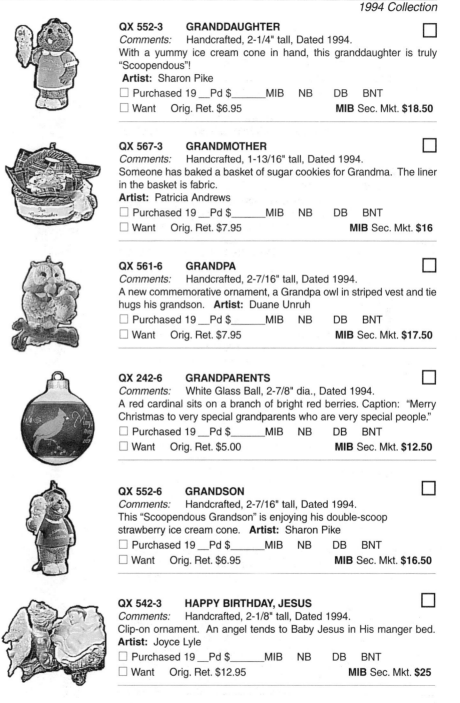

QX 575-3   GARFIELD
Comments: Handcrafted, 2-1/2" tall, Dated 1994.
Garfield is heading off to bed with his teddy, candle and Christmas stocking for Santa to fill.
☐ Purchased 19___Pd $_____MIB   NB   DB   BNT
☐ Want   Orig. Ret. $12.95   **MIB** Sec. Mkt. **$21**

QX 597-3   GENTLE NURSE
Comments: Handcrafted, 2-7/16" tall, Dated 1994.
The nurse has her patient's complete confidence as she bandages his paw.   **Artist:** Joyce Lyle
☐ Purchased 19___Pd $_____MIB   NB   DB   BNT
☐ Want   Orig. Ret. $6.95   **MIB** Sec. Mkt. **$18**

QLX 738-2   GINGERBREAD FANTASY
Comments: Light, Motion and Music, Handcrafted, 4-1/4" tall.
Dated 1994. The gingerbread people, peppermint above the top window and peppermint sticks all turn. Plays "Dance Of The Sugar Plum Fairy." More popular than most past light and motion ornaments. Price down from $85-90 in '96. **Artist:** Don Palmiter
☐ Purchased 19___Pd $_____MIB   NB   DB   BNT
☐ Want   Orig. Ret. $44.00   **MIB** Sec. Mkt. **$80**

QX 445-3   GODCHILD
Comments: Handcrafted, 3-1/2" tall, Dated 1994.
Push gently and the child will swing from the golden star. The caption reads, "A Godchild... a treasure on earth from heaven above."
Artist: Anita Marra Rogers
☐ Purchased 19___Pd $_____MIB   NB   DB   BNT
☐ Want   Orig. Ret. $8.95   **MIB** Sec. Mkt. **$16**

QX 242-3   GODPARENT
Comments: Glass Ball, 2-7/8" dia., Dated 1994.
Mary Hamilton angel designs frame the caption, "A Godparent is a special blessing."
☐ Purchased 19___Pd $_____MIB   NB   DB   BNT
☐ Want   Orig. Ret. $5.00   **MIB** Sec. Mkt. **$19.50**

QX 567-6   GRANDCHILD'S FIRST CHRISTMAS
Comments: Handcrafted, 3" tall, Dated 1994.
This clip-on ornament features a baby mouse sleeping peacefully on a baby blanket.   **Artist:** Duane Unruh
☐ Purchased 19___Pd $_____MIB   NB   DB   BNT
☐ Want   Orig. Ret. $7.95   **MIB** Sec. Mkt. **$16**

QX 552-3   GRANDDAUGHTER
Comments: Handcrafted, 2-1/4" tall, Dated 1994.
With a yummy ice cream cone in hand, this granddaughter is truly "Scoopendous"!
Artist: Sharon Pike
☐ Purchased 19___Pd $_____MIB   NB   DB   BNT
☐ Want   Orig. Ret. $6.95   **MIB** Sec. Mkt. **$18.50**

QX 567-3   GRANDMOTHER
Comments: Handcrafted, 1-13/16" tall, Dated 1994.
Someone has baked a basket of sugar cookies for Grandma. The liner in the basket is fabric.
Artist: Patricia Andrews
☐ Purchased 19___Pd $_____MIB   NB   DB   BNT
☐ Want   Orig. Ret. $7.95   **MIB** Sec. Mkt. **$16**

QX 561-6   GRANDPA
Comments: Handcrafted, 2-7/16" tall, Dated 1994.
A new commemorative ornament, a Grandpa owl in striped vest and tie hugs his grandson.   **Artist:** Duane Unruh
☐ Purchased 19___Pd $_____MIB   NB   DB   BNT
☐ Want   Orig. Ret. $7.95   **MIB** Sec. Mkt. **$17.50**

QX 242-6   GRANDPARENTS
Comments: White Glass Ball, 2-7/8" dia., Dated 1994.
A red cardinal sits on a branch of bright red berries. Caption: "Merry Christmas to very special grandparents who are very special people."
☐ Purchased 19___Pd $_____MIB   NB   DB   BNT
☐ Want   Orig. Ret. $5.00   **MIB** Sec. Mkt. **$12.50**

QX 552-6   GRANDSON
Comments: Handcrafted, 2-7/16" tall, Dated 1994.
This "Scoopendous Grandson" is enjoying his double-scoop strawberry ice cream cone.   **Artist:** Sharon Pike
☐ Purchased 19___Pd $_____MIB   NB   DB   BNT
☐ Want   Orig. Ret. $6.95   **MIB** Sec. Mkt. **$16.50**

QX 542-3   HAPPY BIRTHDAY, JESUS
Comments: Handcrafted, 2-1/8" tall, Dated 1994.
Clip-on ornament. An angel tends to Baby Jesus in His manger bed.
Artist: Joyce Lyle
☐ Purchased 19___Pd $_____MIB   NB   DB   BNT
☐ Want   Orig. Ret. $12.95   **MIB** Sec. Mkt. **$25**

QX 526-6   HEART OF CHRISTMAS   ☐
Comments: **Fifth and Final in Series,** Handcrafted, 2" tall, Dated 1994.
It's Christmas and Mama has a feast in store for her family. **Artist:** Ed Seale
☐ Purchased 19___Pd $_____MIB   NB   DB   BNT
☐ Want   Orig. Ret. $14.95   **MIB** Sec. Mkt. **$21**

QX 440-6   HEARTS IN HARMONY   ☐
Comments: Porcelain, 3" tall, Dated 1994.
Boys and girls of different nationalities join hearts in unity to form a unique snowflake pattern.   **Artist:** Patricia Andrews
☐ Purchased 19___Pd $_____MIB   NB   DB   BNT
☐ Want   Orig. Ret. $10.95   **MIB** Sec. Mkt. **$18**

QX 553-6   HELPFUL SHEPHERD   ☐
Comments: Handcrafted/Brass Staff, 2-11/16" tall.
A shepherd carries his lamb across his shoulders.
Artist: Robert Chad
☐ Purchased 19___Pd $_____MIB   NB   DB   BNT
☐ Want   Orig. Ret. $8.95   **MIB** Sec. Mkt. **$18**

**QX 529-6   HERE COMES SANTA:
MAKIN' TRACTOR TRACKS**   ☐
Comments: **Sixteenth in Series,** Handcrafted, 2-11/16" tall.
Dated 1994. Santa plows the "back forty" with his "Reindeer" tractor. This piece is somewhat scarce. **Artist:** Linda Sickman
☐ Purchased 19___Pd $_____MIB   NB   DB   BNT
☐ Want   Orig. Ret. $14.95   **MIB** Sec. Mkt. **$45**

QX 521-6   HOLIDAY BARBIE™   ☐
Comments: **Second in Series,** Handcrafted, 3-3/8" tall, Dated 1994. Barbie glitters in her gold and ivory gown. She coordinated with the Holiday Barbie Doll which was offered in 1994 and the 1995 Hallmark stocking hanger.
☐ Purchased 19___Pd $_____MIB   NB   DB   BNT
☐ Want   Orig. Ret. $14.95   **MIB** Sec. Mkt. **$55**

QX 582-6   HOLIDAY PATROL   ☐
Comments: Handcrafted, 2-1/2" tall, Dated 1994.
"Stop for Christmas" is the message of this policeman.
Artist: Dill Rhodus
☐ Purchased 19___Pd $_____MIB   NB   DB   BNT
☐ Want   Orig. Ret. $8.95   **MIB** Sec. Mkt. **$15.50**

QXC 482-3   HOLIDAY PURSUIT: KEEPSAKE CLUB   ☐
Comments: Handcrafted, 2-7/8" tall, Dated 1994.
Super sleuth Keepsake Bear is hot on the trail of the 1994 ornaments.
Artist: John Francis (Collin)
☐ Purchased 19___Pd $_____MIB   NB   DB   BNT
☐ Want   Orig. Ret.: Came with Club Membership
    MIB Sec. Mkt. **$22**

QX 594-6   ICE SHOW   ☐
Comments: Handcrafted, 2-7/8" tall, Dated 1994.
A little redbird does amazing tricks skating atop an ice cube. Many of the ice cubes are found with bubbles in them. A perfect cube with no bubble has a projected value of $45.   **Artist:** Patricia Andrews
☐ Purchased 19___Pd $_____MIB   NB   DB   BNT
☐ Want   Orig. Ret. $7.95   **MIB** Sec. Mkt. **$17.50**

QX 576-3   IN THE PINK   ☐
Comments: Handcrafted, 2-3/4" tall, Dated 1994.
A pink flamingo lounges in the shade of a palm tree, sipping his drink.
Artist: Patricia Andrews
☐ Purchased 19___Pd $_____MIB   NB   DB   BNT
☐ Want   Orig. Ret. $9.95   **MIB** Sec. Mkt. **$20**

QX 585-6   IT'S A STRIKE   ☐
Comments: Handcrafted, 2-13/16" tall, Dated 1994.
This monkey will have a perfect score if he continues to bowl strikes at "Santa Claus Lanes." **Artist:** Bob Siedler
☐ Purchased 19___Pd $_____MIB   NB   DB   BNT
☐ Want   Orig. Ret. $8.95   **MIB** Sec. Mkt. **$18**

QX 578-3   JINGLE BELL BAND   ☐
Comments: Handcrafted, 4" tall, Dated 1994.
Our musical mice in the band play the bells -- jingle bells, that is!
Artist: Ken Crow
☐ Purchased 19___Pd $_____MIB   NB   DB   BNT
☐ Want   Orig. Ret. $10.95   **MIB** Sec. Mkt. **$26**

QXC 483-3   JOLLY HOLLY SANTA: KEEPSAKE CLUB   ☐
Comments: Handcrafted/Hand Painted, 3-1/8" tall, Dated 1994, Limited Edition 16,398 pieces produced, Wood Display Stand.
This Santa depicts the essence of a Victorian Christmas with a bag full of toys for all the girls and boys. **Artist:** Joyce A. Lyle
☐ Purchased 19 ___Pd $_____MIB   NB   DB   BNT
☐ Want   Orig. Ret. $22.00   **MIB** Sec. Mkt. **$50**

QX 447-3   JOYOUS SONG ☐
Comments: Handcrafted, 3-9/16" tall, Dated 1994.
An African-American girl in a red choir robe sings a happy melody.
Artist: Patricia Andrews
☐ Purchased 19 __Pd $_____MIB   NB   DB   BNT
☐ Want   Orig. Ret. $8.95   **MIB** Sec. Mkt. **$18.50**

QX 575-6   JUMP-ALONG JACKALOPE ☐
Comments: Handcrafted, 3-7/16" tall, Dated 1994.
The elusive jackalope has been captured in a Keepsake ornament.
Artist: John Francis (Collin)
☐ Purchased 19 __Pd $_____MIB   NB   DB   BNT
☐ Want   Orig. Ret. $8.95   **MIB** Sec. Mkt. **$18**

QX 541-3   KEEP ON MOWIN' ☐
Comments: Handcrafted, 3-1/8" tall, Dated 1994.
Santa, in t-shirt, shorts and sandals, pushes a mower; the wheels and blades of the mower turn freely. **Artist:** Bob Siedler
☐ Purchased 19 __Pd $_____MIB   NB   DB   BNT
☐ Want   Orig. Ret. $8.95   **MIB** Sec. Mkt. **$18**

QX 591-6   KICKIN' ROO ☐
Comments: Handcrafted, 2-11/16" tall, Dated 1994.
A little Roo in his red and white jersey is a big hit on the soccer field.
Artist: Bob Siedler
☐ Purchased 19 __Pd $_____MIB   NB   DB   BNT
☐ Want   Orig. Ret. $7.95   **MIB** Sec. Mkt. **$15**

QX 542-6   KIDDIE CAR CLASSICS: MURRAY® CHAMPION ☐
Comments: ***FIRST IN SERIES***, Cast Metal, 1-7/8" tall.
Dated 1994. This ornament series is similar to the larger Hallmark Kiddie Car Classics. There was a first in series Murray Champion in the mini line in 1995. Very popular! **Artist:** Don Palmiter
☐ Purchased 19 __Pd $_____MIB   NB   DB   BNT
☐ Want   Orig. Ret. $13.95   **MIB** Sec. Mkt. **$50-$60**

QX 541-6   KITTY'S CATAMARAN ☐
Comments: Handcrafted, 4-9/16" tall, Dated 1994.
Kitty is taking his sailboat, the "Cat's Meow," out for a holiday ride.
Artist: Ed Seale
☐ Purchased 19 __Pd $_____MIB   NB   DB   BNT
☐ Want   Orig. Ret. $10.95   **MIB** Sec. Mkt. **$18**

QLX 741-3   KRINGLE TROLLEY ☐
Comments: Light, Handcrafted, 3-5/16" tall, Dated 1994.
Santa's picking up travelers on the "Kringle Christmas Trolley" up and down the "Jingle Bell Lane Snow Express." **Artist:** Ken Crow
☐ Purchased 19 __Pd $_____MIB   NB   DB   BNT
☐ Want   Orig. Ret. $20.00   **MIB** Sec. Mkt. **$45**

QX 588-6   KRINGLE'S KAYAK ☐
Comments: Handcrafted, 1-13/16" tall, Dated 1994.
Some of Santa's deliveries cannot be reached by sleigh, so he takes a kayak. **Artist:** Ed Seale
☐ Purchased 19 __Pd $_____MIB   NB   DB   BNT
☐ Want   Orig. Ret. $7.95   **MIB** Sec. Mkt. **$20**

QX 540-6   LION KING, THE:
               MUFASA AND SIMBA ☐
Comments: Handcrafted, 3" tall.
Father and son enjoy their time together, playing and learning about life in the wild.
☐ Purchased 19 __Pd $_____MIB   NB   DB   BNT
☐ Want   Orig. Ret. $14.95   **MIB** Sec. Mkt. **$28**

QX 530-3   LION KING, THE:
               SIMBA AND NALA ☐
Comments: Handcrafted, 2" tall, 2-3/8" tall.
Set of two hang-together ornaments. The young lion prince and his best friend Nala love to play together.
☐ Purchased 19 __Pd $_____MIB   NB   DB   BNT
☐ Want   Orig. Ret. $12.95   **MIB** Sec. Mkt. **$25**

Ho, Ho, Ho… **Three Santas gathered at the base of Peggy Baer's Hallmark Ornament Christmas tree to wish us all a very Merry Christmas.**

**QLX 751-3   LION KING, THE:
SIMBA, SARABI AND MUFASA**

Comments: Light and Music, Handcrafted, 4-1/4" tall.
Mufasa's family is complete with the birth of the new prince, Simba.
Plays "Circle of Life." With Sound – **Recalled** defective sound. **Artist:**
Ken Crow

☐ Purchased 19 __Pd $_____MIB   NB   DB   BNT
☐ Want   Orig. Ret. $32.00   **MIB** Sec. Mkt. **$35**

**QLX 751-6   LION KING, THE:
SIMBA, SARABI AND MUFASA**

Comments: Lighted, Handcrafted, 4-1/4" tall.
Mufasa's family is complete with the birth of the new prince. No Music.
Artist: Ken Crow

☐ Purchased 19 __Pd $_____MIB   NB   DB   BNT
☐ Want   Orig. Ret. $20.00   **MIB** Sec. Mkt. **$30**

**QX 536-6   LION KING, THE:
TIMON AND PUMBAA**

Comments: Handcrafted, 2-1/4" tall.
The wart hog and his little friend frolic without a care in the world.

☐ Purchased 19 __Pd $_____MIB   NB   DB   BNT
☐ Want   Orig. Ret. $8.95   **MIB** Sec. Mkt. **$22**

**QX 541-5   LOONEY TUNES COLLECTION:
DAFFY DUCK**

Comments: Handcrafted, 3" tall.
Daffy is trying out an angel robe and wings. His halo is brass.
Artist: Don Palmiter

☐ Purchased 19 __Pd $_____MIB   NB   DB   BNT
☐ Want   Orig. Ret. $8.95   **MIB** Sec. Mkt. **$21**

**QX 560-2   LOONEY TUNES COLLECTION:
ROAD RUNNER AND WILE E. COYOTE**

Comments: Handcrafted, 3-1/2" tall.
The crafty coyote has a special gift for the road runner. Watch out!
There's a wire attached! **Artist:** Robert Chad

☐ Purchased 19 __Pd $_____MIB   NB   DB   BNT
☐ Want   Orig. Ret. $12.95   **MIB** Sec. Mkt. **$28**

**QX 534-3   LOONEY TUNES COLLECTION:
SPEEDY GONZALES**

Comments: Handcrafted, 1-5/8" tall.
Speedy is hoping to get even more zip... on his red skis.
Artist: Don Palmiter

☐ Purchased 19 __Pd $_____MIB   NB   DB   BNT
☐ Want   Orig. Ret. $8.95   **MIB** Sec. Mkt. **$19.50**

**QX 560-5   LOONEY TUNES COLLECTION:
TASMANIAN DEVIL**

Comments: Handcrafted, 2-3/8" tall.
Taz is getting ready for Christmas -- right now he's all tangled up in the
lights. It was very popular with Taz collectors and sold out early. It continues to be sought after. **Artist:** Don Palmiter

☐ Purchased 19 __Pd $_____MIB   NB   DB   BNT
☐ Want   Orig. Ret. $8.95   **MIB** Sec. Mkt. **$55**

**QX 534-6   LOONEY TUNES COLLECTION:
YOSEMITE SAM**

Comments: Handcrafted, 2-7/16" tall.
Yosemite Sam is jumpin' up and down with Christmas joy, a candy cane
in each hand. **Artist:** Don Palmiter

☐ Purchased 19 __Pd $_____MIB   NB   DB   BNT
☐ Want   Orig. Ret. $8.95   **MIB** Sec. Mkt. **$18.50**

QX 545-6   LOU RANKIN SEAL

Comments: Handcrafted, 1-1/8" tall.
Lou Rankin's distinctive artistry is shown in this clip-on ornament.
Artist: Ron Bishop

☐ Purchased 19 __Pd $_____MIB   NB   DB   BNT
☐ Want   Orig. Ret. $9.95   **MIB** Sec. Mkt. **$20**

QX 481-3   LUCINDA AND TEDDY

Comments: Special Edition, Handcrafted/Fabric, 2-1/2" tall.
Dated 1994. Lucinda shares a Christmas gift with her favorite teddy.
Artist: Duane Unruh

☐ Purchased 19 __Pd $_____MIB   NB   DB   BNT
☐ Want   Orig. Ret. $21.75   **MIB** Sec. Mkt. **$42**

QX 588-3   MAGIC CARPET RIDE

Comments: Handcrafted, 1-7/8" tall, Dated 1994.
Santa, with his bag of toys, is making his Christmas Eve rounds with-
out his reindeer... he's flying on a magic carpet.
Artist: Ed Seale

☐ Purchased 19 __Pd $_____MIB   NB   DB   BNT
☐ Want   Orig. Ret. $7.95   **MIB** Sec. Mkt. **$22**

**A man wonders what the future will hold in store -
a woman wonders what the stores will hold in the future.**

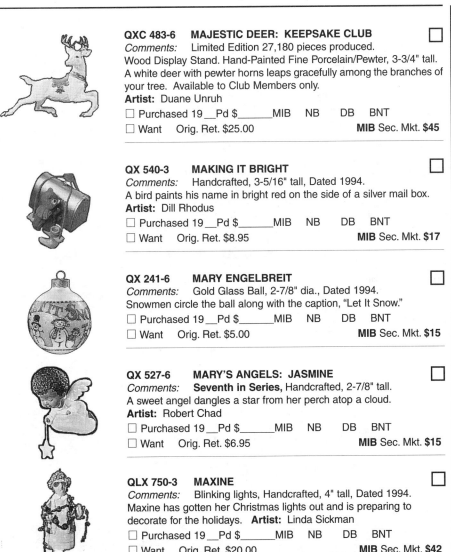

QXC 483-6 MAJESTIC DEER: KEEPSAKE CLUB
Comments: Limited Edition 27,180 pieces produced.
Wood Display Stand. Hand-Painted Fine Porcelain/Pewter, 3-3/4" tall.
A white deer with pewter horns leaps gracefully among the branches of
your tree. Available to Club Members only.
Artist: Duane Unruh
☐ Purchased 19 __ Pd $_____ MIB   NB   DB   BNT
☐ Want   Orig. Ret. $25.00   **MIB** Sec. Mkt. **$45**

QX 540-3 MAKING IT BRIGHT
Comments: Handcrafted, 3-5/16" tall, Dated 1994.
A bird paints his name in bright red on the side of a silver mail box.
Artist: Dill Rhodus
☐ Purchased 19 __ Pd $_____ MIB   NB   DB   BNT
☐ Want   Orig. Ret. $8.95   **MIB** Sec. Mkt. **$17**

QX 241-6 MARY ENGELBREIT
Comments: Gold Glass Ball, 2-7/8" dia., Dated 1994.
Snowmen circle the ball along with the caption, "Let It Snow."
☐ Purchased 19 __ Pd $_____ MIB   NB   DB   BNT
☐ Want   Orig. Ret. $5.00   **MIB** Sec. Mkt. **$15**

QX 527-6 MARY'S ANGELS: JASMINE
Comments: **Seventh in Series,** Handcrafted, 2-7/8" tall.
A sweet angel dangles a star from her perch atop a cloud.
Artist: Robert Chad
☐ Purchased 19 __ Pd $_____ MIB   NB   DB   BNT
☐ Want   Orig. Ret. $6.95   **MIB** Sec. Mkt. **$15**

QLX 750-3 MAXINE
Comments: Blinking lights, Handcrafted, 4" tall, Dated 1994.
Maxine has gotten her Christmas lights out and is preparing to
decorate for the holidays. **Artist:** Linda Sickman
☐ Purchased 19 __ Pd $_____ MIB   NB   DB   BNT
☐ Want   Orig. Ret. $20.00   **MIB** Sec. Mkt. **$42**

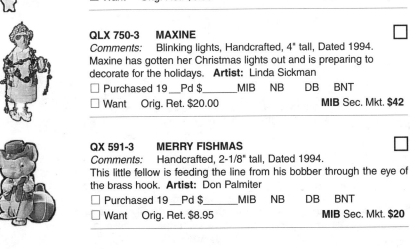

QX 591-3 MERRY FISHMAS
Comments: Handcrafted, 2-1/8" tall, Dated 1994.
This little fellow is feeding the line from his bobber through the eye of
the brass hook. **Artist:** Don Palmiter
☐ Purchased 19 __ Pd $_____ MIB   NB   DB   BNT
☐ Want   Orig. Ret. $8.95   **MIB** Sec. Mkt. **$20**

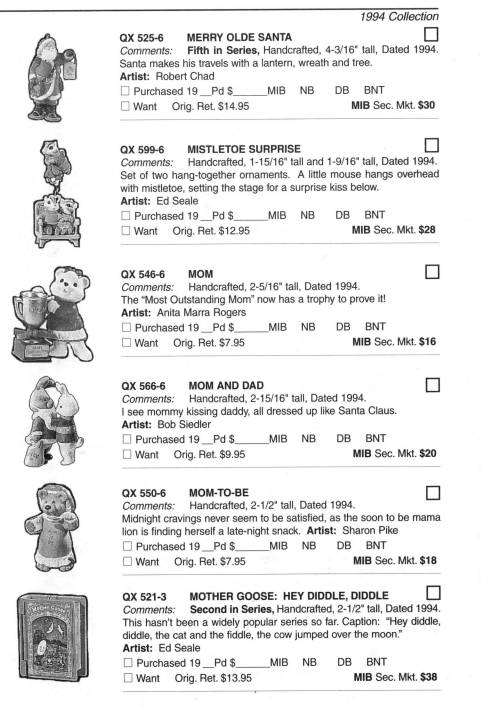

QX 525-6 MERRY OLDE SANTA
Comments: **Fifth in Series,** Handcrafted, 4-3/16" tall, Dated 1994.
Santa makes his travels with a lantern, wreath and tree.
Artist: Robert Chad
☐ Purchased 19 __ Pd $_____ MIB   NB   DB   BNT
☐ Want   Orig. Ret. $14.95   **MIB** Sec. Mkt. **$30**

QX 599-6 MISTLETOE SURPRISE
Comments: Handcrafted, 1-15/16" tall and 1-9/16" tall, Dated 1994.
Set of two hang-together ornaments. A little mouse hangs overhead
with mistletoe, setting the stage for a surprise kiss below.
Artist: Ed Seale
☐ Purchased 19 __ Pd $_____ MIB   NB   DB   BNT
☐ Want   Orig. Ret. $12.95   **MIB** Sec. Mkt. **$28**

QX 546-6 MOM
Comments: Handcrafted, 2-5/16" tall, Dated 1994.
The "Most Outstanding Mom" now has a trophy to prove it!
Artist: Anita Marra Rogers
☐ Purchased 19 __ Pd $_____ MIB   NB   DB   BNT
☐ Want   Orig. Ret. $7.95   **MIB** Sec. Mkt. **$16**

QX 566-6 MOM AND DAD
Comments: Handcrafted, 2-15/16" tall, Dated 1994.
I see mommy kissing daddy, all dressed up like Santa Claus.
Artist: Bob Siedler
☐ Purchased 19 __ Pd $_____ MIB   NB   DB   BNT
☐ Want   Orig. Ret. $9.95   **MIB** Sec. Mkt. **$20**

QX 550-6 MOM-TO-BE
Comments: Handcrafted, 2-1/2" tall, Dated 1994.
Midnight cravings never seem to be satisfied, as the soon to be mama
lion is finding herself a late-night snack. **Artist:** Sharon Pike
☐ Purchased 19 __ Pd $_____ MIB   NB   DB   BNT
☐ Want   Orig. Ret. $7.95   **MIB** Sec. Mkt. **$18**

QX 521-3 MOTHER GOOSE: HEY DIDDLE, DIDDLE
Comments: **Second in Series,** Handcrafted, 2-1/2" tall, Dated 1994.
This hasn't been a widely popular series so far. Caption: "Hey diddle,
diddle, the cat and the fiddle, the cow jumped over the moon."
Artist: Ed Seale
☐ Purchased 19 __ Pd $_____ MIB   NB   DB   BNT
☐ Want   Orig. Ret. $13.95   **MIB** Sec. Mkt. **$38**

QX 528-3 MR. AND MRS. CLAUS:
A HANDWARMING PRESENT
Comments: **Ninth in Series,** Handcrafted, 3-1/4" tall.
Dated 1994. "To Santa." Santa receives a pair of mittens from a loving
Mrs. Claus. **Artist:** Duane Unruh
☐ Purchased 19 __ Pd $_____ MIB   NB   DB   BNT
☐ Want   Orig. Ret. $14.95   **MIB** Sec. Mkt. **$29**

QX 554-6 NEPHEW
Comments: Handcrafted, 1-13/16" tall, Dated 1994.
Santa comes to wish nephew a very merry Christmas.
Artist: John Francis (Collin)
☐ Purchased 19 __ Pd $_____ MIB   NB   DB   BNT
☐ Want   Orig. Ret. $7.95   **MIB** Sec. Mkt. **$14**

QX 566-3 NEW HOME
Comments: Handcrafted, 2-5/16" tall, Dated 1994.
The residents of this acorn home are ready for the holidays as seen by
the window box of poinsettias and the wreath on the door. A plaque on
the home says, "New Home 1994."
Artist: Patricia Andrews
☐ Purchased 19 __ Pd $_____ MIB   NB   DB   BNT
☐ Want   Orig. Ret. $8.95   **MIB** Sec. Mkt. **$22**

QX 554-3 NIECE
Comments: Handcrafted, 1-1/2" tall, Dated 1994.
Mrs. Santa is bringing a special doll to her niece in a cart pulled by a
happy reindeer. **Artist:** John Francis (Collin)
☐ Purchased 19 __ Pd $_____ MIB   NB   DB   BNT
☐ Want   Orig. Ret. $7.95   **MIB** Sec. Mkt. **$18**

QX 241-3 NORMAN ROCKWELL ART
Comments: White Glass Ball, 2-7/8" dia., Dated 1994.
Captions: "Post Cover December 29, 1956" and "Christmas 1994."
Norman Rockwell "Bottom Drawer." A famous cover from
The Saturday Evening Post. **Artist:** Joyce Lyle
☐ Purchased 19 __ Pd $_____ MIB   NB   DB   BNT
☐ Want   Orig. Ret. $5.00   **MIB** Sec. Mkt. **$16**

QX 528-6 NOSTALGIC HOUSES AND SHOPS:
NEIGHBORHOOD DRUGSTORE
Comments: **Eleventh in Series,** Handcrafted, 4-1/16" tall.
Dated 1994. A pharmacy and soda fountain are part of this drugstore.
Artist: Donna Lee
☐ Purchased 19 __ Pd $_____ MIB   NB   DB   BNT
☐ Want   Orig. Ret. $14.95   **MIB** Sec. Mkt. **$32**

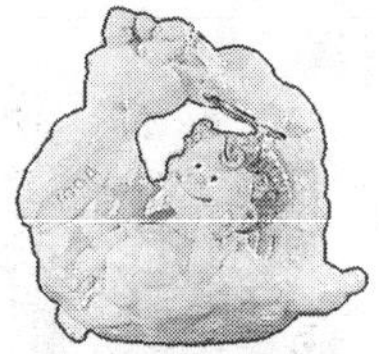

QXC 485-3 ON CLOUD NINE: KEEPSAKE CLUB
Comments: Handcrafted, 2-1/16" tall, Dated 1994.
A little angel relaxes on a cloud. Available to Club Members only.
Artist: Donna Lee
☐ Purchased 19 __ Pd $_____ MIB   NB   DB   BNT
☐ Want   Orig. Ret. $12.00   **MIB** Sec. Mkt. **$28**

QX 569-6 OPEN-AND-SHUT HOLIDAY
Comments: Handcrafted, 3-5/16" tall, Dated 1994.
What better gift for a business associate. The file drawer opens to find
a Christmas surprise inside. **Artist:** Bob Siedler
☐ Purchased 19 __ Pd $_____ MIB   NB   DB   BNT
☐ Want   Orig. Ret. $9.95   **MIB** Sec. Mkt. **$20.50**

QX 481-6 OUR CHRISTMAS TOGETHER
Comments: Handcrafted, 2-3/8" tall, Dated 1994.
A pair of flocked redbirds cuddle together. Their nest of holly leaves
clips to the tree. **Artist:** Anita Marra Rogers
☐ Purchased 19 __ Pd $_____ MIB   NB   DB   BNT
☐ Want   Orig. Ret. $9.95   **MIB** Sec. Mkt. **$20**

QX 557-6 OUR FAMILY: PHOTOHOLDER
Comments: Handcrafted, 3-5/8" dia., Dated 1994.
White poinsettias, gold bells and a red bow on a bright green wreath
form a frame for a favorite family photograph. Caption: "The wonderful
meaning of Christmas is found in the circle of family love."
Artist: Patricia Andrews
☐ Purchased 19 __ Pd $_____ MIB   NB   DB   BNT
☐ Want   Orig. Ret. $7.95   **MIB** Sec. Mkt. **$16**

QX 570-6 OUR FIRST CHRISTMAS TOGETHER
Comments: Handcrafted/Brass, 3-1/8" tall, Dated 1994.
Two bears go for a ride in a sleigh with brass runners. They keep warm
and cozy with their fabric hats and scarves.
Artist: Patricia Andrews
☐ Purchased 19 __ Pd $_____ MIB   NB   DB   BNT
☐ Want   Orig. Ret. $18.95   **MIB** Sec. Mkt. **$39**

QX 564-3 OUR FIRST CHRISTMAS TOGETHER
Comments: Acrylic, 2-5/16" tall, Dated 1994.
A couple shares a kiss as well as gifts. **Artist:** Ron Bishop
☐ Purchased 19 __ Pd $_____ MIB   NB   DB   BNT
☐ Want   Orig. Ret. $9.95   **MIB** Sec. Mkt. **$22**

QX 565-3   OUR FIRST CHRISTMAS TOGETHER:
                PHOTOHOLDER

Comments: Handcrafted, 3-3/4" tall, Dated 1994.
A heart shaped grape vine wreath decorated with holly and red ribbon makes a lovely frame for a favorite photo.
Artist: Don Palmiter

☐ Purchased 19 __Pd $_____MIB   NB   DB   BNT

☐ Want   Orig. Ret. $8.95   **MIB** Sec. Mkt. **$20**

QX 318-6   OUR FIRST CHRISTMAS TOGETHER

Comments: Acrylic, 3-3/16" tall, Dated 1994.
Heart shaped acrylic is etched with a husband and wife's hands and gold foil lettering.   **Artist:** LaDene Votruba

☐ Purchased 19 __Pd $_____MIB   NB   DB   BNT

☐ Want   Orig. Ret. $6.95   **MIB** Sec. Mkt. **$16**

QX 576-6   OUT OF THIS WORLD TEACHER

Comments: Handcrafted, 3-1/2" tall, Dated 1994.
This teacher is sitting on top of the world; it has even been decorated with a red bow! **Artist:** Duane Unruh

☐ Purchased 19 __Pd $_____MIB   NB   DB   BNT

☐ Want   Orig. Ret. $7.95   **MIB** Sec. Mkt. **$18.50**

QX 522-6   OWLIVER

Comments: **Third and Final in Series,** Handcrafted, 2-7/8" tall.
Dated 1994. Owliver and woodpeckers decorate a tree stump for Christmas. **Artist:** Bob Siedler

☐ Purchased 19 __Pd $_____MIB   NB   DB   BNT

☐ Want   Orig. Ret. $7.95   **MIB** Sec. Mkt. **$16**

QLX 740-6   PEANUTS®

Comments: **Fourth in Series,** Flickering Light, Handcrafted.
4-1/8" tall, Dated 1994. Snoopy and Woodstock ring their bells under a flickering street lamp.   **Artist:** Dill Rhodus

☐ Purchased 19 __Pd $_____MIB   NB   DB   BNT

☐ Want   Orig. Ret. $20.00   **MIB** Sec. Mkt. **$44**

QX 520-3   PEANUTS GANG®: LUCY

Comments: **Second in Series,** Handcrafted, 2-7/16" tall.
Dated 1994. Lucy has a special gift for good old Charlie Brown.
Artist: Ron Bishop

☐ Purchased 19 __Pd $_____MIB   NB   DB   BNT

☐ Want   Orig. Ret. $9.95   **MIB** Sec. Mkt. **$22.50**

QLX 742-3   PEEKABOO PUP

Comments: Motion, Handcrafted, 3-7/8" tall, Dated 1994.
The lid on the basket is opening... who is it? It's a cute little pup playing his favorite game! **Artist:** Anita Marra Rogers

☐ Purchased 19 __Pd $_____MIB   NB   DB   BNT

☐ Want   Orig. Ret. $20.00   **MIB** Sec. Mkt. **$32**

QX 586-3   PRACTICE MAKES PERFECT

Comments: Handcrafted, 2-5/16" tall, Dated 1994.
It takes a lot of practice to perfect a tennis game but this little pup is willing to work at it. **Artist:** Don Palmiter

☐ Purchased 19 __Pd $_____MIB   NB   DB   BNT

☐ Want   Orig. Ret. $8.95   **MIB** Sec. Mkt. **$16**

QX 525-3   PUPPY LOVE

Comments: **Fourth in Series,** Handcrafted with Brass Tag.
2-5/16" tall, Dated 1994. A white puppy is entangled in garland.
Artist: Anita Marra Rogers

☐ Purchased 19 __Pd $_____MIB   NB   DB   BNT

☐ Want   Orig. Ret. $7.95   **MIB** Sec. Mkt. **$18.50**

QX 584-3   RED HOT HOLIDAY

Comments: Handcrafted, 2-5/8" tall, Dated 1994.
This would be a great gift for the fireman in your life. He comes prepared with his red fire chief's cap and fire extinguisher.
Artist: Anita Marra Rogers

☐ Purchased 19 __Pd $_____MIB   NB   DB   BNT

☐ Want   Orig. Ret. $7.95   **MIB** Sec. Mkt. **$17**

QX 592-6   REINDEER PRO

Comments: Handcrafted, 3-3/16" tall, Dated 1994.
This reindeer golfer is set to play, rain or shine. **Artist:** Dill Rhodus

☐ Purchased 19 __Pd $_____MIB   NB   DB   BNT

☐ Want   Orig. Ret. $7.95   **MIB** Sec. Mkt. **$18**

QX 535-6   RELAXING MOMENT

Comments: Handcrafted, 2-9/16" tall, Dated 1994.
Santa's taking a break with his favorite beverage, Coca-Cola, as a little fawn sleeps at the base of his chair. **Artist:** John Francis

☐ Purchased 19 __Pd $_____MIB   NB   DB   BNT

☐ Want   Orig. Ret. $14.95   **MIB** Sec. Mkt. **$30**

QLX 740-3   ROCK CANDY MINER ☐

Comments: Flickering Light, Handcrafted, 2-5/8" tall, Dated 1994.
This little gopher is pleased with his progress. He's mined a cart full of
sweet candy from the Rock Candy Mine. **Artist:** Bob Siedler

☐ Purchased 19__Pd $_____MIB   NB   DB   BNT

☐ Want   Orig. Ret. $20.00   **MIB** Sec. Mkt. **$42**

QX 501-6   ROCKING HORSE ☐

Comments: **Fourteenth in Series,** Handcrafted, 3" tall, Dated 1994.
Dark brown with white stockings and brown tail.
Artist: Linda Sickman

☐ Purchased 19__Pd $_____MIB   NB   DB   BNT

☐ Want   Orig. Ret. $10.95   **MIB** Sec. Mkt. **$28**

QX 545-3   SANTA'S LEGO® SLEIGH ☐

Comments: Handcrafted, 1-13/16" tall, Dated 1994.
Santa is making his Christmas deliveries this year in a sleigh built
from LEGO® blocks! Another Lego® ornament debuted in '95!
Artist: Ken Crow

☐ Purchased 19__Pd $_____MIB   NB   DB   BNT

☐ Want   Orig. Ret. $10.95   **MIB** Sec. Mkt. **$28**

QLX 747-3   SANTA'S SING-ALONG ☐

Comments: Light and Music, Handcrafted, 3-15/16" tall, Dated 1994.
Caption: "Sing Along with Santa." Santa is announcing his arrival with
his calliope. Plays "Santa Claus Is Coming To Town."
Artist: Ken Crow

☐ Purchased 19__Pd $_____MIB   NB   DB   BNT

☐ Want   Orig. Ret. $24.00   **MIB** Sec. Mkt. **$52.50**

XPR 945-0   SARAH, PLAIN AND TALL COLLECTION, THE: ☐
COUNTRY CHURCH, THE

Comments: Handcrafted, 5" tall, Dated 1994.
This white-framed, shake-shingled church was where Sarah and Jacob
danced for the first time and later married.

☐ Purchased 19__Pd $_____MIB   NB   DB   BNT

☐ Want   Orig. Ret. $7.95 with any Hallmark Purchase.
                                               MIB Sec. Mkt. **$20**

*True friends are like diamonds, precious but
rare; false friends are like autumn leaves,
found everywhere.*

XPR 945-2   SARAH, PLAIN AND TALL COLLECTION, THE: ☐
HAYS TRAIN STATION, THE

Comments: Handcrafted, 5" tall, Dated 1994.
Sarah arrived from Maine by train. Here at the old train station she met
Jacob Witting.

☐ Purchased 19__Pd $_____MIB   NB   DB   BNT

☐ Want   Orig. Ret. $7.95 with any Hallmark Purchase.
                                               MIB Sec. Mkt. **$20**

XPR 945-1   SARAH, PLAIN AND TALL COLLECTION, THE: ☐
MRS. PARKLEY'S GENERAL STORE

Comments: Handcrafted, 5" tall, Dated 1994.
People met here at the General Store and heard the latest news as they
purchased food, dry goods and other provisions.

☐ Purchased 19__Pd $_____MIB   NB   DB   BNT

☐ Want   Orig. Ret. $7.95 with any Hallmark Purchase.
                                               MIB Sec. Mkt. **$20**

XPR 945-4   SARAH, PLAIN AND TALL COLLECTION, THE: ☐
SARAH'S MAINE HOME

Comments: Handcrafted, 5" tall, Dated 1994.
Sarah lived here off the coast of Maine with her maiden aunts - Mattie,
Harriet and Lou.

☐ Purchased 19__Pd $_____MIB   NB   DB   BNT

☐ Want   Orig. Ret. $7.95 with any Hallmark Purchase.
                                               MIB Sec. Mkt. **$22**

XPR 945-3   SARAH, PLAIN AND TALL COLLECTION, THE: ☐
SARAH'S PRAIRIE HOME

Comments: Handcrafted, 5" tall, Dated 1994.
Sarah, a mail order bride, came to Kansas to live here with Jacob and
his children, Anna and Caleb.

☐ Purchased 19__Pd $_____MIB   NB   DB   BNT

☐ Want   Orig. Ret. $7.95 with any Hallmark Purchase.
                                               MIB Sec. Mkt. **$22**

QX 573-6   SECRET SANTA ☐

Comments: Handcrafted, 2-5/8" tall, Dated 1994.
Who is that masked puppy with reindeer antlers? Why, it's your pal,
Secret Santa! We've had several reports of ornaments being found
with the caption, "From Your Secret Pal." **Artist:** Duane Unruh

☐ Purchased 19__Pd $_____MIB   NB   DB   BNT

☐ Want   Orig. Ret. $7.95   **MIB** Sec. Mkt. **$15**

QX 551-3   SISTER
Comments: Handcrafted, 2-1/8" tall, Dated 1994.
A "Simply Incredible Sister" is really cool in her hot pink convertible.
Artist: Sharon Pike
☐ Purchased 19 __ Pd $_____ MIB   NB   DB   BNT
☐ Want   Orig. Ret. $6.95   **MIB** Sec. Mkt. **$16**

QX 553-3   SISTER TO SISTER
Comments: Handcrafted, 3-1/4" tall, Dated 1994.
Two sisters spend Christmas together inside an acorn. Caption: "Sisters Fill Christmas With Joy." **Artist:** Dill Rhodus
☐ Purchased 19 __ Pd $_____ MIB   NB   DB   BNT
☐ Want   Orig. Ret. $9.95   **MIB** Sec. Mkt. **$18**

QX 562-6   SON
Comments: Handcrafted, 3-3/16" tall, Dated 1994.
What better fun could there be than to skateboard through the holidays? **Artist:** Patricia Andrews
☐ Purchased 19 __ Pd $_____ MIB   NB   DB   BNT
☐ Want   Orig. Ret. $6.95   **MIB** Sec. Mkt. **$15**

QX 560-6   SPECIAL CAT: PHOTOHOLDER
Comments: Acrylic, 3-1/4" tall, Dated 1994.
Kitty gets a place of honor at last... inside the fish bowl!
Artist: Dill Rhodus
☐ Purchased 19 __ Pd $_____ MIB   NB   DB   BNT
☐ Want   Orig. Ret. $7.95   **MIB** Sec. Mkt. **$14**

QX 560-3   SPECIAL DOG: PHOTOHOLDER
Comments: Handcrafted, 1-13/16" tall, Dated 1994.
The "Canine Edition" newspaper features your pet as the Dog of the Year. **Artist:** Dill Rhodus
☐ Purchased 19 __ Pd $_____ MIB   NB   DB   BNT
☐ Want   Orig. Ret. $7.95   **MIB** Sec. Mkt. **$16**

QX 570-3   STAMP OF APPROVAL
Comments: Handcrafted, 1-15/16" tall, Dated 1994.
Little elves help to convey their special message ASAP, "A Santa-Approved Person." **Artist:** Linda Sickman
☐ Purchased 19 __ Pd $_____ MIB   NB   DB   BNT
☐ Want   Orig. Ret. $7.95   **MIB** Sec. Mkt. **$16**

QLX 738-6   STAR TREK®: THE NEXT GENERATION KLINGON BIRD OF PREY™
Comments: Flickering and Glowing Lights, Handcrafted.
2-1/8" tall, Stardated 1994. The Klingon battle cruiser joins the line-up of space craft from The Next Generation. Price dropped considerably from '96 guide. **Artist:** Lynn Norton
☐ Purchased 19 __ Pd $_____ MIB   NB   DB   BNT
☐ Want   Orig. Ret. $24.00   **MIB** Sec. Mkt. **$38**

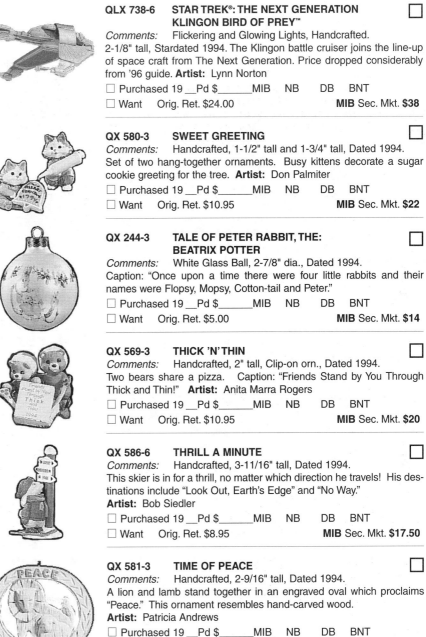

QX 580-3   SWEET GREETING
Comments: Handcrafted, 1-1/2" tall and 1-3/4" tall, Dated 1994.
Set of two hang-together ornaments. Busy kittens decorate a sugar cookie greeting for the tree. **Artist:** Don Palmiter
☐ Purchased 19 __ Pd $_____ MIB   NB   DB   BNT
☐ Want   Orig. Ret. $10.95   **MIB** Sec. Mkt. **$22**

QX 244-3   TALE OF PETER RABBIT, THE: BEATRIX POTTER
Comments: White Glass Ball, 2-7/8" dia., Dated 1994.
Caption: "Once upon a time there were four little rabbits and their names were Flopsy, Mopsy, Cotton-tail and Peter."
☐ Purchased 19 __ Pd $_____ MIB   NB   DB   BNT
☐ Want   Orig. Ret. $5.00   **MIB** Sec. Mkt. **$14**

QX 569-3   THICK 'N' THIN
Comments: Handcrafted, 2" tall, Clip-on orn., Dated 1994.
Two bears share a pizza. Caption: "Friends Stand by You Through Thick and Thin!" **Artist:** Anita Marra Rogers
☐ Purchased 19 __ Pd $_____ MIB   NB   DB   BNT
☐ Want   Orig. Ret. $10.95   **MIB** Sec. Mkt. **$20**

QX 586-6   THRILL A MINUTE
Comments: Handcrafted, 3-11/16" tall, Dated 1994.
This skier is in for a thrill, no matter which direction he travels! His destinations include "Look Out, Earth's Edge" and "No Way."
Artist: Bob Siedler
☐ Purchased 19 __ Pd $_____ MIB   NB   DB   BNT
☐ Want   Orig. Ret. $8.95   **MIB** Sec. Mkt. **$17.50**

QX 581-3   TIME OF PEACE
Comments: Handcrafted, 2-9/16" tall, Dated 1994.
A lion and lamb stand together in an engraved oval which proclaims "Peace." This ornament resembles hand-carved wood.
Artist: Patricia Andrews
☐ Purchased 19 __ Pd $_____ MIB   NB   DB   BNT
☐ Want   Orig. Ret. $7.95   **MIB** Sec. Mkt. **$15**

QX 522-3 TOBIN FRALEY CAROUSEL
Comments: **Third in Series,** Porcelain and Brass, 5-1/4" tall.
Dated 1994. Collectors have questioned the fact that all the horses in this series are white.
Artist: Tobin Fraley

☐ Purchased 19__Pd $_____MIB   NB   DB   BNT
☐ Want   Orig. Ret. $28   **MIB** Sec. Mkt. **$58**

QLX 749-6 TOBIN FRALEY HOLIDAY CAROUSEL
Comments: *FIRST IN SERIES,* Light and Music, Handcrafted.
4-15/16" tall, Dated 1994. A nostalgic carousel is decorated with Santa faces. Plays "Skater's Waltz." **Artist:** Duane Unruh

☐ Purchased 19__Pd $_____MIB   NB   DB   BNT
☐ Want   Orig. Ret. $32.00   **MIB** Sec. Mkt. **$48**

QX 564-6 TOU CAN LOVE
Comments: Handcrafted, 3" tall, Dated 1994.
A pair of gaily colored toucans stand together on a gift.
Caption: "Tou-Can make Christmas more fun!"
Artist: Anita Marra Rogers

☐ Purchased 19__Pd $_____MIB   NB   DB   BNT
☐ Want   Orig. Ret. $8.95   **MIB** Sec. Mkt. **$18**

QX 318-3 TWELVE DAYS OF CHRISTMAS: ELEVEN PIPERS PIPING
Comments: **Eleventh in Series,** Acrylic, 3-3/8" tall, Dated 1994.
A Scotsman in his kilt plays his bagpipe, adding to the Christmas merriment.

☐ Purchased 19__Pd $_____MIB   NB   DB   BNT
☐ Want   Orig. Ret. $6.95   **MIB** Sec. Mkt. **$16**

QX 520-6 U.S. CHRISTMAS STAMPS
Comments: **Second in Series,** Enamel on Copper, 2-5/16" tall.
Dated 1994. Caption: "Christmas 1994 Children Trimming Tree.
Designer: Dollie Tingle Date of Issuance: Oct. 28, 1982; Place of Issuance: Snow, OK." This series ended with the '95 ornament.

☐ Purchased 19__Pd $_____MIB   NB   DB   BNT
☐ Want   Orig. Ret. $10.95   **MIB** Sec. Mkt. **$22**

QLX 744-3 VERY MERRY MINUTES
Comments: Light and Motion, Handcrafted, 4-5/16" tall, Dated 1994.
One little mouse sleeps atop the clock as another swings playfully on the pendulum. **Artist:** LaDene Votruba

☐ Purchased 19__Pd $_____MIB   NB   DB   BNT
☐ Want   Orig. Ret. $24.00   **MIB** Sec. Mkt. **$48**

QLX 746-3 WHITE CHRISTMAS
Comments: Flickering Light/Music, Handcrafted, 3-3/16" tall.
Dated 1994. The world may be covered in white but all is warm and cozy inside. Plays "White Christmas." **Artist:** Donna Lee

☐ Purchased 19__Pd $_____MIB   NB   DB   BNT
☐ Want   Orig. Ret. $28.00   **MIB** Sec. Mkt. **$50**

QX 574-6 WINNIE THE POOH AND TIGGER
Comments: Handcrafted, 2-1/2" tall.
A very excitable, bouncy Tigger has just jumped on Winnie the Pooh, putting him on his back. **Artist:** Bob Siedler

☐ Purchased 19__Pd $_____MIB   NB   DB   BNT
☐ Want   Orig. Ret. $12.95   **MIB** Sec. Mkt. **$35**

QLX 749-3 WINNIE THE POOH PARADE
Comments: Motion and Music, Handcrafted, 4-1/8" tall.
Dated 1994. Pooh twirls as the gang parades around him; Tigger spins on his tail. Plays "Winnie the Pooh Theme." **Artist:** Ken Crow

☐ Purchased 19__Pd $_____MIB   NB   DB   BNT
☐ Want   Orig. Ret. $32.00   **MIB** Sec. Mkt. **$62.50**

QX 544-6 WIZARD OF OZ COLLECTION, THE: COWARDLY LION, THE
Comments: Handcrafted, 3-9/16" tall.
The Cowardly Lion searches for courage with his tail in his hands.
This ornament is highly sought after thus the no box price.
Artist: Patricia Andrews

☐ Purchased 19__Pd $_____MIB   NB   DB   BNT
☐ Want   Orig. Ret. $9.95   **NB** $31.50   **MIB** Sec. Mkt. **$35**

QX 543-3 WIZARD OF OZ COLLECTION, THE: DOROTHY AND TOTO
Comments: Handcrafted, 3-9/16" tall.
Dorothy carries Toto in her arm as she skips down the yellow brick road.
This ornament is highly sought after thus the no box price.
Artist: Joyce Lyle

☐ Purchased 19__Pd $_____MIB   NB   DB   BNT
☐ Want   Orig. Ret. $10.95   **NB** $49.50   **MIB** Sec. Mkt. **$55**

QX 543-6 WIZARD OF OZ COLLECTION, THE: SCARECROW
Comments: Handcrafted, 3-7/8" tall.
Scarecrow looks as if he has been plucked from the fence post.   This ornament is highly sought after thus the no box price.
Artist: Duane Unruh

☐ Purchased 19__Pd $_____MIB   NB   DB   BNT
☐ Want   Orig. Ret. $9.95   **NB** $31.50   **MIB** Sec. Mkt. **$35**

QX 544-3   WIZARD OF OZ COLLECTION, THE:
　　　　　　TIN MAN ☐

Comments: Handcrafted, 3-13/16" tall.
The tin man is reproduced in great detail; he even has his trusty axe. This ornament is highly sought after thus the no box price.
Artist: Duane Unruh

☐ Purchased 19__Pd $_____MIB   NB   DB   BNT
☐ Want   Orig. Ret. $9.95   **NB $31.50**   **MIB** Sec. Mkt. **$35**

QX 531-6   YULETIDE CENTRAL: LOCOMOTIVE ☐
Comments: ***FIRST IN SERIES,*** Pressed Tin, 2-9/16" tall.
Dated 1994. This series will feature different train components and not just locomotives, such as the Tin Locomotive series of the past.
Artist: Linda Sickman

☐ Purchased 19__Pd $_____MIB   NB   DB   BNT
☐ Want   Orig. Ret. $18.95   **MIB** Sec. Mkt. **$45-$52**

Hallmark Keepsake
Personalized Ornaments

No sales found on these ornaments. Any ornament with personal message is unlikely to bring a significant secondary market price.

QP 603-5   BABY BLOCK ☐
Comments: Handcrafted Photoholder, 2-13/16" tall.
Reissued from 1993. **Artist:** John Francis (Collin)

☐ Purchased 19__Pd $_____MIB   NB   DB   BNT
☐ Want Orig. Ret. $14.95   **MIB** Sec. Mkt. **N.E.**

QP 604-6   COMPUTER CAT 'N MOUSE ☐
Comments: Handcrafted, 2-3/4" tall.
A kitten eyes the "mouse" gleefully from atop a computer screen which displays your Christmas message. **Artist:** Ed Seale

☐ Purchased 19__Pd $_____MIB   NB   DB   BNT
☐ Want Orig. Ret. $12.95   **MIB** Sec. Mkt. **N.E.**

QP 607-3   COOKIE TIME ☐
Comments: Handcrafted, 3-1/8" tall.
This iced sugar cookie will be a hit on any Christmas tree. Your message appears as red icing. Yum, yum! **Artist:** LaDene Votruba

☐ Purchased 19__Pd $_____MIB   NB   DB   BNT
☐ Want Orig. Ret. $12.95   **MIB** Sec. Mkt. **N.E.**

Life is full of shadows,
but the sunshine makes them all.

QP 600-6   ETCH-A-SKETCH® ☐
Comments: Handcrafted, 2-1/4" tall.
A little bear plays happily with his Etch-A-Sketch® and shows off his greeting. **Artist:** Ken Crow

☐ Purchased 19 __Pd $_____MIB   NB   DB   BNT
☐ Want Orig. Ret. $12.95   **MIB** Sec. Mkt. **N.E.**

QP 602-5   FESTIVE ALBUM PHOTOHOLDER ☐
Comments: Handcrafted Photoholder, 7-7/16" tall.
Reissued from 1993. Similiar to the '95 (Premiered in July).
Artist: LaDene Votruba

☐ Purchased 19__Pd $_____MIB   NB   DB   BNT
☐ Want Orig. Ret. $12.95   **MIB** Sec. Mkt. **N.E.**

QP 603-6   FROM THE HEART ☐
Comments: Handcrafted, 1-15/16" tall.
A little raccoon has written his greeting in a heart carved in a snow covered tree stump. **Artist:** Dill Rhodus

☐ Purchased 19 __Pd $_____MIB   NB   DB   BNT
☐ Want Orig. Ret. $24.95   **MIB** Sec. Mkt. **N.E.**

QP 602-3   GOIN' FISHIN' ☐
Comments: Handcrafted, 3" tall.
A fisherman's tackle basket is a great spot for a little chipmunk to wish happy holidays. **Artist:** Don Palmiter

☐ Purchased 19__Pd $_____MIB   NB   DB   BNT
☐ Want Orig. Ret. $14.95   **MIB** Sec. Mkt. **N.E.**

QP 601-2   GOING GOLFIN' ☐
Comments: Handcrafted, 2-13/16" tall.
Reissued from 1993. **Artist:** Don Palmiter

☐ Purchased 19__Pd $_____MIB   NB   DB   BNT
☐ Want Orig. Ret. $12.75   **MIB** Sec. Mkt. **N.E.**

QXR 611-6   HOLIDAY HELLO ☐
Comments: Handcrafted, Recordable, 4-1/2" tall.
Just press the button to record your own holiday message on this battery operated telephone. **Artist:** Bob Siedler

☐ Purchased 19__Pd $_____MIB   NB   DB   BNT
☐ Want Orig. Ret. $24.95   **MIB** Sec. Mkt. **N.E.**

Past failures are guideposts for future success.

QP 601-5   MAILBOX DELIVERY ☐

Comments: Handcrafted, 1-7/8" tall.
Introduced in 1993, reissued in '94 and '95. **Artist:** Ken Crow

☐ Purchased 19___ Pd $_____ MIB   NB   DB   BNT
☐ Want   Orig. Ret. $14.95   **MIB** Sec. Mkt. **N.E.**

QP 606-6   NOVEL IDEA ☐

Comments: Handcrafted, 2-7/16" tall.
A little mouse points out a special message written in the pages of a red book. **Artist:** LaDene Votruba

☐ Purchased 19___ Pd $_____ MIB   NB   DB   BNT
☐ Want   Orig. Ret. $12.95   **MIB** Sec. Mkt. **N.E.**

QP 602-2   ON THE BILLBOARD ☐

Comments: Handcrafted, 2-1/8" tall.
Introduced in 1993, reissued in '94 and '95. **Artist:** Ken Crow

☐ Purchased 19___ Pd $_____ MIB   NB   DB   BNT
☐ Want   Orig. Ret. $12.95   **MIB** Sec. Mkt. **N.E.**

QP 603-2   PLAYING BALL ☐

Comments: Handcrafted, 3-11/16" tall.
Introduced in 1993, reissued in '94 and '95.
Artist: John Francis (Collin)

☐ Purchased 19___ Pd $_____ MIB   NB   DB   BNT
☐ Want   Orig. Ret. $12.95   **MIB** Sec. Mkt. **N.E.**

QP 605-6   REINDEER ROOTERS ☐

Comments: Handcrafted, 2-15/16" tall.
Four happy reindeer, with a megaphone and waving banner, will help to send your Christmas greeting. In my opinion, this ornament with a cute saying that complements the '94 Cheery Cyclists ornament found on page 192, may obtain a secondary value faster.
Reissued in '95. **Artist:** Ken Crow

☐ Purchased 19___ Pd $_____ MIB   NB   DB   BNT
☐ Want   Orig. Ret. $12.95   **MIB** Sec. Mkt. **N.E.**

QP 600-5   SANTA SAYS ☐

Comments: Handcrafted, 2-15/16" tall.
Introduced in 1993, reissued in '94. **Artist:** Ed Seale

☐ Purchased 19___ Pd $_____ MIB   NB   DB   BNT
☐ Want   Orig. Ret. $14.95   **MIB** Sec. Mkt. **N.E.**

I love snow!

Hallmark Keepsake Showcase Ornaments
Christmas Lights

QK 112-3   HOME FOR THE HOLIDAYS ☐

Comments: Porcelain Bisque, Lighted, 4-1/16" tall, Dated 1994.
Smoke rises from a snow covered cottage and light glows through the windows. **Artist:** Don Palmiter

☐ Purchased 19___ Pd $_____ MIB   NB   DB   BNT
☐ Want   Orig. Ret. $15.75   **MIB** Sec. Mkt. **N.E.**

QK 111-6   MOONBEAMS ☐

Comments: Porcelain Bisque, Lighted, 4-5/16" tall, Dated 1994.
A star with a moon cut-out dangles from the top of a quarter moon. Light streams from the pin-hole design of this sleepy moon.
Artist: Patricia Andrews

☐ Purchased 19___ Pd $_____ MIB   NB   DB   BNT
☐ Want   Orig. Ret. $15.75   **MIB** Sec. Mkt. **N.E.**

QK 112-6   MOTHER AND CHILD ☐

Comments: Porcelain Bisque, Lighted, 3-1/2" tall, Dated 1994.
A bright shining star stands above the Madonna, attending to her Holy Child. **Artist:** Anita Marra Rogers

☐ Purchased 19___ Pd $_____ MIB   NB   DB   BNT
☐ Want   Orig. Ret. $15.75   **MIB** Sec. Mkt. **N.E.**

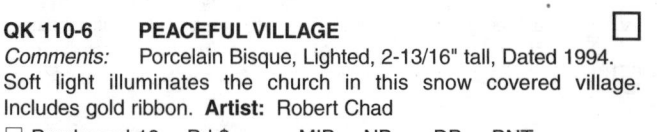

QK 110-6   PEACEFUL VILLAGE ☐

Comments: Porcelain Bisque, Lighted, 2-13/16" tall, Dated 1994.
Soft light illuminates the church in this snow covered village. Includes gold ribbon. **Artist:** Robert Chad

☐ Purchased 19___ Pd $_____ MIB   NB   DB   BNT
☐ Want   Orig. Ret. $15.75   **MIB** Sec. Mkt. **N.E.**

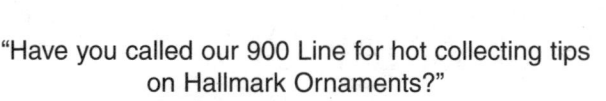

Folk Art Americana

Holiday Favorites

QK 118-3   CATCHING 40 WINKS   ☐
Comments: Wood Look, 1-7/8" tall, Dated 1994.
An elf settles down for a quick snooze among the brightly wrapped packages. **Artist:** Linda Sickman
☐ Purchased 19 __Pd $_____MIB   NB   DB   BNT
☐ Want   Orig. Ret. $16.75   **MIB** Sec. Mkt. **$34**

QK 116-6   GOING TO TOWN   ☐
Comments: Wood Look, 2-7/16" tall, Dated 1994.
Pouches filled with grain, an elf heads to market with his best "pack pig." **Artist:** Linda Sickman
☐ Purchased 19 __Pd $_____MIB   NB   DB   BNT
☐ Want   Orig. Ret. $15.75   **MIB** Sec. Mkt. **$35**

QK 117-3   RACING THROUGH THE SNOW   ☐
Comments: Wood Look, 3-1/16" tall, Dated 1994.
An elf races through the winter landscape astride a rooster on snow-shoes. **Artist:** Linda Sickman
☐ Purchased 19 __Pd $_____MIB   NB   DB   BNT
☐ Want   Orig. Ret. $15.75   **MIB** Sec. Mkt. **$48**

QK 119-3   RARIN' TO GO   ☐
Comments: Wood Look, 2-11/16" tall, Dated 1994.
Hang on tight! This elf is in store for a quick hop through the forest atop a long-eared rabbit. **Artist:** Linda Sickman
☐ Purchased 19 __Pd $_____MIB   NB   DB   BNT
☐ Want   Orig. Ret. $15.75   **MIB** Sec. Mkt. **$36**

QK 117-6   ROUNDUP TIME   ☐
Comments: Wood Look, 2-11/16" tall, Dated 1994.
Wrapped gifts have been tied to this fellow's unique transportation... a cow. Let's get "moo...ving"; Christmas is just around the corner. **Artist:** Linda Sickman
☐ Purchased 19 __Pd $_____MIB   NB   DB   BNT
☐ Want   Orig. Ret. $16.75   **MIB** Sec. Mkt. **$38**

QK 105-3   DAPPER SNOWMAN   ☐
Comments: Crackled Porcelain, 3-5/8" tall, Dated 1994.
This dapper fellow is highlighted with blue accents and a striped candy cane. Includes blue ribbon. **Artist:** LaDene Votruba
☐ Purchased 19 __Pd $_____MIB   NB   DB   BNT
☐ Want   Orig. Ret. $13.75   **MIB** Sec. Mkt. **$17**

QK 103-3   GRACEFUL FAWN   ☐
Comments: Crackled Porcelain, 2-11/16" tall, Dated 1994.
Delicately painted blue leaves circle the fawn's neck. Includes blue ribbon. **Artist:** LaDene Votruba
☐ Purchased 19 __Pd $_____MIB   NB   DB   BNT
☐ Want   Orig. Ret. $11.75   **MIB** Sec. Mkt. **$16**

QK 104-6   JOLLY SANTA   ☐
Comments: Crackled Porcelain, 3-11/16" tall, Dated 1994.
Santa is chuckling a happy "ho, ho, ho!" He's wearing red striped mittens and is holding a miniature tree. Includes red ribbon. **Artist:** LaDene Votruba
☐ Purchased 19 __Pd $_____MIB   NB   DB   BNT
☐ Want   Orig. Ret. $13.75   **MIB** Sec. Mkt. **$25**

QK 103-6   JOYFUL LAMB   ☐
Comments: Crackled Porcelain, 2-5/16" tall, Dated 1994.
A green garland graces the neck of a serene lamb. Includes green ribbon. **Artist:** LaDene Votruba
☐ Purchased 19 __Pd $_____MIB   NB   DB   BNT
☐ Want   Orig. Ret. $11.75   **MIB** Sec. Mkt. **$19**

QK 104-3   PEACEFUL DOVE   ☐
Comments: Crackled Porcelain, 3-5/8" tall, Dated 1994.
Trimmed in blue, this graceful dove will add a touch of grace to any tree. Includes blue ribbon. **Artist:** LaDene Votruba
☐ Purchased 19 __Pd $_____MIB   NB   DB   BNT
☐ Want   Orig. Ret. $11.75   MIB Sec. Mkt. **$15**

Old-World Silver - 1994

QK 102-6   SILVER BELLS ☐
Comments: Silver-Plated, 3-3/16" tall, Dated 1994.
Silver bells ring out the joy of Christmas, depicted in a filigree design.
Artist: Duane Unruh

☐ Purchased 19__Pd $_____MIB   NB   DB   BNT
☐ Want   Orig. Ret. $24.75   **MIB** Sec. Mkt. **$28**

QK 102-3   SILVER BOWS ☐
Comments: Silver-Plated, 3-5/16" tall, Dated 1994.
Delicate bows add a touch of beauty to this intricate old-world ornament. **Artist:** Don Palmiter

☐ Purchased 19__Pd $_____MIB   NB   DB   BNT
☐ Want   Orig. Ret. $24.75   **MIB** Sec. Mkt. **$27**

QK 100-6   SILVER POINSETTIA ☐
Comments: Silver-Plated, 3-1/8" tall, Dated 1994.
A finely detailed poinsettia provides the focal point for this diamond shaped ornament. **Artist:** Duane Unruh

☐ Purchased 19__Pd $_____MIB   NB   DB   BNT
☐ Want   Orig. Ret. $24.75   **MIB** Sec. Mkt. **$34**

QK 101-6   SILVER SNOWFLAKE ☐
Comments: Silver-Plated, 3-1/16" tall, Dated 1994.
Intricate snowflake designs circle the ornament.
Artist: Duane Unruh

☐ Purchased 19__Pd $_____MIB   NB   DB   BNT
☐ Want   Orig. Ret. $24.75   **MIB** Sec. Mkt. **$27**

Specialty Ornament

CRAYOLA CRAYON ORNAMENT ☐
Comments: Handcrafted.
Came as free gift in tin box of Crayola Crayons.

☐ Purchased 19__Pd $ ____ MIB   NB   DB   BNT
☐ Want   Orig. Ret. $5.99-$9.99 (depending on location of purchase)
without tin box **$5-$10**   **MIB** Sec. Mkt. **$10**

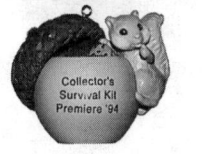

COLLECTOR'S SURVIVAL KIT PREMIERE '94 ☐
Comments: Handcrafted, Dated '94.
Given as a free gift during premiere week of 1994.

☐ Purchased 19__Pd $_____MIB   NB   DB   BNT
☐ Want   **MIB** Sec. Mkt. **$12.50**

Hallmark Expo Ornaments
Expo 1994

The '93 Old-World Silver Ornaments from the Showcase line were finished in a gold color and sold to Expo '94 attendees for $10 each. These were very popular and, by the time of San Francisco Expo, they were sold out. The '94 Bows and Poinsettia Old-World Silver Ornaments were then also dipped in a gold colored finish and sold to lucky Expo attendees.

GOLD BOWS ☐
Comments: '94 Old-World Silver ornament dipped in a gold colored finish with attached ribbon that said Expo '94.

☐ Purchased 19 __Pd $_____MIB   NB   DB   BNT
☐ Want   Orig. Ret. $10.00   **MIB** Sec. Mkt. **$20**

GOLD DOVE OF PEACE ☐
Comments: '93 Old-World Silver ornament dipped in a gold colored finish with attached ribbon that said Expo '94.

☐ Purchased 19 __Pd $_____MIB   NB   DB   BNT
☐ Want   Orig. Ret. $10.00   **MIB** Sec. Mkt. **$20**

GOLD POINSETTIA ☐
Comments: '94 Old-World Silver ornament dipped in a gold colored finish with attached ribbon that said Expo '94.

☐ Purchased 19 __Pd $_____MIB   NB   DB   BNT
☐ Want   Orig. Ret. $10.00   **MIB** Sec. Mkt. **$22**

GOLD SANTA ☐
Comments: '93 Old-World Silver ornament dipped in a gold colored finish with attached ribbon that said Expo '94.

☐ Purchased 19 __Pd $_____MIB   NB   DB   BNT
☐ Want   Orig. Ret. $10.00   **MIB** Sec. Mkt. **$25**

GOLD STAR AND HOLLY ☐
Comments: '93 Old-World Silver ornament dipped in a gold colored finish with attached ribbon that said Expo '94.

☐ Purchased 19 __Pd $_____MIB   NB   DB   BNT
☐ Want   Orig. Ret. $10.00   **MIB** Sec. Mkt. **$20**

QXC 484-3   MRS. CLAUS' CUPBOARD

Comments: Handcrafted, 1994.   Only available at eight 1994 Hallmark Expos held across the USA. Mrs. Claus' Cupboard is filled with delightful surprises... miniature copies of favorite Keepsake ornaments such as *Cheerful Santa, Noah's Ark,* the *1993 Folk Art Polar Bear Adventure,* a *Nativity* and more! Many sales reported in '96.

☐ Purchased 19___   Pd $_____   MIB   NB   DB   BNT

☐ Want   Orig. Ret. $55 with $25 purchase of Keepsake Ornaments

MIB Sec. Mkt. **$175**

Expo '94 Prizes

Available at the '94 Expo were several gifts given to fortunate attendees by entering different drawings. Gifts given included a signed Star Trek ornament, a '94 Looney Tunes set, complete set of all mini ornaments from '94, a signed Mary Engelbreit ball and an original signed artist sketch. Also available by special drawings, the '93 Circle of Friendship (a member's only ornament in '93), Red '94 First Edition Murray Champion ornament (5 given away per each Expo) and the Red '94 Chevy which could have been signed by Don Palmiter at the two Expos he attended.

Coca-Cola Displays

Lois Winker displays her Coca-Cola items around these classic cola glasses.

Audrey Davey made a lamp for her Santa from a Coke Cap and pearl tie tack.

Candie Jones (left) has this little tree covered with Coca-Cola memorabilia.

An elegant way to display this water globe (above) was to place it in the middle of a Hallmark ornament covered wreath with an attractive candle.

Marty & Yoshi Tonomura enjoy displaying Coca-Cola items throughout their home.

1994 Miniature Ornament Collection

A   **QXM 407-3**   **A MERRY FLIGHT**
Handcrafted, 1" tall, Dated 1994. Caption: "Santa's flight is the merriest sight!"
Turn dial with thumb and Santa circles the village. **Artist:** Ken Crow
☐ Purchased 19___ Pd $_____   MIB   NB   DB   BNT
☐ Want   Orig. Retail $5.75

             MIB Sec. Mkt. **$10.50**

B   **QXM 400-3**   **BABY'S FIRST CHRISTMAS**
Handcrafted, 1-1/4" tall, Dated 1994. **Artist:** Joyce Lyle
☐ Purchased 19___ Pd $_____   MIB   NB   DB   BNT
☐ Want   Orig. Retail $5.75

             MIB Sec. Mkt. **$11**

C   **QXM 403-3**   **BAKING TINY TREATS**
Handcrafted, Set of Six, Dated 1994. **Artist:** Ed Seale
A. Merry Mixer, 1-1/8" tall   D. Rollin' Along, 13/16" tall
B. Standin' By, 3/4" tall   E. Scoop, 11/16" tall
C. Just Dozin', 1/2" tall   F. Official Taster, 9/16" tall
☐ Purchased 19___ Pd $_____   MIB   NB   DB   BNT
☐ Want   Orig. Retail $29.00

             MIB Sec. Mkt. **$55**

D   **QXM 407-6**   **BEARY PERFECT TREE**
Handcrafted, 1-3/16" tall, Dated 1994. **Artist:** Ron Bishop
☐ Purchased 19___ Pd $_____   MIB   NB   DB   BNT
☐ Want   Orig. Retail $4.75

             MIB Sec. Mkt. **$8.50**

E   **QXM 513-3**   **BEARYMORES, THE**
Third and Final in Series, Handcrafted, 1-1/8" tall, Dated 1994.
Artist: Anita Marra Rogers
☐ Purchased 19___ Pd $_____   MIB   NB   DB   BNT
☐ Want   Orig. Retail $5.75

             MIB Sec. Mkt. **$17**

F   **QXM 515-3**   **CENTURIES OF SANTA**
FIRST IN SERIES, Handcrafted, 1-1/4" tall, Dated 1994.
Artist: Linda Sickman
☐ Purchased 19___ Pd $_____   MIB   NB   DB   BNT
☐ Want   Orig. Retail $6.00

             MIB Sec. Mkt. **$19.50**

G   **QXM 406-3**   **CORNY ELF**
Handcrafted, 1" tall. **Artist:** Dill Rhodus
☐ Purchased 19___ Pd $_____   MIB   NB   DB   BNT
☐ Want   Orig. Retail $4.50

             MIB Sec. Mkt. **$8**

H   **QXM 410-3**   **CUTE AS A BUTTON**
Handcrafted, 13/16" tall, Dated 1994. **Artist:** Ken Crow
☐ Purchased 19___ Pd $_____   MIB   NB   DB   BNT
☐ Want   Orig. Retail $3.75

             MIB Sec. Mkt. **$10**

I   **QXM 589-1**   **DANCING ANGELS TREE-TOPPER**
Dimensional Brass, 2-7/8" tall, Reissued from 1992.
☐ Purchased 19___ Pd $_____   MIB   NB   DB   BNT
☐ Want   Orig. Retail $9.75

             MIB Sec. Mkt. **$12**

J   **QXM 402-6**   **DAZZLING REINDEER**
Precious Edition, Pewter, 1-3/8" tall.
Artist: LaDene Votruba
☐ Purchased 19___ Pd $_____   MIB   NB   DB   BNT
☐ Want   Orig. Retail $9.75

             MIB Sec. Mkt. **$17.50**

K   **QXM 401-6**   **FRIENDS NEED HUGS**
Handcrafted, 13/16" tall, Dated 1994. **Artist:** Joyce Lyle
☐ Purchased 19___ Pd $_____   MIB   NB   DB   BNT
☐ Want   Orig. Retail $4.50

             MIB Sec. Mkt. **$13.50**

L   **QXM 405-6**   **GRACEFUL CAROUSEL HORSE**
Pewter, 1-1/4" tall, Dated 1994.
☐ Purchased 19___ Pd $_____   MIB   NB   DB   BNT
☐ Want   Orig. Retail $7.75

             MIB Sec. Mkt. **$15**

M   **QXM 516-6**   **HAVE A COOKIE**
Handcrafted, 7/8" tall, Dated 1994, Artist's Favorite.
Artist: Donna Lee
☐ Purchased 19___ Pd $_____   MIB   NB   DB   BNT
☐ Want   Orig. Retail $5.75

             MIB Sec. Mkt. **$12.50**

N   **QXM 400-6**   **HEARTS A-SAIL**
Handcrafted, 15/16" tall, Dated 1994. **Artist:** Ron Bishop
☐ Purchased 19___ Pd $_____   MIB   NB   DB   BNT
☐ Want   Orig. Retail $5.75

             MIB Sec. Mkt. **$12**

A QXM 545-2   **HOLIDAY EXPRESS: REVOLVING TREE BASE**
Handcrafted, 4-1/4" tall. Reissued from 1993.
Train circles track, Miniature tree sold separately.
☐ Purchased 19___ Pd $_____ MIB NB DB BNT
☐ Want Orig. Retail $50.00
MIB Sec. Mkt. **$74**

B QXM 405-3   **JOLLY VISITOR**
Handcrafted, 1" tall, Dated 1994. **Artist:** Linda Sickman
☐ Purchased 19___ Pd $_____ MIB NB DB BNT
☐ Want Orig. Retail $5.75
MIB Sec. Mkt. **$15**

C QXM 409-3   **JOLLY WOLLY SNOWMAN**
Handcrafted, 1" tall, Dated 1994. **Artist:** LaDene Votruba
Snowman wobbles when tapped gently.
☐ Purchased 19___ Pd $_____ MIB NB DB BNT
☐ Want Orig. Retail $3.75
MIB Sec. Mkt. **$8.50**

D QXM 403-6   **JOURNEY TO BETHLEHEM**
Handcrafted, 1-1/4" tall. **Artist:** Joyce Lyle
☐ Purchased 19___ Pd $_____ MIB NB DB BNT
☐ Want Orig. Retail $5.75
MIB Sec. Mkt. **$13.50**

E QXM 408-6   **JUST MY SIZE**
Handcrafted, 1-5/16" tall, Dated 1994. **Artist:** Ron Bishop
☐ Purchased 19___ Pd $_____ MIB NB DB BNT
☐ Want Orig. Retail $3.75
MIB Sec. Mkt. **$8.50**

F QXM 404-3   **LOVE WAS BORN**
Handcrafted, 1-3/16" tall, Dated 1994. **Artist:** Linda Sickman
☐ Purchased 19___ Pd $_____ MIB NB DB BNT
☐ Want Orig. Retail $4.50
MIB Sec. Mkt. **$15**

G QXM 510-6   **MARCH OF THE TEDDY BEARS**
Second in Series, Handcrafted, 1-3/16" tall, Dated 1994.
Artist: Duane Unruh
☐ Purchased 19___ Pd $_____ MIB NB DB BNT
☐ Want Orig. Retail $4.50
MIB Sec. Mkt. **$14**

H QXM 406-6   **MELODIC CHERUB**
Handcrafted, 1-5/16" tall, Dated 1994. **Artist:** Anita Marra Rogers
☐ Purchased 19___ Pd $_____ MIB NB DB BNT
☐ Want Orig. Retail $3.75
MIB Sec. Mkt. **$10**

I QXM 401-3   **MOM**
Handcrafted, 1" tall, Dated 1994. **Artist:** Anita Marra Rogers
☐ Purchased 19___ Pd $_____ MIB NB DB BNT
☐ Want Orig. Retail $4.50
MIB Sec. Mkt. **$10**

J QXM 512-6   **NATURE'S ANGELS**
Fifth in Series, Handcrafted, 1-3/16" tall. **Artist:** LaDene Votruba
☐ Purchased 19___ Pd $_____ MIB NB DB BNT
☐ Want Orig. Retail $4.50
MIB Sec. Mkt. **$12**

K QXM 512-3   **NIGHT BEFORE CHRISTMAS, THE: FATHER**
Third in Series, Handcrafted, 1-3/16" tall, Dated 1994.
Artist: Duane Unruh
☐ Purchased 19___ Pd $_____ MIB NB DB BNT
☐ Want Orig. Retail $4.50
MIB Sec. Mkt. **$13**

L QXM 410-6   **NOAH'S ARK**
Special Edition, Handcrafted, Three piece set.
Ark, 3-1/8" tall: bears, 5/8" tall: seals, 5/8" tall.
Deck lifts off and ladder lowers. Merry Walruses and Playful Penguins were added in '95. African Elephants from '96 complemented the set, although not a part of the series. Price down from '96.
Artist: Linda Sickman
☐ Purchased 19___ Pd $_____ MIB NB DB BNT
☐ Want Orig. Retail $24.50
MIB Sec. Mkt. **$55**

M QXM 511-3   **NOEL R.R.: STOCK CAR**
Sixth in Series, Handcrafted, 13/16" tall, Dated 1994.
Doors slide open and closed. **Artist:** Linda Sickman
☐ Purchased 19___ Pd $_____ MIB NB DB BNT
☐ Want Orig. Retail $7.00
MIB Sec. Mkt. **$16-$20**

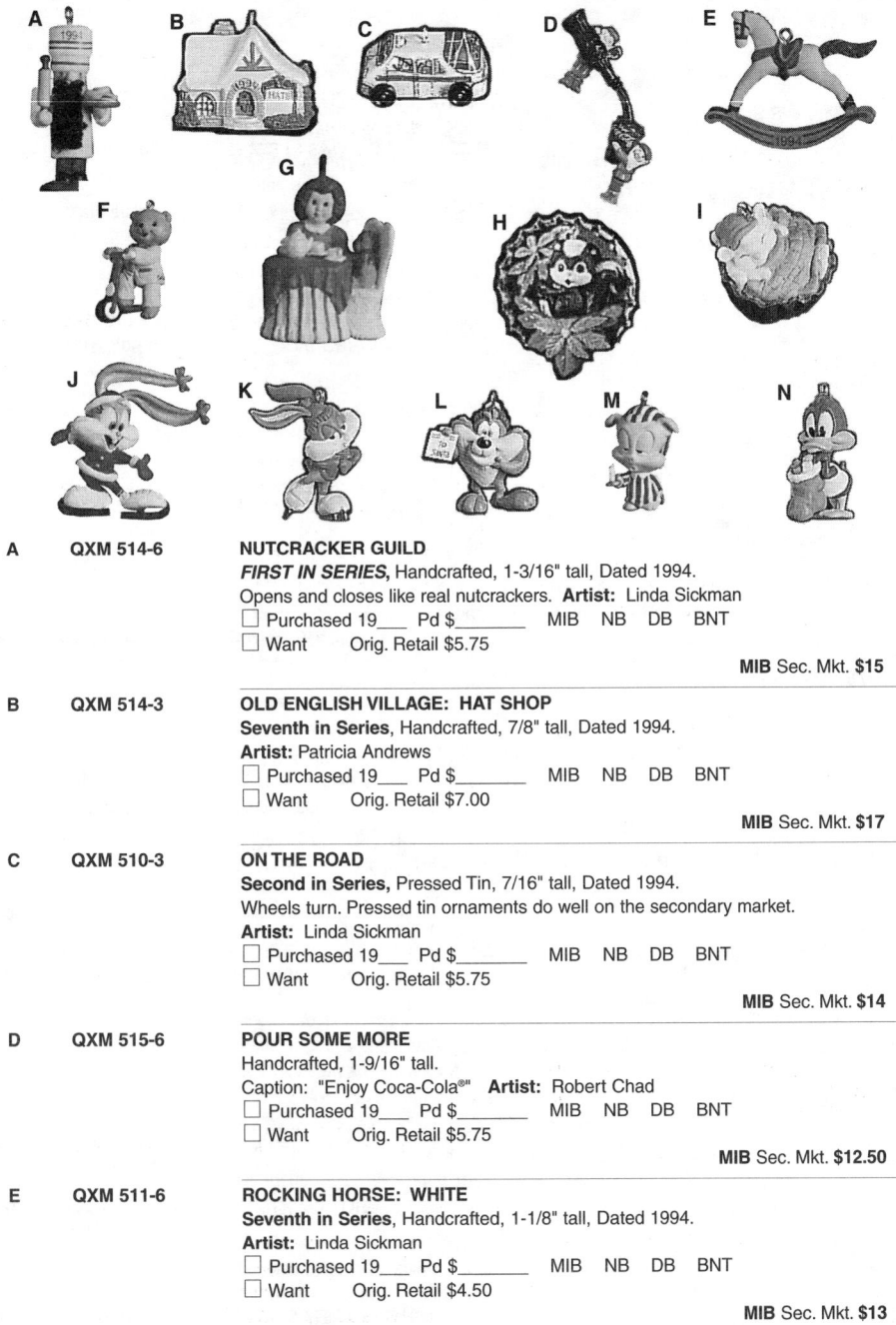

A   QXM 514-6   **NUTCRACKER GUILD**
FIRST IN SERIES, Handcrafted, 1-3/16" tall, Dated 1994.
Opens and closes like real nutcrackers. **Artist:** Linda Sickman
☐ Purchased 19___ Pd $_____   MIB   NB   DB   BNT
☐ Want   Orig. Retail $5.75
                                                    MIB Sec. Mkt. **$15**

B   QXM 514-3   **OLD ENGLISH VILLAGE: HAT SHOP**
Seventh in Series, Handcrafted, 7/8" tall, Dated 1994.
Artist: Patricia Andrews
☐ Purchased 19___ Pd $_____   MIB   NB   DB   BNT
☐ Want   Orig. Retail $7.00
                                                    MIB Sec. Mkt. **$17**

C   QXM 510-3   **ON THE ROAD**
Second in Series, Pressed Tin, 7/16" tall, Dated 1994.
Wheels turn. Pressed tin ornaments do well on the secondary market.
Artist: Linda Sickman
☐ Purchased 19___ Pd $_____   MIB   NB   DB   BNT
☐ Want   Orig. Retail $5.75
                                                    MIB Sec. Mkt. **$14**

D   QXM 515-6   **POUR SOME MORE**
Handcrafted, 1-9/16" tall.
Caption: "Enjoy Coca-Cola®" **Artist:** Robert Chad
☐ Purchased 19___ Pd $_____   MIB   NB   DB   BNT
☐ Want   Orig. Retail $5.75
                                                MIB Sec. Mkt. **$12.50**

E   QXM 511-6   **ROCKING HORSE: WHITE**
Seventh in Series, Handcrafted, 1-1/8" tall, Dated 1994.
Artist: Linda Sickman
☐ Purchased 19___ Pd $_____   MIB   NB   DB   BNT
☐ Want   Orig. Retail $4.50
                                                    MIB Sec. Mkt. **$13**

F   QXM 517-3   **SCOOTING ALONG**
Handcrafted, 1-3/16" tall, Dated 1994, Artist's Favorite.
Artist: John Francis
☐ Purchased 19___ Pd $_____   MIB   NB   DB   BNT
☐ Want   Orig. Retail $6.75
                                                    MIB Sec. Mkt. **$13**

G   QXM 404-6   **TEA WITH TEDDY**
Handcrafted, 15/16" tall, Dated 1994. **Artist:** Anita Marra Rogers
☐ Purchased 19___ Pd $_____   MIB   NB   DB   BNT
☐ Want   Orig. Retail $7.25
                                                    MIB Sec. Mkt. **$13**

H   QXC 480-6   **SWEET BOUQUET: KEEPSAKE COLLECTOR'S CLUB**
Handcrafted, 1-3/16" dia. Caption: "Santa's Club Soda."
☐ Purchased 19___ Pd $_____   MIB   NB   DB   BNT
☐ Want   Orig. Retail - Included with Membership Kit
                                                    MIB Sec. Mkt. **$20**

I   QXM 409-6   **SWEET DREAMS**
Handcrafted, 11/16" tall. **Artist:** Ken Crow
☐ Purchased 19___ Pd $_____   MIB   NB   DB   BNT
☐ Want   Orig. Retail $3.00
                                                    MIB Sec. Mkt. **$12**

J   QXM 411-6   **TINY TOON ADVENTURES: BABS BUNNY**
Handcrafted, 1-5/16" tall. **Artist:** Don Palmiter
☐ Purchased 19___ Pd $_____   MIB   NB   DB   BNT
☐ Want   Orig. Retail $5.75
                                                    MIB Sec. Mkt. **$13**

K   QXM 516-3   **TINY TOON ADVENTURES: BUSTER BUNNY**
Handcrafted, 1-5/16" tall. **Artist:** Don Palmiter
☐ Purchased 19___ Pd $_____   MIB   NB   DB   BNT
☐ Want   Orig. Retail $5.75
                                                    MIB Sec. Mkt. **$12**

L   QXM 413-3   **TINY TOON ADVENTURES: DIZZY DEVIL**
Handcrafted, 15/16" tall. **Artist:** Don Palmiter
☐ Purchased 19___ Pd $_____   MIB   NB   DB   BNT
☐ Want   Orig. Retail $5.75
                                                    MIB Sec. Mkt. **$13**

M   QXM 412-6   **TINY TOON ADVENTURES: HAMTON**
Handcrafted, 1-1/16" tall. **Artist:** Don Palmiter
☐ Purchased 19___ Pd $_____   MIB   NB   DB   BNT
☐ Want   Orig. Retail $5.75
                                                    MIB Sec. Mkt. **$12**

N   QXM 412-3   **TINY TOON ADVENTURES: PLUCKY DUCK**
Handcrafted, 1-1/8" tall. **Artist:** Don Palmiter
☐ Purchased 19___ Pd $_____   MIB   NB   DB   BNT
☐ Want   Orig. Retail $5.75
                                                    MIB Sec. Mkt. **$12**

1994 Easter Ornament Collection

A   QEO 815-3   **BABY'S FIRST EASTER** ☐

Handcrafted, 2" tall, Dated 1994.
Sleeping bunny in basket. **Artist:** John Francis

☐ Purchased 19___   Pd $_____   MIB   NB   DB   BNT

☐ Want   Original Retail $6.75

      MIB Sec. Mkt. **$20**

B   QEO 823-3   **COLLECTOR'S PLATE** ☐

FIRST IN SERIES, Porcelain, 3" dia. **Artist:** LaDene Votruba
Caption: "Gathering Sunny Memories 1994."

☐ Purchased 19___   Pd $_____   MIB   NB   DB   BNT

☐ Want   Original Retail $7.75

      MIB Sec. Mkt. **$32**

C   QEO 816-6   **COLORFUL SPRING** ☐

Handcrafted, 3" tall. Caption: "Crayola® Crayon 1994"
Was very popular. **Artist:** Ken Crow

☐ Purchased 19___   Pd $_____   MIB   NB   DB   BNT

☐ Want   Original Retail $7.75

      MIB Sec. Mkt. **$28**

D   QEO 815-6   **DAUGHTER** ☐

Handcrafted, 2" tall, Dated 1994. **Artist:** Patricia Andrews
Girl bunny in yellow dress.

☐ Purchased 19___   Pd $_____   MIB   NB   DB   BNT

☐ Want   Original Retail $5.75

      MIB Sec. Mkt. **$15**

E   QEO 818-3   **DIVINE DUET** ☐

Handcrafted, 2" tall. Caption: "Easter Hymns." **Artist:** LaDene Votruba

☐ Purchased 19___   Pd $_____   MIB   NB   DB   BNT

☐ Want   Original Retail $6.75

      MIB Sec. Mkt. **$16.50**

F   QEO 819-3   **EASTER ART SHOW** ☐

Handcrafted, 2-1/4" tall, Dated 1994.
Stringer Ornament, hangs from two branches. **Artist:** LaDene Votruba

☐ Purchased 19___   Pd $_____   MIB   NB   DB   BNT

☐ Want   Original Retail $7.75

      MIB Sec. Mkt. **$18.50**

G   QEO 813-6   **EASTER PARADE** ☐

Third and Final in Series, Handcrafted, 1-1/4" tall, Dated '94.
Artist: Dill Rhodus

☐ Purchased 19___   Pd $_____   MIB   NB   DB   BNT

☐ Want   Original Retail $6.75

      MIB Sec. Mkt. **$20**

H   QEO 813-3   **EGGS IN SPORTS** ☐

Third and Final in Series, Handcrafted, 2" tall. Final? Too bad-a great series.
Caption: "Golf Club 94." **Artist:** Bob Siedler

☐ Purchased 19___   Pd $_____   MIB   NB   DB   BNT

☐ Want   Original Retail $6.75

      MIB Sec. Mkt. **$22**

I   **FIRST HELLO** ☐

Handcrafted, Dated '94.

☐ Purchased 19___   Pd $_____   MIB   NB   DB   BNT

☐ Want   Original Retail Free gift to a member who enrolled a
new club member using a special gift application

      MIB Sec. Mkt. **$**

J   QEO 809-3   **HERE COMES EASTER** ☐

FIRST IN SERIES, Handcrafted, 1-3/4" tall.
Caption: "Hop-N-Go 1994." **Artist:** Ken Crow

☐ Purchased 19___   Pd $_____   MIB   NB   DB   BNT

☐ Want   Original Retail $7.75

      MIB Sec. Mkt. **$30**

K   QEO 820-6   **JOYFUL LAMB** ☐

Handcrafted, 1-3/4" tall. **Artist:** Duane Unruh

☐ Purchased 19___   Pd $_____   MIB   NB   DB   BNT

☐ Want   Original Retail $5.75

      MIB Sec. Mkt. **$15**

L   QEO 817-6   **PEANUTS®** ☐

Handcrafted, 2-1/4" tall, Caption: "Easter Beagle 1994."
Was the hottest Easter ornament for 1994.
Artist: Duane Unruh

☐ Purchased 19___   Pd $_____   MIB   NB   DB   BNT

☐ Want   Original Retail $7.75

      MIB Sec. Mkt. **$40**

A   B   C   D   E   F   G   H   I   J   K   L

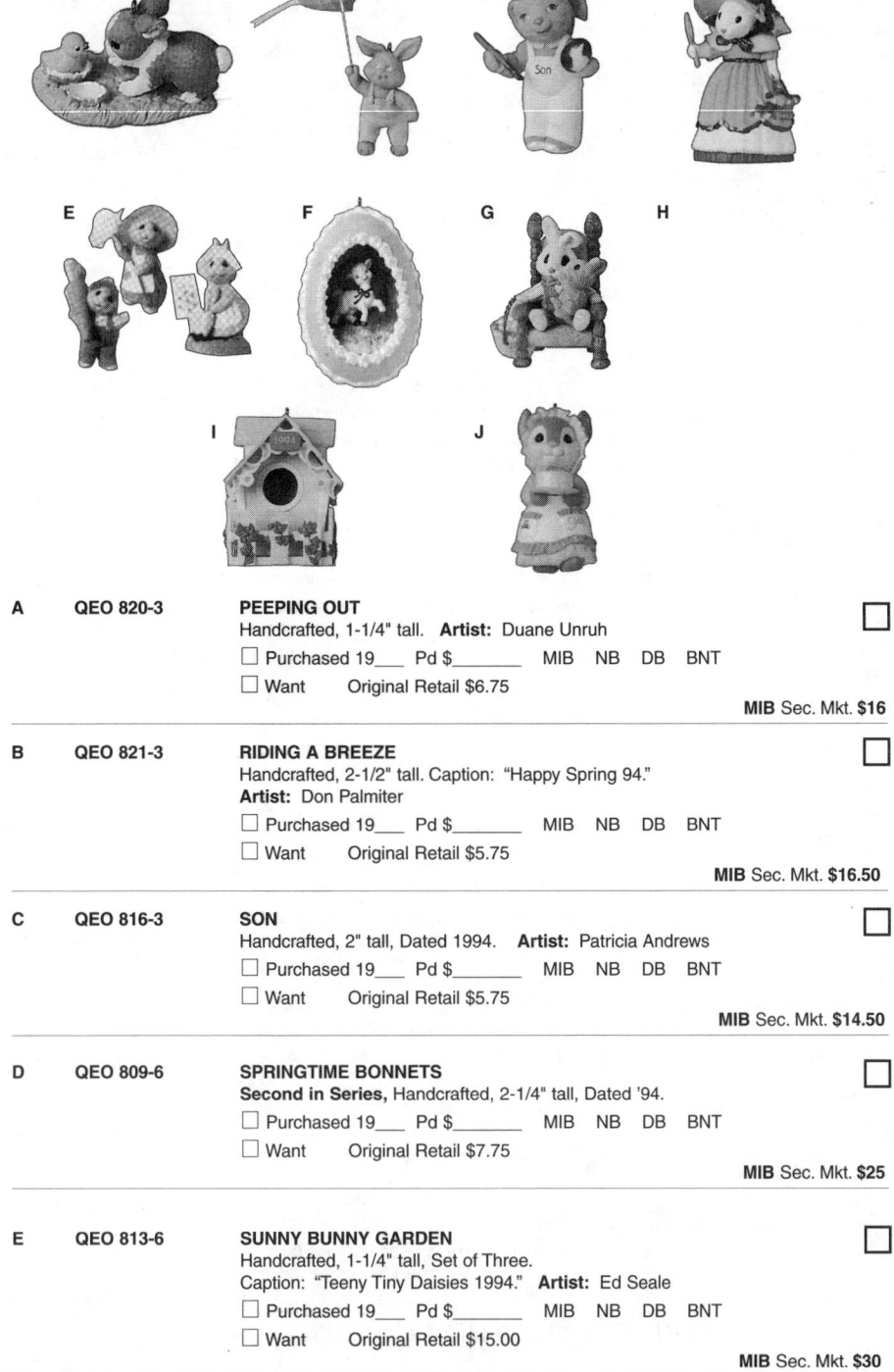

A QEO 820-3   **PEEPING OUT**
Handcrafted, 1-1/4" tall. **Artist:** Duane Unruh
☐ Purchased 19___ Pd $_____   MIB   NB   DB   BNT
☐ Want   Original Retail $6.75
MIB Sec. Mkt. **$16**

B QEO 821-3   **RIDING A BREEZE**
Handcrafted, 2-1/2" tall. Caption: "Happy Spring 94."
Artist: Don Palmiter
☐ Purchased 19___ Pd $_____   MIB   NB   DB   BNT
☐ Want   Original Retail $5.75
MIB Sec. Mkt. **$16.50**

C QEO 816-3   **SON**
Handcrafted, 2" tall, Dated 1994. **Artist:** Patricia Andrews
☐ Purchased 19___ Pd $_____   MIB   NB   DB   BNT
☐ Want   Original Retail $5.75
MIB Sec. Mkt. **$14.50**

D QEO 809-6   **SPRINGTIME BONNETS**
Second in Series, Handcrafted, 2-1/4" tall, Dated '94.
☐ Purchased 19___ Pd $_____   MIB   NB   DB   BNT
☐ Want   Original Retail $7.75
MIB Sec. Mkt. **$25**

E QEO 813-6   **SUNNY BUNNY GARDEN**
Handcrafted, 1-1/4" tall, Set of Three.
Caption: "Teeny Tiny Daisies 1994." **Artist:** Ed Seale
☐ Purchased 19___ Pd $_____   MIB   NB   DB   BNT
☐ Want   Original Retail $15.00
MIB Sec. Mkt. **$30**

F QEO 808-6   **SWEET AS SUGAR**
Handcrafted, 2-3/4" tall, Dated 1994. **Artist:** Anita Marra Rogers
☐ Purchased 19___ Pd $_____   MIB   NB   DB   BNT
☐ Want   Original Retail $8.75
MIB Sec. Mkt. **$20**

G QEO 819-6   **SWEET EASTER WISHES**
Tender Touches, Handcrafted, 2" tall.
Caption: "94 EB." Popular one.
☐ Purchased 19___ Pd $_____   MIB   NB   DB   BNT
☐ Want   Original Retail $8.75
MIB Sec. Mkt. **$28**

H QXC 825-6   **TILLING TIME: CLUB EXCLUSIVE**
Handcrafted,
☐ Purchased 19___ Pd $_____   MIB   NB   DB   BNT
☐ Want   Original Retail $8.75
MIB Sec. Mkt. **$30-$35**

I QEO 818-6   **TREETOP COTTAGE**
Handcrafted, 2" tall, Dated 1994. **Artist:** Linda Sickman
☐ Purchased 19___ Pd $_____   MIB   NB   DB   BNT
☐ Want   Original Retail $9.75
MIB Sec. Mkt. **$21**

J QEO 814-3   **YUMMY RECIPE**
Handcrafted, 2-1/4" tall. Caption: "Anita '94."
Recipe for carrot cake in box. **Artist:** Anita Marra Rogers
☐ Purchased 19___ Pd $_____   MIB   NB   DB   BNT
☐ Want   Original Retail $7.75
MIB Sec. Mkt. **$20**

Miniature ornaments adorn this little tree of Helen Settles.

1995 Collection

Considering the age of the ornaments, NB Prices are not being given for these pieces.

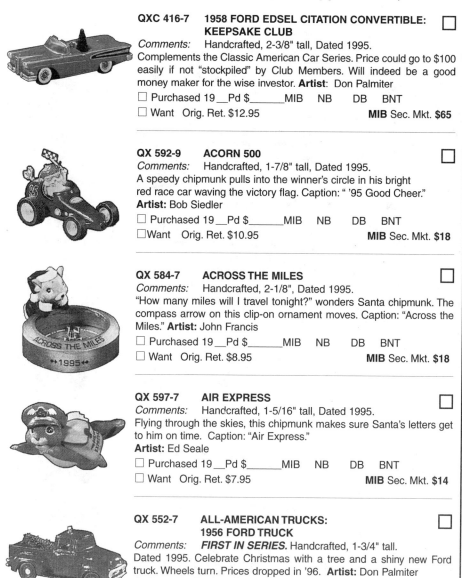

QXC 416-7   1958 FORD EDSEL CITATION CONVERTIBLE: KEEPSAKE CLUB ☐

Comments: Handcrafted, 2-3/8" tall, Dated 1995.
Complements the Classic American Car Series. Price could go to $100 easily if not "stockpiled" by Club Members. Will indeed be a good money maker for the wise investor. **Artist**: Don Palmiter

☐ Purchased 19__Pd $_____MIB   NB   DB   BNT
☐ Want   Orig. Ret. $12.95   **MIB** Sec. Mkt. **$65**

QX 592-9   ACORN 500 ☐

Comments: Handcrafted, 1-7/8" tall, Dated 1995.
A speedy chipmunk pulls into the winner's circle in his bright red race car waving the victory flag. Caption: " '95 Good Cheer."
Artist: Bob Siedler

☐ Purchased 19__Pd $_____MIB   NB   DB   BNT
☐Want   Orig. Ret. $10.95   **MIB** Sec. Mkt. **$18**

QX 584-7   ACROSS THE MILES ☐

Comments: Handcrafted, 2-1/8", Dated 1995.
"How many miles will I travel tonight?" wonders Santa chipmunk. The compass arrow on this clip-on ornament moves. Caption: "Across the Miles." **Artist:** John Francis

☐ Purchased 19__Pd $_____MIB   NB   DB   BNT
☐ Want   Orig. Ret. $8.95   **MIB** Sec. Mkt. **$18**

QX 597-7   AIR EXPRESS ☐

Comments: Handcrafted, 1-5/16" tall, Dated 1995.
Flying through the skies, this chipmunk makes sure Santa's letters get to him on time. Caption: "Air Express."
Artist: Ed Seale

☐ Purchased 19__Pd $_____MIB   NB   DB   BNT
☐ Want   Orig. Ret. $7.95   **MIB** Sec. Mkt. **$14**

QX 552-7   ALL-AMERICAN TRUCKS: 1956 FORD TRUCK ☐

Comments: **FIRST IN SERIES.** Handcrafted, 1-3/4" tall. Dated 1995. Celebrate Christmas with a tree and a shiny new Ford truck. Wheels turn. Prices dropped in '96. **Artist:** Don Palmiter

☐ Purchased 19__Pd $_____MIB   NB   DB   BNT
☐ Want   Orig. Ret. $13.95   **MIB** Sec. Mkt. **$28**

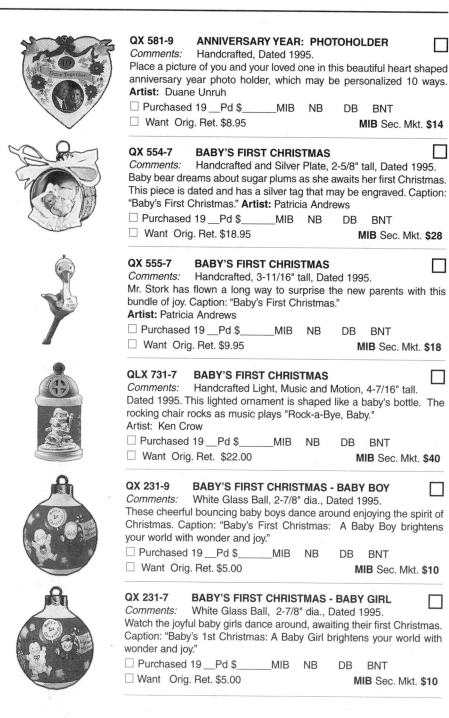

QX 581-9   ANNIVERSARY YEAR: PHOTOHOLDER ☐

Comments: Handcrafted, Dated 1995.
Place a picture of you and your loved one in this beautiful heart shaped anniversary year photo holder, which may be personalized 10 ways.
Artist: Duane Unruh

☐ Purchased 19__Pd $_____MIB   NB   DB   BNT
☐ Want Orig. Ret. $8.95   **MIB** Sec. Mkt. **$14**

QX 554-7   BABY'S FIRST CHRISTMAS ☐

Comments: Handcrafted and Silver Plate, 2-5/8" tall, Dated 1995. Baby bear dreams about sugar plums as she awaits her first Christmas. This piece is dated and has a silver tag that may be engraved. Caption: "Baby's First Christmas." **Artist:** Patricia Andrews

☐ Purchased 19__Pd $_____MIB   NB   DB   BNT
☐ Want Orig. Ret. $18.95   **MIB** Sec. Mkt. **$28**

QX 555-7   BABY'S FIRST CHRISTMAS ☐

Comments: Handcrafted, 3-11/16" tall, Dated 1995.
Mr. Stork has flown a long way to surprise the new parents with this bundle of joy. Caption: "Baby's First Christmas."
Artist: Patricia Andrews

☐ Purchased 19__Pd $_____MIB   NB   DB   BNT
☐ Want Orig. Ret. $9.95   **MIB** Sec. Mkt. **$18**

QLX 731-7   BABY'S FIRST CHRISTMAS ☐

Comments: Handcrafted Light, Music and Motion, 4-7/16" tall. Dated 1995. This lighted ornament is shaped like a baby's bottle. The rocking chair rocks as music plays "Rock-a-Bye, Baby."
Artist: Ken Crow

☐ Purchased 19__Pd $_____MIB   NB   DB   BNT
☐ Want Orig. Ret. $22.00   **MIB** Sec. Mkt. **$40**

QX 231-9   BABY'S FIRST CHRISTMAS - BABY BOY ☐

Comments: White Glass Ball, 2-7/8" dia., Dated 1995.
These cheerful bouncing baby boys dance around enjoying the spirit of Christmas. Caption: "Baby's First Christmas: A Baby Boy brightens your world with wonder and joy."

☐ Purchased 19__Pd $_____MIB   NB   DB   BNT
☐ Want Orig. Ret. $5.00   **MIB** Sec. Mkt. **$10**

QX 231-7   BABY'S FIRST CHRISTMAS - BABY GIRL ☐

Comments: White Glass Ball, 2-7/8" dia., Dated 1995.
Watch the joyful baby girls dance around, awaiting their first Christmas. Caption: "Baby's 1st Christmas: A Baby Girl brightens your world with wonder and joy."

☐ Purchased 19__Pd $_____MIB   NB   DB   BNT
☐ Want   Orig. Ret. $5.00   **MIB** Sec. Mkt. **$10**

QX 554-9   BABY'S FIRST CHRISTMAS: PHOTOHOLDER ☐
Comments: Handcrafted, 4-7/16" tall, Dated 1995.
Place your baby's first Christmas picture in this baby block photoholder. Caption: "Baby's First Christmas."
Artist: LaDene Votruba

☐ Purchased 19 __Pd $_____MIB   NB   DB   BNT
☐ Want   Orig. Ret. $7.95   **MIB** Sec. Mkt. **$16**

QX 555-9   BABY'S FIRST CHRISTMAS: ☐
TEDDY BEAR YEARS COLLECTION
Comments: Handcrafted, 2-3/16" tall, Dated 1995.
Baby celebrates its first Christmas with a stocking and star-shaped Christmas cookie. Design is repeated from 1994. Caption: "Baby's 1st Christmas." **Artist:** Ken Crow

☐ Purchased 19 Pd $_____MIB   NB   DB   BNT
☐ Want Orig. Ret. $7.95   **MIB** Sec. Mkt. **$18**

QX 556-7   BABY'S SECOND CHRISTMAS: ☐
TEDDY BEAR YEARS COLLECTION
Comments: Handcrafted, 2-3/8" tall, Dated 1995
Teddy wears a red and white bow tie and holds a green Christmas stocking with a tree-shaped cookie. Caption: "Baby's 2nd Christmas." Design is repeated from '94. **Artist:** Ken Crow

☐ Purchased 19 __Pd $_____MIB   NB   DB   BNT
☐ Want   Orig. Ret. $7.95   **MIB** Sec. Mkt. **$16**

QXC 539-7   BARBIE™: BRUNETTE DEBUT-1959 ☐
KEEPSAKE CLUB
Comments: Handcrafted, Dated 1995.
This brunette beauty dresses for summer in her black and white bathing suit. Wasn't the most popular Barbie Ornament. **Artist:** Patricia Andrews

☐ Purchased 19 __Pd $_____MIB   NB   DB   BNT
☐ Want   Orig. Ret. $14.95   **MIB** Sec. Mkt. **$40 up**

QXI 504-9   BARBIE™: SOLO IN THE SPOTLIGHT ☐
Comments: **Second in Series.** Handcrafted, 4-3/8" tall, Dated. 1995.
Barbie sings the wonderful sounds of Christmas in her strapless black sequin mermaid dress. Caption: "Solo in the Spotlight 1995 Edition."
Artist: Patricia Andrews

☐ Purchased 19 __Pd $_____MIB   NB   DB   BNT
☐ Want   Orig. Ret. $14.95   **MIB** Sec. Mkt. **$28**

QX 518-9   BARREL-BACK RIDER ☐
Comments: Handcrafted, 2-5/16" tall, Dated 1995.
Cowboy bear is ready for the rodeo! **Artist:** John Francis

☐ Purchased 19 __Pd $_____MIB   NB   DB   BNT
☐ Want   Orig. Ret. $9.95   **MIB** Sec. Mkt. **$22**

QX 502-9   BASEBALL HEROES: LOU GEHRIG ☐
Comments: **Second in Series,** Handcrafted, 3-3/8" dia., Dated 1995.
Caption: "Lou Gehrig '95, 2,130 Consecutive Games American League MVP 1927, Batting Triple Crown 1934, .340 Lifetime Batting Average, Elected to Hall of Fame 1939." **Artist:** Dill Rhodus

☐ Purchased 19 __Pd $_____MIB   NB   DB   BNT
☐ Want   Orig. Ret. $12.95   **MIB** Sec. Mkt. **$18**

QX 573-9   BATMOBILE ☐
Comments: Handcrafted, 1-1/16" tall, Dated 1995.
Batman and Robin rush off in their Batmobile to rescue Gotham City.
Artist: Don Palmiter

☐ Purchased 19 __Pd $_____MIB   NB   DB   BNT
☐ Want   Orig. Ret. $14.95   **MIB** Sec. Mkt. **$25**

QX 541-7   BETTY AND WILMA: THE FLINTSTONES® ☐
Comments: Handcrafted, Dated 1995. Betty and Wilma are headed home from their Christmas shopping spree. **Artist:** Dill Rhodus

☐ Purchased 19 __Pd $_____MIB   NB   DB   BNT
☐ Want   Orig. Ret. $14.95   **MIB** Sec. Mkt. **$22**

QX 525-9   BEVERLY AND TEDDY: SPECIAL EDITION ☐
Comments: Handcrafted, 2-7/8" tall, Dated 1995.
Beverly and Teddy enjoy the true Christmas spirit. Caption: "Carols."
Artist: Duane Unruh

☐ Purchased 19 __Pd $_____MIB   NB   DB   BNT
☐ Want   Orig. Ret. $21.75   **MIB** Sec. Mkt. **$30**

QX 591-9   BINGO BEAR ☐
Comments: Handcrafted, 2-3/4" tall, Dated 1995.
Bingo! Mr. Bear wins with the diagonal 1995. Caption: "Bingo."
Artist: LaDene Votruba

☐ Purchased 19 __Pd $_____MIB   NB   DB   BNT
☐ Want   Orig. Ret. $7.95   **MIB** Sec. Mkt. **$18**

QX 587-9   BOBBIN' ALONG ☐
Comments: Handcrafted, 2-1/4" tall, Dated 1995.
Bucky beaver takes a nap on a mallard decoy, while hoping to catch his dinner at the same time. **Artist:** Ken Crow

☐ Purchased 19 __Pd $_____MIB   NB   DB   BNT
☐ Want   Orig. Ret. $8.95   **MIB** Sec. Mkt. **$35**

QX 567-9   BROTHER ☐
Comments: Handcrafted, 2-9/16" tall, Dated 1995.
Snowboarding brother is the coolest one around in his brightly colored shades and scarf. Caption: "Brother." **Artist:** Joyce Lyle

☐ Purchased 19 __Pd $_____MIB   NB   DB   BNT
☐ Want   Orig. Ret. $6.95   **MIB** Sec. Mkt. **$12**

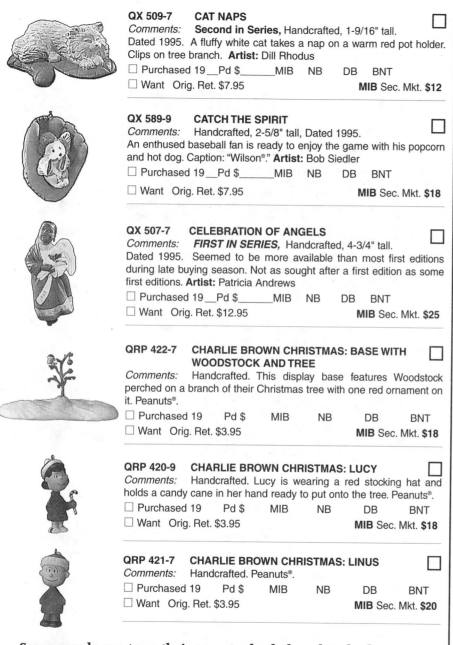

QX 509-7   CAT NAPS

Comments: **Second in Series,** Handcrafted, 1-9/16" tall. Dated 1995. A fluffy white cat takes a nap on a warm red pot holder. Clips on tree branch. **Artist:** Dill Rhodus

☐ Purchased 19__Pd $_____MIB   NB   DB   BNT

☐ Want   Orig. Ret. $7.95   **MIB** Sec. Mkt. **$12**

QX 589-9   CATCH THE SPIRIT

Comments: Handcrafted, 2-5/8" tall, Dated 1995. An enthused baseball fan is ready to enjoy the game with his popcorn and hot dog. Caption: "Wilson." **Artist:** Bob Siedler

☐ Purchased 19__Pd $_____MIB   NB   DB   BNT

☐ Want   Orig. Ret. $7.95   **MIB** Sec. Mkt. **$18**

QX 507-7   CELEBRATION OF ANGELS

Comments: ***FIRST IN SERIES,*** Handcrafted, 4-3/4" tall. Dated 1995. Seemed to be more available than most first editions during late buying season. Not as sought after a first edition as some first editions. **Artist:** Patricia Andrews

☐ Purchased 19__Pd $_____MIB   NB   DB   BNT

☐ Want   Orig. Ret. $12.95   **MIB** Sec. Mkt. **$25**

QRP 422-7   CHARLIE BROWN CHRISTMAS: BASE WITH WOODSTOCK AND TREE

Comments: Handcrafted. This display base features Woodstock perched on a branch of their Christmas tree with one red ornament on it. Peanuts®.

☐ Purchased 19   Pd $ MIB   NB   DB   BNT

☐ Want   Orig. Ret. $3.95   **MIB** Sec. Mkt. **$18**

QRP 420-9   CHARLIE BROWN CHRISTMAS: LUCY

Comments: Handcrafted. Lucy is wearing a red stocking hat and holds a candy cane in her hand ready to put onto the tree. Peanuts®.

☐ Purchased 19   Pd $ MIB   NB   DB   BNT

☐ Want   Orig. Ret. $3.95   **MIB** Sec. Mkt. **$18**

QRP 421-7   CHARLIE BROWN CHRISTMAS: LINUS

Comments: Handcrafted. Peanuts®.

☐ Purchased 19   Pd $ MIB   NB   DB   BNT

☐ Want   Orig. Ret. $3.95   **MIB** Sec. Mkt. **$20**

Some people can trace their ancestry back three hundred years, but they cannot tell where their children were last night.

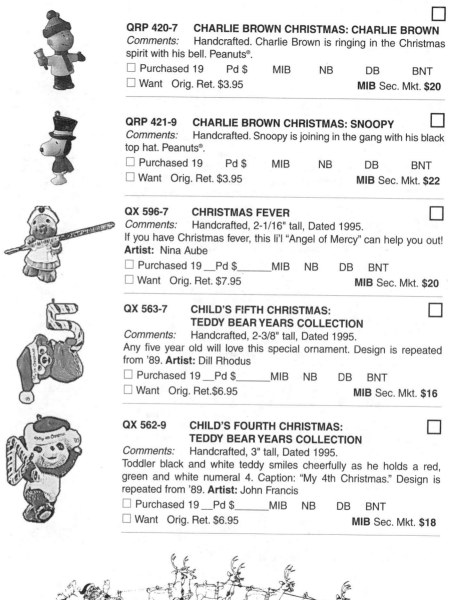

QRP 420-7   CHARLIE BROWN CHRISTMAS: CHARLIE BROWN

Comments: Handcrafted. Charlie Brown is ringing in the Christmas spirit with his bell. Peanuts®.

☐ Purchased 19   Pd $ MIB   NB   DB   BNT

☐ Want   Orig. Ret. $3.95   **MIB** Sec. Mkt. **$20**

QRP 421-9   CHARLIE BROWN CHRISTMAS: SNOOPY

Comments: Handcrafted. Snoopy is joining in the gang with his black top hat. Peanuts®.

☐ Purchased 19   Pd $ MIB   NB   DB   BNT

☐ Want   Orig. Ret. $3.95   **MIB** Sec. Mkt. **$22**

QX 596-7   CHRISTMAS FEVER

Comments: Handcrafted, 2-1/16" tall, Dated 1995. If you have Christmas fever, this li'l "Angel of Mercy" can help you out! **Artist:** Nina Aube

☐ Purchased 19 __Pd $_____MIB   NB   DB   BNT

☐ Want   Orig. Ret. $7.95   **MIB** Sec. Mkt. **$20**

QX 563-7   CHILD'S FIFTH CHRISTMAS: TEDDY BEAR YEARS COLLECTION

Comments: Handcrafted, 2-3/8" tall, Dated 1995. Any five year old will love this special ornament. Design is repeated from '89. **Artist:** Dill Rhodus

☐ Purchased 19 __Pd $_____MIB   NB   DB   BNT

☐ Want   Orig. Ret.$6.95   **MIB** Sec. Mkt. **$16**

QX 562-9   CHILD'S FOURTH CHRISTMAS: TEDDY BEAR YEARS COLLECTION

Comments: Handcrafted, 3" tall, Dated 1995. Toddler black and white teddy smiles cheerfully as he holds a red, green and white numeral 4. Caption: "My 4th Christmas." Design is repeated from '89. **Artist:** John Francis

☐ Purchased 19 __Pd $_____MIB   NB   DB   BNT

☐ Want   Orig. Ret. $6.95   **MIB** Sec. Mkt. **$18**

QX 562-7 CHILD'S THIRD CHRISTMAS: TEDDY BEAR YEARS COLLECTION

Comments: Handcrafted, 2-9/16" tall, Dated 1995.
Teddy holds onto his stocking filled with a frosted bell shaped cookie with the numeral 3 written on it. Caption: "My 3rd Christmas."
Artist: Ken Crow

☐ Purchased 19___ Pd $_____ MIB NB DB BNT
☐ Want Orig. Ret. $7.95   **MIB** Sec. Mkt. **$18**

QLX 730-7 CHRIS MOUSE TREE

Comments: **Eleventh in Series,** Lighted, Handcrafted, 3-5/8" tall. Dated 1995. Chris Mouse climbs to the top of his cheese tree to put his gold star on top. The tree glows. **Artist:** Anita Marra Rogers

☐ Purchased 19___ Pd $_____ MIB NB DB BNT
☐ Want Orig. Ret. $12.50   **MIB** Sec. Mkt. **$25**

QX 599-7 CHRISTMAS MORNING

Comments: Handcrafted, 3-5/16" tall, Dated 1995.
Christmas morning just before the rush! Caption: "How Bright Joys of Christmas, How Warm the Memories." **Artist:** John Francis

☐ Purchased 19___ Pd $_____ MIB NB DB BNT
☐ Want Orig. Ret. $10.95   **MIB** Sec. Mkt. **$18**

QX 595-9 CHRISTMAS PATROL

Comments: Handcrafted, 2-1/8" tall, Dated 1995.
Do you have the Christmas blues? This little car won't let you; he'll pull you over and ticket you for being a scrooge.
Artist: Patricia Andrews

☐ Purchased 19___ Pd $_____ MIB NB DB BNT
☐ Want Orig. Ret. $7.95   **MIB** Sec. Mkt. **$18**

QX 508-7 CHRISTMAS VISITORS: ST. NICHOLAS

Comments: **FIRST IN SERIES,** Handcrafted, 4-9/16" tall.
Dated 1995. St. Nicholas was well known and loved in the 4th century for his kindness and love for children. His staff is brass with a satin brushed finish. **Artist:** Anita Marra Rogers

☐ Purchased 19___ Pd $_____ MIB NB DB BNT
☐ Want Orig. Ret. $14.95   **MIB** Sec. Mkt. **$25**

QX 523-9 CLASSIC AMERICAN CARS: 1969 CHEVROLET CAMARO

Comments: **Fifth in Series,** Handcrafted, 1-5/16" tall, Dated 1995. This classic American car races down the street to get home before anyone wakes up on Christmas morning. The wheels really turn! Many sales reported in '96 below original retail. **Artist:** Don Palmiter

☐ Purchased 19___ Pd $_____ MIB NB DB BNT
☐ Want Orig. Ret. $12.95   **MIB** Sec. Mkt. **$18**

QX 551-9 COLORFUL WORLD: CRAYOLA

Comments: Handcrafted, 3-3/16" tall, Dated 1995.
Multi-Cultural mouse draws his friends with all the colors of the world. Captions: "Crayola® Multi-Cultural 16 Crayons" (front of box), "16 Crayola® Crayons" (side of box), "1995" (back of box).
Artist: Ken Crow

☐ Purchased 19___ Pd $_____ MIB NB DB BNT
☐ Want Orig. Ret. $10.95   **MIB** Sec. Mkt. **$24**

QXC 411-7 COLLECTING MEMORIES: KEEPSAKE CLUB

Comments: Handcrafted, Dated 1995.
Mr. Beaver enjoys displaying his favorite Keepsake Ornaments in a wooden displayer. **Artist:** Bob Siedler

☐ Purchased 19___ Pd $_____ MIB NB DB BNT
☐ Want Membership Fee $20   **MIB** Sec. Mkt. **$18**

QLX 736-9 COMING TO SEE SANTA

Comments: Handcrafted, Light, Motion and Voice, 3-11/16" tall. Dated 1995. Santa says "Ho! Ho! Ho!" when the children come to see him. **Artist:** Don Palmiter

☐ Purchased 19___ Pd $_____ MIB NB DB BNT
☐ Want Orig. Ret. $32.00   **MIB** Sec. Mkt. **$65**

QX 599-9 COWS OF BALI

Comments: Handcrafted, 3" tall, Dated 1995.
Santa's helper cow is ready for an island Christmas celebration in his grass skirt and Christmas tree bikini top. Designed from Shoebox Greetings. **Artist:** Patricia Andrews

☐ Purchased 19___ Pd $_____ MIB NB DB BNT
☐ Want Orig. Ret. $8.95   **MIB** Sec. Mkt. **$16**

QX 524-7 CRAYOLA® CRAYON: BRIGHT 'N SUNNY TEPEE

Comments: **Seventh in Series,** Handcrafted, 2-11/16" tall.
Dated 1995. A little Indian bear peeks out the door of his tepee to give everyone a colorful Christmas hello. Caption: "1995 Crayola® Crayons."
Artist: Patricia Andrews

☐ Purchased 19___ Pd $_____ MIB NB DB BNT
☐ Want Orig. Ret. $10.95   **MIB** Sec. Mkt. **$18**

QX 564-9 DAD

Comments: Handcrafted, Dated 1995.
Dad is ready for Christmas as he pulls the family Christmas tree behind him.
Artist: Bob Siedler

☐ Purchased 19___ Pd $_____ MIB NB DB BNT
☐ Want Orig. Ret. $7.95   **MIB** Sec. Mkt. **$15**

QX 566-7   DAD-TO-BE

Comments: Handcrafted, 1-15/16" tall, Dated 1995.
The dad-to-be reads up on the latest parenting tips.
Caption: "LePaws Dad To Be."
Artist: Dill Rhodus

☐ Purchased 19__ Pd $_____MIB   NB   DB   BNT
☐ Want Orig. Ret. $7.95   **MIB** Sec. Mkt. **$15**

QX 567-7   DAUGHTER

Comments: Handcrafted, 2-3/4" tall, Dated 1995.
This very sharp panda is a great student, but even she can't wait for the Christmas holiday. Caption: "Extra Sharp Daughter."
Artist: Don Palmiter

☐ Purchased 19__ Pd $_____MIB   NB   DB   BNT
☐ Want Orig. Ret. $6.95   **MIB** Sec. Mkt. **$10**

QX 410-7   DELIVERING KISSES

Comments: Handcrafted, Dated 1995.
Two little mice are delivering Hershey's™ Kisses to Santa to fill stockings on Christmas Eve. Name brand ornaments often do sell above the secondary market value. **Artist:** Linda Sickman

☐ Purchased 19__ Pd $_____MIB   NB   DB   BNT
☐ Want Orig. Ret. $10.95   **MIB** Sec. Mkt. **$25**

QX 600-7   DREAM ON

Comments: Handcrafted, 3-3/4" tall, Dated 1995.
The want list is a little too long for Santa. Caption: "I Want."
Artist: John Francis

☐ Purchased 19__ Pd $_____MIB   NB   DB   BNT
☐ Want Orig. Ret. $10.95   **MIB** Sec. Mkt. **$24**

QX 620-9   DUDLEY THE DRAGON

Comments: Handcrafted, 3-3/4" tall, Dated 1995.
Dudley dresses as Santa and passes out gifts to all the good little boys and girls. **Artist:** Sharon Pike

☐ Purchased 19 Pd $_____MIB   NB   DB   BNT
☐ Want Orig. Ret. $10.95   **MIB** Sec. Mkt. **$20**

QX 514-7   FABULOUS DECADE

Comments :   **Sixth in Series,** Handcrafted, 2-5/16" tall, Dated 1995.
An otter relaxes for the winter on the brass date.
Artist: Ed Seale

☐ Purchased 19 Pd $_____MIB   NB   DB   BNT
☐ Want Orig. Ret. $7.95   **MIB** Sec. Mkt. **$16**

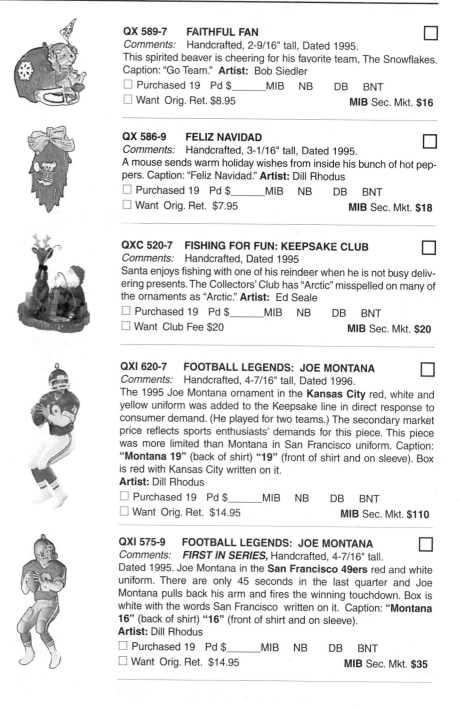

QX 589-7   FAITHFUL FAN

Comments: Handcrafted, 2-9/16" tall, Dated 1995.
This spirited beaver is cheering for his favorite team, The Snowflakes.
Caption: "Go Team." **Artist:** Bob Siedler

☐ Purchased 19 Pd $_____MIB   NB   DB   BNT
☐ Want Orig. Ret. $8.95   **MIB** Sec. Mkt. **$16**

QX 586-9   FELIZ NAVIDAD

Comments: Handcrafted, 3-1/16" tall, Dated 1995.
A mouse sends warm holiday wishes from inside his bunch of hot peppers. Caption: "Feliz Navidad." **Artist:** Dill Rhodus

☐ Purchased 19 Pd $_____MIB   NB   DB   BNT
☐ Want Orig. Ret. $7.95   **MIB** Sec. Mkt. **$18**

QXC 520-7   FISHING FOR FUN: KEEPSAKE CLUB

Comments: Handcrafted, Dated 1995
Santa enjoys fishing with one of his reindeer when he is not busy delivering presents. The Collectors' Club has "Arctic" misspelled on many of the ornaments as "Arctic." **Artist:** Ed Seale

☐ Purchased 19 Pd $_____MIB   NB   DB   BNT
☐ Want Club Fee $20   **MIB** Sec. Mkt. **$20**

QXI 620-7   FOOTBALL LEGENDS: JOE MONTANA

Comments: Handcrafted, 4-7/16" tall, Dated 1996.
The 1995 Joe Montana ornament in the **Kansas City** red, white and yellow uniform was added to the Keepsake line in direct response to consumer demand. (He played for two teams.) The secondary market price reflects sports enthusiasts' demands for this piece. This piece was more limited than Montana in San Francisco uniform. Caption: **"Montana 19"** (back of shirt) **"19"** (front of shirt and on sleeve). Box is red with Kansas City written on it.
Artist: Dill Rhodus

☐ Purchased 19 Pd $_____MIB   NB   DB   BNT
☐ Want Orig. Ret. $14.95   **MIB** Sec. Mkt. **$110**

QXI 575-9   FOOTBALL LEGENDS: JOE MONTANA

Comments: **FIRST IN SERIES,** Handcrafted, 4-7/16" tall.
Dated 1995. Joe Montana in the **San Francisco 49ers** red and white uniform. There are only 45 seconds in the last quarter and Joe Montana pulls back his arm and fires the winning touchdown. Box is white with the words San Francisco written on it. Caption: **"Montana 16"** (back of shirt) **"16"** (front of shirt and on sleeve).
Artist: Dill Rhodus

☐ Purchased 19 Pd $_____MIB   NB   DB   BNT
☐ Want Orig. Ret. $14.95   **MIB** Sec. Mkt. **$35**

QX 572-9   FOR MY GRANDMA: PHOTOHOLDER

Comments: Handcrafted, 4-1/6" tall, Dated 1995.
Keep that special picture of you and your grandma in this
frosted gingerbread house picture frame. Caption: "For My
Grandma, I Love You! From _____."
Artist: Don Palmiter

☐ Purchased 19 Pd $_____ MIB   NB   DB   BNT
☐ Want Orig. Ret. $6.95   **MIB** Sec. Mkt. **$14**

QLX 729-9   FOREST FROLICS

Comments: **Seventh and Final in Series,** Handcrafted, Motion.
4-1/8" tall, Dated 1995. The forest animals enjoy swinging back and
forth on their wooden swing. Caption: "1995 Merry Christmas."
Artist: Sharon Pike

☐ Purchased 19 __Pd $_____ MIB   NB   DB   BNT
☐ Want Orig. Ret.$28.00   **MIB** Sec. Mkt. **$50**

QX 525-8   FOREVER FRIENDS BEAR

Comments: Handcrafted, 2-3/8" tall, Dated 1995.
Give your special friend a bear they will always remember you by. This
bear has holly berries to share with his friends.
Artist: Andrew Brownsword

☐ Purchased 19 Pd $_____ MIB   NB   DB   BNT
☐ Want Orig. Ret.$8.95   **MIB** Sec. Mkt. **$20**

QLX 728-9   FRED AND DINO: THE FLINTSTONES®

Comments: Light, Motion and Sound. Handcrafted, 4-11/16" tall.
Dated 1995. Dino chases Fred while he calls out a holiday message:
"Yabba-Dabba-Doo! Down, Dino, Down! Have a Happy Holiday."
Artist: Dill Rhodus

☐ Purchased 19 Pd $_____ MIB   NB   DB   BNT
☐ Want Orig. Ret. $28.00   **MIB** Sec. Mkt. **$55**

QLX 734-9   FRIENDS SHARE FUN

Comments: Handcrafted, Flickering Light, 2-1/16" tall, Dated 1995.
This clip-on ornament shows two little chipmunks roasting nuts over a
fire. Caption: "Friends are always cooking up holiday fun."
Artist: Anita Marra Rogers

☐ Purchased 19 __Pd $_____ MIB   NB   DB   BNT
☐ Want Orig. Ret. $16.50   **MIB** Sec. Mkt. **$35**

QX 582-7   FRIENDLY BOOST

Comments: Handcrafted and Acrylic, 3-3/16" tall, Dated 1995.
A little penguin gets help from his buddy putting the star atop the
Christmas ice tree.
Artist: Don Palmiter

☐ Purchased 19 __Pd $_____ MIB   NB   DB   BNT
☐ Want Orig. Ret. $8.95   **MIB** Sec. Mkt. **$14**

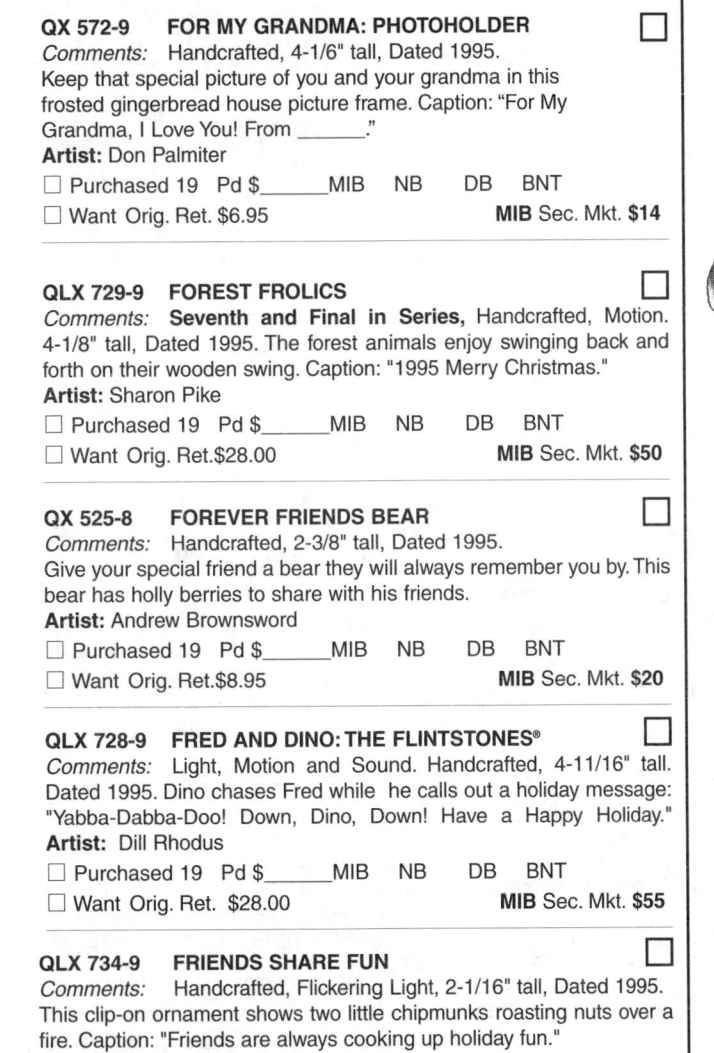

QX 516-9   FROSTY FRIENDS

Comments: **Sixteenth is Series,** Handcrafted, 2-9/16" tall.
Dated 1995. A friendly eskimo takes some presents across the ice on
his snowmobile with a little friend. Caption: "To Santa." How much
longer will this series continue to grow? **Artist:** Ed Seale

☐ Purchased 19 __Pd $_____ MIB   NB   DB   BNT
☐ Want Orig. Ret. $10.95   **MIB** Sec. Mkt. **$28**

QX 500-7   GARFIELD

Comments: Handcrafted, 2-3/16" tall, Dated 1995.
Garfield tries to be a sweet little angel for a minute as he
toots his horn.

☐ Purchased 19 __Pd $·_____ MIB   NB   DB   BNT
☐ Want Orig. Ret.$10.95   **MIB** Sec. Mkt. **$18**

QX 570-7   GODCHILD

Comments: Handcrafted, 2-3/16" tall, Dated 1995.
A little bear angel with brass halo plays Christmas music for his god-
parents. Caption: "Godchild."
Artist: Don Palmiter

☐ Purchased 19 __Pd $_____ MIB   NB   DB   BNT
☐ Want Orig. Ret. $7.95   **MIB** Sec. Mkt. **$14**

QX 241-7   GODPARENT

Comments: White Glass Ball, 2-7/8" dia, Dated 1995.
Little bear angels watch over their godparent. Caption: "A Godparent is
someone special at Christmas time and always."
Artist: LaDene Votruba

☐ Purchased 19 __Pd $_____ MIB   NB   DB   BNT
☐ Want Orig. Ret. $5.00   **MIB** Sec. Mkt. **$8**

QLX 736-7   GOODY GUMBALLS!

Comments: Handcrafted, Lighted, 2-7/8" tall, Dated 1995.
Two little mice raid the red gumball machine. The globe of the gumball
machine glows. **Artist:** Bob Siedler

☐ Purchased 19 __Pd $_____ MIB   NB   DB   BNT
☐ Want Orig. Ret. $12.50   **MIB** Sec. Mkt. **$35**

QX 588-7   GOPHER FUN

Comments: Handcrafted, 3-1/8" tall, Dated 1995.
The little gopher caddy tags along with the golfer to give him his point
of view. Caption: "Score Card '95 Wilson®." **Artist:** Bob Siedler

☐ Purchased 19 __Pd $_____ MIB   NB   DB   BNT
☐ Want Orig. Ret. $9.95   **MIB** Sec. Mkt. **$18**

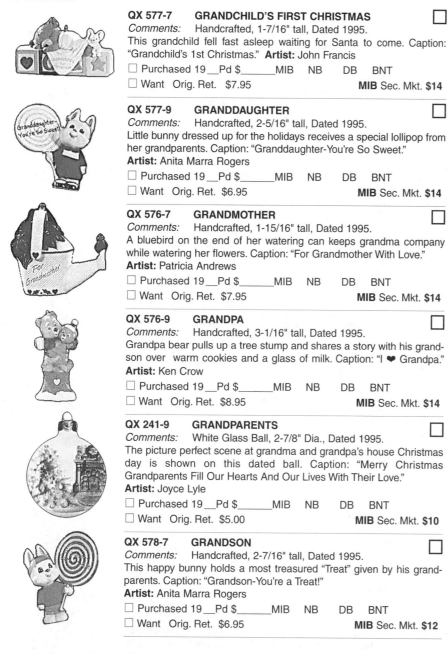

QX 577-7   GRANDCHILD'S FIRST CHRISTMAS   ☐
Comments: Handcrafted, 1-7/16" tall, Dated 1995.
This grandchild fell fast asleep waiting for Santa to come. Caption: "Grandchild's 1st Christmas." **Artist:** John Francis
☐ Purchased 19 __ Pd $_____ MIB   NB   DB   BNT
☐ Want   Orig. Ret. $7.95   **MIB** Sec. Mkt. **$14**

QX 577-9   GRANDDAUGHTER   ☐
Comments: Handcrafted, 2-5/16" tall, Dated 1995.
Little bunny dressed up for the holidays receives a special lollipop from her grandparents. Caption: "Granddaughter-You're So Sweet."
Artist: Anita Marra Rogers
☐ Purchased 19 __ Pd $_____ MIB   NB   DB   BNT
☐ Want   Orig. Ret. $6.95   **MIB** Sec. Mkt. **$14**

QX 576-7   GRANDMOTHER   ☐
Comments: Handcrafted, 1-15/16" tall, Dated 1995.
A bluebird on the end of her watering can keeps grandma company while watering her flowers. Caption: "For Grandmother With Love."
Artist: Patricia Andrews
☐ Purchased 19 __ Pd $_____ MIB   NB   DB   BNT
☐ Want   Orig. Ret. $7.95   **MIB** Sec. Mkt. **$14**

QX 576-9   GRANDPA   ☐
Comments: Handcrafted, 3-1/16" tall, Dated 1995.
Grandpa bear pulls up a tree stump and shares a story with his grandson over warm cookies and a glass of milk. Caption: "I ♥ Grandpa."
Artist: Ken Crow
☐ Purchased 19 __ Pd $_____ MIB   NB   DB   BNT
☐ Want   Orig. Ret. $8.95   **MIB** Sec. Mkt. **$14**

QX 241-9   GRANDPARENTS   ☐
Comments: White Glass Ball, 2-7/8" Dia., Dated 1995.
The picture perfect scene at grandma and grandpa's house Christmas day is shown on this dated ball. Caption: "Merry Christmas Grandparents Fill Our Hearts And Our Lives With Their Love."
Artist: Joyce Lyle
☐ Purchased 19 __ Pd $_____ MIB   NB   DB   BNT
☐ Want   Orig. Ret. $5.00   **MIB** Sec. Mkt. **$10**

QX 578-7   GRANDSON   ☐
Comments: Handcrafted, 2-7/16" tall, Dated 1995.
This happy bunny holds a most treasured "Treat" given by his grandparents. Caption: "Grandson-You're a Treat!"
Artist: Anita Marra Rogers
☐ Purchased 19 __ Pd $_____ MIB   NB   DB   BNT
☐ Want   Orig. Ret. $6.95   **MIB** Sec. Mkt. **$12**

Friendship is one of the greatest luxuries of life.

QX 630-7   HAPPY HOLIDAYS: PHOTOHOLDER   ☐
Comments: Handcrafted, 3-7/16" tall.
Included with this photo album is a photo of Hallmark's Keepsake artists or put your favorite photo inside. A little mouse swings from a ribbon. Was available at ornament premieres in July.
Artist: LaDene Votruba
☐ Purchased 19 __ Pd $_____ MIB   NB   DB   BNT
☐ Want   Orig. Ret. $2.95 with any purchase   **MIB** Sec. Mkt. **$10**

QX 603-7   HAPPY WRAPPERS   ☐
Comments: Handcrafted, 2-1/8" tall, Dated 1995.
Two little elves each wrap a Christmas gift for Santa.
Artist: Ken Crow
☐ Purchased 19 __ Pd $_____ MIB   NB   DB   BNT
☐ Want   Orig. Ret. $10.95   **MIB** Sec. Mkt. **$16**

QLX 732-7   HEADIN' HOME   ☐
Comments: Blinking Lights, Handcrafted, 1-13/16" tall, Dated 1995. Santa flies his reindeer home for the holidays in this red and white airplane. Lights glow on the inside and blink on the wings. Caption: "Polar Air." **Artist:** Julia Lee
☐ Purchased 19 __ Pd $_____ MIB   NB   DB   BNT
☐ Want   Orig. Ret. $22.00   **MIB** Sec. Mkt. **$42**

QX 605-7   HEAVEN'S GIFT   ☐
Comments: Handcrafted, Joseph 4-9/16" tall, Mary/Baby 2-15/16" tall, Dated 1995. The set of two ornaments rejoice in Heaven's gift of life to the world. A shepherd figurine is to debut possibly in '96. **Artist:** Patricia Andrews
☐ Purchased 19 __ Pd $_____ MIB   NB   DB   BNT
☐ Want   Orig. Ret. $20.00   **MIB** Sec. Mkt. **$30**

QX 517-9   HERE COMES SANTA: SANTA'S ROADSTER   ☐
Comments: **Seventeenth in Series,** Handcrafted, 2-13/16" tall Dated 1995. Santa zooms down the highway in his roadster with a Christmas tree for the Elves and Mrs. Claus to decorate.
Caption: "KRUZ-N." **Artist:** Linda Sickman
☐ Purchased 19 __ Pd $_____ MIB   NB   DB   BNT
☐ Want   Orig. Ret. $14.95   **MIB** Sec. Mkt. **$20**

QX 591-7   HOCKEY PUP   ☐
Comments: Handcrafted, 3-5/16" tall, Dated 1995.
Tucked into an oversized ice skate, this Christmas dressed puppy shoots for the winning goal. Caption: "Hockey Pup 1995."
Artist: Ken Crow
☐ Purchased 19 __ Pd $_____ MIB   NB   DB   BNT
☐ Want   Orig. Ret. $9.95   **MIB** Sec. Mkt. **$14**

QXI 505-7   HOLIDAY BARBIE™
Comments: **Third in Series,** Handcrafted, Dated 1995.
Barbie is ready for the holiday parties in her green and white Christmas dress. She accents her gown with little silver and white bulb earrings. Caption: "Holiday Barbie™." Many, many sales found in 1996.
Artist: Patricia Andrews

☐ Purchased 19 __Pd $_____MIB   NB   DB   BNT
☐ Want   Orig. Ret.$14.95   **MIB** Sec. Mkt. **$35**

QLX 731-9   HOLIDAY SWIM
Comments: Lighted, Handcrafted and Acrylic, 3-9/16" tall.
Dated 1995. Delightful aquarium glows while a festive little fish swims among seaweed decorated with red Christmas lights.
Artist: Anita Marra Rogers

☐ Purchased 19 __Pd $_____MIB   NB   DB   BNT
☐ Want   Orig. Ret. $18.50   **MIB** Sec. Mkt. **$34**

QXC 105-9   HOME FROM THE WOODS: KEEPSAKE CLUB
Comments: Handcrafted, 2-1/4" tall, Dated 1995.
A little man is on his way home from cutting down his Christmas tree. Complements the Folk Art Americana Collection.
Artist: Linda Sickman

☐ Purchased 19 __Pd $_____MIB   NB   DB   BNT
☐ Want   Club Fee $15.95   **MIB** Sec. Mkt. **$35**

QXI 551-7   HOOP STARS: SHAQUILLE O'NEAL
Comments: **FIRST IN SERIES,** Handcrafted, 5-1/2" tall, Dated 1995.
It's the last possible shot as Shaq slam dunks the ball for an Orlando Magic win. Caption: "32." With Shaq changing teams to the Lakers perhaps this ornament will become more sought after.

☐ Purchased 19 __Pd $_____MIB   NB   DB   BNT
☐ Want   Orig. Ret. $14.95   **MIB** Sec. Mkt. **$20-$30**

QX 594-7   IMPORTANT MEMO
Comments: Handcrafted, 2-3/16" tall, Dated 1995.
A little mouse is exhausted from the holiday season and takes a nap under an important memo. Caption: "MEMO, Closed for the Holidays 1995." **Artist:** Linda Sickman

☐ Purchased 19 __Pd $_____MIB   NB   DB   BNT
☐ Want   Orig. Ret. $8.95   **MIB** Sec. Mkt. **$16**

QX 581-7   IN A HEARTBEAT
Comments: Handcrafted, Dated 1995. With every heartbeat these two little mice grow closer together. **Artist:** Patricia Andrews

☐ Purchased 19 __Pd $_____MIB   NB   DB   BNT
☐ Want   Orig. Ret. $8.95   **MIB** Sec. Mkt. **$18**

QX 604-9   IN TIME WITH CHRISTMAS
Comments: Handcrafted, 3-3/4" tall, Dated 1995.
It's easy for this little violinist to keep time with the windup movement pendulum. Caption: "Music Makes Christmas Merrier."
Artist: Ken Crow

☐ Purchased 19 __Pd $_____MIB   NB   DB   BNT
☐ Want   Orig. Ret. $12.95   **MIB** Sec. Mkt. **$24**

QX 586-7   JOY TO THE WORLD
Comments: Handcrafted, 3-15/16" tall, Dated 1995.
An African-American choir boy sings the joyful sounds of Christmas.
Artist: Patricia Andrews

☐ Purchased 19 __Pd $_____MIB   NB   DB   BNT
☐ Want   Orig. Ret. $8.95   **MIB** Sec. Mkt. **$18**

QLX 734-7   JUMPING FOR JOY
Comments: Handcrafted, Light and Motion, Dated 1995.
Two little mice jump the barrels. The tree and lamp post light up.
Artist: John Francis

☐ Purchased 19 __Pd $_____MIB   NB   DB   BNT
☐ Want   Orig. Ret. $28.00   **MIB** Sec. Mkt. **$50**

QX 502-7   KIDDIE CAR CLASSICS: MURRAY® FIRE TRUCK
Comments: **Second in Series,** Handcrafted, 1-15/16" tall.
Dated 1995. This bright red fire truck is ready for any emergency. Captions: "1995" (back bumper), "MURRAY 0. CLEVE. O." (on back of seat), "JET·FLOW DRIVE FIRE DEPT." (on sides). This series is Hot
Artist: Don Palmiter

☐ Purchased 19 __Pd $_____MIB   NB   DB   BNT
☐ Want   Orig. Ret. $13.95   **MIB** Sec. Mkt. **$30**

QX 476-9   LEGO® FIREPLACE WITH SANTA
Comments: Handcrafted, 2-5/16" tall, Dated 1995.
Santa comes down this Lego fireplace to find a glass of milk and cookies waiting for him. Caption: "Lego® 1995." **Artist:** Ken Crow

☐ Purchased 19 __Pd $_____MIB   NB   DB   BNT
☐ Want   Orig. Ret. $10.95   **MIB** Sec. Mkt. **$24**

QX 501-9   LOONEY TUNES: BUGS BUNNY
Comments: Handcrafted, 4-1/8" tall, Dated 1995.
Our favorite mischievous Bugs Bunny is at it again!
Artist: Robert Chad

☐ Purchased 19 __Pd $_____MIB   NB   DB   BNT
☐ Want   Orig. Ret. $8.95   **MIB** Sec. Mkt. **$18**

QX 501-7   LOONEY TUNES: SYLVESTER AND TWEETY ☐
Comments: Handcrafted, Sylvester 4-9/16" tall.
Tweety 1-5/8" tall, Dated 1995. Sylvester still has his eye on a
Tweety for dinner. Set of 2 hang-together ornaments.
Artist: Robert Chad
☐ Purchased 19__ Pd $_____ MIB   NB   DB   BNT
☐ Want   Orig. Ret. $13.95   **MIB** Sec. Mkt. **$24**

QX 406-9   LOU RANKIN BEAR ☐
Comments: Handcrafted, 2-5/16" tall, Dated 1995.
This cute and cuddly bear is an ornament that would make anyone
smile. Caption: "Rankin." **Artist:** Bob Siedler
☐ Purchased 19__ Pd $_____ MIB   NB   DB   BNT
☐ Want   Orig. Ret. $9.95   **MIB** Sec. Mkt. **$22**

QX 584-9   MAGIC SCHOOL BUS™, THE ☐
Comments: Handcrafted.
Here they go again on another trip - this time to the North Pole in the
holiday decorated Magic School Bus.
☐ Purchased 19__ Pd $_____ MIB   NB   DB   BNT
☐ Want   Orig. Ret. $10.95   **MIB** Sec. Mkt. **$18**

QX 240-9   MARY ENGELBREIT ☐
Comments: White Glass Ball, Dated 1995.
This brightly colored ball pictures a jolly Santa ready for the holiday
season. Mary Engelbreit collectibles have been more evident in differ-
ent markets recently.
☐ Purchased 19__ Pd $_____ MIB   NB   DB   BNT
☐ Want   Orig. Ret. $5.00   **MIB** Sec. Mkt. **$15**

QX 514-9   MARY'S ANGELS: CAMELLIA ☐
Comments: **Eighth in Series,** Handcrafted/Acrylic, 2-5/8" tall.
Oh, to sing like an angel… Camellia sings a duet with a feathered friend
perched on her finger. Caption: "Mary." **Artist:** Robert Chad
☐ Purchased 19__ Pd $_____ MIB   NB   DB   BNT
☐ Want   Orig. Ret. $6.95   **MIB** Sec. Mkt. **$15**

QX 513-9   MERRY OLDE SANTA ☐
Comments: **Sixth in Series,** Handcrafted, 4-5/16" tall.
Dated 1995. Brass bells on a gold cord enhance Santa as he carries all
his goodies to children's homes. **Artist:** Patricia Andrews
☐ Purchased 19__ Pd $_____ MIB   NB   DB   BNT
☐ Want   Orig. Ret. $14.95   **MIB** Sec. Mkt. **$28**

QX 602-7   MERRY RV ☐
Comments: Handcrafted, 2-1/2" tall, Dated 1995.
Santa and Mrs. Claus begin their trip around the country in their holiday
dressed RV on December 27th. (Santa slept all day on the 26th.)
Caption: "The Claus's Merry-We-Go." **Artist:** Don Palmiter
☐ Purchased 19__ Pd $_____ MIB   NB   DB   BNT
☐ Want   Orig. Ret. $12.95   **MIB** Sec. Mkt. **$28**

QX 564-7   MOM ☐
Comments: Handcrafted, Dated 1995.
Mom is getting ready to decorate her Christmas tree with the popcorn
she is stringing. **Artist:** Bob Siedler
☐ Purchased 19__ Pd $_____ MIB   NB   DB   BNT
☐ Want   Orig. Ret. $7.95   **MIB** Sec. Mkt. **$16**

QX 565-7   MOM AND DAD ☐
Comments: Handcrafted, Dated 1995.
Mom and Dad snowmen snuggle together to keep warm.
Artist: Anita Marra Rogers
☐ Purchased 19__ Pd $_____ MIB   NB   DB   BNT
☐ Want   Orig. Ret. $9.95   **MIB** Sec. Mkt. **$20**

QX 565-9   MOM-TO-BE ☐
Comments: Handcrafted, Dated 1995.
Mom-to-be reads up on the latest bear facts about child bearing.
Artist: Dill Rhodus
☐ Purchased 19__ Pd $_____ MIB   NB   DB   BNT
☐ Want   Orig. Ret. $7.95   **MIB** Sec. Mkt. **$16**

QX 509-9   MOTHER GOOSE: JACK AND JILL ☐
Comments: **Third in Series,** Handcrafted, 2-1/2" tall, Dated 1995.
The Mother Goose book opens to display the verse and a 3-D depic-
tion.   Caption: "Christmas 1995," "Mother Goose," "Nursery Rhymes,"
"Jack and Jill went up the hill …" Many sales reported.
Artist: Ed Seale/LaDene Votruba
☐ Purchased 19__ Pd $_____ MIB   NB   DB   BNT
☐ Want   Orig. Ret. $13.95   **MIB** Sec. Mkt. **$22**

QX 515-7   MR. AND MRS. CLAUS: CHRISTMAS EVE KISS ☐
Comments: **Tenth and Final in Series,** Handcrafted, 3-3/16" tall.
Dated 1995. Mrs. Claus gives her sweetie a kiss before he heads off on
his annual trip around the world. **Artist:** Duane Unruh
☐ Purchased 19__ Pd $_____ MIB   NB   DB   BNT
☐ Want   Orig. Ret. $14.95   **MIB** Sec. Mkt. **$22**

QX 600-9   MULETIDE GREETINGS ☐
Comments: Handcrafted, 3-1/16" tall, Dated 1995.
Mr. Mule takes a rest from delivering gifts this holiday season. Designed from Shoebox Greetings. Caption: "Muletide Greetings."
Artist: Robert Chad
☐ Purchased 19__Pd $_____MIB   NB   DB   BNT
☐ Want   Orig. Ret. $7.95   **MIB** Sec. Mkt. **$18**

QLX 727-9   MY FIRST HOT WHEELS™ ☐
Comments: Light and motion, Handcrafted, 4-1/8" tall, Dated 1995.
Children watch their Hot Wheels go 'round and 'round. Tree lights up and the car goes around the track.
Artist: Ken Crow
☐ Purchased 19__Pd $_____MIB   NB   DB   BNT
☐ Want   Orig. Ret. $28.00   **MIB** Sec. Mkt. **$40**

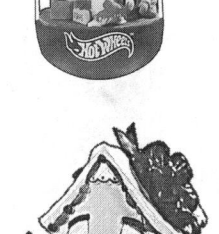

QX 583-9   NEW HOME ☐
Comments: Handcrafted, 2-9/16" tall, Dated 1995.
This cute little house dusts off the welcome mat for anyone who might come visit. Caption: "Welcome New Home 1995." New home ornaments are not readily asked for so those who do buy up extra ask usually double the retail as only a few offer these.
Artist: Patricia Andrews
☐ Purchased 19__Pd $_____MIB   NB   DB   BNT
☐ Want   Orig. Ret. $8.95   **MIB** Sec. Mkt. **$18**

QX 595-7   NORTH POLE 911 ☐
Comments: Handcrafted, 3-7/8" tall, Dated 1995.
Fireman chipmunk is ready for any emergency. "In Case of Emergency" he can break the glass to get a candy cane. Candy cane inside box dangles. Caption: "In Case of Emergency Break Glass."
Artist: Ed Seale
☐ Purchased 19__Pd $_____MIB   NB   DB   BNT
☐ Want   Orig. Ret. $10.95   **MIB** Sec. Mkt. **$20**

QX 508-9   NOSTALGIC HOUSES AND SHOPS: ☐
ACCESSORIES FOR COLLECTOR'S SERIES
Comments: Handcrafted, Street Lamp: 1-9/16" tall.
Evergreen 15/16" tall, Roadster: 13/16" tall, Dated 1995.
These cute accessories will add conversation to any collection of Nostalgic Houses and Shops. **Artist:** Julia Lee
☐ Purchased 19__Pd $_____MIB   NB   DB   BNT
☐ Want   Orig. Ret. $8.95   **MIB** Sec. Mkt. **$12**

QX 515-9   NOSTALGIC HOUSES AND SHOPS: ☐
TOWN CHURCH
Comments: **Twelfth in Series,** Handcrafted, 4-11/16" tall,
Dated 1995. An excellent choice for this favorite series. Easily found.
Artist: Don Palmiter
☐ Purchased 19__Pd $_____MIB   NB   DB   BNT
☐ Want   Orig. Ret. $14.95   **MIB** Sec. Mkt. **$22**

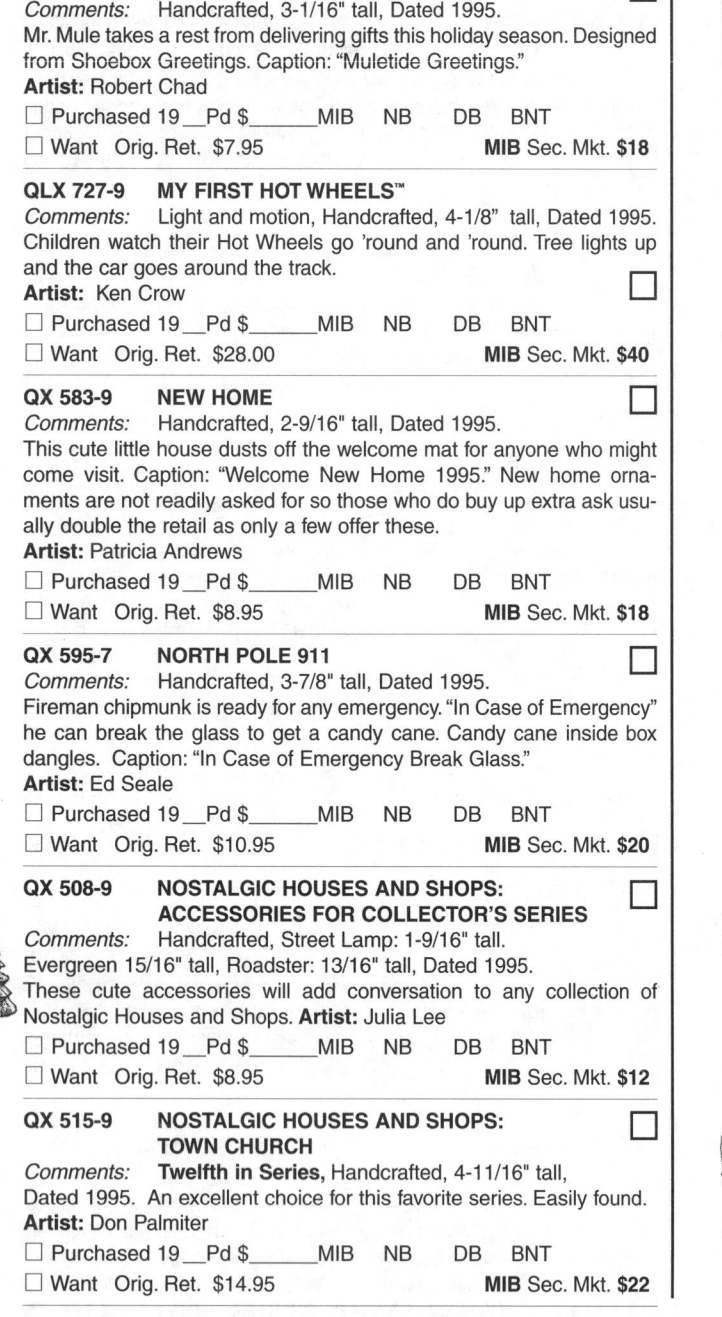

QX 594-9   NUMBER ONE TEACHER ☐
Comments: Handcrafted, 1-11/16" tall, Dated 1995.
This little mouse slides down the bookmark to say, "You're number one in my book." A more outstanding teacher ornament than others.
☐ Purchased 19__Pd $_____MIB   NB   DB   BNT
☐ Want   Orig. Ret. $7.95   **MIB** Sec. Mkt. **$14**

QX316-9   OLYMPIC SPIRIT, THE ☐
CENTENNIAL GAMES ATLANTA 1996
Comments: Acrylic, Dated 1995.
The '96 Olympic Games logo graces this oval acrylic ornament. May go higher this year.
☐ Purchased 19__Pd $_____MIB   NB   DB   BNT
☐ Want   Orig. Ret. $7.95   **MIB** Sec. Mkt. **$18**

QX 604-7   ON THE ICE ☐
Comments: Handcrafted, 2-3/16" tall, Dated 1995.
On a cold winter day this Christmas mouse straps blocks of ice to his feet and enjoys himself. **Artist:** Ken Crow
☐ Purchased 19__Pd $_____MIB   NB   DB   BNT
☐ Want   Orig. Ret. $7.95   **MIB** Sec. Mkt. **$20**

QX 580-9   OUR CHRISTMAS TOGETHER ☐
Comments: Handcrafted, 3-9/16" tall, Dated 1995.
Mr. and Mrs. Bunny decorate their new home for the holidays and their first Christmas together. Caption: "Our Christmas Together."
Artist: Joyce Lyle
☐ Purchased 19__Pd $_____MIB   NB   DB   BNT
☐ Want   Orig. Ret. $9.95   **MIB**Sec. Mkt. **$18**

QX 570-9   OUR FAMILY ☐
Comments: Handcrafted, 3-5/16" tall, Dated 1995.
A treasure trunk full of family mementos and on the outside of the treasure chest you can picture your family. Caption: "Our Family" and "Christmas Is Meant To Be Shared." **Artist:** Robert Chad
☐ Purchased 19__Pd $_____MIB   NB   DB   BNT
☐ Want   Orig. Ret. $7.95   **MIB** Sec. Mkt. **$12**

QX 317-7   OUR FIRST CHRISTMAS TOGETHER ☐
Comments: Acrylic, 3-1/4" tall, Dated 1995.
Heart shaped acrylic ornament is dated to remind you of the first Christmas you spent together. Caption: "Our First Christmas Together."
Artist: Joyce Lyle
☐ Purchased 19__Pd $_____MIB   NB   DB   BNT
☐ Want   Orig. Ret. $6.95   **MIB** Sec. Mkt. **$18**

QX 579-7 OUR FIRST CHRISTMAS TOGETHER ☐
Comments: Handcrafted, 2-3/8" tall, Dated 1995.
These two lovable bears spend their first Christmas together watching the snow fall outside their window. Caption: "Our First Christmas Together." "Christmas dreams come true when they're dreamed by two."
Artist: Joyce Lyle

☐ Purchased 19___Pd $_____MIB   NB   DB   BNT
☐ Want Orig. Ret. $16.95   **MIB** Sec. Mkt. **$30**

QX 579-9 OUR FIRST CHRISTMAS TOGETHER ☐
Comments: Handcrafted Water Globe, 2-15/16" tall, Dated 1995.
Two mice have the key to each others' hearts as they spend their first Christmas together. Caption: "Our First Christmas Together."
Artist: Bob Siedler

☐ Purchased 19___Pd $_____MIB   NB   DB   BNT
☐ Want Orig. Ret. $8.95   **MIB** Sec. Mkt. **$20**

QX 580-7 OUR FIRST CHRISTMAS TOGETHER: ☐
              PHOTOHOLDER
Comments: Handcrafted, 3-11/16" tall, Dated 1995.
Put your favorite picture of you and yours in this "Love Bug" photoholder. Caption: "Our First Christmas Together".
Artist: Ed Seale

☐ Purchased 19___Pd $_____MIB   NB   DB   BNT
☐ Want Orig. Ret. $8.95   **MIB** Sec. Mkt. **$16**

QX 520-9 OUR LITTLE BLESSINGS ☐
Comments: Handcrafted, 3-9/16" tall, Dated 1995.
Two children sit side by side discussing what they want Santa to bring them for Christmas. **Artist:** Ken Crow

☐ Purchased 19___Pd $_____MIB   NB   DB   BNT
☐ Want Orig. Ret. $12.95   **MIB** Sec. Mkt. **$20**

QX 563-9 PACKED WITH MEMORIES: PHOTOHOLDER ☐
Comments: Handcrafted, 3-5/8" tall, Dated 1995.
New commemorative ornament. Keep your child's first school photo in this cute little pouch with a bear peeking out.
Artist: Ed Seale

☐ Purchased 19___Pd $_____MIB   NB   DB   BNT
☐ Want Orig. Ret. $7.95   **MIB** Sec. Mkt. **$12**

QLX 727-7 PEANUTS® ☐
Comments: **Fifth and Final in Series,** Light and Motion. Handcrafted, 4-1/8" tall, Dated 1995. Snoopy spins gracefully on the ice. His message: "Merry Christmas." **Artist:** Dill Rhodus

☐ Purchased 19___Pd $_____MIB   NB   DB   BNT
☐ Want Orig. Ret. $24.50   **MIB** Sec. Mkt. **$45**

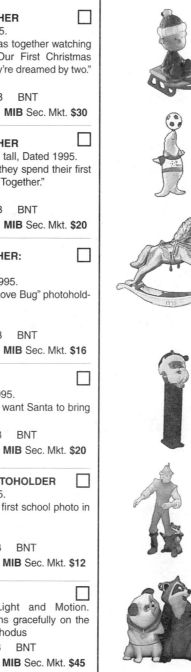

QX 505-9 PEANUTS® GANG ☐
Comments: **Third in Series,** Handcrafted, 2-7/8" tall, Dated 1995. Linus holds onto his sled as he flies down the largest hill in cartoon land. **Artist:** Bob Siedler

☐ Purchased 19___Pd $_____MIB   NB   DB   BNT
☐ Want Orig. Ret. $9.95   **MIB** Sec. Mkt. **$22**

QX 592-7 PERFECT BALANCE ☐
Comments: Handcrafted, 3-11/16" tall, Dated 1995.
A seal from team St. Nicholas shows off his talents spinning a soccer ball on his nose. Caption: "St. Nicks." **Artist:** Bob Siedler

☐ Purchased 19___Pd $_____MIB   NB   DB   BNT
☐ Want Orig. Ret. $7.95   **MIB** Sec. Mkt. **$12**

QX 616-7 PEWTER ROCKING HORSE: ☐
              ANNIVERSARY EDITION
Comments: Handcrafted, 3" tall, Dated 1995.
This anniversary edition pewter rocking horse celebrates 15 years of the Rocking Horse ornament collection. Caption: "1995 15th Year 1981-1995" (each side of rocker). Lots of differing prices.
Artist: Linda Sickman

☐ Purchased 19   Pd $ MIB   NB   DB   BNT
☐ Want Orig. Ret. $20.00   **MIB** Sec. Mkt. **$35**

QX 526-7 PEZ® SANTA ☐
Comments: Handcrafted 3-13/16" tall, Dated 1995.
Your favorite candy treat is now an ornament. Hang PEZ Santa on your tree to make the holiday season even sweeter. Caption: "PEZ®."
Artist: John Francis

☐ Purchased 19___Pd $_____MIB   NB   DB   BNT
☐ Want Orig. Ret. $7.95   **MIB** Sec. Mkt. **$12.50**

QXI 616-9 POCAHONTAS: ☐
               CAPTAIN JOHN SMITH AND MEEKO
Comments: Handcrafted, 4-1/2" tall, Dated 1995.
Meeko steals a biscuit while Captain John Smith watches out for savages. **Artist:** Ken Crow

☐ Purchased 19___Pd $_____MIB   NB   DB   BNT
☐ Want Orig. Ret. $12.95   **MIB** Sec. Mkt. **$18**

QXI 617-9 POCAHONTAS: ☐
               PERCY, FLIT AND MEEKO
Comments: Handcrafted, 1-13/16" tall, Dated 1995.
These three friends love to play, but Percy never likes to have any fun.
Artist: Ken Crow

☐ Purchased 19___Pd $_____MIB   NB   DB   BNT
☐ Want Orig. Ret. $9.95   **MIB** Sec. Mkt. **$18**

QXI 617-7   POCAHONTAS ☐

Comments: Handcrafted, 2-15/16" tall, Dated 1995.
Pocahontas rows "just around the river bend" with her little
hummingbird friend, Flit. **Artist:** Ken Crow

☐ Purchased 19 __Pd $_____MIB   NB   DB   BNT
☐ Want Orig. Ret. $12.95   **MIB** Sec. Mkt. **$20**

QXI 619-7   POCAHONTAS:
POCAHONTAS AND CAPTAIN JOHN SMITH ☐

Comments: Handcrafted, 2-9/16" tall, Dated 1995.
You will fall in love at first sight just like these two did, when you see this
ornament. Many sales found below retail. **Artist:** Ken Crow

☐ Purchased 19 __Pd $_____MIB   NB   DB   BNT
☐ Want Orig. Ret. $14.95   **MIB** Sec. Mkt. **$21**

QX 611-7   POLAR COASTER ☐

Comments: Handcrafted, 2-1/2" tall, Dated 1995.
It's winter fun at its best when this li'l penguin is sliding off his polar bear
friend's back. **Artist:** Ken Crow

☐ Purchased 19 __Pd $_____MIB   NB   DB   BNT
☐ Want Orig. Ret. $8.95   **MIB** Sec. Mkt. **$18**

QX 525-7   POPEYE ☐

Comments: Handcrafted, 3-11/16" tall, Dated 1995.
No turkey or ham for him. Even on Christmas day spinach is the only
thing Popeye eats. Caption: "SPINACH." **Artist:** Robert Chad

☐ Purchased 19 __Pd $_____MIB   NB   DB   BNT
☐ Want Orig. Ret. $10.95   **MIB** Sec. Mkt. **$24**

QX 513-7   PUPPY LOVE ☐

Comments: **Fifth in Series,** Handcrafted, 2-1/16" tall, Dated 1995.
A brown and black puppy tries his best to help with wrapping presents,
but all he really wants to do is play.
Artist: Anita Marra Rogers

☐ Purchased 19 __Pd $_____MIB   NB   DB   BNT
☐ Want Orig. Ret. $7.95   **MIB** Sec. Mkt. **$14**

QX 406-7   REFRESHING GIFT ☐

Comments: Handcrafted, Dated 1995.
Santa stocks up on cold Coca-Cola® for all his little helpers.
Artist: Duane Unruh

☐ Purchased 19 __Pd $_____MIB   NB   DB   BNT
☐Want   Orig. Ret. $14.95   **MIB** Sec. Mkt. **$30**

QX 598-7   REJOICE! ☐

Comments: Handcrafted, 3-15/16" tall, Dated 1995.
Everyone rejoices with the birth of baby Jesus. Caption: "A Child is
Born. The world rejoices!" **Artist:** Joyce Lyle

☐ Purchased 19 __Pd $_____MIB   NB   DB   BNT
☐ Want Orig. Ret. $10.95   **MIB** Sec. Mkt. **$25**

QX 516-7   ROCKING HORSE ☐

Comments: **Fifteenth in Series,** Handcrafted, 3" tall, Dated 1995.
A painted pony with red saddle and green rockers joins this popular
series. **Artist:** Linda Sickman

☐ Purchased 19 __Pd $_____MIB   NB   DB   BNT
☐ Want Orig. Ret. $10.95   **MIB** Sec. Mkt. **$22**

QX 593-7   ROLLER WHIZ ☐

Comments: Handcrafted, 2-1/2" tall, Dated 1995.
Santa turtle roller blades his way home to open the gifts he received.
Artist: Ed Seale

☐ Purchased 19 __Pd $_____MIB   NB   DB   BNT
☐ Want Orig. Ret. $7.95   **MIB** Sec. Mkt. **$18**

QX 587-7   SANTA IN PARIS ☐

Comments: Handcrafted, 3-9/16" tall, Dated 1995.
Santa climbs the Eiffel Tower to decorate it with real garland for
Christmas. Caption: "Joyeux Noel 1995."
Artist: Linda Sickman

☐ Purchased 19 __Pd $_____MIB   NB   DB   BNT
☐ Want Orig. Ret. $8.95   **MIB** Sec. Mkt. **$22**

QLX 733-7   SANTA'S DINER ☐

Comments: Handcrafted, Lighted, 2" tall, Dated 1995.
Santa stands at the door and greets customers into his diner. Sign
glows. Caption: "Santa's Diner."
Artist: LaDene Votruba

☐ Purchased 19 __Pd $_____MIB   NB   DB   BNT
☐Want   Orig. Ret. $24.50   **MIB** Sec. Mkt. **$30**

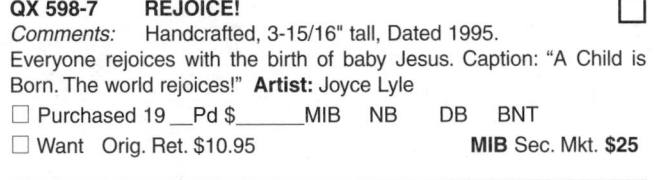

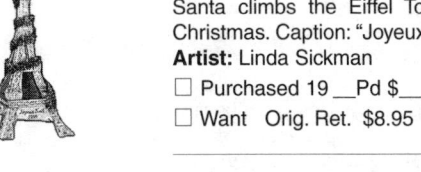
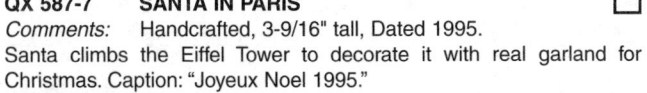

QX 601-7   SANTA'S SERENADE ☐
Comments: Handcrafted, 3" tall, Dated 1995.
Cowboy Santa sings Christmas carols with the help of Mr. Owl on his hat who is playing the harmonica. **Artist:** Ken Crow
☐ Purchased 19___Pd $_____MIB   NB   DB   BNT
☐ Want   Orig. Ret. $8.95   **MIB** Sec. Mkt. **$18**

QX 240-7   SANTA'S VISITORS: NORMAN ROCKWELL ☐
Comments: White Glass Ball, Dated 1995.
Santa makes sure he checks his list for these two little ones as they tell him what they want for Christmas.
Artist: Norman Rockwell
☐ Purchased 19___Pd $_____MIB   NB   DB   BNT
☐Want   Orig. Ret. $5.00   **MIB** Sec. Mkt. **$10**

QX 615-9   SIMBA, PUMBAA, AND TIMON: THE LION KING ☐
Comments: Handcrafted, 3-1/16" tall, Dated 1995.
Simba, Pumbaa and Timon walk across a log singing their favorite song "Hakuna Matata." Caption: "Hakuna Matata."
Artist: Ken Crow
☐ Purchased 19___Pd $_____MIB   NB   DB   BNT
☐ Want   Orig. Ret. $12.95   **MIB** Sec. Mkt. **$14**

QX 568-7   SISTER ☐
Comments: Handcrafted, 2-5/8" tall, Dated 1995.
Skier sister is heading for the slopes. Caption: "Sister."
Artist: Joyce Lyle
☐ Purchased 19___Pd $_____MIB   NB   DB   BNT
☐ Want   Orig. Ret. $6.95   **MIB** Sec. Mkt. **$12**

QX 568-9   SISTER TO SISTER ☐
Comments: Handcrafted, 2-3/4/" tall, Dated 1995.
These two sisters share everything with each other, from secrets to spices. Caption: "SPICES" and "Sisters Add Spice to the Holidays."
Artist: LaDene Votruba
☐ Purchased 19___Pd $_____MIB   NB   DB   BNT
☐ Want   Orig. Ret. $8.00   **MIB** Sec. Mkt. **$16**

QX 566-9   SON ☐
Comments: Handcrafted, 2-13/16" tall, Dated 1995.
This sharp son panda will study hard so there will be no homework during Christmas break. Caption: "Super Sharp Son."
Artist: Don Palmiter
☐ Purchased 19___Pd $_____MIB   NB   DB   BNT
☐ Want   Orig. Ret. $6.95   **MIB**Sec. Mkt. **$16**

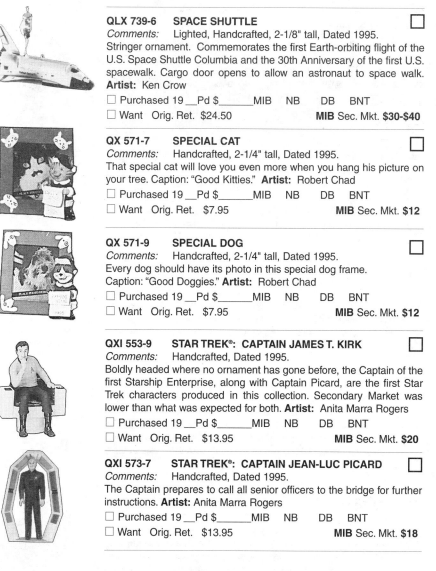

QX 590-9   SKI HOUND ☐
Comments: Handcrafted, 1-15/16" tall, Dated 1995.
One ski, one dachshund – off he goes.
Artist: Dill Rhodus
☐ Purchased 19___Pd $_____MIB   NB   DB   BNT
☐ Want   Orig. Ret. $8.95   **MIB** Sec. Mkt. **$14**

QLX 739-6   SPACE SHUTTLE ☐
Comments: Lighted, Handcrafted, 2-1/8" tall, Dated 1995.
Stringer ornament. Commemorates the first Earth-orbiting flight of the U.S. Space Shuttle Columbia and the 30th Anniversary of the first U.S. spacewalk. Cargo door opens to allow an astronaut to space walk.
Artist: Ken Crow
☐ Purchased 19___Pd $_____MIB   NB   DB   BNT
☐ Want   Orig. Ret. $24.50   **MIB** Sec. Mkt. **$30-$40**

QX 571-7   SPECIAL CAT ☐
Comments: Handcrafted, 2-1/4" tall, Dated 1995.
That special cat will love you even more when you hang his picture on your tree. Caption: "Good Kitties." **Artist:** Robert Chad
☐ Purchased 19___Pd $_____MIB   NB   DB   BNT
☐ Want   Orig. Ret. $7.95   **MIB** Sec. Mkt. **$12**

QX 571-9   SPECIAL DOG ☐
Comments: Handcrafted, 2-1/4" tall, Dated 1995.
Every dog should have its photo in this special dog frame.
Caption: "Good Doggies." **Artist:** Robert Chad
☐ Purchased 19___Pd $_____MIB   NB   DB   BNT
☐ Want   Orig. Ret. $7.95   **MIB** Sec. Mkt. **$12**

QXI 553-9   STAR TREK®: CAPTAIN JAMES T. KIRK ☐
Comments: Handcrafted, Dated 1995.
Boldly headed where no ornament has gone before, the Captain of the first Starship Enterprise, along with Captain Picard, are the first Star Trek characters produced in this collection. Secondary Market was lower than what was expected for both. **Artist:** Anita Marra Rogers
☐ Purchased 19___Pd $_____MIB   NB   DB   BNT
☐ Want   Orig. Ret. $13.95   **MIB** Sec. Mkt. **$20**

QXI 573-7   STAR TREK®: CAPTAIN JEAN-LUC PICARD ☐
Comments: Handcrafted, Dated 1995.
The Captain prepares to call all senior officers to the bridge for further instructions. **Artist:** Anita Marra Rogers
☐ Purchased 19___Pd $_____MIB   NB   DB   BNT
☐ Want   Orig. Ret. $13.95   **MIB** Sec. Mkt. **$18**

**QXI 726-7   STAR TREK THE NEXT GENERATION:
                          ROMULAN WARBIRD™**
Comments: Handcrafted, Lighted, 1-7/8" tall, Dated 1995.
Caption: "Romulans have been the bad guys of the Star Trek universe since the beginning." It looks like this ship forgot its cloaking device.
Artist: Lynn Norton
☐ Purchased 19__ Pd $_____ MIB   NB   DB   BNT
☐ Want   Orig. Ret. $24.00   **MIB** Sec. Mkt. **$28**

QLX 730-9   SUPERMAN™
Comments: Handcrafted, Light and Motion, 5-1/8" tall, Dated 1995.
The sign on top of the telephone booth glows as Clark Kent turns into Superman. (Rotates) **Artist:** Robert Chad
☐ Purchased 19__ Pd $_____ MIB   NB   DB   BNT
☐ Want   Orig. Ret. $28.00   **MIB** Sec. Mkt. **$30**

QX 601-9   SURFIN' SANTA
Comments: Handcrafted, 2-5/8" tall, Dated 1995.
Santa rips a few tides on his break from delivering presents.
Caption: "Yuletide." **Artist:** Ken Crow
☐ Purchased 19__ Pd $_____ MIB   NB   DB   BNT
☐ Want   Orig. Ret. $9.95   **MIB** Sec. Mkt. **$22**

QX 602-9   TAKIN' A HIKE
Comments: Handcrafted, 2-1/16" tall, Dated 1995.
This mouse tags along anywhere you may go on your Christmas journies. **Artist:** John Francis
☐ Purchased 19__ Pd $_____ MIB   NB   DB   BNT
☐ Want   Orig. Ret. $7.95   **MIB** Sec. Mkt. **$18**

QX 590-7   TENNIS, ANYONE?
Comments: Handcrafted, 3-7/8" tall, Dated 1995.
Play tennis with this little mouse; she is sure to help with your game.
Artist: Nina Aube
☐ Purchased 19__ Pd $_____ MIB   NB   DB   BNT
☐ Want   Orig. Ret. $7.95   **MIB** Sec. Mkt. **$18**

**Even Santa reads The Ornament Collector™
for the latest information on
Hallmark ornaments.**

QX 585-7   THOMAS THE TANK ENGINE- NO. 1
Comments: Handcrafted, 1-11/16" tall, Dated 1995.
Thomas the Tank Engine makes it up another hill to teach the young children all about Christmas. **Artist:** Dill Rhodus
☐ Purchased 19__ Pd $_____ MIB   NB   DB   BNT
☐ Want   Orig. Ret. $9.95   **MIB** Sec. Mkt. **$22**

QX 597-9   THREE WISHES
Comments: Handcrafted, 2-5/16" tall, Dated 1995.
The little girl dreams of her three wishes: love, joy and peace.
Caption: "Love Joy Peace." **Artist:** Patricia Andrews
☐ Purchased 19__ Pd $_____ MIB   NB   DB   BNT
☐ Want   Orig. Ret. $7.95   **MIB** Sec. Mkt. **$18**

QX 506-9   TOBIN FRALEY CAROUSEL
Comments: **Fourth and Final in Series,** Handpainted Fine Porcelain. 5-7/8" tall, Dated 1995. This porcelain handpainted carousel is decorated for the Christmas season with its gold star and red and green trimmings. **Artist:** Tobin Fraley
☐ Purchased 19__ Pd $_____ MIB   NB   DB   BNT
☐ Want   Orig. Ret. $28.00   **MIB** Sec. Mkt. **$35**

QLX 726-9   TOBIN FRALEY HOLIDAY CAROUSEL
Comments: **Second in Series,** Handcrafted, Light and Music. 5-9/16" tall. Dated 1995. A horse prances inside a lighted carousel. Plays "Over The Waves." **Artist:** Tobin Fraley
☐ Purchased 19__ Pd $_____ MIB   NB   DB   BNT
☐ Want   Orig. Ret. $32.00   **MIB** Sec. Mkt. **$45**

**QX 300-9   TWELVE DAYS OF CHRISTMAS:
                         TWELVE DRUMMERS DRUMMING**
Comments: **Twelfth and Final in Series,** Handcrafted, 3-7/8" tall. Dated 1995. As soon as you see this piece you will start singing the Twelve Days of Christmas. Caption: "The Twelve Days of Christmas 1995" "…twelve drummers drumming…"
☐ Purchased 19__ Pd $_____ MIB   NB   DB   BNT
☐ Want   Orig. Ret. $6.95   **MIB** Sec. Mkt. **$12**

QX 582-9   TWO FOR TEA
Comments: Handcrafted, 1-11/16" tall, Dated 1995.
Two mice join together in a cup of tea. Caption: "Friendship is a Special Gift." **Artist:** Julia Lee
☐ Purchased 19__ Pd $_____ MIB   NB   DB   BNT
☐ Want   Orig. Ret. $9.95   **MIB** Sec. Mkt. **$28**

QX 506-7   U.S. CHRISTMAS STAMPS
Comments: **Third and Final in Series,** Handcrafted, 3-3/8" tall.
Send your love to anyone with this Christmas greetings postage stamp.
Caption: "25 USA Greetings," "1995 Christmas" and "Christmas Tree."

☐ Purchased 19 __Pd $_____MIB   NB   DB   BNT
☐ Want   Orig. Ret. $10.95   **MIB** Sec. Mkt. **$11**

QX 553-7   VERA THE MOUSE
Comments: Fine Porcelain, 3-7/32" Diameter, Dated 1995.
This fine porcelain Marjolein Bastin collector's plate includes a stand or
it may be hung on your tree. **Artist:** Marjolein Bastin

☐ Purchased 19 __Pd $_____MIB   NB   DB   BNT
☐ Want   Orig. Ret. $8.95   **MIB** Sec. Mkt. **$10**

QLX 735-7   VICTORIAN TOY BOX: SPECIAL EDITION
Comments: Handcrafted, Light, Motion and Music, 4-5/16" tall.
The Christmas tree glows, jack-in-the-box goes up and down, top spins
and Santa wobbles. Plays "Toyland." **Artist:** Joyce Lyle

☐ Purchased 19 __Pd $_____MIB   NB   DB   BNT
☐ Want   Orig. Ret. $42.00   **MIB** Sec. Mkt. **$50**

QX 610-6   WAITING UP FOR SANTA
Comments: Handcrafted, 2-9/16" tall, Dated 1995.
This tired little bear drags his toy bear along while waiting up for Santa.
Artist: Don Palmiter

☐ Purchased 19 __Pd $_____MIB   NB   DB   BNT
☐ Want   Orig. Ret. $8.95   **MIB** Sec. Mkt. **$16**

QX 603-9   WATER SPORTS
Comments: Handcrafted, Boat 1-5/8" tall, Mrs. Claus 1-15/16" tall.
Dated 1995. A set of two clip-on ornaments. Santa takes time from his
busy schedule to enjoy the summer sport of water skiing with Mrs.
Claus. **Artist:** Bob Siedler

☐ Purchased 19 __Pd $_____MIB   NB   DB   BNT
☐ Want   Orig. Ret. $14.95   **MIB** Sec. Mkt. **$28**

QLX 732-9   WEE LITTLE CHRISTMAS
Comments: Lighted, Handcrafted, 3" tall, Dated 1995.
The Christmas tree glows when Santa comes to deliver his gifts. There
is a surprise Christmas scene behind the wall.
Artist: Ken Crow

☐ Purchased 19 __Pd $_____MIB   NB   DB   BNT
☐ Want   Orig. Ret. $22.00   **MIB** Sec. Mkt. **$32**

QX 618-7   WHEEL OF FORTUNE®: ANNIVERSARY EDITION
Comments: Handcrafted, Dated 1995.
Check your luck to see if the letters spell out what you want for
Christmas. Caption: "Wheel of Fortune You're A Winner 1995" and
"Wheel of Fortune 20 Years 1975-1995." Popular ornament.
Artist: Linda Sickman

☐ Purchased 19 __Pd $_____MIB   NB   DB   BNT
☐ Want   Orig. Ret. $12.95   **MIB** Sec. Mkt. **$25**

QX 588-9   WINNING PLAY, THE
Comments: Handcrafted, 1-7/8" tall, Dated 1995.
The athletic mouse takes the court. He dribbles left then right, shoots
and scores. The Christmas mice win the game. **Artist:** Bob Siedler

☐ Purchased 19 __Pd $_____MIB   NB   DB   BNT
☐ Want   Orig. Ret. $7.95   **MIB** Sec. Mkt. **$18**

QX 500-9   WINNIE THE POOH AND TIGGER
Comments: Handcrafted, Dated 1995.
Tigger gives Pooh a boost to put the star atop the tree.
Artist: Bob Siedler

☐ Purchased 19 __Pd $_____MIB   NB   DB   BNT
☐ Want   Orig. Ret. $12.95   **MIB** Sec. Mkt. **$28**

QLX 729-7   WINNIE THE POOH - TOO MUCH HUNNY
Comments: Handcrafted, Motion, 4-1/8" tall, Dated 1995.
Tigger is pulling the hunny loving Pooh through the narrow hole at
"Rabbit's House." **Artist:** Bob Siedler

☐ Purchased 19 __Pd $_____MIB   NB   DB   BNT
☐ Want   Orig. Ret. $24.50   **MIB** Sec. Mkt. **$50**

QX 585-9   WISH LIST: ORNAMENT PREMIERE
Comments: Handcrafted, 2-3/8" tall, Dated 1995.
A small Tender Touches mouse writes a letter "to Santa."
Artist: Ed Seale

☐ Purchased 19 __Pd $_____MIB   NB   DB   BNT
☐ Want   Orig. Ret. $15.00   **MIB** Sec. Mkt. **$22**

**QX 574-9   WIZARD OF OZ™:
GLINDA, WITCH OF THE NORTH**
Comments: Handcrafted, 4-3/8" tall, Dated 1995.
Last year's Wizard of Oz characters were happy to have Glinda join
them in 1995. **Artist:** Joyce Lyle

☐ Purchased 19 __Pd $_____MIB   NB   DB   BNT
☐ Want   Orig. Ret. $13.95   **MIB** Sec. Mkt. **$22**

QX 507-9   YULETIDE CENTRAL
Comments: **Second in Series,** Pressed Tin, 2" tall, Dated 1995.
A little train car carries all of the goodies for children on Christmas Day.
Artist: Linda Sickman
☐ Purchased 19 __ Pd $_____ MIB   NB   DB   BNT
☐ Want   Orig. Ret. $18.95   **MIB** Sec. Mkt. **$22**

Hallmark Personalized Keepsake Ornaments

No sales found on these ornaments. Any ornament with a personal message is not likely to bring a significant secondary market price..

QP 615-7   BABY BEAR
Comments: Handcrafted, 2-5/8 tall, new design.
Personalize this baby bear's bib to commemorate the birth of your little bundle of joy. **Artist:** Patricia Andrews
☐ Purchased 19 __ Pd $_____ MIB   NB   DB   BNT
☐ Want   Orig. Ret. $12.95   **MIB** Sec. Mkt. **N.E.**

QP 612-7   CHAMP, THE
Comments: Handcrafted, 2-9/16" tall.
Baby chipmunk holds on to a winners cup.
Artist: LaDene Votruba
☐ Purchased 19 __ Pd $_____ MIB   NB   DB   BNT
☐ Want   Orig. Ret.$12.95   **MIB** Sec. Mkt. **N.E.**

QP 604-6   COMPUTER CAT 'N MOUSE
Comments: Handcrafted, 2-3/4" tall.
A little white kitten watches over your mouse from the top of the computer. Caption: "Happy Holidata." **Artist:** Ed Seale
☐ Purchased 19 __ Pd $_____ MIB   NB   DB   BNT
☐ Want   Orig. Ret. $12.95   **MIB** Sec. Mkt. **N.E.**

QP 607-3   COOKIE TIME
Comments: Handcrafted, 2-3/4" tall.
An iced Christmas cookie will make your tree even sweeter.
Artist: LaDene Vortruba
☐ Purchased 19 __ Pd $_____ MIB   NB   DB   BNT
☐ Want   Orig. Ret. $12.95   **MIB** Sec. Mkt. **N.E.**

QP 600-6   ETCH-A-SKETCH®
Comments: Handcrafted, 2-1/4" tall.
A little brown bear sketches a warm Christmas wish you. Caption: "Etch-A-Sketch®." **Artist:** Ken Crow
☐ Purchased 19 __ Pd $_____ MIB   NB   DB   BNT
☐ Want   Orig. Ret. $12.95   **MIB** Sec. Mkt. **N.E.**

QP 603-6   FROM THE HEART
Comments: Handcrafted, 1-15/16" tall.
This little raccoon is willing to brave the cold snow to show his sweetheart how much he loves her.
Artist: Dill Rhodus
☐ Purchased 19 __ Pd $_____ MIB   NB   DB   BNT
☐ Want   Orig. Ret. $14.95   **MIB** Sec. Mkt. **N.E.**

QP 614-9   KEY NOTE
Comments: Handcrafted, 2-5/8" tall.
 A li'l mouse holds the golden key to your new home. The tag he sits on can be personalized. **Artist:** Ed Seale
☐ Purchased 19 __ Pd $_____ MIB   NB   DB   BNT
☐ Want   Orig. Ret. $12.95   **MIB** Sec. Mkt. **N.E.**

QP 601-5   MAILBOX DELIVERY
Comments: Handcrafted, 1-7/8" tall.
What a surprise when Mr. Raccoon delivers the mail in person. Mail box opens. **Artist:** Ken Crow
☐ Purchased 19 __ Pd $_____ MIB   NB   DB   BNT
☐ Want   Orig. Ret. $14.95   **MIB** Sec. Mkt. **N.E.**

QP 606-6   NOVEL IDEA
Comments: Handcrafted, 2-7/16" tall.
Mr. Mouse will help deliver your message on this "novel" ornament.
Artist: LaDene Votruba
☐ Purchased 19 __ Pd $_____ MIB   NB   DB   BNT
☐ Want   Orig. Ret. $12.95   **MIB** Sec. Mkt. **N.E.**

QP 602-2   ON THE BILLBOARD
Comments: Handcrafted, 2-1/8" tall.
Have Santa's helper paint a Christmas message on a billboard for you. Caption: "Santa Sign Co." **Artist:** Ken Crow
☐ Purchased 19 __ Pd $_____ MIB   NB   DB   BNT
☐ Want   Orig. Ret. $12.95   **MIB** Sec. Mkt. **N.E.**

QP 603-2   PLAYING BALL ☐
Comments: Handcrafted, 3-11/16" tall.
This little bear is ready to play ball. He carries a bat that can be personalized for your "little winner." **Artist:** John Francis

☐ Purchased 19 __Pd $_____MIB   NB   DB   BNT
☐ Want   Orig. Ret. $12.95   **MIB** Sec. Mkt. **N.E.**

QP 605-6   REINDEER ROOTERS ☐
Comments: Handcrafted, 2-15/16" tall.
Reissued from 1994. This peppy squad of reindeer will help anyone send that special Christmas message. **Artist:**   Ken Crow

☐ Purchased 19 __Pd $_____MIB   NB   DB   BNT
☐ Want   Orig. Ret. $12.95   **MIB** Sec. Mkt. **N.E.**

Hallmark Keepsake
Showcase Ornaments

Offered by Gold Crown Stores only. There has not been enough research to develop a secondary market price.

Turn of the Century Parade

QK 102-7   THE FIREMAN ☐
Comments: ***FIRST IN SERIES,*** Die-cast metal, 3-1/8" tall.
Dated 1995. No fire truck would be complete without a brass bell and red ribbon; the wheels turn and bell rings. I predict this series to end in the near future. **Artist:** Ken Crow

☐ Purchased 19 __Pd $_____MIB   NB   DB   BNT
☐ Want   Orig. Ret. $16.95   **MIB** Sec. Mkt. **$32.50**

Holiday Enchantment

QK 109-7   AWAY IN A MANGER ☐
Comments: Fine Porcelain, 4-5/16" tall, Dated 1995.
Caption: "…The Little Lord Jesus, Asleep on the Hay" "Away in a Manger." **Artist:** LaDene Votruba

☐ Purchased 19 __Pd $_____MIB   NB   DB   BNT
☐ Want   Orig. Ret. $13.95   **MIB** Sec. Mkt. **$23**

QK 109-9   FOLLOWING THE STAR ☐
Comments: Fine Porcelain, 3-7/16" diameter, Dated 1995.
Caption: "…we have seen his star in the east, and are come to worship him. Matthew 2:2." **Artist:** LaDene Votruba

☐ Purchased 19 __Pd $_____MIB   NB   DB   BNT
☐ Want   Orig. Ret. $13.95   **MIB** Sec. Mkt. **$23**

Nature's Sketchbook

QK 106-9   BACKYARD ORCHARD ☐
Comments: Handcrafted, 3-3/16" tall, Dated 1995.
This basket full of fruit feeds everyone from the birds to the butterflies. In '96 Hallmark debuted Marjolein Bastin's "bird" card and accessories. **Artists:** Marjolein Bastin and John Francis

☐ Purchased 19 _Pd $_____MIB   NB   DB   BNT
☐ Want   Orig. Ret. $18.95   **MIB** Sec. Mkt. **$35**

QK 107-7   CHRISTMAS CARDINAL ☐
Comments: Handcrafted, 3-5/8" tall, Dated 1995.
This red cardinal makes a striking contrast to the scenery. **Artists:** Marjolein Bastin and Joyce Lyle

☐ Purchased 19   Pd $_____MIB   NB   DB   BNT
☐ Want   Orig. Ret. $18.95   **MIB** Sec. Mkt. **$45**

QK 106-7   RAISING A FAMILY ☐
Comments: Handcrafted, 3-5/8" diameter, Dated 1995.
This handcrafted ornament pictures mama bird feeding her baby bird. Gorgeous! **Artists:** Marjolein Bastin and Joyce Lyle

☐ Purchased 19 _Pd $_____MIB   NB   DB   BNT
☐ Want   Orig. Ret. $18.95   **MIB** Sec. Mkt. **$35**

QK 107-9   VIOLETS AND BUTTERFLIES ☐
Comments: Handcrafted, 4-1/8" tall, Dated 1995.
This two-sided, handcrafted ornament depicts a lovely spring scene of wildflowers and butterflies. Nice! **Artists:** Marjolein Bastin and Joyce Lyle

☐ Purchased 19 _Pd $_____MIB   NB   DB   BNT
☐ Want   Orig. Ret. $16.95   **MIB** Sec. Mkt. **$35**

Symbols of Christmas

QK 108-7   JOLLY SANTA ☐
Comments;   Handcrafted, Hand Painted, 2-1/4" tall, Dated 1995.
Jolly Santa brings home a Christmas tree for the family to enjoy.

☐ Purchased 19 __Pd $_____MIB   NB   DB   BNT
☐ Want   Orig. Ret. $15.95   **MIB** Sec. Mkt. **$24**

QK 108-9   SWEET SONG ☐
Comments: Handcrafted, Hand Painted, 2-5/16" tall, Dated 1995.
This hand painted caroler sings her favorite Christmas carols.

☐ Purchased 19 __Pd $_____MIB   NB   DB   BNT
☐ Want   Orig. Ret. $15.95   **MIB** Sec. Mkt. **$24**

Invitation To Tea

The handle, spout and removable lid of each ornament are concealed in the design of the teapot.

QK 112-7   COZY COTTAGE TEAPOT ☐
Comments: Handcrafted, 2-7/16" tall, Dated 1995.
A quaint cottage with an ivy covered arch make a lovely teapot design.
Artist: Patricia Andrews
☐ Purchased 19 __ Pd $_____ MIB   NB   DB   BNT
☐ Want   Orig. Ret. $15.95   **MIB** Sec. Mkt. **$24**

QK 112-9   EUROPEAN CASTLE TEAPOT ☐
Comments: Handcrafted, 3-5/16" tall, Dated 1995.
Turrets and balconies add to the charm of this ivory castle.
Artist: Patricia Andrews
☐ Purchased 19 __ Pd $_____ MIB   NB   DB   BNT
☐ Want   Orig. Ret. $15.95   **MIB** Sec. Mkt. **$24**

QX 111-9   VICTORIAN HOME TEAPOT ☐
Comments: Handcrafted, 2-7/16" tall, Dated 1995.
All the elegance and style of a Victorian home are captured in this unique teapot. **Artist:** Patricia Andrews
☐ Purchased 19 __ Pd $_____ MIB   NB   DB   BNT
☐ Want   Orig. Ret. $15.95   **MIB** Sec. Mkt. **$30**

All Is Bright

QK 115-9   ANGEL OF LIGHT ☐
Comments: Handcrafted, 4-9/16" tall, Dated 1995.
Beautiful angel has a holiday golden glow; she dreams of the joy of Christmas. "Gold Leaf" look. **Artist:** Patricia Andrews
☐ Purchased 19 __ Pd $_____ MIB   NB   DB   BNT
☐ Want   Orig. Ret. $11.95   **MIB** Sec. Mkt. **$25**

QK 115-7   GENTLE LULLABY ☐
Comments: Handcrafted, 4-5/16" tall, Dated 1995.
A beautiful golden angel rocks her precious baby to sleep. "Gold Leaf" look. **Artist:** Patricia Andrews
☐ Purchased 19 __ Pd $_____ MIB   NB   DB   BNT
☐ Want   Orig. Ret. $11.95   **MIB** Sec. Mkt. **$25**

Angel Bells

QK 113-9   CAROLE ☐
Comments: Fine Porcelain, 3-5/8" tall, Dated 1995.
A lovely Asian angel, her feet are the clapper for the bell.
Artist: LaDene Votruba
☐ Purchased 19 __ Pd $_____ MIB   NB   DB   BNT
☐ Want   Orig. Ret. $12.95   **MIB** Sec. Mkt. **$22**

QK 113-7   JOY ☐
Comments: Fine Porcelain, 3-1/2" tall, Dated 1995.
The Joy bell ornament seemed to be the hardest one to find. All three were not abundantly produced. Found in box labeled Carole.
Artist: LaDene Votruba
☐ Purchased 19 __ Pd $_____ MIB   NB   DB   BNT
☐ Want   Orig. Ret. $12.95   **MIB** Sec. Mkt. **$30**

QK 114-7   NOELLE ☐
Comments: Fine Porcelain, 3-9/16" tall, Dated 1995.
Noelle is a devout African-American angel. Her feet are the clapper for the bell. **Artist:** LaDene Votruba
☐ Purchased 19 __ Pd $_____ MIB   NB   DB   BNT
☐ Want   Orig. Ret. $12.95   **MIB** Sec. Mkt. **$22**

Folk Art Americana

QK105-7   FETCHING THE FIREWOOD ☐
Comments: Handcrafted, Dated 1995.
A li'l man gives his dog a well-deserved hug after a long day on the trail.
Artist: Linda Sickman
☐ Purchased 19 __ Pd $_____ MIB   NB   DB   BNT
☐ Want   Orig. Ret. $16.95   **MIB** Sec. Mkt. **$38**

QK 103-9   FISHING PARTY ☐
Comments: Handcrafted, 1-7/8" tall, Dated 1995.
Everyone should have a pet walrus. **Artist:** Linda Sickman
☐ Purchased 19 __ Pd $_____ MIB   NB   DB   BNT
☐ Want   Orig. Ret. $15.95   **MIB** Sec. Mkt. **$38**

QK 103-7   GUIDING SANTA ☐
Comments: Handcrafted, 3-3/8" tall, Dated 1995.
A little angel guides Santa as he takes an unusual ride.
Artist: Linda Sickman
☐ Purchased 19 __ Pd $_____ MIB   NB   DB   BNT
☐ Want   Orig. Ret. $18.95 **NB** $24   **MIB** Sec. Mkt. **$48**

QK 104-7   LEARNING TO SKATE ☐
Comments: Handcrafted, 2-1/4" tall, Dated 1995.
Learning to ice skate requires a pillow or two.
Artist: Linda Sickman
☐ Purchased 19 __ Pd $_____ MIB   NB   DB   BNT
☐ Want   Orig. Ret. $14.95   **MIB** Sec. Mkt. **$38**

Expo 1995

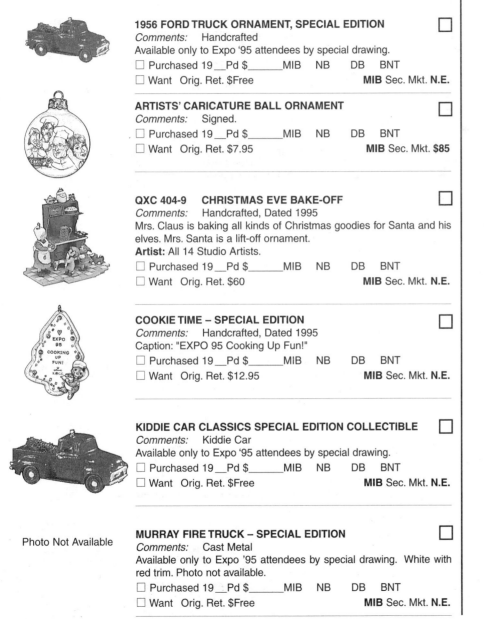

1956 FORD TRUCK ORNAMENT, SPECIAL EDITION ☐
Comments: Handcrafted
Available only to Expo '95 attendees by special drawing.
☐ Purchased 19___Pd $_____MIB   NB   DB   BNT
☐ Want   Orig. Ret. $Free   **MIB** Sec. Mkt. **N.E.**

ARTISTS' CARICATURE BALL ORNAMENT ☐
Comments: Signed.
☐ Purchased 19___Pd $_____MIB   NB   DB   BNT
☐ Want   Orig. Ret. $7.95   **MIB** Sec. Mkt. **$85**

QXC 404-9   CHRISTMAS EVE BAKE-OFF ☐
Comments: Handcrafted, Dated 1995
Mrs. Claus is baking all kinds of Christmas goodies for Santa and his elves. Mrs. Santa is a lift-off ornament.
Artist: All 14 Studio Artists.
☐ Purchased 19___Pd $_____MIB   NB   DB   BNT
☐ Want   Orig. Ret. $60   **MIB** Sec. Mkt. **N.E.**

COOKIE TIME – SPECIAL EDITION ☐
Comments: Handcrafted, Dated 1995
Caption: "EXPO 95 Cooking Up Fun!"
☐ Purchased 19___Pd $_____MIB   NB   DB   BNT
☐ Want   Orig. Ret. $12.95   **MIB** Sec. Mkt. **N.E.**

KIDDIE CAR CLASSICS SPECIAL EDITION COLLECTIBLE ☐
Comments: Kiddie Car
Available only to Expo '95 attendees by special drawing.
☐ Purchased 19___Pd $_____MIB   NB   DB   BNT
☐ Want   Orig. Ret. $Free   **MIB** Sec. Mkt. **N.E.**

Photo Not Available

MURRAY FIRE TRUCK – SPECIAL EDITION ☐
Comments: Cast Metal
Available only to Expo '95 attendees by special drawing. White with red trim. Photo not available.
☐ Purchased 19___Pd $_____MIB   NB   DB   BNT
☐ Want   Orig. Ret. $Free   **MIB** Sec. Mkt. **N.E.**

MURRAY CHAMPION ORNAMENT – SPECIAL EDITION ☐
Comments: Cast Metal Miniature Ornament
Available only to Expo '95 attendees by special drawing.
☐ Purchased 19___Pd $_____MIB   NB   DB   BNT
☐ Want   Orig. Ret. $Free   **MIB** Sec. Mkt. **N.E.**

ROCKING HORSE ORNAMENT – SPECIAL EDITION ☐
Comments: Pewter Miniature Ornament
Hot! Collectors were seeking unwanted redemption forms for this ornament during the Expos!
☐ Purchased 19___Pd $_____MIB   NB   DB   BNT
☐ Want   Orig. Ret. $7.95   **MIB** Sec. Mkt. **$37.50**

Expo '95 Prizes

1995 Keepsake Signature Collection Piece, Signed.
Expo-Exclusive Ball Ornament, Signed.
Kiddie Car Classics Collectible, Expo Special Edition.
Murray® Fire Truck Ornament, Expo Special Edition.
1956 Ford Truck Ornament, Expo Special Edition.
Miniature Murray® Champion Ornament, Expo Special Edition
Holiday Memories™ Barbie® Doll
Regional NFL Ornament Collection
Expo Artists' Caricatures Original Sketch, Signed
When You Care Enough, Book Signed by
Don Hall, Sr. and Don Hall, Jr.

Fred and Coral E. have their tree decorated with just a few ornaments and some Nostalgic Houses at the base of their tree.

1995 Miniature Ornament Collection

Have included a range of prices on several due to the age of ornament being on the market.

A QXC 412-9   **A GIFT FROM RODNEY: KEEPSAKE CLUB** ☐
Handcrafted, Dated 1995.
Artist: Linda Sickman
☐ Purchased 19___ Pd $_____   MIB   NB   DB   BNT
☐ Want   Free with '95 Club Membership
                MIB Sec. Mkt. **$14**

B QXM 483-9   **A MOUSTERSHIRE CHRISTMAS: SPECIAL EDITION** ☐
Handcrafted, 13/16" tall, House 2-5/8" tall, Dated 1995.
A. Moustershire Cottage   C. Violet
B. Robin   D. Dunne
Artist: Dill Rhodus
☐ Purchased 19___ Pd $_____   MIB   NB   DB   BNT
☐ Want   Orig. Retail $24.50
                MIB Sec. Mkt. **$35**

C QXM 477-7   **ALICE IN WONDERLAND** ☐
FIRST IN SERIES, Handcrafted, 1-7/16" tall, Dated 1995.
Artist: Patricia Andrews
☐ Purchased 19___ Pd $_____   MIB   NB   DB   BNT
☐ Want   Orig. Retail $6.75
                MIB Sec. Mkt. **$13.50**

D QXM 402-7   **BABY'S FIRST CHRISTMAS** ☐
Handcrafted, 1-1/16" tall, Dated 1995.
Artist: Ed Seale
☐ Purchased 19___ Pd $_____   MIB   NB   DB   BNT
☐ Want   Orig. Retail $4.75
                MIB Sec. Mkt. **$13**

E QXM 478-9   **CENTURIES OF SANTA** ☐
Second in Series, Handcrafted, 1-1/4" tall, Dated 1995.
Artist: Linda Sickman
☐ Purchased 19___ Pd $_____   MIB   NB   DB   BNT
☐ Want   Orig. Retail $5.75
                MIB Sec. Mkt. **$13.25**

F QXM 400-7   **CHRISTMAS BELLS** ☐
FIRST IN SERIES, Handcrafted and Metal, 1-1/4" tall, Dated 1995.
A popular series! **Artist:** Ed Seale
☐ Purchased 19___ Pd $_____   MIB   NB   DB   BNT
☐ Want   Orig. Retail $4.75
                MIB Sec. Mkt. **$16**

G QXM 408-7   **CHRISTMAS WISHES** ☐
Handcrafted, 1-1/16" tall, Dated 1995.
Need more just like him! Cute! **Artist:** Ed Seale
☐ Purchased 19___ Pd $_____   MIB   NB   DB   BNT
☐ Want   Orig. Retail $3.75
                MIB Sec. Mkt. **$13**

H QXM 401-7   **CLOISONNÉ PARTRIDGE: PRECIOUS EDITION**
Cloisonné, 1" dia. If this had been a "First in Series," the secondary market would have been affected more.
Artist: LaDene Votruba ☐
☐ Purchased 19___ Pd $_____   MIB   NB   DB   BNT
☐ Want   Orig. Retail $9.75
                MIB Sec. Mkt. **$18**

I QXC 445-7   **COOL SANTA: KEEPSAKE CLUB** ☐
Handcrafted, "Coca-Cola®" **Artist:** John Francis
☐ Purchased 19___ Pd $_____   MIB   NB   DB   BNT
☐ Want   Free with '95 Club Membership
                MIB Sec. Mkt. **$16**

J QXC 411-9   **COZY CHRISTMAS: KEEPSAKE COLLECTOR'S CLUB** ☐
Handcrafted, 1-3/16" dia. Caption: "Santa's Club Soda."
☐ Purchased 19___ Pd $_____   MIB   NB   DB   BNT
☐ Want   Orig. Retail - Included with Membership Kit
                MIB Sec. Mkt. **$19**

K QXM 483-7   **DOWNHILL DOUBLE** ☐
Handcrafted, 5/8" tall, Dated 1995. **Artist:** Don Palmiter
☐ Purchased 19___ Pd $_____   MIB   NB   DB   BNT
☐ Want   Orig. Retail $4.75
                MIB Sec. Mkt. **$12.50**

L QXM 401-9   **FRIENDSHIP DUET** ☐
Handcrafted, 1-1/4" tall, Dated 1995. **Artist:** Duane Unruh
☐ Purchased 19___ Pd $_____   MIB   NB   DB   BNT
☐ Want   Orig. Retail $4.75
                MIB Sec. Mkt. **$7.50**

M QXM 482-9   **GRANDPA'S GIFT** ☐
Handcrafted, 1" tall, Dated 1995. **Artist:** Anita Marra Rogers
☐ Purchased 19___ Pd $_____   MIB   NB   DB   BNT
☐ Want   Orig. Retail $5.75
                MIB Sec. Mkt. **$10**

N QXM 403-7   **HEAVENLY PRAISES** ☐
Handcrafted, 1-5/16" tall, Dated 1995. **Artist:** Patricia Andrews
☐ Purchased 19___ Pd $_____   MIB   NB   DB   BNT
☐ Want   Orig. Retail $5.75
                MIB Sec. Mkt. **$12**

A   B   C   D   E

F   G   H   I

J   K   L   M

A   QXM 545-2   HOLIDAY EXPRESS
Miniature Tree Base, able to hold any standard miniature tree.
Train moves on track. 4-1/4" tall. **Artist:** Linda Sickman
☐ Purchased 19___   Pd $_____   MIB   NB   DB   BNT
☐ Want   Orig. Retail $50.00
                                        MIB Sec. Mkt. **$74**

B   QXM 408-9   JOYFUL SANTA
Handcrafted, 1-1/8" tall, Dated 1995.
Artist: Duane Unruh
☐ Purchased 19___   Pd $_____   MIB   NB   DB   BNT
☐ Want   Orig. Retail $4.75
                                        MIB Sec. Mkt. **$12**

C   QXM 479-9   MARCH OF THE TEDDY BEARS
Third in Series, Handcrafted, 1-5/16" tall, Dated 1995.
Artist: Duane Unruh
☐ Purchased 19___   Pd $_____   MIB   NB   DB   BNT
☐ Want   Orig. Retail $4.75
                                        MIB Sec. Mkt. **$12.50**

D   QXM 409-7   MINIATURE CLOTHESPIN SOLDIER
FIRST IN SERIES, Handcrafted, 1-1/8" tall.
Artist: Linda Sickman
☐ Purchased 19___   Pd $_____   MIB   NB   DB   BNT
☐ Want   Orig. Retail $3.75
                                        MIB Sec. Mkt. **$12.50**

E   QXM 407-9   MINIATURE KIDDIE CAR CLASSICS: MURRAY® BLUE "CHAMPION"
FIRST IN SERIES, Cast Metal, 9/16" tall, Dated 1995.
Hot! Disappeared from shelves early in buying season! Secondary market dealers
were big buyers. **Artist:** Don Palmiter
☐ Purchased 19___   Pd $_____   MIB   NB   DB   BNT
☐ Want   Orig. Retail $5.75
                                        MIB Sec. Mkt. **$15**

F   QXM 480-9   NATURE'S ANGELS
Sixth in Series, Handcrafted, Brass Halo, 1-1/8" tall.
Artist: Patricia Andrews
☐ Purchased 19___   Pd $_____   MIB   NB   DB   BNT
☐ Want   Orig. Retail $4.75
                                        MIB Sec. Mkt. **$12.50**

G   QXM 480-7   NIGHT BEFORE CHRISTMAS, THE
Fourth in Series, Handcrafted, 1-1/4" tall, Dated 95.
Artist: Duane Unruh
☐ Purchased 19___   Pd $_____   MIB   NB   DB   BNT
☐ Want   Orig. Retail $4.75
                                        MIB Sec. Mkt. **$16**

H   QXM 405-7   NOAH'S ARK: MERRY WALRUSES
Handcrafted, 9/16" tall. Addition to Noah's Ark Special Edition (1994).
A nice series! **Artist:** Linda Sickman
☐ Purchased 19___   Pd $_____   MIB   NB   DB   BNT
☐ Want   Orig. Retail $5.75
                                        MIB Sec. Mkt. **$15**

I   QXM 405-9   NOAH'S ARK: PLAYFUL PENGUINS
Handcrafted, 11/16" tall. Addition to Noah's Ark Special Edition (1994).
Artist: Linda Sickman
☐ Purchased 19___   Pd $_____   MIB   NB   DB   BNT
☐ Want   Orig. Retail $5.75
                                        MIB Sec. Mkt. **$16**

J   QXM 481-7   NOEL R.R.: MILK TANK CAR
Seventh in Series, Handcrafted, 13/16" tall, Dated 1995.
Artist: Linda Sickman
☐ Purchased 19___   Pd $_____   MIB   NB   DB   BNT
☐ Want   Orig. Retail $6.75
                                        MIB Sec. Mkt. **$16**

K   QXM 478-7   NUTCRACKER GUILD
Second in Series, Handcrafted, 1-1/8" tall, Dated 1995.
Artist: Linda Sickman
☐ Purchased 19___   Pd $_____   MIB   NB   DB   BNT
☐ Want   Orig. Retail $5.75
                                        MIB Sec. Mkt. **$14**

L   QXM 481-9   OLD ENGLISH VILLAGE: TUDOR HOUSE
Eighth in Series, Handcrafted, 1" tall, Dated 1995.
Artist: Julia Lee
☐ Purchased 19___   Pd $_____   MIB   NB   DB   BNT
☐ Want   Orig. Retail $6.75
                                        MIB Sec. Mkt. **$14**

M   QXM 479-7   ON THE ROAD
Third in Series, Pressed Tin, 7/16" tall, Dated 1995.
Artist: Linda Sickman
☐ Purchased 19___   Pd $_____   MIB   NB   DB   BNT
☐ Want   Orig. Retail $5.75
                                        MIB Sec. Mkt. **$12**

Merry Christmas!

A QXM 475-7 **PEBBLES AND BAMM-BAMM: THE FLINTSTONES®**
Handcrafted, 1-1/8" tall. **Artist:** Dill Rhodus
☐ Purchased 19___ Pd $_____ MIB NB DB BNT
☐ Want Orig. Retail $9.75

MIB Sec. Mkt. **$12-$14**

B QXM 407-7 **PRECIOUS CREATIONS**
Handcrafted, 1-1/4" tall, Dated 1995. **Artist:** Linda Sickman
☐ Purchased 19___ Pd $_____ MIB NB DB BNT
☐ Want Orig. Retail $9.75

MIB Sec. Mkt. **$12-$15**

C QXM 482-7 **ROCKING HORSE**
Eighth in Series, Handcrafted, 1-1/8" tall, Dated 1995. **Artist:** Linda Sickman
☐ Purchased 19___ Pd $_____ MIB NB DB BNT
☐ Want Orig. Retail $4.75

MIB Sec. Mkt. **$12-$15**

D QXM 477-9 **SANTA'S LITTLE BIG TOP**
FIRST IN SERIES, Handcrafted, 1-5/8" tall, Dated 1995. **Artist:** Ken Crow
☐ Purchased 19___ Pd $_____ MIB NB DB BNT
☐ Want Orig. Retail $6.75

MIB Sec. Mkt. **$12-$14**

E QXM 404-7 **SANTA'S VISIT**
Lighted, Batteries included, Handcrafted, 1-7/16" tall, Dated 1995. **Artist:** Ken Crow
☐ Purchased 19___ Pd $_____ MIB NB DB BNT
☐ Want Orig. Retail $7.75

MIB Sec. Mkt. **$12-$14**

F QXM 414-1 **SHINING STAR TREE-TOPPER**
Dimensional Brass
☐ Purchased 19___ Pd $_____ MIB NB DB BNT
☐ Want Orig. Retail $9.95

MIB Sec. Mkt. **$10-$12**

G QXI 410-9 **SHIPS OF STAR TREK·, THE**
Set of three, Handcrafted, Dated 1995.
☐ Purchased 19___ Pd $_____ MIB NB DB BNT
☐ Want Orig. Retail $7.75

MIB Sec. Mkt. **$12-$14**

H QXM 403-9 **STARLIT NATIVITY**
Lighted, Batteries included, Handcrafted, 1-7/16" tall, Dated 1995.
Artist: Duane Unruh
☐ Purchased 19___ Pd $_____ MIB NB DB BNT
☐ Want Orig. Retail $7.75

MIB Sec. Mkt. **$17**

I QXM 409-9 **SUGARPLUM DREAMS,**
Handcrafted, 15/16" tall, Dated 1995. **Artist:** Ken Crow
☐ Purchased 19___ Pd $_____ MIB NB DB BNT
☐ Want Orig. Retail $4.75

MIB Sec. Mkt. **$10.50**

J QXM 446-7 **TINY TOON ADVENTURES: CALAMITY COYOTE**
Handcrafted, 1-7/16" tall. **Artist:** Anita Marra Rogers
☐ Purchased 19___ Pd $_____ MIB NB DB BNT
☐ Want Orig. Retail $6.75

MIB Sec. Mkt. **$12-$15**

K QXM 445-9 **TINY TOON ADVENTURES: FURRBALL**
Handcrafted, 7/8" tall.
Artist: Anita Marra Rogers
☐ Purchased 19___ Pd $_____ MIB NB DB BNT
☐ Want Orig. Retail $5.75

MIB Sec. Mkt. **$12-$15**

L QXM 446-9 **TINY TOON ADVENTURES: LITTLE BEEPER**
Handcrafted, 3/4" tall.
Artist: Anita Marra Rogers
☐ Purchased 19___ Pd $_____ MIB NB DB BNT
☐ Want Orig. Retail $5.75

MIB Sec. Mkt. **$12-$15**

M QXM 400-9 **TINY TREASURES**
Set of Six Ornaments, Handcrafted, 5/8" tall to 1-3/8" tall, Dated 1995.
A. Precious Gem   D. Smelling Sweet
B. Glamour Girl   E. All Tied Up
C. Powder Puff Pal   F. Just Reflecting
Many sales below $23 advertised in '96. **Artist:** Ed Seale
☐ Purchased 19___ Pd $_____ MIB NB DB BNT
☐ Want Orig. Retail $29.00

MIB Sec. Mkt. **$35-$40**

N QXM 402-9 **TUNNEL OF LOVE**
Handcrafted, 13/16" tall, Dated 1995. **Artist:** Ken Crow
☐ Purchased 19___ Pd $_____ MIB NB DB BNT
☐ Want Orig. Retail $4.75

MIB Sec. Mkt. **$12**

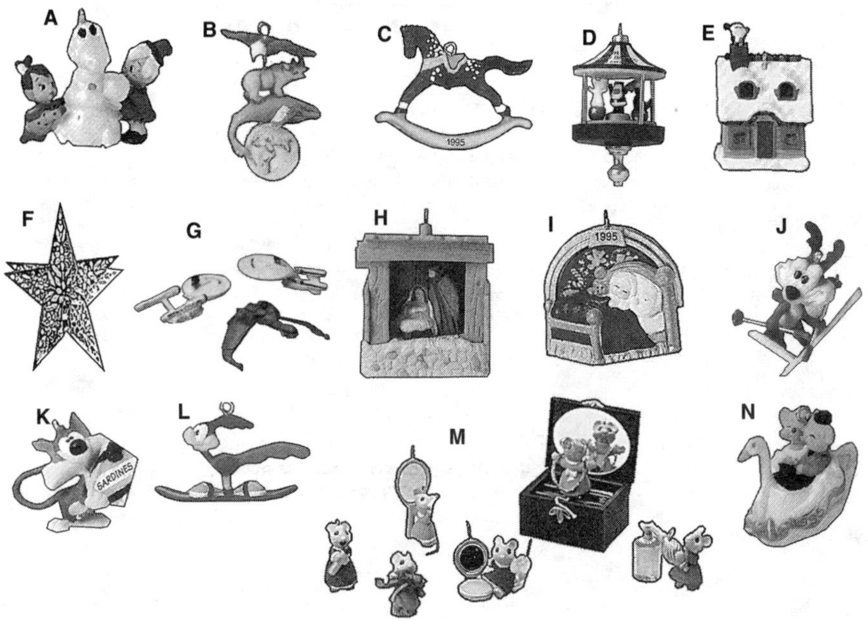

1995 Easter Ornament Collection

A   QEO 820-7   **APPLE BLOSSOM LANE**
FIRST IN SERIES, Handcrafted, Dated 1995.
☐ Purchased 19___ Pd $_____   MIB   NB   DB   BNT
☐ Want   Original Retail $8.95
     MIB Sec. Mkt. **$18.50**

B   QEO 825-3   **APRIL SHOWERS**
Handcrafted, Dated 1995.
☐ Purchased 19___ Pd $_____   MIB   NB   DB   BNT
☐ Want   Original Retail $6.95
     MIB Sec. Mkt. **$14.50**

C   QEO 823-7   **BABY'S FIRST EASTER**
Handcrafted, Dated 1995.
☐ Purchased 19___ Pd $_____   MIB   NB   DB   BNT
☐ Want   Original Retail $7.95
     MIB Sec. Mkt. **$18**

D   QEO 821-9   **COLLECTOR'S PLATE**
Second in Series, Porcelain, Dated 1995.
☐ Purchased 19___ Pd $_____   MIB   NB   DB   BNT
☐ Want   Original Retail $7.95
     MIB Sec. Mkt. **$18**

E   QEO 824-9   **CRAYOLA: BUNNY WITH CRAYONS**
Handcrafted, Dated '95.
☐ Purchased 19___ Pd $_____   MIB   NB   DB   BNT
☐ Want   Original Retail $7.95
     MIB Sec. Mkt. **$18.50**

F   QEO 823-9   **DAUGHTER**
Handcrafted, Dated 1995.
☐ Purchased 19___ Pd $_____   MIB   NB   DB   BNT
☐ Want   Original Retail $5.95
     MIB Sec. Mkt. **$12.50**

G   QEO 820-9   **GARDEN CLUB**
FIRST IN SERIES, Handcrafted, Dated 1995.
☐ Purchased 19___ Pd $_____   MIB   NB   DB   BNT
☐ Want   Original Retail $7.95
     MIB Sec. Mkt. **$21**

Did you know???

Today, more than 22 million households collect ornaments, and more than half of those collect Hallmark Keepsake Ornaments.

H   QEO 827-7   **HAM 'N EGGS**
Handcrafted.
☐ Purchased 19___ Pd $_____   MIB   NB   DB   BNT
☐ Want   Original Retail $7.95
     MIB Sec. Mkt. **$14**

I   QEO 821-7   **HERE COMES EASTER**
Second in Series, Handcrafted, Dated 1995.
☐ Purchased 19___ Pd $_____   MIB   NB   DB   BNT
☐ Want   Original Retail $7.95
     MIB Sec. Mkt. **$18.50**

J   QEO 826-7   **LILY**
Brass.
☐ Purchased 19___ Pd $_____   MIB   NB   DB   BNT
☐ Want   Original Retail $6.95
     MIB Sec. Mkt. **$11**

K   QEO 827-9   **LOONEY TUNES: BUGS BUNNY**
Handcrafted.
☐ Purchased 19___ Pd $_____   MIB   NB   DB   BNT
☐ Want   Original Retail $8.95
     MIB Sec. Mkt. **$16.50**

A QXC 824-6 **MAY FLOWER: SIDEKICK ORNAMENT**
Handcrafted, 1995 Club Edition.
☐ Purchased 19___ Pd $_____ MIB NB DB BNT
☐ Want Original Retail $3.95
MIB Sec. Mkt. **$49**

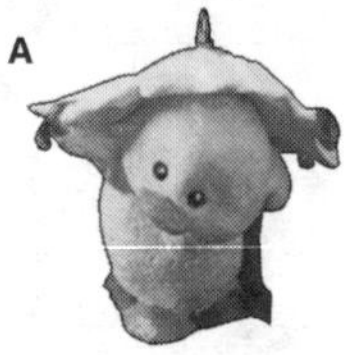

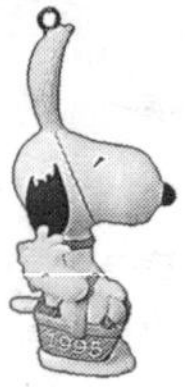

B QEO 826-9 **MINIATURE TRAIN**
Handcrafted, Dated 1995.
☐ Purchased 19___ Pd $_____ MIB NB DB BNT
☐ Want Original Retail $4.95
MIB Sec. Mkt. **$12**

C QEO 825-7 **PEANUTS: EASTER BEAGLE**
Handcrafted, Dated 1995.
☐ Purchased 19___ Pd $_____ MIB NB DB BNT
☐ Want Original Retail $7.95
MIB Sec. Mkt. **$22**

D QEO 824-7 **SON**
Handcrafted, Dated 1995.
☐ Purchased 19___ Pd $_____ MIB NB DB BNT
☐ Want Original Retail $5.95
MIB Sec. Mkt. **$14**

E QEO 806-9 **SPRINGTIME BARBIE**
FIRST IN SERIES, Handcrafted.
☐ Purchased 19___ Pd $_____ MIB NB DB BNT
☐ Want Original Retail $12.95
MIB Sec. Mkt. **$35**

F QEO 822-7 **SPRINGTIME BONNETS**
Third in Series, Handcrafted, Dated '95.
☐ Purchased 19___ Pd $_____ MIB NB DB BNT
☐ Want Original Retail $7.95
MIB Sec. Mkt. **$14**

G QEO 825-9 **TENDER TOUCHES: BUNNY WITH SEED PACKETS**
Handcrafted, Dated 1995.
☐ Purchased 19___ Pd $_____ MIB NB DB BNT
☐ Want Original Retail $8.95
MIB Sec. Mkt. **$18.50**

H QEO 822-9 **THREE FLOWERPOT FRIENDS**
Handcrafted, Dated 1995.
☐ Purchased 19___ Pd $_____ MIB NB DB BNT
☐ Want Original Retail $14.95
MIB Sec. Mkt. **$20**

"It'll be okay pal. Not every player gets to be a Hallmark ornament."

1996 Collection

These may be projected prices but check with last year's guide.
Our projected prices were 99% correct. Insure your pieces at retail until January 1, 1997.
(There's always "sleepers" that become popular when least expected also.)

1937 STEELCRAFT AUBURN BY MURRAY®: KEEPSAKE CLUB ☐
Comments: Die-cast metal, Dated 1996.
Based on a 1935 Auburn pedal car design. Available to club members only. **Artist:** Don Palmiter
☐ Purchased 19__Pd $_____MIB   NB   DB   BNT
☐ Want Orig. Ret. (Club Members)$14.95   **Projected** Sec. Mkt.**$50** up

QX 621-1   A LITTLE SONG AND DANCE ☐
Comments: Handcrafted, Dated 1996.
These two little mice sing and dance as they play their horn.
Artist: Ken Crow
☐ Purchased 19__Pd $_____MIB   NB   DB   BNT
☐ Want Orig. Ret. $9.95   **Projected** Sec. Mkt.**$12**

AIRMAIL FOR SANTA ☐
Comments: Handcrafted, Dated 1996.
A flying red bird carries a special envelope addressed to Mr. and Mrs. S. Claus and Elves. Gift membership bonus ornament available only to current club members who enroll a new member in 1996.
☐ Purchased 19__Pd $_____MIB   NB   DB   BNT
☐ Want Orig. Ret. Membership Bonus   **Projected** Sec. Mkt. **$18**

QX 524-1   ALL-AMERICAN TRUCKS: 1955 CHEVROLET CAMEO ☐
Comments: **Second in Series,** Handcrafted, Dated 1996.
This '55 Chevy is bringing home the Christmas tree for the holidays.
Artist: Don Palmiter
☐ Purchased 19__Pd $_____MIB   NB   DB   BNT
☐ Want Orig. Ret. $13.95   **Projected** Sec. Mkt. **$20-$22**

QX 556-4   ALL GOD'S CHILDREN: CHRISTY ☐
Comments: **FIRST IN SERIES,** Handcrafted, Dated 1996.
A precious black child holds a star which she has painted with great care. **Artist:** M. Root
☐ Purchased 19__Pd $_____MIB   NB   DB   BNT
☐ Want Orig. Ret. $12.95   **Projected** Sec. Mkt. **$18-$20**

QX 550-7   A TREE FOR SNOOPY ☐
Comments: Handcrafted, Dated 1996
Complements "A Tree for WOODSTOCK" Miniature Ornament. Snoopy is bringing home his Christmas tree on his red sled.
Artist: Bob Siedler
☐ Purchased 19__Pd $_____MIB   NB   DB   BNT
☐ Want Orig. Ret. $8.95   **Projected** Sec. Mkt. **$12**

QX 590-1   ANTLERS AWEIGH! ☐
Comments: Handcrafted, Dated 1996.
Those who love the water, will enjoy this reindeer on his wave-runner.
Artist: Robert Chad
☐ Purchased 19__Pd $_____MIB   NB   DB   BNT
☐ Want Orig. Ret. $9.95   **Projected** Sec. Mkt. **$14**

QX 612-1   APPLE FOR TEACHER ☐
Comments: Handcrafted, Dated 1996.
A special gift for that special teacher. **Artist:** Nina Aube
☐ Purchased 19__Pd $_____MIB   NB   DB   BNT
☐ Want Orig. Ret. $7.95   **Projected** Sec. Mkt. **$12.50**

QXI 571-1   AT THE BALL PARK: NOLAN RYAN ☐
Comments: **FIRST IN SERIES,** Handcrafted, Dated 1996
Ryan is up for the final pitch to decide who will win the game.
Artist: Dill Rhodus
☐ Purchased 19__Pd $_____MIB   NB   DB   BNT
☐ Want Orig. Ret. $14.95   **Projected** Sec. Mkt. **$22 up**

QX 575-1   BABY'S FIRST CHRISTMAS ☐
Comments: Fine Porcelain Collector's Plate, Dated 1996.
Artist: Bessie Pease Gutmann
☐ Purchased 19__Pd $_____MIB   NB   DB   BNT
☐ Want Orig. Ret. $10.95   **Projected** Sec. Mkt. **$18**

QX 575-4   BABY'S FIRST CHRISTMAS ☐
Comments: Handcrafted, Dated 1996
An infant's shoe holds the little one's rattle and bear. "Baby's First Christmas" is written on side of shoe. **Artist:** Patricia Andrews
☐ Purchased 19__Pd $_____MIB   NB   DB   BNT
☐ Want Orig. Ret. $9.95   **Projected** Sec. Mkt. **$18**

QX 576-1   BABY'S FIRST CHRISTMAS ☐
Comments: Photo holder, Dated 1996
A yellow diaper pin opens to display a photo of your baby.
Artist: Ed Seale
☐ Purchased 19__Pd $_____MIB   NB   DB   BNT
☐ Want Orig. Ret. $7.95   **Projected** Sec. Mkt. **$10**

**QX 574-4   BABY'S FIRST CHRISTMAS:
BEATRIX POTTER™**

Comments: Fine Porcelain, Dated 1996.
A mama rabbit rocks her little one to sleep. **Artist:** LaDene Votruba

☐ Purchased 19 __Pd $_____MIB   NB   DB   BNT
☐ Want Orig. Ret. $18.95   **Projected** Sec. Mkt. **$25**

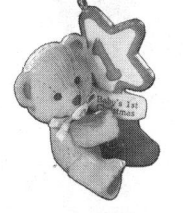

**QX 576-4   BABY'S FIRST CHRISTMAS:
CHILD'S AGE COLLECTION**

Comments: Handcrafted, Dated 1996.
This little bear with a pacifier in its mouth is trying to hold onto its stocking and cookie with a number 1 on it. **Artists:** Ken Crow

☐ Purchased 19 __Pd $_____MIB   NB   DB   BNT
☐ Want Orig. Ret. $7.95   **Projected** Sec. Mkt. **$16**

QLX 740-4   BABY'S FIRST CHRISTMAS

Comments: Light and Music, Dated 1996.
This angel is holding a glowing star "night light" while baby sleeps. Plays "Brahm's Lullaby"
Artist: John "Collins" Francis

☐ Purchased 19 __Pd $_____MIB   NB   DB   BNT
☐ Want Orig. Ret. $22.00   **Projected** Sec. Mkt.**$27**

**QX 577-1   BABY'S SECOND CHRISTMAS:
CHILD'S AGE COLLECTION**

Comments: Handcrafted, Dated 1996.
 A sugar cookie with a number two has been found with this little bear's stocking. **Artist:** Ken Crow

☐ Purchased 19 __Pd $_____MIB   NB   DB   BNT
☐ Want Orig. Ret. $7.95   **Projected** Sec. Mkt. **$12.50**

QXI 654-1   BARBIE™: ENCHANTED EVENING BARBIE® DOLL
Comments: **Third in Series,** Handcrafted, Dated 1996.
Barbie, in one of her favorite evening gowns, is ready for a romantic night on the town. **Artist:** Patricia Andrews

☐ Purchased 19 __Pd $_____MIB   NB   DB   BNT
☐ Want Orig. Ret. $14.95   **Projected** Sec. Mkt. **$20-$22 up**

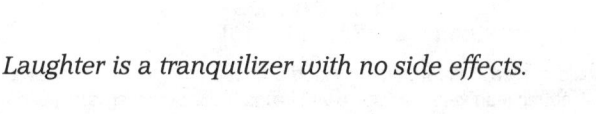

Laughter is a tranquilizer with no side effects.

**BARBIE®: BASED ON THE 1988 HAPPY HOLIDAYS
KEEPSAKE CLUB**

Comments: Handcrafted.
Complements the Keepsake Ornament Holiday Barbie™. Available to club members only. **Artist:** Patricia Andrews

☐ Purchased 19 __Pd $_____MIB   NB   DB   BNT
☐ Want Orig. Ret. (Club Members)$14.95   **Projected** Sec. Mkt.**$25-30**

QX 530-4   BASEBALL HEROES: SATCHEL PAIGE
Comments: **Third in Series,** Handcrafted, Dated 1996.
This series continues with a tribute to baseball great, Satchel Paige.
Artist: Dill Rhodus

☐ Purchased 19 __Pd $_____MIB   NB   DB   BNT
☐ Want Orig. Ret. $12.95   **Projected** Sec. Mkt. **$18**

QX 603-1   BOUNCE PASS
Comments: Handcrafted, Dated 1996.
Look at #96 go down that court. Ball bounces on a spring.
Artist: Bob Siedler

☐ Purchased 19 __Pd $_____MIB   NB   DB   BNT
☐ Want Orig. Ret. $7.95   **Projected** Sec. Mkt. **$12**

QX 601-4   BOWL 'EM OVER
Comments: Handcrafted, Dated 1996
This mouse is going for a strike with his big purple bowling ball.
Artist: Bob Siedler

☐ Purchased 19 __Pd $_____MIB   NB   DB   BNT
☐ Want Orig. Ret. $7.95   **Projected** Sec. Mkt. **$12.50**

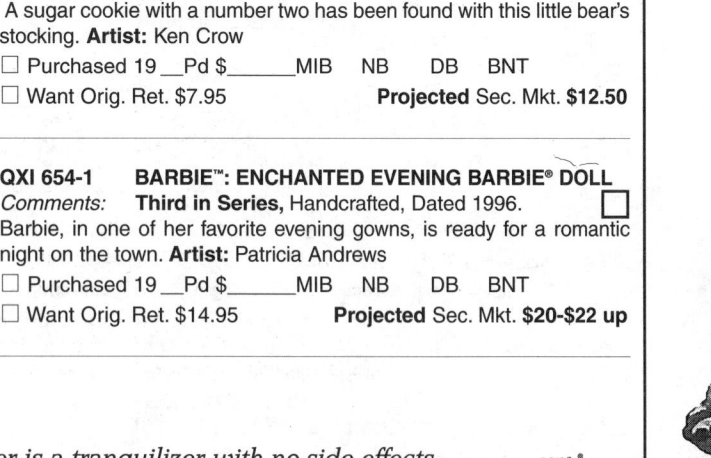

**QX 554-1   BOY SCOUTS OF AMERICA
GROWTH OF A LEADER**

Comments: Ceramic, Dated 1996.
Artwork by Norman Rockwell.

☐ Purchased 19 __Pd $_____MIB   NB   DB   BNT
☐ Want Orig. Ret. $9.95   **Projected** Sec. Mkt. **$12**

QX 564-1   CAT NAPS
Comments: **Third in Series,** Handcrafted, Dated 1996.
This lazy Siamese cat has found her favorite sleeping place in a fabric lined basket.
Artist: Dill Rhodus

☐ Purchased 19 __Pd $_____MIB   NB   DB   BNT
☐ Want Orig. Ret. $7.95   **Projected** Sec. Mkt. **$10**

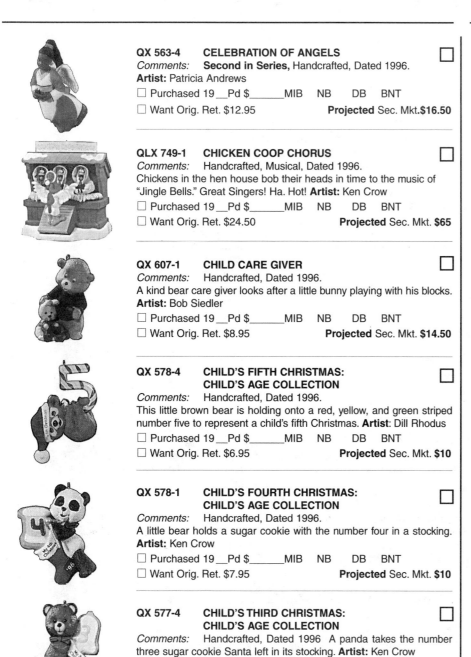

QX 563-4   CELEBRATION OF ANGELS
Comments: **Second in Series,** Handcrafted, Dated 1996.
Artist: Patricia Andrews
☐ Purchased 19 __Pd $_____MIB   NB   DB   BNT
☐ Want Orig. Ret. $12.95   Projected Sec. Mkt.**$16.50**

QLX 749-1   CHICKEN COOP CHORUS
Comments: Handcrafted, Musical, Dated 1996.
Chickens in the hen house bob their heads in time to the music of "Jingle Bells." Great Singers! Ha. Hot! **Artist:** Ken Crow
☐ Purchased 19 __Pd $_____MIB   NB   DB   BNT
☐ Want Orig. Ret. $24.50   Projected Sec. Mkt. **$65**

QX 607-1   CHILD CARE GIVER
Comments: Handcrafted, Dated 1996.
A kind bear care giver looks after a little bunny playing with his blocks.
Artist: Bob Siedler
☐ Purchased 19 __Pd $_____MIB   NB   DB   BNT
☐ Want Orig. Ret. $8.95   Projected Sec. Mkt. **$14.50**

QX 578-4   CHILD'S FIFTH CHRISTMAS:
            CHILD'S AGE COLLECTION
Comments: Handcrafted, Dated 1996.
This little brown bear is holding onto a red, yellow, and green striped number five to represent a child's fifth Christmas. **Artist**: Dill Rhodus
☐ Purchased 19 __Pd $_____MIB   NB   DB   BNT
☐ Want Orig. Ret. $6.95   Projected Sec. Mkt. **$10**

QX 578-1   CHILD'S FOURTH CHRISTMAS:
            CHILD'S AGE COLLECTION
Comments: Handcrafted, Dated 1996.
A little bear holds a sugar cookie with the number four in a stocking.
Artist: Ken Crow
☐ Purchased 19 __Pd $_____MIB   NB   DB   BNT
☐ Want Orig. Ret. $7.95   Projected Sec. Mkt. **$10**

QX 577-4   CHILD'S THIRD CHRISTMAS:
            CHILD'S AGE COLLECTION
Comments: Handcrafted, Dated 1996 A panda takes the number three sugar cookie Santa left in its stocking. **Artist:** Ken Crow
☐ Purchased 19 __Pd $_____MIB   NB   DB   BNT
☐ Want Orig. Ret. $7.95   Projected Sec. Mkt. **$10**

QLX 737-1   CHRIS MOUSE INN
Comments: **Twelfth in Series,** Lighted, Dated 1996.
Chris Mouse has left the light on in his Inn, letting travelers know they can spend the night. **Artist:** Bob Siedler
☐ Purchased 19 __Pd $_____MIB   NB   DB   BNT
☐ Want Orig. Ret. $14.50   Projected Sec. Mkt. **$20**

QX 624-1   CHRISTMAS JOY
Comments   Handcrafted, Dated 1996.
The Holy family celebrates their joy on this wonderful Christmas morning. **Artist:** Duane Unruh
☐ Purchased 19 __Pd $_____MIB   NB   DB   BNT
☐ Want Orig. Ret. $14.95   Projected Sec. Mkt. **$18.50**

QX 621-4   CHRISTMAS SNOWMAN
Comments: Handcrafted, Dated 1996.
Did a child give this snowman a holiday wreath and broom?
Artist: Duane Unruh
☐ Purchased 19 __Pd $_____MIB   NB   DB   BNT
☐ Want Orig. Ret. $9.95   Projected Sec. Mkt. **$12.50**

QX 563-1   CHRISTMAS VISITORS:
            CHRISTKINDL
Comments: **Second in Series,** Handcrafted, Dated 1996.
Christkindl is bringing gifts of joy and happiness.
Artist: LaDene Votruba
☐ Purchased 19 __Pd $_____MIB   NB   DB   BNT
☐ Want Orig. Ret. $14.95   Projected Sec. Mkt. **$16**

QX 538-4   CLASSIC AMERICAN CARS:
            1959 CADILLAC DE VILLE
Comments   **Sixth in Series,** Handcrafted, Dated 1996.
Anyone for a ride in a Classic '59 pink Caddy? **Artist:** Don Palmiter
☐ Purchased 19 __Pd $_____MIB   NB   DB   BNT
☐ Want Orig. Ret. $12.95   Projected Sec. Mkt.**$18-$20**

QX 587-4   CLOSE-KNIT FRIENDS
Comments: Handcrafted, Dated 1996.
Two little kittens have become "Close-Knit Friends" in a knitting basket.
Artist: Katrina Bricker
☐ Purchased 19 __Pd $_____MIB   NB   DB   BNT
☐ Want Orig. Ret. $9.95   Projected Sec. Mkt. **$12**

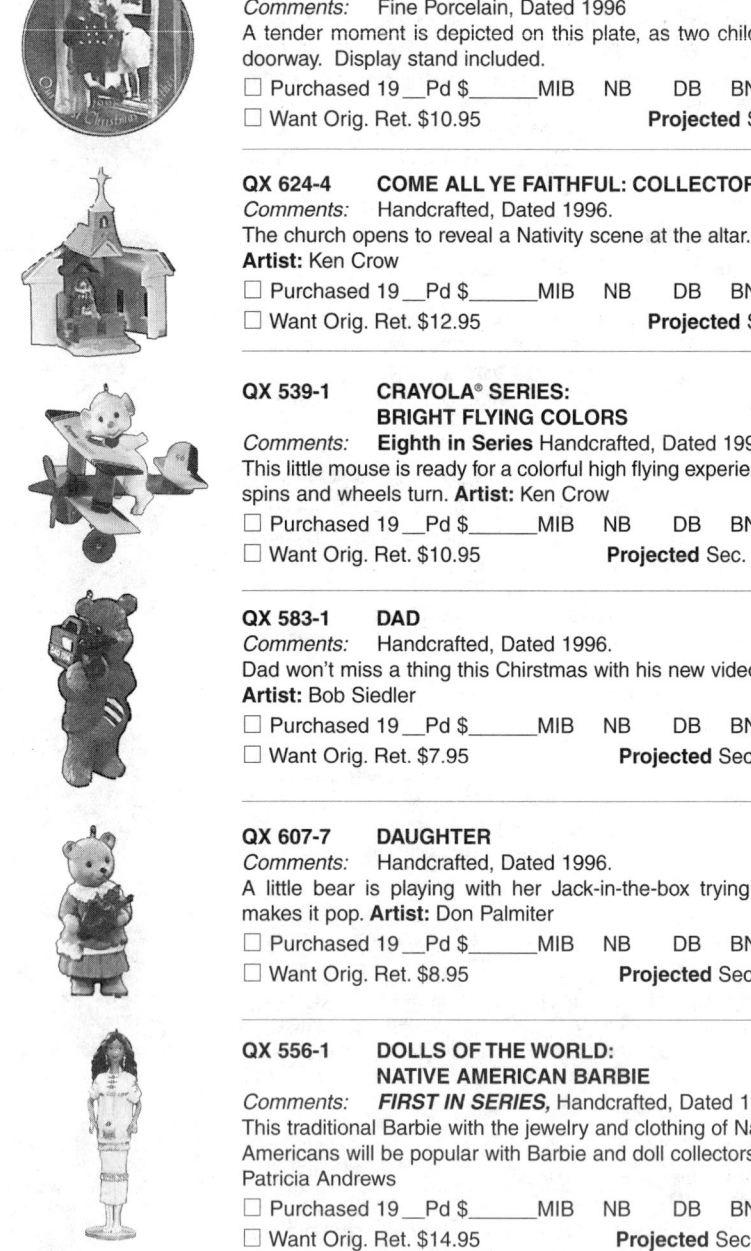

**QX 580-1   COLLECTOR'S PLATE:
OUR FIRST CHRISTMAS TOGETHER**

Comments: Fine Porcelain, Dated 1996
A tender moment is depicted on this plate, as two children kiss in a doorway. Display stand included.

☐ Purchased 19__Pd $_____MIB   NB   DB   BNT
☐ Want Orig. Ret. $10.95   **Projected** Sec. Mkt. **$12**

QX 624-4   COME ALL YE FAITHFUL: COLLECTOR'S CHOICE
Comments: Handcrafted, Dated 1996.
The church opens to reveal a Nativity scene at the altar.
Artist: Ken Crow

☐ Purchased 19__Pd $_____MIB   NB   DB   BNT
☐ Want Orig. Ret. $12.95   **Projected** Sec. Mkt. **$15**

**QX 539-1   CRAYOLA® SERIES:
BRIGHT FLYING COLORS**

Comments: **Eighth in Series** Handcrafted, Dated 1996.
This little mouse is ready for a colorful high flying experience. Propeller spins and wheels turn. **Artist:** Ken Crow

☐ Purchased 19__Pd $_____MIB   NB   DB   BNT
☐ Want Orig. Ret. $10.95   **Projected** Sec. Mkt. **$16-$18**

QX 583-1   DAD
Comments: Handcrafted, Dated 1996.
Dad won't miss a thing this Chirstmas with his new video camera.
Artist: Bob Siedler

☐ Purchased 19__Pd $_____MIB   NB   DB   BNT
☐ Want Orig. Ret. $7.95   **Projected** Sec. Mkt. **$12.50**

QX 607-7   DAUGHTER
Comments: Handcrafted, Dated 1996.
A little bear is playing with her Jack-in-the-box trying to see what makes it pop. **Artist:** Don Palmiter

☐ Purchased 19__Pd $_____MIB   NB   DB   BNT
☐ Want Orig. Ret. $8.95   **Projected** Sec. Mkt. **$12.50**

**QX 556-1   DOLLS OF THE WORLD:
NATIVE AMERICAN BARBIE**

Comments: **FIRST IN SERIES,** Handcrafted, Dated 1996.
This traditional Barbie with the jewelry and clothing of Native Americans will be popular with Barbie and doll collectors alike. **Artist:** Patricia Andrews

☐ Purchased 19__Pd $_____MIB   NB   DB   BNT
☐ Want Orig. Ret. $14.95   **Projected** Sec. Mkt. **$25 up**

QX 571-4   EVERGREEN SANTA: SPECIAL EDITION
Comments: Special Edition, Handcrafted, Dated 1996.
This old fashioned Santa is bringing a tree and star top to a special family. Intricately designed ball shaped ornament. **Artist:** Joyce Lyle

☐ Purchased 19__Pd $_____MIB   NB   DB   BNT
☐ Want Orig. Ret. $22.00   **Projected** Sec. Mkt. **$28**

QX 566-1   FABULOUS DECADE
Comments: **Seventh in Series,** Brass, Handcrafted and Dated 1996.
Fox holding 1996. **Artist:** Ed Seale

☐ Purchased 19__Pd $_____MIB   NB   DB   BNT
☐ Want Orig. Ret. $7.95   **Projected** Sec. Mkt. **$12.50**

QX 592-4   FAN-TASTIC SEASON
Comments: Handcrafted, Dated 1996.
The "all round" sport dog, he's got an ornament for everything!
Artist: Robert Chad

☐ Purchased 19__Pd $_____MIB   NB   DB   BNT
☐ Want Orig. Ret. $9.95   **Projected** Sec. Mkt. **$12-$14**

QLX 739-1   FATHER TIME
Comments: Timepiece, Dated 1996.
Father time is holding a real working timepiece. Battery included. Nice! **Artist:** Robert Chad

☐ Purchased 19__Pd $_____MIB   NB   DB   BNT
☐ Want Orig. Ret. $24.50   **Projected** Sec. Mkt. **$45-$50**

QX 630-4   FELIZ NAVIDAD
Comments: Handcrafted, Dated 1996.
These Mexican mice are celebrating Christmas in their own unique ways. **Artist:** Linda Sickman

☐ Purchased 19__Pd $_____MIB   NB   DB   BNT
☐ Want Orig. Ret. $9.95   **Projected** Sec. Mkt. **$16**

QXI 502-1   FOOTBALL LEGENDS: TROY AIKMAN
Comments: **Second in Series,** Handcrafted.
Troy is waiting to throw that winning touchdown pass.
Artist: Dill Rhodus

☐ Purchased 19__Pd $_____MIB   NB   DB   BNT
☐ Want Orig. Ret. $14.95   **Projected** Sec. Mkt. **$25-$28 up**

QX 568-1   FROSTY FRIENDS ☐
Comments: **Seventeenth in Series,** Handcrafted, Dated 1996.
With icicles for pool cues, these two famous friends play a game of ice pool. **Artist:** Ed Seale
☐ Purchased 19 __Pd $_____MIB   NB   DB   BNT
☐ Want Orig. Ret. $10.95   **Projected** Sec. Mkt. **$14 up**

QX 623-1   GLAD TIDINGS ☐
Comments: Handcrafted, Dated 1996.
This angel is bringing down glad tidings from the heavens above.
Artist: Joyce Lyle
☐ Purchased 19 __Pd $_____MIB   NB   DB   BNT
☐ Want Orig. Ret. $14.95   **Projected** Sec. Mkt. **$18**

QX 600-1   GOAL LINE GLORY ☐
Comments: Handcrafted, Dated 1996.
Set of 2. These penguins are out on the ice playing a little hockey.
Artist: Ed Seale
☐ Purchased 19 __Pd $_____MIB   NB   DB   BNT
☐ Want Orig. Ret. $12.95   **Projected** Sec. Mkt. **$18.50**

QX 584-1   GODCHILD ☐
Comments: Handcrafted, Dated 1996.
A little mouse says his prayers before going to bed.
Artist: Anita Marra Rogers
☐ Purchased 19 __Pd $_____MIB   NB   DB   BNT
☐ Want Orig. Ret. $8.95   **Projected** Sec. Mkt. **$12**

QX 569-7   GRANDDAUGHTER ☐
Comments: Handcrafted, Dated 1996.
A black and white kitten with holly in her bow rides on her sled.
Granddaughter is written on her yellow bow.
Artist: Anita Marra Rogers
☐ Purchased 19 __Pd $_____MIB   NB   DB   BNT
☐ Want Orig. Ret. $7.95   **Projected** Sec. Mkt. **$10**

QX 584-4   GRANDMA ☐
Comments: Handcrafted, Dated 1996.
A little bear gives a special Christmas card to Grandma bear.
Artist: LaDene Votruba
☐ Purchased 19 __Pd $_____MIB   NB   DB   BNT
☐ Want Orig. Ret. $8.95   **Projected** Sec. Mkt. **$12.50-$14**

QX 585-1   GRANDPA ☐
Comments: Handcrafted, Dated 1996.
Hold on tight as Grandpa and Grand "pup" fly down the hill on their red sled. **Artist:** LaDene Votruba
☐ Purchased 19 __Pd $_____MIB   NB   DB   BNT
☐ Want Orig. Ret. $8.95   **Projected** Sec. Mkt. **$12.50-$14**

QX 569-9   GRANDSON ☐
Comments: Handcrafted, Dated 1996.
A Dalmatian puppy with holly in his bow rides on his sled. Grandson is written on his purple bow. **Artist:** Anita Marra Rogers
☐ Purchased 19 __Pd $_____MIB   NB   DB   BNT
☐ Want Orig. Ret. $7.95   **Projected** Sec. Mkt. **$10.50**

QX 590-4   HAPPY HOLI-DOZE ☐
Comments: Handcrafted, Dated 1996.
 After a good holiday meal and game this bear is ready for a long winter nap. **Artist:** Dill Rhodus
☐ Purchased 19 __Pd $_____MIB   NB   DB   BNT
☐ Want Orig. Ret. $9.95   **Projected** Sec. Mkt. **$12.50**

QX 581-4   HEARTS FULL OF LOVE ☐
Comment: Handcrafted, Dated 1996.
These two loveable mice are blowing a big heart full of love. First production had the 1996 printed on the wrong side of the clear acrylic heart and thus backwards. This was corrected. (Errored $25 up)
Artist: Dill Rhodus
☐ Purchased 19 __Pd $_____MIB   NB   DB   BNT
☐ Want Orig. Ret. $9.95   **Projected** Sec. Mkt. **$12.50**

QX 568-4   HERE COMES SANTA: SANTA'S 4X4 ☐
Comments: **Eighteenth in Series,** Handcrafted, Dated 1996.
Here comes Santa in his 4X4; there is no stopping him now.
Artist: Ed Seale
☐ Purchased 19 __Pd $_____MIB   NB   DB   BNT
☐ Want Orig. Ret. $14.95   **Projected** Sec. Mkt. **$22-25**

QX 606-4   HIGH STYLE ☐
Comments: Handcrafted, Dated 1996. This woman is really in the holiday spirit with her Christmas tree hair style. **Artist:** Robert Chad
☐ Purchased 19 __Pd $_____MIB   NB   DB   BNT
☐ Want Orig. Ret. $8.95   **Projected** Sec. Mkt. **$12**

QX 613-4   HILLSIDE EXPRESS   ☐
Comments: Handcrafted, Dated 1996.
A toboggan ride for these forest friends is a lot of fun.
Artist: Nina Aube

☐ Purchased 19 __ Pd $_____ MIB   NB   DB   BNT
☐ Want Orig. Ret. $12.95   **Projected** Sec. Mkt. **$18**

QXI 537-1   HOLIDAY BARBIE   ☐
Comments: **Fourth in Series,** Handcrafted, Dated 1996.
Barbie is dressed in a gold three tier dress with a royal red overcoat trimmed with white fur. Her white fur hat and white muff complete her ensemble.   **Artist:** Patricia Andrews

☐ Purchased 19 __ Pd $_____ MIB   NB   DB   BNT
☐ Want Orig. Ret. $14.95   **Projected** Sec. Mkt. **$20-$22**

QX 620-1   HOLIDAY HAUL   ☐
Comments: Handcrafted, Dated 1996.
One of Santa's reindeer uses his John Deere tractor to haul in his Christmas tree. **Artist:** Linda Sickman

☐ Purchased 19 __ Pd $_____ MIB   NB   DB   BNT
☐ Want Orig. Ret. $14.95   **Projected** Sec. Mkt. **$20-$22**

HOLIDAY WISHES: 101 DALMATIANS   ☐
Comments: Handpainted porcelain, 3-1/4" dia., Dated 1996.
Hallmark and Disney teamed their efforts with this delightful collector's plate ornament, created to commemorate the live-action version of *101 Dalmatians*. Available at participating Hallmark Gold Crown stores. Takes the place of the Reach Program!

☐ Purchased 19 __ Pd $_____ MIB   NB   DB   BNT
☐ Want Orig. Ret. $14.95   **Projected** Sec. Mkt. **$22-$26**

QXI 501-4   HOOP STARS: LARRY BIRD   ☐
Comments: **Second in Series,** Handcrafted.
Bird is up for that three point shot to win the game. **Artist:** Dill Rhodus

☐ Purchased 19 __ Pd $_____ MIB   NB   DB   BNT
☐ Want Orig. Ret. $14.95   **Projected** Sec. Mkt. **$22-$26**

QXI 635-1   HUNCHBACK OF NOTRE DAME, THE: ☐
ESMERALDA AND DJALI
Comments: Handcrafted.
The gypsy girl Esmeralda and her goat Djali dance to entertain us all.
Artist: Ken Crow

☐ Purchased 19 __ Pd $_____ MIB   NB   DB   BNT
☐ Want Orig. Ret. $14.95   **Projected** Sec. Mkt. **$18-$20**

QXI 635-4   HUNCHBACK OF NOTRE DAME, THE: ☐
LAVERNE, VICTOR AND HUGO
Comments: Handcrafted.
Three comedic gargoyle friends of Quasimodo.
Artist: Ken Crow

☐ Purchased 19 __ Pd $_____ MIB   NB   DB   BNT
☐ Want Orig. Ret. $12.95   **Projected** Sec. Mkt. **$15**

QXI 634-1   HUNCHBACK OF NOTRE DAME, THE: ☐
QUASIMODO
Comments: Handcrafted, Dated 1996.
The hunchback, Quasimodo, swings in to wish you a Merry Christmas.
Artist: Ken Crow

☐ Purchased 19 __ Pd $_____ MIB   NB   DB   BNT
☐ Want Orig. Ret. $9.95   **Projected** Sec. Mkt. **$14**

QX 607-4   HURRYING DOWNSTAIRS   ☐
Comments: Handcrafted, Dated 1996.
This little one doesn't want to be last downstairs as he slides down the fire pole.
Artist: John "Collin" Francis

☐ Purchased 19 __ Pd $_____ MIB   NB   DB   BNT
☐ Want Orig. Ret. $8.95   **Projected** Sec. Mkt. **$15**

QX 589-1   I DIG GOLF   ☐
Comments: Clip-on Dated 1996.
This gopher is going to make it in one hole or the other.
Artist: Dill Rhodus

☐ Purchased 19 __ Pd $_____ MIB   NB   DB   BNT
☐ Want Orig. Ret. $10.95   **Projected** Sec. Mkt. **$15**

QXI 653-1   IT'S A WONDERFUL LIFE™   ☐
Comments: Handcrafted, Dated 1996.
Anniversary Edition Celebrating 50 years of this beloved film. The bell rings to show that another angel has received their wings. This ornament debuted late in '96.
Artist: Ken Crow

☐ Purchased 19 __ Pd $_____ MIB   NB   DB   BNT
☐ Want Orig. Ret. $14.95   **Projected** Sec. Mkt. **$18-$20**

QX 591-1   JACKPOT JINGLE   ☐
Comments: Handcrafted, Dated 1996.
A little mouse is playing the slot machine. **Artist:** Bob Siedler
☐ Purchased 19 __Pd $_____MIB   NB   DB   BNT
☐ Want Orig. Ret. $9.95   **Projected** Sec. Mkt. **$12-$14**

QLX 741-1   JETSONS™, THE   ☐
Comments: Lighted, Dated 1996.
The Jetsons are out for a cruise in their car that has flickering exhaust clouds and a lens on the car that glows. **Artist:** Ken Crow
☐ Purchased 19 __Pd $_____MIB   NB   DB   BNT
☐ Want Orig. Ret. $28.00   **Projected** Sec. Mkt. **$38-$40**

QX 622-1   JOLLY WOLLY ARK   ☐
Comments: Handcrafted, Dated 1996.
This ark full of animals will rock to and fro on the high seas.
Artist: Ken Crow
☐ Purchased 19 __Pd $_____MIB   NB   DB   BNT
☐ Want Orig. Ret. $12.95   **Projected** Sec. Mkt. **$16-$18**

QLX 752-4   JOURNEYS INTO SPACE: FREEDOM 7   ☐
Comments: **FIRST IN SERIES,** Light and Sound, Dated 1996.
Celebrating the 35th Anniversary of the first manned space flight. There is an actual countdown then authentic sounds of the rocket's ignition. **Artist:** Ed Seale
☐ Purchased 19 __Pd $_____MIB   NB   DB   BNT
☐ Want Orig. Ret. $24.00   **Projected** Sec. Mkt. **$35-$38**

QLX 733-9   JUKEBOX PARTY   ☐
Comments: Light and Music Dated 1996.
This glowing musical jukebox plays "Rockin' Around the Christmas Tree." by Brenda Lee. **Artist:** Don Palmiter
☐ Purchased 19 __Pd $_____MIB   NB   DB   BNT
☐ Want Orig. Ret. $24.50   **Projected** Sec. Mkt. **$38-$42**

Said the hospital patient when he received his bill for an operation, "Now I know why they wear masks in the operating room."

QX 536-4   KIDDIE CAR CLASSICS: MURRAY® AIRPLANE   ☐
Comments: **Third in Series,** Cast Metal, Dated 1996.
A great ornament! Popular series.
Artist: Don Palmiter
☐ Purchased 19 __Pd $_____MIB   NB   DB   BNT
☐ Want Orig. Ret. $13.95   **Projected** Sec. Mkt. **$18-$24**

QX 627-4   KINDLY SHEPHERD   ☐
Comments: Handcrafted, Dated 1996.
The kind shepherd is bringing one of his lost lambs back to the sheep herd. **Artist:** Patricia Andrews
☐ Purchased 19 __Pd $_____MIB   NB   DB   BNT
☐ Want Orig. Ret. $12.95   **Projected** Sec. Mkt. **$16**

QLX 738-1   LET US ADORE HIM   ☐
Comments: Lighted, Dated 1996.
The wise men have brought their gifts to give to Jesus to show their adoration. **Artist:** Joyce Lyle
☐ Purchased 19 __Pd $_____MIB   NB   DB   BNT
☐ Want Orig. Ret. $16.50   **Projected** Sec. Mkt. **$25**

QX 612-4   LIGHTING THE WAY   ☐
Comments: Handcrafted, Dated 1996.
This angel is lighting the way for all late night travelers.
Artist: Robert Chad
☐ Purchased 19 __Pd $_____MIB   NB   DB   BNT
☐ Want Orig. Ret. $12.95   **Projected** Sec. Mkt. **$15**

QX 553-1   LIONEL®: 700E HUDSON STEAM LOCOMOTIVE   ☐
Comments: **FIRST IN SERIES** Die-cast Metal, Dated 1996.
Replica of the original electric steam power train of the 1900's. Should prove to be popular with train collectors. Plenty for sale in first shipment.
☐ Purchased 19 __Pd $_____MIB   NB   DB   BNT
☐ Want Orig. Ret. $18.95   **Projected** Sec. Mkt. **$30-$40**

QX 550-4   LITTLE SPOONERS ☐
Comments: Handcrafted, Dated 1996.
Artwork by Norman Rockwell. Two fishing love birds watch the sun go down on a beautiful day. **Artist:** Duane Unruh
☐ Purchased 19 __ Pd $ _____ MIB   NB   DB   BNT
☐ Want Orig. Ret. $12.95   **Projected** Sec. Mkt. **$13**

QX 544-4   LOONEY TUNES COLLECTION: ☐
FOGHORN LEGHORN AND HENRY HAWK
Comments: Two Ornaments, Handcrafted.
Celebrating 50 years of Foghorn and Henry. **Artist:** Robert Chad
☐ Purchased 19 __ Pd $ _____ MIB   NB   DB   BNT
☐ Want Orig. Ret. $13.95   **Projected** Sec. Mkt. **$16-$18**

QX 631-1   MADAME ALEXANDER: CINDERELLA - 1995 ☐
Comments: **FIRST IN SERIES,** Handcrafted, Dated 1996.
Madame Alexander dolls are very popular because of their beautiful details. Cinderella is ready for the ball.
Artist: John "Collin" Francis
☐ Purchased 19 __ Pd $ _____ MIB   NB   DB   BNT
☐ Want Orig. Ret. $14.95   **Projected** Sec. Mkt. **$22-$30**

QX 632-4   MADONNA AND CHILD ☐
Comments: Stamped tin, Dated 1996.
This picture of Madonna and Child celebrate peace, love, and hope.
Painted by Jusepe de Ribera. Frame **sculpted** by Linda Sickman
☐ Purchased 19 __ Pd $ _____ MIB   NB   DB   BNT
☐ Want Orig. Ret. $12.95   **Projected** Sec. Mkt. **$14**

QX 627-1   MAKING HIS ROUNDS ☐
Comments: Handcrafted, Dated 1996.
Santa has a full bag of presents to give to all of those children who have been good. **Artist:** John "Collins" Francis
☐ Purchased 19 __ Pd $ _____ MIB   NB   DB   BNT
☐ Want Orig. Ret. $14.95   **Projected** Sec. Mkt. **$18-$20**

QX 545-1   MARVIN THE MARTIAN ☐
Comments: Handcrafted.
Marvin the Martian is trying to learn the earthly tradition of Christmas.
Artist: Robert Chad
☐ Purchased 19 __ Pd $ _____ MIB   NB   DB   BNT
☐ Want Orig. Ret. $10.95   **Projected** Sec. Mkt. **$12-$14**

QX 566-4   MARY'S ANGELS: VIOLET ☐
Comments: **Ninth in Series**, Handcrafted, Dated 1996.
A little angel is taking extra special care of this lost lamb.
Artist: Robert Chad
☐ Purchased 19 __ Pd $ _____ MIB   NB   DB   BNT
☐ Want Orig. Ret. $6.95   **Projected** Sec. Mkt. **$10-$12**

QX 606-1   MATCHLESS MEMORIES ☐
Comments: Handcrafted, Dated 1996.
This little mouse is playing some hot tunes on his "match box" piano! Ornament actually says "Matchless Melodies." **Artist:** Ken Crow
☐ Purchased 19 __ Pd $ _____ MIB   NB   DB   BNT
☐ Want Orig. Ret. $9.95   **Projected** Sec. Mkt. **$**

QX 622-4   MAXINE ☐
Comments: 10th Anniversary of Shoebox Greetings Handcrafted, Dated 1996. Character by John Wagner. Maxine is decked out from head to toe in Christmas clothing. **Artist:** Sharon Pike
☐ Purchased 19 __ Pd $ _____ MIB   NB   DB   BNT
☐ Want Orig. Ret. $9.95   **Projected** Sec. Mkt. **$12-$14**

QX 588-4   MERRY CARPOOLERS ☐
Comments: Handcrafted, Dated 1996. Santa and his reindeer are going to have a little skiing fun after their ride up the ski lift. A li'l crowded. **Artist:** Ken Crow
☐ Purchased 19 __ Pd $ _____ MIB   NB   DB   BNT
☐ Want Orig. Ret. $14.95   **Projected** Sec. Mkt. **$24-$28**

QX 565-4   MERRY OLDE SANTA ☐
Comments: **Seventh in Series** Handcrafted, Dated 1996.
This Santa is all dressed up in Fourth of July style. **Artist:** Ken Crow
☐ Purchased 19 __ Pd $ _____ MIB   NB   DB   BNT
☐ Want Orig. Ret. $14.95   **Projected** Sec. Mkt. **$20-$24**

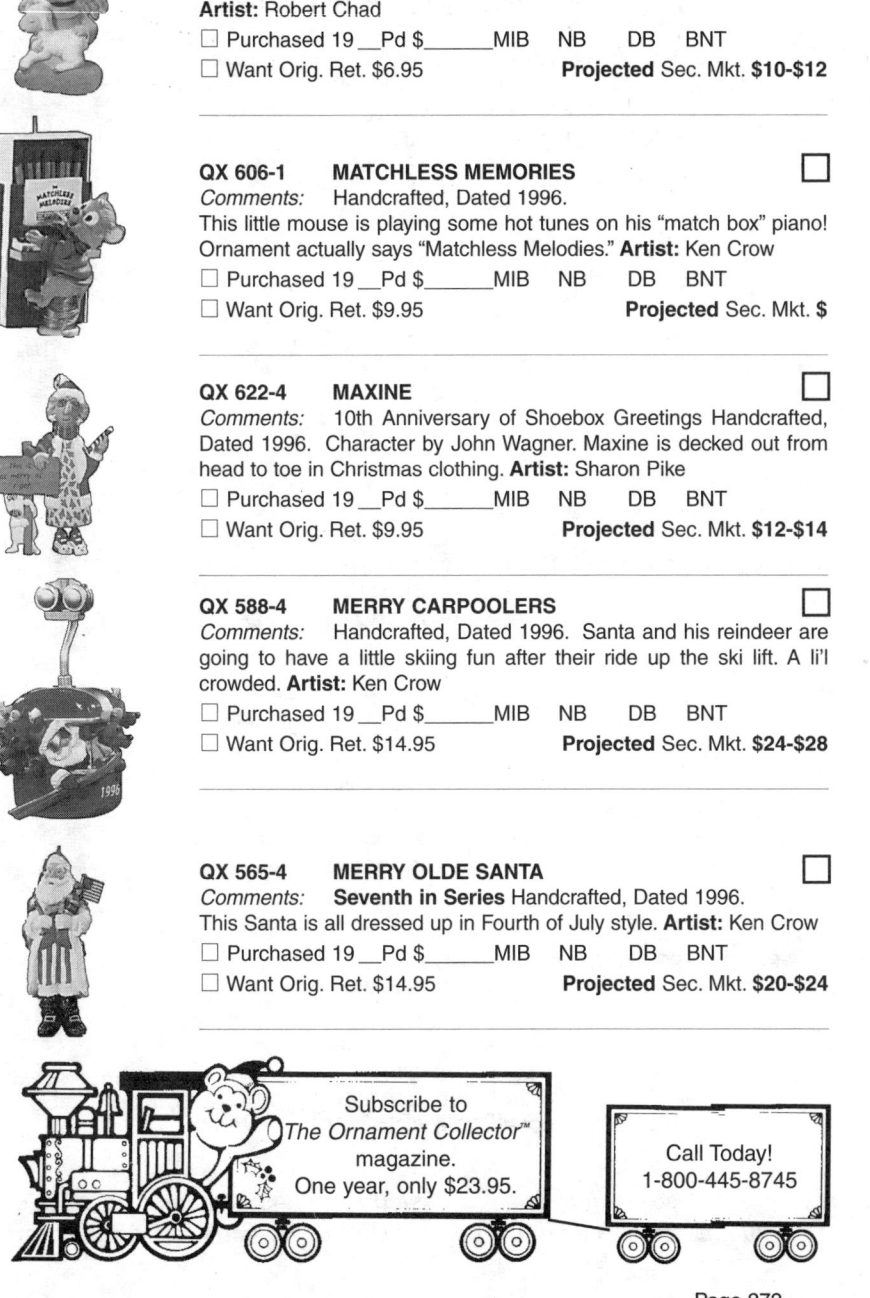

QX 582-4   MOM ☐
Comments: Handcrafted, Dated 1996.
She's trying not to blush with such a large gift that reads "A Mom is a Special Gift 1996." This ornament was found with the signature LaDene on the bottom instead of the correct artist signature. Does anyone have one with the correct signature?
Artist: Joyce Lyle
☐ Purchased 19 __Pd $_____MIB   NB   DB   BNT
☐ Want Orig. Ret. $7.95   **Projected** Sec. Mkt. $

QX 582-1   MOM AND DAD ☐
Comments: Handcrafted, Dated 1996.
Time for a bear hug to show our love. **Artist:** Dill Rhodus
☐ Purchased 19 __Pd $_____MIB   NB   DB   BNT
☐ Want Orig. Ret. $9.95   **Projected** Sec. Mkt. **$14-$18**

QX 579-1   MOM-TO-BE ☐
Comments: Handcrafted, Dated 1996.
This mom is all ready for her special delivery with her bottle and rattle.
Artist: Duane Unruh
☐ Purchased 19 __Pd $_____MIB   NB   DB   BNT
☐ Want Orig. Ret. $7.95   **Projected** Sec. Mkt. **$12.50**

QX 564-4   MOTHER GOOSE: ☐
               MARY HAD A LITTLE LAMB
Comments: **Fourth in Series,** Handcrafted, Dated 1996.
Book opens to display a verse. **Artist:** Ed Seale
☐ Purchased 19 __Pd $_____MIB   NB   DB   BNT
☐ Want Orig. Ret. $13.95   **Projected** Sec. Mkt. **$16**

QX 588-1   NEW HOME ☐
Comments: Handcrafted, Dated 1996.
This little squirrel has found his new home in your mailbox.
Artist: Ed Seale
☐ Purchased 19 __Pd $_____MIB   NB   DB   BNT
☐ Want Orig. Ret. $8.95   **Projected** Sec. Mkt. **$18**

QLX 747-1   NORTH POLE VOLUNTEERS ☐
Comments: Light, Motion and Sound, Dated 1996.
Fire Chief Santa pulls the cord that makes the bell swing and clang. The sirens wail, mascot barks and the wheels turn on this vintage fire engine. **Artist:** Ed Seale
☐ Purchased 19 __Pd $_____MIB   NB   DB   BNT
☐ Want Orig. Ret. $42.00   **Projected** Sec. Mkt. **$65**

QX 567-1   NOSTALGIC HOUSES AND SHOPS: ☐
               VICTORIAN PAINTED LADY
Comments: **Thirteenth in Series,** Dated 1996.
Artist: Don Palmiter
☐ Purchased 19 __Pd $_____MIB   NB   DB   BNT
☐ Want Orig. Ret. $14.95   **Projected** Sec. Mkt. **$18-$20**

QX 548-1   OLIVE OYL AND SWEE' PEA ☐
Comments: Handcrafted
The whimsical look of Olive Oyl holding Swee' Pea brings out the child in all of us. Very colorful! **Artist:** Robert Chad
☐ Purchased 19 __Pd $_____MIB   NB   DB   BNT
☐ Want Orig. Ret. $10.95   **Projected** Sec. Mkt. **$14-$16**

QX 586-1   ON MY WAY PHOTO HOLDER ☐
Comments: Handcrafted, Dated 1996.
Keep your child's school photo in this nifty bus frame.
Artist: Sue Tague
☐ Purchased 19 __Pd $_____MIB   NB   DB   BNT
☐ Want Orig. Ret. $7.95   **Projected** Sec. Mkt. **$10.50**

QX 579-4   OUR CHRISTMAS TOGETHER ☐
Comments: Handcrafted, Dated 1996.
A special couple sit together in this romantic gazebo. Was very popular! **Artist:** Don Palmiter
☐ Purchased 19 __Pd $_____MIB   NB   DB   BNT
☐ Want Orig. Ret. $18.95   **Projected** Sec. Mkt. **$22-$28**

QX 580-4   OUR CHRISTMAS TOGETHER PHOTO HOLDER ☐
Comments: Handcrafted, Dated 1996.
Mr. and Mrs. Claus are at the drive-in theatre where the feature on the big screen happens to be you and that favorite person!
Artist: Ken Crow
☐ Purchased 19 __Pd $_____MIB   NB   DB   BNT
☐ Want Orig. Ret. $8.95   **Projected** Sec. Mkt. **$15**

QX 581-1   OUR FIRST CHRISTMAS TOGETHER ☐
Comments: Handcrafted, Dated 1996.
Two loveable mice are sitting on a sliver of cheese shaped like the moon. **Artist:** Don Palmiter
☐ Purchased 19 __Pd $_____MIB   NB   DB   BNT
☐ Want Orig. Ret. $9.95   **Projected** Sec. Mkt. **$12-$14**

QX 305-1   OUR FIRST CHRISTMAS TOGETHER ☐
Comments: Acrylic, Dated 1996.
Two white doves represent a couple's first Christmas together.
Artist: LaDene Votruba

☐ Purchased 19__ Pd $_____ MIB   NB   DB   BNT
☐ Want Orig. Ret. $6.95   **Projected** Sec. Mkt. **$12.50**

QLX 737-4   OVER THE ROOFTOPS ☐
Comments: Lighted, Dated 1996.
Within this ornament reminiscent of a snow globe, Santa flies over rooftops on Christmas Eve, making his deliveries.
Artist: Ed Seale

☐ Purchased 19__ Pd $_____ MIB   NB   DB   BNT
☐ Want Orig. Ret. $14.50   **Projected** Sec. Mkt. **$18-$22**

QX 538-1   PEANUTS GANG, THE ☐
Comments: **Fourth and Finial in Series** Handcrafted, Dated 1996.
Sally is making out her Christmas wish list for Santa.
Artist: John "Collin" Francis

☐ Purchased 19__ Pd $_____ MIB   NB   DB   BNT
☐ Want Orig. Ret. $9.95   **Projected** Sec. Mkt. **$15-$18**

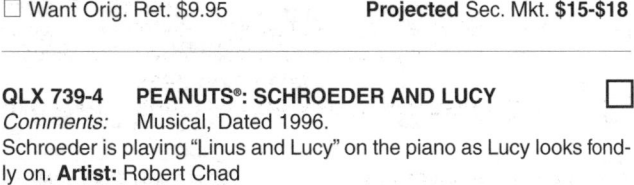

QLX 739-4   PEANUTS®: SCHROEDER AND LUCY ☐
Comments: Musical, Dated 1996.
Schroeder is playing "Linus and Lucy" on the piano as Lucy looks fondly on. **Artist:** Robert Chad

☐ Purchased 19   Pd $ MIB   NB   DB   BNT
☐ Want Orig. Ret. $18.50   **Projected** Sec. Mkt. **$28-$30**

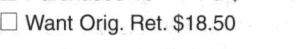

QX 623-4   PEPPERMINT SURPRISE ☐
Comments: Handcrafted, Dated 1996.
Can a mouse be so happy to receive this peppermint candy? From the look on its face it certainly can. **Artist:** Sharon Pike

☐ Purchased 19__ Pd $_____ MIB   NB   DB   BNT
☐ Want Orig. Ret. $7.95   **Projected** Sec. Mkt. **$10-$12**

QX 653-4   PEZ® SNOWMAN ☐
Comments: Handcrafted, Dated 1996.
Anyone for some frozen Pez Candy?

☐ Purchased 19__ Pd $_____ MIB   NB   DB   BNT
☐ Want Orig. Ret. $7.95   **Projected** Sec. Mkt. **$10-$12**

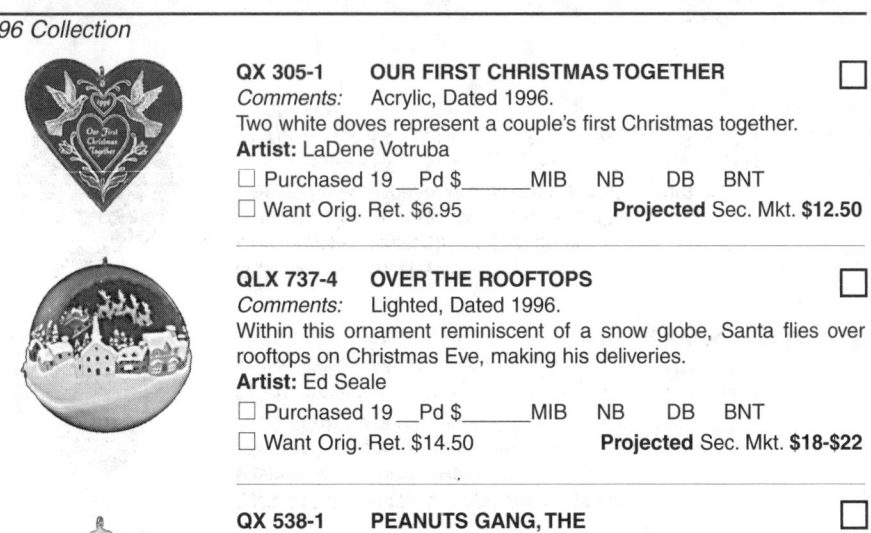

QLX 745-1   PINBALL WONDER ☐
Comments: Light, Sound and Movement, Dated 1996.
Santa is racking up points as he plays this nostalgic pinball machine.
Artist: Ken Crow

☐ Purchased 19__ Pd $_____ MIB   NB   DB   BNT
☐ Want Orig. Ret. $28.00   **Projected** Sec. Mkt. **$35-$40**

QX 603-4   POLAR CYCLE ☐
Comments: Handcrafted, Dated 1996.
A little penguin enjoys his ride on the front of a bicycle ridden by none other than a polar bear. **Artist:** Duane Unruh

☐ Purchased 19__ Pd $_____ MIB   NB   DB   BNT
☐ Want Orig. Ret. $12.95   **Projected** Sec. Mkt. **$18-$21**

QX 626-1   PRAYER FOR PEACE ☐
Comments: Handcrafted, Dated 1996.
A kneeling little girl, her candle and Bible in hand, says her prayers.
Artist: Joyce Lyle

☐ Purchased 19__ Pd $_____ MIB   NB   DB   BNT
☐ Want Orig. Ret. $14.95   **Projected** Sec. Mkt. **$18**

QX 625-1   PRECIOUS CHILD ☐
Comments: Handcrafted, Dated 1996.
The Holy Mother and Child are surrounded by gold on this special ornament. **Artist:** LaDene Votruba

☐ Purchased 19__ Pd $_____ MIB   NB   DB   BNT
☐ Want Orig. Ret. $8.95   **Projected** Sec. Mkt. **$10**

QX 601-1   PUP-TENTING ☐
Comments: Handcrafted, Dated 1996.
The outdoor person will find the humor in this pup and his decorated tent. **Artist:** Don Palmiter

☐ Purchased 19__ Pd $_____ MIB   NB   DB   BNT
☐ Want Orig. Ret. $7.95   **Projected** Sec. Mkt. **$10-$12**

QX 565-1   PUPPY LOVE ☐
Comments: **Sixth in Series,** Handcrafted, Brass tag, Dated 1996.
A brown puppy happily thanks his owner for the bone in his stocking.
Artist: Anita Marra Rogers

☐ Purchased 19__Pd $_____MIB   NB   DB   BNT
☐ Want Orig. Ret. $7.95   **Projected** Sec. Mkt. **$10-$12.50**

QX 620-4   REGAL CARDINAL ☐
Comments: Clip-on, Dated 1996.
This beautiful cardinal is perching on a branch of holly that can be
clipped onto your tree. **Artist:** John "Collins" Francis

☐ Purchased 19__Pd $_____MIB   NB   DB   BNT
☐ Want Orig. Ret. $9.95   **Projected** Sec. Mkt. **$14**

QX 567-4   ROCKING HORSE ☐
Comments: **Sixteenth and Final in Series,** Handcrafted, Dated
1996. This final edition rocking horse is jet black with a white mane
and tail. **Artist:** Linda Sickman

☐ Purchased 19__Pd $_____MIB   NB   DB   BNT
☐ Want Orig. Ret. $10.95   **Projected** Sec. Mkt. **$16-$18**

QXC 734-1   RUDOLPH ® THE RED NOSED REINDEER: ☐
KEEPSAKE CLUB
Comments: Handcrafted, Light, Dated 1996.
Of course, Rudolph's red nose glows! Membership ornament.
Artist: Bob Siedler

☐ Purchased 19__Pd $_____MIB   NB   DB   BNT
☐ Want Orig. Ret. Comes w/Membership
                                Projected Sec. Mkt. **$25-$30**

QXC 416-4   SANTA: KEEPSAKE CLUB ☐
Comments: Handcrafted, Dated 1996.
Santa is giving away candy canes to one and all.
Artist: Bob Siedler

☐ Purchased 19__Pd $_____MIB   NB   DB   BNT
☐ Want Orig. Ret. Comes w/Membership
                                Projected Sec. Mkt. **$20-$22**

QX 592-1   SEW SWEET ☐
Comments: Handcrafted, Dated 1996.
A little bee sits in a red chair, sewing a Christmas pillow for someone
sweet. This was a very popular one! **Artist:** Nina Aube

☐ Purchased 19__Pd $_____MIB   NB   DB   BNT
☐ Want Orig. Ret. $8.95   **Projected** Sec. Mkt. **$15-$18**

QLX 742-4   SHARING A SODA ☐
Comments: Flickering light, Dated 1996.
Santa's giving out soda with his soda machine that has a flickering light
representing "bubbles." **Artist:** Ken Crow

☐ Purchased 19__Pd $_____MIB   NB   DB   BNT
☐ Want Orig. Ret. $24.50   **Projected** Sec. Mkt. **$32-$40**

QX 583-4   SISTER TO SISTER ☐
Comments: Handcrafted, Dated 1996.
Sisters will be reminded of the joys of childhood as these two play at
dressing up for the holiday season. **Artist:** Joyce Lyle

☐ Purchased 19__Pd $_____MIB   NB   DB   BNT
☐ Want Orig. Ret. $9.95   **Projected** Sec. Mkt. **$12-$14**

QX 607-9   SON ☐
Comments: Handcrafted, Dated 1996.
Riding his broom stick horse, this li'l guy pretends to be riding off to dis-
tant places. **Artist:** Don Palmiter

☐ Purchased 19__Pd $_____MIB   NB   DB   BNT
☐ Want Orig. Ret. $8.95   **Projected** Sec. Mkt. **$12-$15**

QX 586-4   SPECIAL DOG PHOTO HOLDER ☐
Comments: Handcrafted, Dated 1996.
Keep your special canine photo in this wreath of dog biscuits.
Artist: Sue Tague

☐ Purchased 19__Pd $_____MIB   NB   DB   BNT
☐ Want Orig. Ret. $7.95   **Projected** Sec. Mkt. **$12-$14**

QX 575-7   SPIDER-MAN ☐
Comments: Handcrafted
Spider-man is out patrolling the limbs of your tree on his "web-lines."
Artist: Robert Chad

☐ Purchased 19__Pd $_____MIB   NB   DB   BNT
☐ Want Orig. Ret. $12.95   **Projected** Sec. Mkt. **$15**

QX 600-4   STAR OF THE SHOW ☐
Comments: Handcrafted, Dated 1996.
This little ballerina bunny is every little girl's dream. **Artist:** Nina Aube

☐ Purchased 19__Pd $_____MIB   NB   DB   BNT
☐ Want Orig. Ret. $8.95   **Projected** Sec. Mkt. **$12.50**

QXI 555-1 STAR TREK® THE NEXT GENERATION™: COMMANDER WILLIAM T. RIKER™
Comments: Handcrafted, Dated 1996.
Commander Riker is poised ready, should danger strike.
Artist: Anita M. Rogers
☐ Purchased 19 __Pd $_____MIB NB DB BNT
☐ Want Orig. Ret. $14.95 **Projected** Sec. Mkt. **$18-$20**

QXI 554-4 STAR TREK®: MR. SPOCK
Comments: Handcrafted, Dated 1996.
Mr. Spock is giving the damage report of the latest Klingon attack.
Artist: Anita M. Rogers
☐ Purchased 19 __Pd $_____MIB NB DB BNT
☐ Want Orig. Ret. $14.95 **Projected** Sec. Mkt. **$20-$24**

QXI 753-4 STAR TREK®: U.S.S. ENTERPRISE™ AND GALILEO SHUTTLECRAFT™
Comments: Die-cast Metal, set of two, Dated 1996.
Galileo Shuttlecraft is getting ready to dock onto the U.S.S. Enterprise.
Artists: Lynn Norton and Dill Rhodus
☐ Purchased 19 __Pd $_____MIB NB DB BNT
☐ Want Orig. Ret. $46.00 **Projected** Sec. Mkt.**$50-$55**

QLX 747-4 STAR WARS™: MILLENNIUM FALCON
Comments: Light, Dated 1996.
The Millennium Falcon is flying through the heavens with lighted thrusters. Seemed to be more popular than some others.
☐ Purchased 19 __Pd $_____MIB NB DB BNT
☐ Want Orig. Ret. $24.00 **Projected** Sec. Mkt. **$30-40**

QLX 742-1 STATUE OF LIBERTY, THE
Comments: Music and Light, Dated 1996.
Lady Liberty's torch and crown light up. Plays "The Star Spangled Banner." Includes special collector's card. Very Nice! **Artist:** Ed Seale
☐ Purchased 19 __Pd $_____MIB NB DB BNT
☐ Want Orig. Ret. $24.50 **Projected** Sec. Mkt. **$30-$35**

QX 630-1 TAMIKA
Comments: Handcrafted, Dated 1996.
Tamika one of the Penda Kids™ celebrates peace, hope and love.
Artists: Cathy Johnson and Katrina Bricker
☐ Purchased 19 __Pd $_____MIB NB DB BNT
☐ Want Orig. Ret. $7.95 **Projected** Sec. Mkt. **$10**

QX 611-4 TENDER LOVIN' CARE
Comments: Handcrafted, Dated 1996.
This little nurse has her stethoscope and thermometer ready to check you out. **Artist:** Ed Seale
☐ Purchased 19 __Pd $_____MIB NB DB BNT
☐ Want Orig. Ret. $7.95 **Projected** Sec. Mkt. **$12-$15**

QX 585-4 THANK YOU, SANTA PHOTO HOLDER
Comments: Handcrafted, Dated 1996.
Place your family photo behind Santa's glass of milk and plate of cookies. **Artist:** Katrina Bricker
☐ Purchased 19 __Pd $_____MIB NB DB BNT
☐ Want Orig. Ret. $7.95 **Projected** Sec. Mkt. **$12-$14**

QX 591-4 THIS BIG!
Comments: Handcrafted, Dated 1996.
Now Santa, don't s-t-r-e-t-c-h the truth about how big that fish was. Cute! **Artist:** Ed Seale
☐ Purchased 19 __Pd $_____MIB NB DB BNT
☐ Want Orig. Ret. $9.95 **Projected** Sec. Mkt. **$14-$16**

QX 631-4 THOMAS THE TANK ENGINE AND FRIENDS™: PERCY THE SMALL ENGINE-NO. 6
Comments: Handcrafted
Percy Small Engine #6 is all steamed up and ready to make that Christmas run. **Artist:** Dill Rhodus
☐ Purchased 19 __Pd $_____MIB NB DB BNT
☐ Want Orig. Ret. $9.95 **Projected** Sec. Mkt. **$14-$16**

QX 546-4 TIME FOR A TREAT
Comments: Handcrafted, Dated 1996.
It's time for a Hershey's chocolate run down the hill. **Artist:** Linda Sickman
☐ Purchased 19 __Pd $_____MIB NB DB BNT
☐ Want Orig. Ret. $11.95 **Projected** Sec. Mkt. **$15-$18**

QLX 746-1 TOBIN FRALEY HOLIDAY CAROUSEL
Comments: **Third and Finial in Series,** Light and Music, Dated 1996. This grey carousel horse plays "On the Beautiful Blue Danube."
Artist: John "Collin" Francis
☐ Purchased 19 __Pd $_____MIB NB DB BNT
☐ Want Orig. Ret. $32.00 **Projected** Sec. Mkt. **$35-$38**

QX 632-1   TONKA® MIGHTY DUMP TRUCK
Comments: Die-cast Metal, Dated 1996.
Replica of the toy many played with as children. Nice!
☐ Purchased 19__ Pd $_____MIB   NB   DB   BNT
☐ Want Orig. Ret. $13.95   **Projected** Sec. Mkt. **$22-$28**

QLX 738-4   TREASURED MEMORIES
Comments: Lighted, Dated 1996.
This design represents the 22 foot Christmas tree at the home of
collector Jim Reid. **Artist:** Linda Sickman
☐ Purchased 19__ Pd $_____MIB   NB   DB   BNT
☐ Want Orig. Ret. $18.50   **Projected** Sec. Mkt. **$20-$22**

QXI 754-4   U.S.S. VOYAGER™: STAR TREK®
Comments: Light, Dated 1996.
The Star ship made famous in the fourth television series of Star
Trek®. **Artist:** Lynn Norton
☐ Purchased 19__ Pd $_____MIB   NB   DB   BNT
☐ Want Orig. Ret. $24.00   **Projected** Sec. Mkt. **$30-$35**

QLX 743-1   VIDEO PARTY
Comments: Light and Changing Screen, Dated 1996.
Two little mice are having fun playing their video game, "Making a
snowman." Different! **Artist:** Bob Siedler
☐ Purchased 19__ Pd $_____MIB   NB   DB   BNT
☐ Want Orig. Ret. $28.00   **Projected** Sec. Mkt. **$35**

QX 539-4   WELCOME GUEST
Comments: Handcrafted, Dated 1996.
Santa welcomes his guests with an ice cold Coca-Cola.
Artist: Duane Uhruh
☐ Purchased 19__ Pd $_____MIB   NB   DB   BNT
☐ Want Orig. Ret. $14.95   **Projected** Sec. Mkt. **$18-$20**

QX 626-4   WELCOME HIM
Comments: Handcrafted, Dated 1996.
The animals are in the manger welcoming the new Baby to the world.
Artist: Sue Tague
☐ Purchased 19__ Pd $_____MIB   NB   DB   BNT
☐ Want Orig. Ret. $8.95   **Projected** Sec. Mkt. **$10-$12**

QX 633-1   WELCOME SIGN: TENDER TOUCHES
Comments: Handcrafted, Dated 1996.
Available only during the Keepsake Ornament Premier July 20-21.
This bear is hanging a wreath in his window to welcome travelers
into his home. **Artist:** Ed Seale
☐ Purchased 19__ Pd $_____MIB   NB   DB   BNT
☐ Want Orig. Ret. $15.00   **Projected** Sec. Mkt. **$18-$22**

QX 545-4   WINNIE THE POOH AND PIGLET
Comments: Handcrafted, Dated 1996.
Winnie the Pooh and Piglet are out for a winter walk, talking about
Pooh's honey supply for the winter. **Artist:** Bob Siedler
☐ Purchased 19__ Pd $_____MIB   NB   DB   BNT
☐ Want Orig. Ret. $12.95   **Projected** Sec. Mkt. **$20-$25**

QLX 741-4   WINNIE THE POOH: SLIPPERY DAY
Comments: Motion, Handcrafted.
Winnie the Pooh, Tigger, Piglet and Eeyore are sliding around on the
ice pond enjoying a wintery day. **Artist:** Bob Siedler
☐ Purchased 19__ Pd $_____MIB   NB   DB   BNT
☐ Want Orig. Ret. $24.50   **Projected** Sec. Mkt. **$50-$55**

QLX 745-4   WIZARD OF OZ™: EMERALD CITY
Comments: Light, motion, and music.
Dorothy and friends spin around on a rotating road with a glowing
Emerald City while playing "We're Off to See the Wizard."
Artist: Ken Crow
☐ Purchased 19__ Pd $_____MIB   NB   DB   BNT
☐ Want Orig. Ret. $32.00   **Projected** Sec. Mkt. **$55-$60**

QX 555-4   WIZARD OF OZ™: WITCH OF THE WEST
Comments: Handcrafted
The wicked witch of the west is ready to cast her awful spell on
Dorothy and her friends. **Artist:** Joyce Lyle
☐ Purchased 19__ Pd $_____MIB   NB   DB   BNT
☐ Want Orig. Ret. $13.95   **Projected** Sec. Mkt. **$15-$18**

**WIZARD OF OZ™: WIZARD
KEEPSAKE CLUB**
Comments: Handcrafted
This ornament depicts a memorable scene from the movie, the
wizard leaving without Dorothy. For Keepsake Club Members Only.
Artist: Anita Marra Rogers
☐ Purchased 19__ Pd $_____MIB   NB   DB   BNT
☐ Want Orig. Ret. $12.95   **Projected** Sec. Mkt. **$50 and up**

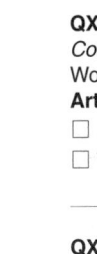

QX 594-1   WONDER WOMAN ☐
Comments: Handcrafted.
Wonder Woman is on the look out for low-down no gooders.
Artist: Anita Marra Rogers
☐ Purchased 19 __ Pd $_____ MIB   NB   DB   BNT
☐ Want Orig. Ret. $12.95   **Projected** Sec. Mkt. **$15-$16**

QX 613-1   WOODLAND SANTA ☐
Comments: Pressed tin.
Santa caries on his shoulder the perfect tree for Mrs. Claus.
Artist: Linda Sickman
☐ Purchased 19 __ Pd $_____ MIB   NB   DB   BNT
☐ Want Orig. Ret. $12.95   **Projected** Sec. Mkt. **$16-$18**

QX 552-1   YOGI BEAR™ AND BOO BOO™ ☐
Comments: Handcrafted
Yogi and Boo Boo can't wait to see what is in the picnic basket that is intended for Mr. Ranger.
Artist: Anita Marra Rogers
☐ Purchased 19 __ Pd $_____ MIB   NB   DB   BNT
☐ Want Orig. Ret. $12.95   **Projected** Sec. Mkt. **$15**

QX 501-1   YULETIDE CENTRAL ☐
Comments: **Third in Series,** Pressed Tin, Dated 1996.
A mail car is next in line on the track of Yuletide Central.
Artist: Linda Sickman
☐ Purchased 19 __ Pd $_____ MIB   NB   DB   BNT
☐ Want Orig. Ret. $18.95   **Projected** Sec. Mkt. **$24**

QX 605-4   YULETIDE CHEER ☐
Comments: Handcrafted, Dated 1996.
This cheerleader is spreading the cheer with her megaphone.
Artist: LaDene Votruba
☐ Purchased 19 __ Pd $_____ MIB   NB   DB   BNT
☐ Want Orig. Ret. $7.95   **Projected** Sec. Mkt. **$10**

QX 652-4   ZIGGY® ☐
Comments: 25th Anniversary Handcrafted, Dated 1996.
Ziggy is all dressed up like Santa. **Artist:** Robert Chad
☐ Purchased 19 __ Pd $_____ MIB   NB   DB   BNT
☐ Want Orig. Ret. $9.95   **Projected** Sec. Mkt. **$15**

Hallmark Keepsake
Showcase Ornaments - 1996

Cookie Jar Friends

QK 116-4   CARMEN ☐
Comments: Porcelain, Dated 1996. Carmen the feline cookie keeper is made like a real cookie jar with a lid that can be lifted.
Artist: Anita Marra Rogers
☐ Purchased 19 __ Pd $_____ MIB   NB   DB   BNT
☐ Want Orig. Ret. $15.95   **Projected** Sec. Mkt. **$20**

QK 116-1   CLYDE ☐
Comments: Porcelain, Dated 1996. Clyde, the canine cookie keeper, is made like a real cookie jar with a lid that can be lifted.
Artist: Nina Aube
☐ Purchased 19 __ Pd $_____ MIB   NB   DB   BNT
☐ Want Orig. Ret. $15.95   **Projected** Sec. Mkt. **$20**

Folk Art Americana

QK 113-4   CAROLING ANGEL ☐
Comments: Handcrafted, Dated 1996.
This angel with wings of stamped copper is singing her praises.
Artist: Linda Sickman
☐ Purchased 19 __ Pd $_____ MIB   NB   DB   BNT
☐ Want Orig. Ret. $16.95   **Projected** Sec. Mkt. **$22**

QK 120-4   MRS. CLAUS ☐
Comments: Handcrafted, Dated 1996.
Mrs. Claus is bringing the last of the gifts to Santa with her copper lantern and bear under her arm. **Artist:** Linda Sickman
☐ Purchased 19 __ Pd $_____ MIB   NB   DB   BNT
☐ Want Orig. Ret. $18.95   **Projected** Sec. Mkt. **$23-$28**

QK 112-4   SANTA'S GIFTS ☐
Comments: Handcrafted, Dated 1996.
This Santa is bringing gifts to the "good little boys and girls" with his brass bells in his hand, train under his arm and an angel with copper wings on his arm. **Artist:** Linda Sickman
☐ Purchased 19 __ Pd $_____ MIB   NB   DB   BNT
☐ Want Orig. Ret. $18.95   **Projected** Sec. Mkt. **$25-$30**

Magi Bells

QK 117-4   BALTHASAR (FRANKINCENSE) ☐
Comments: Fine Porcelain Bell.
Bathasar is bringing his gift of frankincense to the newborn babe.
Artist: LaDene Votruba

☐ Purchased 19 __ Pd $_____ MIB   NB   DB   BNT
☐ Want Orig. Ret. $13.95   **Projected** Sec. Mkt. **$16-$18**

QK 118-4   CASPAR (MYRRH) ☐
Comments: Fine Porcelain Bell.
Caspar is bringing his gift of Myrrh to the newborn babe.
Artist: LaDene Votruba

☐ Purchased 19 __ Pd $_____ MIB   NB   DB   BNT
☐ Want Orig. Ret. $13.95   **Projected** Sec. Mkt. **$16-$18**

QK 118-1   MELCHIOR (GOLD) ☐
Comments: Fine Porcelain Bell
Melchior is bringing his gift of gold to the newborn babe.
Artist: LaDene Votruba

☐ Purchased 19 __ Pd $_____ MIB   NB   DB   BNT
☐ Want Orig. Ret. $13.95   **Projected** Sec. Mkt. **$16-$18**

Nature's Sketchbook

QK 110-4   CHRISTMAS BUNNY ☐
Comments: Handcrafted, Dated 1996.
Design by Marjolein Bastin. This curious rabbit has come to inspect the water jug buried deep in winter's snow. **Artist:** John "Collin" Francis

☐ Purchased 19 __ Pd $_____ MIB   NB   DB   BNT
☐ Want Orig. Ret. $18.95   **Projected** Sec. Mkt. **$24-$26**

QK 111-4   THE BIRDS' CHRISTMAS TREE ☐
Comments: Handcrafted, Dated 1996.
Design by Marjolein Bastin. The birds feed at this lovely Christmas tree decorated especially for them. **Artist:** Duane Unruh

☐ Purchased 19 __ Pd $_____ MIB   NB   DB   BNT
☐ Want Orig. Ret. $18.95   **Projected** Sec. Mkt. **$22-$25**

QK 109-4   THE HOLLY BASKET ☐
Comments: Handcrafted, Dated 1996.
Design by Marjolein Bastin. A bird sits on a basket full of holly.
Artist: Joyce Lyle

☐ Purchased 19 __ Pd $_____ MIB   NB   DB   BNT
☐ Want Orig. Ret. $18.95   **Projected** Sec. Mkt. **$22-$24**

Sacred Masterworks

QK 114-4   MADONNA AND CHILD ☐
Comments: Handcrafted, Dated 1996.
This pays tribute to the19th century lithograph published by Marcus Ward after the painting by Raphael. **Artist:** Linda Sickman

☐ Purchased 19 __ Pd $_____ MIB   NB   DB   BNT
☐ Want Orig. Ret. $15.95   **Projected** Sec. Mkt. **$18-$20**

QK 115-4   PRAYING MADONNA ☐
Comments: Handcrafted, Dated 1996.
This pays tribute to the 19th century lithograph published by Marcus Ward after the painting by Sassoferrato. **Artist:** Linda Sickman

☐ Purchased 19 __ Pd $_____ MIB   NB   DB   BNT
☐ Want Orig. Ret. $15.95   **Projected** Sec. Mkt. **$18-$20**

The Languuage of Flowers

QK 117-1   PANSY ☐
Comments: ***FIRST IN SERIES,*** Handcrafted, Dated 1996.
Pansy is dressed in Victorian tradition carting a delicate Silver plated container filled with the flowers for which she was named.
Artist: Sue Tague

☐ Purchased 19 __ Pd $_____ MIB   NB   DB   BNT
☐ Want Orig. Ret. $15.95   **Projected** Sec. Mkt. **$35-$40**

Turn of the Century Parade

QK 108-4   UNCLE SAM ☐
Comments: **Second in Series,** Dated 1996.
A tribute to mechanical tin toys made with die-cast metal with a brass bell that rings. Dated **Artist:** Ken Crow

☐ Purchased 19 __ Pd $_____ MIB   NB   DB   BNT
☐ Want Orig. Ret. $16.95   **Projected** Sec. Mkt. **$18-$20**

A person cannot be a peacemaker until first he finds peace for himself.

Olympic Ornaments

Prices may increase with the passage of time.

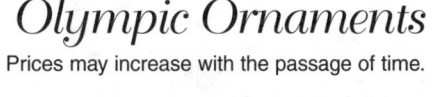

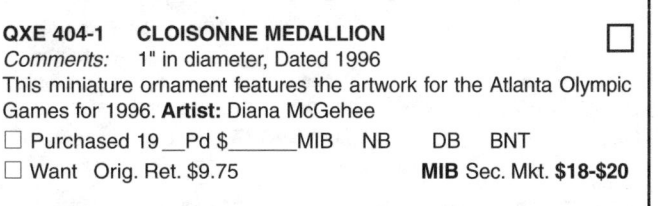

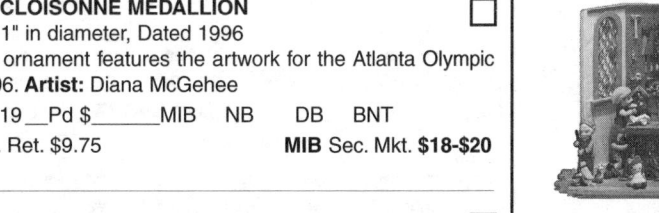

QXE 404-1   CLOISONNE MEDALLION   ☐
Comments: 1" in diameter, Dated 1996
This miniature ornament features the artwork for the Atlanta Olympic Games for 1996. **Artist:** Diana McGehee
☐ Purchased 19 __ Pd $_____ MIB   NB   DB   BNT
☐ Want   Orig. Ret. $9.75   **MIB** Sec. Mkt. **$18-$20**

QXE 551- 1   INVITATION TO THE GAMES   ☐
Comments: 3-1/2" x 2-1/2", Dated 1996
These two ceramic plaque ornaments feature posters from the 1896 and 1996 Olympics. Each comes with display stand and commemorative copy. **Artist:** Diana McGehee
☐ Purchased 19 __ Pd $_____ MIB   NB   DB   BNT
☐ Want   Orig. Ret. $14.95   **MIB** Sec. Mkt. **$16-$20**

QXE 572-4   IZZY – THE MASCOT   ☐
Comments: 3-11/16" x 2-11/16", Dated 1996
Here's Izzy, the official 1996 Olympic mascot.
☐ Purchased 19 __ Pd $_____ MIB   NB   DB   BNT
☐ Want   Orig. Ret. $9.95   **MIB** Sec. Mkt. **$12-$14**

QXE 744-4   LIGHTING THE FLAME   ☐
Comments: 4-15/16" x 2-5/8", battery operated, Dated 1996
Plays Bugler's Dream from the Opening Ceremony. Features commemorative copy and a flickering light. **Artist:** Duane Unruh
☐ Purchased 19 __ Pd $_____ MIB   NB   DB   BNT
☐ Want   Orig. Ret. $28   **MIB** Sec. Mkt. **$30-$35**

QXE 573-1   OLYMPIC TRIUMPH KEEPSAKE ORNAMENT   ☐
Comments: 4-1/16" x 2-13/16", Dated 1996
This sculpted discus thrower includes commemorative copy.
Artist: Ed Seale
☐ Purchased 19 __ Pd $_____ MIB   NB   DB   BNT
☐ Want   Orig. Ret. $10.95   **MIB** Sec. Mkt. **$15-$16**

QXE 574-1   PARADE OF NATIONS   ☐
Comments: 3-3/16" diameter, porcelain, Dated 1996
Includes display stand and features flags from various nations.
☐ Purchased 19 __ Pd $_____ MIB   NB   DB   BNT
☐ Want   Orig. Ret. $10.95   **MIB** Sec. Mkt. **$16-$20**

Artist on Tour 1996

QXC 420-1   SANTA'S TOY SHOP   ☐
Comments: Handcrafted, Dated 1996.
Two Keepsake Ornaments with display. All the elves have their own jobs in preparing Santa for his deliveries.
Artist: all 17 Studio Artists
☐ Purchased 19 __ Pd $_____ MIB   NB   DB   BNT
☐ Want Orig. Ret. $60.00   **Projected** Sec. Mkt. **$100-$125**

TOY SHOP SANTA   ☐
Comments: Handcrafted, Dated 1996.
To complement Santa's Toy Shop.
Artist: Duane Unruh
☐ Purchased 19 __ Pd $_____ MIB   NB   DB   BNT
☐ Want Orig. Ret. $14.95   **Projected** Sec. Mkt. **$30-$35**

24 KT GOLD PLATED ROCKING HORSE   ☐
Comments: Handcrafted, Dated 1996.
Miniature rocking horse.
Artist: Linda Sickman
☐ Purchased 19 __ Pd $_____ MIB   NB   DB   BNT
☐ Want Orig. Ret. $12.95   **Projected** Sec. Mkt. **$25**

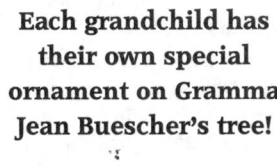

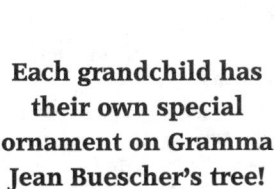

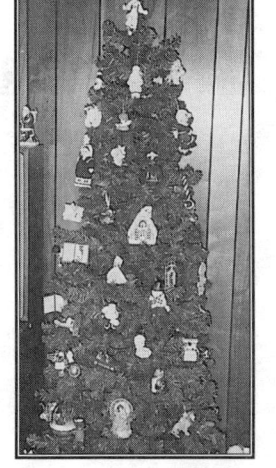

Merry Christmas from Lucille Nevin's brightly lit tree.

Each grandchild has their own special ornament on Gramma Jean Buescher's tree!

1996 Miniature Ornament Collection

A   B   C   D

E   F   G   H   I   J

K   L   M   N   O

Prices are projected ... In the past our projections have been 95% correct!
Keep in touch by reading our other publications in 1997!

A   QXM 423-4   **A CHILD'S GIFTS**   ☐
Handcrafted, Dated 1996. **Artist:** Patricia Andrews
☐ Purchased 19___ Pd $_____ MIB NB DB BNT
☐ Want   Orig. Retail $6.75
Projected Sec. Mkt. **$10**

B   QXM 476-7   **A TREE FOR WOODSTOCK**   ☐
Handcrafted, Dated 1996. **Artist:** Bob Siedler
☐ Purchased 19___ Pd $_____ MIB NB DB BNT
☐ Want   Orig. Retail $5.75
Projected Sec. Mkt. **$10**

C   QXM 422-4   **AFRICAN ELEPHANTS**   ☐
Handcrafted, Complements "Noah's Ark" set. **Artist:** Linda Sickman
☐ Purchased 19___ Pd $_____ MIB NB DB BNT
☐ Want   Orig. Retail $5.75
Projected Sec. Mkt. **$15**

D   QXM 407-4   **ALICE IN WONDERLAND: MAD HATTER**   ☐
Second in Series, Handcrafted, Dated 1996. **Artist:** Patricia Andrews
☐ Purchased 19___ Pd $_____ MIB NB DB BNT
☐ Want   Orig. Retail $6.75
Projected Sec. Mkt. **$10.50**

E   QXM 415-4   **BABY SYLVESTER**   ☐
Handcrafted. **Artist:** Don Palmiter
☐ Purchased 19___ Pd $_____ MIB NB DB BNT
☐ Want   Orig. Retail $5.75
Projected Sec. Mkt. **$8**

F   QXM 401-4   **BABY TWEETY**   ☐
Handcrafted. **Artist:** Don Palmiter
☐ Purchased 19___ Pd $_____ MIB NB DB BNT
☐ Want   Orig. Retail $5.75
Projected Sec. Mkt. **$8**

G   QXM 409-1   **CENTURIES OF SANTA**   ☐
Third in Series, Handcrafted, Dated 1996. **Artist:** Linda Sickman
☐ Purchased 19___ Pd $_____ MIB NB DB BNT
☐ Want   Orig. Retail $5.75
Projected Sec. Mkt. **$12**

H   QXM 424-1   **CHRISTMAS BEAR**   ☐
Handcrafted. **Artist:** Ed Seale This is adorable! Great for earrings!
☐ Purchased 19___ Pd $_____ MIB NB DB BNT
☐ Want   Orig. Retail $4.75
Projected Sec. Mkt. **$9.50**

I   QXM 407-1   **CHRISTMAS BELLS**   ☐
Second in Series Handcrafted, Dated 1996. **Artist:** Ed Seale Very popular!
☐ Purchased 19___ Pd $_____ MIB NB DB BNT
☐ Want   Orig. Retail $4.75
Projected Sec. Mkt. **$10-$12**

J   QXE 404-1   **CLOISONNE MEDALLION: OLYMPIC SPIRIT COLLECTION**   ☐
Handcrafted, Dated "Atlanta 1996." **Artist:** Diana McGehee
☐ Purchased 19___ Pd $_____ MIB NB DB BNT
☐ Want   Orig. Retail $9.75
Projected Sec. Mkt. **$12**

K   QXM 402-1   **COOL DELIVERY COCA-COLA®**   ☐
Handcrafted. **Artist:** Sharon Pike
☐ Purchased 19___ Pd $_____ MIB NB DB BNT
☐ Want   Orig. Retail $5.75
Projected Sec. Mkt. **$9.50**

L   QXM 421-1   **GONE WITH THE WIND™**   ☐
Set of Three, 60th Anniversary, Handcrafted, Dated 1996. **Artist:** Patricia Andrews
☐ Purchased 19___ Pd $_____ MIB NB DB BNT
☐ Want   Orig. Retail $19.95
Projected Sec. Mkt. **$28**

M   QXM 425-1   **HATTIE CHAPEAU**   ☐
Complements "A Moustershire Christmas" set from '95, Handcrafted, Dated 1996.
Artist: Dill Rhodus
☐ Purchased 19___ Pd $_____ MIB NB DB BNT
☐ Want   Orig. Retail $4.75
Projected Sec. Mkt. **$7.50**

N   QXC 419-1   **HOLIDAY BUNNY: KEEPSAKE CLUB**   ☐
'96 Collector's Club, Dated 1996. **Artist:** John Francis
☐ Purchased 19___ Pd $_____ MIB NB DB BNT
☐ Want   Free with '96 Club Membership
Projected Sec. Mkt. **$10.50**

O   QXM 423-1   **JOYOUS ANGEL**   ☐
Handcrafted, Dated 1996. **Artist:** Patricia Andrews
☐ Purchased 19___ Pd $_____ MIB NB DB BNT
☐ Want   Orig. Retail $4.75
Projected Sec. Mkt. **$7.50**

A QXM 424-4 **LONG WINTER'S NAP**
Handcrafted, Dated 1996. **Artist:** Patricia Andrews
☐ Purchased 19___ Pd $_____ MIB NB DB BNT
☐ Want Orig. Retail $5.75
Projected Sec. Mkt. **$8**

B QXM 409-4 **MARCH OF THE TEDDY BEARS**
Fourth and Final in Series, Handcrafted, Dated 1996. **Artist:** Duane Unruh
☐ Purchased 19___ Pd $_____ MIB NB DB BNT
☐ Want Orig. Retail $4.75
Projected Sec. Mkt. **$8.50**

C QXM 425-4 **MESSAGE FOR SANTA**
Handcrafted, Dated 1996. **Artist:** Ed Seale
☐ Purchased 19___ Pd $_____ MIB NB DB BNT
☐ Want Orig. Retail $6.75
Projected Sec. Mkt. **$8.50**

D QXM 414-4 **MINIATURE CLOTHESPIN SOLDIER**
Second in Series, Handcrafted. **Artist:** Linda Sickman
☐ Purchased 19___ Pd $_____ MIB NB DB BNT
☐ Want Orig. Retail $4.75
Projected Sec. Mkt. **$8.50**

E QXM 403-1 **MINIATURE KIDDIE CAR CLASSICS: MURRAY® "FIRE TRUCK"**
Second in Series, Cast Metal, Dated 1996. **Artist:** Don Palmiter
☐ Purchased 19___ Pd $_____ MIB NB DB BNT
☐ Want Orig. Retail $6.75
Projected Sec. Mkt. **$12.50 up**

F QXM 411-1 **NATURE'S ANGELS**
Seventh and Final in Series, Handcrafted. **Artist:** Sharon Pike
☐ Purchased 19___ Pd $_____ MIB NB DB BNT
☐ Want Orig. Retail $4.75
Projected Sec. Mkt. **$8**

G QXM 410-4 **NIGHT BEFORE CHRISTMAS, THE**
Fifth and Final in Series, Handcrafted, Dated 1996. **Artist:** Duane Unruh
☐ Purchased 19___ Pd $_____ MIB NB DB BNT
☐ Want Orig. Retail $5.75
Projected Sec. Mkt. **$7.50**

H QXM 411-4 **NOEL R.R.: COOKIE CAR**
Eighth in Series, Handcrafted, Dated 1996. **Artist:** Linda Sickman
☐ Purchased 19___ Pd $_____ MIB NB DB BNT
☐ Want Orig. Retail $6.75
Projected Sec. Mkt. **$8**

I QXM 406-4 **NUTCRACKER BALLET, THE**
FIRST IN SERIES, Handcrafted, Dated 1996. Comes **with** display stage.
Artist: LaDene Votruba
☐ Purchased 19___ Pd $_____ MIB NB DB BNT
☐ Want Orig. Retail $14.75
Projected Sec. Mkt. **$18.50**

J QXM 408-4 **NUTCRACKER GUILD**
Third in Series, Handcrafted, Dated 1996. **Artist:** Linda Sickman
☐ Purchased 19___ Pd $_____ MIB NB DB BNT
☐ Want Orig. Retail $5.75
Projected Sec. Mkt. **$12.95**

K QXM 420-4 **O HOLY NIGHT**
Set of Four, Handcrafted, Dated 1996. Comes with dated display piece.
Artist: Dill Rhodus
☐ Purchased 19___ Pd $_____ MIB NB DB BNT
☐ Want Orig. Retail $24.50
Projected Sec. Mkt. **$26**

L QXM 412-4 **OLD ENGLISH VILLAGE: VILLAGE MILL**
Ninth in Series, Handcrafted, Dated 1996. **Artist:** Dill Rhodus
☐ Purchased 19___ Pd $_____ MIB NB DB BNT
☐ Want Orig. Retail $6.75
Projected Sec. Mkt. **$9.50**

M QXM 410-1 **ON THE ROAD**
Fourth in Series, Pressed Tin. **Artist:** Linda Sickman
☐ Purchased 19___ Pd $_____ MIB NB DB BNT
☐ Want Orig. Retail $5.75
Projected Sec. Mkt. **$9.50**

N QXM 421-4 **PEACEFUL CHRISTMAS**
Handcrafted, Dated 1996. **Artist:** Duane Unruh
☐ Purchased 19___ Pd $_____ MIB NB DB BNT
☐ Want Orig. Retail $4.75
Projected Sec. Mkt. **$7**

O QXM 412-1 **ROCKING HORSE**
Ninth in Series, Handcrafted, Dated 1996. **Artist:** Linda Sickman
☐ Purchased 19___ Pd $_____ MIB NB DB BNT
☐ Want Orig. Retail $4.75
Projected Sec. Mkt. **$8.50**

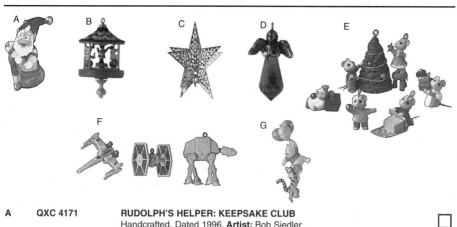

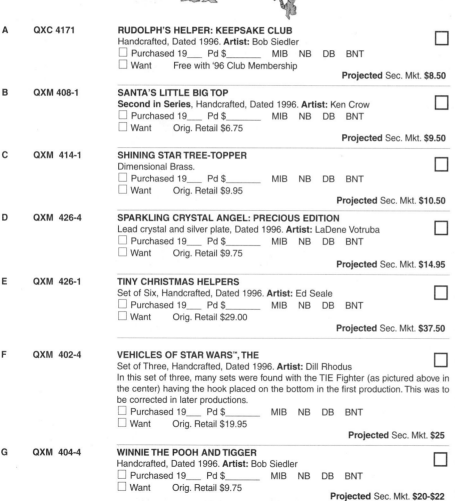

Pat Withall named this her "food" tree. It is decorated with Coca-Cola, M & M's and many other yummy "food" ornaments.

Kathy Schmidt's tree is in front of her scenic bay window. I'm sure there are many people who drive by to view her tree with so many lighted ornaments.

A   QXC 4171   **RUDOLPH'S HELPER: KEEPSAKE CLUB**
Handcrafted, Dated 1996. **Artist:** Bob Siedler
☐ Purchased 19___ Pd $_____   MIB   NB   DB   BNT
☐ Want   Free with '96 Club Membership
Projected Sec. Mkt. **$8.50**

B   QXM 408-1   **SANTA'S LITTLE BIG TOP**
Second in Series, Handcrafted, Dated 1996. **Artist:** Ken Crow
☐ Purchased 19___ Pd $_____   MIB   NB   DB   BNT
☐ Want   Orig. Retail $6.75
Projected Sec. Mkt. **$9.50**

C   QXM 414-1   **SHINING STAR TREE-TOPPER**
Dimensional Brass.
☐ Purchased 19___ Pd $_____   MIB   NB   DB   BNT
☐ Want   Orig. Retail $9.95
Projected Sec. Mkt. **$10.50**

D   QXM 426-4   **SPARKLING CRYSTAL ANGEL: PRECIOUS EDITION**
Lead crystal and silver plate, Dated 1996. **Artist:** LaDene Votruba
☐ Purchased 19___ Pd $_____   MIB   NB   DB   BNT
☐ Want   Orig. Retail $9.75
Projected Sec. Mkt. **$14.95**

E   QXM 426-1   **TINY CHRISTMAS HELPERS**
Set of Six, Handcrafted, Dated 1996. **Artist:** Ed Seale
☐ Purchased 19___ Pd $_____   MIB   NB   DB   BNT
☐ Want   Orig. Retail $29.00
Projected Sec. Mkt. **$37.50**

F   QXM 402-4   **VEHICLES OF STAR WARS™, THE**
Set of Three, Handcrafted, Dated 1996. **Artist:** Dill Rhodus
In this set of three, many sets were found with the TIE Fighter (as pictured above in the center) having the hook placed on the bottom in the first production. This was to be corrected in later productions.
☐ Purchased 19___ Pd $_____   MIB   NB   DB   BNT
☐ Want   Orig. Retail $19.95
Projected Sec. Mkt. **$25**

G   QXM 404-4   **WINNIE THE POOH AND TIGGER**
Handcrafted, Dated 1996. **Artist:** Bob Siedler
☐ Purchased 19___ Pd $_____   MIB   NB   DB   BNT
☐ Want   Orig. Retail $9.75
Projected Sec. Mkt. **$20-$22**

A QEO 808-4 **APPLE BLOSSOM LANE**
Second in Series, Handcrafted, 2-1/2" tall, Dated 1996.
Artist: John Francis
☐ Purchased 19___ Pd $_____ MIB NB DB BNT
☐ Want Orig. Ret. $8.95 **MIB** Sec. Mkt. **$12**

B QEO 822-1 **COLLECTOR'S PLATE: KEEPING A SECRET**
Third in Series, Porcelain Collector's Plate, Handcrafted, 3" tall, Dated 1996.
Artist: LaDene Votruba
☐ Purchased 19___ Pd $_____ MIB NB DB BNT
☐ Want Orig. Ret. $7.95 **MIB** Sec. Mkt. **$12**

C QEO 807-4 **COTTON TAIL EXPRESS: LOCOMOTIVE**
FIRST IN SERIES, Cottontail Express series, Handcrafted 2" tall, Dated 1996.
Additional RR cars may follow. Be sure to get this one autographed by the artist.
Artist: Ken Crow
☐ Purchased 19___ Pd $_____ MIB NB DB BNT
☐ Want Orig. Ret.$8.95 **MIB** Sec. Mkt. **$20**

D QEO 814-4 **CRAYOLA CRAYON: HIPPITY HOP DELIVERY**
Crayola® Crayon, Handcrafted, 2" tall, Dated 1996.
Artist: Ken Crow
☐ Purchased 19___ Pd $_____ MIB NB DB BNT
☐ Want Orig. Ret. $7.95 **MIB** Sec. Mkt. **$14**

E QEO 816-4 **EASTER MORNING**
Handcrafted, 2-1/4" tall, Dated 1996. **Artist:** Duane Unruh
☐ Purchased 19___ Pd $_____ MIB NB DB BNT
☐ Want Orig. Ret. $7.95 **MIB** Sec. Mkt. **$8.50**

F QEO 809-1 **GARDEN CLUB**
Second in Series, Handcrafted, 1-1/4" tall, Dated 1996. **Artist:** Don Palmiter
☐ Purchased 19___ Pd $_____ MIB NB DB BNT
☐ Want Orig. Ret. $7.95 **MIB** Sec. Mkt. **$12**

G QEO 809-4 **HERE COMES EASTER**
Third in Series, Handcrafted, 2" tall, Dated 1996. **Artist:** Ken Crow
☐ Purchased 19___ Pd $_____ MIB NB DB BNT
☐ Want Orig. Ret. $7.95 **MIB** Sec. Mkt. **$12.50**

H QEO 818-4 **JOYFUL ANGELS**
FIRST IN SERIES, 3" tall, Dated 1996. Be sure to get this one! **Artist:** Joyce Lyle
☐ Purchased 19___ Pd $_____ MIB NB DB BNT
☐ Want Orig. Ret. $9.95 **MIB** Sec. Mkt. **$20**

I QEO 818-1 **LOOK WHAT I FOUND!**
Handcrafted, 1-1/2" tall, Dated 1996. **Artist:** John Francis
☐ Purchased 19___ Pd $_____ MIB NB DB BNT
☐ Want Orig. Ret. $7.95 **MIB** Sec. Mkt. **$12**

J QEO 815-4 **LOONEY TUNES™: DAFFY DUCK**
Looney Tunes™, Handcrafted, 2-1/2" tall. Will be popular.
Artist: Anita Rogers
☐ Purchased 19___ Pd $_____ MIB NB DB BNT
☐ Want Orig. Ret. $8.95 **MIB** Sec. Mkt. **$12.50**

K QEO 815-1 **PEANUTS®: PARADE PALS**
Peanuts®, Handcrafted, 2-1/4" tall, Dated 1996. **Artist:** Dill Rhodus
☐ Purchased 19___ Pd $_____ MIB NB DB BNT
☐ Want Orig. Ret. $7.95 **MIB** Sec. Mkt. **$14**

A QEO 807-1

BEATRIX POTTER: PETER RABBIT™
FIRST IN SERIES, Beatrix Potter™ series, Handcrafted, 2-1/2" tall, Dated 1996.
Scarce. Artist: LaDene Votruba

☐ Purchased 19___ Pd $_____ MIB NB DB BNT
☐ Want Orig. Ret. $8.95   **MIB** Sec. Mkt. **$55-65**

B QEO 817-4

PORK 'N BEANS
Handcrafted, 2" tall, Dated 1996. **Artist:** Robert Chad

☐ Purchased 19___ Pd $_____ MIB NB DB BNT
☐ Want Orig. Ret. $7.95   **MIB** Sec. Mkt. **$12**

C QEO 808-1

SPRINGTIME BARBIE
Second in Series, Artist: Patricia Andrews

☐ Purchased 19___ Pd $_____ MIB NB DB BNT
☐ Want Orig. Ret. $12.95   **MIB** Sec. Mkt. **$17.50**

D QEO 813-4

SPRINGTIME BONNETS
Fourth in Series, Artist: Sharon Pike

☐ Purchased 19___ Pd $_____ MIB NB DB BNT
☐ Want Orig. Ret. $7.95   **MIB** Sec. Mkt. **$15-$16**

E QEO 817-1

STRAWBERRY PATCH
Handcrafted, 3" tall, Dated 1996. **Artist:** Ed Seale

☐ Purchased 19___ Pd $_____ MIB NB DB BNT
☐ Want Orig. Ret. $6.95   **MIB** Sec. Mkt. **$12.50**

F QEO 814-1

STRIKE UP THE BAND!
Set of three, Handcrafted, Bugle Bunny: 2-1/4" tall.
Tweedle-Dee Duck: 1-1/2" tall, Nutty Squirrel: 1-1/2" tall, Dated 1996.
Artist: Duane Unruh

☐ Purchased 19___ Pd $_____ MIB NB DB BNT
☐ Want Orig. Ret. $14.95   **MIB** Sec. Mkt. **$18.50**

G QEO 816-1

TENDER TOUCHES: EGGSTRA SPECIAL SURPRISE
Tender Touches, Handcrafted, 2-1/4" tall, Dated 1996. Will be a top seller.
Artist: Ed Seale

☐ Purchased 19___ Pd $_____ MIB NB DB BNT
☐ Want   Orig. Ret. $8.95   **MIB** Sec. Mkt. **$15**

**"My mother said while she's at work
to use my initiative if I needed money,
so I'm selling some of her ornaments!"**

1997 Spring Ornament Collection
Too early to predict as "supply" is not known.

A QEO 871-5 **A PURR-FECT PRINCESS**
Handcrafted, 2-3/16" tall, Dated 1997. **Artist:** Sharon Pike
☐ Purchased 19___ Pd $_____ MIB NB DB BNT
☐ Want Orig. Ret. $7.95

B QEO 866-2 **APPLE BLOSSOM LANE**
Third and Final in Series, Handcrafted, 2-5/16" tall, Dated 1997.
Artist: John "Collin" Francis
☐ Purchased 19___ Pd $_____ MIB NB DB BNT
☐ Want Orig. Ret. $8.95

C QEO 864-5 **BEATRIX POTTER™: JEMIMA PUDDLE-DUCK™**
Second in Series, Handcrafted, 2-1/2" tall, Dated 1997.
Projected pricing… Depends on quantities produced - 1st in Series took retailers by
surprise and never ordered enough. May order too many this year. A waiting game.
Artist: LaDene Votruba
☐ Purchased 19___ Pd $_____ MIB NB DB BNT
☐ Want Orig. Ret. $8.95

D QEO 873-5 **BUMPER CROP – TENDER TOUCHES**
Handcrafted, Set of 3. Grade A Packer -2" tall, First Taster - 1-1/2" tall.
24-Carrot Dreams - 1-5/8" tall. **Artist:** Ed Seale
☐ Purchased 19___ Pd $_____ MIB NB DB BNT
☐ Want Orig. Ret. $14.95

E QEO 863-5 **CHILDREN'S COLLECTOR BARBIE™: BARBIE™ AS RAPUNZEL**
FIRST IN SERIES, Handcrafted, 3-1/2" tall, Dated 1997.
Be sure to get her. May be a very popular series! The second one may be Li'l Bo Beep…
Artist: Anita Marra Rogers
☐ Purchased 19___ Pd $_____ MIB NB DB BNT
☐ Want Orig. Ret. $29.90

F QEO 867-5 **COLLECTOR'S PLATE: SUNNY SUNDAY BEST**
Fourth and Final in Series, Handcrafted, 2-5/8" Diameter, Dated 1997.
Cute! **Artist:** LaDene Votruba
☐ Purchased 19___ Pd $_____ MIB NB DB BNT
☐ Want Orig. Ret. $7.95

G QEO 865-2 **COTTONTAIL EXPRESS: COLORFUL COAL CAR**
Second in Series, Handcrafted, 1¹/2" tall, Dated 1997.
Will be a popular one! **Artist:** Ken Crow
☐ Purchased 19___ Pd $_____ MIB NB DB BNT
☐ Want Orig. Ret. $8.95

H QEO 869-5 **CRAYOLA®: EGGS-PERT ARTIST**
Handcrafted, 1-1/2" tall, Dated 1997. Will be popular **Artist:** Sue Tague
☐ Purchased 19___ Pd $_____ MIB NB DB BNT
☐ Want Orig. Ret. $8.95

I QEO 871-2 **DIGGING IN**
Handcrafted, 2-3/16" tall, Dated 1997. Expensive but cute! **Artist:** Ed Seale
☐ Purchased 19___ Pd $_____ MIB NB DB BNT
☐ Want Orig. Ret. $7.95

J QEO 866-5 **GARDEN CLUB**
Third in Series, Handcrafted, 1-1/2" tall, Dated 1997. **Artist:** Katrina Bricker
☐ Purchased 19___ Pd $_____ MIB NB DB BNT
☐ Want Orig. Ret. $7.95

K QEO 873-2 **GENTLE GUARDIAN**
Handcrafted, 3" tall. **Artist:** Tracy Larsen
☐ Purchased 19___ Pd $_____ MIB NB DB BNT
☐ Want Orig. Ret. $6.95

A   B    C    D

E    F    G

H    I    J    K

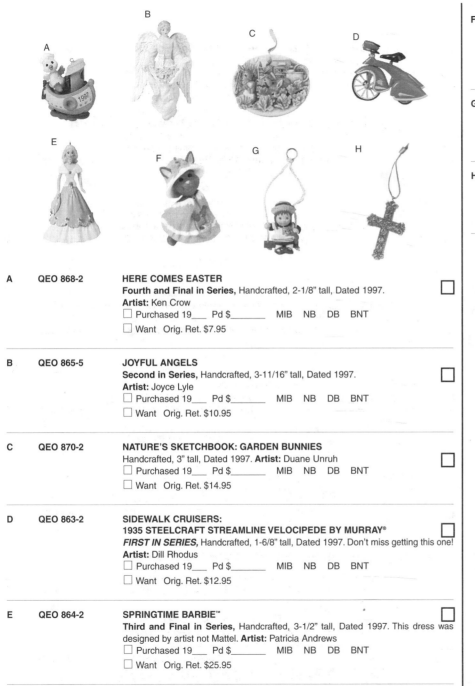

F QEO 867-2   **SPRINGTIME BONNETS**
Fifth and Final in Series, Handcrafted, 2-5/16" tall, Dated 1997. Pretty! Pretty!
Artist: Sharon Pike
☐ Purchased 19___ Pd $_____   MIB NB DB BNT
☐ Want Orig. Ret. $7.95

G QEO 870-5   **SWING-TIME**
Handcrafted, 3-1/4" tall, Dated 1997. **Artist:** Sue Tague
☐ Purchased 19___ Pd $_____   MIB NB DB BNT
☐ Want Orig. Ret. $7.95

H QEO 872-5   **VICTORIAN CROSS**
Pewter, 2-1/4" tall.
☐ Purchased 19___ Pd $_____   MIB NB DB BNT
☐ Want Orig. Ret. $8.95

A QEO 868-2   **HERE COMES EASTER**
Fourth and Final in Series, Handcrafted, 2-1/8" tall, Dated 1997.
Artist: Ken Crow
☐ Purchased 19___ Pd $_____   MIB NB DB BNT
☐ Want Orig. Ret. $7.95

B QEO 865-5   **JOYFUL ANGELS**
Second in Series, Handcrafted, 3-11/16" tall, Dated 1997.
Artist: Joyce Lyle
☐ Purchased 19___ Pd $_____   MIB NB DB BNT
☐ Want Orig. Ret. $10.95

C QEO 870-2   **NATURE'S SKETCHBOOK: GARDEN BUNNIES**
Handcrafted, 3" tall, Dated 1997. **Artist:** Duane Unruh
☐ Purchased 19___ Pd $_____   MIB NB DB BNT
☐ Want Orig. Ret. $14.95

D QEO 863-2   **SIDEWALK CRUISERS:**
1935 STEELCRAFT STREAMLINE VELOCIPEDE BY MURRAY®
FIRST IN SERIES, Handcrafted, 1-6/8" tall, Dated 1997. Don't miss getting this one!
Artist: Dill Rhodus
☐ Purchased 19___ Pd $_____   MIB NB DB BNT
☐ Want Orig. Ret. $12.95

E QEO 864-2   **SPRINGTIME BARBIE™**
Third and Final in Series, Handcrafted, 3-1/2" tall, Dated 1997. This dress was designed by artist not Mattel. **Artist:** Patricia Andrews
☐ Purchased 19___ Pd $_____   MIB NB DB BNT
☐ Want Orig. Ret. $25.95

"Go ahead – make my day."

NFL Ornaments

Pictured are Chicago Bears.
Ten NFL Teams were offered in 1995:

☐ ✱Eagles™   ☐ Panthers™   ☐ Patriots™
☐ ✱Redskins™   ☐ Kansas City Chiefs™ ☐ ✱Dallas Cowboys™
☐ Chicago Bears™   ☐ Vikings™   ☐ ✱Raiders™
☐ ✱San Francisco 49ers™

Not all Hallmark stores carried these. Some only offered "their" area team's logo.

FOOTBALL HELMET ORNAMENTS
Those listed above with the ✱ are highly sought after and command a higher secondary market value of $25-$30. All others would be $20.
Comments: Handcrafted, Dated 1995

☐ Purchased 19__ Pd $_____ MIB   NB   DB   BNT
☐ Want Orig. Ret. $9.95   MIB Sec. Mkt. **$20**

NFL BALL ORNAMENTS
Comments: White Glass Ball, Dated 1995. Quite attractive.

☐ Purchased 19__ Pd $_____ MIB   NB   DB   BNT
☐ Want Orig. Ret. $5.95   MIB Sec. Mkt. **$8-$10**

Thirty NFL Teams were offered in 1996

QSR 648-4 ☐	ARIZONA CARDINALS™		QSR 645-4 ☐	MINNESOTA VIKINGS™
QSR 636-4 ☐	ATLANTA FALCON™		QSR 646-1 ☐	NEW ENGLAND PATRIOTS™
QSR 639-1 ☐	BROWNS™		QSR 646-4 ☐	NEW ORLEANS SAINTS™
QSR 637-1 ☐	BUFFALO BILLS™		QSR 647-1 ☐	NEW YORK GIANTS™
QSR 637-4 ☐	CAROLINA PANTHERS™		QSR 647-4 ☐	NEW YORK JETS™
QSR 638-1 ☐	CHICAGO BEARS™		QSR 644-1 ☐	OAKLAND RAIDERS™
QSR 638-4 ☐	CINCINNATI BENGALS™		QSR 643-4 ☐	OILERS™
QSR 639-4 ☐	DALLAS COWBOYS™		QSR 648-1 ☐	PHILDELPHIA EAGLES™
QSR 641-1 ☐	DENVER BRONCOS™		QSR 649-1 ☐	PITTSBURGH STEELERS™
QSR 641-4 ☐	DETROIT LIONS™		QSR 644-4 ☐	ST LOUIS RAMS™
QSR 642-1 ☐	GREEN BAY PACKERS™		QSR 649-4 ☐	SAN DIEGO CHARGERS™
QSR 643-1 ☐	INDIANAPOLIS COLTS™		QSR 650-1 ☐	SAN FRANCISCO 49ERS™
QSR 643-4 ☐	JACKSONVILLE JAQUARS™		QSR 650-4 ☐	SEATLE SEAHAWKS™
QSR 632-1 ☐	KANSAS CITY CHIEFS™		QSR 651-1 ☐	TAMPA BAY BUCCANEERS™
QSR 645-1 ☐	MIAMI DOLPHINS™		QSR 651-4 ☐	WASHINGTON REDSKINS™

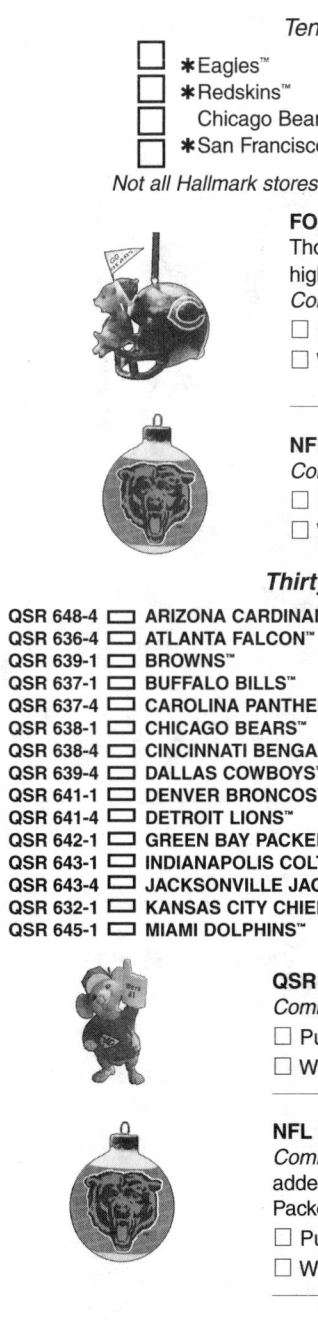

QSR 632-1   KANSAS CITY CHIEFS™
Comments: Handcrafted, Dated 1996. **Artist:** Duane Unruh

☐ Purchased 19__ Pd $_____ MIB   NB   DB   BNT
☐ Want Orig. Ret. $9.95   **MIB.** Sec. Mkt. **N.E.**

NFL BALL ORNAMENTS
Comments: White Glass Ball, Dated 1996. Four other teams were added to the list of ten from 1995. Those teams were Green Bay Packers™, Pittsburgh Steelers™, St. Louis Rams™ and Buffalo Bills™.

☐ Purchased 19__ Pd $_____ MIB   NB   DB   BNT
☐ Want Orig. Ret. $5.95   MIB Sec. Mkt. **N.E.**

Anniversary Ornaments

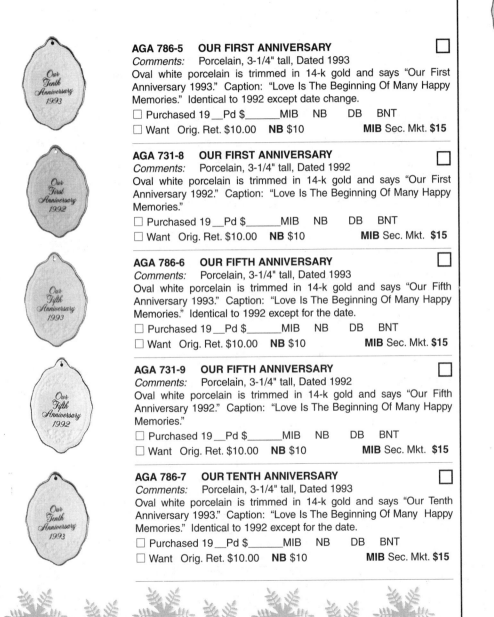

AGA 786-5   OUR FIRST ANNIVERSARY   □
Comments: Porcelain, 3-1/4" tall, Dated 1993
Oval white porcelain is trimmed in 14-k gold and says "Our First Anniversary 1993." Caption: "Love Is The Beginning Of Many Happy Memories." Identical to 1992 except date change.
□ Purchased 19__Pd $_____MIB   NB   DB   BNT
□ Want Orig. Ret. $10.00 **NB** $10   **MIB** Sec. Mkt. **$15**

AGA 731-8   OUR FIRST ANNIVERSARY   □
Comments: Porcelain, 3-1/4" tall, Dated 1992
Oval white porcelain is trimmed in 14-k gold and says "Our First Anniversary 1992." Caption: "Love Is The Beginning Of Many Happy Memories."
□ Purchased 19__Pd $_____MIB   NB   DB   BNT
□ Want Orig. Ret. $10.00 **NB** $10   **MIB** Sec. Mkt. **$15**

AGA 786-6   OUR FIFTH ANNIVERSARY   □
Comments: Porcelain, 3-1/4" tall, Dated 1993
Oval white porcelain is trimmed in 14-k gold and says "Our Fifth Anniversary 1993." Caption: "Love Is The Beginning Of Many Happy Memories." Identical to 1992 except for the date.
□ Purchased 19__Pd $_____MIB   NB   DB   BNT
□ Want Orig. Ret. $10.00 **NB** $10   **MIB** Sec. Mkt. **$15**

AGA 731-9   OUR FIFTH ANNIVERSARY   □
Comments: Porcelain, 3-1/4" tall, Dated 1992
Oval white porcelain is trimmed in 14-k gold and says "Our Fifth Anniversary 1992." Caption: "Love Is The Beginning Of Many Happy Memories."
□ Purchased 19__Pd $_____MIB   NB   DB   BNT
□ Want Orig. Ret. $10.00 **NB** $10   **MIB** Sec. Mkt. **$15**

AGA 786-7   OUR TENTH ANNIVERSARY   □
Comments: Porcelain, 3-1/4" tall, Dated 1993
Oval white porcelain is trimmed in 14-k gold and says "Our Tenth Anniversary 1993." Caption: "Love Is The Beginning Of Many Happy Memories." Identical to 1992 except for the date.
□ Purchased 19__Pd $_____MIB   NB   DB   BNT
□ Want Orig. Ret. $10.00 **NB** $10   **MIB** Sec. Mkt. **$15**

AGA 731-7   OUR TENTH ANNIVERSARY   □
Comments: Porcelain, 3-1/4" tall, Dated 1992
Oval white porcelain is trimmed in 14-k gold and says "Our Tenth Anniversary 1992." Caption: "Love Is The Beginning Of Many Happy Memories."
□ Purchased 19 __Pd $_____MIB   NB   DB   BNT
□ Want Orig. Ret. $10.00 **NB** $10   **MIB** Sec. Mkt. **$15**

AGA 768-6   25 YEARS TOGETHER   □
Comments: Porcelain, 3-1/4" tall, Dated 1993
Oval white porcelain is trimmed in silver and says "25 Years Together 1993." Caption: "Silver Christmas Memories Are Keepsakes Of The Heart." Identical to 1992 except for the date.
□ Purchased 19 __Pd $_____MIB   NB   DB   BNT
□ Want Orig. Ret. $10.00 **NB** $10   **MIB** Sec. Mkt. **$15**

AGA 711-3   25 YEARS TOGETHER   □
Comments: Porcelain, 3-1/4" tall, Dated 1992
Oval white porcelain is trimmed in silver and says "25 Years Together 1992." Caption: "Silver Christmas Memories Are Keepsakes Of The Heart."
□ Purchased 19 __Pd $_____MIB   NB   DB   BNT
□ Want Orig. Ret. $10.00 **NB** $10   **MIB** Sec. Mkt. **$15**

AGA 786-8   40 YEARS TOGETHER   □
Comments: Porcelain, 3-1/4" tall, Dated 1993
Oval white porcelain is trimmed in 14 k gold and says "40 Years Together 1993." Caption: "Love Is The Beginning Of Many Happy Memories." Identical to 1992 except for the date.
□ Purchased 19 __Pd $_____MIB   NB   DB   BNT
□ Want Orig. Ret. $10.00 **NB** $10   **MIB** Sec. Mkt. **$15**

AGA 731-6   40 YEARS TOGETHER   □
Comments: Porcelain, 3-1/4" tall, Dated 1992
Oval white porcelain is trimmed in 14 k gold and says "40 Years Together 1992." Caption: "Love Is The Beginning Of Many Happy Memories."
□ Purchased 19 __Pd $_____MIB   NB   DB   BNT
□ Want Orig. Ret. $10.00 **NB** $10   **MIB** Sec. Mkt. **$15**

AGA 778-7   50 YEARS TOGETHER   □
Comments: Porcelain, 3-1/4" tall, Dated 1993
Oval white porcelain is trimmed in 14 k gold and says "50 Years Together 1993." Caption: "Golden Christmas Memories Are Keepsakes Of The Heart." Identical to 1992 except for the date.
□ Purchased 19 __Pd $_____MIB   NB   DB   BNT
□ Want Orig. Ret. $10.00 **NB** $10   **MIB** Sec. Mkt. **$15**

AGA 721-4   50 YEARS TOGETHER
Comments: Porcelain, 3-1/4" tall, Dated 1992
Oval white porcelain is trimmed in 14 k gold and says "50 Years Together 1992." Caption: "Golden Christmas Memories Are Keepsakes Of The Heart."

☐ Purchased 19__Pd $_____MIB   NB   DB   BNT
☐ Want Orig. Ret. $10.00   **NB** $10   **MIB** Sec. Mkt. **$15**

AGA 768-7   25 YEARS TOGETHER ANNIVERSARY BELL
Comments: Porcelain, 3" tall, Dated 1993
White porcelain bell is trimmed in silver and says "25 Years Together 1993." Caption: "Silver Christmas Memories Are Keepsakes Of The Heart." Identical to 1992 except for the date.

☐ Purchased 19__Pd $_____MIB   NB   DB   BNT
☐ Want Orig. Ret. $10.00   **NB** $10   **MIB** Sec. Mkt. **$15**

AGA 713-4   25 YEARS TOGETHER ANNIVERSARY BELL
Comments: Porcelain, 3" tall, Dated 1992
White porcelain bell is trimmed in silver and says "25 Years Together 1992." Caption: "Silver Christmas Memories Are Keepsakes Of The Heart."

☐ Purchased 19__Pd $_____MIB   NB   DB   BNT
☐ Want Orig. Ret. $10.00   **NB** $10   **MIB** Sec. Mkt. **$15**

AGA 778-8   50 YEARS TOGETHER ANNIVERSARY BELL
Comments: Porcelain, 3" tall, Dated 1993
White porcelain bell is trimmed in 14 k gold and says "50 Years Together 1993." Caption: "Golden Christmas Memories Are Keepsakes Of The Heart." Identical to 1992 except for the date.

☐ Purchased 19__Pd $_____MIB   NB   DB   BNT
☐ Want Orig. Ret. $10.00   **NB** $10   **MIB** Sec. Mkt. **$15**

AGA 723-5   50 YEARS TOGETHER ANNIVERSARY BELL
Comments: Porcelain, 3" tall, Dated 1992
White porcelain bell is trimmed in 14 k gold and says "50 Years Together 1992." Caption: "Golden Christmas Memories Are Keepsakes Of The Heart."

☐ Purchased 19__Pd $_____MIB   NB   DB   BNT
☐ Want Orig. Ret. $10.00   **NB** $10   **MIB** Sec. Mkt. **$15**

Did you know?

The national Hallmark Keepsake Ornament Collector's Club, which was established in 1987, today has more than 160,000 members and ranks as the largest collector's club of its kind in the nation.

Baby Celebrations

1989

A   BBY 132-5   1989 BABY'S CHRISTENING KEEPSAKE
Acrylic, 3-3/4" tall, Dated 1989

☐ Purchased 19___ Pd $_____   MIB   NB   DB   BNT
☐ Want   Original Retail $7.00
                    NB $25   **MIB** Sec. Mkt. **$32-$35**

B   BBY 172-9   1989 BABY'S FIRST BIRTHDAY
Acrylic, 4-1/2" tall, Dated 1989

☐ Purchased 19___ Pd $_____   MIB   NB   DB   BNT
☐ Want   Original Retail $5.50
                    NB $25   **MIB** Sec. Mkt. **$32-$38**

C   BBY 145-3   1989 BABY'S FIRST CHRISTMAS - BABY BOY
Blue Satin Ball, 2-7/8" dia. Identical to QX 272-5, page 120.

☐ Purchased 19___ Pd $_____   MIB   NB   DB   BNT
☐ Want   Original Retail $4.75
                    NB $10   **MIB** Sec. Mkt. **$12-$16**

D   BBY 155-3   1989 BABY'S FIRST CHRISTMAS - BABY GIRL
Pink Satin Ball, 2-7/8" dia. Identical to QX 272-2, page 120.

☐ Purchased 19___ Pd $_____   MIB   NB   DB   BNT
☐ Want   Original Retail $4.75
                    NB $8   **MIB** Sec. Mkt. **$10-$14**

1990

E   BBY 132-6   BABY'S CHRISTENING
Hand-Painted Porcelain, 2-1/4" tall, Dated 1990

☐ Purchased 19___ Pd $_____   MIB   NB   DB   BNT
☐ Want   Original Retail $10.00
                    NB $15   **MIB** Sec. Mkt. **$25-$30**

F   BBY 155-4   BABY'S FIRST CHRISTMAS
Hand-Painted Porcelain, 2-1/8" tall, Dated 1990

☐ Purchased 19___ Pd $_____   MIB   NB   DB   BNT
☐ Want   Original Retail $10.00
                    NB $15   **MIB** Sec. Mkt. **$25-$30**

G   BBY 145-4   BABY'S FIRST CHRISTMAS
Hand-Painted Porcelain, 2-5/8" tall, Dated 1990

☐ Purchased 19___ Pd $_____   MIB   NB   DB   BNT
☐ Want   Original Retail $10.00
                    NB $15   **MIB** Sec. Mkt. **$25-$30**

Baby Celebrations

1991

BBY 131-7   **BABY'S CHRISTENING**
Hand-Painted Porcelain, 2-1/4" tall, Dated 1991, Identical to 1990.
☐ Purchased 19___   Pd $_____   MIB   NB   DB   BNT
☐ Want   Original Retail $10.00
       NB $10   **MIB** Sec. Mkt. **$14-$18**

BBY 151-4   **BABY'S FIRST CHRISTMAS**
Hand-Painted Porcelain, 2-1/8" tall, Dated 1991, Identical to 1990.
☐ Purchased 19___   Pd $_____   MIB   NB   DB   BNT
☐ Want   Original Retail $10.00
       NB $10   **MIB** Sec. Mkt. **$14-$18**

BBY 141-6   **BABY'S FIRST CHRISTMAS**
Hand-Painted Porcelain, 2-5/8" tall, Dated 1991, Identical to 1990.
☐ Purchased 19___   Pd $_____   MIB   NB   DB   BNT
☐ Want   Original Retail $10.00
       NB $10   **MIB** Sec. Mkt. **$14-$18**

A   B 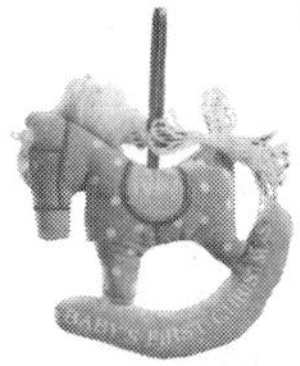   C 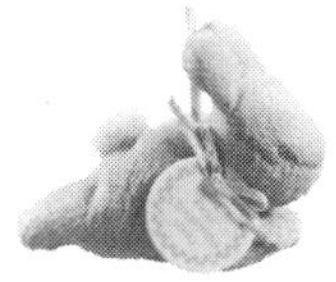   D

1992

A   **BBY 133-1**   **1992 BABY'S CHRISTENING**
Fabric, 4" tall, Dated 1992
☐ Purchased 19___   Pd $_____   MIB   NB   DB   BNT
☐ Want   Original Retail $8.50
       NB $8   **MIB** Sec. Mkt. **$12-$14**

B   **BBY 145-6**   **1992 BABY'S FIRST CHRISTMAS**
Fabric, 4" tall, Dated 1992
☐ Purchased 19___   Pd $_____   MIB   NB   DB   BNT
☐ Want   Original Retail $8.50
       NB $9   **MIB** Sec. Mkt. **$12-$14**

C   **BBY 155-7**   **1992 BABY'S FIRST CHRISTMAS**
Plush, 3" tall, Dated 1992
☐ Purchased 19___   Pd $_____   MIB   NB   DB   BNT
☐ Want   Original Retail $8.50
       NB $8   **MIB** Sec. Mkt. **$10-$12**

1993

D   **BBY 291-7**   **1993 BABY'S CHRISTENING**
Handcrafted, 3-1/16" tall, Dated 1993
☐ Purchased 19___   Pd $_____   MIB   NB   DB   BNT
☐ Want   Original Retail $12.00
       MIB Sec. Mkt. **$14-$16**

E 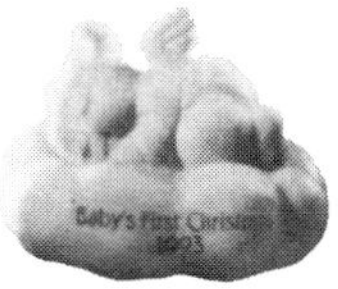   F

H    I    J

E   **BBY 133-5**   **1993 BABY'S CHRISTENING PHOTOHOLDER**
Silver-Plated, 2-3/4" dia., Dated 1993
☐ Purchased 19___   Pd $_____   MIB   NB   DB   BNT
☐ Want   Original Retail $10.00
       MIB Sec. Mkt. **$12-$14**

F   **BBY 291-8**   **1993 BABY'S FIRST CHRISTMAS**
Handcrafted, 1-1/2" tall, Dated 1993
☐ Purchased 19___   Pd $_____   MIB   NB   DB   BNT
☐ Want   Original Retail $12.00
       MIB Sec. Mkt. **$12-$14**

G   **BBY 291-9**   **1993 BABY'S FIRST CHRISTMAS**
Handcrafted, 2-1/4" tall, Dated 1993
☐ Purchased 19___   Pd $_____   MIB   NB   DB   BNT
☐ Want   Original Retail $14.00
       MIB Sec. Mkt. **$16-$18**

H   **BBY 147-0**   **1993 BABY'S FIRST CHRISTMAS PHOTOHOLDER**
Silver-Plated, 2-1/4" dia., Dated 1993
☐ Purchased 19___   Pd $_____   MIB   NB   DB   BNT
☐ Want   Original Retail $10.00
       MIB Sec. Mkt. **$12-$15**

I   **BBY 280-2**   **1993 GRANDDAUGHTER'S FIRST CHRISTMAS**
Handcrafted, 1-7/8" tall, Dated 1993
☐ Purchased 19___   Pd $_____   MIB   NB   DB   BNT
☐ Want   Original Retail $14.00
       MIB Sec. Mkt. **$16-$18**

J   **BBY 280-1**   **1993 GRANDSON'S FIRST CHRISTMAS**
Handcrafted, 1-7/8" tall, Dated 1993
☐ Purchased 19___   Pd $_____   MIB   NB   DB   BNT
☐ Want   Original Retail $14.00
       MIB Sec. Mkt. **$16-$19**

Kiddie Car Classics

A special thanks to Michael Belofsky and David Hamrick for photos and helping with our research of prices for this fabulous popular collectible.

1992

The first five Kiddie Car Classics are considered the "hot ones." Notice how scarcity makes a collectible!

QHG900-3   1941 MURRAY® AIRPLANE ☐
Comments: ***Retired*** October 1993, ***Limited Edition*** 14,500 pieces. With red trim and red wheel covers, this silver plane lands on the top shelf.
☐ Purchased 19__Pd $_____MIB   NB   DB   BNT
☐ Want Orig. Ret. $50.00   **MIB** Sec. Mkt. **$350-$400**
There were approximately 900 pieces produced with a backwards decal.
☐ Purchased 19__Pd $_____MIB   NB   DB   BNT
☐ Want Orig. Ret. $50.00   **MIB** Sec. Mkt. **$700-$800**

QHG901-2   1953 MURRAY® DUMP TRUCK ☐
Comments: ***Retired*** October 1993, ***Limited Edition*** 14,500 pieces. A dumping mechanism is featured on the back of this yellow truck.
☐ Purchased 19__Pd $_____MIB   NB   DB   BNT
☐ Want Orig. Ret. $48.00   **MIB** Sec. Mkt. **$225-$250**

QHG900-8   1955 MURRAY® CHAMPION ☐
Comments: ***Retired*** October 1993, ***Limited Edition*** 14,500 pieces. The favorite of many is the blue Murray® Champion.
☐ Purchased 19__Pd $_____MIB   NB   DB   BNT
☐ Want Orig. Ret. $45.00   **MIB** Sec. Mkt. **$225-$250**

QHG900-1   1955 MURRAY® FIRE TRUCK ☐
Comments: ***Retired*** October 1993, ***Limited Edition*** 14,500 pieces. Red fire truck with a white seat. Listen to the fire bell ring on this truck when you pull the string. The ladders may be easily removed.
☐ Purchased 19__Pd $_____MIB   NB   DB   BNT
☐ Want Orig. Ret.$50.00   **MIB** Sec. Mkt. **$225-$250**
There were approximately 900 pieces produced with a black seat.
☐ Purchased 19__Pd $_____MIB   NB   DB   BNT
☐ Want Orig. Ret .$50.00   **MIB** Sec. Mkt. **$650-$700**

QHG900-4   1955 MURRAY® TRACTOR AND TRAILER ☐
Comments: ***Retired*** December 1993, ***Limited Edition*** 14,500 pieces. Every farm needs this red tractor and trailer which features a dumping mechanism.
☐ Purchased 19__Pd $_____MIB   NB   DB   BNT
☐ Want Orig. Ret. $55.00   **MIB** Sec. Mkt. **$175-$200**

1993

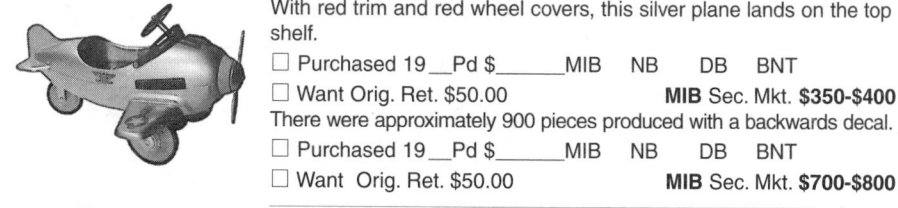

QHG900-6   1955 MURRAY® FIRE CHIEF ☐
Comments: ***Retired*** December 1995, ***Limited Edition*** 19,500 pieces. Listen for the bell, as this white with red trim car comes driving down the road of memories. Special Fire Chief decal on both sides of car.
☐ Purchased 19__Pd $_____MIB   NB   DB   BNT
☐ Want Orig. Ret. $45.00   **MIB** Sec. Mkt. **$150-$175**
There were approximately 15,000 pieces produced with left side decal backwards.
☐ Purchased 19__Pd $_____MIB   NB   DB   BNT
☐ Want Orig. Ret. $45.00   **MIB** Sec. Mkt. **$200**

QHG900-5   1968 MURRAY® BOAT JOLLY ROGER ☐
Comments: ***Retired*** February 1996, ***Limited Edition*** 19,500 pieces. The white boat has red trim and blue wheels.
☐ Purchased 19__Pd $_____MIB   NB   DB   BNT
☐ Want Orig. Ret. $50.00   **MIB.** Sec. Mkt. **$175-$200**

1994

QHG900-7   1955 MURRAY® RANCH WAGON ☐
Comments: ***Retired*** February 1996, ***Limited Edition*** 19,500 pieces. A two tone green wagon which also features a pull down tailgate.
☐ Purchased 19__Pd $_____MIB   NB   DB   BNT
☐ Want Orig. Ret. $48.00   **MIB** Sec. Mkt. **$95-$125**

QHG900-9   1941 STEELCRAFT SPITFIRE AIRPLANE BY MURRAY® ☐
Comments: ***Retired*** February 1996, ***Limited Edition*** 19,500 pieces. Orange wings and trim profile this beige plane of the 40s.
☐ Purchased 19__Pd $_____MIB   NB   DB   BNT
☐ Want Orig. Ret. $50.00   **MIB** Sec. Mkt. **$125-$150**

QHG901-0   1955 MURRAY® FIRE TRUCK ☐
Comments: ***Retired*** January 1996, ***Limited Edition*** 19,500 pieces. White highlights this red fire truck with working bell and movable ladders.
☐ Purchased 19__Pd $_____MIB   NB   DB   BNT
☐ Want Orig. Ret. $50.00   **MIB** Sec. Mkt .**$175-$200**

QHG900-2   1955 MURRAY® RED CHAMPION ☐
Comments: ***Retired*** March 1996, ***Limited Edition***. Limited to 19,500 pieces. Another favorite of many is this Murray® Red Champion. Mine is burgundy. What's color is yours?
☐ Purchased 19__Pd $_____MIB   NB   DB   BNT
☐ Want Orig. Ret. $45.00   **MIB** Sec. Mkt. **$75-$125**

QHX909-4   1956 GARTON® KIDILLAC

Comments: ***Retired*** December 1996. Vintage pink and black Kidillac features side-view mirrors, antenna, spare tire and movable pedals. Antenna found to be easily broken. Not as popular as others.

☐ Purchased 19___ Pd $_____ MIB   NB   DB   BNT

☐ Want Orig. Ret. $55.00   **MIB** Sec. Mkt. **N.E.**

QHG901-1   1955 MURRAY® DUMP TRUCK

Comments: ***Retired*** March 1996, ***Limited Edition*** 19,500 pieces. Black side walls, red hood and dumping mechanism are featured on this dump truck.

☐ Purchased 19___ Pd $_____ MIB   NB   DB   BNT

☐ Want Orig. Ret. $48.00   **MIB** Sec. Mkt. **$100-$150**

QHG901-5   1939 STEELCRAFT LINCOLN ZEPHYR
BY MURRAY®

Comments: ***Retired*** July 1996, ***Limited Edition*** 24,500 pieces. Best seller out of the four released 10/94. This classic black and white Zephyr comes with a French bulb horn.

☐ Purchased 19___ Pd $_____ MIB   NB   DB   BNT

☐ Want Orig. Ret. $50.00   **MIB** Sec. Mkt. **$95-$125 up**

QHG901-6   1956 GARTON® DRAGNET POLICE CAR

Comments: ***Limited Edition*** 24,500 pieces.
White and black trimmed police car has a hood scoop and microphone.

☐ Purchased 19___ Pd $_____ MIB   NB   DB   BNT

☐ Want Orig. Ret. $50.00   **MIB** Sec. Mkt. **N.E.**

QHG901-4   1961 MURRAY® CIRCUS CAR

Comments: ***Limited Edition*** 24,500 pieces.
Tan and red car has gun-sight fender ornaments, and a tailgate that can be opened. Notice production going up?

☐ Purchased 19___ Pd $_____ MIB   NB   DB   BNT

☐ Want Orig. Ret. $48.00   **MIB** Sec. Mkt. **N.E.**

QHG901-3   1961 MURRAY® SPEEDWAY PACE CAR

Comments: ***Limited Edition*** 24,500 pieces.
Starting the collectors' race is this white with red trim pace car. Gun-sight fenders and a special checkered flag decal dress up this classic car.

☐ Purchased 19___ Pd $_____ MIB   NB   DB   BNT

☐ Want Orig. Ret. $45.00   **MIB** Sec. Mkt. **N.E.**

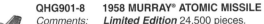

QHG902-2   1956 GARTON® MARK V

Comments: ***Limited Edition*** 24,500 pieces.
The teal painted Mark V features a replica "TOYLAND" license plate; the GARTON® emblem is found above the grille.

☐ Purchased 19 Pd $_____ MIB   NB   DB   BNT

☐ Want Orig. Ret. $45.00   **MIB** Sec. Mkt. **N.E.**

QHG901-8   1958 MURRAY® ATOMIC MISSILE

Comments: ***Limited Edition*** 24,500 pieces.
Gold and white airplane with red seat has a streamline missile design with control knobs and a steering wheel. There are also movable pedals and colorful decals.

☐ Purchased 19 ___ Pd $_____ MIB   NB   DB   BNT

☐ Want Orig. Ret. $55.00   **MIB** Sec. Mkt. **N.E.**

1995

QHG902-0   1950 MURRAY® TORPEDO

Comments: ***Retired*** January 1996. Classic white Torpedo ready for the road.

☐ Purchased 19___ Pd $_____ MIB   NB   DB   BNT

☐ Want Orig. Ret. $50.00   **MIB** Sec. Mkt. **N.E.**

QHG901-7   1959 GARTON® DELUXE KIDILLAC

Comments: ***Retires*** January 1997.
A fully loaded blue and white Kidillac. It has working headlights, side mirrors, decorative trim, non-removable spare tire, hood ornament, and antenna.

☐ Purchased 19 ___ Pd $_____ MIB   NB   DB   BNT

☐ Want Orig. Ret. $55.00   **MIB** Projected Price **$75**

QHG901-9   1961 GARTON® CASEY JONES LOCOMOTIVE

Comments: ***Retires*** January 1997.
A ringing bell, smokestack, cowcatcher and decals adorn this authentic looking red and black locomotive.

☐ Purchased 19 ___ Pd $_____ MIB   NB   DB   BNT

☐ Want Orig. Ret. $55.00   **MIB** Projected Price **$95-$100**

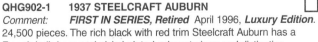

QHG902-1   1937 STEELCRAFT AUBURN

Comment: ***FIRST IN SERIES, Retired*** April 1996, ***Luxury Edition***. 24,500 pieces. The rich black with red trim Steelcraft Auburn has a French bulb horn and nickel-plated exhaust pipes and distinctive windshield. Appears to me to be a favorite!

☐ Purchased 19 ___ Pd $_____ MIB   NB   DB   BNT

☐ Want Orig. Ret. $65.00   **MIB** Sec. Mkt. **$130-$175**

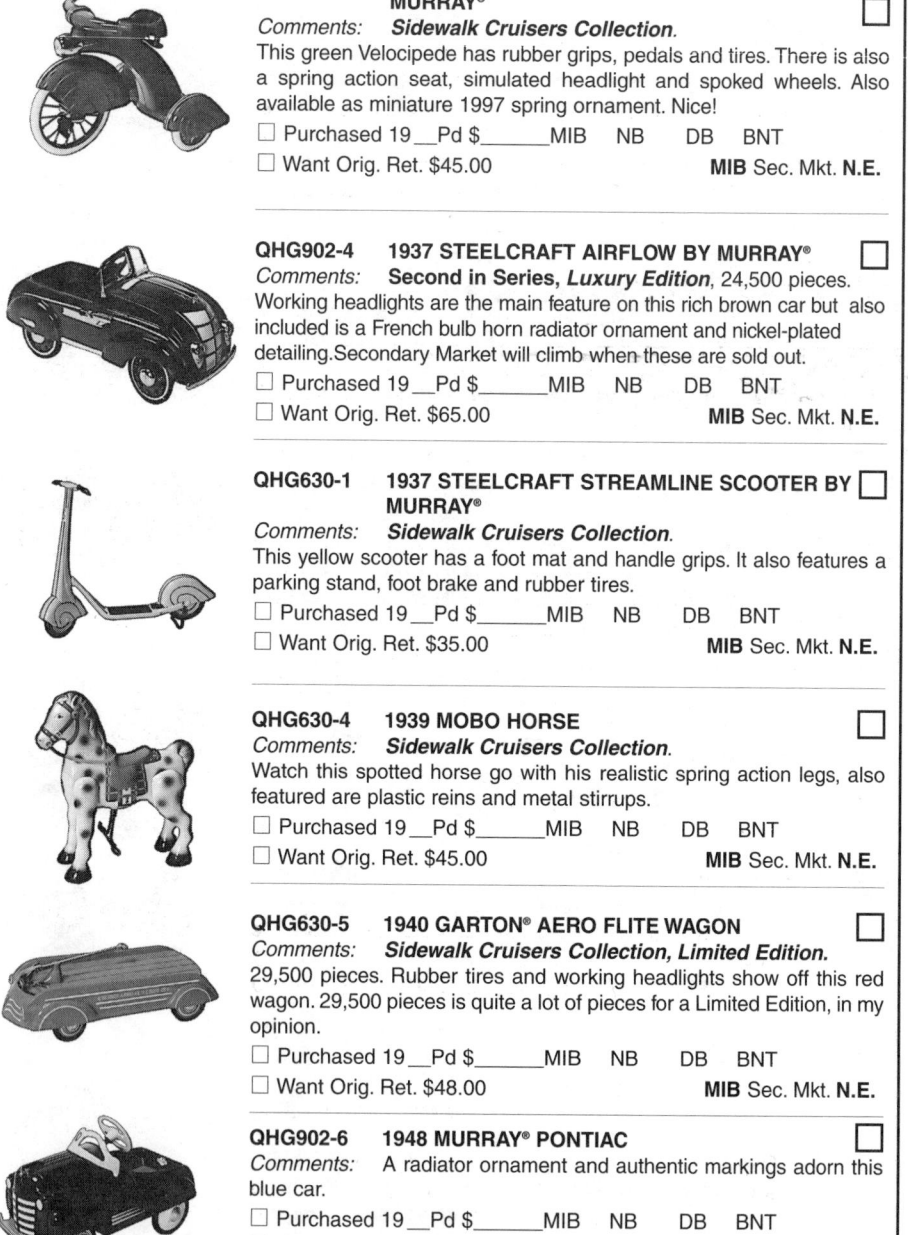

QHG630-6   1935 STEELCRAFT STREAMLINE VELOCIPEDE BY MURRAY® ☐

Comments: Sidewalk Cruisers Collection.
This green Velocipede has rubber grips, pedals and tires. There is also a spring action seat, simulated headlight and spoked wheels. Also available as miniature 1997 spring ornament. Nice!

☐ Purchased 19 __ Pd $_____ MIB   NB   DB   BNT
☐ Want Orig. Ret. $45.00   **MIB** Sec. Mkt. **N.E.**

QHG902-4   1937 STEELCRAFT AIRFLOW BY MURRAY® ☐
*Comments: **Second in Series,** Luxury Edition, 24,500 pieces.*
Working headlights are the main feature on this rich brown car but also included is a French bulb horn radiator ornament and nickel-plated detailing. Secondary Market will climb when these are sold out.

☐ Purchased 19 __ Pd $_____ MIB   NB   DB   BNT
☐ Want Orig. Ret. $65.00   **MIB** Sec. Mkt. **N.E.**

QHG630-1   1937 STEELCRAFT STREAMLINE SCOOTER BY MURRAY® ☐

Comments: Sidewalk Cruisers Collection.
This yellow scooter has a foot mat and handle grips. It also features a parking stand, foot brake and rubber tires.

☐ Purchased 19 __ Pd $_____ MIB   NB   DB   BNT
☐ Want Orig. Ret. $35.00   **MIB** Sec. Mkt. **N.E.**

QHG630-4   1939 MOBO HORSE ☐
Comments: Sidewalk Cruisers Collection.
Watch this spotted horse go with his realistic spring action legs, also featured are plastic reins and metal stirrups.

☐ Purchased 19 __ Pd $_____ MIB   NB   DB   BNT
☐ Want Orig. Ret. $45.00   **MIB** Sec. Mkt. **N.E.**

QHG630-5   1940 GARTON® AERO FLITE WAGON ☐
Comments: Sidewalk Cruisers Collection, Limited Edition.
29,500 pieces. Rubber tires and working headlights show off this red wagon. 29,500 pieces is quite a lot of pieces for a Limited Edition, in my opinion.

☐ Purchased 19 __ Pd $_____ MIB   NB   DB   BNT
☐ Want Orig. Ret. $48.00   **MIB** Sec. Mkt. **N.E.**

QHG902-6   1948 MURRAY® PONTIAC ☐
Comments: A radiator ornament and authentic markings adorn this blue car.

☐ Purchased 19 __ Pd $_____ MIB   NB   DB   BNT
☐ Want Orig. Ret. $50.00   **MIB** Sec. Mkt. **N.E.**

QHG902-5   1955 MURRAY® ROYAL DELUXE ☐
*Comments: **Limited Edition** 29,500 pieces. (Production higher than last year.) Two-tone paint (tan and orange) and continental spare tire make this car very authentic looking. 29,500 seems to be a lot… May take awhile before it is seen on secondary market with the quantity produced.

☐ Purchased 19 __ Pd $_____ MIB   NB   DB   BNT
☐ Want Orig. Ret. $55.00   **MIB** Sec. Mkt. **N.E.**

QHG630-7   1958 MURRAY® POLICE CYCLE ☐
Comments: Sidewalk Cruisers Collection, Limited Edition.
29,500 pieces. Working red spotlight, handle grips with streamers, rear door that open and antenna are featured on this blue, white, and red police cycle.

☐ Purchased 19 __ Pd $_____ MIB   NB   DB   BNT
☐ Want Orig. Ret. $55.00   **MIB** Sec. Mkt. **N.E.**

QHG909-5   1962 MURRAY® SUPER DELUXE FIRE TRUCK ☐
Comments: This fire engine red truck comes complete with blinking red light, bell, detachable ladders and realistic looking markings.

☐ Purchased 19 __ Pd $_____ MIB   NB   DB   BNT
☐ Want Orig. Ret. $55.00   **MIB** Sec. Mkt. **N.E.**

QHG630-3   1963 GARTON® SPEEDSTER ☐
Comments: Sidewalk Cruisers Collection.
A realistic pump-action handle is featured on this blue speedster. I had one similar to this.

☐ Purchased 19 __ Pd $_____ MIB   NB   DB   BNT
☐ Want Orig. Ret. $38.00   **MIB** Sec. Mkt. **N.E.**

QHG902-3   1964 GARTON® TIN LIZZIE ☐
Comments: Old-fashioned green and black Tin Lizzie features running boards and fenders. There is also a French bulb horn and a visor-style windshield. Should do well after retirement.

☐ Purchased 19 __ Pd $_____ MIB   NB   DB   BNT
☐ Want Orig. Ret. $50.00   **MIB** Sec. Mkt. **N.E.**

QHG630-2   1996 GARTON® SUPER-SONDA ☐
Comments: Sidewalk Cruisers Collection.
A special rack on the back of this red scooter can be found along with a banana-style seat and training wheels.

☐ Purchased 19 __ Pd $_____ MIB   NB   DB   BNT
☐ Want Orig. Ret. $45.00   **MIB** Sec. Mkt. **N.E.**

1996

QHG902-9   1935 STEELCRAFT BY MURRAY®

Comments: **Third in Series,** *Luxury Edition* 24,500 pieces. Classic green and black convertible with working headlights, French bulb horn and luggage rack makes this a special car. Nice! Nice! Should go up quickly when sold out.

☐ Purchased 19__Pd $_____MIB   NB   DB   BNT
☐ Want Orig. Ret. $65.00   **MIB.** Sec. Mkt. **N.E.**

QHG630-9   1950 GARTON® DELIVERY CYCLE

Comments: Ringer bell, rubber handle girps, spoked wheels and attached wagon make this a very unique red cycle.

☐ Purchased 19__Pd $_____MIB   NB   DB   BNT
☐ Want Orig. Ret. $38.00   **MIB.** Sec. Mkt. **N.E.**

QHG902-8   1956 GARTON® HOT ROD RACER

Comments: **FIRST IN SERIES,** *Winner's Circle Series.*
First to cross the line is this yellow hot rod racer with nickel-plated hood ornament and hub caps. Always get those first in series!

☐ Purchased 19__Pd $_____MIB   NB   DB   BNT
☐ Want Orig. Ret. $55.00   **MIB.** Sec. Mkt. **N.E.**

QHG902-7   1961 MURRAY® SUPER DELUXE
TRACTOR WITH TRAILER

Comments: At home on any farm is this yellow single front wheeled tractor with detachable trailer which has a tailgait that opens.

☐ Purchased 19__Pd $_____MIB   NB   DB   BNT
☐ Want Orig. Ret. $55.00   **MIB.** Sec. Mkt. **N.E.**

QHG630-8   LATE 1940'S MOBO SULKY

Comments: **Sidewalk Cruisers Collection,** *Limited Edition*. 29,500 pieces. A white horse with red plastic reins pulls this red sulky with wooden seat.

☐ Purchased 19__Pd $_____MIB   NB   DB   BNT
☐ Want Orig. Ret. $48.00   **MIB.** Sec. Mkt. **N.E.**

QHG631-0   1935 AMERICAN AIRFLOW COASTER

Comment: **Sidewalk Cruisers Collection,** *Limited Edition*. 29,500 pieces. Working headlights and a handle that turns the front wheels are featured on this royal blue and cream colored wagon.

☐ Purchased 19__Pd $_____MIB   NB   DB   BNT
☐ Want Orig. Ret. $48.00   **MIB.** Sec. Mkt. **N.E.**

QHG631-1   1935 SKY KING VELOCIPEDE

Comments: **Sidewalk Cruisers Collection.**
This very special tricycle comes complete with a reflective headlight, cruising light, built in step plates and refined wheel hoods.

☐ Purchased 19__Pd $_____MIB   NB   DB   BNT
☐ Want Orig. Ret. $45.00   **MIB.** Sec. Mkt. **N.E.**

QHG903-2   1935 STEELCRAFT AIRPLANE BY MURRAY

Comment: **Limited Edition** 29,500 pieces.
Coming in for a three point landing is this green airplane with white tail, wings and sleek wheel hoods. Features a revolving red propeller.

☐ Purchased 19__Pd $_____MIB   NB   DB   BNT
☐ Want Orig. Ret. $50.00   **MIB.** Sec. Mkt. **N.E.**

QHG631-2   1941 KEYSTONE LOCOMOTIVE

Comments: **Sidewalk Cruisers Collection.**
Take a trip back in time with this old fashioned coal locomotive with its coal tender and rubber tires. May be very popular with train collectors, too.

☐ Purchased 19__Pd $_____MIB   NB   DB   BNT
☐ Want Orig. Ret. $38.00   **MIB.** Sec. Mkt. **N.E.**

QHG903-0   1964¹/₂ FORD MUSTANG

Comments: Side scoops with white racing stripes and wild horse emblems trim this red Ford Mustang.

☐ Purchased 19__Pd $_____MIB   NB   DB   BNT
☐ Want Orig. Ret. $55.00   **MIB.** Sec. Mkt. **N.E.**

Nicholas and Daddy enjoy playing with Kiddie Cars everyday. David, his daddy, is a featured writer in the *Collectors' Bulletin*™ and *The Ornament Collector*™ magazines.

"Oh My! The Auburn Kiddie Car sure did sell out fast!" exclaims 15 month old Nicholas Hamrick, Kiddie Car test driver.

Popular Older Merry Miniatures

Merry Miniatures by Hallmark are a popular collectible. Those pictured are some of the older artplas favorite pieces. Today, many are not produced of artplas but from a "breakable" resin.

In 1994 we published a guide for all the past years Merry Miniatures. We have not found it necessary to reprint as 90% of the prices remain the same, give or take five dollars. Check with your favorite dealer for this guide or call us.

Merry Miniatures have always been an excellent collectible to get children involved in, plus they are a fun collectible for adults, too!

125HPF32 **Ugly Witch** is from the 1977 Halloween collection. Secondary Market Value $185.

300XHA3412 **Penguin** riding on a disc sled is from the 1981 Christmas collection. Secondary Market Value $120.

450XHA5006 **Jolly Tree** is from the 1982 Christmas collection. Secondary Market Value $155.

200VPF3451 **Turtle** with red hearts on its shell is from the 1980 Valentine collection. Secondary Market Value $60.

125XPF131 **Santa** with kitten on shoulder is from the 1976 Christmas collection. Secondary Market Value $80-90.

125XPF122 **Calico Mouse** is from the 1977 Christmas collection. This ornament is patterned after an actual ornament. Secondary Market Value $125.

295THA3433 **Pilgrim Mouse** on orange leaf is from the 1982 Thanksgiving collection. Secondary Market Value $215.

125TPF29 **Indian Boy** with dog is from the 1975 Thanksgiving collection. Secondary Market Value $48.

300SHA3415 **Tumbling Leprechaun** is from the 1981 St. Patrick's Day collection. Secondary Market Value $45-50.

125XPF151 **Betsey Clark** is from the 1976 Christmas collection. Secondary Market Value $265-275.

750XHA3487 **Caroling Animals** is from the 1983 Christmas collection. Secondary Market Value $30.

350 QFM1595 **Mr. Claus** and 350QFM1602 **Mrs. Claus** are from the 1989 Christmas collection. Secondary Market Value is $14.50 each.

Millennium Falcon

U.S.S. Voyager

Hallmark Technical Artist

U.S.S. Enterprise

Lynn Norton

by Kathie Huddleston, Staff

Starship Enterprises

Although Lynn Norton is a member of Hallmark's Keepsake Ornament team of exceptional artists, his job is a little different. While he designs ornaments, he's also one of the technical people who advises the other artists to insure that their creations can be reproduced.

Coming from a strong family tradition of modeling, Lynn has loved working on models since the age of 8. "It all began with my great-grandfather, who handcrafted a large-scale model of a train engine for my uncle when he was a boy," Lynn said.

The Kansas City resident was recruited by Hallmark straight out of high school. He worked for 21 years as an engraver before he went to the Keepsake Ornament department in 1987.

"My primary job is in the prototyping business. I'm called a technical artist and work in the studio with all the other artists. One of the things that we try to do is to intervene very early in the sculpting stages and make sure the project moves along. I see that everything is running smoothly in manufacturing while the product is being developed. We want to make sure it is cost effective in manufacturing. It is very disruptive to develop something all the way through the system and then get it into the manufacturing arena and find out that it

either cannot be made or has to be modified radically."

After 30 years of working at Hallmark, Lynn Norton has become the "Star Trek guy." That has a lot to do with his love of science fiction, and even more to do with the fact that he sculpted the first Star Trek ornament, Starship Enterprise, as well as many Star Trek ships since.

"I'm thrilled because I've been a science fiction fan most of my life. It's very gratifying to be involved in some of the things that I have been excited about in movies or books, and I try to bring that excitement to the product."

The Starship Enterprise ended up being a breakthrough product for Hallmark.

"It was difficult to convince our marketing people it would be that big in the marketplace. It took all of us by surprise. It even took me by surprise because I had been working in the studio for about three years at that point. Everything we had done was based on the strength of tradition and it had to fit into a Christmas theme, more or less, and have Christmas colors. Almost everything we did had a face on it. So that was a breakthrough for us and it paved the way for some other products. When we started realizing the Christmas tree was

becoming a giant diary for people, where they were hanging the icons of their lives; we noted it didn't have to be a specific Christmas item. We're breaking into the realm of interior decorating and other kinds of things."

Designing the ships of Star Trek has offered Lynn a challenge. "I wanted to do something that would be very high quality and a well crafted replica of the studio model as much as possible. We also wanted to make sure that the average consumer would purchase them."

The other challenge Lynn had was finding the Starship Enterprise after it came out, just like everyone else. The ornament was underproduced and was difficult to find. Today, it can bring as much as $300 on the secondary market

"I wish I would have bought more of them. Of course, I was very excited because that was my first ornament and I wanted to purchase them for my friends and relatives and give them as gifts for Christmas. I had just as much trouble as everyone else finding them. Hallmark is generous enough that they give us one of everything that we make, but there are certain products that have high visibility that do not end up in the employee card shop and we have to go into the marketplace

and purchase them like anyone else. I'm guilty of one sin; I found out that there was going to be a delivery at a local department store so I took the day off and opened the store with them. They were all gone by 3 p.m. that day." Lynn promises that he did leave a few for other people.

Despite the fact that Lynn has designed many of the Star Trek ships, including two new ones this year (U.S.S. Voyager™ and the die-cast metal dated U.S.S. Enterprise™), his favorite ornament comes from a different science fiction universe.

"I'd have to say it's the Millennium Falcon (from the Star Wars trilogy). I enjoyed working on that so much. I don't think there has ever been a movie that captured my imagination quicker than that one. I even went out and got the reissued video tapes last year, as I've worn the other ones out. It's amazing. There are very few things in my life that I can look at repetitively and have it still intrigue me. I enjoyed *Star Trek* from a different perspective, as more hard science fiction."

"*Star Wars* is a space fantasy. I think the *Millennium Falcon* was especially exciting because I used to build hot rods when I was a kid and that is what this thing is. The *Millennium Falcon* was a smuggler's ship and they had taken this freighter and turned it into one of the fastest machines in the Galaxy so they could out run the law. I got such a kick out of that and it's a junky looking thing. This thing was a hunk of junk with sheet metal panels on it that looks like it has been repaired and wasn't painted. To make it look even more authentic, they left red and gray primer on. I just love that kind of detail. It looks like the kind of car that I drove in high school."

With re-release of the *Star Wars* trilogy and the new trilogy coming soon, Lynn's hoping more *Star Wars* vehicles are in his future.

"I'm chomping at the bit. I hope I get an opportunity. That's part of being in the studio, too. A person hopes they'll be selected to do these things based on previous performance, but it's a big studio and others may be selected to sculpt some of it. I just have to be willing to deal with that."

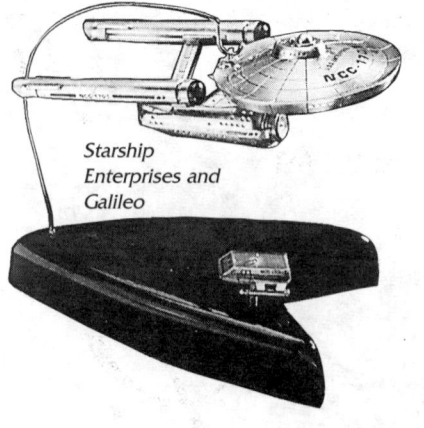

Starship Enterprises and Galileo

"The biggest challenge I face is finding the correct studio version. I get blueprints and drawings from the studio. Sometimes they are good preliminary drawings. But when the model makers actually get in and start crafting things, they make little changes here and there. When that happens I have to study both and kind of extrapolate them. I'd rather have a clear blueprint drawing that has every detail in its right place."

One such problem came when it was time to design the ornament for *Voyager*.

"It is difficult to develop those products in a timely manner because some of them, as we found out with the *Voyager* spaceship from this year, really didn't have images of the ship on screen. They were not ready to be released until about two weeks before the series had debuted. They built their stage sets and actors had been acting for months and months, but the special effects sequence didn't actually get cut until maybe a couple weeks before the thing arrived. So it makes it really hard to develop a product in that kind of environment."

Other difficulties he runs into come from the nature of his job.

"The other big problem we have is that all of our ornaments have to plug into the light string on the Christmas tree. That means they have to intentionally be plugged right into the wall socket. All of our ornaments have to pass Underwriter's Laboratory scrutiny and that is a huge hurdle. We have to make a tasteful rendering so that we can capture the character of the piece by making a large enough cavity to retain the circuit board and all the wiring and everything that is needed to make the ornament go. Even though I'm working with the engineer, taking measurements and trying to make it as good as we can; sometimes we have gotten into manufacturing and ended up having to make things thicker or stretch this or cut that."

While the technical end of his job keeps Lynn on his toes, the people he works with make his job fun.

"The most enjoyable thing for me is working in a studio with so many creative people with marvelous capabilities. It's exciting and a fun job, a laugh around every corner. It is enjoyable to come to work. We all work together in a building that is right across from Hallmark and this gives us a small business culture, where everybody knows everybody. It's just a nice environment to work in. We're all dedicated to the same product so there is a real clean spirit that runs through the place and it will not go away – it just sits there."

Klingon Bird of Prey

One thing Lynn is pleased about is the recent addition of new Hallmark artists. "We're very glad to see that happening. This is a fairly mature studio and we're excited about the new people coming in. They're not only capable, but will be our successors. It's a good feeling to have such excellent people."

It's an environment that creates a spirit of fun. "When I first came in, this one artist had designed a pink flamingo ornament with dangling legs and a Santa hat. All the business people were worried because it was too weird and pink and doesn't go with Christmas, etc. The artists were so inspired by this thing and loved it so much they kept pursuing it and finally the entire studio came around. They came in with pink flamingo noses on. They had a party in the business unit wearing these things and finally the marketing people came in and said okay, and it turned out to be success-

ful. But that's always a challenge. If you're an artist and inspired about something, you have to really sell it to the people that are going to be putting the money into it and are responsible for the financial end of developing the product. We did that and that was very cool."

Lynn finds his inspiration just about everywhere he looks. "I get inspired by everything – art, literature, music, dance. From a focal point, I'm inspired anytime that I see excellence in any arena, whether it is in the marketplace or by the kinds of performances I saw watching the Olympics. Excellence from a human being is what gets me going.

"I have something that I really want to do and hope I can sell it to our product management. It's very much in line with some of things that I've been doing already with the space oriented ornaments. One of the things that has inspired me throughout my life has been man's flight and the fact that we just learned to fly in this century to another planet. That is just the most amazing thing and still amazes me every time I get on an airplane and note how it flies. I would like to do something that would glorify and commemorate man's flight, especially the golden age of flight when the guys were going up in the machine and didn't know whether they would stay up or not and kept pushing the limit."

And that's exactly what Lynn Norton's been doing since he arrived at Hallmark, and more than likely what he'll do in the future.

Romulan Warbird

PEDALING THROUGH THE PAST

By Ed Weirick

Ed Weirick was Hallmark's first primary consultant of Kiddie Car Classics.

During the time I served as Hallmark Card's primary consultant for the popular Kiddie Car Classics and Sidewalk Cruisers collectibles, I traveled about the United States and appeared at many Hallmark stores and secondary shows. As I continue to make appearances, I never stop enjoying sharing the stories and memories of the collectors.

The actual 1950's Murray Sadface Fire Truck was used as a model for the same Kiddie Car Classics model.

I have personally been engaged in building my own collections for years and understand the enthusiasm of a collector. I started collecting antique car parts when I was ten years old. As time passed, you could see me cruising at Harvey's Drive-in Restaurant in Downey, California, in my '23 T-Bucket or my '56 Chevrolet two door hardtop. As a young married man, I restored antique cars, both personally and professionally. For more than 25 years, my family and I have enjoyed the '32 Ford Sports Coupe street rod

that I built. My interest turned to children's pedal cars when I was blessed with the birth of my son.

It all began in Huntington Park, California, on a visit with my mom and dad. Dad was a "collector" but Mom had other names for his habit of bringing home other people's junk. We were watching my son play in the backyard and I mentioned to my dad that I had seen a pedal car in a discount store, but I was concerned about spending so much money for something made mainly of plastic. Dad took me to the back of the garage and showed me two pedal car bodies. He suggested we ship one of the car bodies back to my home in Maine and that I restore it for my son's birthday.

I have to admit that pedal car was easier to move around in the garage than some of the antique cars I had restored. It was fun to watch it come alive under my own hands. At that time, the pedal car craze had not hit the country and I could not find all the replacement parts I needed, so I fabricated what I could not locate. My son's birthday arrived on April 3rd, and he was the most excited little boy in the neighborhood. This restoration project had been a true labor of love, plus I had helped create a lifelong memory for a little boy who is now starting college.

That first restoration for my son started me on a long journey of restorations; buying, selling, collecting and finally becoming the first primary consultant for Hallmark's Kiddie Car Classics.

I am asked repeatedly why I think that restoring pedal cars has become such a craze and/or why Kiddie Car Classics are so popular among collectors. As the owner of an antique shop, I am privileged to meet hundreds of collectors each year. I have learned

that collectors have different reasons for spending their extra dollars on antiques and collectibles. Some folks start collections purely as an investment, but it seems that the majority of collectors are more apt to sustain their interest in collecting if they enjoy the items they collect. Pedal cars bring a great amount of enjoyment to most folks because seeing them stimulates wonderful childhood memories. Kiddie Car Classics collectors relate numerous stories to me. A gentleman from South Carolina saw the first five Kiddie Car Classics released and was suddenly moved to remember the little yellow dump truck he used to pedal around the neighborhood as a child. He went into a dusty old storage area and found the pedal car, which he later shipped to me to restore. It is such a pleasure for me to help him bring back a piece of his childhood.

There is nothing whimsical about a pedal car... it is a real toy, bringing back real memories. Some folks comment to me, "Isn't it nice that the men have something to collect?" However, pedal cars were enjoyed by many girls as well as boys. I meet many ladies who relate stories of their sidewalk adventures. As we were planning Hallmark's Sidewalk Cruisers line, Karen Delff, the product designer, was one of the first to tell me about her own toy *Mobo Horse* that she used to ride.

The most remembered pedal vehicle by collectors seems to be the *Fire Truck*. During the 1950s and 1960s many of the larger toy retailers made

Every child's dream...

pedal fire trucks available at affordable prices for the average family. There were other popular models, but the price tag didn't fit every family's budget.

If you want a pedal car like the one you used to own, in restored or unrestored condition, you should travel to Hershey, PA, in the fall. On the fairgrounds at Hershey, there are at least 13,000 vendors who set up tables to sell automotive items or items that are automotive related. When I first started restoring pedal cars and selling them at Hershey, there were very few vendors displaying pedal cars for sale. I restored original pieces and one-of-a-kind vehicles that I customized. By the mid 1980s the pedal car craze was obvious as you walked about the fairgrounds at Hershey. Now I smile as I see some of the newcomers to the hobby restoring pieces that I helped inspire. The demand for pedal cars has become crazy and the ticket prices have gone up and up. Now there are pedal car publications, a few books, and guys out there who are reproducing those hard-to-find parts that gave me some of these gray hairs.

Hershey, PA, was perhaps the first public unveiling of the first five Kiddie Car Classics. In the fall of 1991, Greg Raymond of Hallmark Cards, Inc., sent me five prototypes to take to Hershey with me. They were a great hit and I was overwhelmed with folks who wanted to buy the models I had on display, but they had to wait for them to come to the retail stores a few weeks later.

I would like to hear from each of you who has a special story about your pedal car memories as a child, or to tell me what makes your pedal car collection special and/or unique. You may send your letters and photos (photos will not be returned) to me at the following address: Ed Weirick, R.F.D. #3-Box 190; Ellsworth, ME 04605. Phone; 207/667-2115.

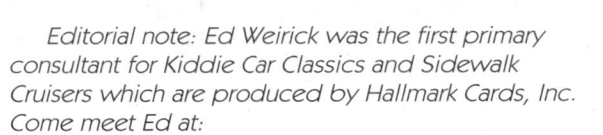

Editorial note: Ed Weirick was the first primary consultant for Kiddie Car Classics and Sidewalk Cruisers which are produced by Hallmark Cards, Inc. Come meet Ed at:

12/7/96 Connie's Hallmark, Wheatridge, CO
4/27/97 Holiday Keepsakes Collector Club, Pittsburgh, PA
July 1997 Party Shop, Warsaw IN
8/3/97 Erie Ornament Collector Show & Sale, Erie PA

It's a Kiddie Car traffic jam as each waits for their turn for restoration.

Playmates

"I met this guy that was nuts about my ornament collection. He traded me this place and some cash to boot for my Kiddie Car Collection."

Collector of the Year

"I look forward to every Issue of The Ornament Collector™ magazine and read it cover to cover many times. I am a fairly new collector (since 1992) and your magazine has helped me enormously to learn about this crazy hobby of collecting and to get in touch with other collectors to purchase ornaments from past years through your Swap N' Sell ads."

Thank you, Joan, for sending us photos of your collections, and for the compliment!

That's quite a grandson you have there.

Hi, Kristoffer!

Joan Phillipson
Mead, WA

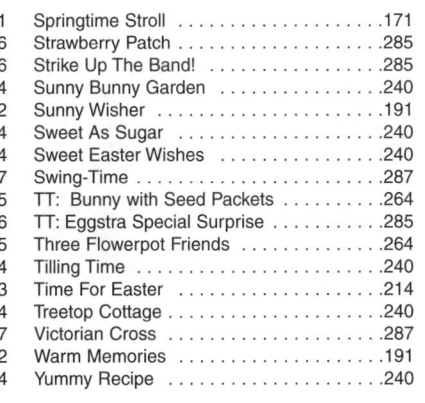

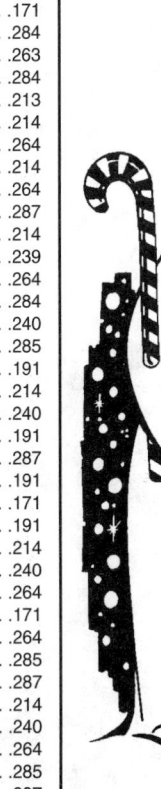

Page 308

Seal

Shoebox Greeting Designs

Signature Figurines

Silver Plate

Sleigh

Snowflake

Snowman

NFL Ornaments

Merry Christmas
to All!

Anniversary Ornaments

Baby Ornaments

Notes

HALLMARK

Several Well Known Artists

Ed Seale

Seale is the creator of some of the most memorable Hallmark Keepsake Ornaments, including the **Frosty Friends** series.

Joyce Lyle

The Holly Basket, one of three hand-crafted ornaments, is based on the work of Dutch artist Marjolein Bastin.

Anita Marra Rogers

Rogers' love of animals can be seen in her 1996 creation – **Puppy Love**, sixth in the series.

Patricia Andrews

Patricia enjoys designing ornaments that convey the innocent, playful emotions that many people associate with childhood.

Bob Siedler

"Each year, we create a completely new line of ornaments. Each one is different, so every assignment presents new challenges."

LaDene Votruba

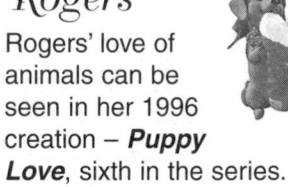

"Many of the things I identify with in my life are reflected in my work. As ornaments, they continue to represent life's treasured moments."

Robert Chad

"I've been waiting to sculpt Marvin for nine years. I consider it a milestone in my career."

Don Palmiter

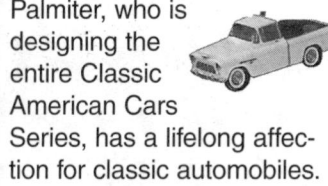

Palmiter, who is designing the entire Classic American Cars Series, has a lifelong affection for classic automobiles.

Duane Unruh

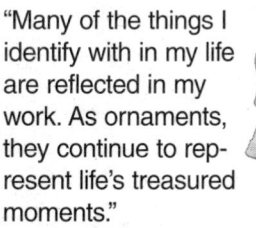

"**Lighting the Flame** is an ornament that's dear to my heart because of my sports background."

Ken Crow

Crow, who grew up 12 miles from Disneyland, is fast becoming known as Hallmark's resident "Disney" Keepsake Ornament artist.

Rosie's Collector Publications

The "Carry Along" Compact Ornament Price Guide

This guide has been reduced in size for you to "Carry Along" wherever you go!

"You'll never leave home without it!"

New Compact Size! 6³⁄₄" x 5¹⁄₄"

Available with attached coupon only!
(Sorry, no duplicating of coupon.)
Available only to those who purchased this large spiral bound guide.

The "Carry Along" guide has the same format as the larger guide without the spiral.

Illinois Residents add 75¢ state tax.

Only $13.25 Includes Shipping

No Phone Orders

coupon

The "Carry Along" Compact Hallmark Ornament Price Guide

6³⁄₄" x 5¹⁄₄"   **$13.25 Includes Shipping!**
(IL Residents add 75¢ sales tax)

When ordering the pocket guide, you must include this coupon.
No phone orders. Redeemable by mail only. Coupon may not be duplicated.

Name_____

Address_____

City_____ St._____ Zip_____

Ph._____

☐ Check
☐ Master/Visa/Discover #_____

  Expires:_____

Store where you purchased this guide:

Name_____

City_____ St._____

Send coupon with payment to:
– No phone calls, please –

Rosie Wells Enterprises, Inc.

22341 E. Wells Rd., Dept. CA, Canton, IL 61520

coupon

Please Return to Desperate Collector

Phone _____

Address _____

Name _____

This Guide Belongs To: